CIVIL WAR GUNS

The complete story of Federal and Confederate small arms: design, manufacture, identification, procurement, issue, employment, effectiveness, and postwar disposal

By
WILLIAM B. EDWARDS

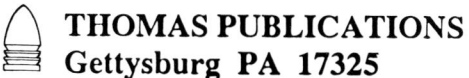
THOMAS PUBLICATIONS
Gettysburg PA 17325

Copyright © 1962, 1990, 1997 William B. Edwards

Printed and bound in the United States of America

1st Edition originally published by Stackpole Books

Library of Congress Catalog Card Number: 62-18172

Published by THOMAS PUBLICATIONS
P.O. Box 3031
Gettysburg, Pa. 17325

All rights reserved. No part of this book may be used or reproduced without written permission of the author and the publisher, except in the case of brief quotations embodied in critical essays and reviews.

ISBN-1-57747-023-0

Cover design by Ryan C. Stouch

Front cover illustration, "The Gray Wall" by Don Troiani.
Photo courtesy Historical Art Prints, Ltd., Southbury, CT.

To the memory of
WILLIAM BENNETT BEAN
SECOND LIEUTENANT, BALTIMORE LIGHT ARTILLERY
(SECOND MARYLAND CSA ARTILLERY)

A Marylander by birth, a Virginian by habits and association, he crossed the Potomac, either by swimming or in a rowboat, to join the battery in Richmond, there to serve with honor through many campaigns. A one-eyed cannoneer, he aimed his guns true in loyalty to the Lost Cause. From him, whom I never knew, I must have inherited my quixotic temperament—to him, therefore, is this volume

Affectionately dedicated by the author

WILLIAM BENNETT EDWARDS

Small door on lock of M1855 series of U.S. arms covers Maynard "tape primer" to allow repeated capping of percussion cone without fumbling with tiny caps. Gun is author's inherited Pistol Carbine, laid over engineer Burton's drawings recently found and now at Harpers Ferry National Historical Park.

Preface

The writing of this book on Civil War guns has occupied bits and pieces of my time from 1955 to the final moments in the summer of 1962.

I am indebted to many friends who have assisted me in the course of research. First and foremost I am indebted to my good friend John Hintlian, of Newington, Conn., who lent me some books in 1955 and has patiently held off demanding their return until I had finished this book. They include sources such as "Correspondence on the Purchase of Arms," Proceedings of the Commission on Ordnance & Ordnance Stores (Ex. Doc. No. 72, 37th, 2nd), Ordnance Contracts (Ex. Doc. No. 99, 40th, 2nd), and the little known Report on Arms Sales 1870 (Report No. 183, 42nd, 2nd), as well as the published libel suit Opdyke vs. Weed which revealed interesting Brooks-Gibbs carbine facts. These are fundamental sources for Civil War Arms study. As this research grew to a close I also discovered the one-time existence of a tabulation of captured Confederate Ordnance and Ordnance Stores sent to the chairman of the House Select Committee on Retrenchment by the Chief of Ordnance in 1866. No trace of this document exists, but should such ever appear, it might justify a sequel volume.

I am indebted to Dr. Stanley Pargellis of the Newberry Library, Chicago, for making available the remarkable resources of this famous depository. Their military collection is too little used, too seldom recognized as being such an extensive library. To Mr. Paul Angle, Mr. Charles Dienethal, and the staff of the Chicago Historical Society my thanks for their courteous aid; within this specialized bracket there was little to find in their files, but they were ever helpful. A few of the photos are of standard guns in the Society's large reference collection.

On numerous trips to Washington, Messrs. Mendel Peterson, Craddock Goins, and the late Captain Carey, always welcomed me, always had time to chat and direct me to some gun or record of value.

Trips abroad, especially to Liege, Belgium, and the distinguished Musee d'Armes de la Ville de Liege, gave me a valuable understanding of the problems of Caleb Huse and Marcellus Hartley. It is not possible even to read about these men comprehendingly until you have also worked in the same gun trades. Mr. Techy of the Musee, and his assistant Mr. Pieters, were always willing to take time and open cases, to allow me to examine unique models or standard arms which had the incomparable merit of having been in the museum for a century. From such friends as Messrs. Paul and Albert Hanquet, and Mr. Ancion, I not only bought guns which had been returned to Belgium from Civil War surplus sales, but gained also knowledge of people, times, places, and methods, which confronted the buyers of North and South a century before in this same city.

Sheer book reference is also important in this work. I have stood for hours in the Newberry's stacks till my feet were sore, leafing through book after book. In Civil War regimental histories, the word "gun" or "firearm" or a brand name like "Maynard" or "Remington" might catch my eye. But mostly, the search was fruitless. Some books such as the Sharpshooter's History, Buell's "The Cannoneer," Semmes "Service Afloat" and many others, which did emphasize the specialized warlike nature of history or actually devoted chapters or passages to weapons, I bought. I do not know whether I should thank Chicago bookseller Dick Barnes for his help in filling out my set of Official Navy Records, and other Civil War books, or he should thank me for buying them. I sold an original plated and fully engraved Winchester Model 1873 rifle that I later found cause to suspect had belonged to Doc Carver, in order to buy a set of Official Records of the Army—then found the set sold; later bought another set from Milwaukee and my Nash was never the same again after bringing those heavy books home in the trunk.

My thanks are most especially due in general— there are too many in particular—to my friends among the various gun collectors associations. The interchange, the swap-buy-sell action at the gun shows, added to my store of lore and incidentally added guns to my collection. Friends such as Val Forgett, Archer Jackson, and Rowland Burmeister, helped materially with the picture end of the book, by supplying essential illustrations or, as Burmeister did, photographing some of my own collection for these pages. Milt

Perry, formerly of West Point's excellent Museum, helped with the loan of photos, while the Smithsonian Institution's Mr. Phillips often was able to squeeze some special chore into a busy schedule over the years and get me a print, or a special enlargement of an old picture. And so it goes . . . the list may not be endless, but it is long.

Cited in the text are many well-known researchers on guns and Civil War topics. I am especially indebted to the pioneering research of Claud Fuller, Col. Berkeley R. Lewis, Richard D. Stewart, and William A. Albaugh III. To Col. Arcadi Gluckman, I am especially grateful for exhaustive studies of U. S. small arms. Col. Lewis by elaborate use of quotes of often obscure original sources, added immensely to the reference lore. Bill Albaugh through his intensive interest in the Southern arms story afforded good background material for the author's C. S. chapters. Many other current books-in-print by my friends Charles Suydam, Harold Peterson, Alden Hatch, Major James Hicks, the late A. Merwin Carey, and Martin Rywell, furnished either reproductions of valuable contemporary documents or current, scholarly research on an item or topic. To all these and many more, my sincere thanks and considerable acknowledgements.

Not always do I agree with earlier researchers; sometimes I am directly at variance. But without their work, this book could not have been written. Verily, what is past is prologue. More specific citations are embodied in the bibliography and index; to these books the reader is directed for an elaborated treatment of individual subjects.

To Mr. E. B. Mann, Editor of GUNS Magazine, I am indebted for permission to use material from my Bannerman story again in Chapter 34, and many of the pictures of standard or non-special arms.

A book like this—this book—has a value that must be gotten across to the reader by the author. It is what the author gradually has learned as a consequence of his study. It is not necessarily the obvious lesson of the book, or the obvious contents. It is something more. For the lesson of history is what people have done, and from this you can conjecture what they will do.

The schooldays prattle about King Cotton and "to keep the Negro in bondage" fall away as you examine the legal causes and justifications for the armed conflict of 1861. The just fears of Southern States that the growing power of the Federal Government would restrict their sovereignty seem very apropos and modern. The same tensions which exist in the nation today with excessive power being drawn more and more into the hands of a central government raise again the eternal questions of Centralist vs. Federalist organization. The average civil rights liberal of 1962 knows as much about the Second Amendment to the Federal Constitution as a hoot owl; but of all the civil rights, this is the one which retains its meaning when all else is gone. The Southern States knew this even in the midst of a war for survival, and ratified the same sentiment into their own Constitution. They recognized that, fighting against the centralist government in Washington to retain their own independence could cause them to become even more authoritarian in their own domestic political structure, and so lose the very liberties for their people that the Montgomery government had gone to war to preserve. This is an oversimplification, but it is not so much of one; and people need to have matters simplified for them because a quick look at the people and the times reveals but mass confusion. So we hope in this book the influence of the guns of the war upon the course of the war will not be deemed too unrealistic a simplification, but merely the necessary one. It is the historian's task, like Theseus in the labyrinth, to lay a clue in a straight path; to carry the simile further, the opening battle of the War was at Bull Run, and the bull has been running ever since.

Evanston, Illinois
October, 1962

WILLIAM B. EDWARDS

Publisher's Preface to Second Edition
Gettysburg, Pa., June 1997

Thomas Publications is honored to present a new edition of *Civil War Guns*, by William Bennett Edwards. This great classic of military literature was first published in 1962. No book of its broad and easyreading coverage has since been written.

When published, *Civil War Guns* was widely and critically acclaimed. But the book now has vanished from second-hand dealers. It commands a high price when found, but it is rarely offered. Owners of early copies use their books. They find meaning for collecting and historical perspectives upon re-reading.

When I learned that Edwards was able to make this new edition possible, it was personally satisfying. In my own writing on arms, I had turned to the pages of my first edition of *Civil War Guns* many times for reference and direction. This new edition is useful to Civil War buffs, skirmishers and re-enactors, living history interpreters, and military historians.

When Edwards, in the 1962 edition, wrote that "the same tensions exist...with excessive power being drawn into the hands of a central government [which raise] the eternal questions of Centralist vs. Federalist organization," he was describing the heritage of the War which today, decades later, still persists. In this, Edwards had a point of view not shared by many, for to him the Civil War was not some event petrified in ancient rocks, but events which were "only yesterday." As a child of five he used to visit an elderly family friend who had himself once been a Civil War drummer boy.

Those long-ago events hold a meaning for American affairs even today. There is a lesson in *Civil War Guns* which has nothing to do with the caliber of arms or the invention of repeating guns. It is the truth that a recourse to violence did not solve America's problems then, nor would it be a solution to domestic or foreign problems today.

The first edition carried a notice about the author. Therefore, I have included a new word about him.

From Edwards' first arms industry job in 1944 as a special weapons operator in a government arsenal to his Federal Firearms Dealer's License renewed to 1999, he has been active in the gun trade. His first FFDL issued in 1947, when he was still a child, cost one dollar.

His interests range from "musket to machine gun." In 1943, he owned a German MP40 submachine gun. Aberdeen Proving Ground's sample lacked a magazine, but Edwards test-fired his gun. This experience began his dossier with the FBI. But in 1959, the Army flew him to Fort Benning, Georgia, where he "showed the Army how to shoot" the new M-14 fully automatic rifle from the shoulder controllably, as a Chicago *Tribune* reporter noted.

His open friendships in the foreign gun trade prompted the CIA Chicago station chief Clarence Perry Oakes to ask Edwards to act as a spy for "his country." After he refused to spy on his friends, the CIA set up his dossier in October 1957, and conducted illegal domestic surveillance of his activities.

In 1957, black powder muzzle loading replica guns drew his interest. In Brescia, Italy, he set up the manufacture of replicas of the Colt Navy 1851 revolver, a principal pistol of the Civil War. His sometime partner, Val Forgett, Jr., of Navy Arms Company has described Edwards as "the dean of American gun writers."

Edwards' numerous gun articles in magazines have been republished in *Gun Digest* and the *Swiss Waffen Digest* annuals. His arms trade work has caused him to be listed in the British, German, and Italian "Who's Who" books. He has been active in many fields, from a 20-year speculation in real estate holding thorium deposit lands, to inventing the world standard SIG P220 pistol with its simple "chamber block to ejection port" locking principle.

In Italy, the replica arms industry he founded may have prevented Italy from "going Communist" and falling behind the Iron Curtain. In 1968, the Gun Control Act embargoed pistol imports and caused terrible financial dislocation in Brescia. The workers, a traditionally well-educated and intelligent class of craftsmen, in such an important industrial center, were hard-hit in their pockets. But it was Edwards' Mississippi Rifle contract of 1969 which helped V. Bernardelli to weather the hard times. The replicas from Rigarmi, Buffoli, San Paolo, Ranson, Euroarms, Zoli, even eventually Beretta, kept the industry going, making guns they could sell into America without damage from GCA68 restrictions. Between 1960, when the Zouave Rifle was begun in replication, and 1970, Edwards estimates that 100,000 had been sold to the U. S., although only 12,500 were made originally in the 1860s! These, plus Colt, Remington, Rogers & Spencer, Confederate copy revolvers, and many other replica models were a major support to the Brescian industry, damaged by the U. S. Embargo.

There is an important change to be noted in the "replica" chapter. The type is left as in the original, on pages 427 and 428, where Edwards criticizes the anti-replica advertising policy of the National Rifle Association in their monthly journal, *The American Rifleman*.

Rejection of replica gun advertising in the Rifleman was caused by Gun Collector Committee advisors James E. Serven, rare gun dealer, and John S. DuMont, wealthy collector. They were "stuck" with a faked Italian replica Walker Colt revolver and advised the NRA not to "promote" such arms. This reactionary policy, among many other backward-looking policies of the NRA, has been changed for the better under newer administration. Gun fans have responded by raising NRA membership from the 400,000 of 1962 to over three million in the 1990s. Edwards' criticism in 1962 helped to make this change.

Edwards now lives in the Blue Ridge mountains of Virginia at Rockfish Gap. He is surrounded by historic sites and battle grounds of America's struggle for freedom. His wife of 43 years is a talented concert piano artist. She has recently published her book on how music influences people and modifies behavior. Their resident cat is 24-year-old Purrierite, named for a former cat, Purrier, and the mineral "perrierite" which contains thorium. Useful for nuclear reactors and atomic bombs, deposits of thorium existed on land Edwards owned for 20 years.

And it is this modern risk of nuclear accident or terrorist outrage that makes the study of America's internal struggle, a study of the arms and the times, 1859-65, of continuing value to the modern citizen.

In the public interest, and to satisfy intense popular curiosity about our arms and our history, Thomas Publications brings you this new edition of *Civil War Guns*.

Other books by William B. Edwards

THE STORY OF COLT'S REVOLVER

THIS IS THE WEST (CHAPTER ON FIREARMS)

CONSPIRACY OF 30: THEIR MISUSE OF MUSIC FROM ARISTOTLE TO ONASSIS *by Virginia Davis Edwards, edited by William B. Edwards*

Forthcoming

UNITED STATES STEAL

Prologue

The Venice air was quiet and clear, invigorating one's spirit by the leisurely atmosphere which was yet infused with energy and briskness. What must seem unreal to so many Americans who have not traveled abroad was quite real to me then in Italy: the incredible gold and azure mosaics facing up the historic old cathedral of St. Marks; the tall tower from which moving figures struck the hours; the pigeons swirling about an old lady who fed them crumbs, and the rich, ruby Dubonnet that moved in my glass as I revolved the stem between thumb and forefinger. What was unreal to me that bright October evening in 1957 was the information a fellow American passed along to me—trouble in Little Rock, segregation, United States Airborne troops dispatched, National Guard units called out.

The whole sorry mess of "the Negro problem" had flared up and I began to wonder if somehow this ancient wound, which four years of war had healed in drastic cautery, was about to open up again. Myself, a grandson of a Southern officer (mine was a lieutenant; somebody had to keep the generals from annoying the sergeants), my parents of a Virginia family, I yet felt no such strong sentiments about states' rights when I could also see plainly that some of the rights sought to be retained by the states were ridiculous, archaic. Perhaps too subtly, I telegraphed the Governor at Little Rock, "Have ten thousand Enfields at eighteen. Do you want? Signed, Huse." Facetiously I paraphrased the sort of cables which Caleb Huse, foreign purchasing agent of the Confederacy, was wont to send almost 100 years before. I doubt that the Honorable Governor Faubus ever saw that cable, but it served to point up not only the ridiculousness of many Southrons' attitudes today, but the striking similarities of history and social life which a hundred years ago seemed justified in culminating in open war.

Today the world has been divided into two armed camps. It is not enough to blame "history" for it, as this is the work of men. Once, too, these United States were also divided. The Union did not fall. Whether it will *long* endure, is the responsibility of present generations. But as what is past is prologue, so a look at the problems of preparing for and fighting a war on the American continent a hundred years ago, may serve to give insight into problems and methods of today. Even in that century past, the United States, both Union and Confederacy, acknowledged themselves to be a part of One World. Hope of the English loan kept the Confederacy in business for years. Ability to ship cotton out to pay, through Fraser, Trenholm & Company, for war materials, kept the Stars and Bars floating over a solvent industrial nation until the last and final accounting at Appomattox. And in the North, which today's history teachers would have us believe was such a beehive of industry and productivity, the troops in blue relied for nearly three of the five war years upon small arms, cannon, ammunition purchased overseas.

In the South, changes also were taking place, the termination of which by force of Union arms left its mark upon the States of Dixie even today. This change was the transition from a Tidewater agricultural society to one including an active iron and steel industry and all the productivity which that implies. Virginia, among the richest of the states, possessed a large capacity for ordnance and armaments production. At Augusta, Georgia the South built the world's largest powder mill. In New Orleans, ridden by "the vomit," yellow fever, and malaria, industry had still managed to gain an ascendancy. Until threat of Union gunboats forced their removal, several key ordnance firms were set up in New Orleans, and their cannon and rifles were in use during the war. The burning of Columbia, South Carolina, appears to be the deliberate destruction of competitive commercial capability, rather than the necessary destruction of railroad stock in use for hauling Confederate war materials. After all, the city had been captured by Sherman, and he was marching on. And the mass destruction of Atlanta, both by Confederates fleeing and by Union occupiers, is a record of destruction of factories which could have constituted a serious threat in the market to Northern manufacturers.

Freeing the slaves was part and parcel of this economic warfare which underlies many of the battles so glamorously recalled today. A slave was a valuable article; the bank account of the South was in its slaves.

These black men in bondage were not all jolly field hands singing in the sun. Many were men of great technical skill. It was the slave who forged the weapons of war at the great Tredegar works; it was the slave at C. S. Robinson's Richmond carbine factory who turned out the stubby copies of the popular Sharps for Southern chivalry; it was the slave in the glow of Southern furnaces who poured the yellow bronze to make the howitzers of the Washington Artillery or the Richmond Greys. And side by side worked their white masters: men like Brooke, of the rifled cannon; or the brothers Cook, musket and carbine makers.

The story of the production and procurement of arms for the South is one of sacrifices and accomplishments. The accomplishments are so great that rarely was the South in want of small arms, after the first scramble to sort out the captures at Harpers Ferry. The accomplishment included building up the tons of salvaged parts into thousands of useful rifle muskets at the Confederate States Arsenal in Richmond. The accomplishment included obtaining a complete factory to fabricate, wholly by machinery, on the most approved system, the No. 1 Interchangeable Enfield, standard arm of the South. While the shipment of tools only got as far as Nassau, the letting of this contract and completion of it was one of the war's minor miracles. And there were men who never laid file to steel, yet supplied more guns in the space of a few months than their contracting capitalist fellows accomplished in the years of the war. These in the North were "Colonel" Schuyler and Marcellus Hartley—given carte blanche to a million dollars; and their counterpart of the South, Caleb Huse, who managed to send through the blockade from the ports of Europe a steady stream of good muskets, good cannon, and good rifles.

Today little remains but monuments and battlefield tours to tell of those days and of this ultimate merging of many states into one National Identity. Like it or not, North and South emerged from the battle as one great nation. But upon the relics of those days still lingers the luster of the men who created the swords from plowshares. Today's collector of old guns and edged weapons borrows a little of this glory in the owning and researching of some pistol or carbine from the Civil War period.

Today, also, we are engaged in a great struggle, to test whether this nation or any nation dedicated to the liberties of man, can long endure. America is an old country today. The New World, in the eyes of many, is past her prime. The nations of Europe are once again new nations: Germany's Constitution since War Two; Italy no longer a monarchy; France lingering in the sunshine of memories of the Great Napoleon yet somehow still strong, still vital; these are the new nations of the world. Ranged beyond them is Russia, a land of revolution still transpiring. America, too, once was a nation of revolutionists. But a revolution that slows down, that dies, is the mark of the end of that revolutionary society. Russia, to all observers, seems to be highballing along with her own revolution working its way with land, life, and people. It is a revolution that differs fundamentally from and sternly challenges the American revolution. Our own was tested many times; most strongly before, by our Civil War.

So far, we have survived.

Contents

	Page
Prologue	
Chapter 1—Old Brown Pulls a Raid	1
Chapter 2—The Militiamen	6
Chapter 3—Ordnance-Industry: Mismatched Team	11
Chapter 4—The Rifle, the Primer, the Ball	13
Chapter 5—Models Perfected	22
Chapter 6—Rifle Muskets: Civil War Scandals	25
Chapter 7—In Justice to Justice	60
Chapter 8—Millions for Muskets	65
Chapter 9—Caleb Huse Incurs Some Debts	82
Chapter 10—Breechloaders of Chicopee	100
Chapter 11—Federal Carbines	110
Chapter 12—Fremont Arms the Western Army	133
Chapter 13—The Dreaded "Horizontal Shot-Tower"	144
Chapter 14—That Damn Yankee Rifle	158
Chapter 15—Remington: Prelude to Conflict	179
Chapter 16—Vulcan's Hammers at Ilion's Forge	190
Chapter 17—The Starr Rises	197
Chapter 18—Manhattan Firearms Goes to War	204
Chapter 19—Sharpshooters	210
Chapter 20—Machine Guns—Masterworks or Monstrosities?	228
Chapter 21—Enfield: The North's Second Rifle	242
Chapter 22—Continental Arms	256
Chapter 23—Yankee Revolvers	273
Chapter 24—The Rifles of Christian Sharps	293
Chapter 25—Colt's Goes to War	304
Chapter 26—From Tredegar to Wilson's Creek	336
Chapter 27—Long Arms for Lee	345
Chapter 28—Sidearms for Southrons	351
Chapter 29—"Sans Guarantie du Gouvernement"	362
Chapter 30—Texas Fights Alone	368
Chapter 31—The Southern Armories and Superintendent Burton	371
Chapter 32—The Southern Pistol—the Derringer	394
Chapter 33—What Happened to the Guns, Post War	400
Chapter 34—What's on Bannerman's Island?	413
Chapter 35—The Rage for Replicas	421
Chapter 36—The War Was for Real	429
Appendix Bibliography	439
Index	440

RULES & REGULATIONS
FOR THE
Workshops of the U.S. Armory.

1. All persons who engage themselves as workmen in the Armory, bind themselves by so doing to obey the Rules and Regulations established by proper authority, and the orders and directions of the Foremen, or other persons authorized to give such directions.

2. As prescribed by the Ordnance Regulations, all workmen are engaged by the day. Every one employed can leave when he pleases, and the commanding officer can cease to employ any one when he pleases. A month's notice will always be given, when possible, if persons are to be stopped for want of work, and workmen intending to leave for other employment are expected, when they can do so, to give a like notice.

3. Punctual attendance is required at bell-ring; all persons who are not present then, will be allowed to work but three-fourths of that day.

4. All workmen are required to occupy themselves *during working hours* with their work; and will not be permitted to break off until the bell rings for ceasing work, without first notifying their Foreman and getting his consent to their leaving.

5. If any person wishes to be absent more than a day, after obtaining the consent of his Foreman he will apply to the Master Armorer, who will authorize his absence for such time as he can be spared.—Persons who absent themselves without giving this notice will be considered as having left the employment.

6. Visitors *who are desirous of seeing the works*, will be allowed to pass through all the Shops, and the Foremen in charge will show them any attention in their power, and will direct the Shop-tenders to accompany them if necessary.

No persons are permitted to visit the Shops for the purpose of transacting *private business* of any kind, or to *interfere* with or *interrupt* the workmen during *working hours*.

Extracts from the Regulations for the Government of the Ordnance Department.

"Whenever at National Armories, Arsenals or Ordnance Depots, any hired workman shall through incompetency, carelessness or design, spoil any piece of work in the execution of which he may be engaged, it shall be the duty of the Commanding Officer to cause the amount of injury to be estimated, and give the necessary orders to the Paymaster to stop the same from the pay of such workman."

"Workmen or others employed by hire in the Ordnance Department, shall be paid only for such days or parts of days as they may actually labor in the service of said department. * * "

"The working hours for hired men at Ordnance Establishments shall be so arranged as to average ten hours a day throughout the year, working by day-light only."

"The public workshops, tools and materials, must be used solely for purposes of public benefit, and all private work in the public buildings, and all other application of public means to any other than public purposes is expressly prohibited."

☞ The above is published for the information of all concerned.

Each Foreman is specially charged to see that these Rules are strictly observed by all under his control.

Commanding Officer's Office,
June 20th, 1853.

BENJ. HUGER,
Col. U. S. A.

"Rules" photo courtesy James Henry Burton Papers, Manuscripts and Archives, Yale University Library.

Regulations for workers and visitors to Harpers Ferry Armory in effect at the time of John Brown's Raid in 1859, indicate that if he and his guerilla chief Col. Hugh (Ugo) Forbes had gone to the front door they would have toured the factory as guests.

CHAPTER 1

Old Brown Pulls a Raid

"John Brown, Aaron C. Stevens, Andrew Coppoc . . . evil minded and traitorous persons . . . not having the fear of God before their eyes, but being moved and seduced by the false and malignant counsel of other evil and traitorous persons and the instigation of the devil . . . are hereby charged with:

"One: Confederating to make rebellion and levy war against the State of Virginia . . .

"Two: Conspiring to induce slaves to make rebellion and insurrection . . .

"Three: With committing murder . . ."

John Brown Obtains His Guns

As the litany of the court droned on, Old Brown, eyes deep-set in recall, thought back over the flaming Kansas years that had brought him to this bar of a lesser justice. Too vividly in memory he knew the hellhole of the arsenal firehouse at Harpers Ferry with the Minié balls poking splintery fingers through the doors, and the thudding battering ram as Colonel Lee's Marines breached the tiny fort; remembered the Kansas years and a Sharps sporting rifle he had once so proudly carried, 'til the 200 Sharps carbines fell into his hands, and the mad dream of a slaves' revolt seemed a possibility. Seemingly from the first, Christian Sharps' destiny and that of John Brown of Ossawattomi were linked, for the rifle used by Brown for hunting on the plains, and left by him with his friend Charles Blair in Collinsville, Connecticut, was one of Sharps' first-made: 1848.

Brown wanted no maker's name on it, this breechloader for Kansas fighting, since there were many who did not care to be identified with his movement. So gunsmith Albert S. Nippes of Philadelphia, licensee of some of the earliest Sharps guns, finished it plain. He carried this rifle during the years when jayhawkers and bushwackers kept the Border States in unrest; perhaps had it with him during the silent but bloody saber-hacking massacre of the Doyles. Yet this monomaniac had strong friends; in his own violent way he was a genius. He planned to arm the slaves who should rise to his standard with pikes, and in the summer of 1859 journeyed to Collinsville, the town made famous by the Collins Axe Company. He stayed at the home of Charles Blair, who had once made weapons, the Elgin cutlass pistol, in 1836, and gave him the old Sharps in token of his help, for Brown had obtained 200 new slant-breech Sharps carbines through the Massachusetts State Committee which he diverted to his military foray into western Virginia.

"I'll carry the war into Africa," Brown once boasted, but his project was doomed. It takes a consciousness of oppression to allow one man, or a nation, to revolt. The slave class in the South as a group did not possess this recognition that they were oppressed, any more than a dog, fed and housed by its master, regrets the loss of freedom of the wilds. Only as generations of slaves were born and grew up in the Southern version of modern European culture, did the Stone Age savage from the Ivory Coast learn he was a victim. Mostly he had a recognition that he received food regularly, was looked after, housed, and did not have to fight superior forces of black enemies in league with Arab or Portuguese slave traders. What had taken the Anglo-Saxon forebears of the Southern whites some centuries to do, wash off their blue-wood dye and become travelers on the Roman road to civilization, Brown hoped to do in a few weeks with the black men of the South.

The sovereign State of Virginia did not view this as any minor foray, but an incitement to insurrection. With memories of the Nat Turner rebellion of three decades past still clear, both Federal and State forces went to the aid of Harpers Ferry Arsenal, which Brown in one fearful morning seemed to have captured; the first casualty one of the very black men whom Brown wanted to free.

Relics of Brown's Raid

In the Maryland Historical Society is one of Brown's Sharps carbines. It is the slant breech Model 1853; the main difference between it and the preceding M1852 is in the link pin that holds the breechblock. Its turning arm, which frees the pin and allows it to be withdrawn sideways from the breech frame, is held by a small spring-loaded plunger fitted into the solid breech frame. (In the 1852 model, a flat spring like the band retaining spring of a musket, is fitted to the wood of the forestock.) The brass band has a widened bottom section, pointing forward, and a brass patch-box on the stock

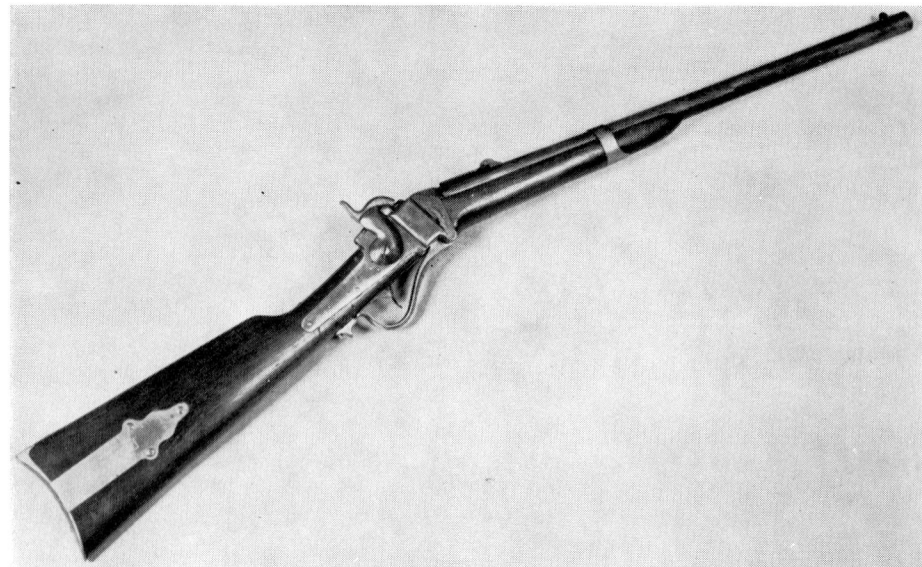

"John Brown" Sharps is M1853 with slant breech, brass trim and sling bar on left side, cal. .54, barrel 21½ inches long. Serial numbers observed (Smith) range between 9179—18602.

right. To the left, a long sling-ring bar is attached to both front band and frame, while the rear sight folds backward toward the breech when not in use for long range shooting. Inscribed on the patch box of this particular carbine are the words: *Captured from insurgents at Harpers Ferry, Va. Oct. 18, 1959, by Col. A. P. Shutt, and presented to his Son Augustus J. C. L. Shutt.*

Colonel Shutt in militia life was commander of the 6th Regiment, Maryland Volunteers. In civil life he earned his wages as an express and passenger train conductor for the Baltimore & Ohio Railroad. The wires carried strange messages of insurgents at Harpers Ferry, and by the morning of October 17, when Negro porter Washington Hayward, at the B & O station near the arsenal, was shot through the body by one of Brown's men, Baltimore perceived that something unusual was happening.

Colonel Shutt, sent to protect the railroad's property and interests, arrived at his post after Brown's capture. He endeavored to restore train service to normal, and using 30 men armed with rifles borrowed from the armory, placed there a temporary guard to prevent rioting, and especially to protect the important covered railroad bridges that spanned the Shenandoah and Potomac rivers. His main job seemed to be to break up the selling of souvenir pikes on the Baltimore & Ohio trains by the inhabitants of Harpers Ferry who would board the train at one place along with sandwich and coffee vendors and disembark a few miles down the line after having disposed of, in total, probably considerably more than the number of pikes which John Brown ever contracted for at Collinsville.

Shutt's carbine came from a cache of arms located at Brown's farmhouse. The day after Brown's arrest, a company of Marines searched the place, recovering 102 Sharps rifles, 102 Massachusetts Arms Company's pistols ("A little under the Navy size," said Brown), 56 Massachusetts Arms Company powder flasks, 4 large powder flasks, 10 kegs of gunpowder, 23,000 percussion rifle caps, 100,000 percussion pistol caps, 1,300 ball cartridges for Sharps rifles (some slightly damaged by water), 160 boxes Sharps primers, 14 lbs. lead balls, one old percussion pistol, 1 major general's sword, 55 old bayonets, 12 old artillery swords, 483 standard spears, 150 broken handles for spears, 16 picks, 40 shovels, 1 tin powder case, 1,500 pikes, together with a large quantity of stationery, clothing, and personal property.

Among the personal property items to which John Brown kept title until his death by hanging, December 2, 1859, was a Sharps carbine and "his belt pistol," both of which he bequeathed to Captain John Avis, jailer at Charlestown prison. Though Captain Avis' men of the Charlestown Irregulars militia had been glad when Old Brown was brought before them at the close of the fighting, bloody and bowed, those few minutes before Brown's death were a time of compassion and weeping. As he gave away the few bits of property—a Bible and some books—the hearts of those assembled to watch him die seemed moved by the message which Brown had tried to preach; blundering, he yet sought recognition for the dignity of men.

Beecher's Bibles

In the North, abolitionist Reverend Henry Ward Beecher thundered in his pulpit even before Brown's death:

"Seventeen men, white men, without a military base, without artillery . . . attacked a State, and undertook to release and lead away an enslaved race." As the congregation of his Plymouth Church in Boston listened, none nodding, for this they knew was history in the making, he roared on: "Seventeen white men surrounded two thousand and held them in duress . . . overawed a town of two thousand brave Virginians, and held them captive until the sun had gone laughing twice around the globe . . ."

While historians may dissect Beecher's personality and his penchant for pushing others along in the cause of Abolition, history shows him to have been on the right side. All have heard how chests of Sharps carbines were shipped out secretly from New England to the west, marked "Bibles," giving rise to the legend for the John Brown Sharps as "a case of Beecher's Bibles." Not at all surprisingly, a case of ordinary King James Bibles packed in clean white wood looks to the gun crank for all the world, and feels, like a case of carbines.

Guns of this ill-fated expedition which, like the Shot at Sarajevo in World War I, effectively may be said to have "started" the Civil War, have long interested collectors. But there exist today few guns having unmistakable association with John Brown's expedition, like the 1848 Nippes Sharps (now property of M. C. Clark of Los Angeles) or the 1853 carbine from the Maryland Historical Society in Baltimore.

As with relics found by archeologists in ground strata, so legitimate regional association will do much to place a gun in its niche in history. Hence Kansas should be a fertile ground today for Sharps guns from this turbulent period. For example, the New England Emigrant Aid Committee's purchasing agent for Kansas obtained 100 carbines from the Sharps Rifle Manufacturing Company in Hartford on March 19, 1856. The price was $30 each less 10 percent. The invoice included 29 packages of Sharps primers at $1 1/8, 20 bullet moulds

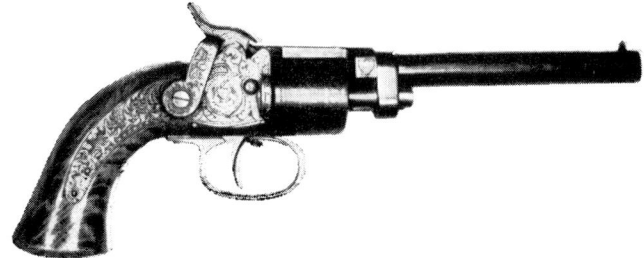

Mass. Arms revolvers cal. .31 designed by Joshua Stevens, with Maynard tape primer, were among weapons taken from Brown's men after capture. Guns sold by Yankee abolitionists to further discord in South were presumably plain; engraved specimen shown was type often presented to free state leaders.

at $1, and was paid in part by a one-day sight draft on Silas Cabot.

The ten boxes of carbines, presumably Model 1853 arms (using Sharps pellet primers instead of the Maynard tape primer coil of the M1855 Carbine mechanism) were sent to Kansas on the Missouri river steamer *Arabia*. The fact of carbines being aboard became known to some pro-slavery passengers and at Lexington, Missouri the ship was boarded by the pro-slavery faction and the carbines taken off. Prior to shipment, Dr. Calvin Cutter acting for General Pomeroy (the Committee's agent), had taken out all the breechblocks

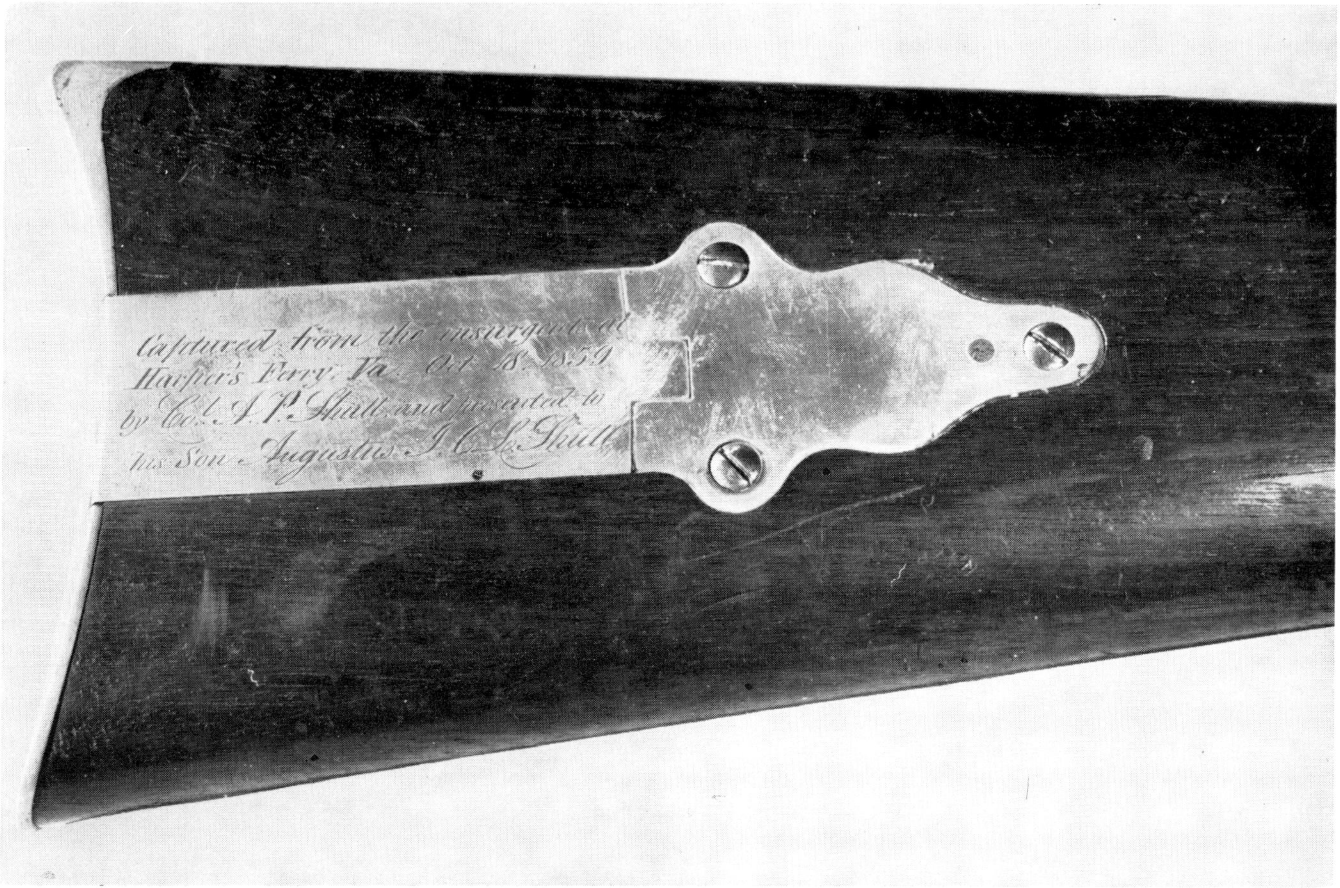

Patchbox of carbine among 102 found on Brown's farm at Harpers Ferry is inscribed with sentiment of presentation from Colonel Shutt of Maryland troops to his son. Shutt was Baltimore & Ohio Railroad man.

and shipped them to Kansas by a different route. The 100 carbines were finally recovered by Free Staters and, according to Martin F. Conway of Lawrence, testifying before a Senate committee 13 February 1860, were in his possession at that time.

Carbines of the Same Type in Belgium

In 1960 in the shop of Mr. Paul Hanquet in Liege, I saw a couple of dozen dirty Model 1853 Sharps carbines, which I was informed had been purchased by an American gun dealer, Turner Kirkland. They were without breechblocks. I now wonder if they were part of Martin Conway's lot of breechblockless guns, sold eventually because of the impossibility of getting the special slant breechblock from the Sharps Company during the war, and by reason of being obsolete after the war.

John Brown's guns came from a similar lot, actually 200 Sharps purchased by the Massachusetts State Committee in August 1856, and shipped out to Kansas. A momentary peace being established by the presence of United States troops along the Kansas border, the carbines, to prevent their seizure by the United States as contraband, were diverted and stored at Tabor, Iowa.

Brown wanted these guns and prevailed upon the Massachusetts abolition authorities to allow him to have them, he being instructed to sell 100 of them at a reduced price of $15 to aid reliable Kansans and use the proceeds to relieve suffering among Free State families attacked by border ruffians. Unknown to the Massachusetts authorities, Brown planned to use these guns for his slave revolt. According to J. H. Kagi, one of the more intelligent and literate of Brown's followers, "The arms in the Arsenal were to be taken to the mountains, with such slaves as joined. As fast as possible other bands besides the original ones were to be formed, and a continuous chain of posts established in the mountains. They were to be supported by provisions taken from the farms of the oppressors. The slaves were to be armed with pikes, scythes, muskets, shotguns, and other simple instruments of defense; the officers, white or black, and such of the men as were skilled and trustworthy, to have the use of the Sharps rifles and revolvers."

Brown was a Guerrilla

The broad plains of Kansas soon to be rippling in wheat, and the wooded hills of western Virginia that a century later would lie scarred and stripped of their tops by mining, were united in Brown's plan; both were the scenes of what today is studied as guerrilla warfare. No man better understood the nature of backwoods warfare than John Brown. A man who, in death, was to lead thousands of soldiers "as his soul goes marching on," led his band almost unseen through a populous countryside, transported into his farmhouse headquarters case after case of munitions, and shipped in steel pike heads to the number of 1,500, within walking distance of one of the nation's most important public military establishments, the United States Arsenal at Harpers Ferry, without arousing suspicion.

Brown's Pistols

Though the Sharps gun and John Brown were linked in the popular mind, another arm, a pistol, figured in this drama. Made by a major firm of this era, these were the Maynard-primed revolvers built by the Massachusetts Arms Company at Chicopee Falls, Massachusetts. As Brown stated, they were "a little under the Navy size." Question has been raised over the exact model and design of these guns, for none are known with Brown's raid association to them. But a Navy-size revolver in the parlance of the period was an arm of .36 caliber, what today is called a .38. An arm of "just under" Navy caliber would, in the phrasing most commonly used, have been a .31 caliber arm. The Massachusetts Arms Company built such a pistol, and the exact model can be deduced from a bill of sale located by collector Albert W. Lindert of Homewood, Illinois, in the hands of Boyd B. Stutler, Charlestown, West Virginia. The original bill of sale was to one George L. Stearns, of Boston, and covered 200 "belt revolvers, 6″ (barrels), with Maynard Primer locks," which were forwarded to Captain John Brown, Iowa City, Iowa, from Chicopee Falls, Massachusetts on May 25, 1857. The price was low, $6.50 each, and the price included "set implements" which would be bullet mould and nipple wrench, also flasks and extra main springs. The bill of sale description "belt revolvers" normally would suggest .36 caliber; but Captain Brown specifically stated "a little under the Navy size." Hence the description ties up the exact model as the Maynard primed revolver, caliber .31, 6-inch barrel, in production at the time. The original Wesson & Leavitt mechanically turned revolver with separate nipples had been discontinued; the declaration they were "Maynard primer" locks definitely rules out the Adams revolvers made about this time by the Massachusetts Arms Company. Remaining, known to collectors, is the Joshua Stevens hand-turned revolver, using one single nipple in the frame, and a tiny hole at the base of each chamber which in succession is carried past the main nipple to allow the flame to discharge the shot.

Whether Brown had all 200 of these revolvers with him at the time of his raid is uncertain, but 102 of them were removed by the Marines officially. A local farmer, John C. Unseld, testified that he opened some of the boxes of materials there and that the guns, carbines and pistols, were taken by "the Baltimore Company" (under Colonel Shutt?) and some other young men who showed up. He estimated that 40 to 50 people got carbines, and most of these got pistols also.

The Allen Breechloader

One rifle never identified with the Brown episode is the Allen & Wheelock. On November 25, 1859, an Allen breechloader was found on the hill near the east end of the railroad bridge, evidently abandoned by one of Brown's men. Unless the gun used was a prototype or early production "patent pending" model, this is not the relatively common .44 caliber rimfire breechloader patented by Ethan Allen in 1860 and made by Allen &

Wheelock in Worcester. It probably was a previous model, very little known, of a "faucet breech" construction. Ethan Allen's patent of 1855, this mechanism has a cylinder lying across the back of the barrel, with a hole bored in it the same size as the bore. A lever on the top of the grip or small of the stock when lifted rotates the cylinder or drum to permit loading the chamber. A side hammer back-action lock fires a percussion cap; the nipple on the breech flashing through channels in the cross-breech drum. The New England firms were engaged in promotional gifts to would-be purchasers on the troubled frontier, and this rifle may have been among them. It was not an item of issue and this is the only reference found to warlike use of this early Allen breechloader.

Colt Navy Revolver Found

Among the personal relics salvaged by Maryland men was an incomplete Colt Navy M1851 revolver; just the barrel was obtained. It was sent to Sam Colt in the fall of 1859 as a memento of the historic occasion.

The remaining arms were taken to the armory and stored there until later capture by the Confederacy. If not lost in the burning of the storehouse of muskets, which collapsed in flames into the basement during Jackson's attack, they may have been salvaged and taken to Richmond, there to be cleaned and issued for Confederate service.

Notables at Brown's Hanging

It was an oddly assorted group of soldiery which converged upon the arsenal firehouse and which followed Old Brown and his boys to incarceration and hanging at Charlestown. The Marines, efficiently under command of Colonel Robert E. Lee, were supported by such men as Maj. Thomas J. Jackson and his company of Virginia Military

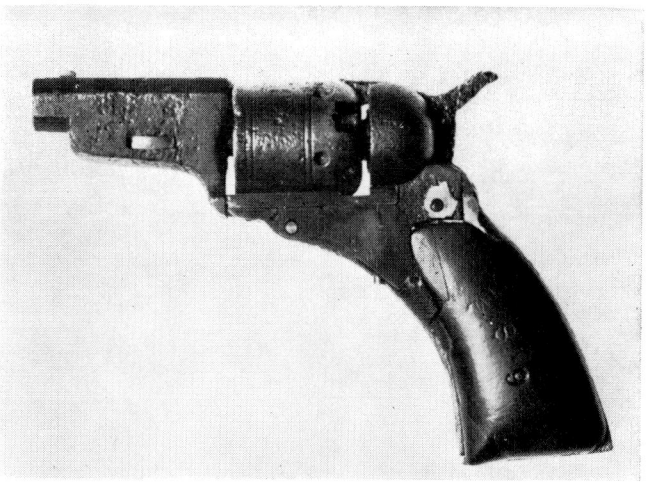

Colt .28 pistol made at Paterson, N.J., 1840, was found at Bolivar Heights overlooking Harpers Ferry recently. Owner George Debo of Altoona, Pa., wonders if it is souvenir of Brown's Raid, characterizes it as "smallest revolver of CW."

Institute artillery cadets. John Wilkes Booth was there in dandy militia uniform. And old Edmund Ruffin, the agriculture expert, came out to see what was happening in western Virginia. He asked to stay on to witness the execution, and stood in a rear rank, draped in a borrowed militia overcoat, as High Sheriff John W. Campbell chopped the latch loose and Brown suddenly dropped in air. A few months later the 66-year-old War of 1812 veteran, in the uniform of a private in the Palmetto Grays, at Charleston pulled a lanyard, snapping the primer on the first gun to bombard Fort Sumter. At Harpers Ferry, at Charlestown, Virginia, many of the actors were now come to the stage. John Brown's foray was the prologue; the play was about to begin.

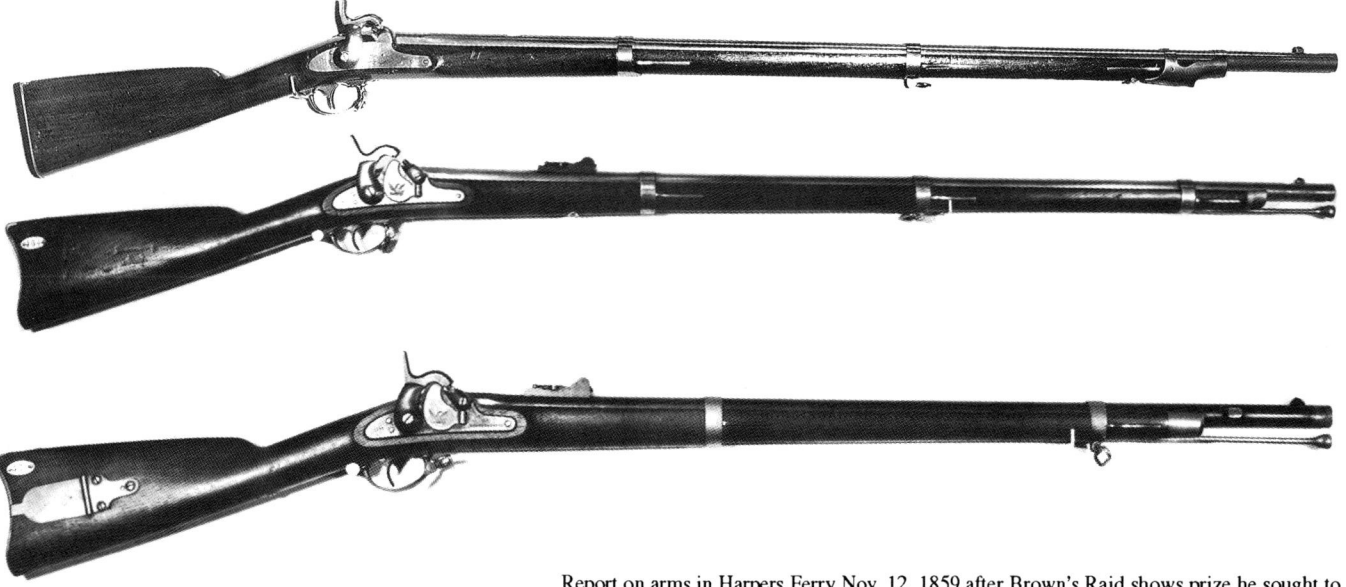

Report on arms in Harpers Ferry Nov. 12, 1859 after Brown's Raid shows prize he sought to arm white non-slave settlers for Blue Ridge guerilla uprising. The list Col. Craig gave Secretary of War J.B. Floyd totaled 18,322: .69 muskets altered to percussion, 149; with Maynard lock, 2; made as percussion .69 (top) 4569; rifled percussion .69, 737; 1855 Rifled Musket .58 (middle) 8599; 1855 Rifles .58 (bottom) 3570; M1841 "Mississippi" rifles .54, 696.

CHAPTER 2

The Militiamen

Few men doubted that war would come. The decision of whether to serve the Union or one's native state was a much more difficult choice to make in 1860 than it might be in 1960.

Taking "the steam cars," the railroad, from one capital to another, was not a certain method of travel throughout the whole settled East. When Jackson's VMI boys went from Lexington to Harpers Ferry and Charleston during the John Brown incident, they traveled by wagon and foot to Staunton, west of Rockfish Creek Gap, and then were able to entrain for the Harpers Ferry. Not even in so settled and prosperous a state as the Old Dominion was there anything like a complete network of railroads between market towns and cities. In the North the situation was somewhat better, but many changes of gauge from one company's line of tracks to another reduced the pleasures of travel. Express men were constantly on the go, and barge men or other members of the water commerce of the nation —canal boatmen, sailors, post coach drivers—were on the go. But the average man was born, lived, and died, without seeing beyond the hills that ringed his farm valley. Such close attachment to one geographical spot was shared by families and towns so that in the recruiting Johnny Reb and Billy Yank set out to see the world all right, but usually in company with dozens of other boys with whom they had grown up and had known all their lives. Only after the fighting got hot and replacements came in, draftees from other regions, did the companies or regiments assume a more cosmopolitan air. Yet companies continued to identify themselves with certain regions and though the regions might be larger now, as from "Illinois," instead of "Chicago," yet the provincial character of national life was preserved.

State Loyalties

It was this easy identification with a certain region in the predominantly agricultural ante-bellum nation that made the choice of State or Union so painful, yet so logical, to so many. Governmentally, the federated states were considered to be sovereign, each and every one; the Constitution of the federation which all named The United States of America specifically reserved to the several States a great many matters of administration within their own borders. Along with administration, went defense. Indians in the East were generally pacified, but in Florida a state of war existed between the Seminoles and the United States until the 1950's, when the first peace treaty was signed. In the West, the fashion of bearing arms was commonplace, for defense against the local savages and also against the savage elements of Eastern society which had located on the westward fringe of the nation. In the general absence of organized police forces before 1850, the citizen owed a duty to his state to come to the aid of his fellows during time of riot or civil insurrection. The John Brown attack on the arsenal was a civil insurrection; numerous were the militia companies from Virginia and nearby Maryland which answered the call and sent troops. Each state also recognized its allegiance to its fellow states in time of war. While warfare between individual states, as between, say, New York and Connecticut, had been renounced as a means of settling differences, in the Federal compact called The Constitution, the need to defend the country as a whole produced a strong emphasis on the militia system.

Origin of the Militia System

In later years it has been the fashion to discuss the value of a militia system, stronger state defense forces, in the United States, and point to the economy of little Switzerland's military establishment in justification of the idea. Curiously, a recent (1955) mimeographed paper distributed by the Swiss Embassy on the subject of the Swiss Army, in answer to so many questions from Americans, gives George Washington great credit for originating this idea. But to neither Washington nor the current generation of Swiss belongs the credit; instead, it belongs to an unsung Colonel Martin who in 1745 published a little tome "A Plan for Establishing and Disciplining a National Militia in Great Britain, Ireland, and in all the British Dominions of America." This book sells for very little in the United States today to bibliophiles; in England they cherish it as valued at some 35 pounds, $100. But Colonel Martin set forth clearly the ideas and the requirements that produced, in the United States, what the Swiss describe as a traditionally American system, a national militia. Oddly,

THE MILITIAMEN

Militiamen delighted in special equipment styled for their own issue. Brass-trimmed US M1855 Rifle was advocated for them because of similarity to French Zouave-issued Minie rifles. Sidearms were also individualized: Colt's M1855 .31 pocket model (top) has stock carved with head of helmeted dragoon.

Colonel Martin gives due credit to the Swiss in his pre-Revolutionary book. The point is not who "invented" the idea, but the implementation, and the implements, which accompanied its fruition in the United States by 1860.

The militia system served important needs in both North and South, though to some extent it is more closely identified with regions of relatively great personal wealth. Hence, while New York and Connecticut boasted important organizations, and the militia of Boston could date their origins in the Revolution, it was in the South that militia flourished as a part of society. In the North, however, there was no militia in being; as, for example, in June of 1863 when Pennsylvania was invaded. Only New York was able to send hastily formed bodies of state militia to Harrisburg.

Workingmen worked hard; farmers' hours were, over the nation, from dawn until dusk. Factories were installing gas lights to lengthen productivity during the winter days. Farmers had to work constantly to get crops in, or to plant, or to carry on the hundred and one affairs of agriculture. If the farmer was rich and owned slaves, so much the worse for him; so much greater the toil. Managerial duties, accounting, planning for shipments, importing the manufactured necessities, took time into the night, long after the field hands were asleep.

Military Training in the South

Though the modern idea seems to be that the Old South was just one long round of fancy balls, common sense if nothing else will inform you that the huge plantation houses now thought of as "typical Southern mansions" were not built by ne'er-do-wells and laggards. Without TV to waste the hours there was still no problem for the energetic of what to do with one's leisure time.

Yet defense of the State was also a social necessity. Supporting full-time military organizations was both costly and unnecessary, for a great many of the whites were organized into companies for local defense. The fear of an insurrection of slaves as the American-born plantation hands got book learning and religion inspired some of the drilling and military exercising. The threat of South Carolina's secession in the 1830's caused other units to spring up, for preparedness. Border troubles with Canada, in the 1840's prompted other units to come into being. And the gala social life of a military ball with its costumed pageantry, and the strains of a military band, caused the ladies to give their blessings to these schoolboy soldiering activities of their husbands and swains. Little did they realize that the same downy-cheeked lads they giggled over, in excruciatingly painful, high stiff collars and befrogged gray jackets, would prove to be some of the best fighting men the world had ever seen.

German-American Militia Rifles

Along the Mississippi, Missouri, and Ohio Rivers, the militia movement took on a distinct color. Made up of men who had fled their native German states to avoid

Colt's New Model Pocket model of Navy caliber (1862) has grips bearing tassel-capped head of Garibaldi, whose exploits in Italy inspired dress of red-shirt militia.

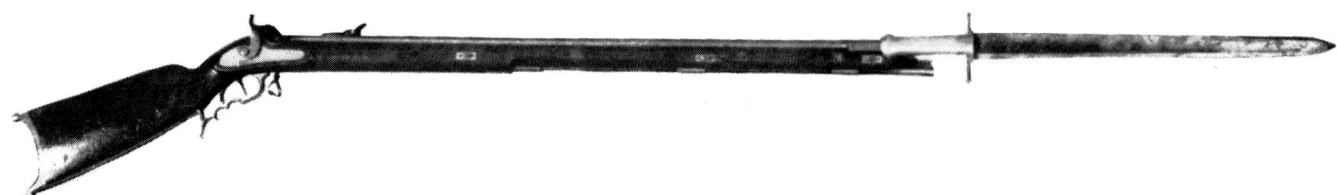

Sword bayonet-fitted Swiss military rifles used for shooting matches according to Army Regulations, had some influence and limited use on Ohio-Mississippi river line by Alpine rifle clubs.

impressment into service, paradoxically many good German-Americans now flocked to join a local militia company. The uniforms were a badge of honor, and the weekly get-togethers fitted in perfectly with their old-time *schuetzenfest* activities.

Special military target rifles were crafted by some of the gunsmiths of Cincinnati, or up in Milwaukee where other large German groups lived, to suit the needs of these dandy companies. A typical Schuetzen militia rifle will have the plain finish associated with the standard "plain" American or Kentucky rifle; sometimes back-action lock, percussion. Drop to the stock will be pronounced and the butt will be pronged in the form we now call "Swiss."

While European military target rifles are often round barreled, the octagon form seems to predominate among the few Ohio rifles examined. At the muzzle either a bayonet stud, or socket a la Swiss, or round-turned muzzle for socket bayonet, indicates the martial nature of the piece. Colonel Martin urged that military meetings be held after church services Sunday. Among those militia groups who adhered to this, grand picnics were the rule, with drills and maneuvers often crisply executed to the tone of commands barked by a local man who often as not had a distinguished war record in 1812 or 1848. Among the German-Swiss shooting societies who took on uniforms in the 1850's, prize shooting offhand at 200 meters, at the 25-ring target, attracted attention in the newspapers and afforded needed weekend relaxation as the golden beer foamed from the kegs.

Putnam Phalanx

In Connecticut, one well known militia association was formed as an honor guard for a special occasion but became preserved through war and peace to survive to this day. It is the Putnam Phalanx, named after old Israel Putnam, famous general of the Revolution.

Like other outfits, it centered on guarding the governor though in this instance it was a favored recent governor to be guarded. Thomas Seymour, Connecticut Governor in 1850-52, had been envoy to the Court of the Czar at St. Petersburg and in 1857 was scheduled to return home. So popular was he among some of the newer citizens, they wanted to do him honor.

The Putnam Phalanx was the answer. Dressed in Continental uniforms, they escorted the envoy's carriage across the green below the capitol, through a triumphal arch which they had caused to be erected in his honor and which stands today across a broad footpath over the green.

French Influence

Typical of the organization and service of a militia regiment was the record of New York's 9th Regiment, Volunteers, known after the name of their colonel as "Hawkins' Zouaves." Their uniform and organization were inspired by the regiments of French riflemen raised for service against the Arabs in North Africa in the 1840's. Many elite troops in the Civil War affected Zouave dress; Ellsworth's Zouaves of Chicago were among the first so raised.

France had abandoned the use of rifled military small arms during their Revolution. A short grooved-bore piece was made at the Versailles factory under direction of Nicolas Noel Boutet, the "carabine de Versailles." Issued to special troops and to soldiers trained to spread out in the front rank or protect the flank of regiments, as skirmishers, its issue ceased by the end of the war when the *levee en masse* had raised huge bodies of troops under Napoleon to be equipped with the common smoothbore musket.

By the 1830's, especially in the United States, sporting gun experiments included the development of elongated projectiles for hunting and target use. But these were not generally in use. France, meanwhile, had embarked upon a venture that required firepower accurately delivered at long range: the conquest of North Africa, in Algiers.

The War with Algiers began in 1830. The African tribes, notable among which were the Kabyles, used lance and swords and long, long, long barreled guns.

The Snaphaunce

Some flintlocks were in use but the majority were of a lock form long since obsolete in Europe, the Spanish-Dutch form of snaphaunce. Variously spelled snapharmce and schnapphaans, this lock form employed the striking action of flint in the jaws of a moving cock, against the rocking plate of a flintlock known as battery (because it battered the sparks from the flint) or frizzen (modern, corrupt). The pan cover was not in one piece with the battery as in the flintlock that superseded it, but was a separate movable slide that had to be pushed back to uncover the priming powder in the pan. Some locks accomplished this mechanically; with others, it was necessary to manually slide the pan cover back before firing. The design spread throughout the Spanish-Dutch trading area, even up to Scotland, and there on the ends of the trade routes, it froze for several centuries. As late as the end of the 19th century, snaphaunce guns of this same description were in production in Liege, Belgium, for trade with the "colonies."

The Kabyles made good use of these guns. Their barrels were sometimes as much as five feet in length; their bores were relatively small, about .50-inch to .75-inch, and the barrel wall was fairly thin. The type of powder used was a fine mealed powder, without much strength, and while lucky sheiks might have owned bullet moulds, more often than not their guns were filled with small shot rendered from a lump of lead hammered flat and cut into cubes with a knife. For wildfowling these weapons were doubtless effective, and against the French when loaded with solid shot they proved devastating. Rarely does any specimen of these ancient guns survive today in good enough condition for the modern shooting researcher to want to try them out. But the record is quite clear: the Arabs with their Long Toms outranged and outshot the best musketeers of France, and the war in Algeria bogged down until rifles capable of shooting more accurately at long range were procured for the French. These first rifles, issued to the Chasseurs d'Orleans, were of the System Delvigne.

The System Delvigne

In 1826 Captain Delvigne proposed a plan which was a variation of the plain round ball, in a rifled bore. After the ball had been pushed to the bottom on top of the powder, it was struck a smart blow or two to upset it into the rifling. Actually, little more than enough upsetting to cause friction between the ball and the bore surface was required. The combustion of gunpowder is at such a rapid rate when confined that its effect upon lead is that of a shock or blow, and if the Delvigne ball was held in place, the firing of the charge would make it upset enough to fill the grooves and gain force and direction as it went on its way.

What was new with Delvigne was his introduction of a conical bullet, the side of which was cylindrical, and the base flat. Early writers speak of this form of bullet, so commonplace nowadays, as "somewhat resembling Sir Isaac Newton's 'solid of least resistance.'"

Following the Delvigne carbine, actually a short rifle for the use of light infantrymen, the Chasseurs received an improved arm with the Thouvenin breech *a tige*. The *tige* of Colonel Thouvenin was a rod set into the inside of the chamber, usually screwed into the breech plug. The rod controlled the limit to which the bullet could be forced, and prevented it from crushing the powder, which fell into the space surrounding the *tige*. The ramrod with Thouvenin's rifle had a large head with a body of about 1 inch length to pass inside the barrel and center the bullet correctly along the axis of the bore. Thouvenin's bullet had a long ogive or front curve, a wide grease groove, and a short base slightly tapered inward.

The *Carabine a tige* with Delvigne or Thouvenin conical projectiles was supplied to the *Chasseurs d'Afrique* in 1846, and seemed capable of pacifying the Kabyles at long range. But the *tige* was liable to become bent; hence a new form of bullet was sought that would obviate the difficulties of being under bore size but could still be fired accurately.

Minié Balls

The proposal of Captain Minié seemed the answer. For by this time experiments had shown that the *tige* was not necessary to upset the bullet, and in Minié's design the bullet alone was the improvement. His bullet could be used in any rifled bore arm to advantage. Being made smaller than the bore of the piece, it could be dropped down a clean barrel onto the powder almost of its own weight. When the bore became fouled it was still possible to fire a greater number of shots with the Minié ball than with a Delvigne carbine. (See Chap. 4). So successful was this rifle of simple construction, that large issues of these were made to the Chasseurs d'Orleans to be used at their Practice School at Vincennes.

A new rifle embodying a relatively short barrel, and two bands, with the muzzle fitted for a sword "yataghan" bayonet, was developed for these crack riflemen. The *Carabine des Chasseurs de Vincennes* was one of the most accurate rifles of the world in the days of muzzle-loaders, and influenced not only the rifle tactics of the day but the design of at least one U.S. rifle, the "Whitneyville Plymouth" naval rifle designed by Captain, later Admiral, John A. Dahlgren.

Zouaves

For service in Africa these dandy troops, some of whom were recruited from among the hardy French settlers farming in Algiers, adopted distinctive uniforms. Closely modeled after those of the Arab world, the Chasseurs d'Afrique typically wore a short jacket, brocaded or otherwise ornamented; a pill-box or kepi, and baggy trousers flaring at the ankle and gathered in a

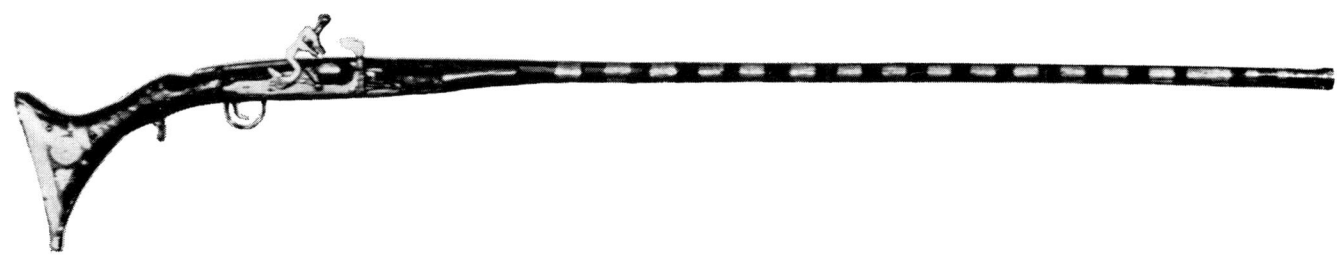

Unwieldy long-barreled snaphaunce smoothbore guns used by Kabyle tribes in North Africa against French troops outranged European muskets. African's superior shooting forced development of rifles. Butt was placed on breastbone, not on shoulder, when shooting.

voluminously bloused effect above the boots. Short buttoned leggins, spats, short boots, or dandy stockings, completed their uniform.

Many armies viewed the hussars or the dragoons as the elite troops, but the tough fighters of the Chasseurs d'Afrique, the "Zouaves," had no doubt that they were tops. Even their martial music had its effect on the culture of *la Patrie;* and into the music of Europe in the 1850's crept strains of oriental pageantry.

The first Zouaves were Kabyles mustered into the service of France when the Delvigne-equipped riflemen had tamed them a little. They proved good fighters, became expert at reloading the muzzle-loading rifle in the prone position. The characteristic dress became identified with bravery and courage. Under their French officers, disciplined as a part of the French Army, they fought against their fellow tribesmen. In 1837 the Kabyle Zouaves corps was divided into three battalions, and rolled up a distinguished battle record. By this time the native element was being eliminated, and by 1840 the Zouaves were almost 100 percent Europeans, uniformed as Arabs with French Army improvements.

New York Zouaves

It was these men who inspired the young militiamen of America. Zouave regiments expressing a variety of details in their uniforms but all borrowing from the Arabian bloused pantaloons, were organized. Early in 1860 a group of New Yorkers including Rush C. Hawkins, Barnett, Parisen, Hammil, Li Baire, Matthew J. Graham, and others, proposed to organize a company, uniformed as were these renowned fighters, to be known as "The New York Zouaves." Committees were formed and the business commenced; on 23 July, 1860 the corps was organized. An address by Rush Hawkins, who was elected colonel and who gave his name to the Regiment as it was later constituted, sets forth some of the spirit and sentiment about these private military units.

"Equality of social feeling should be inculcated to the most unlimited extent," Hawkins said. "Efficiency and good character should be the only recommendation for preferment . . . A feeling of brotherhood and friendliness should be cultivated." About the gay uniform which the corps adopted, Hawkins said, "We should also like to have each man made to feel that a uniform of glaring colors neither makes a man nor a soldier; but that the conduct, efficiency, and bearing of the wearer must decide whether he is a soldier, who knows what he professes, or a fool, wearing a uniform, not knowing why, except that it panders to his vanity, which is satisfied in exciting the ridicule of the sensible, the wonder of small boys, and the admiration of fools."

The precise equipment of this dandy but earnest group of part-time soldiers is not known. Article II of their bylaws reads: "The construction of the uniforms, equipments, and arms shall be similar to that of the French Zouaves." And in case of dispute, Article XI under "Drill-Tactics Adopted" says, "The drill shall be that of the United States Light Infantry, following as near as possible the exercises and discipline of Hardee, and the bayonet exercise of McClellan, except when these authors come in conflict with the drill of the French Zouaves. Then the latter shall prevail."

Captain R. H. K. Whiteley at Governors Island offered the Zouaves the services of Sergeant Louis Benzoni, described as a "consummate manualist" whose exaggerated posturings served to impress upon the young men the necessity for attention to the details of drill.

There were no regularly elected officers as yet and those who commanded the company one day would take their place in the ranks the next. Squads drilled twice weekly, and companies twice weekly. The group moved from provisional headquarters in New York at the Mercer House to a place on the corner of 4th and Thompson Streets. Opposite was the Washington Parade Ground, and the morning and evening maneuvers of the Zouaves were a pleasant and stimulating amusement to strollers during the summer months.

Unfortunately no record exists of the kind of small arms carried by these men prior to the war. Up to the fall of Sumter they were only playing at being soldiers.

When the bulletin boards of the daily papers about noon of April 15, 1861, announced the President's call for volunteers, the men asked their leader, Hawkins, to have him offer the Zouaves to the Government. This was done and on May 4, 1861, the regiment was mustered into Federal service, and designated the 9th New York Volunteer Infantry. The history of this regiment (*The Ninth Regiment, New York Volunteers,* by M. J. Graham) illustrates on its cover one of the Zouaves in full field dress complete with musket. On his head is a natty red Garibaldi cap from which depends a tassel. His hip-length blue jacket is edged in red and on its lapel faces two embroidered bands rise from the bottom ribs to end in a trefoil frog on each shoulder. The bloused blue pantaloons are tucked into white leggings over black shoes, while a "US" initial beltbuckle is backed up by a wide cummerbund or red waist sash. His rifle is, judging from the clear rendering of it in the cover stamping, a U.S. Rifle type 1855-65. Whether it is the Maynard primed 1855 arm or a later type cannot be seen, but the early dates of this company's service suggest they received Maynard primed 1855 rifle muskets. It was after their May federalizing that muskets were issued.

Colonel Hawkins, *after* being mustered into service, made contracts for all the regiment's clothing and equipment, except blankets, overcoats, and arms. It is possible that in the Zouaves' headquarters opposite Washington Parade Ground they only possessed enough rifles—could they have been of the Chasseurs de Vincennes model?—to equip a couple of companies for drill, and these were stored when the regiment went to war, in the interests of using U.S. standard arms, and saving wear and tear on their own.

CHAPTER 3

Ordnance-Industry: Mismatched Team

The militia system was for many years the underpinning of the small-arms procurement system in the United States. Both national armories' output was generally reserved for issue to Regular Army troops. For the militia, six private armories furnished arms under the Militia Act of 1808.

Under this sinecure there was appropriated annually $200,000 to be apportioned among the several states in proportion to the number of militia enrolled. For convenience of accounting, each state had a quota of arms established annually in terms of so many muskets. Thus, for example, South Carolina for 1850 might be allowed 200 muskets, but during the first part of the year had only drawn 100 actual muskets from among the private armories' production in the depot at Governor's Island or Washington Arsenal. South Carolina's militia authorities therefore would have a credit of 100 muskets still due, and could draw their value if desired in harness, cannon, field forges, or other military goods on an approved list of stores for issue under this Act. Sometimes it was possible for a state to carry over a credit to the following year, if an improved model was to be issued, or if a more valuable purchase, such as several batteries of artillery, were contemplated. At other times, states could, if their adjutant generals were persuasive enough, draw in one year materiel against the budget of the ensuing year.

Private Armories

The six private armories achieved quasi-governmental status in 1808, though one or two had been in business for a short time before that. From among all the contractors for arms in the country these six emerged: Asa Waters, of Sutton (now Millbury), Massachusetts, Simeon North of Berlin and later Middletown, Connecticut, Nathan Starr of Middletown, Eli Whitney of Whitneyville, near New Haven, Henry Deringer of Philadelphia, and Lemuel Pomeroy, of Pittsfield, Massachusetts. These private armories were regarded as permanent, having been publicly recognized by the Government as a part of the United States force for the supply of arms. In 1845, when the last contracts expired, the whole system was broken up, without notice. Firms such as Waters and Pomeroy dissolved.

Deringer continued making pistols but ceased to be a factor in armaments. Whitney continued to obtain contracts by reason of the technological excellence of his factory and interchangeable plan. Colonel North, old and in ill health, declined rapidly and upon his death in 1850 his government business ended. But the real reason for the end of the business was the actions of the Chief of Ordnance, Colonel George Talcott, who replaced Colonel George Bomford in 1845.

The Talcott Scandal

Talcott's predecessor, Colonel Bomford, was (like most Chiefs of Ordnance) a man of strong opinions. Practical experience had persuaded him that the flintlock musket was the best arm for the common soldier. Specialized privately patented arms enjoyed success in the hands of elite, trained troops in this country and abroad, such as Harney's Dragoons in Florida with Colt's rifles, and the Chasseurs de Vincennes in France with the earliest military rifles. Nevertheless Bomford did not "hold with the new-fangled patent arms and the rejection of flint and steel." He was instrumental in building up a system of coastal forts and developed for them large-caliber cast-iron shell guns known as "Columbiads."

In 1844, Bomford ordered the building of a Columbiad on a wrought-iron built-up principle. The "Peacemaker" was one of the largest guns in service at that time. Installed aboard the U.S.S. *Princeton,* it was readied for a demonstration before the new Secretary of the Navy, Abel P. Upshur, and President Tyler himself. On the third drill round, the gun burst, smashing a piece of wrought-iron breech into Upshur's chest, killing him, and nearly getting the President.

Bomford's Columbiad was not a success, and it remained for the technology of a later date to perfect a successful wrought-iron cannon.

Colonel Bomford, aging, was retired the following year. In his stead, his subordinate, Talcott, was appointed Chief of Ordnance. With Colonel Bomford having laid the foundations of a Columbiad shell-gun fortress system girding the nation's coast, Talcott was in a position to profit. He profited not from the six private armories, but from another means.

When the contracts for muskets and small arms, and the new Mississippi Rifles made by Whitney, were not renewed, the six private armories were distressed. One of these armorers, Asa Holman Waters, later published (1878) a most interesting document titled "Gunmaking in Sutton & Millbury." In this privately printed book he described the situation under Talcott's regime:

"Since the gunmakers had large capital invested in equipment of no use in anything but arms manufacture, they were distressed. They asked General George Talcott (he was later brevet brigadier), of Ordnance, why their contracts were ended. He replied, 'It was done in obedience to instructions from the Honorable the Secretary of War.' This honorable secretary was Wilkins of Pennsylvania, who soon after retired from office, and when asked why he issued the order, said 'he did not know he had; that Talcott sent in so many papers it was as much as he could do to sign them; he had no time to read them.'

"The condition of things at the department appears to be that while honorable secretaries were coming and going every few months, Talcott remained there in permanence; had been there many years, and had become a perfect autocrat in the office. The only use he had for honorable secretaries was to sign his papers, and if any complaint arose, his uniform reply was, 'Done in obedience to instructions from the Honorable the Secretary of War,' thus making the Secretary a scapegoat for all his sins. But a terrible retribution came at last.

"When President Polk came into power (1846), he appointed as Secretary of War a lawyer from New Orleans by the name of Conrad, whose knowledge of war office business was confined chiefly to the 'code and pistols for two.' He took the customary round of visiting the armories and arsenals, and wherever he went he noticed vast stacks and pyramids of cannon balls. On his return he sent a simple order to (now) General Talcott, to issue no more contracts for cannon ball.

"Not long after, among the papers sent in for him to sign, he happened to notice a new contract for cannon ball. He writes to Talcott to know why it was issued. Talcott replies in his usual style, 'done in obedience to instructions, etc.' Conrad answers that 'so far as being done in obedience, it was in disobedience to instructions, etc.' Talcott, in reply had the presumption to reaffirm his previous statement. Conrad's ire was raised at once; said he did not know much about cannon ball but on matters of veracity he was at home. Being in official station he could not challenge Talcott (to a duel) and so he ordered him to be tried by court martial before a board of which General Winfield Scott was made judge advocate. Much more was proved in the trial than was expected. It appeared in evidence that General Talcott was the owner of a large factory in Richmond, Virginia, devoted to making cannon ball; that it was in charge of his nephew, to whom he issued, from time to time, large contracts upon most favorable terms; that he had become very rich; was the owner of large blocks in Washington, where he was living in the style of an eastern nabob.

"The mystery of the discontinuance of the private armories was now revealed. The moneys intended for their support found their outlet chiefly through this channel.

"General Scott, with his high sense of honor, was greatly shocked that a government official so high in position, a graduate of West Point, a brigadier general in the Army, and Chief of the Ordnance Department, should be found guilty of such corrupt embezzlement. His sentence was terribly severe, almost without precedent. In brief, it was that General Talcott should be removed from the office of Chief of Ordnance, be deprived of his commission of brigadier general, his name erased from the roll of Army officers, and be sent in disgrace out of Washington."

"In Talcott's Footsteps"

While Bomford and Talcott had a profound effect upon the small-arms program of the nation during their tenures of office, I had never given the matter another thought until 1957. Then, during an October meeting of the American Ordnance Association at Aberdeen Proving Ground, I and four thousand other members of this civilian-military league of men concerned with national defense listened to an address on the Ordnance Department's record by Secretary of War Wilber Brucker. I had to stifle my burst of laughter as the Secretary spoke of the men of today's Ordnance Corps "following in the footsteps of the great Bomford and Talcott." Whether the Secretary's speech writer had a most winsome sense of humor, or simply couldn't know any better, I never did find out. Considering the snafus and goof-ups in our ordnance program from small arms through to missiles with which the ensuing years have been marked, I wonder if some unsung scribe in the Secretary's speech-writing staff didn't hit the nail on the head. Historically, the succeeding Chiefs of Ordnance who followed Talcott were a little better. Under Colonel H. K. Craig, through direction of Jefferson Davis, great strides were made in small arms for militia and for the Army. The emphasis swung away either from the private armories supply concept, or from buying cannon balls from the Chief of Ordnance's own foundry, to greater reliance upon the national armories.

The build up at both Harpers Ferry and Springfield, as well as the foundry at Pittsburgh, and the increase of activity restoring old arms, transforming flint muskets to percussion, and building minor stores like gun carriages and holsters at the regional arsenals, was both good and bad. Those establishments which remained in the North worked well for the Union. Those which were in the South constituted reservoirs of technology upon which much of Southern war production was based.

Oddly, General Talcott's buying of excessively large amounts of cannon balls from his Richmond foundry contributed to the improvement in Virginia's ordnance production during the Civil War. For war was coming; even during the 1850's few doubted it.

CHAPTER 4

The Rifle, The Primer, The Ball

The rifle was the major tactical weapon of the war. Rifles were issued to armies both North and South. These were mainly new weapons, of novel pattern. Basic to both fighting forces were Springfield rifles Models 1855 and 1861, and the British 1853-56 Enfields bought by the hundred thousands from abroad. Despite the scarcity of many goods in the South as the conflict dragged on, rifles were usually in ample supply.

But the significant thing was that the rifle, as a weapon of war, was brand new. A rifle could fire a bullet with man-killing accuracy over 800 yards, much farther than the effective range of the smoothbore muskets which had been supplanted by rifles in the infantry for only a half dozen years. And the battles of the War were fought with tactics adapted to musketry engagements. The slaughter created by this mixing of old and new patterns of fighting was terrible, and resulted in making the American Civil War the bloodiest conflict of modern times.

Rifle Effect at Fredericksburg

In Burnside's assault on the high ground south of Fredericksburg, Union troops with fixed bayonets charged a fortified position occupied by 6,000 Confederate troops and 20 guns. Many of these were riflemen. While some troops, notably Meagher's brigade, reached the stone wall at the base of the hill, they were cut to pieces on the way. Meanwhile their supporting columns had become exposed to the longer range canister and case fire of Confederate artillery batteries. The whirling balls delivered in a cannon burst at a thousand yards cut the troops down. Joe Hooker was ordered by Burnside to renew the assault. Hooker's report claimed "the fire of the enemy now became still hotter. The stone wall was a sheet of flame that enveloped the head of the column. Officers and men fell so rapidly that orders could not be passed." Officers with flashing sabers (cost $20, deducted from the officer's pay) and enlisted men with rifles and bayonets fixed (stand complete, $20) charged at the run, as their ancestors had done a century before in Europe, offering to cool marksmen targets two feet wide and five feet high. Only sheer weight of numbers allowed part of the Union lines to reach the emplaced Confederates, and the assault failed. Fredericksburg rated as one of the greatest slaughters of the war.

Rifle Capabilities Already Known

Yet the awful capabilities of the rifle were not unknown to men on both sides. The papers enjoyed publishing incidents of marksmanship matches. *The Baltimore Sun* in March, 1856 recounted an anecdote of the War of 1812. Colonel William Stansbury's First Rifle Regiment "amused themselves in shooting, Captain Ezekiel Burke frequently cutting off small bird's heads, and in a match with a great shot from Kentucky, for $100 at sixty yards off-hand. Burke won, putting three balls in the same hole so that until they were cut out of the tree all thought his last two shots had missed the mark." Unfortunately, wide issue of rifles was not at that time accompanied by any scientific study of the change in field tactics they dictated.

Rifle shooting was popular in some areas of the country. German settlers in the Ohio Valley—men who later were to make up a large part of Franz Sigel's beer-drinking soldiers—were expert riflemen. At a meeting of an Ohio rifle club just before the Civil War, 30 men put 10 shots each inside a 10-inch circle at 300 yards. It is also recorded that at a distance of three-fourths of a mile, many shots had been put inside a flour barrel without a miss.

Examples of Effect of Rifle Fire During the Civil War

There were plenty of individual opportunities for combatants to learn the range of rifle fire. "From a distance of nearly half a mile the Rebel sharpshooters drew a bead on us with a precision which deserved the highest commendation of their officers, but which made us curse the day they were born," wrote William Henry De Forest in *A Volunteer's Adventures*.

"One incident proves, I think," he continued, "that they were able to hit an object further off than they could distinguish its nature. A rubber blanket, hung over the stump of a sapling five feet high, which stood in the center of our bivouac, was pierced by a bullet from this quarter. A minute later a second bullet passed directly over the object and lodged in a tree behind it. I ordered the blanket to be taken down, and then the firing ceased. Evidently the invisible marksman eight hundred yards away had mistaken it for a Yankee."

Even more graphic in the clash of battle is De Forest's description of a fire-fight involving his Twelfth Connecticut opposed by the Second Alabama:

"We laid a line of logs along the crest of the knoll, cut notches in them, and then put on another tier of logs, thus providing ourselves with portholes. With the patience of cats watching for mice the men would peer for hours through the portholes, waiting for a chance to shoot a rebel; and the faintest show of a hat above the hostile fortifications, indistinguishable to the naked eye, would draw a bullet. By dint of continual practice many of our fellows became admirable marksmen. During one of the truces the Confederates called to us, 'Aha, you have some sharpshooters over there!'

"After the surrender an officer of the Second Alabama told me that most of their casualties were cases of shots between the brim of the hat and the top of the head; and that once having held up a hoe handle to test our marksmanship, it was struck by no less than three bullets in as many minutes. The distance from parapet to parapet was not great; our men sighted it on their Enfields as one hundred and fifty yards. . . . Several of our men were shot in the face through the portholes as they were taking aim. One of these unfortunates, I remember, drew his rifle back, set the butt on the ground, leaned the muzzle against the parapet, turned around, and fell lifeless. He had fired at the moment he was hit, and two or three eyewitnesses asserted that his bullet shivered the edge of the opposite porthole, so that in all probability he and his antagonist died together. It must be understood that these openings were just large enough to protrude the barrel of a musket and take sight along it."

Firing from a parapet rest, protected by trench or decline, was something new to ways of war in 1861. Traditional officers, striving to make their volunteers fight "like Regulars," often contributed to the deaths of their command by blind stupidity in obedience to the rule book. De Forest's Twelfth Connecticut were on one occasion ordered to "Halt! Fire by File! Commence Firing!"

"The men could not wait to fire by file," remarked De Forest, "which is a gradual discharge running from right to left of each company; they leveled those five hundred rifles together and sent a grand, crashing volley into the hostile line of smoke which confronted them; for as yet we could see no other sign of an enemy. In the next second everyone was loading his piece as if his life depended on the speed of the operation.

". . . It was the last stop or pause in our advance. We had been drilled long enough under fire, and we broke away from the lieutenant colonel. Once he tried his utmost to make us halt, dress the line and give a volley, as Regulars are said to do in battle. But he might as well have ordered a regiment of screeching devils to halt. On we swept in the teeth of canister and musketry, every man loading and firing as fast as possible. There was such a pressure inward toward the colors that some of my lightweights were crowded out of place, and we were three ranks deep instead of two."

The effect of two charges against hidden riflemen was bloodily typical of such attacks. At the battle of Seven Pines, Townsend requested permission of General Meagher to view the battlefield and relics. "Meagher said, in his musical brogue, that I need only look around," wrote Townsend in *Rustics in Rebellion*.

" 'From the edge of that wood,' he (Meagher) said, 'the Irish brigade charged across this field, and fell upon their faces in the railway cutting below. A regiment of Alabamians lay in the timber beyond, with other Southerners in their rear, and on both flanks. They thought that we were charging bayonets, and reserved their fire till we should approach within butchering distance. On the contrary, I ordered the boys to lie down, and load and fire at will. In the end, sir, we cut them to pieces, and five hundred of them were left along the swamp fence, that you see. There isn't fifty killed and wounded in the whole Irish brigade.' "

But Yankees as well went down before the withering fire of skilled riflemen. While the excitement of battle may have thrown many an untrained soldier into a panic, it also served to steady many an eye and aim by the realization of the earnestness of the business at hand. Especially with the Southern troops, active participation in fire fights was the rule. More than their mechanic and workman counterparts in the Yankee forces, Johnny Rebs were outdoor men, accustomed to eking out their meager livings on poor ridge farms, with the capabilities of their squirrel rifles. They, as infantry soldiers, had a predisposition to shoot, and did.

Townsend gives another example of rifle-fire effect during the Civil War: "A large number of Southern riflemen threw themselves into a corner of wood, considerably advanced from their main position. Their fire was so destructive that General Banks felt it necessary to order a charge. Two brigades, when the signal was given, marched in line of battle, out of a wood, and charged across a field of broken ground toward the projecting corner. As soon as they appeared, sharpshooters darted up from a stretch of scrub cedars on their right, and a battery mowed them down by an oblique fire from the left. The guns up the mountainside threw the shells with beautiful exactness," said Townsend, who was an Englishman and could view the annihilation of Union men with equanimity, "and the concealed riflemen in front poured in deadly showers of bullet and ball. As the men fell by dozens out of line, the survivors closed up the gaps, and pressed forward gallantly. The ground was uneven, however, and a solid order could not be observed throughout. At length, when they had gained a brookside at the very edge of the wood, the column staggered, quailed, fell into disorder, and then fell back. Some of the more desperate dashed singly into the thicket, bayoneting their enemies, and falling in turn in the fierce grapple.

Others of the Confederates ran from the wood, and engaged hand to hand with antagonists and, in places, a score of combatants met sturdily upon the plain, lunging with knife and sabre bayonet, striking with clubbed musket, or discharging revolvers. But at last the broken lines regained the shelter of the timber, and there was a momentary lull in the thunder."

Just how typical were these two charges of standing-up infantry against concealed riflemen is shown by the vital—really vital—Federal statistics of the battle at Cedar Creek.

"Our casualties at Cedar Creek were 569 killed, 3,425 wounded, 1,429 prisoners, and 341 missing, in all 5,764. Early (Lieutenant General Jubal A. Early, CSA) conceded a loss of 1,860 killed and wounded, and we took about 1,200 prisoners, making a total of near 3,100," reported De Forest.

"It must be confessed that we bought our victory at a dear rate," he continued. "For instance, we had 4,000 men hit to the enemy's 1,800, although we were fully double their number, and presumably used twice as many cartridges.

"As I have said before, they were obviously the best shots, and their open-order style of fighting was an economical one. Moreover, when they retreated, they went in a swarm and at full speed, thus presenting a poor mark for musketry. We, on the contrary, sought to retire in regular order, and suffered heavily for it."

Characteristics of the Rifle

What was this wonder weapon of the day? What strange power possessed this not-at-all secret weapon which the United States Army had been considering for some years, and on which the Ordnance Department had comprehensive studies embracing the use, design, and manufacture in detail? Perhaps the power was so simple that military minds did not grasp the full importance of it: with a rifle, a trained marksman could hit where he aimed.

Fundamentally, a rifle is a gun with grooves in the barrel. These grooves run the length of the barrel from breech to muzzle. In very primitive rifles, these grooves may have been straight. Later, the grooves became cut in a spiral so that the bullet spun as it left the bore. The word itself is derived from from an old German word, *riffeln,* "to groove."

The reasons behind the development of rifles are twofold—the first is a self-evident reason; the second, accidental. Straight rifling was created in an attempt to reduce bore friction in charging a muzzle-loading weapon. Old smoothbore muskets were loaded with round balls of lead. The diameter of the bullet was smaller than the diameter of the bore. For example, the common infantry musket of .69 caliber used a bullet .64 inches in diameter. This reduction permitted the gun to be loaded, even though it had a coating of black powder fouling on the bore surface from preceding shots. But as the fouling became heavier from shooting, the muzzle-loading routine became more difficult.

Development of the Rifle and its Bullet

The matchlock muskets used in European warfare in the 1650's were loaded with wooden ramrods. After a number of shots, the wooden ramrods broke and the guns were rendered useless. The employment of a stiff, strong iron ramrod was a distinct invention, and gave the troops of Swedish ruler Gustavus Adolphus supremacy in the field when he first tried steel or iron ramrods. This was one step forward. Another step was to cut away a part of the bore to permit the fouling to collect in the grooves. This was the first straight rifling.

Bullets that were undersized had the habit of bounding down the barrel on discharge, striking first one point on the bore and then another. When the bullet left the muzzle it might strike yards off the target, in any direction, depending on the last bounce it made in its hectic journey from breech to muzzle. This was wholly unpredictable and resulted in poor accuracy. With the grooved barrel, bullets that more closely fitted the bore could be used, with a consequent increase in musket accuracy.

But the straight grooved barrels, occurring very early in arms development in middle Europe, were quickly obsoleted by spiral rifling. The spiral acted on the flight of the bullet as the fletching does to the arrow. By causing the bullet to rotate in the air, a fresh angle of the front of the bullet was constantly exposed to the wind resistance. The rotation of the bullet about its own axis kept the bullet from drifting off its path. The tight fit achieved with part of the rifling cutting into the bullet gave more force by confining the powder for better combustion, high compression, and by avoiding the bounding of the bullet in the barrel, "balloting."

While commercial arms, notably the Tyrolean "Long Jaeger" and the American Kentucky sporting arms, were rifled in the early 1700's, the adoption of rifling by the military powers of the world was put off for more than a century. There was good reason. Rifling was impractical under battle conditions, using solid round bullets. The bullet wrapped in greased cloth patches, like that for the Jaeger or Kentucky rifle bullet, was too slow for military field fighting. When the backwoodsman could select his targets, the Kentucky was supreme. In the melee of the battlefield it was of limited use. Captain Minié made the rifle practical for war. The "minney ball" was the standard rifle bullet of both sides in the conflict.

The Minié Ball

Captain Minié's invention was quite simple, yet it had the advantage of being the first of its kind. Such a thing is patentable, and indeed the astute Frenchman did patent the bullet. As a consequence the British Government paid M. Minié £ 20,000 for the rights to a simple shaping of lead—a bullet of modern conical form, with a hollow base and an iron cup in the base.

Minié's principle was simplicity itself. Round bullets balloted or were too difficult to load. Conical bul-

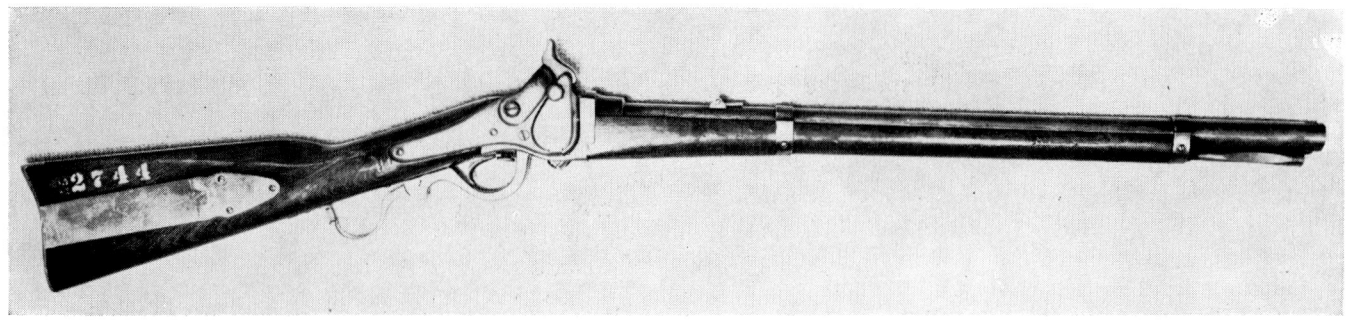

Many tests were conducted under Jefferson Davis' tenure as War Secretary to apply the Maynard tape primer to patent arms of different types. Shown is Symmes under-lever breechloader with dropping block somewhat like the Sharps. Two-band musketoon was styled for dragoons and Navy; few were made.

lets were heavier for the same caliber, and thus would range farther and with more force. Conical bullets were more accurate than round bullets. The problem: to load a conical bullet that would, on firing, completely seal the bore. Minié used the hollow base and iron cup design, built into a bullet that was much smaller than the bore and dropped easily down a clean barrel and a little more stiffly down a dirty barrel.

When gunpowder is ignited in a gun chamber, a very abrupt pressure rise occurs. A peak pressure is reached almost immediately, and then the pressure drops as the bullet travels out the barrel. This pressure rise is so rapid as to be a blow on the base of the bullet. With the Minié ball this blow drove the cup into the soft lead, expanding the skirt of the bullet to bore diameter. The wedge shape of the cup, and the speed at which this happened, kept the bullet centered for accuracy, and yet gave maximum force by completely blocking the rush of gas past a too-small bullet.

Minié was not the first to try this. In 1841, shortly after the adoption of the round-ball "Brunswick rifle" by the British, a Birmingham gunmaker named W. Greener invented an expanding bullet. It was a round ball with a tapered hole in the surface. A plug was stuck in the hole. On loading, the plug was driven down with the last motion of the ramrod, and this expanded the bullet, sealing the bore. Greener's design was published in his book on shooting, in 1841, and the Greener people are of the belief that Captain Minié saw this and copied the expanding plug idea from Greener. In token of his claims to priority, the Crown later awarded Greener a tardy £ 1,000, probably to shut him up rather than as an award for an invention of merit. The truth was that Greener in 1841 was behind the times, designing a round ball for rifles. Here Minié had the advantage, and the Frenchman used a conical or "picket" bullet.

During the war there were two major "minney muskets," the Enfield built in England, and the Springfield pattern of 1855, with wartime modifications.

Jefferson Davis's Influence

It was under Secretary of War Jefferson Davis that the small arms program of the United States underwent a complete transformation. He found the Army's weapons to be muzzle-loading muskets; when he left office, rifled muskets had been developed, mechanical cap-primers built into the lock mechanisms, and extensive trials with breechloaders conducted. Not one to play excessive favorites among manufacturers, he procured sample lots of hundreds each of a number of revolvers and new carbines, to test them in terms of their patentee's claims and the actual needs of the several services.

Davis eventually owned quite a representative collection of small arms, many of them military. Some were received as gifts from arms makers; others he undoubtedly bought or received from friends. One gift survives only in part: a handsome brace of Colt M1851 Navy revolvers complete with detachable shoulder stock. This set very likely was received by him during his tenure as Secretary of War, and was a personal gift from Colt. The outfit was a display for the desk or mantelpiece, constituting, as it did, a set of arms for service, for it was put up in the special glass-topped casing, without partitions, which Colt reserved for very special clients and friends. A complete set like this is a cased rifle and Navy pistol en suite which Colt gave to Elisha Root; this handsome outfit is still preserved in the Colt collection in Hartford. The set of pistols owned by Davis has been scattered; one gun, fitted with the stock studs in the frame, is in the Confederate "White House" memorial museum in Richmond. In another room, the Florida room, is the glass-topped special box, smaller than the Elisha Root chest and without the gold lettering, but unmistakably of the same workmanship. I tried to get Miss India Thomas, the gracious custodian of these items to rejoin the pistol and the case, but she stated this could not be done. Of much greater interest to the collector would be the location of an experimental carbine about which Colt wrote in 1855, saying to Root that he must push along the work on the model arms including the carbine with Maynard tape primer "to please the fancies of the present Secretary of War." If Davis had any favorite, it was the application of the novel Maynard tape primer to musket, pistol, and carbine.

The Maynard Tape Primer

Forerunner of today's toy paper cap for children's pistols, the roll of varnished detonating pellets Dr. Edward Maynard invented made more money for him than a lifetime of pulling teeth. Maynard's title of doctor was evidently as a doctor of dental surgery. Why or how he came to invent his priming device is not recorded, but pelletizing the detonating compound recalls the pelletizing of dental amalgam before the hearty doctor jams it into the tooth cavity he has chopped out, and peens it down with his tools. The musketeer used a small brass cap shaped like a plug hat, with four or six petals in the "brim." The inner top was spread with priming, varnished to make it moisture proof in storage. To prime the gun, the cap was placed on the nipple and the hammer snapped from full cock. Since this miniscule item was not easily pulled from its fleece-lined cap pouch by a man with cold or clumsy fingers, the design left much to be desired. Sportsmen solved the dilemma by inventing a turnip-sized brass magazine to carry 20 or 50 caps which, driven by an internal spring, popped into steel spring fingers at the exit of the magazine. The gunner could easily slip the cap over the nipple and, upon withdrawing the cap magazine, the cap pulled easily free of the retaining fingers. But few military men had the opportunity to acquire such an item and it was not Government issue. Maynard's conception allowed the soldier to charge the musket lock itself with a supply of spare priming, avoiding both the extra operations and the hazards of individually capping for each shot.

Individual prime pellets were stuck on strong paper tape. A thin top layer of tape was glued over this, all well varnished to make it waterproof. The tape was coiled, with 25 primers for pistols and carbines, or 50 primers for the larger locks of muskets and rifles.

Attached to the lock plate forward of the hammer, or built into the lock plate itself if the plate was forged big enough, was a round cavity closed by a swinging trap door. Such a priming magazine was fitted to many of the Sharps guns, 1853 and '55 models, and to the Massachusetts Arms Company revolvers designed by Joshua Stevens. When the hammer is cocked, an attached pawl or hand like in a common revolver moves the cap tape one pellet space and upon pulling the trigger, the hammer in falling shears off the exposed cap shoved out a slit in top of the priming box and explodes it on the nipple. With good caps and a sharp-edged hammer, the Maynard tape primer is a decided improvement upon common musket caps. Perhaps Jefferson Davis thought of the troubles his men had with common caps, in loading their Mississippi Rifles during the Mexican War. At any rate, he was a firm booster of the Maynard primer. Further, he had the approval of past years to guide him, for Maynard's invention had already been applied to Government muskets and sums of money paid out to him for the royalty rights.

In March, 1845, the Ordnance Department contracted with Maynard for the right to apply his lock to 4,000 muskets, paying him $4,000. The contract included the right reserved to the Government to put Maynard locks on 10,000 additional arms for payment of $7,500; or to 20,000 arms for payment of $10,000; or 100,000 arms upon payment of $25,000. If any greater number were desired, the price was to be negotiated, but in no case was to run over 25¢ per arm.

The first lot of guns so altered was 200 Model 1840 flintlock muskets, converted by Daniel Nippes of Philadelphia to percussion (drum conversion) with special flat-shanked hammer and Maynard box attached to the lock plate. These arms were issued in the Ninth Military Department for field trials. On February 9, 1848, Nippes contracted to modify 1,000 muskets to Maynard primer percussion at $4 each and on November 22, 1848, an additional 1,000 at $3. The cover of these primer mechanisms is stamped, MAYNARD'S PATENT WASHINGTON 1845 or EDWARD MAYNARD PATENTEE 1845.

When Jefferson Davis assumed office he felt the Maynard primer deserved a little greater test and accordingly sewed up Maynard by payment of an additional $50,000. For this sum, to be paid in three equal installments (except for the odd penny), Maynard on February 3, 1854 sold to the Government the right to use his design without restriction on Army or Navy small arms.

Remington Arms Company in Ilion having faithfully filled its earlier contracts for U. S. Rifles M1841, the Government again turned to them for the primer conversions. Always an under bidder, Remington received a contract to alter 20,000 muskets to tape primer at $3.15 each, on September 9, 1854. The alteration included a new, somewhat longer lock plate, marked REMINGTON'S/ ILION, NY/ 1857/ US, behind the hammer. Though the hammer spur of this "Remington Maynard Primer" lock is relatively "rabbit eared," that is to say, long, the form of hammer, hinged Maynard magazine door or cover, and cone seat on the barrel, are all quite similar to that shape shortly afterwards standardized by Jefferson Davis when he approved the new model U. S. Rifle Model 1855.

Credit Harpers Ferry Arsenal

No one now can be credited for developing this important design which was to be the basis for production of some million pieces during the war. Probably it took form under direction of Master Armorer Anderson or his assistant, James H. Burton, at Harpers Ferry, though Colonel H. K. Craig, Chief of Ordnance, superseding Talcott, may have had something to do with its styling. The forms of the lock adapted to the Remington conversion entered into it, and the backward-curving hammer was necessary to surround the shape of the Maynard primer magazine. Harpers Ferry Arsenal was preferred in this period to Springfield as a place of development (the U. S. Rifle 1841 had first been developed there) because of its closeness to Washington. To Harpers Ferry Arsenal in Virginia, then, belongs a rather dubious dual credit. It was this arsenal which originated the new standard rifle of the Union. It was this Arsenal that supplied, at first, tools and know-how from which Springfield Armory set up its production lines. It was this arsenal also that supplied the machinery which by capture went to the Richmond Arsenal for use by the Confederacy and it was this arsenal which supplied, in the person of Assistant Master Armorer James H. Burton, a man whose technical skill contributed materially to the strength of the South. As a site for experiments by Ordnance officers acting on direct orders from Washington, it was ideal.

Huger's Tests

Colonel Benjamin Huger (later General Huger, C.S.A.) conducted tests in the winter of 1853-4 with a representative selection of then-modern rifles and muskets from several countries. Some were specially-constructed United States experimental arms applying the *a tige* principle of the Thouvenin system, and others. The experiments by Huger and Lieutenant J. G. Benton both at Harpers Ferry and at Springfield, together with technical extracts from the writings of L. Panot, instructor in riflery at Vincennes, and experiments by Colonel Gordon conducted at the Enfield Royal Small Arms Factory in England in 1853, were ordered printed by Colonel H. K. Craig, "for the use of the Army, and for distribution to the militia, not doubting that it will afford information useful and interesting to both . . ."

For Huger, seven rifles were made at Harpers Ferry in 1852-53 of musket caliber .69, and three of regulation .54 rifle bore. All were rifled with five grooves, commencing at the breech .02 inches deep and lessening in a slight choke to the muzzle at .0125-inch depth. Twists short as one in 4 feet were tried, to one in 6 feet; uniform twist and gain twist. Each rifle had a *tige* fitted inside to the breech plug; and the Thouvenin or Delvigne type solid conical bullet was used, as well as the cup-based bullets of the Minié form.

Nos. 1, 2, 3, and 4, were musket barrels cut to 33 inches (same length for all guns). Nos. 8 and 9 were special barrels, a little heavier, each weighing nearly one pound more than the others. No. 5 rifle had a cast steel barrel from the U. S. 1841 rifle, reamed up to musket caliber, and weighed 4½ ounces more than the first type. Nos. 6 and 7 were also rifle barrels, prepared for the test. Gun No. 10 was a regulation rifle (1841) barrel, without any alteration in its construction. The rifling depth of this bore was uniform, .02-inch, from breech to muzzle. Guns 6 and 7 (rifle caliber .54), were very little used. They were not fitted with the *tige* nor tried with the original Minié bullet which was .69; the first modification of the Minié bullet did not answer in the smaller caliber so these rifles are not listed in the table of experiments.

The five-groove bore was chosen, said Huger, because with expanding bullets there should be an odd number with a groove opposite each land; for when the ball is forced or expanded into the rifling, "each land tends to push the opposite part of the ball into a groove, consequently the ball is less deformed than where the number of grooves is even, when a land would be opposite a land, and a groove opposite a groove." Though modern-day rifle barrel maker G. R. Douglas, whose shop is not far away in Charleston, West Virginia, might be surprised at this technical information (his "ultrarifled" super-accurate barrels are 8-groove), the odd-groove idea was widely believed in the 1850's. Conclusions from these shooting tests, at ranges from 200 to 880 yards, affected the design of the ultimately-adopted 1855 rifle.

It was discovered that a twist greater than 1 turn in 6 feet increased the lateral deviation of the ball at the target. A twist spinning the ball from left to right caused the bullet to go to the right of point of aim; a left twist sent the ball to the left. In the rifles having twists of one turn in 4 or 5 feet, it was found necessary to adjust the sights to compensate for this drift at long distances. Using the regulation 1841 rifle, one in six, the "derivation" as the French called this drift, was not appreciable at 500 yards range. Gain twist, long a favorite of picket-ball riflesmiths for match shooting, and of Sam Colt in his revolvers, did not show up to advantage in these experiments. In the gain twist, the rate of the rifling curve increases rapidly at the muzzle, while seeming to be almost straight at the breech. The idea presumably was to allow the bullet to get well started in the rifling before giving it the rotary motion necessary for top-like stability in flight.

Huger considered the *tige,* while serving to expand the bullet, was inconvenient when cleaning the arm. Fouling would lurk about the *tige* and since the cleaning rod or wiper could not pass all the way to the bottom of the bore, it presented a problem in handling the gun. He also discovered that the ball must not be rammed too much, for deforming it would make it unstable. Too little ramming of course defeated the purpose of the *tige*. The French *tige* projected into the barrel 1.49 inches, with a diameter of .35 inches—presumably those in the U. S. rifles tested measured the same.

Having studied the *tige* system, Huger next turned to the bullet of Captain Minié:

"The balls of this kind, made according to the description of those used in France, did not succeed in our experiments. The cup was often driven so forcibly into the ball as to cause the ball to break. Mr. James H. Burton, the acting master armorer, who conducted the experiments, contrived a different method of expanding the ball by a plug of hard metal. This plug answered the purpose, and the firing at 200 yards was very good. The plug was cast of a mixture of lead and tin and was easily made. The objections to it were that this piece fell out easily after a short flight, and might do injury in firing over our own men; it required a little greater elevation than with the *tige* at the same distances; and the paper of the cartridge around the bottom, forming the patch to the ball, was nipped by the plug being driven up suddenly. Efforts were made to find a better form of plug, and this bullet was not tried at ranges exceeding 200 yards."

A compound bullet, having a plug at the tip which was tapped down by the ramrod, upon seating the projectile, was next tried. The plug expanded the soft lead of the bullet into the rifling. This bullet also gave fairly good results, but the two-part construction was an objection, and the ramming tended to cake the powder. If the gun was fired at once, this was no problem, but if the gun remained loaded for any length of time, the crushed powder tended to attract moisture through the nipple vent and a misfire or weakened explosion resulted, causing inaccuracy.

Huger concluded that a conical bullet with the musket caliber was too much; the bullet would weigh about 1¾ ounce, too much for the soldier to carry ammunition in quantity, and the cost of transportation of supplies to the frontier was increased. With that caliber bullet, the charge must be limited by the practical recoil which the soldier can bear. While this is compounded of form of buttstock, mass of musket, height, weight and shooting style of the soldier, and the excitement of battle or hunt, there were limits. The French rifle charge was about 1/11th the weight of the bullet; with the modified Minié bullets tested the charge was 1/10. Using the rifle caliber (.54) arm, 1/8 weight of the projectile was found "the most efficient charge."

Considering the advantages of using the smaller caliber, Huger and Burton now tried to develop a modified Minié for the 1841 rifle, .54. "After several trials to contrive a plug that would act with certainty, Mr. Burton hit upon the expedient of hollowing out the bottom of the bullet, and making the edges thin enough to be forced outwards by the action of the gas at the instant of the explosion of the charge, thus causing it to fill the grooves and receive its rotary motion."

This plain bullet, used without patch or paper of any kind, became standard for North and South, in many calibers, in the war. Shooting at over 200 yards revealed that this bullet did not hold up well; consequently it was made a little longer. The original short-ogive ball weighed 310 grains, and grouped best with 38 grains musket powder at 200 yards. The improved Burton bullet (all .54 caliber) weighed 400 grains, fired with 50 grains coarse-grained musket powder. It was found that this charge, in the old ratio of 1:8, shot more regularly and fouled the bore less than finer rifle powder.

To be entirely fair in their evaluation of these rifles, Huger and Burton fitted up a new musket, smooth-bored exactly true, with the same rear sight and front sights as used on the test rifles. This musket, fired in the same way against the shoulder and with the forestock on a rest, what today is called "bench rest shooting," proved their work on the rifles worthwhile. "The table of firing," Huger reported, "shows that, at 300 yards, the musket is not so accurate as the new rifle bullet at double the distance; and at 400 yards, the fire of the musket is so uncertain as to be useless."

Huger provisionally concluded these tests with suggesting that if new sights and large-headed ramrods suitable for centering the conical bullet were prepared, muskets could be easily altered to rifles with no more work than the rifling of the bore. Writing from Pikesville Arsenal in Maryland, now (1962) home of the 110th Field Artillery but once the site of extensive small arms development work, Huger on March 18, 1854, indicated that "rifles with new ramrods and breech sights arranged for 150, 300, and 450 yards range, with a supply of cartridges and extra bullets, are submitted for examination and further trials. By direction of the Colonel of Ordnance [Craig], a rifle is also submitted with a sword bayonet attached; the sword to be worn habitually as a sidearm, and in case of need it can be promptly and firmly attached by a very simple lock to the muzzle of the rifle, and used as a bayonet." In this modification of the Harpers Ferry 1841 rifle lay the genesis of the new standard rifle.

About this time, Burton and Huger obtained a copy of tests done at Enfield in England in 1852, prior to adoption of the new British Enfield, .577-inch bore Model 1853 Long Rifle. The British had concluded with three important points: reduction of bore from .69-.70, of their old muskets to .577, making the bullet hollow based without patch or wad, and to use coarse grained powder which seemed to reduce fouling. The improved bullet was smooth, and in actual practice the cartridge paper surrounded it not as a wad to hold it into place, but as a carrier for grease for lubrication. Without allowing the lead to touch the barrel inside, there could be no opportunity for lead fouling to build up, destroying accuracy until cleaned and, if not cleaned, serving to hide destructive rust.

The new English bullet was called the Pritchett, after the inventor. In further tests at Harpers Ferry that October, 1854, Colonel Huger determined that the "Harpers Ferry ball" by Burton was better to a degree than the Pritchett ball or a modified French bullet, and all were far superior to the round ball. Also, most importantly derived from this series of tests, was the conclusion that the number of rifle grooves could be reduced, "if the width of each groove be increased, and its depth diminished." This was a reversal of the traditional belief that the deep grooves held the black powder fouling and so permitted loading a greater number of shots before having to stop and clean the gun. In practice, the fouling built up on top of the lands as well as in the grooves. Three or five grooves were suggested, and during the war that followed, rifles having both numbers of grooves were widely issued in certain makes. The form of grooves was discussed; those having rounded corners seemed to offer advantages, and further trials were ordered.

Mr. Burton spent the winter getting further model arms ready. Springfield Armory now took a share of the work, and commenced to build a lock for the Maynard primer. The Government having bought the full rights to this invention the preceding February, 1854, immediate use was to be made of the idea. The new series of tests to be held in the spring of 1855 were under direction of Lieutenant J. G. Benton, an officer who survived the war and distinguished himself in the Ordnance Corps until his retirement. His project was to reveal four main facts: determine the best mode of rifling the smooth bored arms already on hand; decide if the musket caliber of .69 could be reduced for new muskets and to see if this reduced caliber could be made uniform with all arms, including pistol, and to determine the best form of cavity for the Harpers Ferry bullet. To help him in these tests a special shooting machine was built to hold the rifles and carbines uniformly from shot to shot, avoiding human error. Initially 19 different barrels were tried, with various dimensions of lands and grooves. Most were 1 turn in 6 feet; two had increasing twist, the first ending up with one turn in 2 feet at the muzzle, the second starting with a turn of once in 6 feet and ending with one in 3 feet. New arms were also prepared for the tests; following these patterns:

Altered musket, .69 with Maynard primer lock, Remington pattern, 42-inch barrel, weight 10.87 pounds.

Trial gun No. 1, .6 caliber, a reduction of about 1/10 inch.

Six of these arms were prepared, each with 40-inch barrel, to test the merits of rounded grooves vs sharp cornered grooves, 3 and 5. Improved socket bayonet having a clasp. Weight 11.19 pounds.

Trial gun No. 2, .54 caliber, 40-inch barrel thinner at the muzzle than No. 1 but fitted for sword bayonet. Weight 9.75 pounds.

It is believed Trial Gun No. 1 and 2 had Maynard tape primer locks; the illustration of the shooting machine shows such an arm in place.

Trial carbine, 22-inch barrel, .54 caliber. Four of these were made, to test circular vs square rifling. It is thought these did not have Maynard locks, in view of their most probably resembling the later-adopted Carbine M1855, which did not have the Maynard lock.

Pistol: four of these were prepared. The first, .546 caliber, had an 8-inch barrel rifled with 3 grooves 6 foot twist, rounded. The second was identical, except rifled 4 foot twist. Two more pistols were made, possibly having the Maynard primer, in .58 caliber. One had a 10-inch barrel, the other 12 inches, 3 grooves, 4 foot twist. A cadet musket, percussion type 1852, caliber .57, was also tried.

The pistols proved to be very worthwhile; though they could not be fired from the rest, Benton recorded that "It is shown that the principles of the rifle and expanding ball can be applied to the common cavalry pistol, whose barrel is only 8 inches in length, so as to increase its efficiency from 100 to 500 yards, thus making it a serviceable arm for mounted troops and foot artillery."

The rifle of .6-inch bore having proved quite accurate, while the .54-inch seemed to give moderate recoil, "A size between these two, it is thought, would be most suitable for a uniform caliber." Barrel length of 40 inches was preferred for the new "musket," while the 12-inch pistol barrel "was not found inconvenient to handle." A large cavity was recommended for the pistol bullet so as to ensure complete expansion and bore sealing in the shorter bore; this meant two bullets would be in service, but as they were the same externally, they could be used in an emergency, each in the other gun. Tolerances in rifling the bore were reduced. Smoothbore musket variations from the drawing would be accepted if they were as great as .01 inches above true caliber; with the new rifled arms, tolerance was set at .0025 inches, a fourth as great.

Springfield Armory's master armorer E. S. Allin and master machinist Buckland prepared the model trial arms. The model rifle was made at Harpers Ferry, using the Maynard primer lock "which was not finished at Springfield until quite late in the winter, the completion of this model has been somewhat delayed . . ." By the summer, Colonel Craig was at last able to inform Mr. Davis of the final state of development for the Army's new small arms. A complete program had been started including percussioning of old flint muskets, alteration to Maynard primer of later arms, rifling, and the construction of rifle musket, and pistol with shoulder stock for artillery or cavalry, to all use the Washington dentist's priming pellet tape.

Ordnance Office
Washington, June 26, 1855

To Hon. Jefferson Davis
Secretary of War

Sir: I have the honor to submit the report of the proceedings and recommendations of the Ordnance Board, in regard to the establishment of new models for the small arms of our military service. For reasons assigned by the board, which I think conclusive, a smaller caliber than that of our present musket, but greater than that of our rifle, viz: .58-inch, is proposed for all our small arms; 40 inches is recommended as the length of the musket barrel, 26 inches as that of the sappers musketoon, which will be provided with a sword bayonet, and 10 inches for the barrel of the pistol, which barrel, being also provided with a suitable stock, will answer for a dragoon or artillery carbine, for which a range of 500 yards fits it. One lock, with magazine for 50 Maynard primers, will answer for either musket or musketoon, a smaller lock, with magazine for 25 primers, will serve for either the pistol or artillery carbine. All the barrels of .58 inch caliber to be rifled with three grooves, decreasing depth; the musket and musketoon to have a six-feet twist, and the carbine and pistol barrel a twist of four feet . . . It is recommended by the board, that our present rifles be enlarged in caliber to .58-inch, but no proposition has been made for a new model of this particular arm, in the belief, it is supposed, that the sapper's musketoon may be substituted for it. Concurring as I do with the board in its other recommendations with regard to a new model, and the details which I submit for your sanction, I cannot agree with it in opinion as to the propriety of ceasing the fabrication of the arm now called the rifle. To arrange a new model of this arm in accordance with the main features of the other arms, it will only be necessary to enlarge the calibre from .54 to .58, and arrange the stock for the Maynard musket lock, the other points remaining nearly as at present. For such an arm we have a factory and extensive machinery capable of turning out at least 3,000 per annum. I cannot, therefore, recommend the omission of this arm in our future fabrication.

Very respectfully, your obedient servant,

H. K. Craig,
Colonel of Ordnance

The Rifle, The Primer, The Ball

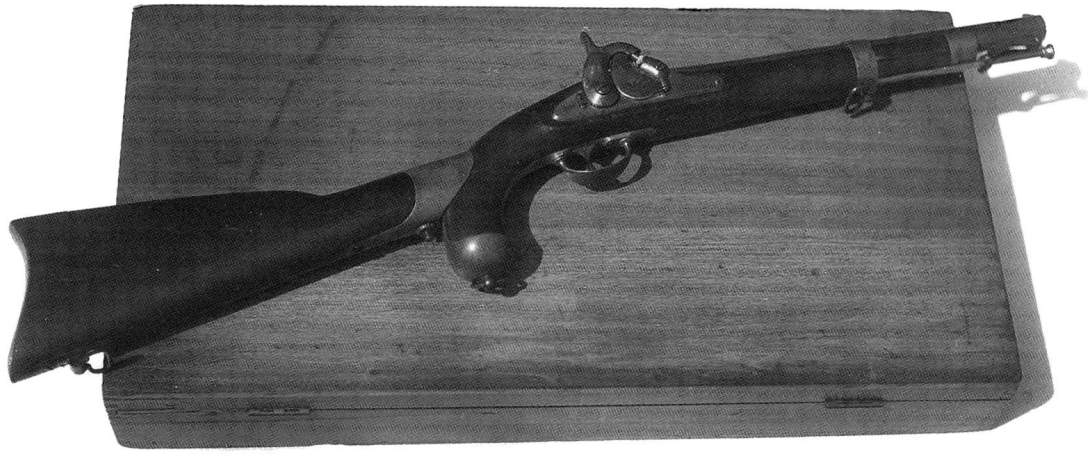

Adopted model of pistol carbine and detachable brass-yoke stock, though pistol barrel was increased to 12 inches from 10 inches. Hinged rammer was attached by swivel similar to those on 1842, 1836 Army pistols.

Within the following ten days, Secretary Davis responded with a specific critique of what Craig had reported, recapitulating the important points, enlarging on some, and approving all:

July 5, 1855

. . . The calibre of .58 of an inch for all small arms, the length of 40 inches for the musket barrel, and of 10 inches for the pistol barrel, with the details of the lock and other component parts, are approved as recommended . . .

The present rifle, modified by the adoption of the new calibre and primerlock, will be continued, and will be issued to the sappers instead of the musketoon, the manufacture of which will be discontinued.

The pistol will be provided with a movable stock, by the application of which, it may be used as a carbine by light artillery and mounted troops.

Jeff'n Davis
Secretary of War

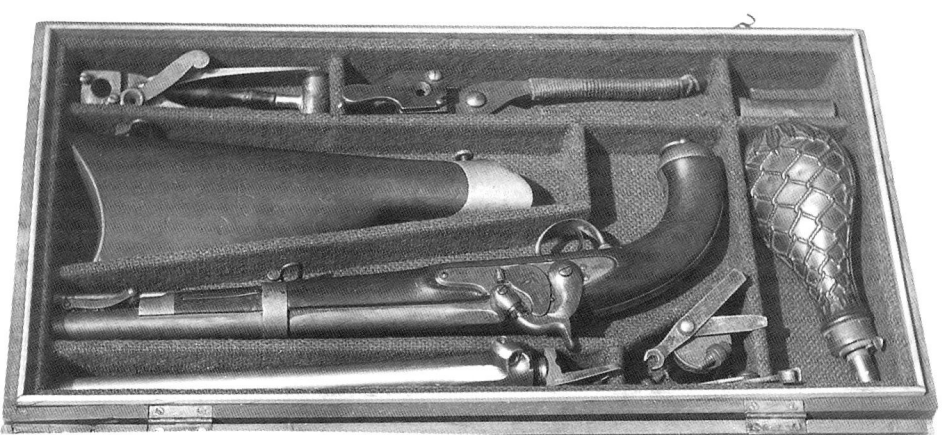

Burton's pistol carbine for Dragoons followed tactic of horsemen fighting dismounted. Detachable stock to fit pistol as carbine is an old idea. Cased set is author's paternal grandfather's gun probably bought by him in the 1880s as "hunter's companion" for $3.50. Below is an 1855 Jenks trial breechloader.

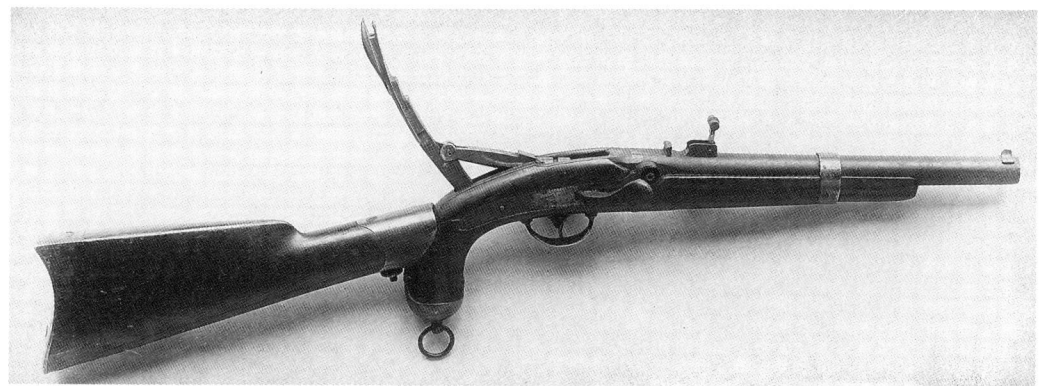

CHAPTER 5

Models Perfected

The new arms which Jefferson Davis had authorized were not fully formed. Neither Burton nor Allin had quite finished with them in both detail and final specifications.

The pistol-carbine barrels as eventually issued were 12 inches long, not 10. And in addition to the "continuation" of the U.S. Rifle M1841, significantly modified, as the M1855 Maynard primed rifle, a new carbine was prepared and a few constructed. The new carbine exists in at least two minor sub-types; both are superficially alike, and both resemble in their furniture and stock shape the discontinued Sappers and Artillery Musketoons, Models of 1847. The lock is common military bar lock, front action, without the new tape primer, but the ramrod is fastened to the muzzle of the barrel by a double swivel somewhat like that which permanently affixed the ramrod to the pistol-carbine barrel. The stock extended only half way to the muzzle, and nose cap and band are like those of the new series, in brass. A ring for the shoulder sling is fitted to the front of the trigger guard, and the guard plate itself is shaped like the early musket form dating all the way back to the 1812 pattern, instead of the simplified M1855 type which was easier to machine. The second type had the sling loop on the rear of the guard.

This rifled carbine, M1855, is a rare arm today and few were made. Judging from the components, it was a model to use up existing parts of the discontinued Sappers Musketoon. The rifle which Craig designed was a much more important arm, having its influence upon many rifles of the Confederacy as well as the special Remington-built rifle of the Union in 1862.

Colonel Craig must be credited with this colorful brass-trimmed Maynard primed rifle. Though relatively scarce in numbers made, and low in survival rate due to being used from the first in the war, its present esteem among collectors is not only due to these causes. It is also a very attractive arm of this period. The lock is hardened in grey-brown mottled colors. The barrel is browned or rust-blued to a satin finish having a bronzy cast. Bands and butt are of brass. The patchbox is slightly smaller in outline than that on the older M1841 rifle, but similar. Inside, the wood is mortised not for patches or tools, but with two intersecting circular cuts which just accommodate a special sniper's front sight. Constructed of two rings, one is about the barrel, the other loops the front sight and holds cross wires in the exact position of the tip of the front sight. It is held, by a set-screw, to the barrel, and is slipped off when not in use. The rather wide brass nose cap, protecting the stock but not holding down the barrel as in earlier rifle front bands, is held on by rivets. The steel ramrod is swell-ended and concaved to match the ogive of Burton's "Harpers Ferry bullet." At first a ladder type rear sight was fitted, the M1855. In 1858 a more compact sight having two folding leaves was introduced and variations of this sight remained in use until after the war.

Tools for the new rifle were prepared for building it at Harpers Ferry, as urged by Craig. The new rifle musket, 40-inch barrel, was also started into production. Because of the importance which these tools later assumed when captured by the Confederacy, it is worthwhile reviewing just what they may have been.

First, the exterior size of the barrel is nearly the same as that of the 1841. The barrel has a stud and guide for attaching a sword bayonet. The breech and cone seat are finished like the same parts of the new rifle musket. The lock is identical with that of the new rifle musket, and the rear sight similar. While the mountings are described as similar, the nose cap was heavier, while the patch box was used on the rifle but seldom on the rifle musket. The ramrod was similar to the rifle musket, but shorter. The sword bayonet had a cast brass hilt, a muzzle loop, and groove on top of the grip for attaching to the rifle stud. Its scabbard was black leather, with brass band or throat and tip. The rifle musket bayonet was of the more usual triangular form, with face and back flutes, and a rotating clasp to hold it firm, locked behind the front-sight fixed base.

Because of these differences, as well as similarities, between the two major arms at Harpers Ferry, duplicate suites of gun machinery existed in part. There was equipment to make both rifle and rifle musket bands and nose caps; but only one set of tools for locks including all their parts. This later was to affect the fitting up of rifles at Fayetteville Arsenal for the North Carolina

Models Perfected

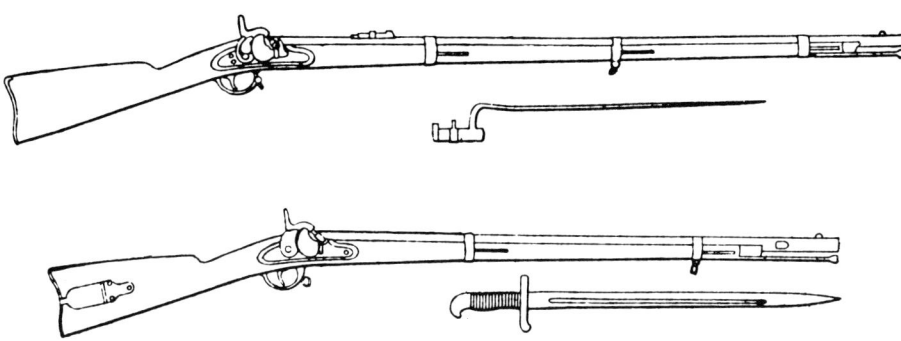

From Official Records Atlas are line drawings of U.S. perfected M1855 Rifle Musket and "Harpers Ferry" Rifle, mistakenly labeled "rifle musket." Rifle was later substantially copied by Remington using style 1841 locks.

troops. A few of the Fayetteville rifles used locks or lock plates from Harpers Ferry which had been originally forged out for the Maynard primer; and U.S.-type hammers. But most of them employed an "S" curved hammer not seen on any other arm but this famous Confederate built-up rifle.

Craig liked the M1855 rifle, and urged its issue to militia. He preferred it to the "patent arms" of the day, and spoke of its shiny fittings inspiring a martial air in the militiamen. But it was Jefferson Davis who signed the final papers on the model, and to him belongs the credit for its authorization.

It was a good, strong weapon. Soon after a few had been made, tests of blow-up strength were tried. Several arms were taken without special selection from piles of finished guns, and loaded with more than one cartridge. With the rifle musket, four charges would get blown out of the barrel, but when five were loaded, the bottom ball melted partially, the second charge fired, and "the entire force of the powder escaped through the vent with a prolonged sound resembling steam at

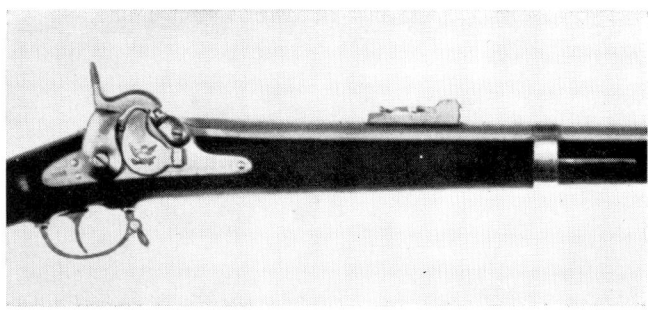

M1855 Rifle Musket as adopted had side-wing leaf sight sometimes called "long range" sight (detail). This sight also fitted to Rifles. Springfield made year later (1859) has improved sight usually associated with 1861 variation, may have been rebarreled during use with later sight.

high pressure. Although all the barrels were rifled, and were mortised and tapped for the sight base, they passed through the firings uninjured. The rifle barrel was made of steel (M1841 bored up to .58), the others (new rifle musket, altered M1842 musket) of iron."

Velocity tests using a 510-grain bullet and 60 grains

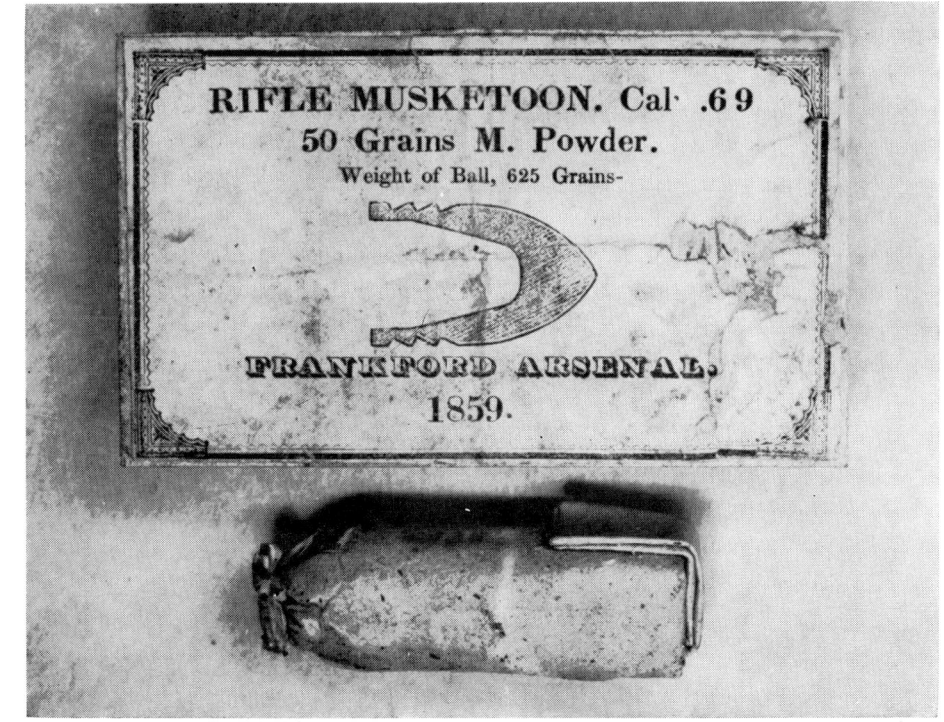

Shape of perfected "minney ball" is shown on package of rifle musketoon ammo in Stu Miller collection. Hollow in base was varied depending on bore to adjust bullet weight for light kick. In loading old muskets, paper tail was torn off to expose powder.

of black powder averaged over 10 shots at 963 feet per second for the new rifle musket, and 914 feet per second for the shorter-barreled M1841 rifle altered to take the new caliber bullet. The grooves cut in the side of the Burton bullet to hold lubricant also make their way heard through the air; standing behind a line of skirmishers there is a solid, deep-toned bumblebee-like "z-z-z-z-z-z-zip" that terminates in the echoing slap of the projectile at the target. Velocities slightly lower than sound made this audible; a higher velocity would have merged the bow-wave sound of the ball with the report. Ten shots with the pistol-carbine, 40-grains powder, 468-grain bullet, averaged only 603 feet per second.

Standardized at last, under a new Administration, the Model 1855 rifle musket was programmed for production. With the election of Abraham Lincoln, the critical post of Secretary of War was given to a supporter from Pennsylvania, the much-maligned Simon Cameron. Recognizing the lack of productive capacity of the national armories, the Government relied heavily upon domestic industry for the production of arms. The withdrawal of South Carolina from that Federal compact of the 1780's; the formation of an autonomous, sovereign, federal government in Montgomery, Alabama; the bombardment at last of the hated Yankee stronghold, brought on the conflict that the war party, the "Black Republicans," seemed to want. And, as volunteers sprang to their respective colors North and South, the manufacturers tendered their services. Arising from the melee of Union Army contracts was a mish-mash of confusion, patronage, and grasping middlemen, and the Civil War rifle musket scandals.

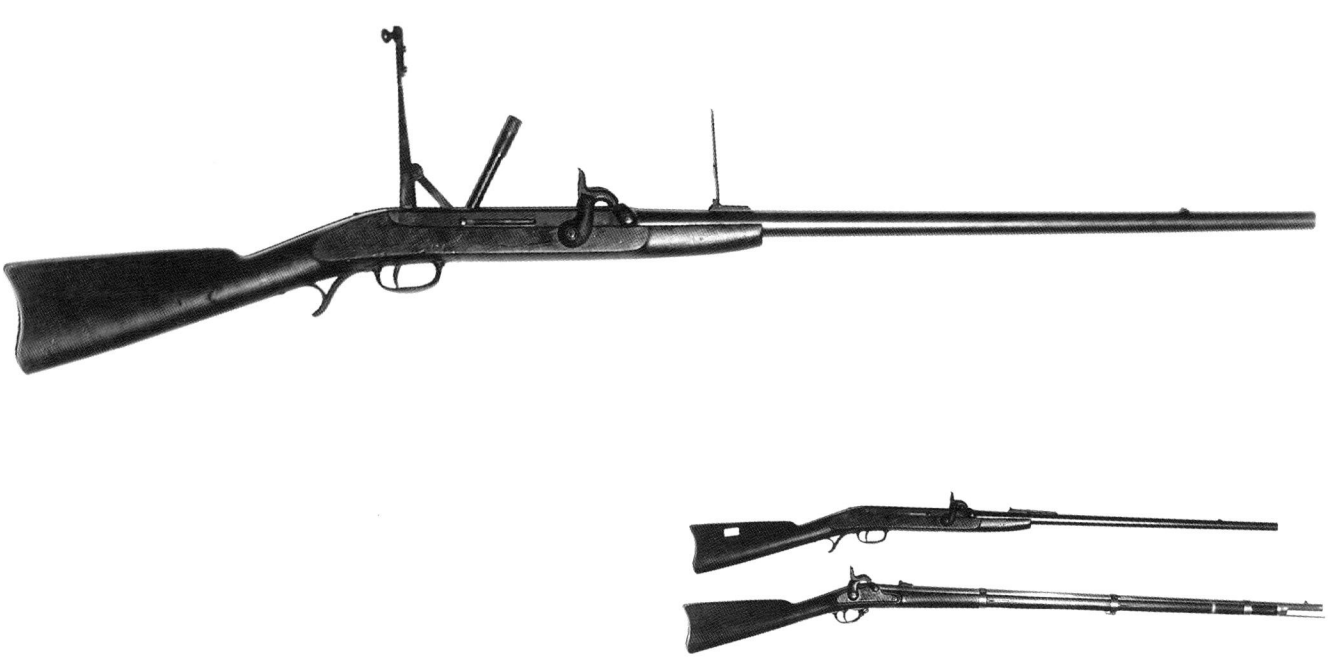

Critics of Ordnance Department claimed that Chiefs stifled innovation, but boots and shoes salesman William Arnold built toggle joint breechloader (Pat. 26,076 of 1859) with armory help as model's details show. Style of 1855 rifle musket is augmented with lever to open breech for bullet stabilized by finned tail (Pat. 23,538) shot through reduced bore to increase velocity. Ideas predated WWII rockets and German HV squeeze-bore AT guns. Concept, ahead of its times, did not lead to production of guns.

CHAPTER 6

Rifle Muskets: Civil War Scandals

"You place me in a most embarrassing position, Mr. Secretary."

"How is that, Mr. Wilkeson?" the gaunt-faced Pennsylvanian queried, the lines of his expression amplified by the fatigue and, somewhat, disappointment with which he laid down his role as Secretary of War for Mr. Lincoln.

"Because, Mr. Cameron," the newspaperman responded, "your contract for rifle muskets with the Eagle Manufacturing Company of Mansfield, Connecticut is for only 25,000 arms, and my friends there, whom I induced to engage in this business in expectation of your issuing a further order, as your assistant Mr. Scott assured me you would, will be sorely embarrassed in their operations on this small amount."

"Indeed this is bad news to me, Mr. Wilkeson," War Secretary Simon Cameron sympathetically observed, as he stuffed papers from his desk drawer into a large portfolio, scanning them briefly, consigning some to the waste basket. "But as you can see, I am leaving office today; I believe Mister Stanton, who replaces me, is the man you will want to see."

"But cannot you issue another order to General Ripley now to have the Eagle works deliver an additional 25,000? These rifle muskets I know will be wanted, and the quantity is about the necessary break-even number to cover their great costs in establishing a works."

Samuel Wilkeson had not come all the way to Washington on behalf of his friend, A. H. Almy, Treasurer of the Eagle Manufacturing Company, to be put off so easily if by being persistent he could gain what he wanted. The order increase to the 50,000 arms which were the terms of almost all the other contracts for Springfield Rifle Muskets, was essential to make the contract a worthwhile venture.

Cameron suddenly drew up the great chair which stood at his desk in the old War Office building, and in exhaustion sank into it, leaning back, staring at Wilkeson who leaned forward, both hands on the edge of the desk, seeking Cameron's approval. The Secretary was tired; the preceding months had been a great strain on him; perhaps he was incompetent as so many of his enemies had said. But he had engaged in long talks with the new Chief of Ordnance, Lieutenant Colonel James W. Ripley, and agreed that two parts of a single arms program were necessary. First, that arms should be bought overseas as rapidly and in as great quantity as possible; and, secondly, that domestic manufacturers, whether they be gunmakers, or makers of plows, railroads, or sewing machines, should be given every encouragement on making the Springfield Rifle Musket which was the best arm in the world for the service.

Now Sam Wilkeson was before him asking him to add one last straw for the critics to seize upon; to increase an order from 25,000 to double the amount, a little matter of half a million dollars.

"There are men in Washington who would put me in jail if they believed it possible," Cameron soberly stated to Wilkeson. "Put yourself in my place. It is your last day, indeed your last hour, in an office of public trust second only to the Presidency. Would you increase the order?"

"No, . . . no, Mr. Cameron, I must confess that I would not do so. . . ."

The conversation is fictional; the statements of fact are from the records. Thus ended the final day in office of one of our most controversial public figures, Simon Cameron, Lincoln's Secretary of War from the beginning days of the conflict until the end of 1861. Perhaps Cameron was "incompetent," yet he set into motion contracts for many hundreds of thousands of arms and although firms like the Eagle Company failed to deliver what was due, others like Colt, Sarson & Roberts, the Trenton Locomotive Works, even Sylvester Mowry and the Savage Repeating Firearms Company, supplied the essential needs of the Union from new manufactures, by the spring campaigns of 1863.

Had Cameron not committed the United States to the procurement of these arms, there would have been little chance for the North in the latter stages of the war. With one of the two Government arsenals, Harpers Ferry, in Southern hands, the musket-making capacity of the North was seriously crippled in the first days of the war. Cameron also sent afield a host of agents to scour the armories of Europe for guns. Many complaints have been leveled at the agents. But principal

The arms: "From floor to ceiling like a mighty organ rise the burnished arms" quoth Longfellow in his poem about Springfield Armory. Production of the improved M1861 Rifle Musket at the National Armory was supplemented by hundreds of thousands of identical interchangeable arms made on contract.

buyers for the North, George Schuyler and later Marcellus Hartley, turned in a record of $4,000,000 spent honestly and thriftily for the Union, procuring hundreds of thousands of rifles and carbines of standard patterns and good quality.

Later Civil War historical writers have taken as literally true many of the contemporary charges that the arms supplied were junk guns, and somehow have assumed that the North went to war incredibly badly prepared. The truth is somewhere in between this exaggerated view and the converse, that there were plenty of good guns on hand, and in time. All this Cameron accomplished before he left office. Yet it is equally certain that the job was too big for him.

So hectic had the corridors of the War Office become with dozens of middlemen scurrying hither and yon with orders seeking a manufacturer, or gunmakers without orders seeking someone with that touch of patronage to get them one, that the new Secretary, Edwin M. Stanton, threw up his arms and ordered a commission to be formed to investigate the whole mess.

A former War Secretary, Judge Joseph Holt and Ohio arms agent Robert Dale Owen, together with Major P. V. Hagner, United States Ordnance inspecting officer at New York, were ordered to form a commission by Stanton's letter of appointment March 18, 1862. Their powers were broad: "to audit and adjust all contracts, orders, and claims on the War Department in respect to ordnance, arms, and ammunition, their decision to be final and conclusive as respects this department, on all questions touching the validity, execution, and sums due or to become due upon such contract . . ." What Holt and Owen concluded was to be law, Stanton ordered, and no claims would be considered by the Department except such as the Commissioners had reported favorably upon. Hagner was to assist them, and the Ordnance or other branch of the War Department were ordered to supply such papers as the Commission might require to verify or study claims. As a last consideration, the Commission was to determine if any "agent or employee of the War Department was directly or indirectly interested in any contract," for if the fact of such interest was established, "it shall be good cause for adjudging the claim to be fraudulent."

Work of the Investigating Commission

Ohioan Owen, Judge Holt, and Major (later General) Hagner, accomplished a monumental task of sifting the claims and evidence and making the settlements in record time. Between 17 March 1862 and 1 July of that summer the Commissioners examined 104 cases* involving claims upon the Government totalling fifty million dollars. The Commissioners accepted some claims, set aside others, cancelled some contracts, rene-

---

* For cases which do not pertain to the subject of small arms and which, therefore, have no meaning for the reader, details are not given. Omitted are: Cases 1, 3, 9, 11, 12, 17, 22, 23, 27, 29, 30, 31, 32, 33, 34, 35, 40, 41, 42, 46, 49, 50, 51, 53, 57, 58, 60, 63, 66, 67, 71, 82, 86, 87, 92, 102, 103, 104, 105, 107.

Simon Cameron was condemned for corrupt contract practices while in office but his opponents studiously ignored fact he managed procurement of several hundred thousand small arms from abroad at time Union was destitute of guns.

gotiated others at lower prices and in the end saved Uncle Sam some $17,000,000.

"In our desire to protect, as far as practicable, the public interests," the Commissioners reported, "no private right has been infringed, nor is it believed that any one of the contractors whose engagements have been the subject of our investigations will, if provident and reasonably skillful in the execution of his contract, suffer loss, or fail to realize a fair profit." But the Commissioners were adamant in objecting to such arrangements as the interest-peddling which went on. "A holder of one of these orders or contracts for Springfield muskets appeared before the Commission, as did a member of the United States Senate, and from their testimony we learned that their order had been obtained from the Secretary of War by the Senator, and that for the service he had charged and is to receive $10,000 . . . For this he holds the notes of the parties, who are responsible, and will no doubt make payment at the maturity of the paper in August and September next."

Because of the number of cases investigated, a full resumé is beyond the scope of this book. The artillery manufacturers' contracts and records are arbitrarily omitted, interesting though they be. This decision had to be taken also in the instance of sword and saber contracts. As nearly as possible, the details of the cases adjusted, together with details of the weapons supplied,

Hard-headed Edwin M. Stanton succeeded Cameron as Secretary of War, cancelled contracts and instituted investigation by Judge Holt and Robert Owen. This expert inquiry into Union arms preparedness of 1862 confirmed many orders let by Cameron but cancelled or disallowed others achieved through influence.

as far as known, will be limited to small arms and no other. Each relevant case is listed below; those more fully dealt with in other chapters, as Colt, or Remington, are noted only, then omitted from detailing in this chapter.

Partial Resume of Cases Investigated

CASE NO. 2. John Pondir, Philadelphia.

He contracted to furnish 10,000 Light Minié Rifles with saber bayonets, at $18.50 each, July 26, 1861. The rifles were described by Pondir as "These are the beautiful Minié, which . . . are at the low price of $18.50." They are a light .58 or .577 French pattern arm, of the Chasseurs de Vincennes style, back action lock, brass trim, made for Pondir under an order he placed at Liege. Barrels are blacked; long range rear sight, weight about 7#, barrel 32¼". The fabricant of these arms is unknown. Deliveries by Pondir on February 3, 19, 20, 27, March 6, and 11, totalled 2,288 arms.

The Commission recommended he be allowed to deliver the full 10,000.

CASE NO. 5. Richardson & Overman, see "Gallager carbines" in Chapter 11.

CASE NO. 6. G. W. Ramsdell, Austrian muskets.

Captain C. K. Garrison of New York, later distinguished as a shipping man and speculator in Civil War surplus, initially presented a specimen musket to General Fremont with an offer of the same at $27. Fremont saw a sample gun while stopping at the Astor House on his way to London to buy arms. To Cameron on 21 July, 1861 he wrote:

Sir: Captain Garrison has shown me a rifled musket of French make (Liege) rough, but well made, which I think is a good, serviceable weapon. I like it much better than the Enfield, or any others I have seen here, and would be glad to have ten thousand of them, for our western force.

A little subterfuge was injected here, for Garrison did not deliver, and his cause was taken up by Ramsdell, who offered October 31 to fill the order given to Garrison at a price $6 less "with an arm equal in every respect to the one he agreed to furnish." Colonel Maynadier accepted the offer November 16, 1861, but it was not until January 13, 1862, that the guns came into the country. Ramsdell had in turn contracted with Samuel B. Smith, a New York lawyer, to obtain the guns; it was Smith who notified the Ordnance office the guns were ready for delivery. He had obtained them through Herman Boker & Company, and they were stored in a warehouse used for guns which Boker, also, had delivered to the Government.

Smith, having advanced money on this matter, was an interested party, though he signed himself "Agent for George Ramsdell." He kept up a flow of letters asking that the arms be accepted and paid for. But Captain Silas Crispin, at the Ordnance Agency in New York, refused to accept the arms proffered; there seemed to be some mistake.

"The sample gun, purporting to come from your office," Crispin wrote January 26, 1862, to Ripley, "is at hand; and I find it, on examination, to be an Austrian rifle, calibre .715, an altered arm, said to be from the model adopted for the use of gun cotton, and known at this office as the Bulkley arm. This arm is of inferior grade, and has been purchased in this market at $10 and $10.50 per gun, about 15,000 having been purchased."

When Holt and Owen tackled the case, a hitherto unknown middleman, James Duffy of Lancaster County, Pennsylvania, emerged briefly. Duffy, it appears, was a sometime employer of Ramsdell, who was a lumberman working for Mehaffy, House & Company of New York, "of which firm I am a member," said Duffy in deposition. Captain Garrison meanwhile asked Duffy if he "could sell an arm like the Chasseur de Vincennes." Duffy took the sample gun to Washington, was informed that $29 was too high a price. Fremont, having seen the Vincennes rifle, okayed the purchase; Garrison brought the telegram to Duffy who again went to Washington to see Secretary Cameron; then he was turned over to Colonel Ripley (Brevet Brigadier General).

"He disparaged the gun," said Duffy; "said he would not pay that price; that neither the gun that Garrison had offered as a sample nor the one I proposed to substitute for it was worth anything; and in answer to the question, 'Whether there was $6 difference between the guns?' replied, 'both together are not worth $6.'"

When Duffy reported this conversation to Assistant Secretary Thomas A. Scott, the rejoinder was, "If the gun business were left to General Ripley, the Government would get no guns."

Duffy thereupon used Ramsdell's name, as the two were sometime partners as well as employee and employer. Holt and Owen unscrambled the matter by getting Smith, who had bought the guns to fill Duffy's contract, for a considerable profit share, off to one side and suggesting that if he wanted to salvage anything out of this tangle he had better make a counter proposition. Smith agreed, and the Commission agreed to accept such of the 10,000 remodeled Austrian rifles as the Ordnance Agency would accept that were in every way equal to the second sample gun. All 10,000 apparently were satisfactory, and payment for them in the sum of $110,000 was made out to Ramsdell on August 29, 1862. Only 9,500 were .71 caliber; 500 were listed as Austrian rifles, caliber .69, but were accepted. Smith in making a counter proposal of $14.50 which the Commissioners reduced to $11 noted that the sample gun was iron mounted; that some, he was informed by Boker, were brass mounted.

The exact model of arm purchased by the Government in lieu of the light and elegant Vincennes "carabine" desired by Fremont is difficult to identify perfectly. But it had a sword bayonet, was an Austrian gun remodeled, and of .71 caliber; yet it resembled the Vincennes arm to some extent. In Chapter 8 is illustrated such an arm, having a Consol-Augustin remodeled lockplate of 1846 vintage, and a musket barrel of 1830 date, percussioned and fitted with stud for saber bayonet. The mountings are of iron and the weapon is a simulation, using Austrian musket parts, of the Vincennes or Enfield short rifles with sword. It is believed to have constituted one of the C. K. Garrison lot as actually delivered by Boker.

This particular rifle was purchased from the firm Ancion-Marx Fabriques d'Armes in Liege in 1961 by the writer. Its peripatetic history is only conjectural, but reasonable: From Boker's store house it went to Fremont; did some service but not much in the Army of the West; was retired and remained in depot in St. Louis until sold about 1867. From there it went back to Liege to the "agent" of Francis Bannerman who in later years was that corporate identity known as Ancion-Marx, amalgamation of the firm Ancion & Cie. with other interests. It remained in Liege, from where it had come, for almost a century. The price paid in 1961 was $23; a mean between the original $26 asked, and the $21 at which Garrison-Ramsdell-Smith-Duffy & Company proposed to sell.

The gun is a good one, cheaply made but hardly inviting the abuse and condemnation which later generations have heaped upon the head of General Fremont. It would be wise to remember that the rifle he

Doctrinaire General James W. Ripley, Union Chief of Ordnance, considered the Springfield Rifle Musket the best arm in the world for infantry. He was right, as events proved. Ripley had been C.O. at Springfield 1841-1854.

approved, and the rifle Ripley, Maynadier, Crispin, Holt, and Owen ultimately supplied to him, were not one and the same quality of arm.

CASE NO. 7. Manhattan Arms Company. See Chapter 23, *Yankee Revolvers*.

CASE NO. 8. Ben Mills.

Mr. Mills was evidently an officer or employee of the machine shop of Ainslee & Cochran, at Louisville, Kentucky. Holt & Owen recommended payment of their account for the full $151.70, for inspecting, repairing, and sighting the arms in the hands of the 19th Regiment, Kentucky Volunteers training at Camp Harrod. Eight men were on the job of making special lathe tools for aligning barrels and sights perfectly, and they worked on the regiment's arms from about 3:30 p.m. of a Saturday, all of Saturday night, and Sunday until 2 p.m., "for which we had to pay double wages," as Ainslee & Cochran complained. Their account was paid in full.

CASE NO. 10. Hedden & Hoey, 50,000 Prussian muskets to be delivered under order from Ripley dated November 23, 1861.

John Hoey, arms importer, in cooperation with Josiah Heddon (who possibly supplied the cash) had proposed to deliver 50,000 muskets within a specified time. Up to the date of termination of their contract they shipped 28,000 which had been accepted by the Government. Of these, 16,000 were shipped to Kentucky and placed in service. Hoey introduced a note from J. F. Speed "of Kentucky," stating that "Our men liked them as well as any guns sent us, except the Springfield musket." During the summer of 1861 he had caused some of them to be rifled, but Speed found this to be a "useless expense," since "the musket is now preferred to the rifle."

"I can say of you," Speed wrote to Hoey, "that at a time when we were sorely pressed for arms, and our state invaded, you rendered us valuable service, and through your instrumentality we procured arms at fair prices and of good quality, for which I desire to thank you."

While Holt and Owen were getting around to the case, in that Ordnance had declined to accept an additional 22,000 muskets offered, Hoey wrote to Lincoln. The President passed on his opinion to Stanton that the arms ought to be accepted, since the time delay was so slight and there appeared to be still need for the muskets. But Stanton would not interject his own opinion into the matter, stating to Holt and Owen, as he enclosed Lincoln's observations, that "Designing that in the action of the department all claims and contracts shall stand on the same ground, this contract is referred to you, with the President's order, to be acted upon according to your judgment and the facts that shall appear in respect to the conformity of the arms, with the terms of the contract." Perhaps Stanton was heavy-handed in many of his methods, but this straight-line backing up of his subordinate appointees reflects an unbending impartiality in his conscience.

The Commissioners had checked into the quality and serviceability of these Prussian guns, arms which very likely George Schuyler had inspected and declined to purchase. H & H were altering the cones to take the smaller U.S. musket cap. Said Captain Crispin, "The arm is the Prussian smoothbore musket, of the model previous to 1839, altered from flintlock to percussion, caliber .70, weight 11 pounds. The plan of alteration from flint to percussion, of both lock and barrel, has, I believe, secured as much strength and durability as can be obtained in an altered arm. The lock appears to be a strong and serviceable one; the barrel is about 41 inches in length, and compares favorably in manufacture with the generality of smoothbore ones. The stock and mountings appear strong. The arm, however, has not been manufactured with much regard to smoothness and neatness of finish. They are all either old or have been in service . . . Permit me to suggest . . . the propriety of using the 'Nessler' ball as a projectile for them. Its weight is about the same as the round ball, and it is stated by reliable European authorities that by its use the smoothbore musket has an accurate and effective range of 300 or 400 yards, or at least double that obtained by using the spherical projectile."

Crispin concluded his remarks by a flattering observation that ". . . the majority of arms heretofore delivered by Messrs. Hedden & Hoey have been pronounced by the inspector, Mr. W. W. Marston, superior to the sample, and the rejections but few." Though Boker had supplied similar muskets at $5.50 each, the H & H price of $7 each was confirmed by the Commissioners. In view of their responsible attitude and conduct, the 10 days lateness was overlooked, and the balance of 22,000 Prussian altered muskets, long ready for delivery, were ordered accepted and paid for.

Between the spring of 1861 and November 5, 1862, John Hoey also delivered thousands of assorted rifles and muskets, Potsdam rifled muskets, Remington-Maynard transformed U.S. rifled muskets, Chasseurs de Vincennes arms and other types, including 8,999 Tower muskets at $7.50 each, to an aggregate value of just under a half million dollars.

Desire to equip U.S. forces uniformly motivated letting of large contracts for Springfield guns by Ripley and Cameron. Platoon of 6th Maine here shown after battle of Fredericksburg was equipped with M1855 RM (3rd from left), Long Enfield .577 (4th & 5th), M1861 RM without patchbox (6th) and, (10th) 1859 2-band Enfield taking socket bayonet, unusual cut-down for short soldier.

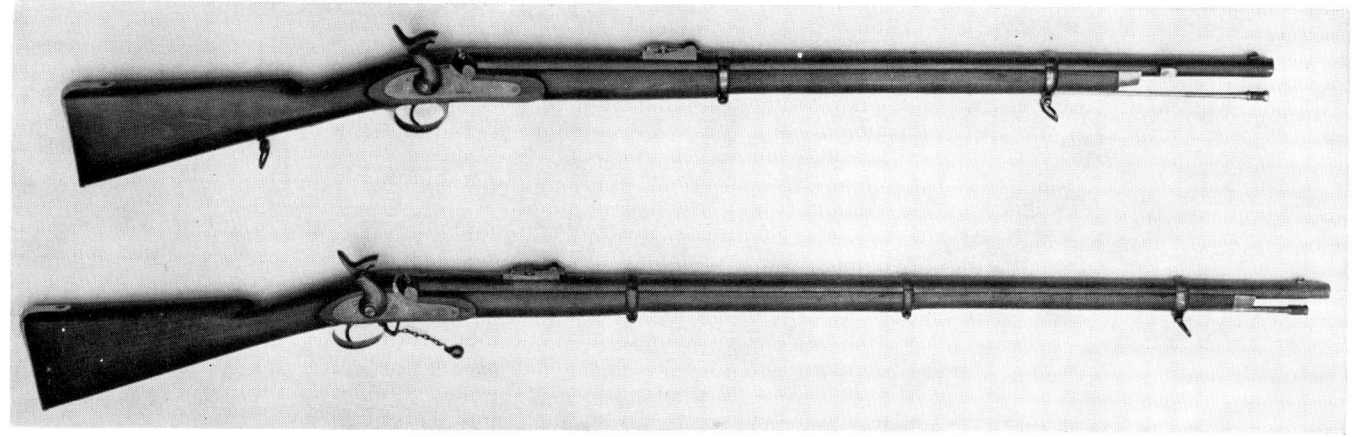

Orison Blunt contracted to deliver Enfield rifles made in the US. Shown is Long Enfield (bottom) by Blunt, fraudulently marked "Tower" and "crown." Proofmark is "Oval around DP over B." Hammer shape, cone seat differ from genuine Tower-Birmingham British government short Enfield shown above it. Barrel, walnut stock, bear serial number "1."

CASE NO. 13. Colt's Arms Company, Rifled muskets. See Chapter 25, *Colt's Goes to War*.

CASE NO. 14. Orison Blunt, Enfield Rifled Muskets.

Orison Blunt, then at 118 Ninth Street, New York, was a practical gunmaker of considerable experience but did not always have sufficient capital. In 1847 he had been called upon to make the prototype revolver under direction of Samuel Colt for approval by Captain Walker, U.S. Mounted Rifles. This large .44 six-shooter, considerably modified from the Blunt model arm, became the celebrated "Walter Colt" and later, still further modified, the pattern for the Dragoon revolvers. At the same time, it appears Blunt was associated with Syms in either importing or fabricating completely in this country, a pepperbox revolver of the basic "Mariette" Franco-Belgian design. A "Blunt & Syms" type pepperbox in the writer's collection is marked on the barrel face "R-C" and "45", suggesting that the machine shop maker was known as "R-C" and the "45" is the serial number, it appearing in several other places. The gun is otherwise unmarked. But Blunt & Syms had a large importing business on Chatham Street, and were otherwise active before the war.

With the outbreak of fighting, Orison Blunt evidently tried to go it alone. He proposed to import 20,000 Enfield rifled muskets, and also during the same delivery period, to furnish 20,000 Enfield rifled muskets, caliber .58, made in the United States. On September 10, 1861, General Ripley informed Blunt the Secretary declined to accept the imported Enfields but would take the U.S.-made guns, "as many as you can manufacture in this country by the first day of January next, at $18 per arm, including appendages." The arms were to be inspected and none would be accepted but those which passed inspection.

With less than four months in which to work, "I immediately commenced preparing my factory building, machinery, and tools," said Blunt, "and have gone to great expense, knowing that the Government would require this arm. I am now all in working order." After the deadline, Blunt reported to Stanton on February 6, 1862, "I can produce 500 to 1,000 per month, like the two I now present, which I have made myself, and which are like the pattern gun filed in the Ordnance office. I am a practical manufacturer of guns and understand it in all its branches, and can make any part of the gun with my own hands. I would respectfully submit that the War Department will extend the time for the manufacture of these guns at least one year, with permission to turn in from 500 to 1,500 per month."

Stanton tossed the ball to Holt and Owen. Blunt further described the details of his preparations. Ripley recommended that Blunt's request be acceded to, to deliver 1,000 per month from January 1862 to January 1863, 12,000 in all. As Blunt understood it, "the parts not to interchange, but to be equal as sample I deposited with you." The Commissioners found for the plaintiff a little differently: they directed that an order be given to him for as many as he could make up to July, 1862, not to exceed 3,000 in all.

The exact model of Enfield supplied by Blunt has been a matter for speculation. There exists a species of 39-inch barrel long Enfield, not usually found with any European marks, marked upon the lockplate with a shield surmounted by an eagle, and the letter "M" in the shield. The meaning of the letter M is unknown; such arms are thought to be of Blunt's fabrication; at least Claud E. Fuller (*The Rifled Musket*) and Robert Riley (essay in *Gun Report*, "A Blunt or What?") examine that belief. But there are some details which do not jibe entirely. Because Blunt later pleaded to be permitted to furnish non-interchangeable guns, these "M" guns would seem to fall within the classification. But several with British (Birmingham and London) proved barrels are known. Others have strange cyphers, not too legible, of interlaced three letters in the location where proof marks are commonly found, left round of breech. This usage seems odd, though not necessarily impossible, for a U.S.-made barrel.

Blunt was quite certain as to the origins of his bar-

Blunt Enfield lock has never been on a genuine Enfield, as screw boss to rear of curved bridle is undrilled. Instead, rear lock screw was passed into plate where hole is shown in line with hammer.

rels, as on January 15 he wrote, "My men are making 300 barrels per week, and can increase to any reasonable extent necessary, so that I am now prepared to furnish the government with from two to five hundred Enfield pattern muskets per month." This suggests Blunt's shop was quite small, though respectable for one-man ownership. His barrel men also had to turn their hands to finishing other parts; say one week to make 300 barrels; then a week to make locks; half a week to make stocks; and the rest of the month putting them together and finishing.

But all these calculations were mere conjectures of rate of production, for Blunt never achieved any particular rate. A very rare and hitherto improperly identified Enfield rifle which most nearly conforms to the Blunt order is shown by Fuller as "The J. P. Moore Rifled Musket," his plate No. XLVII. The illustration shows a clamping band Enfield long rifle, otherwise undistinguished; the lockplate is unmarked outside. Says Fuller in describing this: "It is of the regular Enfield type throughout, but the barrel is 40 inches long, caliber .58, and rifled with three wide lands. The total length is 56 inches, and the weight is 10 pounds, 9 ounces, which is more than a pound and a half heavier than the regular Enfield. The rear sight is of the regular

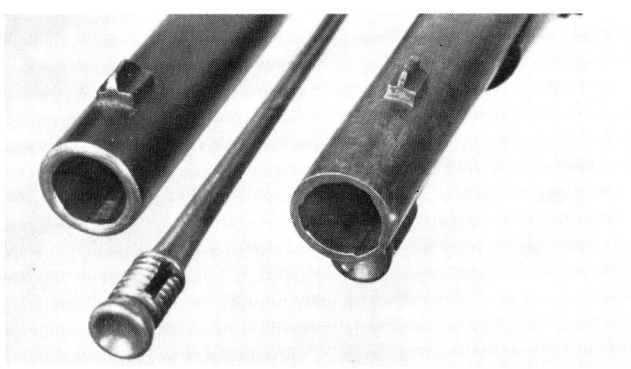

Muzzle of Blunt Enfield three-grooved is contrasted with normal 5-groove rifling at muzzle of new Pryse & Redman British Enfield. Blunt rifling has been deepened slightly at muzzle and barrel is faced off flat and not crowned.

Enfield type, soldered in place, and, in place of the usual British proof marks, the barrel is stamped on the left side near the breech with DP over B in a quarter-inch oval."

With stock of American black walnut, this arm definitely would seem to conform to some U.S. order, but which? Admittedly not knowing, Fuller chooses to place this gun with notes on the John P. Moore order furnished June 10 and June 30, 1862, a total of 1,080 "American rifles, long Enfield pattern, with appendages, $15.00." But more logically, would be rifles marked "M" for Moore, and rifles bearing somewhere a B, for Blunt. Could not the odd proof stamp Fuller notes, a DP over B in an oval, be for something like "Definitive Proved, Blunt"? As Blunt made his own barrels, he would have proof tested them. This unmarked gun has a 40-inch barrel, essential in finding a U.S.-made "Enfield" to conform to the Blunt order. The "M" marked Enfield is with a 39-inch barrel.

Accessory to the notion of unmarked locks is the finding recently by an Eastern gun-parts dealer of a small lot of Enfield lock plates. They were in a box tagged "American" and are of first class machine workmanship, but unmarked and unmounted. They are nicely casehardened, and of especial interest is the screw thread selected for the lockplate "side nails" or stock screws; screws from an English Enfield will not fit. American screws from a Springfield will fit. Could these not be the leftovers from the Blunt order, of which but a very few were ever delivered, possibly only the 500 pieces later mentioned? For Blunt, even after Holt & Owen were done with him, had problems. Ripley and Thornton were determined to throw every block possible into the path of those who continued to want to make nonstandard non-Springfield pattern arms.

By March 31, 1862, Blunt had 200 guns ready for delivery. Ripley told him he would not inspect less than 500. By May 13, six weeks later, Blunt had 500 ready, a production rate of 50 per week or somewhat less than he expected to furnish. Ripley then told Blunt that the model musket was not on hand in the Ordnance Office, and unless Blunt had it, there would be a delay until Major Thornton could be furnished with an approved pattern musket from which to inspect.

Blunt replied to Ripley that if he would look about his office, he would find it, adding:

"The gun was examined and a parchment card tied to the gun, and the Ordnance seal stamped upon it, and I wrote my name on the card. This was all done under the direction and supervision of Colonel Maynadier, and I left it with him. The gun was put into a gray satinet cover, and then put into an India Rubber (waterproof) cover. I think there is no doubt but it is in your office somewhere."

At last the "misplaced" rifle was forwarded to Thornton, in Crispin's office in New York. But the U.S. inspector there, G. G. Saunders, complained that the barrels had been rifled, thus preventing him from proof testing them in the white state for the provisional proof required by the Government. And Thornton

Often confused with Blunt Enfield is mysterious Enfield marked on lock with spread eagle and shield, and "M" in field of shield. Dates to 1863 are seen on lockplate before hammer. Specimen shown is Enfield "eagle-M" short rifle, with notched bayonet stud taking bayonet which has catch that does not lock at rear of stud like regular Enfield bayonet. Long Enfield rifles of this marking are believed to have been supplied by John P. Moore's sons, allegedly made in the U.S. Short rifle shown, in Smithsonian collection, is dated 1863 though preference was for Long Enfields.

sought to inspect each and every part of the arm in detail.

Blunt had three rooms set aside for the use of the inspectors, but he refused to allow this detailed inspection. He claimed it was not in agreement with his order as ratified by Holt and Owen; "neither would I have taken any order for arms if they were to require the above proof and inspection, and it was distinctly understood that my guns were to be inspected when ready for delivery, and to be equal to the sample deposited in the Ordnance office."

But Thornton was firm, and no guns, apparently, were ever received from Blunt. "I consequently stopped my works," he wrote later, in airing the matter through a brochure published by cannoneer Norman Wiard. According to this brochure, quoted by Fuller, Blunt was a gunmaking anachronism in head-on collision with governmental preference for large capital and machine manufacture. Blunt's philosophy is interesting, for he sought to introduce the "setting up" system abandoned by the British during 1855, saying:

I should have adopted the European plan of manufacturing, which is as follows:
Establish a proof house with a government inspector or officer, to test the strength of every barrel, so that any one could make a barrel, take it to the proof house, have it proved and the proof house mark stamped upon it.
Then next, to establish a style of lock and mounting, ramrod, and bayonet. Let any one make the same that could make them according to pattern. The stocker and finisher could purchase barrel, lock, mountings, ramrod, and bayonet, and finish their arms every week with little or no capital invested. The arms would then be all of the same pattern, same kind of mounting, same kind of barrel, same size caliber, and the same length of bayonet, consequently the arms would appear to the eye the same in every particular; and no part should be required to interchange, except the bayonet, ramrod and the cones.
There is no other arm manufactured beside the Springfield Rifled Musket, to any extent, that all the parts interchange, which as experience shows, is unnecessary.
I am satisfied that there is great room for improvement in small arms and ammunition, and the mode of manfacturing them, and I think the day is not far distant when we shall have an entire change in the construction of the same.

CASE No. 15. Herman Boker & Company. For 150,000 muskets. See Chapter 22, *Continental Arms*.

CASE No. 16. W. V. Barkalow, 26,000 English long Enfield rifles.

The commission determined that Barkalow in his nondelivery was an innocent victim of international affairs. He had commenced to fill his contract but the Queen's embargo caused him to suspend further work in England. Upon his return, though he was again able to ship guns, the United States suspended purchases until Stanton's commissioners could look over the contracts. They decreed that since Barkalow was irrevocably committed to "the manufacturers," to take 6,000 Enfields, that the order be confirmed to 8,000, the first delivery of 2,000 to be made before 1 June, 1862, and the final delivery completed on or before 1 September, 1862. Between April 26 and July 18 Barkalow delivered 8,000 guns for the full $160,000 due him, at $20 a gun. They were carried by the "Inman line of (propeller) steamships," the Cunard liners of the day.

CASE No. 17. Horstmann Brothers & Company, Philadelphia, Swords.

CASE No. 18. Silas Dingee & Company, New York, 53,500 Austrian rifles. See *Continental Arms*, Chapter 22.

CASE No. 19. T. Poultney, Smith's patent Carbines. See *Yankee Carbines*, Chapter 11.

CASE No. 20. H. Holthausen, 32,000 foreign muskets. See Chapter 22.

CASE No. 21. Alfred Jenks & Son, Philadelphia, Springfield Rifled Muskets.

Jenks had obtained a contract 13 July, 1861 to furnish 25,000 Springfield Rifled Muskets. Though Model 1855 was spoken of, the primerless 1861 was built. On October 5, 1861, the contract was increased to 50,000 by direction of Cameron, and Jenks accepted, inquiring, "Shall we continue, after the completion of our present contract, to use the present model, or do you design furnishing us with the last improved model?"

This reference was to the 1861 Special Model that Colt and two other contractors were preparing to furnish; the changes would cost Jenks something in tooling and he doubtless assumed any prices would have to be adjusted accordingly. Jenks' firm was called "Bridesburg Machine Works," and 1861 rifle muskets so stamped are of his delivery, fabricated principally at the town of Bridesburg, Pennsylvania, near Philadelphia. However, a few specimens of M1861 Springfields have been observed marked "Philadelphia" in the usual place in front of the hammer. The actual place of manufacture of these muskets has been questioned, but they are believed offered by Jenks under his contract.

As sureties for a second contract issued 15 December 1863, for 50,000 Model 1863 Springfields, Alfred Jenks Sr. and his son Barton, appeared in association with Joseph G. Mitchell and John M. Mitchell, also Robert B. Cabeen, the latter two as sureties on the contract, and one William Whitaker, "a manufacturer."

Whitaker of Philadelphia was surety in the amount of $50,000, which would have been forfeited to the United States if there were delays on the contract. But Whitaker had been called in under unusual conditions; both John Mitchell and Cabeen were also sureties, $50,000 each, as required by the contract law. However, Judge Cadwalader, who took the oaths of the sureties, was not satisfied that these two were each worth enough more than $50,000, to make it possible for them to pay the Government should a claim arise. Therefore Whitaker appeared and testified to the Judge that he was worth $150,000, a great deal more than the sums needed, and his bond was taken in addition.

For Whitaker to have such a great interest suggests that he was a partner financially and possibly production-wise in the Jenks muskets. What he did can only be conjectured, but from Philadelphia on September 27, 1862, Alfred Jenks & Son wrote an enigmatic letter to P. H. Watson, Assistant Secretary of War:

> We have on hand five hundred muskets of our manufacture, complete in every part, which are equally as serviceable as those delivered to the Government. They have, however, marks on the surface, which prevent us from offering them under our contract. They have stood government proof, and are worth eighteen dollars each, but we will dispose of them at seventeen dollars if they will be accepted by the department.

On November 11 Major Hagner reported that "Of 549 offered, 85 are rejected, and 464 are serviceable; of these 132 are worth $17 and 332 not more than $16 each with appendages." On November 15 Colonel Maynadier ordered the guns taken at these figures. Payment was made to Jenks on December 5 for these guns at the rates quoted. Could these have been "Philadelphia" guns? Too few of the Philly-stamped muskets exist to suggest any large quantity existed. Perhaps Jenks had begun to tool up and stamp them "Philadelphia," and had to change to "Bridesburg" in conformity with some Ordnance wish to have the location of the factory actually stamped on the guns? It is possible they were made up for some would-be Government patronage-seeker, perhaps for surety for Whitaker? Jenks did fabricate for other "contractors," a situation which caused him delay and embarrassment in the beginning stages of production. They planned for quantities greater than the first 25,000, and bought tools accordingly. But they ran the risk of forfeit from nondelivery and so came before Holt and Owen at the end of March. Joseph G. Mitchell appeared stating:

> We have [as of March 28, 1862] 14,000 arms passing through our establishment. We have none boxed as yet. We

Soldier's kit might include Hardee's *Rifle & Light Infantry Tactics* if he was bucking for promotion but more essential was Rifle Musket (Norwich contract piece supplied by Mowry shown) with muzzle tompion, ammo, and caps. Drill books were owned by Mayor of Toledo, Ohio, John C. Manor.

> have only one [Government] inspector which is not sufficient. We have been delayed in our work, because a defective model was furnished us from Springfield Armory [Could the Philadelphia-marked guns be first production after the defective model?]. The octagon, cone-seat, and breech pin were defective. We have now six men at Springfield examining machinery, etc.
>
> In five months we will furnish all the guns now overdue on our contract. It takes 13,000 guns on hand to turn out 200 per day. Our establishment can make 240 guns per day of ten hours. We have a contract with John Rice (which see) to furnish stocks and tips for him. We have finished 20 guns interchangeable in all respects except barrels. We are making all of the gun, except the barrel, sight, and stock, for Sarson & Roberts for 25,000. We have delivered to Sarson & Roberts almost everything under this contract.

Deliveries from August 16, 1862, through December 31, 1862, were sporadic in lots of 1,000 which the inspectors broke down into first, second, and third grade arms, paying between $16 and $20. Even the first grade arms were sometimes a shade off; $19.90 instead of the perfection demanded for $20. By January 13, 1863, no more foolishness was tolerated. Jenks was turning out guns right on the button, and they were accepted by the thousands *weekly* at the full price of $20 until the end of the war. Then, some 6,000 which were slightly overdue were accepted at $19 and the Bridesburg Machine Works could look with pride at supplying not only 98,000 accepted Springfields, plus the 464 "with marks upon them," but Saron & Roberts and Rice as well.

CASE No. 24. Alexis Godillot, Paris & New York, Lefaucheux & Perrin revolvers and French rifled muskets. See Chapter 23.

CASE NO. 25. E. Remington & Sons, Ilion, New York, 10,000 Regulation rifles, with sword bayonets. (Special Remington "Zouave" rifle 1862.) See Chapter 25.

CASE NO. 26. Henry J. Ibbotson, New York, 20,000 Enfield rifles. The Commission directed that insofar as Ibbotson had gone to Europe with money, and had shipped a small number of the guns before the Queen's proclamation temporarily cut off shipments, the contract in full was null and void but that the guns he had in the United States if equal to the contract price, should be accepted and paid for. A total of 2,050 Enfield long rifles at $18.28⅛ were accepted May 5, 1862; 87 at the rate of $16.28⅛ the same day; all paid for May 19.

CASE NO. 28. Strobell & Company, Gibbs patent breech-loading carbines. See also *Yankee Carbines,* Chapter 11. Strobell & Company made an offer to fabricate or supply 10,000 Gibbs patent breech-loading carbines to Ripley. The general countered by ordering 5,000. But no contract was actually made. A contract was subsequently made with another party to furnish the carbines. Strobell & Company were left out entirely and received no compensation nor did they deliver any guns.

CASE NO. 36. Lamson, Goodnow and Yale, Springfield rifled muskets, Special pattern 1861.

This is one of the more famous firms to emerge from the Civil War in a stable and prosperous condition. When Robbins & Lawrence failed, in overcapitalizing but not receiving a British contract for 300,000 Enfield rifles, their assets in Windsor, Vermont, were acquired by a triumvirate, E. G. Lamson, A. F. Goodnow, and B. B. Yale, operating as Lamson, Goodnow & Yale. At the close of the war in 1865 Goodnow and Yale bowed out; Lamson carried on as E. G. Lamson & Company, and the writer owned an almost new condition rifle musket dated 1865, marked "E. G. Lamson" instead of the more usual three name company stamp. This did not have the usual inspectors' stamps on the stock, and apparently had not been accepted by the United States Government; though three tiny 1/32 inch-high letter stamps were to be seen on the stock flat opposite lockplate. For a brief time the firm was known as Windsor Mfg. Co.; then in 1869 R. L. Jones joined the firm and ten years later became partner in Jones & Lamson. This firm took over the machine tool business which the three partners had founded in the war to supply other musket makers, and in 1889 removed to Springfield, Vermont, where the company today is one of the nation's largest and most progressive machine tool makers.

On 11 July 1861 L G & Y took a contract issued by Ripley to make 25,000 of the new Colt-pattern rifle muskets, at $20. About 11 September they first received a model musket from Springfield; the 60 days' delay caused them embarrassment, as their contract called for first deliveries in six months; and October 7 they received an increase in the order by another 25,000 arms.

Barrels were ordered from N. Washburn, Worcester, Massachusetts, welded iron, bored and in the rough state, and were processed to finished condition in two works: first at the Bay State Works, Northampton, Massachusetts, and at the barrel mill of Cooper & Hewett. The Bay State Arms Company is listed as working at Oxbridge, Massachusetts, about 1870-75, making single-shot target rifles and pistols. It is probable this gunmaking venture grew out of the Bay State Works venture into barrel making for L G & Y. Bayonets and ramrods were also made for L G & Y at Bay State.

Locks and bands were made at a factory owned by the triumvirate in Shelburn Falls, Massachusetts, a cutlery shop, which on occasion had employed 400 workmen. By February 8, 1862, they reported 25,000 of some parts already finished, and large quantities of other parts ready or in process. Also at Shelburn they had 70 men working on making drop forging tools for this Special Model for Springfield Armory, as at the time it appeared likely that Springfield would put this model into production as soon as it could. As of February, Springfield Armory had six drops in operation forging parts for the 1861 Special Model musket as made by L G & Y. The Windsor works was also busy making up special gauges and other tools for Springfield to use in production work. At Windsor the machine tool manufacture was concentrated, and there they turned out not only equipment needed for their own gun work, but stockmaking machines for Amoskeag (they had turned a stock finished except for ramrod groove by April, 1862 at Windsor) and stock machinery for Providence Tool Company while in musket production. "We are ahead of the armory in this pattern, and we are to get up gauges for the armory while finishing our own," said Mr. Goodnow before the Commissioners.

The decision of Holt and Owen was fair, affirming the contracts, and allowing a grace period on account of the lateness of their receiving the model arm from Springfield. Deliveries between September 24, 1862, and December 10, 1864, indicate payments at $20, $19.90, $19, $18, $17.50, and $16, the Commission taking advantage of the late delivery to the extent of declaring the arms should be assessed at less than contract prices if not perfect. This decision of the Commission was taken upon their being satisfied that $20 allowed an exorbitant profit on any contract exceeding 10,000 or 15,000 arms, and the inspectors in New York cut the prices accordingly. L G & Y delivered their 50,000, and apparently assembled some few later on as E. G. Lamson & Company for private or militia sale.

CASE NO. 37. Providence Tool Company, 50,000 rifle muskets.

This firm also continued in the gun business beyond the span of the war years and made notable contributions to ordnance engineering and to the sporting rifle

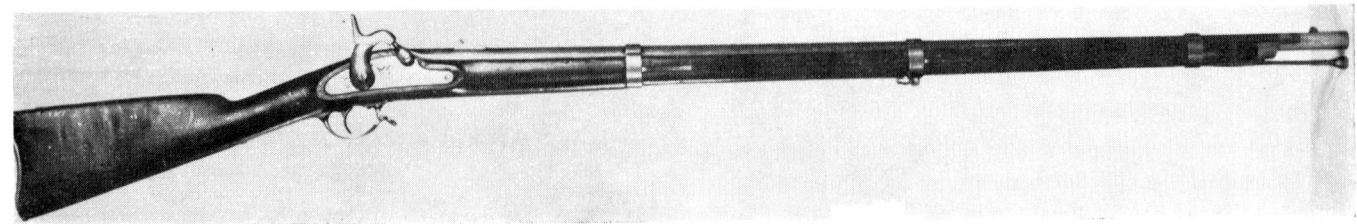

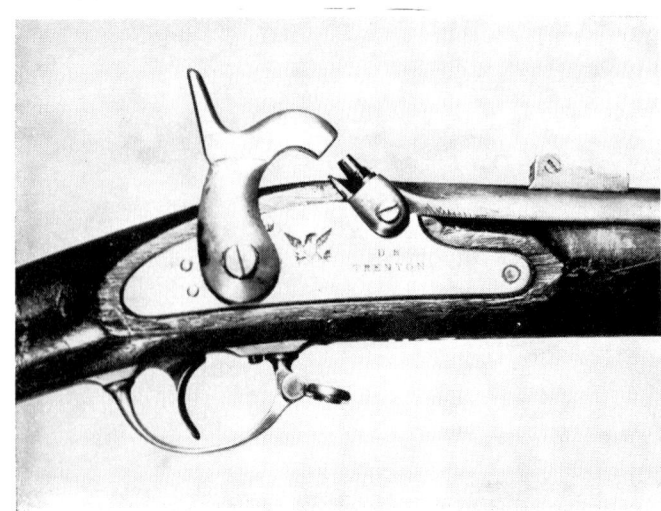

Basic infantry arm of Union was M1861 RM improved over 1855 type by omitting patchbox. Soldiers found primer door cover also objectionable as it flipped loose when catch became weak, rattling and losing caps. Contract piece shown was delivered by either Burt or Hodge, is marked Trenton.

scene. Their Peabody and Peabody-Martini "Creedmoor" long range match rifles were without peer in the target rifle field, achieving the recognition as competitive rifles that the Sharps achieved in the sporting rifle field. They pioneered a practical breechloader and sold many hundreds of thousands of them to Turkey. Modified by the Swiss designer Martini it became the British service rifle and is today still popular wherever usage suggests the propriety of a single shot system.

John B. Anthony, treasurer and prime mover of Providence Tool Company, took a contract for 25,000 rifle muskets, increased by an additional 25,000, on 13 July '61 and 26 November '61. Formerly makers of ship hardware, Providence Tool acquired a new shop and installed complete machinery for gunmaking. They claimed to have the first set of barrel rolling machines in the United States, and had obtained 200 tons of English Marshall iron to replace barrel blanks obtained from Washburn which had proved inferior quality.

Redfield of New York was to furnish the first 3,000-5,000 stocks; afterwards the Windsor machinery from L G & Y would fill the quota. They exclusively contracted the production of a forging and machine shop at Freetown, Massachusetts, for sights. "This shop is under our control, and cannot make for others without our permission." Bayonets and ramrods were made at the ship's chandlery shop in Providence.

For gauges, they hired a machine shop in Springfield and had their own men make up the inspection tools, constantly checking their work against the tools at Springfield Armory. "The pattern guns given out at Springfield are not model guns suitable for making the gauges by, and therefore we have had to start a shop at Springfield, and get opportunities to verify our work by the true models as we could."

Between December 18, 1862, and May 25, 1865, Providence Tool Company delivered 70,000 rifled muskets, the majority being graded Class 1. Most were accepted at $20, others at 10¢ off, $19.90, $19, $18.90. From May, 1864, deliveries were on the third order, a contract for 32,000 arms at $19 each.

Some of these rifles were in 1866 transformed by the tip-down breech of General Benjamin S. Roberts to breechloaders. An almost new specimen of this pattern was purchased from the shop of Mr. Johnson, 16 Quai du Louvre, Paris, by the writer in 1948. The condition of the arm suggested it had been recently removed from a case of muskets, possibly sold to France in 1870.

CASE No. 38. Durrie & Rusher, Enfield rifles.

As no arms were received by the United States under contract, the reader will not be referred to any detailing of this contract in Chapter 22. However, it is interesting to consider that the agent of these men, Mr. Francis Preston, of Manchester, England, did ship about 3,600 long Enfield rifles and 96 short Enfields with sword bayonets, which, as they were refused under their contract, were sold by them at assessed prices on the open market to the U. S. agent at New York, apparently Crispin. Because of late deliveries, occasioned by the Queen's Proclamation, Holt and Owen took the opportunity to wiggle out of validating the contract and it was declared null and void.

CASE No. 39. J. P. Fitch, 75,000 English Enfield rifles.

In this case, too, the Queen's Proclamation having cause nondelivery, the Government in the order having reserved the right to take them or not if delivery was not on schedule, elected through Holt and Owen to not take the rifles, and Fitch's order was cancelled.

CASE No. 43. W. A. Wheeler, 50,000 Rifled Muskets.

This case was decided against Wheeler, and no arms were received. However, the handling of it by Holt, Owen, and ultimately Stanton, was far from objective, though the interests of the Government, that is, cutting off the spiraling supply of contract rifle muskets, were served.

Wheeler was written an order for 50,000 rifle

muskets at $20 December 24, 1861. But this order, though signed by Ripley and ready to go out, was left in Assistant Secretary Thomas Scott's desk when he and Cameron left office. It appeared to the Commissioners, and to Stanton on appeal, that the purpose of the Government being "thus inchoate and unconsummated," the deal was not officially made. Wheeler, in March, 1862, came to the Ordnance office and from the letter book received a certified copy of his "acceptance" order, and then endorsed that to show he had taken the order and was getting to work on it. Holt and Owen did not approve the copy as the original, and Stanton upheld their move. The contract is interesting because of the first statements Wheeler made in his original letter to Cameron proposing to make rifle muskets:

Washington, D. C. November 18, 1861
Sir: I have obtained, in connexion with a number of capitalists in New York, the control of one of the largest manufacturing establishments in the country, which can readily be converted into a manufactory for arms, which enables me to make the following proposition, viz:
I will furnish 100,000 stand of the most approved muskets, with interchangeable parts, equal in every respect to the best Springfield pattern, without the Maynard primer attached to lock, which I learn has been abandoned by the Government—delivery as follows: within six months from the date of the contract, 5,000 in thirty days; thereafter 6,000; and within each succeeding thirty days, 8,000, until the entire number is delivered. The arms to be delivered at Governor's Island, or such other arsenal in or near New York as the Government may direct, and be subject to usual inspection by an officer of the United States Army.
Your obedient Servant,
Wm. A Wheeler

First, Wheeler had control (at least provisionally or temporarily) of a very large plant. His estimated production offers are five to eight times the norm achieved by other factories, even experienced arms firms, as they all seemed to lay their plans for producing 1,000 muskets a month. Wheeler hoped to make 8,000 monthly, an enormous total for those days. A large factory near New York controlled by other speculators was the Trenton Locomotive Machine Shop at Trenton, New Jersey, where a few arms were turned out. One conjecture, from his assertions that he wanted to deliver at New York or near New York, is that he was considering doing the work here.

Second, while he refers to the Springfield without Maynard primer (1861 model) he does not precisely state he will make M1861 Springfield muskets but an interchangeable arm, of the "most approved pattern," which is "equal in every respect to the best Springfield pattern." It is possible to read this sentence with a double entendre, that is, that he proposed to furnish a Springfield musket which would be "equal to" the Springfield pattern musket, of the best finish and detail. But it seems less subtle and more common to interpret this as a claim to making a musket which is like the Springfield in not having the Maynard primer, and is of the most approved pattern, and is "equal" to the Springfield. The only arm of this nature considered in the context of the times is the Enfield long rifled musket. Yet Wheeler does not say flat out, "Enfields." The puzzle may never be unravelled as to the model of arm Wheeler hoped to make, and where he hoped to make it.

CASE No. 44. Wm. F. Brooks of New York, 10,000 Gibbs carbines and 10,000 Springfield rifled muskets. For Gibbs carbines, see *Yankee Carbines,* Chapter 11.

The Springfield musket contract was annulled due to nondelivery. Brooks was associated with William W. Marston, New York gunmaker and inventor of the Marston breech-loading pistols and rifles. His armory though small was complete. He proposed to make the Springfields after he had finished the carbines, using stock tools for the Springfields that had been running on carbine parts. Result was no Springfields, and Brooks lost his chance by order of Holt and Owen.

CASE No. 45. Samuel B. Smith of New York, 40,000 Austrian .54 rifles, reduced by Commissioners to 20,000. This, too, is a short item; Smith proposed to deliver 40,000 arms "as per sample," he having bought the Lorenz rifle *a tige* with leaf sight at Boker's and brought it to Washington. The proposition was accepted by Ripley at $20 a gun, though he was then soon buying the same rifle direct from Boker through Crispin at only $15 each. After kicking the ball back and forth, a compromise was reached at $16 for all up to 20,000. Some "block sights" were in the lot; but leaf and block sighted guns were accepted at $16. A total of 9,667 Austrian rifled muskets and appendages in bond at $16 were paid for to Samuel B. Smith on August 29, 1862, a sum of $154,672.

CASE No. 47, John Hoff, Washington, D. C., and Philadelphia, 20,000 foreign Minié Rifles, Austrian caliber .58, blued barrels. See Chapter 22.

CASE No. 48. Savage Revolving Firearms Company, Middletown, Connecticut. This case is two-fold, the revolver contract part being found herein under *Federal Revolvers,* Chapter 23.

Organized to manufacture revolving breech firearms, handguns, and rifles, of the designs of North and Edward Savage, the firm had as secretary James A. Wheelock. Responding too late to the general scramble for muskets in '61, Wheelock in June of 1862 sought a contract to make 50,000 Springfields at the very low price of $16. Their factory in Middletown, Connecticut, was described by Wheelock as occupied by "practical gunsmiths of long standing—for three quarters of a century." He stated his firm was "the oldest and one of the largest establishments in the country," industrial and corporate successors to the historic firm of Colonel Simeon North's.

Holt, Owen, and Major Hagner thought the proposal a fair price, and that the fabricant had the capability to deliver; but as they had confirmed contracts amounting to over 600,000 guns, they did not think it proper to accept; the Government only wanted 500,000 muskets. Wheelock would not be put off, and on

June 16, 1862, he wrote to the Commissioners of his recent trip to New York. He said that speculators there whose contracts were confirmed had offered him orders up to 200,000 guns, and some would give as much as $19 a gun just to have them manufactured. Wheelock doubted that half the guns that were ordered would be manufactured. To show the Commissioners that he wanted to work for the Government at a fair price out of patriotism, and was not just angling for a contract from any source, he declared that the contract awarded and confirmed to Parker, Snow, Brooks & Company they were willing to assign to Savage Revolving Fire Arms Company! On 9 September 1862 Wheelock's persistence was rewarded by Ripley signing their contract for 25,000 Springfields, deliverable in lots of 2,000 per month after the 6 months tooling-up time, at only $18 per gun. Thirteen thousand five hundred guns were delivered to February '64. A second contract for 12,000 Springfields at $18 was signed 25 February 1864 by General Ramsay and Wheelock, and to November 7, 1864, 12,000 arms were delivered. They were graded out at usually less than contract price, but in exactly what particulars the Class 2, Class 2½, or poorer arms were deficient is not known.

CASE NO. 52. Wigert & Otard, New York, 10,000 French rifles with sword bayonets. Wigert on September 5, 1861 offered to deliver 10,000 Chasseurs de Vincennes rifles in 55 days. George L. Schuyler wrote from Paris on October 10, when queried about this, that Wigert could not fill the order as such guns were not to be had. The price of $23.50 Schuyler supposed would draw inferior guns and recommended a strict inspection at New York. Wigert then wrote for an extension of 8 months. This was after delay granted, and when Holt and Owen came to investigate, the matter stood as before; contract existing but no guns. They withdrew and annulled the order.

CASE NO. 54. Mickles & Hopkins, New York, 60,000 iron mounted muskets "new, never having been used," caliber 17½ mm.

This offer was informally accepted by the War Department, George Schuyler having been directed to inspect them in Antwerp if offered; and, if usable, accept them. But the order was never formally issued to purchase them and it was adjudged that as they were almost certainly Prussian muskets (M & H substituted brass mounted for iron mounted with approval), and the price of $7.65 being too high, the order was generally cancelled.

CASE NO. 55. W. A. Seaver, 50,000 Enfield muskets at $20 equal to "sample with tower mark deposited in Ordnance office by Messrs. Mitchell and Jones." No deliveries; contract annulled.

CASE NO. 56. H. Simon & Son, 5,000 Long Enfield Rifles at $19. No deliveries, contract annulled.

CASE NO. 59. Hewett & Randall, 10,000 Long Enfield Rifles at $20 with $3 forfeit per arm for non-delivery. No deliveries, declared binding on neither party, annulled and forfeiture remitted.

CASE NO. 61. Howland & Aspinwall, 17,000 Enfields. See *Continental Arms,* Chapter 22.

CASE NO. 62. John Rice, Philadelphia, 36,000 Springfield rifle muskets.

This case is a classic one, showing not the machinations of incompetent persons, but the efforts of a sincere and mechanically skilled contractor who proposed to arrange the manufacture of muskets for the Union, but was himself not a skilled gunmaker. There is evidence that all the parts needed for these arms were in fact in existence at the time the matter came before the Commissioners, yet there is no published record of any deliveries.

Rice, a contractor for stonework at the Capitol then being finished, and a carpenter by trade, had many friends in the mechanical industries of Philadelphia. On October 2, 1861 he wrote offering to supply muskets to Cameron, as "I can organize the manufacture of them at various places in Philadelphia, and furnish from ten to twelve thousand inside the time mentioned. This, if accepted, will furnish employment to a large number of workmen who are now idle."

The proposal included delivery in full by 1 July, 1862. Though the "terms appear reasonable and deliveries early," the matter was referred to Ripley who considered that contracts enough were outstanding and that Rice's could not be accepted. Meanwhile, Rice had been checking about in Philadelphia and seemed confident of success. The next month he wrote a new offer, saying he would make Springfields at $20, and deliver 3,000 to 4,000 each month for 12 months, commencing in February, 1862. This proposal Ripley was instructed to accept; by letter a contract was issued 21 November, 1861, ordering 36,000 rifles beginning with 3,000 in February and 3,000 monthly thereafter. "In case of any failure to make the deliveries to the extent and within the times before specified, all the obligations of the United States to receive or pay for any muskets then deliverable under this order shall be cancelled and become null and void," wrote Ripley. Rice accepted these conditions on November 27, 1861. He had but two and a half months before he had to supply the first 3,000 rifles.

To Essler & Brother (later known as C. H. Williams & Co.) of Philadelphia he went for locks, later reported "and I can get them as fast as I want them." Jenks at Bridesburg made his stocks; Rice bought the wood, and it remained at Jenks' waiting requirements for it to be turned and shaped. One thousand five hundred had been finished by Jenks for Rice as of April, 1862, but apparently by that late date when Rice appeared before the Commissioners, no actual guns had been assembled. Rice, due to failures in getting his barrels from Washburn, whose troubles with iron had delayed other makers, felt that deliveries could not be made before July, 1862. Rice had been successful in getting the time of delivery extended to 1 May, 1862, so pushing it up to July did not seem too much more of a problem.

He did not, in all this time, have an actual works or shop in which to assemble the arms. This shop he hoped to obtain somewhere near Springfield, asking if he could deliver for inspection at the Springfield Armory. Meanwhile, he sent several locks up to Springfield for gauging, and also ramrods; the locks were perfect, the ramrods required slight alteration in his own gauges to be made perfect. Between February and April 1, Rice was kept in suspense about the realities of his contract. Did he really have an order? Would the Government designate a place of acceptance and inspection for his guns? To this, Stanton asked, where was his factory? In the breakdown, Rice showed himself an excellent organizer, so long as the Government would give him a little flexibility in time delivery. His muskets were being made by the following parts contractors:

Wm. Mason of Taunton, Massachusetts, barrels, "who reports that he will be ready in time for the delivery."

Hiram Bigelow, New Haven, Connecticut, guard plates, bows, triggers, butt plates, etc. "Will be delivered as per agreement."

Humphreyville Manufacturing Company, Seymour, Connecticut, bayonets. "We can make 600 bayonets per day. In April, and after, there will be no failure to deliver your bayonets as called for in our contract."

E. P. Coleman & Brother, Philadelphia, ramrods, "Now ready to deliver ramrods."

W. F. Nicholson & Company, Providence, sights, bands, swivels, "We see nothing to hinder prompt deliveries."

Cole & Brother, Springfield, Massachusetts, and Pawtucket, Rhode Island, cones, "Will be able to furnish 6,000 by the first of April."

S. Stowe Manufacturing Company, Connecticut, band springs, "We hope to make our first delivery in April 12 to 15 (of gun springs). Hoping they will be in time."

C. B. North, Springfield, Massachusetts, for washers. There were the discs also called, when fancy, "escutcheons," against which the heads of the lock plate side screws bear.

Dwight & Company, Bridgeport, Connecticut, appendages. These men apparently were represented in part by Samuel Norris of Springfield, who reported, "The appendages will be promptly delivered according to contract."

C. H. Williams & Company, Philadelphia, sent a sample lock to Rice, "and trust it will convince him of their ability to fill his contract."

Armed with these statements of condition as of April 1, 1862, Rice made a proposal to the Commissioners for the Government to take the contracts off his hands:

"If I could get the Government to take the prices I have contracted for, I would be glad to be relieved; I can ascertain my liabilities in ten days." But Holt and Owen considered the alternative, that Rice had been faithful in following up the mode of manufacture which was the only one open to him. Their problem was not to criticize the foolishness of the Government in giving him the order in the first place, unless it was truly irregular, but in seeing that the contractor performed according to the best of his ability. While the interests of the Government were to be protected, it was not their job to censure nor condemn diligent contractors, especially a man like Rice who seemed able to corral all the fabricants of New England into making the parts required. Unless he would be permitted to furnish some portion of the number ordered, his loss would be excessive, and the Commission so ordered it:

May 2, 1862
. . . As . . . the government will derive benefit by earlier deliveries than can be promised by manufacturers now starting, it is fair to Mr. Rice to confirm in part the order given him at the price stated therein . . . a number not exceeding in all 25,000 muskets, with the proper appendages, be accepted under the terms and conditions of the order dated November 20, 1861, provided that a first delivery of at least 2,000 be ready prior to July 1, 1862, and that monthly thereafter at least 2,000 per month be delivered until the number ordered is completed . . . (Holt, Owen, Hagner)

The identification of these muskets is lacking. It seems highly probable that Rice, given the grace time he asked for, must have tried to get some guns together. The stocks from Jenks at least had tips, and locks were definitely in existence, and passing gauge at Springfield, in April. Arms of Philadelphia locus, from the marks on them, are "Philadelphia" and "Bridesburg" muskets. The latter are assumed to be Alfred Jenks & Son guns made at their Bridesburg Machine Works. The Philadelphia arms it is conjectured (see Jenks Case above) might be some marked by Jenks in just getting started, and not precisely uniform in stamping with their Bridesburg-marked locks. The possibility also exists that these Philadelphia arms are of the John Rice issue; proof is lacking for either case. Two other marks are known on Springfield rifled muskets which have puzzled Fuller: MILBURY, and WINDSOR LOCKS. Both towns in Connecticut have gunmaking backgrounds; both could have furnished the necessary labor for assembling Rice's muskets. Both are relatively centrally located in the regions where he contracted for the major amount of work, leaving only locks and stocks to come up from Philadelphia. By the time of the Commission's decision to confirm his order to the amount of 25,000 pieces, Rice still had not made up his mind where to assemble, but continued to prefer the area of Springfield, Massachusetts. Windsor Locks, Connecticut, is on the road to Springfield; perhaps Rice was able to get a few arms finished there before defaulting on his second, confirmed contract.

CASE NO. 64. Union Arms Company, New York, and R. S. Gallaher. Springfield rifles and Marsh's patent breech- and muzzle-loading rifles.

Of all the speculative middlemen, Robert S. Gallaher seems to have made one of the best possible arrangements for production and capitalization of a new enterprise. The Union Armory was famous in New York by 1863, and fears were entertained by the authorities that the rioters in the great draft riots of July, 1863, would break in and carry off the arms to create a real civil insurrection. Hundreds of thousands of dollars were paid in by the stockholders—yet apparently of 65,000 Springfields contracted for, of which 25,000 were confirmed by the Commission, and 12,500 Marsh patent rifles, none were ever delivered to the United States. It has been conjectured that some were delivered by Union to state authorities. Fault in this reasoning is that the state authorities supplied men; arms were supplied by the general government. Perhaps not all states turned in their bills to the United States for settlement, but a great many suppliers of arms directly for state issue, in turn came before Holt and Owen for settlement of their accounts. If any state had received any considerable number of either Springfield type arms from Union or Marsh breechloaders, they would have been to satisfy the needs of their three years' volunteers and would almost certainly have been paid for by the United States. Though a full report on Gallaher is lacking, there is a strong suspicion that for all his plausibility, he was able to spend a lot of money without making very many arms. An automobile entrepreneur with many good ideas, it will be remembered, frittered away over ten million dollars in such a fashion in the late 1940's without producing more than a handful of finished autos, though his much-touted engine concepts were implemented in later automobiles.

R. H. Gallaher originally obtained one contract in his own name, for 20,000 "No. 1, Springfield guns, with appendages and angular bayonets," from Ripley on August 31, 1861; delivery to begin in 60 days, at $20. This was extended by a War Department letter, November 26, 1861. Meanwhile, Gallaher and either a brother or father, as John S. Gallaher & Company, obtained a second contract for Springfields, 20,000 of them at $20, on October 11, 1861. Meanwhile, an inventor whose design seems to be the model for what was later celebrated as the E. S. Allin conversion to the Springfield, making a muzzle-loader into a breech-loader, also obtained a contract. Twenty-five thousand Springfield rifles, "in all respects, except the breech-loading attachment, identical with the standard rifle musket made at the United States armory at Springfield, Massachusetts, and are to interchange with it in all their parts, except those pertaining to the breech-loading attachments, and with each other in all their parts," were ordered of inventor S. Wilmer Marsh October 14, 1861. To make these guns, Marsh turned to Gallaher. Needing capital and planning to build for the Union, Gallaher formed a corporation, The Union Fire-arms Company, of New York City. Stockholders and officers included Edward Robinson, James McKay, Linus Scudder, Enoch Chamberlain, John Hays, and Robert H. Gallaher. As the agent of the Union Fire-arms Company, "R. H." now obtained a fourth contract, the Marsh one having been assigned to Union, directly in the name of Union for 25,000 additional Springfields.

On January 3, Cameron agreed, by letter, to the assigning over to Union Fire-arms of all the contracts listed. "It having been shown that the Union Fire-arms Co. . . . have the necessary capital and facilities for manufacturing guns for the government. . . ." By the time of this consolidation into one contract, Gallaher had sold $240,000 worth of stock in the new company, all the capitalized amount, and had put money into the expansion by other sub-contractors of their capacities to make small parts for Springfields.

He approached Daniel J. Young, formerly a works manager of the Harpers Ferry U. S. rifle factory, to obtain some of the more skilled Virginia workmen who had been more or less banished from the state and were looking for work. Gallaher had represented these men from Harpers Ferry in the Congress before the war, and their ability to do the work needed was a part of his plan to make muskets. The Manhattan Firearms Company agreed to sell him some new machines, which they had begun to build for him, and lease him a large number of other machines plus "all small tools and a large amount of vacant room."

Obviously, some part of the Union manufacturing was to be done in the Manhattan armory. W. C. Hicks, superintendent of the Boston Arms Company, agreed to turn over all that firm's machinery and to come to New York with "sixty of the best gun workmen in the United States." Steelmaker R. A. Douglas of New York had ready his rolling mill to roll barrels "as per contract of 500 tons, which I hope you will soon be ready to commence ordering." Charles Hewitt, of Hewitt & Cooper, Trenton Iron Works was ready to roll gun barrels as soon as Gallaher could show him a sample of the moulds as they came from Douglas. Collins & Company were ready to make his bayonets. The ubiquitous C. K. Garrison offered added capital if needed.

The Springfield muzzle-loader was, with all these preparations, not a difficult thing to make, except so far as the precision of work was concerned. Only a little more complicated was the Marsh patent breech- and muzzle-loader, which Union was also to supply. Tested on the West Point ranges by Lieutenant S. V. Benet, later Brigadier General, Chief of Ordnance, and father of the poet Stephen Vincent Benet, the report was quite favorable:

West Point, U.S., August 24, 1861
Sir: Yesterday I superintended the trial of Marsh's breech and muzzle loading rifle, and have the honor to make the following report:
The arm consists of a United States rifle, calibre .58, fitted with a breech attachment. The latter is connected to the upper

edge of the breech of the barrel by a hinge, and consists of a breech plug or bolt, with a gas check at the end next the barrel. The gas check is made of a double ring of steel, breaking joints, that is expanded by means of a steel cone that passes through it, thus closing all escape of gas. The plug or bolt is thrown up by pressing the trigger forward, and exposing the opened barrel to receive the cartridge; it is brought back to its place after loading by a blow of the hand, and is held in position by a steel pin that enters the bolt at its rear extremity.

The ammunition used was of two kinds; a common paper cylinder tied to the United States expanding bullet, and the "seamless skin cartridge," used with the Enfield rifle. The same cartridge serves for both breech and muzzle loading, and no material enlargement as a chamber is therefore made.

Forty-four shots were fired with the common cartridge, loading at the breech. At the seventh round the cartridge could not be inserted, the cartridge paper having been driven into the interior orifice of the vent. This was readily removed with a wire, and the firing continued. At the twenty-eighth round thereafter the bolt moved with difficulty, caused by the escape of gas and consequent fouling. At the forty-first round paper again stuck in the vent; at the forty-fourth fouled and worked with difficulty. The gas check and breech were cleaned, when necessary, by merely rubbing them with a rag or the moistened finger, a very simple, easy and quick operation, that did not materially interrupt the course of the trial.

The breech attachment being thus cleaned, the rifle was fired seventy-seven rounds with Enfield skin cartridge, loading at the breech. At the twenty-eighth round, the breech fouled, and was cleaned with a rag in a moment. At the forty-fifth round it again fouled, and was cleaned. At the fiftieth (or ninety-fourth of the entire firing) the rifle was loaded at the muzzle; the barrel was so foul that the breech was sent home with difficulty. The firing was then continued, loading at the breech, with ease, and so continued to the seventy-seventh, (or one hundred and twenty-first of the entire firing). The last round was loaded at the muzzle with great difficulty, because of the excessive fouling of the barrel. The barrel was not cleaned during the trial.

The gun was fired ten rounds in one minute and fifty seconds.

Conclusions.—The mechanism is very simple and strong, and not easily put out of order. The rifle with which the firing was made is evidently an old one, has been much used, and the bolt that closes the breech not at all firm and solid in its place, the steel pin that enters its rear end working loose. This may account in part for the fouling. The fouling was not very great, and the invention has the great merit of permitting the clogged parts being easily cleaned by the finger moistened with saliva, where a moist rag is not convenient. By this simple expedient the rifle was fired one hundred and twenty-one rounds with no difficulty or detention, although the bore had meanwhile become so foul that loading at the muzzle became a tedious and troublesome operation.

The common cartridge was inserted *entire*, without tearing, the cap exploding the cartridge through the paper without fail. The sticking of the paper in the vent might be easily remedied.

Should, from any cause, the breech attachment fail to work, a few turns of a screw fixes it in its place, and the rifle becomes a muzzle-loader, using the same ammunition.

The invention has undoubtedly great merit, and I believe that a new rifle, with the parts more skillfully fitted, would give more satisfactory results.

Very respectfully, your obedient servant,
S. V. Benet
1st Lieutenant United States Ordnance

Brevet Brigadier General J. W. Ripley
Chief of Ordnance, Washington, D. C.

Faced with the favorable report on this rifle, Holt and Owen could not entirely dismiss the matter. However, their avowed purpose was to reduce the indebtedness of the United States for various kinds of breechloaders, and they suggested to Gallaher that he make some proposals along these lines. He assented, and voluntarily reduced the Springfields to 25,000 in number, surrendering his claim on the United States for the 40,000, and ultimately dropped his demands for the Marsh guns to 12,500 instead of 25,000; the price was reduced to $27.75 instead of $29.75. The Commission's secretary, J. Wise, sent a note on May 1, 1862 to Gallaher to help him quiet his apprehensive backers, saying his contracts would be confirmed, and on May 5 Holt, Owen, and Hagner recapitulated the record of delivery schedules and confirmed the contracts as stated, first deliveries to begin in July. Gallaher was directed to prepare a model musket on Marsh's pattern for Ripley to approve not later than June 15.

Standard ammunition was totally enclosed in paper wrapper, but the Confederate Gardner patent conceived of the idea of crimping the paper into the base of the lead ball. The notion saved paper, however, it was weak, the paper in handling and transportation accidentally breaking at the crimp.

The forfeiture of any guns not delivered on time was to be strictly complied with so as to reduce the number of guns delivered; Gallaher had to put up or shut up.

According to Fuller *(Springfield Muzzle Loading Shoulder Arms)*, only three Springfield muskets were made up by Union Arms and delivered to the United States, probably as samples. No contract deliveries were made, and there is no record of payments. Union did make a few revolvers, of solid-frame percussion system resembling the Whitney small pocket arms. The dissolution of Union Fire-arms Company of New York seems to have been not with a bang, but an inaudible whimper.

Case No. 65. C. W. Durant, Colorado Territory.

Governor Gilpin, to arm the Union citizens of Colorado, bought up an unspecified number of sporting rifles and muskets from Durant, in the amount of $3733.50. "Although the prices for the article are high, yet they do not seem unreasonable," and the Commissioners directed the account to be paid. At the same time it is said the Confederate sympathizers bought up all the percussion caps in town. Thus the rifles and muskets were useless because Rebels controlled the caps. It was a standoff in Colorado!

Case No. 68. Gordon, Castlen & Gordon, Louisville, Kentucky, $1425.00 for Navy pistols and musket caps to arm the regiment of Colonel Jackson, approved by Brigadier General W. T. Sherman. Directed to be paid.

CASE NO. 69. Starr Arms Company, revolvers, carbines, and Springfields. See Chapter 17.

CASE NO. 70. Schuyler, Hartley & Graham, 10,000 Enfield rifle muskets for Ohio.

State agent C. P. Wolcott in New York, acting for the Governor of Ohio, had ordered 10,000 Enfields at $19 from S. H. & G. Five hundred were delivered to him before the Queen's Embargo suspended shipments; the firm's man in Birmingham, Francis Tomes, was told to keep alert and send more guns as soon as he could. This was done, but the state agent no longer having authority to buy, the Maiden Lane partners sold to the United States agent, Captain Crispin, at $20, prevailing market price. Meanwhile more guns arrived, Crispin suspended buying, and some 7,000 arms in all were considered a problem, Schuyler, Hartley & Graham wanting the United States to buy them. They reduced the price finally to $16.25, and the Commission directed they be permitted to deliver up to 7,000 of such arms, including 1,500 contracted for to be made in Suhl, Germany.

While these arms are often described as "Enfields," it is evident from the Commission's decision that they are not, for the words of the decision are, "including the 1,500 made at Suhl, if of equally good quality and similar in calibre and finish." This suggests the arms were only "similar" to the Enfields, and that there was doubt as to whether they might be blued and case-hardened as the Enfields, or finished otherwise.

During May and June, 5,320 Enfields were received and 998 Suhl rifles (Enfield pattern) with appendages, at the arbitrated contract price of $16.25.

CASE NO. 72. William Mason, Taunton, Massachusetts, 50,000 or 100,000 Springfields, at $20, contract letter January 7, 1862.

Manufacturer of machinery for cotton mills, Mason wanted to put his shops at the service of the Government. The glamour of gunmaking seems to have attracted him; he obtained a contract for 50,000 guns, at $20, but persuaded Ripley to endorse it with an additional 50,000, if they were all made in his own shop, and not pieced out here and there. The Federal Government seems to have been highly receptive to the idea that more complete armories than just Springfield and Colt's should exist in the North, and Taunton was well suited for waterpower and manpower, midway between Boston and Providence, for fine machine work. But when Mason had expended about $600,000 in new machines, Holt and Owen put a damper on it.

There seems to have been some confusion over exactly what Ripley did mean in saying the order would be approved for 100,000 guns "if manufactured in your own establishment at Taunton, Mass." The Commissioners took it at face value and interrogated Mason as to where he was having his guns made.

Accessories for CW guns were leather box for percussion caps, thumb-screw vise to cramp spring for stripping lock, pin punch for removing band springs and driving tumbler out of hammer, and combination two-blade screwdriver and nipple wrench. Extra nipple was often carried, together with screw fitting for ramrod to withdraw misfired bullet, and "worm" which held tow for wiping out bore. Wire loop is nipple pick to clear cap debris in case of misfire, while three angle tools are two Colt and one Whitney nipple wrenches.

Washburn, it appears, was supplying the barrels rolled but not finished. Mason planned to finish them, and had promised some finished barrels to John Rice and another contractor, F. L. Bodine. Stock machinery prepared for Eagle Manufacturing Company was taken over by Mason, who planned to fabricate stock tips, buttplates, and ramrods himself. Colman & Company, Providence, engaged to make 50,000 locks and work only for Mason; they were swaging and milling parts in April when Mason was questioned. Some bands were to be made in Fall River, not far from Taunton, under direction of Mason's own superintendent at a private machine shop. Another machinist, Hames, made guards; both parts Mason planned to bring under his own roof as soon as he could. Gauges were being made at Tyler's in Springfield, Massachusetts, and compared with the armory's master gauges. Bayonets only were not arranged for, but as S. H. Waters & Company in Milbury, and one Osgood in Ilion, New York, also Eagle Manufacturing Company, were making them in quantity, he did not see any question about supply; "also Dagget, sabre maker at Attleboro, offers to make bayonets," he concluded.

Mason was a manufacturer of acknowledged responsibility, and a direct dealer, not a middleman. Holt and Owen were faced with the unpleasant task of serving the Government by chopping down this man's orders from 100,000 to something more economical, say 30,000; they spent a lot of wind in arguing the demerits and irregularities of the case, picking on the conflict of "manufactured in your own establishment" meanings, and decreed that the contract should be confirmed for only 30,000. That Mason had a great amount of justice on his side was reflected by the commissioners' accepting 30,000 instead of 25,000. But Mason was not satisfied, and wrote a very carefully and temperately worded appeal to settle for 75,000, which would about break even for him the way he had arranged his affairs. There is a slight hint or suspicion that Mason realized the similarity between gunmaking machinery and cotton gin-making machinery, and had bought a lot of basic tools that were adaptable to several kinds of manufacturing; perhaps Holt and Owen suspected this from Mason's statement that "I do not mean to say that all this machinery or outlay would be lost if the contract were now taken from or refused me," and they rather limply concluded by endorsing his appeal as:

June 10, 1862
Considered by the commission, and it is decided that the number of arms assigned to Mr. Mason is as large as the commission think it proper at this time to assign to one contractor at the price of $20.

J. Holt
Robert Dale Owen
Commissioners

Case No. 73. Burnside Rifle Company, carbines. See Chapter 11.

Case No. 74. Burnside Rifle Company, breech-loading infantry rifles. See Chapter 11.

Case No. 75. C. B. Hoard, Watertown, New York, 50,000 Springfields.

The settlement of this case by Holt and Owen at Hoard's urging is novel; it will, therefore, be given first. The denoument comes second.

Faced with threat of reduction in numbers of guns, Hoard proposed voluntarily to reduce the price of half of them. This was okayed by the Commissioners. Hoard then proposed that the reduction, to $16, would apply to the first 25,000 guns to be delivered, the second 25,000 being taken at $20. This would save him money, for if he failed to make deliveries (as so many contractors expected to do on the early ones,) the losses would only be at $16 per gun instead of $20. This the Commissioners also agreed to, closing the case so far as they were concerned by their report of June 10, 1862, "which confirmation is upon condition that he shall, within *fifteen days* after notice of this decision, execute bond with good and sufficient sureties, in the form and with the stipulations prescribed by law and the regulations for the faithful performance of the contract, as thus modified, resulting from said order and acceptance, and upon his failure or refusal to execute such bond, then the said order shall be declared cancelled and of no effect."

Hoard had achieved the tacit approval of the Commission to his making 50,000 muskets. But apparently he did not want to risk forfeit of even the $16 muskets. He delayed just too long for the order of the Commission to go into effect, and on June 28, 1862 obtained from General Ripley a new contract, in due form, to be sure, but with new terms, to supply 25,000 muskets at $20. Twelve thousand eight hundred were delivered between September 17, 1863 and August 2, 1865, at prices assessed between $16 and $20, the majority at $19 or $18.90.

The Hon. Charles B. Hoard was a steam engine manufacturer with a modern factory at Watertown, New York. On December 4, 1861, he wrote to Simon Cameron asking to obtain a contract for 50,000 Springfields "upon the same terms as to quantity, price, and time for delivery, given to other parties having similar contracts." Accompanying his modest proposal was a rather immodest barrage of letters signed by numerous legislators and representatives, of the State of New York and the United States, persons known to Cameron, who certified to Hoard's ability to undertake this work. "The remaining names, with unimportant exceptions, of members of Congress from New York can be obtained, if desired by the department," Hoard wrote to a colleague who was trying to use his influence in the matter. The night before Christmas General Ripley sent out a little present to Mr. Hoard, the contract letter for 50,000 muskets at $20.

Hoard was a highly respectable citizen, and his business had been interrupted by the suspension of trade with the South. Perhaps his steam engines were a part of the cotton machinery which Mr. Mason made— a steam cotton gin certainly was an ever-increasing and valued farm article in the South, and Hoard's steam engines may have been part of this industry. He also had a half interest in a nearby agricultural implement shop, which lay idle because so much of his trade was with the South. When he heard of Secretary Stanton's order which seemed to throw into disrepute his contract, he at once wrote to the Honorable Preston King, a Washington colleague, to see if Mr. King could do anything for him:

"I am not willing to be ranked with men who would take advantage of the necessities of government, if they could, to profit therefrom," he said to King. "If the Government does not need the guns, certainly I do not desire to make any; but if it does need them, and they are to be made by some one, at a fair price, then I, having a large factory idle, which can be converted into an armory, would like to put its wheels in motion which have been stopped by this rebellion, much to my injury, and convert it to that use."

Detail of india ink stamp of James D. Mowry on side of a Norwich Armories-made M1861 Rifle Musket. Mowry evidently stamped guns obtained by him from other suppliers, which he in turn delivered under his contract to the Union. A Norfolk-made M1861 is also known stamped with name of contractor Welch.

Awaiting the reply, Hoard continued to make his arrangements for gun parts, machinery, and work space.

He bought the other half of the farm tool shop, planning to convert it to the stockmaking works. Washburn as usual was to supply the barrels, 50,000 of them, lumped for cone seats at $1.50 each. Robert Hoe & Company of New York and American Machine Works of Chicopee were scheduled to deliver machinery. This machinery was a large lot of highly specialized gunmaking devices, and useless for any other purpose. They included such set-ups as one lock bedding machine, two barrel bedding machines, one butt-plate bedding, boring, and tapping machine, and one guard plate bedding machine with side apparatus for boring for screws. C. C. Chaffee of Springfield promised nipples and Hoard had sent an engineer to the armory to make drawings of everything, while between $1,000 and $2,000 had been laid out for gauges now being made. In support of the price of the guns, $20, upon which he calculated to make less than his usual 10% profit on steam engines, Hoard offered an unusual calculation of the cost of the Government-made article. This cost basis is the one any private enterprise must go by, figuring in all the overhead before deriving a total cost of the gun. But the Springfield accountants work on the governmental philosophy that if you have a government, you gotta have an armory also. Their computations of the cost of a musket therefore leave out entirely the enormous capital investment at the National Armory, and figure a lot of bare costs without full overhead put in. The calculation Hoard's way was rather stiff:

Supposed cost of Springfield Armory buildings and machinery: $2,000,000. Annual average production, 14,000 arms.
Upon this data, as a basis, and I believe it is very near the truth, it would appear that the annual interest at 6% on the cost is: $120,000
Assuming that the machinery cost one-half of the outlay, which is not far from the fact, and that the natural wear and loss of machinery is ten percent, and when work is prosecuted only during the day, and this is the rate usually calculated upon by manufacturers, and double that when night and day work is performed, the loss on one million of dollars annually is 100,000
The cost for present production of a musket is $14 each, which would be for 14,000 muskets .. 196,000
$416,000

Showing the actual cost to the government, upon this calculation, believed to be even below the truth, to be $29.17.

But Hoard's senatorial friends, his calculations to show the economy of doing business with Hoard's Armory, his letters, even personally laying the matter before Abraham Lincoln, availed him nothing but the conclusions above cited.

CASE NO. 76. James D. Mowry, 30,000 Springfields, order 26 December, 1861.

In association with Frederick W. Carnmann, paper manufacturer James D. Mowry of Norwich, Connecticut engaged to supply Springfields. He at first expected to make them in his father's machine shop in Norwich, but when he received an order for only 30,000 guns, decided to get the parts made here and there and sub-contract the assembly. Samuel Norris in Springfield was to assemble the parts which had all been arranged for by May of 1862 when Mr. Carnmann came before the Commission to give a progress report. Barrels of course came from Washburn, though one Congdon, importer of English hardware, had received samples of British barrel skelps which he was having finished up at the Armory to see if they were suitable. Norris would supply the mountings; stocks to come from their own machinery set up in New York; and locks from either Williams & Company of Philadelphia at $2.25, or Bateman, New York, at $2. Said Mr. Carnmann:

Mr. Norris has agreed . . . to assemble the arms and be responsible for the inspection. Unless I can do better, I will accept this offer. I have had three offers from manufacturers to make these guns complete at their risk; these offers were from $17 to $18.50. My disbursements thus far have been small, and Mr. Mowry's also.

The Commission reduced the number of arms to 20,000, and Mowry went ahead. He solved the problem by procuring arms from two suppliers; two types of Mowry-marked arms exist. As Mr. Carnmann said in explanation before the Commission's decision, "He applied for 50,000 guns, but as he only got 30,000 he decided not to make much—only a part of the work." Mowry supplied guns marked with his name, U.S./JAS. D. MOWRY/NORWICH CONN. on the lock with an eagle, forward of the hammer. While Fuller categorically states "He sublet all parts except the stocks which he made in New York. The arms were assembled at Springfield, Mass." this appears not to be true for the most part. We believe the Mowry-stamped lockplates are fitted to arms fabricated for Mowry, doubtless using his sources of supply and any other sources of parts handy in season, by the Eagle Manufacturing Company at Mansfield, Connecticut. Reference to the contract in proper form which Mowry was directed to execute including bond with sureties for performance, to deliver 20,000 arms, said contract to be executed in 15 days after notice of this decision, indicate the connection.

On June 7, 1862, Mowry of Norwick, as principal, with Carnmann of New York and Albert H. Almy of New York, as sureties, executed a contract with General Ripley to furnish 20,000 muskets. While Carnmann is identified as "interested" with Mowry in the contract, Almy was the Treasurer of the Eagle Manufacturing Company. Though a full history of Eagle is not known to this writer, it is probable the firm maintained executive offices in New York, accounting for Almy's choosing to reside there. With Almy concerned and liable to forfeit $20,000 personally if Mowry defaulted on his contract, the whole resources of Eagle were unquestionably thrown behind the Mowry project. That Mowry was under a positive obligation to Eagle is shown by his signing as surety himself in the sum of $20,000, along with Almy, to a contract which Eagle negotiated later that same month for rifle muskets!

The Mowry-lock muskets were manufactured by Eagle, but deliveries were not in full. Eagle's first delivery was April 14, 1863; Mowry's should have been July, 1862; but they did not get together enough arms to make the first lot of 500 until June 1, 1863. On June 3, Eagle turned in 1,000; on June 15, Mowry delivered 500. Thereafter they alternated, Eagle apparently achieving a production of about 2,000-3,000 arms a month, for on August 29 both contractors delivered 1,000 rifles each. Eagle's last delivery was September 11; Mowry continued to turn in 1,000 fortnightly until November, 1863, by which time he had delivered only 10,000. November, according to the statistical terms of his contract, was the final month for deliveries.

On the 20th Mowry wrote to Stanton asking for permission to extend the time of deliveries. Stanton turned the matter over to Ripley. Though Holt and Owen had used the matter of Mowry's lack of manufacturing facilities to whittle him down, hoping his default would reduce the number of guns the United States would have to pay for, Ripley so liked the Springfield rifle that he okayed the delivery of 2,000 more muskets. These were delivered during December and January of 1864. It is probable these arms are of a most unusual category; fabricated and marked by the Norwich Armories in Norwich, Connecticut, they bear, on the left side of the stock opposite the Norwich-stamped lockplate, a circled ink stamp about 1 inch across, oval in form, the brand of Jas. D. Mowry!

This connection between Mowry and Norwich Armories, though both were in the same town, has not been remarked before. Though only one such arm with this mark is presently known, it seems unlikely that Mowry would fill his requisition with odd lots from here and there. More probably he in turn agreed to take from Norwich Armories completed Springfields of their make to fill his order. The fact that he became in the next year the registered agent of Norwich Arms Company, seems to confirm this supposition.

The balance of Mowry arms bore his stamp on the lockplate, and dates of 1864 will be found. Apparently Norwich supplied these guns to fill his order, we assume, because of his status also as an agent of the company. Mowry delivered in all 22,000 Springfields, some of inferior grades to Class 4 at $16. But the last 10,000 were delivered promptly on schedule in lots of 1,000 accepted at a full $18 re-negotiated price.

CASE NO. 77. Eagle Manufacturing Company, 25,000 muskets, reduced to 20,000 before the Commission.

In this brief compass, we return to the firm concerning which our chapter first opened. With a fictitious interview between Secretary Cameron and newspaperman Wilkeson we set forth Eagle's principal complaint: the small quantity of the contract. The treasurer, A. H. Almy, argued that Colt, and Lamson, Goodnow, and Yale had not only had their first orders confirmed, but upon complaining the totals were not enough to allow economical manufacture, had the totals increased. But the Commissioners were more savvy at the 77th case than at the first. As they elaborated in Mason's case, the price of $20 was entirely sufficient for the Springfield in lots even as small as 15,000 or 20,000. In large lots it should be less. Though Almy sought the intervention of his brother, J. H. Almy, the Assistant Quartermaster General of Connecticut, in writing to Secretary Stanton and the Ordnance officers, he was unable to get an increase in the order. He claimed to be able to deliver guns by July, 1862; it was not until April 14, 1863, that Eagle delivered the first 500 of but 5,500 arms. The collaboration between Eagle and Mowry, and the personnel of Eagle being the same as Norwich Arms Company, suggests that the capital and industrial potential of Eagle and Mowry was ultimately merged with Norwich Armories. By delivering upon Norwich's contracts, apparently both Almy and Mowry stood to profit better. The records show 5,500 delivered between April 1 and September of 1863, not the 20,000 cited as being delivered, according to Fuller. Locks are marked with date at hammer rear, "1863," and eagle, U.S./EAGLEVILLE before the hammer.

CASE NO. 78, James T. Hodge, "Trenton." Contract to supply 50,000 muskets.

CASE NO. 79, Addison M. Burt, "Trenton," contract for 50,000 muskets in conjunction with Hodge.

These gentlemen independently obtained contracts for 50,000 Springfields each, both on December 29, 1861. Honoring the clause voiding the contracts if transferred, they studiously skirted about all hint of business combination by not forming a partnership, logical though such a move would have been. Burt's brother, O. F. Burt, was a partner in the firm of Muir & Company, musket contractor at Windsor Locks, Connecticut. Burt himself had been a spring maker for railroad cars and had to close down his business in Richmond, presumably Virginia, as he speaks of departing from that place in March "and leave all my property there." He was not a mechanic, but a financial and administrative man, apparently the leader or stronger of the two. He asked permission of the Government to form a company, "Burt, Hodge & Company," in connection with their musket contracts. Meanwhile he and Hodge, without forming a partnership which they felt would amount to transferral of their contracts, obtained a charter from New Jersey for a firm, the Trenton Arms Company. Its armory was the shops of the Trenton Locomotive and Machine Manufacturing Company, and its director, A. G. M. Prevost, worked closely with them in sub-contracting their muskets.

Burt capitalized the machinery, which was bought from a dozen makers, some still famous in machine tools. Hodge contracted in turn with Burt to have the parts of his muskets made. And Burt contracted with Trenton Locomotive for some machines, for shop space, and workmen. Burt quite understandably pleaded to be allowed to treat the affair as "Burt, Hodge & Company," but the Commissioners would not agree. The two in their Trenton Arms Company seriously intended to continue the musket making business, not only for Government but for all customers.

The preparations they were making were extensive. While Burt told the Commission they planned to make everything except the rough barrel in Trenton, this was not entirely true. C. H. Williams & Company of Philadelphia proposed to make locks for them, and when Holt and Owen asked for specific details, Williams told Burt that he could commence delivering an order of 20,000 locks by August, 1862. He sent Burt one of the locks, which had passed inspection at Springfield Armory. Samuel Norris had persuaded Major Dyer and Master Armorer E. S. Allin to take four C. H. Williams Philadelphia locks apart and scramble them with four Springfield locks, reassembling at random. They reassembled perfectly. "I think you will have no cause to fear inspection of your work, if the locks you manufacture are as perfect as these. I should also say they fit the gun stock most perfectly," Norris reported for Williams to use as a testimonial.

Washburn of Worcester, the Trenton Iron Company, and Morris, Tasker & Company of Philadelphia, had all been approached about supplying barrels. Which firm finally landed the contract is not known. Burt was not planning to rely indefinitely on Williams for locks, either; the schedule of tooling, approximately $80,000 by that April of 1862 when they came before the Commission, and rapidly increased to over $120,000, is interesting to consider in these days of automation. Today a giant Kingsbury machine will converge from all directions upon a colorless lump of grey forged steel and in a matter of minutes spew forth a glittering, precision jewel of a revolver frame, or a motor block. The process was a little more tedious then. Burt had by April 1862 laid out or committed himself for tools from the following:

Bement & Dougherty, Philadelphia	$23,435.00
Hughes & Phillips, Newark, N. J.	2,650.00
Brown & Sharpe, Providence, Rhode Island	1,449.50
James S. Brown, Pawtucket	2,100.00
Wood, Light & Co., Worcester	1,050.00
George Crompton, Worcester	5,500.00
William Mason, Taunton, Mass.	364.00
Am. Machine Works, Springfield	15,000.00
Hope Iron Co., Providence	3,755.00
W. A. Wheeler, Worcester	4,030.00
Charles Parker, Meriden, Conn.	100.00
...Ames, Chicopee	5,000.00
Massachusetts Arms Company, Chicopee Falls	775.00
George S. Lincoln & Co., Hartford	452.25
Trenton Locomotive Works, Trenton, N. J.	15,791.00
	81,451.75

American Machine Works was making the stocking machines; in addition, they had contracted at a day rate to make all the gauges, adding an estimated $5,000 more to the above total. The investment in machines on hand at the Trenton Armory set aside for Trenton Arms Company was $36,788. While the largest number of like items was 27 vises, it is true that the list, if of machinery in good working order, exclusive of the particular tools and fixtures required in making the muskets, reflected a pretty complete shop for that or any other time.

Though Hodge and Burt had determined to equip a plant supplying 9,000 muskets a month, they admitted their first deliveries scheduled for July would be made partly of purchased components and partly of Trenton-fabricated items.

Doubtless Williams locks were to figure in these early deliveries; it would be interesting to compare the eagle stamps of different contractors such as Welch, Rice, Trenton, Jenks-Bridesburg, and others, to see if it is possible to trace them back to Williams of Philadelphia. Barrels, it appears, were eventually obtained from Dinslow & Chase of Windsor Locks. Paradoxical though it reads, O. T. Burt, Addison M. Burt's brother, had contracted for 25,000 barrels with D & C to begin deliveries in August, 1862. These were not for the William Muir & Company contract in spite of O. T. Burt being a partner in that venture. Muir's barrels were contracted by a steel works on Staten Island, New York. A director, Mr. Andrews, testified to the Commission in connection with the Parker, Snow, Brooke & Company contract, that he had a contract with Muir to make 30,000 barrels for them! Thus the Staten Island barrels went up the river to Windsor Locks; the Windsor Locks barrels floated down to Trenton across the marshes from Staten Island!

The Commission suggested the two non-partners counter with voluntary proposals to decrease their orders to 25,000 each, which they then confirmed subject to forfeitures monthly in the event of non-delivery. Burt and Hodge thereupon executed duplicate contracts with Ripley, on 9 July, 1862, with Burt's brother, O. T. Burt, (whose residence address was Syracuse, New York), and Juan C. DeMeir of New York sureties for both. A. M. Burt's first deliveries from Trenton began March 26, 1863, and until December 30, 1864, he delivered 11,500. Most were $20 guns; many were reduced for defects to $17.

Hodge began deliveries May 14, 1863, and up to December 17, 1864, had turned in 10,500. Though his sub-sub-contract with Burt involved payment only for arms inspected and received by the Government, when received and paid for, it must have been a tightly stressed friendship that survived the drastic inspection cuts in prices for arms; Hodge too was paid for guns as low as $17 for blemishes and imperfect arms. Though the Springfield-pattern arms marked *Trenton* for some reason have been questioned or doubtful in association with Hodge and Burt, this seems groundless in view of their controlling the New Jersey incorporated Trenton Arms Company.

CASE NO. 80. William W. Welch, Norfolk, Connecticut, 18,000 muskets.

This is a rather modest proposal, and Mr. Welch apparently was willing to disclose what Colt and others knew, that a small lot of Springfields could be arranged for at $20 at a fair profit. Welch estimated his net at about $3, somewhat over 15 per cent. For a small manufacturer, he was one of the most consistent in deliveries once he got started. At least the first 500 bore locks by C. H. Williams & Company of Philadelphia. This firm had been makers of sculptured wood mouldings for picture frames and decorative construction trim. In September, 1861 they saw that the house building business was poor, the house dividing business on the upswing, and changed to lock making. By early April, 1862 they had delivered 500 locks to Welch, as well as 500 to John Rice and 500 to "Trenton" Burt. They were preparing to take an order from Mason in Taunton for 50,000 locks, and had 6,000 on hand to fill these customers' early needs. Lockmaker Robert Essler of Williams & Company was experienced in the wood business and had in turn arranged with the Empire Works to make stocks, which he also was to supply to Welch. "We rate the value of lock and stock at $5.35; we cannot furnish for less at present," he informed the Commissioners. Holt and Owen reduced the small number of 18,000 to 16,000 from Welch, provided he signed a contract in due form. Deliveries did not begin until September 23, 1862; from then until December, 1863 they were at the rate of approximately 500 monthly until 16,000 were accepted.

Following, on January 12, 1864, Welch entered into a contract with General Ramsay to supply an additional 2,500 muskets. Two deliveries of 500 each on May 10 and May 31 exhausted the contract. With Welch in these deals were Plumb Brown and Ralph Brown, both of Norwich. They formed a company at the end, Welch, Brown & Company, and undertook a final contract to close out the arms left over; on February 3, 1865 they appealed to Secretary Stanton to be allowed to deliver the last 1,500 guns which had been forfeited under the January 12, 1864 contract. General Dyer, then Chief of Ordnance, recommended that this be permitted, the first class arms to be taken at $18, and the second class at $15. Springfield Arsenal also was authorized to buy Welch's spare parts at suitable prices. On April 21, 1,000 Springfields were accepted at $15; the close-out balance was only 360 arms on May 3, 1865. Marked on the lockplate NORFOLK, there is not considered at present to be any differentiation between W. W. Welch arms and those last few thousand of Welch, Brown & Company. Possibly early 1863-make guns would reveal some tell-tale sign of a Williams lock; a Norfolk rifle is known that is stamped on the left of the stock cheek: W. W. WELCH, NORFOLK, CONN. It is not known if Welch, a conscientious man, ever made more than the barrels in his Norfolk, Connecticut machine shop.

CASE NO. 81. William C. Freeman, 500 Joslyn designed revolvers, improved pattern, not actually manufactured at the time of order August 28, 1861. Order revoked and annulled by Commissioners.

CASE NO. 83. Sarson & Roberts, 25,000 Springfields.

John B. Sarson of New York on August 31, 1861, delivered 90 "cavalry carbines," otherwise unidentified, at $14 each. Thinking the gun business was a profitable one, he sought to get in deeper, and in partnership with William S. Roberts joined the cavalcade to Washington to get on the musket gravy train. In December, 1861, and January, 1862, they delivered 4,900 Potsdam muskets, the Prussian brass-trimmed Model 1830 flintlock transformed to percussion, at $6.50 each. On January 22, 1862, they delivered also 143 long Enfield rifles at $20. But this was a sideline, for since December 26 they had been actively preparing to build Springfields, following the outline of their proposal of July 31, 1861.

Among the first manufacturer-importers to come to their country's call, they offered to make either 25,000 Enfield or Springfield rifle muskets at $18.50, and also "carbines of the Enfield pattern, or of the American standard (not patented arms) at fifteen dollars ($15) each." Their shop at 11 Platt Street, New York, was ready to turn out, they claimed, 500 guns a week "within 30 days from the date of the order."

Ripley accepted their proposal at their terms on August 3, and on that same day Sarson & Roberts wrote asking for three pattern muskets to help speed their preparations. But by November 23, the 30 days had long lapsed with no delivery "owing to the many and great obstacles we have had to overcome in the manufacture of Springfield rifles," as they said. "If we had fully realized the difficulties in the way of making the Springfield gun over the making of the Enfield pattern, with which we were much better acquainted, I do not think we should have ventured to have undertaken so difficult an enterprise."

This is a most revealing statement, in the light of the odd Enfield-form lockplates which were circulated in the antique gun market just one century later, as curiosities.

Sarson and Roberts may have been making some parts for the Enfield; hence they offered to make either the Enfield or the Springfield, rifle musket or carbine form. Ripley of course chose the Springfield and if these lockplates are from Sarson & Roberts they evidently did not make up any Enfields or, as is barely possible, the 143 long Enfields cited as delivered early in 1862.

Because of their difficulties, they asked the War Department to cancel the order of August 3 and issue a new one based on their greater understanding of the manufacturing problems. They wrote now formally to Secretary Cameron, offering to make 25,000 strictly interchangeable Springfields at $20 each, and gave themselves a lead time of two months with first delivery promised February 1, 1862. Ripley received this offer in memorandum from the Secretary and "respectfully returned it" to Cameron, disapproving it not only because of higher price and their previous failure, but because of the precedent it would set. But he was over-ruled and Assistant Secretary Thomas Scott issued the order on that frantic 26 December. They overshot their deadline and by April, 1862, had 200 barrels ready for proving. Letters to the Ordnance office went unanswered but Captain Dyer at Springfield Armory kindly gave them the proof data they required:

> The musket barrels are required to be proved as follows, viz: First charge, 280 grains of powder, one ball weighing 500 grains, and two wads. Second charge, 250 grains of powder, one ball weighing 500 grains, and two wads.

Though slow, they were conscientious and when their case was filed before Holt and Owen it took little time to settle. The order was confirmed in the number of 20,000 rifles, subject to their making a proper contract. This was done June 17, 1862, with Joseph Hall of Staten Island and William Hayes of Brooklyn as sureties. The partners had obtained stocking machinery from Pusey, corner Elm & Pearl Streets, and it was operating in their shop. Jenks of Philadelphia was sub-contractor, making all parts except stock, barrel, and sight. Sights were made by Brown, rough barrels were obtained from Morris, Tasker & Company of Marshall iron from England, finished in the Sarson & Roberts shop on machines made for them by A. & F. Brown, who also made the barrel gauges. Some Pennsylvania iron was used for their barrels, from Craig & Koch at Reading. It was not so light and silvery and did not finish so finely as the Marshall iron, which was celebrated for its beauty as well as serviceability, but it stood proof. First delivery of 340 Springfields was split up into 2d, 3d, and 4th quality arms by Crispin during inspection, and deliveries continued at approximately 300-500 guns a month up to November 20, 1863. To complete their guns, they drew parts from Springfield Armory to the value of $8,434.12. Between hammer and bolster on the Sarson & Roberts locks an eagle is stamped; below the bolster the words U.S./NEW YORK/1862. Only 5,140 were delivered by Sarson & Roberts; the reason for failure to make more is unknown, as monthly totals were reaching a fairly respectable average of 1,000 when they stopped work.

CASE NO. 84. Eli Whitney, of New Haven.

Not the elder Whitney, deceased on January 8, 1825, but his son, Eli Junior, sometimes called The Second, was the principal in this case. He had assumed control of the arms factory and machinery works started by his father for making cotton gins and muskets, several years before Sam Colt came to him in 1847 to make revolvers. Contracts for Mississippi rifles at the same time increased the skill and technological resources of the Whitney works, by the millstream outside New Haven.

The community surrounding the cluster of armory buildings below the dam came to be called "Whitneyville," and as the war began, Eli Junior commenced adding two new factory buildings. In these shops he filled a contract for the State of Connecticut for 5,600 rifles which were, as he said, "nearly like the Springfield." In locks and trim they were close to the M1861 type, but the sight was the 1858 leaf pattern resembling the Remington special or "Zouave" rifle sight, and that on other special arms. This sight base has less metal around the leaf screw, and the base is flat on the edge instead of stepped to protect the folded down leaves, as is the common Springfield sight. The lock is undated and forward of the hammer is marked in small letters E. WHITNEY/N. HAVEN. There are no proof marks and no U. S. nor Connecticut marks. The front sight base which serves as a bayonet stud is wider for the Enfield triangular bayonets with which these rifles were fitted, so Whitney could save a little money with the cheaper imported stickers. A "second model" of this pattern is stamped on the lock with a huge spread eagle and the word WHITNEYVILLE in large shaded letters. The sight is the Springfield pattern, also.

This rifle must have been made some time after April 11, 1862, at which time Whitney informed Holt and Owen that "I am not yet ready to make sights, as I have been using, for the State work, sights of another pattern. I am now forging the Springfield pattern." As of April 11, he had not delivered a final lot of 2,000 of these arms to Connecticut; the first 3,600 had been turned in.

Presumably the big eagle and Springfield sighted guns are of this second batch of 2,000. Though Connecticut did not inspect these arms, except to view them after finishing and see if they were "good and serviceable," Whitney was not afraid of the strict interchangeability required for making the new Springfield. When he heard the price had been fixed for contracts at $20, he wrote on December 17, 1861, offering to make 40,000 at that figure. His offer was accepted by Ripley December 24, but Holt and Owen reduced the number to 25,000, subject to a proper contract.

Whitney himself demurred on accepting this counter-proposal, a whole year during which he completed the 2,000 "nearly Springfields" for the State and took a flyer in a cheapie militia musket which now rates as one of the rarities of the whole Civil War gun field. This is a much misunderstood arm and has been called (and sold at inflated prices as) a "Confederate" arm.

Two versions exist, the long 40-inch barrel rifle and a shorter model conforming to the two-band Enfield sergeant's rifle (33-inch barrel). The lock is of odd non-Springfield form, suggesting some sort of sporting lock plate adapted to the Springfield-contour nipple bolster. It is blued and marked simply E. WHITNEY along the bottom edge forward of hammer. The hammer shape resembles a U. S. 1842 pistol hammer placed in a die for straightening and lengthening the shank to make it fit. The spur is lightly file-checkered, and the lock parts are rust-blued. The trigger guard and plate of Springfield rifle-musket form are of brass;

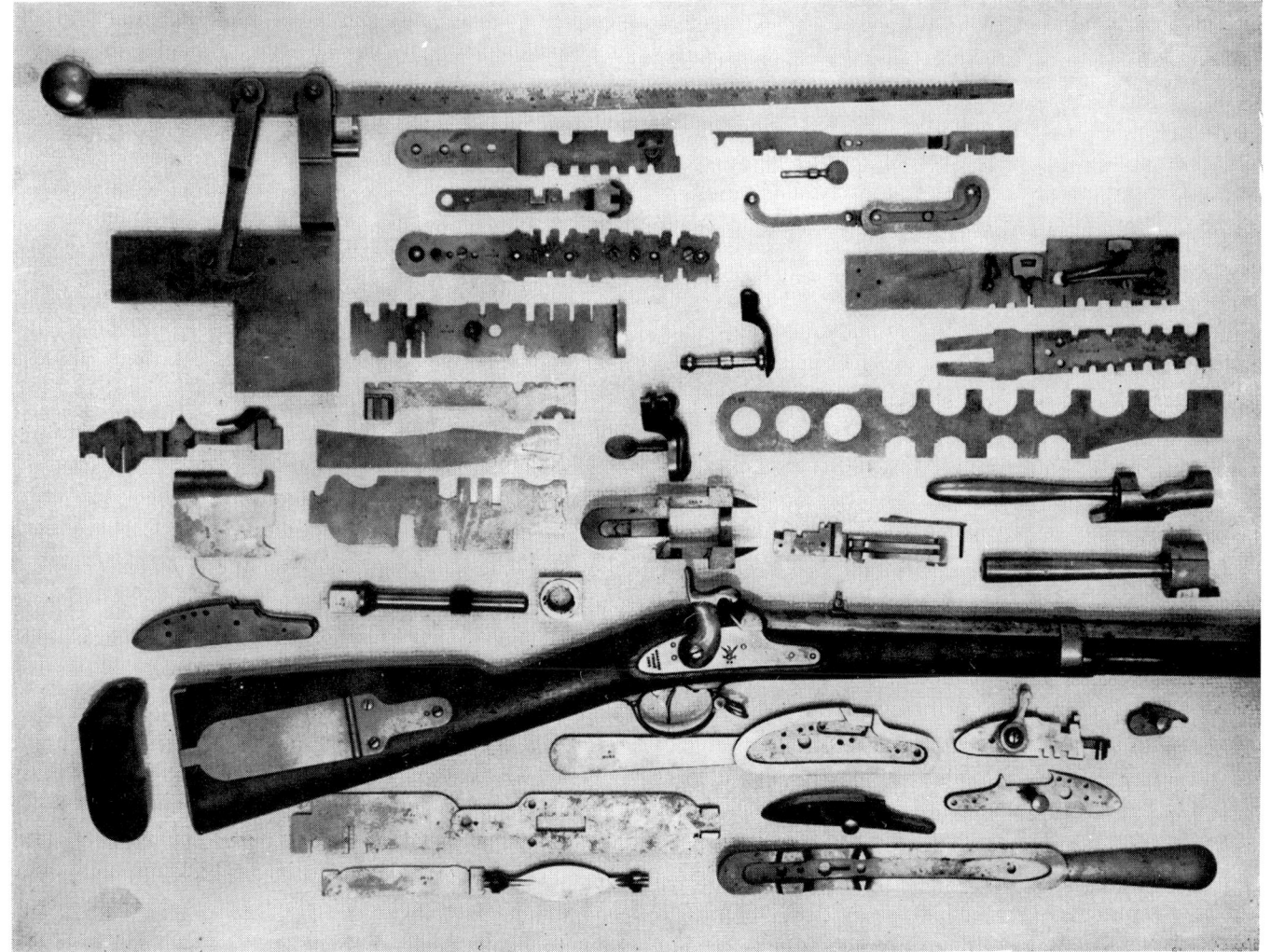

Set of production gauges in A. L. Jackson, Chicago, collection reveal great number of inspections "Mississippi rifle" went through in manufacture. Eli Whitney was pioneer introducing these gauges to commercial arms manufacture and yet turned out some of worst-fitting miscellanies of parts used in the war.

the Enfield-type solid bands held by 1853-pattern springs are finished in a brownish lacquer resembling brass; the butt of steel is similarly "bronzed," but the fore-end cap is of brass. While some specimens are recorded as unnumbered, the specimen in the author's collection, though not proof marked at all, is stamped "166" under the barrel and inside the lockplate. Rifling is three equal lands and grooves, .58 caliber. A short version of this arm is recorded by Fuller as "caliber .61, rifling consists of 7 grooves."

A report exists indicating that Whitney had contracted on 6 June, 1860, with the State of Mississippi, to supply 1,500 "of these rifles with bayonets." The exact description of the arm Whitney was to deliver is contained in a letter by Adjutant General W. L. Sykes of Mississippi to his governor, John J. Pettus, dated January 18, 1861. Sykes says:

> Relative to the Mississippi rifle, it is but justice to state that every effort has been made to procure them within the power of this department. This arm being renowned for the brilliant victories achieved upon the battlefields of Mexico in the hands of the First Regiment of Mississippi Riflemen, has derived the appelation of Mississippi Rifle, and is the principal arm called for by the volunteer corps.

Whitney agreed to make these guns, but it must be remembered that all his Mississippi Rifle making machinery must have been in storage as he had not delivered any of this pattern for some years prior to 1860. He shipped out 60 rifles to Mississippi, but as Sykes noted, "The arms were received and examined and proved to be old guns fixed up. Such an act being a violation of the letter and spirit of the contract, none of the arms were taken as a part of the contract, though the sixty were taken as an experiment."

Sykes was quite certain the 60 rifles received were "old guns fixed up." This does not conform to the Whitney Enfield long and short rifles in collections. The rear sight of the long rifle No. 166 is same pattern as the Connecticut State "Nearly" Springfields, but another hole is drilled forward of the fixed base about ⅞-inch as if for another sight base. The possibility exists that he proposed to fit the sight of the Model 1855 Maynard Primer rifle musket and decided against it as too complicated, filling the base screw hole with lead, blacked over. Such a sight is shown on Whitney's advertisement of November 15, 1862 for these. At any rate, it is an arm entirely different from a refinished Mississippi Rifle and is certainly not a Confederate rifle.

The ad alluded to is a flier or broadside including a testimonial to Whitney's rifles from no less a distinguished personage than Jefferson Davis, who is credited in the fall of 1862 not with being President of the Southern Confederacy, but as ex-colonel, Mississippi riflemen. Pistols only were in regular production at the time and priced; as to the odd "Enfields" of which both short (with patchbox) and long were illustrated, the flier simply said: "For further information with regard to the above, and also with regard to Minnie rifles and Muskets, if wanted, address as above."

Who bought these "Minnie" rifles is not known, with one exception. They may have been used by watch and ward police societies, or by state prison guards and others needing military long arms on short budgets.

But Schuyler, Hartley and Graham was one source for marketing, and some of the "Minnies" were evidently bought by Major Hagner, or Whiteley, or Crispin in open purchase in New York. In the accounts of arms purchased from Schuyler, Hartley and Graham are listed on August 31, 1861, "60 Whitney's Enfields, with sabre bayonets," at $22. Additional "Whitney's short Enfields" were obtained September 6, 80 of them, at the same price. Delivered September 24 were "60 Whitney's short rifles" and on October 4, 1861, 80 more "Whitney's short Enfields, sabre bayonets," all at $22, a total of 280 short Whitney Enfield rifles with sword bayonets. The only listing that *might* refer to Whitney long Enfields is a shipment of December 27, 1861, when 100 Whitney Navy revolvers were received from S. H. & G, together with 180 long Enfield rifles, maker unspecified, at $20. It is possible these were Whitney arms, though omission of the maker's name is not characteristic of the other listings for short rifles.

With the emphasis in the service for the long rifles rather than the short sword bayonet models, of all makes, Whitney probably concentrated on the long model and still had some on hand by November 1862, to judge from the ad.

For the scion of the house who was even then world famous for top quality precision machine work, these "Whitney Enfields" were a pretty poor advertisement. The bands shake, and fitting and finish is very poor, though certainly serviceable. But this little known and much-misunderstood weapon of the war seems to have been the North's "secret weapon." To judge by the workmanship, it was best left that way.

In addition to two different Connecticut State rifles, and two "Enfield" arms which had never been closer than a laugh to Enfield Royal Small Arms Factory, the Whitney Armory fashioned an odd and powerful copy of the French heavy Minie rifle, known as "Carabine a Tige, 1846 model." A specimen "Carabine" in the author's collection dated 1858 was fabricated in Liege for the Brazilian Navy, and has a 34 3/16-inch round barrel shaped at the breech in an octagon (from rear sight back), rifled four grooves, .69 caliber. It takes a brass-hilt yataghan or sword bayonet, and with a 22½-inch curved blade attached it is a formidable puncher for close-in fighting. The guard strap is notched, as are so many French arms, to give a little grip for the hand in thrusting the bayonet. A long-range elevating slide rear sight to graduated 1,000 meters is fitted, and the sling swivels.

Captain John Adolphus Dahlgren, commanding the USS *Plymouth,* was much impressed by this French rifle. The caliber he liked because it permitted a maximum use of buckshot, which was ideal for the close-quarters rough and tumble of deck fighting. He took the French pattern and modified it by the addition of the 1861 type Springfield lock, Springfield butt form, and a special spur behind the guard to give the hand an even better grip in thrusting with the bayonet. All other details he kept as in the French original, including the large headed ramrod designed to thump the solid Delvigne projectile against the *tige* to upset into the rifling. This was no longer necessary using the U. S. hollow-based .69 conical projectile.

Dahlgren's classic *Boat Armament* text of 1856 featured the *Carabine a Tige* M1846; it was not until 1862-3 that he was able to have the model made by Whitney and adopted for the landing and assault boats of the Federal Navy. In general orders to the South Atlantic blockading squadron, penned aboard his flagship the *Philadelphia*, Dahlgren remarked on his pattern of rifle:

> It has frequently happened that the peculiar nature of the duties in this command has required the service of bodies of men to be landed from vessels to act for a short time as infantry, assisted by light field pieces.
> In order to meet similar exigencies commanders of vessels will take pains to select from their crews such men as may seem to have a turn for this kind of duty and have them drilled with small arms until they have attained the necessary proficiency.
> In so doing it is to be borne in mind that the drill and the maneuverings are to be few and exceedingly simple.
> The men should be thoroughly skilled in the loading and firing of their weapon, and firing at a mark is to be encouraged.
> The light infantry drill will be best adapted to this service, and to the habits of the seamen.
> The preferable arm, when it can be had, will be the new navy rifled musket, known as the Plymouth musket, because the first of the kind were made for the U.S. ship *Plymouth*, when under my command, the pattern of which was got up by myself as most suitable for sea service.
> It is a short musket, about 34 inches in the barrel, bore 0.69-inch, and rifled.
> Its special bayonet is a short, broad and stout knife, of the well-known Bowie pattern, the principal use of which I designed to be in the hand in close conflict, such as boarding. In campaigning it would also serve many wants; but it may be fixed and used as a bayonet.
> There is also a sword bayonet similar to that of the French, making the total length of weapon, from butt to point, about equal to that of the army musket with the ordinary bayonet.
> The musket is perfectly balanced for aim when the bayonet is not fixed; and its large bore gives great effect to buckshot, which, at short distances, is always to be preferred.
> As a general rule, we have too much neglected the use of this formidable ammunition for small arms.

It is believed that the first bayonet regularly fitted to this arm was the copy of the French yataghan blade. By 1863 Dahlgren had decided on the use of the bowie-type knife and designed a massive chopper 12 inches long, 1 11/16 inches wide, and thick. It stuck on the end of the barrel but could also be carried as a bowie and was used as the sailor's regular sidearm, constantly with him even if the muskets were locked up. These were made by Ames of Chicopee. Sword bayonets were made by Collins & Company, Hartford, and were numbered to match the rifle. Officially the U. S. Navy Rifle Model 1861, these arms were dated through 1863; Fuller cites a specimen No. 4986 dated 1863. Bowie bayonets were also dated, some in 1864. About 7,000 Whitney Plymouth rifles were made. Being busy on them explains his failure to deliver or attempt to renegotiate an Army contract until a year had passed.

Then, curiously, he signed a contract, on 17 October, 1863 to supply General Ramsay with only 15,000 Springfield rifle muskets at $19. He had been working to get these ready, for his first delivery was three days later, on October 20, 1863. Five hundred Springfields were graded out as 310 class 1, 186 class 2, and 4 class 2½, paid for at $19, $18.90, and $18.50 respectively. In spite of the head start, he delivered but 14,500 of these by January 30, 1865.

CASE NO. 85. William Muir & Company, New York and Windsor Locks.

In this case bargaining achieved the desired end for Muir, confirmation of his contract for a full 30,000 Springfield rifle muskets. He delivered them all.

William Muir on 7 December 1861 received an order from the Secretary of War for 30,000 Springfields at $20. He commenced to sub-contract here and there, ordering 4,000 locks from Essler & Brother in Philadelphia. These locks seem to have given some difficulty among collectors in later identification of the arms supplied by Muir, because in addition to a lock marking, WM. MUIR & CO./WINDSOR LOCKS, CT., there

Man who made most Springfields was Major Alexander B. Dyer, who commanded Armory from 21 August 1861 to 12 September 1864; was later Chief of Ordnance.

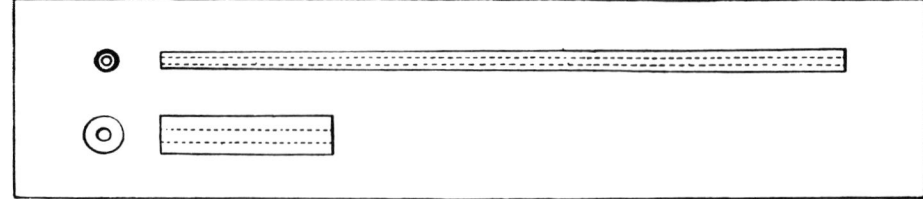

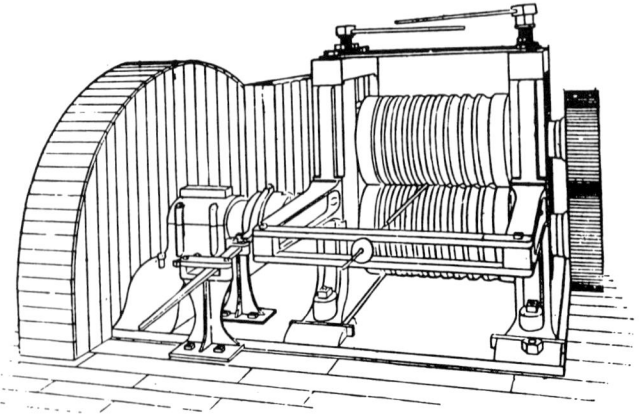

Basic machines of major contractors were similar, often supplied by same machine tool builder like Robbins & Lawrence or Ames. Washburn's barrel rolls looked like this drawing. Barrel began as punched blank called "mould" and while hot was passed through diminishing grooves of rolls till thinned out longer. Mandrels kept hole in center constant.

is another lock marking simply WINDSOR LOCKS and the date and eagle. Whether these Windsor Locks (only) plates are Muir's earliest effort, or residue from the end of his contract, is not known. Both possibilities will be explored; it seems obvious that they have a connection with Muir's operation though oddly, Muir & Company was actually of New York and there is a question as to how many of the rifles were actually made at Windsor Locks. The fine hand of O. T. Burt, who was a surety to the contract of A. M. Burt of Trenton, is seen in the Muir affair.

When Muir bit off the 30,000 musket chaw on December 7, he decided soon he had made a mistake. He asked for the opportunity to have the contract amended to read "Wm. Muir & Company," thus avoiding the later nullifying he risked if he should assign the contract. This was assented to by Cameron and then Stanton and the amended order was dated January 10. Following receipt of the amended order, Muir together with O. T. Burt of Syracuse, New York, (brother of A. M. Burt, Trenton), formed the company Wm. Muir & Company, with Burt as a heavy stockholder. Offices were at 372 Broadway.

O. T. Burt, who had a financial interest in the Hodge-Burt "Trenton" contracts, was also behind the Windsor Locks firm of Dinslow & Chase. This shop proposed to supply Muir with barrels and also was making 25,000 barrels for the Trenton maker. But Dinslow & Chase also possessed capability to make locks. Though Muir proposed to get additional locks from Parker, Snow, Brooks & Company (the predecessors of the famous shotgun firm Parker Brothers), the Trenton makers planned to rely on Dinslow & Chase for locks if need be. The Windsor Locks-marked plates then appear to be of Dinslow & Chase fabrication or assembly. By May 2, 1862, Muir informed Holt and Owen that "We have a few guns assembled," and explained that a flood washing away part of the millrace dike had delayed their works by cutting off the power. It seems possible these first few guns were assembled with Windsor Locks lockplates prior to Muir's incorporating as a company. Those made after the firm was duly established would bear that company name.

Muir was urged to make a proposal to reduce his contract to 20,000 to have it confirmed by Holt and Owen. But he demurred, saying all his contractors were talking about 30,000 pieces and he could not take the loss. Then he had a brainstorm: sell 25,000 at the full $20 and the last 5,000 at only $16. This the Commissioners went for and this was the way Muir filled the order. His contract, formally signed July 9, 1862, contained these terms and the deliveries which began January 22, 1863, and finished November 3, 1864, were paid at that rate: $20 and $16.

O. T. Burt upon completion of the Muir contract sought to get rid of the remaining surplus parts. He notified Major Laidley at Springfield Armory of these items and asked if he wanted to buy them. On November 3 Laidley instructed Master Armorer E. S. Allin and three aides to go to Windsor Locks and inspect and classify the items remaining. Among major parts there were locks, barrels, and ramrods, which Laidley informed Burt he could not take: "The locks are all condemned and have the letter C stamped indelibly upon the different parts. We could not issue such articles to our troops."

But of the barrels, Laidley was less particular. He instructed Springfield workman P. O. Bush to inspect them again and such as could be made useful by cleaning up and removing the "C" were to be taken. Whether the "Windsor Locks" locks were such, having the old Muir marks removed in the cleaning up and renovating, we do not know. Either first or last, they seem certainly to have originated in Dinslow & Chase's shop in Windsor Locks.

CASE NO. 88. Amoskeag Mfg. Company, E. A. Straw, Agent, Manchester, New Hampshire.

This was a simple and short case. Amoskeag was introduced to General Ripley by Hon. C. H. Dalton, who asked for a contract to make 10,000 Springfields. November 18, 1861 Ripley returned Dalton's proposal to Cameron endorsed negatively. But Dalton and E. A.

Straw, the registered agent of Amoskeag, persisted, and on January 7, 1862, Ripley was ordered to send them a letter-order. This he did, 10,000 arms at $20, and Amoskeag got up steam to fill it.

On May 21, after being informed that Amoskeag was a company employing 600 men, representing about $3 million capital, the Commissioners confirmed the order because it was a small one, subject to their taking out a contract. This they did, 17 June, 1862, contracting to furnish 10,000 arms "in all respects identical with the standard rifle-musket made at the United States Armory at Springfield, Mass., and are to interchange with it and with each other in all their parts." Amoskeag claimed they would finish and assemble the rifle complete in their own works, obtaining only the raw materials, rough barrels, and such, outside.

It seems difficult to reconcile their contract with what they actually delivered under its terms. For their muskets were not the Springfield, but the Colt Special Model which is sometimes known as the Springfield Model 1863, but was never made at the Armory, at least not in mass production. Meanwhile, their plant conversion to make the Springfield and also the Lindner carbines (see Chapter 11) continued during the summer and winter and on June 11, 1863, Amoskeag delivered the first 500 arms under their June 17, 1862 contract.

Somehow, in spite of millions of capital and employing regularly 600 men, Amoskeag took longer to deliver their first gun than many of the small shops that had contracts for five times as many. Only 10,001 were delivered. Inferentially, the one extra gun included in the shipment of July 13, 1863, was to replace one held out of the first shipment as an inspection sample. Indeed, how much of the Amoskeag gun was Manchester-made, and how much came from Colt or some other source, like Lamson, Goodnough & Yale, is a moot question.

Amoskeag's second contract, dated November 5, 1865, called for them to make 15,000 Springfields "of the model of 1862, similar to those now being delivered under contract with this department, except that the locks and bands must be case hardened and blued, in the same manner in which those parts are now being finished at the United States Armory, Springfield, Massachusetts."

The first 10,001 were finished "national armory bright," with burnished lockplates, and the barrels longitudinally brushed to a silvery luster. Whether the second lot of Amoskeag Special Models received conformed to the contract or the original inspector's model is not known. So many of these arms were later C & R, cleaned and repaired, that the barrel bands and lockplates may have been brightened up on Amoskeag guns of the second lot originally colored in these parts. By February 28, 1865, 15,000 were received. Meanwhile, on January 6, 1865, Amoskeag's third and last contract shaped up, not as a formal document but as a letter of acceptance of a proposal. John B. Anthony, a principal in the Providence Tool Company, and E. A. Straw of Amoskeag, joined together in a sort of memorial-type letter on 16 December, 1864, to Secretary Stanton, asking to be permitted to finish up their spare parts into complete muskets. General Dyer agreed to this on January 6, and Straw shipped down 2,000 more finished guns made up from overruns of major components. In all, 27,001 arms were delivered and paid for, not one of which conformed to the letter of the contracts.

It is thought possible, but as yet unproved, that Straw may have bought muskets from Colt to supply for the first deliveries, and thus set himself on the trail of making the Special Model instead of the 1861 Springfields for which he contracted.

CASE NO. 89. Green Kendrick, Waterbury, Connecticut. Springfields, no delivery.

An unsuccessful contractor, Green Kendrick earlier had failed in pre-war United States contracts and now tried his hand at arranging the Springfield 1861 rifle muskets. By collaborating with O. T. Burt of Trenton, Muir & Company, and Dinslow & Chase, he hoped to get his parts made along with those for the Muir contract. In addition to the list of sub-contractors, perhaps the most interesting point John Kendrick, Green's son (for the old man was sick and this had delayed his work), reported to Holt and Owen on April 11, is that "His arms are to be finally assembled at Windsor

Vertical four-spindle barrel drill let tool bite down from own weight as cutting face chewed away chips. To drill solid steel barrels, this rig designed by Fred Howe for Robbins & Lawrence at Windsor, Vt. 1852 was probably used by Lamson, Goodnough & Yale for Civil War production of Rifle Muskets.

Locks, Connecticut, by Mr. E. W. Andrews." It is possible that the rare "Windsor Locks" arms are the first few of the Green Kendrick order and that because of Kendrick's sickness and general disability no more were made. No delivery is found on this order, which was issued by letter dated January 10, 1862, calling for 25,000 arms. No formal contract was ever made, as Holt and Owen had required, and the order was annulled by non-compliance.

CASE NO. 90. James Mulholland, 50,000 Springfields.

On January 7, 1862, the superintendent of the Reading Railroad, James Mulholland, obtained a letter order or contract for 50,000 Springfields but was delayed by the failure of Springfield Armory to make a pattern rifle available to him until the middle of February (order of 13 February). Not proposing to capitalize the manufacture of the arm himself, Mulholland went to Parker, Snow, Brooks & Company of Meriden, Connecticut, to do the job, anticipating that he himself would only make the bayonets in a small shop in Meriden. Stocks were to be furnished by H. E. Robbins of Hartford, who operated a musket stock mill at Unionville, capable of making 6,000 stocks per month. Though locks were proposed to be obtained from Williams & Company of Philadelphia, most of them would be made by Parker, Snow, Brooks & Company. Snow was a practical gunmaker of 15 years experience, Parker an inventor of note as manager, quite willing to take on the added liability of the Mulholland contract.

When, in response to the decision of Holt and Owen cutting the quota to 25,000, Mulholland negotiated a formal contract on June 11, 1862, Charles Parker along with B. Rush Petrikin signed it as sureties. E. W. Andrews, who, according to John Kendrick, planned to assemble Green Kendrick's guns at Windsor Locks, was witness to the signature of Charles Parker. Mulholland's first delivery was 500 guns on July 7, 1863; 5,502 arms in all were delivered, almost certainly marked with the lockplate stamping of Parker, Snow & Co. The last delivery was October 31, 1863.

CASE NO. 91. F. L. Bodine, 25,000 Springfields. No delivery.

Though containing an interesting picture of a contractor's efforts at sub-contracting (locks by Williams of Philadelphia, barrels by Mason at Taunton), the Bodine case does not indicate any arms were made. There were no deliveries.

CASE NO. 93. Warren Fisher, Jr. This is the record of the Spencer Repeating Rifle Company, Boston. See Chapter on Spencers.

CASE NO. 94. Merrill, Thomas & Company, Baltimore. Breechloading rifles and carbines. See Chapter 11.

CASE NO. 95. P. S. Justice. See Chapter 7.

CASE NO. 96. A. K. Eaton, New York, New York, 50,000 Springfields. None delivered.

Though introduced to the Secretary of War by the great Peter Cooper himself, Eaton flopped as a musket maker or "arranger of parts." He formed a company, the Syracuse Fire-arms Company, and he had high testimonials from financiers and mechanical people. But erysipelas laid him low and he failed in his contract. Of Eaton, Cooper wrote: "he was a man of high scientific attainments and great ingenuity and skill as a mechanic." Three other firms, including barrel makers Cooper & Hewitt, cited him as "in the front rank as a man of science, and is a thorough mechanic and an inventor of genius." Maitland and Auchincloss described him as "a gentleman of uncommon mechanical skill in the department of firearms." Whether Eaton was once of the firm that Gluckman & Satterlee lists as "Eaton & Kittredge" of Cincinnati, about 1850, is not known. A later Syracuse Arms Company, very likely the heirs of Eaton's enterprise, made hammerless shotguns in Syracuse, New York, presumably not earlier than, say, 1875.

CASE NO. 97. J. Pierpont Morgan. This was the Hall Carbine Affair detailed elsewhere in Chapter 12.

CASE NO. 98. T. Robinson Rogers, 25,000 Springfields. No delivery.

This is an odd one, in the conduct of the principal. Rogers was sent a contract-letter December 24, 1861 and accepted it by his letter in reply January 2, 1862. When Stanton called for copies of documents for Holt and Owen, Rogers promptly complied on February 7, noting he had bought materials and some machinery and expected to be ready. Then, silence. Repeated notes sent to him produced no further response, and on June 18, 1862, the Commissioners agreed to confirm his order for 20,000 arms, provided he signed a contract. But, no Rogers, no contract, no guns.

CASE NO. 99. Rogers & Spencer. Pettingill pistols. See Chapter 23. 25,000 Springfields. None delivered.

This case had its stern aspect, for Hagner dealt very harshly with them though they had acted in good faith. Rogers & Spencer of Willow Vale, Oneida County, New York, had for 25 years operated a machine shop. At the time war began they were making revolvers of the Raymond & Robitaille and Pettingill patents, but obtained an order for 25,000 muskets. Rogers, in Washington in June testifying before the Commission, advised that nothing had been done on the muskets and agreed to relinquish the musket contract to gain approval of the revolver order. This was assented to and the musket order was declared null and void. Relayed to Willow Vale, it produced an immediate response from Courtney Schenck, apparently Rogers & Spencer's works foreman:

New York, June 27, 1862
Gentlemen: I shall protest against any action to cancel the Springfield gun contract issued to Messrs. Rogers, Spencer & Co. I have been for a long while engaged in arranging

Ames stock turning machine was improved by Cyrus Buckland from Thomas Blanchard's original designs at Springfield Armory; was widely used by contractors.

to manufacture these guns, and the parts are now under manufacture and have been for some time. Mr. Rogers, when in Washington, where he had been about one month, was not aware that so much progress had been made, as it has been done principally by one of the other partners, and we expect to deliver guns as soon as any other party . . . I hope if the rumor is true of your intention to annul this contract, you will consider it, and give us a fair chance with the rest of the manufacturers.

Courtney Schenck
Per Rogers, Spencer & Co.

Schenck did not write with authority. To check the correctness of the letter, Hagner cagily wrote directly to Rogers & Spencer in Willow Vale (near Utica), asking for a copy of the letter he had received "from them" on 28 June, which he said had been mislaid. It had of course been "mislaid" on top of the "active" file on his desk. Rogers & Spencer on July 4 confirmed what Hagner had suspected, for he had already on July 1 told Schenck there was no hope for the case. On July 7, Hagner wrote again to Rogers & Spencer, enclosing copies of Schenck's original letter, Hagner's refusal to Schenck of July 1, and the following note which simply does not ring true:

Washington, July 7, 1862
Gentlemen: I enclose copies of letters received and written by the commission. Mr. Holt thought he had lost Mr. Schenck's leter and therefore wrote for a duplicate. It was afterwards found.
This will explain the enigma which puzzled you.
Very respectfully, your obedient servant,
P. V. Hagner,
Major of Ordnance
Messrs. Rogers & Spencer,
Willow Grove, (sic.) Utica, N. Y.

Whether Hagner had qualms of conscience later about this is not told by history, but history does record a rather unusual contract for revolvers which Rogers & Spencer ultimately received. The demand was no longer so great for revolvers, but the Willow Vale firm sold 5,000 revolvers in a quick contract that was of no value to the United States, as shown in Chapter 23. Perhaps this contract was Hagner's doing, to make up for his adamant stand on the muskets. If Schenck was correct, and parts did exist of Rogers & Spencer make, for the Springfields, they were probably absorbed in the manufacture of other arms by other contractors, such as C. B. Hoard at Watertown, New York.

CASE NO. 100. Caspar D. Schubarth, 10,000 breech-loading arms and 20,000 Springfields.

Schubarth described himself as a small gun dealer with a shop in Providence, and stated that he had been engaged in making firearms over seventeen years. Available lists do not reflect his status as a gunsmith in the United States and his expression, "having served my time to the trade" suggests he worked most of this time in Europe, perhaps in his native Norway. However, he had some powerful friends in Rhode Island and one of them, Senator James F. Simmons, gladly took him around Washington and helped him obtain a contract. For this service, Schubarth promised Senator Simmons a commission of five per cent. The gunmaker had been told by Providence friends, machinists Amos D. and J. Y. Smith, with whom he first considered executing the order, that it was customary to offer commissions.

Schubarth proposed to make his own patent breech-loader, but Ripley, without even bothering to learn the name of the man who showed it to him (it was Schubarth himself) quashed that idea. On October 9, Schubarth proposed in writing to make 10,000 breechloaders at $35 (for carbines) and $37.50 (for rifles with bayonets), and 20,000 Springfields at $20. Ripley returned this proposal to Acting Secretary of War Thomas A. Scott, vetoing the breechloaders and saying, as he had on so many other occasions, "Contracts and orders for muskets on prospective deliveries have already been made to a sufficient extent, and I cannot recommend the acceptance of this proposition."

Scott received this memorandum October 10. It is not difficult to imagine what happened: Schubarth and Simmons converged upon the hapless and harassed Secretary.

"My constituent here can make all the Springfields you need; and what if those other contracts for 'prospective delivery' fail, Mr. Scott, what then?" Simmons doubtless argued. The result at any rate was obvious; the day after he recommended refusal of Schubarth's proposal, General Ripley by direction of the Secretary of War issued a letter-contract to Schubarth ordering 20,000 Springfields. His colleagues with whom he at first proposed to arrange the manufacture, Messrs. Amos Smith and J. Y. Smith in Providence, urged him to obtain a larger contract, claiming 20,000 muskets was not enough to get their tools warm. In November, Schubarth returned to Washington and buttonholed Senator Simmons, who again helped him to obtain an extension. On November 26 Ripley ordered an additional 30,000 Springfields from the persistent Caspar.

Behind-the-scenes activities revealed how well grounded Ripley had been in refusing and being cautious in dealing with such men, in spite of the ease with which the Secretary, his superior, ordered arms. For when Schubarth returned to Providence with the expanded order, the Smiths could not or would not cooperate with him. Possessing a big contract, he had to cast about for new partners, and lined up Frederick Griffing of Brooklyn, and James M. Ryder of Pawtucket, to finance him. The three formed a partnership listed as C. D. Schubarth & Company; to it Schubarth contributed his contracts and gunmaking know-how as his one third; the others contributed their money and time. The articles of copartnership contained an interesting limitation, that it existed solely for the musket business, "but said copartnership shall extend to no other undertaking, business, or transaction whatever." Finding any sporting gun or transformed musket legitimately marked "C. D. Schubarth & Company" is therefore most unlikely today. The company, by signed copartnership articles, was formed 15 February, 1862. Subcontracts which Schubarth arranged were:

Barrels, Aston & Co. of Middletown, Connecticut, from rough barrels made by Washburn and Trenton Iron Works.
Locks, 3,000 from Jenks of Philadelphia, the rest from Williams, also of Philadelphia.
Stocks, from Empire Works, New York, foot of East 24th Street.
Mountings, Pecksmith Manufacturing Company of Suddington, Connecticut, to make bayonets, butt plate, stock tip. Guard bow and trigger from Bigelow, Hartford.
Implements, made in Providence under supervision of Schubarth.
Final Assembly, in Providence by Schubarth.

The partners Ryder and Griffing, when they came to learn of the assistance of Senator Simmons, called on him and reached an agreement about the commissions; Simmons received their notes for $10,000; but Schubarth still considered that in all the Senator was due 5% or about $50,000. When Commissioners Holt and Owen came to view the deal, they delved deeply into

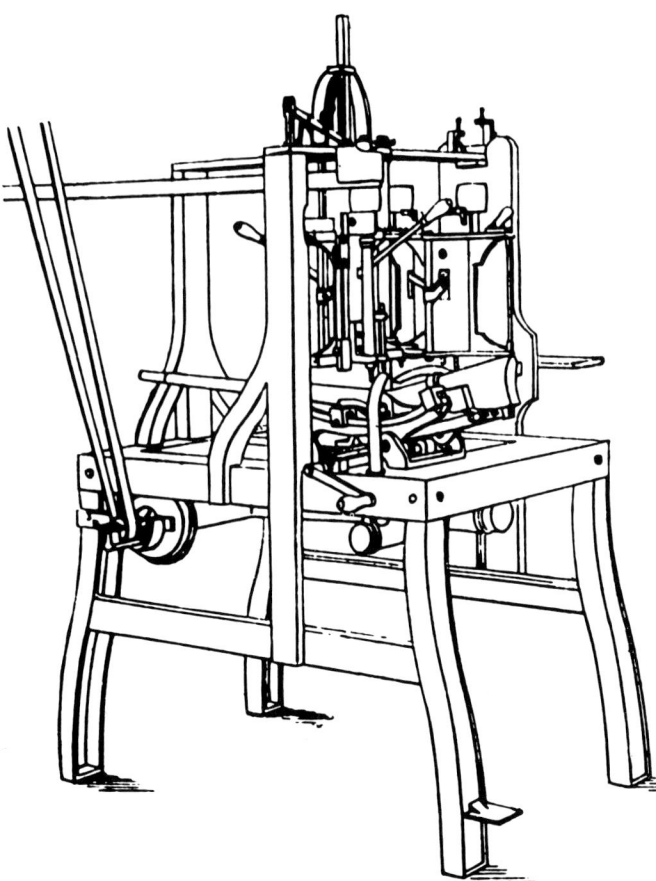

Elaborate guard plate inletting machine did in seconds what good man with chisel did in minutes. Enormous production of war material North and South was result of mechanization of industry which emergency justified.

the fundamental integrity of the senatorial office. The Senate itself resolved to find out what their member from Rhode Island had been up to, and upon their resolution the letters and records of the case were transmitted to the Hon. S. Foote, President of the Senate pro tem.

What Judge Holt and former Congressman Robert Dale Owen had to determine was not only if any laws had been violated by Schubarth and Senator Simmons, but if the deal was contrary to the principles of the Government.

Two statutes bore upon the case, affecting the receiving of compensation by a senator. The first was an Act of April 8, 1808, prohibiting a senator from holding an interest in a contract with the United States. Since payment of the commission by Schubarth was not contingent upon completion of his musket contract, but was for the service of having got the contracts in the first place, it was obvious that the senator held no interest in the contract.

The second Act, of February 26, 1853, prohibited a senator from receiving compensation for acting "as agent or attorney for prosecuting any claim or claims against the United States." Though Senator Simmons' aid might give rise to a claim, as it did in the person of Schubarth before the Commission seeking ratification of his contracts, the Senator's actions were not of themselves pressing any claim of Schubarth's against the United States.

The logic of Judge Holt is seen in the Commission's report: "Senator Simmons, also, we doubt not, regards his action in accepting this compensation as strictly legal, and we cannot, in the present condition of the legislation of Congress upon this subject, contest his opinion."

But the Commission rightly noted that it was not the labor of accompanying Schubarth to chat with Thomas Scott for which Simmons was to be paid, but for his supposed influence over the Executive Branch of the Government.

"If we understand the theory of our government aright," the Commissioners curtly summed up, "the influence which a member of Congress, as such, exercises over the administration of the departments is as much public property as is his vote in the Capitol. While the latter is so carefully protected from being brought into conflict with his personal interests, why is not the former entitled to the same guardianship?" Holt and Owen raised that question on June 2, 1861.

A century later, early in July, 1961, in trying to give a damaged revolver to Senator Paul H. Douglas of Illinois who had promised to investigate the Government's destruction of these arms, I found that such guardianship was actively at work, if not in law at least in morality. Misunderstanding at first what the pistol was, the Senator without even looking at it, said, "Oh, no, I never accept gifts."

In Senator Simmons' day, $50,000 for helping a constituent obtain a contract for needed war supplies was "usual." Holt and Owen had to accept Schubarth's open-faced sincerity, and taking into consideration that others who were American-born had counseled him into making the commission offer, they decided that no blame to either party should be declared. Rather, the evil if such existed, lay with the system. In confirming 30,000 muskets, they required that Schubarth in order to have his contract approved, had to execute a formal contract.

Schubarth's contract for not 30,000 but only 28,000 Springfields was signed 10 July, 1862. As surety, in addition to his partner, Ryder, was Albert H. Almy, of New York, the Treasurer of the Eagle Mfg. Company of Mansfield, Connecticut, an associate of James D. Mowry, and President of Norwich Armories. There is nothing to make it appear that Almy was engaged in anything improper, yet it appears that he had his finger in the supplying of several hundred thousand Springfields, more than any other single person including prime contractor Samuel Colt. To what extent the Schubarth arms were fabricated at Norwich Armories, using Schubarth's 3,000 lockplates already in progress of manufacture by Jenks, is only a conjecture. Schubarth's first delivery, December 19, 1862, was of 500 arms; following deliveries to October, 1863, averaged 1,000 pieces totalling 9,500. Whether Schubarth from the $189,305.10 he received ever paid Senator Simmons for those two visits to the War Department is unrecorded.

Case No. 101. Joseph B. Butterfield, Philadelphia, 50,000 Springfields.

Butterfield began by offering his own version of a sword bayonet Enfield rifle. Though Butterfield was mentioned favorably by Colonel Kingsbury, the War Department preferred to take up his offer of making Springfields. The exact nature of the Butterfield Enfield is not known and no specimen seems to now exist. Butterfield proceeded to push ahead on the Springfields when he received Ripley's letter-contract of December 24, 1861, ordering 50,000 rifle muskets.

Mr. Stephens of the Butterfield firm sent out to raise the money, and had interested a backer when Stanton's order calling for copies of contracts made the backer pull out. Stephens called on Stanton thereafter and was assured that if the arms were made as per contract they would be received. He got another money man interested, but the rumors about annulling contracts after the appointment of the Commission frightened off this one, too. Stephens, having a hard time, turned to Samuel Norris, who was busy making gun parts and sub-contracting at his shop in Springfield, and had turned out some thousands of arms, for Massachusetts. Norris promised to supply Butterfield's muskets if the order was confirmed, and Stephens reported that he could deliver 500 in July. The Commissioners, on June 18, 1862, confirmed the order for 25,000 muskets, but Butterfield failed to execute the contract. No Butterfield-marked muskets are known, nor should there be any.

Case No. 106. Colonel O. De Forrest, see Chapter 23. Concerns Butterfield brass-framed so-called "Confederate" revolvers actually used by Federal troops.

Case No. 107. E. Townsend, shot for cannon. Recommended paid.

Oddly-Marked Rifle Muskets

Versions of U.S.-pattern rifle muskets are thought by this writer to be post-Civil War utilization of unserviceable arms, not issue or volunteer rifles as believed. These include the very few Springfield Rifle Muskets found with lockplates engraved Manton, and those of Springfield pattern variously marked WHITNEY with, in some instances, extra-large eagles or with flat non-beveled lockplates which are usually considered to be cartridge-rifle lockplates.

The Manton arm exists in very few examples. Seemingly identical to the U.S. M1861, it is different as Fuller describes *The Rifled Musket* (Stackpole Co.), p. 176:

No record of this contract is available. This is a regulation U. S. Model 1861 rifled musket, the lockplate of which is marked forward of the hammer MANTON in Gothic print and to the rear of the hammer the date 1862. The barrel has the customary VP and eagle-head proof marks, the eagle head in this case being considerably different from that ordinarily used. In addition to the U. S. proof marks the barrel also has the British proof marks with the numerals 25 like the regular British Enfields were marked.

The US on the tang of the butt plate instead of being the ordinary letters stamped in are heavily shaded letters having the appearance of engraving.

Another specimen seen by this writer was converted to a shotgun after the fashion common after the war.

The firm Joseph Manton & Sons was one of the great gunmakers of London; unfortunately Fuller does not state what British proof marks were present on the specimen he lists, and the shotgun seen by the writer had no such proof marks. If by Joseph Manton & Sons of London make, it should reasonably have a London-proved barrel. But this is not routine in the several examples known.

Suggesting a clue, in the absence of full knowledge of this interesting arm is the record of sales after the war. Then, as for example during March, April, May, and June of 1871, Charles Folsom, 53 Chambers Street, New York was a buyer. Awarded to him during those sales listed was a selection of Colt and other revolvers, unserviceable, 100 Colt "breech stocks" at 40¢ each, evidently for the pistol-carbines, and 17 Henry rifles and 500 Spencer carbines. He also bought 196 pounds of unserviceable spare parts at 35¢ per pound—a valuable assortment.

Later buyers at Government sales numbered Charles Folsom, who is believed to have been associated with H. & D. Folsom in what later became the H. & D. Folsom Arms Company. Registered as a "private brand name" employed by the H. & D. Folsom Arms Company is the name "Manton & Company." This private brand was more or less fraudulently applied to arms to gull the unsuspecting into thinking they were getting a fine gun, of a make dimly remembered as a glorious piece of gun craftsmanship from before the war. Folsom Arms controlled the factory, Crescent Firearms Company, of Norwich, Connecticut, a city where large supplies of surplus Springfield Rifle Musket parts might be logically found in the scrap trade, from the production there of the Norwich and Jas. D. Mowry contract arms 1861-65. We suspect the "Manton"

Forest of machine tools filled Colt's Armory shops. Scene was typical more or less of machine works of 1861. Western buffalo-hide belts slapped over pullies to furnish power derived from steam engine or water wheel.

marked guns are Folsom reworked muskets, marked for sale in locales where the name Manton meant something, including possibly in unsophisticated parts of the United Kingdom where British-proved guns would be mandatory, regardless of mark. Offsetting this conjecture is the very remote possibility that George Schuyler arranged for Manton of London to make the Springfield Rifle Musket and these few pieces which have come to light where preliminary samples for an uncompleted order. Such would have exceeded the authority of Schuyler's orders, and is not mentioned by Schuyler in otherwise detailed correspondence. Manton is not known for the manufacture of military type arms. In later years this firm took on the character of a general sporting goods supply house. The writer once owned a Winchester M1905 self-loading rifle, caliber .401, stamped MANTON & CO., CALCUTTA, their once-owned, later independent Indian agency.

The Whitney arms are difficult to date exactly. How many of several variations upon the main theme of "Springfield rifle musket" are wartime, and how many interim 1866-70 conglomerations for commercial sale, we will never know. But that Whitney sold Springfield pattern arms commercially is a fact. The writer once saw in use on the range of the Associated Gun Clubs of Baltimore, Maryland, about 1948, a Springfield rifle musket bearing the mark on the stock of a large spread eagle and the words in a circle (as remembered), WHITNEY ARMS CO. The barrel was blued. Upon removing it from the stock, the bluing appeared to be old, refinish or new finish, of the same dating as the stock stamp. The lockplate marking is not now recalled, but it was not Whitney. However, a host of "Whitney" lockplate marks exist, some involving the large spread eagle. It seems this was recognized in the arms trade, even far abroad in the Orient, as a trade mark of Eli Whitney's sales organization. Some of these arms, especially short barreled and special model arms, were postwar, put together surplus parts.

Special Model Muskets and two-band rifles seem to be a part of this picture. The contention is often parrotted that these were put together for artillerists, etc. An early quotation in the arms history field on the subject is from Charles W. Sawyer's *Our Rifles*. Published in 1922, this is one of the first references to "special models" and seems to have moulded arms collectors' thinking for years:

> During the Civil War when exigencies demanded more arms than could be issued of the model then under manufacture, spare parts of preceding models were drawn from the storehouses and incorporated with parts of the latest design. Not only was this done in the shops of the Government but also some of the contractors were furnished with extra parts made in the Government shops.

Sawyer then goes on to describe a particular rifle:

> Calibre .58. Weight about 8 pounds. Length of barrel about 33 inches. Two bands. Except for adherence to these specifications the details of this class of arms did not follow a prescribed rule.
>
> These arms were made during 1863, 1864, and 1865 from the left-overs of rifles and muskets of 1865 and preceding years. The specimen shown has a lock of the 1861 pattern bearing the date of 1862; a cut-down barrel dated 1863; a re-shaped model 1841 stock, and a butt plate of 1819 pattern. Some of the specimens of this arm, now in collections, are mounted with brass, and others with iron, and still others with part each. These arms were made during the Civil War when adherence to a standard pattern became a detail of minor importance, because the main object was to get something—anything—that would shoot.
>
> The issue of these arms was to artillerists—field and coast —for personal defense under unusual conditions, and for use when foraging as mounted infantry.

The gobbledygook in the foregoing will reveal to the thoughtful person that Sawyer simply did not know what he was talking about. So far as strict adherence to a standard pattern is concerned, the numerous contracts reproduced in part or in spirit in this section reveal how important Generals Ripley, Ramsay, Dyer, all believed a standard pattern to be. Minor details not affecting service might pass a Springfield Rifled Musket at $19.90 instead of the contract $20, but you can bet your last shinplaster that Springfield looked exactly like 800,000 other of its fellows.

Within the production of the Springfield basic arm there were, it is true, changes. These patterns existed and were used as guides in accepting arms. Contracts negotiated during the 1864-5 period often were filled by arms of the "improved" models. But the short jobs, the 33 inch barreled guns, are unauthorized models. Even when the barrel is tapered at the muzzle to take a bayonet, commercial speculation by surplus arms dealer Francis Bannerman as a "cadet" rifle is the explanation. The majority of such arms, especially those such as the specimen cited by Sawyer with stock of one model and butt of another, are gunsmith put-togethers either for Confederate service or just hopeful sale for bear hunting. No contracts exist for short Springfields, and Civil War photos of artillerists show them equipped with regular rifles. The last sentence of Sawyer's is a malapropism—he says "when foraging as mounted infantry." To have any sense at all the statement must read, "when skirmishing as mounted infantry." And, even then, mounted infantry dismount for purposes of entering the skirmish line (unless the word is used carelessly in describing a cavalry type action). As for foraging, the only enemy battled by foragers were pigs and chickens. Springfield Armory in the hot days of '63 did not produce arms designed for chicken thieves . . . one "snaphance" a millenium is enough.

CHAPTER 7

In Justice to Justice

In justice to Justice, it must be said that a recent examination of one of the muskets, for the supplying of which to the Union he was so villified, proves to be a reasonably well-assembled hodgepodge of surplus parts and at least as strong and reliable as the American parts from which it was built.

But when Philip S. Justice, gunmaker-importer of Philadelphia, tried to get aboard the Federal musket contract gravy train, he both got more than he bargained for—and Holt and Owen conversely gave him less.

Justice Enters the Arena

Justice first came into the rat race with a sale to the United States, of 1,000 caliber .58 Enfield rifles, sword bayonet model (two band M1859), specific maker or marks unknown, which he proposed to deliver during July, 1861. Soon after making his original proposal to General Ripley, Justice offered an additional 500 long Enfields, with angular bayonets. All Enfields were to be delivered by September. These arms, being substitute standard, were not destined for the Regular Army of the United States, but to outfit the newly-authorized 28th Pennsylvania Regiment, recruiting that July at Oxford Park, under command of Colonel John W. Geary. The authorized strength of the 28th having been raised to 1,500 men, Justice offered and Lieutenant James T. Treadwell, inspecting Ordnance officer at Frankford Arsenal in Bridesburg, was authorized to inspect and receive, the added 500 Enfields.

The record shows that Justice delivered actually 700 with angular bayonets by September, 1861, at $18, and another 700 "with swords" at $20.

But the market became competitive that summer of 1861 and Justice turned to other means to supply arms. As an importer, he had the contacts perhaps to obtain some small work done abroad—at least, the trigger guards on his basic .69 caliber rifle and rifle musket are distinctively European in pattern. But whether he bought small parts abroad or made them in Philadelphia is almost academic, for he did manage to obtain a source of supply for condemned Springfield rifled .69 musket tubes, plus old locks, Enfield-type brass stock tips, and brass patchboxes which bear a striking similarity to the Sharps M1853 Carbine patchbox. To all these parts he added his own make of fairly-badly fitting brass split bands, his own make of stock (decried as green wood causing rusting of the locks), and ramrods and bayonets. He may also have made locks which he fitted, or altered U.S. plates to fit. One gun is recorded with a rebuilt Wickham contract lock. Generally the new-made locks are on the .69 rifle-muskets; the altered flint locks are on the sword bayonet rifles. The finished gun is a handsome specimen, very colorful with blacked barrel, lock dulled by case-hardening, warm walnut wood stock, and colorful burnished brass bands, patchbox and guard.

Types of Arms Sold by Justice

Two types of Justice-made arms were offered to and bought by the U.S. Government, for issue to Pennsylvania troops. When the lot was delivered, it included arms of at least five distinct patterns. They were the production outgrowth of his offer made August 12, 1861, to Lieutenant Treadwell, in which he stated:

"I propose to supply the Ordnance Department of the United States with four thousand rifled muskets, caliber 69/100 of an inch, similar in style and finish to the sample deposited with you, at 20 dollars each. In all the month of September, I will deliver one thousand, and each month thereafter, until 1st January, 1862, I will deliver 1,000 of the above arms."

Treadwell was authorized by General Ripley on August 16 to accept the proposition of Justice as to the 4,000 rifled muskets. Justice had also offered Treadwell 680 rifles of the Chasseurs de Vincennes "new pattern," with sword bayonets, 31 inch barrels, .69 caliber, priced in bond at $22.50 each. Ripley refused to make any agreement about arms not yet in port, although these were good quality French arms, but did accept the offer Justice also made to supply 5,000 cavalry sabers. Ripley stipulated they must be delivered and approved after inspection as Justice stated, or else the Government would be relieved of responsibility to take them and might do so or not as the needs of war occurred.

This acceptance was the start of a rhubarb which cost Justice money, vexed the Government, endangered

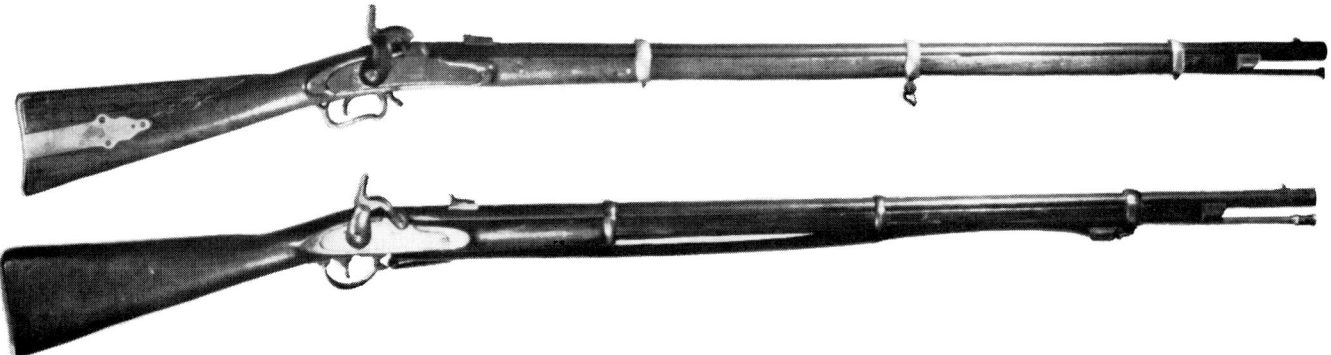

Brass-trimmed P. S. Justice Rifle Musket was .69 cal., used patchbox which resembled M1853 period Sharps, and distinctive curved trigger guard.

At bottom, a Whitney Long Enfield, serial No. 166. Gun resembles Enfield but has no Enfield parts in it. Guard bow is brass on steel plate. Sling is old.

Pennsylvania volunteers to whom the Justice rifles were issued, and left behind as mementos scarce specimens of this most interesting issue, and several illustrations in the Philadelphia-published (J. B. Lippincott) *United States Infantry Tactics,* Lieutenant Colonel H. B. Wilson, 1862. In this book, a two-band rifle, similar in style of patchbox and trigger guard form to the Justice arm, is pictured (viz. "Stack Arms," page 99). Whether this was Justice's effort to publicize his special model rifle, or a conscious effort of Colonel Wilson to illustrate a model of rifle with which the Pennsylvania troops were going to be armed, is unknown. His engraver may merely have sent out to a gun shop "for a musket to use as a model," and fell upon one of the Justice arms which failed to pass Treadwell's eagle eye. At any rate, there it is—one of the first instances of that subtle form of firearms publicity which chooses a particular rifle that the printer or editor or advertiser wants to "push" and uses photos of it as window dressing to an article or book.

Justice built two rifles—a short and a long. Sub-types consisted in each pattern of brass-banded, or iron-banded, rifles. The short rifle had sword bayonet, brass handle. A fifth type, sword bayonet short rifle with cross-pins fastening stock to barrel, was also delivered by Justice. The rifle-muskets were .69 caliber arms; short rifles .58 inch bore. Of the .69 rifle muskets with triangle bayonets, only 2,174 were accepted by Treadwell; only 2,469 were accepted of all three varieties of .58 short rifle. A specimen of the Justice rifle cited by Gluckman has a lockplate stamped US in a shield borne by an eagle.

All Justice arms are stamped in two lines on lock plate and top of barrel breech P. S. JUSTICE/PHILAD^A. On some—possibly on all, but at least on the author's specimen No. P 2584 (.69 RM 39-inch barrel)—the final letter of the maker's name is broken and resembles an F. Not all arms bore an eagle stamp—some, possibly those having new-made locks such as No. P2584 above, are plain except for maker's name. The serial number appears on the trigger guard brass tang behind the bow, and on top of the barrel tang, crosswise. On the guard, the P is above the number; below it, on the barrel tang. No proof mark appears, but the top of the barrel has been slightly struck off at the breech to more nearly match the esthetic line of the stock by the lock. Beneath the barrel is stamped C, for condemned. Justice stated the barrels he used were condemned, done so by reason of being too short for the standard model for which they were intended. The bolster form and general dimensions suggest Model 1842 U.S. Musket, which had a standard barrel length of 42 inches. Oddly, the 1842 barrel's bayonet stud is beneath the barrel; that of the Justice musket is on top, also approximately 1½ inches from the muzzle, and 1 11/16 inches forward of the front sight mortise. The inference is that the bolster was knocked off (or the barrel never originally percussioned) and stocked upside down by Justice to hide that C stamp of condemnation.

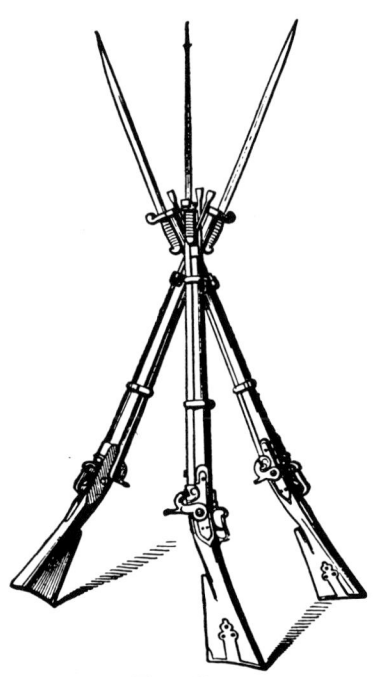

STACK ARMS (No. 410).

Cut from Col. Wilson's drill book shows stand of three Justice rifles, two bands, sword bayonets. Book published in Philadelphia boosted local product, may have been intended for use by Pennsylvania regiments issued Justice guns.

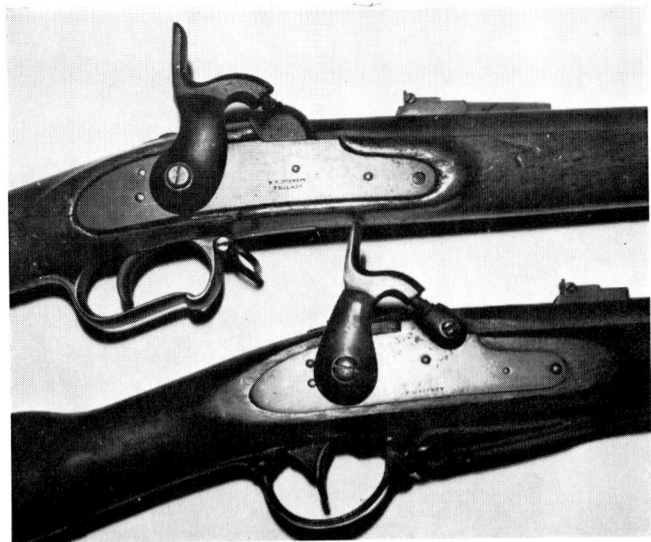

Justice planned no fraud, plainly stamped his mark on lock and barrel. Serial numbers are prefaced by a P, or the P may be below the number. Odd but distinctive guard form is seen. Rear sights on Justice and Whitney Enfield (bottom) are 1859 type. Whitney has barrel like 1861 Springfield; was advertised 1862.

Complaints

Now Justice was a practical gunmaker. He sold various types of arms to the Union, including pistols and revolvers, muskets, swords, and sabers. And of his muskets in particular, issued mostly to the 58th, 88th, and 98th Pennsylvania Volunteers, complaints were many. The least vehement complaint, in the words of Major John Buford, assistant inspector general of the 91st Pennsylvania Volunteers, (commanded by Colonel Gregory), was that they were "unserviceable." Buford obtained the withdrawal of the 91st's Justice muskets, which were returned in late April or early May, 1862 to Washington Arsenal, and an issue was made to the entire regiment of Springfield-made rifle muskets, .58 caliber, 1861 date. Meanwhile, on May 9, Captain Knabb and Lieutenant Wagner of the 88th Pennsylvania Volunteers were detailed to Washington from Regimental headquarters at Aquia Creek, Virginia, to draw arms and accouterments for this command. Inference from the correspondence is, that Knabb and Wagner rode chortlingly back to camp behind a trainload of Justice muskets, glad they had solved their problems of armament so easily—until they opened the cases. Assistant Inspector General R. Jones of the 88th Pennsylvania recapitulated to General Ripley the defects of some 700 muskets inspected, of which all but 130 (by Remington) were stamped on the barrel "Justice, Philadelphia."

Jones declared further:

Of these guns, 423 had the bayonet, and 401 the rammer, either bent or broken; the bands of 262 were so loose as to fall from their places on discharging the guns; 140 had the sights loose, broken off, or otherwise injured; 158 locks were more or less injured; the mainsprings of many being too weak to explode a cap; 14 barrels were bent; and 22 had either burst or were dangerous to fire on account of flaws in the metal.

The stocks of 212 were broken or split, the injuries being mostly at the toe or heel of the butt, or around the lock, and quite a number were broken off at the small of the stock. If was noticed that the sights that had fallen off had been soldered onto the barrel and not secured by a screw; it was also observed that the rifling in many of the guns was so slight as to be scarcely perceptible to either the touch or sight.

A more detailed inspection of arms in store for issue at Fort Monroe Arsenal, Virginia, by Lieut. R. M. Hill, Ordnance Corps, only heaped more abuse upon Justice's products. Absence of interchangeability was decried; even bayonets could not be fitted to guns other than the one whose number they bore. The sights were knocked off, and of those which remained, "imitation screws (are) made upon them," to fill the screw hole, since they all appear to have been of the 1861 type of sight. Hill concluded with, "In consequence of the many defects of this arm, I respectfully recommend that they be not issued to the troops, but be condemned."

A Second Look

Still willing to give Justice the benefit of the doubt, and possibly wondering what Lieut. Treadwell was doing passing as "inspected and approved" so many gross defects, the Commission on Ordnance and Ordnance Stores, through its technical member, Ordnance Major P. V. Hagner, asked Major T. T. S. Laidley at Frankford to take a second look at the sample Justice musket and other Justice arms in the Frankford Arsenal. Laidley was not one bit more encouraging. Out of two boxes of Justice arms, presumably a total of 40 muskets, he found "three barrels which had flaws of considerable size . . . I broke two hammers, which bent back and forth before yielding. I am of the opinion that one, at least, is of cast iron, well annealed . . . The rammers and bayonets are only slightly tempered, and take a set readily . . . Some of the locks were rusted from the green wood stocks, and the bands were, in some cases, loose, as they are upon the sample arm."

Then damning with faint praise, Laidley closed his examination by stating "With the exception of the rifling (very slight, about 0.05 inch, and not as deep as in the sample arm), and some flaws in the barrels, I regard the arm furnished by Mr. Justice that I have inspected equal to the sample arm."

The Commission was not content with field reports; the sample arm from Frankfort was shipped off to the Washington Arsenal, where its commander Lieutenant Colonel George D. Ramsey took a long hard look at what he had on hand. ". . . making the comparison with the sample," he had to admit, "there is no great difference as to service qualities." The sample arm was a three-band rifle musket, angular bayonet, .69 caliber, brass bands. "By comparison with the sample," Ramsey reported to Ripley, "the locks vary in length from 0.5 to 0.9 inches, and the lockplates are variously patched to suit the cone seats . . . one or two [screws] are used, according to length of lockplate . . . The rifling of the barrels varies from three to six grooves; and some of the barrels are reduced by filing down the upper surface at butt to adapt them to the breech screws (plugs). Sights: Some are long, and others short. The long range sights are imperfectly secured, and readily move in the dovetail seat; (see sample arm). The three leaf sights are coarsely riveted on the bands . . . The component parts of these arms are, apparently, with the exception of the brass mountings, of discarded armory work. These arms, in the average, cannot be said to be inferior to the sample arm furnished me, and now before the Commission on Ordnance and Ordnance Stores. They are far, however, from being a first class arm, and, in view of the contract price, $20, are decidedly of inferior quality. The other varieties of the 'Justice arms' on hand referred to are pretty much of the same quality and diversity of parts. The rifles without bands have a coarse notch sight, and are the most inferior of the lot."

Justice's Rebuttal

While the inspectors were criticizing him, Justice did not stand still and absorb the knocks. For one thing, he had coming, at the original price of $20, a balance of $19,171.25. This payment was stopped by the Ordnance Corps when complaints from the field suggested that not all was right with Justice's guns. He, too, informed Commissioners Holt and Owen of his side of the story. And in justice to Justice it must be admitted that he did have some major points in his favor.

First, military arms from Springfield were the peak of perfection of the art of making guns by machinery. Justice had been an importer and maker of sporting guns for 20 years before the war. But, he admitted, he had no experience with military work although then, and since, as is the case today, military small arms are made to higher standards of perfection than common sporting rifles, accuracy excepted.

Justice argued that the sample represented pretty much the best that he could do in the way of a military arm. This seems to be a true statement, not only from the evidence that all inspected were spoken of unkindly, but also because of the circumstances in the small arms trade at the time.

Quantities of surplus United States and contractors' small arms parts were available from the scrap yards. Many gun merchants in the late 1850's seem to have made a point of buying these parts and fitting them up into militia muskets and rifles. Although these arms generally conformed to the United States pattern, there were many differences. The Justice rifles, for example, with sword bayonets and brass fittings, corresponded generally to the U.S. Model 1855 Rifle, although the patchboxes were from surplus old Sharps carbine manufacture, apparently, instead of the smoothly ovaled U.S. style of brass lid. They are rudely finished—perhaps from Sharps' castings, or perhaps new, but following the Sharps M1853 style.

"After much cost," Justice explained to Ripley in Washington, "I made the arrangements (i.e., purchased the junk parts) to manufacture the style of musket of which I showed you the sample. Knowing that I *could*

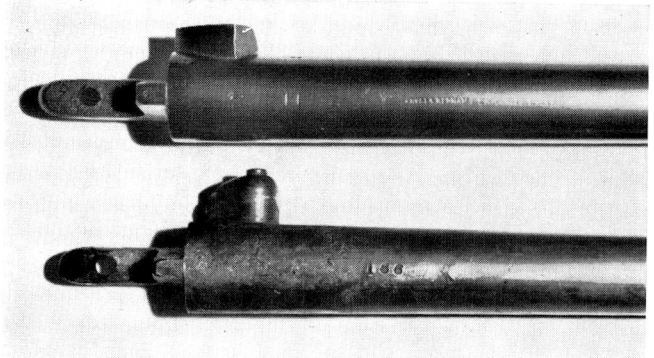

Possibility Whitney Enfield barrels were made in England under Jarvis' supervision for Colt and not used by Colt is suggested but undetermined. Only mark on Whitney barrel is serial number and few cryptic cyphers; regular Enfield (top) is marked by barrel-maker Millward and gunmaker Pryse & Redman.

make *such* arms, I felt *that if your judgment certified to its usefulness,* although it might not meet all your requirements, I was safe in pushing my manufacture to the utmost extent. Your judgment, as expressed through your officers, approved of it, and the order was given, and to this judgment I have always deferred and conformed, because I knew it was the only safe rule for me to follow."

The sample musket, Justice allowed, consisted of a U.S. barrel, bayonet, and flint lock converted to percussion—all the rest of the work was new. He noted that as he gained skill in making the general style of arm, he made improvements, although Lieut. Treadwell told him that he, Treadwell, could not allow any more money for the minor changes. Even at a cost of several thousand dollars ($3,672.50 to be exact), Justice delivered sword-bayonet rifles over and above what had been ordered, in lieu of the .69 rifled muskets, because he gained the impression from Treadwell that they were to be preferred, being more nearly like the U.S. standard rifle.

The soldered rear sights he acknowledged, but he pointed out that not only were they soldered on at the suggestion of Treadwell (drilling for the sight base screw and slotting would weaken the thin barrel) but that the Lieutenant, in examining claims that sights fell off, took a case of twenty arms and hit the sight bases with a hammer to knock them loose. In all cases the metal of the sight was damaged before any tendency to fall off occurred, and not all the sights did fall off.

Justice explained the "dummy screw" charge by noting that since the sight bases had been sweated on, it was only good design and esthetics to close up the old sight base screw holes, which he did by sawing off the threads and soldering the regular sight screw head into place. No attempt to deceive existed, he said. "I believed that the best recommendation I could have for my guns was the fact that they were in part made of government work," he proclaimed. "My muskets I have never invoiced or called as Enfield muskets, as charged, nor have I ever compared them to the Springfield musket, which I hold to be the best military arm extant. I do say emphatically, however, that as a hand made arm, it has been made by me *honestly* and *conscientiously* and as well as it could be made with *the opportunities offered, and is far better than the model in all its parts."*

Justice dismissed the soft bayonet charges and complaints about locks with strongly worded remarks indicating they were, after all, U.S. Government inspected and approved old locks and stickers. The absence of band springs he countered with pointing out that his bands were like the Enfield style and tightened with a screw. Justice compared the soldier's affection for the Springfield gun, as contrasted with his rifle:

I respectfully suggest that as it is natural that each soldier should desire to obtain the Springfield musket, whose qualities are so highly appreciated; they too often abuse the issue of other arms in the hope of condemning the same, and thus have a new chance offered them for obtaining what, perhaps, had been promised them by their officers, to secure their enlistment, as I am cognizant of the promise of Springfield arms having been made to the men in numerous cases of enlistment to aid the object they were striving for. The results of such promises, when broken, are, abuse of the arms and the reputation of the maker. I had nearly been made a sufferer from this very cause, where a complaint was made that the stocks were "rotten," when upon investigation it was found the men had been using the muskets as seats, and thus broken stocks which were afterward acknowledged to be perfectly solid and seasoned.

With cause for complaint in rebuttal, Justice protested the second inspection of guns which had been first inspected and found acceptable, then passed entirely out of his hands and suffered he knew not what manner of deliberate abuse in the hands of soldiers dissatisfied with them. Very much to the point, Justice complained of certain conduct of Government officers in the abstract—if it was permitted the Government to review contracts once made in spite of the model having been acceptable, and inspections made under the conditions he was now exposed to—after guns had been in the hands of troops—it might be seen that any capitalist would be in jeopardy of not being paid by Government in spite of his most careful preparations. Justice cited again his 25 year record as a merchant, reputation "untainted" so far, but if the matter of his gun was not settled fairly, he would be ruined. His money would be lost, and his business ended, "as I shall hereafter be classed amongst the list of 'contractors' whose main effort was to swindle the government they had sworn to support." At the time he wrote to Ripley, April 26, 1862, some $80,000 was unpaid on vouchers for arms received from him and passed by Treadwell's inspectors.

Finding of the Commissioners

Commissioners Holt and Owen considered very carefully Justice's counter-claims. But in their findings, upon the basis of which his accounts were to be settled, they did not agree with him. The actual schedule of deliveries of arms accepted by Treadwell showed considerably less than 1,000 per month of any type arm going into Frankford from Justice. Of 5,035 Justice guns of all five types delivered, 392 were rejected; the accepted proportion of .69 muskets being 2,174 and of the three types of rifles, brass bands, iron bands, and no bands at all, being 2,469. Deliveries were slow, less than scheduled, and continued past the terminal date. Further, many of the defects found to exist were only such as would develop in service. The rusting of the locks and barrels from green wood could not be apparent until the guns have been out on the range, and the sun and dews got to work on the metal. Thin barrels were not only found for a fact by two inspecting officers later on, but several had burst in shooting from such flaws, one from firing a blank cartridge. The variations in rifling, in spite of being, as claimed, "former government work," plus other details, all served to confirm in the Commissioners' minds the opinion that Justice did not supply guns even uniformly up to his own low standards.

They accordingly directed that no contract be considered to exist, as had been declared in a former case, because Justice failed to deliver in time. They did direct that since guns delivered had been accepted and used, they should be paid for. But the pay was adjusted to be only $15 for rifle muskets, and the $20 for rifles with sword bayonets, and that his accounts be settled upon that basis.

From the whole fracas, Justice got odium and scorn, possibly major damage to his business as a firearms dealer, manufacturer, and broker, and $81,990 for his guns.

The name of Justice does not appear actively after the Civil War. He left behind him a strange story, and a few brass mounted guns. These, in spite of the claims made a century ago, are among the prettiest of the Civil War contract pieces with their brass trim, blued barrels, and unique form of trigger guard. Although the Government inspectors seemed to think Justice was as crooked as his oddly shaped trigger guard, we are not entirely sure, from the record, that this is true. He made guns as best he knew how, and, in the dire emergency of 1861, his guns did their part fairly well.

CHAPTER 8

Millions for Muskets

When Secretary Stanton called to the colors a partner of the gun-sales firm of Schuyler, Hartley and Graham of New York, he could have let himself in for a peck of trouble. He proposed to place in Marcellus Hartley's hands virtual control of the supply of arms from abroad. Yet a most searching scrutiny of the record reveals in the person of the youthful Hartley, furnished with the emoluments if not the dignity of a brigadier general, one of the most zealous and honest Union men to emerge from the history of the war. Preceding him as arms buyers were the reckless General Fremont and Colonel George L. Schuyler, whose name is the same as one of Hartley's silent partners, but is not that man.

It was to Colonel Schuyler that Cameron turned first, possibly through recommendation of the Ordnance officers stationed at Governors Island. On June 3, 1861, General Ripley signed his famous letter to Cameron of estimates. Though he was kept in the dark about the other plans for the number of men contemplated being placed in the service, Ripley made a fair guess the Union needed "an aggregate force of 250,000 men of all arms, cavalry, artillery, and infantry," and requested Cameron to instruct him as to his course for obtaining arms. Though a stickler for discipline, realizing his office could not run efficiently unless in an orderly manner, Ripley was not bashful about giving advice. And on June 3 he called the Secretary's attention to the fact that he, Ripley, had suggested, some five weeks before, "when my views on this subject were requested," the propriety of obtaining from abroad from 50,000 to 100,000 small arms and eight batteries of rifled cannon, but that he had no indication any action had been taken on the matter. The suggestion had been made to General Scott; Mr. Daniel Tyler of Connecticut, subsequently General Tyler, was then considered as the agent to send abroad, but no action was taken.

Fremont's Purchases in Europe

The sense of uncertainty created situations which could only lead to abuse. John C. Fremont, that glamorous officer of the Corps of Topographical Engineers, the "Pathfinder," was in Europe that spring. He conferred with the United States Minister in London, Charles Francis Adams, and with Henry Sanford, Minister in Brussels. His belief was that when he returned to the United States to assume command, there would be a great scramble for arms and he did not want to get caught short. He bought quantities of arms at high prices, in one case leading to a scandal of war profiteering which did not easily die: the Hall Carbine Affair. But his foreign purchases were simply standard arms at too-high prices. From John Hoey, an importer with offices in New York, he obtained 100 Enfield rifles on August 31 and another 100 on September 4, at $26.50, as much as ten dollars more than other Enfields later were appraised for. His stop in New York on his return from Europe permitted him to buy, on that same August 18, also from John Hoey, 2,180 "smoothbore muskets, new, brown and bright, at $10." These apparently were Austrian smoothbores, of the 1840 Augustin-lock type which Fremont had to have converted to percussion cone before issuing. He also purchased Colt revolving rifles, perhaps from Hartley's store, for as much as $65, and Colt's carbines at $60, "much more than these arms are worth" as General Ripley complained in evaluating Fremont's irregular conduct. The Colt carbines were issued to Fremont's bodyguard troop of cavalry, the "Fremont Hussars," under command of Hungarian Major Zagonyi. Back in Europe the boats were loading rifles for Fremont, arms purchased in concord with the actions of Minister Sanford, who plunged into the gun buying markets with a will. During the end of 1861 and in 1862, Sanford paid out $446,298 for arms which were among the cheapest arms bought by the Union in the rising market, and the best value for money spent.

Principally from the fabricants of Liege, Sanford obtained 28,364 smoothbore muskets, and 27,648 rifled muskets; and 25 Lefaucheux pistols, ordered by General Fremont. While the description "pistols" could refer to topbreak double barrel pinfire handguns resembling sawed-off shotguns, of small size (9mm or 12mm), they more probably were Lefaucheux military Model 1853 revolvers, 12mm, of the type more commonly recognized as a U. S. secondary martial pistol. The muskets are not fully described; there is a probability that they were the M1840 series of back-action muskets, which had been in the French service and retired owing to wear in the rifling. These guns were rifled about 1847, and new arms made of the same pattern during this time, at the various government factories but also, and principally, at Liege. Though a standard pattern of the French service, it was a popular export model from the Liege fabricants who supplied similar muskets to war departments around the globe. Those which Sanford found he could buy so cheaply, at an average price of $7.96, may have included the Liege muskets, once-rifled, and then reamed up to smoothbore again after wear in the rifling.

The philosophy seems to have been, at least so far as salesmanship goes, better to have a bright-bored smoothbore than a worn rifle. The long-range rear sights which elevated the muzzle to throw the Minie projectile of nominal .70 inch diameter a thousand yards, were melted off; they were attached with soft solder. The muskets being struck up bright, the solder often remained in a smear on top of the barrel to show where the sight had been.

It is believed that these were the arms Sanford found so easily available, weapons which otherwise would have gone into the African or Far Eastern trade for sale to colonial princes and despots. Yet functionally, their back-action locks were superior to the side lock of the U. S. muskets, including the new, vaunted perfect Springfield rifle; they were less likely to be contaminated from the cap smoke on discharge. The bands and barrel proportions were much like the same parts of the common U. S. type 1835-1842 muskets, smoothbores, and the stocks were of good walnut. Sanford, for all the complaints of later commissions, made a fairly good buy. And in the emergency, obviously the merchants would not offer their very best arms first, for it would leave them with unsold arms such as their reworked smoothbores, still on hand. Sanford and Fremont got what was offered, and approximately at the going prices.

Fremont was allowed to keep the arms he had purchased in Europe, to equip his command. But this was not the way to run a war, both Cameron and Ripley agreed. The Ordnance general was particularly miffed by Fremont's irregular purchasing sprees, for he repeatedly referred in his official correspondence to the third section of the Act approved February 8, 1815 . . . "that it shall be the duty of the colonel or senior ordnance officer, under the direction of the Secretary of War, to make contracts and purchases for procuring the necessary supplies of arms, equipments, ordnance and ordnance stores." As Ripley very coldly observed, "These purchases by Major General Fremont or his agents are not in accordance with the stipulations of this act." That Fremont was short-circuiting Ripley's own efforts to buy arms cheaply, for the same ultimate consumer, Uncle Sam, was a matter that Ripley did not choose to make an issue of at the moment.

Schuyler Appointed Central Purchasing Agent

To bring order to the mounting chaos of separate bidders raising prices on arms in the New York market, President Lincoln decided to appoint a single agent. He chose Colonel George L. Schuyler as that man; Schuyler was informed of the choice by Cameron on July 29, 1861: "The President relies upon your integrity and discretion to make such purchases of arms as you may deem advisable upon the very lowest terms compatible with the earliest possible delivery." A credit of $2,000,000 was to be placed to Schuyler's account with Baring Brothers, London bankers, to buy 100,000 rifle muskets with bayonets, 20,000 sabers, 10,000 carbines for cavalry, and 10,000 revolvers.

Foreign arms purchased by Col. Schuyler or Marcellus Hartley were issued in early stages of war to supply Northern levies. Shown at sally port of Union heavy artillery fort near Arlington, Va., is guard with Lorenz Austrian rifle.

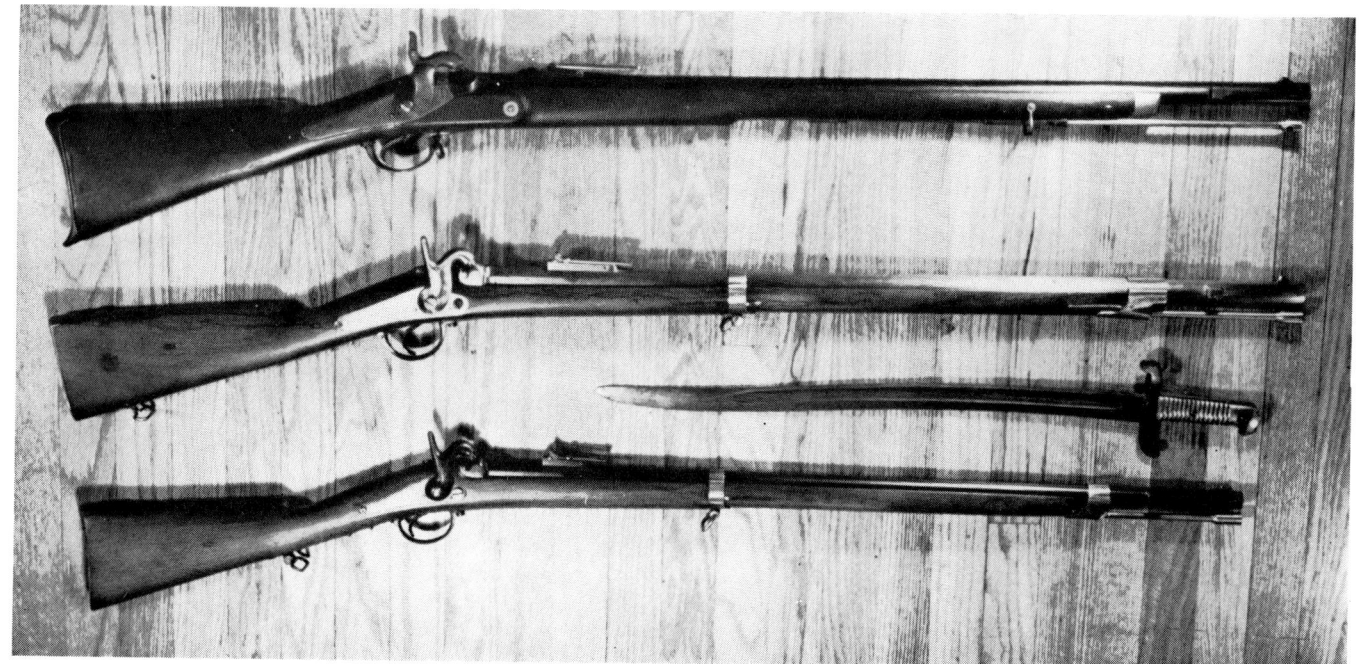

Among best arms bought abroad were Thouvenin system rifles from Dresden, a heavy but accurate .69 round ball gun (top); and French minies. Thouvenin rifle is steel trim, casehardened with blued barrel; Carabine de Chasseurs de Vincennes (middle) is bright with 4-groove .69 bore for minie bullet. At bottom is elegant .58 "beautiful minie," brass trim, blued, weighing 7½ pounds.

While Schuyler could not be limited in detail as to the nomenclature of the arms he should buy, he was quite fully acquainted with the desire for Springfield-quality arms. Ripley had explained to Secretary Cameron that the Enfield rifle as made at the Royal Small Arms Factory in England was largely a result of studies made by British engineers at Springfield Armory; machinery had been bought in Springfield from the same toolmakers who supplied the Armory, and some half dozen of the top Springfield men had been hired to supervise at Enfield—boss of them all as Chief Engineer was James H. Burton of Harpers Ferry. Ripley had confidence in the serviceability of the No. 1 quality machine-made Enfield, if Schuyler would buy them. He was to purchase as many as possible to fill the requirement ready-made, and the rest were to be contracted for, to be delivered in New York not more than six months from the date of his orders.

When Schuyler got to London on August 12, 1861, he scouted around and spent the week fruitlessly discovering that Rebel buyer Caleb Huse, and other agents, including those from the Northern states, had tied up the London and Birmingham factories. The London Armoury, only private machine-made Enfield source, which a short time before had refused to do business with Southern agent Caleb Huse, now turned the cold shoulder to Yankee Schuyler; they were all booked up by the Confederacy. With his inspector, August Rhuleman, he crossed over to France quickly to see what could be learned there. Government arsenals in both England and upon the Continent were full of arms, but they were second-class weapons. They were, however, entirely serviceable and of the class with which the Union eventually fought a large part of the war.

But they did not conform to Colonel Schuyler's instructions. In Paris he conferred with Ministers Dayton and Sanford, who came over from Belgium. These men had been offered 20,000 Carabines de Chasseurs de Vincennes, for about $17 each, but had demurred for want of funds. Now Schuyler took over their offer and was able to line up 28,000 more, in the arsenals of France. Apparently they were possessed by a private firm, perhaps the gun trade in St. Etienne. Half were to be delivered in 30 days, the balance in 60 days from signing of the contract. The inference here is that the firm had a contract with the French Government to supply these arms and had a quantity of work well advanced that they could finish up for the United States, deferring deliveries to La Republique a few months, for possibly slightly higher per gun price.

Back in England, Schuyler wasted no more time in London but took the train to Birmingham, then and now the main gun-making center for the United Kingdom.

Small private makers abounded in this Midlands city, but their productivity was small. Some, such as W. W. Greener on St. Mary's Square, were later to boast of high production on Britain's cartridge rifles for the War Department, but in Schuyler's time they were emphasizing fine shotguns and, to a lesser extent, sporting rifles. Schuyler doubtless stopped in to see the proprietor, W. Greener, authority on shooting and foremost arms writer of the day. Back in New York, shops featured Greener shotguns, fine strong doubles with their barrels marked "Laminated steel warranted

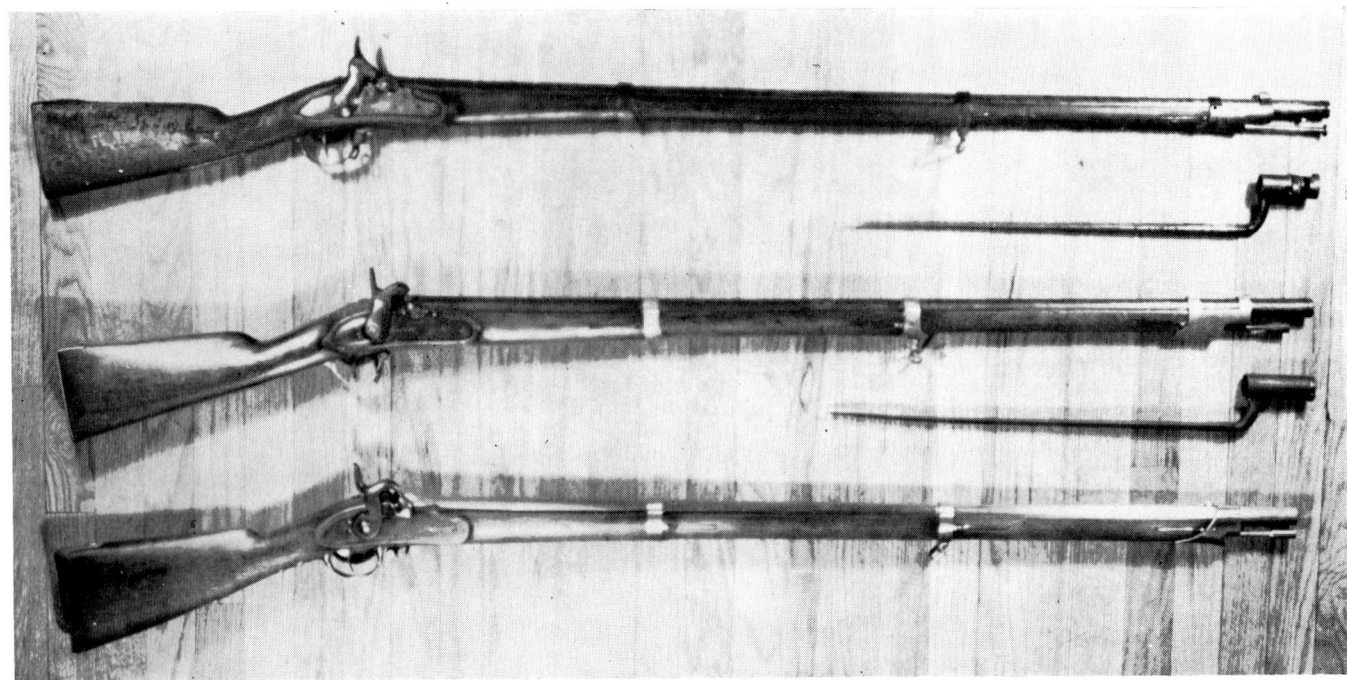

Mediocre arms include Würtemburg musket of French type made at Oberndorf Royal Factory. Gun shown, top, was used by Ill. soldier. Middle, Prussian "Potsdam" marked musket has U.S.-repaired hammer. At bottom is Bavarian .69 smoothbore such as Hartley bought a few of. Gun shown is Liege Museum model.

indestructible by gunpowder." Such guns, chopped a foot or two in the barrel to a handy 20 inches or less, were to be a preferred weapon among many of the Southern chivalry. But Schuyler was not in Birmingham to discuss shotguns.

He was introduced to the members of the newly formed Birmingham Small Arms Trade, a syndicate forerunner to today's famous "B.S.A. Guns, Ltd." arms, cycle, and motor-making corporation. Though the gunmakers of Birmingham had, since the 17th century, been supplying the wants of the Crown and producing for export, their handwork system left much to be desired in efficiency, and their business arrangements likewise were deficient in bargaining power. The start of the Crimean war stimulated 16 of Birmingham's master smiths in 1854 to form the "Birmingham Small Arms Trade Association." Externally, the group formed a united front in bargaining with contractors and buyers. Internally, the group bargained more resolutely with the trade unions. From December 1854 to April 1856 the Birmingham makers supplied 156,000 rifles to the Board of Ordnance, compared to only 75,000 obtained from all other sources including the newly-established Royal Small Arms Factory at Enfield north of London. There, the former barrel mill had been largely increased by the addition of American machinery from Colt's and Robbins & Lawrence, and from the Ames syndicate of Chicopee Falls. Its productive capacity threatened to take from the Birmingham trade all chance they had in future of selling to the Government, for the Crown would not buy handmade guns when it had put up so much money at Enfield to get them by machine. In order to remain competitive and move with the times, the Association in June, 1861, moved to found the Birmingham Small Arms Company, to make guns by machinery.

When Schuyler came to Birmingham he had to present his appeal to the committee of the whole, all 16 shareholders. From them he elicited a promise to obtain 35,000 Enfield rifles within six months from date, as he reported to Cameron on August 20 after signing the contract. To make these rifles the Association drew on its existing handmade capabilities, combined with its developing machine-made potential. Among the first, urgent purchases appears to have been stock-making machinery, and an examination of guns such as those of Pryse & Redman, members of the Trade Association and stockholders in the Arms Company, reveal machine inletting of great precision, "Yankee quality work," in the lock mortises and other cuts. The 16 subscribed initially £24,500. At once £7500 was spent on acquiring 25 acres at Small Heath, where the great BSA-Guns Ltd. was to stand for a century. The factory was not large, costing £17,050. This would compare roughly to a U. S. factory of perhaps double the price or at the prevailing rate of $5 gold to the pound—in New England, a capital of about $170,000. This would compare with the first investments in the U. S. rifle making section of Colt's, for example. The first B.S.A. company was a respectable armory, but not the wonder of the engineering world that the firm was some day to become, employing 28,000 people and, during War Two, producing 1,650 parts of arms *each minute* during the entire six years of war.

Having wrapped up this deal, Schuyler turned to Baring Brothers. Unfortunately, Mr. Chase, Treasury Secretary, had neglected to pass along the appropriate bank credit until one week late. Even then, they lacked the proper signatures. The Birmingham makers, aware that state agents, North and South, were scouring the town for arms, not unnaturally considered this a breach of their agreement and did not deliver to Schuyler. Caleb Huse was in the offing, and by offering 50 per cent more for the arms than the North would have paid, though based on the South's credit through Fraser, Trenholm & Company of Liverpool, he got the deal. The price was 66 shillings a gun; within ten months, normal market prices in Birmingham were to range below 50 shillings, and sometimes as low as 38 shillings, though these were for second class arms, handmade and not of the best finish. Beech or other soft wood was substituted in these cheaper rifles for the straight-grained walnut selected to fit up the machine-made guns and first class handmade arms. Such guns were serviceable, and often bore the "Tower" mark of the Birmingham Tower government inspecting depot and arsenal, but the Association members tried to convince the buyers, at least of the North, that only they controlled the first class arms; all those obtained elsewhere, they said, were the "rejects."

Schuyler did not fret about Birmingham after this failure, but continued on his buying trip. But the French "Vincennes Carbine" deal also was quashed by order from the Emperor, who refused both belligerents the right to buy from the French arsenals. When this became evident to Schuyler about the middle of October, he found that he had not racked up a very distinguished record of purchases in either Britain or France. He had purchased 10,000 pin-fire 12mm revolvers from Lefaucheux of Paris, the large size known as the Model 1853 with side loading gate and fixed trigger guard. At a price of $12.50 each, these were complemented by 200,000 Lefaucheux 12mm cartridges costing $17.45 per thousand. As a comparison for prices, Union Metallic Cartridge Company in the 1870's on an experimental order for the Navy Department offered to make a small quantity of similar cartridges, .38 centerfire for revolver, such as they had never made before, at slightly over $12 per thousand.

Back home the call for 75,000 men to suppress the combinations of states in rebellion had been swelled by the drafts on the loyal states for men. Ripley had promised the Vincennes rifles Schuyler wrote of to various importunate governors for their men; then when Schuyler reported the deal had collapsed, there was embarrassment in Washington.

At Dresden in Saxony, Schuyler was more fortunate. He reported he had purchased 27,055 "Dresden rifles" at $14.04½ each, which were assumed to be, as one writer later stated, "almost identical to the Enfields" except for 1,000 which proved to be Austrian rifles. Unfortunately, what Schuyler purchased was a lot, possibly mixed, of Dresden arms comprising at least two patterns. First, the type he was happy to get "like the Enfields" was wholly unlike the Enfields. It was the somewhat cumbersome Thouvenin system *a tige* of several variations. The short rifle has a back action lock, strongly built, and pin-fastened stock with two wedges. The stock tip has a curved back edge. The forward sling swivel is fastened to a long screw directly through the stock above the front funnel-shaped ramrod pipe. All furniture is iron, gray case-hardened; when made properly the model is a very strong and serviceable weapon, adapted for saber bayonet. The Saxon model rifle *a tige* has a patent breech, the *tige* screwed into the bottom of the chamber. In the riflemusket, some of which were probably obtained in this shipment, the *tige* is screwed directly into the bottom of the breech plug. The new model rifle musket may also have been made available to Schuyler; cleaning difficulties with the *tige* blocking part of the fouled chamber caused the Saxon war minister to revert to the plain chamber, where the bullet is expanded by the explosion. With 40.4-inch barrel, the caliber was .577, four grooves, twist 1 turn in 64½ inches. The rear sight is 4.82 inches from the rear of the barrel, with a fixed leaf sighted for 200 paces or 154 yards, and two leaves; lowest for 400 and highest for 600 paces. The rammer is countersunk for the ball.

Another arm, almost obsolete in Saxony along with the Thouvenin breech *tige* rifles, was the Jaeger rifle. An octagon barrel short carbine with pin-fastened stock and common side lock, percussion or transformed percussion, this model had been modified in 1849 to the Thouvenin *a tige*. The breech was given a conical chamber and the *tige* screwed into the bottom; the ramrod, carried in the stock, was fitted with a head and this, to protect the rifling, with a brass band. Barrel without breech pin was 29.54 inches, eight grooves caliber .577 (actually .576-inch). The "Austrian rifles" received by Ruhlman as inspector on the spot may have been actually these Saxon 1849-transformed Jaeger rifles, or may have been octagon barrel Lorenz 1854-5 Jaeger style rifles, also *a tige* which the Saxon closely resembled.

From Dresden Armory Schuyler went on to Vienna.

The sympathies of the Austro-Hungarian government were with the North. But revealing the liaison which the South had with the forces of the Hapsburgs is the uniform dress of the South. Confederate uniforms are styled after the Austrian pattern, even to the gray, to the same degree that the United States uniforms are copied from the French blues. While the Austrian postal service prepared to refuse correspondence addressed to the secession states, Schuyler closed a deal with the Vienna arsenal for 70,048 Lorenz rifles of the latest model, 1854-5; the price, $15.10 each.

August Ruhlman took a good look at these guns and reported that they could be reamed up from their .54 caliber to .58 without any risk. The Austrian war department assisted in speeding the packing. When Schuyler and Ruhlman first saw the rifles, they were racked in the thousands inside huge, vaulted, dimly lighted arsenal storage rooms, three stories high, some 360 feet long, while four huge armories measured nearly 800 feet in length. Within these dim, dry rooms could be stored hundreds of thousands of rifles; Schuyler was taken to one floor and there he bought what the Austrians wanted him to buy. In eight days 50,000 rifles were packed, and the loaded freight cars shunted from the double tracks which lay alongside the arsenal, to the railroad depot. At the price paid, Schuyler secured new, first class arms; for the price received, the Austrian officers, among the few government officers anywhere with good business sense, probably bought for their own army twice as many arms out of a new lot then under construction at the small arms factory nearby.

Schuyler was not entirely bereft of Vincennes rifles; he shipped 4,558 of these at $17.13 back to Ripley. The Small Arms Association of Birmingham finally released 15,000 Enfields to him at $18.45, and in Bohemia on the way to Vienna he ran across 10,000 cavalry carbines. These at $6 seemed a good bargain; they were .70 caliber, short barrels, and with spur-like extensions to the tangs of the trigger guards. Originally Augustin lock detonators, they had been transformed in Belgium to percussion; Bannerman later sold them to collectors for as much as the Government originally paid for them.

Back home, the colonel wanted to be paid at the rate for his rank. Ripley refused, said he was a civilian employee on per diem, or $1,770.84. Inspector Ruhlman was paid $572.56, and their expense sheets tallied $2,361.55. The account at Baring Brothers was overdrawn $94,334.90. Colonel Schuyler had blown his two million dollars.

Stanton Seeks a Better Purchasing Agent

When Stanton succeeded Cameron after the New Year, 1862, Schuyler's purchases were among the many things with which the irascible but hard-headed new War Secretary was annoyed. The man had done much worse than Stanton supposed a more competent person would have accomplished. The lack of specific instructions on a detailed technical basis as to the types and qualities of arms he should buy contributed to the hodgepodge of Lefaucheux pinfires, Enfields, few and costly, Thouvenin rifles from Saxony, and Bohemian carbines. Stanton wanted to set it up with a true professional.

Meanwhile, the demands for arms were increasing. The New York militia were ready to move as soon as clothing was issued to them; to Governor Tod of Ohio Stanton on May 26 dispatched a telegram:

> We want as many troops as you can raise in the state for the term of three years, or during the war, or for any other term, not less than three months, according as you can raise them quickest.

Quartermaster General George B. Wright promptly replied; said 10,000 men could be raised, and that 7,000 arms would be needed. Wright's was but one of dozens of similar notes; the loyal states had no shortage of men. But they had few arms. Governor Morton of Indiana had sent that state's militia weapons off to war with the troops mustered into Federal service; no replacements had been received. The unsettled affairs in Kentucky made him afraid of border raids; but though he had men, there were no guns. Hon. Robert Dale Owen handed to Stanton the Governor's appeal for arms, saying "Our western men are excellent judges of rifles and know how to use them. If the Government has no good guns to spare, I can make a contract with a responsible New York house for 5,000 first class Enfields at $14.50, deliverable in 40 days, provided the order be given immediately."

Owen was in touch with Marcellus Hartley of Schuyler, Hartley and Graham. Hartley had been informed by his agent, Francis Tomes, then active in Birmingham, that contracts could be made with the Birmingham Small Arms Trade Association at as little as 38 shillings, unloading (including premium on exchange) at as little as $14.50 in bond at New York. But Hartley was fearful of changes in this price structure unless someone tied up the makers with extensive contracts. While Owen awaited a reply from Stanton, Hartley contacted General Ripley, and alluded to the quantities of Enfield rifles which British and Southern private speculators were stockpiling in Nassau warehouses, in the Bahamas, ready to run the blockade into Southern ports for sale. He proposed to Ripley that arms could be bought in Nassau at a low price, rather than causing their owners to risk capture in running the blockade. Said Ripley to Stanton, "It may be advisable for the Government to send out an agent to look into this matter. If so, he should be a reliable, shrewd businessman, to be selected by yourself. His instructions and his mission should be secret, and known to as few as possible, so as to avoid the competition he would otherwise find in making his purchases."

But Ripley was apparently working at the behest of Hartley who, from the will and spirit with which he undertook his eventual assignment, quite obviously wanted such a job. By Ripley suggesting only going to Nassau, he caused contrary-minded Stanton to want to send a man to Europe. By referring to a shrewd businessman to be selected by Stanton, after introducing the fact that Hartley had special knowledge of the availability of arms, he cleverly dangled the bait before Stanton to ask "Who is this man Hartley?" Contradictorily, in this same letter of June 7 to Stanton, Ripley conjectured that "If the fact of an agent having been sent out to purchase should accidentally become public it will probably have the effect of inducing the holders of Enfield arms in New York to come down to the price at which the purchases are limited." (The New York office under Captain Crispin had been instructed to buy 50,000 Enfields at not more than $15; 10,000 only had been obtained; about 2,000 more rifles could be bought privately, most owners holding out for $17.) The need for weapons was continuing acutely; his estimate of the previous summer of 100,000 and eight batteries of guns now was increased:

Ordnance Office, *June 7, 1862*

Hon. E. M. Stanton:

Sir: The number now on hand of good rifled arms, both American and foreign, for issue to troops in service, is about 94,000. The number of such arms which are required to be delivered under existing contracts and orders in the next six months are 138,981 of the Springfield pattern, and 25,000 foreign, in all 163,981, of which the deliveries are not certain and cannot be relied upon. The U. S. Armory at Springfield may be relied on for a supply during the six months of at least 80,000, and probably 90,000 arms. This makes in all, a supply for the six months, which may be confidently calculated on, 174,000, of which there will be ready for issue in this month 107,000; in July, 1862, 13,000; in August, 13,000; in September, 13,500; in October, 13,500; in November, 14,000—174,000. What may be our requirements during this time will depend very much on contingencies that I cannot foresee.

Stanton preferred to hedge his bets. He called in Robert Dale Owen, who seemed to know something about the technical side of weapons; Owen suggested Marcellus Hartley, of "a responsible New York house," and Hartley was called to Washington.

In 1861 Hartley, Schuyler & Graham had two stores, one at 13 Maiden Lane, and another large showroom at 22 John Street. Youthful but most-travelled member of this firm was Marcellus Hartley, who, in 1861, was 34 years old. To the long glass-paneled showroom at John Street came colonels of dandy regiments and pastors of boy's schools, to obtain the fanciest or the simplest in military equipment. Union men admired the patriotically hilted fancy dress swords. But a clandestine copperhead wandering in to buy percussion caps to smuggle south might be amused by another style of sword handle in stock, a kepied officer stabbing a dragon which writhed about to form the handguard. Could it be an allegory of Beauregard slaying the Anaconda, the blockade which Lincoln had set around the Southern coast? In glass fronted cases were racked Smith carbines, Lefaucheux shotguns, the finest of British percussion doubles, and a complete array of Colt's and Remington's arms. A distinctive feature of the Maiden Lane shop was a huge display board upon which were wired percussion Colts "in the white," for Hartley did an extensive business in elaborately engraved arms fitted with specially-cast metal grips by Louis Tiffany.

Hartley had entered the gun business on February 8, 1847, with Francis Tomes & Sons, hardware and gun dealers on Maiden Lane. When business was slack he was sent as a traveller to the west and south to drum up trade. Very valuable experience and knowledge of the gun trade came to him, and remained with him when he left Tomes to go into business for himself. He assumed there was no chance for him to rise to partnership in the Tomes firm and in 1854 began to look about for a new position; preferably a business of his own. He found two like-minded souls, J. Rutsen Schuyler and Malcolm Graham, of Smith, Young & Company, in which Schuyler was a junior partner. They were also hardware and gun dealers. On March 1, 1854, the new firm of Schuyler, Hartley & Graham opened its books at 13 Maiden Lane, almost opposite Tomes and Smith, Young & Company.

Four days later Hartley and Schuyler sailed on the *Baltic* to Europe. They made the grand tour, a tour the modern American gun crank must surely envy. They visited all the gun factories and spent their money on everything that caught their fancy. Hartley, with his experience of "what sells," bought a stock that, after four months abroad, was returned home to bring very handsome prices. The company was in business at last.

During the winter Hartley travelled west, promoting sales to merchants in the Mississippi area, St. Louis, and the Ohio Valley. It is possible that on this trip, 1854-55, Hartley saw something which was later to profoundly influence his life, his business, and the course of American arms making. Someone showed him an early metallic cartridge. Said to have been a rifle cartridge, it is possible he saw a Morse experimental at Harpers Ferry, in western Virginia, or one of the early Maynards. Without expressing his intense curiosity about it he asked for the gadget as a souvenir. This odd copper cartridge later came to mind and led to the formation of the Union Metallic Cartridge Company.

During 1856 and 1857, Hartley made yearly buying trips abroad, but remained in New York during the period 1858-1860. The business had expanded, through the solid connections he had established abroad, to the point where it was the largest of its kind in the country. Not immune to taking a profit when it barked at him, Hartley one day in 1857 passed by a shop in Florence filled with paintings, copies of old masters. Selecting one that took his fancy Hartley asked the price; turned and left when he learned it. The shop-keeper persisted, reducing the price; even following Hartley to the next town to bargain with him. Suddenly Hartley asked the Italian how many pictures he possessed, and how much he wanted for the lot. A bargain was made and munitions-king Marcellus sold the pictures to ante-bellum Southern mansion proprietors to hang in their drawing rooms.

Marcellus Hartley is Appointed

The War Department had informed Minister Sanford in December, 1861, that no new contracts for foreign arms were to be made, the Department hoping that domestic factories would supply the deficit. Hopes were not realized, and Stanton reversed his position several times about procuring more arms from overseas. Then the Government called for 300,000 more men and this put an end to delays. On July 14, Marcellus Hartley got his sailing orders:

WAR DEPARTMENT
Washington, D. C. July 14, 1862

Sir: You are hereby appointed the special and confidential agent of the government, for the purpose of obtaining arms in Europe. . . .

The government desires to obtain abroad . . . rifled muskets with angular bayonets, of the calibre of .577 and .580, and conforming, in their distinguishing characteristics, to the long Enfield rifles.

P. H. WATSON, *Ass't. Secretary of War*

The approval of the Enfield rifle as made in England had resulted in a curious nomenclature being accepted by the War Department. Watson's letter described the kinds of arms Hartley was to buy; grouping them into five classes in descending order of merit:

1. The machine-made English Enfield, with interchangeable parts, manufactured only by the London Armoury Company.
2. The hand-made English Enfield.
3. The Prussian or Dresden Enfield.
4. The St. Etienne or Liege Enfield (misspelled "Tiege" in Ex. Doc. 99).
5. The Vienna and Austrian Enfield.

Hartley was told to get all the L. A. Co. long rifles possible and tie up the firm with contracts until January 1, 1863. Of the last four classes of arms, he was to buy all in the market, at fixed prices, not to exceed 100,000 arms total for the four classes. The prices were: 70/- for 1st class, 60/- for 2nd class, 16 thalers for 3rd class, 60 francs Fr. for 4th and 55 frs. for 5th class.

Watson slipped in a demand that neither Ruhlman nor George Wright, nor Caleb Huse or Major Anderson ever abided by: he ordered that "Every arm—and so all your agreements should provide—must be rigidly inspected in all its parts by an examiner of tried skill and inflexible honesty; and the utmost precaution must be taken to see that after an arm has been accepted another one be not substituted before, during the process of, or after it has been packed. Many frauds were practiced in this way on American buyers last year, and will doubtless be attempted again . . ."

Inspection was rudimentary at best, the United States inspector often merely examining one musket in a case and thus passing thousands. Hartley was instructed to set aside arms that did not pass inspection but if they were otherwise good arms, he could take them at a less price in proportion. He was also instructed in the great secrecy with which this mission was to be accomplished. Hartley must not become known as the agent of the United States Government. As a "free lance" speculator, he could bargain more effectively with the gunmakers, pleading his need to make a profit. All guns were to be shipped to Schuyler, Hartley & Graham, and the War Department promised to see to paying the bills promptly. He could hire clerks and inspectors as needed, expenses would be paid, and he would, at the age of 35, have salary "equal to that of a brigadier general in the United States Army, say $5,000 per annum." Interesting to report is the fact he was never, as Alden Hatch declares in *Remington Arms,* appointed to the rank of brigadier general. Hatch also errs in saying his salary was $2,500 a year; his salary was at the rate of the pay of a brigadier general. Hartley, unlike New York State Militia Colonel Schuyler, held no commission saving that of spending upwards of $2,000,000. Watson's letter of authorization noted that £80,000 would be deposited for him at Baring Brothers—he should advise when more was needed.

Hartley Goes to Europe

Hartley left for England at once, accompanied by his family. He did not get his credit at Baring's for three days. Hatch thinks they diddled him because of alleged Southern sympathies. But this seems doubtful

Hartley became agent for London Armoury Company's Adams revolvers in New York, sold small quantities to U.S. buyers. Top is big 1851 DA Dragoon .50; middle is Adams with Tranter's patent double trigger made by licensee August Francotte; bottom is Beaumont Adams 1856 .450. Same model was also made in U.S. by Mass. Arms.

in view of Barings' almost official status as bankers for the United States in Europe. That he even received the credit within the same month he landed in England, should be accounted a miracle of efficiency under Stanton's direction. Then he hastened to Birmingham, where he took a house at No. 6 St. Mary's Row, not far from Greener, and near Pryse and Redman, the BSA headquarters, Webley & Scott on Weaman Street, and a host of other suppliers grouped between St. Mary's Square and Steelhouse Lane. The shipments began to come back to New York and the drafts on Barings piled up.

The correspondence of Marcellus Hartley is fragmentary, but much on this important period has been preserved and reproduced in the volume *Marcellus Hartley*, by "J. W. H.," believed to be J. W. Hammersly. This book is a memorial volume to Hartley published in 1903 privately after his untimely death. The reports made by Hartley to the War Department sum up his activities that summer and winter of 1862 and the start of 1863:

      6 ST MARY'S ROW,
      BIRMINGHAM, *August 2, 1862*

To Hon. E. M. Stanton,
 Secretary of War

Dear Sir: I arrived in Birmingham Saturday July 26 and found that our agent (Francis Tomes of Lewis & Tomes, his old boss) had secured all the ready-made rifles at prices quoted by me, and the services of nearly all the manufacturers. Nearly all the ready-made guns had been bought up by speculators immediately upon receipt of the news of the want of 300,000 more men. The London market had been cleaned out by speculators for the China trade. In this market Henderson, an American, had made contracts with nearly all the manufacturers at low prices, and is now holding them to it, some 36/— to 40/—, a loss in many instances to the manufacturers; our agent succeeded in obtaining some from them at an advanced price, but as they hope to complete contracts this week and we have secured them, and the arms go to New York, it is better that we should get him out (of) the way.

The Small Arms Company, a combination of manufacturers who produce about 3,000 per week, have given the refusal of their "Combination" to a New York house with hopes of obtaining a government contract at $17. They expect to receive an answer by the mail now due, on receipt of which I hope to close a contract with them before my departure for the Continent. I offered them 47/6, but as they were not in condition to close I withdrew my offer.

In a week or so, when we get things under way and can obtain the control of the "Combination" I hope to send 4,000 to 5,000 per week, and I will swell the amount to 6,000 and upwards when under full headway.

Our agent had secured, before my arrival, some 2,000 ready at 45/ and 46/6. There were some 2,000 more in the hands of speculators, for which they asked 60/ to 63/, which for the present we shall let them hold.

Previous to the news of the want of additional troops, rifles were a drug, and manufacturers took contracts at a low price in order to work up surplus material. The speculators took advantage of it and bound them down. Now when they have to give orders for materials, prices advance, and the greater the pressure the higher the price, so we have to manage quietly, in order to get them under full headway without pressing the material makers too sharply.

Where arms are contracted for and going to New York, I have not interfered, as the sooner we get them out of the way the better, as I have secured the services of the manufacturers. It will not do to pay over $15 in New York; if it is done, it will have the effect of speculators obtaining arms from our manufacturers. I shall not for the present give over 50/ for arms, as the speculators are so combined together that they turn over their guns into one another's hands and thus manage to obtain the highest price.

Most of the arms made and on hand are .577 caliber, and are not of as good quality as I shall have when we get under way and shall make such changes as I can make them agree to, corresponding to our Springfield.

So far everything has worked most successfully for nearly the whole produce of this market, and it will take a little time to get it systematized and under way. I should much prefer to obtain the whole amount in this market of one kind of arms, with such as are ready made on the Continent, than to contract all over the Continent on time.

I was at the London Armoury Company on Wednesday, and they promised to give me an answer this morning how many they could furnish and the price, but they have failed to do so. I shall see them on Monday as I pass through London on my way to Liege.

My credit of £80,000 will soon be exhausted; it will not purchase over 30,000 to 35,000 arms, and if I succeed in purchasing some in Liege, where I have the refusal of a lot, I shall not have more than enough to cover one month's purchases. Please lose no time in sending me an additional credit of at least £100,000, say one hundred thousand pounds same terms as before. Send by return steamer; my house in New York will send it.

The vessels from Liverpool are crowded with freight, so that goods have to be there some days before the arrival of a steamer, in order to secure their turn. I shall make a shipment next week.

Agreeably to instructions, I have detailed to you my first weeks work, and shall continue to inform you of any progress, and hope that nothing will interfere to prevent me from realizing my anticipation, say some 6,000 per week.

      Yours respectfully,
      MARCELLUS HARTLEY

By the same mail Hartley addressed a further note to Assistant Secretary P. H. Watson, for he doubted that Stanton himself would read fully the first note, yet did not want to write more than was formally necessary in it. To Watson he clarified the story a little.

The Henderson who secured in the market at the low prices is the same man who operated for H. (owland) and A. (spinwall) last year. Everything thus far has worked splendidly, and I am only waiting for the Small Arms Company to learn by next mail that the contract they expect is among the things that might have occurred, to secure the entire product of this market. I have remained in the background, allowing our agent, Mr. Tomes, to secure the manufacturers. I have seen several who expect a friend from New York with large government contracts; Tomes, Barkalow, etc. are mentioned. You will please see that I have more credit at once. I do not want to contract beyond the £80,000, as I shall then be held personally responsible, which of course is no risk, yet under the circumstances the government should cover me promptly. I am at work in earnest; it is a laborious job. I shall leave our agent to take care of things until I obtain what are ready made on the Continent. I have the refusal of some 2,000 in Liege.

I enclose two slips cut from the Birmingham "Daily Post" and the London "Times" about shipping munitions of war to Southern States. The steamer Memphis is now loading at Liverpool with munitions of war for Nassau, or some adjacent port convenient to some Southern port; as nearly as I can find out she has about 3,000 rifles on board.

I shall do my utmost to send all arms at once, without

delay. I think I shall be able to obtain all in this market at prices varying from 45/ to 50/, unless orders from some Continental power make them advance, and in that case we may have to allow a little even with those with whom we have contracts made, for the manufacturers are a slippery set.

Respectfully yours,
MARCELLUS HARTLEY

During the nine months that Hartley remained abroad he wrote a great many letters. Unfortunately, W. J. H. in noting that these were wholly on business matters, "to various manufacturers, to his agents, to his bankers," declares that they "possess little interest to the reader." As the copies of these letters were in the files of Schuyler, Hartley and Graham, which remained in the hands of Marcellus Hartley when the firm reorganized as M. Hartley and Company and at the time owned a controlling interest in Remington Arms Company, they were not otherwise in existence; that is, no separate file existed in Ordnance, National Archives, or elsewhere. It is unfortunate that W. J. H. did not make more public their contents, for the type of technical information he deems of little interest is exactly the sort of detail which the student of arms history requires. More recent efforts to locate some of these letters in files of the Remington Arms Company have been without result. In the opinion of an engineering executive of Remington Arms, a "gun nut" type who therefore desires to remain nameless, the files which he examined, searching out just such early correspondence, had the appearance of having been selectively "robbed" of such documents.

Whether some unofficial hand in years gone by purloined Hartley's letters for the secret edification of some rich gun connoisseur whose fancies and purse outweighed his scruples, or whether they were perhaps destroyed on orders of Hartley for some obscure purpose of protecting names or reputations of past associates, cannot now be more than guessed at. Perhaps as so often happens at last, such records will once again come to light. Meanwhile, W. H. J. did preserve some dozen letters filling in a good amount of detail of Hartley's purchases abroad.

Purchases in Germany and Belgium

On October 7, 1862, Hartley was in Berlin, having spent some days in Cologne (Köln) from the armories of which he "liberated" quantities of arms. Liege of course was a common crossroads for his travels; each time he returned to that major arms-making city some one of the fabricants seemed to have a new lot of old arms for him to buy. Stanton had sent to date £380,000 credit, but the letters of credit expired 1 November. These sums included £150,000 just received, and Hartley would have to scramble to spend or commit it before it expired. ". . . I suggest here that it is our right course to secure all arms here in Europe, in order that the South may not obtain them . . ." He explained that apparently the Confederate agents had been buying regardless of prices, and were very active in upsetting the price structure on Enfields which he had set up in England, some of the Birmingham makers refusing to deliver at less than 53/ when four months past they were happy with orders at 35/. "I think if the South has agents purchasing arms, if I can make contracts with the manufacturers to bind them, at prices exceeding your limits, I think it my duty to prevent the arms falling into their hands."

Hartley thus envisioned a two fold nature to his mission: purchase of arms for the Union, and blocking the South from buying arms by outbidding her.

"At Liege I purchased ready made and entirely new arms," he reported to Stanton from Berlin that October 7: "C. Dandoy, 400 French rifled muskets, 69/100, with implements and extra cones—packing boxes no charge, 37 fr.; 120 ditto, No. 2 (i.e., handmade Enfields) 43 fr. From B. M. Tambeur Freres, 2,200 ditto, ditto, No. 2, freight paid to Antwerp (packing boxes 8 fr.),—46.75 fr. From Association of Liege, 2,000 Piedmontese Rifled Muskets, extra cones, implements, freight free to Antwerp (boxes 8 fr.),—48 fr., 1,500 French rifled muskets with implements as above; freight free to Antwerp (boxes 8 fr.),—39 fr.; 800 ditto, with elevated sights—42.50 fr. From Louis Muller, 3,500 French rifled muskets, intended for the Italian Government, all ready for shipment 46 fr."

The report continued:

The above were all made and will be shipped in two weeks, as soon as extra cones and implements can be made. I also ordered 8,000 of the same kind from the Association. Dandoy and Mr. Muller to be ready by the first of November with either quality, they to inform me when the lots are ready for purchasing.

That makes in all ordered in Liege of 69/100, 18,520—all of which will leave Europe on or before, say, the fifth of November.

You will be informed from Birmingham weekly how many are shipped and the amount of drafts.

In Vienna I purchased 20,000 blue barrel with angular bayonet, leaf sight, 58/100, and 10,000 bright barrel with angular bayonet, leaf sight, 54/100—including for each case of 20 guns 10 ball screws, 20 combined wrenches, and 20 extra cones at 26 florins—say 53 francs. The arms are all entirely new, but will have to be carefully inspected and packed, as there is no dependence to be placed upon any of the manufacturers. It will take at least six weeks to ship them all.

I found on arrival in Vienna that Boker had the refusal, or, in other words, the control of the arms. I obtained possession of them by agreeing to pay him 40 kreuzers, or about $16 per gun, he paying all expenses, delivered at the railroad. He will have to pay for packing boxes, viewing (a house will have to be obtained), and banker's commission, which is one-half per cent. All is under the supervision of my Springfield inspector. It is the best arrangement I could make, and under the circumstances very fortunate that he was there, for I should have had to employ someone—a commission house would not have done it except for a commission, and I should be afraid to trust them; my bankers could not do it, and under the circumstances it was very fortunate, as I cannot remain there.

I found that Moses & Co., London house with a Captain or Colonel Hughes [Hartley did not yet know of his antithesis in the Confederate service, Caleb Huse, or how to spell his name], had purchased 50,000 bright barrel Austrian guns, 54/100 caliber, no leaf sight, from the Austrian Government about three weeks since at 26.75 florins, and Mr. Martin of the above firm is now in Vienna attending to the shipment of

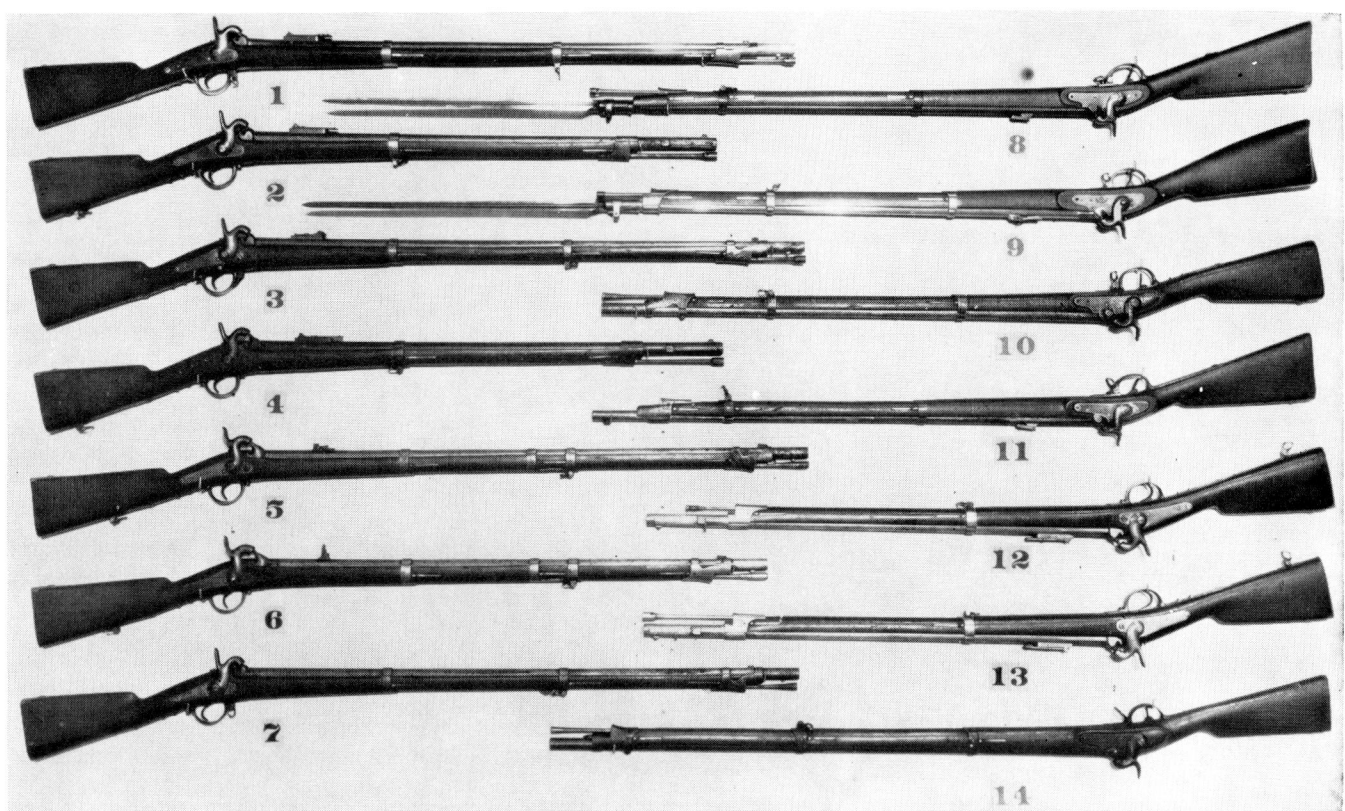

Variety of foreign guns bought by Union is shown in this display once set up in Smithsonian Institution, Washington, D.C. Nos. 1,3,7 are French (Liege make) muskets, No. 3 being rifled with U.S. style sight; Nos. 2,4,12,13 are different makes of Carabine de Vincennes; Nos. 5,6 may be Italian pattern; are not identified. Nos. 8,11 are Austrian Lorenz M1855 rifles; 9 is Bavarian .58 rifle musket; 10 is Italian-type conversion; 14 is iron-mounted Prussian .69.

them. They were in treaty for those I purchased and would no doubt have purchased them in a little time. The Austrian Government refused to sell any more for the present, but Mr. Truberth [sic.: actually Ferdinand Fruwirth, leading Vienna private gunmaker], the manufacturer from which I purchased the arms, the controller of all the manufacturies [i.e., chief inspector] informs me that when the different contractors make deliveries of the "new arm" the Government will no doubt sell more, but it will be some two or three months. He has promised to obtain from the government the refusal of the next lot and inform me.

The South purchased 30,000 in the spring and now 50,000 more. I was informed in London that samples of the Prussian guns were offered there to the South and they thought of purchasing. On inquiry I found that Hughes [Huse] was temporarily absent from Vienna, and thinking that he might be here [i.e., Berlin] I started Sunday for this place. The Government here offer 50,000 rifled Prussian guns, caliber 72/100, nipples too large—in other respects it is a good gun—at 10 Prussian thalers [about $7]. They have already three offers for them—one from Hamburg—but I cannot find out who is offering.

I have carefully inspected the guns and would not hesitate one minute if they were the proper caliber. You instruct me to purchase 69/100 if I cannot obtain smaller, but if 69/100 cannot be obtained you leave it to my judgment to purchase such arms as are serviceable. These arms are serviceable, but the bore is the objection. If I allow them to pass now, the South will have them. They can be used by the militia, and in an emergency by regular troops. The price, 10 thalers, is rather high. They are not worth, at the outside, over $6. Shall I purchase at $7 or not? I have to decide tomorrow. I am a little perplexed. They are scattered in eleven different arsenals throughout Prussia. I shall have to have packing boxes made, employ inspectors and viewers for each place—100,000 thalers to be paid down as a guarantee, the balance at each arsenal on delivery of each lot of guns. Personally I cannot attend to all of it. My Springfield inspector has all he can attend to at Vienna. It would be impossible to have the cones altered here. It would have to be done in New York. All these things are against the arms. Yet I still think it my duty to secure them. The arms, I find, cannot be purchased except by a Prussian subject. This I may arrange with my bankers. I think it advisable to go to one or two of the arsenals—say Stettin and Magdeburg, the nearest—and see the condition they are in before I make an offer.

I now feel the want of more inspectors and trustworthy men. I do not know where to obtain them.

I do not know at present of any more arms of any amount to be obtained in Europe.

I have written to my house in Paris to call upon the French authorities and see if they can or will dispose of any, but there is but little probability of doing anything there. There are some Garibaldis in Hamburg, but they are very inferior. They no doubt will now be sent to New York on speculation.

If I purchase these 50,000 Prussians, the amount purchased by me will be, say, 18,000 in Liege, 30,000 in Vienna, 50,000 in Berlin—98,000 in all.

I send this letter tonight and will endeavor to inform you by same steamer, if possible, in regard to the 50,000.

Yours respectfully,
MARCELLUS HARTLEY

P.S: In reading this letter over, I refer to the Confederates being in treaty for the 30,000 purchased in Vienna, implying that as Boker had the control of them he was the party. They were in treaty with Fruwirth before Boker. Mr. B. informed me that they, Mr. Martin of Moses & Co., had offered them a price for some Garibaldis, but he refused to sell any arms that might go directly or indirectly to the Confederates.

Hartley took a detour via Stettin and examined, as he says, 12,000 of the Prussian rifled 72/100 guns. "They are all in good order, nine-tenths of them never having been used. I have concluded to purchase them, and have made an offer of 8 Thg., 5 silver groschen."

The inspection made by Hartley consisted principally of his being led to one or more large rooms containing racked muskets. Then, as now, the common practice was to have racks two muskets high, and several arms deep. Probably the 12,000 were easily stored in one room not over 50 feet square. Under these jampacked circumstances a detailed examination of even a fair quantity of the arms was not possible, but it is practical for a buyer to make a quick glance and a practiced man such as Hartley could get a good idea of what he was looking at by many extra details.

He would see whether the armorer sergeant had any facilities nearby for routine cleaning and preserving the arms. A talk with the officer who showed him around would often produce unbiased and candid observations on the value of the arms. Two types of arms were in store, the "nine-tenths never having been used" most likely being the Model 1839 percussion musket, and the others earlier patterns, transformed from flint to percussion. Gradual introduction of the breech-loading "zundnadelgewehr" or needle-gun, as Major Mordecai not entirely correctly translated it ("firing pin gun" would have been a more correct translation, logically and semantically), led to the retirement of the muzzle-loaders as the new issues were made. Said Major Mordecai, *Military Commission to Europe,* 1854:

> The alteration of the flint musket is made by inserting a cylindrical cone seat, screwed into the barrel, perpendicular to its axis, in the place of the old vent; this cone seat is bored through the axis, and the outer end of the opening stopped up with a screw; the cone is inserted in the top of this cylinder; the lock is altered in the usual manner; a guide or rear sight is fixed to the tang of the breech pin; the front sight is on the upper band. The bayonet of this musket is fastened on by a spring and catch. The mountings are of brass.
>
> The new percussion musket (model of 1838) is similar to the above, with these exceptions: it has a patent breech, that is to say, a breech piece with a conical chamber, having the cone seat formed out of the same piece of metal, but placed on the right hand side of the barrel so that the hammer requires to be very little bent in order to strike the cone. The priming canal has been pierced through the cone seat perpendicular to the barrel, and the outer end closed with a screw as in the altered musket. The whole arrangement of the breech piece is nearly the same that has been adopted for the alteration of our musket as recently arranged for Maynard's primer. The front sight is brazed on the barrel, and the lower strap of the upper band is cut so as to pass over the sight. The mountings are of brass, except the buttplate, which is of iron; the caliber is the same as that of our smoothbore muskets; the weight of the arm is ten and one third pounds. These new muskets were said to be in process of alteration to rifle muskets.

The external differences of the rifle-muskets, from the preceding plain smoothbore arms, lay only in the construction of the rear sight. This was simple and efficient, similar in form to that later employed in the Mauser Model 1871, having a telescoping or extendable section of the folding leaf. Said Wilcox *(op. cit.)*:

> In 1855 the infantry regiments not provided with the breech-loading needle rifle were armed with rifle muskets having an elevating sight, which is in part fixed and in part moveable; it is lowered to its position on the barrel either to the front or to the rear. The fixed part of the sight gives lines of sight for 150 and 300 yards; the moveable part has a slide. To fire at 400 yards, erect the sight, the slide being lowered, and aim through the notch in its centre; to fire at 600 yards, aim through the notch on its upper edge; at 800 yards, aim through the notch on the upper edge of the moveable arm of the sight; and finally, to fire at 850, 900, 950, and 1,000 yards, aim through the notch on the upper edge of the slide, moving the slide so that its inferior edge shall be on a line with the figures indicating these distances.
>
> The rifle-musket has five grooves of uniform depth and twist, of one turn in 4½ feet; a tron-conic chamber, wedge balls; its weight, 705 grains; charge of powder, 79 grains; total weight with bayonet, 10 lbs.

Hartley may have known all these details; certainly he had at some time made himself familiar generally with the contents of Mordecai's book; and, later, the Van Nostrand edition of Wilcox' *Rifles and Rifle Practice* must have been sold through the store. Not all buttplates were iron; earlier models were brass. But he took a moment to further justify his interest in these arms which were actually rather clumsy and cumbersome, though not defective, in contrast with the Springfields or the "Enfields" of several nationalities which he had been commissioned to buy.

> I examined their cartridge at the arsenal . . . the ball which they use is not larger than our 69/100, and appeared to be lighter. The concave runs nearly to the top, thus making the ball a mere shell. They use an iron cup in the cavity, but the officers said it was of no use, as the powder expanded the ball sufficiently to fill the grooves. I send a ball by this mail, with instructions to send it to you. I am led to make these remarks from what you have written in regard to our troops disliking to shoot the old 69/100. If I remember right, the Minie ball in our cartridge for 69/100 caliber is much heavier than the Prussian 72/100 [U. S. bullet cal. .69 weighed 730 grains].

Hartley concluded his letter by asking the Secretary again for money, rhetorically declaring that if the arms had cost at the beginning ten million dollars, or twenty millions, it would have been worth it if such a move would have deprived the South of weapons. Very foresightedly he asked, "If this war is to continue one year, or two, or more, how long will the arms they now have last them? And when they are gone, where will they obtain more? You will pardon me for referring to this again, but from the exertions they are now making here they will clean the market out, and if so, after that we should take care that they do not have any superior arms."

Hartley did not have to wait long on the Prussian

guns; his offer was accepted for 30,000 of them and he continued on to Liege from where he again reported to Stanton on 16 October. The Association had 1,000 more French rifled .69's for him, and Tanner & Company had 1,500. Muller sold him 2,000 Enfields of Liege make, for the Liege fabricants had orders for the English as well as other governments for Enfield pattern rifles; August Francotte & Company was a large manufacturer, mostly using machinery, of interchangeable Enfields in Liege. B. M. Tambeur Freres offered 10,000 Belgian Government muskets, smoothbore, which they promised to rifle, and 5,000 more which they could rifle and fit with sights, presumably the leaf type with elevating slide. Tambeur also offered a rather enigmatically-named model, "2,000 Untembery (sic) government guns, rifles with sights, implements, cones, and packing boxes, at 40 francs." These we suspect must be "Wurttemberg," which suffered a little as some ancient typist at Remington Arms at the turn of the century, working at the behest of Mr. J. W. H. and doubtless pecking away at an old Remington typewriter, tried to translate the late Marcellus Hartley's manuscript scrawl into legibility for the printer.

The muskets and rifles of Wurttemberg had a distinguished descendant: the rifles of Peter Paul and Wilhelm Mauser. Perhaps on the very muskets which Hartley bought, which evidently had been bought up as smoothbores or sent up to Liege to be rifled, there shone the stamps of "M" of one or the other Mausers as a junior gun craftsman at the Royal Wurttemberg Gun Factory at Oberndorf, on the Neckar river. There in a former Augustinian monastery, muskets of common Napoleonic pattern, iron mounted, were made. The transformations to percussion and rifling made them interesting; the head of the percussion hammer has a rather square shape, unlike the curve of the French-styled percussion hammer. Lockplates, after the filling of flint pan cover spring holes and having been planed flush, may still bear the marks *Kong. Wurt. Fab.* and on top of the barrel, from breech to muzzle, *OBERNDORF*. Caliber is .72; one such musket is known with the mark of W. H. Dow, 64th Illinois Vol. Infy. picked out in tiny nail heads tapped into the stock.

Activities in France

Hartley concluded little business with the French, in this faring no better than his predecessor, Schuyler. His agent at Paris, C. W. May, was instructed to contact M. Poirier, of Poirier Freres, "who has a house in New York, and who has a contract with the French Government to supply all the food and stores for the Mexican expedition, which he does from New York, and knowing the officials and the French Emperor, and being a staunch friend, he might obtain from them what a stranger could not."

In Vienna, Hartley had bought 30,000 rifles; in Berlin, another 30,000; in Liege, first trip, 18,500, and upon his return, 17,500, making 96,000, exclusive of all Enfields which he had shipped from England. He made a very interesting resume of the arms that could be bought or contracted for in the ensuing months in England and on the Continent, in addition to the government orders which the contractors already were working upon; his estimates reflected the increase in productivity which the contractors said they could achieve if pressed with more orders:

Oct. 16, 1862

Statement of the number of arms that probably might be made at the different factories on the Continent and in England in six months:

Vienna $10.40		
80,000 in 6 months at, say, 26 florins at 40 cents..		$832,000
The Government will sell no more until the makers replace what have been sold. These arms may all be 58/100 after the first two months.		
Stahl, in Germany [sic. Suhl? Probably yes] $10.50		
15,000 Enfield in 6 months, at, say 15 thalers at 70 cents		157,500
They are now engaged on Government contracts. They make arms equal to the English.		
Herzberg [Wurzberg?] $11.90		
6,000 Enfields in 6 months, at, say, 17 thalers, 70 cents		71,400
These are good arms.		
Liege:		
30,000 Arms, Enfields and French models assorted, at, say, 55 francs at $11		330,000
The Association have contracts with the English Government and other governments until next summer.		
London:		
50,000 Enfields, at, say 60/, $14.50		725,000
Birmingham:		
140,000 Enfields, at, say 55/, $13.50		1,890,000
France, St. Etienne:		
20,000 Enfields and French model, at, say 60 francs, $12		240,000
341,000		$4,245,900
17,050 packing boxes, $2		34,100
		$4,280,000

The different governments of Europe have contracts out for arms. The calculation above is independent of such contacts, being what can be made besides all government contracts. The calculation is the outside amount.

Hartley Reports on Confederate Purchases

Hartley's espionage was of value to the North. The figures above, coupled with a second memorandum on arms he conjectured would be up for sale in a short time, gave Secretary of War Stanton a close estimate of the small arms available in Europe to the forces of the South. Hartley was not infallible, but the totals he supplied were to be reached in the following years.

Though Stanton did not propose to outbid Southern arms buyer Caleb Huse in the European market, preferring to rely upon the blockade, the fact that this much firepower was available, made Union planners realize they had a fight on their hands. Hartley's second memo supplied a:

Statement of second-hand arms that may be offered for sale in a few months:

Prussia:
Berlin $7.00
22,000 rifled 72/100 at, say, 19 thalers $154,000
Same as the 30,000 purchased.
    Darmstadt $6.30
12,000 rifled 69/100 French model say 9 thalers.   75,600
These may be offered for sale when they receive the new arms now contracted for.
    Wittenberg $6.30
9,000 rifled 69/100 French, say 9 thalers   56,700
When they receive new arms they may be sold.
    Bavaria $6.30
7,000 rifled 69/100 French model, say 9 thalers   44,100
When they receive new arms.

50,000 $330,400
    2,500 packing boxes say $2   5,000

                                                             $335,400

If the party who has the refusal of the 20,000 Prussians [Boker & Co.?] does not take them, they will make the number 70,000.

The English Government has a large number of arms that it wants to dispose of, but refuses to sell any at present to any one. How many, I do not know, but 200,000 at least; they are the old English musket, smooth bore and rifled. She probably will not sell while the war lasts.

The French Government has a large number of old arms. The Emperor has always refused to sell them.

The Russian Government sold over 400,000 arms; they were purchased by a Russian in St. Petersburg. They are very inferior, comprising carbines, etc., all smooth bores and only fit for the ironmonger.

Hartley's Overall Accomplishments

During November and December Hartley worked day and night; by December 20 he was able to report he had been pretty much on his feet for the past sixteen days straight. He had accomplished a great deal. The London Armoury Company at last began to see the light, and was willing to ship some of its fine rifles to the North. Two thousand two hundred "interchangeable Enfields" were sent forward at this time, plus 4,000 of an order for 10,000 he had given to Liege. Of these Enfields, Hartley stated they were "better than any English-made arms, excepting those of the London Armoury Company." He had been diddled by the Birmingham Small Arms Trade group and decided to diddle them in return. Privately writing to Stanton, he alluded to the offers of BSA rifles being made to Washington by Naylor & Company, steel merchants of Sheffield, who earlier had supplied Sam Colt with raw materials, as far back as the Whitneyville Walker contract of 1847. Naylor & Company in 1861 decided to dabble in small arms. Between December 17, 1861, and July 31, 1863, they delivered Enfield pattern arms—long rifles, short rifles, artillery carbines, all .577 caliber, of No. 1 machine-made and No. 2 best handmade qualities, to a total value of $3,810,965.85!

In October 1862, at the very time that Hartley, through his man Tomes, was trying to sew up the Birmingham manufacturers for the benefit of the United States Government, at the low prices of 40-42/-, Naylor was making a proposal to the War Department. The affair was handled by Assistant Secretary P. H. Watson, who somehow should have known better. On October 20, 1862, he accepted a proposition Naylor had made, autocratically reducing the price and thinking he had made a very good deal:

WAR DEPARTMENT
Washington City, D. C. October 20, 1862

Gentlemen: Your offer to supply to the Government of the United States two hundred thousand of the best quality of English hand-made Enfield rifles, to be delivered in New York, subject to the usual inspection, at the rate of not less than 7,000 per week until the whole number (200,000) is supplied, at the price of seventeen dollars and a half for each gun, and sterling exchange above 123 percent added, cannot be accepted by this Department, because the price is deemed exorbitant. The Government will, however, pay for one hundred thousand of these arms, delivered as above, sixteen dollars apiece and sterling exchange above 123 percent, on two pounds fifteen shillings (the assumed cost of the arms) added.

The deliveries to commence not later than the tenth of December.

Very respectfully, your obedient servant,
P. H. WATSON, *Assistant Secretary of War*

The acceptance was addressed to Naylor's man in Washington; by the next available packet boat it went out to London. There the acceptance was rephrased and returned, signed by the firms cooperating to fill the orders. November 7, 1862, was the date of the okay over the imprimaturs of Naylor, Vickers & Company, London, Liverpool and Sheffield, and Naylor & Company, New York, Boston, and Philadelphia. Excepting strikes and such delays, they agreed to deliver the 100,000 Enfield rifles "in about fourteen weeks and a half . . . say by about 21st March, 1863. You will doubtless be gratified to learn that the 100,000 rifles will all be of the well known superior quality manufactured by the Birmingham Small Arms Trade."

Naylor enclosed a letter corroborating their efforts, signed by famed barrel maker J. D. Goodman, who had recently been elected chairman of a committee, the Committee of the Whole becoming too unwieldy in its administrations. While the history of the B. S. A. Guns, Ltd., suggests that the committee was first elected September 30, 1863, there seems to be some discrepancy in the record. Says *The Other Battle*, a record of industrial preparedness of B. S. A. in War Two, "During the first two years of its existence, the company's affairs were administered by a committee consisting of all its shareholders. Not very surprisingly it proved a clumsy form of control and at an extraordinary general meeting held September 30, 1863, there was elected a board consisting of Mr. J. D. Goodman, Chairman; Mr. J. F. Swinburn, Vice-Chairman; Mr. Joseph Wilson, Mr. Samuel Buckley, Mr. Isaac Hollis, Mr. Charles Playfair, Mr. Charles Pryse, Sir John Ratcliff and Mr. Edward Gem.

"By the end of the year preliminary work was begun on the company's first big order—20,000 Enfields for the Turkish Government. This was part of a contract for 50,000 placed with the Birmingham trade and was secured through the good offices of Mr. Goodman."

Perhaps the distinction is one of corporate identity; the B. S. A. Trade Association in 1862 was negotiating, through Mr. Goodman, its Chairman, to supply 100,000 handmade Enfields to the Union. Perhaps the record is correct, needing only to be interpreted that the 20,000 Turkish Enfields were machine made arms, first to be turned out at Small Heath. The Committee members' names are interesting: Goodman, barrel maker; Swinburn of Swinburn & Son, barrel maker; Joseph Wilson, Samuel Buckley, Isaac Hollis of Hollis & Sheath, Charles Playfair of Bentley & Playfair, and Charles Pryse, inventor of the lockwork of the Webley-Pryse service revolver and partner of Pryse and Redmond, all names found on Enfield rifles as makers or parts and barrel contractors.

"I expect to commence deliveries on account of the order forthwith," wrote Mr. Goodman from Birmingham on November 4, "and will certainly complete the quantity within fourteen and a half weeks from 10th December."

This was the large order the Birmingham group had been so anxiously awaiting. Hartley was on the spot and with full powers from the Secretary of War, virtually a Minister Plenipotentiary to treat in the gun trade, but a New York broker was able to swing the deal with Washington. Verily the one hand knoweth not what the other doeth; robbing the public's pockets! Watson's deal with Naylor would have cost the Government about $100,000 more than Hartley was planning to spend on the identical Enfields.

Hartley was aware of the Naylor & Company transaction, and though he was too late to stop it, he managed to get off a note to Stanton on November 29 from Birmingham explaining some of the diddling that was going on. Hartley very reasonably suggested to Stanton, that:

". . . If you have enough arms for immediate use, would it not be as well either to stop purchasing in New York . . . or to reduce the price to, say, $14.50 to $15? I cannot see why we should not as well avail ourselves of the market as to pay the speculators and manufacturers the difference. The Small Arms Company here is up to all dodges. I should like to manage them. Before my arrival here in July a contract could have been made with them at 42/ to 45/; they asked me 65/ on the start, etc. If you do not stop now, prices will rapidly advance again. 42/, exchange at 1.23, would make the cost of guns in New York say $12.13; 45/ at same rate, $13. You pay exchange all above 1.23.

If you put the price down or stop, inform me, and I will stop purchase until I can buy at 42/ to 45/ and purchase all they have in hand, and if it is your desire to continue, I would bind them down, agreeing to take what stock they had at the above price, provided they would agree to give me all they could make in one or two months, at same price. The better plan would be to reduce the price, saying that guns can be bought and are now worth 42/, and tell Mr. Naylor that the Small Arms Company are buying at that. This information must not come from me.

I have referred to the above, as I think, if they are sharp, we should be . . .

Watson had committed the War Department to its dealings with Naylor, and that impartiality which Stanton demanded be enforced in the Holt-Owen investigations was equally at work. He did not try any monkey business with Naylor, and the Enfields piled up in Governor's Island. There was plenty of need for them, though the contract was to run beyond that time when beginning deliveries of domestically produced arms countered the deficit.

By the end of December two last important shipments went out on Hartley's account, to the United States. Via steamer *Hammonia* from Southampton he sent:

1,700 interchangeable Enfield rifles, probably London Armoury make
28,060 hand-made ditto
10,978 Austrian 54/100 and 58/100 calibers.

The steamer *New York* left Southampton on the day before Christmas with the last of Hartley's bundles for America:

500 interchangeable Enfields
7,300 hand-made ditto
13,860 French rifled muskets—69/100

"The above, no doubt, is the largest shipment ever made by one party, or ever obtained at the same time, of first-class Enfields, 37,560," he wrote optimistically to Stanton. "I have used about £110,000 of the last credit. Amount of Enfields shipped to date, 110,140; total amount of arms shipped, 204,848."

Single handed, almost, Hartley had obtained arms for two hundred regiments, in a space of a few months. He relied upon his younger brother, a clergyman, trustworthy, to assist Francis Tomes.

"Of the £580,000 to my credit I have drawn about £490,000, leaving a balance of say £90,000 not used . . . Monday we discovered an error of £288 in our favor, which Barings paid . . ." To the detailed and meticulous resume of money spent and arms shipped, Secretary Stanton observed commendingly that their record was "a model accounting of fiduciary responsibility."

The war for Hartley had its light moments, though sometimes they were not to be made evident until years later. He was constantly alert to Confederate agents at work, dogging his trail or he theirs. The Birmingham Small Arms Company had been shipping arms to an intermediary who in turn delivered them to Nassau to run the blockade. Said Hartley to Stanton, "I would respectfully suggest the increasing of our force in that vicinity." But with Confederate agents in Europe he could take a little more active role.

While he was in Birmingham he learned that Confederate agents had made a contract with a Continental manufacturer for several thousand rifles. J. W. H. recounts this in rather naive fashion, saying that Hartley scurried all over the Continent, "at Vienna, Frankfort and Budapest he was disappointed" in spying them out, "but finally, at Liege, he found, to his joy, the object of his search," the firm with the Confederate contract.

Hartley was too much of an old hand at the European gun game to waste time on such a quest;

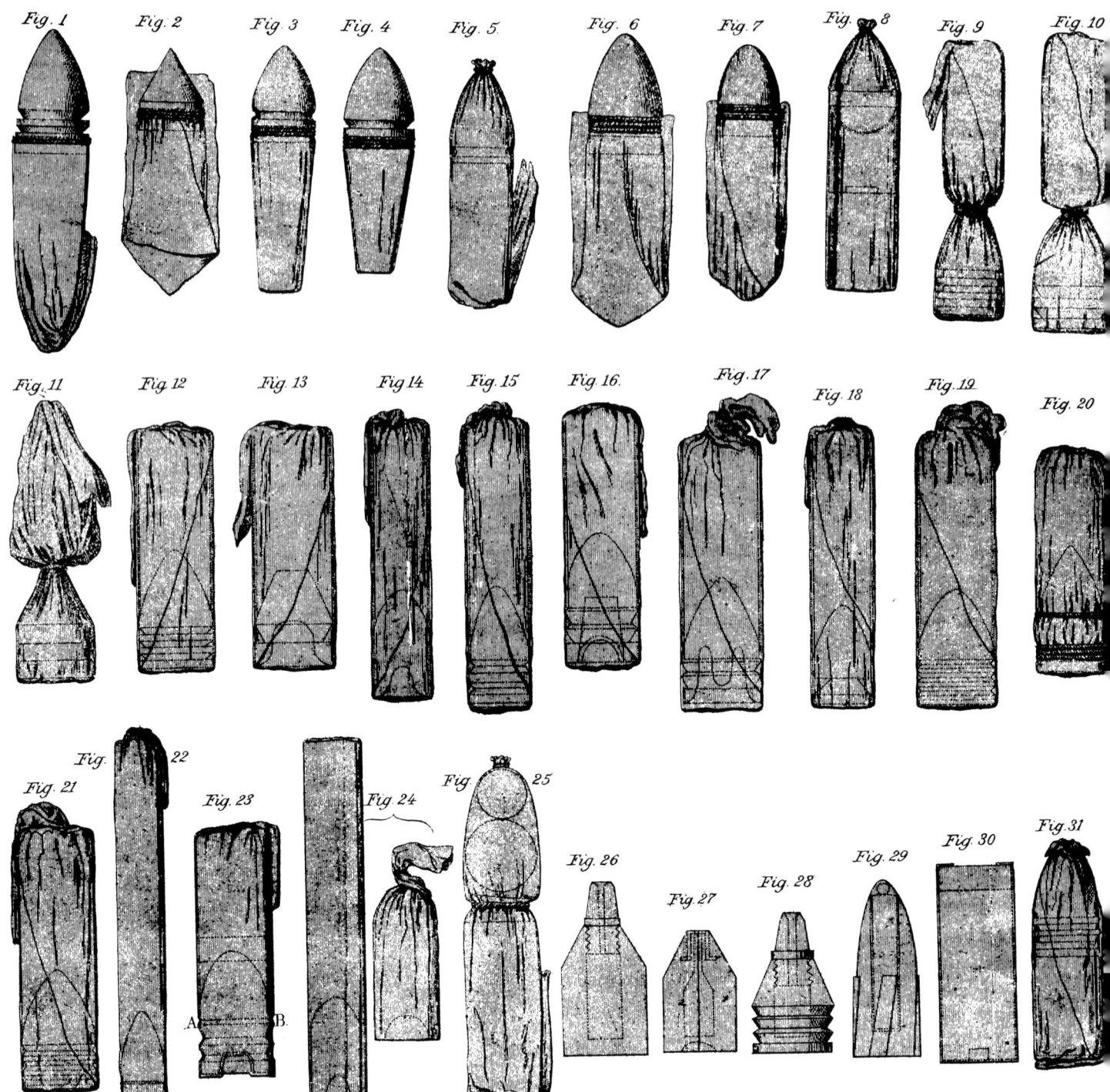

1: Belgian carabine a tige
2: Hanover carbine
3: Mecklenberg tige rifle musket
4: Oldenberg tige rifle musket
5: Saxon tige rifle musket
6: Norwegian breechloader (not used in C.W.)
7: Swedish breechloader (not used in C.W.)
8: Prussian needle gun breechloader. (Not used in C.W.)
9: Bavarian rifle musket
10: Bavarian musket
11: Austrian carbine, Consol-Augustin lock.
12: French carabine a tige
13: French rifle musket
14: Pritchett bullet for Enfield rifle musket
15: Lorenz Austrian rifle
16: Baden rifle musket
17: Belgian rifle musket
18: Dessau rifle musket
19: Nassau rifle musket
20: Russian tige carbine (not used in US)
21: Sardinian carbine (not used)
22: Swiss Federal rifle (not used)
23: Prussian rifle musket
24: English bag-cartridge (not used)
25: Danish multiball (not used)
26: Delvigne explosive ball A (not·used)
27: Delvigne explosive ball B (not used)
28: Delvigne ball, minie form (not used)
29: Jacobs explosive shell (not used)
30: Baden & Würtemburg rocket projectile or "fusee." copper cased (not used CW)
31: U.S. Rifle & RM cartridge

Ammunition was also imported for foreign muskets. Ammo made here in U.S. had characteristics of standard U.S. cartridges in fabrication, differing only in bullet or charge for the different varieties of arms. Foreign ammo came in many different shapes and sizes. From Wilcox's *Rifles & Rifle Practice* a plate is reproduced for the benefit of the cartridge collector, and to give comprehension of the bewildering logistic problem of ammunition supply ca. 1862.

if he heard of a Confederate contract, he went at once, directly, and by the fastest possible conveyance to Liege, if he really wanted to find out about it, for the Liege makers are famous for their traditional impartiality.

"Disclosing his position as the agent of the United States," says J. W. H., though Hartley's instructions from Stanton specifically swore him to secrecy, "he offered to buy the rifles at a small advance over the price for which they had been sold to the agents of the South, and to pay for them on bill-of-lading by drafts on his London bankers. The unscrupulous manufacturers accepted his offer and the arms were turned over to the North."

Some years later Hartley was present in New York at a dinner where one of the guests was a noted banker, John Trenholm of North Carolina. A member of the Southern branch of Fraser, Trenholm & Company of Liverpool, bankers for the Confederacy, Mr. Trenholm rose to give a few words of praise at the warm friendship with which he was received when after the war he took up his abode in the North, and he spoke briefly on his exploits buying arms for the Confederacy in Europe. He observed that at times he seemed just about ready to close a deal when through some agency which he could not explain the guns slipped through his fingers, financially speaking. He remembered one such deal particularly with a rifle maker in Liege.

Their host, Mr. Charles Flint, had heard Hartley relate the tale many times and drew Mr. Trenholm's amazed attention to the fact he was sharing the same table with that mysterious agency. Hartley rose and explained the facts and sat down amid enthusiastic exclamations at the coincidence.

Throughout the War, few knew of his critical role acting for the Union. Thus at last, in a New York salon at a dinner party, Marcellus Hartley received the acclaim due a hero.

CHAPTER 9

Caleb Huse Incurs Some Debts

On the outbreak of war, Caleb Huse was asked to come to Montgomery to confer with General Gorgas on ordnance matters and, accepting a commission as captain, Huse proceeded to go to Europe early in April 1861 to buy arms and cannon for the South. He was equipped with a letter of credit for £10,000 on Fraser, Trenholm & Company of Liverpool, arranged through Confederate States Treasurer Memminger. According to General Gorgas later, "The appointment (of Huse) proved a happy one for he succeeded, with very little money, in buying a good supply, and in running my department in debt for nearly half a million sterling, the very best proof of his fitness for his place, and of a financial ability which supplemented the meagerness of Mr. Memminger's purse."

The young munitions buyer had some adventures and one or two narrow escapes during his travels, but he accomplished his mission to an astonishingly satisfactory degree. He made the Enfield Rifle the standard Confederate arm, aided in obtaining a factory for its production, contracted with English factories for their output, and turned up in the government arsenals and the private storehouses of the Continent a variety of good arms at reasonable prices which he shipped to the South. His method of running the Ordnance Department into debt was partly through issuing warrants for cotton. Though ultimately worthless, these notes of and over Huse's signature sold for a time at a premium in the French banks. A typical cotton warrant read like a long-winded banknote:

The Government of the Confederate States of America hereby engage to deliver to the bearer within forty days after presentation of this warrant at the Treasury of the said Confederate States (follows a sum in pounds weight, f.e.), two millions and sixty eight thousand (2,068,000) pounds weight of cotton of the description and quality called and known in the usual Liverpool classification as Middling Orleans or the equivalent in value of any other description of cotton at the option of the Government . . .

The Confederate Government further agreed to deliver the cotton suitably baled to port, "excepting such port as may be in the hands of the enemy." The warrants were exchangeable for other warrants issued by Huse on other terms, or specifying the sizes of bale as required by the man from whom Huse had bought guns. Each warrant was endorsed by Confederate Commissioner John M. Mason, "As commissioner of the Confederate States of America I approve the above warrant given by Major C. Huse on behalf of the Government of the Confederate States of America. J. M. Mason."

Background of Huse

For Huse to be given such authority at the ripe old age of 31, it must be realized that he was a man of unusual talents. A native of Massachusetts, he had been given a leave of absence from the United States Army upon leaving West Point to take a position as superintendent of the University of Alabama. The reason why a West Pointer was called South to oversee school in Huse's case was the same reason why William Tecumseh Sherman took his job about the same time with the University of Louisiana: student discipline "was almost at an end at the University," as Huse stated. While military drill was taught at many schools and colleges, more as a glamorous "militia company" attraction for the sons of rich families, the Alabama University trustees intended to hold the students in check under military discipline as was done at West Point. "The University of Alabama was a military college so far as concerned discipline," said Huse.

Wrote Huse long afterward, when he had retired and in the winter of his life was living at his home, "The Rocks," on the Hudson, just south of West Point, "I was given a colonel's commission by the Governor of the State, with two assistants, one a major, the other a captain. Tents, arms and infantry equipments were purchased of the United States Government, and a uniform similar to that of the West Point cadets was adopted. The students were assembled on the first of September (1860), and a camp established on the University grounds. Drills were inaugurated at once, and regular camp duties were required and performed."

Huse, who was to do as much as any man for the

Lost Cause, was not beloved by his boy soldiers. A mutiny was planned, and some of the lads, backed by their families, were determined to run him out of the state. Northern-born, he was looked upon as a damn-yankee—this man who spent four years equipping troops commanded by some of these very same Yankee-hating cadets. Huse would have resigned under other circumstances, but he refused to be backed down. He returned to camp and nothing more was heard of the incipient mutiny. Though he makes no mention of exactly what happened, since the camp was under "military discipline" there is a moral certainty that Huse sent out a squad of the guard, arrested the ring-leaders of the mutiny, confined them to quarters, and may even have administered some of the more common punishments of the days such as having them "bucked and gagged," or put to work shovelling manure in the horse barns. Maybe the cadets were persuaded to accept Huse as a sort of Southron by adoption, but feeling was high with the election of Lincoln just two months off and loud talk of secession was around. Under Huse, however, life went on quietly at the University, which is what life was supposed to do there, in the eyes of the faculty and trustees who had installed him as their "Colonel." Accompanying this quiet life was a drain on the funds of the college, since buying muskets and shakos cost money, and these disbursements were extra to the budget. The only hope of obtaining money to meet increased expenses was through a legislative appropriation.

It was proposed to take the cadets to Montgomery to be reviewed by the Governor and the Legislature, but at first this was strongly vetoed. At last, with misgivings, the faculty permitted Huse to take the boys by boat to Montgomery and its fleshpots and alcoholic temptations. As Huse delicately put it, ". . . even the well-meant hospitality of the citizens, which was sure to be generous, would cause trouble." To everyone's surprise except perhaps drillmaster Huse, the boys behaved. They carried their own blankets, evidently going off to the legislature in full field equipment. In Montgomery, they paraded before the Governor and legislature in a grand review, in perfect order, crossed belts clayed to chalky whiteness, their U.S. muskets, probably 1842 percussion arms, burnished to ice-brilliancy, bayonets in glittering line abreast. In the evening after the review, a committee of the legislature called upon Colonel Huse to determine what he wanted. His answer came quickly: An annual appropriation so long as the military organization was maintained at the University.

Yankee Huse and a cousin of a noted New Hampshire abolitionist, who was on the committee, then proceeded to steamroller a bill through the legislature. The next day the rules were suspended and the bill to appropriate funds for Huse's cadets rushed through all its readings, passed to the senate for concurrence that was little more than voluble agreement, and the Governor signed it. Two days after arriving in Montgomery, the Tuscaloosa cadets marched home with money to keep the institution going. Formed without especial thought of war, cadets from Southern schools became a training cadre that spread throughout the Confederate military establishment, producing much of the generalship for which the Southern forces were noted. The boys from Tuscaloosa did their part.

Huse's leave of absence from the United States Army was dated to terminate in May, 1861. So critical had the situation become that in February he received a notice revoking his leave, directing him to report for duty to Washington. "I replied that my leave was granted with the understanding that I was to resign at its expiration, and as I saw no reason to alter my determination," Huse recalled, "I offered my resignation. There was no expectation on my part that my future would be any other than such as my position as professor in the University of Alabama would occasion." Huse tendered his resignation and it was accepted by February 25. Almost as soon as this news leaked south, a telegram was sent by the new Confederate States Navy Secretary Mallory to Huse, telling him to come to Montgomery and take a commission for active service. He received this message April 1, 1861 and started without delay to the Capital.

Nowhere does Huse elaborate upon his feelings about slavery, the problem of States' Rights, or other matters so important in the secession move. He was a Northerner, yet he seemed to identify himself fully with the fortunes of Alabama and the South. Barely had he received indication that his United States commission was void, than he left to take up an analogous commission from the Rebel Government.

In Montgomery he was taken to Davis' Secretary of War Leroy Pope Walker, who told him: "The President has designated you to go to Europe for the purchase of arms and military supplies; when can you go?" Huse had spent six months in Europe in 1859, but outfitting a company of cadets had been his biggest purchase to date. Nevertheless he replied "At once."

He preferred to return home to prepare for the journey, and ten days were granted him. When he returned to Montgomery to report to General Gorgas he found no orders for him and no money, though this latter was not strange since he could not imagine from what source the new Confederate States could at that time have derived revenue. Treasury Secretary Memminger provided him with funds to get to New York, for it was fastest to depart from this port, main stop of the fast steam packet boats which made regular crossings with passengers, mail, and high-value cargoes. In New York, Huse was to receive money for the journey.

He spent a day in the office of President Jefferson Davis, as the latter received callers and answered mail. Between visitors, the two discussed Huse's mission. Davis referred to Huse as "Major," advancing him one rank from his United States Army grade of captain when he was an instructor at West Point. Exactly how familiar with the arms in the strongholds of Europe Davis may have been is unknown; but it was under his supervision as Secretary of War that Captain Alfred Mordecai made his survey of foreign small arms in 1854-5. It is possible that Davis knew a great deal about the then-new arms of the other nations, for he must, as Secretary of War, have had some familiarity with them to properly evaluate the trials of arms which the Ordnance under Colonel Craig had conducted. There were enough officers for field purposes, but Davis needed specialized men. Huse was one.

Huse Goes to New York

The young major traveled north through Charleston, to study the effect of the bombardment on Sumter. Its relatively undamaged condition caused him to speculate on the reason why Anderson surrendered. In his opinion, nothing could have more decisively split the country and forced men to choose sides than this decision by the United States to give up the big square fort in Charleston Bay. At Baltimore, Huse passed through on the day men who had been injured in the great riots were being buried. No rail travel was possible north of that city, so he hired a carriage to take him to York, Pennsylvania, just over the Maryland line. At last, diverting his route to go to Havre de Grace instead, he and other travelers managed to get across to Perryville by flatboat (the ferry steamer having gone to take troops to Annapolis). Though no scheduled trains were running, Huse was in luck; a long troop train came thundering into the station and as the Union soldiers got off, Huse learned that those travelers who wanted to go to Philadelphia could get on. From Philadelphia he took the cars to South Amboy and then to New York by ferry steamer. On this crossing he came face to face with a noted person of his home town, Hon. Caleb Cushing. Huse did not expect to be recognized and was shocked when Cushing with a smile boomed out: "Good morning, Mr. Huse, you are with the South, I understand."

Momentarily frightened, Huse recalled that Cushing had strong Democratic feelings and so risked disclosing his identity: "Yes, sir, what chance do you think the South has?" he responded.

Cushing summed it up tersely: "What chance can it have?" he said, "the money is all in the North, the manufactories are all in the North, the ships are all in the North, the arms and arsenals are all in the North, the arsenals of Europe are within ten days of New York, and they will be open to the United States Government, and closed to the South, and the Southern ports will be blockaded. What possible chance can the South have?"

Huse could not risk any further debate; raising his hat politely he looked Cushing squarely in the eye and said, "Good morning, Mr. Cushing."

The two never met again, yet Cushing lived to recognize in the young major the figure who, acting in England for the Confederacy, negated all the claims to superiority that Cushing attributed to the North. He had no money, but he sold cotton still in Southern warehouses and pledged his young Government's faith for further credit. To supplement existing Southern factories of which Caleb Cushing was unaware, he contracted with the largest private armory in Europe which could make No. 1 standard interchangeable Enfields. For the ships, his colleagues in the Navy Department bought cruisers, outfitted them, and terrified the shippers of the North so that for a time the United States flag all but disappeared from the seas. Large numbers of good small arms had been transferred to the Southern state arsenals before the war, and the supply was by no means as unbalanced as Mr. Cushing supposed. The arsenals of Europe proved to be just as far from Wilmington, North Carolina, and the Bermuda headquarters of the blockade runners, as from New York. And as for arsenals being closed to the South, the Northern agents having so much ready money and being so lavish in their spending had taken many of the older arms for United States troops, while Huse had to play it cautiously and buy only the very best for the least money he could contrive to pay. Huse, typical of the tiny group of some half dozen men, never more, responsible for disbursing over $22 millions of Confederate funds in Europe, proved that the South had a damn good chance. While it may be apocryphal to claim that "the South wore itself out whipping the Yankees," there were plenty of times—witness the New York stock market fluctuations—when the issue was in doubt.

Major Huse had been told to go to the Bank of the Republic in New York, where he would find letters of credit for his trip. On arriving at this bank, he was immediately brought inside and the shades pulled down; fearfully the bank officer asked, "What do you want?" Outside, mobs of angry New Yorkers ranged the streets, attacking any Southern sympathizers they found. Huse realized that not only was he in jeopardy, but he risked the safety of the bank by even being there. And no letters from Montgomery had arrived to establish his status. He left the bank quietly and passed over to the office of Trenholm Brothers.

The Trenholm banking interests were, and are, widespread. The main office at the time was that of John T. Trenholm, in Charleston, South Carolina. In New York, Trenholm Brothers & Company flourished, handling cotton remittances and money affairs in general for Southern merchants in the New York market. Abroad, in Liverpool, Fraser, Trenholm & Company served the cotton growers' financial needs. War Secretary Walker and Navy Secretary Stephen J. Mallory had arranged for the South's foreign finances to be channeled through this one firm.

Somewhere in the welter of scrap paper which remained after the war exists a treasure-trove for the historian, the Trenholm papers. Neither the Liverpool managers nor the Liverpool Public Library have knowledge of these Confederate Civil War records, though the Librarian indicated recently (1959) that several enquiries had been received about them. The present Mr. Trenholm of New York has no information, though he knows generally that his family's firm

Caleb Huse Incurs Some Debts

Accenting finest available for the money, Southern buyer Huse took best of older British muskets (short sea-service shown top, and detail) and best Enfields. Hand-made Pryse & Redman, middle, is 1859 sergeant's rifle, has unmarked lock. Bottom is Enfield carbine engraved London Armoury Co. with Southern-association JS-Anchor stock stamp. Carbine was found in Tennessee. Both Enfields take sword bayonet with iron-trimmed leather scabbard.

had dealings with the South. And the Trenholm papers in the National Archives fall short of expectations. For, every disbursement which Caleb Huse made abroad was by draft or voucher upon Fraser, Trenholm & Company. From these records the names of sellers of arms, nature of arms purchased, and even totals procured, as well as shipping lines or forwarding agents, insurance agents, and all other payments, should be available. The records are nowhere to be found. But the first entry in them, so to speak, is the $500 Huse obtained in New York.

On to England

He went to Trenholm Brothers and asked for the senior partner, Mr. Wellsman. To his dismay, Wellsman had received no word of his coming from Montgomery, and had no authority to extend him any funds. But Huse had traveled with a man also named Wellsman, a sympathetic Southerner, from Baltimore to Havre de Grace, and he gave Mr. Wellsman a personal message, for the traveling Wellsman was the Trenholm Brothers officer's father. Huse acknowledged his status as Confederate officer traveling to Europe to buy arms, and Wellsman, alarmed for Huse's safety, advanced him $500 in gold to travel to Canada. "You must not think of sailing from New York," Wellsman told Huse. "The excitement is very great and if the crowd discovers who you are they will hang you from a lamp post."

The personal message had been enough to establish his "credit" with Wellsman, and with $500 for immediate trip expenses, Huse journeyed on into Canada, found he could not ship immediately at Montreal, and risked re-entering the United States to eventually find a passage from Portland, Maine. While on the trip, at dinner his table mate, a sea captain returning to his ship at Liverpool, casually remarked "I believe you are going to Europe to buy arms for Jeff Davis." Huse had become somewhat accustomed to remarkable statements by seeming strangers and delayed answering, meanwhile chewing on a piece of potato. Then, poker-faced, he responded, "If he wanted arms he would be likely to select a man who knew something about arms." Nothing more was said but Huse was convinced this innocent (as it later proved) question was an example of telepathy.

Dealing with the London Armoury Company

At last in London, the Southern arms man put up at Morley's Hotel, on Trafalgar Square. Described as "a favorite hotel for Americans," the location had some benefit for Huse. It was up the street from Whitehall, so Government decisions could be obtained (if obtainable at all) by a few minutes' walk from the hotel. And farther along at the end of Cannon Street, beyond the Tower, lay London Bridge, and the offices of the London Armoury Company (Limited), 36 King William Street, London Bridge. Not far from there in Bermondsey on Henry Street L. A. Co. promoter Robert Adams had built the new factory for his company in what may

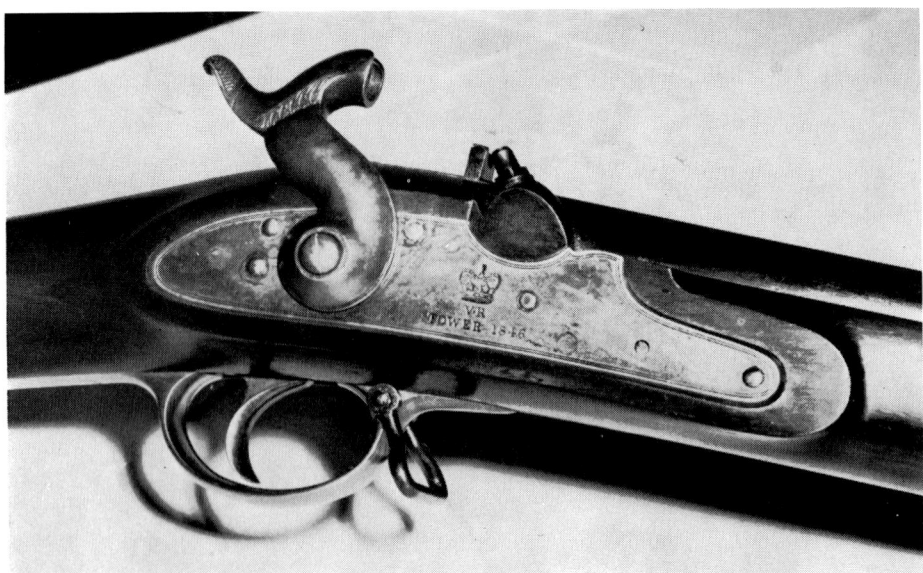

Crisp lock fitting is seen about cone seat of early percussion British sea service musketoon. Gun is model arm transformed from flint, was in Liege gunmakers' museum as a sample for many years. Huse bought similar guns.

have been a former railway shop. The Henry Street address was later spoken of as "the Railway Arches" and since the land was bought from the South Eastern Railway Company it is probable that a standing building was used. Huse was aware that this firm had purchased before the war a plant of gun-stocking machinery from the Ames Manufacturing Company of Chicopee Falls, Massachusetts, and was producing Enfield rifles on the interchangeable plan. The Ames equipment represented the acme of woodworking machinery for that day and the major had hopes the rest of the firm's production might be of this top quality. The next day after getting settled in the hotel Huse visited the armoury offices. His orders at the time were simply to purchase 12,000 rifles and a battery of field artillery (8 guns), and to purchase "one or two guns of larger calibre as models."

"On entering the Superintendent's office at London Armoury," as Huse recalled, "I found there the American engineer (W. F. McFarland) who superintended the erection of the plant. I had known him in Chicopee. Suspecting he might be an agent for the purchase of arms for the United States Government, I asked him bluntly if he was, and added, 'I am buying for the Confederate Government.' Such a disclosure of my business may seem to have been indiscreet, but at that time I thought it my best plan, and the result proved that I was right . . .

"As he had entered the office first, it was in order for me to outstay him, which I did. On his leaving, I asked for a price for all the small arms the Company could manufacture." The major intended, if possible, to secure the entire output of L. A. Co., but Superintendent Robert Adams, revolver inventor, said he could not give a firm price until the next day; nor could the president of the firm, probably Archibald Hamilton, merchant, of Sinclair, Hamilton & Company (who supplied the South with many accessory warlike stores, belts, harness and equipments), say more.

The President took the matter before the directors—Robert Adams, Richard Ashton (merchant), Archibald Cockburn (merchant), William Dray (manufacturer and engineer), George Fry (solicitor) and John Shorter (merchant). The decision was that "the Directors felt they ought to give their present customer the preference over all others." Huse tenaciously refused to give up, even more convinced now that his "competitor" was the Ames Manufacturing Company engineer, working either for the United States or for the State of Massachusetts, buying arms.

McFarland, who had momentarily thwarted Major Huse's efforts, had come over from Ames, in Chicopee Falls, to superintend the installation of the United States-made machinery at the London Armoury Company works. The Confederate buyer's visit to the London Armoury Company offices was late in May, 1861, and he discovered that McFarland had contracted to take 100 Enfield rifles a week, for a period of three months, for Massachusetts.

McFarland was acting under direction of George Schuyler, who in turn was awaiting instructions to contract for more. Meanwhile, a British Government order was taking the balance of the company's production, which in total was about 1,300 rifles a month. Those Huse sought to buy, apparently getting the okay from the London Armoury Company management to the quantity of 10,000, complete with bayonet, scabbard, extra nipple, snap-cap, and stopper, for £3/16/6, or about $19 FOB London. The price was a little higher than Gorgas had authorized him to go, but the major felt the "necessity of arming the Confederacy is so great" that the increased cost was worth it.

Huse Arranges to Buy Enfields

Major Edward C. Anderson, C.S.A., Huse's assistant, wrote on August 11, 1861 to War Secretary L. P. Anderson, describing their purchases:

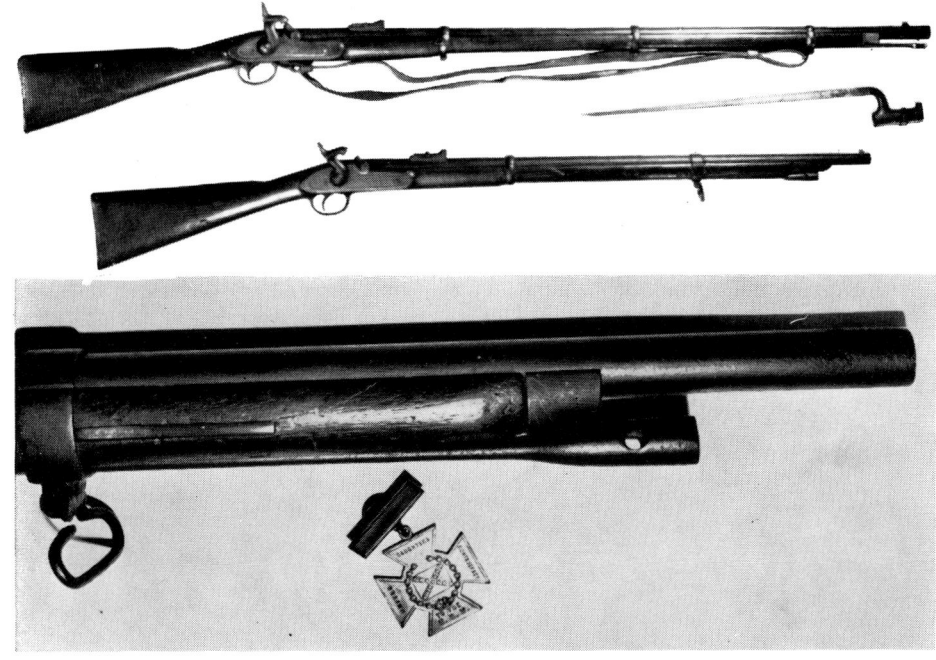

Sinclair, Hamilton & Co. obtained Enfields for Huse. Southern-provenance guns in author's collection include 1863-date Birmingham-proved Long rifle and M1853 spring-band short rifle. Latter was taken from CS soldier by father of man from whom obtained by author. Gun has had repairs (detail), with front band of iron Prussian type and ramrod from Thouvenin rifle. Southern Cross of Honor is associated memento.

When Captain Huse first arrived in England, he met General Fair, late United States Minister to Belgium, and satisfied himself that nothing for immediate service could be obtained from that country. General Fair was certain from personal enquiry that all the establishments at Liege had more than they could do for several months. As the general had made direct inquiry with the view of obtaining arms for the State of Alabama, and as it was known that all through Europe the Liege manufacturers had the reputation of furnishing arms of the worst possible quality, it was deemed best not to give any further attention in that direction for the present.

It was found that the $150,000 which was at first remitted would be well spent in England. Steps were accordingly taken with that end in view. Nothing ready-manufactured was to be found. The attempt to contract with the London Armoury Company failed, as you were informed in a previous dispatch, from Captain Huse, the British Government declining to consent to an extension of time for the completion of their own contract. The principal manager of that company, Mr. Hamilton, of the firm of Sinclair, Hamilton & Company, is a merchant of the highest respectability, and is acquainted with every gunmaker in England.

The connection was fortunate. Hamilton agreed to obtain as many rifles as he could get in England, taking a commission of 2½ per cent on the purchase price for his trouble. Huse and Anderson were happy with the arrangement, since it left them free for other work and Hamilton was well suited to obtain these guns. They were in the hands of many gunmakers all over England, and recognizing the skill of their adversaries —said Alexander, "the agents purchasing for the United States . . . were men quite well informed in their trade" —the Confederates were content to let Hamilton work for them.

The London Armoury Company proprietor did quite well: By February, 1863, a total of 70,980 long Enfield rifles, 9,715 short Enfield rifles, 354 carbine Enfields, rifled, and 20 "small bore" Enfields had been shipped by Huse to the Confederacy. Other British arms completing the list included 21,040 British muskets, and 2,020 Brunswick rifles. The Enfields were current manufacture guns for the most part, the 20 "smallbore" guns almost certainly the Kerr target and Volunteer .45 caliber rifles of the Enfield pattern, which were a proprietary design of the London Armoury Company.

Between August, 1861 and March, 1862, Huse busied himself elsewhere, but kept in touch with the London Armoury Company. Their British Government contract was still going on, but nearing its completion. "I have requested (Hamilton) not to apply for a renewal of it until I can receive instructions from the War Department, and have also requested him to tender to me a proposal for supplying 50,000. I have not received his formal reply, but it will be in substance as follows: The price to be the same as to the British Government, which I think is 60 shillings, say $15; rifles to be delivered in London, payment on delivery.

"It will be necessary in case the contract is made to organize a corps of inspectors of the work as it progresses from the forgings to the finished rifle. I have no doubt that I could secure the services of the same men now acting in the same capacity for the British War Department. In case the General Government or any of the State governments found it necessary to procure a greater number of rifles in England than this company could furnish, the same inspectors would be available for receiving other rifles, and the standard of quality in the minds of these inspectors would be the highest possible."

Involved in these statements, plus Huse's word that he did contract with London Armoury Company for rifles, we find several important facts possibly aiding us to identify "Confederate" rifles. An obvious point is that some London Armoury Company rifles of 1863, all of 1864, and some of 1865, and so dated on the lockplates, would be Confederate States bought and shipped rifles.

A second point of interest follows the first. Since a corps of inspectors was necessary, the probability is that Huse' expectations were carried out, and that the British Government inspectors remained at work for the Confederacy. If so, their workmens' marks would have been the same stamps, a cypher of a crown over a number. Considering that in between the termination of the British contract and the beginning of the Confederate contract, some time in late summer or early fall of 1862, the United States agent Marcellus Hartley was able to get some thousands of London Armoury Company arms, all inspected by the same parties, we now arrive at a collectors' puzzle. How can one determine the Confederate London Armoury Company Enfields from others? William Albaugh feels that Major Anderson obliquely referred to some method of distinguishing these several arms at a glance.

Anderson, writing to War Secretary L. P. Walker from London, August 14, 1861, refers to a sum of money he had which would allow him to buy some muskets being offered. Anderson's letter contains a direct reference to Enfield rifles, stating that "arrangements are in progress" for buying a large number. He then introduces the subject of $100,000 received from the Governor of Georgia to be used for purchasing arms for that State. Says Anderson, "This will enable me to take up many *muskets* which are at this time being offered, a large portion of which, I am inclined to believe, were ordered for the United States Government, but which, for the want of funds in hand, they are unable to obtain from the manufacturers. Some of these guns now in our possession have their viewers' marks upon them, indicating that they had been inspected and accepted by their agents. Of course we subject them to the ordeal of our own standard of excellence."

Anderson did buy guns for Georgia, feeling that every firearm shipped to a Southern state strengthened The Cause just that much.

Now, in trying to puzzle through this thing, just what did Anderson say? His grammar is a little confusing. Albaugh, in publishing this letter passage ("CS or US", *The American Arms Collector,* January 1958, Vol. 2, No. 1, pp. 21, 22), commits a little historical sin, interjecting by way of explanation something which is not in the text. He quotes the critical sentence as ". . . but which, for the want of funds in hand, they (the Yankees) were unable to obtain from the mfgrs." By elucidating the passage this way, Albaugh makes the following references to "their" inspectors' marks suggest that there was some United States inspector's mark on each gun.

But how many men did the North have officially inspecting these guns?

And equally important, how many guns could any one man inspect in a day, sufficient to justify his put-

Killed in the attack of May 19, 1864, Confederate soldier of Ewell's Corps lies in the pockets-robbed indignity of death. His Long Enfield has been artfully laid across his leg. Northern supplies by that date were steady, and apparently it was not necessary to salvage his rifle at once.

ting a stamp on it? Bores would have to be swabbed out, locks taken from the stock, inletting examined to see no hidden cracks existed, and at least one or two other detail studies made with each and every gun, before an inspector could place his reputation and his pocket book in jeopardy on untried goods by putting his stamp on them.

Albaugh also conjectures that this passage meant that, as a corollary, Anderson also had some private inspector's mark on the guns, so he could tell which ones were Confederate. But all this is conjecture, and removed from the text of this fairly interesting letter. Read the letter passages quoted carefully, deny the interjection of "the Yankees" which cannot be "admitted into evidence" as there is no foundation for this particular interpretation, over any other interpretation, and see now what we arrive at.

First, Anderson is not referring to *Enfield rifles* which were so much in demand, virtually unobtainable, and which at that time he was arranging (he hoped) to procure by contract. He specifically mentions Enfields and in the next passage states "muskets." As an officer on Ordnance duty, writing to the secretary of his home War Office, who was vitally interested in whether Anderson was finding *muskets* or nice modern *rifles,* Confederate purchaser Major Anderson wrote "rifles" when he meant rifles, and "muskets" when he meant muskets.

Hence, any particular markings involved must be sought for on British muskets. It will be remembered that up to February, 1863, just 21,040 British muskets had been bought by Huse & Anderson for the Confederate Government. But the number was in an accounting of government, not state funds. Probably, therefore, the $100,000 from Georgia was spent in a purchase of possibly 10,000 additional muskets found in the market.

Flint muskets would not have been taken by the

Confederate agents, even for Georgia. The inference is that the smoothbore percussion musket known as the Model 1842, bar lock like later Enfields but caliber .735-inch, pin-fastened stock with brass nose cap, was the type bought. Furniture is brass, and instead of the stock and barrel being joined by round pins, flat ones or keys were used. Now, Anderson speaks of the guns having "their viewers' marks upon them," which clears the situation not at all. For, does "their" refer to the Yankees, as Albaugh assumes, or does it refer merely to the guns themselves, subjectively? Quite possibly Anderson was familiar with the individual inspectors, whose government-type stamps, a crown over a number, would appear on the guns. But these muskets had, after all, been manufactured several decades before (in 1851 the first British Minie *rifle* was adopted) and would have been viewed and inspected at the time. Anderson continues, saying these marks showed the guns had been accepted by "their agents." While this without a doubt means "Yankee agents," it does not necessarily mean Yankees themselves. Hence, the marks may be indistinguishable from those stamped by the same man inspecting for another purchaser or government, upon similar guns more or less at the same time. For consider this: right before his supposititious remarks about "their marks" and "their agents," Anderson opens his remarks about the muskets which are available, by saying very conditionally that a large portion of these guns, *"I am inclined to believe,"* were ordered for the United States Government. He is far less positive than Albaugh concerning Anderson's reference to the viewers' marks.

Albaugh also infers from Anderson's statement "Of course we subject them to the ordeal of our own standard of excellence," that there was some particular mark and inspection given these guns by the Confederate buyers and that, if such mark were known, we could identify Confederate guns. Unfortunately, it is an Enfield and a Kerr revolver which Albaugh pictures, each bearing a mysterious "JS over anchor" stamp. Remember, in context, the comments Anderson made seem to refer only to muskets of which he ultimately procured, some for Georgia, and do not refer to any other firearm. In order to make the remarks refer to Confederate guns generally, it is necessary to read into Anderson's letter statements and inferences which are not there and, acting on that free basis, I now wonder if perhaps Anderson's observation of "our own standard of excellence" is not just a facetious remark to War Secretary Walker in a moment of glum humor—both men knew how desperate was the need for arms and though the Confederates showed their uniform preference for the Enfield and only Tower or London Armoury Company Enfields at that, the comment seems to express a snobbishness about accepting guns which Anderson did not really feel.

It has been thus necessary to go into the question of marks pro and con because of the importance of the matter to the historian and arms collector. Stamps such as CSA, C.S.A., CS and C.S, CSN, and the JS-anchor are found on weapons with Confederate use proved or assumed. Since one such gun which came to our attention recently is a Lefaucheux second model pinfire revolver, with the solid frame running all the way forward under the cylinder instead of the curious LF design with an L frame on the barrel breech, and since this construction was introduced sometime after the Confederates stopped buying arms, the presence of a large CS stamp on the frame is highly suspect.

The CS has been used on Prussian muskets, also, and we feel improperly in some instances by unscrupulous dealers who blundered ahead on the assumption that "the South used anything they could get their hands on." History proves this is not entirely true so far as procurement goes, and it is questionable if the CS marks would have been punched on later in the war when hands were short at the various Southern arsenals. As the majority of Potsdam muskets were pur-

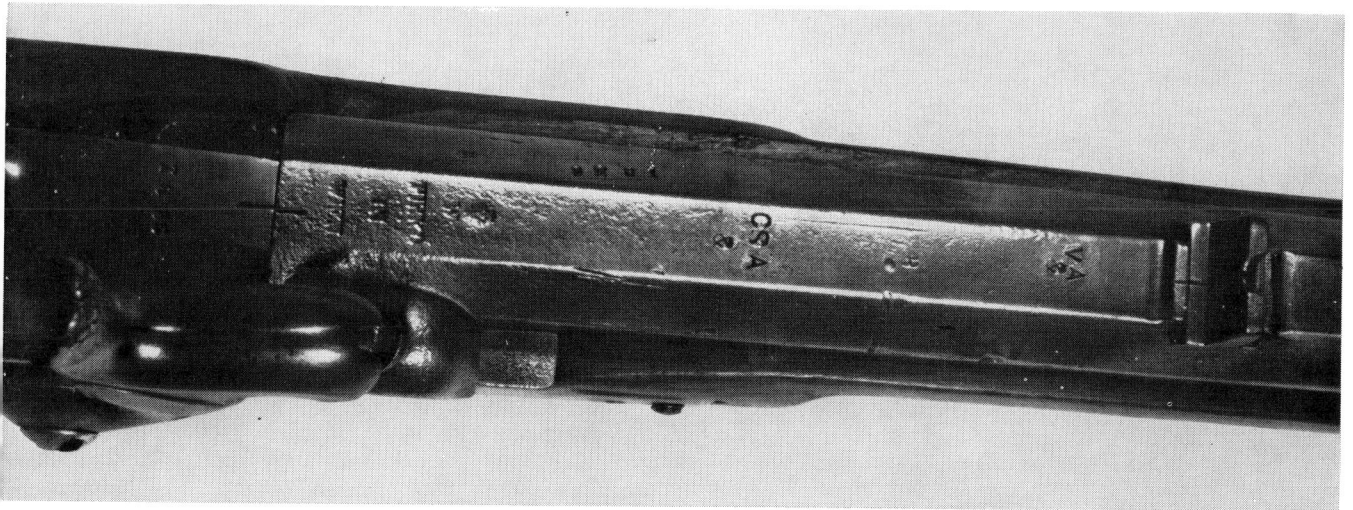

Lorenz 1855 rifle by Pirko, Viennese gunmaker, in collection of Museum of Historical Arms in Florida is stamped VA/& and CSA/&. Museum director Marvin Hoffman doubts authenticity of markings. Made in 1860, gun is numbered 1836.

chased by the scavenging Northern traders, while the South from the first emphasized the Enfield and only secondarily took on the Austrian Lorenz rifles, most other junk muskets with CS or CSA on them are rightly suspect.

Huse's work with the London Armoury proved highly successful; Enfields became the standard pattern arm of the Confederate States forces—Army, Navy, and Marines.

Cryptically, as he described the quelling of the students' mutiny, Huse did not disclose how he achieved his object. There is a hint in his mentioning the delay in correspondence by packet boat; inferentially, McFarland had only inquired about long-time contracts, and had not been able to get a reply. Meanwhile, he had placed an order for 10,000 Enfields; but Huse wanted the rest. He persuaded President Hamilton that a month was a long time to wait for a tentative answer from the authorities of the North. "Within a few days" he reported, "I succeeded in closing a contract under which I was to have all the arms the Company could manufacture, after filling a comparatively small order for the United States agent." Definitively establishing, without equivocation, who the London Armoury worked for between 1861 and 1865, Huse states "This Company, during the remainder of the war, turned all its output of arms over to me for the Confederate Army."

It was the London Armoury Company that, occupying a status akin to official armorers for the Confederacy, supplied the South with its best guns. Emphasis was on the No. 1 quality interchangeable Enfield rifles of "the Railroad Arches" make, and the Kerr revolvers.

The Kerr Revolver

The "Confederate" single action Kerr is of .44 or .450 caliber, called 54-bore. A smaller size, 80-bore or .36 caliber, was also made in limited numbers. Auguste Francotte of Liege was the licensed fabricator and communicant of Kerr and made at least one .36 revolver, marked "1" and clearly of Liege make with full proofs. But the majority were London Armoury guns, and were stamped on the barrel forward of the London view and proof marks, left top quarter flat, with a tiny L.A.C. The frame, to which the barrel was hinged at bottom front, is stamped on the left with an oval LONDON/ARMOURY. The back-action sidelock, detachable from the revolver frame and set into the handle, is engraved by hand with the words LONDON ARMOURY CO. and on the same right side of the frame below cylinder, with KERR'S PATENT and a number. This number, which appears also on the side of the cylinder and is hand engraved, is a mark of final acceptance as it is engraved after all polishing immediately before bluing. The actual serial number of fabrication in the Kerr revolver series is stamped on the front face of cylinder, on the frame flat below cylinder, under the barrel strap over top of cylinder, and in the handle in the lock mortising. On one "JS-Anchor" specimen the engraved number is 9239; the actual stamped serial number, by which pieces were reassembled after being

Southern-association Kerr revolver may have been one imported directly but full story is not yet known. JS-Anchor is stamped on grip and gun was used by Southern man in war. Marked Kerr's Patent 9239 but factory parts No. 813.

Often assumed to be double action guns that don't work. Kerrs are usually single action with a trigger that moves to rear of guard for creepless let-off. Caliber is .450 but .36 Kerrs are known. Some were made in Liege.

taken apart for finishing and then returned from the polishers, is H 813, the H stamped separately from the 813 which from its regularity on the several parts appears to have been stamped in some kind of a jig. The wood under the lock is also stamped "H", but with a bladed tool (screw-driver?) punched three times. On the front side of the handle, immediately at tip of the frame tang, is stamped the initials JS over an anchor.

The identical stamp appears on other Kerr revolvers, and at the rear of the trigger guard tang of a London Armoury .577 carbine in the author's collection, which was bought from a dealer who picked it up "in Tennessee." The lockplate, usually on London Armoury Company guns bearing that imprinted cypher, is hand engraved by the same man who marked the Kerr revolver cited, with *London Armoury*. On the bayonet stud soldered to the side of the barrel, the number 416 is stamped; that number appearing to be the same "1" as is stamped on the Kerr revolver H 813. The carbine barrel is Liege made and proved, over-proofed with London marks.

Although the Kerr revolver was adopted by Portugal, marks denoting Portuguese issue are not now recorded by collectors. It is possible the JS-anchor mark is some Portuguese stamp. But the finding not only of Kerr revolvers, but of Enfield London Armoury carbines from the Border States' backwoods with the same stamp, a stamp in a location denoting final acceptance by the chief inspecting officer, seems to confirm the Southern use of arms so marked. The inference that the JS-anchor is a Southern mark and not the stamp of some other purchaser is argued by a few experts; if so, it may have stood somehow for John Slidell (Confederate Commissioner in Europe) or James Seddon, in honor thereof more than any indication either had personally inspected the arm.

While this is pure speculation, the possibility that the "H" series of Kerr revolver serials were made for Caleb Huse is quite likely. The engraved numbers are not, as usually supposed, actual serial numbers. They are numbers recorded in the firm's books in terms of sale; that is, Adams and Beaumont-Adams revolvers, as well as Kerrs of both calibers and both single and double action, could probably be found in the books with brackets or groups of numbers assigned to be engraved. The stamped metal serial number was for the manufacturing staff to keep track of the current batch of Kerr revolvers; the engraved serial number was in the series of entire Kerr output and ran consecutively without regard to model, a practice common to London gunmakers, Holland, Westley Richards, and Rigby among others. The stamped number is a clue to the quantity made in the batch, lot, order, or contract. It is also a clue as to the ratio of engraved Kerr revolvers to the total output only, regardless of model changes.

Externally the difference between single and double action is hardly visible. The single-action model has the trigger farther forward in the guard, and the rear flange of trigger is more deep in the guard; the DA type is more nearly centered in the guard. Internally, the SA Kerr is designed to keep the trigger, when cocked, in close touch with the hammer to give a crisp and creepless let-off. The rear sight is a huge V in the frame and the front sight a monster brass stud 1/8-inch diameter screwed into the top of the barrel, so the emphasis on fine trigger action seems a little absurd. A hook attached to the trigger on the same pivot as the pawl drops over a stud on the tumbler and, as the tumbler

Enigmatic J-S Anchor. Some experts think that is a Portuguese stamp, others argue that it is a Southern mark, and not the stamp of a purchaser.

is raised when the hammer is thumb-cocked, the trigger flange is drawn back to contact the sear and give a crisp let-off. Incorrectly reassembled, it is possible to assume that somehow the loop is part of a double-action lifting device, reversed, but this is not so.

The Kerr revolvers were made under British patents No. 2896, December 17, 1858, and No. 242, January 26, 1859. Both calibers were five-shot, five-groove, rifling counter-clockwise, barrel 5½ inches. Lockplate, hammer, and loading lever were casehardened; the other parts were blued, and the grips of one-piece walnut coarsely checkered. The center-hung loading lever had a side-springing catch, and the lever like a blade fitted between two sidewise studs under the barrel, avoiding Colt's British patent of 1849.

Sharp Dealers

Though he sought only first class arms, Huse ran into the usual quota of trade sharpies. The French were especially glib in their offerings of inferior quality arms. Back home the din of Bull Run still echoed in the ears of North and South. Though the charge of Colonel Arthur Cummings, commanding the 33rd Virginia which took the Federal battery that was trying to enfilade Jackson, was the turning point of the engagement, the victorious Southern forces did not win because of superior weapons. Of Virginia units, the Hampshire Riflemen from New Creek was a pre-war regiment, well equipped. But the Independent Grays, for example, from Moorefield, Hardy County, had old, altered muskets and flint rifles from Harpers Ferry, possibly the M1803-1814 pattern of half-stock heavy

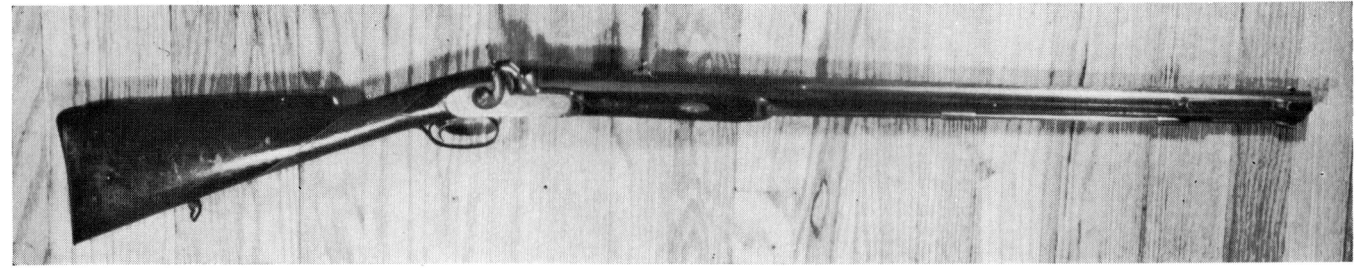

Author's "Jeff Davis" rifle. When former President of Confederacy was captured he had a carbine in his luggage of identical pattern as this but shorter barrel, one ramrod pipe. Sight graduated to 1,000 yards, cal. .69 rifled. Davis' gun now at Springfield Armory Museum. Liege arms museum identifies this pattern incorrectly as "boar hunting rifle" and another specimen more correctly as Carbine of the Guard of Viceroy of Egypt. Takes Yataghan bayonet having two raised lugs pierced for fitting to bayonet studs on muzzle.

.54 round ball rifle. The Potomac Guards, from Springfield, Virginia, had the same equipment; the "Shenandoah Sharpshooters" only flintlock muskets. Mustered into the "Stonewall Brigade," they were opposed that June 21 by the 14th Brooklyn Zouaves and 1st Michigan, which "poured a deadly volley into us." Flint muskets were not the right sort of armament for the South, but Huse found different opinions abroad.

The French agent for the Confederacy wanted to buy flintlocks in Paris, justifying it by saying that U.S. Minister Dayton had bought 30,000 flintlocks in France. Actually, Dayton had bought percussion arms, mostly in Belgium. According to J. B. Jones' *A Rebel War Clerk's Diary*, the French statisticians alleged there was no greater mortality in battle using percussion and rifled arms, than from using smooth bore muskets. "This may be owing to the fact that a shorter range is sought with the latter," opined Jones, but the fact was that the liars were figuring; figuring, that is, how to dump a few tons of flint muskets on the pressed Southern buyers without the need to transform these weapons to percussion. There was great need: "We are not increasing our forces as rapidly as might be desired, for the want of arms," Jones wrote on September 6, 1861, "None have been imported yet." Huse evidently bought none of these flint muskets.

Belgian Muskets

Among Huse' purchases were Belgian rifled muskets. General U. S. Grant had not thought much of these and described the equipment of his forces up to the fall of Vicksburg, when 31,600 prisoners, 172 cannon, and 60,000 muskets, many of them new Enfields, were taken by the Federals.

"Up to this time our troops at the West," wrote Grant in *Century Magazine,* September, 1885, "had been limited to the old United States flintlock, changed into percussion, the Belgian musket imported early in the war (almost as dangerous to the person firing it as the one aimed at) and a few new and improved arms . . . The enemy (Confederates) had generally new arms, which had run the blockade, and were of uniform caliber. After the surrender, I authorized all colonels whose regiments were armed with inferior muskets to place them in the stack of captured arms, and to replace them with the latter."

Writing of *Life in the Confederate Army,* A. P. Ford noted that the South had "old-fashioned Belgian rifles, probably the most antiquated and worthless guns ever put into a modern soldier's hands. But they were all our Government had (aside, perhaps, from the Enfields the Vicksburg defenders possessed?). These rifles could not send a ball beyond 200 yards, and at much shorter range their aim was entirely unreliable."

Yet as late as December of 1864, Belgian muskets were issued to Captain G. L. Buist's Palmetto Guards artillery unit. Four howitzers were reorganized as infantry with their Belgian muskets.

Belgians were issued to Company I, 14th Wisconsin Volunteer Infantry, by March 1862, if a tintype of Private Elisha Stockwell in *Sees The Civil War* is to be believed. Though it could be a "prop" of the photographer's studio, it most likely is Private Stockwell's own Belgian musket, evidently a .69 Minie rifle with back action lock and short elevating leaf rear sight. "We were armed with Belgian rifles," said Stockwell. "They were heavy, but good shooting guns; at least some of them were, when carefully loaded. I saw an Indian of Company F come into camp while here with all the squirrels he could handily carry, all shot in the head. They were gray and fox squirrels. Company F was a big part Indian, and good skirmishers. We had Enfield rifles at Vicksburg, and Springfields the last year and eight months. I liked them the best. I fetched my whole outfit home with me, gave six dollars for it."

Even more enthusiastic about the Belgian arms was a ragged Confederate at Fredericksburg who during the burying truce snatched up a brand new Yankee Belgian musket. A bluecoat officer remonstrated with him for stealing arms under a flag of truce. Without dropping the new musket or slowing down, the Reb looked the Yank slowly over and coldly said, "Never mind, sir! I'll shoot you tomorrow and *get them boots!*" Capture or cargo, the South found use for the "worthless Belgians."

A Liege rifled musket, .69 back action lock with elevator rear sight to 800 yards, has been seen by the author bearing CSA mark. The rear band on this specimen was loose, possibly from another musket. The barrel channel was crudely chiseled out; whether the gun had been rebuilt at some Southern arsenal or not was a question of the moment. The tang of the barrel was stamped "63." On the flat side of the nipple bolster, neatly in 1/16-inch letters, CSA could be read with the "C" uppermost, the "A" near the wood. The legitimacy of this mark was neither argued for, nor against; the owner simply did not know. Unfortunately, while the practice of stamping CSA on an otherwise unimportant old musket vastly enhances its value to the collector, the habit seems more recent than historic. Factories producing for the Confederacy in the South, as opposed to state production, might and sometimes did stamp their guns "CS" or "CSA." On imports, the mark is suspect.

Coastal Steamers Bought Abroad

Besides speculative blockade runners, the Confederate Ordnance Department bought steamers; Huse purchased the *Columbia, R. E. Lee,* the *Merrimac,* and the *Eugenie.* Gorgas locally obtained the *Phantom.* From September 30, 1862 to September 30, 1863, these steamers in addition to heavy goods and uniforms, Blakely guns, and explosives, carried through the "Anaconda" four times as many small arms as were produced at the Richmond, Fayetteville, and Asheville armories. In this Southern fiscal year, 113,504 small arms were imported, making the total of small arms imported to that time about 350,000, including the 100,000 Austrian rifles Huse obtained in Vienna.

These ships were shallow draught coastal steamers, not ocean-going freighters. Their task was to run from Nassau, Havana, or one of the other nearby foreign ports to a Confederate port. Formerly, munitions had been shipped via sailing schooners, but the affair of the *Stephen Hart* ended that. She was American built, but sold to an English house and sailed under the British flag. Still, the proof she was loaded with Confederate war materiel was so overwhelming that the courts declared her, vessel and cargo, forfeit. After that incident, steamers exclusively were used. The outward voyage had little risk, for cargo and vessel usually belonged to bonafide British owners, and were not contraband of war subject to capture and forfeiture by a prize court. But once, a few brass buttons marked C.S.A. were enough to "taint" the cargo of a ship loaded with otherwise innocuous groceries and clothing, the *Springbok,* and the whole ship was condemned as contraband. As Huse recorded:

> To get supplies from "The Islands" to the main land required sea-worthy steamers of light draught and great speed . . . Some . . . had been private yachts, as for example the "Merrimac"; [there were two "Merrimacs"]; some were engaged in trade between British ports, as the "Cornubia"; some were taken from the Channel service between England and France, as the "Eugenie"; and some were built for opium smuggling in China. Later in the war, steamers were built expressly for the service . . ."

His orders had been brought separately to England in the shoe sole of a German traveling on business for the Confederacy, and Huse was enjoying his cloak-and-dagger assignment. He preferred the cloak and went easy on the dagger. The *Fingal* carried the first cargo

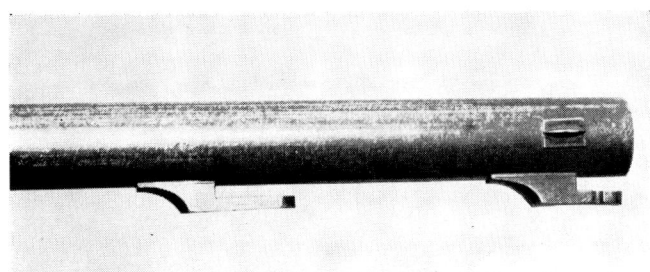

Muzzle of "Jeff Davis" rifle has odd bayonet lugs. One bayonet possibly fitting this gun is shown by Albaugh; at a South Carolina gun show recently a complete cased hunting rifle taking same pattern bayonet but smaller, and a rusty original bayonet, were offered for sale. Possibly Huse bought a few that the Viceroy of Egypt did not take. Carbine shown is marked "Windisch a Nimes," but is Liege made and proved; has hit man target at 300 meters with .69 Minie.

through the blockade, fruits of his labors, and it was necessary to send into Savannah, Georgia, the port for which her chief officer Commander James D. Bulloch had sailed, a set of secret signals in advance. Otherwise, if the *Fingal* did not give the right recognition signs, the heavy shore batteries would blast her out of the water. The messenger, traveling separately, carried a packet of cigars. One was special; said Huse,

> These [signals] were secreted by removing the wrapper of a well-made cigar and carefully replacing it, after rolling the paper containing the signals upon its body. I myself did this bit of cigar work. On arriving off Savannah, Commander Bulloch displayed his signals, which were immediately answered, and he piloted his ship into the harbor with which he was familiar.

Another time, Huse was tempted into an act of piracy, when he got wind of a cargo of Austrian rifles loading at Hamburg for the North. These were Marcellus Hartley's purchases and Huse would dearly have loved to capture them. The *Nashville,* a Charleston-to-New York packet boat, had been bought by the Confederate States Government and outfitted as a cruiser, Captain Pegram, commanding. Though she would have made a ridiculous showing against such mighty vessels as the *Hartford* or the thunder-gunned monitors, she did fly the flag of the Confederate States in Southampton.

Huse had been approached with a cash offer from some people who had either knowledge or interest in a British ship carrying the Austrian guns from Hamburg to New York. If Huse would deposit £10,000 in the Bank of England, in favor of unspecified persons, he could then take out a tug with a gun aboard, and fire a shot across the bow of the British ship. Her captain would have orders to stop her and allow Huse to order her to Charleston as a surrendered vessel. The scheme was not impossible, had Huse held a privateer's commission, and he asked Confederate Commissioner Yancy for a letter of marque and reprisal, thinking also that his status as an officer in the C.S. Army might cover him under international law if he tried it. But Pegram arrived at Southampton and Huse had to leave London to pay him a courtesy call at the docks. The scheme was temporarily suspended and the Austrian guns set sail for New York.

Huse Purchases Vienna Arsenal Surplus

Huse's great coup was the first of his career in Europe, the purchasing of the surplus at the Vienna Arsenal. He had been there in 1859 as a military visitor, with a letter of introduction from the United States War Department. His return was reluctant for, as he put it, he at first "considered the getting of anything from an Imperial Austrian Arsenal as chimerical." He continues:

> But my would-be intermediary (Moses & Company) was so persistent that, finally, I accompanied him to Vienna and, within a few days, closed a contract for 100,000 rifles of the latest Austrian pattern, and ten batteries, of six pieces each, of field artillery, with harness complete, ready for service, and a quantity of ammunition, all to be delivered on ship at Hamburg. The United States Minister, Mr. Motley, protested in vain. He was told that the making of arms was an important industry of Austria; that the same arms had been offered to the United States Government and declined, and that, as belligerents, the Confederate States were, by the usage of nations, lawful buyers. However unsatisfactory this answer may have been to Washington, the arms were delivered, and in due time were shipped to Bermuda from Hamburg. Mr. Motley offered to buy the whole consignment, but was too late. The Austrian Government declined to break faith with the purchasers.
>
> I confess to a glow of pride when I saw those sixty pieces of rifled artillery with caissons, field forges, and battery wagons, complete—some two hundred carriages in all—drawn up in array in the arsenal yard. It was pardonable for a moment to imagine myself in command of a magnificent part of artillery. The explanation of Austria's willingness to dispose of these batteries is that the authorities had decided on the use of gun cotton in the place of powder; and the change involved new guns, although those sold to me were of the latest design for gunpowder. I believe gun cotton was given up not long after.

Though Huse's Austrian rifles from Vienna, described as "of the latest pattern" were of the Lorenz model, he obtained other Austrian-pattern guns from the Liege fabricants. This is revealed by an examination made by Confederate States Ordnance Major Smith Stansbury, in St. George, Bermuda. Stansbury was the commanding officer of the Confederate States Bermuda Ordnance Depot, and under his direction was the shipping house of John Tory Bourne, British commission merchant. A series of letters by Stansbury to Gorgas and Bourne in their excerpts reveal the nature of the guns on hand:

> St. Georges, Bermuda, *July 25, 1863*
> ... We have on hand here (as previously advised) about sixty thousand Austrian muskets, which, judging from the samples I have seen, are also condemned arms, and to us utterly worthless.
>
> * * *
>
> *July 29, 1863*
> ... the *Venus* can be loaded from the *Miriam* with Austrian muskets, which are so much needed at home. After some difficulty, I had one of the cases opened yesterday, and was permitted to inspect one gun. They are new and clumsy muskets, apparently of the manufacture of Liege, but the case examined was in excellent order ...
>
> * * *
>
> *August 11, 1863*
> ... You direct that the boxes be opened, and the arms oiled before shipment. This I fear will be impossible.
>
> * * *
>
> *August 14, 1863*
> ... in relation to Texas cargo ... we have on hand 584 cases of arms, Austrian muskets, which arrived by the *Miriam*, and which are in excellent order ...

That these were Consol-Augustin lock muskets is suggested by the following, relating to the ship upon which it was proposed to ship the Austrian muskets in response to a demand by Texas for arms:

> *August 18, 1863*
> Col. J. Gorgas.
>
> Colonel:
> Unless we receive a supply of percussion caps before the *Ella and Annie* is ready to leave for Texas, I shall with the

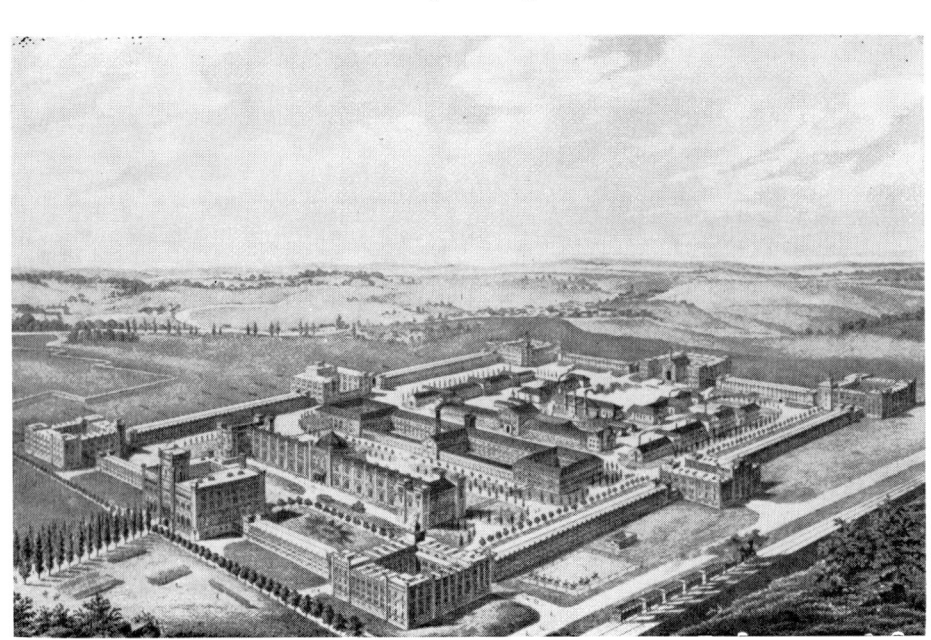

At Vienna Arsenal Huse struck jackpot, bought 100,000 Lorenz rifles virtually from under Hartley's nose. Store rooms 600 feet long contained vast racks of rifles made for armies of Austro-Hungarian Empire in turbulent era of history.

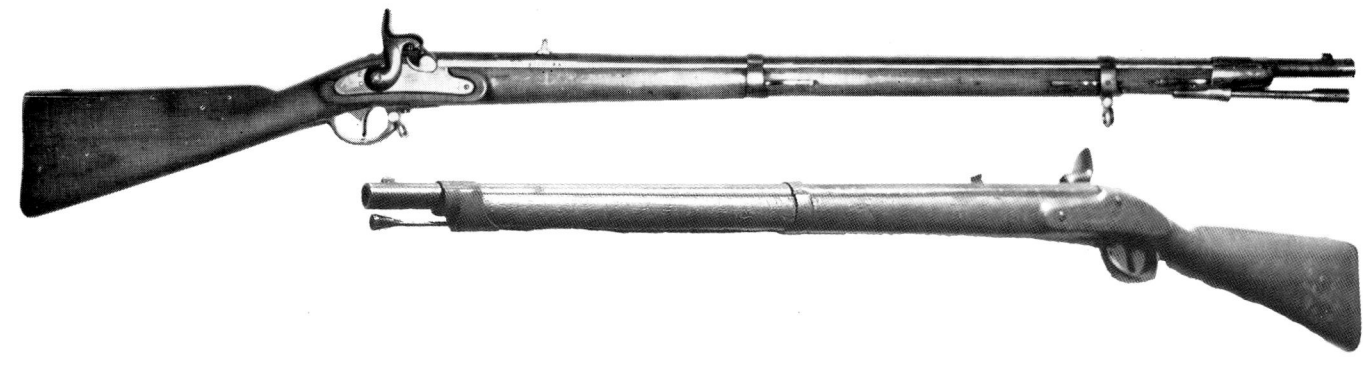

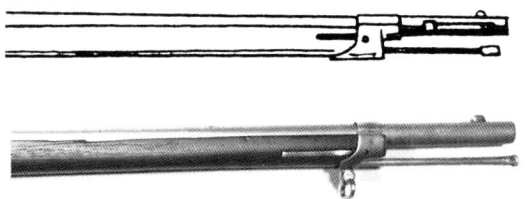

Austrian .54 rifles had block sights and front band with ramrod guide. Middle is Austrian shortened at Tyler, Texas, CS Arsenal; fitted with French front band and muzzle tapered and sight fixed to hold C.W. bayonet M1855. Left, drawing of M1840 front band of guns issued to French troops in Mexico; same band is on Tyler, Texas arsenal rifle (Fuller 818) at Chickamauga and Chattanooga NMP. Detail suggests Napoleon III okayed repair parts sent to Texas arsenal.

concurrence of Major Walker detain her for two or three days.

It is distracting to think that the arms and ammunition sent by her may be almost useless, without a supply of caps.

SMITH STANSBURY, *Major*

P. S. I am very glad to inform you that the Austrian rifles, which were on hand when I arrived, have turned out much better, than the samples I inspected led me to suppose.

With careful cleaning by the soldiers, most of them will, I hope, turn out effective weapons.

Bulloch Also Buys Arms

Buying and collaborating with Huse in Europe were Commander James D. Bulloch, the Confederate States naval representative in England, and Captain James H. North, CSN. Bulloch had been instructed to obtain ships, cannon—at least one Armstrong breechloading gun with pivot carriage for each—and in addition to general stores such as shoes, jackets, pants, certain small arms:

1,000 navy revolvers
   100,000 rounds fixed ammunition
   500,000 percussion caps
1,000 navy carbines
   100,000 rounds of fixed ammunition
   500,000 percussion caps
Bullet moulds, wipers, spare parts for above
1,000 navy cutlasses

Under certain conditions, C.S.N. vessels of war were designated as cargo carriers. A fast screw steam sloopof-war, the *McRae*, 830 tons, armed with one 9-inch pivot gun and six 32-pdrs, 152 men, under command of Lieutenant Huger, was due to arrive in London in early August, and carried a number of despatches for North and Bulloch. They were instructed to purchase at once 10,000 good Enfield rifles, or rifled mustkets with bayonets, "without regard to prices," and send them in the *McRae* on her return trip. Additionally, 2,000 muskets were wanted for the Navy, and powder, "put in large casks like hardware."

If the *McRae* could not be loaded in a British port with this freight, Navy Secretary Mallory suggested that Bulloch arrange to have it lightered aboard outside the zone, or if that failed, ship it to Nassau, New Providence, to the Confederate States shipping agent Henry Adderly, "for and on account of a supercargo on board, who should be some discreet man having our interest at heart." Mallory's instructions were "mellerdramatie" but vital: "Powder in kegs could be shipped in large casks like hardware, as could pistols and Enfield rifles also, apart from their stocks. But the stocks should go in the same casks with their barrels."

Bulloeh set about buying guns. "None of the leading gun factories were in a position to take contracts, except upon a very long time, and I was forced to adopt the plan Captain Huse fell into, of employing a commission house here familiar with the gun trade and d rectors in the London Armoury Company to contract for the sea service rifles my orders called for, with the small makers in Birmingham and elsewhere." One of the directors of the London Armoury Company was Arehibald Hamilton, of Sinelair, Hamilton & Company and it was doubtless this firm which aided Bulloch in his early purchases. One hundred sea-service rifles with eutlass-bayonets attached were contracted for. While these may have been 33-inch short rifles, the mysterious JS-Anchor carbines would also fit the bill. These arms are short, 24-inch Enfield pattern guns, .577 caliber, with 24-inch barrels and folding leaf shortrange rear sights. Such arms were also issued to the British artillery. Identification of these arms is uncertain, but the coincidence of names and facts leads to some possible or reasonable conjectures; suppositions which may be tracked down as fact if enough pieces of the puzzle can be put together.

Bulloch's revolvers were probably 1,000 obtained from London Armoury, of the Kerr pattern. These in the London Armoury Company series or registration number bracket of 9,000 have the cryptic JS-Anchor mark inside the curve of the handle, which has been noticed on Confederate-Association Kerrs. This same mark is seen on the stock of an Enfield 24-inch twoband musketoon, artillery carbine, or, if equipped with cutlass bayonet, sea-service rifle, in the author's colleetion. As previously stated, the meaning of the initials is not known. But there was a London commission merchant with these initials, acting in consonance with a Birmingham gun maker, J. D. Goodman. The firm was known as J. Scholefield, Sons & Goodman, and their agent in the Confederate States was Archibald McLaurin of New Orleans (Fuller misspells the name "Schofield). This worthy was detained by General Ben Butler upon the latter's occupation of the city, and on July 10, 1862, made a sworn statement concerning his activities there in the arms importing trade. In June, 1861, 200 rifles had been shipped by J. Scholefield, Sons & Goodman, to McLaurin but were diverted to Havana. He sold 100 to the "Confederate Guards," deliverable in Havana; these were captured by the United States. About March, 1861, McLaurin also received (at Havana) a sample Wilson's breech-loading rifle.

It is possible that not Archibald Hamilton, but J. Scholefield was the arranger for Bulloch of the sea-service arms and the Kerr revolvers being made under contract for the Confederate States Navy, and that the stamp of their house signifying ships' chandlers and naval stores, was the otherwise inexplicable "JS-Anchor." Such arms could have been made available in the summer of 1861 to Huse and to Bulloch due to the breakdown of their sales outlet in New Orleans, the interned Mr. McLaurin, who (while languishing in a Federal prison) could no longer be expected to receive any shipments from them. JS-Anchor Kerr revolvers tabulated include: No. 2266 (ad. of James Tice in *Shotgun News,* December 15, 1961), No. 3801 (Albaugh, *Confederate Arms,* p. 34); and No. 9239 (a private collector, on loan to the author). In Fuller & Steuart, *Confederate Firearms,* is pictured a Kerr listed as "Used in the Confederate Army," No. 9224. A Kerr in the 10,000's, also single action like No. 9239, is engraved "Bank of England," and has a dovetail large blade foresight. The Albaugh-pictured gun and that in Fuller have triggers the front edges of which just come to the back edge of the trigger guard base; the trigger flange at rear is scant of the deep-curved profile of the single action guns; it is thought these are double action though no mention is made in either book.

But of all the guns, the Fuller pistol has one unaccountable feature: the screw for the loading lever pivot (all enter from the frame right side) is located near to the front curve of the frame (others are in the middle of the frame flat area) and there is less space forward of the cylinder for loading and fouling; the Fuller pistol No. 9224 bullet cut-out is to the rear of a line drawn vertically across the axis and touching the edge of the frame front at the hinge; the others have bullet cuts exactly on that line. The frame end at hinge of the Fuller gun is more rounded than the specimens noted as JS-anchor guns, and there is a difference in shape of the loading lever split lug under barrel.

The significance of these major manufacturing differences between Fuller's Confederate Association "Army" Kerr revolver and others made the same day (if closeness of registration numbers is any indication) also of C.S.A. usage, is not known. Sufficient to say that Kerr revolvers from the 3,000's to the 9,000's are known of Confederate association; one in the 10,-000's is Bank of England, suggesting the end of fabrication for the South, but there is too little understood on serials of known Confederate Kerrs to reveal a full pattern. Probably the registration numbers run consecutively as Kerrs were manufactured, but that batches went to the mysterious "JS" for stamping with his mark, and thence to the Southern Confederacy. Other batches were withdrawn for commercial or military contract sale, as to the Government of Portugal. Inconclusive, it is hoped these cerebrations will help some student of Confederate States arms to find the missing pieces on the incomplete but interesting story of the Confederate Kerr revolvers, for certainly some of Major Huse's purchases were delivered!

The Adams Revolver

London Armoury Company was not exclusively of interest to Confederates. Its revolvers of the Adams design, and those made by the preceding company identities, Deane, Adams, and Deane, and Robert Adams, were rather widely distributed in the North and in Dixie before the war. The first weapon, the Adams revolver, were made in pocket, Navy, and dragoon sizes, while the Adams-Beaumont design was made under license in the United States by the Massachusetts Arms Company of Chicopee Falls, for the Adams Revolving Arms Company of New York. A few in .36 caliber were bought by the United States Government officially, while the small .31 caliber pistol was of limited popularity as an officer's or gentleman's sidearm.

The Army officer who first brought the Adams' revolver to Uncle Sam's attention was Major Alfred Mordecai of the Ordnance Corps. On his trip abroad in 1854, he purchased an Adams revolver made under license by Auguste Francotte, in Liege. Carefully he drew a sketch of the Adams double action which made it possible to fire five shots as quickly as the trigger could be pulled.

"The Deane and Adams revolver differs from Colt's well known pistol, chiefly in the mechanism, by which the simple pulling of the trigger causes the chambered breech to revolve, and cocks and discharges the piece at the same time," said Mordecai. "The workmanship of the pistol is very good, and the arm appears to have met with much favor; but it still wants the test of actual service, and it may be doubted whether it is expedient to arm any part of the troops with a weapon which can be discharged with such exceeding facility and rapidity. It is understood that some of these pistols have been ordered by the Ordnance Department, for trial in our service. At present, they are sold at about 2/3rds of the cost of Colt's revolver."

The Adams revolvers ordered by the United States Government were not foreign-made guns but Massachusetts Arms Company revolvers. While one is known listed as marked "Ames Arms Company, Chicopee

Falls, Massachusetts, (United States Cartridge Company Collection catalog No. 694) the average specimen found is stamped on the top flat of the frame with "Manufactured by/Mass. Arms Co./Chicopee Falls" in three lines. The frame is also marked on the right side "Patent June 3, 1856," and on the left side "Adams Patent May 3, 1858." The loading lever is marked "Kerr's Patent April 14, 1857."

This particular model of revolver made in Massachusetts has two readily visible differences from the Beaumont-Adams of 1856 which was made in London. First, the handle is checkered toward the bottom but has a smooth area of wood near to where it joins the frame. The handle, to the practised eye, is more curved, less backward-slanting, than the regular Adams. In addition, a major improvement has been made in the Adams flat-framed revolver, by the addition of a flange plate on the left side behind the percussion cones. Adams, first large-scale maker of the revolver in Britain, was prevented by Sam Colt's London patent from making a revolver frame which shielded the user from flash-back if an adjoining charge should go off when the barrel charge was fired. This hazard occurred sometimes with Colt's arms, notably with an issue of revolving breech carbines to the Marines in 1841 during the Florida war with the Seminoles. The cylinders had been made from undersized bar stock, jumped up and brazed to close up the fissures. This malpractice produced a cylinder somewhat honeycombed, and fire from one shot could communicate through to the next chamber. This also could occur if a revolver had lain long with powder in the chambers, loaded or uncleaned. Corrosion might pin-hole the cylinder web enough for a second shot to go off. But with the British revolvers an even more common accident might set off adjoining shots. The accident is so easily made that personal experience, in which the author nearly lost the sight of his shooting eye, would condemn the whole class of flat-framed British revolvers as unsafe for shooting, for the firing cap can flash over and by sympathetic detonation or actual fire set off the next shot.

The Adams, and British revolvers which followed it, rotate the charges from left to right. Consequently, those chambers to the right of the bore are empty; those to the left, still loaded. Often it is necessary to pinch the percussion caps slightly to make them fit tightly, if caps of the exact size are not on hand. Further, the shoulders between the nipples are not as high nor the cones as deeply set as Colt's. In shooting a Webley .450, very similar to the Adams Beaumont of the United States trials, the author had the misfortune to see a great orange blossom of flame proceeding back from the left chamber, being left-handed and shooting using his left eye. There was no time but to close the eyes, and this he did, taking the full force of the stinging gas and tiny brass particles in the face. The brass worked its way out of the many tiny cuts but some burning powder tattoo marks still linger about eye and nose.

The discharge happened so rapidly that the barrel bullet was thrown by excessive recoil out of line a foot, striking the top of the target carrier at about 10 yards, and bending into an L. The chamber which discharged threw the ball forward, jamming it against the side-plunger loading lever. The next in line to the left, and the one beside the barrel to the right (starting with a full cylinder) were both heavily washed and eroded with powder gas. That no other shot discharged, quite conclusively proved that charges did not go off because of flash across the muzzles of the chambers, as so many modern day shooters apprehend. But that caps can be flashed if pinched and the priming exposed seems proved.

Regardless of the general literature of the period, this hazard must have been recognized by either an official of Massachuetts Arms Company, or of the Government. Taking the Adams regular flat frame, a milling cut was made to receive the base of an angle iron, the upstanding edge of which was curved slightly to match the cylinder profile. This flange was enough to do what the heavy round bosses do at the back of the Colt frame: protect the shooter in case of accident. As only 600 of this type were procured by the United States, and an unknown number but (evidently few) made for commercial sale in both Navy and the pocket sizes, this is the safest, and among the scarcest, of the Adams pistols. Caliber .36 was chosen for the United States trial guns, although the same frame in England carried a .450 cylinder. Traditionally, double action in the United States Service is associated with naval boarding parties, and these guns may have served for this purpose in the war. In addition, Adams pistols were purchased by both North and South during the war, direct from England.

No specific markings have been noted on Adams guns which might in any way suggest Confederate States or United States use. General "Stonewall" Jackson had an Adams cased set; the U. S. guns were routed through Schuyler, Hartley & Graham of New York. On November 11, 1861, 120 Adams revolvers, double action, were purchased from them by the United States at $18 each. The same type of goods, to judge by the price of $18, again was purchased December 3, 1861, billed as "93 Adams pistols English self-cocking." But on December 13 they delivered a bundle of Christmas cheer consisting of: 7 Adams revolvers, 12 Adams revolvers self-cocking, and 16 Kerr's patent revolvers, all at $18 each; and 26 "Beaumont's revolvers" at $19. The "Adams revolver" is believed to be the original model, which was double action only, having a spurless hammer. But, as S. B. Haw indicated in "The Adams Revolver" (*Army Ordnance*, January-February 1938), quite a bit of work was done during the same period [transition era of 1854-55 when the Beaumont selective single or double action was introduced] in changing over a number of the old self-cocking model to double action, the main features of Beaumont's lock design making this relatively simple. These conversions can be identified easily—the presence of a hammer with a thumb piece together with a butt of the earlier type on the same gun being the most obvious clue. Haw used the words "double action" when he really meant, "single as well as double or self-cocking action."

These first type Adams arms, probably the big Adams "Dragoon" .50 caliber, with hammer spur SA feature, are thought to have been the S.H. & G. plain "7 Adams revolvers." The more common spurless hammer Adams, using double action only, is listed as "self cocking." The Kerr revolvers presumably are *not* JS-Anchor guns—or are they? "Beaumont's revolvers" are the late type Beaumont-Adams, mechanically identical to the guns manufactured under Adams patents by Massachusetts Arms Company. But on December 24, they delivered "115 Adams revolvers, double action," at $18; on January 20, 1862, "25 Adams revolvers, self-cocking," at $18; on February 17, 1862, "144 Adams revolvers" at $18; March 1, "60 Adams revolvers" at $18; March 11, "22 Adams Eng. revolvers" at $18, and on March 14, "25 self-cocking revolvers" at $18. The last shipment of Adams revolvers taken by the United States from Schuyler, Hartley & Graham, was 24 "Adams revolvers" at $18 April 23, 1862. The coincidence of price suggests all these arms were very much the same pattern of gun and, in spite of the dollar extra paid for Beaumont revolvers, when itemized separately, we tend to think these were the more common Beaumont-Adams revolver Model 1856.

Marcellus Hartley, with an eye for fancy goods, made a point of stocking the Maiden Lane store in New York with these arms in fancy cases, elaborately engraved and fitted with solid silver or German-silver flasks, moulds, and accessories. One of these Beaumont-Adams fancy arms (mistakenly identified as a Tranter) is pictured in Albaugh's book, as having been presented to General J. B. Magruder, C.S.A., and is so marked.

There is a distinct probability that this arm was obtained in New York by a Rebel sympathizer directly from Hartley's store and smuggled South—either overland, or bounced by ship from New York to Bermuda or New Providence, and then into a Southern port.

Arms Smuggled South

This system of transshipment was one which Caleb Huse, General Gorgas, Secretary Mallory, and Commodore Bulloch had worked out to a fine art. Their two key men were Major Smith Stansbury of the Confederate States Ordnance Department and a local St. George's, Bermuda, commission merchant, John T. Bourne. Nassau also was an important transshipping point, but Federal cruisers by August of 1862 had made things pretty hot for potential blockade runners, and Huse shifted his shipments to St. George's. In the warehouses of Bourne, of W. L. Penno and J. W. Musson, cases marked "merchandise" or "hardware" loomed high, neatly stacked as only chests holding 20 rifles or muskets can be stacked. "Combustibles" there were, enough stored to blow that wharfside section of town off the map.

From these reserves kept high by shipments from Huse, Stansbury was able to make shipments on the blockade runners in response to the demands of General Gorgas. But the system was not perfect, and through the years the increasing power of the U. S. fleets, as one coastal city after another fell to the boys in blue, gradually shut off the supplies. There was soon to come an end to Major Huse' buying spree. Huse himself summed up the scope of activities in his *Memoirs:*

> During the first two years, the captures were so infrequent that, it may be safely stated, never before was a Government at war so well supplied with arms, munitions, clothing, and medicines—everything, in short, that an army requires—with so little money as was paid by the Confederacy. The shipment from England to the Islands in ordinary tramp steamers; the landing and storage there, and the running of the blockade, cost money; but all that was needed came from cotton practically given to the Confederate Government by its owners.
>
> The supplies were, in every instance, bought at the lowest cash prices by men trained in the work as contractors for the British army. No credit was asked. Merchants having needed supplies were frankly told that our means were limited, and our payments would be made by cheques on Fraser, Trenholm & Co., Liverpool, an old established and conservative house. The effect of such buying was to create confidence on the part of the sellers, which made them more anxious to sell than we were to purchase. When the end came, and some of the largest sellers were ruined, I never heard a word of complaint of their being over-reached or in any manner treated unfairly.

In Defense of Huse

Huse steered a delicate course through the conflicting interests of such firms as Fraser, Trenholm, or S. Isaac, Campbell & Company. He kept them happy, in spite of the final collapse of the Confederacy. During the height of the buying when he handled million of dollars almost without possibility of searching accounting, he apparently played the game straight. He refused subsidiary compensation for his work, saying his commission in the Confederate Army was enough.

Major B. Ficklin, upon his return to the South from a tour of duty abroad, reported to Seddon on January 3, 1863 that he was convinced from things he had seen and heard, that the gun-buying Major was "robbing the Confederate Government in a most shameful manner." He admitted he could not prove this in court, but he felt it his duty as a Confederate citizen to report what he had heard. But Huse had such powerful and respected people on his side as Mason and Slidell. The latter in writing to Confederate States financier McRae in Paris, February 14, 1864, described Huse as being "animated by an anxious desire to perform most scrupulously and consistently, the duties entrusted to him." Huse may have achieved this reputation with Slidell when that gentleman's colleague, James H. Mason, communicated some of Mason's astonishment at being "faced down" by Huse in a firm but courteous manner some months before. As Huse recalls it, their interview went like this:

> Mr. Mason . . . had, for forty years been a prominent member of the United States Senate, and seemed never to be unmindful of the presence and importance of the Honourable

James H. Mason of Virginia . . . I saw but little of Mr. Mason . . . There was in Mr. Mason no magnetism to attract young men, and I do not remember ever to have asked his advice or opinion. In this he presented a strong contrast to all the other Commissioners. Mr. Slidell was as old a man and as experienced in public affairs as Mr. Mason, but he was a genial companion to younger men, and I consulted him quite . . . freely.

One morning I received a note from Mr. Mason's secretary, asking me to call at Mr. Mason's lodgings. I lost no time in obeying the summons, and Mr. Mason lost no time in coming to business.

"Major," he said, "I have sent for you to request you to inspect some army supplies that some of our English friends are sending over under a contract with the War Department."

Without a moment's hesitation, I replied, "Mr. Mason, I will inspect the contract, and if I approve, I will inspect the goods."

I cannot convey an adequate idea of the man's astonishment. It was too great for him to express himself immediately. He was standing in front of the grate. Taking a package of "fine-cut" from his pocket, and removing from his mouth an immense quid which he threw into the grate, he replaced it with a fresh wad and, looking at me, said, "Do you know who I am? Whom do you look upon as your superiors?"

Instantly, but very quietly, I replied, "I believe you are the Honorable James M. Mason, Confederate States Commissioner to England."

"Yes," he replied, "and in a very few days I shall be Minister of the Confederate States to the Court of St. James."

I then said, "I acknowledge no superior on this side of the ocean, in America the Secretary of War and all officers senior to me are my superiors, and especially Colonel Gorgas, from whom I receive my orders. Not only on general principles can I take no orders from you, but I have an order sent me after the Battle of Bull Run, giving me *carte blanche*, and directing me not to allow myself to be governed by political emissaries of the Government. Now, if you are not a political emissary of the Government, I don't know what you are."

Though Huse stated there was no more controversy, the "dispute" lasted some time. But we suspect Huse had a better friend in the self-important Mr. Mason than he realized, for the integrity of Mason was not under fire. He must have appreciated the strict sense of duty which Huse showed by speaking up so quickly and refusing to allow himself to be "pressured"—indeed, the whole interview might have been arranged as a test to determine how Huse would react. Gorgas' continuing faith in the loyalty and correct deportment of his young protege were upheld, and Huse was not interfered with in his special assignment for the "duration."

There is a possible basis for the charges he was feathering his own nest. He may in fact have been doing so, but not at the expense of the Confederate States Government. His travels allowed him to cement relationships with leading men in the arms trade, which six years later he turned to his private account. He was living in New York, at 17 Broad Street. Then, as an American citizen, forgiven his treasonous role in being the keystone in the whole Confederate ordnance "arch," he was permitted to bid in United States surplus arms at the great post-war government auctions. On October 30, 1870, Huse was awarded 13,000 Enfield muskets at $8.50 and 2,600,000 musket cartridges at $16.50 per thousand; these might have been arms which he actually bought and shipped to the South, later to be captured by the North, cleaned and repaired, and ultimately resold to him! November 15, he bought 800 Spencer rifles at $30 each and 324,576 Spencer cartridges at $18/M; and on November 25, 30,000 cartridge boxes and belts at $1.41. Huse also bid on 14,000 new Springfield rifle muskets at $10.75, but was a dollar to two dollars under the winning bids by Austin Baldwin, Herman Boker, and Hartley. Symbolically, this concluded Huse's career in the arms field, for in America in 1870 as in the arms markets of Europe in 1861-65, he was ultimately outbid by Austin Baldwin, Herman Boker, and Marcellus Hartley.

UDC soldier monument at Monterey, Va., commemorates Johnny Reb. CSA troops had .577 cal. muzzleloading Enfields run past blockade from England, but sculptor used an Enfield rifle made ca. WWI. The SMLE or short, magazine, Lee-Enfield, .303 high velocity, ten-shot breechloader, in the hands of good marksman from prone will put 36 shots a minute into 30" circle at 300 yards. With these rifles in the hands of Southern troops, the national capital would be Richmond, Virginia, today!

Note: Caleb Huse's uncle James Tyler Ames, was of the notable Yankee gunmaking family. His brother Samuel Huse was an Acting Volunteer Lieutenant in the U. S. Navy. (Remarked to author by Andrew F. Lustyik, letter 5 April 1963.)

CHAPTER 10

Breechloaders of Chicopee

Ultimately, this was a war between breechloaders. Though the transitions, the development of technology in manufacturing and gun design which permitted abandonment of the single shot muzzle-loader, were rapid in coming, most informed military men realized the replacement of the musket by the rapid fire breechloader was inevitable. In the line, the needs of war for "cannon fodder" caused resistance to novel forms of small arms being used. But in the elite corps, the cavalry, inheritor of the dandy troop reputation of the famous 1st and 2nd Dragoons, considerable variation in equipment was permitted. The enlisted men's uniform for cavalry was similar to that of infantry and the other arms, officially. Instead of the infantry's hip-length blouse the cavalryman wore a waist-long jacket of dark blue laced with yellow; high standing collar and trousers of sky-blue (1857 regulation) or dark blue (1861 regulation) bearing a yellow stripe down each leg. About his waist was wound twice a red silk or worsted sash over which was buckled a wide black leather saber belt. From his left hip two sling straps supported the saber, either Model 1840 dragoon pattern or new light cavalry of 1860 style. A shoulder strap attached to D rings supported the weight of the saber which could be put reversed on a belt hook when not in use. His hat could be that dark-blue forage kind dryly described as "of pattern in the Quartermaster-General's office," but more romantically called "Sherman's bummer cap" by later scribes. For dress he wore a high-crowned stiff dark blue felt hat, "Jeff Davis style" so-called in honor of Secretary of War Davis who authorized it in the 1850's as an improvement over the heavy, sweaty leather shako. But the implement of dress which distinguished him from all others, which proclaimed from a distance that "here stands a cavalryman," was the 2-inch black leather belt crossing his right shoulder and supporting, upside down from a snaffle hook clipped onto a frame-attached ring, one of the many patterns of breech-loading carbines in use.

Activation of Cavalry Units Stimulates Production

Like mushrooms overnight the business of supplying Uncle Sam with breechloaders sprang up. Activation of the cavalry sent heavy demands for small arms to General Ripley's office. Though the good Chief of Ordnance was of the opinion that there was no better arm in the world for ordinary service than the Springfield rifle musket, he acceded to demands for breechloaders for the horse soldiers. And when Ripley bought carbines, he really bought 'em. The cavalry unit commander had upwards of 25 different arms to choose from, each one distinctively different from its competitors in respect of some claim or other of its agent or inventor. Some were notably unsuccessful, such as the Symmes (drop block with Maynard primer), the Schenkl and Schroeder (needle-fire of the Dreyse German patent type) and other experimental and pre-war limited issue test guns. Others were quite successful, either in the field or commercially in being bought in quantities. Some have come down to us as almost household words: Sharps, Spencer, Henry. These were the best, the Big Three of the Union carbines.

Those bought privately, such as the Henry which sold briskly in Cincinnati, and those captured or copied, such as the Sharps made in Richmond, Virginia, did good service for the South as well. While many arms were carbines exclusively, those such as the Sharps were employed in rifle form by the infantry, and the Spencer-armed infantrymen of the Union, Michigan brigades especially, are credited with materially affecting the outcome of battle.

The Maynard

One arm which enjoyed considerable popularity was a tipping barrel breechloader invented by Dr. Maynard. Though but a single shot arm, using an unprimed but perforated-base brass shell cartridge, the Maynard was very practical. Its simplicity made it a favorite of non-mechanical farm boys, while the reloadable brass cartridge could be used in the gun again. It was fired either by roll caps from the Maynard primer magazine or, as on the later models which were made without the primer, using ordinary musket or rifle caps on the nipple. The design of this arm, which moved the barrel slightly forward and allowed it to tip downwards, upon unhinging the under-lever that also served as a trigger guard, influenced the arms of the Stevens Arms Company.

Maynard First Model carbine also supplied as a rifle and, rarely, as a complete sporting outfit with extra barrels of different calibers on same breech. With Maynard primer magazine on frame, this is evidently the rifle of Toby in the "Mississippi army."

This firm succeeded to some of the interests of the Massachusetts Arms Company that in its last days, post-bellum, took the name "Maynard Rifle Company," and in honor of the Washington dentist designated one of their popular cheap little single shots at the turn of the century, the "Maynard, Jr." Though a sensible gun, it was hardly the paragon of armaments virtue which some unsung publicist tried to persuade his Southern readers to believe in *Marginalia,* published in 1864. They were told that:

Toby is a high private in the first regiment of the Mississippi Army. His company is armed with the breech-loading Maynard rifle, warranted to shoot twelve times a minute and to carry a ball effectively 1600 yards. Men who fought at Buena Vista and Monterey call the new-fangled thing a pop gun. To test its efficacy, Toby's captain told the men they must try their guns. In obedience to the command, Toby procured the necessary munitions of war, and started with his pop gun for the woods. Saw a squirrel up a high tree, took aim, fired. Effects of shot immediate and wonderful. Tree effectually topped, and nothing to be found of the squirrel except two broken hairs. Pop gun rose in value—equal to a four-pounder. But Toby wouldn't shoot towards any more trees, afraid of being arrested for cutting down other people's timber. Walked a mile and a quarter to get sight of a hill. By aid of a small telescope, saw hill in distance; saw a large rock on hill; put in a big load; shut both eyes—fired. As soon as breath returned, opened eyes, could see, just could, but couldn't hear; at least couldn't distinguish any sounds; thought Niagara had broken loose or all out-doors gone to drum beating. Determined to see if shot hit.

Borrowed horse and started towards hill. After traveling two days and nights, reached place; saw sun setting through the hill. Knew right away that was where the shot hit. Went closer—stumbled over rocky fragments for half a mile in line of bullet. Came to hole—knew the bullet hit there, because saw lead on the edges—walked in, walked through; saw teamster on the other side, indulging in profane language, in fact, cussin' considerable, because lightning had killed his team. Looked as finger directed, saw six dead oxen in line with the hole through the mountain; knew that was the bullet's work but didn't say so to angry teamster. Thought best to be leaving; in consequence, didn't explore path of bullet any further; therefore don't know where it stopped; don't know whether it stopped at all, in fact, rather think it didn't. Mounted horse, rode back through the hole made by the bullet; but never told captain a word about it; to tell the truth was a little afraid he'd think it was a hoax.

"It is a right big story, boys," said Toby in conclusion, "but it's true, sure as shooting. Nothing to do with Maynard rifle but load her up, turn her north, and pull the trigger; if twenty of them don't clear out all Yankeedom, then I'm a liar, that's all."

While no one would dare accuse Toby of a falsehood, his narrative of the great Maynard Rifle shot does read like an exaggeration of some modern advertising claims for super velocity and magnum sporting rifles. Doubtless the 1st Mississippi (CS) Regiment was invincible, but in this case, at least, the Maynard rifle did not affect the outcome of the war.

Two slightly different Maynard rifles were in service during the war. The earliest follows Maynard's patents of May 27, 1851 (No. 8126) and December 6, 1859 (No. 26364), having a primer magazine on the right of the breech, feeding the pelleted tape forward each time the hammer is cocked. A total of 400 of these were purchased by the United States in 1857. The barrel is pivoted to the action which extends forward of the solid breech several inches, beneath the barrel. When the lever-trigger guard is lowered, the barrel tips down at the hinge, exposing the chamber for loading or unloading. The case, straight-walled in the early models, has a wide flanged base. The barrel being beveled slightly at the rear edges, the fingers can grasp this flange or rim and pull the fired cartridge out. Appleton's *American Annual Cyclopedia* for 1864 eulogizes the dentist's delight thusly:

"Springs, bolts and catches are not used in this rifle, but the ends required are attained by the careful adjustment and excellent finish of the several parts, which work with mathematical precision, and give it the solidity of a mass of steel, which is not affected by any strain to which it can be exposed."

Sounding about as fact-packed as the average modern cigarette ad, this gibberish does hide a really distinctive and distinguished arm. The lever is attached by a movable pivot pin somewhat like that of the Sharps form. The pivot pin's arm being locked back, it also secures the Maynard primer door which is hinged at the bottom edge to swing out and down. The butt plate is unique, being rounded toe and heel, almost symmetrical, and formed to act as base for the "patchbox." The box holds two extra rolls of Maynard caps. While the carbine has a fixed rear sight blade mortised crossways on the barrel above the hinge, some are fitted with early tang sights. A typical U.S. issue carbine has a 20-inch barrel, and the action is stamped "Maynard Arms Co., Washington, Manufactured by Massachusetts Arms Company,

Regular U.S. Cavalry issue Maynard carbine. Patent dates can be seen stamped on left side of receiver. Barrel tips up at hinge to load from rear with flanged metallic cartridge having pierced base, uses cap on center nipple.

Chicopee Falls, Maynard Patentee, September 22, 1845, May 29, 1851, June 17, 1856." Caliber is nominally .50, taking a brass reloadable case with a central flash hole.

The second type of Maynard carbine is far more common, and does not have the Maynard primer magazine. It is the model obtained during the Civil War, of which 20,002 were purchased by the Federal Government, and thousands more by states North and South. With cheerful impartiality, the Massachusetts Arms Company fabricated and Dr. Maynard sold many of the First Model primer guns to the South.

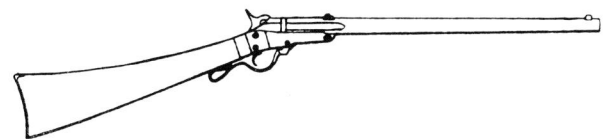

Cut of Maynard issue cavalry carbine, from *Official Records Atlas*.

The Confederate *Field Manual for the Use of Officers on Ordnance Duty* states: "Maynard's carbine has a fixed chamber. There are two calibers in our service. Large size, caliber .52 (.50)-inch. Small size, caliber .36 (.35)-inch. Maynard's primer, attached to this carbine, contains 60 primers in a row, on a tape or ribbon of paper. A primer is moved under the hammer by the act of cocking. The charge is enclosed in a cylinder of sheet brass."

Because of the easily removed barrel, which lifts off the frame when the hinge pin is withdrawn, Maynards were among the first arms to have different calibers and lengths of barrel supplied. One main breech and stock would do for various types of shooting and hunting. But few long barreled Maynards of military form, suitable to be called "rifles" are known; possibly the redoubtable Toby's 1st Mississippi Regiment had carbines, probably of the first type Maynard primer model.

Arms Manufacturers in Massachusetts

The arms-making combine, Massachusetts Arms Company, which produced the Maynard guns, built and also patented arms of other inventors. Within the Chicopee Falls area north of Springfield, Massachusetts, existed several firms which were interlocking in either management or in cooperation. For example, the Smith carbines, of which large numbers were ordered by the Government, were built in part by Massachusetts Arms, and in part by the nearby American Machine Works in Springfield. The odd turning-barrel Greene carbines ordered by the British in 1857 were made by Massachusetts Arms; and there is some reason to suppose the Greene oval-bore breech-loading rifles were also made at Chicopee during the war. Behind this weapons combine lies the little-known person of Daniel Leavett, and an almost unheard of factory entity, the Chicopee Falls Manufacturing Company.

The name of this firm was first brought to the attention of arms men by the noted collector-dealer, W. G. C. Kimball, himself of Woburn, Massachusetts, near Boston. Writing in *The American Rifleman*, September 1948, Kimball pictured an odd light flintlock rifle. "It has a back action flintlock and is marked with the signature 'Chicopee Falls Mfg. Co.' On the barrel of the rifle near the breech is the Government

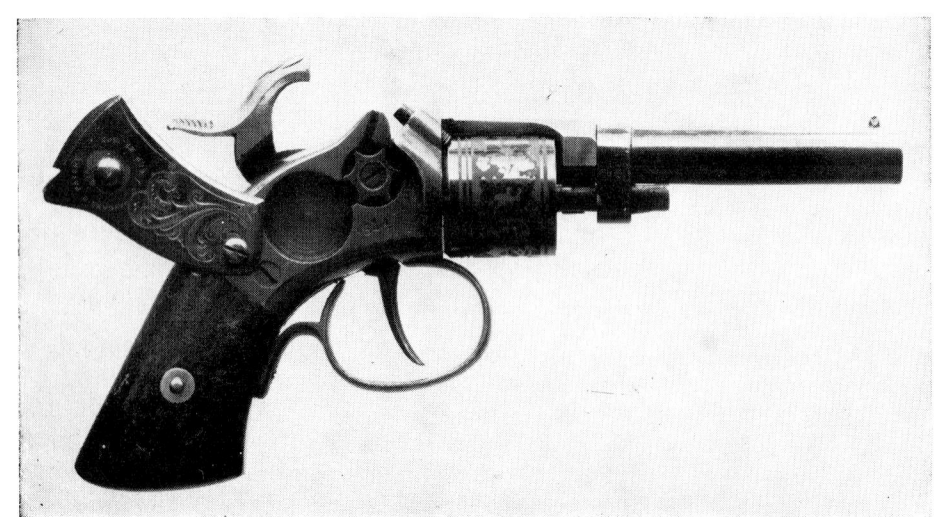

Joshua Stevens designed this Mass. Arms Company revolver with central fixed nipple which flashed fire through chamber holes in cylinder. Cogwheel fed pelleted Maynard primer tape forward into line with hammer as it was cocked. Type received little use, was replaced in firm's line by Robert Adams revolvers.

inspector's initials 'N W P' for N. W. Patch, who was sent out by the Springfield Armory to inspect contract arms between 1839 and 1848," Kimball recounts. While he speculates briefly on the nature of this odd military-type piece, a look at the type of lock tends to reveal its antecedents. The lock is of a type pioneered in the French *fusil a la ligne Mdle* 1840, percussion. The French arm has the lockplate end just forward of the front edge of the hammer. In transforming these arms to smoothbore flintlocks for the African trade, the gunmakers of Liege attached a supplementary plate forward of the hammer, which they had changed to a flint cock, and on the supplementary plate they attached a pan and flint battery or pan cover. (Curiously, a similar lock is on the almost unique Jenks First Model carbines.) The appearance of the musket shown by Kimball suggests that he has a Belgian trade gun using a U.S. barrel. The bands fitted to the arm Kimball shows resemble currently-used cheap bands on trade arms now much sold in the United States. Whether this little-known musket in some fashion served as a model for the Liege trade, or is a case of parallel invention by the American gunsmith, is beside the point. In researching the marks on the gun, Kimball pieced together a good deal of the business background which went into the Massachusetts Arms Company complex. The names are those of famous gunmakers; and their connections are surprising.

Chicopee Falls Concerns

In 1836 monied men of Chicopee organized a company for the manufacture of guns and hardware. The package is not unusual; many companies of that time were organized to include gun-making potential, and never made a gun. Colt's early company at Paterson, New Jersey, formed in 1836, was organized to make "arms, tools and cutlery," but no butcher knives have as yet turned up marked "Patent Arms Mfg. Co., Patterson, N. J." with the city name characteristically misspelled. Few indeed must have been the guns made directly by the Chicopee Falls Manufacturing Company as these gentlemen called their local concern. Incorporated for $25,000, it was raised in 1839 to $100,000. President was T. W. Carter, who was also agent for the Chicopee Manufacturing Company, a textile machinery firm owned by Daniel Leavitt.

It appears possible that the company at first intended to manufacture a revolver based on Leavitt's patent issued April 29, 1837, No. 182 (new series). A hand-turning cylinder gun, this pistol was made as a patent model featuring a military style stock. In the temper of the times, with prospect of war over many issues in the 1830's, if Uncle Sam could only settle in his mind who he planned to fight, military gun-making was a popular, though expensive, form of investment. No pure Daniel Leavitt revolvers were ever produced.

Gluckman does list a percussion cadet musket, back action lock, marked "Chicopee Falls Co." Certainly neither names nor precise manufactured articles are clear in these beginning stages of Chicopee gunmaking. Interested men in the concern were David M. Bryant, an early merchant in Chicopee Falls and Carter's partner; John Chase, Springfield Canal Company manager who would expect to profit from increased trade as the wares of the firm were boated to market; and Benjamin Belcher, T. W. Buckland, and Nathan Peabody Ames.

Ames

Ames owned another arms works, the Ames Manufacturing Company, also in Chicopee. Formed in 1829, the Ames company by 1831 was a primary sword maker for the U.S. Government. By 1836 Ames employed 35 men and removed to a suburb known as Cabotsville. In 1840 the Chicopee Falls Manufacturing Company failed, from "inefficiency and bad management." Early in 1841, Ames, feeling that Government work was more steady, bought the Chicopee Falls Manufacturing Company plant for expansion; then went abroad to study arms manufacture in the centers of Europe. He returned with a reputation as an expert and was able to fabricate the Navy pistol of 1843 for the United States as well as keep a steady supply of the Artillery Swords, M1840, and other edged weapons flowing from his forges. The Mexican War caused an increase over his 1845 work force of 130 men, and Ames turned out swords, carbines, pistols, and was especially noted for manufacture of field and light artillery, the bronze howitzers with which young United States officer Braxton Bragg fought against the Mexicans.

In 1849, Ames decided to confine his work to Cabotsville and dispose of his Chicopee Falls property. Some of the original investors, now increased by Leavitt and Edwin Wesson, of a famous gunmaking family, bought the unhappy firm back from Ames and decided to make it go. Wesson himself had added improvements to the revolver of Leavitt, including mechanically turning the cylinder by the act of cocking the hammer.

Dr. Maynard's priming device seemed about all that was necessary to make it perfect. Rights to use this design were obtained but at about this time, Edwin Wesson died, January 31, 1849. His affairs were taken over by his younger brother, Daniel Baird Wesson, whose name is well known as founder of the present firm Smith & Wesson. The connection between Smith and Wesson may date from this time, instead of several years later as most writers have put it. For it was a man named "Smith" who paid out the money which Massachusetts Arms Company had to remit to Colt in royalty fees for making proved infringements of his revolver patents the following year.

Other Revolver Makers

To begin more or less at the beginning, Wesson and Leavitt commenced production of the Leavitt-modified revolver under Patent No. 6999 issued to Wesson executor E. J. Ripley. As principal workmen they employed William Henry Miller and Joshua Stevens, who in 1848 had worked for Colt's in Hartford. As employees of Sam Colt, under contract to supervise modification of Whitneyville-Walker parts to the 1848 Dragoon type, Miller and Stevens were bound to devote their time while in the shop to Colt's interests. However, due (as they claimed) to slow delivery from workmen who preceded them in the process of manufacture, they found a little spare time on their hands. Being of an inventive turn of mind and much struck by a critical deficiency in the Colt principal of assembly, with the barrel mounted upon a rather weakly fixed cylinder pin, Miller and Stevens decided to improve it.

They took as the basis for their improvement an odd revolving rifle designed by Elija Jacquith in 1838. In the Jacquith design, the cylinder is mounted above the line of barrel and there is a strap which holds barrel to frame below the cylinder. Sight is taken through the hollow cylinder arbor. Few Jacquith revolving guns were ever made, but to Stevens and Miller it seemed to possess fundamental principles they could profitably apply. Their model was the basis for the Massachusetts Arms revolvers.

Then Colt discharged Stevens and Miller. He wrote to Senator Rusk in fear the story might jeopardize his business with the Government, on July 19, 1848, as follows: "I discovered yesterday that two of my principal workmen are engaged with several other persons in getting up a repeating pistol with the hope of avoiding my patents, and that they are in correspondence with the Ordnance Department which encourages them in every way."

The several other persons included Daniel Leavitt, who contributed to the new revolver his own patented concept of a bevel-faced cylinder (according to the theory, so a side flash could not enter an adjoining chamber and set off a second charge accidentally). That July Leavitt traveled to Washington with a model pistol to display to the Ordnance officers, on behalf of the new syndicate. Other partners included the three Wesson brothers: Edwin, Daniel and Frank. Edwin operated a rifle-making shop in Hartford, specializing in heavy match rifles of false-muzzle and bullet-starter type. At least one revolver exists, described by Sawyer (Vol. II, *The Revolver*) and evaluated by Chapel. It is of the general top-strap side lock form of the Wesson & Leavitt guns, but bears the inscription, "Wesson, Stevens & Miller, Jacquith's Patent, Hartford, Ct. 1849." With the establishment of the works once again in Chicopee, being bought back from Ames, and upon the discharge of Stevens and Miller by Colt, the whole project was moved up the river to the Springfield area.

In 1849 additional capital had been pumped into the dormant Chicopee Falls Manufacturing Company. T. W. Carter (again superintendent), James T. Ames (brother of N. P. Ames), John Chase, Thomas Warner, Chester W. Chapin, and R. W. Chapman, incorporated the Massachusetts Arms Company in 1849 to the tune of $70,000. It was formed for the purpose of manufacturing "firearms, sewing machines, and other machinery." And of the names above, Thomas Warner was one of the most important, mechanically. He had once been Colt's employer. On January 18, 1847, as boss of the Whitneyville Armoury, Warner had hired Sam Colt to supervise the manufacture of the Walker pistol lock frames, Colt having assigned the contract in toto to Whitney. Now he was master mechanic in a firm which intended to show the upstart Sam Colt how a set of businessmen ran a pistol company. Now, with the rise of gun making in Chicopee, some of the best men Colt knew were hired to buck him: Warner, who had become a master armorer at Springfield Armory in 1842, was one; Stevens and Miller, Daniel Wesson, and Horace Smith were others.

Career of Horace Smith

How Horace Smith came to be tied up with the Massachusetts Arms Company is a nebulous story, part supposition, part "negative evidence." He was another of the Springfield Armory "alumni" of 1842. It is probable, due to the exceptional mechanical competency of these several men, that he worked in direct association with Master Armorer Thomas Warner. The interchangeable system of manufacture had been introduced by Warner in a highly perfected form in connection with production of the Model 1842 musket. According to Charles W. Fitch, Special Agent of the Census Bureau in 1880, surveying arms manufacture in New England, "In 1840 Thomas Warner, master armorer, introduced improved methods and machinery at the Springfield Armory. He gained interchangeable work by the use of milling machinery, by jig-filing, and by careful inspection. Receiver gauges were used, and it is stated that at this time the locks were not marked for hardening. This improved system was introduced by Warner at Whitneyville in 1842, where, prior to this time, the locks had been assembled and fitted soft and marked for hardening in sets of ten."

Whitney needed Warner's genius to help set up production of the M1841 U.S. rifle or "Jaeger" or "Mississippi" rifle. Colonel Talcott having come into power in 1842 to assist Bomford and replace him, Whitney was beginning to feel the freeze from Washington on the six private armories. He went to the Capital himself in September 1842 and although Talcott was away from the office he evidently succeeded in getting what he wanted. Result, a contract dated October 22, 1842, to supply 7,500 Model 1841 rifles at $13 each, first deliveries to begin by January 1, 1847. Doubtless it was to set up this production that Warner went to Whitneyville. He must have taken along Horace Smith, for Smith is listed as working for Eli Whitney, but from 1851 he is well recorded in his association with Dan Wesson.

Warner went to Massachusetts Arms Company about 1850, probably upon the death of Edwin Wesson, to take over the mechanical supervision of the factory in Chicopee Falls. They turned out approximately 3,500 Wesson & Leavitt revolvers in pocket, Navy, and Dragoon sizes, though the big Dragoon .44 is a very rare, seldom-seen arm.

When Colt realized the magnitude of the business in Chicopee, staffed by his former associates, he at once had his patent attorney, Edward N. Dickerson, bring suit for patent infringement. The trial was a most interesting one; it had its moments of humor and chicanery, as when the Massachusetts Arms Company faked up a "restored" old model of a revolver to prove Colt's was not the first. But the Boston judge found for the plaintiff. The sum of the damages was not a part of the suit, but was to be decided later. After the trial, Dickerson (in Colt's absence) was approached by "Smith" with an offer of $5,000 to settle. Ned just laughed, and Smith upped the ante to $10,000. When he hit $15,000 Dickerson thought it best to grab the deal; it was about a $4 royalty on each mechanically-turning Wesson & Leavitt revolver made, by Dickerson's calculation. He wrote to Colt that, including his fee of $3,000, the costs of the trial came to $9,450, "which left $5,000 profit and sustained the patent."

Smith, apparently financially burned by this, separated his shadowy connection with the Massachusetts Arms Company. He had other fish to fry. If everything Massachusetts Arms was to put on the market was to be tainted by association with Colt's former mechanics, Stevens and Miller, whom Colt now commenced to sue (March-June 1852), Smith preferred to go it alone.

There is a hiatus of some months in the history of Horace Smith. But it is believed that he attended the Great Exhibition in London, opened in May of 1851, and that he also journeyed to France. What is more certain is that one of the things he developed was an evolution from the French "Systeme Flobert" cartridge which was the basis for what a recent scholar on metallic ammunition, Charles R. Suydam, has called *The American Cartridge*. This distinctive rim fire ammunition, it seems on second look, is actually evolved from the Flobert bulleted breech cap, with an assist from Horace Smith and his sometime partner, Daniel Wesson.

Meanwhile, with Smith out of the Massachusetts Arms Company and Daniel Wesson less interested, now that the management had decreed they could afford to make no more Wesson & Leavitt revolvers, the Massachusetts Arms design staff had to prepare new models and look for more business. They did this by contracting to make special patented carbines and rifles, and by tying up Dr. Maynard pretty securely for private industry. A variety of arms were turned out from the Chicopee Falls shops showing the patent stamp in some particular of Dr. Maynard.

Greene's Breechloader

One of the most interesting was the swinging barrel breechloader of Lieutenant Colonel James Durrel Greene, United States Army. Although patented by Colonel Greene November 17, 1857, No. 18,634, this arm is believed to have an improvement upon R. S. Lawrence's rifle of the same basic principle, of which a specimen is shown in the United States Cartridge Company catalog No. 353 patented January 6, 1852, No. 8637. A percussion breechloader, the barrel of the Lawrence and the later Greene arm is supported on a frame pin, and, when it is released from the standing breech, swings to the side around the long axis of the pin, for loading. On the Lawrence rifle, of which very few were made, the latching is a top piece that holds a stud on the barrel. Colonel Greene conceived an easier way to release the barrel. In his carbine, there are two triggers. The front locks the barrel. By pressing the front trigger, the barrel, mounted inside a sleeve, can be rotated to the left, disengaging two massive locking lugs from corresponding fixed frame shoulders. Then the barrel inside the sleeve can be slid forward and the barrel-sleeve unit rocked to the right, exposing the chamber for loading. A combustible cartridge was used. When the barrel was pressed back again to the last rotation for locking, a hollow needle in the face of the breech pierced the cartridge and carried the cap flash into the interior of the charge.

Tests with the Greene by the United States in the 1857 period showed 16-inch penetration of the bullet at 600 yards in pine boards. Test carbines were .45 caliber, for the bullet was .45 inches and the cartridge

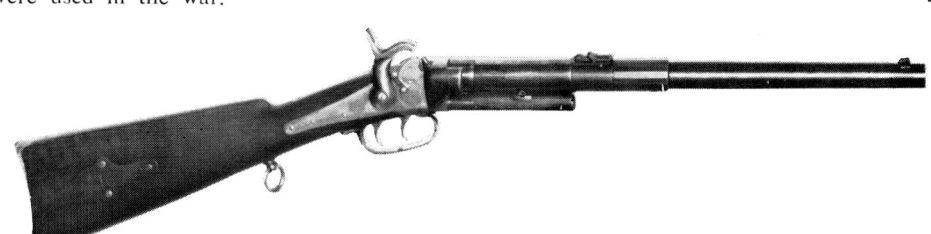

Greene turning-barrel British carbine had Maynard primer. Barrel is released by front trigger to twist and pull forward for loading. About 300 Greenes were bought by U.S. for test 1857; it is doubtful if any were used in the war.

weight complete was 266 grains, loaded with Williams' bullet for bore-scraping. Length overall was 2.25 inches. The common Greene cartridge was 2 inches overall, with a 480 grain bullet of .546-inch diameter, 54 grains of powder. Two production carbines are found of this design. The first is the British contract arm, and may occasionally have been associated with private Civil War use, though by far the greater majority of them are post-World War II surplus sale arms, especially those in fine condition not showing battle use. The second type is similar, does not have British marks, and is United States trial issue.

During 1855 when the British purchasing commissions toured the United States, they gave large orders for small arms and machinery. An order for 2,000 Greene carbines was placed with Massachusetts Arms Company, from whom they also procured gun making machinery. The Greene carbine order gave a boost to the firm's fortunes, which had flagged during the winter of 1852-53 while they recouped their losses from the Colt patent suit payoff.

The lockplates of these British contract guns are stamped before polishing and casehardening with the British "Crown over VR." It would appear that a British inspector or someone especially commissioned to do this inspecting was at hand in Chicopee, since the usual practice was to have the "Crown over VR" stamped on lockplates taken by the manufacturer to the Tower of London for the armorer's viewing. If found acceptable, the part in white would be stamped Crown, Tower, and the queen's initial, then hardened and returned to the Tower for storage and issue to another contractor who would fit them up into complete muskets. At Massachusetts Arms, with all the work being done under one roof, it seems likely British inspectors were on hand to approve and stamp the queen's cypher on the arms.

These British arms have an 18-inch barrel of chunky proportions, and the Maynard tape primer in front of the hammer. A sling loop is fixed to the trigger guard tang. On the lockplate, "Mass. Arms Co./Chicopee Falls/U.S.A./1856" ties down maker and date. Although it is often said some of these 2,000 carbines were "sold back to us during the Civil War," all found have one distinctive characteristic which seems to mitigate against this possibility. They bear the "broad arrow tip to tip" of British ordnance disposal or condemnation sometimes called "Triple cross," and an "S" for "obsolete Service not needing re-proof." The several specimens seen with these marks all conform exactly to a new mint specimen bought by the author in Bapty's in London in 1948 for about ten dollars, suggesting that all were scrapped at the same time; and that date was some time more recently than the Civil War. Those arms sold by the British to United States and Confederate States purchasers in the war did not bear scrap marks; indeed, mention was sometimes made of the boldness with which British agents shipped arms to the Confederates bearing mark of current government issue, the Broad Arrow under a Crown, undefaced! More probable candidates for Civil War use are those Greene carbines tried out by our own government.

Between 1855 and 1857, Greene carbines were purchased by the United States. Major differences include attachment of the sling ring to back of trigger guard, a 22-inch round barrel, and a brass patch box instead of the blued iron box of the British carbine. The first 200 were obtained May 24, 1855, at a cost of $30 each. In 1857, 170 were issued for test by the Army. It is recorded that in all, 300 Greene carbines were purchased between those years. Maynard's primer was of course a principal feature of this Greene carbine, too. Though the Greene is a beautifully constructed weapon, the many surfaces of the sliding barrel turning lug lockup contributed to its failure as a practical weapon in the emergency. Failure to clean a Greene was a quick way to put it out of order. But it did keep the wheels at Massachusetts Arms turning until they teamed up with the Robert Adams interests and Dr. Maynard designed his simple tipping barrel carbine.

Some of the Greene carbines, or perhaps early Maynards, may have gone out to John Brown. In 1856 from Kansas Territory, Brown wrote to Carter, whom he knew from having lived in Springfield, that "I very much want a lot of carbines as soon as I can see my way clear to pay for them and get them through safe." Carter, willing to help the cause of Abolition privately as his company did publicly by its excellent production record during the war, told Brown he could have carbines at 50 per cent reduction because, as Carter replied, he "wished to help . . . in your project of protecting the free state settlers of Kansas and securing their rights in the institutions of free America . . . We have no fear that they will be put to service in your hands for other purposes." Indeed, had old Brown been a better businessman, he might have taken shipments of good guns offered him at an all-heart discount, sold them for whopping big profits right and left, and plowed his proceeds right back into the purchase of even larger supplies of armaments with which he then might have been able to achieve what he desired. Right or wrong, it was an army he needed, and the arms to equip one; not a motley crew of errant slaves and wildly visionary white men waving pikes. He could have bought cheaper Maynard rifles.

At the outbreak of the Civil War, Massachusetts Arms employed 80 men on the Maynard rifle. In 1861 the work force was doubled; by 1864 with improved machinery and the influx of considerable capital from profits, 200 men were at work. While producing 20,002 Maynard carbines for the Union, and additional pieces for commercial and militia, kept the men busy, the major work on which the force was engaged was manufacture of the carbines of Gilbert Smith.

Gilbert Smith's Carbine

Gilbert Smith is believed to be no relation to Horace Smith, coming as he did from Buttermilk Falls, New York, where on August 5, 1856, he obtained his first patent for a breech-loading percussion carbine (No. 15,496). An improvement was patented June 23, 1857, No. 17,644. Smith achieved some notice abroad, and a most unusual and massive breechloader built upon his principles is in the Belgian "Musee de la Porte de Hal," in Brussels. Apparently Smith had been working on his design for some years. W. W. Greener in *The Gun*, 1st Edition, describes the arm and illustrates it. Though not very precisely drawn, Greener illustrates a sporting version with detail differences from the military carbine. Says Greener, "Gilbert Smith's American Rifle. In this arm . . . the barrel drops for the insertion of the cartridge, which is of india-rubber, with a perforated cardboard base. The barrel breaks off in the middle of the chamber, and falls at nearly right angles to the stock . . . The cartridge being flexible, it readily accommodates itself to the fixed portion of the chamber, and the base being perforated, an ordinary cap is sufficient to ignite the charge. This weapon was brought over to England about 1858, and submitted to the British Government; but the escape of gas at the joint—which it was thought would be avoided by having the breech in the center of the cartridge—was sufficient to condemn it. This gun is fastened at the top by means of a horizontally-sliding bar actuated by a small trigger-lever in front of the lock-trigger."

Unsuccessful with a sliding bar lock, Smith modified the design and, as patented in the United States and manufactured, the top bar is a spring member having its front end cut in a rectangular hole. Fixed to the top of the barrel is a stud which neatly fits the hole. In front of the lock-trigger that fires the hammer is a push-pin, which can be raised upward by the top of the trigger finger. This push-pin raises the spring bar from off the stud, allowing the barrel to flop forward.

Proprietor of this invention by 1860 was Thomas Poultney, of Poultney & Trimble, 200 West Baltimore Street, Baltimore, Maryland. Commission merchants, importers of arms and military good, Poultney & Trimble were one of the largest outfitters of the kind in the country before the war and for several years after. In 1860 Thomas Poultney proposed to sell the Ordnance Department a trial lot of 300 Smith carbines at $35. By August of 1861, Poultney had not delivered one gun. Apparently he had tried to get up enough orders to warrant large scale manufacture but had up to that time not succeeded. The advent of war allowed him to proffer his property once more, and he wrote to Assistant Secretary of War Scott, saying (during August '61) that he wanted an order for 25,000 Smith carbines at the price agreed upon, $35. Scott passed the proposal to General Ripley and the Ordnance Chief "respectfully returned" it negatively. The 300 ordered the year before had not been delivered; it was an untried arm, needed a special cartridge, and was too high priced. It was pointed out that "The best of Sharpe's (sic) carbines cost $30 each, including appendages."

Poultney himself was in Washington, hounding the Secretary of War. Ripley's rejection was promptly bounced back along with Poultney's counter-proposal to supply only 10,000 carbines at $35. And again, Ripley rejected it:

ORDNANCE OFFICE
Washington, August 17, 1861
Sir: I have carefully considered the proposition of Mr. T. Poultney to furnish ten thousand of Smith's patent breech-loading carbines at $35 each. I would gladly avail myself of any opportunity of obtaining at this time, at any price not beyond reason, such arms as are required for the troops called into the service. The carbine is only, however, a cavalry arm; it is used only by dragoons when dismounted and fighting on foot, and the orders, in the division of the Potomac, are to arm the cavalry with pistols and sabres only.

Ripley again stated the price was too high, 17,000 carbines of other types had already been contracted for, he doubted the emergency was so great as Mr. Poultney believed, and he asked for specific instructions from the Secretary on the matter. Poultney having already broached the subject to Massachusetts Arms Company and presumably gotten price quotes, he again made a reduction in price, to $32.50. And in response to a note from Poultney clarifying price and delivery schedule to which he proposed to adhere, General Ripley sent him the order:

ORDNANCE OFFICE
Washington, August 27, 1861
Sir: By direction of the Secretary of War, I offer you an order for ten thousand Smith's patent breech loading carbines on the following terms and conditions: The carbines, with appendages, are to be delivered at the factory of the Massachusetts Arms Company, Chicopee Falls, Massachusetts; the first delivery to commence in the month of September next, and other deliveries to continue at the rate of 1,000 per month thereafter, until the whole 10,000 are delivered. The carbines and appendages are to be subject to inspection by such officer as this department may designate for the purpose. In case of a failure to deliver in or within the times before specified, the Government is to be under no obligation to take the arms or appendages, but may or may not do so at its option. Payments are to be made in such funds as the Treasury Department may provide, on certificates of inspection and receipt by the United States inspecting officer, at the rate of thirty-two and a half dollars ($32.50) for each carbine, including appendages.
Please signify, in writing, whether you accept the foregoing order on the terms and conditions specified herein.
Respectfully, your obedient servant,
JAS. W. RIPLEY, *Brevet Brigadier General*
T. Poultney, Esq., Washington, D. C.

The following day Poultney replied with his acceptance and the Smith carbine manufacture got under way full blast. Among the first maker's names in the 10,000 was that of American Machine Works, Springfield, Massachusetts. Stamped almost illegibly MANUFACTURED BY/AM'N M'CH'N WKS/SPRINGFIELD, MASS. this marking appears on the action sideplate, underneath the frame bar on the left, along which the sling ring slides. Above the bar, prominently visible for the cavalryman who might be curious, is the commercial designation: ADDRESS/POULTNEY & TRIMBLE/BALTIMORE U.S.A. The mark SMITH'S PATENT/JUNE 23, 1857 appears also underneath the sling bar.

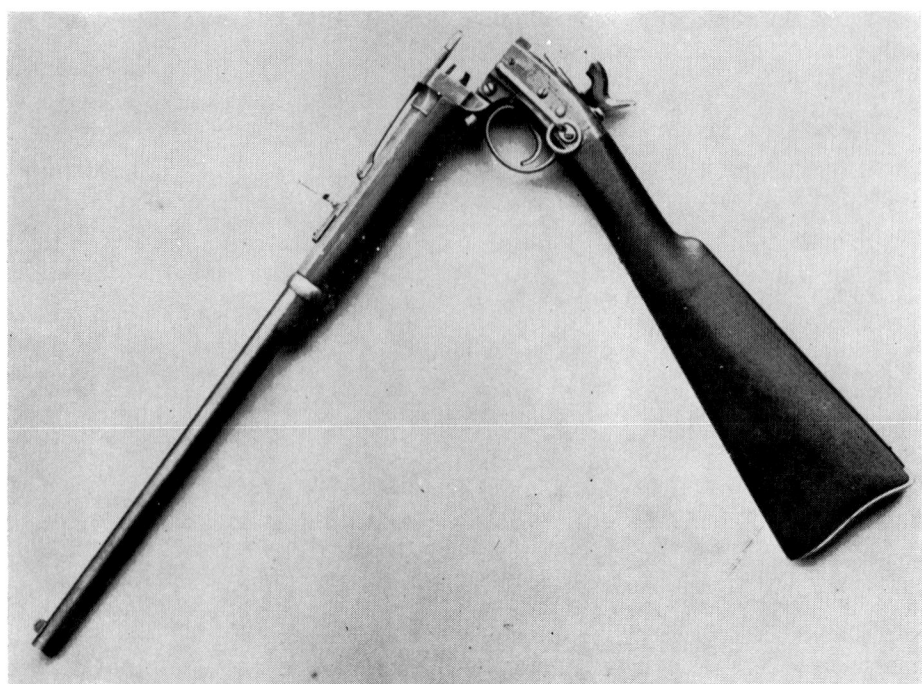

Hinged breech was feature of Gilbert Smith's carbines made by Mass. Arms, American Machine Works of Springfield and American Arms of Chicopee Falls, for Poultney & Trimble of Baltimore who contracted for them with the Government.

The American Machine Works was a tool-making enterprise founded in 1843 by Philos B. Tyler. It is presumed the contract was lived up to, in that American Machine Works guns were taken to Massachusetts Arms Company after finishing, for delivery to the United States inspectors. Closer to the main plant, the American Arms Company of Chicopee Falls also made carbines for Poultney & Trimble; the difference being in the name stamp of the maker.

American Arms was not a fly-by-night outfit, but one which survived for a good many years, from 1861 to 1904. The late A. Merwyn Carey (American Firearms Makers) indicates that although the plant was at Chicopee Falls, the main office was at 103 Milk Street, Boston, from 1866 to 1893. Rollover double barrel cartridge "derringer" pistols were made under patent of Henry F. Wheeler, October 31, 1865; and also Whitmore patent shotguns. The plant was moved to Milwaukee, Wisconsin, 1897 to 1904. Third factory of course was Massachusetts Arms, which Poultney had expected all along would fabricate the carbines. Delivered in all to the United States of the three makes was a total of 30,062 Smith carbines including accouterments priced at $745,645.24, plus 13,861,500 Smith's cartridges of two varieties, rubber and tinfoil, valued at $377,569.78.

Two patterns of Smith's exist, superficially similar but differing in their chambering. Those for the rubber cartridge, adapted only to Smith's carbines, had chambers a trifle larger than those later ones made to use "Poultney's patent" (assigned to him by inventor Silas Crispin) soldered foil and paper cartridges. These had a thinner wall than the rubber cases, though the rubber cases, it was claimed, could be reused 15 times.

Toward the end of the war when Massachusetts Arms and Poultney attempted to adapt the Smith to metallic cartridges, a few were made for test which used the odd Crispin belt-fire copper case. This bulgy load had a priming belt about its middle, and the Smith chamber fore and aft was relieved with a bevel to accommodate the rim. The percussion cone which ordinarily fired the rubber or foil-paper cartridges was replaced by a firing pin striking forward to hit the primer belt. In the Crispin-cartridge model Smith, a significant modification is made in the unlatching; a top thumb lever, pressed down upon the small of the stock, rocks upward at its front end, lifting the latch bar. Confusingly, it was a photo of such an arm which the illustrator used in later years preparing the drawings of U.S. guns for the *Atlas* of the *Official Records*. A Smith carbine is shown, such a carbine as the cavalry never saw.

Instead of the sling bar, Smith carbines could be had with a conventional swivel mounted on the toe of the stock, and on the bottom of the barrel band. Among mechanical details pioneered by the Smith is the attachment of the stock by a single through-belt, with the front of the wood finished off square to fit flush against a flat frame back. This detail is a characteristic of Chicopee Falls guns to this day. But in spite of the Massachusetts Arms' infatuation with the Maynard primer, none was ever fitted to the Smith carbine.

Massachusetts Arms Company is Terminated

With the end of war, having produced approximately 3,000 Greene twist-barrel guns, at least 20,000 Maynards, and 30,000 Smiths for the cavalry, Massachusetts Arms Company was overexpanded. In the sudden cessation of business they were unable to cope with changes in the market. The water-power rights reverted to the Chicopee Manufacturing Company, while the

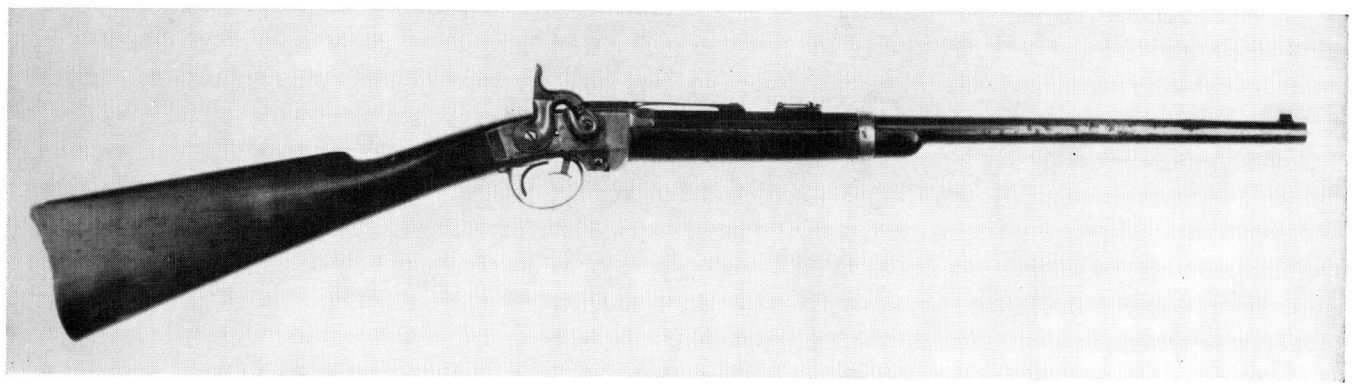

Smith was clean-styled carbine and examples show magnificent machine and finishing characteristic of Chicopee industrial complex. Modern inheritors of this capacity are the Savage Arms Corporation—Stevens—Fox combination.

factory itself was sold to the newly organized Lamb Knitting Machine Company in 1866, and the gun business under the name Massachusetts Arms Company terminated. T. W. Carter retained the rights to make the Maynard rifle, and continued it in production as a quality sporting and target arm until about 1890. The idea of the basic breech to take a selection of barrels resulted in many handsome trunk-type cased sets containing rifles for from rabbits to rhinos, and a shotgun bore to boot, all for installing on the same breech. At the last, William F. McFarland, nemesis of Huse and a former Springfield Armory man, was in charge of production.

More famous to be was Joshua Stevens, who turned to the single-shot cartridge breechloader to found his fortunes, leading ultimately to the great Savage Arms Corporation combine of today. The handful of Yankee mechanics who earned their keep making carbines at Massachusetts Arms learned their trade well.

Though *Appleton's Cyclopedia* (1864) was as obtuse in describing the Smith as in telling of the Maynard, there is truth in its declaration: "There is nothing about it which can get out of order. Its range is 2,000 yards or more and it can be fired ten times a minute (Ordnance tests in 1866 showed it could be fired 14 shots a minute). The cartridge used for this rifle is a metallic one (Poultney's foil) but the case collapses after firing, and can be withdrawn with a single motion of the finger." Whether Smith, Maynard, Stevens, or even Adams or Greene, the epitaph is not too far wrong: "There is nothing about it which can get out of order."

Not so lucky were the two friends, Horace Smith and Daniel Wesson, who left Massachusetts Arms early, when the going got rough, to fend for themselves. They had as principal assets Horace Smith's improvement of the French Flobert metallic cartridge. Before they had finished, they were to found not only two gunmaking firms of lasting fame, but the metallic cartridge industry as well! Their company Smith & Wesson is well known today; less well known are the roles they played in developing the copper self-primed cartridge, and launching Winchester.

CHAPTER 11

Federal Carbines

Fertility of invention bloomed in fitting out the Northern cavalry. By war's end, so many as 44 different breech-loading carbines could be presented to the Ordnance Department for test. Several—the Henry, the Spencer—were old favorites. Others were known by the names of the men who presented them, but reflected the workings of large contractors (Wolcott, of Starr Arms. and E. A. Straw, of Amoskeag) in a bid for postwar business. All proved unsuccessful in attracting the attention of the Federal Army for any re-equipping.

No dangerous enemies were in sight. The greatest army the world had seen marched for three days in review in the Capital of a reunited nation. There were a million Springfields and Enfields on hand. Why bother to get more than the barest essential transformation? Accordingly, the Cavalry wielded the Spencers while the Infantry and Artillery right-shouldered their Allin-transformed M1865, M1866, and later new-make Springfields, with the Civil War dates on the lockplates. But while the patronage of the Government was strong, equally novel, though less diverse, were the creations of the carbine contractors during the war.

Illinois Carbines

The Henry, Sharps, Spencer, Greene, Maynard, Smith. and Starr carbines have all been treated elsewhere in this book. But though these were supplied in numbers of major importance, many state units had their own ideas as to what carbines they wanted. One such weapon was the variously-called "Union," or "Grapevine" (from trigger guard lever form), or "Gross" (after inventor), or "Ohio." Collector-student Thomas B. Rentschler of Hamilton, Ohio (old factory site of the companies making the several styles of carbine mentioned above), declares these names, so commonly used, are quite incorrect when compared with the specimens actually used in the war. He is right; if any name other than the full factory designation should be applied to this family of cavalry arms, it is "Illinois." They first appear in the records with an order from General John Wood of Illinois to Major Hagner, as follows:

HEADQUARTERS QUARTERMASTER GENERAL'S
DEPARTMENT
Springfield, Illinois, December 12, 1861
Major Hagner:
Sir: This will introduce to you Edward Gwyn, esq., of Hamilton, Ohio, who is the manufacturer of the Cosmopolitan breech-loading carbine. This celebrated firearm is the same that I made requisition for at Washington for the Governor's Legion. The order to purchase was sent (to) you without stating the kind of carbine I asked for.
Mr. Gwyn visits you with a view of obtaining the order to furnish this carbine to the Governor's Legion, and I earnestly request that you give him the order to furnish them at once.
JOHN WOOD
Quartermaster General, State of Illinois

Major Hagner asked General Ripley, in strongly flattering terms, to approve. Gwyn offered the 1,140 arms required, with implements, at $27, delivery in 60 days. Stating his views on policy, Hagner noted that he felt he should be permitted to buy arms like the Cosmopolitan, which had been reported on favorably. "Mr. Allyn (sic) at Springfield, reports very favorably to this," he said. "The price, too, is in this offer lower than is usual for this kind of arm."

Cosmopolitan Arms

Still smarting from losses at the battlefronts, Ripley at once agreed to Hagner's two requests: order the Cosmopolitan arms, and order such other arms as Hagner thought necessary "to meet pressing want, reporting what you order in each case immediately to this (Ordnance) office." The formal order of Hagner, one of some dozen officers of the United States Ordnance Department authorized to buy arms in the field, went out:

ORDNANCE OFFICE
No. 55, White Street, New York, December 23, 1861
Gentlemen: In conformity with orders from chief of ordnance, you will please furnish United States ordnance department 1,140 of your cavalry carbines, at the rate of $27 each.
You will alter your pattern gun to make it stronger where you can, and especially use *wrought iron* for the breech box,

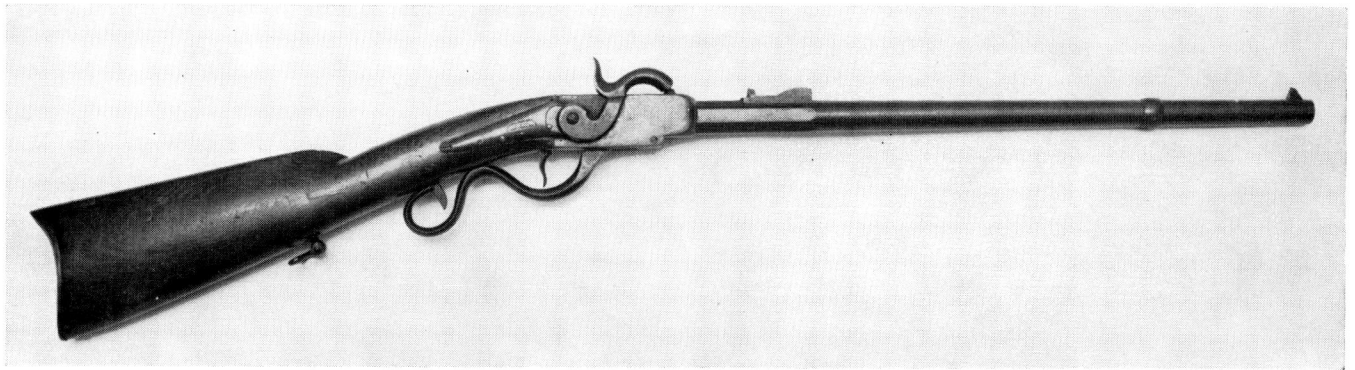

Cosmopolitan No. 1 of military-use arms was pre-production specimen having flat-side hammer and rounded lockplate held deringer-fashion by wood screw. Breech tipped for loading when lever was lowered. Barrel bump is sling band.

instead of malleable; strengthen the pivots of box and box cone; do away with sharp angles and round projections in trigger, tumbler and bridle; and increase the metal around lock screw in front. The arms are to be delivered for inspection to some United States ordnance officer, to be appointed as soon as you may report yourself ready.

I desire that you should prepare, as soon as possible, and send to me, a pattern gun altered from the present, as above suggested, which I will examine and return to you, or retain for a sample.

The arms must be properly boxed, to hold 20 guns each, unless they are required to be issued to troops in your city. It is intended to issue the above number to Governor Yates, of Illinois, as requested by him.

Payment will be made by me upon certificates of inspection, signed by the officer who may be appointed to inspect.

Very respectfully, your obedient servant,
P. V. HAGNER, *Major Ordnance*

To: COSMOPOLITAN ARMS COMPANY, *Hamilton, Ohio*

P.S.—The implements required are screw-driver and cone wrench, spare cone and wiper for each gun, to be furnished without additional charge. Boxes to be paid for, if furnished, at $2 each, to be made like our musket boxes.
P. V. HAGNER, *Major Ordnance*

Messrs. Edward Gwyn and E. C. Campbell, both of Hamilton, began work on the carbines at once. When Stanton called for information about contracts, they responded on February 4, writing on the letterhead of the Cosmopolitan Arms Company, setting forth pretty fairly the fact that the gun should be known by the name of the firm, as "the Cosmopolitan." They supplied Holt and Owen with the facts of the December 23 order. This order was so recent and the term of delivery so indefinite, that Holt and Owen did not choose to investigate the matter; on the face of the record all was in order, and with Major Hagner's approval of the gun there seemed little to occupy their attention. Not only had Master Armorer Allin at Springfield okayed the carbine, but the Navy gave it a shakedown on June 19, 1860, at the Navy Yard.

Undisturbed, Gwyn and Campbell continued to work on the guns, improving and strengthening as Major Hagner directed. First delivery of 840 Cosmopolitan carbines and appendages on June 18, 1862, was paid for a month later at the rate of $27 per gun. The 300 to complete Governor Yates' order came in on July 2, 1862. Then a delay occurred and not until April 11, 1863, were a further 1,000 "Union" carbines accepted by Ordnance. These were the first delivery under a formal contract of August 4, 1862, directly with Gwyn & Campbell for 2,000 Cosmopolitan carbines "to be in all respects identical with a standard pattern carbine to be deposited by the party of the first part, and to be approved by the Chief of Ordnance." One hundred cartridges for each carbine were wanted; $20 each carbine and cartridges $15 per thousand. As surety and possibly subcontractor for parts in this was William Beckett, manufacturer, and also lawyer Alexander F. Hume, both of Butler County, Ohio.

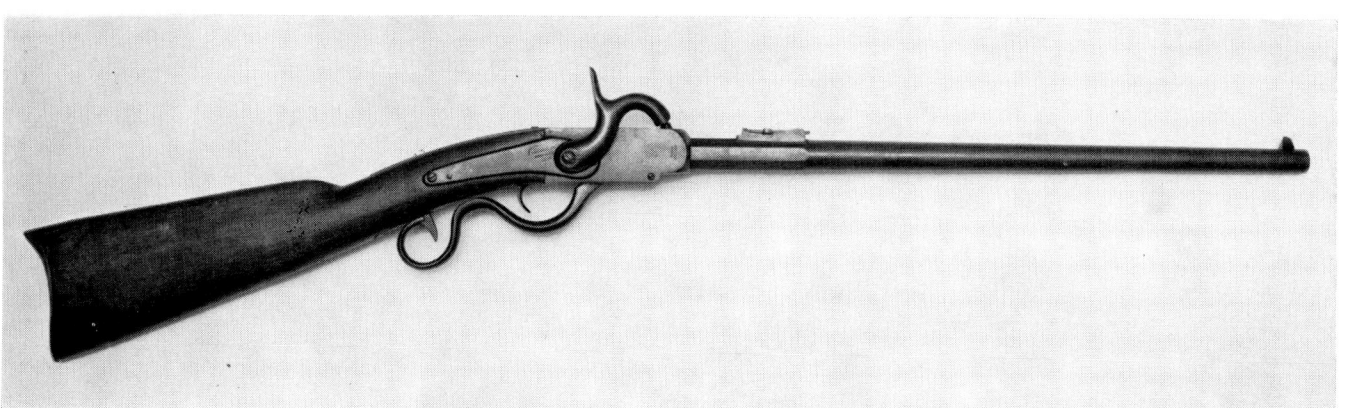

Cosmopolitan No. 2 has rounded hammer, flat lockplate, and head of screw is enclosed by metal of plate. Stamped UNION RIFLE on breech box, this gun was issued to Governor's Legion of Illinois, is marked Gross Patent on lockplate.

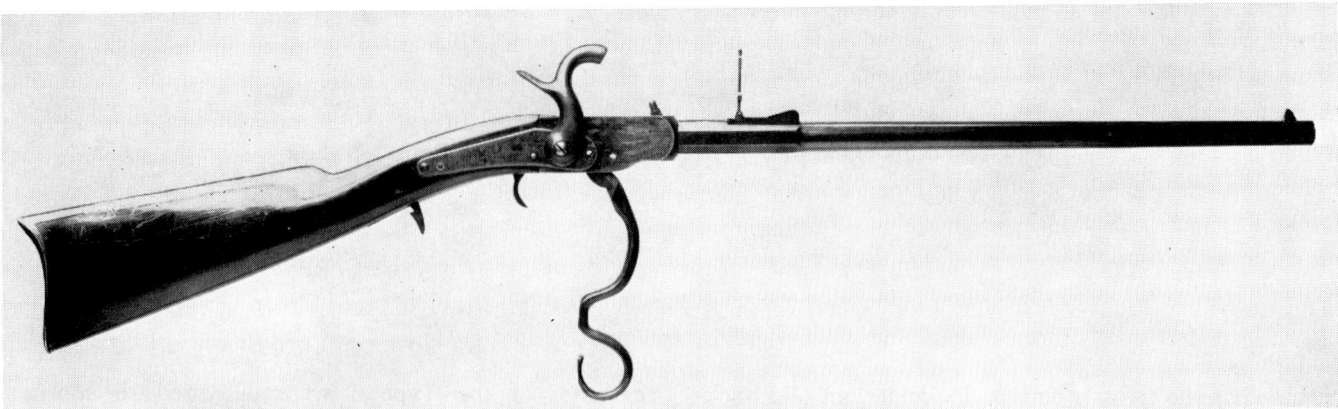

Cosmopolitan No. 3, First type, has same round hammer but breech is Gwyn and Campbell patent though old company name with Gross Patent is still stamped on lock. Lever screw enters from left of breech box. Not marked UNION RIFLE.

Production had so improved, though the firm never achieved high volume, that by April of 1863 the partners offered to furnish 10,000 carbines at $20 if a further contract would be extended. Ripley upon orders from Stanton agreed in principle; he wanted to take all that could be made "ready for inspection by November 1, 1863." His dating was partly from military expediency; such arms might be phased into the cavalry operations in time to do battle before the Army went into winter quarters. Stanton, "fiduciarily" inclined, preferred to bring the accounts up to the end of the calendar year and Ripley bowed to this decision, ordering therefore all the Cosmopolitan carbines which could be delivered up to December 31, 1863.

These 10,000 represented some changes from prior lots as on September 18, 1863, the then assistant Chief of Ordnance, Colonel Ramsay, asked that two sample carbines be sent on, one to the Department and the other to now Lieutenant Colonel Hagner at the new Inspecting Office at 77 East 14th Street, New York.

On 27 February, 1864, a new contract was signed for 3,000 carbines at $20, with cartridges at $18 per thousand. Then a price increase was negotiated during the late summer and on November 18, 1864, a final contract set the price at $22.50 each, and $24 for cartridges. These carbines were of a type evidently covered by the two sample carbines and were specifically referred to as "in all respects identical" with the carbines and appendages of the February 27 contract.

Within the "Cosmopolitan" series are changes which with some certainty can be linked to these contracts and the modifications implicit in the guns by reason of the references or terms of the contracts. The earliest type of course is not even embraced within the contracts, nor is it properly a Civil War arm, being an earlier commercial-military development of the breechloading invention of one Henry Gross.

Gross enters and exits from the history of Gwyn and Campbell early and quick. In connection with Charles B. Gross, believed a brother, he worked in Tiffin, Ohio, between 1852 until the mid 1860's. While he manufactured in 1864 or thereabouts the Gross patent .22 rimfire seven-shot revolvers, his carbine was patented August 30, 1859, No. 25,259.

"In this gun," says collector Tom Rentschler, who has fortunately obtained specimens of this exceedingly rare limited production series, "the paper or linen cartridge is inserted into the breechblock, which moves backward and tilts up (the gun is a lever-action breechloading single shot design). The patent papers also allow for a variation which has the breechblock moving back and down, and the cartridge inserted into an enlarged chamber of the barrel." Rentschler owns No. 19, No. 112, No. 150, and No. 186 of this series, varying slightly in presence or absence of ramrod pipes and detail form of lever and also hammer. No. 19, the earliest, has a lighter breechbox than later patterns, too. It is tinned finish and may have been one prepared for

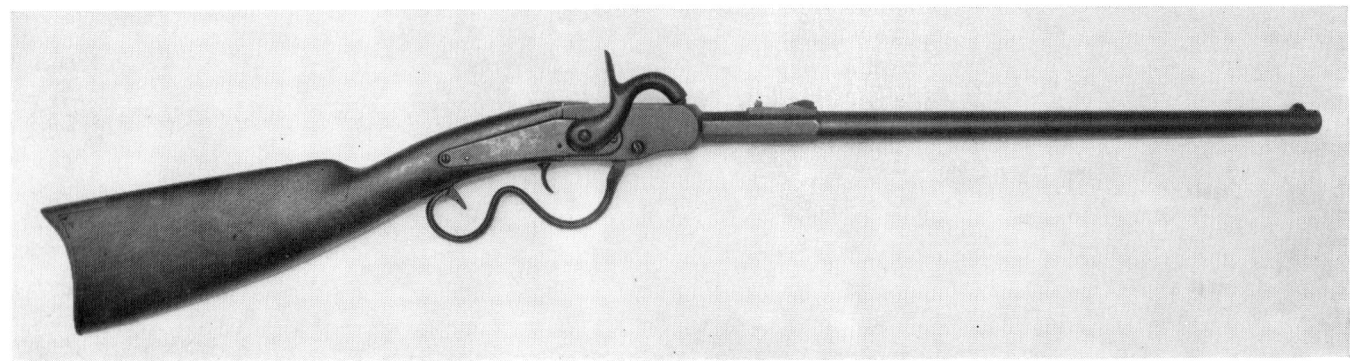

Cosmopolitan No. 3, Second Type, has lever screw from right of frame, and new Gwyn & Campbell mark is stamped on lock. Lever curve does not meet tang of trigger plate on this variation. Gun is rusty but not marked UNION RIFLE.

the Navy tests conducted with some approval and success on June 19, 1860.

Gross and Edward Gwyn together made some firearms in Tiffin, but the venture failed. Apparently Gwyn took as his share the patent rights, and, moving to Hamilton, formed the well-known partnership with Abner C. Campbell. As the Cosmopolitan Arms Company they began to make carbines under Gross' patent. These arms are properly designated the "Cosmopolitan" carbine. It is this arm, Cosmopolitan No. 1, that Hagner wanted strengthened. In his letter he made an obvious mistake; he referred to increasing the "metal around lock screw in front." The Cosmopolitan No. 1 carbine has the Gross rifle type lockplate, an odd back-action pattern with a rounded flat area or pad behind the hammer and with the tang of the plate *at rear* held by the head of a stock screw. Hagner wanted the metal of the plate increased to surround the screw entirely, making a stronger fastening to the stock. The hammer is flat on the body, with a rounded head and spur. While a few of this pattern were made and may have been sold to individual military purchasers locally, The Governor's Legion of Illinois received the Cosmopolitan No. 2 which in its later issue bore the breech stamping (forward on breechbox near barrel) of UNION/RIFLE. With lockplate held at rear by a screw head entirely surrounded by metal, this was the first Gross patent gun to see battle in quantity. The hammer is smoothly curved on body and head. The lockplate is flat, no longer having the pad or flat typical of earlier Gross arms; the bottom edge of lockplate is arched up as other Gross arms. Quickly distinguishing Gross arms from the later design of Gwyn and Campbell (if the workings of the breech innovations are not too clear in your mind) is the location of the leverpivot screw. On Gross guns it is forward of that point where the lever enters the breechbox by nearly 2 inches. On Gwyn & Campbell patent guns, the screw is almost at the point where the lever enters the breechbox, when viewed from the side.

Cosmopolitan No. 3 was made under patent No. 36,709, October 21, 1862, issued to Gwyn and Campbell. Gross's guns have a double cam movement to open the breech, but the G & C patent operates the breech mechanism with a single eccentric cam, dropping the block down and back. Probably this was designed in the spring of 1862 and contracted for August 4, 1862.

Tooling for the improved carbines, which simplified the breech pieces of the Gross and permitted greater production with higher profits and the lower price, was not ready until the winter of 1862-63. First delivery of 1,000 pieces of Cosmopolitan No. 3 was in April 11, 1863. They were stamped UNION/RIFLE and referred to as such in the contract. The rear lock screw head was to the right of the gun; the lever curves were rather open and large on some of this issue. Lockplate shape had been simplified to basically a triangle shape with rounded corners, easy for machining. But 4,200 Union carbines of the Type 3 were delivered to contract expiration 31 December, 1863. Still, Gwyn and Campbell were not satisfied, and they made a final variation, Cosmopolitan No. 4, under their patent.

The No. 4 differed most obviously from No. 3 in the shape of the hammer; it is flat on the shank and flat on the side of the head. The cause is twofold. The round shape of the No. 3 hammer required expansive and slow hand filing to achieve the exact shape. The No. 4 can be roughed out by machine, requiring mostly deburring on the edges to clean up.

The No. 4 lockplate is tapped at the rear for the rear plate screw, which now enters from left of stock. All drill and tap work on the lockplate is done at one time, and there is no need for a separate threaded fitting to anchor the lock screw. The lever latch on the Gross guns, and Cosmopolitans No. 1, 2, and 3, catches the lever which turns forward upon itself in a curl to engage the latch. On No. 4 the catch is simply at the end of the lever.

Tactical changes seem to have modified the machinery a little; Gross guns and No. 3 Cosmopolitan have leaf rear sights slightly like the Enfield, graduated to the optimistic distance of 900 yards. In the No. 3 series 600-yard sights appear and the series of No. 4's is fitted with 600-yard sights. Only 4,502 of the No. 4's were delivered to Uncle Sam, the last 1,000 at an increased price of $22.50. A change not mentioned in the contract but evidently covered by technical advice during production of models for inspection or Ordnance approval was that of caliber size; No. 1 and No. 2 Cosmopolitans are .50 caliber. To make the bore uniform with the Spencers and Sharps the caliber was

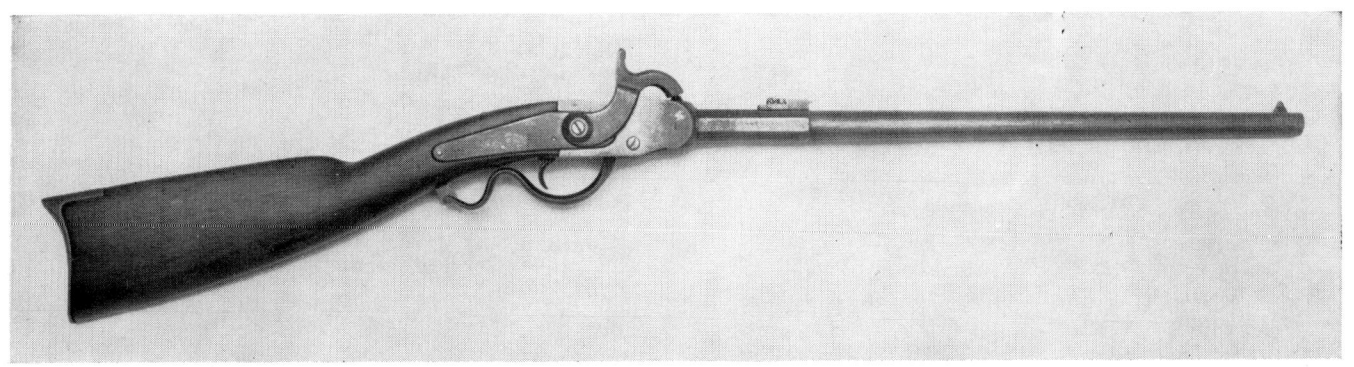

Again marked UNION RIFLE this Cosmopolitan No. 4, last type, has improved carbine rear sight and flat hammer adapted for machining. Lever screw is larger head, from right of breech. Lever has improved rear end catch.

Major General Ambrose Everett Burnside commanded Rhode Island Volunteers armed with his patent breech-loading carbines for the manufacture of which the governor of Rhode Island had signed as a surety on the contract.

increased to .52 in the last No. 3 and 4 series of Gwyn and Campbell design.

Few of these Cosmopolitan arms were made. The partners Gwyn and Campbell seem to have been major pioneers in machine manufacturing methods. Most of the guns made have seen hard service. In design, they contributed nothing to the development of arms generally, but in the engineering lavished upon the models made, they did their share to move the locus of machine industry westward and build a stable self-sustaining economy in the Middle West.

Burnside Rifles

Of 407,734 carbines purchased by the Union from 1861 to 1865, in 19 patterns plus foreign types and musketoons, none was more "colorful" and none better built than the "Burnside." Fifty-five thousand five hundred sixty-seven were received over the war years, of several patterns, and the record of their production embraces the formation and dissolution of two companies.

Of the same species of "breechbox" construction as the Cosmopolitan, the Burnside gun has a receiver to hold the cartridge, like the Hall. An under lever tips the receiver upward to take the foil or copper cartridge, which is loaded from the front of the receiver's chamber. In the final motion of closing, the big ring of metal about the bullet serves as a gas seal between chamber and bore, and a separate percussion cap ignites the flash-hole cartridge, from a nipple placed on top of the receiver, what today would be called the "breechblock."

Designed by Illinoisian Ambrose Everett Burnside, after whom the whiskers called "sideburns" are named, it reflected familiarity with the Hall and its defects, while the inventor was a cadet at the United States Military Academy at West Point. Burnside graduated from West Point in 1847, but became interested in arms design and resigned in 1853. In 1855 he organized the Bristol Firearms Company at Bristol, Rhode Island, to manufacture the breechloader he invented, supposedly while carrying dispatches in 1847.

Early specimens of his sporting rifle have a tape primer, but not the Maynard patent nor design. A strip of pelleted priming tape is fed forward from a slot in the top of the breechbox, and the hammer connects with a cap as it hits the nipple. Burnside was hopeful of far-reaching sales for his gun. Two flashily engraved specimens, Nos. 12 and 34, with short 24-inch carbine barrels, are today in the museum of the Military Academy at Tehran, capital of Iran. Other examples are known of pre-military Burnside rifles, sporting type, finished with varnished "rifle butt plate" stocks and brilliant bluing and fine engraving. An important dis-

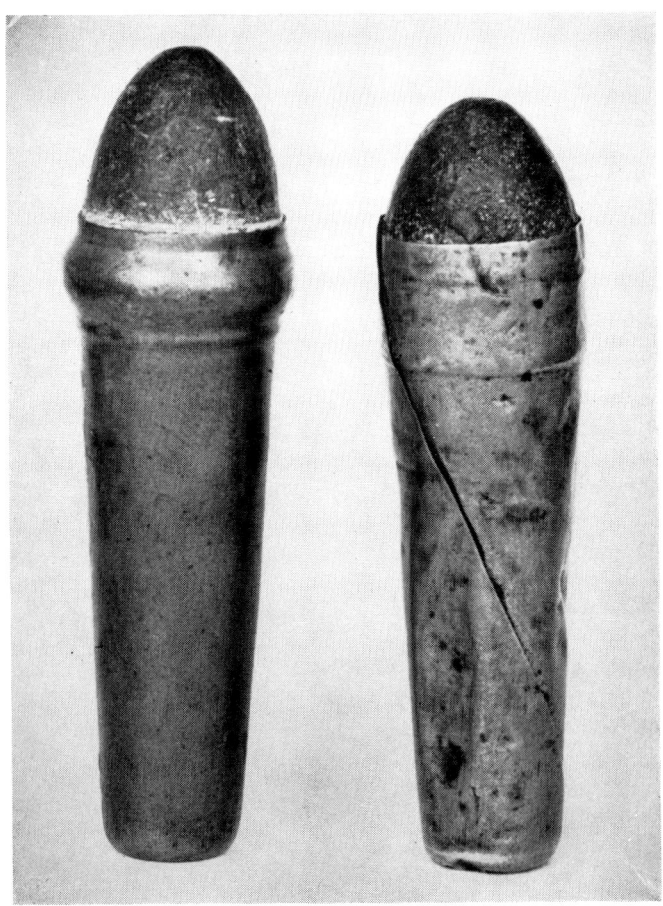

Wrapped foil Burnside cartridge is shown with improved drawn brass type. Case had hole in base, and flash from cap ignited charge. Bulge was at joint of breech and barrel; case extending into barrel helped seal the gas.

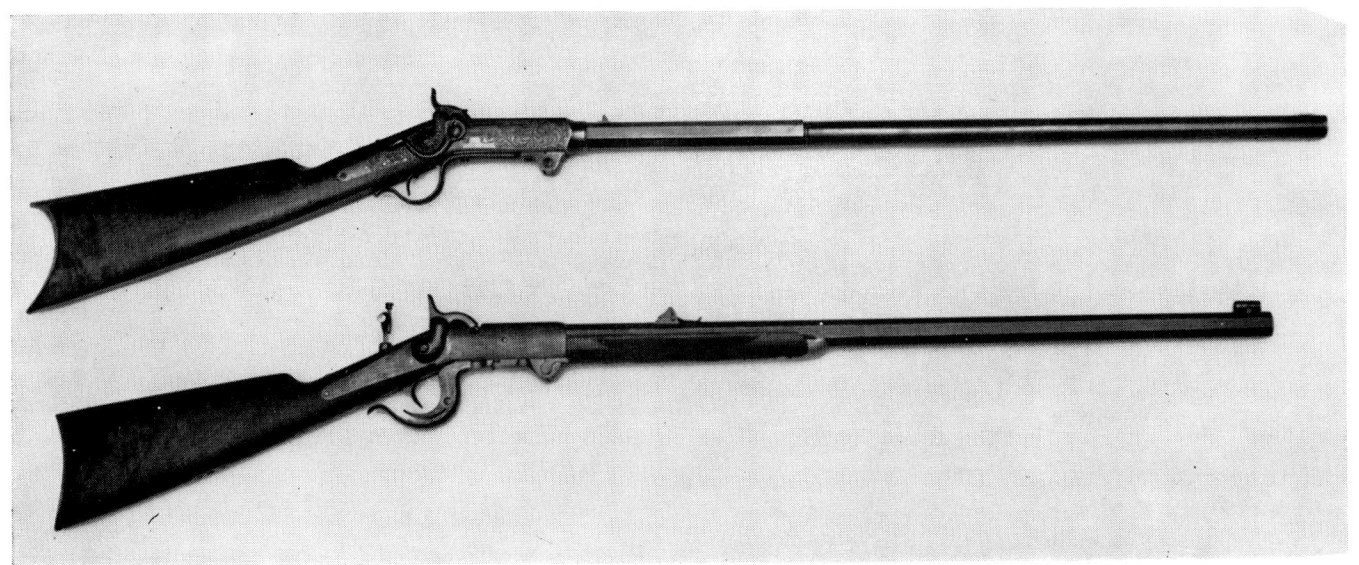

Early Burnside sporter made by Bristol Firearms Co. had safety lever on side of breech box. Inner receiver tips up at front when lever is dropped, to receive tapered metallic cartridge. Postwar sporter (bottom) is unusual combination of last model breech with custom octagon barrel, fine wood.

tinction between early Burnside arms and later mass-produced guns is that the early guns do not have a forestock.

With the coming of war, Burnside ceased to take any part in the affairs of the firm. At the age of 37 he commanded Rhode Island troops, ranking as Major General of United States Volunteers. Though talented, he lacked experience and organizational ability and this served to account for his disastrous charge upon well entrenched Confederates at Marye's Heights in the Battle of Fredericksburg, Virginia. After the war he helped organize and was first president of the National Rifle Association, and was active in Rhode Island politics.

Early sales to the Government were few. On April 21, 1856, 200 Burnside carbines were bought at $30 each. Possibly these had the tape primer, for most of the guns bought under direction of Secretary of War Jefferson Davis had some such feature. Bristol Firearms Company then sold 709 Burnsides to the United States on September 21, 1858, at $35. Details of these specific lots of arms are lacking at present, but it is assumed they were with the tape primer and a side lever lock. Possibly the tape primer serial numbers ran in its own series and the firm started anew with the more or less conventional Burnside as later made.

It is the Second Model Burnside which was the first official war model. The lever and latch were improved by G. P. Foster, Taunton, Massachusetts. A peripatetic contracting gunmaker, Foster had made rifles for Colonel Porter and for New Yorker Philip H. Klein, United States patent communicant of Nicholas von Dreyse, inventor of the Prussian needle gun. He may have been the manufacturing superintendent of Bristol Firearms and the later Burnside Rifle Company, moving to Bristol and then Providence from his earlier location of Taunton, Massachusetts. Foster improved the lever latch of the Burnside carbine by making a rocking curved piece which fitted inside the bow of the lever and naturally unlatched when one's trigger finger was brought against it in a downward motion. A patent was granted Foster April 10, 1860, on this idea, and the date stamp appearing on, for example, No. 378 of the Second Model Burnside carbine without forestock, suggests that but few could have been

Official Records illustration shows second model Burnside carbine with no forestock as made by Bristol Firearms. Some of these were issued early in the war but contracts later specified wooden forearms and one barrel band.

made of this pattern by Bristol before April, 1860.

General Ripley remembered the Burnside gun and when Governor Sprague of Rhode Island requested enough to arm a mounted brigade, the Ordnance general at once sent out the order. It was addressed to Charles Jackson, Treasurer, of Bristol Firearms:

Washington, July 16, 1861

Sir: There are required immediately by this department eight hundred of Burnside's carbines, for which the same price last paid will be allowed. Please inform me of the shortest time possible you are prepared to furnish them.

Jackson during the past two years had perfected the gun, including Foster's lever, and within the past two months had dissolved the old Bristol Company and moved to Providence. "I have recently reorganized, under the name of the Burnside Rifle Company, Isaac Hartshorn, agent," he responded July 18, 1861. "We will take your order for the eight hundred carbines, to be delivered in December next, in whole or in part, probably the whole." The lead time Jackson needed reveals pretty conclusively that the new firm was not in full swing and could not ship from shelf stock.

But the Burnside sales folks were not lazy. Ground was broken for a new armory in Providence in July. Production of about 2,000 per month was the superintendent's program. By December, guns were ready for delivery. Ripley was anxious, Governor Sprague having been pestering him. On November 5, Ripley wrote to Hartshorn, saying "Please have ready for Governor Sprague, as soon as possible, 632 carbines on account of the order to you of the 27th August last." Captain Rodman at Watertown Arsenal, Massachusetts, outside of Boston, was to inspect these guns.

Hartshorn was momentarily disturbed by this notice. The order of 27 August was a large contract which he had obtained to supply 7,500 carbines, but they had some special characteristics different from the forearm-less Second Models which were then in current production. The order of 27 August read:

> The carbines to have steel barrels, twenty-one inches long, *to be half stocked,* bore .54 inch, weight from seven and a quarter to seven and an eighth pounds. . . . Payments . . . $35 for each carbine, including appendages, which are to be one wiping thong and brush, one spare cone, one screw driver and wrench for each arm, and one spring vise and one bullet mould for every ten arms.

Hartshorn, not prepared to introduce the modified model so soon, asked Ripley to consider the carbines for Sprague (Rodman to inspect) as coming under the order of July 16, which was agreed to. Of these unstocked barrel Second Models it appears deliveries were at least as follows:

> October 5 and 12, 1861, 480 on State of Indiana contract of September 21, 1861. December 11, 580 Second Models to Rodman.

More than this number existed at the time Holt and Owen stepped into the case. When Hartshorn reported to Stanton the status of orders, he showed the firm to be in good shape, with an armory capable of 25,000 to 30,000 rifles yearly, and about 1,130 carbines actually on hand in finished state ready for inspection during February and March. Some 6,000 were in progress with delivery estimated commencing April, 1862. Of Second Models made, there were 60 ready for delivery in February, for Rodman to inspect for Governor Sprague. Hartshorn stated that the 1,130 included 520 final lot for State of Indiana contract, assumed by Government, and "will be our first delivery under contract of August 27." These 1,130 must therefore be the first-made Third Model Burnsides with the first appearance of the wooden forearm.

It is fairly conclusive that none of the wood-forearm guns were ever made at Bristol Firearms, but were the second pattern of Burnside made at Providence. The 9½-inch long wooden forearm is held to the barrel by an oval steel band, blued. The barrel to conform to the contract was marked CAST STEEL and sometimes with the date of fabrication. It is supposed from an examination of production delays related to contracts that this pattern without the additional improvements which distinguish the Fourth Model Burnside is one of the rarest of these carbines. But at the moment, the biggest production delay was Holt and Owen.

Robert Owen was not a stranger to this case. Having ordered 1,000 of the Second Model Burnsides for his boss, Governor Oliver P. Morton of Indiana, he knew a little of the business before he dropped his role of arms buying agent and began to assume the judge's robes more usually worn by his colleague Judge Holt. Hartshorn came before them and set forth simply the company's situation.

This situation included two orders for long guns, never filled. On August 28, 1861, Ripley ordered 1,000 Burnside rifle muskets, "to have angular bayonets, steel barrels 37 inches long, full stocked, weight from 9 to 9½ pounds . . . Payments . . . $38.50 for each musket, including appendages, which are to be one wiping thong and brush, one spare cone, one screw-driver and wrench for each arm, and one spring vise and one bullet mould for every ten arms." A following order of November 21, 1861, covered the need for "2,500 Burnside's breech-loading rifles, with sabre bayonets, Harper's Ferry rifle length, calibre .58 inch . . . $38.50." Colonel B. R. Lewis *(Small Arms and Ammunition in the United States Service)* treats the Burnside cartridge as a nominal .54 caliber, but notes that bullets of two types are .565 inch diameter, which is close to .577, which was enough to be considered a

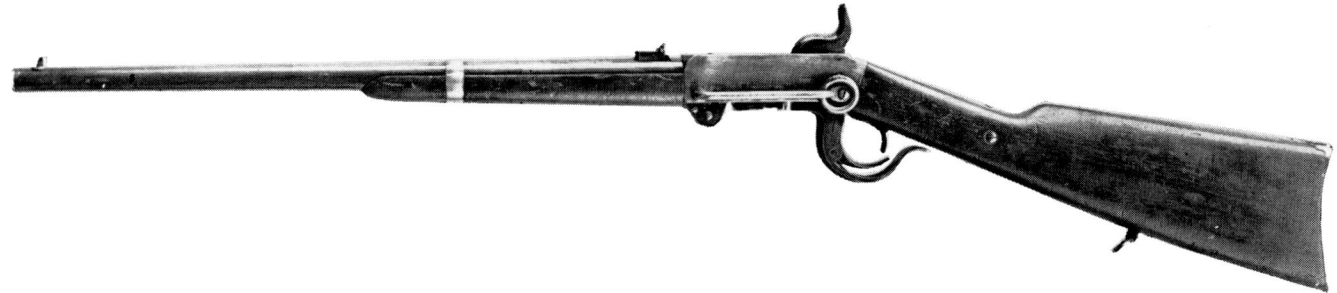

Fourth model carbine had Foster's improved lever, and barrel band held by spring on under side of stock. In fifth type, side screws were added in breech box to guide motion of receiver, which had corresponding cam cuts in its sides.

.58. The likelihood of a beat-up caliber .58 U. S. Rifle Musket being assembled by someone fraudulently about a Burnside breech mechanism now becoming more probable, it would be wise to examine such an arm most carefully, when one proposes to add it to one's collection. Jackson in correspondence was quite certain none of the rifles or rifle muskets had been prepared on these two orders; he did offer to supply cartridges "electro silver-plated cases, at three dollars per hundred. The cases now used (July 18, 1861) are tinned . . ."

During March, 1862, the transition from Second Model to Third took place, and there is a suggestion that the first forms of the Fourth Model were established at that time. To attach the forearm, a band of malleable iron was first used. This simplified manufacture, since the band could be cast to shape and would need only file finishing and possibly internal swedging to form. The cast grey iron was rendered malleable by soaking in a uniform heat for a long time. The rear sight base also was of cast malleable iron. Inspector Major George Balch from Springfield Armory, who was doing Rodman's job of inspecting at the Burnside Rifle Company armory, required changes in the band and sight. The sight change may be the new form of leaf sight now graduated to 100, 300, and 500 yards. Earlier sights were not so marked. A band spring also was added to hold the band in place. Internal changes in the lever, making it bend in two pieces to more easily open and close when fouled, were also devised by the rifle firm's engineers, perhaps Foster. Okayed by Rodman.

"These improvements, with the permission of the department, will be ingrafted upon the arm in a few weeks," wrote Hartshorn to Major Hagner of the Commission on April 7. By April 21, Hartshorn had sorted out the different contracts and overlapping orders and figured out which of earlier patterns he wanted to deliver to whom.

On February 10, 1862 he had delivered to Watertown Arsenal military storekeeper L. Leonard the last of the 640 Second Model carbines for Governor Sprague. On 13 March an added 260 carbines went to Governor Sprague which should (if Hartshorn's statements are correct) have conformed to the Third Model with malleable iron band. The sight leaves may not have been graduated. On 20 March a further lot of 800 Third Models were ready, and by April 21, 530 had been inspected and minor changes made to the wishes of Major Balch. Of these 520 were destined for the Indiana border. And among the 6,000 carbines in various stages of fabrication, 600 had the Third Model locking system. Hartshorn wanted to deliver these on the order for 7,500 carbines and then change to the "ingrafted" improvement of Foster's lever. "In this last type of Burnside carbine," says Gluckman, "the action was improved by double pivoting of the breechblock and the substitution of an easily removed latch hinge pin, at the forward hinge pivot." A further improved or "Fifth Model" has a stud screw in the middle of the breechbox, and a sine-curve cam groove in the chamber block, to prevent jamming on closing.

Price as well as quality came to the minds of Judge Holt and Ohio agent Owen as they conferred with Major Hagner on the Burnside project. Should they confirm the 7,500 order? How should they permit Hartshorn to deliver the various sub-patterns of Third and Fourth Models? They appealed to Ripley for a guide on pricing but the general had no means of estimating the cost of the Burnside carbine and could not therefore, say what price would afford a fair profit to the manufacturers. But Hartshorn, seeing the firm, of which he owned ⅖th share, about to suffer loss, volunteered to surrender the rifle and rifle musket contracts and take a reduction to $30 on the carbines. Assured that the Governor Sprague cavalry really needed his guns, Hartshorn agreed to take out a contract in proper form to cover the 7,500 order. This was signed 19 June, 1862, and so strongly did Governor Sprague feel the need for this locally-made gun, that he signed as a surety to pay the Government indemnity if Burnside Rifle Company should default!

The terms required first delivery of 1,000 guns in June and July, 1862. The guns actually delivered totalled 520 which were accepted June 24 and paid for at $35.75 under the terms of the State of Indiana contract. The same shipment included a further 80 Third Models accepted under the June 19 contract with Ripley at $30. In July, but 200 more Third Models were taken at $30 under the new contract. This finished up the 800 guns which Hartshorn had on hand, but there seems no indication that the remaining 600 of this Third Model, presumably without the double link to the Foster lever, were taken by the United States from Burnside directly. Instead, a delay occurred through the rest of the summer and not until October were 1,000 Fourth Model Burnsides ready for acceptance. Four hundred and eighty-nine were inspected October 20, 1862, and paid for in full; a balance of 11 were second grade guns paid for at $29. Why these guns were worth a dollar less was not recorded, but deliveries of this cut-rate nature continued throughout the production of 5,906 till March 5, 1863, under this contract.

The next contract for Burnside carbines was signed by Hartshorn and Ripley 29 December, 1862, for all the carbines that could be made during nine months after first delivery commencing in February, 1863. Not more than 25,000 carbines could be delivered under this contract, which was at the reduced price of $25. So far as is known, though these arms were to conform to a standard model to be deposited with the Chief of Ordnance, they did not represent any model changes or innovations in manufacture. Hartshorn was preparing a large armory, capable of volume production, and the product did not vary.

In spite of labor shortages, rising costs of materials, and difficulties in getting machinery, the production spiral continued until, after slow deliveries for several months, the Burnside factory was delivering batches of 1,000 Fourth Models regular as clockwork. A peak of 3,000 was delivered in September, 1863; 2,860 in February and 2,500 in March, April, and May of 1864. Two thousand six hundred and fifty-one were shipped in June and in August with the commencement of a last and final order, the enormous total of 3,500 Burnside Fourth Model carbines was delivered. On September 30, 1863, the company's production rate was so favorable that Hartshorn received a further order by letter from General Ramsay, requesting 12,500 carbines with the proviso that deliveries under the prior contract would be completed by January, 1864. The delivery under the order for 12,500 could not be less than 2,500 carbines monthly, at $25. Though Burnside Rifle Company did not quite make the January deadline, the contracts were not interrupted, and the guns continued to flow from the machines.

The Burnside carbine is a handsome piece of manufacture. The gaily mottled casehardened breechbox and lock parts contrast with the deep satin blue-black of the barrel and the burnished blues of the heat-colored bands and screw heads, sparkling highlights to the ensemble. It is to the Burnside Rifle Company production rate of 3,000 guns monthly that the collector owes the existence today of the prized "like new" specimens on hand. Double the production of even the most favorable estimates of 1862 was achieved by the end of 1864; while for precision of manufacture and excellence of finish this company with its absentee inventor yielded supremacy to no gunmaker.

Hartshorn was drunk with the money, there is no doubt about that. In a burst of manufacturing zeal which paralleled the avaricious patriotism of the agents in the good old days of Simon Cameron, the Burnside financier plunged to his fiscal neck into manufacturing not only the breechloaders which gave him his start, but a companion contract for Spencer repeating carbines.

Between April 15, 1865 and October 31, 1865, Burnside Rifle Company delivered 34,496 Spencer carbines. In September alone, 6,000 Spencers were delivered! The contract of 27 June, 1864, called for all the Spencers they could deliver up to 31 August, 1865; evidently the Ordnance Department was willing to continue to accept them until October.

A final contract for 3,000 Burnside carbines was negotiated 6 July, 1864, by Hartshorn, who had been elected president (replacing Earl P. Mason), and General Ramsay. Price was $19 each. Somewhat more than this number were prepared and Charles Jackson, who had been the Bristol Firearms Company treasurer but now took over Hartshorn's duties as registered agent, wrote to Ramsay about them. The general approved Jackson's offer to supply 4,500 first class Burnside carbines at $19 on December 2, 1864. Actually, 9,800 Burnside Fourth Models were accepted at $19 under these two proposals. The saga of Burnside was at an end. Most of the Fourth Model guns were of the sub-type with stud screws in a frame box we have called a "Fifth" model.

Over 55,000 carbines invented by a major general of Volunteers had been purchased by the Union. That they had been ordered mainly to arm Rhode Island troops; that a surety in one of the contracts was the Governor of Rhode Island himself; that their inventor had been appointed a general commanding Rhode Island troops armed with carbines of his own invention, was neither an expression of irregularity in administration nor corruption in conduct. It combined rapid breech-loading with the sturdiness of the metallic cartridge and the reliability of the common percussion cap (not all cartridge primers were reliable then). When war's end pulled the plug on Major General Ambrose Burnside's and his friend Isaac Hartshorn's profits, the company went out of business. To say that it failed is a distinct error, though it did not make its obvious mark on the future of the arms trade. Foster took up with a new design, that of the Howard breechloader surnamed "The Thunderbolt." Though super-streamlined, it was not a success commercially. Foster and the complex of manufacturing know-how faded into the pattern of shops and mills in postwar Providence that were to make the lazy town a Little Sheffield of New England.

Other Carbines

Some half-dozen makes of carbines were bought in

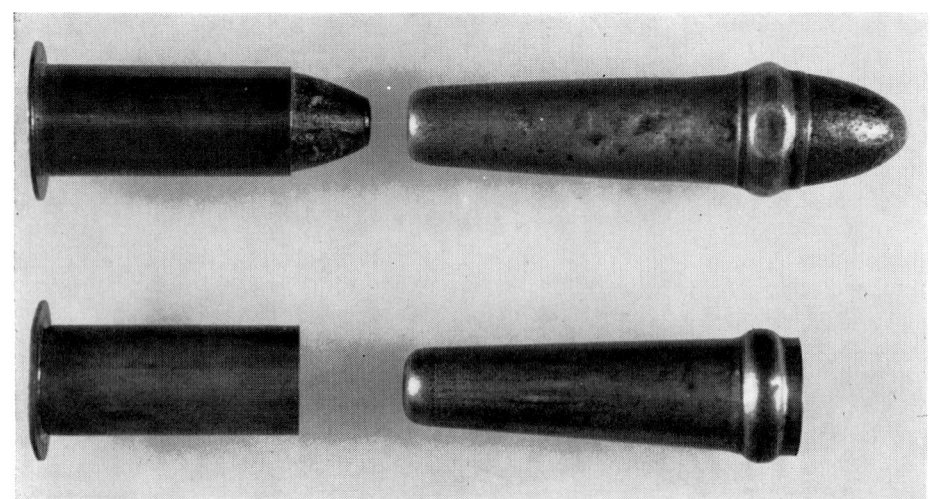

Burnside carbines are popular shooting irons today and scarcity of ammunition has prompted some enthusiasts to turn cases up by hand. Shown are new cases made 1956 for Burnside and Maynard carbines, compared with antique loads.

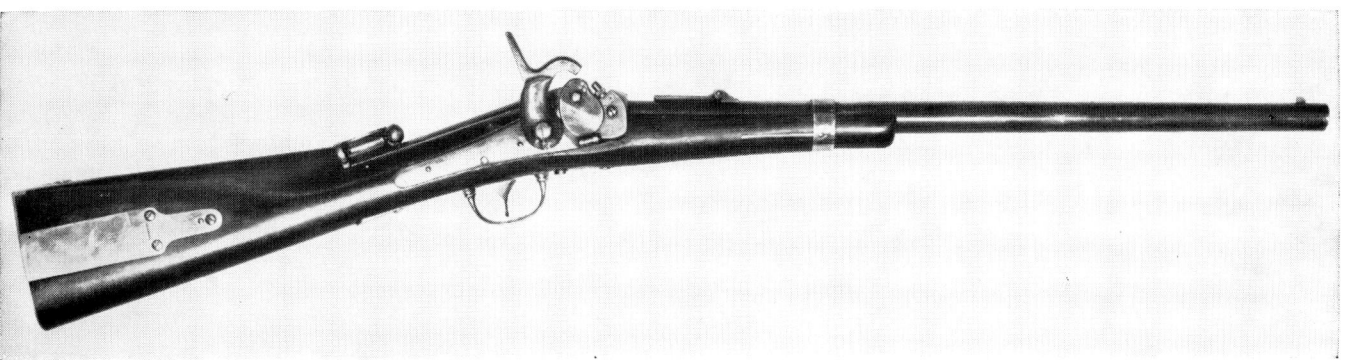

Merrill, Latrobe & Thomas carbines were made by Remington for Government test before the war, to order of proprietors who were Baltimore, Md. firm. Bar on top of stock small lifted up, opening breech. Primer was Maynard's.

a quantity barely sufficient to arm a regiment—approximately 1,000 units more or less for each. These were: Ballard, 1,509; Ball, 1,002; Gibbs, 1,052; Lindner, 892; Palmer, 1,001; Wesson, 151. Of Warner's carbine only 4,001 were obtained, and the Joslyn (11,-261) and Merrill (14,495) must be considered fairly limited in issue in spite of the numbers bought. Only a few of these are shown illustrated in the Atlas of the Official Records. Along with the Sharps slant-breech Model 1859, the Ballard full-stock rifle, Remington's split-breech, and Maynard's tip-barrel carbine, are shown the Burnside Second Model military carbine with Foster's lever but no forestock, and the Merrill capping breechloader. A Smith is also illustrated, but the presence of the thumb-lifter for locking bar on top of the action reveal it to be incorrectly the Model 1865 metallic cartridge Smith instead of the percussion Civil War type. A Starr and a Henry are also shown, and—also mistakenly—the Spencer M1865 two-band postwar rifle. Of these all, the Merrill in both rifle and carbine version is one of the most interesting, and yet little known.

Merrill Weapons

Mechanically, the Merrill is an adaptation of the earlier Jenks system, as made by Ames and Remington. Two patterns of arm exist. The first is known as the Merrill, Latrobe and Thomas carbine, and was fabricated by Remington under contract with the proprietors, who were of Baltimore, Maryland. A faucet breech gun, the rear lever lying a-top the small of the stock upon being lifted pivoted a cross-block and opened the back of the barrel, allowing a cartridge to be inserted. Firing was by percussion side lock. With the ubiquitous Maynard tape primer fitted, 170 of these carbines were bought by the United States on July 26, 1855, for $35 each. While they were marked "Patent Applied For" on top of the receiver, in addition to S. Remington, Ilion, New York, and Merrill, Latrobe & Thomas, Baltimore, Maryland, the patents that covered the final design were issued to James H. Merrill himself July, 1858, and May, 1861. Instead of a turning breech, a reciprocating plunger connected by a toggle link to a forward-folding lever a-top the stock small was used. With the lever forward a latch caught at the rear sight base to lock the lever down. In this position the thrust of the cartridge explosion against the breech plug was distributed in a straight line to the mechanism through the several pivots.

With Philip E. and Lewin W. Thomas, Merrill phased Latrobe out of his business and organized as Merrill, Thomas & Company in Baltimore, with offices and plant at 239 Baltimore Street. "Baltimore St." addresses are today in that sector known as "East Baltimore Street." Where the Merrill carbines once were made and rifle muskets converted to breechloaders, is now a dance hall under the shadow of the Drunk Tank at Central Police Station, Fayette and Fallsway. In Washington, S. P. Dinsmore looked after the business of the company at Clay's Hotel. He offered Assistant Secretary of War Scott these different Merrill arms: caliber .54 rifles weighing 9 lbs. 3 ozs., muskets caliber .58 with 40-inch barrels, and carbines caliber .54. "Selling prices hitherto," i.e., prior to October, 1861, Dinsmore said were $40 for the rifle (with sword bayonet), and $35 for carbine. A price quoted of $28 for musket is probably in error; $48 would be more consistent though actually an excessive cost, as Colt's revolving muskets could be bought for less, and they were repeaters. Production capacity of the works was quoted at 600 rifles, 800 carbines, and 600 muskets per month, beginning delivery within 30 days of order.

The Merrill shop was large, and was increased to make the carbines. At war's end, terminating manufacturing, the Merrill factory was offered for rent, and up to 100 horsepower, steam, was available. Rooms were "light, airy, comfortable, and heated by steam," their for rent ad read.

The Federal officers looked over an assortment of guns sold to the War Department June 5, 1861. The batch consisted of 20 Merrill's carbines, 1 Merrill's Minie musket, 3 Merrill's breech-loading rifles, 3 Remington carbines (Merrill), and 9 Harper's Ferry rifles, (Merrill). Colonel Dichell and General Stoneman were impressed, and Dinsmore made a sale.

"By direction of the Secretary of War," Ripley wrote to Merrill, Thomas & Company on October 25, 1861, "I will purchase 600 of your breechloading carbines, at thirty dollars each, with 600 cartridge boxes, belts, and cap boxes, at $2.50, and 600 slings, at $1, as stated in the letter of the 17th instant from Colonel Dichell and others to General Stoneman; also 60,000 cartridges for these carbines, at $18 per thousand; 80,000 Hick's caps, adapted to the carbine, at $1 per thousand." These 600 carbines were accepted at Washington Arsenal November 5 and paid for in full on November 7, 1861. But Stoneman's cavalrymen in the Army of the Potomac were not the only troops to have Merrills. Invading the western provinces of Cosmopolitan and Burnside, Merrill guns were ordered by Wisconsin and Indiana volunteers in quantity; while locally raised Maryland Union fighters expressed a decided preference for the rifles. Colonels Purnell and Petheridge of the Maryland (U.S.) Volunteers urged the gunmakers to keep writing to Simon Cameron, and inclose price lists of the arms.

Not financial interest nor cupidity but apparently a sincere desire to have the local arms caused Purnell and Petheridge to want the Merrills for their men. Both sword-bayonet rifles and carbines were needed, and Merrill, Thomas & Company's price list to Cameron cited prices as follows:

Carbine, $32.50 each; infantry rifles with sword bayonet, $42.50 each; carbine slings, $1; cartridges, $18 per thousand; caps $1; cavalry cartridge box, belt and cap box per set $2.50; infantry cartridge box, belt and cap box per set $3.

Patent breech-loading rifles were not of much interest to General Ripley, but he had a use for carbines. The night before Christmas he sent likewise to James H. Merrill his order for 5,000 carbines, but he shaded the price a little, possibly in response to negotiations in the interim between Cameron and the proprietors of the design. The contract price was $30. As the stomachs of the New Year's revelers settled down on 2 January, Merrill, Thomas & Company accepted the order at the beginning of 1862. The terms were specific: 500 in 30 days from date of order, (24 December; therefore say 24 January) and another 500 in 60 days (by February 24) and monthly deliveries of not less than 1,000 thereafter till completed. An additional 200 carbines were delivered to General Stoneman through acceptance by the Ordnance Department at Washington Arsenal, who issued them to Colonel Dickel of 1st New York Mounted Rifles. Indiana Volunteer General John A. Dix, stationed in Baltimore, also sought and received 200 of the carbines and his boys liked the design. "Colonel McMillan, of the 21st Regiment Indiana Volunteers," he wrote to the new War Secretary, Stanton, January 31, 1862, "is desirous of procuring Merrill's rifles for his regiment. I know the arm and think very highly of it," Dix noted.

"If 566 (of the carbines) could be exchanged for the larger arm (enough for the 21st Indiana regiment) by arrangement with the Ordnance Department, I would recommend it. Colonel McMillan has 192 of these rifles already and 242 Enfield rifles. The residue of his arms are Belgian and Prussian, for the most part unfit for service and diverse in construction," Dix scornfully concluded.

The swap was suggested to Merrill on his contract for 5,000 and he cheerfully assented to deliver rifles instead of carbines, but he priced the rifles *now* at $45 instead of $42.50 (perhaps labor costs had gone up). Though General Ripley put his endorsement on the order as "I think the charge for the rifles is too high," Dix stuck to his wants, and the arms were made and delivered, the first lot of 40 rifles being accepted April 25 at the full $45 agreed, weeks after Holt and Owen had got their teeth into the case. Wisconsin troops also received these Baltimore breechloaders; Colonel W. A. Barstow during February and March ordered 1,400 carbines for his 3rd Wisconsin Cavalry then training at Janesville, Wisconsin.

When, in response to Secretary Stanton's advertisement for all contractors to come forward and tell of their dealings, Merrill did so. Holt and Owen spent little time on the case. As Merrill apparently had made enough guns, though had only offered 500 for inspection spread over the first two months of production, the commissioners confirmed the contract except for short deliveries. As deliveries rolled on, Merrill made a new offer to sell carbines at $28 and Ripley extended the contract by another 1,400 carbines completed on November 28, 1862. Then, in the dark days of the spring of 1863, "the Department will receive from you as many carbines, Merrill's patent, as you may have ready for inspection, not exceeding 2,800 . . . ." Major Hagner on March 30, 1863 was instructed to inspect and receive these guns. And then from the Army of

Production Merrill carbine had top lever latched at front end to rear sight fixed base. Raising lever pulled back toggle plug in barrel for loading with combustible cartridge. Second type omitted patchbox, changed shape of lever latch piece to round nuts from elaborate filed contours of first type.

Jenks navy carbine made by Remington was among older types of arms converted or remanufactured to Merrill breech-loading system. Harpers Ferry rifles were also converted, and several thousand new Merrill rifles built in 1861-65.

the West came a demand for them; 1,000 were next ordered June 8, 1863, at $25, to be delivered to Major Callender, commanding St. Louis Arsenal, St. Louis, Missouri. An additional 200 were taken under order of July 1, and then 800 more, on July 11.

During the summer Merrill had made some changes in the gun which permitted cheaper manufacture, and proposed to make the carbine at only $22.50. Ripley demurred, but with the prospect of decreasing the price while all about him others were raising theirs, he went after Merrill and got a concession to continue deliveries of the "old model carbines," as they were now called, at the same $22.50. On August 11, 1863, an "all you can manufacture during 1863" order for the old model Merrill at $22.50 was issued by the Ordnance general. But business problems intervened. The Merrill company was reorganized, incorporated as Merrill's Patent Firearms Company, between July 11 and August 11, 1863, when the contract order was given, and deliveries were not regular. Yet Merrill was able to accomplish greater production with economy, and in October he offered to furnish 200 saber bayonet rifles at $30, which was accepted. Then June 8, 1864, a formal contract was signed for delivery of 1,200 "Merrill's improved breech-loading carbines," at $18 each—evidently Merrill was able to cut his prices even more, and General Ramsay, who signed this contract for the Ordnance Department, proved himself as hard a bargainer as his predecessor, Ripley. That this was a distinct new model of arm, one referred to in Merrill's offer to make at $22.50 as declined, is shown by the contract terms requiring two model carbines to be deposited with the Department as guides for inspection. The inspecting was probably to be done by Colonel Hagner.

At present, detailed recognition of the differences between the First and Second Model Merrill carbines appears based on the finger latch, and absence of patchbox. The first has a knurled latch; the second one of button form, cheaply made, and no patchbox.

A total of 10,055 Merrill First and Second model carbines were delivered, with the final 4,100 being delivered of the improved model under the terms of August 11, 1863 contract. Four hundred and six Merrill's breech-loading rifles were also obtained, the last 200 being of the Improved or Second model, delivered 30 November, 1863, by Merrill's Patent Firearms Company as reorganized. The assembly line where James H. Merrill's faithful Union workmen labored is now replaced by the "runway" bar where plump and plush cuties peel to Dixieland jazz.

Objections to the Gallager Carbines

When Thomas Poultney, partner in Poultney & Trimble of Baltimore, and proprietor of the Smith's patent carbine, offered to supply Ripley with 25,000 arms for cavalry, the Ordnance general was not impressed. On August 15, 1861, the debacle of Bull Run having not yet been forgotten, he still resisted, and responded to Assistant Secretary of War Scott's query about the proposal by saying, "This proposition is objectionable on account of its introducing an arm untried in the field, of its requiring a special cartridge, and of the price charged ($32.50); the best of Sharps'

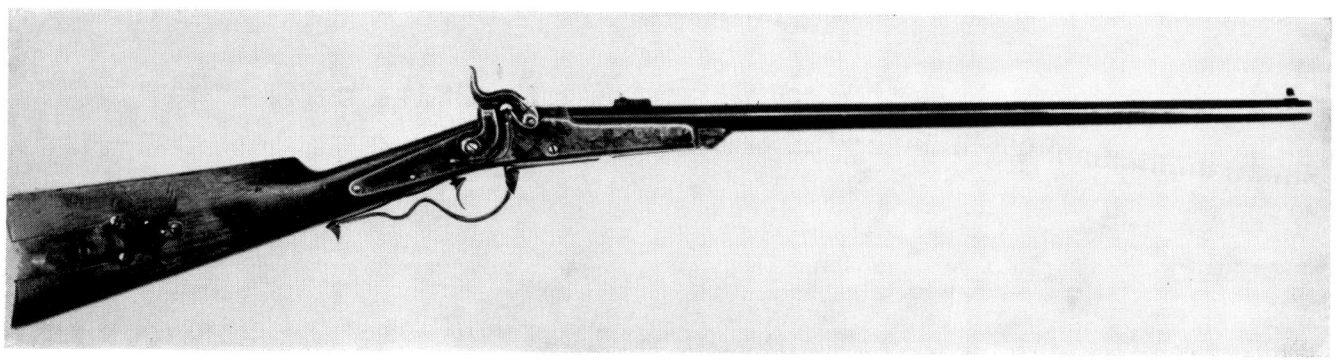

Philadelphians Richardson & Overman supplied carbines designed by Georgian Mahlon Gallagher. Inventor's friends it is believed had approached Colt before the war with proposition to manufacture tipping barrel breechloader in South.

carbines cost $30 each, including appendages." He concluded by referring to recent orders concerning the equipment of the cavalry of The Army of the Potomac: "The orders in this division are, to arm the cavalry with sabres and pistols only." He considered that since orders or contracts for 17,000 carbines had already been let, these would be enough. But when the horse soldiers began to call for harder-hitting arms than a .44 pistol, Ripley's total of 17,000 carbines was soon swelled in contract and order to more than 117,000. Among the lesser known but invaluable guns, which had all the objections that Ripley first voiced against the Smiths, was the Gallager carbine, a contribution of Richardson and Overman, Philadelphia, to winning the war. Including 200 bought in open purchase September 10, 1861, over 20,000 Gallager capping breechloaders taking a special wrapped tinfoil cartridge were bought by the spring of '65. The important design feature of this invention of Georgian Mahlon J. Gallager was the trigger guard lever which, when pressed downwards, swung the barrel forward from the standing breech and allowed it to tip for loading the chamber. Originally, Gallager hoped to manufacture in Georgia. The back-action lock suggested the Cosmopolitan or the Sharps or others in its form, but it was not interchangeable with any other arm. Gallager received Patent No. 29,157 on July 17, 1860, and Richardson & Overman liked it well enough to obtain the rights and commence perfecting the model.

Ripley accepted their proposal on direct orders of Thomas A. Scott who noted "The sample carbine is highly approved. The price is less than offered by others. We should be glad to have 5,000 of these guns provided they can be delivered at the rate of, say, 1,000 by the close of October (1861) and 1,000 each month thereafter." Ripley's order of September 17, 1861, required delivery for inspection at Frankford Arsenal, Philadelphia, in lots of not less than 500 per month. Each carbine was accompanied by 40 metallic cartridges, a screw driver and nipple wrench, and an extra cone and for every ten carbines, a bullet mould, and one loader. A tool existed to reload Gallager ammo.

Ripley's terms were not met, for Richardson & Overman were not actually in production when they submitted the sample to Scott. Months were consumed, and first delivery was 100 guns and 4,000 cartridges on January 23, 1862. Lieutenant Treadwell had taken delivery by March 16 of 840 Gallager carbines and 30,000 rounds of ammunition, when Holt and Owen reviewed the case.

Their decision was to recommend accepting further deliveries, as Richardson & Owen seemed able at last to live up to their promised delivery schedule of 200 a week and had all the forging work finished ready for final machining. George J. Richardson and William W. Overman lived up to their obligations and by the end of their four contracts for Gallager's carbines, were delivering in batches of 1,000 guns.

The first three contracts in addition to Ripley's order were in proper form executed with sureties and totalled 5,000 for the first, as many as they could make for the second, and 10,000 for the third. Under these three contracts plus the Ripley order, a total of 18,748 capping carbines were bought by the time of negotiating for the final Gallager order, the contract of March 11, 1865. Under its terms, 5,000 improved cartridge arms adapted to the Spencer carbine cartridge 56/52 were received and paid for, the last delivered and paid for in June, 1865.

Lindner Guns

One carbine which saw little use in the war still reaped considerable profit from it: the breechloader of Edward Lindner. Patented March 29, 1859, this arm also used a fixed breech and moved the breechblock between barrel and fixed breech by means of a turning sleeve with a thumb piece attached. Often lost or broken off, the thumb piece was necessary to rotate a sleeve over the breech so as to free the breechblock and allow it to be tipped up for loading with a combustible cartridge. The design which seems complicated in description, was actually simple enough though with some defects. The Royal Bavarian Army adopted the system about 1860. In the United States, the Lindner was Amoskeag's entry in the carbine race; added to rifle muskets and the great steam pumper horse-drawn fire engines which clanged down cobbled streets in a thousand towns across the divided nation was Edward Lindner's carbine produced at Manchester, New Hampshire.

Agent for the sale of 892 of these guns to the United States was Samuel B. Smith, a New Yorker headquartering at the Kirkwood House in the suite of A.J.F. Phelan. Smith had plunged heavily in the foreign musket market, scurrying from Cameron to Boker with contracts and buying arms from Boker subject to future delivery and inspection. But with the Lindner guns he was dealing on home ground, with Amoskeag.

As an independent contractor, Smith offered the Lindner guns to Colonel Broadhead's regiment. Secretary Cameron approved the requisition and Colonel Maynadier during a temporary absence of Ripley from the office on November 6, 1861, approved the order for 400 Lindner carbines at $25, and 40,000 cartridges, but all had to be delivered within eight days. Apparently 395 were actually delivered, or 400 of which five failed inspection. They were handed to Lieutenant Colonel Ramsay, commanding Washington Arsenal at the time.

These were not United States purchase guns, but were paid for out of the Militia Appropriation of 1808 which had annually appropriated $200,000 for the purchase and manufacture of small-arms, ordnance, and ordnance stores, to equip the state troops. But Lindner himself got into the act when it appeared that E. A. Straw of Amoskeag was not pushing his guns enough, and Smith, by the Holt and Owen team, had been pushed out of the picture on his foreign musket deal. A year later Maynadier on November 4, 1862, informed Straw that Lindner could deliver all he could

Edward Lindner's patent consisted of a turning barrel sleeve (to which was attached a thumbpiece) then could be rotated to unlatch rear nippled chamber which tipped up for front-loading a combustible cartridge. Amoskeag made guns, in very limited quantity. Design was extensively used abroad in Bavaria.

make up to "the first of December next." Maynadier's time was one calendar year and a part of a month, but Lindner must have been making guns slowly by hand. The delivery on January 9 of 1863 was for but 501 carbines, paid for at $20 each; a total of 892 in all for the Union officially. More state forces may have esteemed the gun but production was extremely limited; Lindner's carbine was little more than experimental, though Straw seems to have "caught the bug" and designed a sliding-forward barrel carbine which he entered in the trials of 1865, without success.

Gibbs Carbines

Small success characterized also the connection between inventor Lucius H. Gibbs, promoter-financier William F. Brooks, and gunmaker W. W. Marston, in the contract for Gibbs' carbines.

Brooks, a brass and flue manufacturer who had done work for Marston, collaborated with Marston in the promotion of the Gibbs carbine. An under-lever sliding barrel capping breechloader, it was patented January 8, 1856, No. 14,057. In 1857 twenty were made, probably by Marston, by hand for test; one was shot with favorable comment by a board of officers in 1858 at West Point. Now Brooks offered to supply 10,000 of the Gibbs guns, together with 10,000 Springfields. The order was issued by Ripley on December 13, 1861 and accepted by Brooks, who was on hand the same day in Washington to make sure there was no slip-up.

He at once began to prepare to meet the need for carbines. Small parts were to be forged by J. Stephenson and sent to Marston for finishing. The famous gunmaker was also to finish up the stocks using his full suite of stocking machinery, capable of turning out fifty buttstocks a day (10 hours). Steel drilled barrels were to be supplied, as rifled and turned blanks, by Dinslow & Chase of Windsor Locks, Connecticut; but by the spring of 1862 Brooks had failed to supply even the model carbine for inspection standard which was required.

Because of machinery delays and other hazards of tooling up in the face of price competition in the Northern war industries, Marston was behind schedule by several months. Holt and Owen persuaded Brooks, who had done nothing toward making his Springfields, to give up that order. Brooks also wanted to surrender the Gibbs order of 13 December and take out a new contract; the time elapsed would be in his favor if renegotiated as to deliveries. The commissioners saw the joker in Brooks' favor but okayed it that way. The contract for 10,000 Gibbs carbines was signed 21 June, 1862, with the provision that the first 1,000 were to be delivered by August, 1862. But Marston still fell far short of expectations.

On December 1, Marston was bought out by George Opdyke, Mayor of New York, with an advance of $65,000 in cash and authority to draw on him, Opdyke, up to $67,000. Loren Jones was factory superintendent, and received a fee of 75¢ on each gun delivered to the United States, plus his salary. Early in January, a new superintendent was called in, John Kane, but the mechanical supervisor or foreman was John W. Keene,

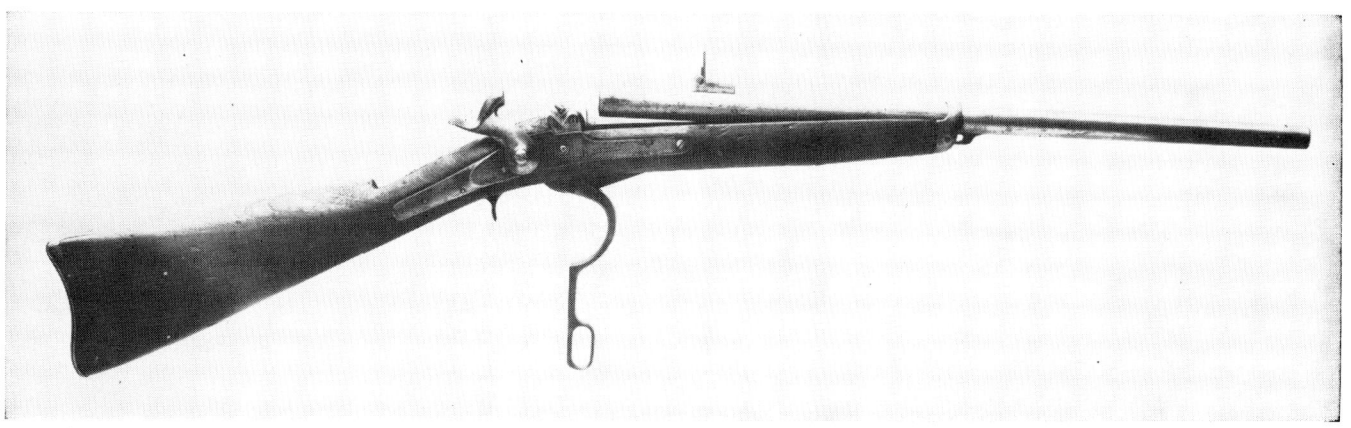

Lucius H. Gibbs invented another tipping barrel capping breechloader which went into production under superintendency of W. W. Marston of New York. Lockplate resembles a cross between front action and back action systems.

Gibbs carbine accepted by Ordnance office in New York was stamped on buttstock with special die impressing, in a circle, the word MODEL and in an arc INSPEC^T OF CONT ARMS.

who actually made the guns. Keene had been 22 years in the gun making trade, and went into the Marston shop (now controlled by Opdyke) in February, 1863, to set things right.

By May 30, a first delivery of 550 Gibbs carbines was accepted by Major Hagner; 502 were ready June 24, and delivered. By July 13, another 500 had been finished in their several parts and were ready for inspection. On that day a great riot was spreading across the city. As Loren Jones recalled it later,

On the 13th, in the morning, I went to the Armory; everything was going on as usual; I went down town for supplies; did not see Mr. Opdyke; got back about 12 o'clock; found 34 policemen there; they said they had come to protect the property; the men were furnished with the guns we were making; each policeman had a gun and ammunition; I furnished them and Mr. Kane furnished them; they were in the lower part of the building; the hands were discharged for the day—some sixty five; they were sent away, as the police were there to defend the building; soon after an attack was made by the mob, who commenced beating on the paneling of the door; the policemen cautioned them to retire, but the mob kept on battering the door, and then the policemen fired through the door; the leading man was killed instantly and two others were wounded, and the mob left immediately.

About two hours after the rioters had fled, the police were ordered to leave. Loren Jones went to Captain Cameron of the 22d Street Station house but was unable to get more protection. Jones then went to the City Hall to see Opdyke but instead found Opdyke's son-in-law, in whose name the ownership of the former Marston Armory was actually listed. G. W. Farlee, the son-in-law, referred Jones to the St. Nicholas Hotel, where Jones found Opdyke but was unable to get him stirred up over the fact the city had withdrawn its defense of the factory; Opdyke was more concerned over the fact he had no lunch, and went out in search of a meal, leaving Jones to return alone to the Armory. When he got back to 22d Street he saw the works in flames, with approximately 6,000 Gibbs carbines in various stages of production inside being consumed, plus the 500 ready for acceptance by the Government inspectors, and materials for the remaining thousands also damaged by fire. Cost of manufacture of the fifty guns daily was $14 each; the Government paid $24.70, and the total loss was about $200,000.

G. W. Farlee put in a claim for the loss before the Commission of Supervisors of New York, studying the claims against the city because of damage from the terrible July Draft Riots. Sitting on the Commission as supervisors, among others, were Orison Blunt, riflemaker, and George Opdyke, Mayor of New York. Before Opdyke came, Farlee who, according to an editorial by Thurlow Weed in the 8 June, 1864 issue of the *Evening Journal,* testified falsely:

G. W. Farlee, Opdyke's son-in-law, made a claim upon the supervisors for damages sustained by the destruction of guns in the process of manufacture under a contract with the Government. Mayor Opdyke was, by virtue of his office, a member of the committee before which the claim was allowed. Opdyke disclaimed any personal interest in the gun claim. Farlee denied in the journals that Opdyke was interested, and made an affidavit, which was submitted to the committee, swearing that *he* was the sole owner of the gun contract. Opdyke, therefore, sat in the committee, investigating the claim of his son-in-law, and at an early day received a check for $190,000.

The explosion which resulted from this and other charges against Opdyke put both Weed and Opdyke into libel court. The searcher can dig deeper by referring to *The Great Libel Case: Opdyke vs. Weed,* which was published by the American News Company, 1865. Sufficient it is to say that no more Gibbs carbines were made.

John W. Keene, as a result of investigating costs for Gibbs guns at Ilion, took employment with Remington Arms as a contractor and remained with them for many years. The Draft Riots ended Marston's Armory.

Ballards

A more solid New York enterprise was that of Merwin & Bray, agents for numerous patent arms, Pond's, Plant's, Smith & Wesson's, and the to-be-famous Ballard carbine. In the mainstream of Ballard production is the theme of the Marlin and Stevens factories of later years. The design of the famous single shot match rifles of the early twentieth century is the almost unchanged conception of Charles H. Ballard of Worcester, Massachusetts. His patent of November 5, 1861, No. 33,631, covers a breechloader with the remarkable concept of having the hammer and sear-trigger hung inside the dropping breechblock so that one stroke of the lever performs the opening, extracting (sometimes, in some models), and half-cocking

1861) and on the left frame side, MERWIN & BRAY AGTS, N. Y., he declares that some were also made by the Ballard Arms Company of Fall River, Massachusetts. Eldon G. Wolff, curator of arms at the Milwaukee Public Museum, in his well organized monograph, *Ballard Rifles in The Henry J. Nunnemacher Collection,* argues that no proof exists of any Ballard Arms Company anywhere, and cites a specimen listed as having been so marked, as not actually having this mark when he examined the particular gun. Satterlee is also unclear on the calibers, saying the "No. 56 Ballard" cartridge was quickly superseded by the .56-56 Spencer, "which is, however, not correct for it." Satterlee was in part referring to such sources as the Rem-

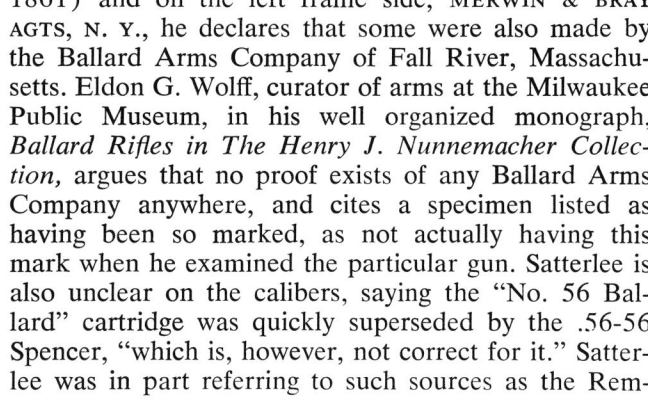

Ballard rifle from *Official Records Atlas* had three bands much like Sharps and Spencer parts; was otherwise unique single shot system with hammer mounted in block that dropped down to open chamber for metallic cartridge.

UMC cartridge catalogs which as late as the winter of 1913-14 listed ".56-.56 Spencer Carbine. Black powder, per 1,000 . . . $40.00 . . . Adapted to Spencer, Ballard, Joslyn, and other carbines . . ." The correct load is slightly longer in the case than the Spencer shell, and is identified by Colonel Lewis as a .54 for what was known during the middle of the war as Ballard's Carbine, O.M., for Old Model.

First producer of the Ballard system was the firm of Ball & Williams, in Worcester. The linkage of the Ballard patent extractor was not used, but a button sliding manually in a groove in the forestock below the barrel was the successful first type of extractor. It attached to the extractor bar which pushed straight back, engaging the cartridge rim at its bottom quadrant. Merwyn & Bray were successful in selling a good many of these arms to the State of Kentucky, claiming in *Harpers Weekly* ads by 1865 that "These rifles were used by Captains Crawford and Fisk on the Overland Expedition to the Pacific, under orders of the United States Government. The General Government and the State of Kentucky have about 20,000 now in active field service, of which the highest testimonials are received."

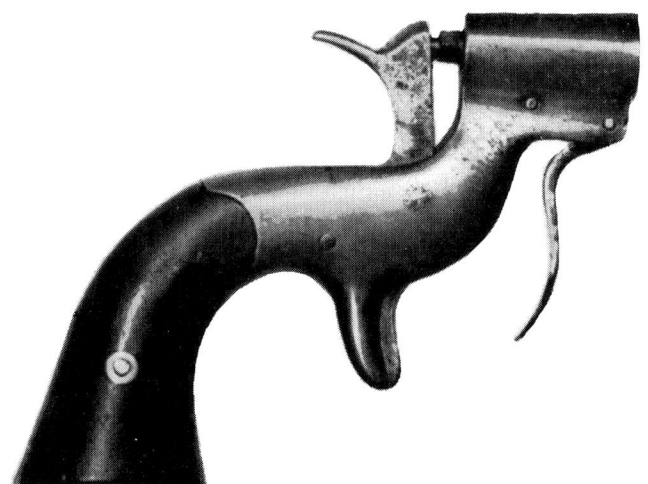

Marston was major gunmaker in New York, spanned period from Allen-type single shots and pepperbox pistols with bar hammers (top) to special breechloading pistol of 1849. During war, Marston made flare pistols.

the hammer. At first a rim fire cartridge design, the shortage of proper ammunition in the field suggested the merit of adapting the gun to percussion cap fire a la Maynard carbine. This modification was patented by Joseph Merwin and Edward P. Bray, Merwin & Bray, agents, on January 5, 1864, No. 41,166 and consisted of a percussion nipple fitted below the striking arc of the rim fire hammer nose. Either the cap could be detonated or the primed rim fire cartridge discharged without any adjustment one to the other, except for capping the nipple.

The first Ballard carbine of the Civil War seems to have been a rather mysterious one which Gluckman lists as caliber .54, rim-fire, 22 inch round rifled barrel, rifled with 5 grooves. Total length 38 inches. Weight 7 pounds. While the listed specimen Gluckman describes as being marked on the right frame side: BALLARD'S PATENT NOVEMBER 5, 1867 (sic, should be

Some of the first Ballards differ in the proportions of the breechblock to the later type; Wolff lists one serial number 223 as having a turned-up hammer ear and a large solid block not fitting into any obviously later models of Ballard. A cut-out on its left side permits the mainspring to be removed. The sear nose of the trigger is sprung into the hammer notch by means of a plunger and coil spring acting against the hammer, and inserted from the front face of the block; later models with the characteristic Ballard split breechblock have a U-shaped spring for the trigger.

In these First Model details, the arm is materially altered from the original patent of Charles Ballard,

Ballard "Kentucky" carbine was sold to U.S. by Merwin & Bray, agents, but made by Ball & Williams in Worcester where inventor lived. Some arms had Merwin & Bray invention of nipple in breechblock for alternative percussion cap fire using metallic cartridges, a la Maynard carbine. Peg below stock is ejector head; pulled back it popped out cartridge case.

which had a single leaf spring acting in a notch in the hammer and a single leaf spring notched into the front of the trigger, bearing against a fixed pin in the block. Spring disassembly in Ballard's patent drawing was from the bottom of the block; in the First Model changes appear which may have been made by Hartley Williams and R. Ball, witnesses to Ballard's first patent.

In spite of the grandiose claims of Merwin and Bray as the war drew to a close, it appears that for the first several years Ballard had a hard time making anything. The rather rare First Model may have been a blind alley in construction and not until the idea of the split breechblock was conceived was it possible to produce the rather tricky Ballard action in quantity. Though the Official Records Atlas illustrates the Ballard 3-band infantry rifle with upturned hammer as an official pattern, none were bought by the Union during the war, only by the state troops, presumably Kentucky.

In the Cavalry Bureau, a study of carbines was under way. A single Ballard carbine was purchased from Merwin and Bray for $25 on September 14, 1863. It was among carbines surveyed by a board of officers which convened September 24. Caliber was probably .54, taking the Ballard cartridge and alternatively but not very well, the Spencer .56-.56 cartridge. Meanwhile, the Springfield Armory experiments leading to the development of the Spencer .56-.52 carbine cartridge were progressing. The Board, under Lieutenant Colonel Hagner, consisted of Major Dyer, Major T. T. S. Laidley, Captain Benton, Captain S. V. Benet, Captain Silas Crispin, and Captain Balch. Each made his individual recommendation for caliber to be adopted but General Ramsay seemed to have the last say-so, boosting for .44 caliber in his letter to Secretary Stanton October 20, largely because it was said that the State of Massachusetts had ordered Spencer carbines in this caliber. The matter was kicked around, and finally .50 caliber settled upon. The Ballard proprietors were notified how to proceed:

ORDNANCE OFFICE, WAR DEPARTMENT
Washington, November 24, 1863

GENTLEMEN: This department, having adopted a general plan for cavalry carbines, has decided that all such carbines as may be ordered in future, shall conform to that plan, the principal features of which are, that the barrel shall be twenty inches long, with a calibre of half an inch, (.50), and that the weight of the arm shall be not over *eight* nor under *six* pounds. With a view to making experiments to determine the best charge for these arms, you will be pleased to make for this department, with the least possible delay, six of these Ballard carbines upon the foregoing general principles—the chamber of each one to be counterbored to fifty-two hundredths of an inch (.52), and of the proper length to receive the cartridges, as follows:

1 for a 35-grain copper cartridge
1 for a 40-grain copper cartridge
1 for a 45-grain copper cartridge
1 for a 50-grain copper cartridge
1 for a 55-grain copper cartridge
1 for a 60-grain copper cartridge

Be pleased to signify your acceptance or non-acceptance of this order, and if you accept, please state the time when the six carbines will be furnished and the cost of each.

Respectfully, your obedient servant,
GEORGE D. RAMSAY
Brigadier General, Chief of Ordnance

Merwin and Bray did not at once deliver the carbines, as difficulty arose over the actual bore diameters to be made. Six Ballard carbines listed as *caliber .44 inch* were accepted from M & B July 2, 1864, under this order of 24 November, and paid for at $28 each. But while the uncertainty of caliber may have existed in the Ordnance Department, Ballard, Ball, and Williams had no such perplexity. They had decided to make the gun in .44 caliber, what today is sometimes noted as ".44 Long Rimfire," and were tooled up at the time of the six-carbine order to fabricate in caliber .44. On January 7, 1864, they prevailed upon General Ramsay to sign a contract ordering 5,000 carbines, .44 caliber. Though delivery was not as per schedule, it was quick and on March 18, 1,000 Ballards were accepted under this contract at $23 each, "with all the appendages required for their use in the service." But the nature of appendages is unspecified; possibly a wiping thong and brush, and a screw driver. The mechanism is a little more slender than the .56 caliber arm; and it appears from the existence of half-stock rifles fitted in a military fashion, with barrel band but a 30-inch half-octagon barrel, stamped KENTUCKY on the top facet of the breech, that the estimated 15,000 rifles made for that state were supplied partly from this Second Type series. With solid breechblocks, though smaller than the .56 (caliber .54 nominally) type, this Second Type military model, including many of the Kentucky state rifles, was made up to about 10,000 serial number.

The Ballard is not looked upon as any kind of Secondary Confederate; but the irregular militia and guerrilla forces in the border states seemed to find its simple mechanism and positive push-plunger extractor a welcome improvement over the percussion Sharps they had preferred a decade before. An interesting manufacturing detail of these early Ballards is the use for the receiver or frame housing of malleable cast iron. This detail was specifically mentioned as a part of the contract of January 7 by Ramsay, who ordered them "with the malleable cast-iron lock frame." Cast-iron frames, cored out to reduce cost of machining, were used through the postwar period, succeeding Merrimack Arms Company, Brown Manufacturing Company, and even into the J. M. Marlin, New Haven, series of Ballard rifles. Made first for war, the Ballard was effectively turned into a tool for peace by the simple addition of adjustable sporting sights.

After the delivery of the 6 special-chamber .44 Ballards, an added lot of 500 in .44 Long Rimfire was accepted from Merwin & Bray under the contract on August 1, 1864. But perhaps the makers in Worcester had scrapped their tools for the larger frame, or in some other way made it difficult for them to compete. The fabrication of .44 cartridges in the winter of 1863, 2,000 of each of the six types, at the Springfield Armory, was not enough to wage a shooting war. Opinion wavered between .50 and the smaller .44, but meanwhile the arms in being were of the .52-.56 series, and these were the calibers in both metallic cartridge and combustible cartridge form that continued to be produced in an accelerating spiral for the war effort. And while Burnside Arms, for example, tooled up and turned out a fantastic number of Spencers for a few months, Ballard failed to get the war recognition that the merits of the design warranted.

Yet Ballard is still with us, while the Spencer is relegated to a collectors' novelty. Under the aegis of John Mahlon Marlin, fanatic for deep-grooved accuracy, the post-war Ballard sporter took on new luster. Its wood-wiping rod model, looking a little like a Hawken of the 1840's, was in the period of 1870 immensely popular as the "Pacific Ballard." The fine rifling imparted high accuracy to sporting calibers which were then under intensive and competitive development. Even today the simple, strong Ballard action is prized for shooting purposes by older riflemen who mix the legend of Ballard accuracy with a modern need for a single shot match rifle. Among the last in war, the Ballard came to achieve a first place in peace in the hearts of riflemen.

Lamson

When Goodnow and Yale saw the last shipping chest of 20 Springfield rifle muskets off by the steam cars for New York, they breathed a sigh of relief. The date was about December 10, 1864, for it was on that date that the final 1,000 arms were accepted at the full contract price of $20 as No. 1 grade Springfields. But though they had finished their participation in the Lamson, Goodnow & Yale contract, their erstwhile partner, Ebenezer G. Lamson, was by no means through with the gun business. He had, sometime before the summer of 1864, bought out their interest and reorganized under the sobriquet "E. G. Lamson & Company." Your author once owned an almost new specimen of E. G. Lamson & Company rifle musket, Springfield pattern, dated on the barrel tang 1865. The stock cheek did not have the U.S. Inspector or Sub-Inspector stamps usually placed there; only the three tiny initials of the parts inspector, so small as to be illegible though perfectly imprinted. Lamson apparently planned to continue in the gun business if he could find a good inventor to team up with and, not being shy, teamed up at first with two of them. On June 20, 1864, Lamson signed contracts with General Ramsay to supply 1,000 each, a sort of field test lot, of .44 caliber cavalry carbines designed by Palmer and by Ball.

New Yorker William Palmer patented December 22, 1863, a turning bolt breech-loading cartridge arm which was to be the first bolt action cartridge arm in the United States service. The only prior model in any way resembling it in operation was the capping breech-loader of James Durrell Greene. The Palmer gun had a conventional back action side lock, the pointed hammer striking the cartridge rim directly. The extractor hook was connected to the top of the bolt. Appendages to be furnished were one brush thong and one screw driver. The guns had to conform to a pattern carbine. Two of these were to be supplied, one for the Ordnance Office and the other for the inspector's office in New York. One carbine only was delivered in addition to the 1,000 contracted for. On June 15, 1865, the shipment was accepted by the inspectors but the guns never saw battle.

Had reports of their use even been filed, the decision to adopt a flip-up breechblock rifle in the transformation work after the war might have been avoided, and the bolt action era, far more versatile in application in terms of strength and magazine loading, have been ushered in 30 years before it was in 1892. (The Krag bolt action rifle was formally adopted after Army and Navy tests with others on a desultory basis during the years following the Civil War).

Lamson's other bet to build an arms empire was equally a failure, though of a clever and practical design. This was the carbine designed by Albert Ball of Worcester, who went to Windsor, Vermont, from his home in Massachusetts, to supervise the manufacture. There is some suggestion here that Ball was of the Ball & Williams firm, though this is not documented. The contract to furnish 1,000 Ball's breech-loading repeating cavalry arm was signed the same date, June 20, 1864, and the guns delivered May 14, 1865. Two additional guns were delivered, samples for inspection, making 1,002 in all.

The Ball gun was a clever design but was damned because of its large caliber, .50, taking the new Springfield Armory designed ".56-.52 Spencer rimfire

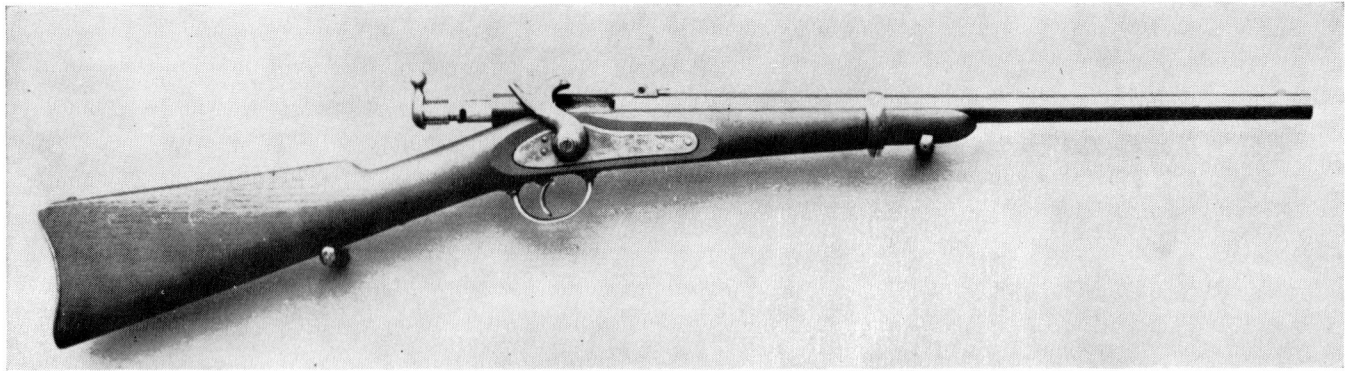

Palmer carbine made by E. G. Lamson after separation from Goodnough and Yale was advanced turning bolt cartridge breechloader. Altogether, 1,001 guns were made but never saw service. Principle was far ahead of its time. Bolt is shown open.

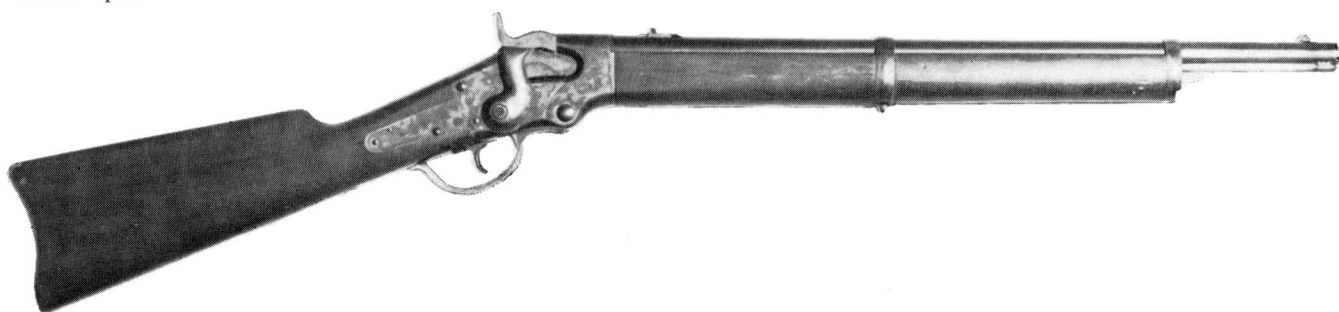

Ball repeater took seven cartridges in under-barrel magazine entirely surrounded by wooden forestock. A total of 1,002 were obtained from Lamson but not issued.

cartridge." Seven of the fat cartridges were stored beneath the barrel in a tube magazine, which was loaded through the ejection port which also served as a loading port. The trigger guard was the charging lever, and the breech housing terminated to the rear in a back action sidelock plate upon which a Spenceresque hammer was hung. Two barrel bands were fitted, the front of slanting shape as a front to the magazine. A useful accessory, a steel wiping rod, ran the length of the barrel. Barrel length was 20½ inches, but Gluckman says some were made in .44 caliber. The statement by Sawyer that this is "Calibre .56, center fire metallic cartridge," is believed an error. While the name of Lamson remained active in Vermont machine tool business, the record of his gunmaking seems to come to a halt at the end of the war.

Four Other Carbines

Four remaining patterns of carbine, the Hall percussion breechloader, the Joslyn transformation, which had some characteristics of a cartridge conversion of a musket, Warner's brass-framed single shot and the tipping barrel light carbine of Frank Wesson, complete the list of United States bought carbines by name. There were two other batches: 10,051 foreign carbines at an average price of $6.50 were obtained, and a miniscule lot of 587 musketoons for $5,815.50 were purchased. Several other makes such as the Triplett & Scott were purchased by state troops on their own account, but were not funded later by the United States. One of the most interesting, the simple little Lee side-swing barrel .44, was the start of the fabulous record of James Paris Lee. From this beginning of 1,000 refused carbines, the total of Lee arms ultimately grew until in 1944 the last Lee rifle, the Russian Nagant Model 1944, was put into production, finis to perhaps 10,000,000 arms in whole or major part designed by Lee. Even afterward, the modern Russian semiautomatic short rifle in its magazine construction embodies features once patented by James Paris Lee. But his first 1,000 arms were refused because of an error in the chamber dimension!

Of the carbines bought by name, the Joslyn was the most numerous. Invented by Benjamin F. Joslyn of Worcester, these arms were made by the Joslyn Fire Arms Company at Stonington, Connecticut. Of a prolific family of arms inventors—a relative, Milton Joslyn, was a top executive in Colt's works—Benjamin F. Joslyn had patented several developments in firearms including the side-hammer Joslyn revolvers made by W. C. Freeman. Why some of these diverse manufacturing interests could not be brought together under one roof for economy in production and to reduce the competition in market for tools and labor is not thoroughly understood. It is possible, however, that the existing labor pool in Worcester was overtaxed by arms factories in or near that city, and that Ball had to go to a labor surplus area, Windsor, Vermont, while Joslyn had to go to another, Stonington, Connecticut, in order to get work done at all.

That Joslyn carbine has a side lock which in postwar versions is a modified Springfield mechanism but

FEDERAL CARBINES

Early Joslyn breechloader was lift-lever type resembling Merrill. Gun was made for Army test by Waters in Millbury, Mass., before the war. Not made in volume.

in the earlier patterns is of Stonington make and bears the company's name. Later Government locks seen on Joslyn breechloading muskets, .50 caliber centerfire, have the name of the armory stamped SP RINGFIELD, with a trace of a gap in spacing between the letters P and R. Others have the word stamped normally, but the 1864 locks seen have the gapped Springfield name—not significant, merely odd.

Joslyn who got off to a late start in the great arms race, managed to get the attention of the Government first by approaching Major Hagner. Empowered to buy arms in the field from sources as he saw fit, Hagner was inclined to take a flier in Joslyn carbines. The breech was simplicity itself. The barrel sat up high and could be loaded easily from the back. The sidelock hammer was bent inward to strike in the center of the block. The block itself was cut with a ring to lock over a groove turned on the back of the barrel, and could be swung easily to one side, exposing the barrel for loading. In practice the knurled finger stud on the right side of the breechblock, that had to be grasped and pulled outward to free the catch and permit the breechblock to be rotated upward and to the side, may have been a little slippery in the heat of combat when one's fingers were slick with blood. Two hundred were purchased by Hagner in November and December of 1861, from Bruff Brothers & Seaver of New York at $35.

Joslyn's first carbine, of which a small number were obtained for United States Army and Navy test in the mid-1850's, was a lifting lever type of breechloader taking a percussion cap. The lever lay on top of the stock small and latched against the front of the comb, like the Fusil Robert of 1836. A. H. Waters made these guns, after the Militia Appropriations had been shut off, but this business was not enough to keep the Waters enterprise alive.

W. C. Freeman also made a few in his Tower

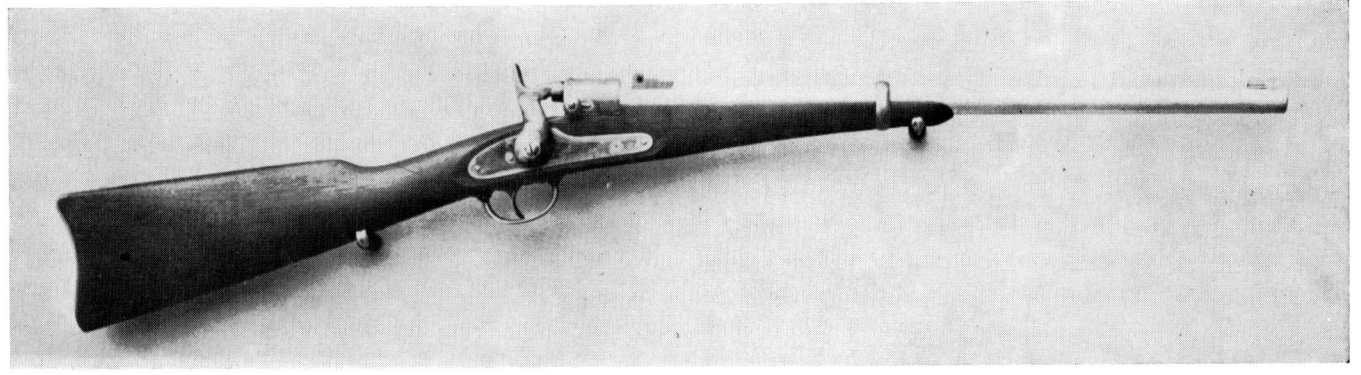

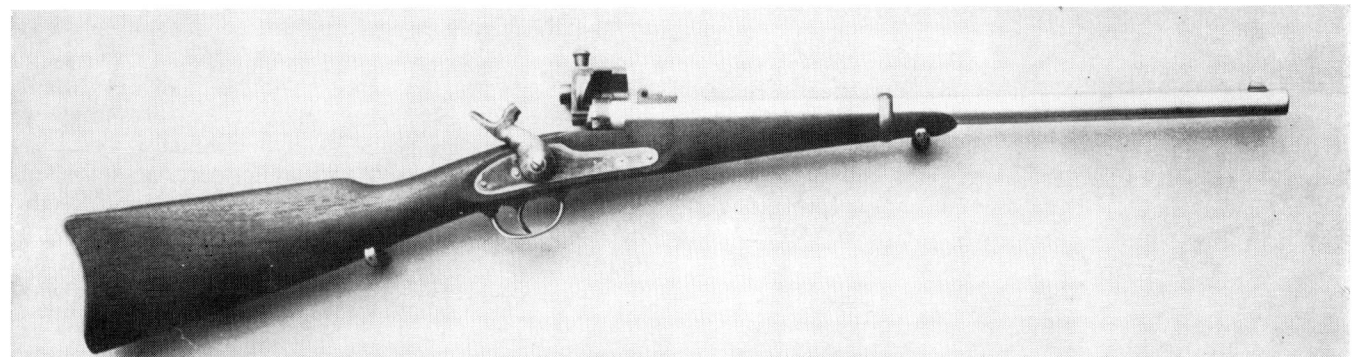

Basic wartime Joslyn was made at Stonington, Conn., to use metallic cartridge. Breechblock when swung aside automatically cammed ejector back. Three-band Rifle Musket was also made, using lockplates marked SP RINGFIELD with a space.

Junction Shop in Worcester, but these are believed to have been the swinging breechblock Joslyn which was ultimately patented October 8, 1861, No. 33435 (improved June 4, 1863, No. 39,407 and March 22, 1864, No. 42,000). Two hundred were bought from Freeman on June 14, 1861, at $35 each. But Freeman had difficulties over his delivery of the Joslyn revolvers, *q.v.*, and it appeared to hamper his business enough to end it. Only 225 Joslyn revolvers at $22.50 were delivered by Freeman through Bruff, Brothers & Seaver and it is possible that the tools and equipment which made the revolvers actually delivered later by Benjamin F. Joslyn included Freeman's carbine equipment.

From Stonington the first delivery of carbines was 100 shipped as an open purchase along with 150 revolvers on January 11, 1862. Thereafter, by the hundreds or less, Joslyn carbines were delivered up to August of 1863. The actual delivery quantities, sometimes twice monthly, of Joslyn carbines, ran 200 (Freeman), 100 (cited), 50, 50, 50, 50, 50, 100, 100, 50, 50, 10, a total of 860. These had been taken by Hagner when offered to him. Then Joslyn worked like mad and made up 1,000 guns for sale. Hagner wrote to General Ramsay suggesting that since these guns had some value to the United States, they ought to take a few under contract. Ramsay agreed and Hagner bought them on August 20, 1863, two months after the offer to make them available had come from Joslyn. Apparently they were sold to the United States before being entirely finished at the Stonington works.

A succeeding contract, of October 26, 1863, for 1,500 carbines was issued by Ramsay but only 1,200 were delivered. Then Joslyn and his general manager R. P. Bruff felt confident enough to push ahead on full-scale production. Backers James I. Day of Stonington and Cyrus S. Bushnell of New Haven had sunk a little money into the firm. Signing as sureties to the contracts gave them some of the joys of participation, but they wanted to see the firm make profits.

On November 18, 1863, Bruff agreed to deliver 15,000 carbines at $23.50; but only 1,000 were actually shipped, on July 2, 1864. Minor changes in the side-swing breechblock latching and extractor seem to have handicapped Joslyn so far as modifying tools and getting quantity production going are concerned. The 14,000 balance was forfeit and no more were taken by the United States. Yet Joslyn persisted, and a final contract of July 6, 1864 was negotiated at the same price. Doubtless from the coincidence of date and delivery of July 2, Joslyn and Bruff argued they could do better and needed only another chance. The quantity was but 7,000 carbines, and the contract was filled. In one month alone, December 1864, 2,000 carbines were delivered. Few if any of these latter carbines were used. Those of the earlier deliveries were issued on state requisitions, but the delivery schedule reveals the smallness of Joslyn's shop. Unlike, say, the Henry arms, of which only approximately 1,700 were bought officially but nearly 10,000 made and used by independent outfits, there is little to suggest that Joslyn was a powerhouse of productivity until the last, and then it was too late. Probably the total of Joslyn carbines made does not much exceed 11,261 bought and paid for by the United States. With the shipment of February 25, 1865, the story of Joslyn's carbine in the Civil War came to an abrupt end.

A good breechloader, concerning which there is very little battle romance in spite of its delivery in time for conflict, is the brass-framed model of James Warner. Fabricated by the Springfield Arms Company as Warner's enterprise in Springfield, Massachusetts, was called, it is in a sense a forebear of the trade named "Springfield" shotguns and rifles fabricated today by the Savage Arms Company in nearby Westfield, Massachusetts. Savage, upon acquiring the Stevens Arms Company factory in Chicopee Falls, Massachusetts during WWII, also acquired the right to the brand name "Springfield Arms Company" which Stevens had used in the 1920's and 1930's. Apparently the Warner interests were absorbed by Stevens after the Civil War —the Warner carbines seem to have been the last arms actually made by Warner himself as Springfield Arms Company. With Warner in their production were Charles O. Chapin of Springfield, and merchant John L. King. Four thousand and one Warner carbines were received but the contracts covering delivery were confused. Warner, one of the most experienced manufacturers in the United States at the time, associated with Chapin, equally experienced in metal working, appears to have made an error of $2 in his price quotation for the guns. On January 13, 1864, Warner obtained a contract for 1,000 of his guns at $18 and delivered one sample carbine at that price purchased January 24. This gun was used by Colonel Thornton as an inspector's model. All the 1,000 were to be turned in by May 1.

By 25 April only 500 more had been delivered, at $18, but the last 500 were accepted June 23. Then Warner delayed some months, building up a parts supply and preparing to put together more guns. Though he did not have a contract he proceeded as if he had an order from Government.

On October 22, 1864, he notified the new Chief of Ordnance, A. B. Dyer, that he had 500 carbines ready for inspection and delivery and sought instructions as to how the boxes should be marked. The tone of his letter suggests he planned to "bull" his way along and get the guns into Thornton's hands and inspected; then with certificates of inspection he presumed he could get payment made without difficulty. Why he would not have wanted to open the question of negotiation for a new contract is not known, but at any rate Dyer on November 11 referred the query to Thornton, "who will please make arrangements for the shipment of the carbines." Dyer treated it as if Warner had an order.

Meanwhile, Warner had been asked on November 5 at what price he would furnish 2,000 carbines, and in promptly replying he advised Dyer the price would

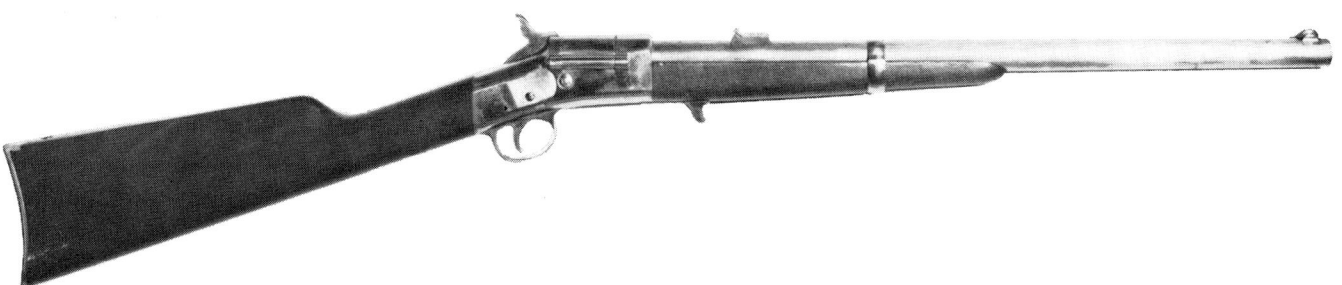

Brass-framed Warner carbine had swinging breechblock that lifts from left side with thumb piece. Action is very much like the Snider later adopted by Britain. Later guns in batch of 2,500 delivered are believed made by Greene.

be $20. When Thornton's order to accept the proffered 500 guns went out, Thornton treated it as a continuation of the old arrangement at $18, and Warner complained. Dyer, less cautious with the Government's money than Holt and Owen, or even Ripley, accepted Warner's arguments and because the okay for accepting the 500 had been issued after Warner's proposal to make them at $20, he upped the ante $2, for $20 each for the 500. Then, disavowing the wish to buy 2,000 at $20, he informed Warner that if he, Warner, would ream the chambers to take the new Spencer carbine cartridge (.56-.50) he would issue an order for 2,500 at $20. This second contract for 2,500 Spencer-chambered Warner guns was dated 26 December, 1864, and all 2,500 were delivered by March 15, 1865.

The Warner has an outside hammer, a back-action lock mechanism and a side-swinging breech astonishingly like the Snider action of 1865. The breech is of brass, the butt being fitted to the back and the 20-inch round carbine barrel, with typical wooden forestock and one band, on front. The early Warners are chambered for a rimfire cartridge of .52-inch chamber diameter, .75-inch long in the case and an overall length of 1.56 inches. The Spencer round was about 1.56-inch overall length also, but the chamber was .56-inch diameter and the cases approximately .88-inch long in the Spencer and Joslyn carbines. Makers' marks of JAMES WARNER SPRINGFIELD MASS WARNER'S PATENT on one model and GREEN RIFLE WORKS, WORCESTER, MASS. PAT. FEB. 1864 are listed. It is thought the last batch of Warners in Spencer caliber are related to the Green marking, for the sureties on his contract are not local Springfield men, Chapin and King, but two men in Yonkers, New York. One, William Warburton Scrugham, was a New York State Supreme Court justice; the other, Dewitt C. Kellinger, was a clerk in Yonkers. Both swore they had property over $5,000 value each and both were interested in the Warner contract. That they were major stockholders in the Green Rifle Works is a possibility, though not proved. The guess is not out of order; in spite of having been part of the mainstream, part of the foundations of the largest gun factory in the United States today, Savage Arms, little is known of James Warner of Springfield and of his simple and efficient brass-framed Civil War carbine.

Even less is known of the carbines of Frank Wesson. A brother of Edwin and Daniel Baird, maker of the revolvers, Frank Wesson ran a small rifle shop in Northboro, Massachusetts. He had designed a tip-down barrel action having a separate barrel releasing "trigger" in its own trigger guard, forward of the regular trigger and guard. The hammer was hung in the middle of the standing breech; the cartridge was a .44 rimfire. Agent for Wesson was Ben Kitteridge of Cincinnati. While 150 of these light rifles—a plain sporter rather than a true military carbine—were purchased by the Union, July 7, 1863, at $23, they were more popular with the guerrillas and irregular troops in the border fighting. In mechanical ways suggesting the Lee—both variations on a theme, so far as breech construction went—the Wessons did not last long in the gun picture. August 1, 1863, one more Wesson was bought from Schuyler, Hartley and Graham for $24.25. After the war Frank continued in the sporting rifle business but though he achieved limited fame in his day for premier

Front "trigger" of Frank Wesson military carbine releases barrel which tips down for loading. Later commercial products of this maker are distinguished by astonishing variety of chamber dimensions. Civil War guns came from agent Ben Kittredge of Cincinnati. Only 151 were bought but numbers run to over 800.

match rifles, in volume his output was among the smallest of any handicraft gunsmith in those early days of mass production.

Unquestionably most sensational of the carbine purchases was the affair of the Hall carbines. It stimulated a Senate investigation of Fremont's command of the Army of the West and led to persistent editorial attacks on the House of Morgan through the ages to the present day. Over-simplified, as the peace-mongers usually are wont to do, the story of the Hall carbines was used with good effect during the 1920's and 1930's. Then, Communist-tinted writers sought to discredit the financier and the arms merchant by pointing to this supposedly nefarious tie-up between money lender John Pierpont Morgan and gun speculator George Eastman in the affair of the Hall carbines. But that, as they say, is another chapter.

CHAPTER 12

Fremont Arms the Western Army

If General Ripley had set out to deliberately embarrass a fellow officer who had reached a zenith in his career, he could not have done it better than by selling the Hall carbines in New York for $3.50. General John Charles Fremont, commander of the Department of the West at St. Louis, the romantically labeled "Pathfinder," who had numerous times crossed the wastes of the Great American Desert in his travels, who had a guiding hand in the short-lived California "Bear Republic" of gold rush days, was stopped as short in his career that might have led (as Grant's did) to the White House, as if he had run into a brick wall. What did it was Fremont's purchase at $22 each of 5,000 Hall carbines obsoleted by order of General Ripley and sold out of Governor's Island (in the midst of a frantic scramble for arms) for only $3.50 each.

That the guns were new, that they were rifled at an additional charge of only a dollar, and then sold to Fremont, served merely to aggravate the situation. Civil War students concerned with personalities and office conflicts may later sort out the problems which beset Fremont when he took command in St. Louis, and how his solutions contributed to his political downfall as well as the side-tracking of a formerly brilliant military career. We are here concerned only with the arms and tactics, and their relation to his status as major defendant in a Senatorial inquisition into the Conduct of the War and its administrative abuses in organizing and equipping the Western Department.

Fremont's First Purchases

This hot potato which Fremont was handed did not come complete with fork and butter to make it palatable; in other words, he had to create literally from nothing an army and its equipment. Fremont left his old command in California for Europe on January 1, 1861, to obtain supplies. He puchased several batteries of cannon together with some muskets and 25 pistols, believed to have been the Lefaucheux Model 1853 12mm pinfire revolver, sometimes erroneously called in the United States service, "the French Tranter." Upon his return to New York he was beset by the agents of many arms makers and speculators, and in one instance at least was shown the light and elegant .58 Chasseurs de Vincennes pattern rifle and when he ordered the guns (at a high price) a cheaper article was fraudulently substituted by the contractor. The substitution was caught up by Holt and Owen but the incident unfortunately reflected little credit on Fremont though it was done without his knowledge or consent. The situation in St. Louis had become desperate. An order for 5,000 arms upon the St. Louis arsenal revealed that the storerooms were bare:

TELEGRAM, QUINCY, ILL., JULY 17, 1861
MAJOR GENERAL FREMONT, NEW YORK:
 I am ordered to hold the Hannibal and St. Joseph railroad. I have three regiments posted along the road, in communication at the west with Iowa troops, for detached service and breaking up camps of rebels. I need better arms than the smooth musket. I have one regiment wholly unarmed in camp here, and can get no arms in St. Louis or Springfield. Can you send me Minies and ammunition?
 S. A. HURLBUT, BRIGADIER GENERAL

TELEGRAM, CHICAGO, JULY 17, 1861
MAJOR GENERAL FREMONT, U.S.A., NEW YORK
 We need specially, to fit out one or two regiments of cavalry, sabres and revolvers. There are absolutely none in this part of the country.
 JOHN POPE, BRIGADIER GENERAL

The call was repeated many times over, and in a flurry of last minute gun buying and partial commitments to contracts, Fremont left New York to assume command in St. Louis. The emergency was severe; the agent of Adams Express cleared the tracks for arms for Fremont by offering to bring them in from New York or Washington Arsenal by fast passenger train. General Nathaniel Lyon (on 10 August 1861 killed in the fighting between Rolla and Springfield, Missouri) urgently needed 5,000 muskets for his men. Given no help by Ripley, who had no rifles to issue, Fremont with the individual determination that had marked his life as an officer took the direct route and bought the guns in the open market. From John Hoey, who in association with Hedden was to sell the United States and particularly General Ripley a large number of arms, Fremont ordered 200 Enfield rifles at $26.50. These were delivered—100 on August 31 and 100 on September 4. With these were 2,180 smoothbore Austrian muskets, "new, brown and bright," as Hoey billed them, at $10 each. As John Hoey is listed as having delivered 1,250 cavalry sabers at $8 each probably at the same time, it is assumed these were also for Fremont, in response to General Pope's urgent plea. Some of these same sabers were put to good use by Major Zagonyi, commander of the fabled and apparently much-maligned Fremont Hussars, the general's bodyguard regiment. These arms went out via Adams Express to Captain F. D. Callender at the St. Louis Arsenal, who receipted for them; and the accounts, briefly held up, were ultimately paid.

The Austrian Muskets

Austrian muskets figured largely in Fremont's command. And as is so often the case, when later tempered judgment can look back at the actions of highly placed executives far from appeal to superiors, Fremont in his purchases of arms can be cleared of charges of incompetence. His acceptance of some 25,000 Austrian muskets, later loudly condemned by field commanders, was a practical move in an emergency. Though he has been criticized for the amount of his expenditures in many ways, including some strong complaints about field fortifications and the alleged dandy dress of his body-guard, Major Charles Zagonyi's "Fremont Hussars," his issue of Austrian guns gave the Army in the West weapons at the time they had none.

The New York import firm, Kruse, Drexel and Schmidt, had on hand in 1861 13,000 new and 12,000 used Austrian Consol-Augustin muskets priced at about $7 each. These were pattern 1841 smoothbores, later sold by Bannerman as "10720. Austrian Army Tube-Lock Musket." They had three bands, the front one with the characteristic tube or pipe for ramrod; 43-inch barrels and of .70 caliber, accepting the new .69 U. S. minie bullet. Bayonets were retained by a spring hook below the barrel. The muskets had been in use a long time in the Austrian army; were obsoleted on adopting the Lorenz rifle 1854.

Fremont and his aide, Colonel I. C. Woods, met the importers in New York and examined samples of these muskets. At first Fremont rejected the idea of buying them, as he had an order from Washington for 7,000 stand of Government-owned arms. Thinking there would be plenty of better small-caliber cap-lock rifle muskets available, the general was miffed when the order had been countermanded. He got Major Hagner to help him, and endeavored to arrange for arms and equipment for a corps of 23,000 men. Fremont and Woods eventually went with the Army to Springfield, then St. Louis, to take up duties. After the Battle of Bull Run, the arms market took a sudden upturn in activity. Fremont's hopes to get better guns failed.

"After General Fremont had arrived in St. Louis, and the Government had issued orders to have all the arms procurable forwarded from New York to Washington, it became impossible to get other arms," Colonel Woods later told the Committee on the Conduct of the War (Part 3, page 198). "These Austrian arms were then bought," he continued, "but upon condition the importers should manufacture, in New York, this percussion primer (which was used on them instead of a percussion cap), in sufficient quantities to answer the purpose for these arms. And as quite a large portion of the Army of the West were foreign soldiers, and a great many of the officers were familiar with the arm, and a great many of the soldiers had before used it, although it took one more motion to prime it than it did to put the cap on our muskets [closing down the detonating pin cover], still, as it took the same bullet—the Minie bullet—that our muskets did, it was decided that it was absolutely necessary to have them."

They planned to issue such arms to key defensive personnel, such as bridge guards, who could count on other support if their primers were expended. The urgent need for guns was much like that in England in 1940, after retreat from Dunkirk, when any revolver, so long as it had five good shells, was enough to arm a Home Guardsman for airport defense.

The Austrian muskets arrived at St. Louis but the primers were not with them, having been shipped separately. "Two boxes of primers were sent out first," Fremont reported to the Committee, "but, in consequence of careless handling, they exploded somewhere near Pittsburg, and killed some two or three men, and that caused some delay." When Colonel Albert of Fremont's staff, who had been in the Austrian Army, saw his old friend the Consol musket, he declared it was "a good weapon." Said Fremont, "I think he used a stronger expression than that, but I will stop with that." The guns were set aside in two lots, 15,000 for issue as tube-locks, and 10,000 to be rifled and altered in the breech to percussion.

Captain Callender, in charge of the St. Louis Arsenal and Fremont's ordnance officer, took out the breech pins of a couple and set them up on his rifling machine. Though he was urgently busy cutting grooves in several thousand Springfield muskets already on hand, he wanted to see how they looked when rifled.

Callender told Fremont's aide, Colonel Wood, that the breech of the Austrian musket was thicker than the Springfield muskets; and rifled better than the United States ones. The St. Louis rifling machine being in use, one Austrian musket was sent to Cincinnati and one to Philadelphia to be altered to percussion, to see which shop did the best work (Kittredge in Cincinnati, Jenks in Philadelphia, or Krider?). On the return of the samples, Fremont preferred the Philadelphia alteration ($5) but Callender recommended the Austrian muskets be sent to Cincinnati for altering and rifling. The cost was less—$4.50. Some were shipped out, others issued immediately to regiments of home guards, who later exchanged their smoothbore Consols for rifled percussion ones.

"One regiment, which was about 15 miles out from Sedalia on the road to Springfield, learning that a carload of these altered arms had arrived, marched in to get these arms, and marched back again the same day," said Colonel Wood. When Callender had finished rifling the several thousand Springfield muskets on hand— his machine had a capacity of 60 per day—he finished up the Austrian guns. Wood declared that, "We looked upon the purchase even at first as being a very excellent one; and when it was found that they could be altered and made a very good weapon, it was looked upon as a very economical purchase in every point of view . . . they cost but about $11.50 each when ready to be put finally into the hands of our soldiers."

Captain Chauncy McKeever (later designer of the McKeever cartridge box used during the Spanish-American War) was an officer of the Regular Army, Adjutant General's Department, stationed with Fremont. His comments on Austrian guns are somewhat less flattering. Acknowledging that the West was unprepared, he said: "The fact is, at this time Lexington was attacked (by General Sterling Price, Missouri Confederate commander), there were scarcely any troops prepared to take the field. They were waiting for arms. I think some 10,000 Austrian muskets had been sent to Cincinnati to be altered and rifled. But I did not consider them a good weapon, even when improved. They did not seem to give satisfaction at all. Complaints were made that the locks were not good; that the guns would go off at half-cock; that the locks would break; that the hammers would break off." Yet McKeever was not at all condemnatory of Fremont as a person, nor of Callender operating under his directions. "Callender," he said, "certainly exerted himself to the utmost, and purchased wherever he could find weapons and whenever he could get the authority to do so." McKeever felt that rumors from the East that Fremont was to be replaced seriously impaired his authority in command, by inference contributing to some of the alleged abuses.

The newspapers, never more active than when there was no real news, made hay of these foreign gun purchases and issues. Fremont received a letter January 21, 1862, from one of his former staff officers still in St. Louis, Captain Hoskins. The captain reported: "Apropos of the long stories concerning the Austrian muskets, &c., which were so freely circulated in the newspapers, it is a very curious commentary on their alleged want of value that I was last week ordered to go to Benton Barracks, on the suggestion of Colonel Callender, to prove some of those very muskets, which had been issued to the troops. I need not say to you that the trial was a very conclusive one, and the two regiments, armed with them, marched next day for Cairo. The men had heard enough against those arms to make them feel very unwilling to take them; but after the proving and trial, I judge they were very much better satisfied. Indeed, if it were not for these same despised weapons many of the regiments would have still remained unarmed; for the Department of Missouri has been much neglected in this respect, as well as the Department of the West, with a fair opportunity to solve the old task-work riddle of making bricks without straw."

Some of Fremont's irregular cavalry units were equipped with Consol-converted Austrian carbines. These guns are of distinctive pattern, locks shaped like the Consol muskets and of .71 caliber, a short 14-inch barrel and stock held by one plain iron band. The iron trigger guard is formed at the rear tang into a sort of semi-pistol grip, while a cavalry sling bar is on the stock left side. Stock wood is often beech or other soft kind, not good walnut, and the guns are cheaply made in general finish though welcome emergency arms when Schuyler bought them. Six varieties of foreign percussion carbines were purchased totalling 10,051 guns for a price of $66,193.00, an average of $6.50 each. They were sold by Bannerman fifty years later as "Rare relics. Only few now to be had. Guns are in perfect order. Price $3.50 each."

Dealings with Stevens and Eastman

Fremont's Austrian guns did their duty for the North, but when Fremont received a wire from one Simon Stevens, his downfall was assured.

56 BROADWAY, NEW YORK, August 5, 1861

J. C. FREMONT,
  Major General Commanding, Cairo, Illinois
Sir: I have five thousand Hall's rifled cast-steel carbines, breech-loading, new, at twenty-two dollars, government standard, fifty-eight. Can I hear from you?
                                                SIMON STEVENS

Fremont replied at once, on August 6, that he would take the whole 5,000 carbines. He instructed Stevens to see the Adams agent and send by express not fast freight, Fremont to pay the extra charges. He told Stevens to send ammunition, and "devote yourself solely to that business today." Without regard for cost, Fremont was determined to save Missouri for the Union. Rather bitterly Fremont, in his deposition justifying his purchases before the Senate committee declared:

The labors of the investigating committee appear to have resulted in a single resolution, in which the purchase of certain arms by myself is made a prominent subject. With respect to the sale of these arms by the government I have nothing to say. They were new, and I am told were sold without being condemned. The contract price at which they were bought by the government was, I believe, $17.50. The price at which they are set down in the ordnance manual is $21. After they had been rifled and otherwise improved, I purchased them at $22. Taking into consideration the advance in price of arms caused by the war, I submit that the purchase is not deserving of special censure.

Fremont furor was kicked off by his purchase of 5,000 Hall carbines of North's improved pattern. Price paid to New York speculator was much inflated over Government sale price but Fremont needed guns in St. Louis.

But history and Fremont's peers all censured him, in spite of his honorable failure to defend himself by commenting on the sale of the arms by the Government. For the sale was concluded during that month of July when he was in New York frantically searching for arms to buy. It was set up in June by active assistance of General Ripley who seemed possessed somehow with an all-consuming desire to rid the United States of the liability of possessing these arms at any price. Yet the need was not, as sometimes dictates surplus sales, for the space in which they were stored. The buyer was permitted to leave the arms where stored, at Governors Island and at Frankford Arsenal, subject to his call or order. And the buyer was not Stevens, but a man-behind-the-scenes named Arthur M. Eastman, of Manchester, New Hampshire.

Stevens himself was a more obvious figure. He and Fremont had come together in New York and Fremont spoke to him concerning arms and forwarding them to him in St. Louis. When Fremont left for the West, Stevens knew Fremont would buy arms from him if he could offer them. He found the Hall carbines and put a price on them which, knowing the state of Fremont's mind so far as arms purchases was concerned, he felt the general would pay. His telegram of August 5 was in his mind and in Fremont's eyes a bona-fide offer to sell arms at a price which Fremont accepted and agreed to pay.

About August 18, because of his doing so much for Fremont in New York, he was appointed to a post on Fremont's staff as a civilian forwarding agent, in New York, looking after Fremont's purchases in Europe and in the East. This caused the Senate investigators and the Commissioners, Holt, Owen, and Hagner, to raise the question, was his purchase of the carbines and resale to Fremont not a definite breach of trust and all claims therefore against the United States invalid?

Collaborating in the financing of this lot were the youthful money man, J. P. Morgan, and a much more respected and well-established firm, the House of Ketchum, whose head, Morris Ketchum, was introduced to the notice of the Commissioners by no less a dignitary than John J. Cisco, Assistant Treasurer of the United States. Of Ketchum, Cisco said to Judge Holt:

". . . The Government has had no more influential, efficient, and courageous supporter in this community than Morris Ketchum. In the hours of greatest gloom and public depression, he has been foremost in rallying capitalists to the support of the Treasury Department. His house . . . has by its energy and boldness in offering for large amounts done more to facilitate the negotiations of our loans and sustain the credit of the Government than any house in the country . . ."

Ketchum and Morgan has collaborated on the financing of the deal, but in a very indirect manner. Yet, as theirs was a security interest in the weapons in question, it was to Morgan that the job of directly submitting the claim fell, when Secretary Stanton suspended all contracts and asked for an accounting. Morgan's claim was for the second half of the carbines:

The United States to J. P. Morgan, Dr.
ORDNANCE STORES
1861
August 7.
2,500 Hall's carbines, at $22	$55,000
5,000 screwdrivers, at 25 cents	1,250
5,000 wipers at 20 cents	1,000
500 spring vises, at 35 cents	175
500 bullet moulds, at 50 cents	250
125 packing boxes, at $4	500
	$58,175

The annexed named ordnance stores have been received in good order.

F. D. CALLENDER
Captain of Ordnance, United States Army

When the full story came out it did not do credit to Ripley or to the disorganized state of the Ordnance Office in the spring of 1861. Basis for the sale was found in an order of Colonel Craig's dated August 25, 1857, authorizing officers to inspect ordnance materiel and classify any as unserviceable that might be found obsolete, damaged, etc. Craig was strict only about the muskets converted to percussion from flint; these he wanted as a war reserve; the miscellany could be sold off, including the various odd patterns of breechloaders and semi-experimental field trial arms bought under direction of Jeff Davis.

Hall Carbines

The reports of arms on hand gathered dust for **four** years, until A. M. Eastman observed there were listed

All Hall guns, rifles or carbines, were rising-chamber breechloaders having either flint cock or percussion hammer mounted in receiver behind chamber. Though not gas-tight, they were used in U.S. Army from 1817 to 1865.

a quantity of the Hall's carbines. These particular guns were mostly new, the Hall-North Model 1843, having North's improved side lever to open the breechblock. With 21-inch round steel-drilled barrels, these .52 caliber carbines were smoothbore. All metal was finished lacquer brown. A sling bar with a ring sliding on it was attached to the left side of the stock, to the rear band, and to the frame. The front band was held by a stud band spring. These guns had been made in 1849-52, and though of nonstandard pattern (with the emphasis more and more to be on metallic cartridge carbines), they leaked no more fire at the breech than did old Sharps and other guns, and in the emergency were certainly serviceable for special issue. But Eastman, up in Manchester, New Hampshire, seemed to sense this before General Ripley, his desk piled high with requisitions for arms.

On May 28 Eastman, who had come to Washington to make this deal, wrote to Ripley a formal offer to buy. He said: "We find reported of Hall's carbines 5,184, and damaged, 1,240 additional . . . I now propose to purchase the entire lot at three dollars each for those entirely in good order, and in proportion for the damaged, upon examination . . ." Eastman himself set a 90-day limit on the deal, cash on delivery, and stated he wanted the entire lot because it would affect the manner in which he would "prepare our works to remodel and alter them . . ." The inference is, that he represented manufacturing interests in Manchester, possibly Amoskeag, though his name does not appear in later Amoskeag contracts and papers. Ripley refused Eastman's price of $3, though similar Hall carbines had been sold for $1 to $2 in small sales prior to the war. He considered the carbines worth $3.50 each, thinking of the past sale prices and calculating what, in his eyes, was a fair appreciation in view of the demand. That he was all out of proportion in his estimates was not to be made clear until later.

Cameron approved the price and ordered all sold that could be taken; Eastman asked for an order on Colonel R. H. K. Whiteley of New York Arsenal. He wanted the order to permit partial delivery in lots of 1,000 with payment on delivery, plus an additional $500 deposit as Eastman's guarantee that the whole lot would be taken away within 90 days.

This arrangement seemed okay and on August 7, Eastman received from Whiteley 4,996 Hall carbines, 4,996 screwdrivers, 4,996 wipers, 499 spring vises, 499 bullet moulds, and 250 packing boxes, all for $3.50 each. Later J. P. Morgan was to charge the United States $4 for the very same chests, containing 20 carbines each and relidded after working on the guns and repacking them.

Between Eastman's visit to Washington in June and his receiving of the whole number of 5,000 guns that he wanted to purchase on 7 August, a new figure had been introduced, Simon Stevens. On 1 August Stevens lent Eastman $20,000 to buy the guns, receiving in return an option for 20 days to in turn buy the guns from Eastman for Stevens' own account. Both knew what a windfall Eastman had walked in to by means of normal procedure in the Ordnance Office.

Probably Stevens beat down Eastman's asking price by referring to the new cost of the guns as but $17.50; Eastman at the time may have assumed Stevens would make but a couple of dollars on each gun, though he had himself cleared $9.50 profit, or about $50,000 on a $20,000 investment. Stevens in turn had obtained funds from J. P. Morgan, advances to pay for rifling and cleaning up the carbines, the high cartage bill on hundreds of cases of carbines, and incidental expenses including commissions on money and services as trustee in handling all the money details of the transaction.

When Fremont told Stevens to get to work on the deal at once, he did not delay; a contract was made August 10, 1861 with W. W. Marston to rifle the guns and enlarge the chambers, to allow the guns to take the .58 musket cartridge. These were done at his shop at 22d Street and Second Avenue and the work went quickly, for it was private business and every day delayed meant a dollar lost. One additional contract was made with Harrison Tweed of the Taunton Locomotive Works to bore out and rifle 1,000 of the guns, which was done for $777.00. The rest of the 5,000 were done by Marston. The initial price was $1—negotiations dropped the balance charges to $0.75.

Fremont wired asking what the delay was, and Stevens told him they were rifling and altering to .58. Fremont answered, "You have done right; go on with the rifling, use despatch, hurry up." On August 23 the first 500 guns went out to St. Louis, arriving in two days; 1,500 guns went in the second lot shipped 26 August, and the last 500 by the end of the month. Captain Callender delayed slightly in getting the payment back to Stevens but finally a check on the assistant treasurer at New York was sent out to Morgan, the actual stake holder, by Adams Express, dated (as Stevens recalled) September 10. The second 2,500 meanwhile had been processed through the rifling and were on their way west, before the 15th of September. By September 24 all the 5,000 remodeled Hall carbines had been issued to troops.

"In the early period of the war," said Lieutenant H. R. Buffington, assisting Captain Callender at St. Louis, "officers complained of these arms, but for many months they are only too willing to use them, as no others have been and apparently cannot be supplied (May 15, 1862); but the impression is, among those who know and those who do not know, that this arm is very inferior to Sharps' carbine."

Buffington gave Holt and Owen details of the Halls which had been turned in for repair, over 10 per cent of them having been damaged in the field since issue. Of 152 then on hand for repair, 18 stocks were broken from the blast of gas at the breech, and two had barrels broken off about 1½ inches from the muzzle. "The parts supplied for repair have been principally tumbler and leaf-spring screws and hammers." The hammer is easily broken off the Hall from its high-up exposed position; the leaf spring screws are easily lost by careless reassembly. It is possible to get one's screwdriver into a position of forcing the screw into place and then it suddenly slips and the screw flies off and is lost, because of being somewhat under tension. But the men of Fremont's and Pope's cavalry were glad to have these guns, in spite of their seeming defects.

In the United States service, as flintlock and later percussion, the Hall system had been "issue" since 1817. Until Craig, it had been a sort of favorite of the Ordnance Department, since Colonel George Bomford, for so many years Chief of Ordnance, was said (by Christopher Colt, Sam Colt's father) to have an "interest" in the Hall patent. The Hall, far from being a junky sort of outmoded piece of scrap, was an entirely serviceable weapon fabricated and considered as Government issue as late as 1851. To justify the prices and the merits of the arms in question as fit for service and worth the sums of the claims, Ketchum fronted for Morgan and submitted depositions from James North and Edward Savage, who had made the guns, and from Marston and also Austin Baldwin, former military storekeeper at Middletown, Connecticut, who had originally received the arms in question from North. These depositions contain first-hand notes of general interest to the arms student, though the events they mention are out of time in the Civil War era; nevertheless they are of merit and two are reproduced in full:

NEW YORK, *May 2, 1862*

STATE OF NEW YORK, City of New York, ss:

William W. Marston, of the city of New York, manufacturer of firearms, doing business corner 21st Street and 2nd Avenue, in said city, being duly sworn according to law, deposes and says: That he is in the fortieth year of his age; that he has been engaged on his own account in the business of manufacturing firearms for the last fifteen years, and that for the last twelve years has had constantly in his employ upwards of fifty men, sometimes upwards of two hundred and fifty, when business pressed; that he is familiar with the manufacture of firearms generally, particularly with pistols, carbines, rifles and muskets; that he is well acquainted with the carbines known as Hall's carbines, manufactured at Middletown, Connecticut; that early in August, 1861, Mr. Simon Stevens called on this affiant at his factory and proposed to contract with this affiant for the rifling and chambering of 5,000 Hall's carbines, steel barrels new; that he made a contract with Mr. Stevens to rifle and chamber the breech of 4,000 carbines, .58 bore, in a good and workmanlike manner; that he received the first thousand carbines, in pursuance of this agreement from J. P. Morgan, on the 10th day of August, 1861, the second thousand on the 21st day of August, the third thousand on the 24th day of August, and the fourth thousand on the 29th day of August, 1861; that he executed the contract faithfully to the best of his ability, and in a good and workmanlike manner, and delivered them to the Adams' Express, upon the order of J. P. Morgan, as rapidly as possible; he finished and delivered the last lot to the Adams' Express on the — day of September, 1861; these four thousand carbines were all new, were of good material and workmanship; they all had upon them the inspector stamps of an ordnance officer and the stamp of the manufacturer, as well as the year in which they were made; they all had side levers with which to raise the breech; that, with the alterations referred to as made by affiant, he considers them a very good and effective weapon for military purposes.

This affiant has been engaged in the manufacture of firearms for over twenty-five years last past, and is now manufacturing arms for the United States Government; that he personally inspected the work he did upon these Hall's carbines, and superintended their packing for shipment.

Some time in November this affiant was applied to by Major P. V. Hagner, United States Army, to assist in the inspection of foreign arms; that this affiant did comply with the request of Major Hagner, and did inspect about sixty thousand arms imported from Europe. The demand for firearms late in July and August, 1861, was greatly enhanced, and the prices were increased very much over the prices in peace times.

This lot of Hall's carbines being new, improved, and effective, as described above, were, in the opinion of this affiant, well worth in the month of August, 1861, about $22; that rifles of the Enfield pattern then readily sold at about from $28 to $30. The same kind of rifles could have been purchased since at from $17 to $20 each.

W. W. MARSTON

The second statement, while signed and prepared by only Edward Savage, was read and concurred in by an endorsement by James North. Curious to note is Savage's statement that only 250 Hall-system rifles were made at the North works in Middletown, though Gluckman records a contract of July, 1829, to North for 1,200 rifles and treats of them as if all were delivered. Savage, with some cause to know, under oath in a deposition before Holt and Owen, in which the background of the Hall carbine technically as well as financially was important, declared otherwise.

STATE OF CONNECTICUT
  City of Middletown, County of Middlesex, ss:

Edward Savage, of the town of Cromwell, County and State aforesaid, late of the firm of North & Savage, contractors with the government of the United States for the manufacture of the celebrated Hall's carbines, and now one of the proprietors of the Savage Revolving Fire-arms Company, located in the city of Middletown aforesaid, being duly sworn, deposes and says: That he is in the sixtieth year of his age; that he has been engaged in the manufacturing of firearms for the last twenty five years; that he was the successor to his father's business, who was the associate of Colonel Simeon North, since deceased, who was the pioneer of government contractors for firearms.

This deponent is informed and believes that Colonel Simeon North commenced manufacturing firearms for the United States Government in the year 1799, in the town of Berlin, State aforesaid; that in the year 1811 or thereabouts, said Simeon North removed his works to the town of Middletown aforesaid, at the request of the Secretary of War, and the Government made large advances to Mr. North to enable him to remove to Middletown and to increase largely the capacity of his works, and at the same time gave him an order for about twenty thousand pistols. It was at this time that Colonel North introduced the system of making all the parts so they would change and interchange with each other with perfect accuracy; for this he was allowed a bonus of $1 per pistol. Subsequently, additional orders of many thousands were received and executed by Colonel North, who associated with him from about 1811 the father of this affiant, Josiah Savage. The said Josiah Savage died in 1831, and, after the settlement of his estate, this affiant, with Colonel Simeon North, was associated with James North, the son of Simeon aforesaid, and continued the manufacture of firearms. About the year 1829 or 1830 Hall's rifles and carbines were introduced into the United States service. The house of Colonel North and of North and Savage made, altogether, about thirty thousand. Only about two hundred and fifty of these arms were rifles; the remaining ones were carbines. They were all iron barrels, with the exception of about five or six thousand of those made in 1848, '49, '50, '51, '52, which were made of steel, with side levers for raising the breech (Savage & North patent). All of these arms were made in a superior manner, with the best of materials and possible workmanship, were all properly inspected by the officers of the government appointed for that purpose, and the last five thousand referred to were received by Colonel Thornton for and in behalf of the United States.

Full particulars of government trials can be had by examining the reports of boards appointed for the purpose between 1830 and 1855. I consider this last lot of five thousand steel barrels, when rifled and with breech enlarged, are now, and have always been, worth as much as any other carbines in use in the Army of the United States.

EDWARD SAVAGE

Austin Baldwin's deposition confirmed what Savage and Marston had said, and added for the edification of Holt and Owen his assertion that the carbines were never manufactured except for the Government. This meant that "It is therefore impossible, in the opinion of this deponent, to fix any price as *their market value*, for market value must at all times be regulated by the supply and demand." Baldwin stated the first cost of the carbines was about $20 but that because of large orders and the prospect of cash payment upon inspection and acceptance, overhead was reduced so the contract price was cut to $17.50.

Owen himself was an old hand in the arms market, and he considered this so much eyewash. The first bill of over half a hundred thousand had been paid; the second bill was the subject of Morgan's claim. Ketchum had come to the financial aid of Morgan in making advances prior to Fremont's anticipated payments, for Marston's rifling and other costs. John C. Palmer, president of Sharps Rifle Company, was interviewed as to the value of the Halls. His guns were being bought in quantity by the United States at $30. Though he did admit that the Halls in August could have been sold for $20 to $22, he added pointedly, "I should not exchange one of our carbines for three of Halls." He observed in comparison that state buyers had offered him up to $50 if he would sell to the states, but his desire to deal only with the United States made him refuse though it lost him money. Stevens was insistent in fixing the $22 value as a fair price for the carbines, and quizzed Palmer himself:

Question by Mr. Stevens: As Hall's carbines cost the Government, when new, $17.50, and Sharps $30, what would be the relative difference in the increase of price owing to the demand in August, when you were offered $50 for your carbines?

Answer: My opinion on that would be very vague, but I should think that our carbine should sell for more than seventy-five percent over Hall's carbine . . .

Stevens had made his point, but Hagner adamantly cut him down. The altered gun, in his own view, was worth only $10 to $12, the price at which Eastman had sold to Stevens at the time he offered to Fremont. In the timing of the transaction lay the crux of the matter. As the Commissioners pointed out, Simon Stevens appeared to have bought the carbines by August 1 when he agreed to lend Eastman the money but actually all he had was an option on them when Eastman went to pick them up. Fremont told Stevens by wire on August 6 that he would buy them all at Stevens' quoted price. His wire, "Devote yourself solely to that business today" clearly intimated that Fremont supposed the guns were ready to roll and he needed them. As the Commission noted, the guns were not delivered until weeks had passed, so no great urgency of the moment which might have justified spending public money to that extent was served by the purchase. Instead, much delay followed and the value declined as the urgency passed. Further, the title to the guns did not pass from the Government, which had offered them, to Eastman, who was the first link in the chain, until the day *after* Fremont, on account of the United States, accepted the offer to sell of Stevens. The Government lost all around as Holt figured it:

> . . . If the purchase made by General Fremont is to be regarded as a valid purchase by the United States, the government not only sold, one day, for seventeen thousand four hundred and eighty six dollars arms which it had agreed, the day before, to repurchase for one hundred and nine thousand nine hundred and twelve dollars—making a loss to the United States on the transaction of ninety-two thousand four hundred and twenty six dollars ($92,426)—but virtually furnished the money to pay itself the seventeen thousand four hundred and eighty-six dollars which it received.

The purchase by Fremont was set aside by the Commission as not binding, in view of the law of 1815 which demanded public bidding on such purchases and required it to be done by authority of the Ordnance Department. But consideration of the daily irregularities in purchasing which in some instances had even been approved by the Commissioners as cases in equity, led them to accept the purchase as a fact and not try somehow to set it aside. The question of Simon Stevens' role then was examined, and it was decided that he deserved no more than the amount he agreed to pay Eastman, plus his out-of-pocket expenses, plus a commission as a broker of 2½ per cent. The basis for this was to contradict even Fremont's own statement that he bought the arms *from* Stevens and not *through* him. Disregarding circumstantial evidence that Stevens was a sort of agent for Fremont so early as August 6, the logic of Judge Holt shone through the Commissioner's ruling:

> Mr. Stevens, however, when he made the offer to General Fremont, knew that the arms he proposed to sell at twenty-two dollars each were at that moment the property of the United States, and that if his (Stevens) offer was accepted, he would have to furnish the funds to buy them, the next day, from the United States, at three dollars and fifty cents each. It is impossible to regard such a transaction as having been entered upon in good faith, and as having, for such reason, an equitable claim to be confirmed.

Accordingly, the best sum the Commissioners could agree upon themselves to pay for these carbines which the Government was itself "financing," was the amount Hagner cited as a fair market value. In support of this were sales, possibly unknown to Austin Baldwin, of April, 1861, in the New York market, of Hall carbines at prices between $6 and $10. And most convincing in fixing value of all the sales was the one from Eastman to Stevens, legitimate or not. "Two shrewd businessmen," as the Commissioners described them, had fixed the price at $12.50, and the most Stevens should be allowed was a brokerage commission in his sale to Fremont.

The added claim of Morgan was therefore disallowed. The amount already paid to Morgan, as the stakeholder in the Stevens-to-Eastman-to-Whiteley buck-passing game, was considered as "on account." The actual price for the carbines was set at the Eastman-to-Stevens price of $12.50, plus packing boxes and accouterments which Eastman had sold to Stevens for $3,695.30 extra (though he failed to pay Whiteley for them upon the latter's tendering a bill), plus the expenses of rifling and a 2½ per cent commission. The full amount was to be paid to Morgan upon the latter's releasing the Government from further claims.

As to Ketchum's part in making advances to Morgan for payment of the rifling and other work, the Commissioners regretted any embarrassment they might cause a loyal banking house. But they pointed out that the second voucher issued from Captain Callender upon which Morgan was trying to collect had not been signed by Fremont and was not valid; so they doubted the House of Ketchum had exercised due caution in its dealings with Morgan and Stevens, no matter in how much good faith they had acted. Ketchum expressed a willingness to accept the Commission's offer to pay the difference, if this would not be construed as a waiver of future rights in claiming the greater balance. The Commission refused, wanting a full and complete settlement, and the money did not get to Stevens until six years later, after the war.

In the fall of 1866 Stevens petitioned the Court of Claims to render judgment in his favor and direct the United States to pay him the sum of the second voucher plus interest from the time he incurred the liability of the second voucher, that is, when he delivered the second 2,500 guns in September, 1861. Ripley and Eastman were not called in, but Stevens, Fremont, and Ketchum among others were questioned. The United States defended its position on three points:

1. That Fremont did not have the authority by virtue of his office to purchase arms.

2. That Fremont did not have any special instructions from the President (such as had been given to Schuyler and Hartley) to buy arms.

3. That Stevens had already been paid a fair price for the guns.

A judgment was handed down favoring Stevens by a three to one majority. The opinion of the Court decided that since the Chief Ordnance Officer under Fremont's command could have procured the arms, the general was able in law to do what his subordinate could do. As to asking his subordinate to try and get arms, Fremont knew there were none to be had from the Ordnance Department, and he was excused by the Court because "the law does not require the performance of a useless act." Fair market value was held to be the $22 and not the $12—it is worth considering that Fremont fixed the market value by his demand and willingness to pay $22. Stevens filed the Court of Claims judgment with the Treasury for payment and on August 24, after an appeal by the United States was dismissed, he was paid the amount of Morgan's claim in full plus interest at 5 per cent from the time the judgment was filed.

Fremont's Hussars

The Hall carbines alone did not "cashier" Fremont. Among other highly controversial matters in his conduct was the equipment and dress of the Fremont Hussars, his bodyguard regiment.

Officered by Hungarian cavalryman Charles Zagonyi, this elite body of troopers has been pictured as gaily caparisoned and living a life of luxurious ease in St. Louis at headquarters. Zagonyi, who had fought in the Hungarian revolution of 1848 against the combined Russian and Austrian armies, was a tough little man who had a great deal of respect and loyalty to Fremont. Though he had come to the United States to live a quiet life, he seemed stimulated by patriotic zeal as he saw the Union cleft in twain. At first captain, later major, he served with Fremont from July 12 to November 6, 1861, commanding four companies of cavalry. Though it has been said that these men carried Colt revolving rifles, Zagonyi only states their equipment was "a revolver, and generally a sabre, and about two thirds had carbines." Some of these were unquestionably the Hall carbines issued during September by Callender.

Organized along Continental lines, what Zagonyi had recommended to be just one company, recognized as Fremont's "bodyguard" but really a cadre for training officers, was swollen by enlistees to the four companies he at last commanded.

"This cavalry . . . did every kind of duty in St. Louis," Zagonyi declared. "I have been ordered out many times in the middle of the night . . . We did regular duty . . . We were everywhere scouting, reconnoitering, performing night-guard duty. Everything of that kind was done by my three companies, so that we never had twelve hours' rest at any time, no man of us." The "Hussars," dressed not in gold bullion and fourrageres, but in plain Army blue with gilt buttons, did double duty as provost marshal's men in troubled St. Louis where every second man on the street was a Seccesh or a bushwhacker. And in combat they turned in a terrible and devastating account of themselves.

Zagonyi was a pitiless drill master, knowing that only through excellence could his men hope to survive. In an action on the road to Springfield, beyond the town of Warsaw, Missouri, the Hussars acquitted themselves bravely. When bullets started whistling about his ears, Zagonyi realized he could either advance or retreat, and the latter was out of the question. He at first ordered his men into a trot down a lane but in 200 yards about 40 had been unhorsed by Confederate riflemen. He then breached a fence and regrouped in a field, standing in the stirrups, sword point at chest height, and leading a charge. In five seconds, Zagonyi said, the Rebels had broken and fled; "In that single attack I lost fifteen men killed . . . and the enemy's dead men on the ground were 106." From raw recruits, in six weeks Zagonyi had made first class swordsmen of them.

> We Hungarian cavalrymen teach our soldiers never to use the revolver, as they are of very little use. The sabre is the only arm the cavalry need if they are well drilled. There were no swords of my men that were not bloody; and I saw swords from which the blood was running down on the hand . . . (To learn the sabre) we worked from the time the sun was up until the sun went down; and in the evening I gave extra hours to my officers and non-commissioned officers, so that I had hardly four or five hours to myself nights; and I never saw that the general slept more. He beat me in work every day . . .

The dead, Zagonyi reported, all had sabre cuts in the head, and of the Rebel wounded, many more were rumored seriously injured and dying. Of his own men, Zagonyi had nothing but praise; in the words of this peppery officer one can sense the devotion which he must have inspired in his 300 troopers that day before Springfield: "I stated to them that when I started, I expected to find about 300 or 400 of the enemy; but instead of that, the probability was that there were about 1,900 of the enemy. I told them I had made up my mind to attack the enemy, and I promised victory; but, I said that I did not want to throw away any lives, and I asked those who felt tired to step forward two steps, and I would put them on extra duty; but not one single man showed any tired or sickness; and every one of them, I saw their eyes grow big like your fist, every one . . ."

These men of iron that Zagonyi had recruited, elite in spirit and fighting courage if not in uniform and arms, were thrown away by their dismissal, discharged in disgrace. The cause: because of utterances claimed to be treasonous in their charge at Springfield. Zagonyi, following established custom for millenia, had given the men a battle cry: "the Union" and the name of their general, "Fremont." Washington thought this showed an attempt to set up Fremont as a higher officer and that sentiment was building up to establish a western republic with its center in Iowa. Zagonyi thought the idea ridiculous, and there is nothing in the Commission's inquiry to show the truth was otherwise.

Birge's Sharpshooters

Another group of good men who went down with Fremont were the Birge's Sharpshooters. A regiment recruited along the same lines as the Berdan regiment of the east, these squirrel hunters, if disciplined along military lines, could have done great damage to the irregular Confederate forces. Their arms were obtained under contract for 1,000 pieces with Horace E. Dimick, a displaced Yankee gunsmith who had achieved fame and prosperity in St. Louis. He had in 1848 considered making Colt's patent revolvers under license from the inventor to supply the western market. Now he turned his talents to buying guns. Headed "1,000 rifles with sword bayonets," Dimick's contract was embodied in letters proposing to furnish rifles and Callender's acceptance of the terms on September 18, 1861.

"I can furnish the regiment of Colonel Birge with 1,000 rifles of the same general character as samples exhibited at headquarters," Dimick wrote to Fremont on September 11. He declared a difference in barrel lengths of not more than 3 inches should be allowed, and bullet weights to range from a half ounce to an ounce. He proposed to purchase them from gunsmiths "in the different cities in the west," offering his services to undertake this commission. He had 150 such rifles in stock, and calculated a price of $25 on an average would do the job. To close the deal he agreed to supply a bullet mould and ball screw and wiper with each gun, and 10 extra ball screws and 10 spring vises to every 100 rifles. The rifles to be sighted, "and to be equal in every respect to the sample which Colonel Birge has, and to be subject to his inspection . . . and only those

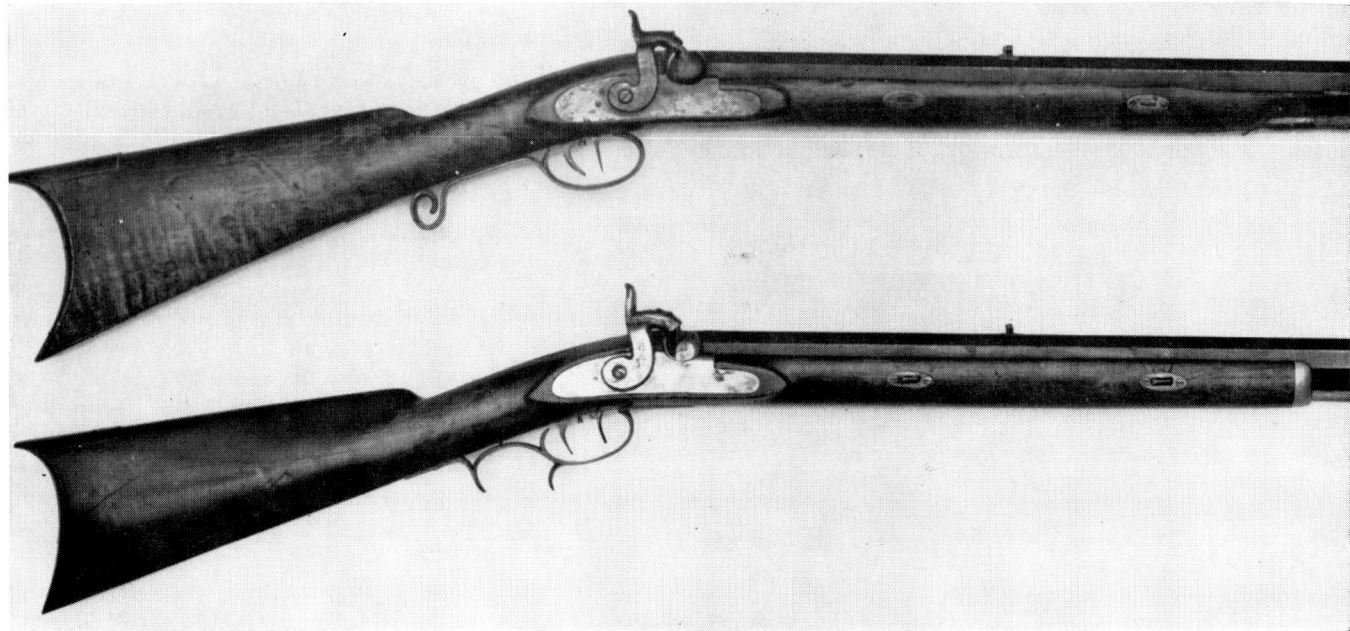

Percussion sporting rifles were also obtained by Fremont while commander at St. Louis. Shown are two typical St. Louis rifles by Hawken compared (full view) with Harpers Ferry U.S. Model 1803 half-stock rifle. Two-wedge style of forearm is typical of St. Louis rifles.

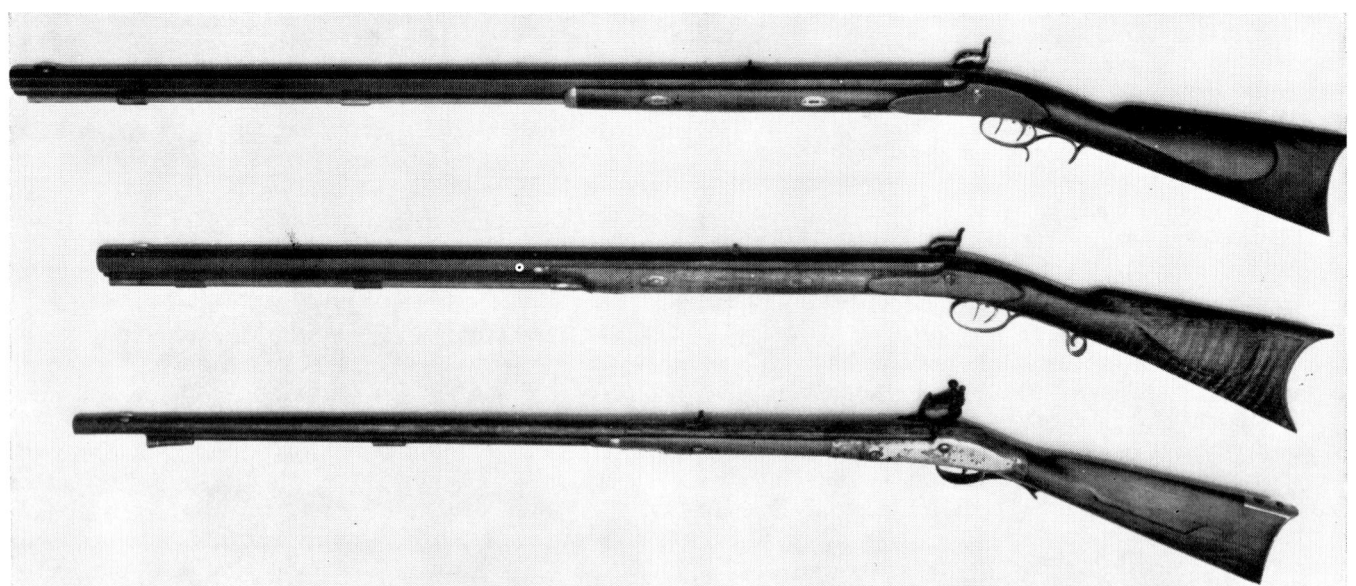

Full view of two Hawkens and Harpers Ferry M1803 rifle. U.S. gun has had brass sheath repair to stock skillfully applied. Horace E. Dimick was contractor who supplied General Fremont with 472 sporting rifles for Birge's Sharpshooter regiment. Order called for "with sword bayonets" but collectors believe lot was mixture of many sporting and militia arms Dimick delivered.

accepted by him shall be paid for . . ." Dimick promised in writing.

The specific character of rifles Dimick promised to get is difficult to assess, conforming as they must to a long discarded sample rifle once in Colonel Birge's care. By April 27, 1862, Dimick had delivered 472 sporting rifles at $25 each; the account was paid May 20. But, considering the irregularities in getting funds out to Fremont, and the fact Dimick had 150 guns actually on hand in September, it is no libel to suppose he had actually delivered at least the 150 by the end of September. We believe these arms included para-military target rifles of the prong butt style affected by the German-Swiss *schuetzen* clubs of the middle west in the 1850's. Often they were fitted for bayonet—socket, clasp, or sword—to conform to a special shooting match for military target work. Some of these special rifles, adapted for fighting, and for accurate shooting, were what Dimick obtained. When Birge's Sharpshooters were disbanded and translated into the 67th Regiment Illinois Volunteers, a colorful corps of men vanished from history. Their patron, General Fremont, nearly did, too. Yet his faults in the armaments race were three:

He equipped his men with 5,000 new breech-loading .58 caliber carbines when there were none to be had at any price.

He established a training cadre that in six weeks turned plow jockeys into tiger-mad swordsmen willing to follow a crazy, but valiant little Hungarian saddle tramp into the gates of Hell.

He set up a corps of trained, expert woodsmen, dressed in forest green and wielding bayoneted target rifles capable of placing a bullet into a Reb's belt buckle ten times out of ten at 200 meters.

With these errors, the record of Fremont in the West was ended.

CHAPTER 13

The Dreaded "Horizontal Shot-Tower"

Christopher Miner Spencer created a pretty good rifle, built a highly profitable business, became one of the leading men in the machine tool industry, was a friend of President Lincoln, and in one sense made the "rifle that ended the Civil War." All of which is doing pretty well for a young man of 27.

Number of Spencers Purchased

Spencer was born at Manchester, Connecticut, June 20, 1833; he remained identified with Connecticut industry all his life and died there, prosperous and founder of the famous Billings & Spencer firm, manufacturers of drop forging tools, on January 14, 1922. Patentee of designs in silk-winding machinery, automatic screw machines and turret lathes, he is known for his development of the seven-shot Spencer repeating rifle and carbine. Buckeridge estimates 230,000 Spencer arms were used in the war; Harold Peterson in a profile on Spencer appearing in *American Rifleman,* more conservatively noted that 200,000 Spencer rifles and carbines are thought to have been employed in combat. The number is quite large, so large as to suggest error. Some 94,196 Spencer carbines are listed as procured in the war at a cost of $2,393,633.82; and 12,471 Spencer rifles, costing $467,390.56. Spencer cartridges totalling 58,238,294 were bought for $1,419,277.16. These purchases, by the Ordnance Department, spanned the period January 1, 1861 to June 30 (end fiscal year) 1866. They do not include the Navy's early purchase of 700 Spencer rifles at the beginning of the war.

Types of Spencers

Two basic Spencer arms were used during the war; in one of them, the rifle, there are two detail variations. The carbine and rifle are of the same design exactly from the breech of the barrel to the buttstock; forward, the rifle has a 30-inch barrel, a long forestock held by band springs and three iron bands. Beneath the rifle barrel at the muzzle is a bayonet stud for sword bayonet, on those rifles delivered for the Navy. The Army pattern takes the regular socket bayonet, triangular blade, as used on the Sharps. The carbine has a 20-inch barrel, one band. In many of the parts, there are similar or identical dimensions to like parts in the Sharps arms, reflecting the assistance both technical and production given to Spencer by R. S. Lawrence, contractor on Sharps Rifle Company work in Hartford during the war. The Spencer for the Army, the rifle, is largest of all Spencer arms in the bore, taking the No. 56-56 Spencer cartridge. Some confusion in nomenclature has existed over the various Spencer calibers, but Colonel B. R. Lewis is satisfied in his own researches that the Civil War Spencer must be the No. 56-56 straight-cased cartridge, not the No. 56-52, which is slightly tapered or bottlenecked, and of nominally smaller .52-inch bore.

Three general classes of arms exist that were made under Spencer's direction. The earliest are sporting rifles and a few semi-military small-caliber carbines, made and marked in Hartford, Connecticut. The main factory for Spencer production was subsequently established in the premises of the Chickering Piano Company building in Boston, on Tremont Street. The "Boston" Spencer is the rifle of the war. At the close of the war, the Burnside Rifle Company of Providence, Rhode Island, contracted to build and remodel Spencer arms; they turned out rifles which saw service for a brief time in the Indian wars. It is supposed by some that Custer's dash and heedlessness, armed as he was later, with single-shot Springfields, might have stemmed from the firepower efficiency of his Michigan troopers who carried Spencer 7-shooters in the war.

Early Spencer Models

Spencer's first gun patent of March 6, 1860, No. 27393, reveals how early he had turned his talents to arms inventions. His was no sudden desire to capitalize on the need for arms, though certainly a boyhood enthusiasm for guns had matured in the martial spirit of the times. A second patent of July 29, 1862, No. 36062, described and claimed the "perfected" Boston Spencer.

Certainly by the end of 1859, Spencer had built his first models. While the exact location of his shop is not known, it seems probable that they were made in the Robbins and Lawrence works managed by R. S. Lawrence in Hartford. Small frame arms adapted to the just-developed .44 rimfires, like the .44 Henry, were Spencer's first output. Specimens in the Winchester Museum

Small frame Hartford-made Spencer carbine cal. .44RF has Lawrence sight of type fitted to Sharps guns; reveals Sharps contractor's interest in Chris Spencer's new repeater: 19½-inch barrel carbine is serial 5, one of few made.

suggest there is a sequence of design, judging from the gradual discontinuance of unnecessary furbelows as the arm was refined. All lever action rifles made by Spencer had 7-shot tubular magazines inserted into the buttstock. All had a rolling breechblock moved by an under lever, to charge the chamber and eject the empty shell.

All had side back-action locks and side hammers manually cocked for each shot. Sporting rifles and military arms were made, in two frame sizes.

The .44's and .36's are the earliest arms of the Spencer system. They are "tool room models." A ring-ended lever specimen numbered "15" on left side of breechblock and forward end of finger lever bears the mark C. M. SPENCER HARTFORD, CT. PAT^D MAR. 6, 1860 atop the breech. Caliber is .36 rimfire; 24⅝-inch octagonal barrel, browned. The extractor is made like a segment of a buzz saw, that is, the type shown in the original patent drawing. Whether fabrication of this and other arms was not commenced until the patent was issued, or was begun some months before and marked prior to case-hardening and finishing, is not known. Neither is it known for sure what were Spencer's plans for production. Did he hope to put across a .36 or .44 rifle or carbine for militia, or was he simply thinking of it as a practical sporting rifle, carry-

Simple and strong rolling breech design was unlocked by pulling down lever, which withdrew top section of block from engagement at rear with receiver, and permitted whole assembly to roll back. Cartridges fed from butt tube and emerged into space beside sling bar base, to be pushed into chamber on closing breechblock.

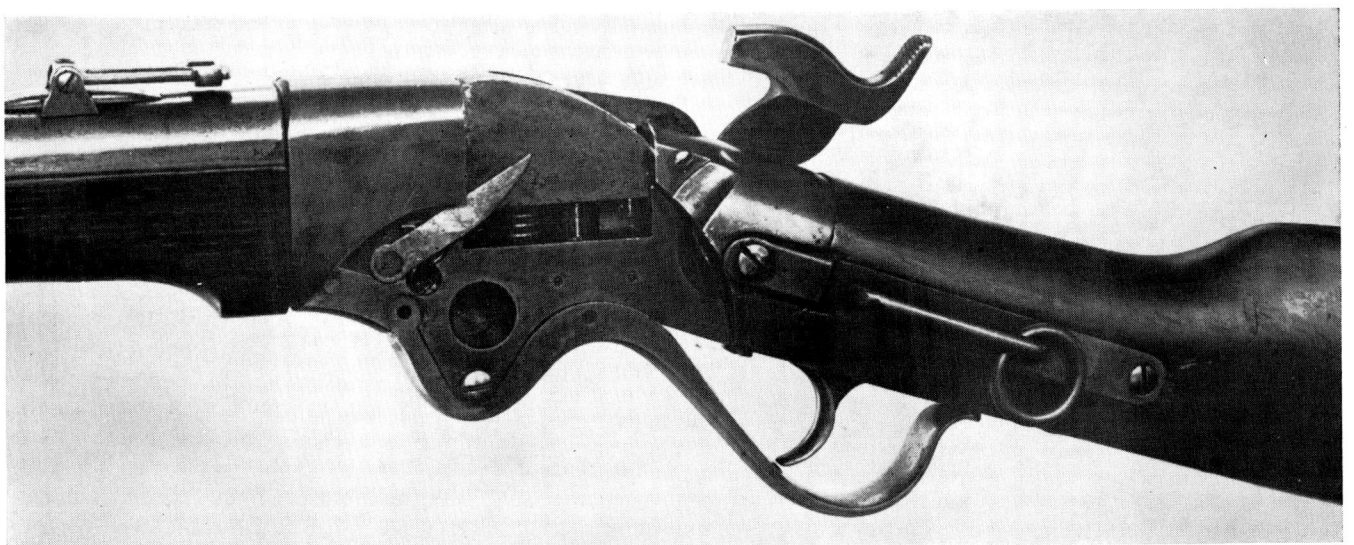

ing a day's supply of shots without the need for flask or bullet pouch? Except for the detail of the extractor, this arm is identical to one illustrated in the *Scientific American* January 25, 1862. No big frame gun is known marked "Hartford." A carbine of military form, small framed, caliber .44 long rimfire, 19½-inch barrel, is also in the Winchester museum. It is number 5. In addition to the C. M. Spencer marking as above, the rear sight base is marked R. S. LAWRENCE/PATENTED/FEB. 15, 1859, some tangible evidence of Lawrence's aid to Spencer; the sight base is the same as that found on Sharps New Model 1859 and 1863 rifles and carbines.

Spencer Finds a Factory

Between his patent of March 6, 1860, and the summer of the following year, Spencer found capital and organized a factory. His mentor was Charles Cheney, owner of silk mills in Manchester where he (Spencer) had got his start and where he returned after a brief period working at Colt's.

Cheney had lived next door in Hartford to Gideon Welles, who in 1861 was Secretary of the United States Navy. With the irony that characterizes the crosscurrents of interest and patronage in government, it is amusing to note that lovingly preserved today (by Massachusetts collector Gerald Fox) is a handsome Henry rifle, one of the first made, serial number 9, inscribed "Gideon Welles - Secretary - Navy." But the gift to Welles availed Winchester nothing.

With Spencer, it was a different story. Cheney introduced Spencer to Welles and a test of the new gun was arranged at the Washington Navy Yard. A trial board under Captain, later Admiral Dalhgren, test-fired the weapon in June, 1861, and reported:

The mechanism is compact and strong. The piece was fired five hundred times in succession, partly divided between two mornings. There was but one failure to fire, supposed to be due to the absence of fulminate. In every other instance, the operation was complete. The mechanism was not cleaned, and yet worked throughout as at first. Not the least foulness on the outside, and very little within. The least time of firing seven rounds was ten seconds.

Government Contracts

Within weeks, Spencer received an order for two rifles; a week later, there arrived a Navy Department order for 700 adapted for the sword bayonet.

Frank Cheney and Christopher Spencer went to Boston to supervise the manufacture of these first Navy rifles in leased premises of the idle Chickering Piano plant. "It was the beginning of struggles and troubles," Spencer later told his children. "The installation of the machinery, building a forging shop, making of tools, fixtures, gauges, and many special machines, and finishing the first of the Navy guns, all within a year, was a Herculean task."

Though the Navy required but 700 rifles, apparently Spencer was willing to make 1,000 in the first lot; his daughter, Mrs. Vesta Spencer Taylor, recalls that from the Navy Yard tests came "an order from the Navy Department for one thousand guns." It is likely that Spencer would speak of making "one thousand guns" and also of making "guns for the Navy," and it is equally likely that given an order for 700, he would plan to make 300 additional for profitable speculative sale. But 1,000 arms was not enough to justify the expenditure of half a million dollars capital and, again, politics was resorted to in order to obtain Government business. Through James G. Blaine, Speaker of the House of Representatives, a requirement for an additional 10,000 rifles was passed to the Secretary of War by the Navy. But the matter was not without its technical and official sanction; the rifles were obtained only after official favorable tests, ordered by General McClellan.

According to Special Order No. 311, Major General McClellan appointed Captain Alfred Pleasonton, Captain A. Sully, and Lieutenant S. C. Bradford, all Regular Army, to test the Spencer rifle. Colonel C. P. Kingsbury, after whom the present Kingsbury Ordnance Works in Indiana is named, was then Chief of Ordnance on McClellan's staff, Army of the Potomac. He had written his opinion of the rival Henry rifle on November 16, 1861, saying: "As I have no doubts of the merits of 'Henry's Repeating Rifle,' compared with other breechloaders, I think it would be well to purchase a number sufficient for one regiment." Making an invidious distinction between it and the Spencer, he said, "Henry's rifle appears to be . . . superior to others in that it may be fired 15 times without reloading . . ."

Spencer Company agent Warren Fisher got after the McClellan crowd. The test board under Pleasonton, who was to become a major general and organizer of the highly effective Union cavalry later in the war, convened on November 22 at the Washington Arsenal, and rendered its decision: "The Rifle is simple and compact in construction, and (taking a slap at the Henry with its exposed magazine spring) less liable to get out of order than any other breech-loading arm now in use." The board also tested the new .56-56 carbine, and was "particularly pleased with it," recommending it as "a very useful arm for the Mounted Service." It was discovered by Pleasonton that the Spencer could be held beneath the arm, pressed against the body, and the lever worked, cycling cartridges into the chamber, the hammer being thumb-cocked. The Spencer firm made hay of this in a later catalog, stating "Its special aptitude for the Cavalry Service may be inferred from the single fact that but one hand is required to load and fire it." Kingsbury was whipped into line, evidently, for the same catalog also noted after the November 22 tests that "Colonel Kingsbury . . . concurred substantially in the foregoing opinions, and as the result of these several examinations, trials, and tests, the War Department ordered ten thousand of the rifles for the United States Service."

Following the November 22, 1861 tests, Spencer was informed that he should write directly to the Secretary of War and tell him how rapidly Spencer rifles could be furnished, and at what price. That the arm was satisfactory, was now established. The day after Christmas, Simon Cameron was handed a letter by Warren Fisher, Jr., who was in Washington personally to get the order:

Washington, December 18, 1861

Sir: The proprietors of the Spencer repeating rifle propose to contract with the United States for the manufacture and delivery of ten thousand of said arms, with triangular bayonet, and the usual appendages for service, at the rate of ($40) forty dollars for each rifle complete. The whole number of rifles to be delivered for inspection at the manufactory in Boston within the year 1862, as follows: 500 in the month of March; 1,000 in each of the months of April, May, June, July, August, September, October, November; 1,500 in the month of December.

Your obedient servant
Warren Fisher, Jr.
One of the proprietors of the Spencer repeating rifle

To: Hon. Simon Cameron,
Secretary of War

Ordnance General Ripley is always held up as the bugaboo of independent arms inventors, but on the same day Fisher sent the above note around to the Secretary of War, Ripley received and acted on his instructions, which were to accept the proposal and buy the rifles. Had Ripley honestly felt the purchase of 10,000 new-fangled Spencer repeaters was a bad thing for the service, he likely would have objected to these instructions.

Cameron was a political appointee, given the post of War Secretary in token of his political support of Lincoln, not because he was especially well versed in military affairs like one of his predecessors, Jefferson Davis. Cameron often did bow to Ripley's judgment, not in any degree servile, but as an executive of the company might rely upon a trusted employee's technical counsel. The delay between receipt and reading of the Fisher proposal, and the issue by Ripley of the order, could not have consumed more than a couple of hours:

Ordnance Office
Washington, December 26, 1861

Sir: By direction of the Secretary of War, I offer you an order for ten thousand (10,000) Spencer breech-loading magazine rifles, with angular bayonets and appendages, on the following terms and conditions, viz: These rifles are all to be of the same pattern, and of the calibre .58-inch, and are to be subject to inspection and proof by such inspectors as the department may designate . . . Payments are to be made . . . at the rate of forty dollars ($40) for each arm complete . . .

Respectfully, your obedient servant
James W. Ripley,
Brigadier General

To
Warren Fisher, Jr., Esqr.
Boston, Massachusetts

Fisher returned to Boston and, receiving the Ripley letter on the 31st, immediately accepted. The description of the rifle obtained is also quite clear: a "Boston" Spencer, adapted for angular bayonet, not with the sword stud; and in caliber .58. The cartridge that the Spencer actually used is known as the "56-56", listed as late as 1914, in a Winchester Cartridge catalog as: ".56-.56, adapted to Spencer, Ballard, and Joslyn carbines; powder . . . 45 grains; bullets . . . 350 grains; per 1,000, $40." Above this listing is that of the bottleneck, later-developed Spencer round, .56-.52, with the legend "Adapted to Spencer military and other rifles." This has led recent researchers to conclude the Spencer Military of the war is a .52, whereas it is in fact the

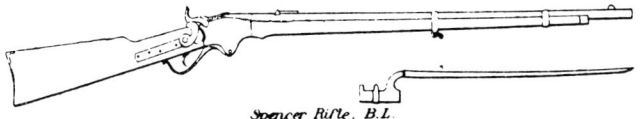

First U.S.-bought Spencers were rifles, though illustration in *Official Records Atlas* omits third (rear) barrel band. Socket bayonet was same pattern but not interchangeable with U.S. Rifle Musket bayonet. Caliber ordered was .58 (.56).

.56, conforming, with the loose tolerance of the day, to General Ripley's specification of "calibre .58 inch." As the number of Spencer rifles bought during the war was only 12,471, it would seem the long arm had less effect on the course of battles than the carbine. This is not quite true, for Wilder's brigade and other mounted infantry units were armed with the long rifle, though the newly organized cavalry, among them the Michigan regiments including one under General Custer, carried carbines as well as some rifles. But for a time it looked as if the 10,000-gun order was going to be cut off completely by Joseph Holt and Robert Dale Owen.

Upon their appeal to all parties to furnish them with copies of contracts, Warren Fisher responded quickly with a letter detailing the status of his work on the 10,000 Spencer rifle order. Alexander H. Rice was his first intermediary to whom he sent contract papers, asking Mr. Rice to deliver them to Holt and Owen on March 22, 1852. Then on April 24, Fisher sought out his representative, J. Hooper from Boston, and had him write a letter introducing Fisher to Holt and Owen personally. As a result of this he was asked to detail in a sort of memorandum what the Company had accomplished. Fisher stated that when Cameron retired from the cabinet, he had written to Washington to make sure nothing had interfered with the contract of December 26, 1861. The Assistant Secretary, on January 25, 1862, had reassured him in writing that all was well: "The gun is good, and needed for our sharpshooters—an arm of the service for which it is intended."

When on January 29 Stanton ordered copies of contracts from the contractors, Fisher prepared his and sent them in by February 4-5. Meanwhile Ripley had requested that Fisher supply a Spencer machine-made military rifle of the exact pattern he was proposing to furnish, so it could be studied at the Ordnance Office and approved. Earlier guns tested had been made generally by hand and Ripley always wanted the exact article as a pattern. Fisher had obtained specimens of all the parts for the rifle and they were assembled in April, though the sample gun was not proof-tested.

On February 24 he went to Washington to deliver the pattern rifle to Ripley and also to see Holt and Owen. While Ripley momentarily objected to the pattern rifle, suspecting that the receiver was made of malleable iron, he approved the pattern when reassured that the receiver was in fact a solid forging, machined. Holt and Owen also were cordial, did not intimate to Fisher that any interference in the contract might occur. Then, while in Washington again on 15 May, they indicated their intention to review the order to the Spencer Repeating Rifle Company and reduce the quantities or suggest that a delivery of Springfield rifle muskets be substituted for repeating Spencer guns. Fisher objected most strenuously to either idea. Quite well informed concerning the money his company had paid out for special tools to build the repeater, he at once countered with a "buy me out" proposal as one fair solution; also that the Government pay the actual amount expended for tools, as determined from an appraisal and examination of vouchers and receipts. Secondly, he proposed that the order be changed from rifles to carbines for cavalry; 6,500 carbines of large size (.56-.56) and 6,500 small size carbines, caliber .44 rimfire, apparently, as Fisher said, weighing about 6½ pounds. He offered 1,000 a month, deliveries to begin in August 1862; but the pattern rifle had not at that time been approved and its approval was delaying the work. Holt and Owen accordingly summed up the matter with their decision of May 31, 1862.

Finding that deliveries scheduled for March, April, and May, amounting to 2,500 guns, had not been made, they relieved the Government of the responsibility of taking them and reduced the Spencer order to 7,500 rifles. Of these, first delivery was to be 1,000 in June and 1,000 monthly thereafter until 7,500 were taken. Ripley at last approved the pattern rifle on June 9. Fisher asked Holt and Owen, because of this delay, to extend the time of delivery to August, but they remained firm. Actual delivery of rifles began December 1862. First were 600 rifles accepted by Naval Sub-Inspector Mr. Griffith. On December 4 he inspected the 600 guns, proof-testing 700 barrels, of which but one burst. The proof charge was a cylindrical bullet, first with 280 grains of powder, and second with 250 grains. The burst barrel was discovered to have a flaw causing the failure; this was the fault of the steel maker, not of Spencer's armorers. The parts were then inspected by Griffiths, and after all the rifles were assembled, he returned on the 10th and fired each rifle about 10 times. In 6,000 shots only 4 of the Spencer-made cartridges failed to fire. The charge was 34 grains of powder, contrasted with Spencer's direct competitor, the Sharps New Model 1859 Navy rifle which, according to Naval Inspector Captain John S. Chauncy, carried a 64-grain charge. Chauncy inferred that the excellent ballistic performance of the Spencer round came in part from the fulminate inside the cartridge case.

The Navy order was ready for shipping by December 25, 1862, packed in chests of ten guns each, plus sword bayonets, brushes, cleaning rods, and screw drivers. Presumably the final 100 guns to complete the order were assembled when Spencer had a barrel ready to replace the burst one, and this may have taken a week or ten days.

These rifles were ultimately issued to the Mississippi flotilla of gunboats and "cotton clads." They proved effective counters to the fire of Confederate sharpshooters from overhanging river bluffs, who liked to drop minie balls inside open-topped gun turrets.

By the end of December, the rifles for the Army were also being boxed and shipped out; presumably 20 per chest as General Ripley desired. By the summer of 1863, several thousand of these infantry arms had given a good account of themselves.

Spencers Used in the War

General Norton in 1872 (*American Breechloading Small Arms*) conservatively estimated, and most realistically, that of the Spencer gun "over 100,000 arms of this system have been in use in the Army of the United States." Perhaps the first of such arms was a gun—we do not know whether it was a rifle or carbine—that Spencer shipped to his friend Sergeant Francis O. Lombard, with the 1st Massachusetts Cavalry, who was a former Smith & Wesson gunsmith. Eventually Massachusetts ordered 1,500 Spencer arms. Sergeant Lombard used this gun, shots fired in anger, at Cumberland, Maryland, in a skirmish occurring on October 16, 1862.

Production of parts was speeding up and rifles were beginning to be put together for the Navy. Spencer felt it was a good time to be off on a selling trip. He wanted to emphasize the carbine, because although he charged less for it, it was also less expensive and so could be produced in greater numbers more quickly. The barrel, which Spencer drilled from solid steel, took half the time and half the cost to make, as did the rifle barrel. The armies in the late fall were getting into winter quarters, and the busy impresario-engineer took a swing through the lines in Northern Virginia and then went west to visit Grant and the Army of the Tennessee.

Grant himself could not order the purchase of any arms. His men did not get new rifles until July of 1863 when after the fall of Vicksburg they were re-equipped with captured Southern Enfields, discarding their smoothbore Springfield muskets of 1842 and earlier patterns.

Spencer had some luck with individual commanders and with men who were willing to buy rifles with their own pocket money. From lieutenants who ordered at company or battalion level to colonels on brigade command duty who ordered thousands at a time, he found a ready acceptance not only because his was a repeating rifle, but because he *was ready to deliver it*. By the spring and summer of 1863, Spencer rifles and carbines had been in use on many fronts, and the reports began to come in.

Captain G. M. Barber, Ohio Sharpshooters, Murfreesboro, Tennessee, May 19, 1863, noted: "I have

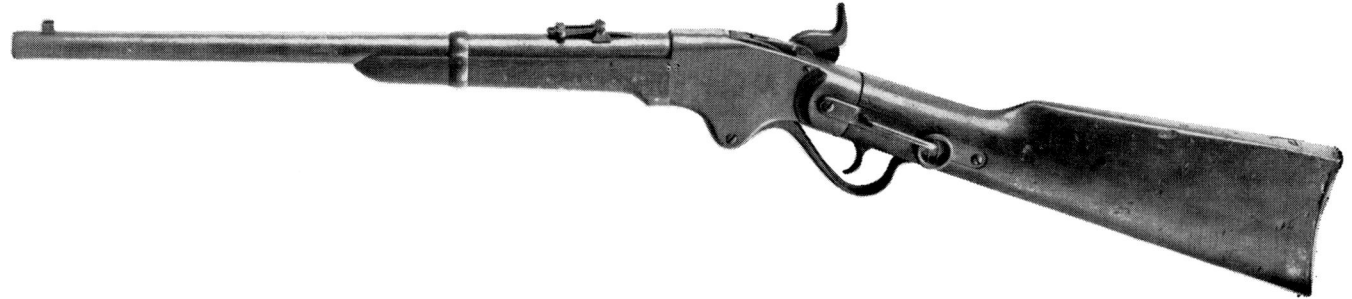

Standard Spencer carbine was made by Boston firm in old Chickering Piano Factory building, had improved Lawrence rear sight, was rather clubby in shape but strongly built. Protected magazine in butt was deemed superior to Henry.

been drilling my battalion together with some companies of the 10th Ohio Infantry, in target practice for some time past, and it has given me a fine opportunity to test your rifle and compare it with the 'Enfield' (of the 10th Ohio) and the result is more than forty per cent in favor of the Spencer Rifle. It is admitted by all who have witnessed our practice that we have the best gun in the Army . . . On long ranges they exceed our expectations . . ."

Specimen carbines were also distributed to officers who could hit the mark and report. "Yesterday Colonel Wass and myself went out with our pickets," wrote Colonel T. E. Chickering, 41st Massachusetts, and possibly of the piano family, in a letter dated Baton Rouge, Louisiana, January 13, 1863. "(I took) my carbine along, for amusement. We fired at targets at musket range. The target was about 5 feet long 18 inches wide. I hit the target every shot, and put one ball through the very centre of the bullseye, beating the whole party. The little gun shoots most admirably, and is all the Rifle Company claims for it."

At Norfolk, Virginia, where General King's regiment was digging out of its winter quarters, his A.A.G. Captain R. Chandler wrote to Spencer, "In every particular, it surpasses all breech-loading arms I have yet seen, and must eventually supersede the old musket for war purposes."

The man who did the most to spread the fame of the Spencers, the man who caused the Confederates to talk of it as the "horizontal shot tower" so formidable was its output of hot lead as fired by a regiment armed with Spencers, the man who fired his guns so fast and furiously that bewildered Rebels marched in as prisoners asked "What kind of hell-fire guns have you got?", didn't want Spencers in the first place. Colonel John Thomas Wilder, commanding 1st Mounted Brigade of the 17th Indiana Volunteers, passed a request for prices of Henry rifles to Oliver Winchester under date of March 20, 1863. Two of his regiments had received their horses and were exercising with them as mounted infantry, fighting mainly on foot, and arriving at the battle site on horses. The men were willing to buy repeaters, so Wilder, probably as much from curiosity as any special partiality to the Henry arm, asked the New Haven Arms Company to state prices for 900 rifles, with slings, without ammunition (they would draw on the Government for ammunition). The men were willing and able to pay for these arms from their $13 monthly wages; Wilder himself, proprietor of an hydraulic machinery works, would guarantee the amount. The ammunition not only came from Frankford Arsenal ammunition works near Philadelphia, but from firms like C. D. Leet & Company of Springfield, Massachusetts, and Smith & Wesson who by 1865 had produced millions of cartridges for the Spencers.

And at the "Metallic Cartridge Manufactory" of Crittenden & Tibbals in South Coventry, Connecticut, an unusual endurance record was taking place. The .56-.56 cartridges were supplied by this firm early in production of the big rifle, and they obtained in April, 1862, one rifle for ammunition testing. In use for 2½ years, it was fired by their count at least 16,000 times, not being cleaned more than three times, and as of September 10, 1864 it was "now in good working order."

So durable an arm was Wilder's second choice, and Spencer was quick to supply his requirements. By the time the Henry people had informed them that they could not deliver the rifles needed in time, Wilder's brigade included other regiments that wanted repeaters. The order was passed to Spencer for 2,000 rifles, to be usd by Wilder's Mounted Infantry, the celebrated "Lightning Brigade," sometimes called "Hatchet Brigade" because he armed them with axes as camp equipment and to cut breastworks rapidly from brush in the field.

During April or May, 1863, Wilder's Brigade received its issue of Spencer rifles. These were not carbines, but the long 30-inch barrel .56-.56 rifles, adapted for angular bayonet. "My Brigade of Mounted Infantry have repeatedly routed and driven largely superior forces of rebels, in some instances five or six times our number and this result is mainly due to our being armed with the Spencer repeating rifle," wrote Wilder to Warren Fisher. "Since using this gun we have never been driven a single rod by any kind of force or number of the enemy. At Hoover's Gap, in Tennessee, on June 24, 1863, one of my regiments fairly defeated a rebel brigade of five regiments, they admitting a loss of over 500, whilst our loss was 47 . . . No line of men, who come within fifty yards of another force armed with the Spencer repeating rifles, can either get away alive, or reach them with a charge, as in either case they are certain to be destroyed by the terrible fire poured into their ranks by cool men thus armed. My men feel as if it is impossible to be whipped, and the confidence inspired by these arms added to their terribly destructive capacity, fully quadruples the effectiveness of my command."

Spencer, during his sojourn in Hartford with Colt, had learned the value of testimonials. Officers in these days were less likely to cover up their opinions, too, and many like Wilder were quite outspoken in their favoritism for special rifles. But even such old time Regulars as General O. O. Howard ("I prefer it to any other repeating rifle") or Joseph R. Hawley of Connecticut, long time friend of Sam Colt ("the terrible roll that the Spencer carbines beat had utterly routed them") were willing to stand on their statements in favor of the Spencer. Though personal data is scanty, Spencer it seems quite obviously desired the general junking of the Springfield rifle musket, muzzle loading, percussion cap, and the obtaining of a sufficient number of his rifles to arm the Union. In this, the sentiments such as expressed by General Hawley supported him: "Our army has . . . thrown away an advantage equal to 50 per cent of its force, in not arming every man with a breechloader, and if possible a magazine rifle with a metallic cartridge . . . It is as easy to bring along ammunition wagons as wagons with rations, and as easy to have a detail to bring up cartridges, as one to carry stretchers."

The Spencer in Battle

Gettysburg has been called the high-water mark of the Confederacy. But some researchers have chosen to title their essays provocatively "Who Won At Gettysburg?" In the North, it was viewed as a defeat for the South. Only in armchair generalling can it be unquestionably asserted that it is a high-water mark. A good case can be made out for a dozen different "turning points" or decisive moments during the battle, which, though not recorded in history, might have resulted in the battle going the other way. Longstreet's hesitation of an extra five minutes because of the sudden bewildering fire from Berdan's Sharpshooters armed with Sharps Rifle and the Colt Rifle, is such a moment; so, too, is the moment of destiny ascribed to the Federal troops armed with Spencer's seven-shooter. The echoes of July in Pennsylvania had sobbed into memory when the *Boston Journal* for October 21, 1863, published a most laudatory essay on the Spencer rifle at Gettysburg:

> In the Army of the Potomac it is equally well known. The daring and dashing feats of the 5th and 7th Michigan Cavalry, under the lead of the intrepid Kilpatrick, have become historic. In the great Battle of Gettysburg these regiments achieved the most enduring renown by the success with which they foiled all the efforts of Stuart to get into our rear, to cut our communications or to capture and destroy our ammunition and supply trains. And in the pursuit of Lee, until he escaped across the Potomac, these regiments were constantly upon his heels, and their brilliant charge upon his rear guard at Falling Waters (where they captured more prisoners than their own number) must be fresh in the memory of our readers.

As Pleasonton's cavalry unpleasantly pursued the fleeing forces of Lee along the Rapidan, trooper Robert Trouax distinguished himself "with his Seven Shooting Spencer rifle, killing six rebels as they were crossing the river."

An unknown chronicler who addressed a report on Gettysburg to the *Scientific American* (published December 26, 1863) stated:

> After the battle at Gettysburg whilst our cavalry were pursuing the Rebels, our regiment was employed as skirmishers; some of our boys got into a mill, the Rebels holding a stone wall opposite; these hearing our guns go off would rise up thinking they would find us unloaded, but would fall back carrying rather more lead than was agreeable. The "Johnnies" couldn't stand this long, and retired. Shortly after this we took a captured officer across this part of the field to the rear. When he saw his men lying there he began to complain bitterly against our barbarity. He was asked to explain, when he pointed to his dead, saying "Almost all are shot through the head," implying that they had been murdered after surrendering; but when he was shown one of our rifles he only wondered "that more were not shot."
> One day as our line of skirmishers was advancing, one of the Johnnies yelled out, "Helloa Yanks, have you got them damned guns loaded to the muzzle again?" Whilst the cavalry was picketing along Robertson's River, skirmishing was frequent along the line, but when our regiment took its turn we exchanged but a few shots with them when they offered the following propositions:—"Say there, if you'ns won't shoot, wee'ns won't shoot," and peace existed along the lines as long as our regiment remained.

A hopeful editorial appearing about this time in another Boston paper suggested that Spencer's repeater was an instrument of peace. So certain was it in dealing death, "the sooner fighting comes to be the certain

Repeater dubbed "horizontal shot tower" was adopted as corps insignia by cavalryman Wilson.

annihilation of one or both of the contending parties, the sooner fighting will be abandoned as a useless waste of human life . . . People will think twice before resorting to deadly weapons, when those weapons are the assurance of nothing short of certain death."

Apparently at least one Rebel soldier held to this view though the closeness with which the shots clustered about him might suggest he had strong persuasion at work: "I was under good cover (at Gettysburg) but when exposing myself was fired upon; thinking I had drawn their fire I stepped out when another ball just missed me; I thought that perhaps they had a double barreled gun and I had him sure. I stepped out again when another ball grazed me; then I thought there must be two of them in front of me. I then stepped entirely from under my cover, determined to have my chance for a shot, and was wounded by a fourth shot. While I was lying there I heard three more shots in rapid succession from the same gun, when our boys fell back and (the Yankees) came up and sent me prisoner to the rear. There's no use fighting against such guns . . ." The Yanks would try this ruse often, once they got the hang of it: a volley, to simulate the discharge of a number of Springfield rifled muskets; then hold fire till the Confederates exposed themselves and give them sure, aimed shots.

Spencer Sees Lincoln

With such a battle record, Spencer decided to again go to Washington. The plum he apparently sought was the complete arming of all Union forces with his repeating rifle, and the abandonment of Springfield rifle musket production. The 7th New Hampshire, once issued some Spencers, was to have their repeaters called in and defective Springfields issued, causing them to lose a battle. Such a thing Spencer hoped to avoid, for he intended to go to the highest authority. He went to Gideon Welles and this time met the President.

There is a fascinating legend attached to this interview. It relates how young Spencer, his rejected rifle presumably under his arm, was disconsolately wandering the halls of the War Office building trying to find someone who would listen to him and order some guns. We are given a picture of a lad barely out of his teens, a truly quixotic figure. A kindly old Negro porter is said to have taken pity on him, and to have told Spencer, "You come with me, I'll take you to someone who will take a look at your rifle." And so he takes Spencer to the White House and introduces him to President Lincoln quite unofficially. Thereafter follows the celebrated shooting match at the shingle, on the White House lawn, and as proof of the story, the shingle preserved in a museum is cited as evidence.

There is some truth to this story. Spencer did see Lincoln, but not so naively as the story suggests. And in two published accounts of this meeting, there are differences which though detailed, suggest inaccuracies in either the recollections of Spencer's daughter, or the reporting of J. O. Buckeridge as cited in *Saturday Evening Post* "Abe and His 'Secret' Weapon," March 31, 1956. Spencer's daughter, Vesta Spencer Taylor, published "A Personal Reminiscence" appended to Harold Peterson's article "The Repeater Lincoln Tested," in *The American Gun*, Vol. 1, No. 1, Winter 1961. In both essays, a lengthy quotation directly attributed to C. M. Spencer is published. Although Harold Peterson was quite incensed over editorial changes made in his manuscript by the publishers, which may have been necessary in the interests of shortening it but which also introduced technical errors of fact which Peterson had not made, it seems doubtful if any changes of wording would be made in so valuable a source document as C. M. Spencer's own words describing his visit with Lincoln. It is therefore reproduced here verbatim from that source:

> On the 18th of August, 1863, I arrived at the White House with the rifle in hand, and was immediately ushered into the executive room. I found the President alone. With brief introduction I took the rifle from its case and presented it to him. Looking it over carefully and handling it as one familiar with firearms, he requested me to take it apart to show the "Inwardness of the thing." It was soon dissected, and laid on the table before him. After a careful examination and his emphatic approval, I was asked if I had any engagement for the following day. When I replied that I was at his command, he requested that I "Come over tomorrow at 2 o'clock, and we will go out and see the thing shoot."

Here was no sudden secret interview; Lincoln was expecting Spencer, and had put aside a few minutes for him to determine if there was any purpose in spending the time of the Government in Spencer's interest. Convinced, upon superficial examination, there was, he was then willing to arrange time on the morrow to shoot the gun. The reports of officers were only confirming what he would himself discover, if it seemed as good as it looked, as a repeating rifle.

Spencer continues:

> Arriving at the appointed time, I found all in readiness to proceed to the shooting place, which was about where now stands the Washington Monument. (Buckeridge also places the site for shooting at the Mall, but states it was 1862. We prefer Spencer's version). Accompanying us was his son, Robert, and one of the officers of the Navy Department who carried the target and rifle, with the ammunition. Arriving at a point opposite the War Department the President requested Robert to go over and ask Mr. Stanton to come and see this new gun fired. Robert soon returned and reported Mr. Stanton too busy to attend. "Well," says the President, in his humorous way, "they do pretty much as they have a mind to over there."
>
> While we were waiting for Robert, Mr. Lincoln discovered that one of the pockets in his black alpaca coat was torn open. Taking a pin from his waistcoat, he proceeded to mend it, remarking, "It seems to me that that don't look quite right for the Chief Magistrate of this Mighty Republic, Ha! Ha! Ha!"
>
> Arriving at the shooting ground, Mr. Lincoln, looking down the field, said, "It seems to me, I discover the carcass of a colored gentleman down yonder," and ordered the target placed so as to avoid accidents. The target was a board about six inches wide, and three feet long, with a black spot near each end. The rifle contained seven cartridges. Mr. Lincoln's first shot was low, but the next hit the bullseye, and the other five were close around it. "Now," says he, "we will let the inventor try it." Being in almost daily practice, I naturally beat the President a little. "Well," he said, "you are younger than I am, have a better eye, and a steadier nerve."
>
> The end of the board which the President had shot at was cut off by the Navy official, and handed to me when we parted on the steps of the White House. I kept it until 1883 when at the request of one of the staff of the *Army and Navy Journal*, it was sent to Springfield, Illinois, to be placed in the collection of relics.

The following evening Lincoln, having retained the rifle, went out to shoot again. He and Spencer, together with a clerk in the War Department, John Hay, did the firing. According to Hay, "This evening and yesterday evening an hour was spent by the President in shooting with Spencer's new repeating rifle. A wonderful gun,

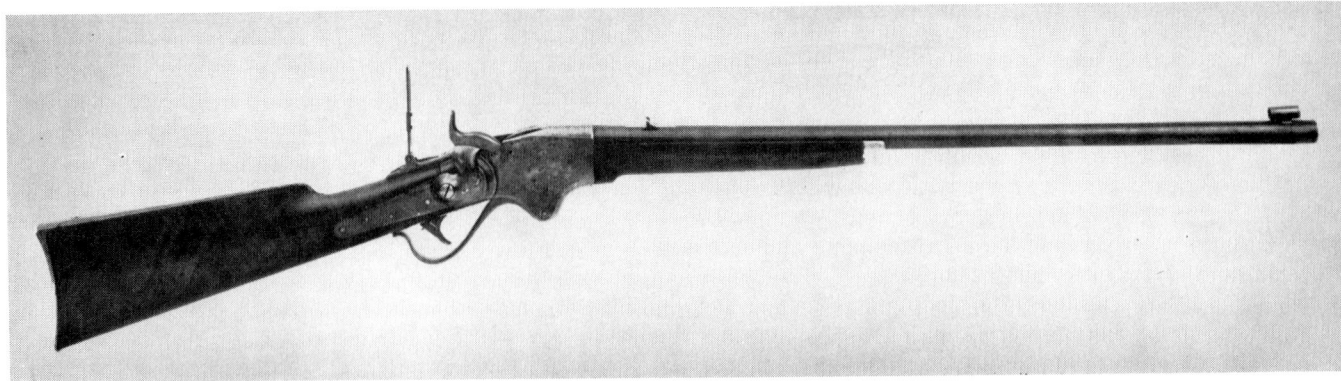

Author's sporting Boston Spencer .56-.46 is fitted with de luxe wood but uses some military parts in its assembly. Basic serial number is 8386, but number believed to be its place in "sporter" series is 7 on major parts. Set trigger is unusual accessory. Few other sporters, one other set trigger are known.

loading with absolutely contemptible simplicity and ease with seven balls & firing the whole readily and deliberately in less than half a minute. The President made some pretty good shots. Spencer, the inventor, a quiet little Yankee who sold himself in relentless slavery to his idea for six weary years before it was perfect, did some splendid shooting. My eyes are gradually failing. I can scarcely see the target two inches wide at thirty yards."

Hay reports the trio had some kibitzers absolutely fantastic in their repartee. "An irrepressible patriot came up and talked about his son John, who, when lying on his belly on a hilltop at Gettysburg, feeling the shot fly over him, like to lost his breath—felt himself puffing up like a toad—thought he would bust. Another, seeing the gun recoil slightly, said it wouldn't do, too much powder: a good *piece of audience* should not *rekyle;* if it did at all, it should rekyle a little *forrid*."

I have met shooting experts of this type in my own days on the range; they are a prolific breed.

The target board at which Lincoln fired, that was given to Spencer, was sent to General John A. Logan for that worthy's collection of Civil War relics in the State Capitol in Springfield, Illinois. According to Miss Margaret A. Flint, Assistant State Historian (1961), "When the General John A. Logan Memorial Collection was transferred from the Illinois Adjutant General's custody to this library in 1956 it was reported to contain such a relic. Unfortunately, we were never able to locate it or any information regarding it."

Discovering this lost shingle would be a most interesting thing for collectors, as it might identify beyond all question precisely what rifle was used by Spencer in his shooting match with Lincoln. Was it a regular military rifle, of a type just being made and of which no actual deliveries had been accomplished to the United States until December of 1862? Or could it have been one of the very rare Spencer sporting rifles which were listed in the sales catalog in 1865 but which evidence suggests were actually in existence during the Boston production period? Suydam (Charles R. Suydam, *The American Cartridge,* 1960) says that the .56-.46, one of the few genuinely bottlenecked rimfires, was fired from Spencer sporting rifles and light carbines, using cartridges manufactured by the Spencer company. Similar ammunition was made by other manufacturers during the years 1862-1900.

Source for most Spencer sporting rifle information is Spencer's 1866 catalog, but this is unclear. Though a light .44 carbine was pictured and offered for sale, none have as yet been found which are not early Hartford Spencers. Of the Boston rifles, made on the regular Spencer frame, taking the .56-46 which is a bottleneck adaptation of the big .56-.56 case and dimensions, very few exist. They are of the same general form, and a careful measurement of his sporting rifle was made by collector C. Harald Sebenius of Altadena, California:

Bore measurement over lands	.443"
Number of grooves	6
Length of barrel, muzzle: chamber front	24⅜"
Length of barrel to rear of chamber	26"
Length of chamber	¾"
Chamber at rear, diameter of ⅞" part	.56"
Chamber at front, diameter of ¾" part	.443"

Overall length of rifle is 43⅞" or 44"

Receiver marked on top in three lines with:

SPENCER REPEATING

RIFLE CO. BOSTON, MASS.

PAT^d MARCH 6, 1860

A similar specimen in the author's collection is also a round 26-inch barrel (Spencer offered 28-inch and 30-inch, 50¢ each inch additional extra). A unique single set trigger is fitted, appearing to be of Spencer design. (Another example of this Spencer trigger has come to light.) Pushing the back bar of the trigger sets it. The tip of the bar protrudes through the trigger itself and is fired by a light touch on this protruding tip of the set bar. The entire trigger then flips up under spring tension, knocking loose the sear to fire. The original Spencer back sight is a vertical bar with a sliding screw-locked peep hole block. One sight mounting screw cuts through the serial number, which is stamped on top of the receiver tang behind the breechblock, and the sight base completely obscures it. The first digit of the number is restamped a little out of line, thus: 8386, and appears to have been done at the factory. This suggests the receiver is one of those made on the first 10,000 order of .56-.56 rifles for the Army; other specimens of this model bear widely spaced numbers, apparently not consecutive. The hammer of No. 8386 bears a "D" of the United States sub-inspector, somewhat burnished down as if refinished subsequent to stamping for acceptance. As a theory for the production of these sporting rifles, it seems logical that a few were put up on condemned United States actions which were not accepted by the inspector and thus gave Spencer an opportunity to try out the market with a sporting gun. On forestock, lever, breechblock, underside of barrel, and other parts is the tiny assembly or sub-serial number "7". Numbers in the mid-250's have been noted on these parts. The mid-barrel sight, instead of being a Lawrence elevating type, is a single range sporting notch made on a base cut to fill the slot for the elevating sight base. There is a small flat fore and aft of this slot for the Lawrence-type sight leaf spring. The cartridge for this arm was later listed as ".56-.46," and actual specimens measure between .460 inches and .488 inches bullet diameter. This is a tight but not unrealistic squeeze down the barrel for the slightly hardened lead bullets of the old time cartridges.

Checking into the differences between the sporting rifle, first listed in 1865-66 but actually in existence as early as 1863, to judge by numbers, leads to a not unnatural but wild surmise.

With what kind of rifle did Lincoln fire at the wood board? Was it the regular heavy .56-.56 military rifle with its somewhat cumbersome 30-inch barrel? Or might it have been the lighter, more elegantly finished sporting rifle, with better sights and the reduced "rekyl" of the lighter .56-.46 cartridge? If the board could be found or a precisely scaled photograph of the board measured, some interesting facts as to the gun Spencer showed the President might come to light.

". . . I took the rifle from its case and presented it to him," Spencer wrote later. Buckeridge's version uses the expression "cloth case." This is unlikely, but not impossible. The habit of carrying arms in canvas or heavy duck cases was not well established until after the end of the war. It is doubtful if Spencer would have entrusted such an important "secret weapon" to the mercies of baggage porters and freight forwarders wrapped so insecurely as in a simple cloth case.

My opinion is, in view of Lincoln asking Spencer to disassemble the gun, and Spencer's readily coming up with a screwdriver, that he had the rifle in a conventional wood or leather trunk box. It most likely was compartmented with spaces for ammunition and cleaning tools, and a screw driver and, if any cloth case was featured, he may have had the rifle further wrapped in a light flannelette or doeskin cloth like a sword cover. We have a hunch that Lincoln shot a sporting rifle,

Special Spencer sporting rear sight is unique pattern with these rare arms, does not have large disc peep so characteristic of sights of following decade. Gun is listed in 1866 catalog but is believed to date from early in the war. Flange on butt plate is end of loading tube which, turned aside, is pulled out to insert seven cartridges into magazine. Design was heavy, but foolproof. The loading tube (not shown) is carried in a recess in the stock, and inserted through the butt plate.

one of the first Spencer had made on the .56-.56 production line. If so, could he have chosen No. 7 as his "lucky seven?" A photograph exists of the board, incised with a sharp point with the words "7 consecutive shots made by the President of the United States with a Spencer rifle at a distance of forty yards. Washington, D. C., August 18, 1863." Until the board itself is located, formerly in the John A. Logan Collection in Springfield, Illinois, the mystery of what rifle Spencer gave the President will remain unsolved.

Other Evidence Favoring the Spencer

The heavy casualties at Chickamauga had sealed the value of the repeater in war. Under Wilder's command and cooperating with the terrible fire of double-shotted canister Parrott rifles at point-blank range, the Lightning Brigade had chopped a red valley through the Confederate ranks of Longstreet's desperate, battle-hardened veterans.

On Saturday, September 19, 1863, Van Cleve's and Davis's corps had been separated by Longstreet's yelling "foot cavalry" who knifed between them with triumphant hurrahs, confident of victory. A portion of them had crossed a small field and charged toward a grove in which Wilder's mounted infantry lay dismounted, quietly cuddling their deadly Spencers. Through the woods ran a drainage ditch five or six feet deep to carry off water of a nearby swamp. Wilder's account follows:

> As the rebels entered this field, in heavy masses fully exposed, the mounted infantry, with their seven-shooting Spencer rifles, kept up a continuous blast of fire upon them, while Lilly with his Indiana Battery, hurled through them double shotted canister from his ten-pounder rifles at less than three hundred yards. The effect was awful. Every shot seemed to tell. The head of the column, as it was pushed on by those behind, appeared to melt away or sink into the earth, for though continually moving it got no nearer. It broke at last, and fell back in great disorder. It was rallied and came on again, and with desperate resolution pushed through the solid fire to the ditch. Here, all who could get it took shelter. Instantly Lilly whirled two of his guns and poured right down the length of the ditch his horrible double canister. Hardly a man got out of it alive.
>
> When the firing ceased, one could have walked for two hundred yards down that ditch on dead rebels, without ever touching the ground.

While Wilder did not claim that his brigade defeated Longstreet, he thought that 2,000 Confederates were killed and wounded in the immediate front he commanded. Wilder, two hundred times under fire by that September, later said "At this point it actually seemed a pity to kill men so. They fell in heaps, and I had it in my heart to order the firing to cease to end the awful sight."

Results of the Interview with Lincoln

The result of Spencer's interview had been characterized as a highly successful one, and after that it is said that he made all the guns his company could turn out for the Union. The facts are somewhat different. Orders for Spencer arms amounted to 10,000, which number had been reduced by Holt and Owen to 7,500. At the price of $40 each, this contract was quite comparable to Springfield Rifle Muskets contracts for twice the number, and there were quite a few contractors who did not get additional orders until they had commenced to deliver in quantity on their original orders. The requirement of the rifle to arm the Sharpshooters had long passed and the need for the long gun was not so pressing, with increased production of the National Armory and the musket contractors, and the increase of special arms for mounted riflemen and other skirmishers-type infantry. The need was for the new cavalry organized under direction of General Pleasonton, and the most important thing in Spencer's future was the record of the carbine tested by the McClellan Board at the Washington Arsenal in November of 1861. Now it was the cavalry that demanded the gun, and it was the Michigan troops with which the stubby Spencer carbine especially became identified.

The Model Adopted

The model adopted for the cavalry was 22 inches in the barrel, blued and casehardened, 3-groove rifling, and firing the .56-.56 cartridge. The caliber is often listed as .52, using the No. 56 Spencer rimfire cartridge. Bullet diameters of the round for this and the Spencer CW rifle listed by Suydam run: .535 inch, .551 inch, .541 inch, .555 inch, and .545 inch, indicating considerable leeway in tolerances. The earliest of this charge used a long, heavy one-ounce conical bullet resembling in ogive the U. S. M1855 rifle minie ball and is evidently Spencer's idea of a "calibre .58-inch metallic cartridge." The carbine receiver top has the usual "Boston" marking. Added is a short sling bar on the left side of the receiver, based on a small plate let into the small of the stock, along which a sling ring slides freely for attaching the snaffle hook of the trooper's cross-shoulder carbine sling. Carried this way, the carbine is inverted along the left side of the trooper when mounted, its muzzle down and forward underneath the leg, and the muzzle itself caught in a short leather socket to keep it from flopping around.

A special cartridge box was invented by Blakeslee to carry ten additional loaded Spencer magazines. Of leather over wood, six-sided, it was carried strapped on the trooper's back and gave him a quick supply of 70 spare shots. Though the tubes were pre-loaded and therefore expendable, he probably had to do extra duty at camp if he was so careless as to lose them in a skirmish.

Michigan forces became famous with their Spencers. Though Wilson's cavalry brigade adopted the Spencer carbine as their badge or emblem, many of the troopers carried the infantry rifle, to the extent that Wilder in 1864 when asked his opinion of the Spencer suggested that the rifle, which he deemed superior for mounted infantry, should be fitted with a sling ring to enable it to be carried like the carbine. Apparently the rifle was carried slung across the trooper's back by means

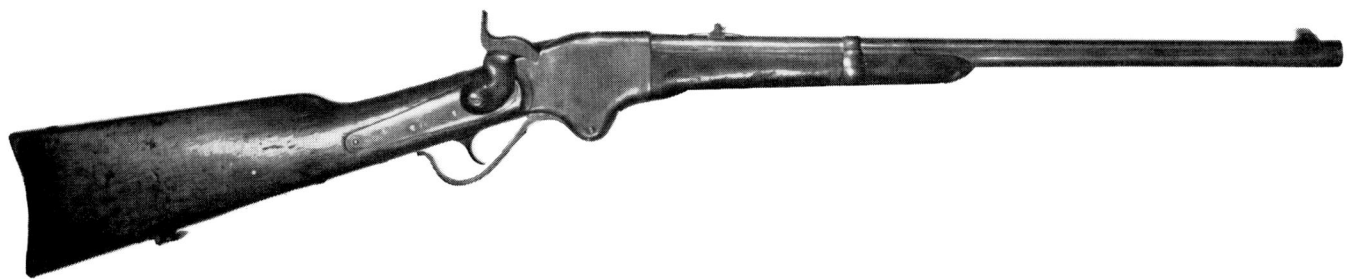

Some Spencers had sling swivel of ordinary form mounted in toe of buttstock. Regular finish was linseed-oiled wood, case-hardened frame, lock and hammer in mottled colors, and rust-blued barrel. Small work was usually brightly polished and heat-blued. Burnside Rifle Co. of Providence made over 30,000 Spencer carbines in last days of war.

of the swivel-fastened ordinary sling or, in more alert moments, balanced across the saddle bow across the knees. While the McClellan saddle lacked the lasso horn of the earlier prairie or Spanish saddle, over which frontiersmen sometimes slipped a double leather rifle loop, it had D rings to which the rifle could be thonged and jerked loose in an instant. Many of the Michigan regiments with the firepower of their Spencers proved equal to much more numerous Confederate units.

Headquarters Cavalry Corps, Army of the Potomac
May 14, 1864

Mr. F. Cheney

Dear Sir:—Being in command of a Brigade of Cavalry which is armed throughout with the Spencer Carbine and Rifle, I take pleasure in testifying to their superiority over all other weapons. I am firmly of the opinion that 1500 men armed with the Spencer Carbine are more than a match for 2500 armed with any other firearm. I know this to be true from actual experiment.

Very respectfully &c.
G. A. Custer,
Brigadier General

In June, the general of the flowing locks got a chance to prove that his testimonial was in good faith:

New York Herald, June 2nd, 1864
Torbert's Division.

As the fight waxed hottest, between two and three o'clock, Custer's brigade of Michiganders was ordered in to assist Davies' and Gregg's brigades, who already had the enemy weakening, putting him to rout. This command is completely armed with Spencer rifles and the enemy would rather see the devil coming at them than these. As Custer marched up the road and dismounted his men, Davies opened a gap in his line to make way for the Michigan brigade. The line was immediately joined and a furious assault commenced. It was just in the nick of time, for at the same moment, a brigade of fresh troops reinforced the enemy. But nothing could withstand the terrible volume of iron hail which our boys now poured into their ranks. Back they went, South Carolinians and all, for a mile and a half, with fearful loss. At five o'clock the battle was ended, and we had the field. Three of our brigades had whipped their whole corps.

The Confederate estimation of the Spencer was quite as flattering, all things considered, as the Yankee approbation. An editorial in the *Richmond Sentinel*, December 8, 1864, after remarking on the general issue of breechloaders to the Union cavalry, and especially citing the Spencer rifles and carbines, went on to say:

The captures which we have made from the enemy embrace a large number of these Spencer rifles. It would be eminently desirable to arm our cavalry with them and thus remove that inequality between the opposing lines which told so heavily against us in the cavalry encounters in the past campaign. A practical difficulty exists, however, which we are informed has not yet been removed. We call it to the attention of our Ordnance Department, that the ingenuity which has won so many triumphs in obviating other difficulties may perform a similar service in this case. The Spencer rifle cannot be used with any cartridge yet furnished to our soldiers. The cartridges are put up in copper cases of peculiar mechanism, which we have not yet undertaken to make. Hence our valuable captures are stacked away in our armories, as so much dead weight. The thing needed is the manufacture of cartridges for the Spencer rifle . . . A large number of (the best breechloaders)

Resplendent in "Jeff Davis" cap and shoulder scales, sergeant of Federal cavalry posed in 1864 for Q.M. Corps picture holding issue Spencer carbine. Snaffle hook snapped to ring on sling bar, hung carbine from shoulder while trooper was in the saddle. Muzzle of carbine rested in leather socket strapped to McClellan saddle rig behind leg; was swung free with off hand when dismounting or mounting.

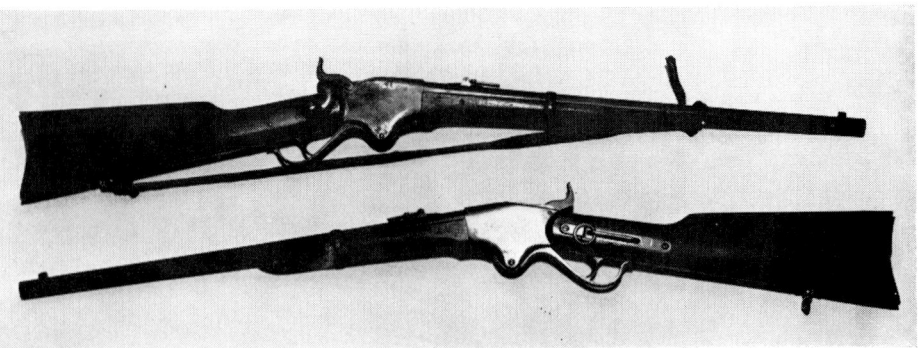

Pair of Boston Spencers owned by John Wilkes Booth and used by him at time of Lincoln murder. Ironic twist in Spencer story was capture of Jeff Davis by Michigan trooper armed with Spencer carbine. Booth guns are now in Ford's Theatre museum.

the world has yet produced, are in our possession, but idle for want of cartridges. So we are informed by cavalrymen—will the Ordnance Department please to take notice?"

This wholly gratuitous piece of scribbling did nothing to cheer up harassed and much-overworked General J. G. Rains, CSA. As superintendent of the Confederate powder mill at Augusta and Chief of the Nitre and Mining Bureau, he had enough to do in trying to supply the want of ordinary combustibles for muzzle-loading arms. Collecting of night soil from which to render nitrogen salts for making gunpowder was but one of his chores; another was the calling in from the hills of every copper "worm" he could find. No modern "revenooer" was ever so diligent in seeking out the sources of untaxed beverages as was Rains and his men in calling upon the patriotism of Southern hill planters to give up their copper coil stills. The precious metal was needed, not for cartridge cases, too costly a luxury for the South, but simple copper percussion caps. A hundred could be punched from the same metal that would make one Spencer cartridge. If the South could manage to capture a depot of Spencer ammunition, the issue of the rifles would be quite worthwhile. But though they were the best the world had produced, they lay idle for want of raw, red copper—precious ore of Mars that is found in many places, but most economically mined in areas controlled by the North. A cartridge-loading plant was finally begun by the Confederacy but too late to affect the outcome of the war.

Influence on Tactics

The issue of breechloaders like the Spencer gave rise to several tactics which were new to warfare. Among them was the trick of firing a volley, waiting until the enemy began a charge, then mowing them down. Another "modern" tactic was moving or assault fire, which Custer tried when he went between Davies' and Gregg's brigades and moved upon the South Carolinians.

The repeaters lent an aura of invincibility to the regiments which carried them; without them they lost heart. "The 7th New Hampshire had so deadly a fire poured at them that they broke and fell back in confusion" reported the New York *Tribune* of the Union defeat at Olustee, Florida, in March of 1864. "Dissatisfaction had been created among the men by depriving them of the Spencer repeating rifle and by issuing, in lieu of this formidable weapon, Springfield muskets in a damaged condition. Unable to protect themselves with such guns, one wing of the regiment gave way and could not be rallied, while the other wing, which still retained the repeating rifle maintained its position until the ammunition was exhausted, when it too was obliged to fall back." As the Confederate correspondent in the Richmond paper indicated, not all the Union troops armed with the Spencer were invincible: "A large number of the best the world has produced are in our possession."

The Spencer did not win the war; on the other hand its contribution to the Union cause was substantial. Up to December 31, 1865, the Ordnance Department had bought 77,181 Spencer carbines, in addition to the 1,500 bought by Massachusetts (probably rifles) and the tens of thousands bought by other State troops. Of these arms, at least 30,496 were received under a contract issued to the Burnside Rifle Company in June, 1864, for 35,000 Spencer carbines. The Tremont Street Armory was taxed to capacity, and the Burnside Company expanded their production. These are marked on top of the frame with the words, MODEL 1865 and SPENCER REPEATING RIFLE/PATENTED MARCH 6, 1860/MANUFD AT PROV. R. I. BY BURNSIDE RIFLE CO. and the serial number. The Burnside Spencer had a 20-inch barrel, and the new .56-.50 rimfire cartridge, a bottleneck case of .50 caliber. Bullet diameters measured by Suydam range from .476 inches to .528 inches but the head of the case forward of the rim is more regular: .556 inches to .558 inches; they would all fit the Burnside Spencer chamber. These carbines were delivered too late for use in the war, but received a shaking out in the Indian campaigns which followed.

The last use of a Spencer carbine in anger was by a play actor at Ford's Theater. Booth used a tiny pistol to do the deed, but in his secondary armament, cached here and there should he be holed up and have to fight off pursuit, were at least two Boston Spencer carbines. They are now preserved and are still in good serviceable condition. One was carried by Booth when he was shot at Garrett's barn; it has a thong tied to the butt swivel and around the barrel to carry it by. The other was picked up at Lloyd's Tavern where Booth had hidden it.

There is a recent and possibly well founded belief that War Secretary Stanton had much to do with the death of Lincoln; that he put Booth up to it. The actor was truly an actor in a play staged by others, some have it. Ironically, the weapons which Booth received, cavalry Spencer carbines, with which to defend himself were the very arms which Stanton had been too busy to witness being fired in August of 1863. Verily, as the Chief Executive then remarked, "They do pretty much as they have a mind to over at the War Office."

The corollary incident looms less bright in history, for it was a quieter sort of activity: the capture of President Jefferson Davis. For many years in the G.A.R. room of the Chicago Public Library was preserved a Spencer carbine said to have been carried by a Michigan trooper on the occasion of the Confederate President's apprehension.

In the 1865 Model a peaceful note was intruded into the mechanism. Quaker inventor Edward M. Stabler of Maryland invented a turning lever to cut off the magazine and stop the "hose like" discharge of cartridges. Placed before the trigger, it impeded the movement of the breechblock enough to keep the following cartridge from popping forward to be chambered as the lever was closed. Turning the Spencer repeater into a single shooter had its advantage, for it permitted loading the chamber shot by shot, holding the full magazine in reserve.

After the War

The denouement of Spencer and his rifle story came after the War, as Spencer had created by his diligent production so much war surplus that he put himself out of business. By 1869 the firm was placed up for auction, and its assets sold to Oliver Winchester. The big Spencer breech could hold a .52-inch bullet; it was cumbersome when adapted directly by bottleneck cartridge to any smaller round. The Henry rifle could not conveniently be adapted up to .50 or larger, but it was a dandy saddle rifle in a straight .44 case. So the Henry prospered in sporting rifle sales, having made but 10,000 during the war, while Spencer, making 10 times as many, had produced himself out of the market. Spencer continued with his other mechanical interests. He founded the Billings & Spencer Company, which is still in business, and tried several flyers again in the arms field, with Sylvester Roper's unsuccessful shotgun-rifle combination, and later on with his own slide-action guns and rifles. Mechanically successful, one was used by Annie Oakley, but sales were not achieved and again he failed. He also adapted his slide action mechanism for the Lee box magazine in the late 1880's for military purposes, but the Spencer-Lee rifles were built only in prototype, and never produced.

Christopher Miner Spencer died in 1922. His work in machine tools has produced happiness and prosperity for thousands in New England industries, but he is best known for his death-dealing "horizontal shot-tower," Spencer's Seven-Shooting Rifle.

CHAPTER 14

That Damn Yankee Rifle

In sunny California a lady built a house. To San Jose in 1881 after the death of her husband and only child, came Mrs. Sarah Winchester, wife of William Wirt Winchester, son of gun company founder, Oliver. Her husband had been secretary and vice president of "Winchester." In San Jose she bought a modest eight-room house, and without rhyme or reason began at once to add rooms and remodel. Thirty years later she died leaving a crew of 16 or more carpenters busily adding on or tearing down portions of a structure which had grown to the enormous total of 160 rooms. Says Williamson in his book *Winchester:*

> Spread over six acres, within an estate of 160 acres, the house is a hodgepodge. In one room inside windows are barred, outside ones are not. There are screens on blank walls; exterior water faucets extend beneath second story windows; a balcony or skylight may be found in the middle of a room. Narrow passages and stairs with steps one or two inches high lead from one room and one level to another. Some stairways lead to blank walls, others open out into space. There is a gas light operated by an electric push button, and one room has four tiled fireplaces and four hot air registers . . .

There is no adequate explanation of Mrs. Winchester's actions. The legend grew that she was a spiritualist and that she was told by the spirits that she would live as long as her house was not completed. An alternate version is that she was afraid of being haunted by the ghosts of individuals shot by Winchester guns and ammunition.

Origin of Winchester

Born in the furnaces of conflict, the New Haven Arms Company (renamed Winchester Repeating Arms Company in 1866) grew to become a part of the American Legend. Bought by Union soldiers with hard-earned private funds, at prices equivalent to a couple of months' pay, the Henry repeater, forerunner of the Winchester, was liked but not much by the Southrons. Major Joel W. Cloudman, 1st D. C. Cavalry, all of whom were armed with Henrys, wrote to Oliver Winchester telling him a captured Southerner had protested, "Give us anything but that damned Yankee rifle that can be loaded on Sunday and fired all week."

Cloudman also wrote of an action of the 1st D. C. (Baker's Cavalry) on August 25, 1864, near Ream's Station, where his unit was dismounted and withstood a charge of Rebels, and "easily repulsed the foe, while the infantry were broken and swept from their well constructed breastworks." The later history of the war is sprinkled with such anecdotes.

Popular in the border states, the Henry was bought by Colonel Netter's Kentucky Volunteers. Near Owensboro, Kentucky, 15 Henry-armed men on a scout repulsed 240 Confederates, wrote P. K. Williams and W. W. Gardner to Winchester: "They were attacked in an open lane where there was no shelter, in March 1863. These must have been among the earliest Henrys to be issued, for production was by no means able to equal the demand. Owing to their capacity to maintain a rapid and continuous fire, they successfully repulsed and drove from the field the entire Rebel force."

Beatty recalls in his diary on March 23, 1863 that, "Colonels Wilder and Funkhauser called. We had just disposed of a bottle of wine when Colonel Harker made his appearance, and we entered forthwith upon another. Colonel Wilder expects to accomplish a great work with his mounted infantry. He is endeavoring to arm them with the Henry rifle, a gun which, with a slight twist of the wrist, will throw sixteen bullets in almost that many seconds."

The Henry Rifle

This prodigy of small arms, the Henry rifle, was the first really successful rifle to be manufactured by Oliver Fisher Winchester.

All Henrys had the hand-loop lever extension of the trigger guard, to work the gun and fire as fast as the hand could be flicked and the trigger touched off. The 16-shot magazine, and the blunt, heavy ".44 Henry Flat" bullets, in rapid fire made it the best repeater of the war. Approximately 10,000 Henrys were made, 1,731 bought officially at a cost of $63,953.26 by the Ordnance Department; the rest were used by soldiers rich enough to buy them privately.

Priced at $40, a Henry cost a lot of money to a private soldier. This high capital investment may have accounted for some of the sentiment about arms which

Southrons felt the Yankees possessed. It was generally realized that during the war anyone wanting guns could go up to Nashville and buy all he wanted for Confederate gold. Even the Yankee soldiers, the Rebs somehow believed, might be induced to sell their guns. "Are you not afraid of going to war?" a Southern countryman was asked. "No," he replied, "if I should see a Yankee with his gun leveled and looking right at me, I would draw out my pocket-book and ask him what

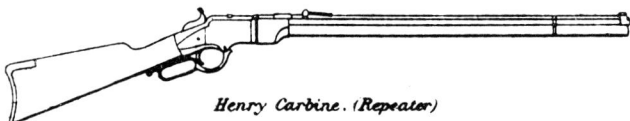
Henry Carbine. (Repeater)

"Damned Yankee rifle" loaded on Sunday and fired all week was Henry M1860, first successful rifle built by Winchester. *Official Records* pictured gun, tabulated over 1,700 bought by U.S. of 10,000 produced to war's end.

he would take for his gun, and the fight would end right there." Through *Marginalia, An Army Note Book, 1864* is more anecdotal than hard-case history, this sketch illustrates an attitude of the times.

Pride of possession in his purchase was revealed by one of Sherman's soldiers who wrote in his journal on May 11, 1864, "I got a Henry rifle—a 16 shooter—yesterday . . . I gave 35 dollars, all the money I had, for it . . . I am glad I could get it. They are good shooters and I like to think I have so many shots in reserve." Ten months later he noted "I think the Johnnys are getting rattled; they are afraid of our repeating rifles. They say we are not fair, that we have guns that we load up on Sunday and shoot all the rest of the week. This I know, I feel a good deal more confidence in myself with a 16 shooter in my hands than I used to with a single shot rifle." (Quoted from Oscar C. Winther, *With Sherman to the Sea*).

In *Letters from Lee's Army* the Southern point of view was summed up well, "We never did secure the Winchester (Henry) whose repeating qualities made the enemy's cavalry so formidable towards the end of the war."

Exploits of the Henry

Formidable was a mild word for it. Sales boosters, firearms merchants, company agents, all told of the Henry's remarkable firepower. It was proclaimed by a large broadside of the Henry, "which could be obtained from Jno. W. Brown, Gen'l Agt, Columbus, Ohio," that sixty shots per minute could be fired. Henry's Patent Repeating Rifle was said to be "The most effective weapon in the world." Considering that it was also a good deer gun, agent Brown conceded that "For a House or Sporting Arm it has No Equal." But Ohio was full of Copperheads, and conflict between Southron and Yankee stalked the streets, pistol in hand. Agent Brown described the power: "Penetration at 100 yards is 8 inches; at 400 yards 5 inches; and it carries with force sufficient to kill at 1,000 yards." Set in bold face type was the clincher: "A resolute man, armed with one of these Rifles, particularly if on horseback, CANNOT BE CAPTURED."

Putting this claim to the test, Kentuckian James M. Wilson saved his skin and created a legendary exploit of the war, good also for sales propaganda for Winchester. Wilson, Captain of Company M, 12th Kentucky (U.S.) Cavalry, was described as "an unconditional Union man, living in a strongly disloyal section of Kentucky." He had been threatened by his neighbors:

Majority of Henrys made saw war use, from Copperheads alleged to have "total of 30,000" stashed away in Chicago, to this specimen inscribed to show use by Fifth Tennessee Cavalry. Gun now owned by Thomas Suter of Colorado.

In consequence of this, Captain Wilson had fitted up a log crib across the road from his front door as a sort of arsenal, where he had his Henry rifle, Colt's revolver, etc. One day, while at home dining with his family, seven mounted guerrillas rode up, dismounted, and burst into his dining room and commenced firing upon him with revolvers. The attack was so sudden that the first shot struck a glass of water his wife was raising to her lips, breaking the glass. Several other shots were fired without effect, when Captain Wilson sprang to his feet, exclaiming. "For God's sake, gentlemen, if you wish to murder me, do not do it at my own table in the presence of my family."

This caused a parley, resulting in their consent that he might go outdoors to be shot. The moment he reached his front door, he sprang for his cover, and his assailants commenced firing at him. Several shots passed through his hat, and more through his clothing, but none took effect upon his person. He thus reached his cover and seized his Henry rifle, turned upon his foes, and in five shots killed five of them; the other two sprang for their horses. As the sixth man threw his hand over the pommel of his saddle, the sixth shot took off four of his fingers; notwithstanding this he got his saddle, but the seventh shot killed him; then starting out, Captain Wilson killed the seventh man with the eighth shot.

Wilson's exhibition persuaded the Kentucky authorities that the gun was a good one for war; in token of this feat they armed his company with Henrys. Less flattering is this anecdote to the vaunted Southern chivalry which not only was composed strictly of centaurs, but of impeccable marksmen, as well. To blaze around in Wilson's front parlour and not get the captain when firing at drawing-room distances speaks poorly for the shooting eye of Rebel Kentuckians.

By one of those wry quirks of fate which so often

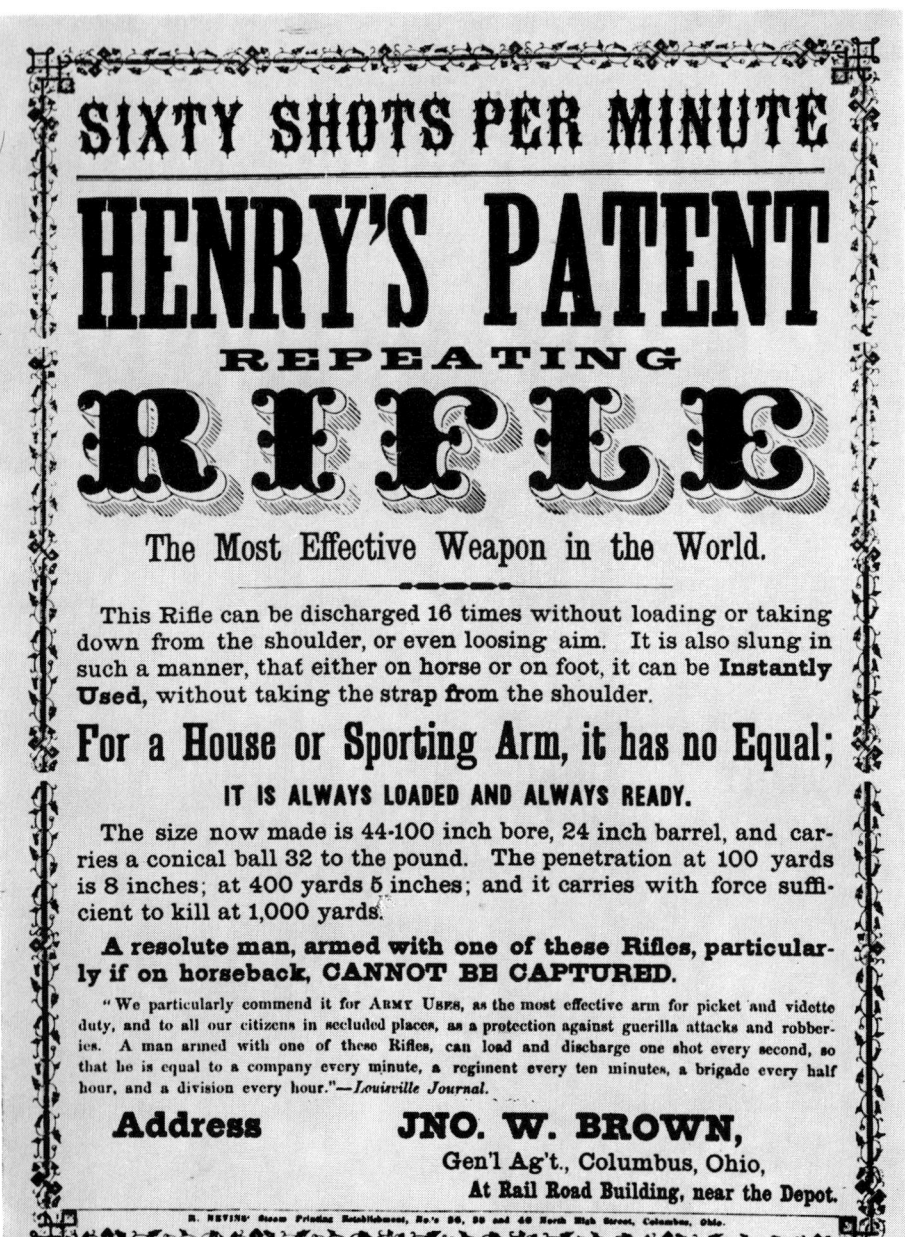

First class publicity, worthy of Winchester Public Relations writer of today, stimulated popular demand for fast-acting 16-shooter; began to shape up "western" image of lever action types because of heavy distribution in the area west of Appalachian mountains. Warlike capability is accented in ad poster for Henry which became No. 1 American sporting arm in era after war.

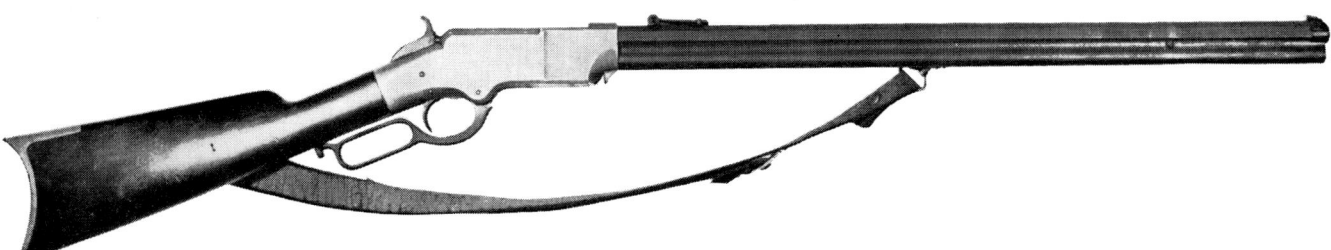

Sling for Henry was hooked to fixed loop on side of barrel-magazine assembly and to loop swivel based in side of stock. Rifle was carried by mounted men across back, instead of by usual carbine sling with saddle boot for muzzle.

happen when sales managers are more ingenious than they are honest, battle accounts of the Henry's strongest competitor, the seven-shot Spencer, appeared in the 1865 Winchester catalog to boost his own guns. The incident is ironic because instead of getting the Henrys which he applied for, Brigadier General John T. Wilder was supplied with Spencer carbines. Wilder's Brigade distinguished itself in battle with the Spencers, but the Winchester people, perhaps expressing a sales aggressiveness which caused the firm to triumph over their competitors, stole Spencer's thunder for their own puff sheet. Wilder had in fact first applied to New Haven for weapons:

HQ. 1ST BRIGADE, 5TH DIV., 14TH ARMY CORPS
Murfreesboro, Tenn., March 20th, 1863
Proprietors New Haven Arms Co.,
 Gentlemen:
At what price will you furnish me nine hundred of your "Henry's Rifles," delivered at Cincinnati, Ohio, without ammunition, with gun slings attached? Two of my regiments, now mounted, have signified their willingness to purchase these arms, at their own expense, if they do not cost more than has been represented to them. My two other regiments will be mounted soon, and will, doubtless, go into the same measures. It is of course desirable to get them at as low figures as possible, as the men are receiving from the government only thirteen dollars per month. How much additional expense would it be to have an extra spiral spring for each gun, to replace any that may be broken, or when worn out?
You will please afford the desired information at your earliest convenience. and oblige,
 Yours respectfully,
 J. T. WILDER
 Col. Commanding

Though Winchester published Wilder's letter, the firm was unable to supply so large a number as 900 in the short time available. Only 53 employees were at work during the last half of 1863, a drop of 15 hands since the firm started up in 1860. By January, 1863, Williamson (Harold F. Williamson, *Winchester*) estimates that 1,500 rifles had been made and delivered, produced during the preceding seven months. After 1863, production was stepped up about 25 per cent, from about 215 rifles monthly to about 260. At this rate, between 200 and 300 rifles monthly, it appears Winchester was unable to supply Wilder's order, and the Spencer salesman stepped in and took it. Wilder's Brigade did excellent service with the Spencer, but because his report used the non-specific term "armed with the breech-loading repeating rifle," it was grist for Winchester salesmen. Perhaps the Winchester company believed they "owned" Wilder's report on the Spencer —by 1875, when Winchester used the famous letter of Wilder in advertising, they had absorbed the Spencer Company.

One regiment more realistically reporting on its full complement of Henry rifles was Colonel Lafayette C. Baker's 1st Washington, D.C. Cavalry. It was the only regiment of the Army of the Potomac so well equipped. A single battalion raised in the District of Columbia for special duty under command of Colonel L. C. Baker, provost marshal of the War Department, formed the nucleus of this regiment, whose work for Secretary Stanton resembled activities of the "Gestapo." It was familiarly known as "Baker's Mounted Rangers." Formed for the military defense of the Capital, it was employed as a mounted police force, the "terror of evil doers," quoth Baker's memoirs, *United States Secret Service*. Writing in 1890, after Winchester had triumphed and Spencer gone under, Baker chose to beat a dead horse in his praises: "After having witnessed the effectiveness of this weapon (the Henry Rifle), one is not surprised at the remark said to have been made by the guerrilla chief, Mosby, after an encounter with some of our men, that 'he did not care for the common gun, or for Spencer's seven shooter, but as for these guns, that they could wind up on Sunday, and shoot all the week, it was useless to fight against them.' "

The 1st D.C. Cavalry was attached to General Kautz's cavalry division on a raid in May, 1863. It was one of the earliest engagements in which about 800 Maine enlistees fought. These Down-Easterners had enlisted under the assurance they were destined for active combat, and they had been simmering under their relatively peaceful duty status around Washington. "At half-past two o'clock on the afternoon of the 7th, he . . . struck the Weldon Railroad just in time to intercept a body of Rebel troops on their way to Petersburg. A thunderbolt from a clear sky could hardly have been more astounding to the enemy . . . In an incredibly short time the action was over, the enemy was whipped, the railroad was cut, the public buildings were in flames, and the gallant Kautz was again on his march, with some sixty prisoners in his train . . . The bravery of the men and the efficiency of the sixteen shooters, were put to the test . . . Some of the prisoners said they thought we must have had a whole army, from the way the bullets flew. One lieutenant asked if we loaded up over night and then fired all day. He

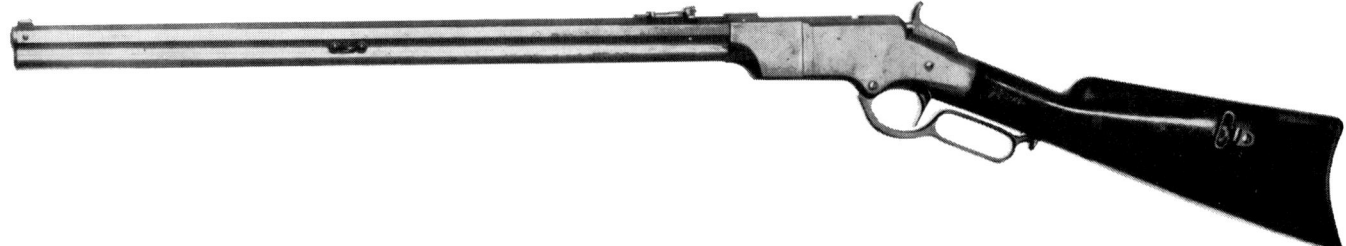

Side position of Henry sling fittings are more clearly seen in this left side elevation. Brass frame was easily machined, but production was slow and not until 1863 were deliveries fairly regular.

said he thought, by the way the bullets came into the bridge, they must have been fired by the basketful."

Kautz' command continued its raiding perambulations in the Valley. Approaching Petersburg, Virginia, three days later, the six mounted companies of the 1st D.C. Cavalry trotted down the Jerusalem Turnpike. Lieutenant Colonel Conger, commanding, ordered Major Curtis to dismount his battalion and charge the enemy's works as infantry. This was not an unusual request, as the 1st Dee-Cee were organized as "mounted infantry," whose use of the horse was to convey the trooper to the scene of battle, after which he would fight on foot.

The troopers moved out, their Henrys at the ready, every fourth man holding the horses. The battalion moved steadily forward, firing rapidly as they advanced. It was one of history's earliest effective uses of the storm trooper and moving assault fire so important to battlefield tactics of the modern "human sea" war. The Confederate position was overrun by the walking horse-soldiers. They then discovered the defending force, behind breastworks, had been three times their number. "With the common arm," Baker remarked in describing this victory, "This would hardly have been possible. Some of the prisoners said, 'Your rapid firing confused our men; they thought the devil helped you, and it was of no use to fight.'"

Henrys on the defensive were powerful, too. Some of Baker's men attacked a community south of Washington known as Cox's Mills. A slight breastwork had been thrown up on a rise commanding a bridge. Rebel horse was sighted, and the Dee Ceers formed behind the breastwork:

"A heavy force of mounted rebels had crossed the bridge, and with wild yells was charging up the hill, outnumbering our men two to one. On, on they came, expecting an easy victory. Coolly our men waited. Not a shot was fired till they were within easy range. Then a few volleys from the sixteen shooters sent them back in confusion. A second time they charged, with the same result. This time they did not return."

The story of a few men prevailing against great odds was the rule when Henry repeaters were on the smaller side, and then-conventional single-shot muzzle-loaders the equipment of the larger force. In the incident at Cox's Mills, Baker's boys were later surrounded, the Confederates having got into their baggage train and dressed in Union uniforms as a ruse. But when the Henrys had a fair chance, they won out as long as the ammunition lasted. The 1st D. C.'s report to General Dyer, when the latter was Chief of Ordnance in 1865, is of special interest in view of the battles listed in which Henry rifles took part:

HEADQUARTERS 1ST D. C. CAVALRY
In the field before Richmond, Va.
January 20th, 1865

Major Genl A. B. Dyer, Chief of Ordnance
Sir:

In connection with the accompanying report, I would beg leave to make the following remarks in regard to the merits and demerits of Henry's Repeating Rifle, as an arm for the cavalry soldier.

My regiment has been fully armed with these rifles, ever since their first organization, which was in June, 1863. The rifles now in use in my command are the same that were issued to us at the time of our organization, and since that time they have been in constant use, most of the time in active service in the field, and they are now with a very few exceptions, as serviceable and efficient as they were when they were placed in the hands of the regiment. These rifles have been well and thoroughly tested in the following battles and raids during the last summer campaign:

General Kautz's first raid in the month of May.
Battle at White's Bridge, on the 8th of May.
Gen. Kautz's second raid in Southern Virginia in the month of May. An engagement with the enemy near Fort Pride on the Bermuda front on the 1st of June.
The first attack on Petersburg on the 16th of June.
Gen. Wilson's raid in Southern Virginia in the month of June and July.
The battle at Roanoke Bridge on the 27th of June.
The first battle at Ream's Station on the 29th of June.
The first battle at Deep Bottom on the 25th, 26th, and 27th of July.
At the battle on the Weldon Railroad on the 21st, 22nd and 23rd of August.
The battle at Ream's Station on the 25th of August.
The affair at Sycamore Church on the 16th of September.
Engagement on the Darbytown Road near Richmond on the 7th of October.

From the experience I have had with this rifle, in the engagements above mentioned, and in numerous other affairs and skirmishes on the picket lines, I have no hesitation in saying that I consider it one of the most effective weapons now in use in the Army.

The remarkable rapidity and accuracy with which the gun can be discharged, renders it an invaluable weapon to the Army. Under ordinary circumstances, I believe it utterly impossible to make a successful charge on troops armed with them. At the battle of Ream's station on the 25th of August, repeated attempts were made by the enemy in large numbers to charge a position held by my regiment (they being dismounted) and at each attempt they were repulsed with heavy loss. On one occasion there were several officers of high rank from the Cavalry Corps and the 2nd Army Corps present, and noticed the destructive effect of my fire upon the enemy. But notwithstanding my high opinion of this arm when in the hands of dismounted men, I do not think it a suitable weapon for cavalry. I consider it too heavy; the barrel is also too long for the mounted service; the coil spring used in the magazine is also liable in the cavalry to become foul with sand and mud, and this, for the time being, renders the arm unserviceable. I do not think they get out of repair any more easily than most of the carbines now in use in the Army.

They carry with great accuracy; in target practice I have ascertained that an ordinary marksman can put two balls out of the three inside a ring two feet in diameter at a distance of from six to seven hundred yards.

For the cavalry service I prefer arms of calibre .44 in preference to those of larger calibre.

Very respectfully, your ob't servant,
J. S. BAKER,
Maj. Comd'g Reg't

This lengthy endorsement, which may have cost him no more than the gift of a rifle, was one of many Oliver Winchester obtained. General Kautz summed up his opinion of the Dee Cee'rs by saying: "The 1st District of Columbia cavalry was in my command during the past year, and was exceedingly efficient; and had the discipline of the regiment been in proportion to the arm they carried, which is the 'Henry rifle,' the efficiency of the regiment would have been still greater. The valuable service which the regiment performed was, in the main, due to the superiority of the arm they carried."

And in spite of an exposed magazine spring and consequent failures in service, the superiority of the Henry was directly due to the cartridge which it used.

While B. Tyler Henry receives main credit for the big .44 shell his rifle fired, to Horace Smith of Massachusetts Arms Company and his friend Dan Wesson go some of the credit. And the credit for the inspiration goes to a virtually unknown French *armurier,* Flobert.

Louis Flobert

Louis Nicholas Auguste Flobert is a man little recorded in the annals of firearms inventors, though his name is among the best known of all—his last name, that is, for his first is never mentioned. Pollard in *A History of Firearms,* speaks of his invention of the metallic cartridge as early as 1836, making him a contemporary of Lefaucheux. But Blanch *(A History of Guns)* dates him 1847 and damns him with faint praise, saying "even if he did not invent" the metallic cartridge. Flobert's date is more correctly set by the Swiss gun writer Captain Rudolph Schmidt, who sets it at "1845," seemingly logical as Flobert is listed as having exhibited "muskets, rifles, and pistols" of his design at the London Great Exhibition in 1851.

But the catalog does not describe these arms, and gives Flobert's address as 3 Rue Racine, apparently incorrect; nor does it give his full name.

For a man who was ignored, his designs swept the gun world like a storm. Gunsmiths in Paris, Liege, Suhl, and even in the Connecticut Valley, were soon turning out Flobert-design arms, mostly small-caliber rook rifles or target or "saloon" pistols. I have heard glib gun dealers, trying to peddle junk, inform their gullible customers that the "saloon pistol or rifle" was designed for use in saloons, to be used for impromptu

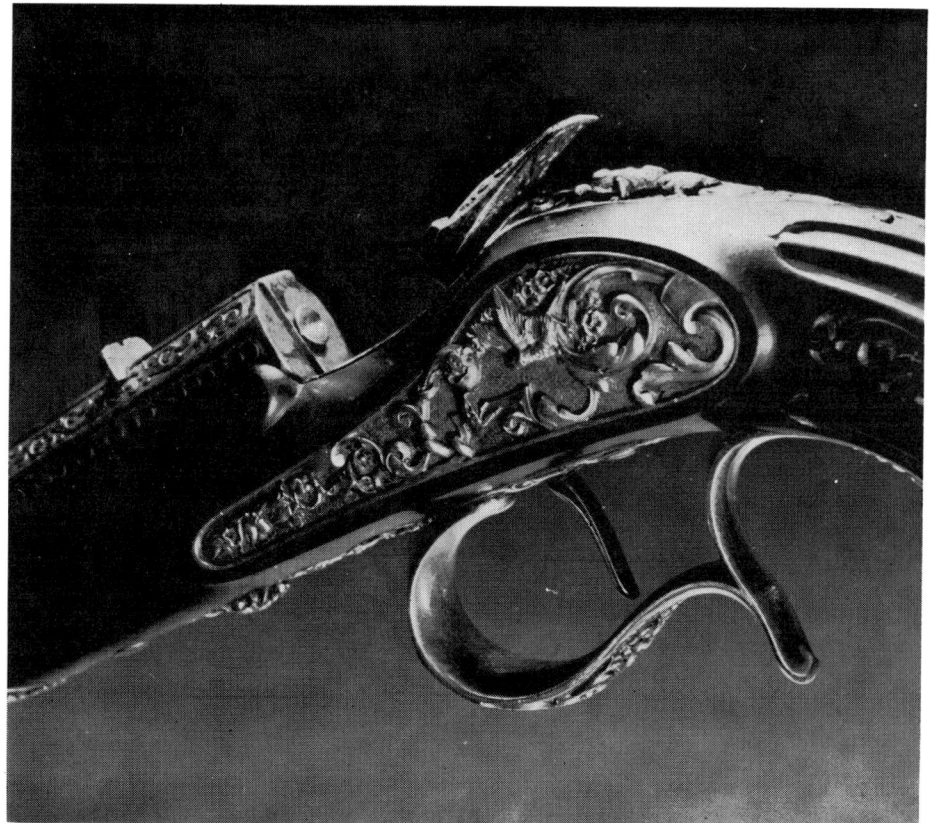

Flobert bulleted-breech cap .22 used in "saloon pistol" of 1845 was predecessor of cartridge which made Henry rifle practical. French design was known to Horace Smith, inventor who had hand in evolution of perfected Winchester-built Henry Civil War rifle. Flobert gun shown had rib on hammer face to ensure complete ignition of inside priming by denting entire diameter of cartridge base.

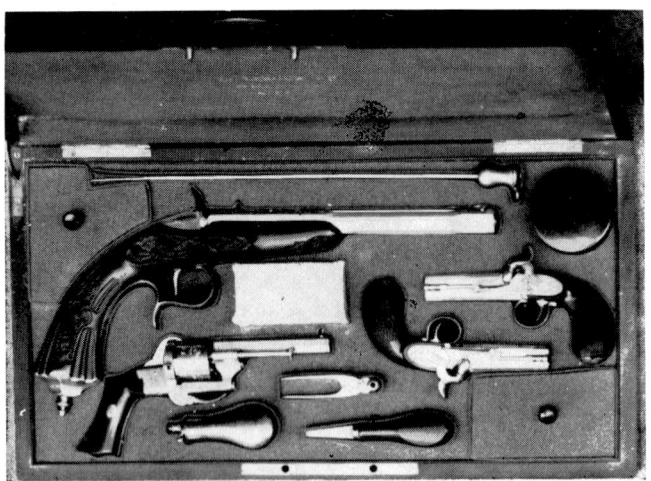

Cased gunmaker's display set is in white, unfinished, ready for finishing to customer's order. Set includes Flobert pistol of 1845 and Lefaucheux pinfire of type identical to those sold by Marcellus Hartley during Civil War in New York store. Set typifies contemporaneous dating of Floberts, pinfires, and regular percussion pistols in period of rapid evolution from which emerged perfected U.S. cartridge designs of Smith and B. Tyler Henry. Case shown from Sig Shore, Chicago, collection.

shooting matches to settle wagers. The speaker seems to have confused the sober English game of darts played in the pub, for an anglicization of "salon," a room or chamber; literally, "pistolet de salon," or shooting gallery pistol.

The "saloon" in which Flobert's arms were used was usually such a pretentious shooting emporium as that of the celebrated gunmaker Gastinne Renette, at Rond Point au Champs Elysees. Here Paris gallants could repair of an afternoon to fire ten meters at steel sheet profiles of a dandy in top hat and tails; practice for the duel.

Flobert's arms took the form of subcaliber or practice pistols for the deadly business of defending one's honor, or that of one's lady, on the Continent.

His arms, imported by Hartley, had a vogue antebellum, and doubtless some dashing Southern cavalry officer owed his unerring aim with his Richmond-made carbine, to practice with a "Flobert." Following the war, Flobert-System smallbore breechloaders supplanted the caplock plain American rifle in the hands of the people, just as his metallic cartridge conception, matured through the improvements of Horace Smith and Dan Wesson, had supplanted the muzzle-loader.

Horace Smith is recorded as having manufactured Flobert-type pistols in 1851 and 1852. According to Williamson this fact was brought out "In The Matter of the Application Sarah E. Allen, Executive, for the Extension of Letters Patent issued to Ethan Allen, Etc.", a brief on file in the United States Patent Office. The statement is interesting; missing are known examples of pistols to corroborate this declaration, at least, of obvious Flobert principle. Recently discovered examples of a single-shot pistol having butt frame and other characteristics have led the owners to suppose they were "early Smith & Wesson single shots." It is possible these arms are the Floberts to which the deposition of Sarah Allen refers. Yet this brief allusion furnishes the missing link between the rimfire cartridge of the partners Smith and Wesson, and the European progenitors, Flobert and, one suspects, even Houillier.

Louis Flobert was born in Paris in 1819. He died in the town of Gagny (Seine-et-Oise Departement) in 1894. With whom or where he served his apprenticeship is not known. Presumably he was articled to a master gunmaker until his 21st birthday, as was the custom. Then he may have sought employment in either his master's shop or in another, working as a journeyman. Young Flobert's name first appears in print in his 25th year in the Paris City Directory as "armurier, 6 Rue Racine," between the Boulevard St. Michel and the Place de l'Odeon. He must have been working on his breech-loading gun at the time, but his

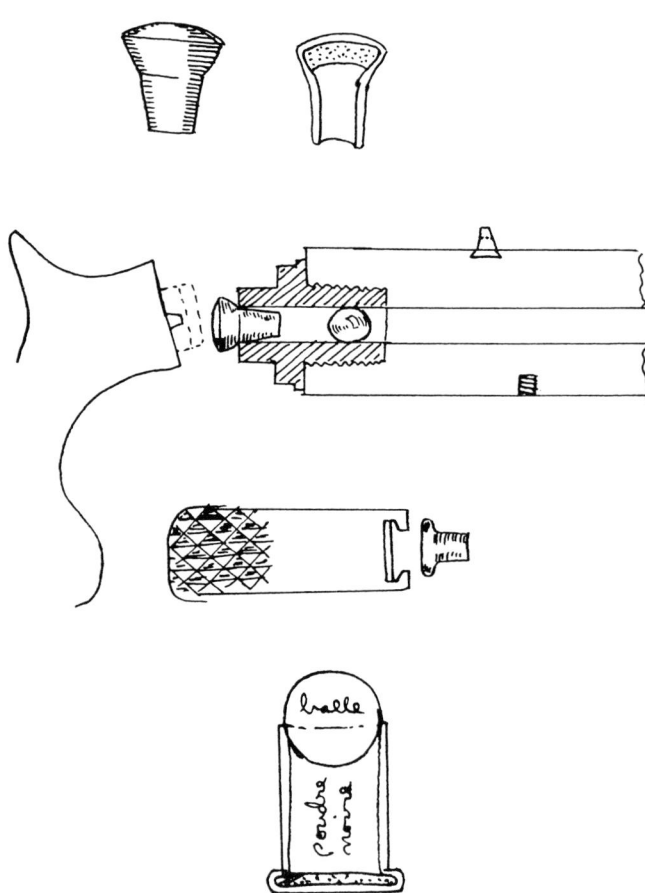

First Flobert concept was to use percussion cap much like ordinary type, flared at back to support it, with ball loaded from muzzle. Design shown has hooked hammer face to pull cap free after force of explosion bulges it out into cuts of hooks. Idea was patented 17 July, 1846, No. 3589 in Paris. Second idea to evolve (inset cut) was regular drawn metallic cartridge of modern form, charged with black powder. Though shaped with a rim, case had fulminate across entire base for special Flobert ridge striker. A ridge striker instead of firing pin is used today in Gevarm semiauto rifles .22. Flobert cartridge patent was filed 20 July 1849 and issued 4 October that year.

first patent of 1846 refers to a special kind of percussion cap and nipple, not necessarily a true breech-loading arm at all. From the French patent specification of 17 July, 1846, No. 3589, issued to Flobert and to his friend Antoine Paul Regnier du Tillet, we read: "System of priming firearms by semiconical capsule which one places in the interior of the percussion cone."

The cone evidently could accommodate a common outside cap, but was bored rather large at its back end and tapered slightly. The special Flobert-Tillet cap was drawn a little closer at the mouth, with a head slightly bulged and filled with priming. It looked a little like a Parker House roll. The rim was bulged out wider when fired and was grasped by hooks on either side of the hammer face, which pulled it free. While the idea could be employed with common powder-and-ball muzzle-loaders, Flobert discovered that important in his invention "is the result obtained with an indoor target pistol (pistolet de salon), thus one introduces into the percussion nipple a No. 4 ball (4 mms) and on this ball an ordinary cap rendered conique, one obtains a distance of the shot of 100 paces." Though ball and case were as yet separate, Flobert was on his way to inventing the inside primed metallic cartridge, and with it, his famous breechloader.

The next patent was granted to Flobert alone, still at 6 Rue Racine, on October 4, 1849, No. 8618 (French). For the first time he described "A new type of firearm: This invention consists of a new mechanism or hammer ('percuttor') which permits me to make a great saving of price in new guns, that is to say musket, rifle, pistol, from the littlest calibers to the biggest muskets, *combined with metallic cartridges* (emphasis supplied) in which the power is derived from fulminating powder with addition of sporting gunpowder."

The drawing illustrates the hammer and breech-block in one piece, with hooks for catching the cartridge rim, familiar to those who have seen the Flobert pistols. The cartridges are quite clearly pictured; in one the round ball fits at its diameter into the metallic case which carries not only priming in the base but in Flobert's own hand the words "poudre noire," black powder, inside. A shot cartridge was also pictured, and table-top re-loading apparatus.

Smith and Wesson's Cartridge

It was this cartridge which Horace Smith and Daniel Wesson used as the basis for their "Improved cartridge for Pistols, Rifles or other firearms," granted U. S. Patent No. 11, 496 on August 8, 1854, and applied for 10 May, 1853. The Smith and Wesson cartridge illustrated is the Flobert "bulleted breech cap" or BB Cap, taking 4mm or BB-size round ball.

Two innovations are introduced by the partners. First, the ball rests upon an impervious disk which covers all the powder, and between which and the back of the round ball the tallow lubrication is placed. This is an "inside lubricated" cartridge, first of its type apparently, but not especially claimed as such. What is claimed, by Smith & Wesson, is the construction of an internal backing plate to hold the primer pellet against the force of the central-fire pin; in this lies their "invention." The words of the patent quite clearly describe an inside primed central fire cartridge, suggesting that the base of the case be made "very thin and yielding, or of some substance easily punctured by a blunt point or needle driven against it, and this for the purpose of causing priming to be inflamed either by the effect of a smart blow given on such end of the cartridge by the cock of a gun, or by a blunt needle driven smartly through the end of the cartridge and against the priming while the latter is resting on the seat-piece or disk *f*."

To the Flobert cartridge with its priming generally spread over the end of the case, Smith & Wesson had introduced not novelty, but impossibility. Their conception was, in small sizes at the time, too difficult to manufacture and imperfectly conceived in the first place. Flobert's firing device was not a pin, which would pierce the copper case leaking corrosive gases into the mechanism, but a heavy rib or bar straight across the face of the hammer. It passed across the center of the case, and over the rim at both sides. It is true that Flobert's idea had deficiencies. The priming may not have been evenly spread over the inside of the case and into the rim areas, and irregular ignition from first one side and then the next, of succeeding cartridges, might give varying impacts of the bullets due to variations in burning caused by differences in ignition. Smith and Wesson stated in their patent the purpose of "our said arrangement of the disk and priming affording an excellent opportunity for applying the force of the blow by which the priming is inflamed, such force being applied in the line of the axis of the cartridge."

So far as is known, the partners never made a gun to take this unusual central fire small-caliber cartridge. But that it merely is an alteration and doubtful improvement of the Flobert, is obvious. How Smith came to know of Flobert is not conclusively determined, but it has been said that Smith visited France. *When* he visited France, it is very difficult to determine. For certain it is that by 1852 Smith had teamed up with Wesson and was working independently on an improved firearm, the gun which ultimately became the Henry and finally the Winchester, basis of a great series.

Hunt, Volcanic, Allen, Brown & Luther, are names that sparkle through this narrative like fireflies on a summer's eve. To pick a starting point, it is Jennings; the single shot breechloader of Lewis Jennings, manufactured by Robbins & Lawrence, Windsor, Vermont, and modified during that production period to be a repeating magazine rifle, using the patent of Horace Smith. The nature of the Smith invention is as a modification on an arm that was in very limited production; the mechanical characteristics seem to indicate Smith himself was working at Robbins & Lawrence in connection with this design improvement. Safety-pin in-

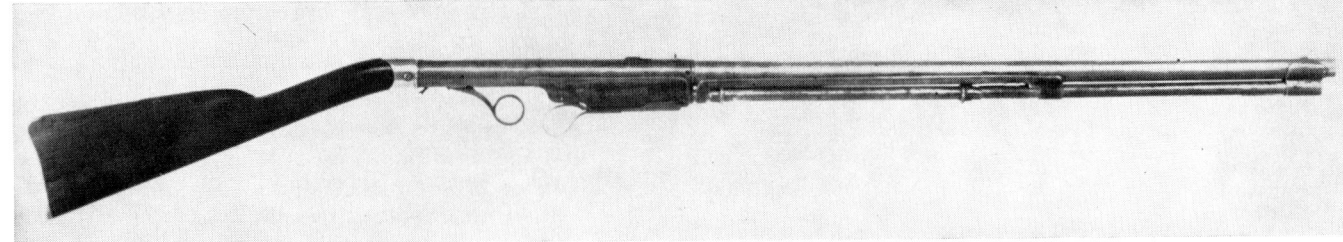

Walter Hunt designed lever action .54-inch "rocket ball" repeating rifle in summer of 1847 but patent was not granted until 1849. Design was not produced, but inventor laid first stepping stone to Winchester rifle success.

ventor Walter Hunt must be blamed for this tangle of associations for it was his "rocket ball" patented August 10, 1848, and his unsuccessful repeating rifle (filed Steptember 17, 1847; granted August 21, 1849) to take this self-propelled projectile that initiated the events.

Hunt's Rocket Ball

Hunt had accomplished in his loaded bullet idea two things. First, the propelling charge and primer were contained in the one unit, far handier than conventional combustible paper envelope cartridges needing to be capped separately. Secondly, since the charge itself was inside the pointed bullet, the skirt had to be made thinner, expanding a la Minié and sealing the bore against frontwards gas escape. Though Hunt's gun was a breechloader, the idea had its merits in theory, permitting a bullet to more easily enter a fouled chamber and wiping the fouling forward with each shot, avoiding an accuracy-destroying build-up. Hunt's bullet was not used to any extent in the Civil War, except as it may have figured in incidental uses of the later Volcanic-brand repeating pistols adapted to use bullets of his patent.

Hunt, it is believed, made only one model of his rifle, a patent model now preserved by the Winchester Museum. With a 25⅝-inch barrel of rifle caliber, .54, it measures 52¼ inches overall including a slim, tubular-form receiver 11¼ inches long. An underlever protrudes forward of the position where the trigger finger would normally rest; is pulled back to function on the loading and firing. While the rifle is complicated to operate, the appearance is modern, with no protrusions or unnecessary gadgets hanging out. Hunt's was the second gun patented in the United States to load from a tubular magazine beneath the barrel; his carried 12 loaded bullets.

The Jennings Repeater

Jennings filed for a patent on August 2, 1848: "My invention relates to that class of firearms in which loaded balls are used and inserted in a tubular magazine below and parallel with the barrel."

A shorter rifle than the Hunt model, the first-type Jennings was not particularly successful as a repeater; is more commonly found with the repeating function out of order, as a single shot. In function the Jennings is ingenious. A breechblock reciprocates fore and aft under influence of a slidable ring trigger. The trigger is fitted to a rack-gear bar. The bottom of the breechblock is also rack-toothed. A pinion idler gear unites the motions of the two. When the trigger is pushed forward inside the large loop guard, the breechblock draws back. When the trigger is pulled back, the block moves forward. At its closed position, further motion on the trigger wedges a special plate upwards, locking the plate between block and receiver, supporting the force of the explosion at that moment. The hammer has a long needle nose (inspiration for Horace Smith?) which strikes through the receiver top to impact against a priming pellet which has been deposited in the priming cavity on the breechblock in its final stage of closing. When the block is open, a Hunt rocket ball is placed inside on the carrier and chambered as the block or bolt closes. There is no provision for extraction. Military sales were looked for, though the War with Mexico had just ended. Caliber was .54 and agent C. P. Dixon of New York contrived to obtain favorable endorsements from the New York State Militia to help boost trade.

Jennings' repeater proved too complicated, says Winchester historian Tom Hall, so the first lot were finished as single-shot rifles. Apparently serials ran in sequence; No. 250 in the Winchester Museum is an incompleted repeater functioning as a single shot. The friction in the rack-and-pinion must have been great, when fouled from firing, as no secure obturator (breech sealer) had as yet been devised.

It remained for Horace Smith's ultimate application of a copper metal cartridge by expanding to accomplish the first effective sealing of the breech against back flash and ordinary powder fouling. It was this among other problems which confronted Horace Smith, then living in Norwich, Connecticut, when he took up his tools to modify the Jennings system. His patent, which covered the second type Jennings that was actually built in some quantity as a repeater, is dated August 26, 1851.

The principle of a prop-up block behind the true breechblock, to lock it, was retained. A direct-acting lever extended up from the pivoted loop trigger, and this lever moved the breechblock back and forth as the trigger loop was moved. The prop-block, now pivoted at its back end in permanent fashion on the frame, and free at its front end to jam up against the breechblock, appears to be the genesis of the collapsing toggle link later patented by the partners in their

Smith & Wesson "Volcanic"-type pistols. The prop block engaged the rocking trigger by a simple hook and the arrangement reduced inner friction so the shooter had some strength left in his trigger finger to raise the cartridge lifter and carry a fresh loaded ball from the under-barrel magazine tube into line with the chamber. The same pellet primer atop the breech was used, possibly a concession to agent Dixon and some unknown ordnance buff in the military department at Albany, as the pellet primer in the United States is associated with New York state arms. This improved arm received highly favorable publicity in the papers, the *Mechanics Reporter* for Thursday, February 20, 1851, declaring:

A new rifle: This rifle, known as Jenning's patent rifle, is designed to be an almost endless repeater, and to avoid the difficulty of capping or priming each load, and also to be uncommonly free from dirt . . . By a simple contrivance within this breech, the breech-pin is withdrawn as the gun is cocked. A cartridge (of which we shall speak) is placed in this opening and, on pulling the trigger, the pin closes the barrel tight, a strong block of steel falls behind it, and the gun primes itself and is discharged in one motion . . . By this contrivance a rifle is made capable of being loaded at the breech as often as it is fired off, and as rapidly as a man's hand can move to throw in the cartridges. This is at the rate of twelve shots per minute, for a person not acquainted with the gun, a velocity sufficient to make one man fully equal to a dozen armed with ordinary rifles. Another variety of the same gun is now completed and nearly perfected by the patentees, which differs not at all from this in external appearance, except that, in place of a ramrod, is a tube of the same size, capable of containing thirty cartridges, which, by a very simple contrivance, are so arranged that they are placed in the barrel one by one, and fired successively without any interruption. The moment that the thirtieth ball is fired, this gun may be used as the first one, loaded at the breech, and be fired at the rate of fifteen a minute. But the chief strength of this formidable weapon rests on the cartridge which is used. This cartridge, which is also patented, is simply a loaded ball. A bullet elongated on one side to a hollow cylinder of about an inch in length, is filled with powder, and the end covered with a thin piece of cork, through the center of which is a small hole, to admit fire from the priming. As each ball goes out of the barrel, the cork cap remains in the barrel, and is carried out in front of the next ball, sweeping thoroughly all the dirt with it. The gun may thus be discharged from sixty to seventy times in good weather, without needing a swab. The barrel (held by a cross pin through the frame) may be detached at a single blow of a hammer or stone, and a swab run through it in a moment at any time, the operation of cleaning occupying no longer than the ordinary loading of a common gun. The priming of the rifle is in small pills, of which one hundred are placed in a box, from which the gun supplies itself without fail.

The description is substantially accurate, though it seems the magazine tubes are generally a little larger than the ramrod tube on Jennings' first single shot. To fill the tube, it was necessary to remove the end cap, withdraw the long coil spring and follower, and then, after filling with cartridges, replace all. Thirty cartridges seems a rather fanciful number; examples of Second Type Jennings' rifles have 26-inch barrels as a standard length, limiting the length of the magazine tube. Twelve or thirteen is a more reasonable number of cartridges "of about an inch in length" for the Jennings. Serials on Second Type or repeater Smith-patent Jennings rifles suggest serial numbering started over again at the beginning. Mechanically, the two are quite different.

Contractor for the Jennings was Robbins and Lawrence, a machine works established at Windsor, Vermont about 1847. The firm began with the association of Richard S. Lawrence with Nicanor Kendall at Windsor, in 1843. Kendall had, since 1835, been manufacturing guns using contract labor from the local prison, with free mechanics on hire finishing up the work. A sliding bar five-shooter is known of N. Kendall's make, and it is believed he obtained some of his barrels from Remington. Richard Lawrence was born 1817 at Chester, Vermont, and became employed by Kendall in 1838 at a salary of $100 per year. In 1842 Kendall & Company ceased business and the partnership of Kendall and Lawrence began. In 1844 they were joined by added capital of S. E. Robbins, and became known as Robbins, Kendall & Lawrence. It was in this form that the company undertook a contract for M1841 Mississippi rifles, agreeing February 18, 1845, to deliver 10,000 rifles at $11.90 each in five years' time. The contract was completed 18 months *ahead* of time. In 1847, Kendall bowed out, and the reorganized firm worked under the name of Robbins & Lawrence. One of Kendall's earlier partners

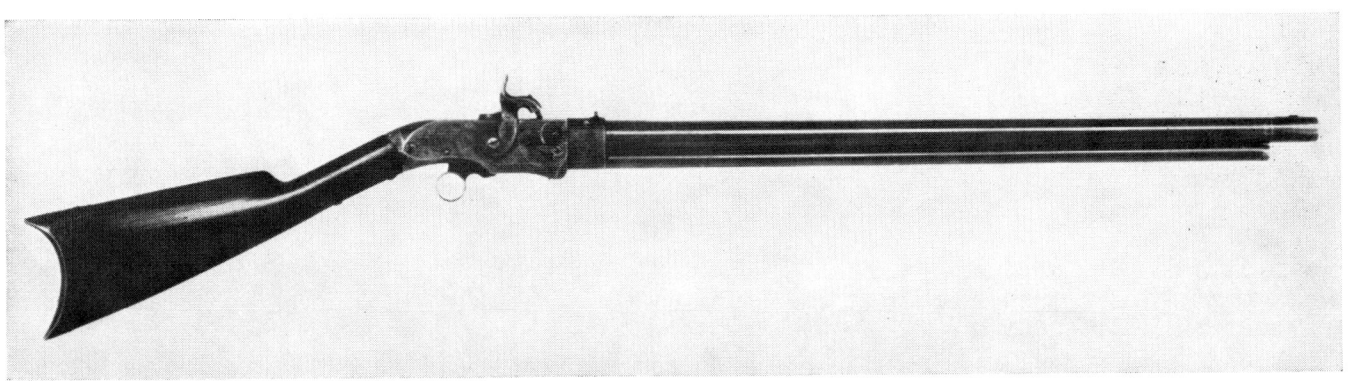

Tube repeater of Lewis Jennings was improvement over Hunt designs and in turn was modified by Horace Smith. Short ring lever for cocking was carried over into pistols and carbines designed by Smith made by Winchester.

when doing business as N. Kendall & Company is listed as "Smith." No further identification is given for him (Gluckman and Satterlee, *American Gunmakers*, 1953).

Robbins & Lawrence accepted a further contract for 15,000 M1841 rifles January 5, 1848, price $12.87½ each, to be delivered at Springfield, Massachusetts. Their record delivery schedule on the first batch and their competency to deliver the second was based upon their introduction of full inspection through the use of snap gauges of all parts in all stages of manufacture. They also were foremost in developing specialized machines to perform special functions in manufacturing, and supplied machine tools to other domestic gunmakers and for export to foreign arsenals. It was in this spirit that they took on the job offered by New York capitalists of making a new repeating rifle.

Hunt, in developing his first rifle and cartridge, had lacked funds to exploit it fully. He assigned his patents to a fellow New Yorker, George A. Arrowsmith. Arrowsmith was a model maker and machinist, for whom Lewis Jennings worked. It was Jennings who got the job of improving the Hunt designs and within a few months succeeded in redoing Hunt's ideas into his own patented form protected December 1849, U.S. Pat. 6973. Seeking financing, Arrowsmith contacted Courtlandt Palmer, one time president of the Stonington & Providence Railroad, and a hardware dealer of New York who would profit handsomely from being the exclusive proprietor of the Jennings repeater (if it worked). Palmer went to Robbins & Lawrence, noted as fabricators of the famous M1841 rifle which in the hands of Jeff Davis's Mississippi Volunteers in the Mexican War had earned the sobriquet "Mississippi rifles."

Robbins & Lawrence agreed in 1850 to build 5,000 Jennings rifles. In their employ at the time was Daniel Wesson, who had completed experimental work he did for Wesson & Leavitt, and to him came the project of cleaning up the Jennings rifle for production. Every biographical source commonly consulted refers to Horace Smith meeting Daniel Wesson in 1852. The statement most often read is that "The association of Smith and Wesson had begun while both were in the employ of Allen, Brown & Luther, rifle makers of Worcester, Massachusetts, in 1852." It is true that Frederick Allen, Andrew J. Brown, and John Luther, were in business making rifle barrels in Worcester, but Williamson *(Winchester)* places the connection with Smith positively at Robbins & Lawrence, in connection with the Jennings rifle design. He is also quite certain, based on Mrs. Sarah (Ethan) Allen's statements, that Smith made Flobert pistols in "1851 and 1852." Suddenly, checking dates, and considering the role of these men in the arms industry of the time, Smith is seen to have a spare moment when he could go to France, and reasons for so doing. One reason could have been for him to visit the London Great Exhibition of 1851 and make a survey of small arms design on the Continent at that time.

The Great Exhibition opened on 1 May, 1851. Smith's patent for modifying the Jennings gun was not to be issued until that August, but he had long since finished with his share of the development and model making. As the *"Mechanics Reporter"* said in February, 1851, "Another variety of the same gun is now completed and nearly perfected by the patentees." By April, Smith must have been free to go to London. Robbins & Lawrence proposed to exhibit their Mississippi rifles there, manufactured by machinery on the interchangeable plan. Smith, obviously one of their star engineers, was shipped over, we believe, with Palmer paying the bill, to see what he could find of use in the European market. He found two things: the Flobert bulleted breech cap and, possibly, as Graham Burnside argues, ("The Volcanic Quandary," *The Gun Report,* December 1958) an entire breechloading pistol mechanism for which he was to either obtain the rights or pirate whole, to solve deficiencies of the Jennings-Smith system.

Flobert attended the Great Exibition. The rifles and muskets one wonders at; did Flobert make a cartridge so large as 17mm for a breech-loading or transformed musket? The making of a copper cartridge case all in one piece of that size, if Flobert really had one, suggests he was a man of exceptional mechanical skill in fundamental engineering. Whether he conceived of deep drawing to shape a one-piece cartridge or rested content with soldered or riveted-on bases as some of his contemporaries did, is an unanswered puzzle in arms history. But if Smith got near to the Great Exhibition, it is a certainty that he met Flobert, since both were exhibitors. Smith had made a few breech-loading magazine pistols designed by Orville Percival at Moodus, Connecticut; they are known to have been made by "H. Smith, Norwich, Ct." Using separate magazines for powder and ball, which hung teat-like below the breech machinery like teats on a cow udder, this was a notably unsuccessful invention. Smith must have been eager to find mechanical ideas which could be refined to practical applications. The Flobert was one; the Vendetti was another.

The Vendetti Pistol

There has come to the attention of American pistol collectors in the past few years since World War II a group of unusual arms, some of which bear the marks "Vendetti Brevettato," or Vendetti patent. It is assumed these pistols are "Italian," though from which of the Italian states of approximately 1850 has not been determined. The name of the supposed inventor is obviously Vendetti, and he apparently obtained a patent on his pistol. It, and the design patented by Horace Smith and Daniel B. Wesson February 14, 1854, are almost identical in construction.

Says Graham Burnside, in his very interesting and admittedly speculative essay on the Volcanic of Smith & Wesson, and the Vendetti, "This leads one to wonder where the Volcanic pistol came from."

"Maybe the gun came to us from Europe," he con-

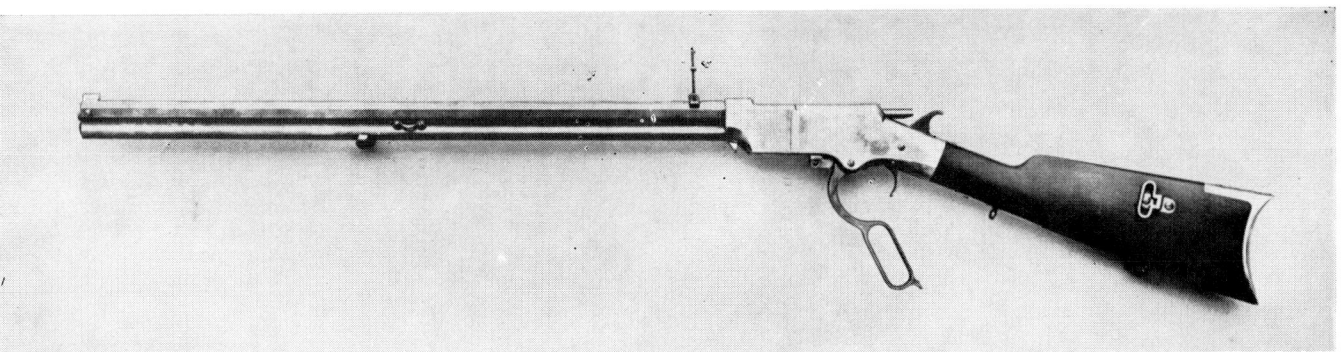

US Government test report of Henry rifle pictured gun complete, showing lever in down position and breech bolt withdrawn which cocked gun, and also all parts. Double pieces near lower left of disassembled view are toggle links that collapse when lever is moved. Principle is identical to enigmatic Italian Vendetti pistol, suggesting missing link which designer Horace Smith found overseas.

tinues, "where it was a parlour arm (c.f. saloon pistol) using self-contained cartridges like the Loron and the Gaupillat.

"Loron was working with self-contained ammunition back in the late 1830's and early 1840's. Strangely enough we know of arms that look like copies of the Volcanic, that are made to handle the Loron and Gaupillat cartridges. We cannot prove that these foreign gallery pistols were made before the Volcanic but we can prove that they used ammunition that was earlier than Volcanic ammunition.

"When viewing a foreign product like the system Vendetti pistols one gets a strange sensation. Here is a 'Volcanic' that works, and works well. The whole thing seems to be designed expressly for the saloon cartridge that it shoots, and the saloon cartridge is older than the American Volcanic patent. The Vendetti not only has a 'system' which is identical in design to

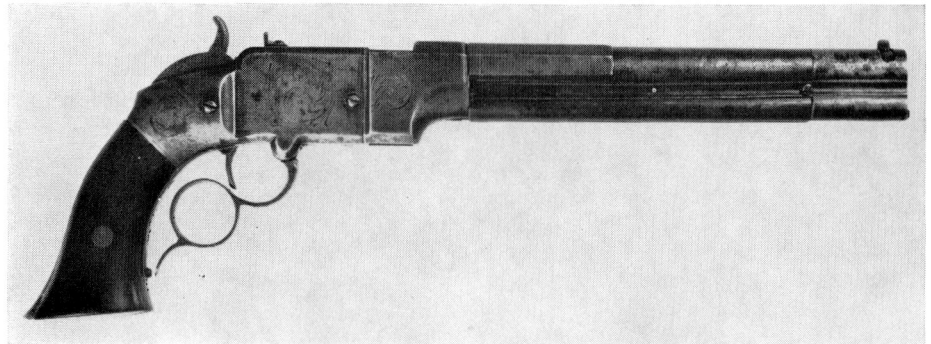

Early lever pistol made by Smith & Wesson in Norwich is distinguished from later "Volcanic" arms by iron frame, and hump behind hammer. Spur to loop is also early S & W motif. Front section of barrel swings to side exposing end of magazine tube for loading, after follower and spring has been pulled up into front section below barrel.

the Volcanic, but the contours of the pistol leave no doubt that one or the other is a copy.

"We also have seen Vendetti pistols that appear almost identical in function to the Volcanics, that have a chamber to accept a cartridge case. I do not know of such a cartridge (Burnside's field of arms scholarship is cartridge history) . . . but it is obvious that it was a rimfire type utilizing a double striker. This ties in with Smith and Wesson's intended cartridge, and even the double striker as used in the later Henry rifles. The odds are, that these Vendetti pistols are earlier than our American Volcanic."

There is much sense in Burnside's speculation, determined on a study of the drawings of the Smith and Wesson design of 1854, and a reading of the claims of the patent. Structurally, the most obvious element in the Vendetti, Volcanic, and the "damn Yankee" rifle that fired all week, when the sideplates are taken off, is the collapsing breechlocking toggle joint. The breechpin, to use Jennings' term, is slidable. At its back end it is connected by an assembly crosspin to one of two linked arms which are themselves fastened at the far end of the rear link to an assembly pin in the frame. Cut inside each rear link is a cam track. The finger lever, not divorced from the added function of triggering off the hammer, has an engagement with this cam groove or track. When the finger lever is thrown down and forward, its upper end connected to the rear link is pushed back and down, pulling the rear link out of its "stiff knee" alignment with the breechpin. With the collapse of the toggle links a consequent shortening of their fore-and-aft dimensions takes place, withdrawing the breechpin from its forward position. At the same time the finger lever further activates a lifting lever that raises a platform, originally in line with the magazine, to a line with the barrel. The breechpin on the return stroke passes through a trough in this platform pushing ahead of it the cartridge, "rocket ball" or metallic, into the barrel.

It was this design which occupied Smith upon his completion of the Jennings modification. Williamson, in speaking of this new arm, a product of joint efforts between Smith, Wesson, and Courtlandt Palmer who furnished the money, is quite definite: "Out of this experimentation came a new patent (U.S. 10,535) granted to Smith & Wesson in February, 1854. The most important feature of this rifle (the patent shows a pistol) was the mechanism that moved the bolt and locked it in position with its head supporting the cartridge. It was a simple mechanism and, for cartridges of medium power, a highly satisfactory method of obtaining reciprocal movement in the carrier and locking the block in its forward position. This improvement, added to the tubular magazine and the rising breechblock of earlier models, completed the essential mechanical features that were subsequently incorporated in the early Winchester rifles."

A look at the patent reveals Williamson's conjecture to be in error, for the toggle joint, "the most important feature," is not patented by Smith & Wesson. The illustrations include views of a pistol, of the form later known as "The Volcanic." There are eleven claims; not one claims the toggle link construction for locking the breech and imparting motion to the breech pin. The second claim is a Flobert-type claim, "In combination with an extractor for drawing the shell out of the chamber, a device arranged to strike the shell or cartridge and expel the same from the arm." The first claim is also, when taken with the extractors, which were two hooks, one on either side of the breechpin, a Flobert conception: "The combination of the percussion hammer (used in sense of percussive force, not percussion detonating cap), the sliding breechpiece, and the barrel, substantially as described, whereby the breechpin H, shall serve both as a breech to hold the cartridge in the barrel, and as a means of conveying the force of the blow of the hammer to the cartridge, substantially as set forth."

There was no firing pin as we think of it today, in this first Smith & Wesson repeater but, instead, a solid part of the breechblock, containing the extractor hooks, was hit on its rear end by the fall of the hammer and by means of a "billiard ball" shock transmission the primer was detonated. The cartridge shown in this patent is not claimed and, as was so often the fact, the really important key to the construction was held up in patenting for a longer time, to give that much added real protection of patents to the article made for sale.

The gun and ammunition package Smith and Wesson wanted to make featured a Flobert type cartridge in its inception. But the toggle link breechlocking device, not found in the same form in any other American firearm, is not claimed for protection. Closest to it is the fourth claim: "The combination of the hammer and the breechpiece H, with the operating lever G, whereby the hammer may be cocked by the movement of the operating lever, substantially as described." The operating lever G is the loop finger lever that serves also as a trigger guard; the breechpiece H is the breechblock or bolt on the front end of which are hooks r-r acting as cartridge case extractors.

The other claims, which in one sense or another mention the movement of the breechpiece in combination with the operating lever, do not expressly claim the collapsing toggle joint as a breechlock but relate to handling metallic cartridges in the gun. It might be argued by the sophisticated patent expert that a toggle joint is a common mechanical principle and could not have been patented. But toggle joints are not patented as common mechanical principles; what would be patentable, in the absence of other arms of the same construction, would be a toggle joint acting as a breechlock; a common mechanical principle in a special application.

It is an axiom of patent law, in the words of contemporary patent expert Ned Dickerson, that "you can describe your elephant, and talk about your elephant, but if you do not claim him, he is not your elephant." Smith and Wesson did not claim their elephant; probably because they knew it to have appeared in another firearm elsewhere—the saloon pistol "Vendetti." Whether it was Smith who returned from Europe with a Vendetti in his pocket, that inspired the new gun, or B. Tyler Henry who helped the two while at Robbins & Lawrence, to perfect the toggle link, the fact remains that the most obvious feature of the new weapon, basis for a long line of Winchesters, is not patented by the "inventors."

Benjamin Tyler Henry

Benjamin Tyler Henry was another ex-Springfield Armory man. That shop in Windsor must have seemed like a friendly frat house for these mechanical lads who served their time at Springfield. Henry had long been interested in repeaters. He served his apprenticeship with J. B. and R. B. Ripley, gunsmiths of his home town, Claremont, New Hampshire, where he was born March 22, 1821. R. B. Ripley, Lebbeus Baily, and William B. Smith had patented a "waterproof rifle," an underhammer magazine gun inspired by the breechblock of the Hall and thought by some to be an "intermediate" step between the Hall and the Spencer butt-loaded repeater of the war. This wild idea, fundamentally sound, was patented February 20, 1839. To polish off his training as master machinist, Henry went to Springfield Armory. He left there in 1842, suggesting his employment was also in connection with the retooling for the new interchangeable muskets and, when that was finished, there was no work for him in the production line. He returned to his home area, to nearby Windsor, there to work for Nicanor Kendall. When Kendall became Kendall, Robbins & Lawrence, and later Robbins & Lawrence, Henry remained. His background of work at Springfield probably fitted him for planning out the machinery with which Kendall, Robbins & Lawrence prepared their first "Mississippi" rifle on the interchangeable plan. It is probable that Henry went on to Norwich, Connecticut, when Wesson formed the association with Smith and took the work to Smith's gunshop in Norwich. Certainly Henry knew Smith at Springfield Armory, and the continuing business association of friends is not at all unusual.

By June of 1854, Palmer and the mechanics were ready to make some terms. On the 20th a limited partnership was formed of Smith, Wesson, and Palmer. They owned the Hunt, Jennings, Smith improvement, and the February 1854 Smith and Wesson patents; their shop was at central wharf in Norwich, Connecticut.

Smith & Wesson

Which came first, is always a subject of interest to the arms collector who may like to have one of "the first series" produced of any famous make. The Smith & Wesson (Norwich) repeating pistols were built in two basic frame sizes, their No. 1, .30-inch (sometimes called .31), and No. 2 or Navy size, .38 (sometimes called .41). Both had iron frames, often lightly scroll engraved with coarse, cheap patterns quickly executed. We believe the smallest No. 1 frame type, .30, was issued first, having as it does certain "primitive" characteristics. Barrel is half octagon at breech, round forward; and the finger lever has a little tang, like the patent picture; though this little tang is not found on all the smallest pistols. The butt is of pepperbox form similar to the common Allen pistols, and the half-octagon barrels are also very reminiscent of the single shot target pistols made by the Allen clan; with whom, it will be remembered, Smith had previously had some connection. Allen and Thurber, for example, made pepperboxes in Norwich, Connecticut, a form of gun manufacture with which Smith was certainly familiar, he having worked for them until 1846, off and on.

Taking a certain risk, we would like to set forth a theory of development behind the external forms of these Smith and Wesson pistols. Logically, we have worked backwards from the later designs, discarding or adding as circumstances seem to dictate, till we arrive at the primitive form. The theory is this:

First in production were the smallest pistols. In final form, their date of issue is less important than when they were actually made. This we believe to have been earlier by some months than the filing date of the St. Valentine's Day patent 1854, which was May 24, 1853. The patent illustration shows one of the .41 caliber pistols, square butt as might be expected, in a large frame gun. This was because the small pistols did not work out so well and models of the larger guns had to be built, and ammunition made up for them, to prove the system.

Smith was responsible for the small pistols. Evidencing pepperbox details, including the ring lever (found on Blunt's and other types including the Continental Mariette), and some fanciful shaping to the outside of the receiver, they are more "hand made" than the bigger arms. Small, they took less metal to make; in those days cost of raw materials was much higher compared with labor than today, and the added labor of working with the smaller pieces in fitting and then assembly of the .30 calibers was offset by the savings in materials, especially laboriously hook-rifled barrels. Smith was 17 years older than Wesson, certainly the dominant figure in the partnership at first. The little pistol was Smith's production, made largely by hand using frame castings probably bought from Allen & Thurber. The sideplate construction of the Smith & Wesson guns reveals Allen-type technology, as well.

Whether Smith proposed to use the Hunt rocket ball, or the Flobert cap, in the first pistols, is not known. But apparently some difficulties occurred for there are minor functional changes between the round butt guns and the bigger square butt pistols of the patent. A "prawl" or hump to the frame is added. This more solidly positions the frame in the hand when working the finger lever, something which it seems is almost impossible to do one-handed. The muscles of the fingers are better adapted to pulling in than they are to pushing out. The ammunition for the guns, on the other hand, seems to be a concession to Wesson's point of view. For Smith, it would appear, definitely wanted to make the guns to use a metallic cartridge.

Experiments continued even after setting the form of the small pistol into production. Ultimately the larger pistol was made up, and test metallic cartridges hand-made for it, we assume from viewing the patent of February 1854. By that spring of 1853 the largest frame gun existed, fully equipped with extractors and ejectors to handle metallic cartridges of centerfire construction having a rim. The tube magazine was clever, also. The plug that followed the cartridges back to the action, had a button on it which slid along the tube in a slot on the bottom. When the button was slid all the way out with the spring compressed, it was possible to turn aside several inches of sleeve about the muzzle, into which the spring and plug had been compressed, allowing filling the magazine tube from the front end. By turning the front sleeve back in line, the cartridges were put under spring tension to feed them one at a time to the cartridge carrier or

Iron frame, style treatment of handles, on Allen & Thurber pepperbox of 1840's made in Norwich, Conn. at shop employing also Horace Smith suggests relationship between technology Smith learned making pepper box frames, and first of the Smith & Wesson lever pistols. Small caliber S & W lever pistols have round butts, grip plates, cast frames much like Allen pepperboxes.

lifter. J. Carrier of Baltimore displayed one of their new pistols at the annual Fair of the Maryland Institute for the Promotion of Mechanical Arts in 1854. The two men were quite proud to receive a Gold Medal of the Institute, for "a self loader, and works remarkably well; it is a good invention, and we think it will be extensively used, and is entitled to notice."

Courtlandt Palmer's hopes for sales from such publicity were not to be fully realized; and in ten years Baltimore men in Maryland Confederate regiments would rue the day they were confronted with that "damn Yankee rifle" which they had helped along by voting its originators a gold medal.

The Flobert cartridges of Smith were not suitable for use in the lever action pistol. With fulminate spread over the entire base inside, a considerable force was developed on the interior of the soft copper case head. Bulging and jamming of the extracting mechanism must have plagued the little Smith-Norwich pistols. They turned to the Hunt bullet, perhaps at the urging of junior partner Dan Wesson; perhaps, and more likely, at the insistence of financier Palmer, that they get up something to sell.

The exact form of bullet used in the Smith & Wesson pistols differed somewhat in construction from Hunt's original form. It became known as the "Volcanic" bullet, and though all Smith & Wesson and later "Volcanic" pistols were made to use this, it never worked well. According to engineer William C. Hicks, who was concerned with improvements in the Smith & Wesson pistol design:

> Its cartridge was of lead and hollow, what has been termed a loaded ball. Black powder was put in the cavity and the end was closed with a metallic disc and cork containing fulminate between them, the only part exposed being the cork. A blunt instrument projecting centrally from the breechpin was pressed through this cork when the breech was closed against the cartridge. This mashed the fulminate against the steel disc, where it was fired by a blow given the end of the breechpin by the hammer. The ball never extracted if there was a misfire, you had to push it out with a ramrod. The steel disc in the cartridge on firing, went out the muzzle sometimes, and sometimes came back and caused trouble. The cork was drawn back by the breechpin into which the cork had been forced by the explosion; the old type had a recess in the breechpin for this purpose. The cork was pushed off by the rising carrier block. The cartridge did not extract if the gun was not fired. Later a cap was added by Smith & Wesson, covering the cork and disc around the edges, leaving a circular hole in the center and holding the steel disc by a flange. The new cap made a more solid end to the ball and brought the steel disc back with the cork.
>
> Crittenden & Tibbals made the balls for the Smith & Wesson Volcanic. The cartridge first used a hollow based bullet, which was filled with powder, then closed with a steel and cork disc holding the fulminate. As originally made, the bullet was first charged, then the steel disc placed, next the fulminate added, then the cork placed, and the bullet closed at the rear. After assembly, the ball was grooved and greased. Later a metal cap was used to cover the cork. Then the disc, fulminate, cork, and cap were assembled, and put into the bullet as a unit. The end was then swaged and varnished. The cork base was used before August 1855. Then a copper cap was added and used till December 1855. Thereafter, brass was used to facilitate extraction. The brass cap used on the No. 1 size had the same size hole as before, but that used on the No. 2 size had a smaller hole, which improved extraction.

It was a loaded ball of this complex construction, with an extraction of residue dependent upon little more than the friction of the "blunt instrument," a firing pin, with the cork gas seal, that Smith & Wesson had built for Palmer to sell by the summer of 1854. The bullet construction was issued a patent eventually January 22, 1856, No. 14,147, though it was already obsolete at the time.

Sales had been good, but disappointments and complaints even more than they expected. The mechanism of the gun with its rocket ball was no more odd than a dozen other competitive firearms on the market. The shooting man of 1854 was by no means so hidebound in his acceptance of new things as the shooter is today. But he did know the difference between a gun that shot rapidly and well, and a pistol that misfired and could not then be easily cleared without a ramrod to poke the bullet out. At least with one of Colt's percussion revolvers, if one charge failed, you could go on to the next. Not so with the Smith & Wesson— you had to get the dud out before firing another. And misfires were common. While the primer pellet was neatly protected by the cork wad from sideways displacement, according to engineer Hicks, it was mashed by the firing pin when the breech was closed. In other words, the firing pin, which did not move separately like a modern pin, was in actual contact with the priming pellet. If the pellet was a little large, and the pin pushed heavily on it, the primer might be crushed. In modern handloading where the shooting hobbyist introduces variables, avoidance of too much pressure on seating the primer, which might crush it, is important. Crushed primers lack sensitivity, will not fire most of the time. The transmission of shock without moving the firing pin from hammer to primer, which was a principal ingredient in the Smith & Wesson pistol, was also its main defect. But financiers could not know that. As the complaints piled up, so did interested inquiries from other financiers, less well informed in arms design. Among them was shirtmaker Oliver Fisher Winchester, of New Haven.

Smith & Wesson Shop Sold

Sale of the Smith & Wesson shop at Norwich was consummated in June of 1855 to a newly organized stock company having Winchester as one of the active members. The new Volcanic Repeating Arms Company paid the partners $65,000 in cash, plus 2,800 shares of stock, for the partnership assets including their machinery and stock on hand.

During August, 1855, said Winchester, the machinery, tools, and fixtures, and arms, finished and unfinished, were removed from Norwich to New Haven. "Among these assets purchased were about 300 pistols of both sizes, finished and unfinished, and the parts of some 280 or 300 more pistols, not as-

Beginnings of mighty Winchester-Western armaments empire were small. This two-story brick house on Orange Street, north of Grove Street, New Haven, was first office for Volcanic Arms Co.

sembled. The (Volcanic) company was occupied, in part, nearly or quite a year in overhauling and repairing and assembling these 600 pistols, more or less, and manufacturing a new model, and the tools and fixtures for that model. The (Volcanic) company continued for the remaining six months of its existence in finishing and selling pistols of this new model until February 3, 1856, when they passed a vote to go into insolvency and made an assignment accordingly."

The Volcanic Repeating Arms Company of New Haven was capitalized at $150,000 with 6,000 shares of common stock at $25 a share. The partnership of Smith, Wesson, and Palmer held almost a majority share with 2,800 shares at $70,000. Among other stockholders was William C. Hicks, and Green Kendrick, who in 1862 obtained a contract for but did not deliver any Springfield rifle muskets. Winchester owned 80 shares. President of the firm, one of the largest stockholders, was Nelson H. Gaston of New Haven. Perhaps some of the $65,000 cash went to pay off Palmer, for he faded from the scene. Smith for a time served as superintendent, but left after what may have been only a few weeks, moving up to Springfield where he kept a livery stable with his brother-in-law, William Collins, on Market Street. Daniel Wesson then assumed the superintendency. Some conflict may be assumed to have occurred between him and stockholder Hicks, for Hicks felt the extracting difficulties could be solved by adding a slight hook to the end of the firing pin or as it was sometimes called, "nipple." Says Hicks, "My new hook extractor was added about February 1, 1856, to all new arms being made. All small-size pistols brought back for repairs after about October 1, 1855, were altered." Says Winchester, ". . . the 3rd of February, 1856, when they passed a vote to go into insolvency . . ." Says Samuel L. Talcott, a stockholder and secretary of the Volcanic Repeating Arms Company:

New Haven, February 8, 1856

Daniel Baird Wesson
  Dear Sir:
    By vote of the Board of Directors of "The Volcanic Repeating Arms Company" I am hereby instructed to inform you of their acceptance of your resignation of the office of Superintendent of Said Company, to take effect on Monday next. And also acknowledge their appreciation of your services as a mechanic, and the conscientious discharge of your duties as a man(ager?). With respect, I am
      Very truly yours,
        Samuel L. Talcott, Secretary

Why this flight of talent and capital from the Volcanic Company? Personalities may have been part of the answer; Dan Wesson himself was a pretty firm personality for a young man, and may have tangled with Hicks. The letter of Talcott reads a little like a recommendation as well as an acceptance of resignation. He felt it necessary to speak of Wesson's abilities as a mechanic, as if they had been called into question, rather than simply accept the resignation. Whatever the cause, the situation was aggravated by the death of Nelson Gaston. Floundering management was set on a firm footing by minority stockholder Winchester.

Oliver F. Winchester

"O. F." owned but $4,000 worth of the Volcanic Company, but he was no featherweight in business, finance, and manufacturing. Born November 10, 1810 in Boston, his father died when he was one, and he had been brought up early to accept responsibility. At seven he went to work on a farm; at 14 he was apprenticed to a carpenter. When he was 20, as a master, he went to Baltimore and worked as a building contractor. He was prospering; after three years he changed his career and worked in a local dry goods store. At 24 he had founded enough of an estate to consider marriage a safe proposition, and at the same time opened his own retail men's furnishings store in Baltimore. As one of his customers for the fancier grades of goods, he might have had young Sam Colt, who was traveling about the country as "Dr. Coult, of London and Calcutta." Colt worked as a traveling showman, raising money for early revolving pistol model-making. Winchester may have later remembered this early friendship when he proposed contracting with Colt's for the manufacture of his perfected Henry-modified Smith & Wesson design as a rifle.

Winchester was a man of considerable intellectual curiosity. He was also a man to turn a profit. Farm boy, carpenter, clothing merchant; in 1847 he patented a method of cutting men's shirts to avoid pull on the neckband, and in 1848 moved back north, to New Haven, where labor was cheaper, and started a shirt factory.

He took as partner John M. Davies, clothing jobber of New York, in 1849, and while textile machinery magnate Daniel Leavitt was backing Edwin Wesson and Joshua Stevens in Chicopee, the man to be the most famous riflemaker of the world was betting his shirt on a shirt factory of grand proportions. Before

Volcanic .41 was reputed to have astonishing accuracy but modern researchers computed chances of hitting target as reported in 1850's to be against large odds.

1853. Winchester employed 800 people to cut shirts and the parts were sent out to about five thousand workers to sew at home by hand. In 1853, sewing machines were installed—five hundred of them. With a works force exceeding 1,000, Oliver Winchester was one of the big men of New England. He became president in December, 1856, upon Nelson Gaston's untimely death, of a tiny works near the corner of Orange and Grove Streets, New Haven. Fifty people were at work, under direction of William C. Hicks, who had succeeded Wesson as superintendent in February.

Williamson makes an interesting statement about Hicks: "Little is known of Hicks' early life and training, but he appears to have been an experienced mechanic. There is nothing, however, to indicate *that he knew very much about guns.*" (Emphasis supplied). Neither, for that matter, did Smith or Wesson know very much about guns. Their whole history to date seems to have been in connection with mechanically unsuccessful ventures, in spite of the big cash settlement Volcanic paid them. First the Jennings rifles, then Flobert single shots, or the Massachusetts Arms Company guns that were proved infringements of another's patents . . . all these had cost money, though as practical mechanics there seems to be no quarrel with their talents. Now, they pull out of the Volcanic enterprise, voluntarily or by request, leaving it in a sinking condition.

The truth is, nobody in those days knew anything about guns, any more than any person today can honestly be said to "know about guns." The standards are relative; the ideas seemed good, but the times needed something a little better. Publicity and promotion often replaced mechanical perfection in launching a product, then as today. The papers were kinder to the "Volcanic." Six days after the company was voted into bankruptcy, the New Haven *Journal-Courier* (quoting the New York *Tribune)* said: "The Volcanic pistol and rifle seem the very perfection of firearms, and must be favorites with the public when they are fully known. We understand that orders crowd in upon the company from all quarters." By November 17, 1856, the *Journal-Courier,* again quoting the *Tribune,* described under "Tall Pistol Shooting" a rather unbelievable performance by Colonel Hay of the British Army.

"The (Volcanic) pistol used on the occasion was an 8-inch barrel, which discharged nine balls in rapid succession. The colonel fired shots which would do credit to a rifleman. He fired at an 8-inch diameter target at 100 yards, putting 9 balls inside the ring. He then moved back to a distance of 200 yards, and fired 9 balls more, hitting the target seven times. He then moved back 100 yards further, a distance of 300 yards from the mark, and placed five of the nine balls inside the ring, and hitting the bullseye twice. The man who beats that may brag."

The ballisticians of the modern-day Winchester firm studied this opus and concluded after some analysis that Hay's chances against putting 9 x 9 into an 8-inch target at 100 yards were about 11 to 1. The odds against 7 x 9 at 200 yards, about 70 to 1; and at 300 yards, one chance in 7,140 of doing what was claimed.

I recall in 1944 meeting a Marine Corps sergeant in an antique gun store in Baltimore, who might shed some light upon this feat of "tall shooting." He told me that he did not want to sell any of his Volcanic bullets, as he still used the pistol for shooting.

With Volcanic voted into bankruptcy, there was an interregnum when men remained at work but no company existed to carry forward the design, manufacturing, and sales. O. F. had advanced some $25,000 to the Volcanic firm to keep it going, and money had come in from some of its sales agents, notably Post and Wheeler of New York who had ordered $11,000 worth. These guns had been delivered to Post and Wheeler during the summer and autumn of 1856, and presumably included some of the Smith & Wesson guns and parts made at Norwich. Many claims existed against the Volcanic firm from its stockholders and raw material suppliers, but as late as May of 1857 "The settlement of the affairs of the Volcanic Repeating Arms Company is now being delayed by claims at law . . . occasioned by the inferior quality of the workmanship of the arms sent Messrs. Post and Wheeler during the last summer and autumn."

Exactly what the "inferior workmanship" was, is not specified, but a look at Hicks' role in the firm reveals some clues. Defect in the Volcanic pistol was still the ammunition, which Hicks tried to remedy by adapting the gun to handle the Smith & Wesson loaded bullet. Also, there was no proper chamber in the Volcanic,

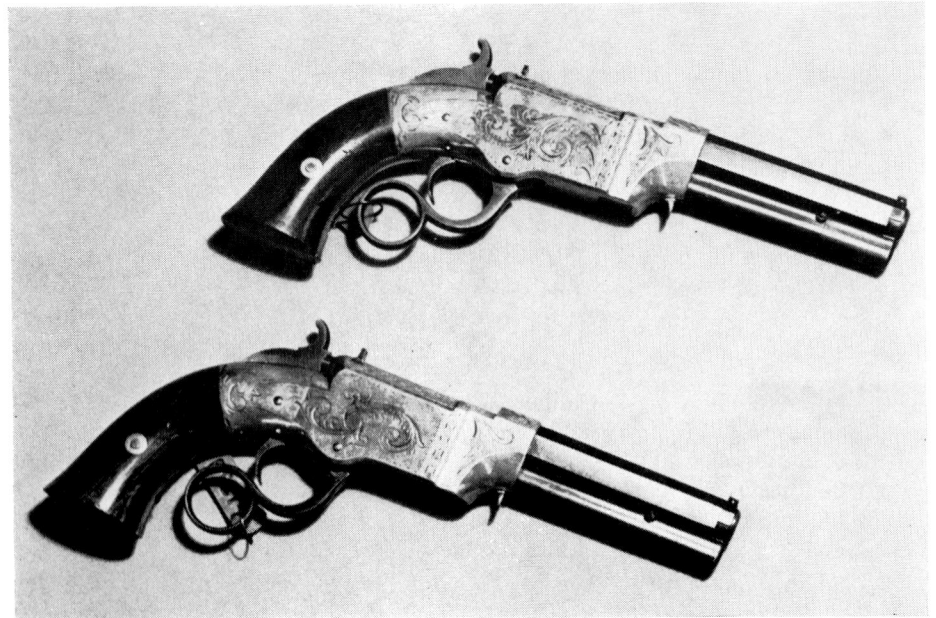

Handsome pair of .31 caliber Volcanic pistols are lightly engraved on brass frames. Style of gun is somewhat more sophisticated artistically than iron-frame S & Ws, but mechanism is fundamentally same. Guns are new, having been preserved in Winchester collection to this day. Larger sizes and a pistol-carbine with detachable stock were also made, as well as rifles.

just a bored-out groove-depth section at the breech. The rifling alone was not enough resistance to the entrance of the loaded bullet to position it regularly all the time. Sometimes it would be shoved too far forward, and that would cause a misfire. At other times it conceivably could fire upon closing the lever smartly. Also, ignition of all the cartridges in the magazine tube, Roman-candle fashion, it is said was possible with the Volcanic.

As much as he could, Hicks tried to correct things. For the firing pin or nipple, he designed a hook, that caught inside the cork and metal plate assembly and removed it upon withdrawing the breechpin. New arms made after February 1, 1856, had Hicks' improvement on them, and small pistols which had been sent in for repairs, actually a readjustment to make sure they were working correctly, were modified before returning to customers, after October 1, 1855. It was before this that the large lot of arms was sent out to Post and Wheeler, arms that were of "bad workmanship." Presumably, the Post and Wheeler arms would not extract properly.

"We first made a single nipple or hook," said Hicks, "then single with two prongs, finally a double nipple or hook. The hook works as follows: On firing, the lower side of the primer (disc) moves forward, often through 90 degrees, leaving the primer (disc) engaged on the bill of the hook by the rear side of the hole in the disc cover. It is then withdrawn and removed by the rising carrier block. The single prong hook was used on the small pistol and the double prong hook on the large size, after the winter of 1855-56 . . . I fired twenty balls each in twenty arms every day for months. The gun needed very little cleaning." What it did need was a decent cartridge.

Meanwhile, Winchester had formed a new organization, the New Haven Arms Company. He proposed to carry on Volcanic production under his management. He seems to have been bitten by the "gun bug" and perhaps delighted in this paradoxical industry as a sort of hobby, a respite so to speak, from making money making shirts.

Volcanic stumbled along and failed to meet some notes at the bank. Upon petition by the Tradesman's Bank of New Haven, Volcanic was declared insolvent on February 18, 1857. Talcott and R. B. Bennett

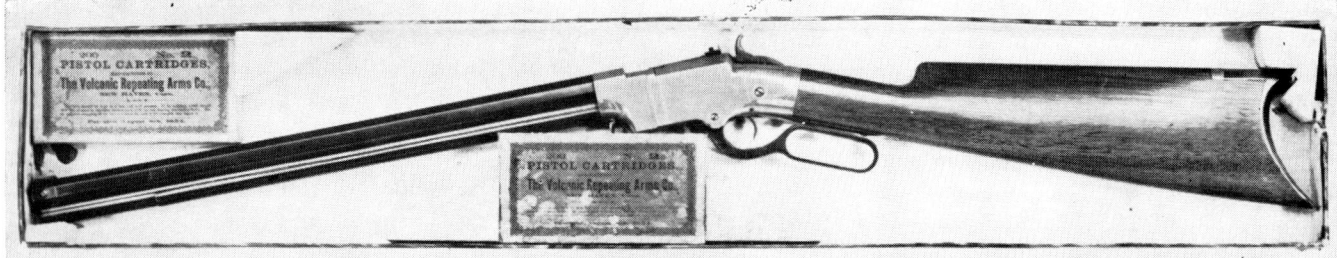

Volcanic carbines and ammunition in original boxes remained in storage at Volcanic Arms Co. when firm went into liquidation in February, 1857. Guns were discovered in attic of Winchester in 1920's or '30's, and placed by the main gate for employees who wanted to buy one as souvenir. Guard was instructed to collect twenty five cents from each employee for each carbine taken. Specimen shown, cal. 38 taking "No. 2" Volcanic cartridges, from Winchester Museum, would today bring perhaps $2,500.

Substantial factory was put up to turn out New Haven Arms Co. pistols and carbines and then Henry rifles in 1860. Though firm had considerable technical talent, production on improved cartridge repeater of B. Tyler Henry's was slow in getting started at this plant.

were appointed trustees; Eli Whitney, Jr., Henry Newson, and Charles Ball, to make an inventory of the assets. Irony indeed, for Eli Whitney, Jr. had his own firm, the internationally famous Whitneyville Armoury, which Oliver Winchester's company was to buy up when it in turn failed a few decades hence.

Winchester arranged with the Tradesman's Bank, and with the heirs of Nelson Gaston, to take over their claims. By order of the court, on March 15, 1857, Winchester for $39,000 obtained title to the entire assets of the Volcanic Arms Company. There was nothing left over for the stockholders, not even for the 2,800 shares held by Smith and Wesson. On April 3, 1857, the New Haven Arms Company articles of association were signed. Winchester had brought along seven shareholders who had lost money in Volcanic, and four new ones. He turned over to the New Haven Arms Company all the Volcanic assets: guns, tools, and patent rights, for 800 of the 2,000 shares of stock (par $25), and $20,000 in cash. He did not sell the patents which he acquired, but only assigned the right to manufacture, to the New Haven firm.

The guns made by all three firms, Smith & Wesson, Volcanic, and New Haven Arms, are fundamentally alike internally. Outside, there are differences. Though rifles are not listed as of Smith & Wesson make, there do exist specimens of Smith & Wesson marked Norwich lever rifles, including one handsome experimental piece in .50 rimfire, serial number 8. This evidently did not take the rocket ball cartridge, but it was not made up for general sale and possibly Winchester himself never got to see this specimen or recognize it for what it was, until later. J. W. Post, Volcanic agent at 23 John Street, New York, advertised "Volcanic repeating rifles, carbines, and pistols will fire 30 shots per minute." But actual production shoulder arms of either Smith & Wesson, or Volcanic, are not to be found. Only when Winchester formed New Haven Arms Company did actual shoulder-stocked guns get into production, though Volcanic had attached stocks temporarily and made up pistol-carbines or "hunter's companion" guns. A tabulation made by Colonel B. R. Lewis of these regularly produced arms includes:

Smith & Wesson, Norwich, Ct., 1853-55

Caliber	Weapon
.30	4" pistol
.38	8" pistol ("Navy")

Volcanic Repeating Arms Co., New Haven, 1856-7

.30	4" pistol
.30	6" pistol
.38	6" pistol
.38	8" pistol
.38	8" pistol with stock
.38	16½", 21", 25" carbines and rifles.

New Haven Arms Co., New Haven, 1857-60

.30	4" pistol
.30	6" pistol
.40	6" pistol
.40	8" pistol
.40	16½", 21", 25" carbines and rifles.

A price list of the New Haven Arms Company stated the number of charges each of their guns would hold was: 4-inch pistol, 6 balls; 6-inch pistol for target practice, 10 balls; 6-inch Navy pistol, 8 balls; 8-inch Navy pistol, 10 balls, 16½-inch carbine, 20 balls; 20-inch carbine, 25 balls; 25-inch carbine, 30 balls. The carbine lengths are from measured specimens, though the factory listed them at 16 inches, 20 inches, and 24 inches. But Winchester had got himself stuck with the same product that Smith & Wesson and the then stockholders of Volcanic had dumped.

"After buying the Smith & Wesson patents in 1855," he reported later, "I was never able to make the 'improvements' in their February 14 and October 10, 1854 (reissue) patents work reliably, but used the hollow ball. It was for this reason that I hired Henry to work out a practical system."

B. Tyler Henry was responsible for the ultimate development of the Winchester repeater. He at first made minor refinements. Brass was instituted for the receivers of the Volcanics instead of cast iron. Iron had to be blued, an added operation and if the blueing was poorly done, it had to be repolished and reblued. Brass could be polished once, lacquered, and left alone. Once sold, it was up to the customer to keep it polished if he desired. The barrel, which Smith liked turned round at the muzzle, like the single shot pistols of his mentors Allen and Thurber, was left full octagon. This saved an operation or two at the lathe and re-

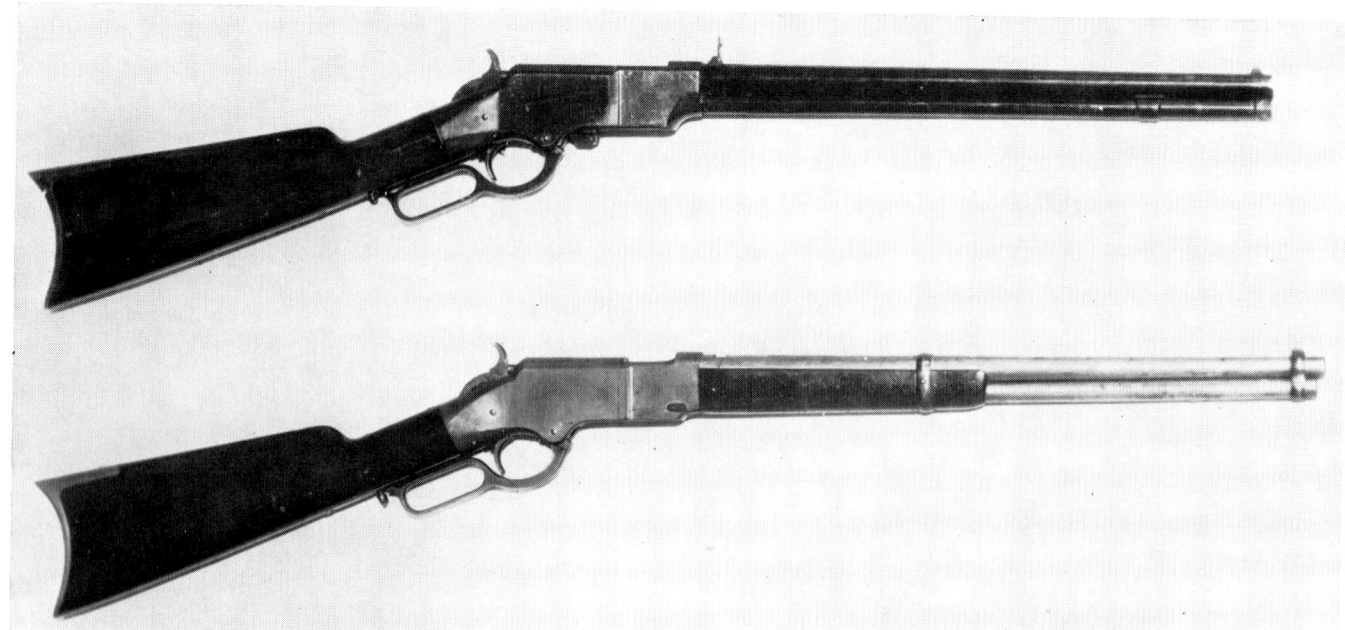
Toward end of war, Henry and Winchester improved design by adapting system to .50 caliber and using loading gate attached to bottom of frame. Lower rifle resembled succeeding "King's Improved" Model 1866 but gun shown, from Smithsonian patent office collection, is still a true "Henry" though with wooden forestock.

duced the cost of the arm a trifle. But it was in solving the problem of the cartridge that Henry showed his true ability as a mechanic.

With the growing tension throughout the nation, work was pushed forward and he applied for a patent upon his improvement to the Volcanic. Winchester had obtained, as a consequence of the Smith & Wesson deal, certain parallel rights to Smith & Wesson patents. That is, he as well as Smith & Wesson had the right to use certain S & W patents. Important to this agreement was the Flobert-transformed cartridge, the inside primed centerfire, patented by them on August of 1854. Their agreement gave to the Volcanic company, and therefore to Winchester by his obtaining the Volcanic assets, ". . . the exclusive use and control of all patents and patent rights which the said Smith and the said Wesson or either of them can or may hereafter obtain or acquire for inventions or improvements in firearms or ammunition."

Such a sweeping assignment seems not to have ever been invoked by Winchester except in the metallic cartridge efforts of his workman, Henry. For what Henry was doing was giving some sense to the little inside primed cartridge by making it bigger, easier to handle in drawing presses and in priming, and stronger because of the increased wall thickness possible. Issued October 16, 1860, with the election of the Illinois lawyer growing near, Henry's patent No. 30446, ". . . relates to improvements in a repeating breechloading gun, designed and arranged for the exclusive use of a hollow loaded ball, with a primer inserted at the base. My improvements are designed to remove the objection heretofore existing . . . adapting the arm to the use of a solid ball, enclosed in a metal cartridge, thus greatly increasing the power and certainty of fire of the arms."

The leverage of the odd finger lever must have troubled Henry and Winchester, too. No more would the flat, graceful, but almost unmanageable pocket pistols appear. The New Haven Arms Company began to devote itself to getting up the tools to build a flashy brass-framed octagon barreled rifle, a repeater taking a heavy, solid bullet of .44 caliber, backed by a meaningful charge of 40 grains more or less of black powder. Machines for spinning the empty cartridge case in loading had been devised, and a drop of safely wet fulminate placed on the center of the case head inside would soon spread itself out to the rim, to dry there permanently. Misfires were uncommon but could occur with the Henry rifle, when the firing pin, moveable now and separate in the breechpin, hit a "dead space" of the rim where there was no fulminate. But at last an extractor, big enough and adapted to the one purpose of hooking the rim to pull the shell out, was to be found. For the first time Smith & Wesson's original patented pistol was to be manufactured as a rifle, and Benjamin Tyler Henry was to receive the credit.

On the base of rimfire cartridges made by Winchester, a small "H" began to appear. This stood for Henry, master mechanic and the man who fashioned the first Winchester. Why Winchester chose to remain in the background is a mystery. He obviously liked to piddle along with these things. For five years he was losing money as fast as his shirt firm could make it. Perhaps he envisioned war profits when the conflict should at last begin. But in spite of his sales sense and political connections, he definitely did not act the role of the "profiteer."

CHAPTER 15

Remington: Prelude to Conflict

The little smithy at Ilion Gulph by 1861 had grown into one of the major industrial complexes of midstate New York. The influence of this entity, founded by Eliphalet Remington and carried on by his sons Eli Jr. and Samuel in 1861 has never been thoroughly explored. An adequate personal, mechanical, and industrial history of Remington Arms has yet to be written. But it is certain that shortly before the Civil War began, Remington's engineers had effected some radical improvements and innovations in manufacturing methods. To a degree they were without much local competition in the specialized labor market of arms trade workmen. It is true that they apparently paid slightly less than they might have done; Colt lured away one of their barrel straighteners by higher wages, and the man traveled many hundreds of miles to his new job. This job mobility is not uncommon now, but was very unusual then, except perhaps in the arms trade and its related machine tool industry. The loss was not crippling to the family rifle business founded approximately in 1814 as a sporting rifle shop, but it was a handicap. For 600 workmen and a million dollars in tools then, there might be as many as two or three barrel straighteners. With mass production and automation, with the most modern electronic inspecting gear in this second half of the 20th century, the art of the barrel straightener, by hand and by eye, remains supreme. When it is considered that rifle barrels by Remington demanded a premium, were highly esteemed in the trade, and that so-called gunsmiths all over the country built their reputation on Remington barrels to which they affixed their "maker's mark," it may be seen that Remington could ill afford to lose such a key employee.

Barrel Straightening

Early in the development of gun barrel making, it became obvious that inaccuracies in shooting were due to bores which were not straight. A method described in antiquity used a straight string, held taut by a slim bow of wood, the string inside the barrel. By looking through the barrel at a light source, the shadow of the string could be seen as a wiggle where the bore was dented, and as a straight line where it was straight. Hammer and anvil came into play and the skill to correct crooked barrels was built into the workman through experience. The next stage was the discovery that a straight line, externally, could be trusted to perform the same job. In the second method, possible only after bores had begun to be mirror finished inside, the workman simply viewed a straight line, such as the edge of a window, through the bore, and its reflection was seen along the bore surface. As many efforts were made to improve this, ultimately a special barrel-straightening machine was developed, now com-

Eli Remington, Jr., as a lad built a rifle at Ilion Gulph which was first firearm in series of possibly 30,000,000 made to date. Gun's ignition type has remained puzzle for modern researchers.

mon in all countries. Instead of the barrel being hit externally to offset the kink or bend revealed in inspection, it is supported on two rests, and midway a grooved press is caused to act by spinning a screw-wheel that moves the press down (to affect the barrel) or up to release. By shifting the wheel slightly and rapidly, the operator can rotate the barrel in the rest while looking through it to perceive the changes in shadow that revealed the changes in straightness.

Existing descriptions of barrel manufacture during and immediately after the Civil War do not describe this machine; it evidently was a carefully guarded secret. The reputation of Remington barrels for straightness and good shooting qualities suggests that the Ilion works had a rudimentary device of this kind in use; the premium on Remington barrel straighteners placed by Colt's hiring one suggests the trick was not generally known in the trade, but worth knowing.

At Remington other work was in progress to have a profound effect on arms manufacturing during the war. Revolvers of first quality had been developed there, and methods in turning out rifles and muskets existed which permitted considerable economy in production. This led to some revision in contract prices and caused a competitor to drastically cut his own profits to meet the Remington price.

Remington Zouave Rifle

One of the most colorful of Civil War arms is the so-called "Remington Zouave rifle," caliber .58. The order to supply 10,000 of these was sent by Ripley on 30 July, 1861. Though listed as an order for 10,000 "regulation rifles with sword bayonets," the article produced was in fact not regulation at all. It was a special model following the order:

These rifles are to be .58 inch calibre, and to have a three leaf rear sight, and a cupped ramrod, with sword bayonet stud similar to those of the Harpers Ferry rifle, Model of 1855, in other respects of the pattern of rifles without bayonets heretofore made by you for this department.

The order was acknowledged and agreed to, at $20 per rifle, on August 6 by Remington, and they at once got to work to prepare the prototype for approval.

The rifle design established used a stock of M1855 configuration, two brass bands and fore-end cap, and a brass box in the stock for spare nipple, ball screw, or screwdriver. The barrel was heavier than the normal United States rifle musket, and the rifles of the first order filled were rifled with 5 grooves. The lock is similar to the U.S. M1841 or Harpers Ferry rifle "heretofore made by you for government," as Ripley put it. Normal finish was casehardened colored lock, bright brass trim, and blued barrel. At the same time J. Remington showed Ripley, upon the recommendation of Major Hagner, a .36 caliber "Beals" Navy revolver, then currently in production at Ilion.

"I am procuring all of them I can for the western army," Hagner told Ripley, "and hope to hear I can get all I may need. I have seen no revolver I like as well, and the price is nearer the cost than some others." Hagner endorsed the good work of Remington heartily to the Department.

New Remington Army Model .44 Revolver

Acting upon these and other recommendations from his men in the field, as well as his knowledge of the past deliveries and quality of work of the Remington establishment, Ripley issued an order for a non-existent revolver:

ORDNANCE OFFICE
Washington, July 29, 1861
GENTLEMEN: Please make for this department, with the greatest possible despatch, five thousand revolver pistols of the same description as the sample you showed here, but of the calibre of the Army pistol, .44 inch . . .

Remington accepted the order by J. Remington in Washington that same date, at $15 each, and thus the great New Model Remington Army .44 was born. While General Ripley has been latterly characterized as an old fuddy-duddy and a reactionary who consistently refused to listen to inventors and held back arms progress for decades, he was in fact a man of often rapid but not hastily-considered decisions, who had a very good grasp of the needs of the service and acted within this framework for supply. Giving Remington fairly substantial orders for non-existent patterns of arms (one of them the patented revolvers which Ripley is supposed to have hated so much, as some careless writers have put it), reveals him to be able to make a quick choice and a good one. Remington's past performances were well known at the Department.

Remington Background

These past performances stand out with certain dates importantly in mind. Their significance is that they tend to profile the importance of the Remington estab-

"First rifle" often pictured in Remington literature is actually percussion half-stock American sporter of 1840's and was made several decades after Eli Jr. founded gun firm. Cheekpiece on right as well as left of stock is sometimes found on Remington-built early rifles.

Another rifle often pictured as Remington's first is shown being fired in "competition" with modern Remington .280 Model 740 autoloading sporting rifle. The flintlock handled by the "Dan'l Boone" character is a fraud, having a Common Rifle lock of military type glued into an 1840-pattern sporter with putty and plastic wood to fill the gaps. Gun originally had common percussion lock.

lishment in the upper Mohawk Valley, much as the Colt and Whitney enterprises affected industry in their Connecticut Valley ethos. The gun collector and the student of engineering history finds in the Remington saga some puzzling paradoxes, and some incomplete details. A major mystery in the arms history of industrial America is the origin of the enterprise that became Remington Arms.

Among many things not clear are a few certain items; 1816 marks the date of fabrication of a rifle by Eliphalet Remington Jr. The senior Remington was a farmer, having emigrated to the Mohawk Valley from Connecticut about 1800 and taken up 300 acres of good land at a locale known as Ilion Gulph. Operating such a manor required a decent forge and the acquisition of metal working skills by the thrifty farmer and the boys of the family. Young "Lite" excelled in such skills. Some time before 1816, at the occasion of the marriage of his sister, he was sent to Herkimer with a bag full of silver dollars to have them made into a set of table silver. The young man, just reaching maturity, saw in the hammering and cutting of the silversmith nothing beyond his own capabilities and returned to the homestead with the same silver dollars and no spoons. Instead, with his own hands he hammered the coins into sheet metal and cut the spoons, some of which, simple but well made, are still preserved by the Remington family.

In 1816 when the farmer's son was 23, he asked his father for money with which to buy a rifle. Though the Pennsylvania smiths were turning out first class Long Rifles, New York was the trade center to which Ilion Gulph looked, not Lancaster, Pennsylvania, and in New York rifles were only found as imports. In 1816 few indeed were imported; the majority of arms characteristic of the New York region were smoothbore muskets doubling as duck guns or extra-long barreled sporting arms, musketlike in style of fittings, known as "long fowlers." By that date the United States Army itself had only a few thousand rifles, half-stock arms resembling a cross between the British sporting rifles and the Kentucky rifles. Rifles had been made in New England, but they were not common articles of trade. The story that father Eliphalet refused young Lite the money because they were too poor, did not gain much currency until the early part of the 20th century. The Remingtons were in fact quite rich. Father Remington's land purchases commenced with 50 acres bought March 22, 1779, from James Smith in Litchfield, New York, for $275. Times and fortunes moved slowly for over 20 years; then on 20 April 1807 he obtained 195 acres for $585 from Samuel Merry, and the next year bought 71 acres more. The Remington homestead was rapidly growing, for in addition to farming, the Remingtons had turned their manor smithy to good account making farm tools and metal repairs for the surrounding community of farms. But as an example of how legends grow, we refer to published accounts of the building of the first Remington rifle—the first of perhaps thirty million arms manufactured since then at one or more Remington Arms Company plants.

A most interesting account appears in *The Remington Centennial Book,* 1816-1916. Perhaps the most authoritative text about the building of that first Remington rifle is one said to have been typed on Remington Typewriter No. 1. In 1916 this anonymous typescript was in the possession of Philo Remington's daughter, so the author is reputed to have had his facts straight. He did not embroider the matter too much, but it is suggested that Philo himself or one of Eli Junior's generation may have written the essay, as it speaks of family land purchases, pre-1800, in some detail.

The narrative first recites the story of a young man who improvised a gun with which to shoot a bear. Then it goes on to recount the history of "a young man residing in Litchfield whose inclinations pressed him in the same direction as the young man already spoken of." A footnote in this typescript refers to the boy who shot a bear. Confusion in chronicles caused Irving Crump in his highly glamorized *How A Boy Made The First Remington,* also published in 1916, to make out that Lite Remington himself made the gun and shot a bear. Mr. Crump is in error, comparing with the more ancient scriptures.

What actually happened is subject to conjecture, nothing more. The young man who refused to patronize the silversmith because he could take raw metal and do as good a job cheaper, now turned his talents to making a rifle. In 1816 there was strong sentiment at the close of the War of 1812 to "buy American." Youthful Lite Remington's patriotic ardor first vented itself in poems; he was a scholarly lad and possessed a faculty for memorizing. But the need to build the rifle kept pushing itself forward. Some say his father refused him the money to buy one. This may be true; prices after the War of 1812 on imported commodities so far in the hinterland must have been sky-high. Competent craftsmen that they were, the Remingtons may have scorned to buy something which they could make better and cheaper. But another item rings the bell of memory, makes the arms scholar think that the demand for his guns was based upon Remington's adoption, even momentarily, of one technological advance which occurred in arms making at this time—the use of the detonating pill-lock.

The First Remington Rifle

Remington lore has it that Remington's first rifle was a flintlock rifle. Surviving in collections of Kentucky rifles produced by hand in far fewer numbers than the Remingtons must have made guns are flintlocks of scores of little-known but skilled makers. If the Remingtons followed the ordinary path, between 1816 and 1830 they would have made enough rifles for at least one specimen to have turned up showing its flintlock origin origins, no matter how much transformed. Alas, the only Remington flintlock rifle in existence is a fraud, made into a flinter by the Remington Arms Company at some time in its existence for promotional purposes. The arm is a plain half-stock rifle of simple form, the cheapest of the Remington mass-produced single shot sporters of 1840. It has two ramrod thimbles, open "buckhorn" sight and blade front, and double set triggers. Unusual is the lock; rounded at the rear but without marks, it resembles the flintlock from a Common Rifle. The inletting about the plate once accommodated a differently shaped and slightly larger percussion lock; indeed, one of America's most famous rifles is seen to be a "reconverted" fake. More probably a "first" is another rifle shown in Centennial (1916) Remington literature as "The First Remington Rifle." This arm has a shadbelly stock curve, and cheek piece on the right side of stock, possibly right and left cheek pieces as came to be almost a sculptured trade mark of the Herkimer output. The common side lock has a drum in barrel to support the nipple and is a simple original percussion of the 1830-50 style. But it could also have been pill-lock.

Pill-lock Rifles

The pill-lock rifle is a little-studied phenomenon associated with the New York State rifle industry. When in 1807 Rev. Alexander Forsyth in Scotland shot down his first goose using a detonating compound to ignite the main charge, he ushered in not an era of firearms advance, but an era of confusion and experiment. By 1814 Captain Joshua Shaw of Philadelphia had formed iron and later copper capsules, open at one end, containing detonating or priming compound in their closed end. The capsule was slipped over a steel tube leading to the main charge, and when the hammer struck it, the flash passed through the tube to ignite the main charge. Though Shaw's innovation caught on, not all sportsmen recognized it as the universal solution to applying a detonator to gunfire. Shaw's device required the fabrication of caps to carry the detonator compound. Inventors such as Joseph Manton believed the primer could best be handled as a tiny pellet of mixture and binder, applied directly to the gun in a sort of basin or hole. By the 1830's one J. Miller had patented a revolving breech rifle. It was a pill-lock, the surface of the cylinder having small holes into which the priming pellets were placed. A long nose on the hammer punched the pellets securely into the holes and detonated them. As some claim that gum arabic was used in making the pellets, it is possible they had a tacky quality to cause them to adhere to the Miller gun's cylinder. Gunmaker

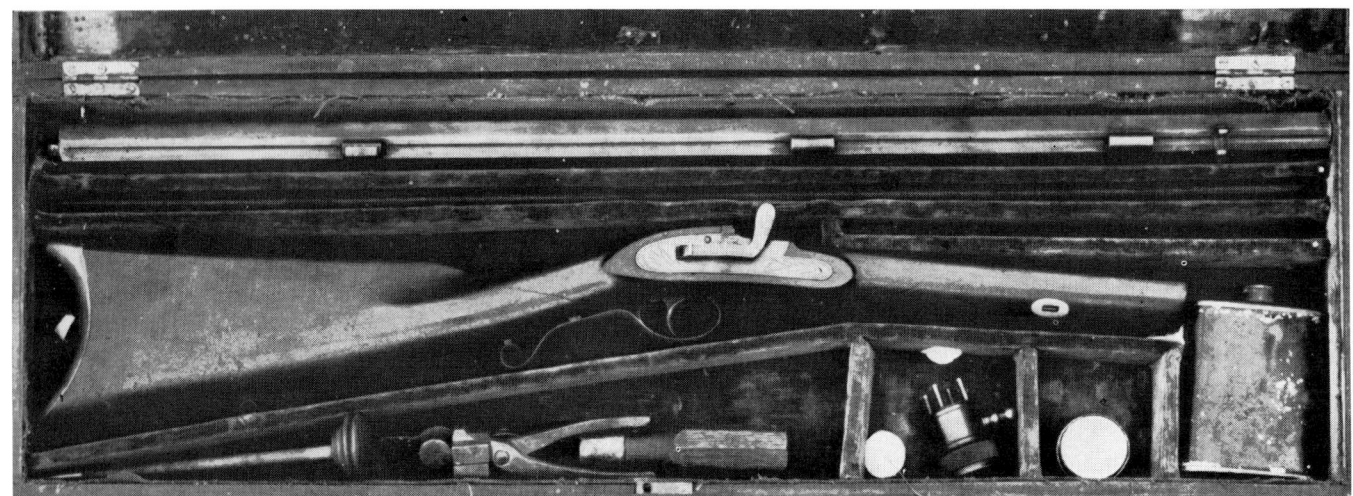

Pill lock ignition with striker on side of lock is found on some New York State rifles like this handsome Albany rifle of 1840's with Clark patent false muzzle. Design resembles Jenks sidehammer percussion arms made by Remington for Navy, suggests first rifle of Remington history may have been novelty to shooters in that it was percussion system or pill lock.

Billinghurst of Rochester, New York, made a number of these arms; Jonathan Browning, father of J. M. B., also used this design. The pill-lock in America is almost invariably associated with New York State guns.

Perhaps the reason there are no flintlock Remington rifles in existence after a century and a half of searching is that none were made. Early Remington arms were pill-lock, quickly converted to percussion by the drum alteration method. Later Remington arms obsoleted the pill-lock as the cap lock caught on, and following the vogue of the day, were naturally percussion.

Remington's First Barrels

In the Remington story, certain dates are significant. In 1816 Remington made his first rifle barrel. Alden Hatch in his romantic book *Remington Arms* describes the activity in detail:

The job was done at last. Lite had a tightly wound spiral of metal some forty-two inches long with a .40 of an inch hole running through it. Once more he laid it in the bed of coals and this time brought it to white heat. Then he sprinkled borax and sand on it (sic) to make it weld, and seizing it in his tong pounded it vigorously on the stone floor. This was called "jumping." It jarred the malleable edges of the spiral strip against each other so the heat-activated molecules, running together, were welded into a solid tube of iron. Because only eight inches could be heated at once, Remington repeated this process six times. There was the rough barrel of the gun.

In addition to confusing the fabrication of a Damascus or wire twist barrel with what must certainly have been a simple wrought-iron lap-welded barrel, Hatch compounds his error and the error of "old hands" at Remington Arms by describing a method of using a plumb line to test for barrel straightness; such a method almost never existed. The important thing is that straightness of the barrel was acknowledged by all sources, secondary and tertiary though they be, as important in the commercial success of Remington's first gun.

A commercial success it was; idyllic essays on winning shooting matches, or dramatic corruptions of record that Remington shot a bear with his first gun, do not gloss over the fact that other folks wanted one. He made them. If the first had a lockplate salvaged from scrap and, as the anonymous Remington Typewriter scribe said, "The spring and other parts wanting he made himself," the business that emerged from the flare of the forge at Ilion Gulph was a hard, sound, commercial success.

The date of 1816 coincided with a move by the Remingtons, father and son, to a new and enlarged shop. Tradition has it that young Lite walked over the hills 15 miles to Utica to have his barrels rifled by a gunsmith there. But if there was a genuine gunsmith in Utica, he would have been able to supply the wants of the communities even as far off as Ilion. Tradition also links the name of Morgan James of Utica with that of Remington, and declares that James rifled the First Rifle Barrel. Hatch makes out Morgan James to be quite a gray-beard, possessed of sage advice and wisdom on gunmaking for the stripling riflemaker. Actually, James was from Litchfield, Connecticut, and had moved to the region near that other Litchfield, of New York, to engage in gunsmithing about 1820. Satterlee and Gluckman date him in Utica as early as 1820, and at the corner of Fayette and Seneca Streets in 1859-1866. Prior to 1859 he was for a time associated with George H. Ferris as James & Ferris, specializing in heavy match rifles with scope sights. James, if he was in Utica in 1816, was no wise old gaffer; he was a green young man, doubtless a journeyman gunmaker, hardly two years Remington's senior. Apparently this was a case of two sharp lads getting together to fill the market, and turn out rifles. Remington had the forge and grindstones, furnaces, and hammers, to shape out the tubes. James, if he did not have a rifling machine, knew how to make one from wood using steel pegs in a spiral channel on the outside of a drum, to turn the rifling cutter through its spiralling arc.

Tradition continues to note that Remington got orders from neighbors, hammered out more barrels, went over to Utica to have them rifled, and brought them back. The trip was 30 miles on foot. Six or seven barrel skelps, say 10 pounds each in the rough for a load of 70 pounds, gave Remington a mighty hefty pack to tote for the march. Production was limited to the number of barrels he could carry— hardly more than ten or twenty barrels a week and certainly not that many finished rifles.

But business continued, and Remington looked upon it as a sober means of livelihood. Though most arms historians have supposed that Remington was famous for barrels only, there seems little doubt that he made complete rifles. The economics of the frontier, together with the breakthrough in transportation afforded by the new Erie Canal, now gave him a water level route to a wide market in the state. Not only gunmaking but other metal goods such as farming tools, continued to be made in the Remington shops. By 1828 father Remington bought a large farm in Ilion itself and there, on the canal, the present plant of Remington Arms Corporation was founded. Eliphalet Remington senior died that year, his son Lite succeeding to managership of the factory.

The First Factory

Factory it was, this stone foundation mill with two upper floors of frame construction. A list was apparently in existence in 1916, quoted in *The Remington Centennial Book,* of machinery installed in the new works under Lite Remington's watchful eye: "A big tilt hammer, several trip hammers, boring and rifling machines, grindstones, and so on." The elusive catchphrase "and so on" we hope has damned this booklet writer to a perdition of unending research, for it would be exceedingly interesting to know exactly what potential for arms making Remington possessed in that new and enlarged factory, first in Ilion. But by 1828 the percussion system was generally in vogue

Morgan James rifle made by Remington's Sons at Ilion Gulph and stamped on barrel UTICA N Y/ M JAMES in two lines with city on top. While arm now on display at Remington museum from author's collection confirms link between two famous men, gun's construction dates it as 1840's. Hammer is only percussion hammer fitted by Remington Arms in 20th Century due to loss of original when rifle was sent to factory for display.

among the better gunmakers, though for military arms flintlock held on for two decades more. Assuming that the first Remingtons were pill-lock, almost all must have been converted to percussion system as soon as their owners could rely on getting the new fangled percussion caps. It was more expensive but less dangerous than rolling pellets of detonating compound oneself.

We are informed by *The Remington Centennial Book* that "The lapwelded barrel was standard until 1850, and he got together a battery of trip hammers for forging and welding his barrels. Finer dimensions became a factor in his business when the output grew large enough to warrant carrying a stock of spare parts for his customers, and so he improved those parts in ways that gave at least the beginnings of interchangeability." No claim can be made that Remington invented interchangeable parts, but the development of a small arms factory can be read between the lines. By 1836 Remington's barrels had become known in Baltimore and New Jersey. Sam Colt, laying in barrels for his rifles to be made at Paterson, New Jersey, wrote about "the barrel maker in Litchfield." While we had followed John E. Parsons in supposing this related to some Connecticut barrel maker, we tend now to wonder if, in the absence of further facts, this did not refer to the lad from Litchfield, Lite Remington.

By 1846 Remington had matured considerably in skills and technology. In that year he first exhibited a barrel solid-drilled from a steel rod, less likely to develop weakness such as happened along the seam of weld. But it appears he may have applied this technology somewhat earlier, for he had experience in fabricating 5,000 U.S. Rifles, Model 1841, our first truly interchangeable military arm. In 1844 Lite Remington took into partnership his son, Philo, changing the name to E. Remington & Son. In 1845 the firm landed a contract for M1841 rifles which had been defaulted by the original contractor, John Griffiths, of Cincinnati, Ohio. Since obtaining the contract in December 6, 1842, Griffiths had not delivered one gun. The Remingtons filled this order so well that a second order was obtained in their own name for 7,500 M-1841 rifles, which they duly filled. Meanwhile, casting around for more work, during 1846-7 they arranged to take on a contract held by N. P. Ames for Jenks carbines.

Jenks Carbine

The Navy's breech-loading carbine designed by William Jenks of Columbia, South Carolina, was like other arms familiar to the New York gunmakers. It used a New York State type side hammer, although in prototype form some few fitted with a back-action flint lock are known. As perfected, and made in several slightly different styles by several contractors, the Jenks had a sliding breechblock and a finger lever on the top of the small of the stock. The side-striking hammer had a hook or curve at the top edge that, when the hammer was snapped, served to lock over the breech. Generally if the breech was partly open, the hammer would not reach the side-placed nipple to fire.

Sidehammer plain sporting rifles, with full stocks of the Kentucky or common American style of 1830, are known bearing New York or upper Pennsylvania association and marks. One of these formerly in the noted Independence Hall Association exhibition in Chicago on Devon Avenue had a pill-lock ignition, definitely a New York State rifle and perhaps a Remington. Whether these sidehammer guns are before or after the Jenks gun is a moot point. But the carbines Remington finished for the Navy were all sidehammer. N. P. Ames probably sold the contract for a profit, since Ames was noted as a conscientious contractor. Remington's version incorporated the Maynard tape primer in the lockplate. It is said that Jenks, reputed to be a competent mechanic, came with the contract to Herkimer County. As Hatch puts this episode, it becomes a curiously garbled mixture of documented fact and old wives' tales—or old workmen's tales, than which there is nothing more unreliable:

At Chicopee Falls, in Massachusetts, (Eli Remington) visited the plant of the N. P. Ames Company . . . Recently they had gone into gunmaking with a Navy contract for a new-fangled breech-loading carbine invented by William Jenks. Mr. Ames was not happy with his experiment. He had no experience with the manufacture of firearms, and was rapidly acquiring too much experience with governmental red tape. He was ready to listen to a proposition. Remington looked at the excellent Ames machinery and coveted it. He examined the Jenks carbine, and decided that it was a practical mechanism. With his inventor's perception, he saw that he could make it into the best breechloader yet seen. And he took an instant liking to William Jenks.

Jenks was a Yankee, of Welsh descent, with curly hair, round eager eyes, a straight chiseled nose, and a thin, unhappy mouth. He looked like a minor poet, but his appearance of delicacy was strangely deceptive. For Jenks had the fire and imagination of a true genius, and a resilient inner core that had enabled him to buck bureaucratic indolence and red tape for nearly a decade, until by sheer perseverance (plus the excellence of his invention) he had dragooned the Navy into ordering a few of his guns. In Remington, he saw a chance to realize his ambitious dreams.

The upshot of Remington's visit to Chicopee Falls was that he bought the whole Ames gun business, including machinery, contracts, guns in all stages of completion, and, most important of all, the services of William Jenks. The price was exceedingly moderate. In addition to a small down payment, Remington gave Ames two notes on the Phoenix Bank of New York payable in eight and ten months. Each note was for $1,290.50, making a total of $2,581.00.

Hatch concludes this passage by noting that there was a momentary delay in production while Lite and Philo Remington, at the insistence of the Government, filled a "hurry-up order of ancient flintlocks—the last ever issued to American troops!" Like the Unicorn and the Dodo, these alleged flintlock muskets by Remington are no longer with us, nor were they ever; no such arms are on record as having been ordered, no record exists at Remington to indicate they were fabricated, and no specimens exist in any collections in this or any other land.

But these are not the only catches in the Hatch story of Jenks. That he was a Yankee may be agreed, if of the "galvanized" kind, he coming from South Carolina in the preceding decade where he invented his breech mechanism. As to Remington perceiving it could be made into the "best breechloader ever," there seems little need to say that Remington made what the Secretary of the Navy and the Board of Navy Commissioners ordered. And that Ames, who remained a faithful and diligent Government contractor through the war and whose corporate identity still survives (in somewhat reorganized form) today, was filled up with red tape is absurd. Ames, at the time he relinquished the Jenks contract, was on the verge of completing or had completed his contract for fabricating the novel Model 1843 U. S. Navy pistol or "boxlock pistol." Perhaps Remington had gotten the barrel drilling method down pat and figured he could buy Ames out and still make a small profit, and at the same time end up with vastly increased production power. No great virtues need be attached to William Jenks coming along for the ride, though Lite Remington gave house room to every stray cat of an inventor who had an idea.

Such philanthropy seldom paid off, but the typewriter was a notable conception. If Jenks left his mark by improving machinery and processes, it will take a lot more digging to substantiate it. He fades from sight, there in his new home on the canal in Ilion, while beside the original armory building of 1828 a new works goes up, far more impressive in size and power. A new mill race is put in, and the Ames machinery, including stock-turning machines of the most advanced patterns of Thomas Blanchard, begin to spew their fine red dust as they chew out the shapes of the gun stocks.

Sporting Rifles

Remington continued production of common American sporting rifles in at least four basic sizes. Shipped South, they became essential armament in 1861 for volunteers; in the North, some match rifles were carried by Sharpshooters.

The smallest size is a buggy rifle or possibly a boy's rifle, having a barrel less than 30 inches and with a slim stock. Calibers are not uniform and are as yet uncatalogued as to bore; perhaps barrels that did not finish well to one size were cut up to the next size, lacking uniformity, but all with a proper ball mould for each barrel.

Next in size would be described as the Basic Sporter. Such a rifle in this writer's collection is utterly plain in finish, but very well made. The lock is plain outside, with old or original fire-blacking to its surface. Inside in a tiny arc the initials "B. FA Co" are placed between fixed limb of spring and arm of tumbler, in British fashion.

The cognomen "X Fire Arms Co." was not too common in the British trade of the time; not one in-

Long strip on top of Jenks carbine lifts up by hook thumbpiece to uncover trough for loading combustible cartridge. Hammer must be cocked by pulling on hook end. Gun was designed for Navy use.

stance comes to mind of traditional maker or parts supplier being known by that title in the 1840's. In the United States the custom had greater use, and there is little doubt that this is an American-made lock, essentially hand made but well finished. It has an unusually long limb to the tumbler, to which the spring stirrup is attached, and this gives a good and easy action to the striking of the hammer. The half-cock notch on the striking motion is protected by a hardened steel flipper or "fly" to guide the sear out of catching in the notch. The bridle itself, which supports the tumbler and the sear, is of forged and either swedged or milled construction. Along the edge there are two ridges where some sort of tool came together. It may have been the end of arc of some curved punch which blanked out the bridle in several operations, but more likely it is the edge remaining where shaped cutters imperfectly continued the arc made by a preceding cutter on the adjoining edge. A combination of machine work and hand work can be seen; not so fine as a typical No. 1 Enfield lock, but as good as thousands of first-class imported locks used in shotguns and sporting rifles. The inletting of the lock is not machine made, except possibly for the outline. The stock itself appears shaped by machine; finished by hand. The butt plate screws for example are slightly

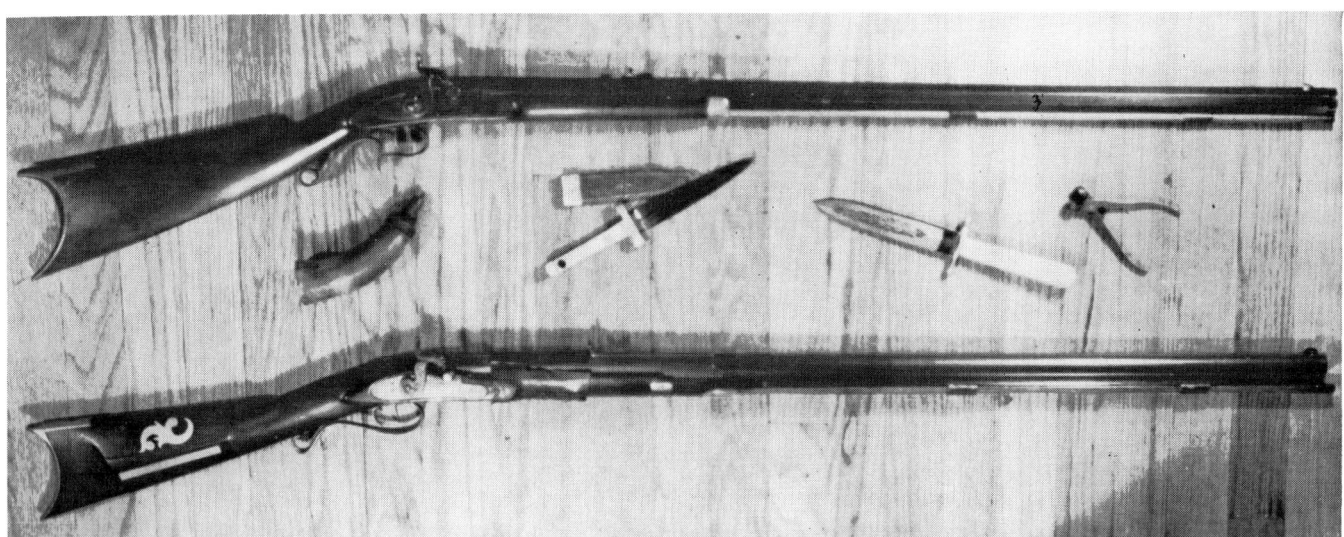

Top short rifle is buggy or boy's rifle, smallest seen of Remington-Ilion fabrication. Next is medium weight full octagon sporter with bullet starter. Rear peep sight is turned sidewise to show shape. Bottom is long plain sporter, a work rifle, with back-action lock. Same character of arm is shown in second cut on wood background in which top arm is M. James rifle (with hammer on it before loss) compared with fancy Remington-made match rifle having barrel turned round. Flattened planes on round breech section are called "Rigby flats" after British maker who affected this style. Medium-heavy match rifle takes bullet starting cone over muzzle. Stamped Devendorf, of Cedarville, Pa., this gun is unquestionably Remington-built in its entirety. Powder horn, hunting knife and celluloid-handled "Dont sheathe me without honour" gentlemen's fighting knife and round ball mould are associated items.

off center and filed into unique positions; one would not interchange with any other. The oval escutcheon on top of the small of stock with a threaded hole for the screw-disc rear peep sight is held by two screws, their grooves filed almost away.

Among possible suppliers of locks marked "B. FA Co.," which is also listed (by Gluckman and Satterlee) as "B.F.A.," are Joseph and Robert S. Bartless, Binghamton, New York. Between 1829 and 1834 they made flintlock Kentucky rifles and then percussion arms. If Gluckman's recording of this is accurate, the dates may bracket a general change from flintlock or even pill-lock to the common percussion system among New York State gunmakers. At first located on Court Street, they moved to larger premises when the site of the first shop was taken over for a Canal project. At their new building on Franklin Street (now renamed Washington) they employed as many as 25 hands. If "B. FA Co." is in fact their maker's mark, a not unlikely conjecture, then there may be Remington barrels fitted to arms bearing their names as makers.

To the stock and lock, Remington fitted a barrel 33½ inches long exactly, 1 inch across the muzzle, 1⅛ inches across the breech, tapered octagonal, and bored 14/32-inch or .45-inch caliber, seven equal grooves and lands, twist one turn in 24½ inches. The muzzle for 5/16-inch is turned round, to accommodate a brass sleeve inside which a plunger fits for starting the bullet. Each rifling groove is filed out a trifle on the muzzle end to help the patch start without cutting. The combination of statistics suggests use of a picket ball at fairly high black-powder velocity. A scope may once have been fitted; located 11½ inches, 12 inches, and 12½ inches from the breech face are three ⅛-inch holes, plugged, on top of the barrel. A rear mount at that place could have been used with a mount in front dovetailing into the front sight slot. The present gunmetal base and blade is cut in 1 1/16 inches from the muzzle face; at 13/16-inch from the muzzle a line is scribed across the top flat, and a zero line scribed in the centerline of the flat, with divisions for windage right and left marked in with lines and tiny prick-punch dots. The front sight and present rear sight appear to have been fitted when the gun was expertly refinished sometime before the turn of the century. The rear sight of buckhorn sporting type with elevating wedge is machine made and appears like the Remington, Lyman, or Winchester sights of the 1880's. Near the breech the bottom flat of the barrel in a not very precise fashion bears faintly the mark REMINGTON. On top, located 5 inches from the breech, in two lines with the city address uppermost, is stamped UTICA. NY/M. JAMES. Unquestionably, Morgan James knew the Remingtons, at least as business clients; he sold their rifles.

This same basic sidelock rifle can be found in a heavier barrel model, with general characteristics similar including the peep sight. Sometimes the rear peep stem screws directly into the end of the breech tang; on others it fitted to an escutcheon on top of the stock. Where a sight stem is threaded into the tang, an escutcheon may be fitted as a decorative initial plate, for the owner's cypher.

The plainest form of this rifle has only a brass butt plate and a white metal fore-end cap; there are no stock escutcheons for the cross bar that holds barrel to wood. Perhaps on order, optional extra, or simply a logical innovation in the regular production, Remington soon fitted little plates on each side of the stock for the wedge to bear in, strengthening the stock in recoil. About the time the gun collector is ready to observe these plates were "characteristically rectangular with mitred corners," in shape, a rifle fitted with long oval plates turns up. In this same standard rifle size, locks can be either bar style, or back action. More likely the back action locks were fitted as an improvement late in the 1840's after the back action style became common from the French inspiration in their infantry muskets, *Fusil a la Ligne Mdle 1840, systeme á piston,* or percussion. In heavy barreled styles, sometimes two wedges were used to hold stock and barrel together. A patent breech was also used, and a very odd Remington rifle in the writer's collection has "Rigby flats" on a round barrel, turned smaller for false muzzle.

This arm gives evidence of its Remington origins in two ways: the first is the form, but we will revert to this point later on. The bottom of the barrel also bears faintly . . . INGTON, showing the barrel has been set back slightly and re-breeched. As this arm has a patent breech permanently screwed into the stock, with the barrel breechplug keying into it, the breech may be an addition to take up the space if the back was cut off, removing the REM of the maker's name.

This handsome rifle has seen better days but still shows its original high quality. All furniture, instead of being common yellow brass, is bright German silver. The rifle-style butt is cut with double cheek pieces, one for each side. On each cheek flat is inset a floral silver cut-out; along each cheek flat is a stylistic groove; below each is a silver strip 4 inches long. The round barrel is 34 1/16 inches from muzzle to breech. Extending forward 10½ inches from the breech are flats; one on top and one each side. These flats are not parts of any octagonal form; the round shape of the barrel is projected between each flat all the way to the breech. This is a cylindrical barrel with three tables or pads shaped integral, that on Ballard rifles of the 1880's had come to be called "Rigby flats." It is thought that John Rigby & Company, Dublin and London, first affected this cross between the round and octagon in their rifles, but the flatted areas were much smaller and close to the breech than on this handsome Remington match rifle. The barrel tapers from 1¼ inches at the breech to 1 1/16 inches at muzzle; the round for starter is 1 inch across. Rifling is .50-inch, 6-groove; it has been relined. On the top flat, 1⅞ inches from breech, partially covered by an old Indian or frontier rawhide sleeve stock repair, is the stamp of L. DEVENDORF/CEDARVILLE. Louis Devendorf of Cedarville, New York, is listed as having made "percussion target rifles." On one at least, he put his sales stamp; the rifle was made by Remington.

Among little details of outline and shaping which come to spell "Remington" to the collector's eye is a shape of the stock that is characteristic. Not all Remingtons have this shape; but of all rifles seen with this shape, of the half-stock percussion "American sporting rifle" type, all were in some part identified "Remington." The inescapable conclusion is that the arm complete was made by E. Remington & Son, Ilion, New York, using bought locks and sometimes bought hardware, but own-make barrels, ironware, and stocks. This detail is the unusually tapered "teat" shape to the stock cheeks on either side; on the right where the bar lock sets in, and on the reverse where there may be a simple escutcheon for the cheap single lock-screw that holds on the hardware company lock. The M. James rifle has an odd liver shaped escutcheon; the Devendorf rifle a fancy scrolled silver plate. To fill Devendorf's order, Lite Remington bought a lock from WARREN/ALBANY as the outside is incised. But Warren, sometimes in association with a partner, as Warren & Steele, is known to have used English parts in his own gunmaking. Perhaps, to judge from the jammed-up position of the names compared with the spread out cheap engraving, this was an imported lock they marked and then sold.

Remington Arms was soon to fill a large role in the greatest war on the North American continent. To prepare for it, the family, the sons of Eli Remington II, needed more preparation than desultory rifle barrel making.

The fact is that E. Remington & Sons from the time in 1832 when only 20 men were at work to the mid-1850's had achieved success and production capacity by making sporting rifles. They had made and by the friendly Erie Canal shipped thousands of them; an average annual production capacity of even 1,000 common sporting rifles from 1830 to 1850 would yield a total of 20,000 rifles actually produced and sold by the time Colonels Talcott and then Craig turned to the Herkimer County firm as a contractor. A total of 12,500 M1841 rifles were turned out, and Remington passed from the handicraft stage to machine production. The Jenks contract was bought from Ames and with it stock turning equipment of high production. Transformation of 20,000 Springfield pattern muskets to Rifled Muskets, .69, with special Remington made Maynard locks shows the firm had more than nominal capacity. It was under date of September 9, 1854, that E. Remington signed a contract to alter 20,000 flintlock muskets to Maynard primer at $3.15 per musket. The new "Remington primer lock" was slightly different from the usual Maynard linkage inside but was under Maynard's recent agreement (of February 3, 1854) permitting unrestricted use of his invention by the Army and Navy, upon payment of $50,000. The new locks made by Remington, who would hardly have undertaken a lock contract unless they had extensive lock making machinery already on hand, was marked REMINGTON'S/ILION. N. Y./1857/US behind the hammer.

The "Rigby flatted" barrels exist on larger sizes of rifles; one absolutely plain specimen, but with double cheek piece, examined at an Ohio gun collectors convention, is a gut-buster weighing about 25 pounds and measuring just under 2 inches across flats. Caliber as

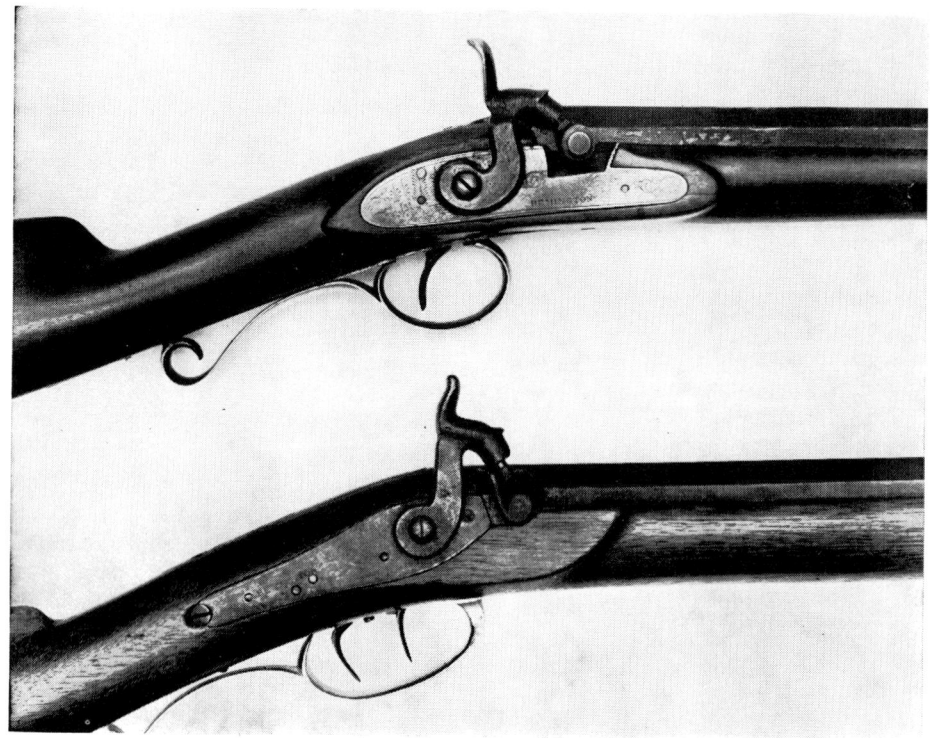

Closeup of locks from boy's rifle and long back-action sporter of preceding plate show REMINGTON lock markings. Boy's rifle lock and guard resemble same parts on pill-lock rifle shown previously, though lock probably is not a conversion but is original percussion. Remington had extensive lock-making machinery at work by time of Maynard primer government contract.

recalled is about .50-inch, not exceptionally large. It was turned for false muzzle and had the unusual long Rigby flats, on an otherwise round ribbed barrel. A full stock Remington sporter is not known, though such may exist. Superposed rifles, fitted with back action percussion locks, engraved Remington and finished in other details like those described, have been handled. In the Remington Arms Company offices sharing dishonors with the fraudulently flinted percussion rifle, is an honest old side-by-side rifle and shotgun, twist barrels, back action locks, with a fanciful Germanic-style trigger guard. A combination rifle and shotgun, side by side, believed of Remington make, appears to have the barrels bored parallel from a single block of cast steel.

To the statement that Remington made a great number of sporting rifles, noted rifleman and arms authority John T. Amber, editor of *The Gun Digest,* snorted, "If Remington made so many rifles, where are they?" The answer is only now beginning to be searched out; they are behind the misleading lock marks like "Warren, Albany" or the retail salesmen's stamps like UTICA, N. Y./M. JAMES.

Any gunmaker worth his salt could slave over spokeshave and drawfile until he had created by hand a masterpiece of artistry for the discriminating customer, all by himself. But with the dawn of the Industrial Revolution in upper New York State, young Lite Remington harnessed the tumbling water race of a brook in Ilion Gulph to his dream and turned out as yet uncounted thousands of good, and often fancy, standard American rifles for frontiersmen who wanted the best but could not afford to pay for needless foofurraw. To these men Remington offered his arms with the marks hidden on the bottom of the barrel. Let the local gunmaker gain the trade and the credit; Remington knew that soon the postman would bring in another order and onto the canal boat as it passed beneath the Remington dock the Remington shipping clerk would drop not one rifle but perhaps a dozen, addressed to "L. Devendorf, Cedarville," or "Utica N. Y., M. James."

CHAPTER 16

Vulcan Hammers at Ilion's Forge

When Ripley gave Eli Remington II the contract for 10,000 rifles with sword bayonets, he set in motion the wheels of industry that were brought to a shattering halt by Secretary Stanton's proclamation. Like everyone going up unto his own city to be taxed, the arms makers descended upon the chambers of Holt and Owen in Washington. In jeopardy was the contract for 10,000 rifles and 5,000 .44 caliber revolvers. The firm—for E. Remington & Sons no longer boasted the steady and patriarchal hand of Eli II at the helm, he having died in August, 1861—was about to suffer much loss. Philo, the eldest son, born 1816, was the inventive one, and later was responsible for the breech-loading Remington rifle upon which the firm rode the postwar tide. His younger brother Samuel was the general agent, making selling contracts and concluding purchases of materials and machines but also doing design work. Eliphalet Remington, later also to be called "Junior," was the youngest of the three brothers. Known for his command of language and skill in penmanship, he had charge of the correspondence of the firm and the accounting. The three brothers had been taken into partnership in 1856 with the extra "s" added to "& Son." Now it fell to Samuel to confer with Messrs. Holt, Owen, and his friend Major Hagner, as to the outcome of their small but precious contracts.

Remington War Contracts

While Colt had tackled the matter first and foremost, and set the $20 price for all Springfield musket contracts, Samuel went at it in a different manner. He had Eli calculate the smallest margin they could work on with profit, jacked it up a little for profitable padding, and then journeyed to Washington to pull the skids out from under the competition. Instead of clamoring for 50,000 or 100,000 Springfields in addition to their other guns, Remington simply offered to make 40,000 Springfields at a nominal $16 each, four bucks less than Government price, and for this he promised first-class arms. He told the commissioners that the 5,000 pistols were well under way by May, 1862, and the 10,000 rifles in parts were going through the works. The brothers had plowed back $100,000 into enlarging the factory and "they are working zealously and extra hours to expedite their work."

Remington stated that he desired to commit his factory entirely to the uses of the Government (for obviously the sporting rifle business had just gone out the window with the cannon shot at Sumter). He offered to make an additional 40,000 M1855 ('41 type) rifles with sword bayonet, or 40,000 Springfield rifled muskets, $17 for the rifles with sword bayonets, $16 for Springfields. If the first 10,000 rifles were confirmed to them, they would then charge in all only $17; and if the 5,000 revolver order was confirmed, he would be willing to include it as part of any larger order and at the same price of $12 each (Colt was still getting $25 for his New Model Army).

With this sort of hard bargaining in cash terms staring them in the face it did not take the commissioners long to decide. They confirmed the Harpers Ferry-type rifle order for 10,000, and the 5,000 of what collectors now call the Beals Model .44, and added 40,000 Springfields at $16 and 20,000 revolvers at $12. Hagner urged that General Ripley approve all this. In making his report to the War Department, Judge Holt asked Samuel Remington's permission to use his name in connection with fixing this low contract price. Characteristically self-effacing, for individuals do not stand out in the galaxy of stars at Ilion like the nebulae of Sam Colt in Hartford, came back the reply:

OFFICE OF REMINGTON'S ARMORY
Ilion, New York, June 25, 1862
SIR: We have your favor of the 20th instant, addressed to one Mr. S. Remington, and, in reply, have to say that we have no objection to your using our name, as suggested, in your report to the Secretary of War in connexion with the manufacturing of Springfield muskets, &c.
We are, very respectfully, your obedient servants,
E. REMINGTON & SONS

Though Eliphalet Remington III penned the letter, not a hint of personal achievement or setting one brother above another was permitted to issue from Ilion's new armory buildings. The oldest gunmaker in America was determined that the firm should continue,

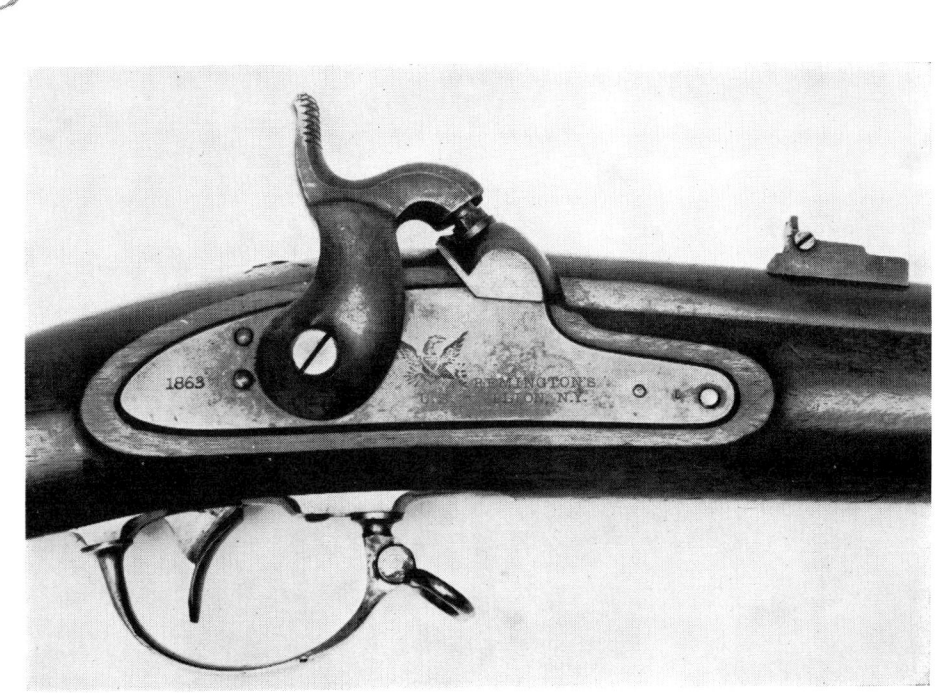

Detail of Remington "Harpers Ferry" rifle shows similarity of lock and cone seat to M1841; rest of rifle was finished like U.S. M1855. First delivered were five-groove rifling; later were three-groove. Sight is type found on Whitney militia rifles. Design probably was originated for Southern order.

not dependent upon the glamor of a single person. Come in with the low dollar and produce up to a maximum standard of quality—then the Springfield Rifled Musket—came to be a sort of trade mark of the Remington line henceforth.

The contracts given were confirmed, and the Remingtons entered into new contracts during the war. Sureties on these documents are George Tuckerman and H. H. Fish—their names may be significant on any Remington arms. One Abraham Fish is listed as an early village officer, "poundmaster" of Ilion. Possibly Henry H. Fish was of his family, though in 1862 of Utica. The tabulation of contracts is as follows:

Contract	Delivered
13 June 1862	
5,000 Navy revolvers cal. 36 @ $12.	4,000 (plus 8,251)
13 June 1862	
20,000 Army revolvers cal. .44 @ $12. Of these, 5,000 were to be of the first model already deposited; the 15,000 "after a pattern to be deposited."	12,505 (5,102; 14,402) March 31, 1862—June 22, 1863
11 August 1862	
10,000 "Harpers Ferry" rifles with sword bayonets @ $17.	10,001—April 18, 1863—January 8, 1864
6 July 1863	
"All the army .44 revolvers they can deliver within the present year (i. e., until December 31, 1863) @ $12."	13,908—July 8, 1863—November 10, 1863
21 November 1863	
64,900 army revolvers cal. .44 @ $12.	62,003—November 23, 1863—December 31, 1864
13 December 1863	
2,500 "Harper's Ferry" rifles with sword bayonets @ $17.	2,500
14 December 1863	
40,000 Springfield rifle muskets with appendages at $18 (not $16)	40,000—May 31, 1864—May 24, 1866
24 October 1864	
15,000 Remington breech-loading carbines at $23	15,000—September 30, 1864—May 24, 1866
24 October 1864	
20,000 Army revolvers cal. .44, same as the 64,900 delivered, but at $15.50	20,000— January 12, 1865—March 23, 1865

To final payments in May of 1866 for arms contracted for and delivered during the war, Remington received a total of $2,837,332.26.

Of 12,251 Navy revolvers delivered and paid for, most were accepted at the $15 original price and renegotiated $12 contract price. But a few were taken with blemishes or minor defects not functional in nature, at $11. Of 114,513 Army revolvers of both types accepted, most were paid for at $12; a few at $11.82. While condemned work was not common at Remington's, it did exist. Uncle Sam paid out $1,191.65 in labor of Government inspectors for examining pistols at Remington that were not accepted by the Government. A rejection rate of less than 1 per cent is a commendable record under those conditions; about $1 an arm was budgeted for the labor of Government inspection.

Possibly as many as 5,100 of the first or "Beals Model" Army .44's were delivered; 4,250 at $12 on contract and 850 earlier at $15.0368(!). Immediately after that, a lot of 502 Army revolvers is listed (December 31, 1862. This doubtless included two sample revolvers of the second series of 15,000 new model to complete the first confirmed contract of 20,000 pieces. While the Navy revolvers never achieved great production, only about 5,000 of each of several patterns being made, the Army .44's topped 140,000 in quantity with sales being made through Schuyler, Hartley & Graham and other firms to the trade and to military men who preferred to own their handguns. Most of these pistols were full blued finish with varnished walnut grips for commercial sale and plain oiled dark walnut, with the inspector's stamps on each plate, for the military arms. Sub-inspectors' initials also appear on minor parts, typically on the frame near the barrel and on the barrel flat at that point; also on the cylinder near one shoulder.

Four Basic Remington Handguns

Collectors confuse terminology slightly because of dates in describing these revolvers. There are four basic Civil War Remington handguns; of the second pattern there are again two variations, tabbed generally "1861" and "New Model 1863"; in all, six distinctly different handguns in two calibers, .36 and .44. The name of inventor Fordyce Beals is attached to these guns, all made under his basic "Beals Patent September 14, 1858," as it is usually stamped along the barrel top flat. This patent applied to the use of the hinged lever as a retainer for the cylinder pin. Beals could not patent the solid frame of his revolver, certainly its most important practical feature. Colt in 1850 had anticipated solid frame patents by making and claiming in shadowy fashion some Dragoons modified with top straps and hinges on the barrels top and bottom. But a solid frame,

Symbolizing the role of Remington in arming the North is photo of original nickle and ivory-handle New Model .44 laid across Civil War map of Union successes. Pistol is in collection of and photo by Don Simmons.

Fordyce Beals developed tiny solid frame revolver before war that had screw-in barrel and cylinder pin taken out from front. Shown is original outfit in cardboard box with mould, flask, loading plunger. Handle is "gutta percha."

as in the sidehammer 1855 series of Colt pocket pistols, meant the cylinder pin had to be withdrawn somehow. Colt's cylinder pin was removed from the back; ergo, Beals removed his from the front of the frame. There was no patentable distinction in this detail; Beals was but following his mentor, Eli Whitney Jr., once Colt's partner (in the Walker pistol contract), and soon thereafter Colt's competitor in the pistol business. It was Whitney who set up the basic solid frame which Beals later used in his Remington arms; and Whitney's first solid frame guns, much like the Colt in outline but with the important innovation of grip straps in one piece with the frame, also had pins that removed from the front, below the barrel. Whitney did not achieve a good loading lever with this combination; hence his arms were not successful as percussion guns.

Beals joined the lever to the base pin; it was held in the frame by means of a cross screw through the frame below the barrel. He then modified this to use a T-head pin, locked into place by the butt end of the loading lever when latched up. The lever was independently hinged and, when dropped, the pin could be pulled forward to free the cylinder. It was this basic construction, using a somewhat simplified single action lockwork, that grew into the Beals Remington Army and Navy revolver after a diversionary and diverting but highly impractical series of pocket revolvers with external cylinder turning hands and jazzy new fangled gutta-percha grips.

These big pistols were heralded to the trade as "A New And Superior Revolver" in a brochure of 1857. Though Major Hagner wanted "all he could get for the western army" they did not catch on commercially and when Sam Remington went to Washington, it was to sell these guns to the Ordnance Department.

A sale to the State of South Carolina of 1,000 Remington revolvers in 1860 is recorded (C. L. Karr, Jr., *Remington Handguns*). Karr notes it as "Beals .44(?)." Remington informed Judge Holt they had turned down trade orders from the South after November, 1860. A contract offered by Jefferson Davis to Remington to make "5,000 rifles for the State of Mississippi, in November, 1860 . . . was also peremptorily declined." Meanwhile, the Beals loading lever in production on the big solid frame .36 and .44 revolvers was soon to be shelved in favor of an improved lever, designed by Wm. H. Elliott. Beals, who had come to Remington's in 1846 in connection with the Jenks carbine contract, evidently possessed general mechanical skill. He may have remained as a superintendent or subcontractor within the Remington Armory on pistols, but Elliott's design supplanted his in the lever-pin arrangement.

The Elliott lever was more symmetrical in form, not square but streamlined in a curve beneath the barrel. The solid frame was basic Beals-Whitney, from the inventor's tenure of service in working out a special revolver for Whitney in 1854. But the T-headed cylinder pin was shaped to fit on either side of the top of the lever, which itself was cut away slightly to permit

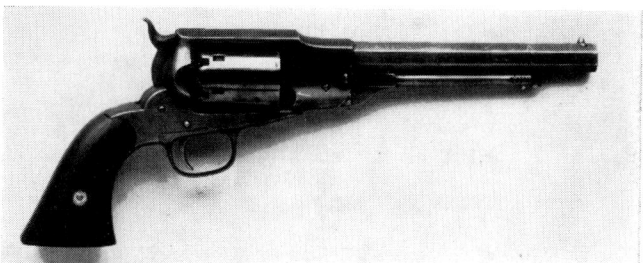

Beals type pistol is distinguished by frame covering back of barrel and square shank of loading lever. Arm was sold to Union in .36 and .44 sizes, identical in design but differing in size.

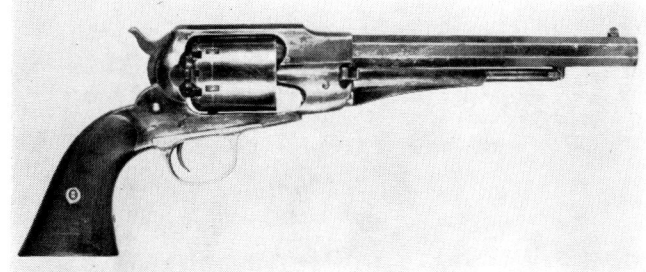

New Model .44 was introduced about 1863 at new reduced prices. Remington sold handguns lower than most other contractors. Full blue finish. Specimen shown has inspection stamp of Major James Hagner on grip.

pulling the pin forward. This allowed dropping the cylinder without unhinging the lever. It would have an advantage in reloading on horseback, using a freshly-loaded spare cylinder. Both Beals' 1858 and Elliott's 1861 revolvers had cylinders without the safety-stop notches introduced on the third "New Model" pattern.

The pin that could be withdrawn without dropping the lever was not such a good idea. Although two pistols apparently of this pattern were supplied as models along with a delivery of 500 arms on December 31, 1862, the design was very soon modified to prevent entirely the slipping forward of the pin unless the lever was hinged down. Too commonly the pin would jump forward from recoil inertia, jamming cylinder rotation and causing a stoppage of firing. Elliott's design to ease out the cylinder was not a success. The odd result of this was the abandonment of the only patented feature on Remington's big military handguns and the delivery throughout the war of almost a hundred and a half thousand first-class firearms featuring details which were all in the public domain!

Details distinguishing between these three types and two calibers are:

Beals M1858

    Front sight: dovetail, brass or German silver cone.
    Frame, solid, shrouds barrel threads completely.
    Loading lever: Square at back end with web of streamline form connecting it to loading plunger. Must be dropped to withdraw T-head cylinder pin.
    Cylinder: Smooth, no safety notches, nipple cuts narrow as seen from side.
    Calibers: .36 and .44.
    Barrel: Octagon, 8-inch in Army, 7½-inch in Navy. Marked BEALS PATENT SEPT. 14, 1858 MANUFACTURED BY REMINGTON'S ILION NEW YORK.

Elliott M1861

    Front sight: dovetail, brass or German silver cone.
    Frame: Solid, transitional, may expose threads of barrel end, or may be flush with face of cylinder.
    Loading lever: Web runs forward to reenforce beneath cut-out rear section where cylinder pin rides when drawn forward. T-head cylinder pin specially grooved to slide over lever.
    Cylinder: Smooth; no safety notches.
    Calibers: .36 and .44.
    Barrel: Octagon, 8-inch in Army, 7½-inch in Navy. Marked: PATENTED DEC. 17, 1861. MANUFACTURED BY REMINGTON'S ILION N. Y.

New Model 1863

    Front sight: Iron blade cut by scooping sides of a cylindrical piece which is screwed into place; not dovetailed.
    Frame: Solid, does not shroud barrel threads.
    Loading lever: Must be dropped to pull T-head cylinder pin forward. No slot in cylinder pin head.
    Cylinder: Smooth. Safety notch between each chamber for nose of hammer to rest when chambers are capped. Nipple cut-outs seem wider when viewed from side.
    Calibers: .36 and .44.
    Barrel: Octagon, 8-inch in Army, 7½-inch in Navy (sometimes 7 3/8-inches, perhaps cause for government inspection rejection?). Marked: PATENTED SEPT. 14, 1858. E. REMINGTON & SONS, ILION, NEW YORK, U.S.A. NEW MODEL.

While the detail differences noted above caused patent claims to come and go, the major improvement in the Remington system was the manufacturing economy. Remington's claimed they could make the Colt gun as cheaply as their own; in this they were not mistaken, but made a boast not strictly true. The Colt construction with major groups: barrel with lever, cylinder, lock frame, AND back strap and trigger guard, represents more machine and set-up time than the simple slabbed Remington barrel plus lever, forged frame of shape encompassing both handle straps that were separate pieces on the Colt, and the non-engraved cylinder. Remington made one part do what Colt used three parts for, and by reason of the advanced state of machine technology, drawing from Colt's the lessons learned in producing the more archaic pattern, Remington built the more "modern" handgun at a less price. Although there were noncritical areas inside the Remington frame for hasty manufacture, such contours as the grip straps fore and aft were closely controlled; Remington-make replacement handles from century-old war surplus storehouses fit snappily and accurately to old Remington frames. Remington likewise joined the cylinder stop bolt and trigger onto the one pin or screw, instead of staggering them on two screws as in the Colt

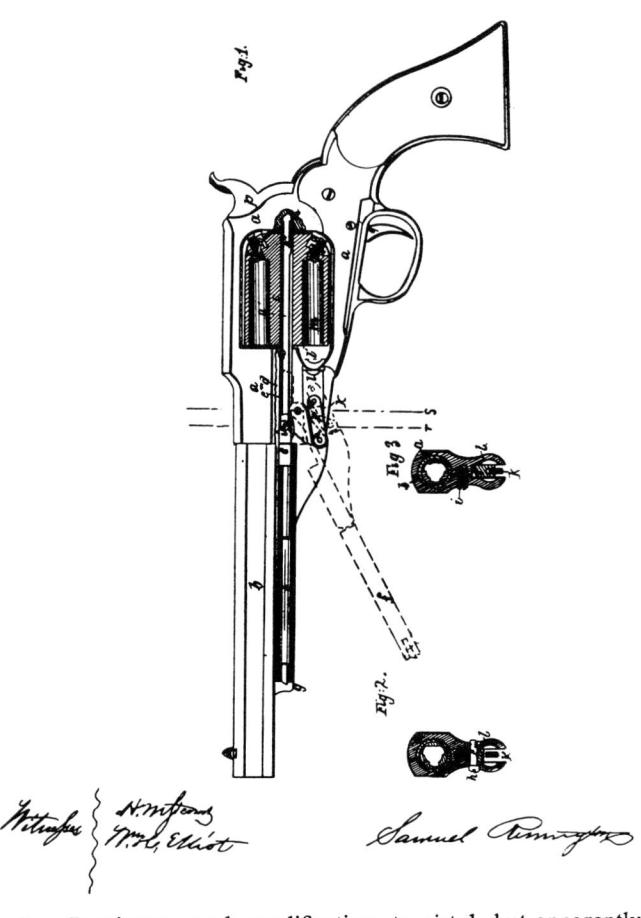

Sam Remington made modifications to pistols but apparently this improvement of loading lever-cylinder pin linkage was not produced. Patent No. 37921 dated March 17, 1863, pictured Beals Navy revolver as model.

Split-breech carbine is shown with block partially rolled back. Arm was contracted for by Sam Norris but not actually delivered until after war. With Rider's improvements, design became famous Remington Rolling Block single shot.

frame. Not patentable, these simplicities greatly reduced cost, made the quiet and unassuming Ilion gunmakers still challengers in quality and price.

Geiger's Rolling Block

While Beals had his brief day at Remington, and Elliott remained to prepare cartridge designs of variant novelty, the greatest man at the Ilion forge outside of the firm's founder was to be Leonard M. Geiger. Hatch does not indicate where Geiger came from. Gluckman and Satterlee list a V. Geiger in Towanda, Pennsylvania, in the "late flintlock period," say 1830. Conceivably this could have been a forebear of Leonard Geiger, the man who invented the famous Remington Rolling Block single-shot rifle and pistol breech mechanism.

In its perfected form the rolling block system appeared markedly modified by Remington engineer Joseph Rider. But as the pioneer gets the credit for opening the wilderness, not the man who builds the homes, so Geiger it is who should reap the credit for this milestone in musket making: the rolling block system.

Geiger's breech system had a hinged block that swung up and down behind the chamber. The frame was L shaped, with the foot of the L upright into which the barrel screwed. Hung in this was the rolling breechblock, and the hammer which supported it in the fired position. The hammer in Geiger's original design acted directly to lock the block, and was shrouded inside the rear curve of the block; hence the modern cognomen "split breech Remington." It was this pattern of breechloader that Remington proffered to the Government; Leonard Geiger did not have the distinction of even obtaining a patent directly upon it. The carbines made under Dyer's contract with Remington's agent Samuel Norris of Springfield, on 24 October 1864 were marked on the breech tang: REMINGTON'S ILION, N. Y. PAT. DEC. 23, 1863, MAY 9 & NOV. 16, 1864. Joseph Rider had refined the Geiger design and patented it, all in the name of Remington Arms, of course, December 8, 1863, No. 40,887, reissued May 3, 1864, No. 1663, and Patent No. 54,123 of November 15, 1864. Chambered for the .56-.50 Spencer rimfire cartridge, 14,999 Geiger split-breech carbines were shipped out of Ilion beginning with 1,000 delivered September 30, 1864, up to May 24, 1866. An additional 5,000 similar carbines in caliber .46 rimfire were delivered between March 30 and June 30, 1865. The .56-.50s were at contract price of $23; for the last 5,000 Eli Remington dropped the price to only $17.

Remington's War Contribution

But it was not carbines, but rifles and muskets of the more conventional form, on which Remington's contribution to the Union cause must stand. It was on the Harpers Ferry modified, sometimes called "1862 Remington rifle" and the Springfields at $17, that Remington in causing prices to fall all along the line made his presence felt.

First came the famous Zouave rifles. Though most Zouave regiments went into battle in 1861 and 1862

Rider also designed double action system applied to Navy frame of "New Model" characteristics. First issue had fluted cylinders; later type were round, caliber .36. Cased sets were popular with officers in the field.

with foreign arms or transformed Springfields, the title "Zouave rifle" has clung to this special weapon. It is much like the elegant French "Chasseurs de Vincennes" rifle in style and bright brass trim, so the name is apt if the association is not. Actual issue of the special Remingtons is not properly documented at this writing; a suspiciously large number of them seem to have found their way in brand new condition to the shops of Liege in the post-war trade, there to become bored smooth for shot and shipped out to Africa or South America at prices cheaper than junk guns cost to make. Like so many others of the special or limited issue weapons ordered in the first days of the war, they may have served most of the time reposing quietly in their arms chests, awaiting a call to duty that never came. Exactly 10,001 of these rifles and sword bayonets complete were delivered between April 18, 1863, and January 8, 1864. Though the contract price was $17, nearly 10 per cent were accepted only as arms of the second class at $16.90. The second contract for 2,500 rifles apparently was to insure acceptance of rifles otherwise forfeited by reason of failure of the contractor to deliver in time, as provided by the confirmed contract for 10,000. The extra rifle is inferentially the model arm held by the inspector at the New York Ordnance office.

More important were the 40,000 Springfields. In production Remington experienced difficulty in meeting the Government standards. Of the total delivered between May 31, 1864 and March 24, 1866, 326 were accepted only as 4th class arms, and a considerable number of each delivery, again about 10 per cent, were taken as arms not equal to the standard, and at lower prices.

In spite of Hagner's haggling over the values of muskets, Remington's did not exactly suffer from want of work during the war. Once, back in 1835-40, the entire machine shop of the Remington works comprised one turning lathe, one stocking, and four milling machines; the fixtures and tools had to be changed about as occasion demanded.

Now, a great corporation had emerged from the fires of war. Incorporated under the laws of New York, with capital stock owned by the Remingtons, and Philo's son-in-law, W. C. Squires, save for a few hundred shares to qualify local citizens as board members, E. Remington & Sons, Inc. took its place in the world January 1, 1865. Philo Remington was of course president, go-getter Samuel vice president, and Eli secretary and treasurer.

During the war, production of 3,000 revolvers a month had been achieved. Soon after the close of war, the Remington Rolling Block rifle proved a ready seller in the hands of Samuel Remington, who was elected president to give him more prestige in traveling through the war ministries of the world. Five years after the war ended and hard times seemed to settle upon the country, E. Remington & Sons, Inc., and 1,400 workmen labored two shifts 20 hours at 400 milling machines to produce a *daily* sustained total of ONE THOUSAND FIVE HUNDRED THIRTY RIFLES, tallying 155,000 rifles shipped to one customer (France) between May and September, 1870. Whether flintlock or pill-lock or percussion, whether lap welded or spiraled around a mandrel, whether tested by surprise at a bear or at a target match, or on a deer, Lite Remington's little rifle had scored a bullseye in America's history.

Remington assembler learned to fit parts from studying cutaway revolver (above). At right, pair of New Model Remington .44s and case were in baggage of Confederate President Jefferson Davis when seized at Irwin, Georgia, during flight from Richmond. Remingtons served both sides, though Davis' pistols were U.S. inspected, C.S. captured.

Davis' pistols photo courtesy New Market (Va.) Battlefield Military Museum.

CHAPTER 17

The Starr Rises

From the catalog of Wallis and Wallis, British gun auctioneers (1962) at Lewes in Sussex, we read of the sale of a Starr revolver:

Lot 1060 . . . A 6 shot .44 Starr SA Army Perc Rev 14", brl 8", No. 51594, the top strap bearing old engraving "Col. Colt Address New York," Good Condition but action As Found & frame screw not orig.

Eben T. Starr of Yonkers, New York, might not have smiled at this latter day whimsey. Marking his revolver with the name of the man he dared challenge by launching a new revolving pistol business in 1858 was to him not funny. Though the modern gun bug who fraudulently marked this in the hope someone would "bite" on it as a hitherto unknown Colt double action revolver we trust was unsuccessful in his piracy, perhaps the buyer at the Wallis and Wallis auction cherishes his purchase for what it is: one of the best and most "modern" revolvers of the Civil War era. Though complex inside at first glance, its parts are well thought out and reveal Starr as an exceptionally gifted inventor.

To generations of gun collectors who pored over Bannerman's catalogs, Starr is best known as the proprietor of a factory subsequently taken over by a mysterious merchant known only as "Jones of Binghamton. He Pays The Freight." Few have bothered to find out who Jones was, but history should do better by Starr. His double action revolver was a rugged and successful handgun; his breech-loading percussion carbine resembling the Sharps was a distinct improvement upon that famous arm. Adapted later to cartridge, the Starr carbine had leverage in closing to make it chamber even dented ammunition in a dirty gun. But with the flood of surplus arms, the westward expansion away from sources of metallic ammunition and business recessions attacking the fortunes of firms not otherwise diversified, Starr folded, and Jones stepped in. While active, Starr gave Colt a run for his money and produced thousands of good arms that saw battle and were of great value to the North.

Starr's First Patents

Starr in 1856 obtained his first patent. Though the drawings illustrate a pepperbox firearm, the patent date was to be stamped on the frame right side below the cylinder of all Starr revolvers: STARR'S PATENT JAN. 15, 1856. The claims referred to two features unique with Starr. First, the actual trigger was but a stub behind a "lifter lever" of form similar to our accepted idea of trigger shape today. The sear was one end of the trigger, and the construction is somewhat like the modern Harrington & Richardson or Iver Johnson separate sear behind the "lifter lever" trigger. Secondly, the lifter lever had a sliding piece on its rear curve to restrict the motion at will of the shooter. It could be set to permit continued firing by straight-through double action, or it would allow the lifter to raise the hammer to full cock and then the stub of a trigger could be pulled by a firm and steady single-action pull. This mechanism is little understood by the modern collector for two reasons: good manners and a desire to avoid battering the percussion cones denies the modern Starr owner a chance to try out his gun by snapping it and, secondly, seldom is the sliding lifter piece working easily.

Starr's second patent No. 30843, issued December 4, 1860, illustrated the perfected type of Starr double-action revolver, the .36 Navy size.

Starr assigned his two patents plus a further patent on the breech-loading carbine to a group of New York financiers headed by H. H. Woolcott and Everett Clapp. The former was president of the Starr Arms Company, while Clapp was treasurer. T. B. Stout was secretary; in addition, the group including Starr and one more, F. J. Clark, formed the trustees of the patents. As sureties on some of their contracts with the United States, John Mack of New York signed as a "freeholder with property valued at over $40,000." The syndicate by the spring of 1862 had paid Starr $200,000 for the patents and an added $90,000 as commission or salary for his employment in perfecting the mechanical aspects of the design.

The first factory was at Binghamton, and by 1858 Starr had begun to deliver guns.

"We had only made one thousand for the Government in 1858," declared Treasurer Clapp before the War Contracts Commission on April 10, 1862, "and five hundred for the trade," prior to August of 1861. These arms were .36 caliber double-action types of the form patented in 1860.

First Contracts

By August of 1861, the Starr Armory in Binghamton employed 225 men and represented an investment in machinery of $140,000. At this time a somewhat enlarged version of the in-production Navy revolver was prepared as a prototype for the Government's approval and forwarded to Washington:

NEW YORK, *August 31, 1861*

The Starr Arms Company, located at Binghamton, New York, propose and agree to deliver to the United States Government *twelve thousand* (12,000) of their *army pistols,* like sample herewith submitted, with the appendages, consisting of bulletmould, screw-driver, and cone-wrench to each pistol, for *twenty five dollars* each . . .

Clapp set forth the schedule of delivery, 500 each month October through December, and 1,000 thereafter until June when all deliveries were to be complete. Though from that October the Binghamton plant went on night shift, they did not make their deadlines.

In September Starr proposed to increase the order to 20,000 and offered to reduce the price to $23. Ripley was directed by Cameron to use his judgment. Conservatively, though the Union needed arms, he made the contract for only 12,000. On February 5, 1862 the first 1,000 were delivered of the new double action Army .44. An additional 600 were delivered to inspecting officer R. H. K. Whiteley on 24 February.

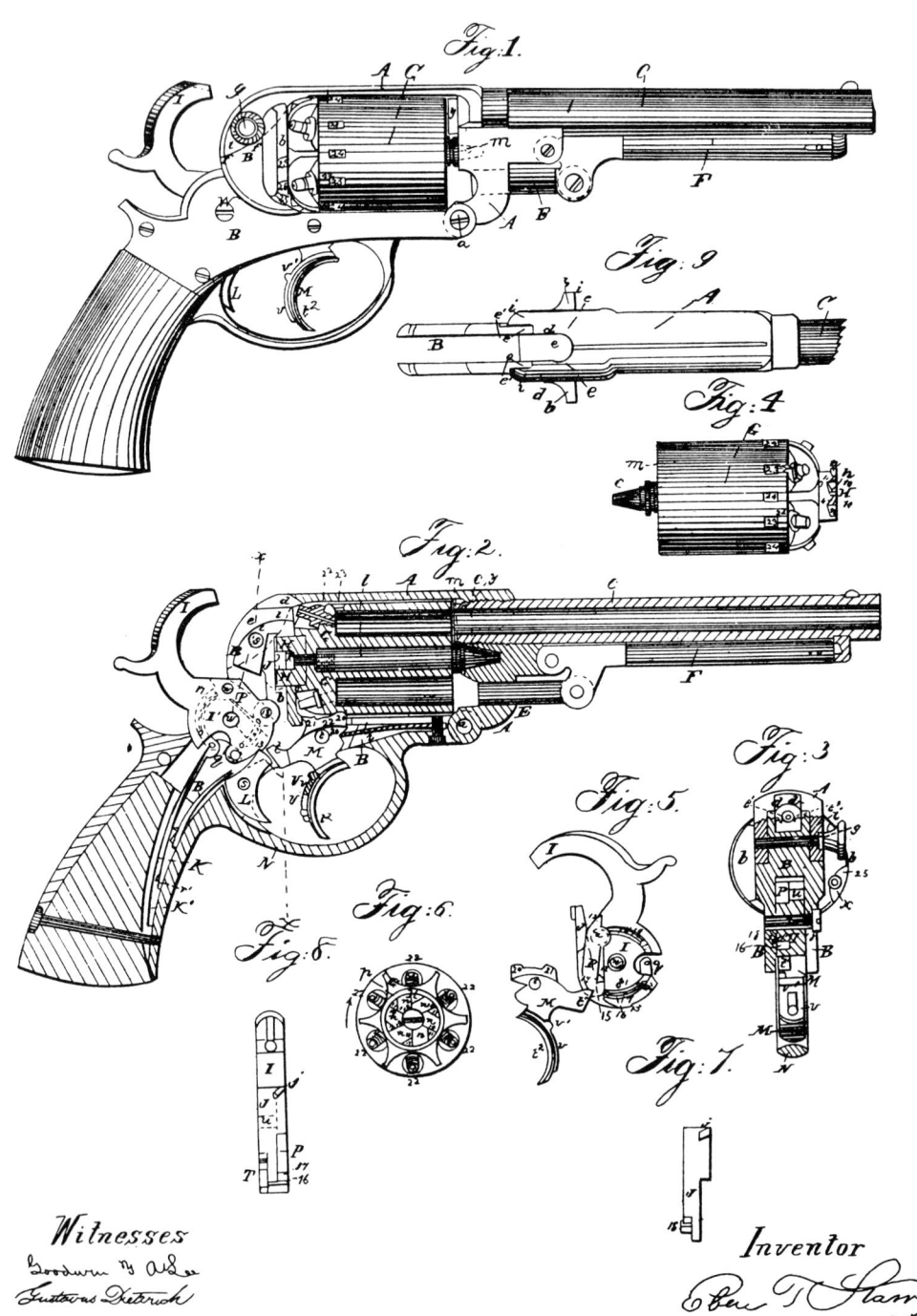

Starr's first produced revolver was .36 caliber of hybrid double-and-single action. Barrel frame detail of curved section near hinge is immediate distinction between large-framed .36 and .44's which were introduced soon after. Fouling was reduced by cylinder pin integral at front with cylinder itself.

Among deliveries on first contract for 20,000 DA .44's was this specimen in new condition, No. 6596, preserved at West Point Museum. Case-hardened colored frame is unusual on Starr revolvers, suggests either special order or old Government refinishing.

While Starr was working under the extended contract which Ripley oddly issued on January 11, 1862 at the full price of $25 though he increased the number to 20,000 pieces, Whiteley did not pay for the guns. The order of Secretary Stanton suddenly clamped down and even though these guns had been inspected and bore the stamps of the inspecting officers on the sides of the wood stock, Starr's money men were whistling for their $40,000.

President Woolcott stepped into the fray and presented a polite and reasoned appeal to the Commissioners that had much weight. He described their enterprise as one of the largest armories in the country, being specific in saying that "the armory in Binghamton is employed exclusively in the manufacture of pistols." To fulfill expectations concerning a contract for carbines, and a hoped-for order of rifle muskets, a second armory had been erected rapidly in Yonkers at great cost, in spite of frost and bad weather. At Yonkers, the carbine and musket factory of Starr, "the extent (of this works) is exceeded only by the Colt establishment, in Hartford." In detailing both failures to deliver revolvers and noting actual arms they did deliver, Mr. Clapp testified:

> We were not ready to deliver in October (1861), but we sold to Major Hagner, in New York, 500, navy size, at $20, in that month. We also sold in like manner, 250, navy size, in November, and in the same month we sold 250, navy size, to the agent of Ohio. We have delivered and received certificates for 1,000, army size, in January; 600, army size in February; 1,400, army size, in March, and we notified the department that we had 1,000 ready for inspection March 28 or 29. The department immediately sent inspectors, who are now (April 10, 1862) at work.

The fact that .36 caliber arms predominantly were bought in 1858 (such purchases as the Adams revolvers of Massachusetts Arms Company and the Colt Navy pistol carbines for Dragoons), together with the explicit separate mention of "army size" in Treasurer Clapp's testimony, leads us to believe that the .44 double-action Starr was preceded in manufacture by the .36. The .44 apparently did not come along until the offer to Ripley was tendered together with a sample; it seems that had the sample been identical to those formerly made for the Government, Ripley would have mentioned it in his order to further be explicit as to the arms desired. It was the quantity above referred to by Clapp which, inspected but not yet received and paid for, by Hagner, was causing Starr Arms Company such embarrassment.

Starr also obtained a contract for 10,000 breech-loading carbines (his patent No. 21,523 of 14 September 1858) on November 27, 1861, to meet the "exigencies of our cavalry service," price $29. With expansion into the shoulder arm manufacture now assured, Wolcott again sought for further orders and was granted a contract along with others on December 24, to furnish 50,000 Springfield rifle muskets at $20. The Binghamton works being taxed to the utmost in revolver manufacture, Starr Arms Company erected a sizable works in Yonkers where they "proposed to make the whole Springfield gun, including the barrel." Large orders were given to machinery firms.

"We will make barrels from steel rods" said Wolcott, declaring that one set of barrel machinery was already in operation on carbine work and another ordered from Hewes & Phillips of Newark, New Jersey. Lysander Wright of Newark was preparing a full set of stock turning machinery, which Starr was committed to accept; one set of four eccentric lathes and shapers was already in the carbine factory, but it "turns out the work so that it requires more hand work than the Springfield musket machines ought to do." For the Springfield rifle work as well as carbine parts, Starr contracted for 130 milling machines; 40 from Springfield contractors Parker, Snow Brooks & Company of Meriden, Connecticut, 20 from the Fishkill Landing Company and 50 from Putnam Machine Company. Twenty millers were already at work in the carbine factory, obtained from Parker, Snow Brooks & Company. The revolvers cost, laid down at the factory, between $14 and $15, nearly twice as much as Colt's revolvers; the Springfields, including interest on investment, wear and tear, in Wolcott's experience would come to about $17.

"Should the order for carbines be filled, we could turn all our stock, machinery &c. to work upon the muskets without important loss. We are arms makers, have all our capital so engaged, and expect to continue in the business, having been at it now (April 15, 1861) for three years. We therefore must seek this kind of work, even if the Government do not employ us," Wolcott explained to the Commissioners.

Adverse Action by Commissioners

When Stanton called a screeching halt to the war contracts, for Holt and Owen to examine them, Ripley recognized that a severe dislocation in the arms business and in his sources of supply would occur. He at once requested permission from Stanton to continue to receive all the arms outstanding under certain orders and contracts for a period of three months. During this time Holt and Owen could examine the facts and by the end of this time through either affirming or denying the contracts, bring order into the chaos. But the names which Ripley gave to Stanton in his letter of 15 March, 1861, did not include Starr. Colt's, Sharps, J. T. Ames for cannon and swords, Knapp, Rudd & Company at Pittsburgh for shells, R. P. Parrott at West Point for heavy guns, and Cyrus Alger in Boston for field artillery, were the firms listed as "regular manufacturers for this department" and from whom Ripley wished special orders permitting receipt under existing contracts for arms during the next three months unless specially revoked.

The failure to mention Starr in the list worked against them before in their dealings with the Commissioners. Perhaps most telling against them was Major Hagner, who willingly bought their pistols in the open market but denied them the right to continue uninterruptedly, on the grounds that his chief had noted they were not "regular manufacturers."

The price of $20 for Navy .36 double action revolvers which Starr sold to Hagner and the agent for Ohio also worked against them. The Major suggested to Wolcott that he make some proposal for reducing their commitments for arms. Since the Springfield rifle musket preparations were less advanced, they could the easiest be disposed of, and the existing or to be delivered machinery put into the Yonkers works. Wolcott made the proposal that the increase to 20,000 on the pistol order be confirmed and he would reduce the price to $20; the carbine contract for 10,000 pieces at $29 be confirmed, and he would therefore surrender hi rights under the Springfield musket order, diverting th materials to the carbine fulfillment. Judge Holt ⸺me back with a further reduction, and the Commissi ⸺'s decision stood at not more than 15,000 revolvers, at $20, and the 10,000 carbines, at $29.

In explaining his decision to Secretary Stanton, Holt pointed out that the claim for payment at the rate of $25 each for the 1,600 inspected but not accepted revolvers had to be considered as within the scope of the Commission's decision, and therefore the bill at $25 was disallowed and payment made at the $20 rate thenceforth.

The record reveals actual deliveries and payments as follows:

> October 15, 1861, 500 Navy revolvers purchased at $20.
> November 19, 1861, 500 Navy revolvers purchased at $20.
> December 18, 1861, 250 Navy revolvers purchased at $20 (for State of Ohio).
> Army revolvers at $25 were accepted and paid for as follows:
> February 22, 1862, 1,000 Army revolvers contract at $25.
> March 25, 1862, 600 Army revolvers contract at $25.
> March 25, 1862, 1,400 Army revolvers contract at $25.

First Deliveries

First deliveries of the double-action revolver "costing twice as much as Colt's" at the renegotiated price of $20 began on June 25, 1862, with a minimum shipment of 1,200 pieces as per Holt and Owen's order. Unexplained is a drop in delivery rate to 500 on January 13, 1863, the preceding lot of 1,300 having been accepted two months prior on November 26, 1862.

A New Factory

Possibly an expansion of revolver making facilities was begun, transferring the pistol business to the new and enlarged Yonkers, New York factory which had been especially built for them. A delay in production might be expected as work and machines were being set up anew. The new factory was a block-long standard factory building others of which, as shrines to the beginnings of industrial revolution, still stand, often abandoned, in the mill valleys of New England.

Two stories with a heavy machinery ground floor and a skylighted loft for parts storage, the Starr building conformed to the flow of materials patterns of manufactures at that time. Raw stock went in on the ground floor. Centrally located, to equalize friction losses on both sides of the system, was the steam engine which powered overhead shafting. Mounted in ceiling braces, the steel shafts ran outward from the fixture, above the giant flywheel, and from these shafts, slapping in a constant din of flapping leather, the buffalo-hide power belts ran to reducing pulleys at each machine. To start his lathe, the operator shifted a lever which moved the belt sideways from an idler pulley to another of the same dimension, a driving pulley, geared to the lathe. Except for new gray paint, red-lined electrical switches for safety recognition and shields and safety devices not thought necessary in those earlier days of more skilled labor, the scene in the Starr factory might be any job shop of good size of today.

Automation is a fancy new word, but to the handicraft technology of the last century, the fine new Blanchard lathes on their fancy cast iron "Victorian" bird feet and griffon's legs painted a glossy black were miracles of mass production. Even in Wolcott's observations about the suite of four stocking machines for the carbine stocks, which left much handwork for finishing, he implied the sentiment of "automation" when he spoke of a superior and more elaborate set of tools to make the Springfield stocks, without hand labor except for final sanding and oiling.

From the first floor where the heavy drops or forges stood, the parts in their rough state would move up to the machining floors. The top floor had space for final assembly, to use the last of the day's light streaming in the windows. At Starr the gas lights flickered late, to give the second shift equal advantages. A thorough comparison of production problems in 1862 with those of 1962 is hardly possible now, for much ephemeral information is lost; how did the men react to the necessities of a second shift; what were the problems of two ten-hour shifts versus the three-shift eight-hour schedule and did quality suffer from lack of daylight? The four hours when Starr turned down the fires were not moments of idleness; the trouble shooters went in and readjusted the machines, made repairs to worn bearings and cutters, serviced the indispensable steam engine and the belting. Thus was the war won in Yonkers.

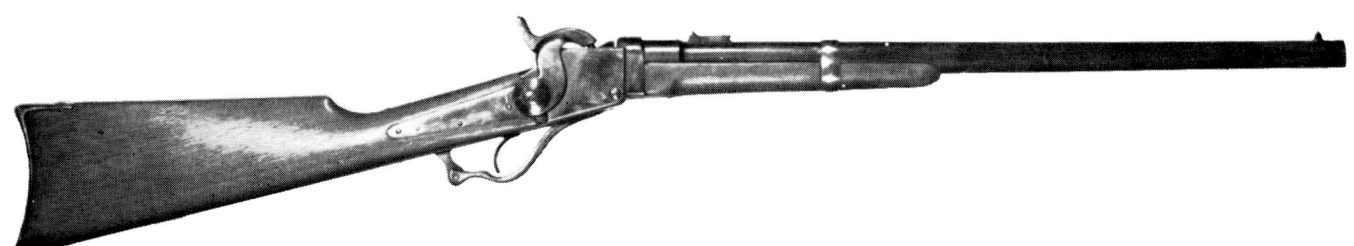

Large modern armory was built by Starr firm in Yonkers to build Springfield Rifle Muskets, but order was not confirmed and plant was phased into production of Starr carbines and revolvers. Shop is typical institutional architecture of period, for hospital, school, or city hall. Materials flow began in forging shops on first floor, ended at assembly room under skylights.

Starr Carbines

Starr had delivered 16,100 Army double-action .44 revolvers when their time ran out, by May 4, 1863. Production was well begun on carbines and the first lot of 600 was received on July 30, 1863, as an open purchase at $25.

These carbines, though at a lower price, had been delivered under the original contract for 10,000 pieces at $29. While parts piled up in the Yonkers armory, Wolcott and Starr Treasurer Stout negotiated anew with Ordnance, signing a contract with General Ramsay September 22, 1863, to deliver 20,000 carbines at $23.50, deliveries to begin in October. Regularly, in lots of 1,000, Starr turned out the guns, delivering the last lot of 1,000 on August 20, 1864. One additional carbine, evidently to use as a model, was delivered September 12, 1863, as a purchase at $25. Total percussion Starr carbines delivered to the United States at all prices, only 20,601.

Price of Revolvers Reduced

With efforts no longer diverted by the musket business, that contract having been surrendered by Wolcott, the Starr Armory turned to the little matter of profit on their revolvers. Starr himself continued to manage the mechanical side of the business and with the double action system costing them twice as much as a single action, Starr turned to a solution. Beginning with a delivery of December 19, 1863, Starr's Army pistols took a sudden drop in price, to $12. Since the cost of the earlier model at the factory, as Everett Clapp testified to Holt and Owen, was between $14 and $15 in

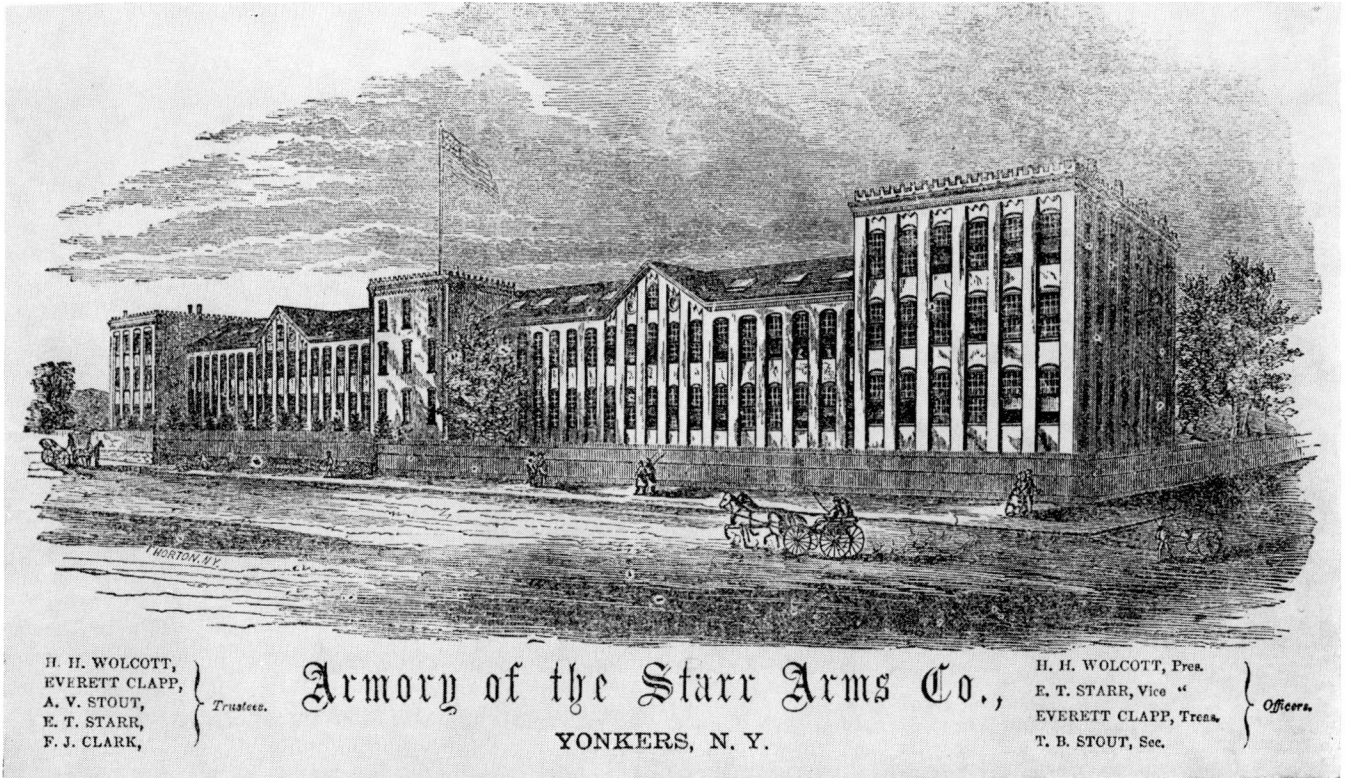

First model percussion carbine had brass band, hammer resembling late type "Union Rifle" part. Breech dropped and tilted back when lever was lowered, then cammed tightly forward on closing to effect gas seal superior to Sharps. Metallic cartridge model was almost identical; the later percussion and cartridge arms had iron bands. Breech and lock were case-hardened, barrel blued.

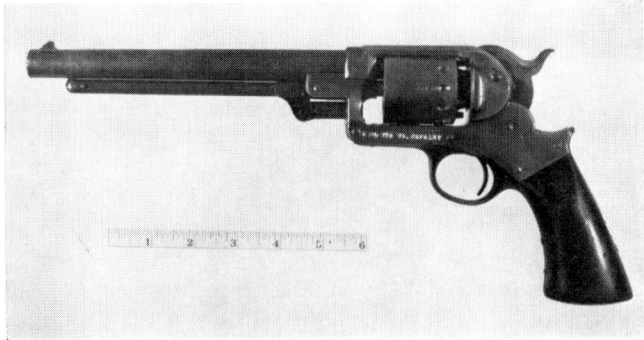

Second Model .44 was single action with 8" barrel to be uniform with Colt's and Remington's arms. The Ordnance obtained 25,000, plus two cutaway inspection models. Specimen shown, from Ed Louer collection (Ill.) is marked "Va. Cavalry," but 77th Regiment is not mentioned in *Official Records* Index.

1862, with no prospect but that of labor, materials, and machinery increasing in price, it is not reasonable to assume Starr was in the business of giving away two-dollar bills with each pistol sold. The price therefore seems conclusively to prove what was first suspected in print by C. Meade Patterson ("Starr's Self-Cocking Revolver," *The Gun Report,* January 1959) that the single action Starr is the succeeding and final model of this revolver. While Gluckman dismisses this second model with "This Army revolver was also made in a single-action model with eight-inch barrel," the pistol referred to was obtained in larger quantity than the double actions. A total of 25,000 were obtained in regular deliveries of 1,000, plus 2 for inspectors' models attached to the delivery of January 24, 1864. Final delivery was December 22, 1864, all under another contract of 22 September 1863. In this document the pattern of pistol is noted as "improved Army pistol" indicating changes from the former. To the Army, the simplification of the rather indeterminate double-or-is-it-single action of the First Model Starr to a more straightforward single action style would be considered

Regular Army .44 DA Starr was full blued on frame as well as barrel and cylinder. Inspector's stamp on both sides of grip denotes acceptance and delivery to the U.S., but some exist having only one grip mark. These may be partially inspected, but not accepted by Hagner's suspending work until Holt and Owen adjudicated the case. Widget slides on false trigger, is means for releasing hammer by pressing against real trigger stub at back of guard.

an improvement. For some years in the collection of E. Page Guilette of Baltimore, Maryland, there reposed a handsome old Starr Second Model Army .44 with the frame cut to reveal the mechanism. It bore full inspector's marks and presumably could have been one of the two arms delivered in January, 1864.

Starr's Accomplishments

Starr's final endeavor for the cause of the Union was the transformation of his percussion carbine design to metallic cartridge. Ordnance gave him a contract 21 February 1865 to furnish 3,000 carbines "adapted to the use of the metallic cartridges as now used in the Spencer carbines," at $20 each carbine. One extra model carbine was delivered March 28, 1865, and another on April 11, 1865. Chief of Ordnance General A. B. Dyer ordered by letter 2,000 carbines at $20, "calibre .52, adapted to the Spencer cartridge," increasing the total of cartridge Starrs to 5,001.

With the final delivery of .52 carbines May 25, 1865, the wheels of the big Yonkers steam engine slowly spun to a halt. Five basic arms had been produced. These were the Navy .36 and Army .44 First Model Double Action; the First Model Percussion Carbine, the Second Model .44 Army Single Action, and the final Cartridge Second Model Carbine. All three revolvers, though they differed in lock work, featured two details of importance. Starr in his 1856 and 1860 patents did not claim the hinged frame and it is incorrect to say that he invented the break-open revolver; if anybody did, it was Colt who in a manner of speaking claimed such a construction in his 1850 Dragoon patents. But the mortising of the top strap to fit over the standing breech, distributing the stresses of firing, was Starr's innovation and claimed by him. It made an exceedingly strong two-piece frame.

Secondly, the construction of the cylinder, with ratchet separate, was not entirely novel, but the form of the ratchet teeth was unique and the fixture of the cylinder pin rigidly in the cylinder, turning in a seat in the frame below the barrel, was also patented. Starr had viewed the Navy as the best market for his pistols at first, and his commercial catalog "With Reports and Recommendations" issued in 1864 reflects their favorable responses. Testing Starr D. A. revolver No. 9002, Lieutenant Commander J. S. Skerrett in March, 1863, praised the unitized center-pin, which prevented fouling inside the central bore of the cylinder, so long a hazard with the Colt design. Colt's had a spiral fouling groove to reduce friction. Others, such as Remington and Beals, had tried to overcome the binding by reducing the diameter of the cylinder pin. Starr instead shut off fouling from the cylinder and permitted it only at the front bearing end of the center pin. To clean this was easy and Commander Skerrett noted how simple it was to unscrew the cross bolt and "break" the pistol to remove the cylinder pin. As one who has shot the Starr a little, however, I feel it is worth noting that the cylinder must be carefully aligned again to permit closing the top strap smartly; otherwise it may hang up in back on the ratchet or frame seat for the ratchet. The design was not to allow switching to fresh loaded cylinders to keep up a volume of fire, but with the hinged lever ramrod (a copy of Colt's of 1847-49 but with button front latch) Skerrett evidently did all right, consuming 5,500 .44 combustible cartridges supplied by the Starr company. He then drew 814 rounds of Navy cartridges for Colt's .44 and shot them up, finally reporting to Admiral Dahlgren that although "The hammer never failed to explode the cap, 22 caps failed to explode the charge. This pistol has stood the test remarkably well, and required no cleaning during the trial." As a fair commentary on the high standards of performance of firearms during the Civil War, it should be noted here that in 1962 the current standard of experimental test for the automatic rifles adopted by the United States Government is that they should fire 6,000 rounds without failure. Starr's revolver, with good percussion caps, meets today's automatic rifle standards.

What Starr Company made up in quality they definitely lacked in salesmanship. No outstanding showman like Sam Colt, no leading international magnate like Hartley, no suave handler of Eastern potentates like Samuel Remington arose to join Starr in the firmament of post-war arms makers. By 1867 the company dissolved, selling the Binghamton plant to scale-maker General Edward F. Jones. General Jones had commanded the Massachusetts regiment that was fired upon by rioters in Baltimore in the early days of the war.

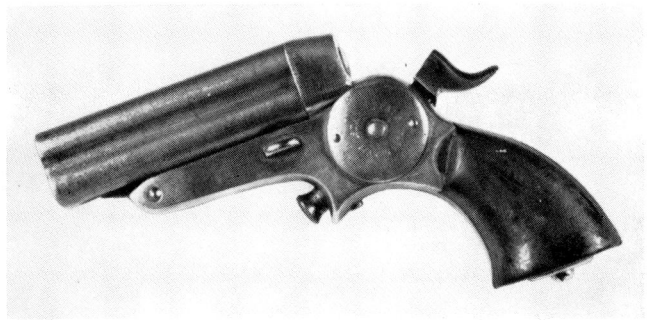

Pocket pistols of Sharps form with improved striker system by Starr were not enough to keep wheels of industry turning at close of war. Gun was closely styled after and competitive to Sharps & Hankins type of 4-barreled "derringer."

Starr revolvers rarely exist in presentation guise, cased and engraved with ivory grips. Silver plated sets are known; one Starr D. A. with a stock fitted as a short rifle exists, possibly factory work though this is doubtful.

While most of the post-war arms sold found their way to France in 1870, some Starrs exist with .44 five-shot cartridge cylinders, transformed in Belgium, it is said for sale to Germany. But the saga of Eben T. Starr winked out when Jones began to pay the freight.

CHAPTER 18

Manhattan Firearms Goes To War

Almost unrecorded is the important part which a company more distinguished for making "copies" of famous guns played in making an original contribution to manufacturing in the North. This firm, the Manhattan Firearms Company, variously of Norwich, Connecticut, and later of Newark, New Jersey, fabricated single-shot pistols and pepperbox arms quite similar in appearance to the Allen guns built by its neighbor firm of Allen & Thurber, of Norwich. Then, with the cessation of Colt's exclusive patent rights in 1857-8, Manhattan turned to manufacturing .31 and .36 percussion revolvers that closely resembled Colt's arms but which contained many patented detail improvements. And lastly, in 1860 Manhattan introduced a 7-shot .22 square butt tip-up revolver which was a dead ringer for the tip-up Smith & Wesson. Though the big octagon-barrelel .36 Manhattans are commonly called "secondary U. S. martial pistols," in that they are the size most to be expected in the hands of troops buying for their own use, the only actual purchase by the Union of Manhattan arms yet traced deals not with the big military-caliber Navy Manhattan revolver, but relates instead to the tiny vest-pocked sized seven shooters!

Confiscated Arms

In September of 1861 the United States surveyor of the Port of New Albany, Indiana, Jacob Anthony, had seized a large quantity of arms as contraband. Among these was a shipment of Manhattan revolvers and ammunition consigned to the company's sales agent, S. H. Harrington at New Albany; 36 revolvers caliber .22.

Governor Oliver P. Morton was frantically sending telegrams to General Ripley and to anyone else who could, he thought, supply his state troops with arms and ammunition. When he learned that Mr. Anthony had a lot of arms, he wired Salmon P. Chase, Secretary of the Treasury, and got Chase's permission to have from Anthony, "all revolvers in his hands not absolutely needed for effective discharge of office duties."

Anthony retained two pistols and 400 cartridges presumably for "office duties" and delivered to Governor Morton 33 pistols. The one pistol different was later the subject of some conjecture, but as there was no record or trace of it the matter was not delved into very deeply. Morton also received 4,600 pistol cartridges. A claim was made against the United States by the Manhattan Firearms Company for $423.80 under the premise that the pistols having been incorrectly seized should be returned or paid for. It was stated that the pistols were sent as samples to Stephen H. Harrington as agent.

"Facts have come to my knowledge which satisfy me beyond all doubt that this box of pistols was never intended for Rebel use, the owners being loyal; and this box was a sample which this agent was using in effecting sales to Union men," reported the United States district attorney John Hanna to Secretary Chase. "I therefore unhesitatingly state that the amount realized by the governor ought, in justice to the claimant and owner, to be paid, as the pistols received in exchange are now in the service of the United States."

While these pistols of Manhattan make were technically "military pistols" by reason of circumstance, Morton was not entirely satisfied with their caliber. "Shortly after they were received, I exchanged them for Navy revolvers, now in the service of the United States," Governor Morton wrote to Chase on December 7, 1861.

In order to obtain redress of this loss, for the pistols had been dispersed by Morton's use and later exchange,

Model IV Manhattan revolver is common version of .36 five-shooter which many collectors look upon as a "secondary martial" pistol. Made from April 1864 to June, 1867, approximately 24,000 of this later variation were sold. The Union did not buy any.

possibly with some Ordnance office, for Navy pistols, Manhattan sought to get payment for the guns. To do this it was necessary for the works manager, Albert Beach, who was at this time also secretary, to make a deposition as to the nature of the guns and their value, which he testified was $378.60.

The money in question did not total millions, but it was dear to the heart of Manhattan's president, Frederick H. Smith of Newark, and he went to Washington to see Mr. Chase upon the matter of settlement. The case had the distinction of being the last one of the many controversial disputes over ordnance and ordnance stores to be brought routinely to Secretary of War Stanton's notice. Following the Manhattan case, No. 7 as it was listed by the Commission on War Claims, Major Hagner issued an informational order, "By direction of the Secretary of War the reports in future are to be addressed to the chief of ordnance for execution, without reference to the War Department." Stanton did not want to be bothered by such favorable reports as the Commissioners sent in: ". . . they find the prices charged are reasonable, and they therefore recommend that this account be paid to the full amount of the claim, $423.80."

Imitations of a Smith & Wesson

These little pistols, the only ones which can lay claim to having been (so far as is presently known) officially purchased by the United States, were not the only arms made by Manhattan. But they were among the most controversial. They are substantial imitations of Smith & Wesson's First Model of 1858, and are of a bored-through cylinder construction to be considered an infringement of the famous Rollin White patent. Of a number of firearms fabricants brought into the courts by the litigious Rollin White in protecting his patent rights assigned to Smith & Wesson, Manhattan was the only firm to make an almost literal copy. Other arms such as the Moore which resembled the Colt pocket model, infringed in a detail of construction; a cylinder bored to load at the rear end for cartridges. But Manhattan was not named directly though was an indirect party in an action brought by White against Herman Boker.

Boker had apparently wanted to secure an agency for the main "big" companies of the time, for United States and possibly for foreign sales. But although he sold Uncle Sam over two million dollars worth of guns, only 22 were United States make: Sharps carbines. Of revolvers, he sold but 52 Lefaucheux revolvers to the Government in five years. Waldo E. Nutter, author of the comprehensive volume *Manhattan Firearms*, conjectures that Boker was "hurting" because he didn't have a good line of handguns to sell, and that soon after the Manhattan Company was organized in 1855 by a group of New York and New Jersey industrialists, he sought them out and signed them up with him as New York agent. When Smith & Wesson brought out their first cartridge revolver, it was phenomenally successful but Boker, familiar with the European market, was in Nutter's opinion convinced that the Rollin White patent was a fraud. He knew of a host of continental revolvers loading their cylinders at the back end and believed that White had no patent of value. "We suspect that Boker was influential in the initial decision to manufacture the .22-caliber revolvers," says Nutter.

Beginning in 1859, Manhattan moved their office to Boker's address at 50 Cliff Street, New York. Some of the first of the little cartridge pistols which Boker had to market were not stamped on the barrel at all—were plain. While many questions could be raised about the existence of the unmarked Manhattans, we also would like to "suspect" something: that prior to the actual shooting at Fort Sumter, Manhattan was not adverse to shipping their pistols South, but appreciated the anti-North sentiment that would be aroused by a stamping of any name so closely identified with New York as "Manhattan," and purposely left the tops of the barrel ribs blank. Soon there was no longer a need for disguises, and the familiar horseshoe name-address stamp, also found on bullet moulds for Manhattan percussion revolvers, made its appearance at the widened part of the barrel at the hinge. "Decorative engraving stands out as one of the distinctive characteristics of Manhattan's First Model .22 caliber revolvers," notes Nutter in a brief description of the salient features of their wartime pistol. "The vertical flats of the barrels were hand engraved with a scroll design . . . Barrels were usually finished blue, occasionally were silver plated; the seven-shot cylinders, ⅝ inches in length, were not engraved, had only one cylinder stop per chamber, with no provision for safety rests and were finished blue. The cylinder stop (in the frame top strap) has a nose which is set at an angle to the nose on the hammer, so that cocking the latter raises the former (lifting the locking stud out of the cylinder notch), but, in firing, the two noses pass one another."

The top of the cylinder stop release also served as the rear sight; it was an improvement upon the tiny groove in the top of the corollary Smith & Wesson top-frame cylinder stop. Hammers were case-hardened in colors; the iron frames and grip straps were usually silver plated and the grips of walnut or rosewood were varnished and polished to a high finish. Serial numbers of very small size were stamped on the breech of the barrel, on the rear of the cylinder, and on the grip frame, underneath the grips; the inside surface of one grip was marked with the serial number, usually in pencil but occasionally die-stamped in the higher ranges of serial numbers.

Variations of early production are noted; a first type of the First Model is considered to have a frame plate of iron instead of brass, and the tension screw to set up the mainspring, usually located in the inside handle strap, may be lacking. The front cylinder bearing is a round pin instead of the adjustable round-head screw. Rifling is six grooves right hand, instead of three grooves as is almost the rule in later .22 Manhattans, and the barrel may lack the company name. Many other minor engineering changes can be traced through the production of this little pistol, to its unhappy demise at the hands of Rollin White vs. Herman Boker in litigations.

A Second Model

A second model .22 having a distinctive flat frame of brass, usually silver plated, was made between June of 1861 and October 1862. Most distinctive feature of this arm was the cylinder stamping scene, a fight between settlers and Indians showing one of the settlers' hair being lifted. About 8,000 of this second model were made up to the time of the court's decision against Boker.

White and Smith & Wesson sued Boker under the terms that one selling could be liable to prosecution for patent infringement, as well as one making the article said to be an infringement. Why Smith & Wesson did not go after Manhattan is not known; Nutter thinks Boker was a more prosperous target for White to collect damages from, and they launched into the German-American gun merchant with a will. White claimed Boker had sold 12,000 pistols for a profit of $60,000 since November of 1856; and that "All consisted of extended chambers through the rear of the cylinder for the purpose of loading them at the breech from behind, either by hand or by self-acting chargers from a magazine placed in the rear of said cylinder." (Nutter quoting Colonel Roy Kuhn's extract from case record.) The 12,000 revolvers estimate is probably close to the actual quantity; Nutter dismisses the $60,-000 profit as ridiculously high. An impressive battery of witnesses was paraded before the court, including Charles H. Pond, B. F. Hart (whose name appears on a Bacon-manufactured revolver as an agent or sales outlet), William J. Syms of Blunt & Syms, John J. Spies a prominent gun importer, Joseph Cooper, Marcellus Hartley, Charles Folsom, George G. Moore, Jacob Rutsen Schuyler, Jubal Harrington, Thomas P. Wheelock, Ben Kittredge, James Warner, Bacon of Manhattan, William Reed (Boston gun merchant), Christian Sharps, and John P. Lower.

A permanent stop order was issued by Chief Justice Roger B. Taney, October 31, 1862, restraining Boker from infringing White's patent by making or selling guns of the Manhattan kind. Whether White ever received damages is not known; apparently not, since none were credited to White by Smith & Wesson on this account. But the trial did have a salutary effect so far as Smith & Wesson was concerned. Other cartridge pistol makers now came to terms with the Springfield pistolmen and paid the royalties demanded or surrendered their pistols to be marked "Made for Smith & Wesson." No Manhattan gun is known with this mark, so evidently the firm of Fred Smith and Albert Beach did not comply to that extent with the court's order.

Other Business

An aura of immunity in some respects surrounded Manhattan, for their principal business was not simply firearms manufacture. They also made the highly specialized machinery for fabricating guns. One of their star designers, a Swiss, Augustus Rebetey, is credited (Patent 26, 641 Dec. 27, 1859) with designing the intermediate or double cylinder stops on the Manhattan percussion revolvers. In fashion worthy of the nonsense drawing of Sam Colt's reconstructed 1836 patent specification, in which the picture is more difficult to understand than the broadness of the claims, Rebetey and co-inventor Joseph Gruler neglect to make a full drawing of the details of their invention. They claim very clearly:

> The use of the intermediate recesses, r r, in combination with the stop d, actuated by the hammer, in pistols where the cylinder is revolved in the act of cocking the pistol, as herein described, thereby effecting a self-acting lock of the cylinder, midway or otherwise between any two cones.

The artist however did not show the double stops familiar to the gun collector; he illustrated only one stop per chamber. The drawing does nothing to alert the patent searcher for a competitive pistol firm, to the novelty in the patent. Apparently Manhattan did not believe in giving unnecessary publicity, even through the necessary publication by means of a patent, to some of their ideas.

More important in their scheme of business was their machine tool fabrication. Andrew R. Arnold, formerly a top level workman or contractor for Colts, was "General Superintendent of the Manhattan Company's mechanical business," as he testified in the case of White vs. Boker. Nutter seems to make this out as some hint that Manhattan was engaged in matters other than their chartered gun-making business. This theory is not at all necessary to explain Arnold's choice of words; he very simply was the general superintendent in charge of the mechanical aspect of Manhattan. Sales, billing, contracts, and all the routine of business affairs exclusive of design and manufacture, were handled by other people, Mr. Arnold would inform us.

Arnold sought to buy from Colt's a drop hammer of a type recently invented by Elisha King Root. His letter to Colt's is couched in friendly terms and refers to his past association with the firm. Whether Colt's sold Arnold the drop forging hammer he wanted is not known, but it appears likely that they were not exactly trade enemies. A degree of cooperation appears to have existed in connection with an unusual Manhattan pistol known as the London Pistol Company revolver.

"London Pistols" were Manhattans

Briefly, collectors had long noticed the existence of a Colt-like percussion revolver having a cast iron frame and removable sideplate like the Manhattan arms, and with extra intermediate cylinder stops on the cylinder to lock it between chambers as a safety precaution. The barrel marking is LONDON PISTOL COMPANY and the octagon barrel with hinged loading lever is a dead ringer for the barrels manufactured by Colt in the midfifties on pocket pistols, such as the London pocket model fabricated at the Colt factory at Thames Bank.

"London Pistol Co." was Manhattan trade mark stamped on this flared grip .31 five shooter. Supplementary cylinder stop slots were for safety allowing capped cylinder to be locked between chambers with hammer down. Cast iron frames were often engraved.

Pimlico, London, England. There a factory was in operation between 1853 and December, 1856. Along with Navy revolvers and experimental rifles, just over 10,000 pocket .31 revolvers distinguished by having iron handle straps were made. The company closed down manufacturing, the Hartford plant having enough productive capacity directly under Colt's personal supervision to satisfy the world needs, and British workmen being difficult to get along with. Many dealers had parrotted the belief that the left-over parts were sold to a firm which assembled them for a time under the cognomen of "London Pistol Company." It was not until after World War II that collector-researcher Sam Smith, of Markesan, Wisconsin, thought to determine why, if these pistols were London manufacture, there were no British proof marks on them? Proof house laws were quite strict; a British make gun, or one to be sold in the United Kingdom, had to have British proof marks. The London Pistol Company arms simply bore a patent date; on the frame under the cylinder is stamped "Patented Dec. 27, 1859." When Sam Smith got his 25¢ copy of the patent he had solved a riddle of the ages. It was the patent to Gruler and Augustus Rebetey for the extra cylinder stops, and was assigned to Manhattan Firearms Company. The "London Pistol Company" guns were at last recognized as being American work, but the source of the rumor remained to be identified by Sam Smith. Quoting Major H. B. C. Pollard, a prolific and pioneer but not always accurate British gun writer, Smith noted Pollard as stating in "A History of Firearms" (p. 135) that: "Colt's invasion (of the British gun trade) was not a success, and the London factory was closed in 1857. The relics were taken over, and a small company appears to have used up the surplus of parts, as The London Pistol Company, a name I have seen impressed over an almost obliterated London Colt stamp."

Says Smith in conclusion, but slightly in error, "I believe we may judge from that that the true English London Pistol Company product is one of leftover Colt parts and that few were manufactured. It is significant that J. N. George's book, *English Pistols and Revolvers*, the best book on that subject, makes no mention of the London Pistol Company which succeeded Colt."

Smith makes a fundamental error in considering that there was any firm other than a Colt firm in London, which "succeeded" Colt's closing down of the London factory.

The stopping of the engines at Thames Bank did not stop the business entity of Colt in London. The offices and warehouse at 14 Pall Mall continued to be used for a number of years thereafter. The depot was a customs-bonded storage area at the 14 Pall Mall building, in which without payment of duty Colt's workmen and sales agents could manipulate guns, do reblueing and rebuilding, conversions to cartridge, repack and reship for export, and all manner of business activities. A complete stock of parts was maintained also for repairs, and there was absolutely no question but that Colt under no conditions and under no circumstances would have sold his actual Colt patent parts to some London handy man for marketing in direct competition with the identical article still fabricated in Hartford and finished for the London export trade.

That London fabricated parts were returned to Hartford is suggested by the existence of a barrel for a 5-inch pocket pistol which was broken from a mass of fused scrap that later was salvaged from the ruins of the Colt fire in Hartford in 1864. The barrel has the regular ADDRESS COL. COLT/LONDON stamping though the word "London" is all but obscured by a blob of fused brass trigger guard. The barrel is finished through the filed stage, rifled; and the bore, except for scale, is perfect. That it is not a second hand barrel returned for some cause is revealed by the absence of the front sight pin; instead, the hole for the sight is perfectly clean. If there had been a pin, in spite of the molten heat, the brass of the sight would have remained smeared at the front sight hole. This is an unfinished London Colt barrel, from storage in the parts wareroom at Hartford in 1864.

Given this fact we must return to the observed great similarity between the London Pistol Company barrels and the Colt barrels, and to Major Pollard's statement, incredible though it is. We need not try to deny the existence of a London-based "London Pistol Company," for the absence of this name in all listings of British arms firms is sufficient. But Major Pollard states categorically and not as supposition, that he has seen this marking "impressed over an almost obliterated London Colt stamp." It may be that this is the shape of the story:

Colt could not by snapping his fingers cause the dissolution of the Manhattan Firearms Company. As he was engaged in hiring principal workmen from other firms, such as a barrel straightener from Remington, so others found it desirable to hire key workmen away from Colt. It was in the nature of the trade. Hence, Andrew R. Arnold left Colts for perhaps Norwich first; then to the Newark enterprise of Manhattan. With him he may have taken some top level information, such as the contents of the Colt parts storerooms, including the large amount of finished and semi-finished work returned from London. (There is enough documentation for the return of many key Colt parts from London, in addition to the pocket London barrel cited, to lay low once and for all the notion any firm other than Colt's in London assembled Colts parts there.) Possibly the pocket barrels could be bought from Colt's? Arnold seems not afraid to ask for a critical gun manufacturing tool of great value, e. g. Root's drop hammer, from his former associates. Purchase of the odd scrap from London, if otherwise valuable, might have been negotiated. No mass buying was done, only the obviously London parts. Those parts not bearing a London stamp, such as cylinders or frames, could easily be used in the Hartford production. But perhaps the London barrels existed in a quantity surplus to estimated use. Purchase by Manhattan of London barrels from the Hartford pistolmakers would account for the ephemeral but sometimes reported barrel stamping of London Pistol Company "over an almost obliterated London Colt stamp."

Why this name was used is puzzled over by Nutter. He has examined many of these guns (though probably not over 1,000 were made with the London Pistol Company mark) and concluded these were assembled from seconds or rejected parts not incorporated in Manhattan's first line pistols. While certainly minor defects seem to exist in the London Pistol Company guns that Nutter examined, it would be very difficult for this to be the case, that the guns represent a conscious culling out of these defective parts. Rather, since we are open to speculation in this deal, it is equally possible that the marking was Manhattan's tentative bid for British trade. By identifying the Colt-made barrels as "London make" through linking them always with the London Pistol Company stamp, Manhattan, through Boker or anybody else, would gain a commercial advantage by shipping them into the United Kingdom. Their value at which duty would be paid would not include the value of the barrel, since the barrel was already of British make and could be shown as such, supported by affidavits. Perhaps a few London Colt barrels were purposely not fully polished, so as to prove beyond all doubt this fact. Today, the only way to prove it would be by polishing and etching the top barrel flats of a series of these guns to try and raise any latent Colt-London stampings which may have been erased. Collectors will wait long and in vain for a group of public spirited Manhattan enthusiasts to douse their pistols with acid, disproving or proving this conjecture. Equally plausible is that these guns may have been marked for Manhattan's bid for Southern trade, fabricated as they were in 1859-60 period of the "cold war," and that they were dumped on the Northern market when it appeared that the Southern states were not to be allowed to depart peacefully from the Union. Nutter concludes that Smith's estimate of quantity produced is less than 1,000: "estimate that only a very few hundred were so marked." This would seem to lend credibility to the idea that it represented a tentative effort of the Manhattan marketing endeavor suddenly disrupted, as if by the beginning of war.

War did not bring to Manhattan the unmitigated flow of profits that some fabricants enjoyed. During the spring of 1862, after the hard knocks from Rollin White's team, they were in a sense looking for work. Rifle musket contractor R. H. Gallaher came to them with a proposition that they cooperate with him in the fabrication of the Springfield rifle. Gallaher, president of the newly-formed Union Firearms Company, was offered a large quantity of machinery and space in the Newark plant. It is tabulated here to show the nature of equipment in a typical middle-sized gun factory of the time:

List of machinery ready to be turned over by the Manhattan Arms Company to the Union Fire-arms Company

6 milling machines
3 four-spindle drill presses, finished
1 rifling machine
2 edging machines, finished
4 screw and cone machines, ready April 1, 1862
6 plain engine lathes, ready April 20, 1862
4 drilling lathes, ready April 20, 1862
4 small drill presses, ready April 15, 1862
3 edging machines, ready April 20, 1862
3 screw and cone machines, ready May 1, 1862
1 quadruple drop (four drops) ready May 1, 1862
1 polishing machine (6 spindles) finished
1 machine for tapping lock-plate, finished
1 tumbler milling machine, finished
4 cone lathes for drilling cones, ready April 20, 1862
30 milling machines, ready May 1, 1862
New York, March 24, 1862

The above tabulation clearly indicates Manhattan included among its "mechanical business" affairs the fabrication of gunmaking machinery on a large scale. Thirty milling machines are promised within two months; many other tools were finished or nearly so. Specialized equipment good only for the U.S. rifle musket, such as lockplate drilling machine and tumbler milling machine are finished, ready for Gallaher's call. The things which set these machines apart from ordinary machine tools of lathe and drill nature are the specialized fixtures attached or in-built adapting them to work on the U.S. rifle musket. The "edging machine" is believed to be a profile miller, perhaps a vertical double spindle type. Gallaher was hardly the first or only customer of Manhattan in this field.

A second list "of machinery in the pistol factory of the Manhattan Arms Company ready for use by the Union Firearms Company" included non-specialized machinery otherwise similar to that noted above, and also "All small tools and a large amount of vacant room." It would seem that Judge Taney's order severely curbed their pistol manufacturing for the time being, though causing them to emphasize machine tool manufacturing.

Late Manhattan Pistols

Throughout the remainder of the war years, in the absence of any more detailed records, it seems safe to assume that Beach, Rebetey, Gruler, Arnold, and Smith concentrated on the design and construction of machine tools. Ultimate change of Manhattan into a company known as The American Standard Tool Company in Newark at the close of the war reveals this to be a reasonable assumption. But percussion revolvers were safer than cartridge arms, and Manhattan stressed also manufacture of fine .36 caliber pistols, lighter and more elegant in frame than the Colt but of similar form.

Western agent Ben Kittredge of Cincinnati, Ohio, took out a patent on a novel attachment for these mid-war period .36 revolvers of Manhattan's. He conceived of the application of a steel plate behind the percussion cylinder, so arranged (as the patent specification #41.848, March 8, 1864) "between the cock and the nipple to throw the fire laterally from the nipple." The patent claim was an odd one, since discharge of more than one shot from a percussion gun in good condition had generally gone the way of the dodo and the aurochs when the compound loading lever had been applied by Colt in 1839-40. The great merit of Kittredge's plate is overlooked in the patent, but may have been appreciated by users in combat. By fitting a plate between hammer face and nipple, the inventor prevented broken cap fragments from working back into the hammer cut. A flattened bit of cap on the frame where the hammer curve comes to rest would halt the hammer short of detonating the next cap, causing a misfire. Or a fragment of brass wedged inside the lock frame could snap the thin limbs of the stop bolt or cause a real jam. The Kittredge plate prevented this accident, otherwise common with percussion revolvers.

Some of these later .36 caliber Manhattans were sold in England. The arms are London proved. Apparently Boker found a market. One of these larger .36 revolvers, a handsomely engraved specimen encased with an unusual eagle-pattern flask, was presented to General Grant in 1863. In August, Grant went to New Orleans to confer with General Banks about changes in Army organization and regimental assignments.

"During this visit," Grant wrote in his *Memoirs*, "I reviewed Banks' army a short distance above Carrolton. The horse I rode was vicious and but little used, and on my return to New Orleans ran away and, shying at a locomotive in the street, fell, probably on me. I was rendered insensible, and when I regained consciousness I found myself in a hotel nearby with several doctors attending me." It was when the great commander was laid up in sick bay that the Manhattan revolver, ordered by the officers and men of Company B, 21st Regiment Illinois Volunteer Infantry, caught up to him and was presented. This regiment was Grant's first command of the war, and was known as "Grant's Own."

A pistol possibly having a little more active career than the Grant Manhattan, which is now preserved in the collection of William Locke, is one of the tiny .22's the backstrap of which is engraved *O. Moulton from his Friend C. B. Whiting/Apr. 13, 1861*. Though there is no guarantee of the men being one and the same, there was an Orson Moulton, a captain of Massachusetts cavalry, mentioned a number of times in dispatches and reports. From New Berne, North Carolina, on 24 July, 1862, he, together with two companies of the 25th Massachusetts, two of the 27th, one section of artillery and 20 cavalrymen under his command, moved out on the road to Trenton. Perhaps it was en route to this place bearing the name of another New Jersey town that Captain Moulton carried his Newark-made Manhattan revolver.

CHAPTER 19

Sharpshooters

"Very soon after the outbreak of the war for the Union," opens Colonel William Ripley's *Vermont Riflemen* in what was undoubtedly the understatement of the war, "it became painfully apparent that, however inferior the rank and file of the Confederate armies were in education and general intelligence to the men who composed the armies of the Union, however imperfect and rude their equipment and materiel, man for man they were the superiors of their Northern antagonists in the use of arms."

In a war which opened with victory to the rifleman in the early campaigns, Johnny Reb, who lived on corn pone and boiled squirrel, brought down with his long mountain rifle, was a far more effective soldier than the Yankee mechanic. Beef roast obtained from the butcher shop does not sharpen the eye and aim like possum and quail for vittles. Southern levies, whether the first dandy troops composed of sons of gentlemen who had done nothing much in their 20 years but learn to ride and shoot, or the last dregs of manhood drafted in 1865, were composed largely of men skilled in the practical use of arms.

Berdan's Sharpshooters Organized

To combat the superior skill of the average Southern soldier, the U.S. War Department early in the summer of 1861 authorized a New York amateur target shooter, Hiram Berdan, to enlist a regiment of skilled riflemen. The regiment was to be called the First Regiment of United States Sharpshooters, and was to be composed of the best shooters in the Northern states. To make sure they were the best, it was decreed that no man should be enlisted in Berdan's outfit who had not proved his skill with a rifle through practical test. A recruit, before he was enlisted, had to shoot ten shots at 200 yards inside a ten-inch ring. Any style of rifle was allowed, but telescope sights could not be used. Any position was permitted, variations of the off-hand (standing) or prone positions, kneeling or squatting, except that the rifle had to be against the shoulder.

From Vermont, Company F, First United States Sharpshooters was the first company mustered into service on September 13, 1861, at Randolph. That day the company, 113 men under command of Captain Edmund Weston and Lieutenants C. W. Seaton and M. V. B. Bronson, left Vermont by train, bound for the Sharpshooter's encampment at Weehawken Heights, near New York.

Sharpshooters' Training Camp

The Weehawken camp was the center of attraction for many New Yorkers, for while other regiments presented scenes in camp of either little activity or dull marching drill, the Sharpshooters constantly engaged in target practice. However, they had not yet been issued their military rifles. Weapons fired at Weehawken were a motley lot, some good, some not so good. A few were fine heavy octagon-barreled target rifles with false muzzles, so that in loading from the front the bullet would not be deformed and would be exactly centered in the bore. The false muzzle was a section of barrel which had been cut off after rifling during manufacture, and fitted with four pins to exactly match the rifling when it was re-fitted to the muzzle. Pushing a lead, patched bullet through this false muzzle sized the projectile and protected the sharp edges of the rifling from damage by wear or the cleaning or loading rod striking the edge. Then, when ready to fire, the false muzzle was removed, aim taken, and the shot fired. Doubtless the first false muzzle, patented by Clark in 1848, did not have a sight obscurer. But after Mr. Clark fired a shot with the false muzzle still installed, and saw it disappear down range, he soon discovered that the way to avoid this accident was to put a small plate or peg on the muzzle which would block the line of sights. With the muzzle attached, aim could not be taken.

A more common type of New England rifle used especially by the Vermont men was the heavy off-hand match rifle with a section of the muzzle turned round. This was to permit a brass cast bullet starter to be slipped over the muzzle. The starter, while used with the false muzzle rifles, was also often used on guns which were not designed for false muzzle pieces. With the starter in place, the riflemen would give the round knob a blow with the palm of his hand and drive the bullet down below the level of the muzzle an inch or two. Then the wooden ramrod could easily push it all the way down.

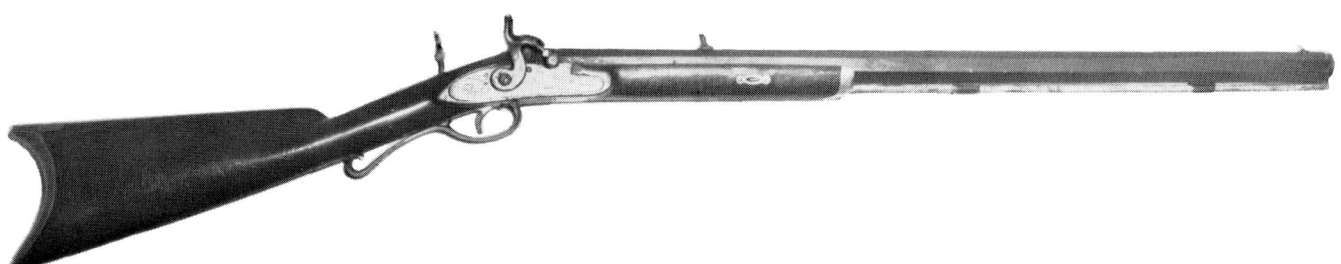

One Sharpshooter downed 50 men with this American sporting rifle now preserved in Fred Elliott collection, N.Y. rifle appears to be a light Remington Sons sporter, adapted for bullet starter, but bears mark of gunshop at Mayville, N.Y. Some Sharpshooters used own rifles.

The men of the Sharpshooter Regiment were all good shots, even down to the chaplain of the Second Regiment, the Reverend Lorenzo Barber. He was "the beau ideal of an Army chaplain . . . beating the best marksmen at the targets . . . His *faith* was in the 'Sword of the Lord and of Gideon,' but his best *work* was put in with a twenty-pound telescopic rifle which he used with wonderful effect."

The original plan of arming the Sharpshooters had been to let them use exclusively target or sporting rifles. The soldiers had brought along their favorite weapons, being told that the Government would pay for them at the rate of $60 each. The Sharpshooters who chose to use issue weapons would receive the best obtainable, and they were promised breechloaders, with telescopic sights, hair triggers, "and all the requisites for the most perfect shooting that the most skillful marksman could desire."

With their own rifles some good practice was made in camp. Men who formerly had been acknowledged good shots, steadily improved under systematic practice with a purpose. In camp outside Washington on Thanksgiving Day, November 28, 1861, Vermonter Al Brown, 3rd Corporal of Company F, won the 200 yard off-hand match, and $5 for the shortest two-shot string. His two shots measured 4¼ inches, or each within 2⅛ inches of the center. The following week a Michigan man won the match, three shots off-hand at 200 yards measuring only 6 inches.

Target Shooting

The string system of measuring shots is an odd one, and a method which could not successfully be used today. The small number of shots used to score, two and three, compares interestingly with the usual 5-shot string or 10-shot string of today. Because of the large amount of black powder being burned in barrels which were made of low-carbon steel or iron, the barrels heated up rapidly. Modern rifle barrels undergo a stress-relieving operation during manufacture so they will not warp from the heat of firing and change their shooting. But the old match rifles, while highly accurate, had their limitations. They could not be fired often without overheating. Therefore two or three shots was more common a target than one of many shots. As methods of working metals became more scientific, and riflemakers discovered how to make barrels which would not warp, targets were often fired composed of as many as fifty shots. These targets were often used in advertising of the period, and corresponded somewhat to today's automobile catalog which has vital statistics of "0 to 60 m.p.h. in umpteen seconds flat." To fire a large number of shots and have them all strike in the bullseye was almost an unheard of thing.

The string measurement was used because a circular bullseye was not always the shape of mark shot at, and because it offered a statistical evaluation which had some realism to it. A figure of merit which is merely how far apart the widest placed shots are, is a good test of the rifle but not of the man. A rifle making a small "group" may be a good rifle, but for Berdan's Sharpshooters to spend their time just making groups was a waste of ammunition. Accordingly, they tried to hit the bullseye or aiming point, which had a center. Their shots were measured by, sometimes, an actual piece of string, laid off to see how far away from the center the shots were. Each shot was measured and the total was the figure of merit for the match. A "string" of 4 inches for two shots could mean that both shots were touching each other or almost in the same hole, and both struck about 2 inches away from the target center, or it could mean that each shot struck on an opposite side of the target, but just 2 inches each from the center.

To the modern target shooter this might seem to be an unfair method of scoring, giving the palm to a man who made a better "string" but a wider group. This is true, and the modern system of bullseye scoring based on the German ring target arose out of this primitive but widely used "string" system.

In the Sharpshooters' camp before Washington, target practice was a constant amusement. Unfortunately, Colonel Berdan, who had merely been commissioned for the purpose of raising the regiment and was not a Regular Army officer, ran into continual opposition to his plans from official circles. Springfield Armory was rolling day and night but only 13,802 of the new rifle muskets had been made in 1861 to the time of authorizing the Sharpshooters, and there simply were not enough arms on hand to equip the regiment for the field. Some smoothbore muskets were issued from stores, and used for guard duty. Two companies also retained their personal target rifles, but the men of both regiments were anxiously awaiting their issue of Sharps military breechloaders.

They had suffered some disappointment at learning

that the promises of the Government to pay for their fine target rifles at $60 each was without authorization. They were even more disgruntled to learn that no new rifles had been provided for them. A man who did have a light target rifle was in an enviable position at first since such a weapon, about the weight of a common sporting rifle, was at least as handy in the field as a musket. Consequently men having such rifles were well armed. But those who had brought along cased bench rest rifles, weighing upwards of 20 pounds, found their target shooting pets wholly unsuited for maneuvers and work in the field.

While in camp at Weehawken Heights, the agents of all the patent gun makers had besieged the men, showing them the virtues of this and that breechloader or repeater. Apparently a considerable number of the men settled, in their own minds, that they were to have Sharps rifles. But months passed and they remained in camp near Washington, becoming highly skilled in the school of the skirmish, but not getting their guns.

Influence of President Lincoln

President Lincoln himself was directly responsible for the Sharpshooters' rifles. At "Camp Instruction" near Washington one day Colonel Berdan and the regiment were treated to a visit by President Lincoln, General McClellan, and Assistant Secretary of War Colonel Thomas A. Scott.

Berdan turned out the men to show what they could do. A target, representing two Zouaves painted on canvas, was set up at 600 yards. One hundred men with their heavy target rifles were placed in a pit, where each fired one shot. When the bullet holes were counted, it was found that each shot had struck within the outlines of the figures. Lincoln fired three shots from a "globe rifle" belonging to H. J. Peck of Company F. The rifle was equipped with a round aperture-type front sight which circled the target, and had a post or bead sticking up from the bottom of the circle for a front sight. Lincoln proved entirely at ease with a rifle, and resting a gun across a tree he called out "Boys, this reminds me of old-time shooting." The soldiers waved their hats and cheered.

The obvious favor of the President brought forth the jealousy which Assistant Secretary of War Thomas A. Scott had evidenced about Berdan's whole operation. Scott, echoing the attitude of Ripley, the Ordnance chief, didn't like this kind of special service troop set-up. He asked Berdan in an impudent, sarcastic manner, what he knew about guns and "that I should set up my opinion against all these officials, and ended by challenging me to fire, thinking doubtless I would decline or, if I accepted, to get the laugh on me by making a bad shot." Berdan, however, was as skilled with a rifle as any man in the regiment, and luckier than most. At 600 yards a man-target was set up, with the words "Jeff Davis" painted above its head. Lincoln laughed at the idea. "Colonel," the President said, "If you make a good shot it will serve him right."

The target was set up and Berdan called for the sergeant major's rifle which he knew to be sighted in for the range. Baited by Scott, who prevented Berdan from assuming the natural prone position for such shooting, the colonel stepped to the line and brought the gun to his cheek. "What point are you going to fire at?" queried Scott. "The head," Berdan replied. "Fire at the right eye," Scott shouted, doing his best to rattle the marksman. Berdan fired, and the heavy Morgan James scope-sighted rifle bounced with the recoil. In all, the colonel fired three times, calling his shots each time. When the target was brought in, the shots were in the places he had called—head, right breast, left thigh. Incredible to relate, the head shot cut Davis's right eye, and knocked the pupil clean out. "No man knew better than President Lincoln how to turn what he knew to be an accident to good account," related Berdan later. "He began to laugh and kept on laughing until he got into his carriage and then said: 'Colonel, come down tomorrow, and I will give you the order for the breechloaders'."

It is not clear exactly what kind of "breechloaders" Lincoln spoke of. The visit to Camp Instruction was very likely not an expression of the President's general interest in firearms—he was a pretty busy man to spend a day at the range—but was the result of conflict within the War Department which he alone could reconcile.

Colt Rifles Are Issued

Colonel Ripley, the Chief of Ordnance, was against the idea of arming the Sharpshooters with anything but common muskets or rifles of Springfield armory manufacture. The men of the Sharpshooter regiments apparently wanted to have the Sharps rifle. Yet Berdan himself must have been in favor of the Colt, to have them the first pattern issued.

Doing business with the Army in the early days of the Civil War was to do business with a hydra—if you couldn't sell to one head, you could always count on cooperation from another. The secretary of the Colt Company, Hugh Harbison, was in Washington seeing officers of new regiments and endeavoring to either sell them Colt guns directly or have them requisition them from the Ordnance Department. Harbison reported the whole Berdan business to Sam Colt early in December, with great success. Aiding Harbison was Colt's friend Randolph Barnes Marcy, formerly of the Topographical Engineers and a fan of the Colt rifle since 1856. Marcy in 1861 was chief of staff for McClellan, and as the executive officer of the Army of the Potomac, authorized to order and requisition arms.

Head Quarters, Army of the Potomac
Washington Dec. 2, 61

Hon. S. Cameron
Secretary of War

Sir:

Genl. McClellan is desirous that the 1st Regiment of Col. Berdan's Sharp Shooters should be armed with Colt's improved pattern repeating Rifles, which have been offered to the Govt at $45.00 each and which offer through Col. Berdan's efforts is $7.50 less than he charged the Govt. This price is very low for this arm and Genl McClellan would be glad to have it ordered as soon as practicable.

Very respectfully,
Your obt Servt
R. B. Marcy
Chief of Staff

Marcy's letter received the endorsement of the President on December 4th: "Understanding this to be substantially an order of Genl McClellan, let it be executed —A. Lincoln."

Harbison immediately went to Washington to make sure that this order, which amounted to $45,000, did not get cancelled or shelved by Colt's opponents in the Government. From the famous Willard's Hotel where all the Congressmen and visiting dignitaries stayed, Harbison wrote to Sam Colt on December 7, 1861:

Magnificent Whittmore offhand match rifle was presented to General Grant by "Citizens of Providence, R.I." after the war. Set is typical, though luxurious, of fine rifles used by marksmen who enlisted in Berdan's regiment. Loading picket ball through false muzzle ensured its being aligned with axis of bore. Muzzle is shown removed in view of rifle kit and in place, below, on barrel of arm. Hammer and lock detail with "snail" shield by cone seat suggest shapes associated with Greener, England, guns of 1850's. Gold and silver decorations are lavish but basic style of arm is typical of best match or hunting rifles of period.

My dear Colonel,

I arrived here last evening after a long and tiresome ride. This morning I went out to see Col. Berdan. When I arrived I found he was in the City. On my return I called at General Marcy's office and while there I met Col. Berdan and made arrangements to meet him at Willards. I did not see Genl. Marcy. I met the Colonel according to agreement and had a long interview with him. He feels very anxious about the rifles but says he must have them no matter what the consequences are. To show you what has been done, I enclose a copy of a letter (above quoted) which Genl Marcy addressed to the Secretary of War, also a copy of the endorsement of the president on said letter which will speak for themselves. Genl. McClellan has agreed to take hold of the matter himself today if time will permit. Secy Cameron referred the letter to his Assistant Secy and he (the Asst Secy) sent for General Ripley. After they had an interview together they called on Genl. McClellan and proposed to him that Col. Berdan's Regiment be armed with the Springfield rifles, to which the General consented (Col. Berdan says that the only reason he can give for the General's action is: that the whole matter had been arranged by General Marcy and himself and that Gen. McClellan was not familiar with the arrangement) and Colonel Berdan was at once notified to that effect. On its receipt the Colonel immediately started for the President and procured his endorsement. He then called upon Genl McClellan and had an interview with him. He told him that the rifles were positively promised to him by the chief of his staff (Gen. Marcy) and that he (Col.) had promised Colt's Rifles to his men and that the President had also approved the action. Genl. McClellan then said that the rifles must be procured and that he would call upon the Secty of War himself and arrange the matter if possible. Col. Berdan says that Ripley is determined that the rifles shall not be ordered and Genl Marcy and himself are determined that they shall be ordered. So the matter stands at present. Col Berdan desires me to say to you that he has been fighting this matter for the past six weeks with all the energy that he could muster and he is determined not to give it up until he obtains what he wants. Should Genl McClellan fail to secure the order, he (Berdan) intends to still go further. The Colonel wanted to know if you would furnish him the rifles without an order from the Ordnance or War Department—provided he procured an order from Genl McClellan for the liberty of arming his Regiment with Colt's rifles, said Rifles to be paid for within 30 or 60 days and in case they are not paid for he (Berdan) will agree to return them to you in good order and if you require it. He will furnish you personal security for the fulfillment of said agreement (in order that he may carry out his own and Genl Marcy's wishes) but he hopes it will not be necessary to enter into such an arrangement. I told him I shall submit the matter to you for consideration. The Colonel further states that with the letters to (&c) which he has in his possession he can obtain an appropriation from Congress to pay for them and if he is compelled to take the latter course he will make it for a much larger number as he really wants 2,400 in lieu of 1,000 but in order to do this, the rifles must be on the spot. He has shown the sample to every member of Congress (both branches), that has visited his regiment and there has been quite a number of them out to see him and his men. His Regiment has a target shooting every Saturday and he gave me a very pressing invitation to go out and spend the day with him and see it, but money matters prevented. I have agreed to see him on Monday or Tuesday. I have now given you an outline of our interview and would request that you give me definite instructions about the rifles—in case that an order cannot be obtained from the proper parties. I should like to receive it before I see him again. After I got through with Berdan I immediately started for the Treasury department but had to wait some time before I could see Mr. Harrington, the Asst Secty of the Treasury. In our interview Mr. H. did not give much encouragement in reference to immediate payments. I insisted that you must have the money.

He finally told me that he would see what could be done and asked me to call again next week Tuesday. If I have my health I shall pay my respects to him Tuesday morning and in the meantime I shall try and present your letter to Mr. Cameron; also get forward all the items I can and if possible get them into his (Harrington's) department.

If the Navy bills on the Boston and New York yards are received and you will send them forward together with the ones that are in one of the drawers of my desk (Mr. Sheldon will know where they are) I will try and get them through if possible.

The Navy Department are very anxious that the pistols which are ordered by them shall be forwarded at the earliest moment possible. It might be well to give this matter attention and have them delivered as soon as possible.

With kind regards to yourself, Mrs. C. and the young ladies, I remain

Yours faithfully,
Hugh Harbison

Harbison's letter reveals Berdan's strong liking for the Colt rifles. Eventually these arms were replaced by Sharps rifles in the hands of the Sharpshooters, but whatever may have been the real wants of the men, several points seem to be true. First, Berdan promised his men that they would be issued Colt rifles. Second, they were not issued the rifles at once. Then, after some groundwork by Marcy, Harbison, and Berdan, Lincoln paid a visit to the camp near Washington. An order for the Colt rifles was forthcoming and Berdan did not have to buy the rifles on terms as he suggested. Between January 1, 1861 and June 30, 1866, a total of 4,612 Colt's revolving rifles were bought for $204,487, an average of slightly less than $45 each. This price was high, despite Colonel Berdan's supposed "efforts" in getting the price down from $52.50 to $45 for the infantry rifle in .56 caliber. The "Army pattern" Colt revolving rifle, with a 31 5/16-inch barrel, weighing nine pounds, fifteen ounces, listed in 1860 at $43.50. It is unlikely that the bayonet would cost as much as $9 extra. There is a strong inference that Colonel Berdan was on "Colt's side" in his fights with the Army Ordnance purchasing agents. Berdan's rifles appear to have been delivered between December 7 and December 31, 1861, a total of 886 having been received at year's end, including 70 from C. J. Brockway December 5, 1861.

Colt's rifles have been vigorously condemned on the grounds that more than one chamber might go off at once. Not one instance of this is recorded by the unit historian, Captain Spencer. But the Colts were easy to put out of commission. The Berdan riflemen were accustomed to stripping their guns to the last screw and pin in cleaning them after firing. The lockwork of the Colt revolving rifle with its hammer on the side and many small parts is tricky to reassemble. While there were many good features of the Colt, it should not have been taken apart by the soldier in camp. But Berdan's camp, with its dozens of cased sets of fine target rifles replete with screwdrivers of every description, was a basement mechanic's delight. In ordinary service, the Colts would have stood up well. But no mechanism on earth can be designed so it is proof against the wiles of a determined putterer with a screwdriver. The Colts, if they failed at all, failed on the camp ground, not in battle.

The reception of the Colt rifles by the Sharpshooters seems, from the officers at least, to have been characterized by mixed emotions. Lieutenant Colonel Ripley (of Vermont, not the Ordnance Ripley) wrote:

"The War Department (agreed) to arm the regiment with revolving rifles of the Colt pattern, and had sent the guns to the camp for issue to the men with promise of exchanging them for Sharps rifles at a later day. They were five-chambered breechloaders, very pretty to look at, but upon examination and test they were found inaccurate and unreliable, prone to get out of order and even dangerous to the user. They were not satisfactory to the men, who knew what they wanted, and were fully confident of their ability to use such guns as they had been led by repeated promises to expect, to good advantage. When, however, news came that the rebels had evacuated Manassas, and that the campaign was about to open up in earnest, they took up these toys, for after all they were hardly more, and turned their faces southward. Co F was the first company in the regiment to receive their arms . . ."

The Vermonters' morale boost on issuing Colts saved the regiment. Discontent over not being paid for their own rifles, and not receiving scope-sighted Sharps rifles as promised, had led the men to the brink of rioting. "Discontent became general and demoralization began to show itself in an alarming form," reported Lieutenant Colonel Ripley. But with the issue of Colts, the discontent was stilled.

Captain C. A. Stevens, historian of the Survivors Association of the Sharpshooters and author of their official history, considered the Colts in a more gentle light.

"The regiment, except the two companies having target rifles, were armed with Colts five-shot revolving rifles, the long promised Sharps not having arrived. It was thought at first that these Colts would not shoot true. This proved not exactly the case, as they were pretty good line shooters, although there was some danger of all the chambers exploding at once. The shooting qualities of this arm were tested in several instances before getting into action, and some good shots were noted. Andrew J. Pierce, of Company G, a very clean and tasty soldier, while on the way down the Potomac made a trial shot of the five chambers in the presence of the regimental officers, at a buoy bobbing up in the river some 400 yards distant. The result was thus announced by Colonel Berdan, who, with the other officers, was intently watching with their field glasses:

" 'There, that will do, sir. You have struck the buoy twice, and it was well done.'

"Pierce had not an opportunity heretofore to make any targets, on account of the Wisconsin company having no arms in the Camp of Instruction, and this, his first chance to draw a bead, was very satisfactory to the officers mentioned."

First Combat

Let us hope the practice was satisfactory to the man from Wisconsin, too, for it was not a pleasant prospect to enter battle with a new weapon, and one untried by the soldier. Pierce and his fellows soon had a chance to warm up their Colts, at Yorktown, April 5, 1862.

In the morning of that day, the Sharpshooters were given the order to advance. Rain greyed the sky but did not dampen the enthusiasm of the target shooters for combat. Suddenly, through the drizzle, a Confederate gun opened on them, a field piece possibly firing lead-flanged Hotchkiss shells. The screaming shell passed high above them and dropped into a field beyond the line. But every man instinctively ducked as the sound hit him—so sudden did the noise occur that the motion of ducking was as if an order had been given, right down the line. Captain Stevens continues:

"As the riflemen pressed forward, the enemy fell hurriedly back, and soon after, far in advance, approached within sight of the formidable-looking earth works next to York river, computed by our battery men 1,800 yards distant, and which were well mounted with guns of large caliber. These forces were commanded by Gen. J. B. Magruder.

"Leaving the road on the right, the Wisconsin men with the Swiss company deployed out in an open field, the latter on the right of the line, where they remained upwards of an hour in support of Weeden's battery, which had hurried up, taken position, and opened fire, and which was afterwards joined by Griffin's battery on their right . . . The Wisconsin company was finally assembled and marched to some buildings in a peach orchard on the left of the road, where they rested under arms an hour . . .

"From the peach orchard fence the Sharpshooters proved themselves. In a very short time they succeeded in silencing a number of cannon on their front, which the enemy were unable to load, so fast and thick did Colt, Sharps, and target-rifle bullets come in upon them. Their futile attempts to man their guns, their excited gestures running to and fro, were plainly to be seen by our men, and with cheers they drove them off, or dropped them, whenever they came forward. They were completely silenced, and the Sharpshooters thus demonstrated their efficiency for such an occasion.

"There was but one Sharps rifle in the regiment at the time, which was the personal property of Truman Head, better known as "Old Californy," or "California Joe," a member of Company C, who gave most convincing proofs of his skill as a marksman. This particular Sharps rifle was purchased at Camp of Instruction and had a sabre bayonet and single trigger. But the men, after a careful examination of the outfit, while they unanimously endorsed the rifle, decided they would rather have the angular bayonet as less cumbersome and more to the point."

They preferred the Sharps over the Colt, but those who carried the five-shooters realized the value of firepower under special conditions. The Rebel cavalry, determined to make an attack on the peach orchard snipers, came out from behind the protection of their barricades, preparing to make a charge, . . . "they drew up in line, threatening to ride down the five-shooting riflemen by the roadside, and cut off those in the orchard. The men with the Colts quietly awaited their coming, and had the enemy made the rash attempt but few would ever have returned. With five shots from every man at close quarters, death and destruction would have awaited them." But a shell from a Union gun burst near to them, scattering the formation as the horses bucked from shell fragments, and the charge did not materialize.

There were few casualties that day among the Sharpshooters. The first man dead, Private John S. M. Ide of New Hampshire, had been using a scope-sighted target rifle. He had exchanged shots from an exposed position in front of an old building with a Confederate sniper placed in a tree, and taken a Rebel bullet in the forehead.

When Lieutenant Colonel Ripley learned that one of his men had fallen, he walked out alone to where Ide lay and picked up his rifle. "With a quick step, but erect, this good officer advanced, the admiration of hundreds of eyewitnesses, while bullets ploughed and dusted the ground around him."

As cool as if he had been on the range, Ripley picked up Ide's rifle. "I'll try him a shot at one notch higher, anyway," the colonel said, as he adjusted the scope sight one turn more of elevation, thinking Ide had been shooting under. Then, taking position, the man in the tree top was discovered, and a quick exchange of shots followed. Ripley escaped injury as the bullets spattered the log wall behind him. After an instant, no more shots came from the tree top.

This sort of activity was summarized dryly by General Porter who reported that: "The Sharpshooters under Colonel Berdan were busily engaged as skirmishers, and did good service in picking off the enemy's skirmishers and artillerists whenever they should show themselves."

California Joe

The papers attributed practically every remarkable shot fired by the regiment to colorful California Joe. But he was far from the figure of a popular hero. Truman Head resembled pretty much the average modern target shooter, give or take a bit. "Entirely free from brag and bluster, an unassuming man, past the middle age, short in stature and light in weight, and a true gentleman in every sense of the word, he was always a special favorite with the entire command."

Joe had never married. A Philadelphian, he apparently had loved a lass of one of the better families, and her father had disapproved of the marriage. So Joe left for California, and remained a bachelor. He had made a reasonable fortune, however, and upon enlisting he made a will leaving $50,000 to the Philadelphia Old Soldiers Home. But though he was looked on with affection as an "old gent" by his comrades in the U.S. Sharpshooters, Truman Head was a highly skilled rifleman and a professional killer—the deadliest kind, for he did not brag, was self-effacing, and did not like the whole business to begin with. This all made him more than ordinarily efficient.

The kind of stories he hated most were those circulated about him. That he ever "shot a man out of a tree two miles off, just at daybreak, first pop," was not only untrue, but the story made him quite angry. His genuine skill with the single-trigger Sharps was quite good enough without the sort of embellishment which the gunmakers put in their catalogs.

Joe scored one down when he shot a Confederate cavalry officer, but the distance is unspecified. "The officer in command fell—it was claimed he received the contents of the Sharps rifle—his white bosom presenting a blood stained mark as he tumbled from his horse, which was reported as plainly discernible through one of the strong rifle telescopes brought into use."

Once the report circulated that "Joe is killed." The camp was aroused and ready to take on the whole Army of Northern Virginia, but they quieted down when it turned out that Joe had only been slightly wounded, with his own gun. A Rebel bullet had struck the Sharps, and broken one of the bands, which flew off and struck Joe in the nose.

California Joe Head's service as a Sharpshooter ended with the Peninsular campaign, because of ill health and failing eyesight. Honorably discharged in the fall of 1862, he returned to California, where he died in 1888. The California papers made much of the passing of a famous and heroic citizen, and in San Francisco a monument was erected to his memory— California Joe, the only man in Berdan's Sharpshooters who was originally armed with a Sharps.

Stories About Sharpshooters

Not all was glory with the Sharpshooters, and one man, Joe Durkee of "C," was killed while on a scout within 40 yards of a Rebel rifle pit. In such an exposed position, Durkee's body could not be recovered during daylight, and he lay there with his Colt rifle beside him. Came nighttime, and the Sharpshooters went out to get him. Instead of the .56 Colt they found a note, stating which Southern regiment had it, and declaring the Confederates' intention to have them all before long. They were evidently elated to know they had killed a Sharpshooter. The boaster's promise was never kept. The 5th Wisconsin in its famous bayonet charge against the 5th North Carolina recovered the Colt rifle. Its possessor was just one more K.I.A. on Confederate rolls.

The Petersburg (Va.) *Express* drew the longbow in telling of this incident:

"A McClellan Sharpshooter had been picked off by a Kentucky hunter, at two hundred yards distance, and on approaching the pit where the Sharpshooter lay, it was found to contain a cushioned arm chair, choice liquors and segars, and food of the best description."

Riflemen performed unusual military tasks in the war. While the pious hope had been expressed that all the Sharpshooters would kill one Confederate for each shot fired, more practical yet more unusual duties were also demanded of them.

Rifles against cannon proved to be more than a match for the big boys. Not firepower, nor yet weight of metal thrown, but shrewdness, sometimes balanced things in favor of the riflemen. One group of Berdan's regiment, under command of Lieutenant Bronson of Company F, managed to blow up a cannon with rifle fire. This was one of the Confederate big guns dubbed "Petersburg" by the Sharpshooters, and it had been making life difficult for them. Bronson, formerly an artilleryman with Greble's battery, had learned that sand or gravel thrown into a cannon muzzle after it is loaded will very likely cause it to burst. On April 30, 1861, Bronson noticed that the muzzle of "Petersburg" was surrounded with sand bags. The big gun was rolled back inside the revetment, and loaded. As soon as it was loaded, while being run up to fire, Bronson ordered his men to fire at the sand bags so as to splash sand into the muzzle. After the 13th shot, with the Sharpshooters still peppering the sand bags, the gun went into the air. The Sharpshooters had really exploded the cannon.

"Old Seth" from New Hampshire was another Sharpshooter who captured a cannon. He was a dyed-in-the-wool shooter who had been complaining about camp duty and his inability to be up in the front of the fighting. When a call came from Colonel Berdan "to select a special detail of sharp shots for important service," Old Seth was in his element. The group of skirmishers moved out, Seth with them, equipped with his single shot scope-sighted match rifle. Most of the other men were from another company, and carried Colts.

Seth took up a position in a rifle pit, somewhat in advance of the other men. When the Johnnies woke up to the fact that the pit the Yankee rifleman was occupying was one dug the night before by one of their

Sharpshooters served in a special capacity as skirmishers, or were detached to cause harassing fire on the enemy's flank and headquarters positions. This famous photo by Timothy O'Sullivan shows a dead Confederate infantryman in a "sharpshooter" position in the "Devil's Den" at Gettysburg. The body was moved about forty yards to this location. The U.S. rifle musket is an Alexander Gardner prop. Battlefield scavengers would not have left a serviceable weapon when fighting was done.

own men, but not yet occupied, they commenced throwing everything they had at Old Seth.

The New Hampshire man would have had no chance with his slow-firing target rifle, except for the fact that he was backed up by the fast-firing Colt repeaters. The Confederates were quickly silenced by the rifle fire, and Old Seth turned his rifle on larger game. A huge cannon had been firing at him for sometime, breaking its shells

Yankee gun flanking Peachtree St. outside of Atlanta is emplaced similarly to cannon called "Petersburg" by Sharpshooters. Rifleman Bronson caused gun to burst by kicking sand from revetment into muzzle from rifle bullet hits.

all around him without effect. Seth concluded he was in a tight spot, until he thought on the fact that the cannon was a muzzle-loader and the Confederates had to load it. As soon as one of the crew stepped up to the muzzle with a swab, Seth got off a shot. The rebel gunner dropped. Another took his place in the embrasure. Seth fired again.

So successfully did he place his shots around the big gun, that it was not long before firing ceased, and he virtually had the cannon captured. It was to all intents and purposes his gun—they couldn't load it. From that time until the siege was over, two days after, the Sharpshooter held his place, keeping the cannon quiet. Day and night he remained at his post; he had got away from camp and was just in his glory, with plenty of ammunition.

The First Issue of Sharps

On May 8, 1862, the regiment received a first issue of the long-awaited Sharps rifles. Only 100 were received as a first consignment, and they were immediately issued to Company F, the Vermont troops, in regard for their valor and conduct. The Colts were, according to Captain Stevens, "found defective in many respects, and they gladly turned in the five-shooters. On receiving the new arms, the men were impatient to get again within shooting distance of the enemy. These rifles shot both linen and skin cartridges, of .52 caliber, and also had primers, little, round, flat coppered things, which were inserted below the hammer; but the Regular Army or hat cap was more generally used, as the primers were not always a sure thing; also it carried the angular bayonet."

Description of the Rifle and Ammunition

The single-shot Sharps rifles differed considerably from the Colts. The barrel was open at the rear and a sliding block moved vertically to cover the bore and uncover it for loading. The block carried the percussion cap cone or nipple, and was pierced with a channel which angled into the position coincident with the axis of the bore and just behind the cartridge when inserted.

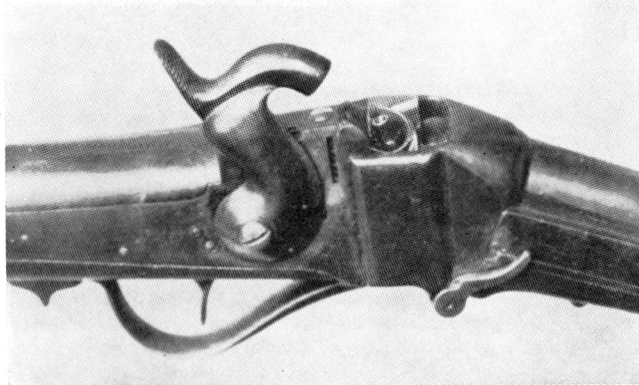

Sharps breechblock was lowered to expose bore and chamber at back, allowing rapid reloading with a combustible glazed linen cartridge. Sharps primer was column of copper wafers in front of hammer which were mechanically fed to nipple at instant hammer fell. Sharpshooters used Sharps rifles but name was old term for accurate marksmen.

Thus the flash from the cap, when struck by the hammer on the side of the gun, was carried into the chamber to fire the cartridge.

The breechblock was moved up and down by a lever below the arm, which was curved as a trigger guard. A few of these rifles are known which are fitted with double triggers. In these, the second trigger is pulled back and clicked. This makes the front trigger "set," just as a mouse trap is set. When the front trigger is touched, the rear trigger is released and under spring tension it flies up and strikes the sear which holds the hammer cocked. This fires the gun, and since a very light touch is all that is necessary, the aim is not disturbed.

Cartridges used with the Sharps were made of linen, rolled into a tube, glued, and filled with powder with a bullet at one end. When the breech was closed while being loaded, a sharp knife edge on top of the breechblock sheared off the rear of the cartridge, exposing the powder to the flash from the cap. The skin cartridge used was a transparent envelope round made from gold beaters' skin, the tissue lining of intestine. This, when wet, could be shaped and stretched, much as wet leather is handled. When dry it was stiff like rawhide. Moulded into capsule form, skin cartridges were used like the linen cartridges in the Sharps.

The Sharps in Combat

Single-shot rifles they were, but their breech-loading system gave them greater firepower than the rifle muskets and smoothbores of the Confederate troops. At the battle of Malvern Hill, Berdan's men, armed with their new 100 Sharps rifles, gave a good show, described by Stevens:

"At about half past two the Confederate artillery fire eased up, and suddenly bursting from the edge of the forest a heavy line of skirmishers came at a run, heedless of the Yankee troops on their front. Company F's bugler was ordered to sound the 'commence firing' signal.

". . . the Sharpshooters sent across the field and into the line of the oncoming Rebels a storm of lead from their breech-loading rifles that soon checked their advance and sent them back to the cover of the woods in great confusion and with serious loss."

The Sharpshooters were forced to retire when the Confederates charged again and again, although more and more gray dead remained behind on the field. But the Sharpshooters held their ground, "and by the greater accuracy of their fire, combined with the advantage of greater rapidity given by breechloaders over muzzle-loaders, kept the Rebels well under cover."

Then the Sharpshooters got the chance to show what aimed fire could do. They repeated the target made at Hythe in 1856, but this time it was not a painted light battery but a real artillery unit they fired on, the famous Richmond Howitzers. This unit was a dandy troop, its members being sons of some of the most distinguished men of the city, and literally the flower of Southern chivalry. "Suddenly there burst out of the dense foliage

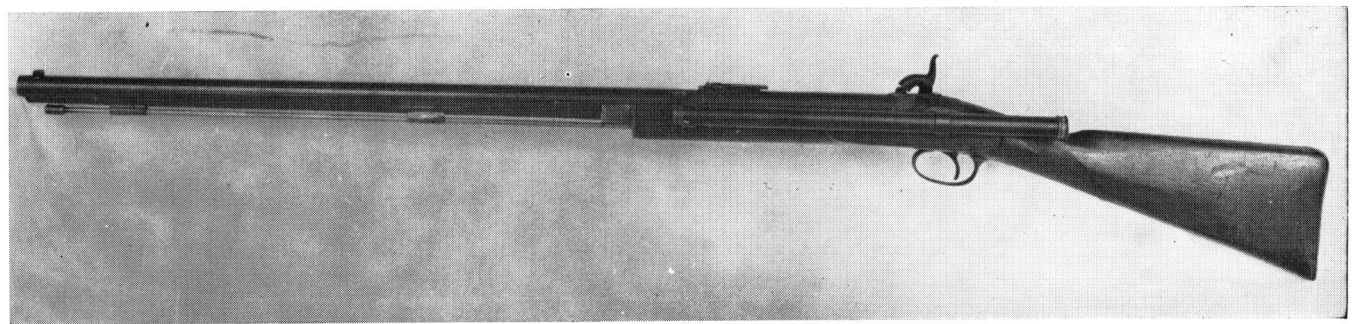

Whitworth sniper rifle in Battle Abbey museum, Richmond, has been much altered to sporting stock but retains original side-mounted scope sight. Leaf sight is unusual Minie type found on some Whitworths in conjunction with vernier screw adjustment for fine shifting of aim at long ranges.

four magnificent gray horses, and behind them, whirled along like a child's toy, the gun. Another and another followed, sweeping out into the plain. As the head of the column turned to the right to go into battery, every rifle within range was brought to bear, and horses and men began to fall rapidly. Still they pressed on, and when there were no longer horses to haul the guns, the gunners sought to put their pieces into battery by hand; nothing, however, could stand before that terrible storm of lead, and after ten minutes of gallant effort the few survivors, leaving their guns in the open field, took shelter in the friendly woods."

"We went in a battery and came out a wreck," said one of that gallant band which escaped decimation. "We stayed ten minutes by the watch and came out with one gun, ten men, and two horses, without firing a shot." That was not the first nor the last time that individual aimed rifle fire was to prove superior to heavier equipment, in that and later wars.

Confederate Long-Range Rifles

The Yankees were not the only ones with long-range rifles. During the siege of Charleston, South Carolina, the Union forces were under continual small arms fire from long range. Their artillery batteries were pounding the city, but one by one a blue-clad sponger and rammer would drop suddenly, a bullet through his head as he stood beside the smoking muzzle of his cannon. The 144th Regiment New York Volunteer Infantry served in this fighting. Some men stationed in Fort Wagner, a Union artillery strong point from which Charleston was being shelled, complained "Nor was the danger alone from (Confederate) shells, for on a Rebel picket line among the sand hills in front of Fort Wagner the sharp shooters had established themselves. These sharp shooters were provided with the Whitworth rifle with telescopic attachment and from their little sand-bag batteries, established in the sand hills, they watched through the hours of the day for the opportunity to pick off the Union soldiers. These guns were able to reach with fatal result at a distance of 1,500 yards. The casualties averaged about two killed and eight wounded each day during the siege."

By Act of Congress in Richmond in 1862, a formal Confederate sharpshooter regiment was organized on the same basis as the 1st and 2nd U.S. Sharpshooters. But many skilled marksmen in the Confederate Army

Fine cased Whitworth of Dr. L. P. Clarke collection, Sheffield, England, has full assortment of loading tools, bullet mould and flask, and elaborate cleaning rod heads. Typical of most Whitworths is round steel patch box, three bands, and checkered grip and forestock. Lock has safety slide.

Long hexagonal bullets designed by Sir Joseph Whitworth had great sectional density and retained velocity and accuracy at long ranges. Paper patching prevented lead from fouling bore and kept rifle cleaner for more shots. While bullets were sometimes wrapped separately, complete cartridges were also used. When rolled they resembled those for standard Enfield M1853 Long Rifle (shown, bottom) but slight ridges on sides revealed bullet shape to eye and finger.

were also issued superior rifles, the English-made Whitworths, capable of fantastic accuracy at long range. The claim of "fatal results at 1,500 yards" was no foolish boast.

This "wonder rifle," accurate at seven times the range of the average musket, was the development of Sir Joseph Whitworth, engineer, steel maker, and one of the leading scientific men of his age. A modified Minie rifle had been adopted for the British service in 1853, but the combination of soft lead bullet expanding into the bore, and the irregularities of barrel manufacture, led to difficulties. The Commander-in-Chief, Lord Hardinge, asked Whitworth to experiment with rifles and come up with something better. He devised a long, hexagonal bullet of hard cast lead, which would expand in the bore slightly and fill the corners of the hexagonally rifled barrel. There were no rifle grooves. The bore was a long hexagonal prism which turned once in 20 inches, twice as fast a twist as the usual musket rifling. Whitworth reduced the bore to .450 inches from .577 inches of the Enfield, but retained the same bullet weight. The long, heavy bullet had excellent "sectional density," as the cross-section area to weight ratio is called, and because of the reduced air resistance of the reduced frontal area, it continued to carry well beyond ordinary Enfield ranges.

At short ranges the Enfield and Whitworth rifles were nearly equal. It was at ranges beyond 500 yards —two and a half city blocks—that the long Whitworth hex slug showed its value. At 500 yards the Whitworth required 1° 15′ of elevation; the Enfield, 1° 32′. Mean deviation from the point of aim for the Whitworth was but .37 feet; of the Enfield, 2.25 feet. At 1,100 yards, Whitworth elevation was but 3° 8′; that for the Enfield, 4° 12′. Mean deviation for the Whitworth was just 2.62 feet, and of the Enfield three times as much, 8 feet. Beyond 1,100 yards the Enfield would not group on the target. At 1,400 yards the Whitworth with five degrees of elevation exactly would give a mean deviation of 4.62 feet. At 1,800 yards, over a mile, with 6° 40′ elevation, the Whitworth would strike within a mean deviation of 11.62 feet.

Whitworth rifles weren't British general issue, but a quantity were made at the Enfield Royal Arsenal. The Rifle Brigade was for a time armed with them. The Whitworth "sniper" rifle differed from the usual Enfield. The metal of the barrel was Sir Joseph Whitworth's own invention—molten steel, cast into a bar and compressed while in the fluid state. The compression set up internal stresses which resisted the force of the explosion.

Fittings on his rifles were like those of the standard 3-band Enfield, and the muzzle would take the socket triangular bayonet. The small of the stock was often checkered, and the wood was of good quality, with usually some figure in the butt.

The scope sights fitted were less cumbersome than those on the heavy Union rifles and therefore less liable to damage in campaigning. Regular iron sights were also attached, but the scope was short, with the front end where the elevation adjustment was made attached to a plate at the rear barrel band. The ocular lens was nearly six inches to the *rear* of the hammer. These rifles could, when the sniper was able to recline comfortably, be shot from the back position with the head supported by the elbow of the left arm and the muzzle resting on the thigh or between the feet of the marksman. A thin cross wire served as the reticule. Both ocular and objective lenses were of the same diameter and as a consequence the light gathering power of the scope was poor. Looking through a Civil War rifle scope is a little like peering into a dark tunnel. At the other end the image looms more or less clear, depending on whether spiders have crept into the tube past the non-sealed lenses, or the last man who had the rifle before hadn't fooled with the equipment out of curiosity.

The Metcalf Legend

Among the many stories of the sharpshooters' exploits, none stands out more than the vaunted accomplishment of Captain John H. Metcalf, who is said to have killed a Confederate general with a picket ball rifle at the enormous distance of one mile, 187 feet range. That no "Captain John H. Metcalf III" existed, or that the one Captain Metcalf of some distinction to be found in the *Official Records* was not a sharpshooter

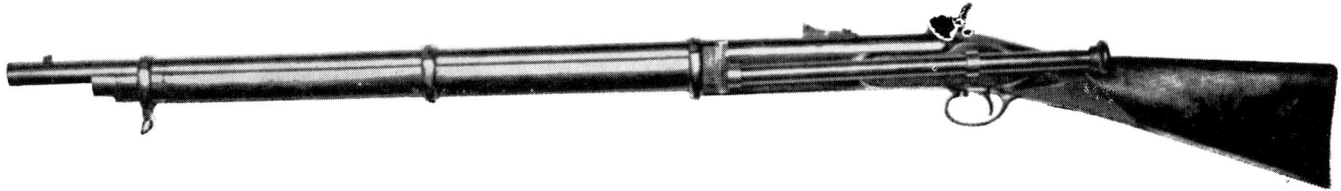

Left side of full stock Whitworth shows slightly different scope but position is same as on Battle Abbey Confederate specimen. Long eye-relief tube was located so because rifle was shot from "back position," with muzzle balanced between shooter's crossed feet and butt near cheek, lying on one's back. Rifle shown, in N.R.A. (British) museum, has Enfield-type rear sight.

and did not earn his honors as a rifleman, seems not to have worried latter-day retellers of this fabulous story. In *True Magazine* for January, 1961, Robert M. Debevic tells dramatically of the "Mile-Long Shot To Kill." To sum up the incidents it will be enough to briefly give the conclusion of Debevic's essay:

"It was during the Red River Campaign in Louisiana that Metcalf got his chance . . . The fateful morning had come. He blinked his eyes wearily. The preparations had been a strain, but this waiting at dawn was worse. Where was that Rebel general?

"Metcalf blinked again. The tent fly had suddenly opened. He tensed as a man, in the distinctive field uniform of a Confederate general, stepped out of the distant tent into the morning sunlight. The general looked up at the sky. He was bearded and gray. He was smiling.

"Metcalf felt a great emptiness at the pit of his stomach.

"He touched his finger gently to the cold, curved steel of the trigger—and slowly squeezed. The super load of black powder roared and echoed in the hills.

"A lieutenant pressed the button on his stopwatch (sic!) and counted nervously: '. . . three . . . four . . . fi . . .'

"Metcalf watched fascinated as the general spun around, fell to the ground, tried to rise and then fell flat on his back. Amazed officers and men rushed to his side.

"Capt. John Metcalf allowed the great weariness he'd been fighting off so long to settle over him as he watched the Northern army break from cover and swarm across the valley. The victory was quick and overwhelming. The commendation which was issued shortly afterwards read: 'To Captain John T. Metcalf for coolness and courage in the Red River Campaign, Louisiana, April, 1864.' "

While Debevic does a creditable job of evoking the image of the scene before our eyes, he is quite weak on history and even weaker on gun knowledge, though he does "draw the long bow" very well. His essay is a mixed-up rewrite of a fiction piece by Charles Winthrop Sawyer, noted arms writer of yesteryear. Sawyer's essay does not make any claim to truth, but merely to a slight confusion which is a common if unpardonable trick in a work of otherwise historical fact: his book, *Our Rifles*.

On page 89 Sawyer describes "No. 3, Heavy Target Rifle. A scientist's instrument, rather than a mere rifle. It was not held in the hands when fired, but lay on a bench or stout table, supported, at the forward end, by the steel bracket, or foot, shown; and at the rear by the set screw beneath the breech resting on an inclined plane of metal; or by an apparatus which was capable of vertical and horizontal adjustment secured beneath the breech by means of the set-screw and the adjacent steel dowel. The shooter sat behind the rifle and a little to one side; and could put either shoulder to the butt, because the stock has a cheek piece on either side. The recoil, however, was not severe. Its weight is thirty-seven pounds; its caliber about .68; its rifling has six ratchet grooves; the pitch is of the gain twist variety, beginning at the breech with one turn in 5 feet and ending with one turn in 3 feet. The owner had at least a dozen different bullet moulds casting a great variety of elongated bullets, cannelured and smooth, long and short for, and not for, use with patch; and also the hollow base variety such as the Army used in the rifle musket . . . The telescope, of about 25 power, is so light and has such a large field that it rivals a best modern one (ca. 1920: Ed.). The scale on its mountings, which are adjustable both vertically and horizontally, reads in minutes of angle. The barrel is marked 'Abe Williams, Maker.' On an ornamental insert in the top of the butt is engraved *Little George Lainhart*. On the left side of the stock are two gold hearts, close together . . ."

Sawyer saw in this handsome rifle, an arm which actually existed and which he illustrates by photo, quite a romance. He tied its Civil War use, as he imagined it, in with a romantic narrative which he had already published in an earlier journal, the history of *John Metcalf, Old-Time American Rifleman*. Sawyer recreated in his fictional John Metcalf an archetypical American frontiersman, user of the Kentucky Long Rifle and moulder of our historic destinies in the 1770's. The entire purpose of his essay is summed up in its opening sentence: "In times of long ago, in the settlement of Wayback, somewhere in New England, there lived a young man whose skill with firearms had wide renown . . ." His choice of "Wayback" as the name of the settlement reveals the purpose of the story; it is pure fiction.

In carrying the narrative of "Metcalf" forward in time, Sawyer jumps a generation, lands on "John Metcalf 3rd, graduate of West Point, officer and gentleman, who was a better specimen of man than his grandfather." Says Sawyer in preamble, "Thus John 3rd was able to use mind and knowledge in a way impossible to his ancestor; and with a special weapon of (t)his

Use of the "heavies," the 30-40 pound bench-rest rifles, was reserved to the best and coolest shots who acted independently of the Regiment. Here in a sequence of photos cool and independent shooter John T. Amber, editor of *Gun Digest*, re-enacts loading and sighting of a "heavy."

False muzzle is put on, to protect end of rifling from ramrod wear and deliver bullet from muzzle with greatest precision. Thumb-blade is to obscure vision through scope when muzzle piece is installed so accidental shot will not throw it down range and damage rifle.

later period, he was able to perform a feat hitherto unparalleled and even on a par with the best that we, his descendants, find to be about our limit."

Sawyer, knowing of the existence of the real heavy match or accuracy test rifle marked "Little George Lainhart," has one of his characters of the same name; the Confederate general, specifically. His story is substantially as *True's* writer Debevic has retold it. In the *Official Records*, Debevic finds not denial, but substantiation, for the Sawyer fiction. Locating a Captain John T. Metcalf in the *O.R.*, Debevic ignores the fact that such a famous general as "Little George Lainhart" is not listed, simply because he is a figment of Sawyer's imagination. Nor does Debevic care to examine the Heitman's *Register of Officers* of the United States Army and Navy, 1776-1876, to discover the name Metcalf appears, but not one John Metcalf III. Instead, substance is given, erroneously, to the legend by discovering that attached to the staff of Brigadier General Jas. W. McMillan in the Red River Campaign was a Metcalf; McMillan's report (*OR* I, XXXIV, Part 1, page 419) refers to Metcalf and also to a Captain Lynch: ". . . My staff did their duty well, and I cannot in justice omit to mention Capt. J. A. Lynch, 26th Massachusetts, and acting assistant inspector-general, and John T. Metcalf, my volunteer aide, for coolness and courage displayed in the discharge of their duties . . ."

McMillan does not single Metcalf out for any special mention in token of his extra-duty accomplishment of the long range rifle shot, an incident which would have made history as, according to both Sawyer and Debevic, it turned the tide of battle and broke a stalemate. Instead, it is Lynch who is mentioned in some detail as to accomplishment: "I also beg leave to state, for the information of the Brigadier General commanding, that he owes much to Captain Lynch's persistent bravery in getting the battery into position, that finally, by a few well-directed shots, expelled the Rebels from the ford."

It was in fact artillery under Captain Lynch and not rifle shooting by Metcalf, that dislodged the enemy facing the Yankees in this incident at Pleasant Hill.

Next, powder is carefully measured and poured in. Flask could throw charge directly but greatest precision is gained by using funnel. Some funnels had long tubes to place powder carefully at breech, avoiding loss of weight from individual grains adhering to bore.

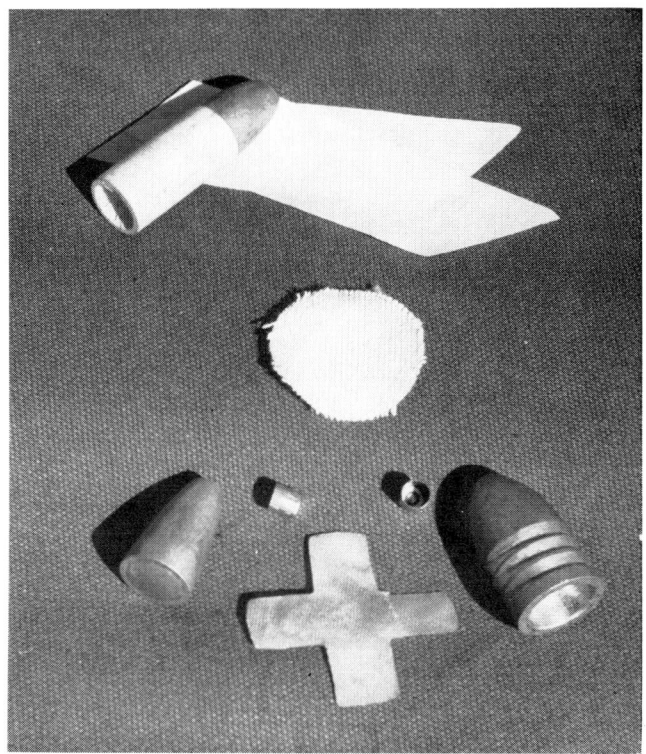

Bond paper carefully cut into strips with diagonal ends is used to patch long slug; shorter sugar-loaf "picket ball" is often seated into cross-patch or ordinary round patch. Some "heavies" were same caliber as U.S. Rifle, and used common grease-grooved minie ball at rifleman's option.

Aligned, smart blow with palm starts bullet evenly and centrally in bore. Concentricity of bullet in bore gives maximum accuracy because influence of air resistance does not tend to deflect it as it screws evenly through the air. Eccentric motion would develop increasing spiral motion on way to target.

Bullet seater fits over end of false muzzle and movable center plunger guides bullet into bore. Rifling in false muzzle is cut a little loose to allow patched bullet to center itself.

Aside from the odd history of this anecdote, which since the *True* publication is sure to crop up again and again in increasingly authoritative publications about the war, what was there about the big rifles which created such a legend?

These big scope rifles were called "the heavies" among the Sharpshooters. The heaviest one in the 1st Regiment U.S. Sharpshooters was carried by James Heath of Michigan. It weighed 34 pounds. "The giving of these telescope rifles, but few of which were now carried," writes Stephens, "at this period of our service, was in the nature of a mark of honor. The sharpshooter thus armed was considered an independent character, used only for special service, with the privilege of going to any part of the line where in his own judgment he could do the most good. It is therefore sufficient, in naming the men who carried these ponderous rifles, to show that they were among our most trusty soldiers and best shots." Evidently Private Heath did not have the "Abe Williams" rifle of Little George Lainhart. There is an Abraham Williams listed as a general gunsmith at Covington, Kentucky, about 1845, but the finish and style of the rifle Sawyer pictures suggests it was made by Abe Williams, Owego, New York, in the late 1850's. The gun and bullets used have been pictured, and the one which is "such as the kind

Bullet is seated firmly but not heavily on powder by brisk motion of stiff bore-fitting ramrod. Hickory is used for ramrod to avoid damaging rifling as barrels were iron or soft steel.

used in the rifle musket" is shown. This appears identical with the .58 regulation bullet, and since many of the sniper rifles made for the Army were in the .58 caliber, to use standard issue ammunition as well as special bullets cast from moulds for each gun, there is a strong suspicion that Mr. Sawyer's .68 caliber is a typographical error. Such a caliber would be an unusually large caliber for a match rifle of this kind.

The bullet used is important. A long, heavy bullet which had a considerable cylindrical section at the base is called a "slug." Rifles known as "slug guns" are not thought of as common until some years after the war. The usual match rifle projectile was the "picket" bullet, a pointed bullet with only a slight bearing surface at the base. While accurate at a fair range, the expectation of hitting a man target at over one mile range is quite doubtful. The Whitworth rifles, true slug guns, and far in advance of their time in 1860, could not shoot with any degree of precision at such formidable ranges.

Other Snipers

But snipers did not need fairy stories to build them up when the chips were down. Even the common rifle muskets, in the hands of a man who knew how to use the inverted wedge front sights and had the patience to aim carefully, could account for a fantastic number of individual enemy soldiers. The dead Confederate sniper immortalized in the picture taken by Brady at the Devil's Den at Gettysburg used a common Rifle Musket.

The 2d Regiment of Colonel Henry A. Post also had been issued Colt's rifles, .56 caliber, fitted with two bands and a triangular bayonet. The 2d has not come down in history with the popular name of the 1st, but was nonetheless distinguished in combat throughout the war. Their first skirmish with the Confederates came at Falmouth, Virginia, April 18, 1862.

"Advancing ahead of Augur's brigade they met the Confederate fire with their five-shooters in a manner that evidently surprised the foe, who little expected such rapid firing. The revolving chambers of the Colts were soon heated up, and right there a most favorable opportunity was presented to test these heretofore doubtful arms; and the boys were compelled to admit that they were not so bad after all, having done good work with them." Yet the 2nd, returning to Fredericksburg after the end of May, exchanged their well-used Colts rifles for the Sharps also issued to the 1st Regiment.

Two companies of Andrews Sharpshooters raised in Massachusetts, who adopted the name of their governor as a unit designation, were attached to Berdan's regiment. The colonel offered to outfit them with Sharps rifles, but they preferred to retain their heavy telescopic rifles such as they used for target shooting. Sometimes these heavier weapons were carried in the baggage train and the men marched without arms. Thus their affection for the heavier rifles can be understood. But there proved to be some major disadvantages in not having weapons fitted with bayonets. One company of Andrews Sharpshooters was with Gorman's Brigade of the 2nd Corps at Antietam.

"The company was badly cut up in a close engagement where quick shooting with them was out of the question, their guns being little better in that affair than clubs, they losing 26 with their captain and a lieutenant among the killed." But General Gorman commended them for their work in silencing "one of the enemy's batteries and kept it so, driving the cannoneers from it every time they attempted to load." Countless times throughout the war the individual rifleman showed his ability to immobilize field artillery by accurate, aimed fire. But the heavy rifles had to take a back seat to the Sharps in combat.

The first sergeants of each company were issued telescope sighted rifles, to be used for special occasions, but these were finally turned in because they were too heavy to carry around, and of little use in a skirmish line. "These rifles were all right in a fixed position— a good rest—and did great work at long range, particularly among the enemy's batteries," wrote Captain Stevens in 1892. "But for hurried off-hand shooting, skirmishing, or in line of battle, the open sights could be brought to the eye quicker, and even the muzzle-loading muskets with which the infantry were armed could be loaded quicker, while the breech-loading Sharps were far ahead of all, for rapid firing.

"The great improvements made in the breech-loading system since the war of the Rebellion, particularly in the metallic ammunition, have caused the muzzle-loaders to be discarded. A line of battle of breech-loaders lying down can shoot faster and do more execu-

With muzzle piece safely removed, rifle is capped and placed on table ready to fire. Here writer-rifleman Amber takes aim at imaginary Confederate general in general vicinity of University of Chicago Campus near where he lived. Scope mount has delicate screw windage and elevation adjustments.

tion on a charging column, than heretofore when the bite and tear cartridge and rammer were used, besides causing less exposure in the men. A charging column at the present day must needs be very brave, to face a line of breechloaders, as they will hardly get there. It was owing to the success attained by the Berdan Sharpshooters, in developing the superiority of the Sharps breech-loading rifle over any other known weapon in use, in point of safety to the men as well as execution in firing, for I never knew of an accident occurring by premature discharge of a Sharps rifle, that caused so soon after the war the substitution of the breech-loading system, improved upon, in all manner of firearms.

"The American manufacturers opened their eyes to the fact that a safer and better gun could be loaded at the breech, in shotguns as well as rifles. To Colonel Berdan's persistency in urging the Government to furnish his command with these arms while at Camp of Instruction, in response to the demands of the members of both regiments, is the credit largely due for the general substitution after the war of the breech-loading gun."

The Sharpshooters at Gettysburg

Sharpshooter against sharpshooter should have meant a sniping match, with life instead of the Wimbleton Cup to the winner and death to the loser. But at the Devil's Den at Gettysburg the Berdan Sharpshooters served as shock troops. A small force of Confederate riflemen, armed mainly with conventional but well-aimed rifle muskets, had settled themselves along the crest of the rocky knoll. Their sniping had been very annoying to the Union officers within range. But so well concealed were they, that rifle fire could not dislodge them. Sergeant Richard W. Tyler of Company K detailed 20 "volunteers" to help him take the position. They raced across the marsh, routed the Confederate pickets at the foot of the hill, and closed in, capturing 20 snipers. The Confederate sharpshooters were terrified because they believed that they would be hanged, but on learning that it was Berdan's men which had taken them prisoner, their spirits changed from fear to complete happiness. Not one of the Union soldiers in this charge received a wound. They seemed to dodge through the fast flying Rebel bullets—one lost a frying pan, another caught a ball on his gun stock. But they accomplished their mission.

At Gettysburg the Sharpshooters are credited with having delayed Longstreet 40 minutes—a critical figure, since Longstreet claimed that if he had only been delayed 35 minutes, his corps would not have been repulsed. The green-clad riflemen frequently heard the cry "Sharpshooters to the front" and responded with speed which was typical more of the intense esprit de corps among the men rather than any unusual quality of bravery or daring. Only 100 of Berdan's men were engaged in what proved to be a delaying action of a handful against 30,000.

About 11:30 a.m. on July 2, prior to Longstreet's flank march, General Birney ordered Berdan to take 100 Sharpshooters and, accompanied by 200 musket-armed infantrymen of the 3rd Maine, reconnoiter the Confederate right flank. Part of Anderson's division was approaching Pitzer's Wood, to the west of the Emmitsburg road, which was in front of the Union lines stretching from Little Round Top, where Birney's division held the left of the Union line. The Sharpshooters moved off across the Emmitsburg road and deployed through a peach orchard to the northwest, past some farm buildings. A young boy warned the green-coated marksmen that they should "Look out! there are lots of Rebels in there, in rows," pointing towards the woods.

The soldiers did not believe the young boy, thinking he knew little of fighting. The Sharpshooters suddenly discovered that the lad had made the understatement of the day; they discovered three columns of infantry on the rear edge of the woods, the west slope of Seminary Ridge near Pitzer's Run. Berdan sent Captain Briscoe to warn Birney and Sickles; then, in command of hardly three companies of men against regiments, gave the order to "advance firing." The Sharpshooters attacked the enemy on the flank, piling them up and creating confusion, "doing great execution with their reliable breechloaders—catching it hot meanwhile from the volleys received." Berdan's line held back a regiment in a "bold and audacious venture," as their generals said. The green coats were pressed hard by the enemy and eventually retired, but in complete command of the situation, not in retreat. Colonel M. B. Lakeman of the 3rd Maine reported that "The enemy showed himself in overwhelming force; but so well did we hold our position that his advance was much checked and very disastrous, and not until ordered by Colonel Berdan to fall back, did a single man leave the ranks."

The one small incident could have been magnified to one of the most amazing fights of the whole campaign, had all of Berdan's two regiments been there. His order to "advance firing" was a turning point in combat tactics. Moving fire was an uncommon tactic in the formal repertory of war. A volley, then fix bayonets and charge, continued to be the routine for decades after Berdan's order. Yet his command could have come down in history as more famous than "don't fire till you see the whites of their eyes."

The breechloader-equipped green coats were able to keep up a rate of fire proportionately so much greater than the musket-equipped Southern infantry that with their small force they actually halted a division for an instant.

Longstreet admitted that the delay was critical—"That five minutes saved the day for the Army of the Potomac," and put on record one of the first instances of troops advancing under cover of their own marching fire. Captain Stevens records that "All the generals who went over the historic field at a meeting of ex-officers and soldiers 23 years after the battle, declared that the spot where Colonel Berdan's command attacked Wilcox's brigade was the turning point of the war."

The effect on the Confederates was great. Wilcox's lines were temporarily sent into a turmoil and the Sharp Shooters poured fire into the huddled masses of soldiers while the Sharps barrels burned their hands and the white smoke hung thick in front of them. In the 10th and 11th Alabama at the end of the line, receiving most of the Sharps bullets, more than 56 men were killed in the few minutes of firing. Forty gray dead lay close together and later the common grave was found to be over 100 yards long. General Wilcox in dispatches spoke of being under fire from "two Federal regiments," deceived by the rapid firing of the breechloaders and the casualties during the short time they were engaged.

Unable to retreat or take cover from the merciless rain of lead from Berdan's men, who on an average had fired some 95 shots, Colonel Forney of the 10th Alabama gave the order to charge but did not succeed in breaking up Berdan's formation. The execution of the Sharps on the Confederate ranks was witnessed by a captured Berdan soldier, Peter Kipp of Company D. "We started for the rear, and passed through where Longstreet's men had halted. It is impossible for me to describe the slaughter we had made in their ranks . . . It beat all I had ever seen for the number engaged and for so short a time. They were piled in heaps and across each other . . . I found hundreds of wounded men. The doctor would hardly believe there were so few of us fighting them, thought we had a corps, as he said he never saw lead so thick in his life as it was in those woods."

Certainly the officers of the Sharpshooters never worried about their men not shooting. Less than five rounds per man was counted in their cartridge boxes when the company formed after withdrawal.

After Gettysburg on the 23rd the Third Corps was ordered to feel the enemy at Manassas Gap, resulting in the severe skirmish known as "Wapping Heights." The Berdan Sharpshooters opened the engagement and bore most of the fighting, driving the Confederates through the gap and beyond the mountains. They inflicted severe losses on the Confederate troops, and collected some prisoners. In one capture, a man from the Sharpshooters, armed with his breech-loading Sharps, suddenly discovered a gray soldier levelling his rifle at him, at very short range. He swung his Sharps to his shoulder and both fired simultaneously. Neither shot struck the mark. With guns unloaded, they were now on equal terms but each supposed himself at a disadvantage, since the cartridges were the last ones possessed by either soldier.

"Yankee cheek was too much for the innocent Johnnie," says Ripley in *Company F,* "for the Sharpshooter, with a great show of reloading his rifle, advanced on the Rebel demanding his surrender. He threw down his gun with bad grace, saying as he did so: 'If I had another cartridge I would never surrender.' 'All right, Johnnie,' said the Yankee, 'If I had another you may be sure I would not ask you to surrender.' But Johnnie came in a prisoner. In this action the Sharpshooters expended the full complement of sixty rounds of ammunition per man, thus verifying the assertion of their ancient enemy in the Ordnance Department that 'the breechloaders would use up ammunition at an alarming rate;' both he and others were by this time forced to admit, however, that the ammunition was expended to a very useful purpose."

At Spotsylvania

An occasion for expending ammunition profitably occurred later on during the Union advance toward Spotsylvania. The Po river had to be forded and the engineers were making preparations to cross while occasional exchanges of artillery fire broke the monotony of the day. The artillery fire was not really effective, but a Rebel signal post was spotted some 1,500 yards off, observing the Union lines. Federal guns opened fire on the observation point, a clump of trees from the upper branches of which wig-wag flag signals could be seen, but the range was too great for canister, and shell was wholly ineffective.

Some men of Company F watched the proceedings, and then tried their hand at long range work. They were reasonably skilled at up to 1,000 yards, although under 400 yards was considered a reasonable maximum range for individual targets. But the rifles were not sighted to elevate for this range. "They therefore cut and fitted sticks to increase the elevation of their sights and a few selected men were directed to open fire, while a staff officer with his field glass watched the result. It was apparent from the way the men in the distant tree top looked *down* when the Sharps bullets began to whistle near them that the men were shooting under still, so more and longer sticks were fitted to still further elevate the sights; now the Rebels began to look *upward,* and the inference was at once drawn that the bullets were passing over them. Another adjustment of the sticks, and the rebels began to dodge, first to one side and then to another, and it was announced that the range was found. Screened as they were by the foliage of the trees in which they were perched, it was not possible to see the persons of the men with the naked eye; their position could only be determined by the tell-tale flags; but when all the rifles had been properly sighted and the whole twenty-three opened, the surprised rebels evacuated that signal station with great alacrity."

Repartee

Confederates under fire, like their Blue-legged compatriots, often kept a sense of humor in the presence of death. Some of Berdan's men had quietly settled themselves in the basement of a Virginia gentleman's home from the windows of which they had a good short-range view of the Southern lines. A captured Alabama soldier later paid tribute to their cool efficiency. "It was only necessary to hold up your hand to get a furlough," he said, "and you were lucky if you could get to the rear without an extension."

Repartee verging on friendship sparked frequent temporary truces called by men in opposing sections of the lines. To boil coffee or cook a meal, the pickets would often call "time" and for a half hour contented sounds of dinner would be the only noises to break the stillness. Then, after an appropriate interval, someone would call "time" again and the men return to their diggings. One overly confident Southern lad who had just been poured his ration of scalding hot coffee was less lively than most. Believing himself out of sight, he sat munching some bread and blowing on his brimming tin cup to cool the coffee. One of the Sharpshooters, less bloodthirsty than most, called out, "I say, Johnny, time is up, get into your hole." "All right," replied the butternut figure, still blowing on his coffee to cool it, and not moving. "Just hold that cup still," hollered the Sharpshooter, "and I will show you whether it is all right or not." The Southern soldier suddenly became apprehensive that he really was visible, and froze for an instant, the cup still, giving the Union rifleman the chance he had been waiting for. A shot rang out, a white puff of smoke drifted from the concealed Sharpshooter, and the Rebel's tin cup was knocked from his hand. The surprised coffee hound scrambled for cover, to the tune of laughter and jeers from his own comrades.

These incidents paint a curious picture of the men engaged in mortal combat, laughing and joking one minute, firing for record the next. The Sharpshooter was a curious personality. "Sharpshooting is the squirrel hunting of the war," explained Ripley. "It is wonderful to see how self-forgetful the marksman grows— to see with what sportsmanlike eyes he seeks out the grander game, and with what coolness and accuracy he brings it down. At the moment he grows utterly indifferent to human life or human suffering, and seems intent only on cruelty and destruction; to make a good shot and hit his man, brings for the time being a feeling of intense satisfaction."

Ripley's comment has touched on one aspect of sharpshooting which is unique with this version of the rifle sport. The common soldier lacks the nerve and too often has been educated by a gentler society into abhorring the taking of life. This is good, for society most of the time is not so oriented that killing constitutes survival. But in the peculiar state of society which is war, when killing becomes of importance, the man who can take the life of another without either a relish bordering on insane fanaticism, nor the conflicts and inner doubts which result in a personality estrangement as serious as the former, is in an enviable position. To him, war becomes a game, but instead of the gamble of his skill at the target range, the rifleman is gambling his life on his ability to kill before he is killed. Seek, find, destroy, are the aims of the combat rifleman. In wars subsequent to the American Civil War the importance of this kind of man has been belatedly recognized, but always too late to make use of them in war to the best advantage. Snipers and marksmen have been made cooks and bakers, and truck drivers and clothes clerks have been made BAR-men or handed scope-sighted Springfields and M-1's. Only in the Civil War has conscious use been made of these men of sharpshooting ability—in that, the War stands unique. Later attempts to train snipers were uncoordinated, and distinguished by the issue of miserable equipment such as the abortive telescopic Warner & Swazey "musket sight" of World War I, or the unfortunate mass-produced Springfield M1903A3 with a cheap small-game scope hung on it that passed for a sniper rifle, in the Second International Debate. It has been nearly a century since specialists' weapons have been intelligently issued to riflemen who were trained to kill. The damage they did to the enemy, in battle and encounter without number, should have proved the point, but the lesson seems to have been forgotten as soon as the war was won.

Note: The real George Lainhart, a close friend of riflesmith Abe Williams, was married to a daughter of Walter Ogden, "Owego's most prolific gunmaker." Lainhart, who did not serve in the Civil War, died about 1904. Williams, who died in 1909, boarded with Lainhart's widow at the last. (Letter to author from Richard D. Barton, Apalachain, NY, 23 February 1963.)

CHAPTER 20

Machine Guns—Masterworks or Monstrosities?

The origin of rapid fire weapons equal to the machine gun of the paper cartridge era is lost in antiquity. There are Biblical references to weapons shooting many arrows, and Leonardo da Vinci, millenia later, planned a device of that class of arm known as *orgue des bombards,* or organ of bombards (small guns). In the ordinary "organ" of the late medieval ages, a row of barrels was placed parallel, or with breeches converging, to be fired by a single touch of the match in a volley. Tactically, this primitive device and the "machine guns" used by the North in 1862 were virtually identical in purpose.

The machine gun as employed by regular forces was looked upon as a "fortress or flank defense gun," a sort of large buckshot cannon to be placed within the outer defences of a fortress, and turned loose in the event enemy soldiers breached the walls. The *orgue des bombards* of the Middle Ages was such an arm, intended for use inside the castle outer wall or at the head of steps, to sweep it clear.

Not until the development of Dr. Gatling's gun began during the Civil War did a sense of the field and attack values of the machine gun occur to modern military men. Even then, the principles of the old "orgue" kept their sights limited, although the original purpose of the volley gun was to serve a defense need vital in the America of 1860. Today, full comprehension of that first role of the American machine gun is held only by the historical buffs who preserve the lore and artifact of old covered bridges. But in 1860, to keep storms from scaring horses through guard rails, nearly every bridge was covered and dark inside. To suit this situation, gunmaker Billinghurst at the behest of inventor Requa resurrected the *orgue des bombards.*

Requa's and Billinghurst's Machine Gun

The first gun made was not full sized, but a tiny working model about 10 inches broad in the wheel track. Five octagon pistol barrels some six inches long were mounted with a very slight dispersion onto the frame plate. Behind their open breeches was mounted a sliding breechblock or bar in which was mounted a single percussion nipple. The sliding bar was shoved forward by toggle joint handles, which blocked the chambers at the back after loading. This model stood in the window of Billinghurst's store in Rochester, New York, for many years.

The full sized gun showed greater ingenuity. The secret of its rapid fire was the "piano hinge" cartridge clip. A hinged strip of metal was perforated 25 times on each limb. The side next to the chambers had holes of the same diameter as the body of the special flanged metallic cartridge. The reverse side had smaller holes, enough to allow the cap flash to penetrate the tiny center flash hole of each cartridge, a la Maynard cartridge. Twenty-five round barrels of carbine length were mounted between the normal light carriage wheels. A single percussion nipple was mounted in the sliding breech bar, and the hammer was a simple lanyard-flipped type without sear, springs, or complexity.

To Requa and Billinghurst this must have seemed the answer to a munitions maker's prayer, for every covered bridge would need one of these, safely and secretly tucked inside, to repel Rebel horse. Unfortunately, most of the covered bridges were in the North; their market was therefore relatively limited. Suppose one of these guns ever got into battle in a covered bridge, in the way it was supposed to be used! The carnage, as screaming mounts piled up, jammed by the troopers rushing on from behind in mistaken eagerness to succor their fallen comrades, would have increased until the whole squadron of cavalry writhed inside the bridge. Unseen by any observer, the dying mass of men and animals, riddled by the Billinghurst-Requa bullets, would have injected into the history of the war a most shocking episode.

First Use

Instead, the Requa guns, five in all, purchased at a cost of $5,482.72 or about $1,100 each, were used by the Federal besiegers of Battery Wagner in front of Charleston, South Carolina, in August 1863. The guns must have made a sort of ripping noise as the fire traveled outward in each direction from the middle, igniting successively each pair of cartridges till the last. They gave the Confederates very little trouble. A ser-

Requa battery gun discharged scythe-sweep of lead which would interdict passage of covered bridge by horse or footmen. Early "machine gun" was not a repeater except so far as fresh clips of cartridges could be loaded, for simultaneous discharge.

geant of the 25th South Carolina Infantry, then in Fort Wagner, reported that they were outranged by the rifles of the garrison. "They seem to have caused so little notice," writes Aiken Simons, in *Army Ordnance*, November-December 1934, "that one otherwise very accurate writer attributes them to the Confederate defense. At all events," Simons concludes, giving them their due claim to fame, "they were the first machine guns with metallic cartridges used in actual combat."

Whether the Confederates ever used such a gun is difficult to say now authoritatively. Colonel G. M. Chinn, (*The Machine Gun*, Vol. I) declares positively "There is a record of possession by the Confederate forces of a gun of this design on a fort at Charleston, South Carolina. As it was used for defensive purposes only, and there was no problem of mobility, it was heavier than the field piece type of the North. The Confederate weapon weighed 1,382 pounds, and was of considerably larger caliber than the Northern version." Whether Chinn is correct or not, the Requa gun did not achieve any great popularity, despite demonstrations with it by the makers on the steps of the New York Stock Exchange Building late in 1861. With a crew of three men, the gun could be fired at the rate of 7 volleys or 175 shots per minute. The effective range of the .58 caliber projectiles was 1,200 yards.

These curious piano-hinge organs whose song was death were not used to any extent to judge from the purchases made. From David Smith, 36 Liberty Street, New York, Captain Crispin obtained Billinghurst and Requa battery guns and ammunition. The first purchase is listed as December 23, 1862, for 600 cartridge holders and 15,000 cartridge cases, unloaded; inferentially, as many as six guns were already in service, say 100 cartridge holders per gun. But later, the nomenclature is "cartridge clamps," 550 being bought on July 24, 1864, at $40 per 100, a reduction in price of $10 per hundred. Five guns at $1,000 each were received June 20, 1863; and an additional two guns July 24, 1864, at the same price. Skin cartridges for loading into the metallic cases, percussion caps ("Eley's double waterproof") and at one time 600 pounds of "No. 54 swedged bullets" were bought to feed the batteries. David Smith, perhaps a business agent for Rochester-based Billinghurst, received in all $9,724.75 for the seven guns and accessories. From this brief deviation from the trend of rapid fire arms development, at least two or three of the original seven have survived the rigors of war.

Ager's Volley Gun

One of the best guns to see service was little spoken of after the war. Of simple design, the principle may have added nothing radically new to repeating arm construction, but it was a good gun, the Union volley gun of Wilson Ager. Sometimes called, after the fact it had a cartridge hopper like the hopper on a grinder, the "coffee mill gun," this .58 steel-charger repeater was regularly supplied with two barrels. They were supposed to be alternated during use to prevent them from getting too hot; actually in test one of the guns was fired till the barrel glowed and bits of metal issued from the muzzle with each shot.

It used an open chamber, a cylinder the chambers of which were but grooves into which the steel cartridge would fall from the drum. At the back the steel cartridge had a musket nipple and could be recapped and reloaded and used many times. The drum was turned by means of the hand crank, and as each loaded groove came opposite the barrel, it was blocked up and fired.

President Lincoln was originally persuaded to order ten of these guns from contractors Woodward & Cox of New York, at the price of $1,300 each. They were ordered November 2, 1861, and paid for November 4,

Model of Prof. Requa's gun was made by Rochester gunmaker William Billinghurst using short sections of octagon rifle barrel. Lever moved breech closed. Single percussion cap fired all barrels. Gun was demonstrated on steps of New York Stock Exchange, legend says.

1861, presumably the date of delivery. Two more Union guns were purchased and paid for on November 25, 1861, and another brace on June 20, 1862, at $1,500 each, all from Woodward & Cox. Significantly, the Chief of Ordnance later noted that the documents relating to the original order were not on file at his office.

In December of 1861, J. D. Mills, representing Carr & Avery, of New York, somehow also agents for the Ager gun, visited Washington. He contacted the President, but Lincoln in response to Mills' entreaties stated that he did not intend to order more Union guns unless General McClellan distinctly indicated in writing that he wanted them ordered. Mills, stopping at Willard's Hotel, immediately sent off a note to McClellan (12 December 1861) asking that he order more guns.

The general considered the price of $2,300 too high, but was willing to allow the manufacturer a fair cost for fabrication, plus 20 per cent margin for profit; this was considerably more generous than War Two's "cost plus 10%" contract profit figure.

McClellan considered that 50 of the Mills guns would be useful if they could be obtained on these terms. On December 19, the word went out: "Let the fifty guns be ordered on the terms above recommended by General McClellan, and not otherwise. A. Lincoln." By July 8, 1862, a bill for 28 of these guns had been filed with the Ordnance Department, including delivery of at least this number. The costs of the components is an interesting schedule of manufactured values at the time:

Estimated cost of iron and woodwork of one Union Repeating Gun and carriage:

IRON

Two cast steel barrels	$30.00
Sights	6.00
Cylinder	18.00
Slide, and fixtures pertaining thereto	33.00
Fitting-up castings	25.00
Elevating screw and box	4.00
Shield	4.00
Hopper	6.00
Charging tool (loader)	5.00
Irons for woodwork	60.00
Tools and implements	4.00
384 chambers, at 87½ cents	336.00
16 brass boxes	16.00 $547.00

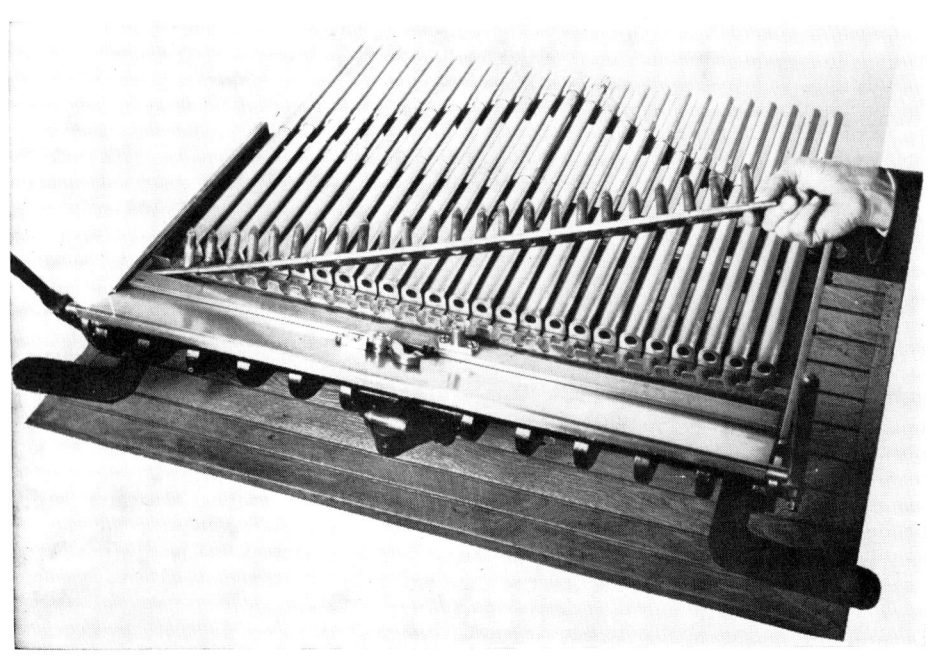

Piano hinge clip held 25 caliber .52 base-fired metal cartridges. When breech was closed, common musket cap detonated central cartridge while fire flashed in rear channel to succeeding outer charges. Confederates may have used such a gun but seven "Requas" were bought from New Yorker David Smith by Union officers.

Lincoln okayed McClellan's order of "Union" repeaters. Design had one major defect: it could be fired so fast through single barrel the steel would melt. Hopper held preloaded, reusable steel cartridges. Serial No. 2 of few cal. .58 guns bought by Union is now in Springfield Armory museum.

WOOD

Four wheels	24.00	
One limber, with chest	20.00	
One carriage	20.00	
Two linen covers for chests	1.50	65.50
Total		$612.50
Add twenty percent		122.50
		$735.00

That these guns saw active service is beyond question, but their influence, as with the Gatlings and the Confederate repeaters, on the outcome of even minor engagements was very slight. The two barrels mentioned in the bill of materials could have made a major tactical improvement in the use of volley firing guns. The spare barrel was to be held in reserve and switched when the first barrel became hot.

The first Union repeating gun from Carr & Avery was received on April 21, 1862. Makers Carr & Avery, (whom J. D. Mills represented), apparently expected to be paid the $1,200 asking price. After McClellan's remarks about cost plus 20 per cent, two more shipments of guns were received; 28 guns were received after the order of July 8, 1862, and paid for at the $735 price July 9, 1862. The second batch of 22 guns came in a day or two later and was paid for July 14, 1862. Mr. Mills' first sample gun remained in an accounting limbo until finally paid for on August 3, 1865—at the $735 valuation. At Ream's Station, Confederates had one of these guns—took a shot at a Yankee observation balloon; then limbered up and disappeared. Whether it had been captured, or bought in the North and smuggled South, is not known.

Confederate Machine Cannon

On the Confederate side, attempts to increase rate of fire, even as General Rains pleaded for more copper to make percussion caps, continued with all the ingenuity at their command. General Gorgas distinguished himself by the innovation of a repeating small-bore cannon, 1.25-inch, of the turret principle. The pancake turret held 18 copper-lined muzzle-loaded chambers, radiating outward spoke-like. The inner ring of the pancake held the percussion nipples. A cam arrangement loaded and tripped a striker successively as the turret was turned. Of special importance was a loading groove in the cast-iron gun chassis to the right of the barrel, in line with the direction of rotation of the pancake. Inserting cartridges at this point and working the charging lever, the gunner's assistant could keep the turret constantly loaded. Apparently only one was made; none were used in the field.

A straightforward approach to machine cannon design was used by the South in the siege of Petersburg. This particular piece, a cast-and-wrought iron five-chamber 2-inch revolver cannon, was captured 27 April 1865 at Danville, Virginia, and sent by the Union troops to the Ordnance Laboratory at West Point for study. Mounted on cast-iron wheels resembling the frame of a plow or harrow, this hand-crank percussion cap fired repeater was not particularly successful; it did little for the South.

More widely publicized, less practical, was the "celebrated gun presented by Robison (sic) and Cottam of London to Governor Vance of North Carolina." This gun caused General Holloway to detour via Bull's Gap ordnance depot on April 25, 1865, where reposed the big brass cannon-like repeater which the Yankees had captured. The joke in a sense was upon the North at last. For nearly four years Union officers had steadfastly refused to accept this cumbersome breechloader; now it was theirs as a booty of war!

The inventor, General O. Vandenberg, was an American but he went to Britain to try and market his design. Before the Royal United Service Institute he gave an address 9 May 1862 on his "new system of artillery, for projecting a group or cluster of shot." The gun which General Holloway saw was of 85 barrels, caliber .54. Other Vandenberg guns had as many as 451 barrels.

The breechpiece contained the charges, in individual chambers, at the front of which each time the gun was loaded, the gunner placed little copper sleeves for effecting a gas seal. When the breech was screwed into place the sleeves forced into the backs of the barrels and kept the action free from smoke—or so Vandenberg hoped. There was a loading machine to charge all chambers at once with powder, and another to put in the bullets and ram them down.

While the center charge was ignited by the single percussion cap and fired all charges simultaneously, there were vents to be plugged that could restrict the fire. Thus only a portion of the shots could be discharged, and then the vents were opened and the piece was recapped, ready for a second discharge. As with the Gorgas gun, and the revolving 2-inch cannon, true sustained fire was not possible.

Vandenberg tried unsuccessfully to get the United States to buy his guns. On 18 February 1864 he addressed General Ramsay, saying he would send or bring three of his guns to the United States and present them to the President or the Secretary of War as "an offering to our country and government." Three guns were shipped over, and tested by Captain Benton, who reported adversely on them. Being a thorough man and believer in the axiom "Never let the sun go down on an uncleaned gun," Benton had the test Vandenberg gun cleaned. He found it took one man a total of 9 hours to adequately clean the barrels and action of the piece, which was sufficient cause for condemnation.

The three guns were eventually shipped back to Vandenberg in London in an effort to get rid of them. But the fates ruled otherwise. In April 1865, cavalry under Major General George Stoneman at Salisbury, North Carolina, captured the gun which the fair-minded Vandenberg had sent to Governor Vance (why play favorites?) and routed it up to West Point. Today, it reposes in solitary brass-burnished splendor in the museum, edification for the cadets as well as labor for whoever polishes the brass. Another Vandenberg gun is in the Rotunda Museum of the Woolwich Arsenal near London. The guns were made by Robinson & Cottam, of London, not generally recognized as armaments makers. Perhaps they were brass founders or general machinists.

The most effective of the Confederate guns was the Williams single-barreled rapid fire cannon. It was not a true machine gun but because of its cranked fore-and-aft breechblock was capable of being fired, using combustible cartridges of 1.56-inch caliber, at a rate of 65 shots per minute. Invented by Captain D. R. Williams, C.S.A., of Covington, Kentucky, it has been called the first machine gun successfully used in battle, but it was not properly a machine gun for it had no attached feeding mechanism nor multiplicity of barrels to give it rapid fire. The loader had to be quick, that's all.

A hand crank on the right of the breech opened and closed the breechblock, firing the cap as the cartridge was shoved into the chamber. When the barrel heated

Spare barrel and anti-rifle fire shield was supplied with Union guns. Cartridges fell from hopper into open-chambered drum rotated by simple crank. One of these guns is recorded as having been used by Confederates against a Union observation balloon.

Repeating turret magazine cannon of small bore and considerable ingenuity is credited to invention of Confederate Ordnance General Josiah Gorgas. South used several repeaters and rapid fire breech-loading Williams gun also.

up, expansion sometimes prevented complete closing, stopping firing until the metal had cooled down.

A battery of six of these guns was in use by Giltner's brigade of Texas troops under command of Captain T. M. Freeman. On 3 May, 1862, at the Battle of Seven Pines, Virginia, a battery attached to Pickett's brigade created havoc among the Yankees. The guns were directed by the inventor. Some captured Union officers later asked to see these new Confederate "secret weapons"; their firepower had made a great effect.

Captain T. T. Allen, 7th Ohio Cavalry, expressed amazement at the rapid fire and devastation of the little guns at the battle of Blue Springs, East Tennessee, on 10 October, 1863. For all this success, only a few of these cannon were made. Two batteries of six guns each were made at Lynchburg, Virginia, and the Tredegar Works cast four batteries, 24 guns. One set of six was made at Mobile, Alabama, and served in the artillery of General Simon Bolivar Buckner, C.S.A. One of these latter guns with accessories was captured at Danville in 1865. The breech obturating plug served, according to Chinn, as the basis for the first breech-loading field gun adopted by the U. S. Army.

The Gatling Gun

Ager, Williams, Vandenberg, these have faded into history. The repeating gun most remembered from the war, and yet one which had a very confusing record of use therein, is that of Dr. Richard Jordan Gatling. I had the pleasure of witnessing how effectively Dr. Gatling had built when I attended a meeting of the American Ordnance Association at Aberdeen the fall of 1957. Mounted on a testing stand was a small bundle of barrels, dwarfed in seeming firepower by the huge cannon flanking it. But when the gunner pushed the button and that mighty mite whirred into action with a high-pitched snarling roar so rapidly that no individual explosions could even be sensed, I knew I had witnessed not only the world's fastest-firing machine gun, and the world's heaviest gun in weight of metal fired (a ton and a half in one minute), but a gun that was directly inspired by the Civil War special artillery General Butler bought from Dr. Gatling.

The revolving bundle of barrels to which Dr. Gatling attached a hopper feed for steel chargers solved many of the problems then plaguing machine gun designers. First, the hopper permitted the sustained fire desired. With sustained fire, as in the Ager or Williams gun, came hazards; expansion from over heating and either jamming, or erosion of the bore. Gatling solved this by adding barrels. The time delay between the firing of succeeding shots in any one barrel, as it revolved about to return to its place before the firing mechanism, was enough to permit some cooling. Originally Gatling conceived of an enclosed barrel group with a cylinder about the barrels to hold cooling materials. This was found to be not necessary and the Gatling guns from first until the brass-jacket M1883 were exposed barrel models.

It can be answered with some degree of certainty why Gatling invented his gun. That is, in the lives of many other inventors, statements of purpose are often lacking. Some may have invented such-and-such for patriotic motives, to get rich quick, or some other mundane, prosaic reason. Dr. Gatling, independently wealthy at the start of the war, has chosen to set forth his own reasons quite clearly.

In 1877, Gatling lived in Hartford, Connecticut next door to Mrs. Colt, widow of the late Samuel Colt at whose factory the Gatling Gun Company now contracted the manufacture of their guns. Mrs. Colt's little niece, Elizabeth Jarvis, was a frequent visitor to the Gatling's hospitable residence, and Gatling explained to her his beliefs at the time he developed the guns:

Hartford, June 15th, 1877

My Dear Friend.

It may be interesting to you to know how I came to invent the gun which bears my name; I will tell you: In 1861, during the opening events of the war, (residing at that time in Indianapolis, Ind.,) I witnessed almost daily the departure of troops to the front and the return of the wounded, sick, and dead. The most of the latter lost their lives, not in battle, but by sickness and exposure incident to the service. It occurred to me if I could invent a machine—a gun—which could by its rapidity of fire, enable one man to do as much battle duty as a hundred, that it would, to a great extent, supersede the necessity of large armies, and consequently, exposure to battle and disease be greatly diminished. I thought over the subject and finally this idea took practical form in the invention of the Gatling Gun.

Yours truly,
R. J. Gatling

By the time of Gatling's elderly years, the story had grown slightly in nobility; as his granddaughter, Mrs.

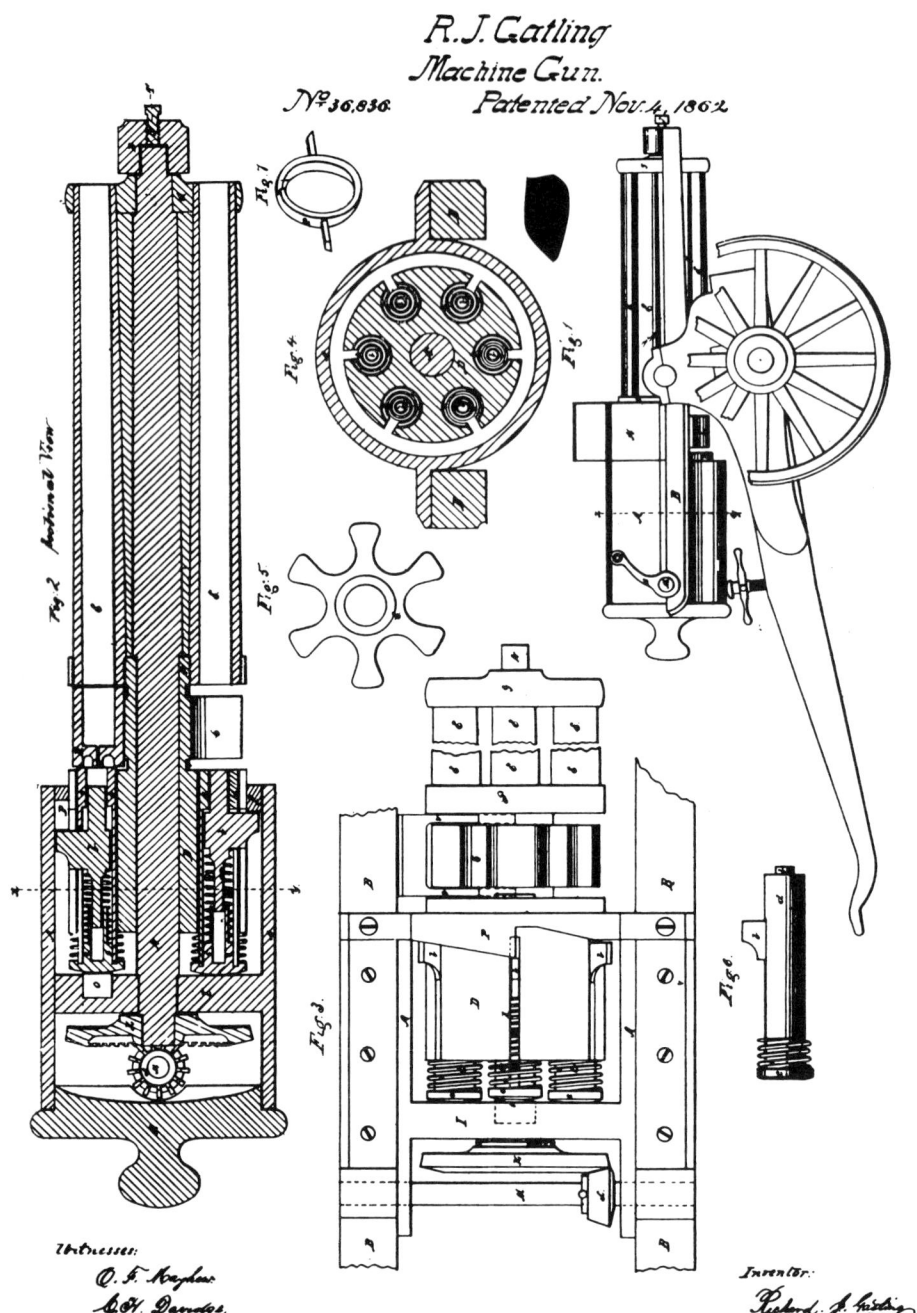

First of Gatling's guns was bulky wheeled carriage "cannon" of six barrels, made by Miles Greenwood & Co. of Cincinnati. Actual arms were destroyed by fire but patent drawing probably pictures these first specimens. Weapon used steel chargers of "Union" type.

Albert Newcombe, remembers it. "He was a most peace-loving soul, and I remember that his reason for inventing that then-lethal gun, was to make war so horrible that it would end wars."

But Gatling's own written words seem to be less glamorous, for in 1864 he touched somewhat on his motives in a letter to President Lincoln. "The arm in question is an invention of no ordinary character," he wrote from Indianapolis to the President on February 18, 1864. "It is regarded by all who have seen it operate, as the most effective implement of warfare invented during the war, and *it is just the thing needed to aid in crushing the present rebellion.*" (Emphasis supplied by Dr. Gatling). Taking a swipe at the Ager gun in a postscript, Gatling concluded his appeal to Lincoln to have the gun adopted by the Army with:

"I have seen an inferior arm known as the 'coffee mill gun,' which I am informed has not given satisfaction in practical tests on the battlefield. I assure you my invention is no 'coffee mill gun,'—but is entirely a different arm, and is entirely free from the accidents and objections raised against that arm."

There is in this a hint of the efficiency, the veritable "automation" which Gatling, a mechanical scientist first and always, sought to bring to the battlefront. His first gun was patented November 4, 1862, but was in existence, working well on July 14, 1862. That day, T. A. Morris, A. Ballweg, and D. G. Rose certified to the working of the gun which they had tested at direction of Governor Oliver P. Morton of Indiana. "The discharge can be made with all desirable accuracy as rapidly as 150 times a minute, and may be continued for hours without danger, as we think, from over heating."

But Morris, Ballweg, and Rose admitted that only field service would prove the point; they recommended that Morton order enough be made for testing in battle.

The Governor was unwilling to risk state funds at the time, and so sent Gatling to Washington with a letter of introduction to P. H. Watson, the new Assistant Secretary of War under Stanton. His letter is dated December 2, 1862; Gatling must have arrived there not much later than the 4th or 5th, allowing even for delays en route. With him he had a gun.

What kind of gun this was is the subject of some dispute among arms historians. By the fall of 1862, prior to the issue of his patent, Gatling had contracted on his own account to have six guns made at the works of Miles Greenwood & Company in Cincinnati. This firm was recognized by the Ordnance Department as a firm loyal to the North. They supplied between August 30, 1861, and December 24, 1862, many bronze smoothbore and rifled guns and howitzers, and 2,500 lances with pennons, for a total value delivered of $84,157.68. That Miles Greenwood could deliver to Gatling the guns he required seems true, but the factory was destroyed by fire and with it, Gatling's models and the partly finished battery of guns. The date of the fire is carelessly passed over in the record, and we have not been able to tie it down; yet it would seem to have been about the New Year's, 1863. The sample gun was made either by a private model maker to Gatling's order, or by Miles Greenwood and delivered to the doctor in time for his trip to Washington. Most likely, he would have taken one of the six, if finished in time, asking the factory to store the others until he should know whether to send them to Washington or to some commander in the field. There was said to have been a Gatling gun dated 1862 in the Washington Arsenal for some years after the war. The models of Gatling guns must therefore be said to consist of patterns as follows:

Type I: Wooden breech actually made and deposited with the initial filing for the patent. This shortened mechanical model of wood was in existence in the 1940's and photographed, but its location is not known now to this writer.

Type IA: the gun detailed more clearly in the final issued patent specification of November 4, 1862, No. 36836. Of six barrels mounted in plates at muzzle and breech, this piece set the style for subsequent models having long trunnion arms reaching forward to support the barrel group on a cross member at the front. The back plate has the cascabel knob of one of Miles Greenwood's cannon; it is not the round knob containing aiming or safety mechanism that is found on later Gatling guns. Elevation was a simple screw jack in a box between the trail arms; the gun trunnions were mounted in pillow blocks on top of the cheeks of the trail and, perhaps a draughting error or perhaps a designing error, the caps of the pillow block slanted to the rear, suggesting the ease with which the gun could jump out of its seat if recoil was excessive.

The barrel group axle passed entirely through the breech to the rear, just inside the cascable plate. There, a gear engaged a cog on the right-mounted hand crank, to turn the barrels and breechblocks. From a centrally mounted hopper, steel cartridge cases using individual percussion caps on musket nipples, dropped into a cylinder exactly like the Ager cylinder.

Gatling considered the Ager gun to be competition and obliquely referred to it in his patent: "I do not claim the use of the grooved or fluted revolving carrier separately considered, and when the same is made to revolve separately and independently of the barrels and breech, the same being an old device," he deprecatingly put it. The group of barrels and locks revolving together with him were new.

It is possible that this type of gun was going with him to Washington. But the record is not entirely clear. "My first guns were built in Cincinnati (Miles Greenwood), and were able to fire 150 to 250 shots per minute. Six had been completed when the factory burned down and the guns were destroyed," he reported in an interview to a New York reporter, recorded later in an obituary column on his life. "Following this accident," as Dr. Gatling categorically calls the fire, "I had thirteen guns made at what is now the type foundry in Cincinnati, and those I sent on by my partner, a wealthy merchant of Cincinnati, to Washington to persuade the Government to introduce them. He took them to Baltimore, where he left twelve, and went with the other to Washington. The Chief of Ordnance at the time was an old fogey. He received him coldly, told him he had no faith in his gun, and that he believed flintlock muskets were on the whole the best weapons for warfare. In short, he would have nothing to do with him. My partner then left Washington and returned to Baltimore. Ben Butler was there with his troops. He had heard of the guns and had asked to see them work. As soon as he had done so he said he would buy them on his own responsibility, and did so, giving his voucher for $12,000 for them. My partner had this cashed, but at this time there was a great fall in pork, and 50,000 hogs which he had packed in Chicago in expectation of a rise had to be sold. In a word the break in the market ruined him, and my money went with him. So, for the first twenty guns I had made at a great cost to myself, I received nothing. Ben Butler took the guns he had with him to the Battle of Petersburg and fired them himself upon the rebels. They created great consternation and slaughter, and the news of them went all over the world . . ."

The autobiographical *Butler's Book* in its several volumes neglects to mention this colorful use of an important novel weapon of war by the loquacious major general. Major Frederick V. Longstaff in *The Machine*

Gun (1917) notes the oft-repeated tale that Gatling's guns were demonstrated "on the field of battle" by either Dr. Gatling or one of his crew, but says little more than that of the alleged Civil War use of the arm. An early reference to Ben Butler and the guns is made by General Norton, who was in 1872 not only a close friend of Gatling's but possibly a paid publicist. His cover ornament for *American Breechloading Small Arms* is a beautiful stamping of a horse carrying a Gatling gun, over the legend, "The Gatling Gun," while the back of the book is devoted to a very thorough essay on the Gatling, with emphasis on its successful use after adoption by the United States and manufacture in 1865-66 by contractors Cooper and Colt.

Says Norton briefly, "Some of them did get into service before the close of the American war, and were used effectively in repelling rebel attacks upon the Union Forces, under command of General Butler, near Richmond, Virginia." To check with the facts, these guns had to be in service between June 1864 and April 1865, during which time several battles or campaigns involving fighting at Petersburg are dated. The letter of February 18, 1864, of Gatling to Lincoln makes it quite clear that no guns were delivered to the United States Army or Navy before that time. Yet during the New York draft riots of July, 1863, right after Gettysburg, several Gatling guns were ensconced in the windows of Horace Greeley's *New York Tribune* headquarters, and on one occasion at least turned away a serious threat of attack by the mobs. Reference to this is found lately in *July 1863* a novelized version of the time by Irving Werstein, whose sources for the Gatlings seem to confirm their existence there in Greeley's windows.

We therefore have to assume that at least two or three of the Cincinnati type foundry guns had been completed by June of 1863, and that Gatling sent them out to Greeley for publicity purposes. These presumably were returned to Gatling in Cincinnati, where they remained until February of 1864, when, as he said to President Lincoln, "Messrs. McWhinny and Rindge, partners of mine in the manufacture and sale of the gun, are now in Washington with a sample gun and I hope ere long to hear of its adoption by the War Department."

Robert V. Bruce in *Lincoln and the Tools of War* is equally uncertain about this matter of the use of Gatlings. There was an easy chance in the records to confuse them with the Ager or Union Repeating Gun, which may have accounted for Gatling's vehemence in declaring to Lincoln that his was no "coffee mill gun." For example, Bruce reveals that the coffee mill guns died hard. In October 1863 John H. Schenck, an associate of Edward Nugent, announced himself as their new proprietor and complained that those ordered by Rosecrans had not yet reached that officer's successor, General George H. Thomas, "who highly approves of them."

Although 16 of the coffee mill guns remained at the Washington Arsenal, the Ordnance Office ignored Schenck's complaints, as well as his suggestion that the guns be carried on horseback by cavalry and mounted

Improved styling is present in second series of Gatling repeaters which also used steel .58 chargers. McWhinney, Rindge & Co. were partners with Gatling in manufacture of second series of guns at Cincinnati Type Foundry. Gun shown is No. 205, preserved at Springfield Armory.

infantry, ready for swift dismounting and use. Ten were sent to General Butler in February 1864 when he requested them for use on boat service upon the James river (op. cit., p. 282). These it must be assumed are those "Gatling's" sometimes spoken of as in service in the James River squadron; actually, they were Ager coffee mill guns. But later on (pp. 290-91), Bruce says Admiral Porter actually acquired one Gatling gun for his Mississippi squadron and General Butler used eight Gatling guns on gunboats and two in the Petersburg lines. Bruce himself seems confused in the issue; even more confusing is the statement from John W. Gatling, grandson of the inventor, to this author on June 21, 1957:

"No one seems to know any anecdotes on the Civil War use of the gun. General Ben Butler, with his own money, had the first gun made after my grandfather had been turned down by the Army. They were made at Cincinnati at a brass foundry that did work of this nature on contract. How my grandfather came to know him I don't know, but they were very close friends. This factory was destroyed by fire, but I don't believe it was anything but an accident and in no way connected with the war or guns."

Here we have a very interesting piece of family legend, in which there may lurk some shades of history. *If* Butler advanced money to Gatling for the manufacture of the guns at Miles Greenwood & Company, then Butler was a party to the manufacture of an invention which he later, exercising the prerogative of a commander, purchased for use after rejection by the Government. He may have been quite reluctant, in view of history not also noticing the event, to have made much of any employment of the Gatling guns if he did in fact have any in his command. Dr. Gatling was quite sure that Butler bought the 12 guns his partner had taken to Baltimore, but there appears to have been contemporary confusion over the use of the expression "coffee mill guns" that made soldiers and commanders interchange the Union repeater and the Gatling Battery Gun under the same heading. Later, in his writings during which he makes claim to other innovations, Butler's failure to mention his alleged purchase of the Gatlings is conspicuous.

That Butler had an "interest" in the Gatlings, paying for "the first gun made after Gatling was turned down by the Army," is beyond proof today.

Aside from the Butler references, it was not until May, 1863, that Gatling was able to get much notice taken of his development. Meanwhile, the fire had destroyed his factory and he began again, in association with McWhinny, Rindge & Company. Neither McWhinny or Rindge are listed as gunmakers, contractors for ordnance and ordnance stores, nor in tabulations of gunsmiths and like suppliers. It is assumed they owned or represented an establishment in Indianapolis, which Dr. Gatling made his headquarters after the fire at Miles Greenwood. One gun tested by the Navy appears to be a transition model, in that it necessarily still used the steel cylinder percussion cap-charges, but had an improvement in the form of the breech casing which is reflected in the construction of the several existing percussion-cap Gatlings now in Government museums. In other words, it was a model not shown in any patent, but somewhat less bulky in the breech than the 1862 model. During May, 1863, the Navy tested the gun:

NAVY ORDNANCE YARD
Washington City, May 20th, 1863

Rear Admiral John A. Dahlgren, Chief of Bureau of Ordnance:

Sir: In relation to the "Gatling gun or battery," I have to report as follows:

Mounted on light field artillery carriage, rapid fire .58 Gatling gun may be one of few bought by Ben Butler, though records are exceedingly hazy on this alleged use of Gatling's design in Civil War. Family says Butler backed Gatling in manufacture of arms for government use.

The gun consists of six rifle barrels, of 58/100-inch calibre; each barrel is firmly connected to a breech-piece by a screw of 1 inch in length. The breech-piece is composed of one solid piece, which is made secure to a shaft 1⅜-inch in diameter. The barrels are inserted in the breech-piece around the shaft, on a parallel line with the axes of said shaft, and held in a proper position by a muzzle-piece, bored by the same gauge as the holes for the breech-piece for the reception of the barrels. The breech-piece is also bored in the rear end, for the reception of the locks, on a parallel line with the barrels, each barrel having its own independent lock, revolving simultaneously, so that in case one lock or barrel becomes disabled, those remaining can be used effectively.

Between the locks and barrels is a receptacle for the charges on a parallel line with the locks and barrels. As the entire gun revolves, the charges find their way through a hopper, containing any given number, fed from cases, instantaneously. The breech-piece contains the locks, and is entirely protected by a heavy casing of gun-metal (brass alloy), made fast to a wrought-iron frame resting on trunnions 1½ inches in diameter. It is screwed to the frame by four bolts. Inside this casing is attached an inclined ring, which the hammers of the locks ride as the gun revolves, until coming to the point of fire, when the discharge takes place. The locks are composed of three pieces and one spiral spring, and are entirely protected from dust or any injury. The gun is mounted as other field-pieces, with limber attached.

The gun or battery has stood the limited test given it admirably, has proved itself to be a very effective arm at short range; is well constructed, and calculated to withstand the usage to which it would necessarily be subjected. It is suggested that an improvement in the rifling of the barrels would be advantageous.

Respectfully submitted,
J. S. Skerrett,
Lt. Commander U. S. N.

Admiral Dahlgren gave permission to commanders of fleets and squadrons to requisition such guns as they might require. As Gatling wrote to Lincoln, on February 18, 1864, "Since which time a number of requisitions have been sent in for the guns by different naval officers, but none of said requisitions have been granted to my knowledge."

The delay in patronizing the Indianapolis physician, who was known to be of Southern descent, lay with the belief that he belonged to the Organization of American Knights. While some principles of this secret society flourishing in the western and border states were very fundamentalist American, what in calmer times might have been called truly patriotic, in the present schism they served merely to rock the boat. For one thing, as a goal for some of the members, they proposed to unite the states west of the Mississippi in a third nation, a Western Confederacy, sympathetic to the Southern and withdrawing the support of these regions from the war machine of the North. Further, they proposed to bring Illinois, Indiana, and Ohio into the war on the Southern side; secret agents reporting to Federal Provost Marshal Colonel J. P. Sanderson at St. Louis even referred to Confederate volunteer regiments of Indiana as being at least nominally in existence.

A report filed with Sanderson some time between April 18, 1864, and May 25, 1864, by an unnamed informant, listed among members of the Order of American Knights "in different localities as far as known to date," one "Dr. Gatling, inventor of gun so called."

The report circulated, and Brigadier General Henry B. Carrington, U.S. Volunteers, conveyed the information in a report to Captain C. H. Potter who was assistant adjutant general of Ohio, at Columbus. Carrington sought to advise Captain Potter how widespread the conspiracy was, and especially the current threat of an uprising of Southern sympathizers, well armed, at the occasion of a forthcoming convention and speech in Chicago by C. L. Vallandigham, the grand commander of the Order. "If numbers, money, and oaths can give them the power and will to strike," Carrington wrote June 6, 1864, "they are a dangerous body of men and it will pay to be ferreted out . . . Dr. Gatling, inventor of the gun so called, is a member of the order."

During the year preceding, a celebrated incident of the war had occurred that Colonel Chinn thinks may have some direct bearing on why Gatling's guns were not made and used before this. The incident is Morgan's Raid, up into Ohio and Indiana. That Morgan was in direct contact with the Knights of the Golden Circle, as the Order of American Knights was sometimes called, is indicated by voluminous correspondence and testimony. Most directly, a letter noted by James D. Horan in *Confederate Agent*, written July 10, 1863, by Conrad Baker, Acting Provost Marshal General of Indiana, to Colonel Fry, Acting Provost Marshal of Indianapolis, states: "In consequence of Morgan's raid into this state and the fears I entertain that there is an understanding between him and the Knights of the Golden Circle."

For a fuller exposition of the scope of this fantastic but almost-successful series of insurrections proposed by the Confederate secret service, we would refer the reader to Horan's book. That Morgan was in league with the Knights is quite certain. The purpose of his raid, therefore, is what fascinates Chinn. Did Gatling contract to have his guns made by Miles Greenwood in order to have them captured by Morgan thus saving him from the embarrassment of openly supplying the guns to the South? Or did Morgan push on toward Indianapolis partly to capture the new lot of guns being made under direction of McWhinny and Rindge? Exactly when were Gatling's guns actually burned, and did the whole factory of Miles Greenwood go, or only the Gatlings? It would seem probable that only the latter occurred.

There is room here for a book, resolving the seeming paradox that while Gatling was accused of being a sympathizer and member of the organization working to destroy the Northern government, he also sought to supply the North with his guns. Such duplicity is not unheard of, but it does not fit Gatling's character as later revealed by those who knew him.

He was definitely not a sympathizer with the slavery of the South, and at the same time recent researchers have made out a fair case that to be a member of the Knights of the Golden Circle was not necessarily to be disloyal.

During War, Gatling's guns influenced no battle, won no conflict. At war's end contract was let to Colt's who supplied 50 guns in 1″ caliber for fortress defense. Here three of this order are shown on river front at Washington Arsenal on Potomac.

Gatling was of a temperament to side with the Southern cause for a time, at the same instant being a firm "Jacksonian Democrat," a fundamentalist, a Constitution-man in an age when interpretations of the Constitution varied widely.

"My grandfather abhorred war, force, and was most peace loving," his grandson John W. Gatling notes as a recollection of family lore, John W. having been born about two years after Richard J.'s death. "You could not impose on him, for he was very firm and strong about his 'rights,' but differences were to be settled by negotiation, and people were to be free, unregimented, and individuals." The charge that Dr. Gatling was of the Order is plausible and possible; that he was genuinely disloyal, implausible.

Gatling's contribution to the war effort of either side was negligible. But he persisted in seeking government patronage and continued to perfect his designs. To adapt the percussion cap guns to metallic cartridge, he effected a modification of the breech bolt to a double-edge firing pin, and at the same time substituted cylindrical steel chambers individually charged with rimfire .58 musket cartridges. But this was a makeshift and did not last long. The patent of 1865 reveals a four-barrel gun, slower rate of fire, and a genuine novelty in cooling system; the barrel group is cased in a sealed canister, into which water or cooling liquids, or plaster of paris for cooling, could be introduced. It takes little imagination to see that the first time the plaster of paris was put in and then later someone carelessly added water, the concept was found to have practical defects. Gatling for the time dropped the barrel casing, and increased the barrels to a minimum of five, a maximum of ten.

Transition guns were experimentally chambered for the .58 rimfire musket cartridge at the end of the war, and further changes were due. After the tests of January-February 1865, General Dyer suggested constructing a 1-inch gun, and special ammunition for this caliber was made at Frankford Arsenal. The contract was given to the Cooper Firearms Manufacturing Company of Philadelphia, where eight were built in 1-inch caliber, ten barreled. Tests continued, more for the fun of shooting the thing, we suspect, than from the need to really learn anything new. Captain T. G. Baylor at Fort Monroe, firing the 1-inch gun in comparison with the 24-pdr. flank defense howitzer loaded with langrage, reported what Gatling long since knew and had often said: "The moral effect of the Gatling gun would be very great in repelling an assault, as there is not a second of time for the assailants to advance between the discharges."

Reported on July 14, 1866, it was at last decided to really adopt the Gatling gun as a part of the arsenal of the United States. An order for Gatlings not previously recognized is that given by General A. B. Dyer. Dated August 24, 1866, was the order to Talbot, Jones & Company of Indianapolis, for 100 guns, half .50 caliber and half 1-inch caliber, "each gun to have six steel barrels, rifled." The gun carriages were to be of seasoned white oak, the limbers and ammunition chests to be identical, except for interior arrangement of the ammo boxes, with the limbers for field carriages. Barrels were to be browned, a blue-black rusting process; other iron or steel parts to be blued. In proof each gun was to be fired 96 times, 16 from each barrel. The order was to be completed in 12 months, the guns to be delivered "at the manufactury." Price was $2,000 each 1-inch gun and $1,500 each .50 caliber gun.

Col. Mel Johnson in 1949 took regular M1883 Gatling and hooked up electric motor drive to achieve fantastic rate of fire. Notion led to development of electric Vulcan gun for F105 jet fighter armament.

Talbot, Jones & Company subcontracted this work to the Colt's Patent Firearms Manufacturing Company of Hartford, and the guns were completed there. Deliveries and payments to Talbot Jones spread over the spring and summer of 1867; first deliveries in April 20 of five .50 caliber guns were paid for promptly on May 1. Deducted from the payment was the sum of $525, evidently an advance against materials or work, by the United States. Additional advances totalled over $11,000, but work lagged slightly on the 1-inch guns until the day before deadline, 35 1-inch guns were presented for inspection and acceptance on August 23, 1867. The contract totalling $175,000 at last was paid; Gatling had begun to reap a return from his endeavors. But the gun he developed to make war more economical, so that fewer soldiers would be called upon to fall ill from the diseases of the camp and field, had quite the opposite effect.

Gatling's Later Career

Rapid fire inventions followed at a rapid pace. The nations of the world sought out Gatling and he was royally received wherever he went. His host Czar Nicholas treated him to a game of chess, and cautioned his best chess player to "let the Doctor win once or twice." The master chessman later reported to the Czar that it was all he could do to win against the shrewd playing of the quiet physician who dealt in death.

Russian General Gorloff was sent to Hartford to supervise the fabrication of the Gatling guns for the Czar. In the Colt plant a special section had been set aside to handle the increasing contracts of the Gatling Gun Company of Hartford. The good doctor moved up to Farmington Avenue, and bought a big house next door to Mrs. Colt's Italian villa with the big plaster Uffizi dogs at the porte cochiere. In Hartford lived Gideon Welles, late Secretary of the Navy in Lincoln's cabinet. He took a major interest in the Gatling Gun Company and became its Secretary and Treasurer. Down in the South Meadows Armoury, General Gorloff inspected the revolving battery guns in detail and stamped each with his mark of approval, his name in Russian, "Gorloff."

Back in the Russian Empire the Gatling guns became important to the Czar's artillery. The name "Gorloff" was all that the cyrillic-reading Russkies could see to understand, and they dubbed the new bundle of barrels light artillery "Gorloffs." The gun went into production in a Russian Arsenal, possibly Tula or Sestoretsky, rifle factories where the rifle designed by the American Colonel Berdan, of the Sharpshooter regiment, was being made. The usual story is that the Gatling gun was "pirated" by the Russians. The relations between Dr. Gatling and the Czar, who practically gave him the keys to the Winter Palace, suggest a more gentlemanly attitude toward the rights of inventors. It is known, for example, that the contract with Smith and Wesson called for complete sets of gauges for inspecting the work of manufacturing the so-called "Russian Model" .44 revolvers. And in England, all the tools for inspecting the Berdan II rifle were fabricated as a part of the contract and shipped out to Russia along with the specimen rifles. In such open and aboveboard dealings it seems most likely that the Russians also paid for the right to manufacture for their own needs, the designs of the Smith & Wesson, the Berdan II, and the "Gorloff" Gatling guns.

Dr. Gatling reaped the rewards of genius, business acumen, and hard work; an income exceeding $2,000,000 in the space of 30 years from his revolving barrel

Electric Vulcan aircraft 20mm cannon described in patent as "Improvement on Gatling Gun" is shown in test stand at Air Armament Center, Eglin AFB, Florida. Six-barrel gun fires up to 8,000 rounds per minute with motor drive.

"battery gun" that was to shorten the Civil War. But Gatling, though no active Southron sympathizer, was robbed by a species of carpet-bagger which infested the North in those halcyon days of national expansion: the railroad stock promoters. Gatling invested heavily in railroads that never went anywhere except to take him to the cleaners. Bad investments and further development of heavy artillery taxed his resources but he remained all his life a gentle man, firm and of strong convictions, but one who lived on in the hearts of his family.

When he had married, his wife received a slave as a wedding present. The senior Gatling, farmer though he was, dependent upon slave labor for his income, had freed 100 slaves before the war at a financial loss which may have amounted to more than $100,000. Dr. Gatling shared his father's dislike of the "peculiar institution" and on their wedding day he and his new bride, "Jimmy," (Jemima) freed their slave. The good black woman remained with them as a paid servant until her death in the 1890's. Thereupon ensued a brief scandal, for Dr. Gatling wanted to bury his faithful cook in the family burial plot in Indianapolis. "She is a member of the Gatling family," he sternly proclaimed, and would not budge an inch from his declaration. Prevailing against the uncharitable souls who managed Crown Hill Cemetery, the first Negro to be buried there was laid to rest by Dr. Gatling beside his father and his mother in the Gatling family plot.

The big house in Hartford was a beloved retreat for the globe-trotting inventor-medic. He loved the big parlor upholstered in pale blue satin. It had a magnificent crystal chandelier sparkling with the light of a hundred candles as he wined and dined the Russian general, or the representative of the Khedive of Egypt, or the King of Italy, or perhaps the taciturn J. G. Accles who was to establish a dynasty in the metal industries of England, Accles & Pollock, tube benders, offshoot of Accles' fabrication in England of the Gatling Gun to supply the Crown. Across the hall was a reception room all done in deep red. From some jaunt the doctor had brought back a mechanical bird that nested in its glass pedestal case, and when wound up would sing and turn its head to stare with unwinking eyes at the observer. It was in this house full of memories that Gatling breathed his last.

His granddaughter, Peggy (Mrs. Albert Newcombe), was with him in these moments.

"Grandfather died in my arms when I was about 16, as nearly as I can remember the time. He had just returned from downtown in New York City at noontime," Mrs. Newcombe wrote to this author. "As was his custom, he said he would have a cat nap before lunch. He cat-napped all through his life. He seemed very old to me, but alert and with a twinkle in his eyes. I covered him up on the couch in my father's study and left him to snooze, and went down the long hall of the apartment to join Grandmother at our lunch. They had been living with us for some time. I believe at that time Grandfather was out of money, as he'd been spending it to develop a new large gun I remember hearing about. While at lunch the phone rang in my father's study, and I ran down the hall to answer it. As I lifted it off the hook, I glanced at Grandfather and he seemed to be gasping for breath. It proved to be my father, on the phone, and I asked him to hold on, as Grandfather was on the couch, and looked queer to me. I went to him and lifted up his shoulders. In my arms he gave a big sigh and collapsed. Somehow I knew he had died. I told my father on the phone that Grandfather had just died. He passed away as gently as he lived, for I remember him as gentle voiced and sweet natured. He had the softest, silky white hair, straight and fine; as a child I always loved to stroke it which always made him laugh. He had a very sweet tooth and used to put five lumps of sugar in his cup of tea and also a spot of butter."

Thus ended the inventor of the Gatling Gun; but not the gun itself. In a way this simple construction, for there is nothing very complicated in the gun's design—has proved as elemental as the wheel. Inaugurated in the 1950's, a half-century after the inventor's death, is the modern-day Gatling gun styled by the Air Force "Vulcan." Delivering a snarling hurricane of steel at the rate of 8,000 shots per minute, the six barrelled air-to-air combat gun is but Dr. Gatling's basic model, electrified. In 1893 Gatling put an electric motor on his gun, with contra-rotating field coils for the double purpose of reducing the rotational speed to a mere 3,000 shots per minute, and also acting as a brake instantly, by reversing polarity. Both these ingredients were taken into account in designing the modern Vulcan which is, as the patent says, "a Gatling Gun." The inventor, remembered as a kindly old man, has long since passed into dust, but his Civil War battery gun is still in the Arsenal of the Union.

CHAPTER 21

Enfield: The North's Second Rifle

For the first three years of the Civil War, foreign-made weapons were bought, imported, and issued to Union and Confederate troops. Several arms became co-standard U. S. service arms, and are so indicated in the Atlas to the Official Records. Others were liberally damned in correspondence and battlefield reports by officers envious of the fine Springfield rifles of other regiments, but the record seems to indicate that, despite congressional investigations of their procurement and issue, foreign muskets put firepower into the hands of front line troops at a time when North and South were starved for infantry weapons.

The foremost foreign arm was the British service rifle, made at Enfield RSAF and by private shops.

The general pattern of Enfield Rifle, three-band rifled musket with band springs, adopted about 1853 by Great Britain, is found in a variety of forms which superficially are alike but which differ subtly. A detailed examination of three "typical" Enfield-pattern specimens reveals a number of detail dissimilarities among them.

The Birmingham Tower Enfield

First to be studied was a Birmingham-made "Tower" two-band artillery rifle, fitted with stud for sword bayonet. Brass buttplate, brass trigger guard (without provision for any swivel or sling loop), and brass nosecap, are bright; the iron barrel and iron bands are blued, the latter brightly polished and heat blued and the barrel rust "browned." Lockplate and hammer were case hardened in mottled colors. The escutcheons at the side nails or screws were brass and bright, side nails hardened. The front band bore a sling swivel; the rear swivel base terminated in a wood screw and was twisted into the stock, which was of light beechwood.

The lock outside mark is standard for military Birmingham arms, a crown over V ★ R (Fig. 1) behind the hammer, with the word TOWER below the bolster cut, the date *1862* surmounting TOWER, and in front of this, midway between the Tower mark and the hole for mainspring positioning pin or stud, the mark of government acceptance, a simple crown over an inverted Broad Arrow (Fig. 2). Inside the lockplate, the maker's mark ORD, with the first letter defaced by another inspection stamp, appears above the fixed lump that stops the rigid limb of the mainspring. Forward of the tumbler-spring stirrup position is the Government lockplate inspector's stamp, presumably as the mechanism is accepted into the government storehouses at the Birmingham Tower government arsenal. This mark is shown in Fig. 3. Toward the front edge of the plate, inside, is a tiny view mark indicating the lockplate passed gauge to fit into a government stock: (Fig. 4). And to the right of this "crown-S" stamp is the letter H in ¼-inch size stamp, which mark also appears on stock and barrel. The H was punched into the lock metal after it was finished and hardened, and no further mechanical work was done to the lock. It is the contractor's mark, the symbol of the firm which "set up" these parts to fill a government order. The inside curve of the hammer bears another stamp similar to the storehouse mark, "crown-L-2." It is a crown-B-51 stamp, similarly arranged.

The barrel of this Birmingham Tower gun does not bear any commercial Gunmaker's Company proof marks; only the government marks. Most interesting in the barrel markings is the hardly discernible mark, in italic script, about ⅛-inch high characters, of *John Field Swinburn*. His name sometimes incorrectly written "Swinburne," he was one of the major government contractors who grouped together in 1861 to form the Birmingham Small Arms Company which is today still in existence, a capital stock corporation, with its gunmaking activities conducted under the title of BSA-Guns, Ltd.

Barrelmaker Swinburn, organized as Swinburn & Son, supplied a tube to the Tower contractor "H" which had been used once before, and bore the row of marks of former Government proof. These marks now appear on a quadrant of the breech covered by the stock. Swinburn's mark is located four inches from the breech edge, on the underside. It has been partially defaced by an overstamped workman's initials *TT* and partly by striking up for refinishing. The percussion lump on its rear flat contiguous with the breech face bears the percussioner's initial A. The proof house number of the barrel, *945*, and the final fitter-up mark, a big "H," are hidden traces of the gun's history.

The bore is rifled with five narrow lands, each having a slightly lowered edge step, because of inferior rifling

Co. E of 22d N.Y. State Militia on duty at Harpers Ferry after capture of Arsenal by Jackson and removal of this portion of Union's armaments production to South was equipped with imported Enfield short rifles.

and a damaged rifling cutter. Since each groove was rifled separately in sequence, a damaged or chipped cutter tooth would have duplicated its mark all around. Four inches from the muzzle a bayonet stud without guide rib is fitted. The stud face bears the stamp S&S, Swinburn's company mark, and numbers. The arrangement is: $\frac{\text{S\&S } 44}{801}$. The larger number is possibly Swinburn's own factory serial number for the barrel, indicating he had supplied at least 801 barrels for the two-band rifle with bayonet stud to the Birmingham Tower. The number 44 may be a model or type designation or, most likely, a workman's number.

The stock reveals the same sort of many-fingered-pie history. On the left side flat opposite the lockplate, at the rear, is stamped the same H found on barrel bottom and inside the lockplate. It is believed to be the mark of the fitter-up or contractor, as mentioned, who supplied the finished gun to the Birmingham Tower. The barrel groove and lock inletting are clearly hand work. Especially in the lock inletting does it differ from the machine-made London guns. Except for two marks of the wood bit which are relieved for the bridle screws of the lock, the recess is cut away cleanly with knife and chisel. This sort of recess actually weakens the stock more than the machine-cut recess, which is inletted just enough to accommodate the metal in all its free motion, but no more. The handmade stock is just chopped out. The stock contractor's name HERBERT is stamped near the location of the rear band in the ramrod groove. The Government inspector's initials J. P. are an inch farther forward, and the man who inletted the barrel took up his ¼-inch straight-edge chisel and struck two notches, also in the ramrod groove, to correspond with the double file mark he put on the barrel after he fitted the stock to it. The barrel double file mark, since the inletter was in the establishment of "H," is near to that initial on the barrel.

Then the whole works were put together, and stamped by the Birmingham Tower proof authorities with the government test marks, the barrel once, and later the second time as a finished gun. These impressions appear on the top of the barrel at left of the barrel flat, being the marks of the several inspectors and workmen responsible for the final completion and acceptance of the gun.

On the stock, at the tang of the brass guard, the stamp shown in Fig. 5 is imprinted twice. There are no regimental markings.

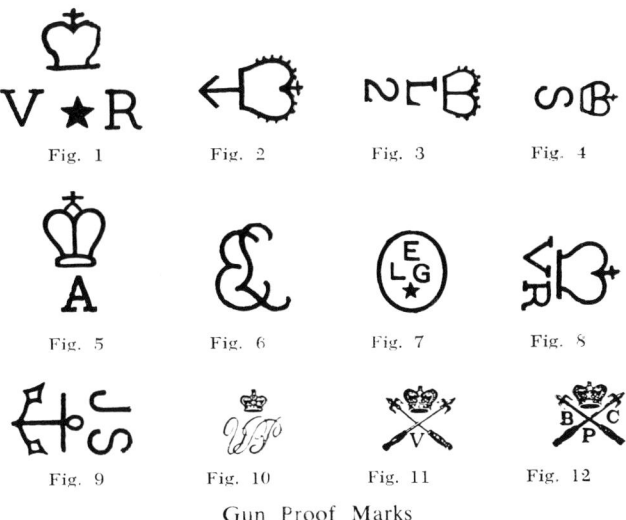

Gun Proof Marks

The Potts & Hunt Gun

Somewhat simpler is the complex of marks and stamps on a machine-made Potts & Hunt short rifle of similar design, but London made.

The 33-inch barrel does not have a bayonet stud; instead, the stock is approximately four inches longer, the nose cap fitted 1⅜-inches from the muzzle. The front band is fixed with both screw tightener and a cross pin, and the bayonet lug is forged integral and machined out of the band metal. Located 7⅝ inches

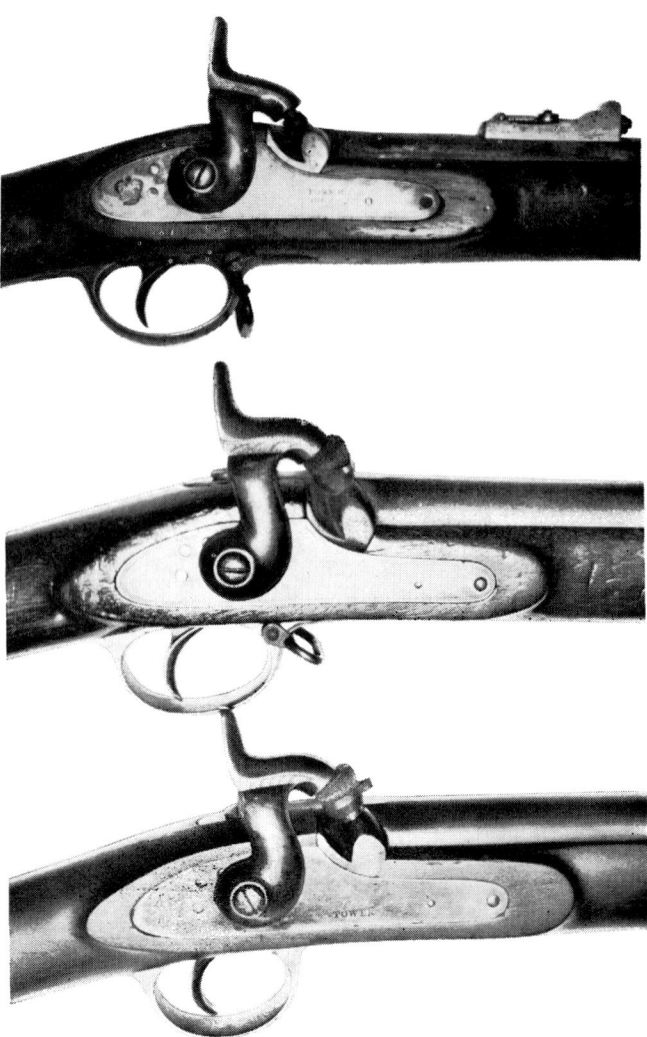

Breech detail of three different Enfield rifles. Top is long Enfield with rear sight near to line drawn forward of lockplate; bottom two are short two-band sword bayonet rifles, 33" barrels, which have sights farther forward out of photo view. Word TOWER may be above or below date; numerals may be Arabic or Italic, though latter is associated with Bagot Road Government factory in Birmingham also called "Tower." Non-British government guns without Broad Arrow mark usually do not have VR under Crown, though Crown is always used. Washer devices on nipples are leather-padded snap caps for aiming and trigger pull practice, usually attached to rifle by link chain.

a works in Birmingham and a shop in London for some time during the early part of the 19th century.

The Potts & Hunt barrel is a Birmingham tube, stamped underneath six inches from the breech, MILLWARD. Charles Millward was a prominent member of the Birmingham gun trade. In 1859 he was a member of the Board of Guardians of the Proof House; he and W. L. Harrison were the company auditors. Charles and Ezra Millward conducted an extensive business in military barrels, and supplied a great many to the Colt enterprise during the Civil War.

The Potts & Hunt gun number, probably of a lot of one dozen or twenty guns which were fitted up by the same set of workmen in their factory, is 8. The numeral appears on the barrel and close by on the bottom edge of the barrel plug wedge. It is also scribed VIII in Roman characters on the barrel bottom, and again with narrow chisel, in the ramrod groove to match tube with the stock for which it was inletted. The initials P&H are on the bottom of the barrel, mostly for edification of the Proof House in London, and on the top left edge of the barrel breech appear the London provisional, definitive proof marks, and view marks, all of the Gunmakers Company. The government crown over an inspector numeral, 22, appears on the back face of the barrel and fitted plug, and again on the plug below the tang, but there is no other evidence of any government inspection of the gun.

All the locks appear fundamentally similar, but will not interchange in the stocks without slight fitting. This may be due to age and shrinkage, as they are very close. Original stock tolerances might have been enough to allow the locks to interchange. Interior workmanship is good on all locks.

The stock maker of the Potts & Hunt gun stamped his name P. WEDGE clearly in the ramrod groove closest to the rear band. A second workman J. WICKS fitted barrel to stock. Between these two marks appears the stamp, in small ⅛-inch characters, of POTTS & HUNT. The initials J. N. appear once on lock inside, bottom of barrel, and at the rear edge of the stock face opposite

from the breech (7½ inches on the Tower-Birmingham rifle) is the rear sight fixed base. Both short rifles have identical sights, calibrated on the right wing with elevation marks to 400 yards (1, 2, 3, 4) and on the raised leaf up to 1100 (11). The Tower sight is unmarked otherwise, except for the Government "crown-B-36" inspector stamp at the root of the raised leaf near to the cross pin. The Potts & Hunt sight does not have this mark.

On the right wing of the Potts & Hunt sight is a maker's cypher, W&S, possibly for Robert Wheeler & Sons, a firm which subscribed £100 for aiding to build the Birmingham Proof House in 1813 and maintained

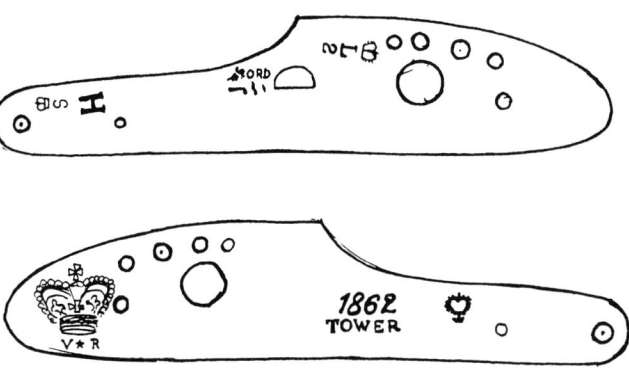

Lock marks on both sides of Birmingham "Tower" two-band short rifle. This arm appears to be refinished, but years ago, as bore is in perfect condition. It may be what was denoted in records as "cleaned and refinished," or "C & R." Italic date is unusual. Lockmaker's name is —ORD, possibly Ford, but inspector's mark has defaced initial letter.

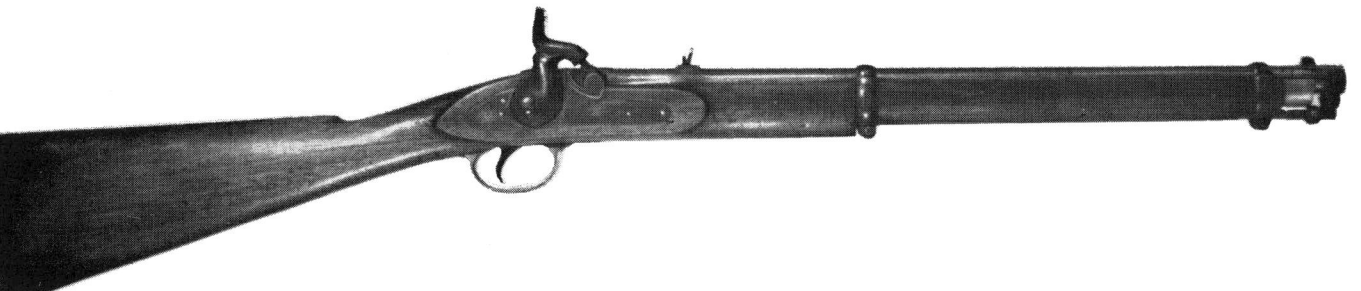

Tower-mark cavalry carbine had swivel to attach ramrod to muzzle so it would not get lost while reloading on horseback. Rifles regularly had spring "spoon" in stock to hold ramrods in by friction. Very few short Enfields of any type were used by North.

the lock. This is evidently the mark of the final inspector in the Potts & Hunt shop.

The London Armoury Gun

The third Enfield is a short 24-inch barrel musketoon, two bands, fitted with bayonet stud on the barrel. The stud has a short guide rib. (Front band is missing, but had a swivel.) It is unusual because, although marked as made by the London Armoury Company, it has a Belgian barrel. Beneath, the bottom is stamped (see Fig. 6) and on the top left quadrant, mingled with the British government crown and number stamps, is the mark of the Liege proof house: (see Fig. 7). The tube bears the London Proof House stamp 403, and, on top, the crown over crossed flags or pennons of the Enfield proof. The barrel on the bottom is also stamped L.A.C. in small letters, and the gun assembly or work number is 22, on both barrel and plug. The percussioning was done in England, and the lump bears a mark crown over A, while the top quadrant has a similar crown over VR (see Fig. 8). Erosion and flash pitting confounds the marks with false traces of other marks on the breech, but the top of the breech, as on all Enfields, is clearly stamped with the distinctive crowns and lines on both tang of plug and breech of barrel, on the top flat, as well as a visible draw mark.

Inside, the lock is unmarked except for a tiny stamp L.A.C. while outside, it is border line engraved and forward of the hammer is engraved LONDON ARMOURY.

The stock is machine inletted and, as is also the case with the Potts & Hunt inletting, all possible wood is permitted to remain in the lock mortise. Only the wood essential to be removed for free motion of the lock parts is taken away; the rest left untouched for maximum strength. The construction of lock inletting in both Potts & Hunt and London Armoury guns suggests a possibility that the Potts & Hunt stock was in fact inletted by London Armoury. Both stocks are of walnut, unlike the soft-wood Birmingham Tower gun stock.

The barrel inletter, whose initial B is stamped in the barrel groove, made a mistake in reassembling the guns. He selected barrel No. VII and put it with stock No. VIII, his own initial B having obscured slightly one of the Roman I's. The ramrod groove, though bored through, has only a narrow slot from rear band to nosecap, too narrow to stamp the stock maker's name in. The only stock mark of interest is an anchor and JS stamped at the tang of the brass guard on the small of the stock: (Fig. 9). The same stamp also is found on the stocks of Kerr revolvers, L.A.C. manufacture. The London Armoury butt plate, of brass, is engraved on the heel tang *242*. Sight is the carbine leaf sight with fixed leaf at 100, and folding leaves for 200 and 300 yards.

Deceptive Marking

The mark "Tower" on an Enfield-type arm was apparently used more or less to deceive Northern purchasers as well as those of the South. It apears hand-stamped, without fixed location, on the locks forward of the hammer. The date may be either above or below the mark or, indeed, on some other part of the lock entirely. So far as can be determined, several of the Birmingham Gun Trade used "Tower" locks promiscuously on rifles and rifle muskets which they assembled for export. The export "Enfield" generally can be told from those made for the British Government, by the absence of the Broad Arrow mark on lockplate and barrel breech. Those barrels which bear the provisional (Fig. 10), the number 25 for gauge mark, then the definitive view mark (Fig. 11), another 25, and the definitive proof mark (Fig. 12), all Birming-

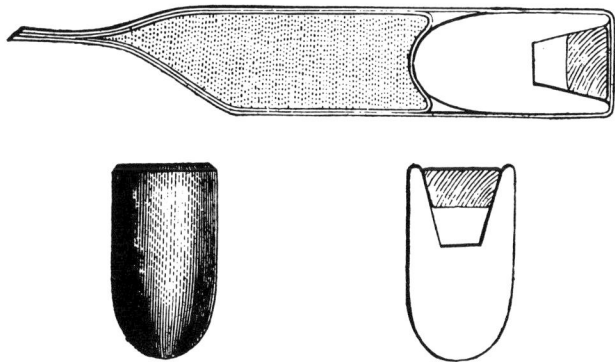

Enfield cartridge's powder was held in smaller bag inside larger one. Bullet held wood plug supposed to be driven forward by force of explosion to expand lead into rifling, but later simple cavity was found to work as well. "Tail" was folded over in rolling cartridge, later torn off with teeth to pour powder into bore. Bullet end of loaded round was dipped in hot wax mixture of mutton tallow and beeswax as lubricant; the paper acted as patching.

ham Gun Barrel Proof House marks, may be assumed to be commercially exported rifles made for sale abroad. The presence of such barrels on Enfield arms found in the United States which have "country origins," such as many of the rustier ones that turn up in the Middle West, may be assumed to be United States or Confederate Enfields, regardless of makers marks, with some exceptions.

A Birmingham short rifle seems to fall into this class of arm. Marked "TOWER" beneath "1861" it has proofs as above. The barrel maker was *Beasley & Son*. Inside, the lock maker's mark arcs about the boss for retaining the mainspring fixed leaf: SPITTLE & BROS. The lock, inside, above the fixed leaf and upside down, is stamped with the same small W & S sometimes found on other small parts, such as sight bases. The actual fitter-up, DG, marked stock between side nails, lock above fixed leaf, and barrel underside. Barrel and breech screw both are marked *2* but the barrel bayonet lug is boldly stamped 11. The ramrod groove bears the small stamps of workmen and stock maker, but they are unclear.

Unusual Details

An unusual detail about the above-cited rifle is the state of finish on the metal. The surface is rust-pitted and brushed more or less bright, but when the bands were removed, the metal underneath was seen to be smooth and bright originally. Then the barrel was unstocked and on closer look it could be seen that the original finish was definitely Enfield-style, rust-browned or blacked. The bands, too, showed heat blue tints inside. But the underside of the barrel definitely was bright and had been struck bright long ago—so long ago that the top part, unprotected, had again weathered dull and rough.

The inference here may be that this rifle during the Civil War was put into "serviceable" shape by some armory unit—whether Confederate or Union cannot be determined—and this included polishing the barrel again to conform to the current standard since it was probably impracticable to reblack the barrel in the state of the emergency. If the gun had shown better condition, one might assume that those "cleaned & repaired" Enfields offered for sale after the war were also struck up "national armory bright." But this gun definitely shows use and field abuse after the polishing. It was picked up by a Union soldier after the retreat of Confederate forces.

Generalizations on the basis of one specimen are absurd; but often a good guess will be corroborated later by wider study of the subject, once the student of arms learns what he might be looking for. Certainly, in categorizing and typing the wide number of variations among Enfields, possession of a specimen different from all others you own does not mean you have some rare, unique prize. More often than not, any generalizations you may infer from the arm you possess will apply equally to some tens of thousands of others, substantially identical, to what you may now construe to be a "rarity."

Slings and Ramrods

As a rule, all Enfields were fitted for slings. The M1853 long Enfield used a special sling, running from the loop attached to the front band, all the way back to the trigger guard. The later 1856 type of long Enfield has a similar sling arrangement, though the bands were screw fastened instead of spring held. The 1859 short rifle made use of the 1856 type of brass guard swivel, and a front band swivel as well. But some 1859 short rifles did not have the guard pierced for swivel loop. Instead, a wood screw was capped with a swivel and turned into the stock belly about midway between rear guard tang and buttplate. This was also generally true of carbines and musketoons of this style; the rear swivel was screwed into the butt stock, not attached to the trigger guard.

Nearly all Enfields had ramrods held in by a spoon in the stock, and pushed out of line at the stock fore tip by a slightly raised aspect of the nose cap. This tended to grip the ramrod snug, but without the objections of a mechanical locking such as a notch that would foul with rust or jam the rammer in tightly.

The Long Rifle was Most Important

The short rifle is the most colorful of the Enfield arms, and also the rarest, as used in the United States service. Only "8,034 Enfield rifles, short, calibre .577, sword bayonet," are listed as having been procured at a cost of $187,915.09. But the long Enfield, three iron bands and a 39-inch barrel of .577 or .58 caliber, was unquestionably the most important. Not only were 428,292 of them purchased by Schuyler, Hartley, or Naylor and Company, but many of those fine London Armoury guns shipped by Major Huse in blockade runners fell prey to "the anaconda" and were delivered to New York. First shipments were of the M1853 model, obsolescent because of the spring bands.

Enfields Made in America

The M1853 Enfield long rifle was first manufactured in the United States. In 1853 a revolution was in progress—a revolution in manufacturing. That same Major Anderson, who later was Southern agent in Birmingham was, at the time, master armorer of Enfield. This factory had existed for a number of years principally as a barrel mill and parts storehouse. The trouble leading up to the Crimean War suggested to the Crown the advisability of putting arms procurement more directly under control of the government, by expanding the Enfield establishment and introducing machinery and mass production. The example of the Colt factory in Pimlico, and the growth of machine tool firms like Naysmith, Whitworth, and others, showed that the time was right for mass production.

The "Enfield Commission" visited the Springfield Armory and toured the Yankee gun mills. Of particular interest to the British experts was the Robbins & Lawrence works in Windsor, Vermont. The Enfield Commissioners were following up an initial order for Enfields which the Robbins & Lawrence firm is said to have completed. No specimen of this contract, reported to have been 20,000 rifles, has come to the attention of the author, but it is believed to be the 1851 Tower Minie rifle.

This contract, it is thought, was completed, and the rifles delivered. The war in the Crimea does not record many uses of rifled British muskets, but a few of the new .577 Enfield type did get into service and when used, were very effective with their long range accuracy potential. Certainly when the Enfield Commission came to the United States, Robbins & Lawrence had every reason to expect some business. They were given another contract, this time for 25,000 rifles. The locks were marked WINDSOR, the crown, and 1856. Presumably these were the M1853 long Enfield, with bands spring-fastened; a specimen in the author's collection is a short sergeant's rifle. They pushed ahead with the work and laid plans to turn out a further order of 300,000 rifles, but the order never materialized.

Robbins & Lawrence supplied machinery to the Enfield works in England. This was the source of their own collapse, since the Royal Small Arms Factory took over the job for the Crown, and Robbins & Lawrence did not have either the agents to promote nor the facilities to cheapen their work, to compete with the Birmingham and Liege trades. The month to six weeks minimum shipping delay alone cut them out of the European-Eastern-African market, and their interests were placed in bankruptcy and sold at auction to Lamson, Goodnough & Yale.

Other machine companies in New England contributed to the Enfield works. Operating by 1857, Enfield was turning out, by machinery, long rifles of excellent quality. They became the standard by which others were to be judged.

Importance of the Enfield

Long Enfields of .577 and .58 caliber were issued to United States troops interchangeably with the Springfield rifle musket. In the same squad one might find M1855 Rifled Muskets with M1859 patchboxes, 1855 or 1861 types, long Enfields, and perhaps a special model from Colt, Lamson, or Amoskeag.

Volunteers by the spring of 1863 were being issued Enfields and Springfields, all new from the armory or contract shops. Enfields continued to be important in the issues to troops, in spite of the decline in purchases and import contracts after 1863. Oddly, almost none seem to have ever born any mark indicating Enfield Royal Small Arms Factory origin—most were Birmingham; a few were London contractor guns, or those from the London Armoury Company.

Turning out these and more guns for the belligerents of the American war brought prosperity to Birmingham. Even London-marked guns shared their honors with the Midlands city, since so many of the barrels, including those proved in London, were made in Birmingham.

"The high-water mark was reached during the American Civil War," writes Clive Harris in *History of the Proof House,* "when in 1861 over 700,000 arms were exported, and the incomes of some of the skilled workers rose to fabulous figures.

"Some astounding stories of these earnings are related by the 'old timers.' £20 a week was considered commonplace (average wage maximum before the war was about £3 weekly.) In some instances barrelmakers had earned as much as £50 in a single week . . . This sudden stimulus given to the trade by the American Civil War led to much profligacy among the Birmingham gun trade workers. Stories are common of these men bombastically lighting expensive cigars with £5 notes in public-houses. None would consider paying less than 2s. 6d. for a cigar—and this at a time when the average price of tobacco was about 1½d. an ounce!

"One of the local men (who could have as easily walked), an expert percussioner, invariably came to work on horseback, stabling his horse in Whittal Street. Most of the workers, however, travelled to and from their work in hansom cabs; and it is related of one (for whose custom two cabbies had fallen out) that he engaged both by boarding the cab of the first, and, tossing his hat into that of the second, instructed

Warlike quartet of Yankee nicotine addicts relaxes in camp of New York Zouaves by leaning on their Long Enfields. Guns are M1853, having spring-fastened bands, snap caps, long slings for shoulder carry, and brass-end muzzle stoppers or tompions to keep out morning dews. Some soldiers kept mountain dew in barrels, removing stopper to quaff a snort. Revolver in belt is .31 Pocket Colt, type of 1849, a favorite with men at the front as on the frontier.

the driver to follow to the *Gunmaker's Arms,* where great carousals nightly took place."

During 1861-64, North and South were Birmingham's best customers. Finished guns were exported. Minor elements in its trading pattern were gun parts, particularly locks and barrels. The Liege, Belgium, trade worked with Birmingham to supply arms to Americans.

Enfields were delivered by many firms, mostly importers in New York. Unlike some who ran around the corner to Herman Boker & Company to fill their contracts for French or German guns, the Enfield importers almost all had their direct agents in the Birmingham or London trades. Holt and Owen stopped or disallowed a number of the early contracts and more blatant speculators, but the delivery of Enfields reached a peak, not in the first years of the war, but in 1863.

Buckley & Company, New York, delivered dribs and drabs of Enfields, 1,160 in all, at prices from $12.64¾ to $22.32, as a result of open purchase between December 24, 1862 and May 28, 1863. Samuel Bulkley & Company, also New York, delivered on November 13, 1861 "660 long English rifles," presumably Enfields, with angular bayonets, at $22.50. An additional 160 were turned over to the New York Ordnance office at $15 to $20. W. V. Barkalow contracted on November 2, 1862, and did deliver in all, 8,000 long Enfields at $20. Brown Brothers & Company started out selling short Enfields in August 1862 but the Government's preference was for long rifles, which they delivered after February 3, 1863, all caliber .577. Boker of course sold Enfields; his dealings are more fully dealt with elsewhere. Bailey & Company of Philadelphia sold 260 Enfields *minus cones*—fitting the wrong-thread U. S. musket nipples into these arms must have given Billy Yank quite a headache when they popped out and snapped off the hammers.

Colt delivered a number of Enfields to the United States and sold more to state governments. While Potts & Hunt is characterized by Albaugh as "probably confederate," Colt was a contractor with Potts & Hunt and more likely the Potts & Hunt Enfields in the Civil War came to the North through Colt. The "Inman line of propeller steamships," on which line Hartley was instructed to ship his purchased guns, got into the great money musket scramble. Between August 13, 1862, and January 29, 1863, E. Cunard imported and delivered 8,980 long Enfields at prices from $13.75 to $23.44. Cooper & Pond, New York, after deliveries of "Beals" revolvers, possibly either Remingtons or Whitneys, sold 1,740 long Enfields to the United States between December 5, 1862 and June 30, 1863. But one of the most enigmatic listings which deserves more research is the purchase of 200 long Enfield rifles in bond at $14.62¾ from B. J. Calisher "of New York."

B. J. Calisher and William Terry, English gunsmith and inventor, perfected a capping breech-loading rifle that was tested in 1858 in England for ship's use and found effective. While J. H. Walsh ("Stonehenge") disapproved of the principle of breech operation, a notice by Terry spoke of trials by "authorities at Enfield, Hythe, and Woolwich, and it appears to have undergone the severest test with complete success."

Behind the hammer, which is mounted on a lockplate of conventional Enfield form, lies a hinged bar, under spring tension to remain flat against the rear part of the barrel which is extended rather far back over the small of the stock. Unfolding this bar makes it into a torque arm, the end of which is attached to a breech bolt. The breech bolt on its rear end has two locking lugs; at the front, it passes a loading port into which the special Terry patent tallow wad lubricated cartridge is placed. Dropping a cartridge into the loading port, shoving the bolt home, and rotating the hinged handle 90°, then folding it flat alongside and placing a cap on the nipple, completed the loading operation. The cartridge was self-consuming, and was ignited in the middle by cap flash. This left the wad in the back, to be pushed forward by the bullet of the next round, thus giving ample lubrication each discharge.

Army test guns were caliber .577, rifled Enfield style, with three grooves but a faster twist, once in four feet while in 1859 the Enfield twist was once in 6½ feet. Unfortunately for Calisher, who must have had some money invested in Terry's design, a similar but perhaps a simpler breechloader by Westley Richards was adopted and issued in 1861 for trials in England. With military sales dim for Calisher & Terry, Mr. Calisher's presence in New York may be accounted for by his desire to sell what rifles he had on hand to the United States. With transoceanic passage at the time costing about $100 to $150 one way, it is possible that the speculation of bringing 200 of his own rifles over and selling them, without payment of duty, at the figure of $14.62¾, would have been attractive to him. Whether they were simply common Enfields, or were of the Terry patent, is not specifically revealed. In view of the grandiose claims by gun dealers of the present times for the Calisher & Terry as a "Confederate" arm merely because Jeb Stuart and Jeff Davis each owned one, the sale of Calisher should be considered carefully as showing a Yankee sympathy, or at least a sympathy on the part of Calisher for the Yankee dollar. Terry carbines were issued to New Zealand Constabulary in quantity.

Jeb Stuart's "Terry carbine" (most references of the time are to Terry, not Calisher) was marked "Thomas Blisset, Liverpool." Whether Blisset finished it or merely bought it from Calisher's factory has not been determined. But Stuart, who was the official Confederate States cavalry carbine tester, having a "Terry," can hardly be construed as indicating that the Calisher & Terry Carbines were in any way a Confederate issue piece. Whether Calisher's "long Enfields" were Terry patent or simply common rifle muskets is not now known. That Calisher sold to the Union is a matter of record.

Deliveries from the following New York firms and individuals consisted of Enfield rifles or carbines: E. W.

Canning, Durrie & Rusher, Goddard & Brother, and C. K. Garrison.

Garrison after the war insisted he knew nothing about guns, that he would rather do almost anything than "ship batteries of cannon." In 1861 he knew enough to charge $27 each, and deliver 2,800 Enfield muskets on November 20; his delivery of 3,200 Enfields on December 11, 1861, at $27 was reduced to $20 and paid for at that rate.

John Gill, John Hoey, and Howland & Aspinwall—all of New York—offered to deliver 17,000 Enfield long rifles at $19 "of the best English manufacture," in bond, at the rate of not less than 2,000 a month. Just 8,000 had been delivered by the time Holt and Owen reviewed the case, and they decided because of apparent failure to complete the contract, that future purchases should be made in open market, at prices prevailing, consistent with the needs of the service. But unknown to them, additional guns had been offered and accepted by Ripley; and a letter had been sent by Ripley saying they could deliver as soon as possible, "thus virtually renewing the order," and meaning that no decision of the Commissioners was required on the case. Purchases at market rates seemed to be the rule, after a big lot of 9,040 were delivered April, 1862, and during the next months to May of 1863, Howland & Aspinwall sold in bunches from 100 to thousands at prices ranging upward from $12.64¾. For example, 100 were delivered on May 4, 1863, that must have been positive knockouts for some reason. They were supremely excellent, for they were bought in the open market at the fantastically high price (for the time) of $25.07¾ each.

Howland & Aspinwall also sold 92 LeFaucheux revolvers at $22 each, 50 "carbines" of undisclosed nature at $22.50, 1 "naval rifle" $24.50, 1 French carbine $15, and 1 Whitney rifle, possibly the "Enfield" type, at $10.50.

Samuel Haskell sold 420 long Enfield rifles $27.50 each. Marcellus Hartley bought and shipped, between August 13, 1862 and December 18, 1862, 6,500 interchangeable Enfield muskets at an average price of $14.91 and 103,924 Enfield rifle muskets at $12.04. H. J. Ibbotson sold 2,137 long Enfield rifles on May

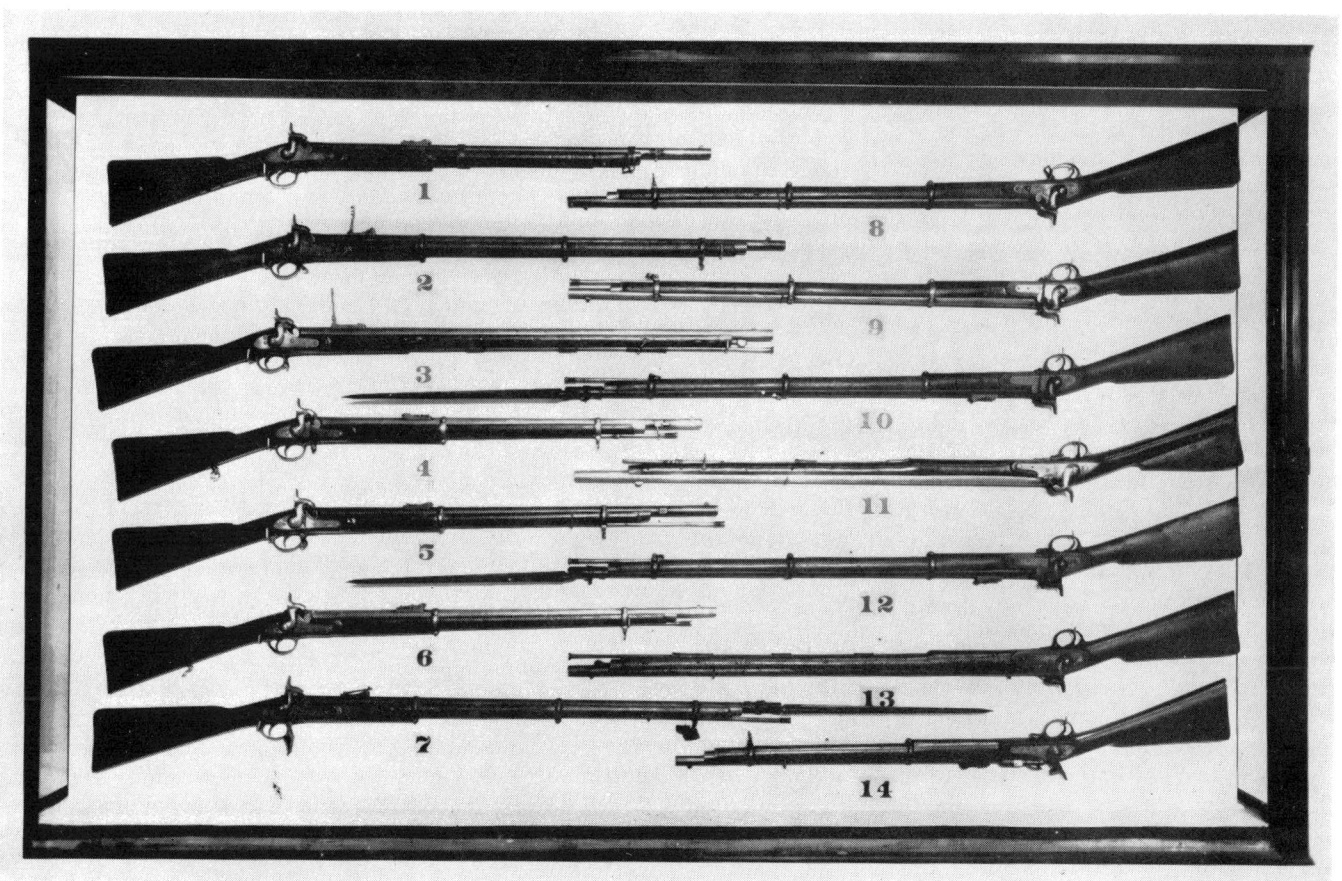

Many Enfield-type arms were obtained by the North as a second-line rifle. In this plate only No. 14 is post-war, a Snider breechloading M1866 conversion. Item 3 is a Tower Minie rifle M1851, while Item 13 is same pattern by Barnett of London but does not have long range rear sight. No. 4 is 1862 Tower gun but there is no VR under lockplate crown, and vendor's name *W. E. Brown, Gloucester,* is engraved on edge of lockplate. Brown evidently fitted special bayonet stud with short guide rib, differing from regular two-band export Tower 1861 rifle No. 5. Item 10 is No. 1 machine-made London Armoury long Enfield stamped 1862/L.A.Co. on lock, and seal of firm on stock. Gun is possibly one of initial contract made by McFarland for State of Massachusetts. No. 11 is early flintlock Tower-marked trade musket sold by Birmingham smiths after percussioning at inflated prices to Yankee buyers.

Alleged breechloading Civil War rifles are (top) Westley Richards M1860, .450 Whitworth caliber, with bayonet stud on front band; Wilson's sea-service or sergeant's rifle with bayonet stud on barrel, and, bottom, "Breechloading Gun Co." .577 Leetch patent short rifle with side-swing block. Bayonet stud resembles that for Sharps, Spencer rifles.

5, 1862. Richard Irwin & Company, New York, sold 1,020 Enfields, August-September 1862.

Philip S. Justice may seem to have had a rough deal (see Chapter 7) but it was a case of what he made on the peanuts he lost on the dam' banan'. Defraying his losses on the special models of rifles and muskets he made for the United States, were his sales of Enfield imported rifles and muskets at top prices, almost all above $20, many including short rifles at $27.50. He was also a major commercial source for Whitney's revolvers at retail prices which somehow the United States seemed unable to obtain directly from the old patriot's factory until later in the war.

Charles W. D. Jefferys, New York, sold 1,920 long Enfield rifles, caliber .577, on August 5, 1862, at $15.52½ each.

J. Kirkpatrick, New York, sold 80 long Enfields, at about $16, on September 12, 1862.

J. B. Kinsman on January 2 and 13, 1862, delivered a total of 200 "breech-loading rifles" at $40 each. The exact nature of these arms is not known; however, we think it possible these were the rifles of James S. Leetch, patented in England September 23, 1853. Certain "facts" exist in the foregoing description of arms. First, they were probably not of continental make, for Major Hagner or Captain Crispin would never (to judge from their evidenced attitude) have paid $40 for a French, Belgian, or German breechloader. Second, they were not long rifle or rifle muskets, but simply "rifles," which pretty definitely requires, in the parlance of the time, that they be of rifle length, i.e., about a 33-inch barrel. That they had military usefulness is without saying, from the very high price. To be worth that, they were probably standard caliber. That they were mechanically operated and of a certain standard of finish and excellence, is attested to by the price of $40—in the purchasing officer's eyes they must have been about the equal of a Sharps rifle bought in open market. Had they been American—Smith's, Burnside, etc.—it would be stated. Since the great probability is that they were English, of the Enfield short rifle form and .577 caliber, and worth $40, it is reasonable to seek among Enfield-like breech-loading arms in a hope of finding some hint of what they might have been, these elusive and rare 200 "breech-loading rifles."

The Leetch Gun

Such a rifle with Connecticut provenance and the appearance of having been used in the field, is Leetch patent breechloader in the author's collection numbered "162." A short type 1859 Enfield-like rifle, the Leetch gun has a light back-action lock and a receiver housing or breech box, into which the barrel is screwed. The breech box is open to the right side, and along its bottom edge is a hinge pin, on which swings a receiver of the same conception as the Hall, but rotating on the hinge, instead of swinging upward. The receiver carries the nipple, and the breech box is notched at the back so the nipple is in line with the hammer when the breech is closed. A folding lever on the receiver, when pivoted out, uncams the receiver from its joint with the barrel, and allows it to be swung outward. The charge goes into the front of the receiver. Then, swung closed, the cam forces the receiver tightly forward when the lever is folded down along side of the receiver. An added safety is a push-pull pin or rod linked to the hammer (which is of elegant form) that passes into a hole on the rear of the receiver. If the receiver is not closed in line with the bore, the pin is arrested on the blind face of the receiver casing at rear, and the hammer cannot hit the cone, nor fire. Enfield rifle sights are mounted; light scroll engraving covers the metal parts. A saber bayonet stud is hung beneath the barrel, forward of the buffalo horn fore-tip. While the lockplate bears the words LEETCH'S PATENT/COMPANY, the top of the breech box is engraved BREECH LOADING GUN COMPANY/ 29 GT PORTLAND ST LONDON and below, POWDER 2½ DRS./BULLET .577. The barrel is from Birmingham maker John Clive, but is London proved. Each part bears the number 162, the only distinctive thing being the "1" from which the left serif at the foot is missing. It is not the identical "1" with which the obvious serial number is stamped. This number, also 162, appears on the trigger plate guard tang behind the rear screw hole, and it is stamped, not (as so often found) hand engraved. The other marks are hand engraved. The marking, "Breechloading Gun Company" conforms to the description of 200 guns bought, and the serial number is within the range. Finding the rifle in Connecticut makes it likely that the Leetch gun was from this lot of 200. Other Leetch guns are recorded by other writers, as Lewis Winant; and a Leetch gun is shown in Golden State Arms' *World's Guns*. Even purchase of a Leetch gun in England in recent years does not necessarily mitigate

Breech views showing actions open on Leetch, Westley Richards, and Wilson rifles. Author doubts latter two were employed in war at all, while Leetch rifle may be hitherto unsuspected Yankee issue rifle. Cartridge enters front of .577 Leetch chamber.

Common ruled foolscap tablet was used by inspector at U.S. Ordnance Agency in New York to list the parts detail of a sample Enfield rifle musket. Most parts were "serviceable," but several "required light repairs." Gun was one of 10,000 in shipment. Case mark H.C. suggests Marcellus Hartley company destination, later Hartley & Graham. C.W. document is not fancy, but is incredibly rare. These papers were invariably destroyed as of no use later on.

against that rifle's being used in the American Civil War, so much surplus was shipped back overseas at the close of the conflict. J. H. Walsh, writing as "Stonehenge" in *The Shotgun & Sporting Rifle,* London, 1859, notes that:

Mr. Leetch, of Great-Portland-street, London, has exhibited for the last three or four years a breech-loading rifle, which is constructed on the principle of the revolver, but without more than one chamber . . . (follows a description of the breech). This plan is very simple, and I have seen extremely good practice made at short ranges; but there must of necessity be an escape of gas quite as great as in the revolver, which has the advantage of permitting five or six shots in rapid succession. If, therefore, the escape is not objectionable to the sportsman, I should advise a revolving rifle with five or six chambers in preference to this, with only one. Still, Mr. Leetch's rifle has the advantage of using the Government ammunition, and on that account it will be valuable to sportsmen on distant stations.

In shooting by the author with the Leetch rifle at 50 meters, consistent grouping the size of a man's chest was obtained on the target, achieving a rate of fire about 18 shots in a minute, using flask and Lyman mould "minie ball." Gas did escape at the breech, but evidently Mr. Walsh had not seen the camming design of the Leetch invention, for in the last stroke of closing, the lever shoves a wedge of steel behind the receiver, forcing a Savage-like cone on the receiver at the chamber mouth against the barrel. The gun was not noticeably dirtier to shoot than a common musket, with its attendant cap fouling and blow-back of smoke through the nipple.

Other Imported Guns

Not only Leetch and Calisher seem to have had friends here, but gunmakers outside of New York speculated on foreign imports, large and small. For example, F. H. Lawson, Cincinnati, delivered 100 Enfield sword bayonet rifles at $22 on December 18, 1861. W. Baily Lang & Company, New York, from June 1862 through April, 1863, delivered $93,537.92 worth of Enfields. John P. Moore's Sons, New York, delivered a steady flow of small lots of two basic types, the long and short; and of two basic origins, English and U. S. make. On June 10, 1862, 840 guns and on June 30, 240 more priced at $15 each were delivered under the designation of "American rifle, long Enfield pattern, and appendages."

Final identification of these rare American rifles, delivered by Moore, is uncertain, but it seems probable that a variety of Enfield arms, bearing on the lockplate behind the hammer a spread eagle surmounting a Federal shield, with the initial M in the field of stars, is the Moore-delivered rifle. These arms have dates of 1861, 1862, and 1863 observed forward of the hammer on the locks, which are conventional Enfield locks in form, with the typical double-line engraved edge border. A carefully detailed analysis of one such long rifle, three clamping bands, was made by Bob Riley in *The Gun Report,* January 1960. He found a small stamp looking like a B with the bottom curve broken away, on virtually every part, usually in association with an arrow-like stamp made of three incisions or punch marks, which could be a simulation of either the British Broad Arrow or the Liege proof mark. These evidently were assembly marks and appear inconspicuously inside.

Very visible on the barrel breech in the location where a British proof mark might be, is a cypher seemingly composed from two or three interlaced initials. Riley suggests that, by filling in the broken parts of the die stamp, the initials "N B" could be made out. On the barrel this is stamped 1 inch forward of the back flat. But on Riley's gun the same mark appears on the stock, ½ inch behind the trigger guard tang.

Fuller (*Firearms of the Confederacy,* by Fuller and Stewart) notes that he found a part case of these guns, "all badly damaged, but not showing any particularly hard wear." He concluded these were the Blunt rifle, of which Orison Blunt of New York had 500 ready for delivery, but never had them accepted by the Union. He states categorically "the barrel carries the regular British proof marks, all indicating that the completed barrel was an importation."

Fuller's statement doubtless reflects what he thought was correct, but that he did not know what he was talking about is shown on the face of the statement. There are no marks affixed to British-made firearms which by any stretch of the imagination can be characterized as simply "the *regular* British proof marks." There are in fact the special markings denoting proof at the Worshipful Company of Gunmakers of London, and also marks denoting proof at the Proof House in Birmingham. And there are British military proof marks. None of these are common, one set to the other. The cypher Riley describes resembles the interlaced script letters *VBP* for Birmingham Provisional Proof stamped on the barrel when presented for proof in the finished state, ready also for Definitive Proof. Our opinion is that the cypher on the "Eagle M" muskets is a fraudulent simulation by J. P. Moore of the Birmingham proof. Viewed upside down, it appears to be EPU in script. As to mysterious marks, Fuller cites one eagle-M Enfield which on the brass trigger guard tang is "stamped L. S. M. in heavy, crude letters." While this is supposed to mean "Louisiana State Militia" it could also mean "Logan Square Mercury," an automobile dealer in Chicago—the verification at this moment is as valid for either meaning. This author has seen Birmingham-proved barrels on guns with "Eagle-M" locks. The locks and barrels did not fit each other at the cone seats. Inference: they were Birmingham Long Enfields with Eagle-M locks recently attached to enhance the price. The story is still not complete. Three styles of this rifle are noted:

1. Dated 1861, barrel 34½ inches, with a long knob for saber bayonet on right side of muzzle.

2. Dated 1862, 31½-inch barrel, no bayonet knob. Inside lockplate is stamped "250."

3. Dated 1863, 39-inch barrel rifle musket, at Na-

tional Military Park, Fredericksburg, Virginia. Inside of lockplate is marked "100."

All have brass butt-plates and guards; and iron bands. While Fuller surmises the "M" could mean Mississippi, or Marshall, or McElwaine, for Confederate factories, it seems more reasonable that it means "Moore," and that these rifles, plainly marked "American rifles"—for do they not have the Yankee eagle and shield adapted from the National emblems? —were of the 1,080 supplied in June, 1862. Later dates are not conflicting; obviously Moore, finding it possible to sell them to the Ordnance Department buyers, also was able to sell a few to state and Volunteer purchasers. With the flood of contract Springfields available in 1864, it is not surprising to find the latest date to be but 1863. Most of the regular Enfields also tapered off in deliveries after 1863.

Additional purchases:

Samuel McLean & Company, New York, 80 Enfield rifle muskets and appendages, in two parcels on May 5 and July 25, 1863.

J. Meyer, New York, about $41,000 worth of sabers but including 166 long Enfield rifles and appendages at $20 and $19.65, December 1861-January 1862.

John T. Mitchell, New York, 780 Enfield rifle muskets, August 6, 1861, at $19.

Naylor & Company, New York. Between December 7, 1861 and July 23, 1863, this firm, a steel maker principally who supplied steel to Sam Colt for the early Dragoon revolvers, in Sheffield, shipped 192,677 of privately purchased Enfields to the North. Enfields in several styles other than the tens of thousands of long rifle muskets, were imported by Naylor as follows:

February 1, 1862	197 short Enfield rifles (195 at $20)	$18.00 & 20.00
June 23, 1862	179 Enfield artillery carbines	14.83½
	1 Enfield artillery carbine	12.83½
December 6, 1862	200 Enfield cavalry carbines and appendages	19.68
	280 short Enfield rifles and appendages	19.68
	240 Enfield artillery carbines and apendages	19.68
	40 Enfield sapper's and miner's carbines and appendages	19.68

First delivery listed simply as "1840 rifles" on August 21 were by way of open purchase, Major Hagner, R. H. K. Whitely, or Captain Silas Crispin officiating. But in the Birmingham Gun Trade Association, presided over by Mr. J. D. Goodman as chairman, a stirring of prosperity was felt with a desire to compete with the machine-made London Armoury guns.

Up to October, 1862, Naylor had shipped in 33,000 Enfields. An adjustment in price was agreed upon by the Secretary of War, acting through the Assistant Secretary, P. H. Watson. For Class 2 Enfields, Naylor (actually Naylor & Company of New York, Boston and Philadelphia, and Naylor, Vickers, & Company, London, Liverpool and Sheffield) received a bonus due to their losses in exchange of 2 shillings more; for first class Enfields, (of which they delivered the most: 25,000 against 8,000, second class) they received 5s. extra.

Naylor became confident that the war was to drag on a good deal longer than it first appeared. The Queen's embargo on shipment of arms to America was lifted, and the British Government made no moves to recognize the South as a nation, only recognizing their rights to receive arms as belligerents. Naylor with Goodman and the Birmingham Association made a proposal to furnish the North with 200,000 "of the best quality of hand-made Enfield rifles, to be delivered in New York, subject to the usual inspection, at the rate of not less than 7,000 per week until the whole number (200,000) is supplied, at the price of $17.50 for each gun, and sterling exchange above 123 per cent added." Assistant Secretary Watson rejected this offer on October 20, but stated in reply that the United States *would* take 100,000 at $16, plus sterling exchange adjustment.

Watson's letter was at once referred to the head office of Naylor, Vickers & Company in London and one of their men took the cars up to see Goodman. At Birmingham, Goodman gave the Naylor, Vickers man a letter of confirmation, accepting the order for the Birmingham Small Arms Trade. The letter was directly addressed to the War Department, and treated as if Naylor was merely bringing the order to Birmingham as some sort of agent. Said Goodman on November 4, 1862, to the Secretary of War: "I hereby agree, subject to the exceptions of strikes, accidents, &c. as mentioned in Messrs. Naylor & Co.'s said letter of 17 Oct., to execute your valued order through the medium of Messrs. Naylor & Co., New York. I expect to commence deliveries on account of the order forthwith, and will certainly complete the quantity within fourteen and a half weeks from 10th December."

Goodman's letter was endorsed by Watson November 29, authorizing the Chief of Ordnance to furnish Captain Crispin with the necessary instructions for receiving the arms and inspecting them. A shipment of 99,720 long Enfields was received by Crispin under this order, plus additional guns accepted in open purchase, almost another 100,000 of them. Naylor had previously been commended for delivering guns which were superior at the price the United States was allowing for "medium quality Enfields," which was another way of speaking of good handmade (non-interchangeable) guns. Many of the 99,720 were accepted at prices higher than the contract; others for slightly less. That Crispin or his sub-inspectors personally inspected each rifle seems very probable; deliveries show a breakdown on 7,260 arms total, with 4 priced at one level, 54 at another, and 26 at a third lower price; 7,176 were paid for at $21.25, which was higher by reason of the compensating figure on the exchange Naylor had demanded.

While in Birmingham, Marcellus Hartley complained of the interference by Naylor buying Enfields. Doubtless unknown to him, Goodman had committed himself to the 100,000 guns for Naylor on November 4. Three weeks later, the day after this deal was approved by Watson, November 28, Hartley was in Birmingham. Writing to Secretary Stanton 29 November, he urged that Naylor be told that Enfields were only worth 42 shillings ($10.50). But Hartley was due back in the United States—his usefulness was at an end. The stop-gap emergency arms shortage which it was his job to cover, had been covered. Now the Union could rely on Small Arms Trade Association guns from Naylor & Company.

Arms from the Association

Arms from the Association were from various makers. No special tabulation now exists by which a name could be connected with this order. Records show barrels passing proof at Birmingham as follows:

1856	384,900
1857	490,037
1858	333,478
1859	450,753
1860	486,617
1861	656,605
1862	1,131,306
1863	No record
1864	No record
1865	552,109

The pre-war years and 1865 indicate the norm for the Trade was about a half million barrels annually. A large proportion of these were common sporting gun and rifle barrels; presumably, also, pistols. But the rise in 1860-61 was caused by the excitement in England that they might go to war with France at any minute. A Volunteer Rifle movement swept the United Kingdom and yoemanry regiments were formed overnight. Equipped at private expense, their rifles were finely finished. For this market the Whitworth and Kerr sharpshooter rifles were aimed.

The Volunteer Rifle movement tapered off into the shooting association of Great Britain, but the Confederate and Yankee purchasers came along to fan the flames of Birmingham barrel forges higher. The increase of 500,000 barrels over 1861 for 1862 was entirely of Enfield type barrels, for the warring purchasers. Why no records are found for 1863 and 1864 is not known —they would be of great interest, if they existed. How much more the United States paid for Enfields from Naylor, than if Stanton had let Hartley remain another six months abroad, is a simple problem of arithmetic which others can solve. The record of history shows that Naylor sent in guns regularly, in quantities promised, and of good quality, often better than expected. That a great many of these guns never got to the fighting fronts, and troops maneuvered in the morass of a southern winter carrying smoothbore muskets, is the fault of official Washington and failures of transportation, not of the Ordnance to contract and buy, nor of Naylor or other contractors to deliver.

Records of Other Purchases

State of New York, October 1, 1862, 10,737 long Enfield rifle muskets; $185,505.59, plus "Amount of commission and cost of inspection of 10,737 rifles. $3,825.37."

Frank Otard, New York, 775 long Enfield rifles, June-August 1862.

F. Otard and Arthur Wigert, New York, 2,554 Enfields, between September 30, 1862 and January 1863. Arthur Wigert had obtained an order 5 September 1861, to deliver 10,000 rifles of the Chasseurs de Vincennes pattern at $23.50, in 55 days. Schuyler in Paris wrote to Secretary Cameron October 10, 1861, saying "He cannot, of course, fulfill. Such arms do not exist in the markets at any price." Wigert asked for an extension of time to eight months, but Ripley refused on 24 October. Wigert then on 26 October wrote to the Secretary, offering 10,000 Chasseurs de Vincennes rifles, in eight months, the same proposal he had failed with in Ripley's care. Assistant Secretary Thomas A. Scott endorsed this letter with "The Secretary desires the guns referred to shall be secured," and as Ripley bluntly put it, "and that contract now stands." Holt and Owen, finding no deliveries, annulled the order under date of April 24, 1862. Wigert turned to Enfields for speculation and it was the popular and historically essential Enfield rifle musket that they delivered.

Perkins & Livingston, New York, 120 Enfields October 15, 1862-March 1863.

John Pondir, Philadelphia, 1,269 Enfields, September, October 1862, January 1863.

H. Simons & Sons, 480 Enfield rifles, October-December 1862.

John Stuart, 30 Enfield rifles, October 28, 1861.

Searer & Hay, 200 Enfield rifles, January 9, 1862.

Schuyler, Hartley & Graham, New York. Between first delivery of 140 Enfield rifles, saber bayonets, (short) at $26.50 on July 31, 1862, and last deliveries of bayonets for Enfields September 26, 1863, Schuyler, Hartley & Graham delivered a variety of Enfield pattern arms. These included 60 Enfield rifles, short, with saber bayonets, for artillery. The 24-inch barreled two-band artillery carbine which in regiments of Volunteers equipped with regular 33-inch rifles, was sometimes issued to sergeants or color guards. Very few of these short 24-inch barrel sword bayonet Enfields were bought by the North, not more than a few hundred in all. The very high prices which Schuyler, Hartley & Graham realized on their sales suggests that they delivered nothing but the London Armoury interchangeable Enfields, for even in the vastly inflated New York market that August of 1861 the peak prices for Enfields were $26 delivered. That Schuyler, Hartley & Graham did business with London Armoury is proved by their delivery December 13, 1861, of 7 Adams', 12 "Adams' revolvers, self-cocking," 16 Kerr, and 26 Beaumont

(Beaumont-Adams) revolvers at $18, for all but the Beaumonts at $19. The suggestion is strong here that the mysterious JS-anchor stamp seen on London Armoury guns of "Southern" origins is the stamp of senior partner J. Rutsen Schuyler, as many researchers have surmised it to be "a shipping house mark."

Another Enfield rifle of Schuyler, Hartley & Graham's importation is the mysterious "Suhl rifle (Enfield pattern) and appendages," of which 1,273 were obtained from them by the New York buying officers. Deliveries were May-July 1862, at $16.25 except the last 275 at $15. We have never seen an Enfield rifle of Suhl manufacture; however, the gun trade in Suhl was much like that of Birmingham, Liege, or even the Vienna-Ferlach complex of artisans. For a price, they would make anything. The Liege trade naturally specialized in the French-style arms, but also fabricated the Enfield, both as private speculation and for government contract work. Many of the smaller nations of the world flocked to these gunmaking centers in historically industrial regions, and a single gunmaker (as the London Armoury Company) might have contracts for warring powers, simultaneously. Evidently Hartley was able to buy up a part of some Enfield-type rifle musket contracts in Suhl. Remotely possible is the notion that he actually had, say, 1,500 Enfields fabricated in Suhl. Aside from our guess they might bear fraudulent "TOWER" marks, there is no information on the marking of these rifles.

William J. Syrus & Brother, New York, delivered 740 regular Enfields and 180 Enfield rifles (Belgian). The probability is that the Belgian Enfields were by August Francotte, who not only was a principal "fitter up" in the Liege trade but one of the largest privately owned machine shops. Francotte, whose initials "Crown over AF" are to be found on a host of widely different Liege-marked arms, was a maker of interchangeable Enfields including some for the British Government. Syrus' delivery, in May, 1862, of these at $16 and $18, suggests they were good rifles. A Francotte Enfield examined a century later in the shop of the Liege agent of Bannerman, to whom it had returned via surplus dealings, was noted as being marked forward of the hammer with A. FRANCOTTE & CIE.

Sarson & Roberts, New York. On January 22, 1862, long before their first delivery of Springfields under terms of contract, they sold 143 long Enfield rifles at $20 to the Ordnance Department.

Tomes, Son & Melvain, New York. Marcellus Hartley's old friends and sometime business partner got into the act, Tomes himself serving at Hartley's agent in Birmingham. Between October 30, 1861 and May 23, 1863, this firm delivered several thousand Enfields. But Tomes found 4,500 ramrods at 60¢ plus 714 angular bayonets, for Enfields, at $1.62, were neat little sideline profit makers. A ramrod possibly from such a source is now in the Blunt Pattern Musket (see page . .), marked near the head DEELEY.

Tiffany & Company, New York. This exclusive Gotham firm more noted today for jewelry than cold steel, delivered a formidable array, though small in numbers, of munitions in the war. Approximately 4,500 long Enfields were received from Tiffany, and 480 short Enfields. But most enigmatic is the item "40 engineers rifles" which were delivered December 2, 1861, priced at $17, in a shipment of short Enfields at $22 and a few second class at $18. The model of gun we suppose is the Enfield, but not adapted for a bayonet, the $1 possibly being dictated by Crispin's or Whiteley's concept of the value of a bayonet lug. As a practical measure, we suppose these rifles should complement an earlier invoice of October 9, 1861, which included "10 short swords with saw backs," at $4.50. Equipping engineer troops, also called pioneers or sappers, with sidearms that could double as tools was an old idea in Europe. What practical use these saw-swords were put to is not known. It is said by men who have used saw-bayonets in battle (I have no practical experience, myself) that the saw edge is a damn nuisance as it makes thrusting with the bayonet difficult because the saw edges usually cut on forward stroke. The basic purpose of the saw-sword is as a saw for offense or defense. On the defense, it can be used to cut wood for breastworks; on the offense, it could cut, say, bridge pilings, which then could be pulled away to cause the bridge to collapse. Bridge burning was far more practical a trick for Yank and Reb alike, except when the bridges were of stone. Though used in Swiss and German armies, the saw-sword or bayonet never achieved acceptance by the American armies. These 40 "engineers" rifles are the only such listed, as purchased by the Union.

United States District Court, eastern district of Pennsylvania, supplied 1,299 Enfield rifle muskets September 30, 1862, and 20 more on October 10, 1862.

Union Defense Committee, New York. 428 Enfield rifles, August 1861, $22.50.

W. W. Woodcock, 809 Enfield rifles, November-December, 1862.

Jeremiah M. Wardwell, November 9, 1861, 4,000 long Enfield rifles, $23.

CHAPTER 22

Continental Arms

In records of arms purchased by the Union, the reference to "Springfield pattern German rifled muskets" is an enigma to arms students. Listed as No. 181 in the collection of the U.S. Cartridge Company is a "United States Model of 1861, Rifled Percussion Musket, caliber .58. Stamped on the lock 1861, U.S. and an eagle (the USCC catalog illustrates an eagle facing to the eagle's right, whereas the German guns known show eagles facing to their left); curly-maple stock. Made for the United States Government during the first year of the Civil War, in Germany. Note—A very rare arm."

The description is complete, defining the typical spring-band rifle musket, three bands, hammer curved originally to follow the Maynard primer lid, but the primer mechanism omitted during manufacture. Three examples of this gun are presently known. One is in the West Point Military Academy Museum, numbered "8" on all parts, including screw heads; and the barrel where it is let into the wood is marked SUHL. The manufacturer as marked on one specimen's barrel is Chr. Funk, of Suhl. The arm was one of two lots imported by William Hahn, contractor or merchant of New York, who delivered to Major Hagner by purchase 179 "German muskets, Springfield pattern, caliber .58 inch, in bond," at $16.50 for a total payment of $2,953.50.

The arms were received and Hahn paid March 26, 1862. A further lot of 302 "German rifled muskets, Springfield pattern, caliber .58 inch" were signed over to Major Hagner in bond on July 15, 1862, for $14.60. Payment of $4,409.20 for these arms was made July 19. During this time Hahn also supplied 335 cavalry sabers in various stages of finish. Information is lacking of the issue of these weapons. They were retained by the Government and carried on the books as arms for issue, judging from the 1865 "Instructions for making Quarterly Returns of Ordnance & Ordnance Stores."

Under "Small Arms, Muskets & Rifles, Foreign Manufacture" is the item: "Rifled Muskets, Springfield model, *German,* calibre .58." The shape of the hammer, having been made some by hand is not a perfect copy of the machine-made Springfield gun hammer. Metal finish, while good, shows hand work. Yet, according to Milt Perry (former West Point arms curator), the parts of the gun interchange with the standard Springfield rifle musket. West Point's sample, though the records are not clear, probably was one of the pattern or sample arms used by Hagner in inspection, if the number "8" is a serial as well as individual assembly number. Another German Springfield, No. 22, is in the collection of C. N. Wynkoop of Tulsa, Oklahoma. A third example was in the collection of Floyd Garrett, North Quincy, Massachusetts.

The Austrian Lorenz

Second in importance to the British Enfields to both sides were rifles obtained from Austria. Both Caleb Huse and later Union buyers scoured the arsenals and arms trade firms, buying weapons. Huse later recalled that he arranged to import 100,000 weapons, while among the North's imports were listed 226,924 Austrian rifles to a gross value of $2,640,704.41. These rifles existed in several varieties, although they were all of the pattern nominally called "Lorenz Model 1854." Because the shape of the lockplate suggested the British 1853 rifle, and because the barrels and fittings of some Austrian rifles were colored with a rust-process to a blue black finish like the Enfields, they were occasionally called "Austrian Enfields," by both vendors and the troops.

Graded as arms of the second class by the U. S. Ordnance, they were lumped as inferior to United States percussion altered rifle muskets .69 and Remington-Maynard arms and P. S. Justice's miscellany obtained from his Philadelphia depot. Austrian rifles, properly titled "rifle muskets," were obtained in the following descriptions:

Rifle muskets, Austrian, leaf sight, quadrangular
    bayonet ....Caliber .59
Rifle muskets, Austrian, leaf sight, quadrangular
    bayonet ....Caliber .58
Rifle muskets, Austrian, block sight, quadrangular
    bayonet ....Caliber .58
Rifle muskets, Austrian, leaf sight, quadrangular
    bayonet ....Caliber .57
Rifle muskets, Austrian, block sight, quadrangular
    bayonet ....Caliber .577
Rifle muskets, Austrian, quadrangular bayonet ..Caliber .55
Rifle muskets, Austrian, quadrangular bayonet ..Caliber .54

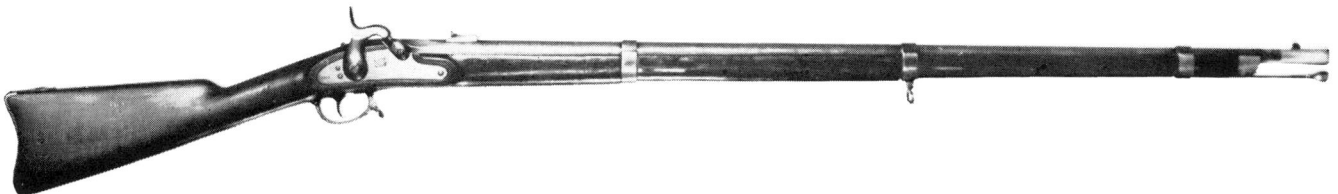

Springfield rifle copy believed imported by William Hahn is dead ringer for U.S. regulation rifle but it is not known if maker had U.S. gauges or simply did a good job copying.

All these weapons were of one basic pattern, newly adopted by the Austrian Army in 1854. Supplies were obtained from three principal sources: the Government arsenal in Vienna, the gun shops and local Vienna factories such as that of Johann and Ferdinand Fruwirth, and Pirko, and arms made by the gunmakers of Ferlach in the western Austro-Hungarian Empire province of Carinthia, due north of Venice (near today's Italian border). This town is still a thriving center of the gun trade, producing sporting rifles and shotguns for the world markets. Originally settled by 400 Belgian gunmakers who were transplanted from Liege to Ferlach (where iron ore and water power was abundant) about 1500, the town during the Napoleonic wars turned out hundreds of thousands of muskets and pistols. Study of Austrian arms will undoubtedly reveal Ferlach marks of origin on many.

Calibers between .59 and .54 existed because these rifles were adopted in .54 by Austria, later offered by speculators bored out to various sizes. Those bored out were supposed to be so enlarged as to take the United States Government .58 Minie bullet, but not all the gunsmiths had the same idea on dimensions. When imported shipments were eventually examined and classified, caliber differences served to place almost all of those not right on .58 caliber into reserve stores. The original Lorenz rifle bullet was a sugar-loaf slug of 450 grains, designed by London riflemaker Wilkinson, tested at Enfield in 1852. It had two grease grooves, .54 caliber, was propelled by 62 grains of powder. The rifle barrel is 37⅛ inches long from tang line at breech to muzzle. Shape is octagon at breech, blending into round about 8 to 10 inches from tang line, about 2 inches forward of rear sight base. Rounded-end, beveled lockplate 5½ inches long, cut for nipple bolster which is forged to barrel. Iron musket butt plate, cheek-piece raised on left of butt. Counter plate plain. Guard bow oval, tangs rounded, extreme length of tang ends 10¼ inches along stock curve. Rear band iron, spring fastened, widened to protect stock where ramrod enters. Band placed 13¼ inches from tang line, ⅝-inch wide. Middle band placed 27⅛ inches from tang line, retained by a spring pegged into a hole, spring to rear. Swivel for a 1⅝-inch sling permanently riveted to guard bow and middle band. Middle band also widened along ramrod channel. Front band located 31¾ inches from tang line, shaped to shroud stock tip, rounded to funnel ramrod into stock groove, and formed to top of barrel with relief cut at front edge to permit disassembly, band being slid forward off the muzzle over the bayonet-stud sight base. Front band also retained by peg spring to rear. Front sight stud of unique form, a long oval placed diagonally on barrel, with foresight blade shaped integral in line with barrel.

The cockeyed shape is characteristic of Austrian quadrangular bayonet rifles, as the bayonet has slanted groove to attach. Ramrod for .54-inch Lorenz rifle has elongated head protected by a brass band to seat original bullet; the original ramrod or .58 Springfield pattern rod could be found in these guns, the latter seeming proof of issue and use with .58 cartridges during Civil War, if of bored out pattern. Furniture all iron; both bright and blued mountings are found. Barrel blued or bright. Lock hardened; case color may exist on new specimens but most of those in the Smithsonian and Rock Island Arsenals, and Liege museums are bright polished. Typical specimen has following marks: On lock—Austrian eagle and "860," believed to be "1860," the date of manufacture. Bands are numbered on left "13"; front band with six-pointed star in circle, middle band with circled symbol over punch dot, number "13" only on rear band. Left breech stamped with a tiny "L." Name on top of breech flat is indistinct, —DER clear, believed to be name of contractor "Werder," Bavarian arms maker Johann Ludwig Werder (1808-1885) who later developed the breech-loading "Lightning" pistols and

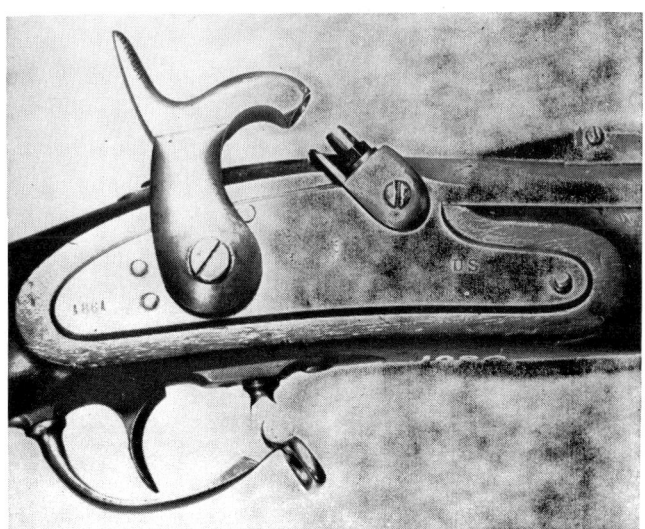

German-made Springfield rifle in West Point Museum bears number 8 on most parts including cone seat clean-out screw. Hammer nose is rounded while date numerals appear individually stamped.

Serial number 22 appears on various parts of this example of German Springfield. Barrel was made in and is stamped SUHL but modern-day record searchers are stymied by Iron Curtain and document losses of many wars. No. 22 is in collection of Charles Wynkoop of Tulsa.

carbines for Austrian service. The basic Lorenz 1854 rifle musket is 53 inches long, the stocks on most are of good walnut. Though interchangeability has not been tested, the introduction of machinery in the manufacture of small arms in Austria took place during the early years of the 1850's, and probably most parts will interchange.

The quadrangular bayonet is a clasp type similar to that of the Springfield and Enfield, but the 19½-inch blade, sharply pointed, is shaped like a cross the width as it parallels the line of bore being wider than the thickness rib. At its widest it measures about 1 1/16 inches, tapering to the point, and is encased in a wooden, leather-covered scabbard tipped with iron. The groove for the muzzle stud is on a bias or angle curving to the left or counterclockwise, blade to the right when installed on the gun. A typical bayonet is stamped on the arm where blade joins socket (evidently welded) with a "T" in a circle, "3," and an "S" with an arrow struck through it. The issue number is stamped on the other side.

Aside from calibers, only one of which is the original boring (.54 inch), the sights distinguish the two basic patterns of Lorenz arms. The rifle musket issued to third rank men in the Austrian Army (file closers and skirmishers), was sighted to 820 yards with a curved leaf which elevated. The plain infantry musket had a fixed sight blade graduated to 245 yards. Though a feature of Lorenz's design was the *tige* to aid in upsetting the bullet to bore-size in loading, the rifle muskets did not have the *tige* fitted.

The Jaeger

This was reserved for the Jaeger carbine, one of the more unusual of the imported weapons since it is illustrated in the Atlas of the *Official Records* and is considered as a United States substitute standard weapon.

The records show that 29,850 of the Jaeger carbines were imported. Fruwirth's name stamped in a sunken oval about ¾ of an inch long at the breech is on some guns. "Joh-Fruwirth a Wienn" is also found.

A typical Jaeger is 43½ inches overall, with a 26-inch octagon barrel. From the muzzle back 4½ inches the barrel is turned round to accommodate an unusual socket bayonet resembling the Brown Bess sword bayonet, and has a clasp. The bayonet stud is beneath the barrel; front sight is brass, rear sight in two patterns. The bayonet is distinctive because of its diagonal slot, and because the blade is wide and flat, about 1¾ inches wide, single edged as a sword. Except near the point both edges are sharp. There is no guard or hilt. Total length is 23 inches. Caliber standard, .54.

Significant ballistic difference between the Jaeger carbine and the rifle musket is that the Jaeger has a *tige* inside the breech. Boring is four grooves, uniform depth, grooves and lands equal width, and the twist is one turn in 5 feet 2 inches. Range and accuracy of this Lorenz short rifle was remarkable as Austrian Army tests showed 95 per cent hits on the target at 820 yards; at 984 yards, 65 per cent struck the target; at 1,230 yards, 49 per cent hits, the target being six feet by 55 feet long, a company front target. At 246 yards, 100 bullets were fired, all inside a 6-inch diameter bull. At extreme effective range of 1,640 yards, the conical bullet pierced three poplar boards 1.02 inches thick placed one foot apart in line. Some Jaeger carbines have the *tige*, others are without it. Noncommissioned officers, men of the third rank who by their tactics are skirmishers, and the best marksmen of the battalions in Austria, were issued with the *tige* carbines. They may be distinguished externally by their

Fruwirth Jaeger carbine bears Federal eagle mark thought to indicate Wisconsin regiment which had a mascot eagle "Old Abe" who flew into battle above them. Gun shown was in Liege arms museum 1961, had been sent to Europe in post-Civil War sales of surplus arms.

rear sights graduated up to 1,000 yards. The *tige* in the Austrian carbine is used simply to support the bullet, leaving an interval between it and the powder; it was not intended to assist the taps of the rammer in expanding the ball into the grooves. The Jaeger rammer is carried separately. Jaeger carbines without *tige* had sights graduated to 770 yards, and were issued to ordinary line infantrymen. The *tige* carbine was the more accurate.

The Lorenz designs also were bought by the combatants in 1861 in musketoon form, corresponding more closely to the design of a short rifle, two banded. Basically the same gun as the rifle musket, the Lorenz short rifle had the front band set back and the rear band fitted with the sling swivel. The rear swivel base was screwed by two screws to the underside of the buttstock to the rear of the trigger guard plate. A small three-leaf rear sight similar to that on Enfield carbines was mounted.

Dingee's Austrian Rifles

Silas Dingee originally offered Austrian make rifles which seem definitely to have been of the late Model 1854 Lorenz pattern, of the *tige* or skirmisher's type with long range rear sight, and the line infantry model with plain sight. These sights are described variously as "short sight" and "long sight," and "leaf sight" and "block sight." Calibers of the arms supplied were .58, and also .577, as well as .54, .55, and .59. The model arm was bright; those to be delivered were to be "browned," that is, finished with the cold-rust process to a satiny blue-black. The order specified arms of .58 caliber. Because of the differences, the matter ultimately was brought before Lincoln. He directed that the arms be assessed based on the contract price for arms equal to the standard, at $19, and all others should be valued accordingly. The prices eventually ranged between $16 and $17, as agreed upon by Major Hagner and Dingee's office. By the middle of March, 1862, 8,000 to 9,000 of some 12,000 inspected had been delivered to the Government.

"These arms were much needed, and were urgently called for by General McClellan," said Dingee, about 45,000 in all having arrived. The rest were on the way, and Dingee hoped the contract would be honored by Holt and Owen. To help wind up the deal, as possibly Dingee found he could turn his guns over to Boker if indeed he was not actually getting them through Boker, his counsel O. S. Halsted, Jr., suggested to General Ripley (June 6, 1862) that the balance of the contract could be filled by Dingee, with Enfield rifles, "to the number yet due under their contract, at the same price, $19."

Halsted apparently had the good ear of some folks in high places; a fortnight later having had no favorable word from Ripley as to the final inspection and acceptance of some 3,060 guns of Dingee's which were in Crispin's store rooms, nor approval of the Enfield switch, he said to the Ordnance general, "Should it be deemed necessary to see the President again, I will cheerfully accompany the General, or get the Presi-

Pvt. Geo. Atkinson, born Yorkshire, England, enlisted in Yankee army at age 41 on 21 Aug. '62 at Ft. Snelling, Minn. in Co. F, 9th Minn. Vol. Infy, as a 3-years man. He was issued at that time an Austrian Lorenz M1854-5 rifle *a tige* with leaf rear sight and typical quadrangular bayonet. Photo from Kay Fritz Archive collection.

dent to make an appointment to see us together at an early day."

Holt and Owen sifted the arguments, came up with a reasonable solution. They recommended accepting Enfields to fill out the order, at $19, but in consideration of paying a premium price for Enfields then worth $15 in bond in the market, they declared no extension of time should be allowed on the contract. Time was sought by Dingee, as his agents had not been able to adhere to the very strict schedule of shipments which he had set up and which formed a part of the original contract. No Enfields were received from Dingee by Crispin; of some 45,000 guns presented for that worthy officer's inspection, 21,915 were accepted at prices of $19 (for 540 only) down to $16.15. Precisely why nearly half the lot were refused, is not known.

Consol Weapons

Of secondary importance to the Lorenz arms but of major interest to the arms collector and historian were another class of Austrian guns, the Consol-primed muskets, rifles, and pistols which were imported by the North. A few of these unusual weapons, erroneously termed "pill lock" by collectors, may have been used by the South. But Confederate supplies of even regular percussion caps were always strained—the special tube-like detonators used in the Consol lock guns would have been almost impossible to supply. The North was in better shape, and the tally at war's end listed "249,641,400 percussion primers, Austrian, &c......$11,683.50" as having been procured for the Consol-lock guns.

Hermann Boker & Company, "Guns & Hardware," of 50 Cliff Street, New York, Liege, and Birmingham, England, was the principal source for Consol muskets, though General Fremont acquired 25,000. Boker, until after the turn of the century an active New York export-import munitions firm and jobber of Borchardt automatic pistols, worked closely with a Belgian agent who also seems to have been tied up with the later international junk armaments dealer ALFA, Adolph Frank, Hamburg, and with the post-Civil War United States arms dealer Francis Bannerman. Bannerman, whose Belgian addresss in 1900 was 79, rue Lairesse, Liege, pictured the Consol lock guns in his catalog, saying: "Our agent in Belgium acted for the firm of Hermann Boker & Co. . . . He informed me that he altered over 60,000 Austrian tube-lock guns into regular percussion cap muskets, which were used to arm the Union Army Volunteers, 1861-65. . . ." M. Ancion of Ancion-Marx in 1961 told this writer his firm had been agents for Bannerman in Liege.

Major Alfred Mordecai, on a military mission to Europe in 1854, noted the issue of this form of musket lock. "In Austria the greater part of the foot troops are still armed with the smoothbore musket, altered from flint to percussion, and adapted to a peculiar kind of priming," he wrote. "This priming consists of percussion powder placed in a copper tube of such size

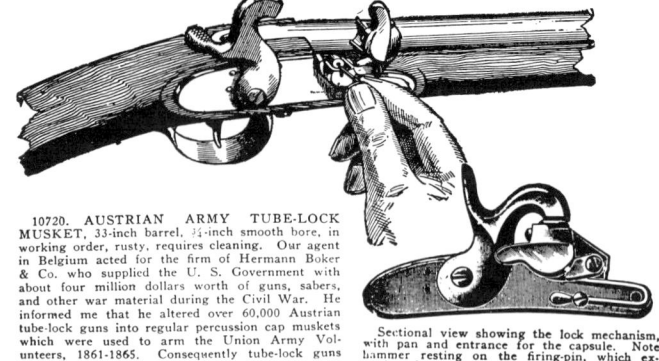

10720. AUSTRIAN ARMY TUBE-LOCK MUSKET, 33-inch barrel, ¾-inch smooth bore, in working order, rusty, requires cleaning. Our agent in Belgium acted for the firm of Hermann Boker & Co. who supplied the U. S. Government with about four million dollars worth of guns, sabers, and other war material during the Civil War. He informed me that he altered over 60,000 Austrian tube-lock guns into regular percussion cap muskets which were used to arm the Union Army Volunteers, 1861-1865. Consequently tube-lock guns are now rare, every gun collector needs one to show evolution in fire arms. Offered complete.

Sectional view showing the lock mechanism, with pan and entrance for the capsule. Note hammer resting on the firing-pin, which explodes the pill-like fulminating charge when struck by the hammer.

Augustin version of Consol lock used tube primer and had protective hood that closed down over it like "frizzen" over flintlock pan. Firing pin in cover hit primer to detonate. Many were used by North with imported primers.

that it can be introduced into the vent of the flint musket. Thus inserted, the primer lies in the groove of an iron seat which is substituted for the pan of the old musket; it is there protected by a cover which corresponds to the lower part of the flint 'battery,' and is held down by the battery spring; the percussion hammer, substituted for the flint cock, strikes on the top of this cover, and causes a point which projects from the cover into the pan to strike the tube of percussion powder, and thus fires the charge."

Mordecai noted also that both smoothbores and rifles of the same caliber .70, were issued, rifled guns to noncommissioned officers "and some of the men in each company," probably the more proficient marksmen as was the case five years later when the several styles of Lorenz rifles had been adopted. The Consol rifle "is constructed on the Delvigne plan; the ball resting on the mouth of a chamber, where it is expanded by a blow from a heavy rammer," wrote Mordecai.

Two varieties of Consol lock existed. The 1835 pattern of Milanese inventor Giuseppe Consol was a true conversion from flintlock. An improved form was designed by General Baron Vincent Augustin. The latter, vintage Model 1841, was the pattern most widespread in the Austrian Army, an evolution from the Consol flint conversion, and perhaps preferred by Austrian authorities over the new percussion cap system because of its similarity in handling to the flint priming manual, with which hundreds of thousands of soldiers were already familiar, and also because the spring cap held the primer secure against loss yet ready to fire with the hammer cocked.

The original Consol cartridge had a primer fastened to a sort of button by two fine brass wires from primer through the holes in the button. The button was rolled into the paper cartridge tube when making ammunition. Placing it in the primer groove, the protective cap was closed down, cutting the strings and then the cartridge was torn and rammed in conventional fashion. The undersized bullet, upset in the Delvigne system rifles, was retained by wads top and bottom in the musket load.

Augustin's improvement consisted of placing a small firing pin in the protective top, hit directly by the hammer and thus making ignition more certain. The Augustin locks, flat beveled edge and with rounded ends much like the later Lorenz locks, were those most commonly bought by wartime speculators and government agents, and of which Bannerman's Belgian friend converted 60,000 to caplock for Boker.

The Army's 1865 "Instructions for making Quarterly Returns of Ordnance & Ordnance Stores" under items of Class VI list a number of Boker guns. Designations are by sample number, as "Boker's No. 1, Nos. 6 and 7," up to No. 13. Reference is to a number of sample muskets deposited with the Ordnance Corps in 1861 when Hermann Boker undertook to supply weapons to Uncle Sam, and later referred to by inspecting Captain Silas Crispin in his report of February 13, 1862 to the Commission on Ordnance & Ordnance Stores. Austrian converted muskets were among this lot.

Said Crispin of Sample No. 1: "This arm is caliber .70, rifled with four very light grooves, the lands broader than the grooves. The length of the barrel is 34.5 inches. The stock is of white wood, common to the Austrian manufacture of arms. The lock is inferior in finish, but the material appears to be good. From the indications around the cone-seat, I believe this to be an altered arm, from flint lock to percussion (actually Consol-lock to percussion). It is furnished with the angular bayonet, the provision for securing which is a steel spring or catch riveted on the barrel; its weight is 9.25 pounds. This gun is the Austrian smoothbore musket rifled. It is furnished with an elevating sight, which turns down on the barrel, and has several notches for different ranges up to 900 paces. The implements accompanying these arms are screwdrivers and cone

Detonator lock of Guiseppe Consol was modified by Austrian engineers and named after Austro-Hungarian Ordnance General Vincent Augustin. System is type 1840; is here shown fitted to smoothbore musket. Holes left in lock after side assembly is removed in converting to percussion give rise to supposition arm was "originally flintlock." Belief is, M. Ancion & Co. converted 60,000 in Liege for Boker to sell to U.S.

wrenches, and wipers of the Austrian pattern. No ball screws, spare cones or spring vises are furnished, 10,268 of these arms have been received."

No. 2 Boker arm was the Austrian Lorenz 1854 rifle musket, both sights. Up to February, 1862, 15,528 had been received, 12,384 of the fixed sight type, 3,144 balance with elevating rear sight ranging up to about 800 yards. One bayonet sample was soft, incorrectly hardened, and Crispin was cautioned about inspecting them, but considered the gun, .54 caliber (he called it .55) "on the whole, fair . . . serviceable."

No. 3 Broker arm was the same Lorenz rifle musket bored out to .58. Crispin noted the similar external dimensions, deduced this to be bored up to .58 and re-rifled. Same equipments as No. 1. Of the No. 3 kind, 984 had been received to that date.

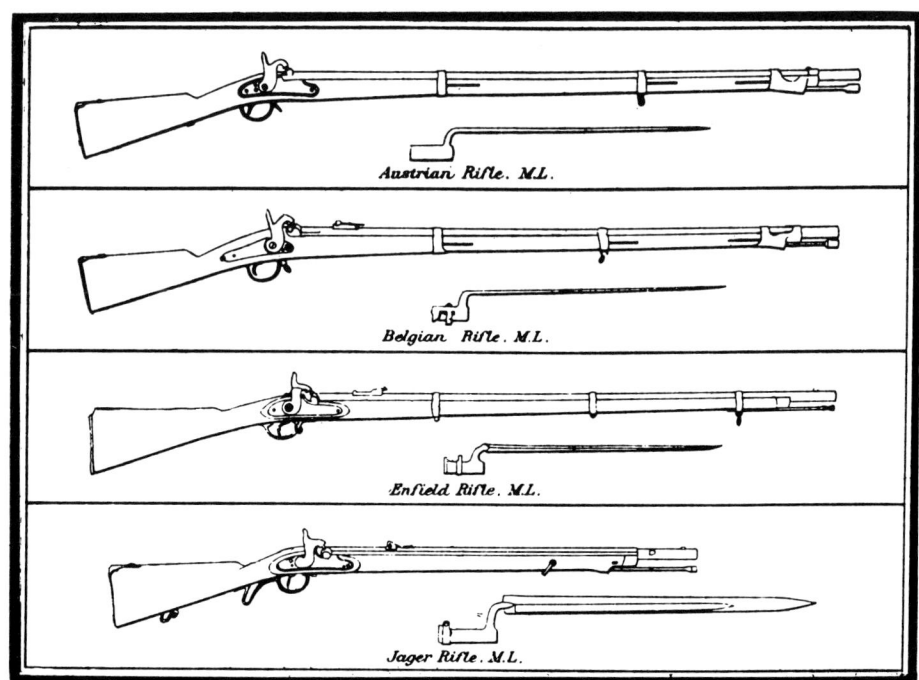

Official Records illustrated Austrian musket of Augustin lock type converted to percussion, Belgian minie rifle also bought as smoothbores, regular Enfield, and Lorenz Jaeger rifle with broad single edge bayonet.

The No. 4 Boker gun was also the Lorenz rifle musket, bored to .58 inch. "It is finished, in some respects," stated Crispin, "in imitation of the Enfield rifle; barrel and lock blued, and tompion [tampion] and snap cap attached; the bayonet the usual Austrian model," and identical, Crispin said, to No. 2 and 3, but "somewhat superior, in every respect, to these (2 and 3) samples." Exactly 7,376 No. 4's had been received.

French and Belgian Arms

French and Belgian materiel was considered next best to the Enfields, though the types and calibers were more varied than either Enfield or Austrian Lorenz arms. Basic pattern for the best rifles of both France and Belgium was the "carabine" of Captain Minie.

Minie's designs had exerted profound changes in the world's small arms armament. That change was ably summed up by lexicographer Thomas Wilhelm after the war when he prepared his military dictionary. Said Wilhelm, "Minie Rifle. A species of fire-arm, invented by Capt. Minie, from whom it receives its name. It is certain in aim, and fatal in its results at 800 yards."

The claim was, if anything, inferior to the real capability of the Minie rifle.

France in 1861 possessed a surplus of many arms. During the 1840's the temporary procurement of guns designed by Thouvenin, Pontchara, Minie, and others kept the arsenals busy and the soldiers active testing them. Then came the Crimean War and France's involvement on the side of Great Britain and Turkey against Russia. Soldiers of the Republic to the number of 309,258 embarked for the Black Sea battlefields, and with them went vast quantities of munitions. Small arms were in production at the factories in France: Charleville, Mutzig, St. Etienne, Maubeuge, Chatellerault. These weapons remained in storage after the Crimean War ended in 1856, and were a constant article of trade among arms speculators who never hefted a gun nor opened a case of muskets personally. Some lots of arms in government arsenals changed hands several times without being being shipped. Three basic rifled shoulder arms were issued to French troops in the Crimea: the rifled musket with *tige,* the Carabine with *tige* Model 1846, and the Carabine of the Cents Gardes. Other French guns were bought by Northern officers and the Ordnance Department. Exactly 200 "French carbines" for $4,800 were purchased, as well as 44,250 "French rifles" for $757,-416.69, an average of $17.11 2/3. This lot at that price would have consisted of good quality rifles. French long guns were also among 162,533 "Boker's rifles" bought for $2,267,834, and one single lot of 25,000 "Boker's rifles, sword bayonet," purchased for an average of about $5.50; for $139,254.

As with the Austrian arms, the French were evaluated according to caliber as to their serviceability. First class French guns included rifled muskets, French, triangular bayonet, caliber .58. These most nearly conformed to the Springfield pattern in style and shooting. Also of first class category were rifles, light French, saber bayonet, caliber .577. Second class arms included rifled muskets, French, triangular bayonet, caliber .71, and rifled muskets, French brass-mounted, triangular bayonet, caliber .69. Bright-steel mounted muskets of the same caliber were also obtained, graded second class. Third class arms were of decidedly inferior grade for military purposes. Among U. S.-made guns so classified were percussion sporting rifles, various calibers, shootable but definitely not of the uniform nature demanded for efficient maintenance in the field. Two types of French smoothbore muskets were in this grade, calibers .69 and .70. In the fourth class "Rifles a *tige,* French, sabre bayonet . . . calibre .63" and Rifles a *tige,* French . . . calibre .58" were included, as were the 25,000 Boker rifles described as "Rifles, French, Boker's Vincennes, sword bayonet, steel scabbards . . . calibre .69."

The most highly developed shoulder arm from France in 1861 was the *Carabine a tige,* Model 1846. The Chasseurs de Vincennes, a regiment of skilled marksmen, were among the units armed with this rifle. Zouaves and the Infantry of the Guard were armed with a musket form of the *Carabine a tige,* up until 1858; then rifled muskets with tige were called in and the *Carabine* issued.

The French percussion muskets Model 1842, graded as third class guns by U. S. Ordnance, were three-band percussion guns; overall length, 47¾ inches; barrel length 43 inches; weight about 8½ pounds. The iron mounted gun had three bands; retained by springs. The rear band was held by a spring before it and the band bottom flared a little to protect the stock where the ramrod entered. The middle band, to which was riveted a sling swivel, was also held by a spring in the stock. The front band was double; the bayonet stud a lug beneath the muzzle, the band held by a rearward spring locking into a hole in the band. Caliber was .69 and .70, the latter possibly because rusted guns might have been "freshed out" in French service to a slightly oversize bore.

Most distinctive feature of this model and all subsequent French arms imported by Union agencies was the lock. Designed on the back-action principle, it was a common percussion mechanism with a massive hammer, but with the main spring placed at the rear of the tumbler instead of in front as in the Springfield gun. The lockplate was held to the stock by screws fore and aft, the heads of which were drilled for a two-pronged split screwdriver.

This type of fitting was designed to discourage the soldier from disassembling his gun unless under the supervision of a noncommissioned officer, who would issue the special screwdriver and call it in again after the cleaning session was over. Since the lock was inletted entirely into the wood without any part touching the barrel, and could not be contaminated by smoke from firing, there would usually be no need for the soldier to take off the lock. This was a step toward more simple maintenance. A typical lock marking

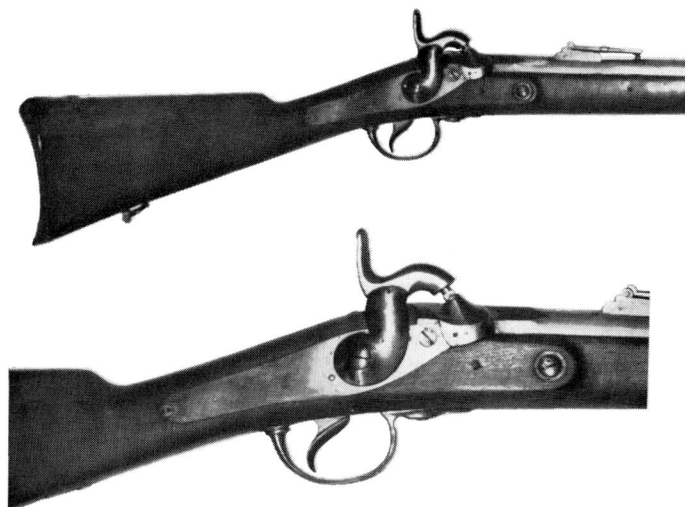

Thouvenin rifle had a *tige* in breech. Caliber .69 rifle used round ball. Innovation of early 1840's, gun was matured in style by French ordnance who held stock and barrel together by bands instead of pins as Thouvenin gun, and called improved model *carabine a tige*. Minie ball then was used.

would be MRE RLE DE ST ETIENNE, indicating the gun was made at the large Government arms factory in the city of St. Etienne, about 200 miles southwest of Paris. As these guns were smoothbore, there were no rear sights; front sights were brass lumps on the front bands.

Predecessors to the Model 1842 percussion back-action lock muskets were those of models extending as far back as the 1777 flint muskets copied by Springfield Armory in designing our own arms of the 1820's. These guns existed converted to percussion. Their brass trim did not add to their martial usefulness in the mid-1800's where concealment and tactics as skirmishers made concealment of troops desirable in the field. In 1855, according to Major Mordecai's report, "The great body of infantry of the line (French Army) are still armed with the simple percussion musket (new or altered from flint-lock), and use the spherical ball. The caliber of this musket has been lately increased to 0.708 inch, and the old arms have been reamed out to correspond with the new one, carrying a round ball of one ounce; but this change is regretted on account of the increased difficulty of altering the arms to rifle muskets for carrying the elongated balls now generally adopted. This alteration has, however, been made in some of the muskets by inserting a *tige* in the breech pin, and cutting four broad and shallow grooves in the barrel, adding a high sight graduated up to 800 meters. The grooves, which are of equal width with the lands, are 0.02 inch deep at the breech, diminishing to 0.004 inch at the muzzle; the twist is one turn in two meters, or about six and a half feet. The ball weighs seven hundred and twenty grains, and the charge of musket powder is seventy grains. This arm was used by the infantry of the guard in the Crimea. An old soldier said the recoil was not inconveniently great. The infantry of the Imperial Guard are armed with a rifle musket like the above, but without the *tige*. The ball for this arm is cylindro-conical, with a cavity at the base, but without a 'culot' or expanding cup. The Chasseurs are armed with the *carabine a tige* which is constructed on the same principle as the *tige* musket above mentioned. The barrel is thirty four inches long, and the ball and charge are the same as for the musket. The sight is graduated to 1,200 meters." The musket of course took a triangular socket bayonet of clasp form.

Three years after Mordecai wrote his report, the French Zouaves were rearmed with the *Carabine a tige,* turning in their three-band rifled muskets.

The Carabine, actually a short rifle with two bands like many rifles of the world's great powers, was fitted with a sword-like bayonet having a brass hilt and one curved quillon, the quillon opposite the flat of the back being circular to slip over the muzzle. The hilt was grooved to receive a long lug soldered to the side of the muzzle, and a spring catch in the pommel locked the bayonet onto the gun. Its curved blade is variously called "saber" and "sword," neither description of which is really correct. The French called it more correctly, "yataghan," after the Turkish sword which it copied. The single edged blade was sharpened sometimes on both edges of the tip. Length of 22½ inches gave the Carabine a total length which was 3½ inches shorter than the infantry musket or rifled musket.

"The weight, length, and form of this bayonet renders it a formidable weapon in hand-to-hand contests," wrote Wilson in his *Tactics*. "The handling of the carbine in the bayonet exercises is superior to that of the rifle musket, owing to its less length; with bayonet off, the length is only 49½ inches, which renders it highly favorable for light troops." The yataghan bayonet is called by one authority (Liege museum catalog) "Model 1847."

Boker's sample guns Nos. 8 and 9, as described in Captain Crispin's report of February 13, 1862, were French weapons. No. 8, said Crispin, "is of French manufacture, .71 calibre, weight 10.25 pounds, length of barrel 41 inches, rifled with four grooves. The lock is a back action, and the sear and main spring are in one. This is a solid and substantial arm, well made in lock, stock, and barrel. The bayonet is of the angular form, with clasp; the rammer is not cupped for the accommodation of the elongated ball; and a simple notched projection at the breech pin constitutes the rear sight. No appendages are furnished with this arm. The large caliber renders, of course, this arm objectionable; but in other respects it is acceptable. We have received 6,940."

According to Wilcox, this is the standard French rifle musket, apparently with Delvigne breech, no *tige*,

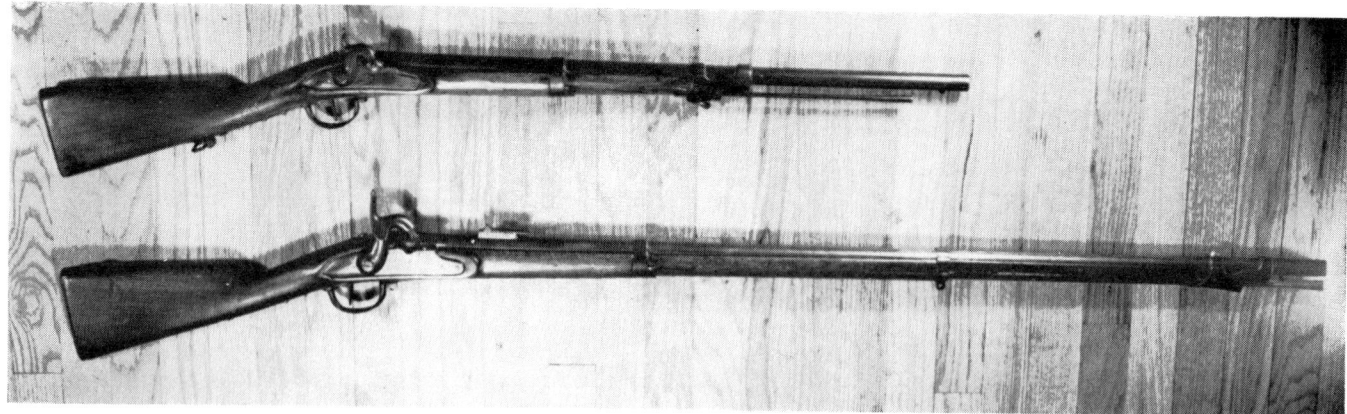

French flintlock carbine of 1822 has been transformed to percussion by a German gunmaker using clean-out screw type cone seat. Bottom arm is French musket of 1825 transformed to percussion 1842 and then rifled with long range 800 meter rear sight fitted 1857. Called *Mousqueton de gendarmerie,* or "State Police Musket," long gun with full charge and Lyman .69 Minie ball seems to shoot point blank up to 100 yards. U.S. Minister Dayton obtained such arms from Belgian fabricants who wanted to sell older models first before such experts as Hartley and Huse got around to demanding Enfields.

firing a round ball. He said, "The rifle musket has no *elevating sight;* the rear sight is fixed. To aim at 200 yards, or under, the rear sight is used; but beyond that the soldier places his thumb across the barrel, and sights over the nail, or, to give a greater elevation, aims over the joint of the thumb." According to Wilcox, writing in 1859 with the storm of war brewing, and rushing to get his manuscript off to Van Nostrand and into print to sell to militia officers, the French feared the elevating rear sight in the hands of infantry would cause them to fire beyond the accurate range of their rifled muskets. Wilcox noted that this seemed a difficult thing to justify, by implication referring to the entire field of improved arms and tactics being developed, but recognizing also that the French had studied the elevating rear sight thoroughly in battle, he cautioned that "it would be well to study the matter thoroughly before venturing to disapprove."

The Delvigne musket with round ball developed 1408 fps MV, while the heavier cylindro-conical bullet fired from the *tige* musket of the same caliber reached only 1023 fps MV. A thousand of Wilcox's books were bought from Van Nostrand by order of June 29, 1859, from the Adjutant General, and it would be strange if Crispin was not thoroughly familiar with the shooting lieutenant's opinions and information, so handy to him as inspecting Ordnance officer at the small arms bottleneck of the Port of New York.

Sample No. 9 appears to have been an altered flintlock with front action lock. According to Crispin: "This is the same style musket as the French rifle muskets *a Liege,* being the same calibre. (.71 inch); about the same weight, (10.5 pounds); and the same length of barrel (41 inches). It is equal in make and finish to No. 8, and differs but little from it, except the lock, which is front action. The rammer is cupped to suit the elongated ball. No implements are furnished with them. 1,320 of them have been received."

It is very probable that this gun is the model known in France as the *Mousqueton de gendarmerie,* model 1825-42-57, caliber 17.6mm, an iron mounted 3-band musket of the latest flint pattern. The gun was converted to percussion in 1842, subsequently rifled, and fitted with a new rammer adapted for elongated Minie bullet. The gun was probably newly breeched as well, with a *tige,* though Crispin does not seem to have pulled the plugs on any during his cursory inspection. In France, due to the age of the gun and the number of alterations it has passed through, the type was not classed as fit for front line service. Instead, it was issued to the gendarmes who, in the 1850's, were auxiliary troops composed of ex-soldiers who had served their tours of duty in the Regular Army and were now in the active reserve. With the adoption of new rifles, and the realization by the French authorities in 1861 that breechloaders were just around the corner, large quantities of these obsolescent rifled muskets were made available in Government warehouses to eager Federal and Confederate arms speculators. Unpacked in New York, inspectors graded them as arms of the second class.

German and Austrian Arms

Among Prussian arms specially imported, Boker delivered his share. Sample No. 10 described by Crispin was .69, weight 10.55 pounds, the Prussian new-model musket rifled four grooves, without the long range sight, and having a front action lock. "A well made arm, with a strong, substantial lock," said Crispin. "Its great defect, of couse, is its large caliber." The only accouterments (which fitted the ramrod) were ball screw, and worm for the twist of tow or flannel rag that would be used to wipe out the bore. By February, 848 had been received.

Sample No. 11 was the Austrian rifle, with broad sword bayonet, also called Lorenz Jaeger carbine. The original Model 1854, caliber .54, had no ramrod, the rammer being a separate accessory. Said Crispin, "the arms imported by the Messrs. Boker & Co. have been bored in the stock to receive a steel rammer." No spring was installed to secure the rammers, as is done in the Enfield or Springfield. Crispin supposed that as "these arms are well made," they might do for artillery or,

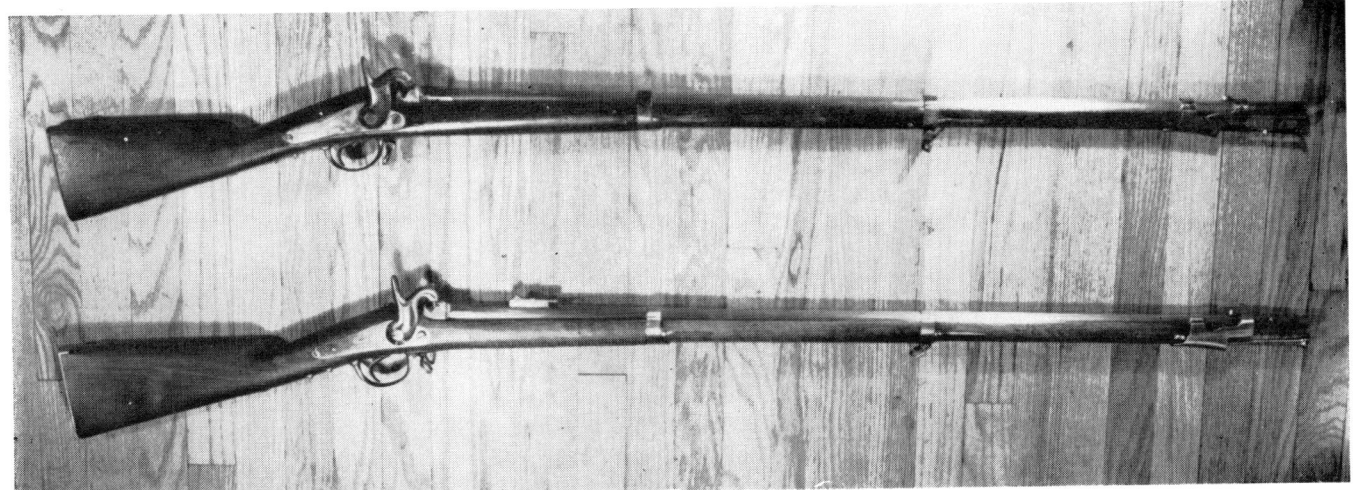

without sword bayonets, for cavalry. By February 13, 1862, 1,488 had been received.

A specimen of the Boker-modified Lorenz Jaeger carbine in the author's collection is bright finish, stamped FERD. FRUWIRTH in a circle on top flat of octagon barrel about ½ inch from breech. A draw mark is incised on top of the breech and plug tang, to index after unbreeching. The nipple bolster is of approximate Enfield form. The barrel is held by two cross wedges, pinned to the stock to avoid losing them; and by the screw for front "jaeger type" sling swivel. The rear swivel is on a two-screw base and mounted on the belly of the stock. Iron trigger guard has the usual Austrian deep curve before the tang. The muzzle is turned round for about 4½ inches, and the bayonet socket fits over the muzzle, a spiralling cut in the socket conforming to the inclination of the front sight base and bayonet stud. Near to the octagon there is another stud on right side of barrel, against which the ring wedges when the bayonet is locked on. The broad flat blood-gutter single-edge blade is sharpened on top of the point for about 5 inches. The fore-end cap and ramrod thimble are two pieces, and the well-cut screw threads of the cap will not fit the screw threads of the screw that holds the ramrod thimble on, and vice versa. Differences in the two screws, which are actually very similar, suggest the thimble is not a Fruwirth factory addition. The ramrod is a shortened ordinary Lorenz rifle rod, with egg-shaped head having a hole through it, and threads very casually grooved on the tip. The hole through the head is for a torque arm supplied normally as part of the implements, to help withdraw the stuck bullet in case of misfire. A common blade front sight is mated with an elaborate curved incline rear sight, open notch it is true, but of the same principle as the sight on the U. S. Army Garand rifle 1936-60. A thumb screw on the right of the sight base clamps the sight curve leaf in proper elevation. Sight and nipple are blued; all else is bright.

That this is one of Boker's guns is fairly conclusively proved by the fitting of a brass shield on top of the stock small, having an eagle on it. The plate has

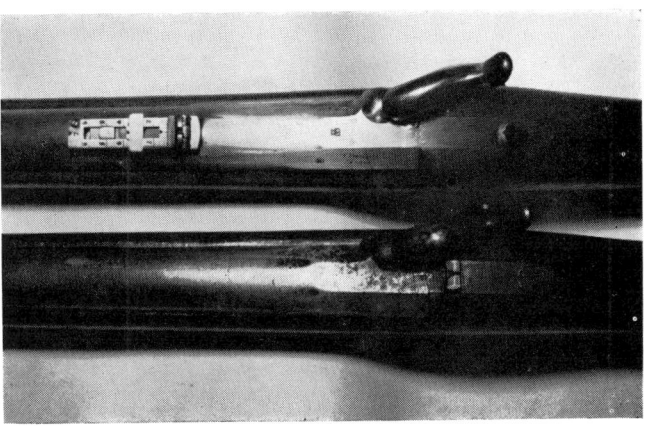

French Delvigne musket with long range rear sight is compared with identical arm bored smooth. Top gun originally was rifled with same type sight but this has been removed, leaving traces of solder and file marks on barrel. Bore was cut out smooth to remove pitting when sold off as surplus after several years of hard shooting practice. New musket type sight is on tang of barrel.

been stamped in a double die, the male die not so crisply cut as the female die once doubtless was—it is now much rubbed. Of yellow brass, this shield-eagle has been noted on one other foreign gun. Though it is thought the other gun was an Enfield-like arm also branded OHIO, it has been suggested this eagle (which is unmistakably Federal, olive branch, arrows, and Washington's arms) is the insignia of the famous Wisconsin "Eagles" regiment, whose mascot was an American bald eagle. If so, the "Eagles" turned this Lorenz carbine over to the surplus property officers and after the war it was sold off as a serviceable gun. Thousands were returned to Europe, mostly to Belgium. There, being transformed into Wanzel-system flip breech-loaders was the fate of some; being falsely fitted with flint cock and pans, the fate of others. This one escaped such a fate and was presented to the new Musee d'Armes de Liege in the old palace on the Quai de Maastricht. It was No. 853 in the old listing, a gift of Monsieur A. Simonis, believed a gunmaker of Liege. In June, 1961, the author bought at an auction of some duplicates from the Museum this interesting carbine

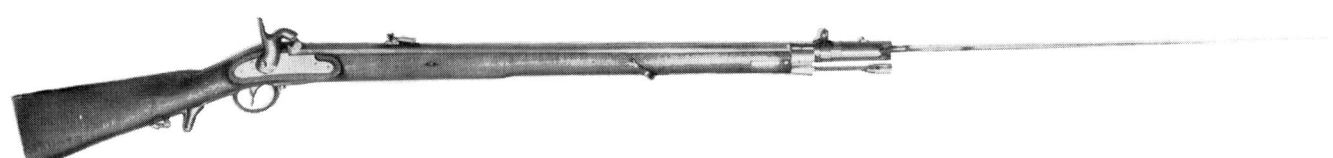

Garibaldi rifles were strongly made but clumsy, and non-standard .71 caliber. Records state only 5995 Garibaldi rifles were purchased. Style similar to Lorenz Jaeger carbine but barrel is round and special front band holds ramrod.

Brazilian light Minie combined characteristics of Enfield and Minie .577 rifles. Arms are found with OHIO on stock and several are to be seen in U.S. Government Civil War collections.

Majority of Boker guns were brass mounted Prussian smoothbore muskets, model 1831 converted to percussion.

and returned it to the middle west where it now reposes in a place of honor on the gun rack above the front door. Yet this is doubtless not the first of Boker's guns to make the westward trip across the Atlantic twice.

Three patterns of arms are not well described by anything in any official records, but are definitely Civil War Northern issue. One resembled the Enfield, may actually be the "Belgian Enfields" mentioned with William J. Syrus & Brother's imports. The gun is actually the Brazilian light Minie rifle, made in Liege for the Emperor Dom Pedro of Brazil. The butt stock, butt plate, trigger guard and lock with nipple bolster, are plain Enfield 1853 model. The rear band and front nose-cap are straight from the light .58 French Minie, and the yataghan sword bayonet is also of the light French .58 Minie form, brass hilted, almost straight blade, slanting away from line of bore when fitted. It attaches to the right of muzzle with a guide rib. The same bayonet seems to fit certain Colts, and possibly Sharps and other .58 rifles having rather large muzzle diameter. The rear sight of this composite rifle is long Minie form, not Enfield. The lockplate bears simply the stamp of an anchor, flanked by the initials D and G or, as it sometimes seems to appear, C. The bayonet is also stamped thus, a smaller punch, on the right of the blade, and on the left, one example bears the initials S&K. Albaugh & Simmons identify this as Schnitzler & Kirschbauer of Solingen, Prussia, whose initials appear on many Civil War items—both North and South.

The first example of this gun seen was in the Marine Corps Museum at Quantico, Virginia. Museum chief Lieutenant Colonel John H. Magruder informed us the rifle had been located with and was in association with a Plymouth rifle and a Mississippi rifle, and had been with them for a long time. Though it is possible the Marine Corps made some shooting tests of this rifle in competition with the others, no record has so far been found. As a rifle for boat crews, it would be useful. The second specimen seen was in the Liege museum, identified as "Bresil." The third seen was at an Ohio Gun Collectors Association convention, offered for sale modestly. The stock small was branded OHIO and appeared entirely legitimate, the gun showing signs of honest use.

Bavarian Guns

The second and third patterns are found with the same makers' names on them, as well as yet other makers: *Cranpin, Herzberg*. One is Bavarian, a huge single-shot musket of 1832-40 pattern having an odd center-hung percussion hammer. The hammer when cocked has a hole in it through which the front and rear sights may be viewed. The barrel, of about .70 calibre, is rifled and of striped or twist steel, so called Damascus but not figured. The stock has an iron tip, funnel-shaped front thimble to which the front swivel is attached, and a rear thimble running into the wood somewhat like the fittings of the Old Brown Bess. Three cross wedges hold stock and barrel together; at the breech, the stock has flat paneled sides like a Lindsey musket. The rear swivel is on the trigger guard. Mountings are brass.

Though the "cyclops Bavarian" with the hole in the head like a great eye is the most outstandingly clumsy-appearing musket ever seen, it was far from being unserviceable. The very ruggedness of the parts, the utter simplicity of manufacture and maintenance, made it as useful as many more elegant rifles. Hung inboard, the hammer is as well protected as any musket from that bugaboo of all soldiers, dropping the gun on a hard surface and snapping the hammer off.

The "Garibaldi," a massive chunk of musket, is strongly and precisely made; the Liege standards on government work were high. Boker's agents were willing to sell the United States almost anything, but they did require that the guns be serviceable. The price of $18 Boker offered the guns for was entirely beside the point; he had every wish to profit. But to deliver good guns was his intention, though he fell short of his goal by about a million dollars.

Complaints guns were no good, did not register too well on men who fought the war with them. After the war, Fred Elliott bought his musket about 1865 for $2.50, and used it for shooting rabbits. Grandson Fred took photo 1899, was noted trick shooter with Colt's .22 rifles. Musket shown has Danzig lock.

The third type gun resembles the above, but has a side lock with the lockplate extending from the front screw hole right up to make a square-section or area forward of the nipple bolster. This particular lock is of the same form as that used on the Swiss cavalry pistol Model 1842, and the cone seat is curved before and behind. The ramrod has a fancy onion-shaped head surmounted by a cylinder which is cupped for the ball. Brass mounts are like the foregoing "cyclops Bavarian," and examples are known marked *Cranpin, Herzberg,* in script on the lockplate. Caliber is also .70, and the barrel may be a twist barrel, though bright specimens are known. One in the U. S. Cartridge Company catalog is listed as having been made by LeMille of Liege. This arm conforms exactly to one in the Rock Island Arsenal Museum long labeled "Garibaldi." It is believed that the North Italian states which were involved in the Garibaldi revolutions used some of these rifles, doubtless obtained from the Liege trade, and the name stuck. One basic pattern of arm could be issued to a number of different nations, and sometimes be known by their different names. Both "Garibaldi" and "cyclops Bavarian" take socket bayonets.

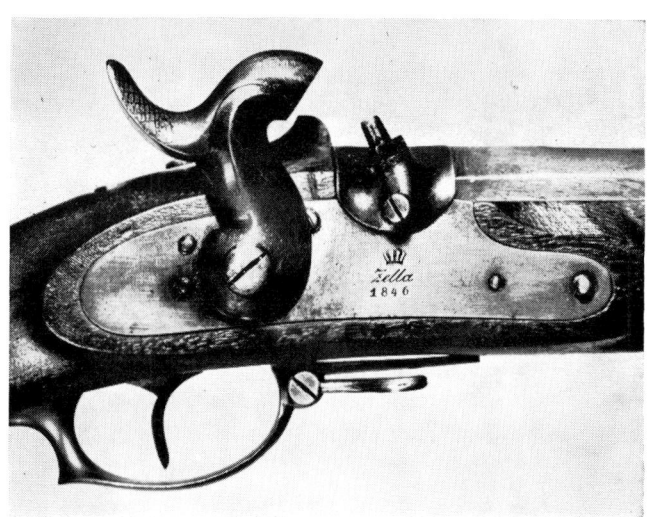

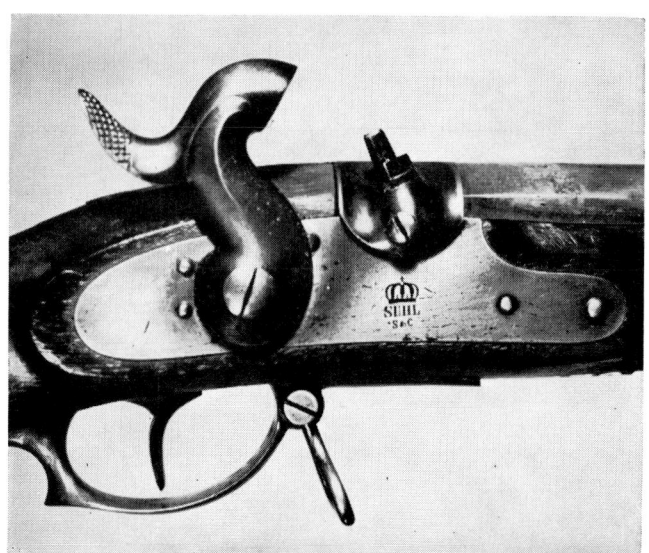

Superior Prussian muskets were the Model 1839, shown here with locks of Zella (twin cities Zella-Mehlis are gunmaking towns) and Suhl. Cone seat is patent breech that unscrews from barrel. Guns were surplus in 1861 because of German states' rearming with new "needle gun" breechloader.

Weapons Offered by Boker

On September 4, 1861, Boker's New York man wrote to Simon Cameron, offering 100,000 "rifled percussion muskets, new and in good condition," which they now controlled in Europe by having made advances on them. Cameron was thrown into a tizzy, rushed quickly to his friend Lincoln, who quietly and incisively endorsed the Boker proposal with:

> I approve the carrying this through, carefully, cautiously, and expeditiously. Avoid conflicts and interference.
> A. LINCOLN

Boker had set a price of $18 each on the guns, subject to inspection and approval of an armorer which Cameron was to appoint to accompany their authorized agent. Cameron agreed, issuing a letter-contract September 5, 1861 setting New York as the place of payment, upon inspection certificates of the United States inspector in Europe, on delivery. He also at once wrote to Minister Henry Sanford at Brussels, asking him to cooperate to the fullest with Boker's men. Civilian Ordnance employee George Wright, a master armorer from the Washington Arsenal who had received some $1,500 as a special royalty on a patent for casting fuses, was appointed to acompany Boker's man to Europe. General Ripley put him on full pay during the absence, and his expenses to and in Europe and return were to be paid by Boker.

Cursory Inspections

Instructions to Wright as to inspection reveal how cursory was to be the examination he gave many of the guns with which Captain Crispin later found much fault, as has been recounted. Ripley said,

> All the firearms are to be of one or other of the calibres .58 or .69 inch, or with such slight shades of difference that they will take one ammunition for these calibres. Without exacting all the accuracy and nicety observed in the inspection of our own arms, it will be necessary to see that the arms you are to inspect are of good and suitable material in all respects, and are altogether serviceable . . . It is not necessary to go into minute details of instruction on these points, as your own experience and familiarity with the manufacture of arms, and their quality, will enable you to see that none but good, serviceable arms are accepted for government use . . .

Ripley, the watchdog of Government quality, the aficionado of the Springfield Rifle Musket as the finest military rifle in the world—as much from the supreme excellence of its manufacture as from its design—Ripley gave instructions to George Wright that would have almost permitted acceptance of cases of 20 yellow tom cats instead of muskets for Government issue.

The warning of trouble came when Boker's New York man asked Cameron to vary the conditions of the letter order, agreeing to accept smoothbore muskets, caliber .70 and .72. He explained that these were the best arms shown to them; that rifled muskets caliber .58 and .69 had to be contracted for in advance, and that Wright concurred in the opinion that the smoothbore musket loaded with buck and ball "is far more serviceable than any ordinary rifled piece."

Still, Ripley plunged in deeper; he agreed (October 22, 1861), hoping that .70 would be the maximum but that .72 could be accepted; and that "The cones of the arms should fit our regular percussion caps, if it be possible to obtain arms with such sized cones . . ."

By November 23, Boker in New York had been advised by all the other Bokers in Liege, Solingen, Remsched, Birmingham, Bonn, that 125,000 stand of arms had been purchased on the order plus 28,000 sabers, being shipped as fast as space on the steamers could be found for them. The contract called for Boker to present the arms for inspection to Wright within 60 days—which 60 days had expired on 11 November.

Instead of presenting the guns to Wright for inspection, they had been presenting Wright to the guns. With scarcely a good night's sleep he had been to different arsenals in France, Belgium, Prussia, and Austria. Because of distance and the time consumed in travel he had been able to inspect only a portion of the arms.

Minister Sanford had asked him to return to Vienna to inspect arms Sanford had contracted for there, and Wright, writing from Cologne (Koln) November 24, expressed the hope his actions would be met with favor for he certainly had been hard at work. Boker, meanwhile, had made contracts to deliver in equal amounts January, February, March, and April, a total of 50,000 rifled muskets, "new, caliber .58, with angular bayonets, at $18." One shipment into New York November 7 was accompanied by George Wright's inspection certificate for:

400 rifle muskets, calibre .69, Liege (Arrived Nov. 7).
1,680 rifle muskets, calibre .69, Liege (960 Nov. 7, Balance to come).
5,000 rifle muskets, calibre .69, Cologne (4,080 arrived Nov. 7, balance to come).

Hagner's Outcry

Major Hagner received the arms, which went directly from the docks to his warehouses, Collector of Customs Hiram Barney having been instructed to pass Boker's goods, destined to the United States, free. The November 7 shipment was distributed to troops by Hagner at once. A following shipment arrived via the *Saxonia* from Hamburg, about 10,000 rifle muskets (these apparently were Austrian guns, mentioned by Caleb Huse). Of these, 2,300 Austrian .69 and 1,656 French .69 were issued to the State of New York. At once a minor sort of hell broke out and Hagner asked Ripley querulously "Are the arms to be accepted by me without inspection?"

The State of New York had returned a few specimens of what were in the Boker arms cases, and the "French" proved to be old arms, some rifled but without sights, and one model altered from flint with patent breech, with sights. "As both are roughly made and second hand, since alteration, their value here should not exceed $7 and $8." The Austrian arms were an even more mixed lot:

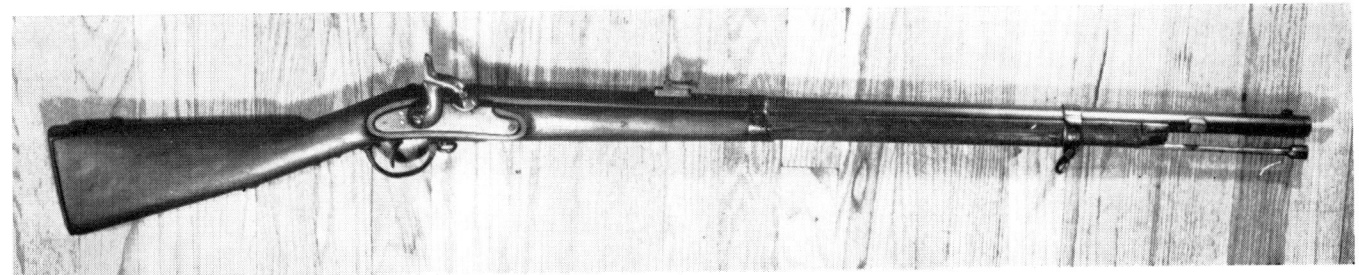

Rifles that Hagner and New York authorities complained of were altered and secondhand. Gun shown is believed typical of this lot, caliber .69 rifled with 1830 dated flint barrel and Augustin lock transformed to percussion using cast iron hammer roughly finished. Piece is reasonably good in appearance, and presence of stampings on bands resembling fraudulent Mexican Eagle marks registered as trade insignia of a Liege firm suggest gun was built for sale to Mexican state governor and diverted into lucrative American trade. Gun uses Austrian components but is finished like an Enfield.

. . . bayonets, locks and rods very common; three modes of attachment for the bayonets; locks old flint, patched in some cases; rods of iron, and some with small ends; Barrels, old flint with small cone-seat brazed on and rivetted, plug in old vent. Mixed with the barrels of usual length are many short barrels, 33 inches long. Such guns are of little or no value and ought not to be imported. Some of the French arms were issued yesterday (Dec. 1) to a regiment before departing, but I have requested General Welch to detain the Austrian until I receive your instructions. Wright's certificates of inspection embrace, I believe, all of these arms, but it is evident that no proper inspection was made, as one of the bayonets snapped into three pieces upon very slight pressure in my hands . . .

Ripley did not answer the heavy-handed Major Hagner, who the next week wrote again crying "I now have three large storehouses filled or filling with arms." Still, no answer, and Boker kept on passing guns through customs and into Hagner's warehouses. Prior shipments, which he had tried to issue, choked them to the ceilings. From the lot of Austrians which the State of New York refused, he had culled out 1,524 short Austrian muskets, triangular bayonets, .70 caliber 33-inch barrels.

"They are altered from flintlock by priming and brazing on the cone seat," he mistakenly reported, apparently being not too familiar with the Consol-Augustin locks. Transformation of the Augustin lock guns (which Austria had been phasing out of service with the issue of the new Lorenz original percussion series) produced an altered lockplate which the average gun expert might identify as a "flintlock, now altered."

Boker, meanwhile, wanted to be paid for their guns. The deliveries were regular and tons of arms were piling up in Hagner's warehouses for their account. By January 10, 1862 Ripley got around to writing to Cameron asking for a copy of the Boker contract, actually Cameron's letter of 5 September. On February 10 Boker, shocked perhaps but being entirely businesslike, sent to the new Secretary of War, Edwin M. Stanton, copies of all correspondence and documents relative to their order. At once an inspection was ordered of the different types of arms Boker had so far delivered, and it was then that Major Crispin examined 11 different samples and made his report of February 13, 1862, from which descriptions have already been cited.

Boker Gets Desperate

Boker's situation was rapidly becoming desperate. Though the enterprise founded by Herman Boker had been in business 30 years, guns and hardware, he was not possessed of unlimited capital. It seems likely he had obtained many of the guns on consignment, having to pay his numerous suppliers in a specified time. By March 13, 1862, the need for money was urgent, and Boker of New York offered to adjust the prices of arms if desired, but that the United States should please send him half a million dollars needed to tide him over a tight situation.

The accounts rendered by us for arms since December 21, 1861, and the delivery of arms since that date to your ordonance [sic] officer in New York amount to upwards of *one million and a half dollars. To save our credit,* which we value beyond profit, we require *this week* $500,000 . . . By our proposition, we evince our readiness to risk our legitimate profits *to save our credit,* which is dearer to us than anything else in business; but the offer also demonstrates our confidence that you will deal uprightly and fairly with us . . .

Stanton directed Hagner to strike up a balance on the Boker deal and (including advances made by Sanford of $402,895.00) found that about $252,000 was still owing Boker. Stanton tossed the whole bundle to Holt and Owen who at once sent notice out to Sanford not to pay any more on Boker's arms, and not to buy any more guns himself. Then they turned to sorting out the mess.

On March 24, the New York agent of Boker, Mr. Schlesscher, offered to settle the whole deal for cost plus 2½ per cent commission, so urgently did they need the money to pay their European accounts. The proposition was contingent on the United States making an immediate advance of $500,000. The Commission did not dally, and on March 27 made its provisional finding, directing the half million to be paid on account. But Holt and Owen now began to sift the evidence.

Wright Was Given a Superhuman Task

George Wright was principally to blame, except for the simple fact that he was only human, faced with a superhuman task. Inspecting over 100,000 muskets and about 38,000 sabers in a couple of months time was beyond the abilities of a Hercules. Had Wright

Array of rear sights mostly on imported guns reveals complications in training caused by variety of otherwise ordinary foreign arms. Guns are, left to right, Smith carbine, Austrian converted .69 short rifle, U.S. Springfield, Enfield 1856, Thouvenin French rifle, Belgian *carabine a tige,* French rifle musket 1825-42-57, and stub sight on Danzig Prussian musket.

been more of an administrator, he might have hired help. Major Hagner, if assigned to the task of inspection, would almost certainly have surrounded himself with a flock of paid sub-inspectors, all drawing salaries from Boker & Company. Wright, trained as a tinsmith and self-taught as an armorer repairing muskets at Washington Arsenal, was virtually alone and friendless in not just one but a number of countries, and did not think of doing this. His own responsibility he failed to recognize. For it was actually Wright, and not Minister Sanford, nor Colonel Schuyler, nor Herman Boker, who was supplying arms to the Union from Europe; it was George Wright's certificates of inspection, without which the arms might not be accepted and paid for.

General Ripley wrote to Wright in unmistakable terms, on December 7, 1861, that the Secretary of War directed him to "remain subject to the instructions of Mr. Sanford, United States Minister at Belgium, until all the guns ordered by him, Mr. Schuyler, and Mr. Boker are inspected and shipped to this country." Wright had tried to discharge this duty fully. When he arrived at Liverpool 22 September, he had been met by Herman Boker's partner, Mr. Funke, and in company with him had toured the arsenals of the Continent. He formed an affection for Funke and a respect for his integrity and, in the failure of letters from the Department to reach him promptly, was often guided by Funke's advice, which later proved to be corroborated by Ripley's letters, Boker's "pipeline" from the Department to Europe being faster than official channels.

The two went to "Liege or Cologne, where I commenced duty," as Wright put it. "I found at Cologne samples which were submitted to me of lots of guns ready for inspection," Wright told the Commission. These were apparently at Boker's office, for he took from the samples, presumably specimens of every type of gun available, "such as I considered might answer," and went to Liege to inspect.

"My course of inspection," Wright continued, "was to take up a gun from the box, requiring a box here and there to be opened for me, to feel the strength of the mainspring, the fit and spring of the ramrod, the fit and the material of the bayonet. I did not take a lock off, except once. I suppose I have taken off a dozen barrels and taken out the breech pins, to see about the rifling. I went away in such haste I had nothing to inspect a gun with except a taper gauge for caliber."

The number of boxes Wright would open depended on the nature of the arms offered and their location. "In Vienna 25,000 .55 calibre, from the government arsenal, were examined but little; I took off no barrels and no locks, as they were in the government arsenal; and I only handled a few of them, feeling satisfied that they had been thoroughly inspected by the Austrian government." Noting the stamping on the lockplates, of "860, 861, 862," Wright correctly observed "These arms were made in 1860-'62. Mr. Schuyler bought a lot of the same arms from the same storehouse before, and Mr. Rhuleman had inspected them, as I heard, and I believe rejected none.

"Of the other lots of guns inspected at Vienna, I handled at least 30 percent. I do not know how many I inspected there and I can form no estimate. I do not intend to say that I took off the locks or took out the barrels or the breech pins of any. I have visited often the shops of manufacturers in Vienna and examined barrels, locks and stocks. . . ."

One rifle noted as "the Marseilles arm" proved particularly offensive to Captain Crispin, in the sense that he felt the United States had been imposed upon. Represented as a Chasseurs de Vincennes carbine of .69 caliber, it appears Wright had little chance to really

see if this were true. He went to Marseilles, after having seen a specimen of the rifle in Paris. There, in the Marseilles railroad freight depot he "only opened a few cases." Wright admitted his inspection was faulty, that he might not have accepted the rifles if he had looked at them closely enough to find the defects which Crispin observed. Crispin's main objections were based on the failure of the rifle to be a Chasseurs de Vincennes carbine. Instead, 8,689 had been released from customs, were counted, and awaited receiving, in one of Hagner's bulging warehouses. Criticized Crispin:

> These guns, I find, are all old and have evidently seen long and hard service. They are a French model, caliber .708, and in peculiarities of shape of lock, stock and barrel, and dimensions, are about the same as the present French rifle, well known as the French carbine. They are, however, a chambered one, the old and abandoned plan of M. Delvigne, for destroying windage, using the round ball—relics of the past in the history of rifled arms.
> The ramrod is cupped for the round ball, as of course should be expected.
> The hausse is a simple standing sight and leaf folding on the barrel with notches for different ranges, a clumsy and inefficient sight as compared with the present model. I should judge the barrel to have belonged to the French smoothbore musket, and been altered at the time when Delvigne's plan was in vogue. The most peculiar feature of the arms, if they are all like the samples examined, is, however, that they are lightly grooved, straight, or if any twist at all exists, it cannot be detected with the eye.
> As they are grooved, but so grooved as to be incapable of giving rotary motion to the ball, I can neither call them a rifled arm nor a smoothbore musket. From the above, it would appear that the arms are old, of an abandoned model, and inferior, if anything, to a smoothbore musket in consideration of the chamber and the straight grooves; and in consequence, if received, should only be used in cases where the emergency of the service demanded their issue . . .

So much at variance with the terms of Boker's order offering arms that were "new and in good condition" were these Delvigne modified short muskets, that Crispin declined to accept any on his own responsibility. Major Hagner took the responsibility, issuing his order June 10, 1862, from his desk at the Ordnance Office: "The commission direct that these arms be accepted, as having been shipped upon certificate of inspection given by George Wright; they are embraced in the number to be paid for by the United States." He then concluded his examination and conferences with Mr. Schlesscher and M. H. Boker, Jr., and took their accounts for study.

From these records of purchases they had negotiated

Only Spanish-made arm with Civil War use known to author is this short two-band Enfield-style rifle, bearing arsenal mark on lock, MADRID and date 1861. Unusual rear sight allows regulating gun on test stand for any choice of bullet, then clamping sight base fingers tight and cutting stock inletting to receive sight in new location. Style of sight (middle) is uncommon, but resembles modification of U.S. Rifled Musket 1840-42 style shown on Pomeroy .69 gun (bottom) or Remington sight fitted to experimental Lee .50 caliber single shot musket about 1870 (top). Neat .58 caliber short rifle is adapted for socket bayonet, has brass banded ramrod similar to Brazilian sea-service "Enfield" musket rod. Workmanship on metal and wood is superior, not trade junk. Now in author's collection, gun was obtained after checking alleged use by troops (North, South?) raised in Louisville, Ky.

emerged a tabulation of 20 individual lots of arms, each lot having been purchased at a different price. Far from the $18 each which Boker had offered, the guns averaged between $5 and $7 in cost. Because of the scarcity of complete information on these Boker guns, the tabulation is given in full.

The Civil War historian must remember that these arms were the *principal equipment* for the Union and especially for Volunteers outfitted in the vicinity of New York, for the year 1862-63. Though far from being Springfield Rifled Muskets, their mere possession by the Union gave greater confidence to the overall strategy and prevented many losses which a more retiring policy might have permitted, if weapons had been in such short supply at they were that September

5th when Herman Boker proposed to arm the North. The prices in Hagner's list were given in French gold francs, and later translated to dollars, giving the odd fractions:

Herman Boker & Co. Firearms (Muskets & Rifles) 1861-62

Class	1	4,440 at	$5.13	$22,777.20
Class	2	600 at	5.47⅕	3,283.20
Class	3	1,992 at	5.70	11,354.40
Class	4	7,931 at	6.27	49,727.37
Class	5	12,332 at	6.84	84,350.88
Class	6	5,488 at	7.98	43,794.24
Class	7	4,588 at	8.66⅔	39,750.43
Class	8	847 at	10.26	8,690.22
Class	9	3,928 at	10.48⅘	41,196.86
Class	10	6,940 at	10.71⅗	74,369.04
Class	11	4,100 at	11.40	46,740.00
Class	12	9,350 at	11.51⅖	107,655.90
Class	13	236 at	12.54	2,959.44
Class	14	3,486 at	12.82½	44,707.95
Class	15	21,945 at	13.11	287,698.95
Class	16	1,824 at	13.68	24,952.32
Class	17	25,247 at	14.52½	366,965.14
Class	18	2,272 at	14.82	33,671.04
Class	19	51,819 at	15.67½	812,262.82
Class	20	18,689 at	16.40	306,499.60

Total, 188,054 rifles and rifle muskets to a value of $2,413,407.04

This and the other accounts of Boker for sabers was ordered paid, with the shipping charges and 2½ per cent commission, and an adjustment for difference in exchange between the hard currencies of Europe and the falling value of the American dollar.

Wright Accomplished a Miracle

It was charged at the time and has been parrotted since, that the refuse of all the armories of Europe was poured into the United States, and vast "investigations" clamored for. But the tabulation above shows that Boker's cost in Europe for 125,000 of the guns—Classes 14 through 20—equalled the cost at Springfield Armory for a rifle. Of the 188,000 arms delivered, at least half were comparable in the market to the Springfield Rifle Musket. Calibers for the most part were .69-.72, but Ripley caused that to be accepted by George Wright. With inadequate briefing on his duties and also on his authority, such as the possibility of hiring viewers in England, which Wright certainly could have done, he accomplished a minor miracle. Though it was Boker who offered, and Cameron and Ripley who accepted the deal, it was George Wright who armed the Union that dreary winter of 1861. It may be categorically stated that the one man who signed certificates of inspection for more rifle muskets than any other did not put a mark on the guns. His tools were not the majesty of international commerce, nor the belching chimneys of a hundred factories, but a tapered plug of steel with scratch marks on the side to show its diameters . . . a bore gauge.

Zouave dandies in studio of "Obermuller & Son, 28 Cooper Square, New York" carry foreign muskets apparently of unconverted detonator side lock type, Consol-Augustin, with sword bayonets. Ancient tintype is dim, but revolvers holstered for cross draw are sported by both corporals.

CHAPTER 23

Yankee Revolvers

For half a century the halls of official Washington resounded with the clamor of disappointed inventors of revolving breech firearms. Seeking the patronage of the War Department or Navy Department, they thronged the anterooms of the respective Bureaus of Ordnance, but to no avail. Elisha Collier, inventing his revolver in 1813, had to take the idea to England to find capital and manufacturers. A mysterious Mr. Chambers, who appears to have developed a "Roman candle" type of load for fighting tops of warships, received so little recognition that the physical description of his invention is lost. Persistently, unfailing (but he failed), a Mr. Cochran tried to have his turret-chambered revolver adopted. Even Colt failed for 15 years, before at length, in 1847, some measure of success in having his revolvers adopted by the Army brought him modest riches and the beginnings of fame and fortune. Then, suddenly, the War Department seemed convinced that the rotating chambered breech firearm was here to stay. By the time the First Regiment of United States Dragoons was reorganized into the First Regiment United States Cavalry in 1861, official Washington was willing to buy virtually any type of cylinder-breech hand arm offered. In one or two cases influence seemed necessary, commissions were paid to members of Congress, and scandals arose, but in the main, anybody with a decent pattern of repeater and some hope of a factory could get a contract.

The list of officially purchased revolvers and pistols is not large but it embraces a number of distinctly different types. Curiously, the most "modern" of all, the Smith & Wesson, is not listed. For reasons best known to themselves, but perhaps principally that policy of conservatism and refusal to over-expand, that marks the firm's policies even today, Smith & Wesson deliberately held out on their larger military revolvers and did not launch one into production until the war was well over. Next best were the imported arms, especially the Lefaucheux and the Raphael and Perrin types. But among the standard brands in use by the cavalry were old favorites: the Colts of Army and Navy sizes, the Whitneys, Remingtons, Starrs, and Adams. Four hundred and fifteen Adams revolvers were bought, seemingly obtained all from Schuyler, Hartley & Graham, and in several different patterns. Of arms discussed in this chapter, the following were obtained:

536	Allen's revolvers	$9,130.50
1,100	Joslyn revolvers	24,793.00
2,001	Pettengill's revolvers	40,287.10
11,284	Savage's revolvers	221,355.75
5,000	Rogers & Spencer's revolvers	60,739.90
11,214	Whitney revolvers	139,690.39
200	Horse pistols	1,400.00
348	Signal pistols	1,938.50

Of foreign handguns, the following were obtained not otherwise listed:

200	Perrin's revolvers	$4,000.00
12,374	Lefaucheux revolvers	167,489.99
978	Raphael's revolvers	16,181.73
100	Foreign pistols	1,000.00

In addition, notes of Ordnance purchases include the following handguns:

- 346 Cavalry pistols
- 68 French revolvers
- 772 Percussion lock holster pistols
- 453 U. S. holster pistols

The exact nature of these different arms will be considered; the first to be mentioned is a revolver which is in fact not a U. S. military arm at all, the Freeman revolver of C. B. Hoard.

The Freeman Revolver

Hoard had obtained ratification of his Springfield contract, but as his testimony before Holt and Owen indicated, he felt that revolvers offered greater profits. Much of the machinery listed on the large bill which he presented to the Commissioners, in arguing that his musket contract should be confirmed, was doubtless capable of manufacturing revolver parts as well. To obtain a revolver design he went to Binghamton where Austin T. Freeman worked. To judge from the handle configuration of the revolver eventually made under Freeman's patents, Freeman worked at the Starr Armory and either openly or secretly was

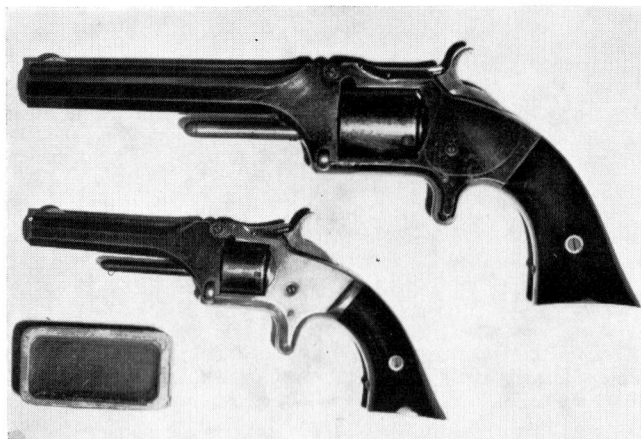

Smith & Wesson's revolvers were made in quantity but firm preferred to sell smallbore .32s and .22s to private soldiers than engage in government work. Top gun, known as No. 2 Army, was used by officers to some extent. Indiana cavalryman Col. Edward Anderson owned pearl-handled specimen with 6" barrel with which he executed over 50 suspected Confederate spies or guerrillas.

intending to effect an improvement by preparing a single-action style of revolver. The location of the rear screw in frame, hammer pivot screw, and a screw near the front edge of the wood handle, are much the same in the Starr and the Freeman guns. Freeman's design has a full handle strap instead of the one-piece grip of the Starr. The Freeman revolver has two-piece grips held by a center screw and escutcheon in ordinary fashion. But the cylinder without recesses for the cones and with the back turned to a bevel shape, like the Starr, where it runs in the lock, suggests how strongly Freeman was influenced by Starr. The front of the frame is pure Remington, and the frame is solidly joined to a rounded standing breech, instead of the concave-flared standing breech of the Starr. The Freeman loading lever latch is similar to that of the Starr, which is unlike any other arm of the time. Not necessarily significant, the Starrs and Freemans have six groove rifling. Freeman's patent of December 9, 1862 (No. 37091) is stamped on all known Freeman revolvers, so the gun could not have been in production much before that time, and none sold without the mark.

Manufacturer was C. B. Hoard, who produced a very small number of these 7½-inch barrel .44 six-

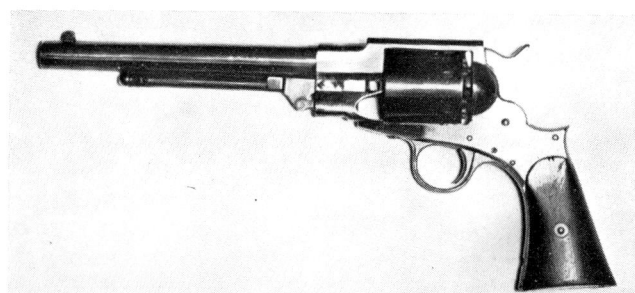

C. B. Hoard at Watertown, N.Y., made Freeman revolver which has strong resemblance in frame to Starr design. Design of Freeman was probably swapped to Rogers & Spencer for their stock of Springfield musket parts.

shooters at his Watertown, New York, remodeled farm tool works. Serials over 1700 have been noticed but none bear U. S. inspectors' marks and none are listed as having been bought by the United States. No State of New York or other purchases are at present known. Superintendent was W. A. Roberts, formerly of Remington. It is possible that the manufacture of the Freeman began to be more a headache than a profit to Hoard, who must have found that producing the Springfield was not all moonlight and roses. The Hoard revolver thereupon disappears from the scene, and the Rogers and Spencer bursts upon the market. In between was the brief and accepted military revolver, the Pettengill, produced by Hoard's neighbors at Willow Vale, Rogers and Spencer. A "pepperbox" with revolver frame, it is the only hammerless percussion revolver bought by the United States.

The Pettengill

The patent genealogy of the Pettengill (often misspelled Pettingill) was threefold. The basic pepperbox design with inside striker was the invention of C. S. Pettengill of New Haven No. 15,388 dated 22 July, 1856. Edward A. Raymond and Charles Robitaille, Brooklyn, New York, further improved the gun, taking out patent No. 21,054, July 27, 1858. Refinement for production was accomplished by Henry S. Rogers, of Rogers & Spencer, patent No. 36,861, November 4, 1862. Because of the close similarity between the Pettengill barrel, frame front and loading lever, as manufactured, and the eventual Rogers & Spencer revolver, it seems likely the form in which the Pettengill was made was due to Rogers.

By December, 1861, Rogers & Spencer had established a shop in Millvale, Oneida County, New York, where they were making the Pettengill pistol in pocket .31, and belt .34 calibers. They asked Secretary Cameron for an order, stating:

. . . we are making the Pettingill (sic) pistol, a very superior arm for cavalry, belt or any other army service, of any size, of finish and material equal to the sample we present for your inspection . . . We are prepared to manufacture these pistols, army size, at the rate of 1,000 in ninety days, and 1,000 per month thereafter; and at this rate we should be glad to receive so large an order as the government please to give . . . We will make and deliver, of the army size, any number, for $20 each pistol, at times above indicated . . .

The lead time of three months pretty definitely establishes that Rogers & Spencer did not have the .44 Pettengill in production at the time; their misspelling of their patentee's name suggests that Pettengill himself had long since lost any rights or authority in the control of his patent. Ripley ordered 5,000 on December 26, 1861, at $20, first delivery 90 days. Before the Commission in June, 1862, Rogers and Spencer themselves declare "It was upon the presentation by us of a pair of the Pettengill pistols, belt size, that the order for 5,000 of the same, army size, was issued to us." The belt size they specifically describe as .34 caliber.

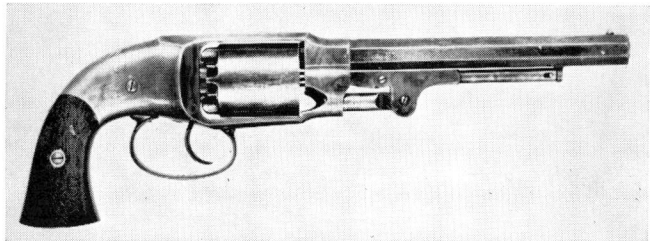

Pistol invented by Pettengill, Raymond and Robitaille was further improved by Henry Rogers of Rogers & Spencer. Inside striker principle dated from 1856 patent but form of loading lever and frame front resembles the Civil War R & S revolvers; was probably engineering refinement of Rogers himself. Casehardened frame contrasted with blued cylinder, barrel. 2,000 were ordered by Ordnance in .44 caliber.

But Rogers & Spencer were to receive a decided shock in their production expectations. Having gotten about 1,000 ready for the assembly room, about 2,000 in the machinery, and the fourth 1,000 just going into the factory as raw materials, they learned that orders had been given not to accept any of their pistols, that they were "not satisfactory."

Rogers and Spencer had asked their partner, George C. Tallman, of Washington, D. C. to deliver a pistol to the Secretary of War as a sample and to ask an extension of time, their 90 days having run out. It had taken that long to get the special tools ready to produce the Army size, and it was their wish to supply an exact duplicate of the production guns, made on the same machinery, for all the Pettengills were to be fully interchangeable. George Tallman's son, Henry, called upon Secretary Stanton and received assurances that the extension was okay; his nephew, Edward D. Tallman, was the one who delivered the sample pistol to the War Department.

When the Commission came to consider whether the Pettengill contract should be ratified, the question was raised as to whether the sample required in Ripley's letter had ever been received and approved after inspection. Major Hagner concluded that it had been received but never approved, so there was that much doubt at least as to the validity of the Rogers & Spencer claim. But, wanting to be fair, Hagner recommended to Ripley that the sample pistol be tested by Major Dyer at Springfield Armory. Mr. Tallman, possibly nephew Edward, arrived at Springfield about the first week in May, Dyer said:

SPRINGFIELD ARMORY,
May 20, 1862

General Ripley,

SIR: In compliance with your instructions to me, dated April 14, 1862, directing me to "examine and try the sample Pettengill pistol which will be presented," and to report to the commission on ordnance stores through your office my opinion "of its sufficiency and suitableness in all respects for the purpose for which it was designed," I have the honor to report that Mr. Tallman presented the sample pistol to me for trial about three weeks since; that I carefully examined the workmanship and found it to be good, the parts being as little liable to get out of order as those of any other revolving pistol I have seen.

The firing was accurate, and the penetration good, the balls penetrating three white pine boards one inch thick and embedding themselves in the fourth, at a distance of fifty yards. The calibre of the pistol is .44. The charge 24 grains of powder and a conical ball weighing 218 grains. As many as sixty shots were fired. The cylinder which contains the charges is revolved and the pistol is cocked and discharged by pulling the trigger. I regard this as a serious objection and do not see how it can be corrected. The great distance to be passed over by the trigger in revolving the cylinder and discharging the pistol makes it impossible, even when the pistol is clean, to fire rapidly with ease, and after a few discharges it becomes foul and heated, and the firing is done with great difficulty. I sometimes found it impossible to revolve the cylinder by means of the trigger.

Mr. Tallman was of opinion that the objections could be removed, and asked to be allowed to withdraw the sample pistol in order to have the necessary alteration made. This was allowed. Mr. Tallman returned about two weeks since with the pistol, and it was again tried. When clean it was fired with less difficulty, but after a few discharges it was almost impossible to revolve the cylinder by means of the trigger, and the pistol was again withdrawn.

It was again presented for trial a few days since, and has been fired more than 100 times. It has worked better than on either of the former occasions; still it has not been free from the objections named above. In my opinion, it is not "suitable in all respects" for the military service.

Respectfully, your obedient servant,
A. B. DYER, *Captain of Ordnance*

As a consequence of this report, Hagner directed Rogers & Spencer to suspend manufacture, and to indicate when an improved sample would be ready for trial. Rogers was especially hurt by this directive, for his was the responsibility of the final form of the pistol. With about $25,000 invested in tooling, and their money lenders doubtful of returns when stop work orders issued so freely from the Commission, Rogers went to Washington to try and get the matter adjusted.

He pointed out that the "serious objection" of double action firing was in fact the distinguishing feature of the Pettengill, and was present in the .34 caliber samples which had been in Washington at the start of the whole contract. The Navy had pronounced it "the perfection of arms," and Rogers stated he could not have anticipated Hagner's or Dyer's objections under the terms of their order, with which terms he

Boxed middle-size Pettengill had been pronounced by Navy "the perfection of arms" but trial at Springfield Armory revealed defective trigger relationship to handle making too-long a double action pull. Caliber is called .36 but contemporary documents refer to it as .34". Paper boxes from last century are very rare firearms "accessory." From Shore collection, Chicago.

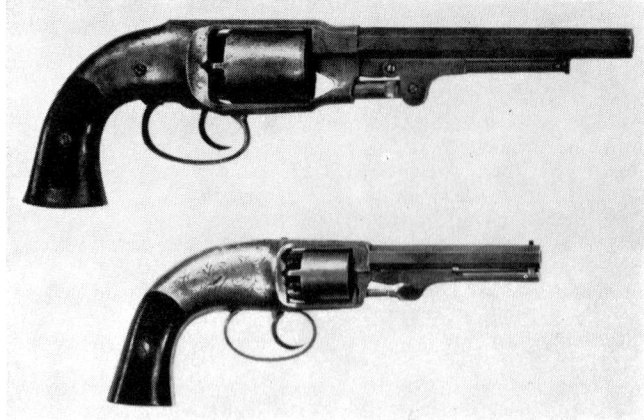

Comparison of Army .44 sixshooter and small Pettengill in .31 caliber shows not only difference in size but difference in loading lever latching. Bottom pistol had two studs and lever arm was cramped between them when not in use.

had tried to comply. To compromise, Rogers offered to surrender a parallel contract for 25,000 Springfields, upon which Tallman said nothing had been done, and to deliver instead 2,000 Pettengills slightly modified. The anti-fouling extension should be on the cylinder instead of part of the frame, to keep the smoke from jamming the cylinder pin. "We will also, if it is desired, substitute for the thumb screw, which holds the centre-piece in place, one with smaller head, and nicked for screwdriver . . ."

Most Pettengills seen have the thumb screw, so apparently this was not required; the change in the cylinder was directed by the Commissioners and on June 27, 1862, a contract in due form was executed between Amos Rogers, Julius A. Spencer, and George Tallman, partners in Rogers & Spencer, and General Ripley, for 2,000 Pettengill .44 revolvers. First delivery was October 20, 1862. The last delivery January 17, 1863, of 401 arms (total 2,001) included a replacement for the pistol held out of the first lot by the inspector.

Battlefield use of these arms is not well recorded; most specimens seen show considerable use and it appears they definitely were issued. One gun formerly in the U. S. Cartridge Company collection was a first-issue Pettengill, "from the battle-field of Gettysburg, Pa., July 1st-4th, 1863." The distinction is not one of model, but of frame stamping. First-issue Pettengills with lower serials are marked on top of the frame in two lines on each side of the sighting groove, PETTENGILLS PATENT 1856 and RAYMOND & ROBITAILLE PATENTED 1858. Second-issue Pettengills have slightly different marking: PETTENGILLS PATENT 1856, and PATENT JULY 22 1856 & JULY 27 1858. The underside of the frame is stamped PATENTED/NOV. 4, 1862.

When Rogers & Spencer confirmed their Pettengill business it was mainly to use up what parts they had nearly finished, to avoid loss. Aside from obvious profit motive, there is a rather pitiable element of patriotism shining through their pleas to gain a contract. Before the Commission they said on June 4, 1862:

We have no disposition to urge upon our government an arm it does not want; but the present shape of the matter is disastrous to us in the extreme, and we therefore request you to consider whether some relief should not be afforded us. Cannot we make for the government some army pistol that we would be at liberty to make, and of which the government is in need, for such prices as are paid to other parties, and on such terms as to time as will enable us to manufacture them advantageously? Our preparations for this work are good. We can do it to the extent of their capacity as cheaply as other parties. Such as arrangement would enable us to work up a large amount of partly-wrought stock which otherwise will be lost.

At the time, Major Hagner could only urge the acceptance of the 2,000 order, but it was to appear in the record later than the Ordnance Department had a heart. Meanwhile, Rogers was left with partly-wrought work to get rid of. The expression is important, for he said not "cast" but "wrought," which means, forged. The frames of the Pettengill are made of malleable iron. Such parts if only cast represented little investment; if finished, it is believed their total number dictated the number of Pettengills actually contracted for. Serial numbers have been seen between 1600 to 4600 range, but the three partners may have had much more laid up in their steel loft, such as barrels and loading lever forgings, "wrought work." There must have been a displacement of their 180 workmen, but not until November, 1864 did they again get an order from Government. Possibly the interim was occupied in finishing the 2,600 additional Pettengills for civilian sale, though they earlier closed down their New York sales office to devote their entire production to Government work.

They were ready to go again and make "some army pistol," this time a new model. In November Rogers & Spencer proposed to supply more guns, and General Dyer, who remembered his role in helping kill their commercial chances in 1862, had the pleasure of righting a wrong:

ORDNANCE OFFICE, WAR DEPARTMENT,
Washington, November 29, 1864

GENTLEMEN: I have to acknowledge yours of the 25th instant, offering to furnish army pistols, and hereby give you an order to deliver to the inspector of contract arms, subject to the usual inspection, 5,000 revolving pistols, for which you will be paid, for all such as pass inspection, at the rate of twelve (12) dollars for each pistol, to include all the necessary appendages. Deliveries to be 500 in the month of January, 1865, and 500 per month thereafter.

Respectfully &c
A. B. DYER
Brigadier General, Chief of Ordnance
Messrs. ROGERS & SPENCER
Utica, New York

The arm which Rogers now prepared was made under patents obtained from C. B. Hoard. It was the short-lived revolver of Austin Freeman. Rogers adapted to it the Pettengill barrel, loading lever, pin front sight, and top strap with sighting groove. The resultant model was marked on the top strap on each side of the sight groove, ROGERS & SPENCER and UTICA, N. Y. Though hundreds of thousands of other revolvers,

Standard Rogers & Spencer revolver is apparently covered by no special patents though right to use single action design is attributed to deal with Hoard's Armory on Freeman revolver. 5,000 new guns remained in storage until sold off by Government as scrap in 1900. Big .44s were among best, strongest design of War but never saw battle.

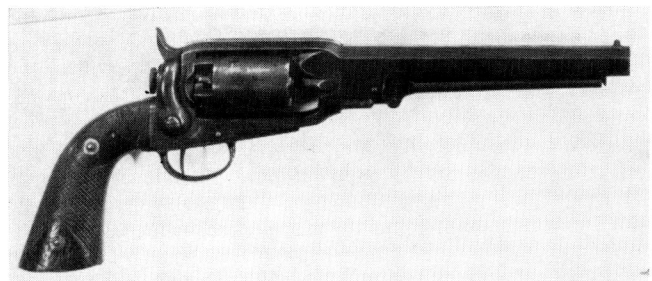

Sidehammer design of Ben Joslyn was rather bulky. Layout strongly suggested prototype Root revolvers made secretly by Colt in late 1850s but never produced. W. C. Freeman of Worcester was the contractor.

especially Colts and Remingtons, were pouring into Government storehouses, Ordnance inspector Captain Robert P. Barry stopped from his labors at Starr or Remington to take a look and stamped 5,000 of the guns on the left grip with his inspector's cartouche. Deliveries were prompt; from January 30 to September 26, 1865, Rogers & Spencer delivered 5,000 arms at $12, a cost to the United States and the taxpayer of $60,000 for guns which at that late date had very little military value.

The pistols remained in storage at New York Arsenal and on October 17, 1870 were among arms offered for public sale by sealed bid. The Ordnance Department reserved the right to reject any or all bids "which may not be deemed sufficient or satisfactory." A lot of 20,000 Starr revolvers put up at the same time was sold for $8 each to Austin Baldwin & Company but the Rogers & Spencers were not sold then. By March, 1904 they had been sold to Bannerman of New York, at the turn-of-the-century scrap sale of all Civil War surplus.

"We had the entire lot of 5,000 that was contracted for by the United States Government," said Bannerman, "which were considered so good that they were held in reserve . . . Revolvers were never out of their original cases . . . We have sold off all the surplus, reserving enough for our customers (100 offered) who are collecting rare weapons. Price, $2.85 each."

Ironically, the $60,000 worth of revolvers in 1865 had probably been worth at least $30,000 in 1870 when Starr revolvers, used, went at $8 each. But General Dyer felt so attached to them that he refused to sell for a low bid and the guns stayed in storage. By 1900 they were worth approximately the price of scrap iron, and for that price Bannerman bought them, said to have been 25¢ each. But to the taxpayer's dismay, this is the common story in the way our Government handles its surplus arms problem: refusing to sell when buyers can be found, then dumping later at a fraction of the possible return. Though among the first absolutely brand new guns to be sold that way, the Rogers & Spencers, alas, are not the last.

For the right to make these revolvers, which they sold for $12 and which the United States ultimately sold for scrap, Rogers & Spencer possibly traded off some scrap—parts for Springfield rifles. Though Rogers was willing to cede the 25,000 Springfield rifle contract, one of the sub-contractors, Courtney Schenck, was not so pleased. He declared that a large amount of work had been got up, and that Rogers & Spencer would be embarrassed by the cancellation. If Schenck was correct, even though speaking without authorization, it is likely that the deal involving the Freeman rights included an exchange of the Rogers & Spencer parts which then went into Hoard's muskets to make up his delivery of 12,500.

The Joslyn

Less successful with the Government was another Freeman, W. C. Freeman, of Worcester, Massachusetts. Though he consciously used a United States Senator, the Hon. W. S. Williams, to act in his behalf in Washington, he failed to get what he wanted.

Freeman offered through Williams on June 7, 1861, to make for the Army the revolver designed by Benjamin F. Joslyn at $25 each. A .44 caliber solid frame five-shooter, its side hammer and rear-removing cylinder pin reveal the influence of Root and Colt's designs. The barrel is octagonal, screwing into the frame, and shaped with a lump at the rear for the pivot screw of the hinged loading lever. The barrel is stamped with B. F. JOSLYN/PAT^D MAY 4TH 1858, in two lines. Some have a Navy anchor stamped in the butt or in the underside of the barrel, but none have U. S. inspectors' initials on the grips, because the order of 500 guns given to Freeman by Ripley was annulled.

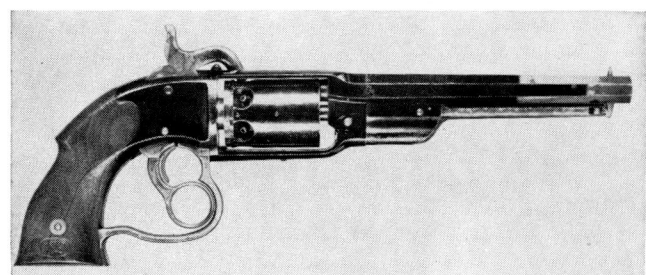

Big Savage reciprocating cylinder revolver was noted as "Navy" because of .36 caliber but many were bought by Army. Handsome full-blue pistol with case hardened colored hammer, lever and guard was expensive gun to make. Ring lever turned and shifted cylinder; separate trigger released hammer.

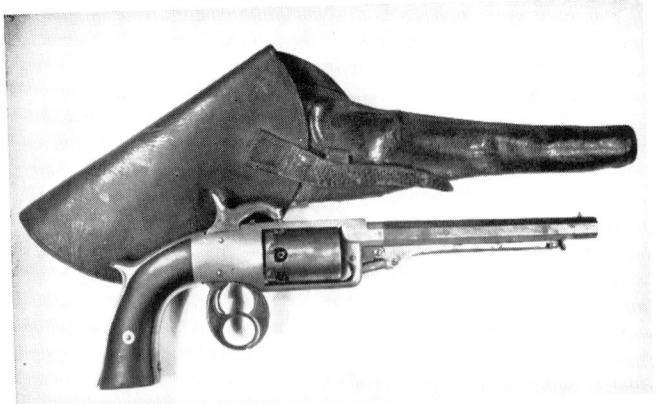

Predecessor to Civil War model was "Figure Eight" Savage Navy revolver so called because of front guard shape matching lever to make an "8." Hinged lever was later abandoned for creeping lever that was infringement upon Root's patent owned by Colt. Figure-8 guns have brass frames.

Freeman stated to the Commissioners in explaining his reasons for non-delivery, that "The delivery has been delayed by our desire to give the Government a good article (the pistols then on hand not being in all respects what the government needed)" and by failures to obtain machinery which the makers diverted to Springfield Armory. Holt and Owen decided to annul the contract and no guns were to be obtained of the Joslyn make except in open purchase at not more than $15.

Apparently the inventor was a man of no mean manufacturing and organizational skill, and he became tired of Freeman's failures in working with his guns. Freeman had obtained through Williams a contract in 1860 for 1,000 Joslyn carbines and had been able to deliver only 200. Now Joslyn took over the business and moved the works to Stonington to his own Joslyn Firearms Company. Eight hundred and seventy-five Joslyn patent revolvers caliber .44 were bought from Joslyn himself at $22.50 each, between January and May, 1862. An additional 225 appear to have been a Navy purchase. Private sales, mostly of Stonington make, may have totalled 2,000; serials up to about 3,000 have been seen. Williams' supposed influence availed Joslyn and Freeman little in the way of selling guns to Government.

North & Savage

A firm that fared better with an intermediary was that of Edward Savage, founder and co-partner with Henry S. North in the firm of North & Savage. At Middletown, Connecticut for three-quarters of a century, the name of North had been the byword for gun-making. Formerly S. North, Middletown, the company had been changed to North & Savage during the mid-fifties. It took on a new shot of capital with the commencement of hostilities. The Savage Revolving Firearms Company of Middletown was organized in 1860 and August 12, 1861, Charles R. Sebor was elected president. Secretary and Treasurer for several years was James A. Wheelock. Edward Savage, patentee of the "figure eight" .36 caliber revolver, together with Henry Savage North, seems to have had less and less to do with the managing of the firm. Their work appears ended when they finally brought the revolver to a state of "perfection."

Figure 8 Savage

The start of the North and Savage revolvers appears to have coincided with the decline of the North interests as contractor for the United States in 1851. At that time Henry S. North and Chauncy D. Skinner patented a bar-hammer revolving breech arm illustrated in the patent as a handgun (incomplete) but apparently only made as a rifle. Cocking the hammer and rotating the cylinder was accomplished by pulling down on the trigger guard. Importantly, this wedged the cylinder against the barrel to seal off gas. The guard at the front was mounted on a frame strap which went below the cylinder, and was hinged at its front end to the barrel. The guts-falling-out mechanism rather suggests the later Winchester (Browning designed) Model 1894 series of rifles. Patent No. 8,982 of June 1, 1852, covered this first step. "The World's Revolver" appears hopefully stamped on one example of this unsuccessful rifle.

Defective commercially and mechanically, this first design was abandoned by North who concentrated on revolver pistol design. On June 17, 1856, he was ready to buck Sam Colt's patent expiration by having a new style of arm which resembled a pepperbox in internal principles, with a cylinder and barrel attached. The cylinder was surrounded by a solid frame. No loading lever was illustrated, and a prototype semi-finished pistol of this form in the William Locke collection has no lever. The lever which works the mechanism is a ring-trigger, with a separate small trigger for dropping the hammer. This real trigger is hung in a slot in the ring trigger, above the ring—the index finger sears off the shot; the middle finger rotates the cylinder and cocks the piece. Though Smith & Wesson had thoroughly proved how clumsy this principle was in their defunct Volcanic arms which Oliver Winchester was having B. Tyler Henry elaborately re-design at this very time, North seemed to like the idea. Apparently many of the shooting experts, not yet shown what the main line of small arms development would be, were not sure the ring trigger was such a bad idea; Colt, ultimately to win out in setting the style for the century, had abandoned the idea in 1842, and had never applied it to handguns. Edward Savage bent his mind to the problem and on May 15, 1860, patent No. 28,331 was issued to Savage and H. S. North jointly on what is known to collectors as the "Figure 8 Savage" revolver.

The exact details of incorporation of the Savage Revolving Firearms Company we do not know, but it seems reasonable to assume that the major share of inspiration in the Figure 8 pistol was Savage's and that his was the ownership of the capital that he and North contributed to the new corporate identity; else there seems to be no good commercial reason for abandoning the North name, good since 1799 on U.S. firearms, and introducing a new one. The cognomen "Figure 8" is from the shape of trigger, the ring trigger mating a curved guard in front; the real trigger is at the back of a complementary ring in the upper portion, the whole assembly looking like an 8. Distinctive also is the spur at back of grip, the frame otherwise having much in common with pepperbox-making practice of the era. Well perfected in this design is the forward-back shifting cylinder, the chambers of which fit over the end of the barrel to seal off the gas escape when firing. The build-up of black powder fouling was gradually a problem, but the high heat of the discharge at that point by the chamber kept this at a minimum.

The idea has current use in the Model 1895 Nagant revolver used by Russian forces until the Korean War. The difference between the chamber sealed, and unsealed, is the difference between 1100 feet per second and about 750 feet per second, muzzle velocity for the .30 caliber long revolver cartridge. Closing off that escape of gas at the breech of a revolver has always been the desire of the inventor, probably no one more than North and Savage due to their experience with an identical sort of gas escape, in the Hall breech-loading carbines and rifles.

As nearly as can be determined from a study of existing specimens, the rounded brass frame is the earliest in the Savage-North Figure 8 series of revolvers. The early arms have a hinged loading lever with the plunger not well supported and incapable of seating a conical bullet really concentrically. One specimen, unnumbered, in the Locke collection, has the ends of chambers finished to protrude inside the barrel, instead of the barrel coned to fit inside the chambers. This seems to have been an experimental variation and no benefits were obtained by the more complicated form of manufacture. Numbered in the same series as the brass framed Figure 8's was the round iron-framed issue which appears to have been introduced after several hundred had been made with brass frames.

Henry S. North patented a rack-pinion type of creeping lever for his revolvers April 6, 1858, No. 19868. Though the 1860 patent for the Figure 8 shows a hinged rammer with an eccentric guide groove in the lever and a pin in plunger, by which the plunger is given a straight line motion, it seems probable that the 1858 patent has some relation to the dates of actual manufacture of these arms and that on a job-shop basis, Savage and North were working out the bugs and trying to produce, with the use of modest capital, an acceptable revolver. Apparently the Figure 8's were more or less available some time after 1858. With the use of the creeping lever, a more shrouded frame element beneath the barrel was used. changing the profile of the pistol.

The round frame not being quite the answer, North and Savage modified the design to use a flat frame, with boss turned at the back like the Colt behind the cylinder. Brass was again used for the frame, and the spur at back of grip was considerably shortened to a hump or, as the British call it, a "prawl." The idea was to help the hand hold its position while working the finger lever. The use of brass has been common

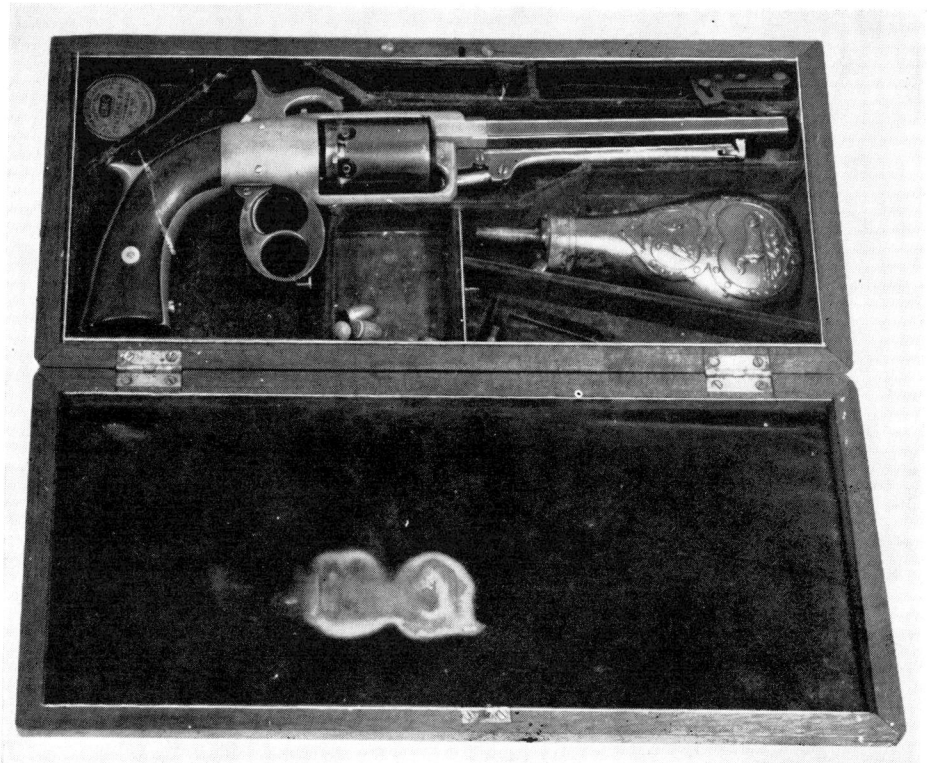

Casing believed contemporaneous holds only known set of Savage Figure-8 revolver with accessories. Flask is type also supplied with Remington .36s, while bullet mould casts ball like Colt's Belt .36 moulds. Gun now in famous Independence Hall, Chicago, gun collection.

in machine production as a method of proving the tools. Details of set-up can be examined without the need for the heavy chopping incidental to roughing out steel or iron parts, since brass is much softer and easier on the cutters. The scarcity of the brass-framed Savages and their placement prior to iron-framed, with the change back to brass when a major manufacturing modification occurs, seems to confirm the reason for its use. The end of production of the Figure 8 series was a flat iron-framed, creeping lever rammer pistol.

The Alsop Series

Apparently during the winter of 1859 and the spring of 1860, one of the chief workmen at the Savage establishment in Middletown, once the scene of Colonel North's carbine factory, was Charles R. Alsop. The May, 1860 North and Savage patent shows pin and groove loading lever suggesting that fitted to Alsop revolvers also marked "Middletown," and on May 22, 1860, Charles R. Alsop patented a shoulder stock attachment for the Figure 8 Savage revolver. In addition, his own patents of July 17 and August 7, 1860, May 14, 1861 and November 26, 1861, and January 21, 1862, all relate to the small five-shot Alsop series of spur trigger revolvers; revolvers which have an unmistakable relation to the North and Savage series of arms.

Alsop remained associated with the Edward Savage enterprise for at least the first several years of the war, and it is probable that the arms of Savage, Alsop, and Savage Revolving Firearms Company, including their rifle muskets, were all made in the same shops, Colonel North's old works.

Alsop's shoulder stock, the assignment of which was to J. R. Alsop of New York, was fitted first to the round iron-framed Figure 8 and then experimentally to one of the final series of arms, the Savage Navy Revolver. Edward Savage also turned his talents to the stock idea, and patented April 9, 1861, No. 32,003 (reissue 999) a brass-yoked stock hooking into the top of the handle, suggesting the form of the Colt shoulder stock. Apparently Alsop's connection with Savage extended from the 1858 or 1859 to about 1863, if not later.

The Savage Navy Revolver

The perfected Savage Navy Revolver was with the flat iron frame and a shrouded loading lever, but of more conventional hinged lever form, not creeping type. The cylinder reciprocated to seal off gas escape. Improvements in manufacturing the frame had been made; no longer was the breech turned with a rounded boss, but was just a flat lip or flange to protect in case of multiple discharge. This last was quite improbable, and the nipples were set into recesses like the Wesson and Leavitts, well protected, with the hammer nose striking downward through the top of the frame. A full trigger guard now surrounded the ring trigger, and extended back in a strip to the handle frame. This model by the fall of 1861 was confirmed for production. A .36 caliber six-shooter, it is spoken of as a "Navy" revolver only because of the caliber. It was Savage's hope to sell these to the Army.

Savage's Status

Within the company, Savage's position was an odd one. A director, inventor, factory owner, and stockholder, he appears not to have had executive status.

Savage wanted to go to Washington to get the contract for the company; James Wheelock wanted to retain Thomas Dyer, of Washington, who had been a middleman in the first large beef contract handed out when the war started, to get the orders for them. Direct application to Washington seemed not to have proved fruitful for Wheelock, who testified that "all our (Wheelock's) personal efforts to procure such a contract from the War Department had failed." Dyer was authorized by Wheelock by his letter of September 9, 1861, to obtain an order for 5,000 Savage pistols at $20 each, guaranteed deliveries 500 in October, 700 November, 1,000 in December 1861, and 1,500 per month thereafter.

But at some date just before then, Savage, perhaps exasperated at Wheelock's insistence on handling the business himself, wrote to General Ripley. He was well known in Washington and the letter must have come as no surprise; Ripley on September 10, 1861, replied, apparently by telegram, ordering 5,000 "of your cavalry revolvers," provided they be delivered at the rate of 1,000 per month. Savage in Middletown on the same day, 10 September, replied to Ripley accepting his terms. Secretary Wheelock and President Sebor refused to accept Savage's contract, especially since he wanted compensation for it; they had committed themselves to paying $2 more or less to Dyer. Dyer originally wanted them to fix $22.50 as their contract price, saying he had in mind to apply for a pistol contract at that price. He implied he would then scout around and resell it by assignment to someone who manufactured pistols. Wheelock retorted their pistols weren't worth more than $20 and that was the price they wanted to sell them for. Dyer was reassured on September 16 that he and he alone was authorized to treat for the Savage Revolving Firearms Company in the matter of a pistol contract.

On October 11, 1861, General Ripley in accordance with the one-month proviso in his letter to Savage now notified the inventor that since the one month had elapsed with no deliveries, the order was annulled.

Contracts and Deliveries

Meanwhile Dyer was at work and on October 16, 1861, received an order for 5,000 to include 1,000 which Ripley had verbally ordered from Dyer earlier. The terms were as Dyer had been instructed, 500 in October, 700 in November, 1,000 in December and 1,500 monthly until filled. The ice broken, Wheelock lost no time in writing Secretary Cameron October 25 offering him 10,000 pistols at $20. When Ripley got to endorsing it with his recommendation, on October 31, it was negative because the "Savage pistol is not, in my opinion, a desirable arm for the service, and not such a one as I would supply, unless in case of emergency." Meanwhile, under the wire for the October deadline, Wheelock turned over to Army Captain Balch's inspectors 500 of the Savage Navy Revolvers, on October 28. Then Wheelock repeated his request, on November 19, to furnish 10,000 pistols. Assistant Secretary Scott on November 21 referred it to Ripley "for such action as may be necessary in the premises."

The war had turned into a long, cold winter and the requirements of the new cavalry brigades were to be great; Ripley on November 28, 1861, ordered from Wheelock a second 5,000 pistols. To speed up Captain Balch in his duties of inspection, Ripley forwarded to him February 26, 1862, a letter from Wheelock dated 22 February in which it was stated that the first 5,000 would be finished for inspection "in the next two weeks," and asking that the inspectors (three on duty, who could inspect 400 pistols weekly) should be continued on the second lot of 5,000. Captain Balch quickly pointed out that only 4,500 had been delivered; that the November delivery had defaulted. Though it appears Captain Balch himself failed to complete that month's inspection, the record stood, and he recommended that the 500 under terms of the October 11 order not be accepted. But no reply was returned from Washington and Wheelock stood ready with the last 500 guns, which Balch duly accepted on March 11, 1862. On that same day, Ripley sent out a letter following instructions of Secretary Stanton, to suspend inspections and acceptances of arms; but it was too late; Balch had already taken the final 500. Thomas Dyer, we suspect, was as influential with Stanton as he had been with Cameron.

Ripley informed Balch by letter dated March 17, 1862, that no arms were to be received without the special permission of Stanton. But on March 20, Balch accepted 500 more "North's patent pistols" under the order of November 28, by special instructions of the Secretary. It was thus that matters stood when Wheelock appeared before Holt and Owen seeking ratification of the second order.

He proposed to deliver the 4,500 remaining pistols at $19. As Ripley seemed to feel the pistol shortage acutely, the Commission's decree confirmed this new arrangement, but introduced the technical evaluation that "this arm should be made in future free from malleable iron (the frame) and at a lower price than $19." In detailing the behind-the-scenes conduct which led to his receiving these orders, Wheelock not only spoke quite openly about Dyer's work in getting the first order, but brought in for the first time mention of Henry Wycoff as a middleman. He openly visited Wheelock at Middletown, and asked if they wanted a contract. Wheelock was willing to pay $2 each to obtain a contract for 5,000 at $20. Wycoff left, and soon after Ripley sent out his order of 28 November. At the time the Commission disposed of the case, Wheelock was not certain to what extent he would pay Wycoff the $2, in view of the order having had the price reduced to $19. By June 10, 1862, the last of the Savage revolvers had been delivered at $19, a total 10,000 in all.

Wheelock apparently fooled about with Alsop for a time, but the manufacture of these arms seemed unprofitable. The Savage Revolving Arms Company turned its manufacturing talents to the Springfield rifles and on September 9, 1862, signed a contract to make 25,000 of the Model 1861 Springfield. They gained the approval of Holt and Owen to this in a rather remarkable way: by determining that Parker, Snow, Brooks & Company (who were swamped with sub-contract work at fair prices) would transfer their contract to the Savage firm. With this knowledge that he could obtain a contract from a "speculator," Wheelock asked if Holt and Owen could not give him some encouragement in that respect. As ace in the hole he offered to make 50,000 such guns at $16 each. Holt and Owen had to decline recommending that any contract be made in such an irregular fashion, but by September the tide of battle had ebbed to a serious low point. Losses of muskets were high, replacements needed, new arms in desperate shortage. The Ordnance Department agreed to split the difference, and Wheelock signed up to make 25,000 at $18.

A further contract was issued to Savage Revolving Firearms Company on 25 February 1864, for 12,000 more Springfields M1861. Edward Savage signed as surety in addition to Samuel L. Warner; Wheelock was still Secretary. Savage delivered 13,500 under their first contract; all 12,000 for the last. Stamped SAVAGE R.F.A. CO. on the locks, they reveal nothing of the struggles which went on to achieve recognition for the revolver of Henry Savage North, last pistol to bear the North name and then only rarely.

Savage Revolver Not a Success

The Savage revolver was unappreciated when it was in service; without the glowing testimonials of a dozen officers flattered to find themselves in print, it was not a commercial success. Called "Navy," the majority were employed by the Army. Of these, hundreds which had been issued and turned in dirty and rusty, were bought out of New York Arsenal by Bannerman and peddled off at 25¢ each. But of the lot, some were brand new, in the original packing cases. For these Bannerman wanted a little more. With Colt .44 New Model Army's at $2.85, and Whitney's complete with bullet moulds and 100 caps for $3, Bannerman had the unmitigated gall to ask—and eventually to get—$16 apiece for these revolvers which had cost the United States only $19 a half century before. The odd slab-sided pistol with the gas-seal cylinder seemed better liked in the dingy store of Bannerman on lower Broadway than it ever was in the Ordnance Office in Washington.

Allen & Wheelock Revolvers

Listed among the "Pistols" obtained for the war is a lot of 536 Allen's revolvers at a total cost of

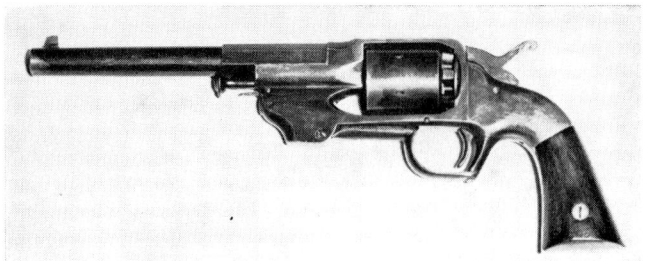

Big Allen's revolver used trigger guard hinging forward to rack back a loading plunger with enormous force, to seat bullets. Percussion arm was fundamentally well designed and built in spite of bulk.

$9,130.50. Of these, 198 were bought from William Read & Sons of Boston, December 31, 1861, for $22 each. More correctly known as Allen & Wheelock, they were produced in Worcester, Massachusetts by Ethan Allen and his brother-in-law, Thomas P. Wheelock. Allen, pioneer gunmaker (no relation to Ethan Allen of Ticonderoga fame) patented features of the gun January 13, 1857 (No. 16,367), December 15, 1857 (No. 18,836), and September 7, 1858 (No. 21,400). A .44 caliber percussion six-shooter, the Allen & Wheelock is a single action gun having a creeping lever ramrod of distinctive form; the lever arm is bent around to form the trigger guard, pivoted in the frame below the barrel, and working on the bottom side of the loading plunger. The principle is the same as the Savage and Root patent creeping levers; the means are quite differently arranged.

A solid and strongly built gun, the Allen & Wheelock had no official use, only the few purchased, though Allen's salesmen were active in the South in early '61. It is presumed the Reed pistols were .44's; a .36 "Navy size" was also made, and a .31, using the same loading lever but with a side hammer, the

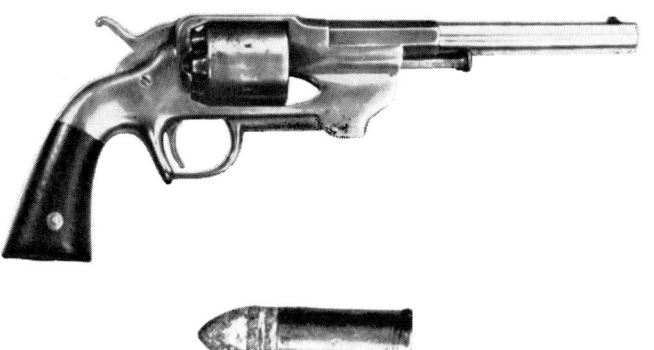

Compared with lip-fire cartridge model Allen revolvers also produced during the War is regular Allen percussion Army .44. Special cartridge used had flange which fitted into notch seen in cylinder rim, while frame on .44 size was modified in production to allow side plunger for extracting fired cartridges. Only recently has lipfire .44 been identified as distinct model, not a conversion, though frame, hammer, lever differences are obvious in comparison.

cylinder pin withdrawing from the rear of the frame like the Joslyn and Colt. In the .44 A & W, the cylinder pin removes from the front, above the lever plunger. The .44 nipples were in line with bore; in the sidehammer, recessed in holes. A final model of cartridge side-hammer A & W appeared toward the end of the war.

The Butterfield

One of the battle-worn limited issue revolvers ignored by Ordnance buyers is that of Josiah B. Butterfield. A brass-framed percussion six-shooter using the patented Butterfield pellet primer device, this gun originated during the time when Jefferson Davis wanted guns to be self priming. Perhaps it is this erstwhile

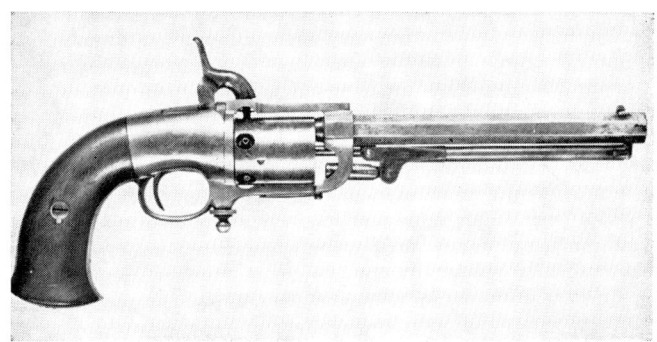

Pellet primer revolver of Josiah Butterfield was bought on authorization of Dr. Rowand who wanted to help out. Fifth New York Cavalry carried some, and Confederate use is also alleged. Firm Beauregard & Slidell are said to have sold a few in the Carolinas presumably during "cold war" period.

Confederate association which has caused the Butterfield to be listed as "Confederate," for there is no record of its having been used by Confederate forces. But as a Yankee revolver specially ordered for the Ira Harris Guard Regiment of the 5th New York Cavalry, it certainly deserves recognition.

The Ira Harris Guard, under command of Colonel O. De Forest, was raised as a volunteer force during the fall of 1861. Colonel De Forest received authorizations during the months of September, October, and November from General Ripley, to buy horse equipments and revolver pistols aggregating 2,280 arms. Assisting Colonel De Forest in the organization of the regiment was Dr. Charles L. Rowand who, thinking himself authorized to do so, and seeking to relieve De Forest of unnecessary details, placed the pistol order with Josiah B. Butterfield & Company of Philadelphia.

When the Commission on Ordnance Stores stood ready to receive copies of contracts and adjust claims, a letter over De Forest's signature was sent to the Secretary of War, Stanton, dated Camp Harris, Annapolis, Maryland, the camp of instruction of the "Guards," which stated categorically that De Forest "contracted with J. B. Butterfield & Company for the delivery of 2,280 pistols." This letter was sent on to

Major Hagner by General Ripley, "to be read in connection with the De Forest case."

Though De Forest failed to answer a summons of the Commission to give evidence, he sent word over from Major Maynadier's office on May 31 that he was there and would like to see the papers on his case. As Major Hagner declared in the finding statement of the Commission, on June 24, 1862, Colonel De Forest read the letter saying *he* had contracted with Butterfield, and repudiated it as not having been written by him. Thereafter, De Forest learned that Dr. Rowand had made the Butterfield contract in his name, and so again contacted the Commission saying that the Butterfields were "an article of superior value and which should be adopted by our government. He informs me that they have never been received by you, but are ready (June 18, 1862) for delivery. Will you do me the favor to have them inspected and paid for?"

Hagner and Judge Holt could not find it in their power to do De Forest any such large favor, which would have amounted to say $45,000, and their negative decision was binding:

> No obligation rests upon the government, however, to carry out an agreement not made by its orders, but under an error by an unauthorized agent. The commission therefore direct that nothing be received under such contract or agreement, but that should it be deemed advisable to purchase the pistols stated to have been made, it shall be done, after proper trial and in open market, at such price, compared with the present prices of revolvers, as may be fair and just.

Water, water, all around, and not a drop to drink, was the situation Butterfield faced. A small businessman, he had sunk $10,000 in tools and materials to make the few thousand pistols for De Forest. Refused by Government, though he had contracted in good faith, Butterfield fades from the scene. Behind, he left about 2,000 .44 revolvers having one unusual feature: a spring-loaded column of priming pellets in front of the trigger guard, which fed flat detonating discs into the path of the hammer on the down stroke. The percussion nipples are at right angles to the axis of the cylinder, like a pepperbox, and are not well adapted to carrying percussion caps since the shock of discharge would cause loose caps to fall off. It was the Butterfield's fate, like that of the Walch that follows, not to be in the path of the development of modern arms.

Walch Revolvers

The revolvers of John Walch of New York City require more than passing mention. He felt a man could never be too well armed, especially in lawless New York, where the Metropolitan Police had been organized only a couple of years before and were still not sure who would rule the roost: the Tammany Tiger, the Tenderloin element, or Law and Order. (Come to think of it, the same problems exist today in New York or any city!)

Walch cured the problem of being undergunned by designing a six-shooter and then jamming six more

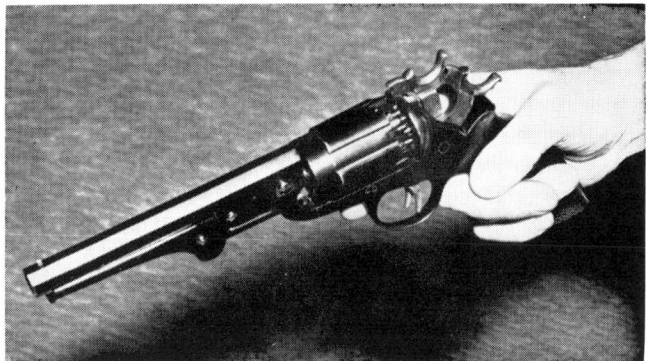

Walch revolver of unique two-hammer design discharged first one shot, then a second, from same chamber before rotating cylinder one index notch as both hammers were recocked. View of pistol in Independence Hall, Chicago, collection shows two triggers but both charges could be fired at once with safety, manufacturer claimed.

shots into the elongated chambers. His patent model was a little less sophisticated. Starting at front with a conventional 6-inch barrel probably robbed from a Pocket Colt, he created a hand-chiseled frame holding a strange cylinder with conventional in-line nipples at the back and a strange bevel belt midway into which six more nipples were stuck. Two hammers hung on the same hammer screw were installed; one with a tip to reach forward and swat the front row of cones. Shades of John Pearson and Ethan Allen! Walch proposed to cover the cylinder with a steel sheath held by a screw on the frame; two orifices gave access to capping the nipples of both rows. He soon learned how impractical this could be and though he deposited the pistol when he filed for Patent No. 22,905, granted February 8, 1859, he had already improved the concept to allow a more streamlined form of ignition system. As finally perfected, it involved a not unesthetic rounded rib on each chamber which was drilled from the rear for the second nipple and at the front, presumably accessible from the mouth of the chamber, a subsidiary touch hole was drilled to allow the flame to fire the front charge.

Walch's first design used a single trigger to fire; then in the 12-shot .36 "Navy" Walch pistol, two triggers are used. Later, a single trigger improved by John P. Lindsay of New Haven was used for the small pocket .31 ten-shot Walch revolver, and for a series

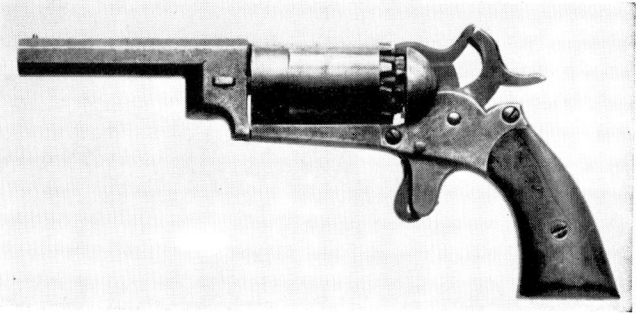

Single trigger improvement of John P. Lindsay was employed on small Walch five-chambered ten-shooter, cal. .31.

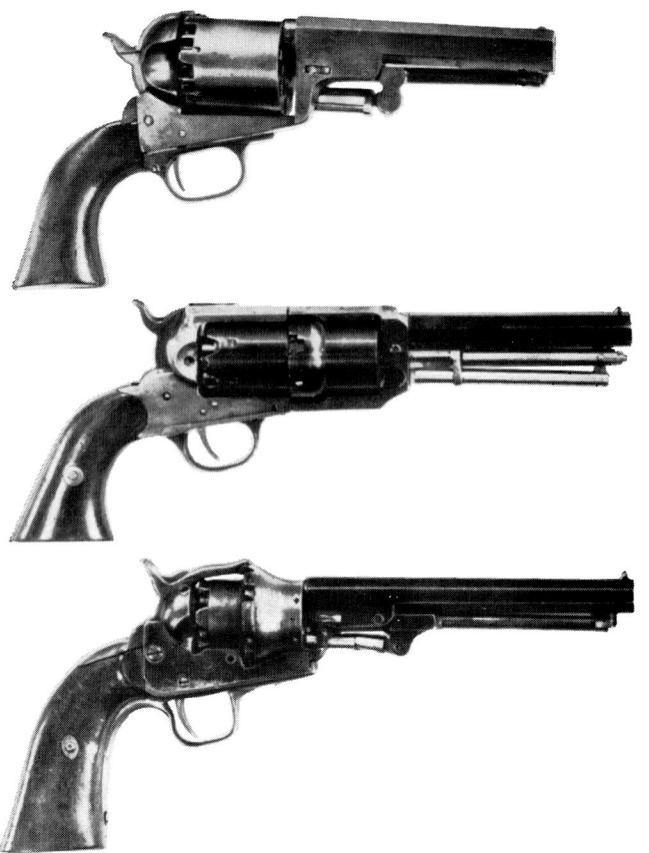

Multishot designs were ingenious. A. C. Vaughn built Colt-type pistol cal. .24 with concentric rows of chambers, two loading lever plungers. G. H. Gardner patented supplementary cylinder and special loading plungers on modified Beals-type pistol. Walch in patent model went hog wild with belted cylinder, special frame. 12-shot model has barrel like .31 Colt but is recorded as .30 caliber.

of single barreled two-shot pistols ranging from tiny "derringer" to large .44 caliber smoothbore holster pistol size. These single barrel two-shooters with the improved single trigger, and a Springfield-type rifle musket made to the same design, are known by the name of inventor Lindsay who apparently manufactured them. The revolvers marketed by the Walch Firearms Company had a limited vogue in the Army. To manufacturer Lindsay, Lieutenant B. W. Hornbeck, Company I, 9th Michigan Infantry, wrote from Camp Muldrow's Hill, West Point, Kentucky, on December 2, 1861: "My company of the 9th Regiment Michigan Infantry have supplied themselves with your 10-shooters and are highly pleased with them. I am frank to say it is the most *reliable* (in orig.) revolver I have ever seen."

The lieutenant's enthusiasm was not shared by Private Elisha Stockwell, Company I, 14th Wisconsin Volunteer Regiment, in the Army of the Tennessee. Said Stockwell in his biography, ". . . south of Holly Springs . . . I went out with George Reeder to get some fresh meat . . . Reeder had a small revolver he borrowed from one of the boys. It shot ten times out of five barrels in the cylinder, all muzzle loaded . . . Reeder shot several times before he would give up. That gun wouldn't kill a hog, and the pigs got so wild we couldn't get near them . . . So we went to camp without any meat, and I wouldn't go with him any more."

J. P. Lindsay

While the 10-shooters and double pistols were in production by 1861, as evidenced by a broadside featuring comments of officers dated that year, the .36 caliber was probably introduced soon after, and during 1862 Lindsay got to work on a rifle musket. While the rifle musket may be assumed to belong in that chapter, the design is wedded to its origins in the Walch revolver, as made by Lindsay.

The site of the Walch-Lindsay factory is open to conjecture, according to some authorities. Gluckman declares the Lindsay double muskets "were probably made for Lindsay on contract by Cyrus Manville, whose plant was at 208 Orange Street, the site of the old Volcanic factory." This address is usually given for the J. P. Lindsay Manufacturing Company, in New Haven. But the broadside alluded to above, which includes statements from such notables as Colonel George L. Schuyler, now back from Europe and acting as aide de camp to General Wool of the New York State troops, declares quite clearly: "The J. P. LINDSAY MANUF'G CO., of Naugatuck, Connecticut, are sole Manufacturers of Lindsay's Patent Fire-Arms; also, Manufacturers of Camp Knives, Forks and Spoons, Knives and Forks, and Bowie Knives for Army Use." However, Colonel B. R. Lewis (somewhat in error) states: "About 1860 the Springfield Armory made 1,000 Lindsay double shot rifle muskets, firing superimposed charges." He is wrong in the date; and in citing Springfield Armory draws most probably upon references in Bannerman's old catalogs. On one page familiar to most readers, Bannerman illustrates a series of photos of model and experimental breech arms, including a Lindsay double

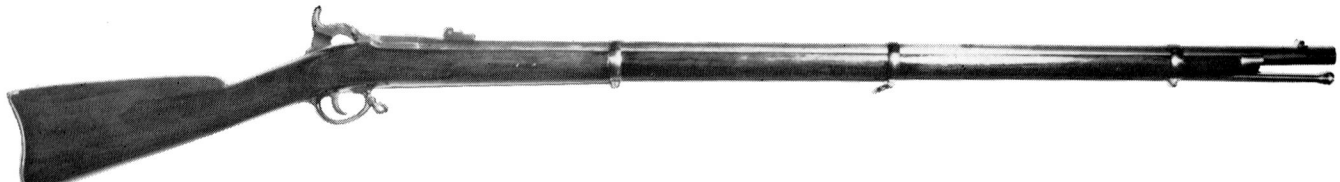

Lindsay Double Musket was obtained on contract from inventor. Arm was identical to regular Springfield except for patent breech screwed onto back of barrel and stock specially inletted for new mechanism.

LINDSAY'S PATENT
Double Shooting Fire Arms.

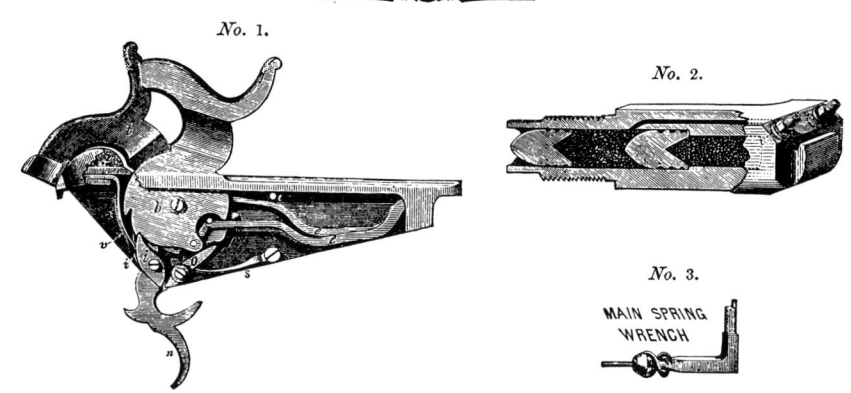

Cut No. 1 represents interior of Lock, *b b* Hammers, *e e* Main Spring, *i i* Scears, *v v* Scear Springs, *r* Screw, which holds *scear spring* and *cap* in place, *n* Trigger, *o* Detent, which *prevents* both hammers falling by a *single* pull of the trigger, *s* Detent Spring, *t* Main Spring *Wrench* hole.

Cut No. 2 represents the inner section of breech, with two charges in position.

GENERAL FORMATION. The double lock is inserted into the stock directly in *rear* of barrel. The barrel breach is provided with *two* cones and *two* vents, which communicate with the *separate* charges of powder— the *right* one with *front* charge, the *left* one with *rear* charge. Both charges are loaded into, and fired from *one* barrel separately. By these simple means a *double gun* is obtained *without* necessary *additional weight* above a single barrel arm.

CONSTRUCTION. The *bottom* of the bore is *decreased* in size, forming a chamber. (See cut No. 2.) This *chamber* receives *powder only from one cartridge*. The *rear* or first ball rests upon the edges of this chamber, completely *sealing up the powder* in the chamber. Upon this *rear ball* the *second* charge of *powder* and ball rests. The vent to the *front* charge passes from *right* hand cone through the metal to a point *between* the balls. The vent to the rear charge passes from left hand cone directly into small chamber.

AMMUNITION used should *always* be the *regular Springfield paper pressed ball* cartridge. *Full size* for caliber $\frac{58}{100}$. *Grooves* in ball should be *filled* with lubrication. Fire *cannot* pass back to rear charge, if the *grooves* in the ball are properly *filled with lubrication*, and balls thoroughly "*rammed home*."

Double musket used two regulation .58 charges. Right hammer fired front ball but by accident or deliberately left hammer could safely discharge both shots.

musket. Of this gun he says: "United States Muzzle Loading Repeating Rifle (two shots from one barrel), made at United States armory during the Civil War. Intended for use of troops firing two balls without reloading. Rifle is .58 caliber; has two hammers, two nipples, only one trigger. Gun did not prove a success, so only a few were made, which makes them valuable to collectors. The lead bullet of the first cartridge is intended to act as the breech for the second cartridge. Those guns can only be had from us. We bid higher than all competitors and secured the lot. Gun is complete, with bayonets and in fair order; barrel and mountings are polished bright; walnut stock. Very rare. This rifle is a U. S. Government gun, made at Springfield."

How far back into history the Springfield Armory story goes we cannot say; we can only trace it to Sawyer's *Our Rifles* first published 1920. He says, "The inventor was J. P. Lindsay, an employee at the Springfield Armory. Five hundred of these rifles were made at the Springfield Armory and issued to troops for trial . . . According to tradition, Mr. Lindsay's brother, a soldier, was killed by Indians, who pursued their usual tactics of drawing the fire of a small outpost and then charging in overwhelming numbers, before the soldiers could reload their single shot arms, and massacring the entire company. The Lindsay two-shooter with the appearance of a single shooter was intended to offer the sort of surprise that would discourage repetition of such tactics."

It is such tales as this that make one of the regrets of my young life the fact that I never knew Mr. Sawyer. He was before my time. It must have been the joy of a winter's eve to sit before a friendly fireplace with Mr. Sawyer rambling on and on with these fascinating anecdotes about arms lore and history.

On December 17, 1863, John P. Lindsay of New Haven entered into a contract "with the United States to furnish 1,000 Lindsay double-muskets," at a price of $25 each, interchangeable, inspected, and delivered within four months from date. Eight months later almost to the day, Lindsay handed over to the inspector 1,000 double muskets, received August 16, 1864, and paid for in full August 25. These muskets

Principle of two-shooter was applied by Lindsay to big "horse pistol" but arm is exceedingly rare today, so few were made.

had been ordered as a consequence of a trial held by Captain S. V. Benet at West Point about August 26, presumably 1863.

Benet's letter to Ripley reporting the results describes the musket and its purpose in detail; and was reproduced on a brochure or flier advertising "Lindsay's Patent Double Shooting Fire Arms" and giving instructions and illustrating the parts of the Double Musket:

> The object of the invention is to be enabled to load the musket with two charges of powder and ball, and fire them separately thus having all the advantages of a double barrel weapon. The bottom of the bore is supplied with a chamber to hold a charge of powder, the sides of the chamber supporting the first bullet that is inserted. A tap with the rammer fixes this bullet in place, and prevents the flame from the forward charge, when ignited, from igniting the powder in the chamber. Upon this first bullet the second charge loose powder and the naked bullet is placed. The gun is provided with two vents, the left one communicating directly with the chamber, as in ordinary cases, the right one passing through the metal by the side of the bore, and entering it in front of the rear bullet, the edge of the chamber fixing this rear bullet always in the same place. The gun has two hammers, both worked by one trigger; both hammers being cocked, the trigger acts upon the right hand one, firing off the forward charge; a second pull at the trigger fires the second or rear charge. By cocking the left hammer only, the trigger will fire the rear charge, discharging both charges and emptying the barrel. The mechanism of the lock is simple and strong, made of few pieces, and not liable to get out of order. The gun was fired *sixty rounds without cleaning;* the first thirty with bullets 58 diameter, the last thirty with bullets 57 diameter. The gun fouled considerably, but not so much, in my opinion, as with a single cartridge from a service rifle musket. I attribute this to the fact that the explosion of the front charge forces the rear bullet hard against the bottom of the grooves, filling the bore completely, and that this bullet, when fired, carries with it much of the accumulated foulness. Of the sixty rounds, or *thirty loads,* both charges were fired separately in each case, and the gun was in perfect working order to the end. The inventor having expressed the opinion that the grease around the rear bullet was necessary to prevent the passage of the flame from the front charge to the powder in the chamber, several bullets were cleaned of all grease, and wiped perfectly dry, but they worked as perfectly as when greased. Twelve rounds, six loads, were fired at a target for accuracy, the record of which is herewith enclosed. In my opinion, the invention *is a success.*

Regrettably, Lindsay did not reproduce the target fired from his sample musket at West Point. It would have been interesting to know what Benet considered good accuracy and, also, since it appears to have been the first and last time the Double Musket was fired in the Army, the record deserves perpetuation. As nearly as can be determined, the Lindsays served out the war snoozing peacefully in their armory packing chests.

Who made them, remains something of a mystery, but a clue may be furnished by the contract. Surety for Lindsay was one Cornelius S. Bushnell of New Haven, who also appears as surety in connection with Joslyn carbine contracts. In matters as touchy as firearms contracts, especially with the hazardous record of cancellations and annulments meted out by Holt and Owen, sureties were not usually mere money lenders.

The name of a man guaranteeing the contract's fulfillment was usually the name of a man who had an administrative or manufacturing interest in the production of the items covered. In some dim recess of fallible memory, we recall being told the Lindsay muskets were assembled by parts-maker and subcontractor Samuel Norris, whose shop in Springfield, Massachusetts, was the scene of many activities behind the scenes of Civil War production. Lindsay may have made up the breech parts and hammers in either his Naugatuck factory or at the Joslyn works in Stonington, and then had Norris take semi-finished Springfield stocks, not inletted for locks, and let in the Lindsay-breeched barrel (otherwise standard, cut off behind the rear sight for the patent breech) and the Lindsay two-hammer lock assembly. Confirmation of this is lacking; but Lindsay taking eight months to produce suggests he ran into difficulties. One thing is virtually certain, that he did not tool up to manufacture the Springfield Double Musket complete, but that he bought all parts, except his own, from one of the major fabricators, and had them put together to fill the contract. That he was a workman at Springfield Armory may be true; that his brother fought Indians seems possible. But double shot guns existed through arms history long before Indians were ever a factor in warfare; Lindsay offered only a mechanical variation, patentable, not unique. The story is probably mere legend, invented probably by Bannerman to sell his otherwise unsalable brand new Lindsay Double Muskets, last gasp of an idea that began as the Walch revolver.

The Whitney Navy .36

The welter of assorted and sordid revolvers which burst upon the Ordnance Department's attention must have palled upon General Ripley after a time. Though contracts with Colt, with Remington, and others were going well, he still needed good, solid revolvers. One make that his field inspector-buyer officers had been picking up from the large jobbers was the Whitney Navy .36. A Beals'-designed solid frame six-shooter, it resembled the Remington and was a well-made and sturdy pistol. From Schuyler, Hartley & Graham, for example, on August 7, August 15, and August 26, his men in New York had bought a total of 360 Whitney Navys at $17. Time rolled on; why not go to the source?

On May 15, 1862, Ordnance bought by purchase most of the on-hand stock of finished revolvers at Whitneyville, 600 of them at the modest price of $15.03 each. June 9, 1862, Whitney and General Ripley closed the deal and drew up the contract for 6,000 Whitney Navy Revolvers at "$10 for each musket complete." Whether the typesetter made the error or whether it was a quirk of the contract form in that the word "musket" was not erased and "revolver" substituted, is not known. Nor is it explained why Whitney for the first 1,000 delivered June 27, 1862, was paid $12 each, $2 over the contract price.

Concluding on February 28, 1863, Whitney in all delivered 7,002 to the Ordnance Department on this contract. In addition many thousands were bought by state troops, though how the Whitneys marked "NJ" for New Jersey are tabulated is not known. According to the usage of the day, state troops mustered into Federal service had the value of their equipments reimbursed to the state authorities, and their guns were carried on the books as bought by the United States. Possibly, but not definitely known, the 600 purchased were for some special purpose for New Jersey, and the large order led to Ripley's issuing the formal contract. A popular arm, about 30,000 Whitney Navy revolvers were made.

Early examples have a curious cylinder stamping scene, of a coat of arms made from half the British and half the American arms, flanked by a lion and an eagle. This is stamped twice on the cylinder in early arms; later guns have one coat of arms substituted with a naval scene. The meaning of this cannot even be guessed at. In the Colt Museum there is a Colt-made pistol, Navy size, unique in having two-piece wood grips. The cylinder is grooved where the bolt drags and scars the surface. And upon the cylinder, stamped by machine, is a similar heraldic scene, the British and American arms halved; while to the left is a Federal eagle and on the right, paws crossed, a Trafalgar lion. No Colt mark appears on this pistol, and the serial numbers are all stamped upside down.

Whether Colt and Whitney vied for some odd contract, and the Whitney was preferred, is the only hint of the meaning of this odd cylinder decoration. The Whitney Navy pistols are stamped on the top barrel flat with the noncommittal E. WHITNEY/N. HAVEN. Some were finished in tin, a hot-dip finish, it is believed, akin to galvanizing. Certain of these bear a Navy anchor stamped on the top barrel flat forward of the frame. With Ames brass cup-hilted cutlasses at one side the men of the Western Flotilla or damning the torpedoes in a hundred water engagements wore their Whitneys in the short-ended Navy holster on their right hip.

Pocket pistol used bullet with gas-seal tallow groove, and special mould cast bullet in that shape. This specimen is about new, an extremely rare sidetrack down the path of arms development in America. Photo of gun from Shore collection.

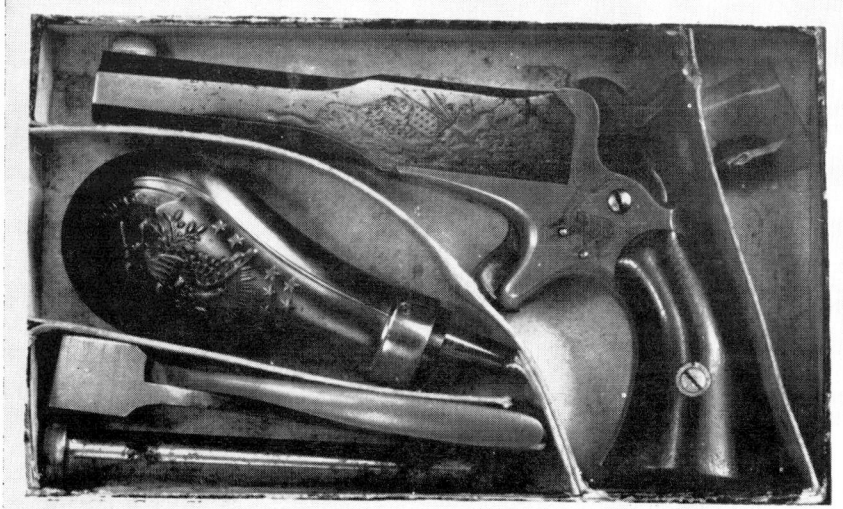

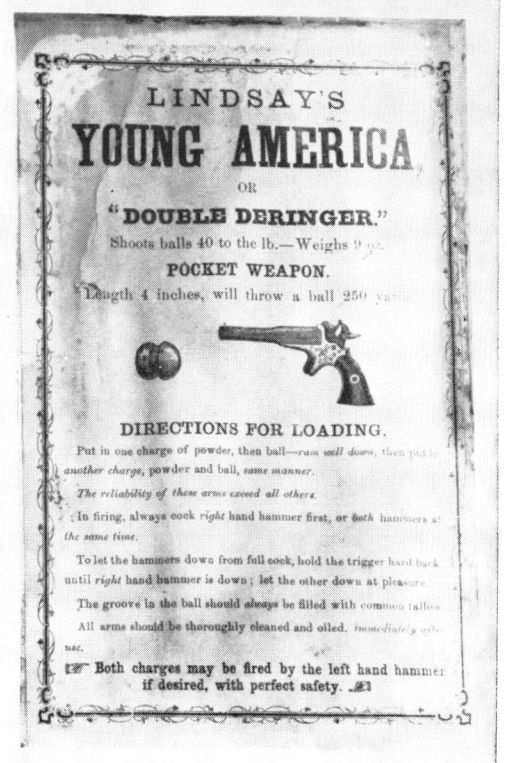

Navy .36 of Eli Whitney's was solid, reliable arm combining features of Colt and Remington-Beals designs. Cylinder had eagle-lion engraving scene. Pistols taken by Navy have anchor stamped on barrel top flat at frame.

Foreign Revolvers

Three of the foreign revolvers rate as very important U.S. martial arms. The Lefaucheux or, as the American patent documents sometimes list them, Lefaucheaux, 12mm pinfire revolvers were most plentiful. Colonel Schuyler bought 10,000 at $12.50 each, and 200,000 cartridges at $17.45. Minister Sanford in Belgium also sent over 25 of the Lefaucheux, average price $7.96 4/10; a misleading price, as they were averaged out with 55,000 smoothbore and rifled muskets. Civil War pistols imported seem to range from approximately 25,000 to about 37,000 serials. The gun, introduced about 1853 in France, was popular; in 1863 it was adopted as the Swedish artillery pistol. Two basic types existed; single action and double action. The single action frames are curved at the back; the double action have a hump or prawl. While the 12mm DA type has a rounded trigger guard, the smaller calibers (9mm, 7mm) often have folding triggers,

Odd Colt-made Navy .36 has similar lion-eagle cylinder stamping with experimental groove between stop slots, and two piece handle. Barrel is unmarked; serial number on usual parts is 302, stamped upside down.

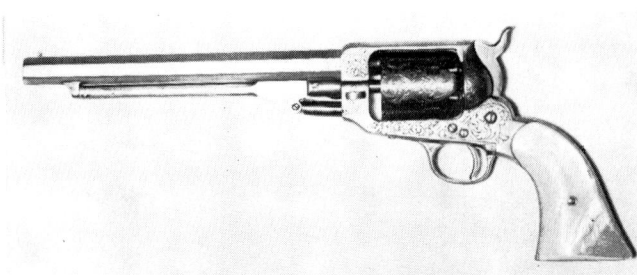

Fancy Whitney's were scarce; this engraving is much worn and plated over but may be original with period of gun's use. Grips are pearl.

hinged forward for easy pocket concealment. Some of these were sold through Schuyler, Hartley & Graham, commercially. The single action is the basic U.S. martial revolver, and almost all were imported of the "cavalry" form of trigger guard, with a small spur as an extension of the square-back form. The spur is to place the trigger finger while mounted, in a charge or otherwise riding, after the order to cock the pistol has been given. The arm is carried in the position of "Raise, PISTOL," the finger *outside* of the guard. A side rod ejector pushes the empty cartridges back out of the cylinder when the loading gate is swung open. The barrel extends in a frame section underneath the cylinder, which is open at top with no frame above. Stamped on the frame, usually to the left by the serial number, is the mark "LF under a shotgun action, broken." E. Lefaucheux' most famous design was the innovation of a bottom lever top break action breech-loading shotgun, and that became his trademark symbol.

The revolvers and to a lesser extent the shot gun of Lefaucheux figured in the early days of the war. As early as 1836, Lefaucheux had developed a copper based shotshell cartridge, of rolled paper. Inside the base was a common percussion cap at right angles to the line of bore, and entering the cap through paper and base metal was a copper pin which protruded from the side of the shell about ¼ inch. For this cartridge, Lefaucheux devised the break-open shotgun and though simpler hinges have since been designed, his was the first. A lever extending forward under the forearm beneath the barrels pushed to one side, disengaging the barrel group and permitting it to flop downwards exposing the breech. The side hammers had flat ends that slammed the cartridge pins in, detonating the cap and the charge. These hammers had to be set on half cock before the barrels would open; then the fired shells could be extracted by one's fingers. Metallic ammunition was not too plentiful in the ordinary trade. Nevertheless, Schuyler, Hartley & Graham had sold these guns since Hartley's prewar trips to Europe, and, as with other premium and special guns, they had a limited vogue, especially among the French sportsmen resident in Louisiana, many of whom could send regularly to friends or family to get more ammunition on the next packet boat.

Lefaucheux also designed a rotating breech pistol, with a side loading gate for pushing the cartridges in from the rear. The military model of this arm in 12mm was probably the gun imported at $17 by Godillot, as well as by Schuyler and Hartley later. The lockwork was a single action design of the Belgian inventor, Mariette.

Numerous LeFaucheux shotguns and revolvers exist with other makers' names upon them; the guns were actually made by Lefaucheux in Paris, though some were licensed to Liege gunmakers, as evidenced by proof marks. A like-new specimen of the U.S. Lefaucheux single action cavalry revolver in the author's collection is nicely engraved by the seller, whose name, elaborately etched on top the barrel, is:

Capt. Julius W. Adams, USA, carried this Whitney .36 until his death in November, 1865, from exposure and effects of wounds. Battles in which he fought were carved on ivory grips.

LEPAGE FRERES A PARIS 12 RUE D'ENGHIEN. On the right of the barrel frame is the LF trademark and the number 7411, stamped after final polishing. The cylinder is bright on the rear face and is stamped between chambers "D" and "55." On the loading gate when swung open can be seen the same small "D" and 55, evidently an assembly number. Unscrewing the front trigger-guard screw releases the barrel, which then can be unscrewed from the fixed cylinder pin. On the barrel frame left side is the factory stamp in an arc, INVOR E LEFAUCHEUX/BREVETE sgdg (PARIS), settling the spelling of his name, at least. Set on half cock, the cylinder is free for loading. Barrel and cylinder are a rich deep dark blue; frame casehardened.

Augustus Buell in *The Cannoneer,* at Cedar Creek in the Valley Campaign under Sheridan speaks of being armed with a Lefaucheux pistol:

In our right and center sections, there were 23 or 24 cannoneers, four or five non-commissioned officers and Lieut. Baldwin, and none of us had any arms except revolvers. It was, therefore, a question whether about 30 artillerymen, with revolvers, could repulse a heavy skirmish line of veteran infantry, backed up by a main line of battle less than 20 rods behind them.

I freely confess that when I had pulled the lanyard the last time my impulse was to run; but when I saw Serg'ts Yoder and Beckhardt, and Corp's Kennedy, Benham and Knorr, and Cannoneers Pike, Marean, Hummel, Gresser, Hunt, Callahan and others pull their revolvers to stand their ground, I did not see how I could consistently desert them, and so I pulled, too, and began shooting at the Johnnies coming up out of the ravine. The usual revolvers for the cannoneers was the Navy Remington or the Colt, but the one I had was a "French Tranter," as they were called, which I had bought from Corp'l Ray, of the 10th New York Cavalry, who had taken it from the body of a Confederate lieutenant killed at Brandy Station the year before. I used to say that "I captured it," but as a matter of fact I captured it with a $5 bill. However, it was a captured weapon, by proxy if not in person. Of course all six loads were gone out of it in as many seconds. My last shot hit the Rebel lieutenant who was leading his men, and knocked him down. He was captured later in the day. He had on a hat that was too large for him and he had stuffed some paper or pasteboard under the leather sweat band to make it fit, and as he happened to have it pulled down over his eyes, my ball struck it just over the left temple and was deflected by the paper wadding in his hat; otherwise it must have gone through his head. He was so close when I fired that my flash singed his eyelashes and blew his left cheek full of powder.

Buell was handicapped by the special ammunition needed for his pistol. During a lull in the fight it occurred to him he had better reload his revolver; his cartridge box had been shot away, and "It was a serious loss to me because my revolver used the pin fire metallic cartridge, which I had to buy, as the Government did not issue them, and I had recently filled the cartridge box at a cost of 10¢ per cartridge."

Buell's revolver came from a "Rebel lieutenant." Perhaps it was one of the 500 "lost" by Godillot, as the vessel aboard which his guns were shipped appears to have been captured on the high seas. But others of the French Tranters saw good service. At the Gettysburg battlefield one Yankee lieutenant of artillery lost one of two revolvers he owned. The other eventually wound up in the Gettysburg museum. It is in good serviceable condition. Its mate was recovered from the mould underneath the tree where the lieutenant had stood 90 years before. Rusty but still recognizable, the two 12mm Lefaucheuxs are reunited in the museum, as the nation is in fact.

Most of these arms now in collections originated with a lot of 500 that Bannerman offered for sale in the 1904 catalog, "with box of surefire ball cartridges, $1.95." Paradoxically, immediately below this claim that the ancient pinfires were "sure fire" Bannerman notes, "we do not guarantee any firearms or cartridges." More accurately, said he, "purchased in France to equip U. S. Army officers and cavalrymen during the Civil War." The cut illustrates the identical single action Lefaucheux so there is no mistake. United States contractor to supply these arms was Alexis Godillot of Paris and Liege.

Though his antecedents are not known, Godillot was represented in the United States by one J. B. King of New York and spent time between New York and Paris in arranging his business. On 16 December Godillot wrote to Cameron offering 1,000 Perrin revolvers at $20, "like sample deposited (with Hagner), with ordnance office seal attached." Hagner accepted the order on 19 December; Godillot requested it modified to include 2,000 Lefaucheux revolvers, with 50 cartridges each, at $17, which Hagner did 20 December, including also 1,500 French rifle muskets with 18 inch bayonets, at $15.

Of Perrin revolvers, 550 only had been shipped. These, including those in bond ordered accepted according to Hagner's letter, were delivered as follows: January 6, 1862, 350; March 28, 1862, 100; May 31, 1862, 100.

Of the Lefaucheux revolvers, six were received by Major Hagner and 1,500 had been shipped awaiting acceptance. An additional 500, evidently sent in a different boat, were lost in the passage, and 600 had been then shipped, of a different pattern valued at $15.90 each, to fill the order. Commissioners Holt, Owen, and Hagner decreed the 1,500 should be accepted; they were received May 31, 1862, and paid for at $17. The balance of the 600 were referred to General Ripley who, judging by their absence from

CHAPTER XI.

DEVASTATION OF THE VALLEY — SIXTH CORPS STARTS FOR PETERSBURG — RECALLED TO THE FRONT — CEDAR CREEK — ADVANCED TROOPS SURPRISED AND OVERWHELMED — THE SIXTH CORPS TAKES THE BRUNT — DESPERATE FIGHTING BY GETTY'S DIVISION — FREE USE OF THE COLD STEEL — THE UNCONQUERABLE VERMONTERS — THEY RESCUE BATTERY M — WE ARE COMPLIMENTED BY GEN. LEWIS A. GRANT — TOTAL WRECK OF EARLY'S ARMY — BATTLEFIELD AMENITIES.

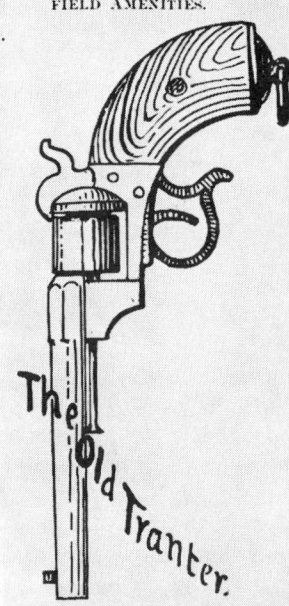

FROM Fisher's Hill Sheridan's army moved rapidly up the Valley, encountering no resistance worth mentioning. As for ourselves, we did not go beyond Harrisonburg, but halted until the army began to retrace its steps to Kernstown. Concerning the devastation of the Valley during this retrograde movement I have little to say. We of the artillery had no hand in it, except to kill a few pigs and chickens for our own use. Of course it was a proper military measure, and was designed to prevent the subsistence of the Rebel army there. But one of my saddest memories is the recollection of the poor women and children looking hopelessly at the destruction of everything they had to eat, the burning of their grain stacks, barns, mills, and frequently their houses, which, though not intentionally set on fire, would frequently be involved in the conflagration of their outbuildings. However, the most of this business was done by the cavalry which brought up the rear, and was stretched across the whole Valley, from mountain to mountain, and absolutely left a desert in its track. Returning to Kernstown we lay there until about the 10th of October, when the Sixth Corps got orders to return to Petersburg, and the next day we marched to Berryville. Here, just as we were about to cross the fords in front of the gap, en route

Erroneously called "the old French Tranter," the Lefaucheux 12mm pinfire U.S. service revolver was sketched by Augustus Buell in "The Cannoneer." Actual model 1853 revolver Schuyler, others, bought is shown together with Lefaucheux break open long gun: engraved cased revolver is rare, and gun is not common shotgun, but double rifle, pinfire cal. 58.

the list of arms purchased, refused to take them as not in accordance with the letter of the letter. At that, Godillot was dealt with more leniently than others; all his rifle muskets were accepted.

The Perrin revolvers, one of the war's rarities, were competitive to the Lefaucheux. Open top, these centerfire .45 revolvers by Perrin & Company of Paris are double action, resembling the Lefaucheux frame and barrel, but of unique design. There is no hammer spur, and the guard is given an angle at the back, making it look slightly squareback. The right side-loading gate swings upwards and back. The grip is squared at the top edge somewhat like a Beaumont-Adams, and the cylinder pin has a central "poker" which removes to push the fired cases out. Backed by a small 6-grain powder charge, the .438 Perrin 268 grain bullet seems hardly to have been a threat to the South. Possibly the 6 grains of powder were an early nitro powder charge. The cartridge is distinctive in having not a rim, but a belt about the base which serves as a rim. Inside the belt is the anvil for the inside central fire primer. Chamber diameter is .465 inches, cartridge length over all .98 inches. We have seen but one Perrin revolver though know it from pictures; and that one, a deluxe cased specimen, engraved and bright steel, was bought in Paris by a Southern martial pistol collector in 1957.

More common than the Perrin, if examples in collections are any indication, are the pistols of George Raphael. As listed on December 11, 1861, for $16 each he sold the United States 806 "revolvers." But reference to the Document 99 tabulation reveals an interesting conjecture: these "revolvers" at $16 are but the common Army 12mm Lefaucheux pistols. For that tabulation shows, as received from Raphael in New York, the following:

September 21, 1861	106 breech-loading revolvers and appendages	$26.33
November 30, 1861	806 revolvers and appendages	16.00
March 8, 1862	138 Lefaucheux (sic) revolvers	16.00

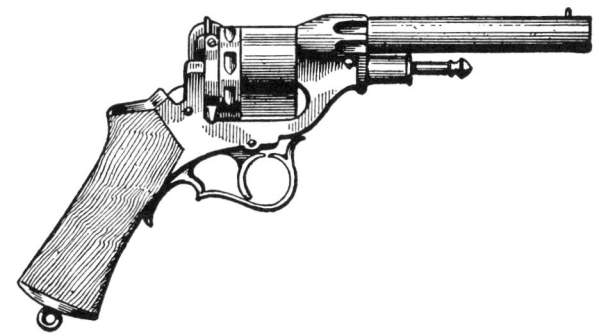

Perrin revolver is one of war's rarities; 550 were received by New York ordnance officers from Paris gun seller Alexis Godillot. Center pin removed to poke out fired cartridge cases.

Open-top "Raphael" revolver may be one of 106 actually purchased from George Raphael in New York. Maker or inventor of design is unknown but gun used special centralfire inside primed cartridge, and was double action.

Between November and March the identity of the Lefaucheux revolver had become fixed in the minds of Crispin, Hagner, and the other officers concerned with buying, and they so listed them. The 806 arms therefore are thought to have been simply Lefaucheux revolvers of the type imported and issued in quantity. It is the lot of September 21, 1861, that is of special interest, for several examples of what is believed to be guns of this lot have been seen in collections and sales. Most have a worn brown finish, indicating originally that they were blued. They have the appearance, if not obviously polished, of having seen service. A special rimless metallic cartridge case .53 inches long (loaded round .95 inches long) was used, having an inside anvil for centerfire. Except for absence of case taper, the round resembles the later Thuer cartridge, or perhaps a long-based "gas check" .44 of modern days. The primer is of course not visible. The chamber of Raphael's revolver was cut with a shoulder and the cartridge bottomed on the front of the shell, the same principle that is used in the Thompson Submachine Gun and other arms using rimless cartridges today. Raphael himself was not the inventor; it seems likely that the lockwork is the Mangeot-Comblain double action system of 1854 though absence of any documentation on the pistols and scarcity of model makes this difficult to check. The cylinder and a rotating back-plate are connected during firing; when the gun is set to load, the plate is turned to a position when the loading gate segment can be opened, and then the cylinder turns freely, allowing the spent cases to be emptied. The back-plate has six deeply coned firing pin holes and the nose of the hammer is a long pin. The two-piece wood grips come up on each side of the frame to the back edge of the cylinder, and the double action trigger is curved and well-located. In spite of the absence of information on this scarce revolver, it seems to have been in the mainstream of revolver development abroad. The rear sight, like the Lefaucheux, is notched across the rear top of the 5½ inch barrel. Unmarked, the gun like the cartridge seems to defy investigation. As a guess, to explain the high price of $26.33 (if enthusiasm to buy and emergency need is not enough justification), it is thought the "appendages" mentioned could have been tools for reloading the special cartridges.

Horse Pistols

Among relative rarities are also the few single shot European horse pistols bought by the North in the dark days of 1861. Philip S. Justice delivered 96 on September 4, 1861, and an additional 250 (125 pairs), September 19, at $8 a pair, $4 each. Without confirmation, we think these are the Model 1859 Austrian cavalry pistol, system Lorenz, caliber .54. A standard percussion pistol, these have a special hammer-safe which is raised up in front of the hammer to hold it off the capped nipple. No spur on the guard; you are supposed to hold your finger inside in the charge, and when you cock the gun and set it half-cock, the hammer block will prevent discharging if the gun is accidentally dropped from horseback. The barrel band is steel; lock and band are case hardened; other parts rust blued. A specimen in the author's collection stamped on top of the barrel PIRKO is dated "864" on

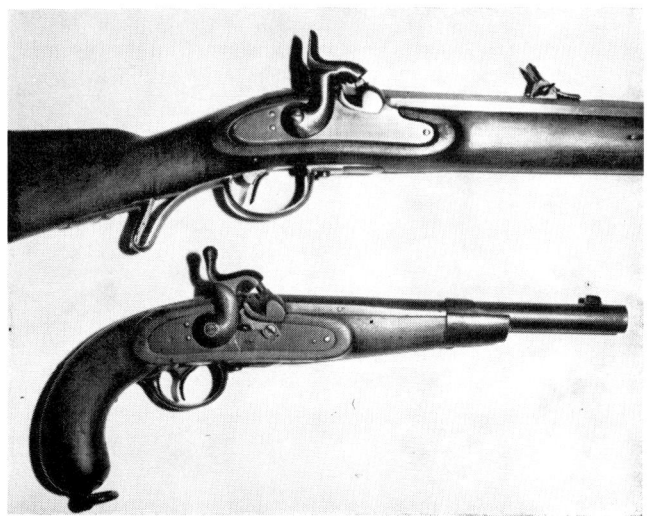

Pirko in Wien made this M1859 Lorenz horse pistol, shown with Lorenz Jaeger carbine ("Wisconsin Eagles" carbine illustrated elsewhere.) Justice may have sold a few such pistols, and Huse might have obtained some from Vienna Arsenal later in the war. Actual issue is not proved.

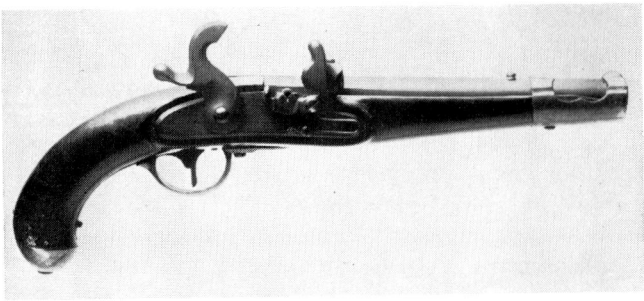

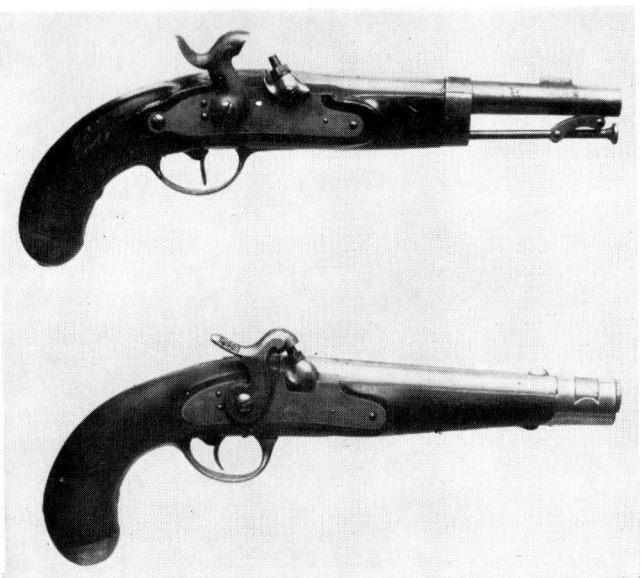

Model 1842 Augustin-lock Austrian cavalry pistol is shown with (below) Prussian dragoon pistol having linked rammer and Bavarian horse pistol made at Amberg Arsenal. These arms are preserved in Smithsonian Institution collection as specimens from U.S. Civil War purchases, but very few "horse pistols" were ever imported for either North or South. Proof of use in battle should be demanded with "Civil War gun" offering today from dealer or collector.

the lock, date for Justice but not too late for some state agent in spite of the gradual retirement of foreign guns by 1863-4 and the issue of the new contract-made arms.

A prior model of Austrian pistol also saw limited service: the M1842 percussion with Augustin primer lock. The front band is a distinctive double band of brass. In the Austrian service, the model before this was the M1798 Dragoon pistol having a conventional French-type double neck cock flintlock. These arms were transformed to the first percussion Consol system about 1836 and the new model Consol lock, named after General Augustin, was introduced in 1842. By the mid-fifties the Imperial and Royal Austro-Hungarian Cavalry had decided these primer-locks were for the birds and changed over with the 1859 Lorenz pistol to common percussion. The Lorenz M1859 pistol barrel breech is shaped almost exactly like the Enfield nipple bolster. A sight groove is cut on top of the barrel breech. Rifling is four grooves, slightly wider than the lands. Whether the M1859 is the only Austrian model to see service is debatable; American museums preserve examples of the Model 1842 Augustin pistol as well, apparently from Government purchases. It is well these big holster pistols were so sturdily constructed; most were doubtless thrown at the enemy in exasperation as the dandy gray-coated Rebel cavalry, which had taken the precaution to arm itself by frequent telegrams to Colt's, with the latest in .44 Army revolvers, triumphantly rode over the Yankee horsemen. Not until the revolvers of the later contracts did the Northern cavalry have some parity in equipment with the South cavalry which, though irregularly raised, was by choice equipped with double shotguns, and new revolvers. Fremont's captain of cavalry Charles Zagonyi, who scorned the revolver and preferred the saber, was an exception in the history of the revolver and pistol as used by the Federals.

CHAPTER 24

The Rifles of Christian Sharps

The rifles and carbines of Christian Sharps fought the great battle, and won. The North bought 80,512 Sharps carbines and 9,141 Sharps rifles, yet the Sharps company did not suffer the fate of the Spencer firm, which mass-produced itself out of the market. Many postwar models kept the Sharps company solvent through the buffalo years. While the factory hummed, at several locations including Hartford, Bridgeport, and Philadelphia, the name of Sharps was a household word and, more importantly, a word heard frequently in the old red brick War Department building in Washington. Christian Sharps, who had worked for John Hall at Harpers Ferry, patented his first breechloader as a military rifle September 12, 1848. This patent date appeared on all the guns through the Civil War.

Basic Features of the Sharps

The basic principle of toggle-linking trigger guard-lever and vertically sliding breechblock dated from that

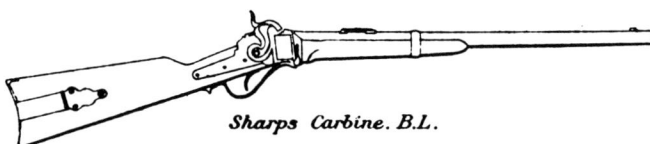

Sharps New Model 1859 carbine illustrated in *Official Records* typified over 80,000 of this type bought by the North from Hartford gunmaker.

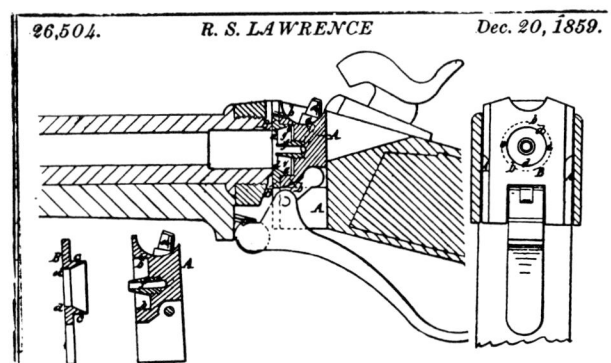

Basic Sharps design had vertical sliding breechblock. Here, patent drawing for Lawrence gas-check ring or plate shows also Sharps breech. Design is patent No. 26504 of Dec. 20, 1859, and appeared in all Civil War Sharps carbines and rifles with sliding breech.

patent. Sharps' sliding wedge breechblock is still with us; on artillery, as a rifle mechanism, and the lever-link-breech construction of the Sharps rifle, with its slide milled out on each side to reduce friction, is the genesis of the spring lever-toggle-breech action of the Borchardt-Luger automatic pistol.

No finer piece of precision manufacturing in steel and wood was available in the world in 1861 than a U. S. contract carbine; and among the best of these was the Sharps.

The "Model 1859" was the basis for the Civil War Sharps. If complete and original, perhaps its easiest detail for recognition is the R. S. Lawrence folding leaf rear sight, the spring-base of which is stamped R. S. LAWRENCE/ PATENTED/FEB. 15th 1859. The carbine sight leaf is short, not less in range, but short because of the short barrel requiring less drop at the breech to get the same elevation. It does not fall over the base spring retaining screw, as does the rifle leaf, and is graduated 2-8 for hundreds of yards. The slot is square-ended, as is the New Model 1859 Rifle sight leaf slot; the leaf is graduated 1-7. In 1863 the rifle was re-regulated, a leaf of substantially the same proportions now being used, graduated 1-8, and the slot rounded to slip over the base spring screw to let the leaf lie flat when set at battle sight. Mechanically, the 1859-63 lockplates have the pellet primer patented by Sharps October 5, 1852, and modified by R. S. Lawrence's pellet feed shut-off, to conserve the pellet primers, patented April 12, 1859. Sharps' basic patent 1848 is stamped on the receiver left; the primer patents on the lockplates. On the barrel to the rear of the sight is NEW MODEL 1859 or NEW MODEL 1863, and in front, the company marking SHARP RIFLE/ MANUFG CO/HARTFORD CONN. Serials numbers are on the top tang of the action body, to rear of the loading trough.

Winston O. Smith's *The Sharps Rifle* (Morrow & Company, 1943) gives some details of mechanical changes:

The tumblers in the models prior to 1855 were too small for the weight of the hammer and strength of the main spring and frequently broke. Often the separate sear springs in these same models also broke. The tumblers were made much

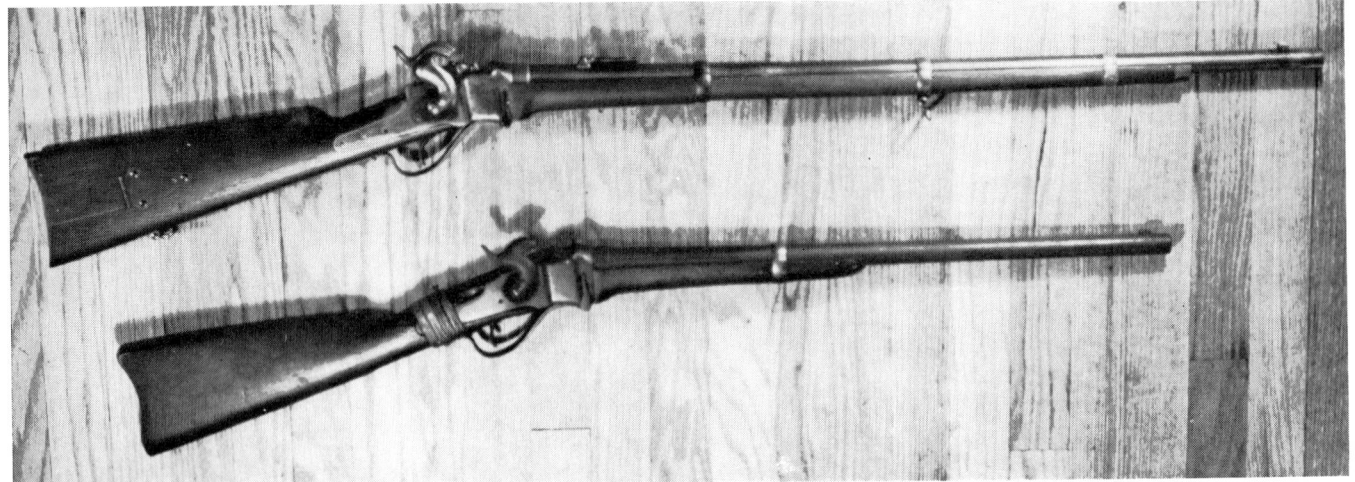
New Sharps-made parts from Civil War surplus stores still being sold were used in 1960's by author to complete stripped barrel-breech unit of New Model 1863 rifle (top). Below is Sharps New Model 1863 Carbine which has had Indian use, and butt is replaced by section of Springfield Rifle Musket butt, held by rawhide repair.

stronger in the 1859 model, and the separate sear spring was eliminated from the models of 1855 and after, a thin extension of the lower branch of the mainspring serving as a sear spring.

To make possible the cleaning of the central section of the (flash) tube, a hole was drilled into it from the side of the block and normally closed by a small headless screw. The slot in this screw was too small, and when the threads inside became gummed with powder . . . it was . . . impossible to remove the screw, and the screwdriver would strip the screw slot. In 1863 a screw with a large filaster (sic) head was (used).

The Sharps Rifle Manufacturing Company used special machines, tools, jigs, fixtures and gauges in making each particular part of the gun, and the parts of each model from 1851 to 1855 are interchangeable to a very great extent. The parts appear to be almost perfectly interchangeable for all percussion arms manufactured in 1859 and after.

It is interesting to note that the tumblers, bridles, mainsprings, and mainspring swivels of these later models (1859 and after) are interchangeable with the corresponding parts of the Models 1860 and 1865 Spencer repeating rifles and carbines, and the Sharps sear can also be interchanged by first grinding off part of the sear arm.

In 1961, almost a century after it was made, I bought a used Sharps New Model 1863 barreled action. To this basic assembly I attached a used breechblock, and all new lock and stock parts, completing an "almost new" Sharps rifle from spare bits and pieces. Two details needed filing: the tumbler square, to receive the hammer, needed dressing down; and the stock and rear band required some compensating removal of metal. Otherwise, each part fitted the other as perfectly as if it had originally been put together that way, a tribute to the way in which President John C. Palmer's Sharps Rifle Company workmen did their job under the U. S. Contract system.

First Sharps Rifles for the Union

Three Sharps long guns were made in Hartford for the Union. Rarest was the rifle musket, a 36-inch barrel arm without patchbox measuring 53 inches overall, in the new Model 1859 series. The Rifle with 30-inch barrel measured 47 inches overall, and the 22-inch barrel Carbine, about 39 inches. Early 1859 carbines have patchbox, butt plate, and band of brass; in the New Model 1859 series, casehardened iron was substituted. A brass patchbox combined with an iron buttplate or band does not seem to have appeared as factory issue. M1859 numbers (with the Sharps series, with some exceptions, starting in 1851 with "1") range according to Smith's records of numbers, 21788 to 31047. New Model 1859's range 32833 to 73602. An overlap of numbers occurred in 1863 when that "New Model 1863" was introduced, the major distinction in manufacturing being the improved fillister head cleanout screw, the model stamping, and sight change; externally, the patchbox was usually omitted in the carbines following contract terms which will be mentioned later. New Model 1863 numbers have been observed as low as 71149, ranging up to 100,000. At this point the C series began, running from C,1 up to approximately C,49999—gun number C,50012 is recorded by Smith as being a "New Model 1866" metallic cartridge carbine. Gun number C,4 was sold in 1961 at a gun show near Chicago; it was a carbine, New Model 1863, without patchbox.

All Civil War Sharps arms were percussion cap, using a combustible cartridge of glazed linen. In the front of the breechblock was set a plate having a slight motion front to back under the influence of gas pressure. The top edge, on closing the breech, sheared off the cartridge end to expose the powder. Adjusted properly, the gas pressure would slide the plate forward against the breech of the barrel, making (it was hoped) a gastight seal. More or less gas did escape from the Sharps breech, but not until it had been much used, did this become serious.

In the author's collection is a Sharps 30-inch New Model 1863 rifle C,35515, which has suffered an "explosion" accident that could occur to Sharps guns. In the event of a misfire, with the breech being dropped to unload, some of the powder inside the gas-seal recess of the breechblock will be dropped forward into the

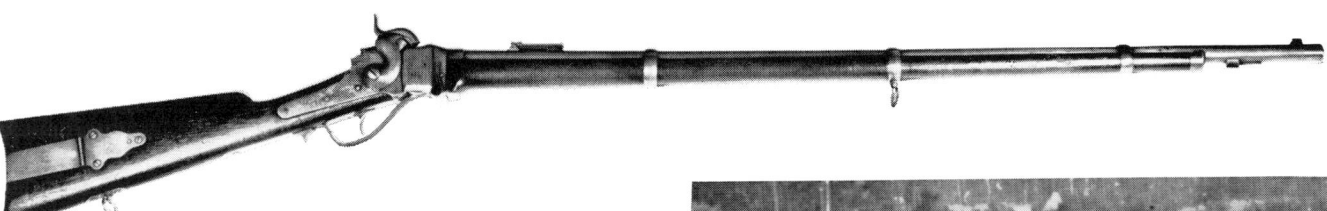

Extremely rare M1859 Musket with 36" barrel was sometimes issued to artillery, when adapted for taking sword bayonet. Shown is same model gun in redoubt of Union heavy artillery before the battle of Fair Oaks.

stock mortise surrounding the block spring, underneath the barrel. This can build up and if a trace of hot gas escapes downwards to ignite this, the wood of the stock at that point will be blown out. On C,35515 cited, wood up to the stock screw escutcheon is popped out, and the escutcheon and screw missing as if blown out.

The excitement of Bull Run caused many changes in Northern plans. Refusing to fight with cornstalks, General Ripley wired President Palmer at Sharps in Hartford, on June 25, 1861, "For what price will you make 10,000 Sharpe's (sic) carbines and how fast can you deliver them?" Palmer replied instantly, "$30 and ten months." On June 29 and July 4 following, Ripley then ordered 3,000 and 3,000 carbines, 6,000 total, to be delivered in "the shortest time possible." As formal as Ripley was to become in later months, Palmer replied:

SHARPS RIFLE MANUFACTURING COMPANY
Hartford, July 9, 1861

Sir: I have the honor to acknowledge the receipt of your order for six thousand carbines, and I forward a sample arm for your approval, to be stamped and returned here as a model for the sub-inspection.

It is our understanding that each arm is accompanied by one thong, one brush, one cone wrench and screw driver, one cartridge stick, 1 extra cone, one extra primer spring, and one ball mould to every five arms—packed in cases of ten. Price of arms and appendages as above, thirty dollars each; ditto of arms chests, two dollars and fifty cents each at our armory . . .

Respectfully &c
J. C. PALMER, President.

General J. W. RIPLEY
Chief of Ordnance

By March 8, 1862, starting with 300 carbines delivered September 13, 1861, Palmer had turned in 8,800 accepted carbines. Deliveries were so much according to schedule and quality so high, that Ripley named Sharps Rifle Manufacturing Company in his letter of March 15, 1862, asking that such arms as might be presented for inspection by them during the following three months, under existing orders, be accepted if of satisfactory inspection quality. Secretary Stanton approved.

Palmer did not have to come to Washington to defend himself against Holt and Owen in their relentless cutting of contract totals, for Ripley was quite sold on

the merits of the Sharps guns. Though Colt in his controversial way had once urged his agent in the west (James D. Alden in Arizona) to report all the accidents that happened with the Burnside and Sharps guns, calling them "humbug arms," the Army buying agents were less biased. They bought the Sharps when and where offered.

General Ben Butler upon taking command in Baltimore immediately purchased 200 New Model 1859 rifles adapted to sword bayonet, with stud soldered beneath the muzzle for the bayonet handle clip. These were bought from C. C. Bean of New York by contract of 7 June, Bean to deliver the guns on July 1, complete with 110 saber bayonets, balance of 90 saber bayonets to be furnished; terms, complete with equipments (as Palmer described for carbines), $40.45 each rifle, $5 for saber bayonet and $3 for "a steel bayonet, not the sabre pattern, but of the latest improved pattern . . . There being in all 590 of both kinds of bayonets."

For a lawyer, Ben Butler drew up a cloudy contract.

Regular New Model rifles either 1859 or 1863 type are externally almost identical but have minor lock and sight differences not affecting interchangeability of major components. Socket bayonet model was preferred by the Berdan and Post Sharpshooter regiments.

We are not certain if he took all of Bean's 500 Sharps rifles, which were lying then at Fortress Monroe, and therefore wanted 200 with saber bayonets but if the saber bayonets were not suitable he wanted to make sure he had also 500 bayonets of socket type for all the rifles, or if he wanted 90 more saber bayonets, and for some purpose as yet undetermined, desired 500 additional "steel bayonets, not of the sabre pattern." On July 13, Bean is listed as delivering the 110 rifles "with swords" under this order of Ben Butler's. He also sold to New York buyers, possibly Major Hagner or Silas Crispin, 100 Sharps carbines.

Palmer sold directly to the United States 100 sword bayonet rifles on September 17. Tiffany & Company sold only 5 on September 23, and Ben Kittredge scoured the warehouses of Cincinnati to deliver 816 on November 8, 1861, at the "all-heart" price of $50 each. Orison Blunt, whose whole desire was to build non-interchangeable but serviceable Enfields for the Union fast, was able to sell but three guns for the cause of the Republic; three interchangeable machine-made Sharps carbines, at $30 each, bought in New York on December 13, 1861.

Bean ultimately delivered 100 carbines at $30 on June 11 together with "109 long range rifles with bayonets," one rifle having been taken as the inspection sample, we suppose, at the signing of the purchase contract. On March 10, 1862, he was able to deliver the balance of 288 Sharps rifles and appendages, but no bayonets, to Butler. There they joined the famous Duryea's Zouaves regiment stationed on Federal Hill covering Baltimore. Colonel G. K. Warren, commanding, on October 15, 1861, had been sent 25 saber bayonets by Palmer. The long, wicked swords must have inspired a fearful respect for the police authority of General Nathaniel Banks' "U. S. Police" force which supplanted the suspected secessionists of the regular Baltimore Police Department. An additional 150 saber bayonets were ordered sent to Washington Arsenal on December 7, presumably for rifles there.

The 6,000 carbines Palmer was making were inspected in an unusual fashion, for contract arms. They were not inspected in detail, but only after final assembly. Palmer was instructed (July 4, 1861) to have them assembled, "observing strictly all the government regulations in regard to proof, testing and gauging, and passing nothing which is not of standard quality in all respects. Report as soon as the arms . . . are ready for inspection, and an officer will be sent to inspect them . . ."

This should refer to a new Model 1859 carbine without detailed inspectors' marks under the finishing on small parts, but with the stock "cartouche" of the chief Army inspector, possibly Captain Robert S. LaMott (*RSL*). At least 6,000 carbines may be indicated in this inspection variation. But Major R. H. K. Whiteley (*RHKW*) was referred to in Ripley's "full steam ahead order" of December 21, 1861. Ripley instructed Palmer to "continue to supply this Department with Sharps carbines, to the utmost capacity of your factory, until further orders. Major Whiteley has been informed of my wishes, and will retain his sub-inspectors where they are for the present." Orders continued to flow from Washington like manna from heaven, and Sharps Rifle Manufacturing Company worked round the clock supplying the demand for the cavalry, especially in Kentucky. Carbine orders were:

February 15, 1862: send "soon as made" 343 Sharps carbines to Lt. Col. Harvey Hogg, 2nd Batt., 2nd Ill. Cavalry, at Paducah, Kentucky.

June 26, 1862: "all the Sharps carbines you can manufacture for the ensuing three months" at $30. Major W. A. Thornton, inspector.

September 9, 1862: "all the Sharps carbines you can manufacture for the three months next ensuing after the expiration of your present order, namely, the 26th instant," at $30, Major P. V. Hagner, inspector.

December 19, 1862: "all you can deliver for three months" commencing Jany. 1, 1863, at $30, Major Hagner, inspector.

Six-cavity Sharps rifle or carbine mould cast .52 cal. conical bullets but user had to trim excess lead off bases.

Carbines by Sharps had been tested by the U.S. since first 1851 Maynard primed model with inside hammer like Ames "boxlock" pistol (top) but volume production did not begin until War when M1859-63 types (middle) were produced. First 1859's had brass patchbox, trim; later ones were iron, color hardened. Then in April, 1863 the New Model series was altered to a lower priced gun without patchbox (bottom) and several tools omitted, lowering price. Guns without patchbox began at C,1 to about C,50,000.

The New Model 1863

During the late winter and spring of 1863 the New Model 1863 was developed. Minor manufacturing changes plus the omission of the patchbox in the stock of the carbines marked this "new" arm. With the change in pattern, Palmer was concerned over the existing parts which had been manufactured; he asked Ripley to continue to receive those on hand until used up during this transition period, at the old price before commencing the New Model at the reduced price. The order read:

ORDNANCE OFFICE, *April 1, 1863*
Sir: By authority of the Secretary of War, this department will receive from you, at the current price of $30 for each carbine and appendages, all such carbines of the present pattern (i.e., New Model 1859) as you may now have completed, or in process of construction, with the parts deemed unessential, and to be omitted in those hereafter to be fabricated and bought at the reduced rate. All to be subject to inspection as heretofore. Major Hagner, inspector of contract arms, has been furnished with a copy of this order . . .
JAMES W. RIPLEY
Brigadier General, Chief of Ordnance

J. C. PALMER, ESQ.
President Sharp's Rifle Company, Hartford, Connecticut

The "parts deemed unessential and to be omitted hereafter" were mentioned in Ripley's accompanying April 1 order: "The said carbines to be without patchbox, and to be provided with no other appendages than one cone wrench and screwdriver, and one brush and leather thong, to each carbine." Sharps pellet "primes" were thenceforth not to be used, and the spare primer magazine springs omitted; bullet moulds also were no longer required, the supplies of factory-made combustible ammunition being ample. And the patchbox to hold the spare cone and springs, was left off. The new low price was to be $28.25, a decrease of $1.75.

Between May 15 and June 23 six shipments of second class arms marked "special" at only $28, totalling 1,000 carbines, are recorded. During the same period, under the April 1 order to finish up old stock, 5,614 "with appendages" at $30 were received. Then deliveries are itemized as "less patchbox" at the contract price of $28.75, 9,601 being received to December 31, 1863. Still the demands of Mars were insatiable; in service with Regulars and Volunteers from New Hampshire to Wisconsin to Kentucky, the carbines were essential arms for the Army of the Cumberland in its border states campaigns. On January 26, 1864, an "all you can deliver" to 31 August 1864 contract

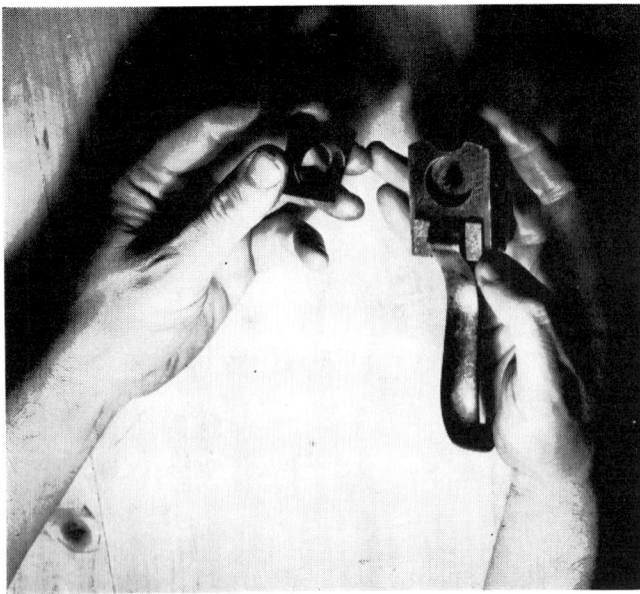

Lawrence ring plate could be removed for cleaning. For modern shooting, back can be shimmed up and front surface ground smooth to improve gas-sealing qualities by cleaning off eroded area.

was signed for carbines, less bullet moulds, at $24; 17,993 were delivered. The last carbine contract was then dated September 24, 1864, and under this which ordered 15,000 arms, also at $24, 15,001 were actually received, the last one all by itself March 15, 1865.

Deliveries were regular in thousands, but on December 21, immediately following a delivery on 20 December of 1,000 carbines at the contract price of $24, 1,000 more guns were received at a special price of $22. As Sharps guns go, these are rarities, not only in number, but from causes, for these were reject or "factory seconds." During the prior production of the Sharps, in spite of the strictest attention to manufacturing, the eagle-eyed U. S. inspectors had set aside parts or finished guns for some cause or other. Whether such rejects had been sold commercially or simply gathered dust in the lofts of the armory, is not known. That it was financially irksome, is obvious. The September 20, 1864 contract specifically provided:

Should any portion of the carbines herein contracted for be accepted by the inspector of small arms as second class, (the parts excepting barrels and springs having slight defects or flaws which will not in any way affect the serviceable qualities of the arm), the price of such second class arms is to be $22.

The 1,000 second-class arms delivered must have been saved up since the preceding delivery on June 25, of 50 second-class "special" priced at $28.

Rifles from Sharps were numbered in with the carbines, and are to be found in far fewer numbers than the short guns; yet the collectors seem frantic to buy carbines these days assembled from left-over new parts at fancy prices, and disdain the long guns. Such was not the case in 1862:

(Telegram)

ORDNANCE OFFICE, *January 27, 1862*
J. C. PALMER & Co. Hartford, Connecticut:
Send 1,000 Sharp's rifles, with accoutrements, and 100,000 cartridges, to Washington arsenal for Berdan's sharpshooters. More by mail. Send as soon as possible.
JAS. W. RIPLEY, Brigadier General

An additional order for 1,000 more rifles, identical to the Berdan guns, was issued by Ripley February 6, 1862. These went to Colonel Henry Post of the 2d Regiment U. S. Sharpshooters. Deliveries were in parcels of 500, and the timelag of two months indicates that the rifles were not in stock, but had to be manufactured. During February, Palmer made great efforts to assemble carbines in order to get a little ahead. He delivered 2,633, leaving the assembly room clean for putting up the rifles. They were received in four lots, April 21, May 2, 14, and 24. The dates are important, and the fact of their regular delivery as assembled, because they tend to bracket the probable serial numbers of the Berdan regiment's rifles.

Considering these were socket bayonet rifles, taking triangular bayonets (see Chapter 19), and that they were numbered in with the New Model 1859 Carbine series, we can conjecture their number range. Assuming Winston O. Smith to be accurate when he lists #32833 as the low and #73602 as the high to the New Model 1859 arms, and an overlap low of #71149 to #100,000 on the New Model 1863 production, certain deductions are easy. Prior to the first acceptance of patchboxless New Model 1863 Carbines under the April 1 contract, and since the Berdan deliveries, 25,015 Sharps arms were received by the Government. Palmer was quite particular (in testimony before Holt and Owen concerning Hall's carbines, for which see

Navy ordnance insignia was inscribed on silver plate fitted to New Model 1863 rifle No. 35515 by Marine or sailor who seemed to have more time than fighting on his hands. Gun is embellished with mother-of-pearl and silver inlays, dog chasing fox, bear, and cutlass on stock, but has government inspection marks also.

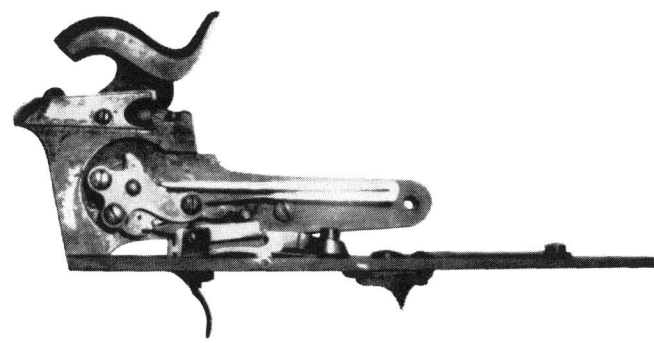

Set triggers do not a Berdan Sharps make, no matter how glamorous they seem. No mention of set triggers is made in Berdan records and if any were used they must have been individual gunsmithing jobs. Shown is trigger from rifle in the C,38,000 range, definitely not a Berdan regiment gun. Workmanship appears to be Germanic.

Chapter 12) that he delivered only to the United States and had turned down state offers at $50 in order to sell to Government at $30. Allowing that he may have made some private sales through the trade in the same period, we do arrive at a serial #46,134 as the lowest carbine number *following* the delivery of the four parcels of 500 each rifles.

From the other side, by adding the number of Sharps arms including rifles delivered since the start of the war, we find 10,533 added to the serial at the commencement of the war, viz: low-number New Model 1859 of 32,833, gives us #44,366. While there may be evidence later to prove this in error, it appears that simple arithmetic leaves us with a serial number bracket of about 44,000 to 46,000, plus or minus perhaps 1,000, for the Berdan rifles and the second thousand required for Post's 2d Regiment.

Existing Sharps triangular bayonet rifles which have double set triggers fitted, seem not necessarily to be Berdan rifles, but simply Army surplus fitted with the post war type of trigger plate in hopes of pushing their sale. But one such rifle in the Lutiger collection, Chicago, has a special handmade set of trigger of obvious Germanic execution in the forms of its springs and parts. Creation of a professional gunsmith, such a trigger might be imagined to be the work of a winter's bivouac for some Wisconsin member of the Berdan Regiment. Serial number of this rifle, unfortunately for romance, is in the C38,000 range, on a New Model 1863.

The Sharps Was Highly Regarded

Among Sharps Rifle Manufacturing Company executives during 1854 to 1861 were William Jarvis, Samuel Colt's brother-in-law, and Elisha Colt, Samuel Colt's financier uncle who had supported the revolver maker in 1848 by a letter of credit of up to $14,000, helping him to get established in Hartford. W. J. Hamersley, Colt's journalistically prolific friend, and eloquent speaker, was also a director. The influence on these men of the way Colt managed things seems to have had its effect. Impressed on their minds was the battery of letters which Colt obtained in the early 1850's lauding his revolvers, from some 39 officers of the Army, Navy, and Marine Corps. On the force of these letters, in a petition to Congress, Colt obtained the adoption of his revolvers as standard U.S. sidearms.

Palmer decided to go the late Colonel Colt not one, but several dozen better. He obtained from the following officers letters praising Sharps rifles. Since some of these men were long time friends of the Colt firm, it seems their willingness to write letters was simply their desire to see their names in print. These officers, some of whom are listed with their units, give a good idea of the scope of distribution of Sharps arms in the war. Were there but a few names, no excuse for prolixity would be necessary. We beg indulgence for reproducing all these names, but do so because there is an impressive list:

General W. T. Sherman; Lieutenant General Sheridan; Major Generals Robert Anderson, Don Carlos Buell, Rosecrans, Thomas, McCook, Nelson, Crittenden, Gilbert, Granger, Smith, Wood, Howard, Stanley, Schofield, Rosseau, Palmer, Davis, Hooker, Slocum, McPherson, Butler, Hancock, Meade, Burnside (impartial, that one!), Custar (sic), McLarnard, Logan, Steadman, Merritt, Heintzelman, Robinson, Terry; Brigadier Generals Morgan, Schoff, R. S. Granger, Judah, Gillman, Bramlett, Burbridge, D. McCook, R. McCook, Van Cleave, Murray, Mott of New York, Brannar, Pry, Manson, Smith, Crupt, Boyle, Shackleford, Hobson, Terry of Michigan, Whitaker, Farnsworth; Colonels T. Wolford, 1st Kentucky Cavalry, Jackson, 2d Kentucky Cavalry, Bayles, 4th Kentucky Cavalry, Cooper, 4th Kentucky Cavalry, Haggard, 5th Kentucky Cavalry, Watkins, 6th Kentucky Cavalry, Shackleford, 8th Kentucky Cavalry; Bt. Brigadier Generals Bristow, 8th Kentucky Cavalry, Holloway, 8th Kentucky Cavalry, E. M. McCook, 2d Indiana Cavalry, B. B. G., (and later governor of Colorado Territory); Stewart, 2d Indiana Cavalry, Kennett, 4th Ohio Cavalry, Wynkoop, 7th Pennsylvania Cavalry, Williams, 9th Pennsylvania Cavalry, Berdan of Sharpshooters, McGowan of Berdan Sharpshooters, Fenke of Berdan Sharpshooters, Ross, 20th Connecticut, Slocum, 2d Rhode Island; Lieutenant Colonels King and Moore; Majors Clay, Murray, Shacklett, Thomas, 1st Veteran Cavalry, Wolfley, Braithett, White, Alston, 3d New Jersey Cavalry; Captains McMurdy, 41st New York, Shister, 2d Pennsylvania Cavalry, Cummings, Joniett; Colonels E. E. Cross, New Hampshire Volunteers, Leonidas Metcalf, Kentucky Volunteers, Hurlburt E. Payne, 4th Wisconsin Volunteers, Gillman Marston, 2d New Hampshire Volunteers, H. A. V. Post, 2d Sharpshooters; Lieutenant Colonel S. C. Griffin, New Hampshire Volunteers; Majors C. H. Larabee, Wisconsin Volunteers and J. I. Dimock, 2d New York State Militia; Captains Charles S. Watrous, 76th New York, J. W. Carr, 2d New Hampshire, B. Giroux, Sharpshooters, J. B. Brookland, 9th Pennsylvania, E. P. Darlington, 9th Pennsylvania, W. T. Partridge, 5th New York, C. H. Craig, 105th Pennsylvania, George Charpenning, Pennsylvania Rifles, Ed. A. Hamilton, Sacramento Sharp Shooters, Ira Wright of Ira Harris Cavalry, Milton B. Pierce, Sharpshooters, H. Bowen, Jr., 151st New York, A. E. Niles, 1st Pennsylvania Rifles, Wm. D. Glass, 6th Illinois Cavalry.

Typical of the sentiments of all these officers were the words of General Joseph R. Hawley who, as a young Justice of the Peace for Hartford in 1853, had witnessed the transfer of land to Sharps Rifle Company by which the then new firm had become established in Connecticut. Commanding Connecticut troops at St. Helena Island, South Carolina, (November 27, 1863), Hawley wrote: "Sharps Rifle is the best made

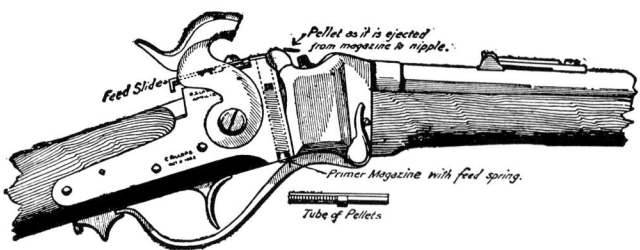

Schematic drawing of Sharps priming motions from Bannerman's catalog shows pellet primer descending on nipple; actually hammer would not be back, but forward, at this instant of priming and firing cycle. In spite of delicate springs, last batch of NM1863 rifles to be made were ordered with Sharps primers.

arm that I have seen in the service. Ours have been now about 26½ months in the hands of the men, nearly all the time right by, and sometimes in salt water, and they are in excellent condition. They have refuted, by actual tests, in battle and in camp, the objections so frequently made by old-fashioned people against breech-loading weapons."

On September 12, 1861, approximately 26½ months prior to the date of Hawley's letter, Sharps Rifle Company delivered 100 Army rifles, sword bayonets and appendages, at $42.50. It is probable these were turned over to Hawley's volunteers from Connecticut; that these same arms should have remained in service for 26 months is a remarkable achievement, in that or any war before or since.

In addition to Sharps rifles purchased from wholesalers, General Dyer ordered 150 on December 1, 1864, at a low price of $38; Colonel William A. Thornton, inspector. A long-time fan of the Sharps arms, Thornton it is believed suggested the sliding cut-off plate in the Sharps primer lock whereby the primers could be held in reserve, the soldier to simply use musket caps. For fast firing, the 50-pellet magazine of "Sharps primes" as they were called was valuable, but the labor of loading it was complicated and tedious:

TO CHARGE THE LOCK WITH "SHARPS' PRIMES," cock the Arm, shove back the magazine cover on the top surface of the lockplate, by pressing the left thumb against the screw head beneath the cup of the hammer. Withdraw the tack nail from the charging tube, insert the primer's end of this tube in the magazine with the left hand, the slot in the tube in line with the slot in the face of the lockplate, and press it down as far as the spiral spring will admit, then with the right hand thrust the tack nail through the slots in the tube and lockplate above the primes, withdraw the tube, bring the lock to half cock and withdraw the tack nail. The priming magazine charged, the cover must not be moved back, lest the primes escape. Nor should the hammer be worked, between half cock and full cock, for the same reason.

In spite of the limited success of these primers, there remained a demand for them. On January 7, 1865, 1,000 additional rifles with triangular bayonets were ordered at $36, and an additional 5,000 at $33 on March 7. Of the last lot of 5,000, it was specifically noted that "These rifles are to be adapted to use Sharps primers." These last 6,000 Rifles are on C-series carbine frames, and if my arithmetic is correct, should be numbered about C,43,000 to C,49,000 plus or minus. Of some special interest is the one lot of 150 rifles ordered December 1, 1864. Reading backward in serials, this lot is about 10,000 before the end of production of the C, series percussion arms, or prior to No. C,40,000. They were delivered February 6, 1865. A regular New Model 1863 rifle believed to be of this lot, evidently delivered to the Navy Department, is in the author's collection, numbered C,35515. It has been owned by a man who had more leisure time than fighting time on his hands, suggesting guard duty with plenty of coffee breaks.

No. 2270. SHARP'S CIVIL WAR COFFEE MILL CARBINE. During the Civil War a workman, employed at the St. Louis Arsenal, devised a plan to incorporate a coffee mill on the butt stock of the gun. Sharp's carbine was selected. The grease box on the butt stock was retained as one of the side plates; the handle was detachable, and easily carried in the pocket. Several models of the carbines were altered in this way. It was intended to issue one of these carbines to each company; they are now very scarce; sold to museum.

Coffee mill fitted to butt of Sharps is rare prize for collector. One in collection of Bob Zellmer of Milwaukee is New Model 1863 No. 55787. Work appears to be largely hand-made, is said to have been performed at St. Louis Arsenal as experiment early in War. Sketch from Bannerman's catalog illustrates general layout in which coffee beans were poured into hole and crank turned to issue ground coffee from slot in side plate. Device works as is shown by former Springfield Armory museum director Bill Murphy.

THE RIFLES OF CHRISTIAN SHARPS

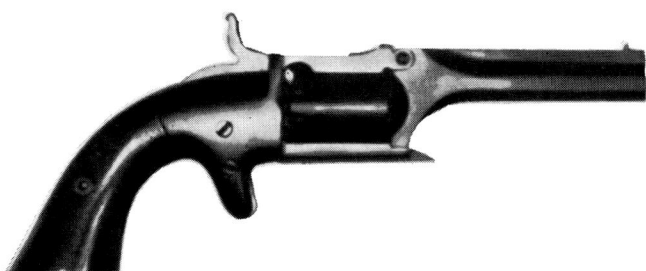

Rare Sharps percussion revolver using tip-up barrel like Smith & Wesson was digression from main business of rifles and carbines which inventor engaged in at new establishment in Philadelphia.

Who ever the Navy man or Marine was who owned it, he had a background as a cabinet maker schooled in the German tradition. Elaborate geometric patterns of mother of pearl and ivory are inlaid in the stock; silver and coin-nickel silver inlays decorate the wood, with a dog running a fox and an inlaid bear in silver worked into the right of the stock. On the comb is a fierce cutlass-like dagger, while on the left of the stock, beside the almost illegible inspection stamp, is inlaid a neat shield possibly cut from a dime, engraved with the crossed cannon and anchor symbol of our Navy Department.

Though Palmer claimed he manufactured only for the United States Government, fragmentary records of the firm remaining today attest to the facts being otherwise. In 1863 the following numbers of arms were shipped to commercial and private accounts, to list a few: Schuyler, Hartley & Graham, 457; Cooper & Pond, 171; J. C. Grubb & Co., 109; A. W. Spies, 19, and Spies, Kissam & Co., 50. Wm. Read & Son got 32 in 1865, the Government of Spain 28 in 1863, and of especial interest, Thurlow Weed received 78 shipped August 10, 1863, which we believe were either to strengthen the shaky conditions of the New York Police Department after the disastrous draft riots of July 1863, or to protect his newspaper offices.

Apparently Palmer did not deprive the commercial market of a few second quality arms, while he delivered as fast as accepted to the United States on his contracts and orders.

Postwar Record

The record of Sharps Rifle Company after the war is beyond the scope of this book; summed up, it enjoyed great favor as a buffalo killer, Indian fighter, and long range target rifle. Why it ultimately failed as a commercial venture is a question we cannot answer. Expert shooters, favorable journalists, a packed "jury" among the military of the nation, all gave it devoted service. Perhaps the cause of failure was economic and overcapitalization. The tremendous factory which had delivered as much as 3,000 carbines in one month, could not be supported by peacetime sporting goods trade. With the passing of the buffalo, the Sharps rifle passed from the sporting scene, without having gained any major acceptance in the postwar scramble for foreign contracts.

Sharps and Hankins

Christian Sharps' personal career had separated from that of Palmer and the Sharps Rifle Company a decade before the war. In 1853 Sharps moved to Philadelphia, doing business as "C. Sharps & Co." In association with Nathan A. Bolles and Ira B. Eddy he moved into a large four story 140 by 40-feet brick factory building on 30th street at the western end of a wire suspension bridge. Today, the double decked Spring Garden Street bridge passes the same point, over the Schuylkill river. Forging was done in the basement, the second floor was used for barrel drilling, the third for tool and small parts making, and the top floor, making best use of the last rays of light each day, for assembly and finishing. A 75 HP steam engine moved the machinery, and in 1859 the capacity of the factory was described (Edwin T. Freedley, *Philadelphia and Its Manufactures, 1859*) as 1,000 rifles a month. The rifles hopefully referred to by Sharps, who doubtless was the source of information, were patented January 25, 1859, No. 22752 and July 9, 1861, No. 32790. In 1862 Sharps had gone into partnership with William C. Hankins and it is by the firm name of Sharps & Hankins that these unusual Civil War rifles and carbines are known.

Using a rimfire metallic cartridge, they were breech-loading single shots, in which the frame extended far under the barrel, and when the lever was swung down from its position of forming the trigger guard, the barrel slid forward for loading. Small pocket pistols were made generally on this form. Sharps also, some time subsequent to the introduction of the Smith &

The Walch-Lindsay pistols described on page 283. The .36 caliber or Navy size revolver has ridges on the cylinder that carry the flash forward to the charge.

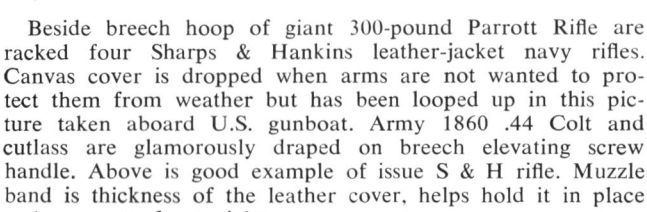

Beside breech hoop of giant 300-pound Parrott Rifle are racked four Sharps & Hankins leather-jacket navy rifles. Canvas cover is dropped when arms are not wanted to protect them from weather but has been looped up in this picture taken aboard U.S. gunboat. Army 1860 .44 Colt and cutlass are glamorously draped on breech elevating screw handle. Above is good example of issue S & H rifle. Muzzle band is thickness of the leather cover, helps hold it in place and supports front sight.

Wesson small revolvers, made such an arm but in percussion, not cartridge, form. Otherwise it looks much like a tip-up .32 rimfire Smith & Wesson. The Sharps pistols, while of much interest to collectors, were no more significant than any of a host of other small personal firearms made before or during the war. It is the Sharps & Hankins rifles and carbines, sometimes spoken of as Navy rifles, that are of main interest.

Sometime in the summer of 1862, as Holt and Owen mercilessly hewed away at the huge pile of arms contracts, Sharps and Hankins got their works in order and began to turn out long guns. Their offer to the new Secretary, Stanton, was very modest, and it was accepted. Ripley thereupon gave instructions to Major T. T. S. Laidley at Bridesburg Arsenal, as Frankford Arsenal was then known, in Philadelphia, to inspect 250 "of their improved carbines." He was also told to get 200 cartridges for each, "a peculiar kind being required." The carbines were $25, cartridges $20 per thousand. A year was to pass before the Army again ordered any, these being listed as "Sharp's new pattern for metallic primed cartridges." The order of September 12, 1863 issued by Major Laidley, specified price at $25 and 480,000 cartridges at $22.50 per thousand. The first lot of 250 was received September 9, 1862; the second lot November 5, 1863. The next Sharps & Hankins guns received by the Army were a milestone order of December 15, 1863, which lists the first .30-caliber shoulder arms to be obtained by our Army. They were delivered in 1865 some 30 years *before* the general issue of the "new" Krag-Jorgensen rifles of the 1890's:

ORDNANCE OFFICE, WAR DEPARTMENT
Washington, December 15, 1863

Gentlemen: Your letter of the 12th instant is received. Please send the six carbines of three-tenths inch calibre of ball to Springfeld Armory, direct addressed to Major Dyer. You may also send there the six carbines of .44 barrel, .52 chamber, .46 ball, with 1,000 rounds of cartridges of your own make for each gun, or such as you can prepare with the space allotted by the lever. Please prepare, with as much despatch as possible, four (or six if you can get the cartridge into the bore in these of 55 or 60 grains) prepared for a ball of .4375 diameter, and in which the diameter of the chamber will be .44, for a ball arranged thus (diagram here) the bore will be .42. No cartridges will be required. Please advise this office when you can forward each lot. The last one is wanted at as early a day as possible, and will be sent to Major Dyer, who will advise you of the depth of counter boring for each of the changes required.

Respectfully &c.,
GEORGE D. RAMSAY,
Brigadier General, Chief of Ordnance

Messrs. SHARP & HANKINS
Philadelphia, Pennsylvania

The projectile shown is a long .44 bullet having an ogive of about two diameters, and a total length of at least three diameters. Three grease grooves of the V shape like the original Burton-bullet Minie are turned on the base, and the heel of the bullet is reduced to .4175. We once were shown an odd rimfire cartridge by Graham Burnside and tended to scoff at it as being made up out of a Krag gallery practice bullet, as it resembled that projectile very much. The Sharps & Hankins Springfield Armory designed .4375 carbine bullet also closely resembles the Krag gallery practice ball, except for being .44 instead of .30. Might not Sharps & Hankins have used the same style of ball, longer with better sectional density, in getting up their ammunition for the carbines of "three-tenths inch caliber?" A total of 17 special carbines were received January 2, 1865, and paid for January 17, 1865. One listed mistakenly as "Sharps & Hankins Rimfire Sporting Carbine introduced 1868" by Phil Sharpe was in L.D. Satterlee's collection, serial 6220, and marked (as instructed by Major Dyer) on the barrel ".55 gr." The carbine-length barrel is partly leather covered.

Four basic Sharps & Hankins long guns have been noted; caliber is a nominal .52, taking the "No. 56" cartridge. The rifle bullet diameter was .55, that for the carbine only .54; as Colonel Lewis opines it was to reduce recoil in the lighter guns. ". . . the Sharps & Hankins types shown (there were others) both had linen patches on the base of the bullets, the patch coming flush with the mouth of the case when the bullet was seated," Colonel Lewis notes. "One variety of Sharps & Hankins had a round post in the middle of its base to center the patch, which had a corresponding hole."

The S & H Rifle had a 32½-inch round barrel, with a forestock held by three oval bands. The bayonet stud below the muzzle was for the Dahlgren bowie knife bayonet or a brass-hilted saber bayonet of the basic French "light Minie" brass-hilted pattern which was made in Europe or by Collins or other makers, almost a standard and interchangeable pattern between foreign arms and the Colts, Sharps, Sharps & Hankins, etc. The muzzle socket of the Plymouth sword bayonet of course is much too big for these arms, being adapted to a .69 caliber arm. According to Sharpe, "Records show that some of these were on hand at the Navy Yard December 1866 and these were sold off at auction under an advertisement August 12, 1876."

The "improved" Sharps & Hankins is improperly identified, but it is thought that the leather covering of the barrel was an "improvement" since tinned-finish exposed barrel carbines have also been observed. The hot dip tinning was certainly a more primitive finish, historically, and the leather covered barrel guns are much more numerous. The most common is the Navy carbine, having a barrel covered with leather and a muzzle ring of the thickness of the leather, to protect it at the front end. The buttstock is of well oiled walnut, and a sling swivel in almost all cases is set into the belly of the butt. The plate is curved brass; frame steel, casehardened. The carbine length barrel was 24 inches. But an Army tinned-finish carbine, with steel barrel burnished bright but with no traces of leather cover, and front sight fitted neatly to the uniform-diameter barrel, was sold at auction in Chicago about 1958 (Shore Galleries). The number is not recorded, but the barrel was noted as 22 inches long, original length.

These make three basic Sharps & Hankins guns, the long 32½-inch blued or browned barrel three-band Navy Rifle fitted for sword bayonet, the Navy or Army carbine, 24 inch leather-covered barrel, and the short 22-inch Army carbine with sling ring on the side of the frame. All are chambered for the Sharps & Hankins rimfire .52 cartridge. The fourth model of Sharps & Hankins seems to have been the 17 assorted special carbines in three basically different calibers: .30, .44, and .42, taking a bullet of unspecified diameter, of .46 diameter, and of .4375 diameter. The first and last are probably straight cased; the .44-46 being a bottleneck round on the standard .52 rimfire base.

Death of Sharps

Christian Sharps died aged 64 in Hartford, March 12, 1874. The brief obituary in the Hartford *Courant* for Sunday, March 14, contains a sentence which, for reasons still not clear, must be his epitaph:

As an inventor he was one of the greatest, not confining himself to firearms—though he produced several models—but covering the peaceful arts as well, and in whatever he undertook in this direction he displayed a great fertility of resource; yet somehow failed to secure a decided practical advantage out of any of the valuable products of his brain-work.

In Philadelphia, scene of his last gunmaking activities, the papers noted this failing, saying he "never derived from his inventions the pecuniary share to which he was entitled." Inventor of the most famous breech-loading rifle in the world, though produced in far fewer numbers than some more financially successful, Christian Sharps at his death was described as a man of peace, "a decided spiritualist," without the slightest fear of death. He left behind his wife, Sarah, a daughter, Satella, a son, Leon Stewart Sharps, and an estate of $341.25.

CHAPTER 25

Colt's Goes To War

The role of Colt in the Civil War might be considered by some as an enviable one. The company had by the late 1850's "attained the status of a National Work," according to Secretary of War John B. Floyd; and it was to grow even larger. But the stress of war was a real thing to man and machines. Sam Colt, weakened by illness, was killed by the pace of war.

From the fall of Sumter to Appomattox, Colt's Armory turned out a prodigious quantity of war materiel. A total of 129,730 Colt's Army revolvers, "New Model Revolving Holster Pistols," to a value of $2,296,112.49, and 17,110 Colt's Navy revolvers costing $446,068.13 were delivered to the general government for issue during the war. In addition, a constant supply of pistols and patent rifles for volunteers, officers, and soldiers, who were buying totin' pistols, were routed from Hartford through wholesalers as far west as Cincinnati and St. Louis.

Filling orders of Southern purchasers directly, Colt himself was willing to make special efforts to fill special requirements. "I desire Mr. Colt to send me two pair of pistols, one pair 12-inch, the other 14-inch barrels; I desire to test them. I shall need some 25 pairs as soon as my company decides as to which they will prefer. I desired each pair to be sent in a double case (two pistols in a case) with all the accompaniments, flasks, wrenches, etc." So wrote Felix Tait from the Adjutant General's office at Montgomery, Alabama, February 18, 1860.

Colonel Colt endorsed on this letter, "I think this order can be complied with by using the 12-inch barrels we have on hand and by measuring from the rear end of the cylinder. In the one we will have a 14-inch barrel or gun then by cutting off the barrels 2 inches, the 10 inches left added to the cylinder will answer for the 12-inch pistols."

Perhaps a Colt's Navy pistol owned by Massachusetts collector, Gerald Fox, may be one of these arms; numbered 91750, it has a 10-inch barrel and is with an original flap leather holster. The unnumbered loading lever, to my recollection, was supplied by me to a former owner before the gun was sold, as the lever which had been attached to it originally for many years was numbered but not matching the gun. A dated Navy pistol of this year is No. 95844, given by Colt to Andrew B. Moore, Governor of Alabama, in December of 1860. No general issue of such long-barreled arms is known; an early special 10-inch barreled Navy was sold in 1851, when No. 618 was made up for Colonel Jack Hays. This pistol has never been found.

Colt responded in more ways to the call for arms. One was his offer to form a regiment of volunteers— the short-lived "1st Regiment Colt's Revolving Rifles

Portrait, painted in 1857, of pistol inventor Samuel Colt.

of Connecticut." Cynicism, not patriotism, has been argued as the motive. Without being too partisan, we urge this is an unfair appraisal of the man. Colt had always wanted to have the actual rank of colonel. This was his chance.

Colt Had Military Ambition

Back in 1837, the legislature of New Jersey, when young Sam Colt then managed a primitive factory for making his guns, passed an act authorizing the raising and equipping of a regiment of volunteers, to be armed with Colt's Paterson revolving rifles or carbines. The legislature neglected to appropriate the funds to buy these rifles, and no regiment was raised; but Sam made known his wish to be the officer commanding, for he felt convinced the firepower of his rifles would prove devastating against troops with conventional arms. In the dark and slim-pursed years of the early 1840's, his younger brother, James B. Colt, later a judge in St. Louis and at the time of the war in 1861 an employee of Colt's in Hartford, chided him about his wish. Several letters (at a time when there was no war and Colt held no commission) from Jamie are addressed to him as "Col. Colt." The title was facetious, based on Colt's wish for a command in the field, a deep-seated desire.

After Sumter he proposed to Governor Buckingham to equip a regiment. "His other proposition is to give the use of a sufficient number of rifles to arm an entire regiment," wrote J. D. Williams of the Adjutant General's office to the Governor on April 25, 1861, "to be called the 1st Connecticut Regiment Colt's Revolving Rifles, to be officered by Army officers and West Point cadets of Connecticut origin, for the field, and as many captains as can be procured —he mentioned Major (Wm. B.) Hartley and others— the regiment to be enlisted for the War and offered to the President. He can make 100 rifles a week after the second week, so that enough to arm the Regiment could be made in nine weeks, if authority is given for enlistments. He will furnish officers to drill the recruits as fast as they come in."

Colt's offer was accepted by Governor Buckingham the day it was received, April 26, and May 1 in addressing the legislature the Governor spoke of the type of arms to be issued as with saber bayonets; the two-band rifles, evidently, instead of the long muskets. One thousand of them to equip 10 companies, the Governor appraised at over $50,000 cash—to be furnished without charge to the Government for the duration. Enlistments began on May 14 and on May 16 Colt's orders were cut for the war:

View of Colt's famous arms factory, which achieved the status of a "national works."

GHQ State of Connecticut
*Adjutant Gen'l Ofc.
Hfd May 16, 1861*

Special Orders No. 83
Sam Colt, Esquire, of Hartford is appointed Colonel 1st Regiment Colts Revolving Rifles of Connecticut.
By order of the Commander in Chief
*J. D. Williams,
Adjutant General*

The regiment was almost at once fully manned. Standards were high; five feet seven was the minimum and many groups which came in from different communities of the state to enroll averaged five nine or better. Aside from the physical stamina which these larger, healthier troops might be presumed to have, Colt's organizational intentions can be deduced from the rifles which the Governor indicated were being made for them. These were the sword bayonet rifle, not musket, probably .56 caliber taking either Colt's solid bullets or the Government minie bullet in an emergency, barrels 27 inches, weight 9 pounds 11 ounces, $40.50 plus sword bayonet. They indicate that the regiment was to train as light infantry, a special force relying on Colt's five-shooter firepower to clear the way for regular musket-armed infantry. The 1st Connecticut Revolving Rifles were the world's first storm troopers.

As light infantry they were "active, strong men carefully selected from the rest of the regiment. Selected and trained for rapid evolutions; often employed to cover and assist other troops," they had a mission as skirmishers. *Hardee's Tactics* tells us what characteristics skirmishers had:

1. The movements of skirmishers shall be subjected to such rules as will give to the commander the means of moving them in any direction with the greatest promptitude.
2. * * *
3. When skirmishers are thrown out to clear the way for, and to protect the advance of, the main corps, their movements should be so regulated by this corps, as to keep it constantly covered.

* * *

8. The movements of skirmishers will be executed in quick, or double quick time. The run will be resorted to only in cases of urgent necessity.
9. Skirmishers will be permitted to carry their pieces in the manner most convenient to them.

These were the shock troops, the men on point; these were something new in formal warfare. Uniformed as Regulars, the Revolving Rifles were an elite corps. On the South Meadows their ranks could be seen late in May, arms smartly swinging in cadence, the broad blades of the white Collins-made bayonets glittering like a field of steely wheat rippling in the sun. Major Hartley was in command, Colt himself being too ill to take an active part in the maneuvers. But the guidance behind the training of the regiment was his. Too soon was it ended.

Perhaps the Governor became miffed because of the highly personal title of the unit; perhaps there was pressure based upon the issue of the non-issue re-

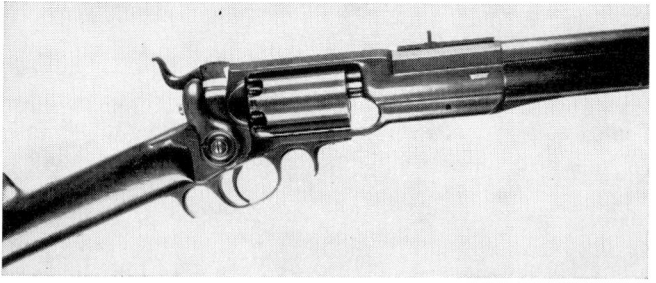

In 1857 about 300 cal. .44 revolving rifles had been bought for field trial issue; specimen shown has hooks to place supporting hand in firing. Inspection stamp of William A. Thornton, *WAT*, is on side of stock.

volving rifles. Three hundred Colt revolving rifles had been issued in 1857; there was then another President, another Secretary of War. Whatever the reason, the blow came barely a month after the reigment had been organized: General Orders No. 307 dated June 20, 1861, declared: "The 1st Regiment Colt's Revolving Rifles of Connecticut is hereby disbanded and all commissions issued to officers in said regiment are revoked." All arms, equipment, uniforms, and other property of the State were directed to be returned at once to the State Quartermaster General. Presumably, Colt's revolving rifles were returned to the armory for cleaning and storage. How many there were was suggested by the original proposal.

Colt offered to start making 100 guns a week, one week after approval was given. Between organization and disbanding, five weeks had elapsed. Allowing for the finishing up of arms in preparation the final week, a run of 400 sword bayonet rifles appears to have been made up for the Revolving Rifles Regiment. That a week had to elapse before any guns could be made, indicates that the "production line" for the revolving rifles was temporarily set aside, and the week's delay was set-up time for putting the tools back onto the machines to get things going again. Though Colt obviously did not intend to lead the regiment in the field—he was too valuable running the factory to spend his time midst shot and shell—the sudden termination of a life-long dream that had been within his grasp must have been a bitter shock to him in his sickness. He was defeated in his vanity, the most important vanity of a man, the vanity of a belief in the value of his career. Colt had developed his revolvers, had made them in all sizes, had sold them around the world, because he believed that greater firepower would revolutionize defensive warfare. They had "terrorized the Indians of the Sierra Madres into honest habits" in Gold Rush days; what the full-sized repeating rifles would do in "modern" war, he was never to find out.

The First Government Contracts

The records reveal the instant response of "Colonel" Sam Colt to the President's call for volunteers. But on the production front he was equally responsive. Without a single tool in his armory adapted to the production of United States Rifle Muskets, Colt nevertheless was the first private arms manufacturer to receive a rifle order from the Government.

On July 5, 1861, Samuel Colt contracted with Brigadier General James W. Ripley, Chief of Ordnance, to supply 25,000 rifle muskets, Model 1855, with the first delivery to be 1,000 muskets in six months. It must have given General Ripley a certain sense of satisfaction to have the upstart revolver maker producing Ripley's pet, the "Springfield." Certainly the price which Colt was to get, $20 for each musket with "appendages," gave the worthy Hartford gunmaker considerable satisfaction, too.

Lincoln called for 75,000 volunteers for three months. Colt, amateur student of war, and professional supplier of weapons of war, foresaw a million men under arms for five years. When he received the rifle musket contract, he laid his plans accordingly. But he was a manufacturer competing in a market for workmen and equipment that was rapidly becoming flooded with other manufacturers, each possessing an arms contract from Ripley. While worry gnawed at him, more so did "inflammatory rheumatism," a syphilitic condition of the leg and arm joints.

In February of 1861 he had taken a leisurely trip to Cuba on a steamer chartered for a pleasure cruise. The voyage was not entirely profitless leisure. In addition to relishing the warm weather instead of the bitter chill of Hartford, he had a chance to take the temperature of the nation on his way South. "Run the Armory night and day with double sets of hands" he instructed Elisha Root and Horace Lord, his works superintendents, February 18, 1861, "until we get 5,000 or 10,000 ahead of each kind. I had rather have an accumulation of our arms, than to have money lying idle, and we cannot have too many on hand to meet the exigencies of the times." The warmth invigorated the Colonel and he returned ready to push ahead.

But April 20, 1861, with the shots over Sumter shattering the nation, found him putting up at the St. Nicholas Hotel, his favorite hostelry in New York, writing to Navy Secretary Gideon Welles, an old Hartford man; "I started for Washington with the purpose of ascertaining to what extent the Federal Government might desire to employ the forces of our manufactory in Hartford and am stopped here by sickness. We can produce if required 100,000 military arms this year, which amount may be afterwards increased to an indefinite number." Though the War Department replied to this query seeking to learn exactly what kind of arm Colt designated by the expression "military arms," single shot rifles appear to have been the theme.

A single shot "Colt" was first proposed by Major Wm. B. Hartley during a February 7, 1860 visit to Richmond. Virginia proposed resurrecting the defunct State Arsenal and equipping it to make guns—what kind, they were not sure, though proposals were many. Hartley urged Colt to consider leasing the Richmond Arsenal to assemble Hartford-made arms that could be finished and marked in Virginia. "A cheap rifle should be made for the militia at from $10 to $15 each, say .52 or .50 caliber, and I believe many thousands would be ordered."

There is a strong indication in later correspondence that Colt took the major's suggestion and a model arm and tools were prepared. For one year later, writing from Havana, on February 18, 1861, Colt instructed the factory that "it is not unlikely we will soon be changing to the machinery of *the plain rifles* of the sword bayonets . . . make hay while the sun shines." Colt's choice of the word "plain" is a strong hint he meant exactly that, a plain rifle, not a Colt's Patent Repeating Rifle with Rotating Chambered Breech, but a plain militia rifle, adapted to sword bayonet. Though no general issue of such a rifle is known, the absence of what might be no more than a half dozen prototypes from the ken of collectors is not strange. For, if such a rifle existed, it was modified considerably before Colt's first produced a single shot arm.

A New Factory

Apparently, he planned on going ahead in his new musket armory to build not only the U. S. musket, but militia rifles of an Enfield pattern. Yet the record is confusing, with the increasing severity of his illness incapacitating him from work. From the master bedroom at Armsmear overlooking the great expanse of nearly 300 acres of green valley he had reclaimed from the spring ravages of the Connecticut River, to his new buildings being added to the factory by the dyke, Colt falteringly ruled his armsmaking empire. Daily conferences with Major Hartley; with James Dean Alden, captain in the Light Guard and Colt's personal secretary; with Hugh Harbison, secretary of the firm, kept affairs moving. While the fires of Mars glowed bright on the hearths of New England industry, work at the Colt factory was seriously hampered by Colt's indecision.

Three large buildings totaling 160,000 square feet had been erected at the rear of the original pistol making buildings put up in 1854. Of Portland stone, they rose four stories, internally braced upon a novelty in construction, one of the world's first buildings to use steel reinforcing. Actually, they were pillars of rolled wrought iron, made in four long troughs and riveted together along the side flanges. They stood until demolished by wrecking crews about 1956. About $100,000 had been spent on construction plus an additional $300,000 for steam engines, production machinery, and special tools. Building the tools, which was done in Colt's extensive pattern department where many great names of the New England gun trade first learned their craft, was hampered by an order from the War Department requesting Colt to turn out revolving pistols as fast as they could. This put every man on production work and there was no one left to build machinery for making muskets. The company had to buy machinery from other firms, such as American Machine Works in Chicopee Falls, but most important on the list of necessities was barrel rolling equipment. To make his pistol barrels, Colt used rough forged blanks approximately the shape of the barrel. To make his revolving rifles, he used blanks of cast steel bought from the steel suppliers, often foreign, such as Thomas Firth & Sons of Sheffield. But for making the long U. S. rifle muskets at the rate of a thousand a week he had to plan things differently and go into the primary barrel making business. This required rolls.

An iron barrel was welded from a flat chunky plate of iron, heated to sparkling forging heat and bent around a mandrel and welded along the lap. This length, perhaps three or four inches in diameter, round, with a hole in it, and a foot long, was called a "mould." Heated to welding heat again with a cold mandrel inserted, the mould was passed between two workmen, holding tongs, on opposite sides of special grooved rollers. The grooves in the rollers were some six or seven, and of "cam shape" in profile; that is, they had a lift or change in dimension resembling a cam if cut through at that part. The rolls were water cooled internally and in constant motion when geared to the power source which was flume or steam engine belting. Their diameters were calculated to give circumferences equal to the finished length of the barrels.

This process had been patented in England by barrel maker Osborne who was shortly afterwards confronted by more than a thousand hand barrel makers with their blacksmith's hammers in their hands threatening to tear down his Birmingham works. The rioters were dispersed, the barrel makers shifted to the pace of the new technology, and Osborne flourished. Barrel rolling became the accepted method of putting a hole in a long barrel before boring, reaming, and rifling.

Colt needed three sets of this machinery; England was the place to get it. He also planned to turn out a militia musket for private sale, because without the exacting full inspection of the Springfield musket he knew he could make considerable savings and yet get substantially the same retail price. The cast brass "heel plate" of the English pattern was cheaper than the more elaborately profiled iron U. S. butt plate, while the Enfield trigger guard was a one-piece brass casting including tangs for setting into the stock. The U. S. guard assembly, of machined iron, had a bow, trigger plate, two nuts to hold the bow to the plate, and required more finishing than the Enfield. Barrels were somewhat different. He proposed to get both Enfield barrels and barrels in rough form to finish up to Springfield rifled muskets, for he expected to obtain a contract for the Springfield type guns as well as engage in Enfield sales and service on his own.

Purchases in Europe

To accomplish this, Colonel Colt delegated authority to his brother-in-law, John S. Jarvis, to go to England and arrange many matters. Mitchell (James H. Mitchell, *Colt, the Man, the Arms, the Armory,* 1959) reproduces a great many interesting letters in full from this period. They reveal a picture of a man, Jarvis, not fully briefed by Colt, and of Colt fatigued and harassed by so many different demands upon his attention, and pulled out of his activities for a month or two by illness, that Jarvis wound up quite confused. In the letters there is more than hint of displeasure of the Colonel at some of Jarvis' actions; yet between one condemning letter the pace of events moved so rapidly and the boom in arms buying increased so much that the next letter rescinds the first. The Mitchell letters must be integrated with the correspondence, offers, and contracts, of Colt to the Ordnance Department, to determine what he really had on his mind.

At first it appears he sent Jarvis abroad to lay in small parts for making his militia musket. That he definitely intended to engage in manufacture of an Enfield pattern gun is revealed by his order of April 26, 1861 to Jarvis who was at the Depot 14 Pall Mall address in London. He told Jarvis to contract for all the Enfield barrels he could find in England and on the Continent, to make up into a gun "of the Springfield pattern." Jarvis had with him a bright Springfield 1855 musket with Maynard tape primer. The expression, "of the Springfield pattern," is clarified later on when it becomes evident that what Colt meant, or what Jarvis assumed, was to make a bright Enfield arm, steel mounted. He was instructed to buy all the plain military percussion locks he could find "suitable for making a good plain rifle like our Springfield or Enfield pattern."

More explicitly, Colt wrote (April 30, 1861): "In contracting for military percussion rifle locks to be used upon the arms we make here, you must be very careful to select a fine, strong simple model which is or can be got up cheap, and have them so uniform in size of lockplate and general arrangement that they can all be let into the wooden stocks by machinery."

While instructing Jarvis elaborately in lengthy epistles on what he should and should not do, Colt failed to realize the time lag in getting letters to Jarvis and in obtaining action and then replies. On May 10 he detailed his wishes on Jarvis' getting three sets of barrel rolling machinery—sometimes he wanted them shipped to the U. S. and other times he wanted them set up there and the barrels "bored, turned and proved at the Government works," though it is not stated whether the Enfield or the Birmingham Tower is meant.

The Mitchell-Colt letters indicate certain basic facts. Jarvis was authorized to buy ready-made Enfields. He purchased 1,000 upon his arrival in England and forwarded them to New York. Upon examination, Hugh Harbison, Secretary of Colts, informed Jarvis August 16, 1861, what Jarvis must have already known, that "In the lot of one thousand long Enfields received we find 115 second-hand guns besides a great variety of calibres." It is conceivable that in this lot there were .450 Kerr or Whitworth rifles, Enfield Royal Small Arms Factory Whitworths, and .577's and possibly a few .58's which both the London and Birmingham trade were beginning to turn out for the Yankee speculators.

By May 24, Colt wrote hoping that Jarvis had contracted for a large lot of locks, and also that Jarvis should send over Enfield barrels and small parts, to be finished up in Hartford and stocked there. But he changed his mind in the same letter, and urged Jarvis to have the fitting-up done in England or Belgium. Meanwhile, Jarvis did obtain locks, and shipped them; Harbison's letter of June 10, 1861, reflects receipt by the factory from Jarvis of 2,500 locks. This was first installment of 6,000 locks, since Colt on June 26, 1861, stated, "It is not probable I will want any more of these locks made in Europe after these first 6,000 are completed." The remainder of 4,500 locks remained in England subject to Jarvis' direction, and were fitted up into special Colt-Enfield Rifle Muskets. These arms were to have bayonets of the American pattern (letter June 14, 1861), but this was modified by Colt on June 21, "if time can be saved in getting the supply, viz. 2,500 (guns) which I authorized you to contract for."

The bands were to be split bands, no springs to the stocks; the lock and cone seat "may be the same as those made at the Enfield armory," (June 21 letter) but "Be sure while you make this change (cone seat to Enfield pattern) not to make the length of the barrels you order made any shorter than those made at Springfield and have all of them made like the Springfield in every other particular except the cone seat as I have before written (June 10, 1861). All the metallic parts must be finished bright like the Springfield pattern. The heel plate and Trigger Guard to be of iron . . . the locks must be brightened on the outside after case hardening as well as all the other mountings, except the trigger and sights. You must look carefully to your Springfield model for all the little details and have our arms look just like it, except so far as I have directed changes . . . (June 14, 1861)."

We therefore have an indication Jarvis managed the fabrication of 2,500 Enfield rifles, with barrels of Springfield length, 40 inch instead of 39 inch, fitted with the Enfield bayonet probably, and with iron mountings instead of brass, all finished bright except for the sights, cones, and triggers. These rifles took a year to finish and deliver. On March 31, 1862, Thomas J. Fales, the new secretary of Colt's who replaced Hugh Harbison, addressed an offer to Ripley:

> We have in port in New York in bond three thousand rifled muskets of choice quality and of the U. S. Government caliber, say 600 Long Enfield rifles complete, brown finish, bayonets, etc., and 2400 rifles bright finish of the U. S. Springfield pattern in length, caliber and finish, with regulation bayonets, snapcaps, and muzzle stoppers. These are the guns made after the sample you furnished us.

Fales offered the guns at $20 but the next mention is a telegram from Colts dated April 18, saying "they have received an application" for the Enfields, now numbering 5,000 in bond, and seeking to know if the Government wanted them. Apparently the Government did not want them, and some state or private purchaser took them. Whether these identical guns turned up

Colt in London in 1854 had experimented with Enfield rifles and understood the cost of fabrication. Specimen shown is Tower gun rebuilt at Colt's London factory with Colt patent rear sight and Colt patent oiler on ramrod. In middle is Potts & Hunt iron-mounted short Enfield, believed one of 1940 arms sold by Colt of 2,000 specially contracted for abroad. At bottom is Colt Special Model 1861, rifle actually manufactured in Hartford for the Union. Arm shown has had breech slotted and banded for very primitive experimental Colt cartridge conversion, but is otherwise regular for the model. Bright finish, or blued bands with color-hardened locks, were supplied under different contracts throughout the War.

later in some other importer-contractor's deliveries to the U. S. is not certain from studying the records.

Finished Enfields were sold by Colt to the Union. Jarvis had orders to buy "all the finished rifles you can find of the Enfield or any good military pattern at a cost not exceeding three pounds sterling each" (Colt to Jarvis, April 26, 1861). One thousand finished Enfields were shipped, plus 2,200 "Smoothbore Birmingham Muskets," as Colt named them, saying "they are the poorest lot of arms so far as yet received I have ever seen." Three hundred saber bayonet Enfield rifles were also obtained. It appears that Colt dumped these in the market somewhere, possibly at a loss, for no listings seem to reflect their being purchased by the North. He was not happy with them.

Jarvis also followed the colonel's instructions in contracting for "all the Enfield rifles you can get made in three months on the best terms you can get and at a price not exceeding two pounds ten shillings Sterling each." (April 26, 1861) On May 22, Jarvis wrote to Colt stating what contracts had been made, and Colt in reply June 10 after receiving this information stated that he approved. On July 9, Colt wrote a letter which was carried to Jarvis personally by the subject of the note, Davis Brown, "late superintendent of the barrel department at Enfield who I have engaged to return to Europe and take charge of the inspecting department on the finished arms which you have contracted for, and also the barrels, under your direction. He will no doubt require several assistants to keep the manufacturers up to the full standard of the Springfield or Enfield work, as no other quality of work must be received or paid for."

Colt urged Jarvis to condemn bad work liberally, and notes he (Colt) "shall not be in the least grieved if at least half of them are found so faulty that you cannot receive them." The arms that Brown was to inspect, rejecting all that would not pass inspection at Springfield Armory as to quality, were made under several exclusive contracts for Colt.

In the London trade, Potts & Hunt were Colt's prime suppliers in the summer months of 1861 and on into 1862. They made 4,000 Enfields with 39-inch barrels, price 65 shillings, which Colt approved "provided they are well made of the Springfield calibre and the delivery is made punctually." Potts & Hunt also were ordered to make 2,000 short rifles with sword bayonets, at 100 shillings, about twice what Colt authorized Jarvis to spend. Jarvis contracted for 6,000 long Enfields with the Birmingham Small Arms Trade, through Mr. J. D. Goodman at 65 shillings, approved by Colt "provided the calibre of bore is precisely the same as that of the U. S. Springfield Model you took out with you. . . . If it should so happen that the barrels of these arms are finished to the Enfield size and that alteration to the size of our U. S. Springfield pattern cannot be made, then they had better be laid aside and others of the right bore size substituted." Colt was quite sure he wanted only .58 Enfields, not .577. The difference in a clean, sharp bore, is not too much; a .58 U. S. regulation bullet slides down a .577 bore snugly, and in a .58 bore there is perceptible side-play. But when fouled, the .577 is difficult to load though the skirt and grooves of the .58 U. S. bullet tend to fold or collapse, allowing loading if one uses force on the ramrod. The Potts & Hunt sword bayonet rifles were too high-priced, and Harbison wrote to Jarvis August 20, 1861, saying:

> There is no prospect of getting rid of the short Enfields with sword bayonet in this country at a profit, and the Colonel again desires us to state that the short rifles with sword bayonets must not be forwarded to this Country, and he hopes that you have been able to dispose of them at cost or a small advance.

General Ripley had informed Colt's officially that Major Hagner "at the 5th Avenue Hotel" was authorized to purchase arms, and that they should call his attention to the fact they had Enfields for sale. In sudden inspiration, Colt sent a telegram to Ripley, offering the 10,000 long Enfields at $22.50 and the short sword bayonet Enfields, same price, "they are a number one article." Ripley replied at once by telegram accepting the Enfields, and followed up by a letter setting up the conditions for acceptance "if they pass inspection at New York Arsenal as good and serviceable arms." The letter accepted the short as well as the long Enfields. A following letter from Ripley dated August 31, to Colt's, refers to the "12,000 Enfield rifles purchased from you to be paid for in bond." Ill and in bed though he was, the nutmeg colonel still had effected a sale of the short rifles in spite of the general trend away from sword bayonet arms to long rifle muskets.

Harbison's letter of August 20 telling Jarvis to dump the Potts & Hunt short rifles was therefore followed up quickly by one August 27:

> My object in writing by this mail is simply to state that the Colonel has sold the 10,000 long Enfield rifles and the 2,000 short Enfield rifles to the U. S. gov't.

Rather wryly, he postscripts, "excuse all blunders."

While Jarvis had told Goodman rather sternly that since he was behind in deliveries with the Birmingham Small Arms Trade guns, Colt's would have to annul the contract, Colonel Colt was much disturbed at this prospect. It is not likely that Jarvis was able to salvage the deal. Early in September, 660 long Enfields and 440 short sword bayonet Enfields were received for Colt's account in New York. Six hundred of the long, 400 of the short, were delivered to Major Hagner September 11, 1861, and somehow Colt persuaded the major to accept the swords at an extra $2.50 for the short rifles were paid for at $25 each. A total of 2,680 long Enfields and 1940 short Enfields was sold by Colt to the United States from the Potts & Hunt order. But then Enfield sales by Colt cease, and no more are listed as being delivered to the United States. If Jarvis was able to rescue the Birmingham contract, the 6,000 long Enfields would have gone into the general trade in New York. It seems unlikely that Jarvis did rescue the sale, and Colt's Birmingham Enfields went into the melting pot of deliveries to Schuyler or Hartley or Howland & Aspinwall.

These Potts & Hunt arms are distinguished from British Government purchases by having the commercial London Company's proof marks on the barrel, including the provisional proof stamped on barrels which were in the state to also receive definitive proof, e.g., fully finished. A Potts & Hunt short Enfield in the author's collection with a New York provenance is stamped on the top flat of the breech "48," which may have been Jarvis' or inspector Davis Brown's serial number of the lot. The breech plug has been unscrewed, apparently a long time ago, and might have been done so by Hagner in inspecting the bores. The stud for bayonet is unusual, which is forged as a lump on the front band, the stock continued near to the muzzle. The fittings are all iron, not too common for Enfields; a snap cap is attached to the eye-pin on front tang of the guard. Of Enfield type arms obtained specially for Colt and actually delivered, it appears Jarvis shipped:

2,200 Birmingham bright smoothbore muskets, caliber, maker, model unknown.
2,680 long iron-mounted Enfields caliber .58, by Potts & Hunt (possibly 4,000 in all accepted, but perhaps also Davis Brown rejected the balance).
1,940 short iron mounted Enfields with sword bayonets, by Potts & Hunt.
600 long Enfield rifles, brown finish, maker unspecified (balance of the Potts & Hunt guns, most likely).
2,400 Bright finish rifles polished like the Springfield, iron trim. The maker is unspecified; probably it was also Potts & Hunt, since Colt had so heavily contracted with them, through Jarvis. If the locks bear any special markings, none have come to the attention of the writer at this time. Enfields engraved "Colt's" etc. should obviously hereafter be viewed with deep suspicion.
2,500 locks only, probably Enfield pattern.

Jarvis had further the responsibility to contract for large lots of barrels and for the manufacture of three sets of barrel rolling machinery. A lot of 10,000 barrels had been contracted for by LeMille of Liege, while 30,000 barrels were to be supplied by Millward of Birmingham. It was considered desirable by Colt for the English barrels to bear the Birmingham proof marks, as he supposed this would help him sell the finished arms to the United States. It was proposed to fit these barrels, finished up at Hartford, into Springfield rifle muskets. Liege barrels not proving to the liking of the United States, Colt directed Jarvis and their Liege agent, Baron Friedrich August Kunow Waldemar von Oppen, to sell the barrels. Mention is made of a possible sale to "Mr. Schuyler," so perhaps Colonel George Schuyler managed to buy the barrels put up into Liege arms, anyway. But another possible Schuyler is J. Rutsen Schuyler, and it is on a London Armory Enfield 24-inch carbine fitted with a Liege proved barrel, underneath the London Proofs, that the enigmatic stamp "JS-Anchor" appears. Could J.

Rutsen Schuyler have arranged for some Liege barrels to go to London from the abandoned Colt contract for fitting into special-order short carbines? But this is a digression, raising insoluble problems in history.

The barrels which Charles Millward had made for Colt were in the rough bored and turned state, not finished. They had passed provisional proof at Birmingham, and by September 17, 2,500 had been received in New York. But to comprehend the details of the rifles which Colt at last did make in the United States, it is necessary to revert to events of some months prior. On July 5, 1861, Colt agreed to make 25,000 Springfield rifle muskets, described as "of the exact pattern of the muskets made at the U. S. armory in Springfield, according to sample to be furnished to the contracting party," at $20 each. But the rifle muskets that Colt delivered under this and subsequent contracts was quite different from the Model 1855, or even the modified M1861 that was undergoing a facelifting for economy production that spring and summer of 1861.

Colt Methods

To the field of musket-making, Sam Colt brought novel engineering and quick, and large, profits.

Collectors have lately been surprised that the Colt Special Model rifle musket resembles the British Enfield. Harking back to the ill-fated Robbins & Lawrence project on Enfields for the British Government, they seek to explain this resemblance by suggesting that Colt used spare parts which he could buy cheaply from the junk dealers. They also suggest that Lamson, Goodnow & Yale, successors to Robbins & Lawrence, and Amoskeag, who worked in the same technical "atmosphere" as the famed and defunct Windsor makers, could somehow use the R & L Enfield tools in the production of the Special Model which they undertook. All this is unreasonable to the reasonably informed mechanical person.

Tools of Robbins & Lawrence, made for the 1853 Interchangeable Enfield, will produce only components of the M1853 Interchangeable Enfield, and no other. They would not produce an arm similar, but different. No, the differences in spite of the similarity prove the Colt Special Model as made by Colt, and by the more northern contractors, were produced on new tools made from new drawings of a new arm. But, why was it so close to the Enfield? The answer, we feel sure, lay in what today is known as cost-accounting or analysis.

In those days it was roughly known as figuring your profits. Too easily a competent gunsmith but incompetent accountant could figure his profits wrong and manufacture himself right into the poor house. Colt had done it a little differently. For in his vaults, at the time his country needed his technical skills, there reposed a complete set of drawings of the Interchangeable Enfield, and all the costing of each and every part. This is known to have been the case because Colt in 1854, testifying before the Parliamentary Investigating Committee which was studying the Gun

Trade in England, made a boast. It was not an idle nor a little boast; it undercut the Government price on muskets by an astonishing degree. In a formal letter to the British Board of Ordnance sometime before March, 1854, Colt wrote indicating his estimate of what the Enfield rifle could be made for, not, as he stated, with a view to obtaining a contract, but with a view to giving comparative values between properly capitalized manufacturers, and the then current system of hand fabrication.

"So confident am I that this system of manufacturing firearms is correct," he wrote, "and the only one by which arms can be made the one like the other, with economy, that I am free to say, what I have before verbally stated, that with one hundred thousand pounds expended in machinery, tools and etc., one million of rifled muskets can be produced at an expense of thirty shillings each. . . . (but) if you desire me to do so, at the prices above named, thirty shillings; and I would endeavor to do all the work in this country unless I should be interrupted by combinations of operatives claiming from me more than the present price of manual labor."

Colt did not make his offer to entice the British Government into giving him a contract; but if they should call his bluff, he was ready and willing to do the job at the price quoted, labor remaining the same. This means beyond question that he had broken his costs down into such definite terms as machine time to make a part of specific form and, in 1861, if he could persuade the United States to accept a part of specific form, that is, Enfield form, in a "new pattern musket," he would have a great jump over his competition in estimating his own costs. A thirty shilling musket ($7.50 equivalent) might be worth as much as $10 or $12 with the smaller quantities, higher proportional capitalization, and higher cost of labor, in the United States. But if he could adopt a pattern that would use certain hard-to-make Enfield parts, that he could obtain at low prices from specialists in the English gun trade, he would be still ahead of the pack on profits. Comparisons between an Enfield, the Springfield 1855, modified 1861, and the Colt Special Musket reveals some of the profit making similarities, and some of the engineering improvements.

Colt Characteristics

The lock differences are most pronounced. Colt's design is 100 per cent Enfield in the interior, and the hammer form is influenced by the Enfield shape, but is stronger, less liable to damage if dropped on the spur. Enfield and Colt musket springs will interchange, giving to Colt at once, without additional capital invested, all the spring resources of the English spring specialists in London and Birmingham. The "bridle," that part which supports the pivot of the hammer tumbler, and the sear screw, is heavier on the Colt model at the upper lockplate screw, than in the Enfield. Sears are about identical. The round stud of the Enfield plate, inside, which is cut across its diameter and against which the fixed limb of the mainspring bears, is much altered in the Colt plate. The Enfield piece is actually pressed into the plate as a separate piece; is liable to loosening or shearing straight across. In Colt's plate, the base stud for the spring is a solid rectangular lump made integral with the forging of the plate, and machined and filed-squared to give the strongest possible support for the spring. At the rear lock screw or "side nail," to use the English term, the Enfield plate has a threaded boss fitted into the plate itself, to give more threads than the simple thickness

Bright 40" barrel Enfield rifles Jarvis had made for Colt to sell have never been identified by collectors, but this wartime photo of Co. E, 4th U.S. Colored Infantry at Fort Lincoln, shows such arms issued in hands of troops. Close examination with magnifying glass confirms that bright barrels and bands are reflecting light and are not just retouched. Enfields held by first and second men in line compare with bright Colt Special Model held by third man.

of the plate will admit. This gives a more secure fastening of the lockplate screws. But, this boss is a cylindrical block like the spring stud which is pressed into the plate and welded before hardening and finishing. The plate is thin here and rejected Enfield locks often show a tiny crack in the plate itself at the top, thinnest portion, above the screw boss. The Colt plate is shaped with a wider outline at this point to increase its strength; also, the Colt plate is thicker with a bevel, giving added strength to the support of the tumbler. While main holes in the Colt plate will almost coincide with Enfield plate holes, as for tumbler, spring-fixing pins, sears, and screws, the outline of the Colt plate is different.

Its main changes are in areas where trouble was experienced with the Enfields because of their plate outline. For example, all side lock guns of the bar action type, with spring before the hammer, have trouble with the stock wood being damaged if for some mischance the mainspring should flex too much when the hammer is let down. On the Enfield, the hammer comes to rest with the tail of the tumbler bearing against the lockplate screw boss, and the mainspring hook, attached to the tumbler stirrup, at the bottom edge of the lockplate.

On badly fitted guns or those which wore in service, this point might cause trouble, with the spring hitting the stock wood itself, breaking the stock at the bottom of the plate. Colt's plate was increased at this point by $\frac{1}{8}$ of an inch to allow for excess motion in the main spring—"tolerance," we call it today, in manufactures.

In stock form, the Colt Special Model musket resembles the usual United States pattern, there being little to choose from between the esthetics of the Enfield pattern and that from Springfield. The butt plate also is standard U. S. Colt could buy this from subcontractors, from Springfield Armory itself, or could make it in his own works if practicable; the cost was not too important. The bands of the Colt gun are like the Second Type Enfield, split bands, fastened by a screw instead of solid held by a spring. The split bands reflected some special experience of the British in issuing the original Enfield with solid bands, spring-held.

Using a smoothbore musket with an undersized round ball, inaccuracy resulted from what is known as "balloting in the bore." That is to say, the ball would rest upon the bottom of the barrel, with its "windage" or loading clearance, at the top of the ball. Upon firing, the hammer-like blow of the powder burning would be transmitted to the ball and through it, as by a hammer, to the bottom of the bore. In cannon, this point was known as the "ball seat" and, using hard cast-iron cannon balls, a dished place soon appeared which required reboring of the cannon to a larger size to restore smoothbore accuracy. With a musket, as with a cannon, the effect upon the ball was to cause it to rebound from the elasticity of the barrel metal, throwing it upwards at the same time it passed along the bore. In bore time, the ball might strike three or four different parts of the barrel as it bounded along and out the muzzle. The direction it took on its last bounce affected greatly its direction of flight at the muzzle. To correct this, bore-fitting solid bullets were devised and the bores grooved, rifled, to afford stability by spinning to the elongated bullets in use. Balloting was no longer a problem.

During balloting, no constant stress was imposed upon the bore. Bands could encircle the barrel closely to grasp it to the stock. And simple spring clips could hold those bands against shoulders cut in the stock wood, with some assurance they would remain tight. Suddenly the armies of the world engaged in mass riflings of their old smoothbore muskets, to take tight fitting bullets. The Enfield with the solid Pritchett bullet was put into service in the Crimea. And the bands loosened up. Nothing could tighten them up again. The solid bullets in passing down the bore made an imperceptible but energetic "goose egg" passing the whole length of the bore. When the bullet came opposite each band, the hammer blow stretched the band a trifle. Repeated firing made this stretched band take on a permanent set, enlarged oversize. With a rifle, if you had *solid* bands, you had to put up with *loose* bands if you wanted rifle accuracy. Of course, as the barrel then loosened in the stock, you had to tighten it up again. The sensible way was to cut the band and fit an adjustable screw to draw the ends of the bands tighter together. Springfield Armory (as is so often the case) did not discover this sensible solution until the war had progressed for several years. In "mixed model muskets" using components from several basic patterns, split bands appear, and with the thicker wall ratios of .50-70 barrels post-war, this band permanent set became less important. But Colt introduced it from the first.

The purpose was not to make a superior musket; it was because he had costed-out precisely the work needed to make the Enfield split band in his boast to Parliament, and he knew how much profit he could make on that item. It was the Enfield split band he put on the Colt Special Model musket, minutely different in shape, but identical in cost, machine time, labor of polishing and finishing, and about the same in materials. And screws were cheaper to machine by the ton than special L-shaped springs that also needed precision stock drilling to fit them properly. It was better, cheaper, and could be sold for the same price as the Springfield pattern.

In the barrels he also made innovations which were better and cheaper, and could be sold for the same price. Along with small parts, he proposed to supply his barrel needs from England and Liege. The Liege barrels had been sold, and the English barrels of Marshall iron were so finished that final machining about the cone seat and rifling had to be done, and final outside work. On 20,000 of these, breech plugs were fitted in England. Locks also were made in England, though by whom and of what model is not conclusively determined. By June 10, 1861, Hugh Harbison was able to speak of the 2,500 locks Jarvis had already sent them. Later letters speak of not wanting more than the 6,000 contracted for, and the context is, they are speaking of the bright Enfield rifles, locks for Enfields.

By September 16, 1861, Colt's secretary, Thomas Fales, was able to write to Jarvis in recapitulation of the transactions, noting that they had received "per 'City of Baltimore' 1 box 4A containing 755 gun locks." It seems probable these locks were referred to by Colt in an earlier letter to the Honorable George Ashmun, dated July 15, 1861. Colt, to escape the heat of town and relieve his knee joints' inflammation by bathing in the mineral springs, had gone to St. Catherine Springs, "Upper Canada." He sought Ashmun's help in furthering the contract, and in getting Ripley to okay sending a United States Ordnance inspector to England. "The last mail brought me the important intelligence," he wrote to Ashmun, "that the parties who contracted to furnish me with my rifle barrels and a part of the locks to make the Springfield Rifled Muskets, are about ready to submit them to the regular Enfield proof and inspection, and as it is my privilege to have an inspector present to detect any imperfections, I feel that it is of the greatest importance to both the Government and myself that this work and especially the barrels, be thoroughly inspected at the manufacturers before shipment."

Ripley declined to send a Government inspector to England, and even to examine the semi-finished barrels when they came into New York. Though he perhaps felt he was setting Colt's mind at ease when he stated it was not required to have the 25,000 musket barrels made at any one place, just that they should pass proof and inspection in the usual manner. Since Colt had in the lot before him then, only 2,500 barrels, it is possible he did not import too many more in that state. As to the locks, nothing more appears on them, unofficially or officially.

Colt's Chief Workman

Chief engineer Elisha King Root had been with Colt since 1849. He became president of the company after Colt's death, January, 1862. Root was a quiet and methodical person, but a go-getter in his way. He had plenty of work cut out for him; Sam Colt on December 26, 1861, had signed an additional contract for 25,000 muskets, although not one had been delivered on the first contract by that time. No arms had been produced, but the Colt factory had not been idle. Three large buildings totalling 160,000 square feet had been erected to the rear of the original pistol making buildings which dated from 1854. But Colt's machinery suppliers were not always prompt and the entire rifle musket program was far behind schedule, complicated by the second contract for 25,000 guns, which Root agreed to accept as soon as Colt's death put the decision in his hands.

By February of 1862, 1,500 men were at work day and night on two 10-hour shifts. The massive flywheel

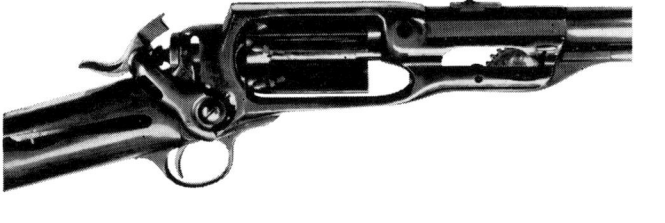

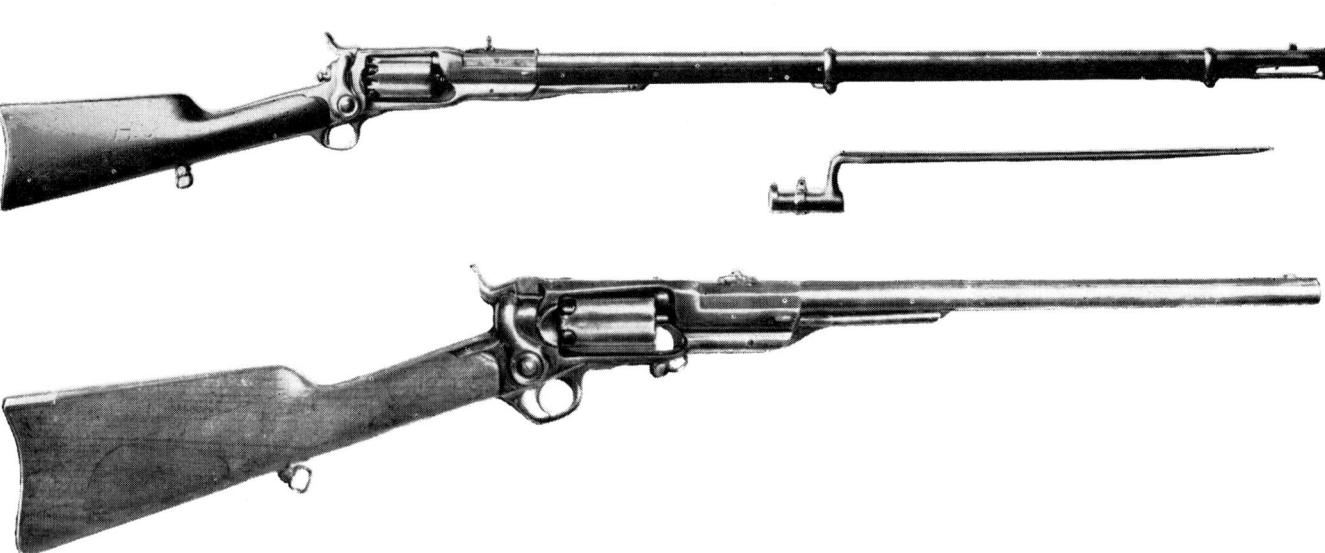

Sidehammer rifle design is attributed to Root though patents on most details were issued to Colt. Only Root patent element is creeping lever believed developed first in December 1849 but not protected until later. Cutaway model shows pinion gear teeth for lever and cylinder turning pawl in slot behind hammer, which acts on head of cylinder pin in reverse motion upon cocking. Long rifle is Heavy Military Musket nominally caliber .56 but can be loaded with .58 U.S. bullet. Angular bayonet type was believed used by Berdan's Sharpshooters though Colt Guard (5th Conn. Revolving Rifles) had sword bayonet version comparable to short Enfields. Bottom carbine is military .44 six-shot on light military frame. Latch is pre-war button type on lever end. Southern militia in "cold war" period bought hundreds of these.

measuring 30 feet in diameter ran constantly as the big 50 horse power steam engine drove the belting which ran the lathes and drills in the factory. The flywheel had been made by Colt's pattern men. It was so perfectly balanced that although it was sunk nearly 15 feet below the level of the engine house floor, the wheel did not appear to be moving when seen from the edge at top speed. "We have now received most of the machinery needed for the production of at last 1,000 muskets per week," wrote Eli Root to Secretary Stanton in February of 1862, "and the remainder will be delivered in a few days. Our small tools are completed, and we shall be ready to turn out arms as soon as the stocking machinery is delivered to us."

Root was writing to gain an extension of both contracts from Stanton. Despite the delay, it was easy for Root to satisfy Messrs. Holt and Owen that not only was Colts Company doing their best, but that they had the capacity to do much better. While the tools were readying, Root had been engaged in procuring materials for the guns. On March 26, 1862, the Colt factory president reported to the commissioners that "we have engaged 54,000 skelps of Marshall iron; have on hand 19,000; also have engaged 25,000 barrels of steel, solid, to be bored, and by us; we have also 20,000 barrels made in England, rough bored and first smooth bored; they have turned breech pins fitted. These breech pins may each interchange, although we ordered them by the Springfield pattern for this order. We have also ordered bar steel for 25,000 barrels in case our iron will not answer. Have machinery enough to roll over 1,500 barrels per week and to finish over 1,000 guns per week, (except in stocking machines which we are now extending). Have been much delayed on this work thinking that the Secretary's order annulled the contracts . . . Some of our order to Mr. Ames was taken by the Springfield Armory and this had delayed us. (I think) $20 per gun as low a price as the Springfield musket can be made for a profit, and consider that an order for 50,000 required for that price."

The original contract with the Ordnance Department contained a clause which voided it if Colt's did not supply the muskets on time. Because of the expense, not to speak of the profit, Root was anxious to have an extension of time granted. On May 16, 1862, Commissioners Holt and Owen recommended that the original contracts of July 5 and December 26 be confirmed and that they be allowed time to fill the order. Accordingly, on September 26, 1862, nearly a year after the first deliveries were due, a thousand rifle muskets were trucked by Colt's to Governors Island for inspection and acceptance.

It is significant that in speaking of the progress of operations, Root did not mention the locks, either from foreign sources or of his own make. The locks, it appears, were in arrears. Lamson, Goodnow & Yale had fallen heir to the Windsor, Vermont, factory of Robbins & Lawrence, which included the Robbins & Lawrence British-contract Enfield rifle M1853 machinery. They had a gold mine in the tooling, which according to Mitchell resulted in their selling off "lots of surplus Enfield rifle bayonet machinery for more than they paid for the entire plant. It was here, also," Mitchell continues, "that Whitney procured the machinery to make his 'Enfield' pattern arm which he tried unsuccessfully to sell to the State of Mississippi." We have shown that Whitney did not try to sell Mississippi any Enfield pattern arm, but that the Whitney Enfield appears to have been a bad job all around and was sold to a limited extent to the United States through Schuyler, Hartley & Graham. That Whitney might have obtained, say, barrel band die stamps, of this refuse equipment, is possible, for the Whitney "Enfield" has bands of the 1853 pattern—and that's about all of the Whitney Enfield that is from the Enfield model, too, while of the Special Model locks, not one part will interchange with the Windsor-stamped Robbins & Lawrence Enfield rifle lock, without major file fitting.

L, G & Y boasted that in spite of receiving the new model musket 60 days after signing the contract, they would have their work far enough ahead to get up gauges for the Springfield production of this gun; as they said, "we shall turn out the new gun before they do at Springfield." They were also making stocking machines for Amoskeag, and barrel finishing machinery.

In spite of this outside labor, they were prepared to deliver 1,000 finished rifle muskets two days prior to Colt's own delivery.

Amoskeag, of Manchester, New Hampshire, also built the Special Model '61. Their first delivery was August 25, 1863.

Early Troubles

Why Colt had so much trouble in turning in the first muskets cannot now be surmised. In the development stages, everything went smoothly. On April 19, the day after Fort Sumter was bombarded, Colt took the cars to Washington, but was stopped in New York by a flare-up of his sickness. He wrote to his friend Gideon Welles, offering the services of his factory, saying he would send Root to see him, and "shall suspend individual orders for military arms." The mails were interrupted but Welles queried his peer, Cameron, on the matter and Cameron responded that he could not say until he knew what kinds of arms Colt proposed to make, but that of his revolving pistols, "it is the opinion of the department that a sufficient supply should be kept constantly on hand, and we have none now."

Meanwhile, Colt had secured a Springfield rifle musket for his brother-in-law Jarvis to take to England as a pattern. That it was a Maynard primed gun is suggested by the express instruction that Jarvis was to get all the plain military locks he could—in our experience, all military locks are "plain," unless they be "patent," such as the Maynard or Sharps lockplates.

But at Springfield Armory on May 18, 1860, a board of officers had recommended changes in the M1855 pattern. While they approved the use of the patchbox, suggesting adoption of an improved round form, this was later rescinded. But they did suggest abandoning the Maynard primer, and "that no more arms of this kind be made after those in progress are finished." That the change was not at once instituted is shown by the existence of a very few dated 1861 Maynard primed Springfield and Harpers Ferry lockplates. Springfield superintendent George Dwight noted on April 30, 1861, that the Armory was on an 11½ hour shift, and:

> The omission of the Maynard Primer will not retard the production of arms and the machinery will be adapted without embarrassment to change for the percussion locks.
> The production is now 60 muskets per day. By the change the number will be much increased.

Colt then wrote to Ripley, having heard of these changes, and asked on May 13 if he could have three pattern muskets sent over. These were to have "such modifications and improvements as have been made by your department to guide us." At this time, Colt still did not have a contract to manufacture, but he was proceeding as if he did; his assurance was based on the realization that he could get a contract, and if he couldn't get a contract (for some fantastic and unforeseeable reason) he could still sell them to the states. At present, the amount of his risk was three Springfield percussion muskets, which he offered to pay for or return, at Ripley's pleasure.

Between then and May 10, the Special Model was taking form. On May 10, Sam Colt informed Jarvis he should have the barrels in England of "the Enfield pattern so far as the cone seat is concerned." This was because the Government had stopped the Maynard primer production, "and hence the cone seats will hereafter be made more like the Enfield barrels, and the cones located nearer the barrels." The reasoning behind this Colt also stated: "This avoids the necessity of forging so great a projection upon the butt of the barrel for the cone seat, and it will reduce the labor and expense of forging and making the barrels.

"I think in one of your letters," Colt reminded Jarvis, "you say that the barrel makers charged you one shilling extra for this very part being required to correspond with our Springfield pattern."

Economy in barrel making, cheaper split bands with no extra springs, lock parts some of which could be obtained from England and on which he knew costs to a mill; all these totaled the "improved" Special Model 1861 for Colt.

Elisha Root prepared a model musket for discussion with Ripley and Dwight; while the latter, following Ripley's orders, had been preparing a model musket of his own. Ripley suggested the lockplate should be flush with the stock, setting the cone further in, making a more direct flash to the charge. The only extant arms which would conform to this pattern are the odd Whitney special type-1861 muskets and short rifles. As a special hammer is necessary to strike in the correct alignment with the cone, using the new special barrel with improved cone seat, it is not reasonable to assume these Whitney arms are "mixed models." They are a distinct pattern and may reflect the intent of Springfield to make a thin lockplate arm with lock set flush, as a distinct model. Special '61 barrels do not fit regular '61 locks, nor vice versa. But with the pressure of production for war upon them, changing the lock tools was obviously undesirable; while reducing the thickness of the plate also was bad, since it reduced the bearing of the tumbler.

First actual mention of this Special Model officially is in General Ripley's letter to Springfield superintendent Dwight of June 15, in which he refers to making the lockplate flush without Maynard primer, band "after the fashion of the English," and any other modifications that might be advantageous. Dwight was to take all this into consideration and incorporate them into a model musket for Ripley to examine. As Colt was "about to commence" making similar guns, Ripley suggested that Master Armorer E. S. Allin and Root should confer on these changes to avoid delay and inconvenience, *"and use the result of their joint consultation in making up the new musket,"* Ripley concluded.

By June 29, Root had finished a sample musket in Colt's armory, which he was planning to send to Dwight for examination. Dwight also had made a model arm. It is probable both guns incorporated the modified Enfield bands, used the regular M1861 butts and trigger guards, and may have had two different locks. It is logical to think Dwight would have followed Ripley's suggestions; while Root would have used the Enfield parts inside the lockplate. But of interest is the fact that Ripley's suggestions seem to have originated with Colt in an interview. After being laid low by an attack of "inflammatory rheumatism" on April 20, Colt had recuperated somewhat and some time before June 15 visited Washington. On June 29 Colt telegraphed to Ripley that Hon. George Ashmun was acting in his behalf. Ashmun was authorized to "arrange a contract for rifled muskets of a pattern to be established for *future* make at Springfield and by us." As to the model musket, Colt promised to send Root down to Washington with "a sample of the Springfield Rifle which we have just finished with the alterations *suggested by you when I was in Washington.*"

Colt and Root went to New York; then Root continued July 1 on to Washington, taking the Colt Armory model musket. Ripley suggested one or two further points of change—what, exactly, cannot now be surmised. Root departed with the model musket, to call on Dwight and Allin at Springfield.

"When they have reached satisfactory conclusions in regard to all points, let a model musket be made, and send to this office for authorization, and a duplicate of it be retained at the armory," ordered Ripley. Root carried more than the musket, that July 5; he carried also the contract signed by General Ripley, calling for 25,000 rifle muskets "of the exact pattern of the muskets made at the United States armory at Springfield, according to sample to be furnished to the contracting party." Sam Colt signed the paper July 8, and the deal was made. To deliver, took more time.

As Root later testified before the Commissioners, the work force was turned to making pistols and they could not devote the manpower needed for making tools; hence had to buy them outside. Jarvis had managed to send over portions of the three sets of barrel rolling machinery, but not all the bits and pieces were in each shipment. Setting-up instructions were lacking, and this caused much transoceanic correspondence and further delay. Uncertainty caused by the colonel's ill-health contributed, and the armory force was partly diverted by remodelling Harpers Ferry rifles.

As Root's engineers readied the works for full-scale production of the new Special Model 1861 Rifle Musket, the colonel dabbled in altering surplus arms. A rifle which Colt remodelled is the U. S. Rifle, Caliber .54, Model 1841. Variously known as Mississippi Rifle, Yaeger, Yanger, Yerger, Windsor rifle, Whitney rifle, Kentucky rifle, this popular, highly accurate round-ball military arm was due for a face lifting wherever found from 1855 on. Adoption of the new .58 caliber caused many of the M1841 arms to be called in to one or another shop and there rebored and rifled to .58 Minie, fitted with the 1855 type long range rear sight, and either with or without stock changes, being fitted often with a front bayonet stud for the 1855 sword bayonet.

Colt-modified Guns

The demand for arms was great that spring of '61, and Colt obtained a sample "old Harpers Ferry rifle" as he wired Ripley on June 22, "and on hasty examination believe they can be bored up with sword bayonets so as to be useful to Mi(li)tia." Asking the price, he was told by Ripley he could have those on hand in the various arsenals at $10 each. Colt's letter of the next day, June 23, asked for a box of rifles to be sent from each place where stored. Coloney Ripley so ordered, telling Colonel Colt there were 11,500 of the rifles on hand at Watertown, Watervleit, Governors Island, and Washington arsenals.

Colt followed up with a request for more arms; then Ripley wrote in some heat that rumors had reached him Colt was offering these same rifles, unaltered and without bayonets, in the open market. Since the express understanding had been that by converting them Colt would increase the store of rifles generally available for war, a service for which he might reasonably also expect a profit, Ripley asked that Colt at once take steps to fill his offer by reboring and fitting bayonets as he had promised. Colt immediately disavowed any general intent to peddle the arms, but did confess August 2, 1861, "that the only Rifles I purchased of Your Department which have yet been sold are 468 upon which Sabre or Sword bayonets were attached. These were sold to our own State without a change of Caliber but altered to correspond with some they had on hand in order to make up enough to arm the 5th Connecticut Regiment uniformally (sic), which have just entered the service." Colt continued to say that sword bayonets for additional rifles had been started in production, presumably at Collinsville although he does say "are already in the works" as if he meant in his own factory. He promised to "soon begin to put them on and be ready to offer the altered Rifles for sale to our Volunteer Troops." During this period the 10th of January, 1862 passed, and with it Colt's death.

Toward the end of the month Ripley decided he wanted the rifles back, and was willing to pay the company for the added cost of the converting and bayonets. Three officers were recommended to mediate the value of the work: Colt's good friend Brigadier General Marcy, Major Thornton of the Contract Office, shortly to move into Colt's old New York premises at 240 Broadway, and Major Rodman, who may have been the only impartial man of the trio. Root on March 5 wrote that the Government's offer was agreeable and they had 5,000 rifles to deliver. Ripley thereafter authorized the commanding officer at Springfield Armory "to visit the Armory of the Colt's Arms Manufacturing Company at Hartford, Connecticut, and inspect the rifles cal. .58 with sword bayonets, which are to be taken by the U. States . . ." By May 4, the 5,000 Colt-modified Harpers Ferry rifles were shipped to St. Louis for the Army of the West. There is in fact indication that Colt had not just 5,000 of these rifles, but the whole 10,000. Late in 1864, Hartley, Schuyler & Graham wrote to Colt's, asking if they still had any Mississippi Rifles, as they, H. S. & G., had a stock of bayonets to which they wished to fit rifles and so dispose of them. Colt's answer is not known.

Two types of Colt-Mississippi rifles thus may exist. Specimens of the M1841 have been observed fitted with the Colt double leaf rear sight, such as was fitted to the Revolving Rifles. Whether these arms had bayonet studs is not certain; they were in use by North-South Skirmish shooters at Camp Perry, August, 1959. But from the record it would seem likely the Colt-sighted gun is the one to look for; those in original .54-inch bore would logically be of the 468 sold to the State of Connecticut for the 5th Regiment. The .58 caliber arms, especially if of a St. Louis or Missouri provenance, must be of the first 5,000. Whether additional arms exist is uncertain. The .58 caliber weapons at least may bear the marks of inspectors from Springfield Armory ca. 1862.

Special Model Colts

Of Special Models, Colt's fabricated 75,000 which they delivered under their own contracts:

5 July, 1861	25,000 contracted	25,000 delivered
5 June, 1863	50,000 contracted	12,500 delivered
19 March, 1864	37,500 contracted	37,500 delivered

In Haven & Belden's *A History of the Colt Revolver* it is stated that they delivered 75,000 on contract, and "nearly forty thousand more on sub-contracts for others who could not fill their orders."

Not usually reliable on esoteric bits of information, H & B drew this data from Prof. Barnard (*Armsmear*) who presumably in 1866 had some accurate sources. Such a flat statement is not opposed by contradictory evidence; it is probable that Amoskeag drew heavily on Colt for assistance, since Lamson, Goodnow & Yale were quite clear in their arrangements for parts and forgings.

That Colt was willing and able to make additional guns is reflected by a query from Major T. T. S. Laidley, then stationed at Springfield Armory, to Elisha Root on November 10, 1864. Laidley was authorized to purchase "such spare parts of muskets as you may *have on hand*, and may be required for repairs of the muskets of that model."

Root on November 18 countered with an *offer to fabricate* spare parts as might be needed. He enclosed a bill of parts and cited the quantities he could produce, based on delivering the "quantity named within three to four months." Laidley apparently did not buy any parts; and from the tenor of Root's letter it is clear that he had no vast stock of spare parts. The parts were, at the end of 1864, useless except to the Government.

Root's strict sense of economy that vastly increased the fortunes of the company he had been handed by the death of his friend would never have permitted so many as 10,000 sets of guard assemblies, butt plates, etc. to accumulate; while the offer of 20,000 to 22,000 lockplates and 25,000 to 27,000 hammers quite clearly indicates a proposal to manufacture to Laidley's order, not an offer of parts on hand. Having 25,000 hammers on hand as refuse work has given rise to the unrealistic suggestion that these were rejected parts, or that one third of Colt's machine production in the hammer and lock department was defective! While Colt replaced cylinders of the New Model Army revolver, or complete pistols, which proved defective, as well as violently complaining about the quality of arms issued from the assembly department at one time, the proportion is too high—Colt had no left-overs after the rifle muskets were delivered, so far as evidence today shows.

The New Model Colt

Colt's greatest contribution to the Union was the production of the New Model Army 1860 revolver, .44 caliber. This big-handled 8-inch round barrel six-pistol was carried in the fight at Brandy Station, saw service in the hands of Major General Custer; was a gift of supreme elegance to General Andrew Porter, General McClellan, and others "from the Inventor," and has been a favorite of cap-and-ball shooters in this century, as it was a weapon of necessity in the last. Early in September, 1861 General Ripley realized there was going to be one hell of a scrap to "save the Union." He began issuing purchase orders and telegrams which had the force of contracts.

> Ordnance Office, *Washington, September 17, 1861*
> Samuel Colt, Hartford, Connecticut:
> Deliver weekly, until further orders, as many of your pistols, holsters, new pattern, as you can make.
> James W. Ripley

Honor and Death

It must have been a source of great satisfaction to Colonel Colt to be thus at last recognized. Genuine disease, not disappointments, brought him to his death bed. On January 10, 1862, he breathed his last.

Sam was not one of Hartford's favorite sons—he was in fact looked upon as being quite an upstart, and his smelly factory a blot on the idyllic, pastoral status of Hartford as a genteel state capital. Sam once symbolized this forceful mating of peaceful old days and the songs of steel, in adapting special wood to pistol grips. This had come from the saintly Charter Oak, a tree in which legend had it the Charter of the Colony of Connecticut had been hidden, and in whose boughs and boles since then the legends of Hartford's gentility had become enshrined.

When a bolt of practical lightning laid the ancient tree low, the man on whose land it stood, I. W. Stuart, presented fragments of it to Colt who made pistol grips of the bits. These pistols, sometimes inscribed "Charter Oak Stock," were given to friends; but the friends sometimes had more than especial significance, as the handsome sidehammer pistol given to J. P. Moore, for it was Moore and the other "allies," Colt's trade distributing organization, which accomplished the measure of his riches in the last years before the war.

In the chill dawn of a New England winter, the mantle of death stilled the restless mind of Samuel Colt. Yet in his honor much was forgiven, and the office buildings and public flagpoles flew the old flag for which Colt had been among the first to give their lives, at half mast. The Putnam Phalanx militia company formed a double line through which his friends carried the colonel's bier, their rifles reversed at present arms. But though Colt himself was dead, the factory which he had created, the projects in being, rolled on to inevitable conclusions. His hand at the helm was Colt's associate of some thirteen years, and boyhood mentor, Elisha King Root, the genius of Collinsville.

The New Model Series

The 1860 Army was but one of a series of handguns in all calibers, characterized by the creeping lever and usually by a round "streamlined" barrel.

The creeping lever was designed by Elisha Root in 1849, and he applied for a patent on December 3. The patent was withdrawn and Colt for some years after that dallied with inadvertent slips of publicizing the design of his employee, Root, by picturing or suggesting it in patents but never quite saying it. At last in 1855 he allowed Root to take out a patent on a solid frame spur trigger revolver which embodied as its patentable features a system of rotating the cylinder that was not very practical, and on reissue, the creeping loading lever.

The lever as fitted to the Army had six studs which bore in sequence in cavities drilled along the underside of the barrel, a rack and pinion device. At any given moment in the working of the lever maximum thrust was concentrated on one stud. Hardened, these studs

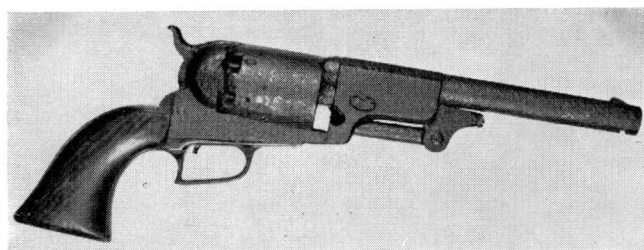

Some Colt's stayed South. This rusty relic Dragoon was obtained by author because it was such a wreck, and because it was a militia issue pistol from Massachusetts (MS) and because its serial number 10,500 was smack dab in the middle of Dragoon production, approximately 21,000 in all having been made. Gun is regular for type, with Dragoon latch (lever broken) and rectangular cylinder stops. Frozen tight when found in South Carolina, pistol through cleaning using Branson Instruments ultrasonic equipment has been restored to shooting condition.

pressed hard into the steel barrel and sometimes raised dents inside on the rifling.

The Army 1860 weighing two pounds 11 ounces was the production end of a three year search for lighter weight arms for the Dragoons and Cavalry. Originally in 1847-50, the huge .44 caliber Colt Dragoon models were issued for the use of mounted men. But four pounds is heavy for a pistol and the Dragoon revolvers never achieved the popularity of the 2½ pound Navy Colt M1851, though the latter was much lighter in caliber, being only a .36. To reduce weight was always a prime object.

Some time late in 1858 or early 1859 Colt had several experimental Dragoon revolvers made up. Their cylinders were fluted full length; forward of the trigger and bolt screws the frames were scalloped or reduced in width, while the barrel lug also was thinned out below the barrel wedge. The barrel breech instead of being octagonal was rounded to a continuation of the ordinary round barrel. The fluting of the cylinder, to reduce weight, seems to have also been an effort to equalize stresses in the chamber walls upon firing. According to Manly Wade Wellman, author of *Giant In Gray*, the subject of his biography, General Wade Hampton, CSA, originated this idea: ". . . the pattern of grooves on revolver cylinders, which, as I believe, was first suggested to the Colt factory by Wade Hampton of South Carolina."

According to Glenn E. Davis, quoted in *Butler And His Cavalry in the War of Secession*, General Hampton said that before the war he had used a Colt's revolver frequently in his hunting. The old style of pistol then had smooth cylinders. On one occasion this cylinder burst when Hampton was shooting it. "He saw that if the cylinders were grooved, the pressure when fired would be more equalized and the danger of bursting would be obviated. General Hampton then wrote to Colt, and explained fully his ideas, telling him if he agreed with him he could use the suggestion as his own. Colt patented the invention and sent General Hampton a very fine pistol specially made and thanked him for the idea."

The Navy frame from the .36 belt pistol was selected for improvement. Using a cylinder of enlarged front diameter, and a tapered inner chamber, it was possible to fit a .44 cylinder to a .36 frame. The fluted "rebated" cylinder first appeared on a model Navy pistol, the barrel of which had been pieced up by silver soldering lumps at the breech, to permit moving the barrel a little forward along a longer cylinder pin, and give adequate clearance for the .44 bullet loading cut. A Navy hinged rammer was fitted, the .44 cal. 7½-inch barrel being rounded, somewhat resembling the Dragoon barrel. This first experimental pistol proved a .44 was practical with rebated cylinder. Next, a small-guard Navy frame was taken, and cut for the fluted rebated cylinder. The barrel, partly machined, had been further pieced up with silver-soldered inserts to permit shaping a dirt shroud over the loading lever plunger. The lever, to give a "patent" claim to the arms (for Colt's other patents had just expired), was the Root patent creeping lever ramrod. The shroud about the lever plunger had a dual purpose: it kept dirt from getting in to jam the plunger, and it also could be tightened up by hitting with a mallet, to tighten the sideplay of the plunger, in factory fitting. It also was a streamlined, esthetic style point, highly distinctive and giving a "new look" to the old Navy frame.

This pistol was marked "M" on barrel, frame, and trigger guard, where numbers ordinarily appear, and was the model for the New Model Army .44. We understand it was "salvaged" during the transfer of Colt's irreplaceable museum from the Colt factory to the State Library about 1957-8, and is in the hands of a private collector now. The use of the small guard was not important, event though the New Model Army .44 was not made with a small guard. Adequate tools existed for making the correct large guard, and the use of the small guard appears to have been accidental economy in the model room.

On pistol "M," Nos. 37, and 78, the small Navy handle is fitted. It appears the issue up to perhaps 100 or more had the Navy handles, while Colt was getting

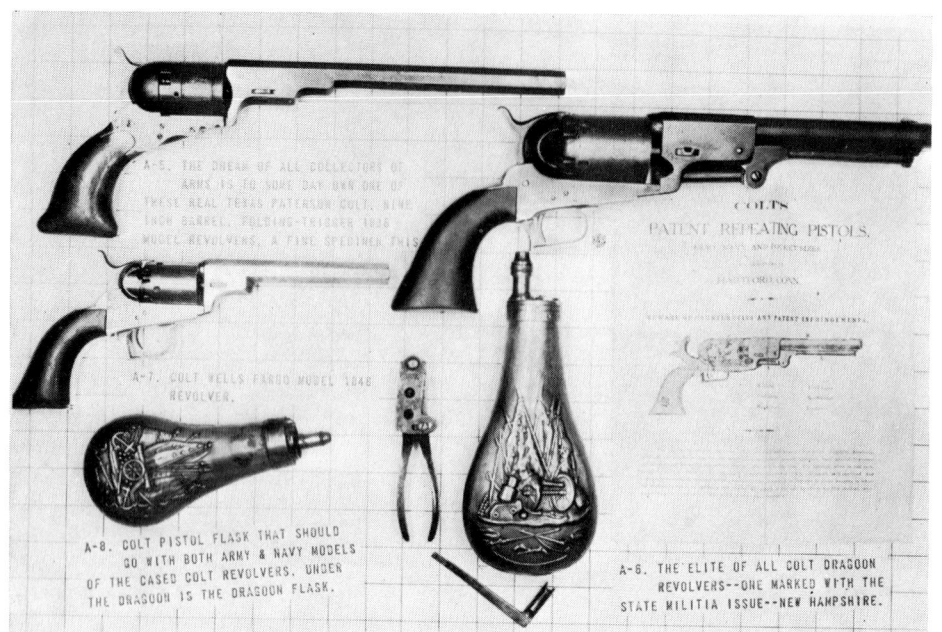

Somewhat superior condition Dragoon, but same Second Model, is this specimen marked on left of barrel flat NEW HAMPSHIRE. Arrayed with piece is special Dragoon powder flask, usual cone wrench and a late iron Colt bullet mould. Instruction sheet is of the period. Grip is marked WAT for inspector Thornton. Wade Hampton is said to have suggested way to reduce weight of big pistol.

tools ready for the increased handle desired by the Dragoons. Barrel length, originally 7½ inches, was also made optional at 8 inches during early production. Of the three pieces cited above, only "M" has the full fluted cylinder; the other two have a round cylinder, on which a naval battle scene is engraved, as is the ordinary New Model Army of later production. Generally, cylinders up to 6,500 were full fluted, and in most cases the flutes were stamped with the serial number in one, and in another, the fine mark PAT. SEPT 10th 1850. At the high end of this range, one pistol, 8-inch No. 5891 in the author's collection, has a round navy scene cylinder, though general experience suggests it should be full fluted. These round cylinders are, we believe, the exception that proved a rule of Colt's: replace the defective part or the pistol at once, and send the bad one to Hartford for examination and repair, at no charge. Old No. 5891 came from New Mexico, and certainly was one of the first year issue, in late 1860 or early 1861; a "secondary Confederate," from period and provenance. Perhaps it was one sent out to Texas agents for Colt, H. D. Norton & Brothers, in San Antonio. On March 25, 1861, they informed Hugh Harbison that they had seen a New Model Army "with the cylinder burst. It blew out at the place in the cylinder where the catch enters. Two of the places are entirely out and another one raised. The thinness of the cylinder here has been often urged as an objection to them and if many of them do it they will not sell at all."

Colt's endorsement on this letter set factory policy for the time and for a long time to come: "Replace the injured parts at once free of charge and if necessary furnish a new pistol and send the defective parts to us without delay. We are quite sure that this will not prove to be a general or serious difficulty." By April 16, 1861, Norton had returned 120 of the New Model

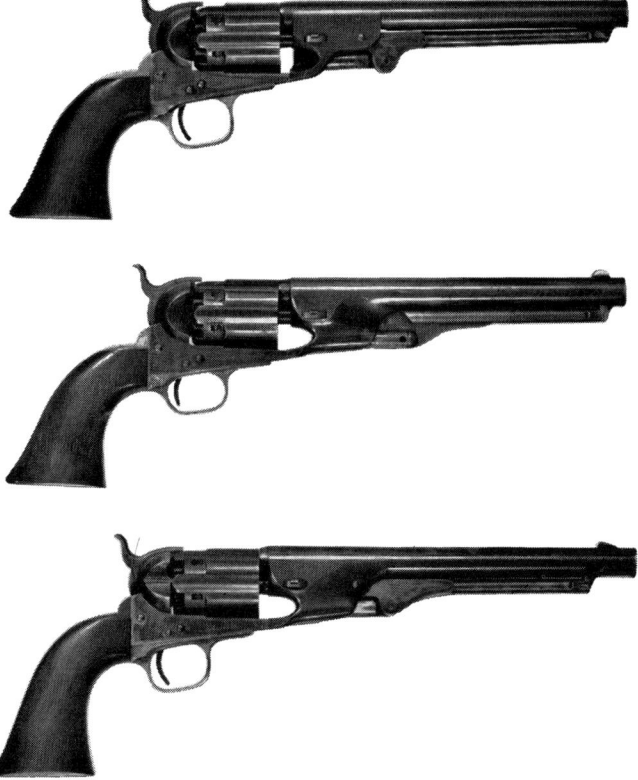

First experiment seems to have been using Navy frame with special fluted cylinder and barrel pieced up in manufacture to allow longer .44 bullet cut out. Middle pistol is "perfected" New Model Army .44 which is stamped M for model. Area of barrel which sheathes loading lever plunger has been added by carefully fitting pieces with silver solder. Bottom is test pistol reverting to hinged lever rammer, with 8" barrel but Navy handle which has been pieced up to increase to new Army length. Stop slots on fluted cylinder do not have the guides for stop bolt. While several versions of this hinged lever "M1860 Army" exist, the type was not placed into production.

cylinders to Hartford for "Mr. Lord's attention." It is the author's opinion that not only cylinders were returned, but complete pistols. In the case of salesman's samples such as No. 78 might have been, the gun was refinished entirely to extra quality blue and fitted with a cylinder that was actually a replacement. In the case of No. 37, this bears a date of presentation privately, "Capt. L. P. Richmond to Lieut. D. S. Remington Roanoke II, April 8, 1862." The finish is aged nickel plating, and the gun was almost certainly one "dumped" through Schuyler, Hartley & Graham or another one of the Allies, after the pattern had been changed to the larger Army-size handle. In the light of circumstances, it seems the gun was sold, then turned in with the cylinder burst, fitted with a new Navy cylinder, and then sent out to the Trade. By frame No. 153 an innovation had occurred; the long handle strap was "issue" and the frame had one extra screw in it for a stock recoil stud.

The long handle frame appears to have been pioneered on the hinged lever New Model pistols; at least, one of them in the Wadsworth Athenaeum collection, formerly in Colt's home, had the front strap lengthened from a Navy-size guard plate to accommodate the new iron backstrap. Not all of the hinged lever special Armies have frames cut for stock; those that do, are four-screw, and all fluted cylinder. Apparently the hinged lever Army was a bypath never followed up, for the creeping lever remained constant on the New Model series. The frame notches in the standing breech were for attaching Colt's patent "attachable carbine breech," a pistol-carbine concept of interest to the Dragoons in their training program.

The Dragoon trained as a mounted infantryman, using the horse to get him to the scene of conflict in a hurry (or get away from it if necessary!). He then dismounted and fought on foot as a rifle skirmisher. The buttstock attached to the pistol was a Southern influenced idea. First approved by Jefferson Davis when Secretary of War, for the single shot Springfield pistol carbine, it was later employed by frontier regiments of the Dragoons as an attachment for the Colt revolvers, Dragoon size .44, and later Navy .36, bought for the mounted service. Then in May, 1860, a Trial Board at the Washington Arsenal of frontier-trained officers convened: Brevet Colonel J. E. Johnston and Major W. H. Emory of 1st Cavalry, Captain W. Maynadier of Ordnance, and Captain J. W. Davisson, 1st Dragoons. On the 19th they filed a report of their tests between the 7½-inch barrel New Model Army .44, one with an 8-inch barrel weighing but a half ounce more, in competition with a 3d model Dragoon. The 8-inch barrel New Model pattern won out. Among tests was one often repeated, but never enough for the facts to sink in to the brains of the hoi polloi: an attempt was made to cause multiple discharge: "The arms were loaded and capped, and then loose powder was scattered around the percussion caps, and also around the balls, when they were so fired without producing any premature discharge, or communication of fire from one chamber to another."

The author once tried an even more severe test, loading a Colt .56 revolving rifle cylinder with full charges of FFg Black powder and the Government .58 minie ball, rammed down unlubricated. Caps were put on the cones. The cylinder was placed on the roof, and gunpowder poured over the cylinder face until all chambers were completely obscured; then fired with a long match. The powder "whooshed" up, but all bullets remained in place. A Colt's revolver, loaded with proper bullets rammed home, is as safe from accidental discharge or communication of fire from one chamber to another, as is an ordinary metallic cartridge .38 Police Positive Special. In cases where multiple discharges do occur, other causes must be found, such as corrosion pitting joining two chambers, or sympathetic detonation across two adjoining caps. Excess cylinder slap with possibility of shock from the standing breech setting off a cap is another cause; all mechanical defects which condemn the maintenance, not the design.

"There are a few minor points requiring modification, to which the manufacturer's notice has been called, and to which he should be required to attend in any arms he may furnish for the Government use. With these modifications, the Board are satisfied that the New Model Revolver, with the 8-inch barrel, will make the most superior cavalry arm we have ever had, and they recommend the adoption of this New Model, and its issue to all the mounted troops."

We think these minor points requiring modification embraced the Board's study of the fluted Navy handled 7½-inch barrel pistol, and the 8-inch experimental hinged rammer pistol, some of which were adapted for shoulder stock use, and one of which had a rear sight raised in a lump on the barrel rear.

After the trial, Colt adjourned with Secretary of War John B. Floyd to the Old Soldiers Home. There the Secretary tried a few volleys, and approved the arm with the changes. On June 9, 1860, Colt informed Floyd:

> I shall send to Col. May a specimen of this new arm so soon as it can possibly be got ready, that he may learn the changes which have been made which you so highly approve, which I hope will reach him for trial by the Mounted Men of the frontier before his official report is made to you.
> I shall have the perfected model embracing the suggestions made by the board officers & approved by you ready in a very short time, & will send or bring it to you for your approval to govern me in manufacturing to meet the wants of Government.

These improvements seem to include: fitting four screws and lengthening stock for attachable carbine breech; grooving the capping cut-out to help guide the caps easily onto the cones when mounted and trying to reload; 8-inch barrel. The creeping lever was acceptable and in production for commercial reasons, and it was this model that General Ripley ordered.

In 1857 and 1858, Colt produced a slight surplus of arms, 39,164 in '57 and 39,059 in '58. In 1859 in spite of the state militia anxiety, the competition of Manhattan, Volcanic, and Massachusetts Arms all cut into business; only 37,616 pistols were made. In 1860 the total dropped in production, but in that period Colt managed to sell surplus arms from prior production. For 1860, only 27,374 pistols were produced. Colt also was readying the tools for the New Model series, and with the manufacture of the great .44, production jumped way up: 69,655 pistols fabricated in 1861, of which 14,000 were the New Model Army, variously called "Colt's dragoon pistol, new pattern," and "new model army pistol," delivered to the U. S. directly by Colonel Colt. Less than 1,000 of the NMA had been made, bearing the ADDRESS COL COLT HARTFORD CT barrel stamping when Hartley wrote his warning letter of 18 November, 1860, cautioning about use of the Hartford stamp on guns destined for Southern purchasers (see page 331). The die was changed to read ADDRESS COL SAML COLT NEW-YORK U.S. AMERICA, but the exact break from the "Hartford" stamp is not pinned down; also, 7½-inch barrels alternate with 8-inch barrels in the second thousand series, and possibly before, though all the Hartford-stamped barrels seen were 7½ inches. Neither the Type One stamp of Hartford nor the Type Two stamp of New York have the customary dashes at ends. This second type name stamp is about

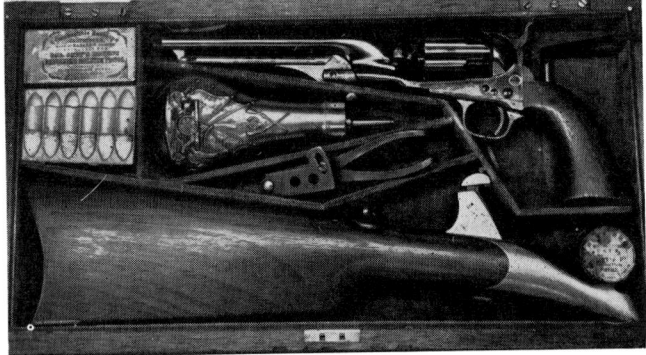

Production specimen New Model Army was cut for stock, fluted cylinder with fourth screw in frame for stock recoil. Serial No. 893 is typical of pistols made up to about 6500, though barrels 8" long predominated after first 1000. Barrel markings varied, Hartford stamp being abandoned early. Cased set shows same gun with stock, regular Army-size flask and "bowlegged" iron mould usually stamped 44H on side. Cartridge packet was invention of Roots but Colt invented opening string like red tape on cigarette package used today.

2½ inches long. No. 2948, for example, is regular in all details, fluted cylinder with "2948" reading from front in one flute, 7½-inch barrel of early side shaping, small New York name, no end bars, measuring 2½ inches in length, and 4-screw frame, fitted with cap screws. No. 3947 is also 4-screw, with date stamp PATD SEPT 10, 1850 in one flute as was customarily found, early barrel, but the third name stamp: —ADDRESS COL. SAML COLT NEW-YORK US AMERICA— about 3-9/16 inches in length with dash terminals.

No. 3712 is a fluted cylinder gun, lightly scroll engraved, and suspect as it has a 3-screw frame. The barrel is of the second type streamline profile, and 8 inches. The backstrap has been inspected by a Government inspector and bears the T mark—so the pistol is doubly suspect with its light engraving.

No. 6144 has a number only on the frame, other marks erased, round cylinder with a once obviously Navy scene engraved. The fourth frame hole is fitted with cap screws, not studs for stock. The majority of all four screw guns were supplied alone, not with stocks attached.

No. 12120 is a Government pistol, 4-screw, 8-inch butt with early barrel side.

No. 17678 over "o", once was fitted with a stock, the grips showing the marks, and the studs being old. The pistol has been reblued but appears to be first type barrel side, 8-inch. Name is type 3, 3-9/16 inches long, as commonly found on most specimens.

No. 17704 over "o" (an actual "o", not a zero as in the serial) had cap screws in 4-screw frame, early 8-inch barrel side. The round cylinder is mis-matched, but stamped with the full number, 21192. The first "2" interferes with the "o" in the COLT'S PATENT NO marking. Somewhat above this number the practice of stamping the last four digits of the serial became customary, and in some instances at the last, only three digits. Approaching 30,000 serial, the fourth stock screw was omitted. The extra labor of drilling, tapping, and assembling the two additional parts cost Colt's money. They were confronted with competition. They paid workmen more than Remington, but were being undersold by Remington, who complained that their gun was refused at $15, while Colt's were getting $25 for all they could make. At once Colt's negotiated a contract for $14.50. Chronologically, the time is about when Root would have made these minor economies to shave pennies off cost. They still made money, but not so much as before!

Thenceforth the regular New Model Army had an 8-inch barrel, frame cuts (for the stock if any commanders should insist upon it, but no stock studs as they were not essential,) and a plain Navy-scene round cylinder. The stock studs took up recoil of the pistol in the stock, preventing bending of the backstrap; as well, preventing bending if the gun should be accidentally dropped upon the butt stock. But the growing supply of a bewildering variety of carbines by Starr, Sharps, Cosmopolitan, Spencer, Jenks, Burnside, Greene, etc., caused the combination pistol-carbine, once thought so

Several thousand 4-screw round cylinder pistols were bought by U.S. and by Kentucky with attachable stocks but majority made up to about 30,000 serial number were supplied with cap screws in fourth hole.

highly of in Jeff Davis' tenure as War Secretary, to decline in popularity. Two pistols in the belt and two at the saddle bow was about all the rough and ready riders of the fighting forces could handle; a carbine buttstock was just in the way!

First and foremost a cavalryman's pistol, the New Model .44 was the subject of early printed instructions on loading and shooting. As the "Cavalry Manual" for 1863 noted:

The trooper having been well instructed in the manual on foot, should be made to repeat it mounted, first at a halt and afterwards at the different gaits, but the progress of instruction should be slow. Every trooper should be made to execute all the motions well (i.e., loading and firing) at each gait before passing to a more rapid gait.

Aiming, and especially at right gaits, requires some remark. Aiming should be practiced to the right, left, front, and rear. In aiming to the right, left, or front at a gallop, or at speed, the trooper should rise a little in the stirrups and incline the body a little to the front; the arm should be half extended, and the body turned in the direction of the object aimed at. In aiming to the rear, the right shoulder should be well thrown back and the right arm extended to its full length.

Firing should, at first, be executed with the greatest care and deliberation. The target should be 8 feet high and 3 feet wide, with a vertical and horizontal line, each an inch wide, intersecting at the height of five feet. The vertical line should pass through the center of the target. The troopers should be formed in front of, facing, and at a distance of 100 paces from the target. The firing should, at first, be executed at a distance of ten paces, but the distance should be gradually increased to 40 paces. A peg in front of the target will mark the point from which the trooper is to fire.

To commence firing, the instructor will cause the trooper on the right to move five paces to the front, turn to the right, move 30 paces to the front, turn to the left, move to the front until he arrives abreast of the peg in front of the target, turn towards it, cock the pistol, aim and fire deliberately; then turn to the left, move 30 paces to the front, turn to the left again, and pass to the rear of the troop, reload and take his place on the left of the rank.

To fire to the right the trooper executes what he did in firing to the front, except that he does not turn towards the target when he comes in front of it. To fire to the left the instructor causes the trooper on the left to execute, inversely, what the trooper on the right executed in firing to the right. To fire to the rear, the trooper on the right executes what he did in firing to the front, except that he turned from the target instead of towards it, and aims to the rear. The points where the troopers are required to turn in the exercise will be marked by pegs.

At first but one chamber of the pistol should be discharged by each trooper, and great care should be taken to guard against frightening the horses. The troopers should be cautioned to be gentle with them, and soothe them when excited. When a young horse is very timid, he should be accompanied by one which has courage. When the troopers are sufficiently instructed in the exercise, and control their horses well, three or more targets should be used. They should at first be placed on the same line, and 100 paces apart; but the distance should be gradually reduced to 50 paces.

Regular deliveries of the New Model Army to the Army commenced with Colt's offer of 500 finished pistols early in May, 1861. On May 4, Lieutenant Colonel Ripley ordered Lt. Col. Sam to deliver the pistols to Major William A. Thornton at New York Arsenal. The inference is, that as old "Wat" was assigned as Inspector of Contract Arms, these guns were accepted in the finished state and bear *only* Thornton's famous initials on the wood handle; not the detail inspection stamps on each piece of sub-inspectors. Within two weeks, Colt had finished 500 more New Model Armys, and again offered them to Ripley. Major Hagner was ordered to inspect them, as he was nearby at Hazardville, doubtless conferring with Colonel Hazard about gunpowder and ammunition. Hazard's Powder Mills fabricated pre-loaded percussion ammunition of the "fixed" variety, bullet attached to envelope of gold-beater's skin or other combustible envelope, containing the powder. A steady supplier to Colt's, for assembling into the ammunition which the girls put up in the fancy printed packages in the tiny Colt's ammunition works, Hazard also made cartridges on their own for many types of small arms. Hagner was ordered to inspect the 500 at Colt's, and Colt was

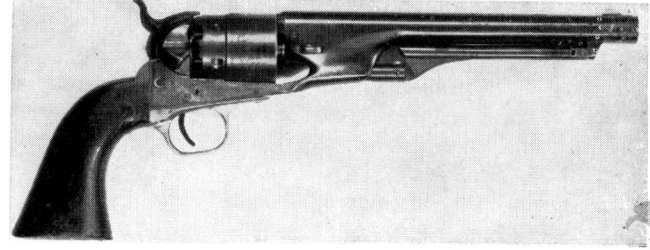

Regular New Model Army shown is G.I. with inspection stamp JT on stock. Dull finish replaced high blue polish in later production as Colt cut costs to compete with $15 Remingtons.

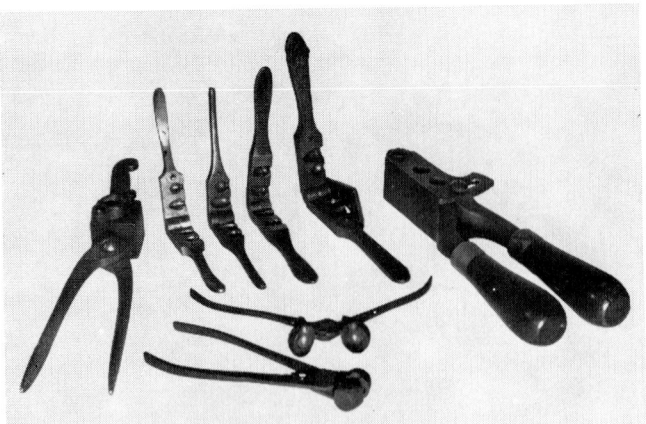

Moulds for Civil War arms include big .56 Colt rifle mould with wood handles and next to it double cavity Navy size iron mould from factory fire scrap heap. Mould casting two split bullets is evidently for Walch or Lindsay type, probably .31 pocket revolver; next is pepperbox mould casting one round and an odd oval bullet, and left in center a tiny brass Colt-type mould for .28 pocket revolver, make unknown. Left end mould is French for Light Minie .577 rifle. Opened and closed in front are round ball moulds for American sporting rifles.

directed to make 500 more, and Hagner would inspect them also, or as many as Colt had ready. Actually, Hagner inspected the lot of 500, plus only 300 more, which Colt delivered June 4, at $25.

The price was the old price fixed in Walker Colt days when Sam was planning to make only 1,000 pistols, and calculated his costs accordingly. There is reason to believe the Walker pistols cost only $11 each to make, leaving a fair profit to say the least. With the increase in capital, mechanization, and skills, the .44 New Model Army can hardly have cost as much as $8 —pocket model Colts representing a fair amount of machine work and finishing retailed at $9 and $10 in 1860, so the comparison is not out of line. There are those who marvel that Colt made so much money in so short a time, once he got going. There is little to wonder at—with his profit picture, selling $10 pistols for $25, it was better than stealing.

The requisitions from the field were piling up, and June 12, 1861, Ripley ordered 5,000 Colt's revolvers "of the latest pattern. The pistols are to undergo inspections and the price will be the same as allowed for the same kind of pistols recently furnished by you."

Between these and a purchase in March, 1862, exactly 23,300 New Model Armys had been delivered to Ordnance under several orders and contracts. Recently discovered shipping ledgers that were recovered from a dusty corner of Colt's by an employee of the "new regimen," Louis Hafner, who immediately recognized their great worth, shed new light on the Civil War orders. Summed up by John E. Parsons in "New Light On Old Colts," *The Texas Gun Collector*, No. 57, March 1955, it appears that in spite of charges against Colt of favoring the South, he sided with the North at the instant the lines were drawn. Shipments south of the Mason and Dixon line were halted with a final dispatch of 500 NMA's to Peter Williams & Co. of Richmond, Virginia, April 15, the day Lincoln called for volunteers and four days after the bombardment of Sumter began. However, prior bulk shipments of the New Model Army to Southern merchants included:

300 New Model Army shipped December 27, 1860 to Georgia
50 " " " " January 15, 1861 William M. Sage of Charleston, South Carolina
160 " " " " (with 80 stocks) January 17, 1861 William T. Martin, Natchez, Mississippi

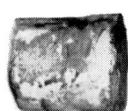
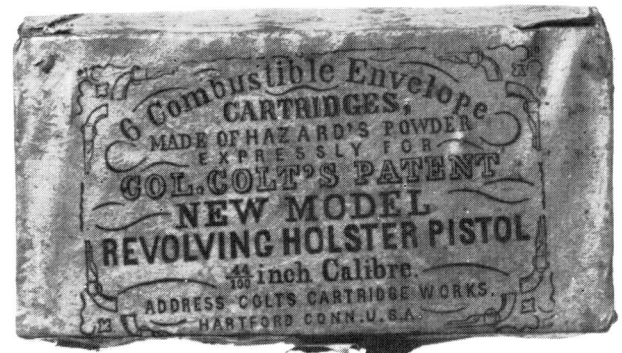

Cartridges for Colt's included tailed rolled government style loads for .36 but most .44's and larger calibers used pre-fabricated ammo of Colt patent made usually by Hazard's Powder Works or in Colt's own cartridge works. Shotguns had charge in two increments, shot wrapped separately. Commercial New Model Army ammo came in fancy package with pistols stamped in corners, but government contractors made plainly labeled packets showing different arms the loads were adapted for.

120	"	"	"	"	(prior to April 16, 1861) H. D. Norton & Brother, San Antonio, Texas
1100	"	"	"	"	(up to) April 9, 1861 Kittredge & Folsom, New Orleans
500	"	"	"	"	April 15, 1861 to Peter Williams & Company, Richmond, Virginia

A total of 2230 New Model Armys shipped up to April 15, 1861, in bulk orders South, as recorded.

More may have been so shipped, while numerous standard orders were shipped in case lots or assorted sizes to the "Allies." While the number of "Allies," that is, jobbers who signed Colt's agreements to handle Colt's arms primarily or exclusively, varied slightly, in 1861 they were: Joseph C. Grubb & Company of Philadelphia, Ben Kittredge & Company of Cincinnati, A. W. Spies & Company, Schuyler, Hartley & Graham, Cooper & Pond and Smith, Crane and Company, all of New York. There was of course John P. Moore's Sons of New York who aparently were Colt's New York customs brokers and import agents, and in Boston, William Read & Sons. Not previously recognized but shown in the dusted-off shipping ledgers was F. B. Loney & Company of Baltimore, and Child, Pratt & Fox of St. Louis. Cincinnati, Baltimore, and St. Louis shipments undoubtedly helped arm the South. The majority of these guns are in the "fluted cylinder series" of first production of the NMA, justifying the belief they rate as a "secondary Confederate martial pistol"; that is, not of C.S.A. manufacture but still widely used in the South. One of these pistols, unfortunately, has lost its identity since it was not offered by serial number listing; but about 1900 the catalog of the Great Western Arms Company of Pittsburgh offered for sale the Colt's Army revolver that killed General Zollicoffer. That it was an early 8-inch fluted 4-screw Army is listed, and the tale has its odd quirk of fate, for Congressman Felix Zollicoffer in 1859 had opposed Sam Colt's pleas for an extension of his basic patent.

In a petition to Congress, during consideration of which Colt stated privately that he would pay $50,000 to gain the extension and that it must be equally divided between the members of the House and Senate, Zollicoffer stood to block his way. Ultimately Colt was compelled to employ the Creeping Lever Ramrod in order to justify the claim of a patent, and to mark the revolver cylinder with a not terribly important patent, the September 10, 1850 protection (almost nearing expiration) concerning the rectangular stop slots and the small lead grooves into the slot itself. Zollicoffer resisted granting the extension of the mechanically-turning-the-cylinder basic claims of Colt's already once-extended patent, and the matter fell through. In the fall of 1861 the Kentucky State Guard split, many of the Confederates rallying around their general Simon Bolivar Buckner at Bowling Green, Kentucky. The Union men joined up with General William Nelson, reorganizing the Home Guard at Camp Dick Robinson, near Lexington. It was presumably at Lexington that the Ballard "Kentucky" carbines were issued, while to Frankfort in the next year a shipment of 1,000 Colt's New Model Armys with 500 shoulder stocks was sent August 25, 1862, to the Quartermaster General of the Union state forces.

But it was one of the early Colts that brought about the death of Zollicoffer, in an incident typifying the confusion of the period when uniforms were all of the "cadet gray" type and the efforts to issue distinctive field dress had not yet been successful. On October 21, 1861, Zollicoffer, now a Confederate general in command of Rebel Kentucky troops and Tennesseans, was defeated at Wild Cat Mountain. By the middle of January, Zollicoffer remained the only Southern resistance opposing Buell, and the drive was on. At Mill Springs on the Cumberland River in Eastern Kentucky on January 18, 1862, Zollicoffer was in command of four regiments, including the Ninth Tennessee. At the rear of this unit which was opposing the Fourth Kentucky (Union) with a brisk fire, Zollicoffer became convinced the Kentucky regiment was a Southern outfit and ordered the Tennesseans to hold their fire. He then rode to the front, where he met Colonel Fry, the commander of the 4th Kentucky. Zollicoffer stated to Fry that both commands belonged "to the same side" and that firing should stop. Fry assented and was about to order the 4th Kentucky to cease fire when one of Zollicoffer's aides rode up and, seeing that Fry was a Federal officer, opened fire, wounding Fry's horse. Fry returned the fire, shooting Zollicoffer in the heart. Whether Fry's revolver was one bought in the East, or from Kittredge in Cincinnati, or an issue from the Home Guards, the records do not reveal.

When Ripley ordered that the 5,000 pistols undergo inspection, the Ordnance Officer in New York by direction of Major Hagner and Captain Whiteley detailed individual workmen to act as sub-inspectors at Colt's Armory. A system of gauges to judge the critical surfaces and locating points, size of chambers, and align-

Pistols attributed to ownership of celebrated Connecticut soldier and governor, Joseph R. Hawley, are magnificently engraved pair of New Model Armys. Double casing shown is "standard," if such a collector's prize may be called standard.

ment with bore, indexing, fit and finish, almost certainly was set up. Similar gauges exist from the production of the M1873 Frontier Army revolver, and the Springfield Armory system of gauging involved such operations. The individual major pieces of the New Model Army bear sub-inspector's marks on the parts, but no gauges now seem to exist for this pistol, though other arms' gauges are owned by collectors, for the Mississippi Rifle, the M1842 Holster Pistol, and the M1855 Harpers Ferry Rifle. By March 1, 1862, 23,300 Army-ordered New Model .44's had been gauged; while on May 9, 1861, the New York Navy Yard was shipped 250 NMA's, presumably with fluted cylinders but not absolutely known; and to the Boston Navy Yard shipments totaled 250 on May 22, 1861, and 250 on June 8, 1861. On June 14, 1861, Ohio Governor William Dennison finally received 500 NMA's ordered in November of 1860. On March 1, 1,000 "Colt's dragoon pistol carbines, new model, each $31" were purchased. The listing describes the 4-screw Army with shoulder stock, $6 extra; serials were between 16,000 and 22,000.

The 1,000 with 500 stocks shipped to Quartermaster General of Kentucky at Frankfort August 25, 1862, list serials between 16,000 to 60,000. It is presumed numbers above 30,000 were not stock-stud 4-screw guns, though the stock itself could be hooked to either pistol. A last order to Kentucky, sent September 10, 1862, was for 100 pairs of pistols, fifty pairs (100 guns) having solid stocks, and 50 pairs having stocks with canteens. Colt had made some stocks with a tin lining, the spout with a screw cap (secured by a chain) issuing from the point of the comb. With a little untaxed bourbon mellowing in the canteen a Federal Kentucky trooper was a formidable opponent in a fire-fight.

Parsons has made an estimate of total New Model Army with stock orders, totalling 2,600 pistols of

Pocket model 1849 cal. .31" continued to be produced during the war and was quite popular as secondary sidearm for officers and enlisted men North and South. Blue and case-hardened pistol, bottom, is contemporaneously engraved (1862) on buttstrap, *W. Edwards;* was present to author from Navy Arms Co. owner Val Forgett who found it in South Carolina collection in 1960. Serial is 141896. Author also obtained recently full nickle plated '49-er No. 140512, made same month about 1862. Whether nickle is original at time of fabrication or redone for post-war sale has long been puzzle to collectors. Author believes this specimen is wartime nickle, but such finish is very rare.

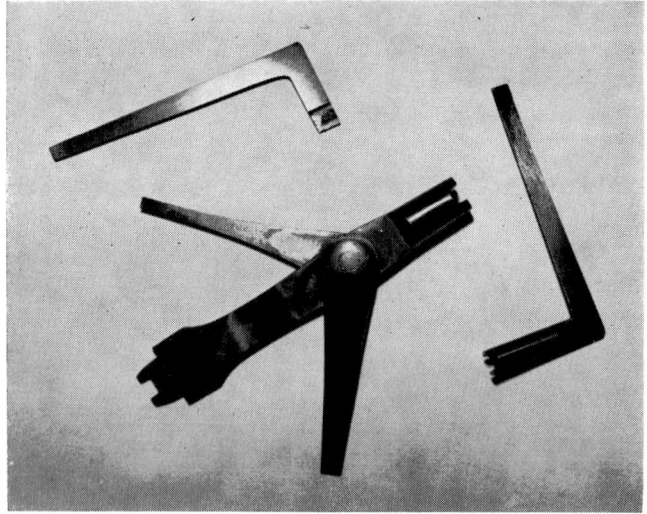

Angle screwdrivers were typical Colt accessory, round one having cone wrench for Army size and flattened one being for sidehammer pistols with cones integral with cylinder. Leggy job in center is almost unique Colt Revolving Rifle tool; end has been notched for later use in removing common rifle guard nuts.

which 1,900 had stocks attached (80 of these with canteens). Fifteen hundred were accounted for by the U.S. Ordnance and Kentucky State orders. Stocked Armys from December 1861 to August 1862 ranged 16,000-25,000, and 49,000-50,000. In 1863, 30 New Model Armys were put up for the London Agency, with stocks, in the 94,000 serial range, while 150 listed after 1866 were grouped in the 156,000's, 157,000's, 163,000's and 168,000's. Among great rarities in New Model .44 variations are 12 with six-inch barrels tabulated in the 46,600 range May, 1862. An earlier 6-inch N.M.A. pistol was presented by Colt about March 15, 1861, engraved "To Lieut. Nelson U. S. Navy from Col. Colt."

A hiatus in New Model deliveries occurred after 32,500 "dragoon pistols" had been delivered to Ordnance by April 15, 1862. Thereafter the works force was busy on Harpers Ferry rifles, remodeling, re-rifling, and fitting sword bayonets. Between February and June, 1862, exactly 9,900 of the .58 rifles had been okayed by the Ordnance team of Marcy, Thornton, and Rodman. May 31 and June 4 deliveries were 300 and 200 of the same, but without designation of caliber, suggesting they were unaltered .54's, all at $18.50. The sword bayonets fitted had a value of from $2.50 to $4; rifling of Hall carbines was done for 75¢ so Colt's could have done the Harpers Ferry rifles for about twice that, double the length of bore to cut. Base cost of $10 still leaves a profit of possibly $5—up to Colt's usual figuring. Then Root turned his eye once again to the New Model series. It appears that during this time sales of the 4-screw framed Army as a regular pistol were being made to commercial outlets; sometime prior to

June 6, 1862, Root altered the model omitting the fourth screw and got the okay of the inspectors to this change.

On June 6, Root and Ripley signed a contract for Colt's to deliver 15,000 Army revolvers caliber .44, "to be identical in all respects to a pattern to be deposited and approved by the Chief of Ordnance." The pattern was rapidly deposited and Root, racing to make delivery under the 10-day period allowed by the contract, shoved a whole 1,000 pistols at the inspectors who accepted them June 9. A new price had been negotiated, and it is thought that the reduction to $14.50 was not only because of the influence of Remington, competitively, but partly through reducing the machining on the frame and allowing a little less brilliant finish over all. The degree of polish on new-condition New Model 3-screw pistols of this issue is almost exactly like that of the Model 1917 Colt issued in vast numbers during a later war. Apparently the extra polish cost more and could be omitted to help eke out the $14.50 price Root agreed to, in cutting Remington's price half a buck. These, believed to be first of the 3-screw, were "holster pistols, new model." A second major contract was agreed to for 30,000 revolvers on August 14, 1862, at only $14. The last 1,000 of the $14.50 pistols was received August 15; the first 1,000 of the $14 pistols was delivered August 21. Though a pattern pistol was called for on this order as well, it is not believed there was any change in manufacturing to warrant the lower price, just the tremendous steamroller of mass production that Elisha King Root, who was bending 100 per cent of his will to the task, was building up.

When Sam Colt died, the local poet laureate and belle of Hartford society, Mrs. Lydia Huntley Sigourney, penned a wistful epitaph, ending "The like of him we lose today, we may not see again." She was to see Colt's like again, in the driving energy, the determination, of Elisha Root. That he was a more taciturn, self-effacing fellow, made him unlike Colt in some personal characteristics. In drive to get the job done and determination to stick to it, they were as brothers. A total of 24,800 were delivered under the 30,000 pistol contract, and Root applied for a further order, January 30, 1863. For 30,000 more pistols, this contract referred to the guns delivered under the contract August 14, 1862, and used for the first time in a Colt revolver contract, the terms, "They are to interchange in all their parts." The only prior Colt revolver contract referring to degree of interchangeability was that negotiated by Sam Colt in 1847 on the Walker pistol. These big guns, predecessor of the Dragoon .44 series, were "to interchange with slight or no fitting." The labors of Root at the big Old Armory along the dyke were best summed up in this unequivocating contract clause. All 30,000 were delivered.

The succeeding contract for the first time specifies what had been noted as "with the regular appendages" in the earlier documents. These were, "one extra cone, and one screw-driver and cone wrench to each revolver, and one bullet mould casting two balls to every two revolvers, and one bullet mould casting two balls to every two revolvers, and one bullet mould casting six balls to every fifty revolvers," as enumerated in the contract of May 25, 1863, for 20,000 Army-size revolvers. The last of the 20,000 was delivered to Major Hagner November 10, 1863; immediately thereafter, Root petitioned to be allowed to deliver a few more pistols. Hagner replied:

> Office of Inspector of Contract Arms
> No. 77 East 14th Street, New York
> November 14, 1863
> Sirs: You will please furnish 155 revolvers in excess of your contract, so as to fill order for supplies No. 8738, at same price (given verbally in Hartford).
> Very respectfully, your obedient servant,
> P. V. Hagner
> Lieutenant Colonel of Ordnance, Inspector

These 155 pistols at the special price of $13.73, 52¢ being allowed on each brace since no moulds were supplied, were received by Hagner November 10, with the last 1,000 on the contract, and the letter of the 14th was to regularize the purchase and set forth authorization for payment which apparently accompanied the letter to Colt's. From November 14 to the fire in February, no more New Model Armys were delivered.

Cessation of Revolver Production

It is odd that "the man who invented the revolver" kept his factory going by making single shot muskets. But deliveries from the Hartford works reveal a cessation of revolver production for the Government with a last delivery of 955 Colt's holster pistols, new model, at $14; 155 of them being without bullet moulds at only $13.73. These arms were received November 10, 1863; no more are shown as bought by the North from

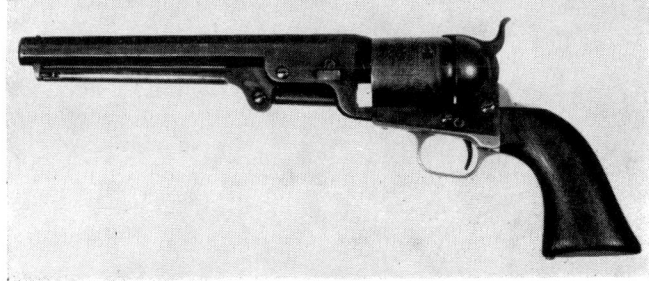

Military Navy Colt is US stamped on frame and bears inspection seal on grips. Backstrap of this pistol now owned by Tom Parvin of Illinois is inscribed to Col. Pleasants who was supervisor of the Crater mining in Union siege of Petersburg, Va. Pistol is said to have been presented to Pleasants while he was Provost Marshal of Lexington, Ky., by the "citizens."

Placed across old photo of destroyed Colt's Armory is bullet mould and London-stamped Pocket Model barrel, relics of fire salvaged from fused scrap. Old match box is symbolic of suspected Confederate arson though fire hazard conditions in factory made blaze of February, 1864, not totally unexpected.

that time forward. A great fire destroyed the pistol section of the factory, and collectors have thought the fire terminated production of the New Model Army revolver. But the fire was not until three months after the last of the New Model Armys had been made.

The Old Armory Fire

About 7 a.m. February 5, 1864, a fire was discovered in one of the drying lofts where wood cured under the skylighted roof of the Old Armory. The flames glinted through, shattered the skylights and the draught roared like a Bessemer, light spattered against the dark winter's dawn. Within the armory, the hungry tongues of flame raced as fast as a man could walk along the oil-soaked floors, curled in hot embrace around the riveted wrought-iron columns, and blistered the buff-colored Portland stone. The great steam flywheel slowly spun to a halt as smoke and flame crossed to the power house roof and licked avidly at the tallow-soaked oxhide belting. A veritable fuse pattern throughout the building, daubed with lubricant and tracing a lane from flammable roof to floor to each machine, the belting burned. In the parts room heat rose to melt brass, but not iron. Handle straps, bullet moulds, loading plungers, and trim, fused into glowing putty that meshed in the matrix cylinders from Dragoons, nipple wrenches, Navy moulds, and pocket model barrels returned from London and held as spares. The lard oil used to drench the machine-tool cutters, the sperm oil in the bluing department, the heavy grease in the maintenance room blended in a towering pyre of flame that seemed a belated pagan send-off to the soul of the late colonel, who in his lifetime had never carried insurance—and never had a fire.

With the ice-choked Connecticut River a stone's throw away, the fire fighting equipment somehow was not on hand when needed. With a great crash and sparks seen miles away the three top floors of the Old Armory subsided into the basements, while tons of irreplaceable machinery and essential patterns were consumed in the blaze. And so Colt's Armory burned. Behind the fire lines, stood thousands of Hartfordites, warmed by the flames. Root was there, and Richard Jarvis, muffled up and still in his night-clothes.

The H-construction of the factory with the New Armory or musket factory as the second limb of the letter, connected only by a thin passageway, saved the rifle muskets. Only the original armory built in 1855 along the river was destroyed, and much of the office building adjoining on Van Dyke Avenue. While Jarvis calculated the actual loss at about ¾ of a million dollars, the stock on hand was vastly more valuable, and as he put it, they would not have taken a million dollars in cash for the armory the night before, for what was destroyed was the production line for the New Model Army .44, "the best pistol by all odds I (Colt) have ever made for military purposes." In 1863 Colt had made 136,579 pistols; in 1864 by the end of the year, the Old Armory, rebuilt, turned out 10,406.

As previously described, in 1864 Colt's factory burned to the ground. Photos of the ruins reveal the total destruction of the world's biggest private armory. The New Model Army revolver equipment was totally destroyed, but the emergency continued. From the ruins, with the assistance of many of the models and papers saved in the nearby office and in the lofts of the musket buildings which did not burn, the great pistol was returned to production.

Close examination has not narrowed down the serial of the first "post fire" NMA, but it should be in the range of about 150,000. Soon after this the so-called "Civilian Model" made its appearance. While this model is actually a clear concession to the fact Uncle Sam wasn't buying any more shoulder stocks, collectors have confused it with the idea the gun was designed, stockless, for "civilians and officers." The type was merely regular production after the fire. Closer study of serials should narrow this fact. One example in the 90,000 series is known; but 90,495 is cut! But the shoulder stock idea died hard. No. 176660 is fitted with a stock numbered 17660, which does not hook under the breech like the true Colt's Patent stocks. Instead, it has a small steel hook that notches into the backstrap, and the Colt-type bottom catch for the butt. The gun is apparently post-fire, "Civilian Model," and whether the stock was fitted at Colt's in 1865, or many years later, is impossible at present to say truly.

Post-fire, the barrel stamp appears a little "larger" in appearance but almost identical in dimensions. Dash terminals end it, and the marking reads the same. A very few Colts 1860 New Model Army are also found numbered with an "L" preceding the serial, and stamped ADDRESS COL COLT LONDON. These were marked for sale through the Colt London agency managed until after the war by Charles Frederick Dennett and Baron von Oppen.

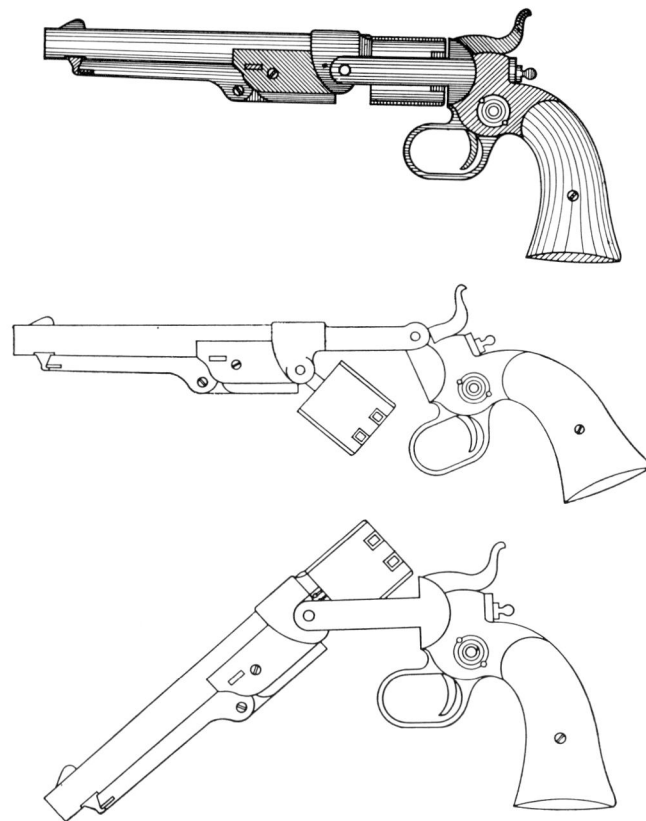

These modern drawings are ink reconstructions from fragmentary engineering drawings in pencil made at Colt's Armory during the war. They show prototype forms of army-sized hinged frame revolvers having long handle required by Board of Officers of 1860 but sidehammer design and stronger frame. No models appear to exist; drawings only survived the fire but author suggests this was planned to replace the M1860 pistol in production after November, 1863. From Hintlian document collection.

The New Model Army died hard. Favorite with frontiersmen, it was transformed by Springfield Armory and Colt's factory to cartridge shooting. Modified, it became a distinctive cartridge pistol, the Model 1872. And while the factory went back to the Navy handle for the great Frontier, not everybody approved the choice. Special long Army-like handles were fitted to target frontiers. And the Bisley handle strap is very much the proportions of the Army strap turned inside out!

Was it a bad gun? To the engineer interested in technical details, in contrast with the solid frame models of the competition, yes. But there were no kicks from the using services. The Yankee cavalry were glad to "give 'em a jolt with a Colt." The competition was more dangerous, and also, Root and Horace Lord, works superintendent replacing Root when the latter was elected president, had forced a gosh-awful lot of New Model Armys down Uncle Sam's throat.

For the first time reproduced in any firearms history book are the reconstruction drawings appended hereto, of the never-issued New Model .44 holster revolver that would have combined solid frame accuracy and strength, and metallic cartridge breech-loading capability in one basic construction. These drawings are our own completion of pencil and ink sketches preserved from destruction during one of the periodical pulpings of Colt factory records which depleted our historical sources along the Connecticut River from time to time. These sketches contain nothing basic which do not occur in the original drawings, but the originals from the John Hintlian Collection of Arms Memorabilia are too faint for reproduction.

They form the "missing link," we believe, to what Root and Lord were doing before the fire.

They were readying the works to fabricate a new model of arm, a model so secret that it could not be heralded in advance until prototypes had been built and pilot production run through. Admittedly, this supposition sounds like the guff penned some twenty-five years ago to sell four or five fraudulent "Paterson Walker" so-called "Colts," but we have nothing here to sell; just pencil drawings to which we have taken the liberty of adding completed barrel assemblies where a percussion gun is obviously drawn, or the hammer profile from one incomplete sketch to another more complete. It was to be a sidehammer revolver, of the type Root liked, though the patents on the earlier sidehammer revolvers produced by Colt's were not taken out nor invented by him. In the grip form and location of the trigger guard, the relation to the New Model Army proportions at once becomes evident. While both are illustrated as percussion cylinders, the potential for fitting cartridge cylinders is obvious. The rammer is apparently hinged, but of the profile of the New Model series. The barrel is fixed by a cross wedge in the front frame, as in the other sidehammer pistols. Releasing the cylinder for tipping the barrel down, or upwards, is apparently accomplished by pulling back on the center pin, the knob of which is shown behind the hammer spur. The sideplate and hammer are arranged as in the other sidehammer guns.

This frame conception is an advance upon the earlier sidehammer military pistols, being less bulky and more consistent with the approved form of the New Model .44. The solid handle frame with grips in two pieces is unusual but not unique for a Colt of this period, but the shape of the handles suggests a Remington, Rogers and Spencer, or any one of several other competitive makes. The proportions of the pistol indicate it is .44; the engineering drawings, which were full scale, show it to be about the same size as the New Model Army. The facts about this 8-inch pistol, no model of which is known, seem to have been one of the bits of Coltiana which actually did perish in the fire.

What the causes may have been for the failure of Root to sell more Armys to the Government is unknown. The musket works hummed day and night but pistol production in 1864 was a bare 10,406. The Trade had been hit hard with the sudden collapse of Colt's as a supplier. By the end of April at least they had not yet delivered any guns. From Louisville, Kentucky, wholesaler John Griffith & Son wrote on April

28, 1864: "We would take it as a favor if you would inform us about the time that you will probably be prepared to fill orders for pistols."

The lack of endorsement on this letter prevents any supposition as to when they *could* deliver, but the totals shipped that year make delivery prior to September, 1864, very unlikely. That some service was maintained is shown by a letter to Elisha Colt, Sam's uncle who had a financial interest in the endeavor and apparently rallied to help the old firm in its emergency. Sidehammer pocket pistol owner William Reed from Maine asked to obtain, for his gun No. 17637, "a small key with wedge to hold the cylinder pin in." Elisha was apparently a little new at the game and endorsed this, "Do not understand your description. Please send pistol and we will repair it at once."

The wartime output of Colt's in the New Model Series included the following patterns:

1. The New Navy .36, a streamlined creeping lever pistol en suite with the Army .44, but of course Navy size handle. A very few of these, probably under 100, had been made up with a special pattern of full fluted cylinder, when the change occurred to the smooth Navy-scene stamped cylinder in the Army series, so the Navy was changed to the Old Model cylinder to keep it uniform. Military deliveries included 1,000 New Model Navy at $22.50 February 17, 1862, and 1,000 more April 2. An added 56 were bought January 26, 1863, at $15, while commercial arms already in the trade were taken at varying retail prices when needed by the purchasing officers. About 40,000 New Model Navys were made.

2. New Model Police Pistol and New Model Pocket Pistol of Navy Caliber. Though appearing in two forms, this is, we believe, a basic model which was supplied during the war indiscriminately. The basic

New Model Pocket Pistol of Navy Caliber was .36 design built on .31 Pocket '49 frame by same size-increasing tricks as used in NMA .44 on .36 frame. Round cylinder is usually linked with octagon barrel but barrel lengths in ½" sizes (4½,5½,6½) allowed this secondary pattern to be shipped on same orders as new improved round barrel fluted cylinder pistol which had creeping lever and was also offered with 4½,5½,6½-inch barrels.

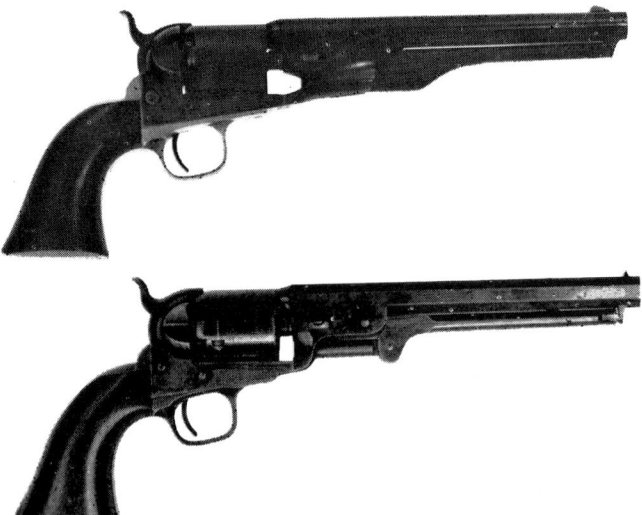

Production during war included large-guard M1851 Navy .36 with octagon barrel and streamlined New Navy .36 using barrel and lever of New Model Army. The barrel shaping setups are almost identical except for diameters to the NMA .44 and loading lever and plunger interchange, except the .36 plunger end is turned smaller.

pistol is the Pocket Model 1849 with rebated cylinder. In the New Model streamlined barrel, the loading levers are esthetically uniform with the 7½-inch Navy and first type Army pattern; the small framed barrels are all to half-inch lengths, viz.: 4½-inch, 5½-inch, 6½-inch. The rebated cylinder allowed fitting 5-shot chambers of .36 caliber, and the bores enlarged to this size. The factory designation was simply "New Model Small .36 Cal."

That this pistol, called by collectors "Model 1862," was ready in 1860 is reflected by a letter from Colt to Commodore James Smith, U.S.N., Chief of the Bureau of Yards and Docks at Washington. Dated April 25, 1860, the note refers to "one of our new model increased caliber," and states: "I caused to be got ready the pocket pistol for you with all the necessary fixings some two months since . . ." The round barrel creeping lever rammer pistols of this type seem uniformly to have cylinders partly fluted between chambers, on the enlarged portion of the cylinder body. A variant of this rebated frame is what, after the war, Colt's parts lists shows was termed "New Model Pocket Pistol of Navy Caliber." The cylinder is rebated, smooth, with stage-coach scene, octagon barrel. It is suggested by reading the voluminous numbers of orders from buyers all over the country who ordered these pistols by barrel lengths, to differentiate one model from another, as "NM 4½-inch" could not be mistaken for any other pistol, that both variations are the same factory model. It is believed Colt shipped both types indiscriminately to purchasers at the same price, and though both types seem to run to about 38,000 serial numbers, and both have low numbers, no *duplicate numbers* have as yet been noticed. The inference they were numbered in the same series is inescapable.

It was to the original creeping lever "New Model Small .36" that a great honor almost occurred, in January of 1861. During the fall preceding, Colt campaigned on the Stephen A. Douglas ticket for the governorship of Connecticut. He resisted the notion that

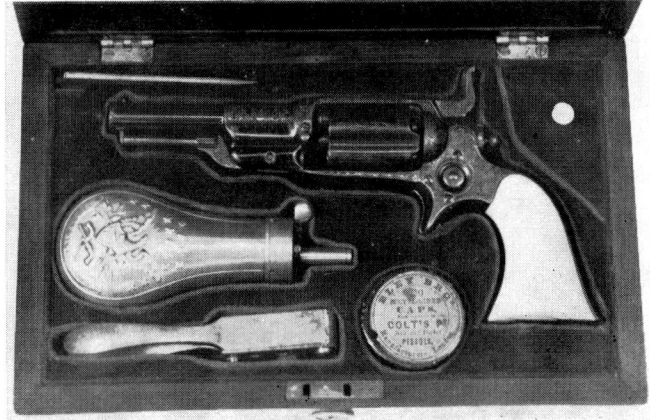

Elisha Root supported worthy causes, donated sidehammer pistol to Metropolitan Fair in New York conducted by U.S. Sanitary Commission, the "Red Cross" of the American Civil War. French-type casing may have been obtained from Schuyler, Hartley & Graham.

there would be war; preparations for the New Armory that was to make muskets were made in the faith that a "cold war" would give him rich profits. His efforts to line up parts and barrels through Jarvis for a militia musket showed his earlier thinking. Since 1808, the Federal Congress had appropriated annually $200,000 "for equipping and arming the militia." Colt had gotten his share of that in the mid-50's. But with the breaking away of the Southern states, with each state planning to set up its own army, muskets would be needed. Not only Colt, but P. S. Justice, Orison Blunt, Henry, Whitney and others, seem to have acted in this assumption, preparing prototypes or limited issue militia muskets which met with more or less success, as the Cold War turned to hot. Colt felt that Democratic leadership in Washington would do much to allow the Southern states, who were adamant, to go their way in peace, and to hold many of those, such as the great Old Dominion of Virginia, that were not so hotly tempered. His willingness to change the barrel marking from "Hartford" back to New York reveals his sensitivity to political matters.

He made a survey of the principal workmen in his armory, setting opposite each name in a little book a red mark for "Black Republican" or a blue mark for the Democrats. But his donations, his campaigning, though it polled him over 80,000 votes, did not bring him the governorship. Never one to enter a race in despair, he had intended to give his colleagues and assistants as the first token of victory, when he should be inaugurated in Hartford on the New Year's, a handsome cased pistol. The gun was the ordinary New Model Small .36 Cal., but the case was no ordinary case. Handsomely bound in embossed gold-stamped leather, it had the presentation marking "Jany 1st 1861" and "Dedicated by the Author to . . ." The title, sentiments which gave Colt 80,000 Connecticut votes, and lost him the governor's chair: "Colt on the Constitution, Higher Law, and Irrepressible Conflict." Few indeed were the book-cases ever presented, and the occasions sad ones, for they were tokens of aid, and remembrances of failure.

That Colt was politically sensitive, as just stated, is revealed by his action in the case of the Hartford name stamps. The first of the New Model Armys had the Hartford barrel stamp, but they were not unique. This mark was applied uniformly to all of Colt's arms —then changed back to the New York stamping.

A puzzle to collectors has been the presence of the words ADDRESS COL. COLT—HARTFORD on barrels for the octagon pocket pistols—Old Model Pocket and New Model Pocket Pistol of Navy caliber, and upon the Navy 1851 barrels of pre-Civil War manufacture. One historian, Perry Schumaker, *(Colt's Pocket Pistols,* Fadco, Cal.) suggested the Hartford guns were refinished arms actually of British manufacture, and that they were so marked that Sam could determine if those made of "English steel" were satisfactory or not, by the frequency of the word Hartford appearing in connection with repairs. That this is not necessarily a true solution is shown by London agent Charles Dennett's letter of December 21, 1860, addressed to one of the allies, John P. Moore & Sons of New York. Dennett, in following Sam Colt's instructions, had boxed up and prepared to ship to Moore "all the American manufactured Colts arms . . . I have sent 49 cases marked [CC] #1/49 J. P. Moore & Sons New York, containing 2,000 Navy revolvers & etc. . . . I will add for your guidance that the first 16 cases were part of 1 to 41 inclusive sent as nearly as I can ascertan (by invoice) on or about 1st of July, 1857, by the New York steamer to Bremen, consigned to Charles Caesar . . ."

Of this lot, some were parts of arms and were reshipped back to New York later, while 16 cases remained to become part of the invoice to J. P. Moore. These 16 cases contained an assortment of arms:

"These pistols, viz, 300 Navys & 750 Small (Pocket Pistols, probably 4-inch) are Hartford make & bear the stamp ADDRESS COL COLT HARTFORD—

"The 1,700 with moulds & wrenches in cases #17/49 are also American make—but stamp ADDRESS COL COLT LONDON—& have been refinished here by hand & proved here—but are of American manufacture . . ."

A solution to the problem of the different Hartford vs New York marking is suggested in Lieutenant (later Major) William B. Hartley's letter to Col. Colt from Washington of November 18, 1860. Hartley, along

Marcellus Hartley offered morale-boosting, gaudily decorated pistols in his wartime catalog. Special cast handles were made by Louis Tiffany, noted N.Y. sculptor. Handle detail (inset) shows allegorical figure on cast silver handle of New Model Police Pistol presented to Ibrahim Pasha, Governor of Adrianople, by Abraham Lincoln. Set of guns is now in Roosevelt Hyde Park Library; handle is by another sculptor, Ward.

with his adroit prosecution of Colt's arms and welfare among the military men in the Capital, also gathered information on the temper of the times which he relayed back to Hartford.

"You may rely upon it that not only will numbers of Southern states secede, but that they will pass retaliatory laws with reference to all the states that have prevented the execution of the fugitive slave law by their pennal (sic) bills. It will become therefore a matter of grave consideration for you to decide as to (the) policy of having Colts arms hail from the City of New York, rather than from the State of Connecticut—from the very town where *Wide Awakes* originated . . ."

Hartley's fear was a very real one of commercial uncertainty. In those insular days when the provincial, narrow outlook was the norm, the dread effect of boycott might be brought to bear on goods labeled as to some origin that proved noxious in the consumer's mind. If Colt, in going to a normal trade stamping of ADDRESS COL. COLT—HARTFORD, which serial numbers on Pocket Pistols and the Navy model indicate he did do about 1858, was risking loss of business in the South, Hartley felt it essential to call his attention to the fact. The Wide Awakes, a group of youthful Republican boosters whose distinguishing mark was the wearing of the wide-brimmed soft low-crown felt hat of the same name, had been organized in September, 1860, in Hartford. Wide Awake groups sprang up in many other Northern towns, parading, arousing martial spirit, damning the Southern Democrats and secession sentiment.

In urging the colonel to take care lest he lose supremacy in the Southern market, Hartley was not being disloyal to the Union cause. The temper of the times moved rapidly in those days of 1860, and not all wanted war, on either the side of the North, or the South. Many hoped that moderate tempers would pre-

Lincoln presented most beautifully decorated Armies in world to King of Norway and Sweden, and to King of Denmark. One of Swedish pair is shown. Gold inlay is highest quality. Grip carving is Scandinavian symbolism. Beehive signifies industry; anchor and scythe: fishing and farming. Cased pair stolen from Stockholm in 1967 and are still missing in 1997.

vail and, if secession occurred, that it would occur in peace. Manufacturers of all goods were looking to a continuance of their markets. Colt's factory and supply program was geared to an existing expanding market. A sudden contraction of it by means of an unpredictable Southern boycott on his Hartford-stamped guns would have put him near bankruptcy. His business correspondence often indicated how important to him the solvency of his accounts receivable were on the first and fifteenth of every month, when his large payroll fell due. His trade agreements were all made with a view to receiving payments regularly to enable him to meet that payroll. Having a lot of unsold guns thrown back upon him would endanger his payroll and cash reserve, causing him to lose workmen. A strict manager, Colt demanded that his men work for him a full ten hours a day "during the running of the (steam) engine," and "anyone who dus not care to do so, need not apply for wirk." Equally, he demanded of himself the same strict, just accountability to his men, and he would meet his payroll.

The safest thing was to restore the stamping of New York, which he did on pocket and Navy arms, keeping it through the duration and for some dozen years thereafter until the introduction of cartridge models again required new barrel stamps and the management felt sectional passions were subsided enough to risk the true office address on the barrels. The new mark, in one line, was: ADDRESS COL. SAML COLT, NEW YORK, US AMERICA.

Arms seen with the Hartford mark include the New Model .44 Army revolvers as well as the Navy '51 and the Pocket series. Dennett may have returned some of these Army .44 Hartford guns to Hartford during that December of 1860. As stated, on December 21 he wrote of shipping 300 Navys made in Hartford and stamped ADDRESS COL. COLT HARTFORD, along with 750 pocket pistols of the same Hartford-stamped nature. After Christmas, Dennett wrote to Colt concerning a following shipment to go out "by the Asia to New York on the 5th of January, contents: 150 Armys, 450 Navys, 510 4-inch (unfinished—276 proved), 250 5-inch, 150 6-inch, 1,510 in all, with mould and wrenches . . ." No mention is made of Hartford marking in this lot and it is possible the only pistols received in London were those Dennett returned in December of 1860, they having lain unopened in Bremen and London since being shipped from Hartford in December of 1858. But it is possible, in view of the efficiency with which Colt often supplied the London office with a quantity hot off the machines of the latest models, that the "150 Armys" listed were fluted cylinder New Model Armys—for some of these are known bearing Hartford barrel stamps.

Those guns sent to Moore, one of the Colt Allies, very likely went into the trade with some destined for the South. "I fear our Allies have been indulging their Southern customers to their fullest ability," wrote Hartley to Colt, without any trace of fear of any kind in his letter. Swords and belts, ordered from

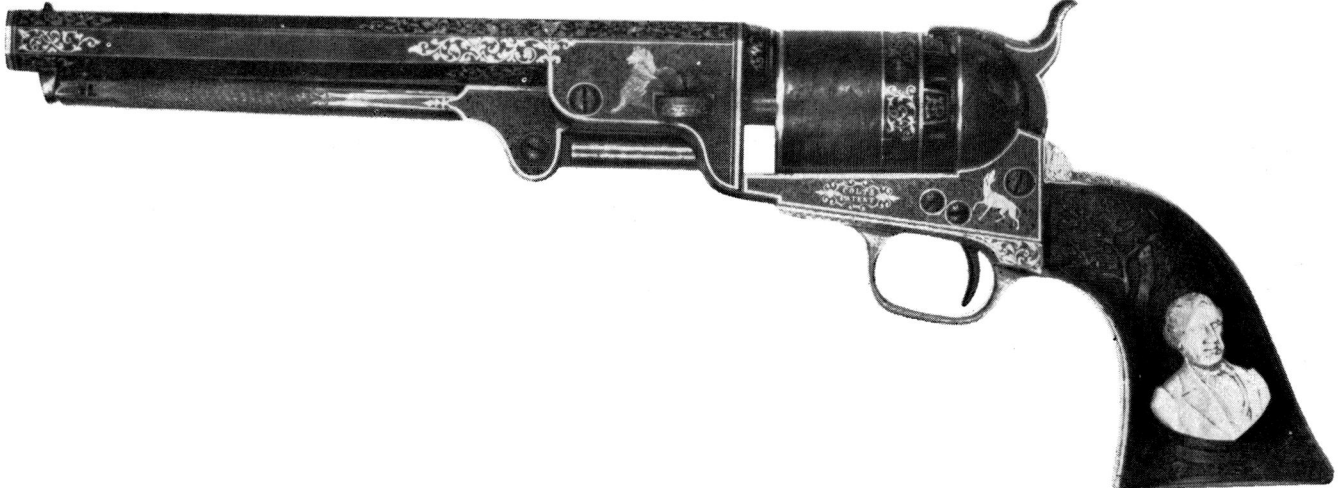

Navy 1851 was elaborately engraved and inlaid in mid-fifties but is supposed to have been planned for presentation to Abraham Lincoln. Special carved grip was not completed until war president's death, so ribbon presumably to bear dates of his service in office is marked with day of assassination.

Ames, by Moore, were to be shipped on South, said Hartley, "to Lamar, at Savannah, by steamer from New York, & the pistols if you get his answer. Please instruct J. P. Moore & Sons if he is to insure or not. Lamar will probably write an answer as to cannon, and if required, Ames will make them at 40¢ (40¢ per pound) . . ." So many of the fluted cylinder Army .44's, Hartford and New York stamp, have turned up in Southern museums or from Southern sources as to cause some experts to consider it almost a "Secondary Confederate pistol" by association.

In the Pocket Pistols, Schumaker suggests not more than 6,000 Hartford-stamped guns were made, in 4-inch, 5-inch, and 6-inch lengths. The earliest Hartford stamp observed was #164,816, while the highest he observed was #205,975. He rightly places the production period embracing this range from 1858 to

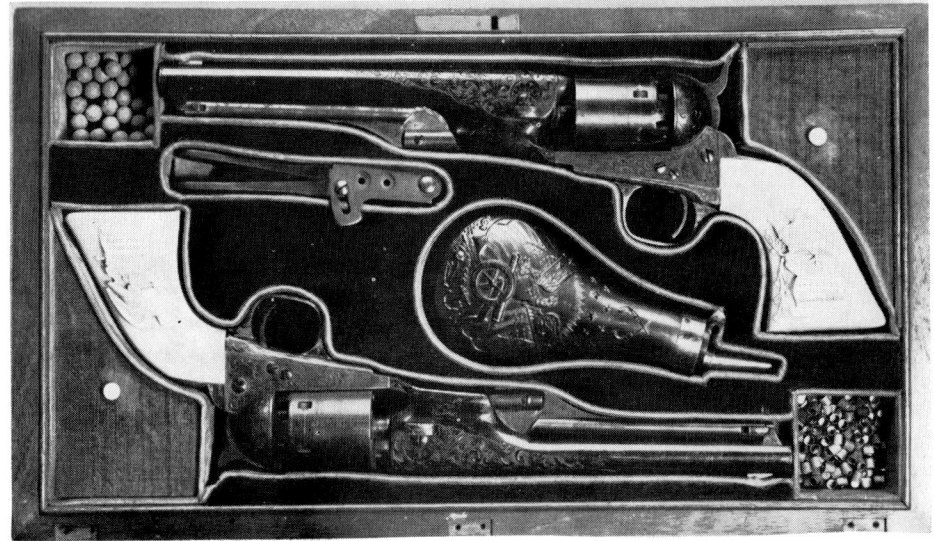

Cases for Colts varied. Top set of wartime Navy 36's is enigmatically marked "Division Aide-De-Camp." Original owner is unknown (from Jonathan Peck colln). Center is set of New Model Navys belonging to Gen. Phil Sheridan. Both this set and Navy 51's above have proper Navy Colt flask with set. Eagle handles are carved with names of battles in which Sheridan fought: Booneville, Chaplin Hills,

Stone's River. Bottom set, in Chernoff collection, is said to have belonged to Gen. George A. Custer during war. Pistols are New Model Navy 1861 caliber .36, but cased with Army size flask and U.S.-inspected government bullet mould, subsequently silver plated. Absence of Navy scene on cylinders suggests casing was done outside Colt factory, perhaps at Schuyler, Hartley & Graham.

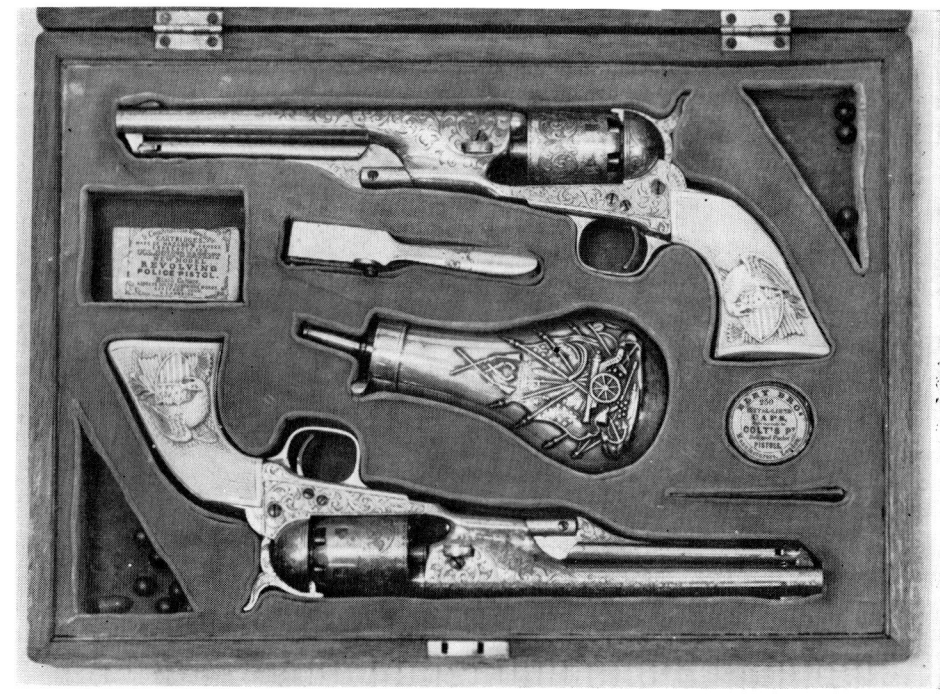

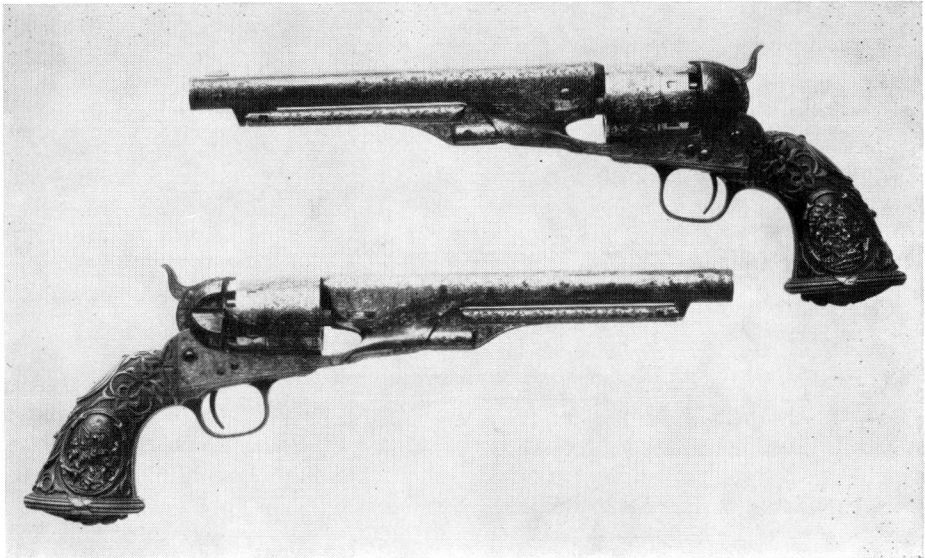

Post-fire New Model Army .44's are "civilian models" without cut in breech for stock. Highly finished pair in Smithsonian Institution have Tiffany grips with scenes of Union cavalry victorious in battle.

some time in 1861. Two sub-types of Hartford pocket pistols are tabulated: those with large rounded brass trigger guards spanning the production range, while some with large iron trigger guards have been observed in the brackets 185,200 to 186,000, and again in the 205,000 group. Though the subject is rife with bad guesses at best, those in the lowest group would appear to have included 750 shipped to Caesar at Bremen, thence reshipped still packed to London and two years later returned, still in their original cases, to New York for sale by J. P. Moore & Sons. The Hartford-stamped guns of 1861 "production" may have included some of the parts of arms shipped abroad and given the same runaround, for as Dennett wrote (December 21, 1860), "Cases 21 to 41, parts of arms, were re-shipped direct from Bremen to New York by Messrs. Miner & Co. December 1858 by order of Mr. Good . . . " And in the arms which he returned to Moore in December of 1860, as stated, were "510 4-inch, unfinished, 276 proved."

These are not more precisely described, so it is impossible to say whether they bore the name stamping or not. If they did bear London stamping, and were numbered, they may have included pistols that were to become oddities, two-line London-stamped guns of obviously non-London make, numbered in the Hartford-factory series (one #143,631 is known in the Art Livingston collection), and unproved since they never were issued from the British agency. Of the 510, 276 Dennett stated were proved—but evidently still in the white state, not blued. The remainder without British proof marks would not have been additionally stamped, merely blued and sold, after their receipt in Hartford. The demand for Colt's arms was so great, and the stamping of the name so deep, that it seems doubtful Colt would have bothered to erase the London stamping if already affixed, before finishing for the American market.

Some London-stamped guns made such a lengthy itinerary in their transshipping that their freight must have eaten up all of Sam's profits! As to the Hartford-stamped pocket models, at least one Sam Colt found a ready sale for in the "South." It was a 4-inch 6-shot .31, serial number not now recorded, with the engraving on the butt of *U. S. Police Balto Md.* Sam sold the gun to be used by the special police set up by General Nathaniel Banks when in 1861 his troops "saved Maryland for the Union." The Baltimore police proved adept at sequestering guns which Banks had ordered turned in, and they had to be replaced with more reliable law enforcers. In this interregnum, a newspaper reporter penned a plea to Colonel Colt asking for one of his pistols to protect said reporter in "this most miserably governed city," but Colt answered by what must have been a small sale of Hartford-stamped Pocket '49's to General Banks' men. Not even the very town where "Wide Awakes originated" could exceed the anathema in which the Yankees were held by the Baltimoreans.

It is said, "The credit for the revolver goes to Colt; to the way they were made, to Root." The labors of Elisha Root took their toll on him as they did on Colt and on July 5, 1865 Root died. Though he helped Colt to make revolvers, it was to him alone that credit for the Rifle Muskets goes. The date was symbolic, for it was the fourth anniversary of Colt's rifle musket contract. As it was said of another, so were both Colt and Root: "First in war."

CHAPTER 26

From Tredegar to Wilson's Creek

When Abraham Lincoln stood aboard the Federal gunboat steaming up the James River to Richmond, he glimpsed along the shore the broken shells of long brick buildings which had lately housed one of the world's most formidable ordnance establishments: the Richmond Arsenal, the Carbine Factory, the C. S. Laboratory, Richmond, and the great Tredegar Iron Works. In addition to private gunsmith contractors like Samuel Sutherland of Richmond, or fabricators large and small like the man at Wytheville who is thought to have remodeled the Hall rifles to muzzle-loaders, the Virginia capability to wage war was equal to the capacity of any ordnance establishment of like size in any nation on the globe.

Though the secession of the western part of the state prevented any rebuilding of the burned United States Arsenal at Harpers Ferry, Virginia had acquired a good share of the machinery for rifle muskets, and at the Tredegar Works possessed a facility for expanding production that was limited more by available manpower, than by intrinsic restrictions such as capital or know-how. What Lincoln saw had been systematically destroyed, by the Yankee captors of the vanquished citadel of the Lost Cause, and by the Confederate defenders themselves in the last days.

In a holocaust the like of which was perhaps not seen until the last days of Berlin in World War II, the most important capital enterprise of the Confederacy, the highly industrialized city of Richmond, was blasted into a Reconstruction Era from which it has taken many decades to recover. The removal of the Confederate seat of government from relatively well protected Montgomery, to Richmond, soon after the Virginia Legislature signed the Ordinance of Secession on April 17, 1861, was a move of double importance. Not only was Richmond the capital city of the richest and most populous state of the Confederacy, but she was also the center of capital, a great trading and shipping port, and possessed unusual manufacturing potential from the very first. Richmond and the Capital were synonymous—they would be defended to the very last!

Arms Fabrication in the Old Dominion

Even before organization of the Tredegar Works of Joseph R. Anderson, Virginia had a long history of efficient arms fabrication from Revolutionary times. The South was undergoing by 1860 an industrial revolution which the war accelerated. More than 1,600 mechanics were employed in iron works in Richmond by 1860; by 1855 at least 41 locomotives built in the Tredegar works were running on Southern rails; three other locomotive shops existed in Richmond, while in the western part of the state, at Wheeling, were two rolling mills. Five more rolling mills plus one at the Tredegar existed in the Southern states; two of these had been completed in Georgia in 1856 and 1858.

The South was not, as is often parroted by grade school children and their teachers, a purely agricultural society under "King Cotton," fighting the industrial North. During the decade preceding 1860, Southern politicians promoted Southern industry; the Norfolk Navy Yard was a ship factory of major importance, with a boiler shop that was a significant contribution to the Southern cause. From it were obtained 1,200 pieces of ordnance, more than 50 of them big Dahlgren "pop bottle" naval guns of the latest type, which were rich prizes of war for the Confederacy. Young Lieutenants Catesby Ap Jones and George T. Sinclair, formerly USN, now CSN, Friday night, April 19, 1861, spirited away safely 1,300 barrels of gunpowder sent to Richmond and another 1,500 barrels secreted inland, without the knowledge of the commander of the Navy Yard. It was from Norfolk eventually that the iron-plated steam frigate *Merrimac* ventured forth to revolutionize naval warfare.

"Great as was the loss of the ships," wrote Admiral David D. Porter, USN, later, "it was much less than the loss of guns." The essential heavy ordnance was shipped to many parts of the Confederacy. Porter had cause to rue their loss, for it was such great guns at Forts St. Philip and Jackson on the Mississippi that he later had to pass in reaching and taking New Orleans.

A contract for artillery destined for Fortress Monroe across the water from Norfolk was held by Dr. Junius L. Archer of the Bellona Foundry, near Richmond. A million dollars having been appropriated January 29, 1861, by the Virginia legislature for the defense of the Commonwealth, it was decided to pay off Dr.

Archer and refund to Washington the money paid to Archer by the Federal Government. Then the guns were taken possession of by the superintendent of the State Armory who deposited them therein "for safe keeping." The Tredegar was not the only cannon foundry in Virginia, but it was the greatest in all the South.

An enterprise of considerable size, the Tredegar Works was organized and rolled its first iron in 1837, just a few years after the first iron was puddled and rolled at Pittsburgh. Next were founded the Shockoe Manufacturing Company, later the great machine shops of the South, and the Virginia Foundry Company, and two more rolling mills. The Tredegar promoter, Deane, now took over the Virginia Foundry Company as a stock company in 1838, but the enterprise stumbled from lack of business foresight and was in real trouble when Joseph Reid Anderson stepped in, recently schooled at West Point and virtually a beardless youth (though he may have worn a mustache). Graduate of the Class of 1836, Anderson resigned in 1837 to become Chief Engineer of the Shenandoah Valley Turnpike, and built the road between Staunton and Winchester.

That a West Pointer should resign from the Army to take up a civilian career was not unusual in those days, regardless of placement in his Class or opportunities for promotion. West Point was nearly the only scientific school in the United States, and its graduates had a profound influence upon the industries of the United States from the earliest days. Anderson successfully saved the Tredegar by competing in Northern and foreign markets with English and Yankee ironmasters. Serving first as registered agent, he became in 1848 sole owner of the Tredegar Works. One of four major founders who supplied the United States with heavy ordnance, Anderson before 1860 had built the ironclad U. S. Revenue Cutters *Polk* and *Colorado,* and furnished the United States with 1,200 cannon. Tredegar iron was recognized as one of three leading American charcoal irons, superior to the English.

When a visitor in September, 1860, strolled through the Tredegar Works he beheld the Krupp of the South. Two rolling mills were busy supplying rails for the South; separate foundries were at work pouring artillery, railroad car wheels, and water pipe for Richmond. The blacksmith's shop had a steam hammer and 25 forges; the locomotive shops were finishing shiny engines for Southern railroads, while marine, stationary, and other applications of steam engine were being constructed. An engine and sawmill had been boxed up for shipment to Cuba, a new market for the expanding and flourishing Southern industrial economy. The existing shops were from 140 to 180 feet long; there were two great machine shop buildings three stories and four stories high; the noise of tools at work in them deafening.

Nearby, a whole new plant for making cast steel, metal precious as diamonds for small arms manufacture, was being erected. Business troubles had shaken the Tredegar in 1859, but Anderson, quick thinking as a secessionist, and enterprising to take advantage of the demand for state armies, sent out a circular letter to the governors of ten Southern states, offering them his foundry and twenty years experience. "Will make anything you like, prices same as to United States Government" was its sentiment. Five days later South Carolina declared itself an independent country.

The record of the Tredegar in the years that fol-

Blackened shell of Richmond industrial center greeted eyes of Union President Lincoln as he arrived at capital of South in 1865. View shows rail sheds at left, Tredegar partially visible in background right. Destruction by Union guns and official C.S. burning was complete as any saturation bombing attack on a city in WWII.

Virginia State Armory was activated 1860, fitted out with new machinery and phased into Richmond's war production to make Rifle Muskets of the latest Springfield pattern. Arms made and finished there were top quality.

lowed was impressive. The powder rolls for the great gunpowder works which General Rains set up at Augusta, largest powder factory in the world, were made here. The plate of the *Merrimac*, rolled two inches thick and too tough to punch—it had to be drilled for the rivet holes—was the most famous production. But naval torpedoes, and Brooke guns, the iron "Napoleons" which replaced the brass cannon in C. S. service, were developed at Tredegar, as well as the Williams repeating cannon. To the rank and file, Colonel Anderson's greatest contribution was in the machinery which he prepared to re-activate the State Armory in 1861. During an enlargement of the Armory in 1862, Tredegar supplied the boiler equipment and machine-base castings. On these tools, with partly captured fixtures and partly new fixtures designed and made by draughtsmen and machinists at Tredegar, General Gorgas built the Richmond Rifle Muskets and Carbines, and later the Sharps Carbines, with which the South opposed the might of the North. Between July 1, 1861, and January 1, 1865, the Richmond Arsenal issued 323,231 rifle muskets cleaned, repaired, renovated, and actually made there (estimated at about 40,000), and 30,067 cavalry arms, carbines principally. This was the spirit of Richmond.

Ordnance Status in Virginia in 1861

On the day Virginia signed the Ordinance of Secession, Adjutant General Richardson reported to Governor Letcher on the condition of the state forces. Seven troops of cavalry had been formed, armed with sabers and cavalry percussion pistols, 350 men in all. One hundred men, two troops, had sabers and cavalry musketoons. Thirty-six troops, 1,800 men, had sabers and revolvers, almost certainly the Colt Navy pattern of 1851, while 22 troops, 1,100 men, had sabers only; and 29 troops had been formed, 1,450, which had no arms at all. The artillery was in an equally irregular state so far as equipment went. Twelve companies of 600 men were armed with 6-pounder field guns with carriages and implements complete, but only 11 companies had artillery swords. One company, 50 men, had 6-pounders, swords, and sappers and miners' musketoons. One company, armed with 6-pounders, had artillery musketoons, while one was a full battery of six 12-pound howitzers, the men equipped with light artillery sabers. Seven infantry companies had been formed, armed with rifled muskets, 440 men. Eighty-one companies had percussion rifles, 1,400 men. Twenty-six companies, comprising 1,300 men, had flint muskets, while five companies were without arms; in all, 6,040 light infantry. Forty-two companies of riflemen were armed, four with long-range rifles of the U. S. Harpers Ferry M1859 pattern; 28 companies of 1,400 men had percussion rifles, and ten companies, 500 men, carried flint lock rifles of the Virginia Manufactory pattern, presumably. In addition, 76 companies had been formed awaiting arms, a total of 6,030 riflemen.

Before Bull Run or First Manassas, the Army of Northern Virginia was in bad shape for ammunition, being limited to four rounds per man, for want of percussion caps. Captain Louis Zimmer, sent by Commodore Maury to buy 1,000,000 caps, drew $10,000 gold from a Baltimore bank and belted it on. Then he travelled to New York and bought the caps at "a store on Liberty Street."

The caps were seized an hour later by the authorities, but were finally cleared to Zimmer's friend in Philadelphia to whom they had been consigned. At Philadelphia they were received by the friend, "in care of the Mayor," but were finally turned over to the Southern sympathizer. Then they were packed in several trunks and by various means smuggled across the Potomac past Yankee guards and gunboats. In all, 800,000 of the caps were delivered, with a trunk containing 200,000 being lost when a Yankee gunboat took after the rowboat ferrying the stuff over the Potomac, and the rowboat sailors dumped the trunk overboard. But the 800,000 caps were distributed to the Army of Northern Virginia and materially affected their successes in their first engagement.

Foreign Purchases

Two of the most important men in the Confederacy assumed their posts during April. On April 8, 1861, Special Order No. 17 issued by C. S. Adjutant General Samuel Cooper at Montgomery declared "Major Josiah Gorgas, of the Corps of Artillery and Ordnance, is assigned to duty as Chief of the Bureau of Ordnance." Placed under his command on April 15, was Captain Caleb Huse, directed to proceed to Europe to buy arms. About December, 1861, arms began to come in through the purchases of Huse, and there were a good many Enfields in the hands of Confederate troops at Shiloh. The shipment of arms resulting from Commodore Bulloch's work in England, via the *Fingal*, was among the most important single boat-loads of arms to be sent over. Aboard the *Fingal* were:

On Account of the War Department—10,000 Enfield rifles, 1,000,000 ball cartridges, and 2,000,000 percussion caps; 3,000 cavalry sabers, with suitable accouterments, a large quantity of material for clothing, and a large supply of medical stores.

On account of the Navy Department—1,000 short rifles, with cutlass bayonets, and 1,000 rounds of ammunition per rifle; 500 revolvers, with suitable ammunition; two 4½-inch muzzle-loading rifled guns, with traversing carriages, all necessary gear, and 200 made-up cartridges, shot and shell, per gun; two breech-loading 2½-inch steel rifled guns for boats or field service, with 200 rounds of ammunition per gun; 400 barrels of coarse cannon powder, and a large quantity of made-up clothing for seamen.

For the State of Georgia—3,000 Enfield rifles.
For the State of Louisiana—1,000 Enfield rifles.

"No single ship ever took into the Confederacy a cargo so entirely composed of military and naval supplies, and the pressing need of them made it necessary to get the *Fingal* off with quick dispatch, and to use every possible effort to get her into a port having railway communication through to Virginia, because the Confederate army, then covering Richmond, was very poorly armed, and was distressingly deficient in all field necessaries," reported Commodore Bulloch in his biographical narrative, *Secret Service of the Confederate States,* London, 1883.

The new Confederate Secretary of War, Leroy Pope Walker, exhibited a charming capacity for haggling in the market place, in an exchange of telegrams with an arms broker in Washington. The C. S. Government was still in Montgomery, and the war clouds had not burst to rain their curtain of death for four years over the scene, so Walker dallied with the following arms order:

Washington, April 9, 1861
Hon. L. P. Walker:
Have ordered 2,000 Colt new army pistols, at $25; Sharps carbines, new (army) improvement, held at $30; Sharps rifle, with sword bayonet, $42.50; Colt carbine, $30. Two hundred to three hundred tons Hazard's (Government) powder offered at 20 cents. Answer immediately.
John Forsyth

Walker replied the same day that "The rifles are too high. Would take 2,000 Sharps rifles, with sword bayonets, at $30. Do not want the other guns; if the powder has been tested and is cannon powder, will take it. You had better ascertain and know certainly all about it. Answer fully."

The Secretary showed remarkable aplomb, or stupidity, in refusing Colt's revolvers at $25 when soon the wires between Washington and Hartford were to hum with messages demanding all the factory could turn out "until further notice" for the Union. But at the time neither Colt's plant nor the Federal army were committed to the course which opened before them within ten days, when Sumter was fired upon. On April 9, all was hustle and bustle, but somehow the reality of war seemed distant; a tone of "they'll never do it; it can't happen *here*" prevailed.

Munitions magnate Forsyth wired promptly back, setting Walker straight on the conditions of the market. He told Walker the prices were lowest market; subject to immediate acceptance; "Probably they could not be had twenty-four hours hence." Walker must have spent the afternoon checking with local arms dealers, for it dawned on him that the newest army model of Colt was a pretty good buy then at $25, and he also accepted the Sharps rifles.

Missing from the records is Forsyth's letter of reply indicating how the arms were to be delivered. On the following day, Walker agreed to buy gunpowder from Forsyth, who replied stating he had arranged for the cannon powder "to be delivered in same manner as the pistols."

How these particular Colt pistols were delivered is and may remain a mystery. There is a strong inference here that at least 2,000 of the full fluted cylinder New Model Armies were sold to Walker while operating out of the Montgomery war office.

The combination of industrialization of the South and the success of Huse's imports by 1863 was maintaining the balance between the new nation and the old, in the opinion of observers in the Confederacy. Apparently, the South was not in want of arms, though measures had to be kept up to maintain the supply. In *Three Months in the Southern States,* by the Englishman, Fremantle, published by S. H. Goetzel, Mobile, 1864, he noted that on June 20, 1863, a Saturday, as he changed cars at Gordonsville, Virginia, en route to Culpeper, there was "an enormous pile of excellent rifles rotting in the open air. These had been captured at Chancellorsville; but the Confederates have already such a superabundant stock of rifles that apparently they can let them spoil."

"The Confederate troops are now entirely armed with excellent rifles," Fremantle wrote, from a rather limited vantage point, "mostly Enfields. When they first turned out they were in the habit of wearing numerous revolvers, and bowie knives. General Lee is said to have mildly remarked, 'Gentlemen, I think you will find an Enfield Rifle, a bayonet, and sixty rounds of ammunition as much as you can conveniently carry in the way of arms.' They laughed, and thought they knew better, but the six-shooters and bowie knives gradually disappeared and now (June 1863) none are to be seen among the infantry."

Not all the Enfields got to the South, of course. Diversion of Confederate shipments by capture raises a pedantic question for the collector. It has been noted there are three types of "Confederate guns," the Primary, the Secondary, and the Probable. These are defined as, first, one "made under Confederate contract, by private contractor or by the government itself to be issued directly to Confederate troops. A Secondary Confederate (arm) is one which might have been made for any purpose, but which was purchased by the Confederate Government for issuance to its troops after it was made. A Probable Confederate is that which, through Southern markings or method of finding, one can be reasonably sure was carried by a Confederate soldier and used in the Civil War." Where in this definition we find the arms of the 144th Regiment New York Volunteer Infantry we cannot say. At Elmira, New York, on the way to the seat of war in 1862, the regiment received Enfields: "Those issued to us were intended by the English makers of them for the Confederate service; but the blockade runner having them on board was captured in its effort to reach Charleston and so were appropriated by the War Department to meet a pressing need in arming Northern soldiers."

Not all Southern soldiers were so lucky as to receive Enfields. Perhaps Johnny Reb who was supposed to get an Enfield from the blockade runner captured as cited above, was issued instead a Belgian musket. These arms, of the same description as the identical make and patterns of guns issued to the North, were about as well liked in the South as by the Northerners. As A. P. Ford, *Life in the Confederate Army,* recalled in 1905, his outfit was "armed with old-fashioned Belgian rifles, probably the most antiquated and worthless guns ever put into a modern soldier's hands. But they were all our government had. These rifles could not send a ball beyond 200 yards, and at much shorter range their aim was entirely unreliable." Failure of a bullet to reach a mere 200 yards suggests A. P. Ford was so stupid he loaded his rifle with .58 bullets in a .69 caliber barrel, thus losing most of the force of the gunpowder past the bullet. But the Belgians continued in service; in December of 1864, Captain G. L. Buist's Palmetto Guards artillery unit of four howitzers was reorganized as infantry and issued Belgian muskets.

Useless Weapons

Later reports pro and con confused the issue in retrospect, but the merits of different arms was questioned by many soldiers at the time.

As Carlton McCarthy of the Richmond Howitzers, Army of Northern Virginia, wrote later in the *Southern Historical Society Papers*:

> Revolvers were found to be about as useless and heavy lumber as a private soldier could carry, and early in the war were sent home to be used by the women and children in protecting themselves from insult and violence at the hands of ruffians who prowled about the country shirking duty.
>
> The infantry found out that bayonets were not of much use, and did not hesitate to throw them, with the scabbard, away.
>
> The artillerymen, who started out with heavy sabers hanging to their belts, stuck them up in the mud as they marched, and left them for the ordinance (sic) officers to pick up and turn over to the cavalry.
>
> The cavalrymen found sabers very tiresome when swung to the belt, and adopted the plan of fastening them to the saddle on the left side, with the hilt in front and in reach of the hand. Finally, sabers got very scarce even among cavalrymen, who relied more and more on their short rifles.

Impressions of a Confederate New Yorker

Perhaps one of the most authoritative opinions of Confederate preparedness came from "An Impressed New Yorker," otherwise unnamed, who published in 1862 *Thirteen Months in the Rebel Army.* The prevailing attitude was one of great optimism, the success of Southern arms, and ultimate recognition of the Southern Confederacy by the great nations of Europe:

> During the six weeks I was attached to the Ordnance Department (as a brevet second lieutenant) I learned some facts which it were well for the North to know. Since reaching home I hear wonder expressed at two things: the vast energy of the South; and their unexpected resources, especially in the procuring of cannon, small-arms and ammunition. How have they secured and manufactured an adequate supply of these, during such a protracted and destructive struggle?
>
> In answer to this enquiry let me say: The immense supply of cannon—to speak of them first—which that stupendous thief Floyd traitorously placed in the Southern forts and arsenals during his term of office, made a very good beginning for this branch of the service. It was also said by Southern officers that a large number of guns used in the Mexican War were still stored in the South, I have heard, at Point Isabel. These were soon brought into use. Many old Mexican and Spanish brass guns were recast into modern field pieces. These were said to have made the finest guns in the Rebel service because of the large percentage of silver contained in the metal.
>
> Very early in the Rebellion an extensive establishment for the manufacture of field artillery existed in New Orleans, which sent out beautiful batteries. These batteries I saw in various parts of the army. This factory was under the superintendence of Northern and foreign mechanics. Memphis supplied some 32 and 64 pounders, also a number of iron Parrott guns. These were cast in the navy yard firm of Street & Hungerford. At Nashville, Tennessee, the firm of T. Brennan & Co. turned out a large amount of iron light artillery of every description; and shortly before Nashville was evacuated, they perfected a fine machine for rifling cannon, which I examined. They sent a spy north, who obtained, it was said, at the Fort Pitt foundry the drawings and specifications which enabled their workmen to put up this machine. This expensive, and to them valuable machine was removed to Atlanta, Georgia. In escaping home I came through Nashville a few weeks since and saw about a dozen large cannon still lying in this foundry, which the sudden flight of the rebels from Nashville had prevented them from rifling or carrying away. All know that the Tredegar Iron Works in Richmond, Va., is an extensive manufacturer of guns of large caliber. Indeed, every city of the South having a foundry of any size, boasts of furnishing some cannon.
>
> Many of these guns were defective and even dangerous. One battery from the Memphis foundry lost three guns in a month by bursting, one of them at the Battle of Belmont, November 7. After the Rebel reverses at Forts Henry and Donelson, and the retreat from Bowling Green and Nashville, when General Beauregard took command of the Army of the Mississippi Valley, he issued a call to the citizens for bells of every description. Courthouses, factories, public institutions and plantations sent on theirs. And the people furnished large quantities of old brass of every description, andirons, candlesticks, gas fixtures, and even door knobs. I have seen wagon loads of these at the railroad depots, waiting shipment to the foundries. *The rebels are in earnest.*
>
> But the finest cannon have been received from England. Several magnificent guns of the Whitworth and Blakeley patents I have seen, or heard described as doing good execution among the "Yankees." How many have been imported I cannot tell, but surely a large number.
>
> As to small arms, the energies of the South have been more fully developed in their manufacture than is dreamed of by the North. As early as April, 1861, Memphis had commenced the alteration of immense quantities of flintlock muskets, sent south during Floyd's term as Secretary of War. I saw this work progressing, even before secession was a completed fact there. New Orleans turned out the best rifles I ever saw in the South. They were similar to the French Minie rifle, furnished with fine sword bayonets. The Louisiana troops were mostly armed with these. At Nashville, and Gallatin, Tennessee, rifles were also made, and I suppose in every considerable city in the South. In addition, it should be known that thousands of Government arms were in the hands of the people, all through the Southern states; how they procured them, I do not know. These were gathered up and altered or

improved and issued to the troops. Many of the regiments went into the field armed with every description of guns, from the small-bore squirrel rifle and double barreled shotgun to the ponderous Queen Bess musket and clumsy but effective German Yager. The regiments were furnished as fast as possible with arms of one kind, and the others returned to the factories to be classified and issued again. Sword bayonets were fitted to double barreled shotguns, making them a very effective weapon. Others were cut down to a uniform length of about twenty-four inches, and issued to the cavalry. Common hunting rifles were bored out to carry a Minie ball, twenty to the pound, and sword bayonets fitted to them. One entire brigade of Tennesseans, under General William H. Carroll, was armed with these guns.

When recovering from sickness at Nashville I spent hours of investigation in the basement of the capitol, used as an armory, where an immense amount of this work has been done. At Bowling Green I saw many thousands of rifles and shotguns which had been collected for alteration, and the machine shop of the Louisville and Nashville Railroad was used as an armory. Many of these guns were destroyed and others left when the town was evacuated. Nor should it be forgotten that almost every man of any position owned a pair of Colt's repeaters, many of them of the Army and Navy size. These were eagerly bought up by the Confederate authorities, who paid from thirty to sixty dollars apiece for them. They were for the cavalry service. Add to these facts, that every country blacksmith made cutlasses from old files, & etc most of them clumsy but serviceable weapons in a close encounter. Artillery and cavalry sabers were manufactured at New Orleans, Memphis, and Nashville, and probably at other places.

In short, at the beginning of the year 1862, there was rather a surfeit than any scarcity of arms all over the South . . . the largest supply of small arms comes from England and France. I have repeatedly heard it said that 300,000 stand of arms have been received from abroad; that 65,000 came in one load by the *Bermuda*.

The imported guns are principally Enfield, Minie, and Belgian rifles. The first Enfields received had been used somewhat, probably in the Crimean and Indian wars. The crown marks on the first importations were stamped out with the initials of those who had bought them from the government; the later arrivals *exhibit the crown marks uneffaced*. I have seen Enfield rifles of the manufacture of 1861 and 1862, with the stamp of the "Tower" on the lockplate! Officers, in opening and examining cases of these, would nod significantly to each other, as much as to say, *"see the proof of England's neutrality!"* The French and Belgian rifles, among the best arms made, are mostly of recent manufacture, and elegantly finished . . . with the cargoes of arms, ammunition was supplied at the rate of a thousand rounds for each gun . . . I often issued boxes of ammunition, which were put up in London for the Enfield rifle. The fixed ammunition of England is said by Southern officers to be the finest in the world. But much was also made at home. The largest laboratory for making cartridges, of which I had any knowledge, was in Memphis, afterward removed to Grenada, Mississippi. Powder mills were established at various points, one of the largest at Dahlonega, Georgia; and old saltpeter caves were opened, the government offering forty-five cents per pound for saltpeter, and exempting all persons employed in its manufacture from military duty. Percussion caps were made in Richmond early in 1861, and great numbers were smuggled through the lines, in the early part of the war. As to the supply of ammunition, my opinion is, that the South will not lack while the rebellion lasts.

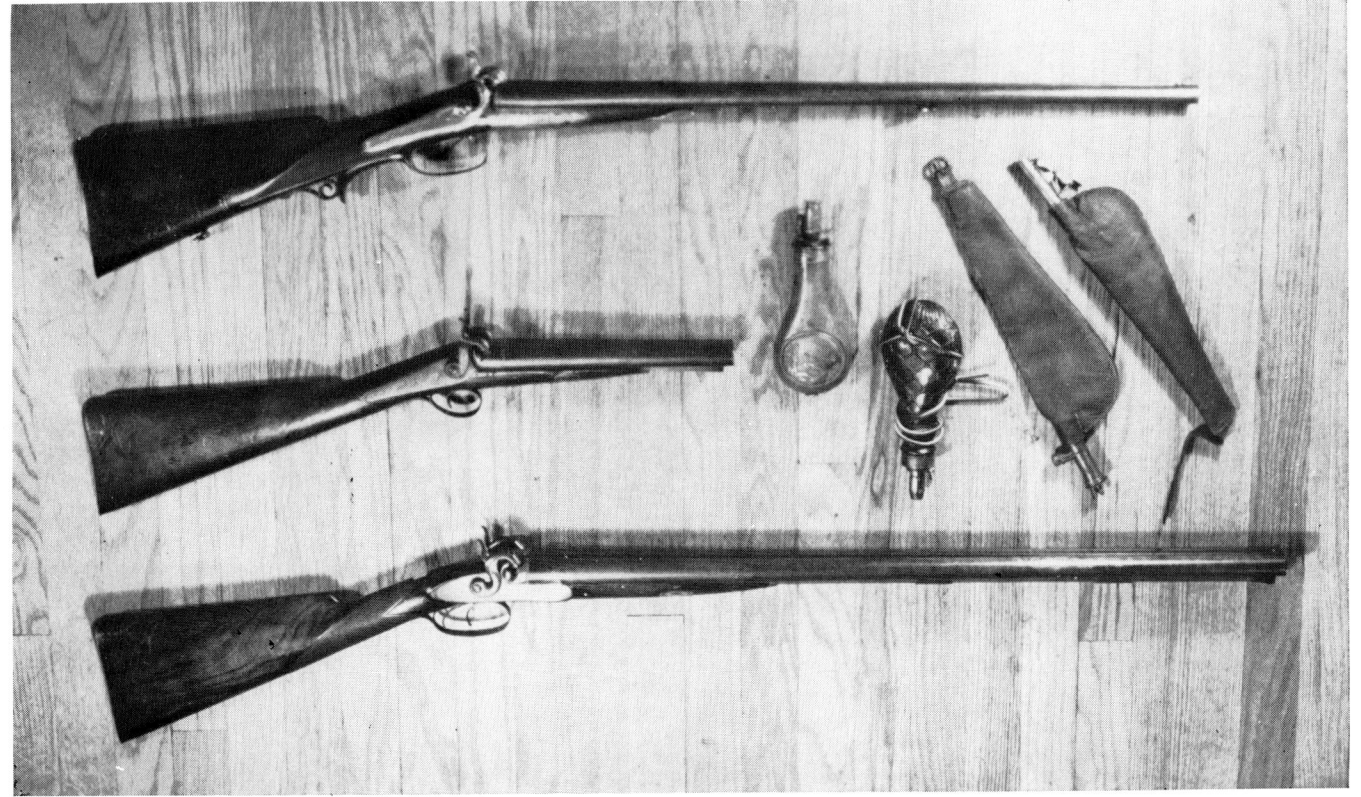

Regiments went into battle armed with shotguns. Ranged beside two shot pouches and two typical sporting powder flasks are Lefaucheux double pinfire gun such as achieved limited sale pre-war through New York agents Hartley, Schuyler and Graham, and was esteemed by French-ancestry Southrons resident in Louisiana. Middle is true "sawed off shotgun" by Ezekiel Baker, having heavy 10″ barrels bored for shot or ball. Piece has single non-selective trigger, made in 1850! Bottom is Greener 10 bore waterfowler popular along eastern shore and Mississippi flyway. Cut to 20″ and occasionally fitted with bayonet, such first quality sporting arms made Southern cavalryman formidable fighter.

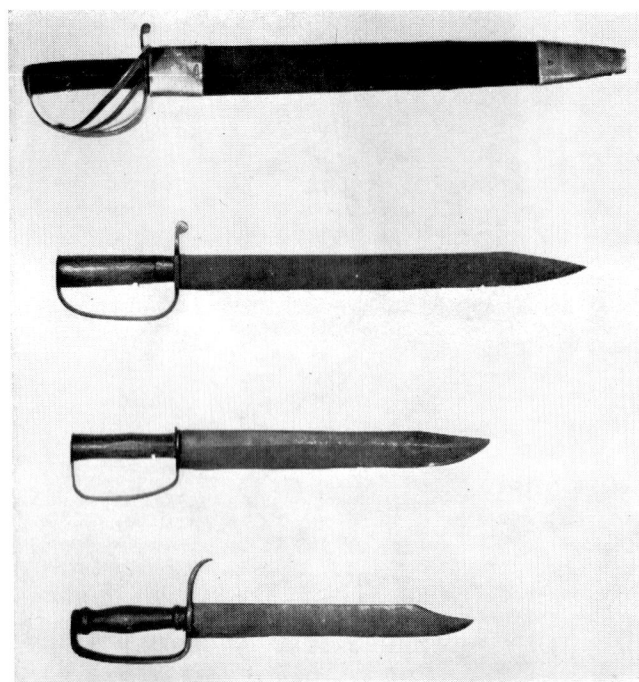

Country blacksmiths beat out old files into "side knives" which every Confederate wore to show how ferocious he was. Occasionally regiments went into battle with nothing but knives until they got good sense. Basket hilt sword is cutlass copying British pattern adopted by C.S.N.

Salvaged Arms

Salvage from the field was a major item in resupply: the Battle of Fredericksburg had material compensations for the Southern side. Lieutenant Colonel Briscoe Baldwin, Chief of Ordnance of the Army of Northern Virginia, reported 9,091 rifles and muskets with 255,-000 rounds of assorted small-arms cartridges were recovered by Confederate scavenging parties after the battles of the 12th and 13th of December, 1862. The breakdown illustrates somewhat the equipment of the Union forces thrown against the Gray lines at the crest of the hill.

Newtype Springfield rifles were in the minority, 250 only having been taken. Improved muskets, those of the M1842 original percussion construction, tallied 3,148, with the cap-and-ball altered muskets of older patterns amount to 1,136 captured. Austrian rifles enough to equip a regiment were picked up, 772 of them. Only 78 Belgian muskets were recovered, and 42 Springfield muskets. This may have revealed a tendency to cull out Springfield-made arms from lots of, say, 1842 pattern guns which would also bear contractors' marks. Mississippi rifles, the M1841 pattern, totalled 478. Original flint muskets were in the minority, 13 being recovered, and a few large-bore Enfield muskets, .67 caliber, possibly of the so-called "sea service" type, and 59 Enfield rifles of the .57 caliber, were among the salvage. Eighty thousand caliber .69 cartridges, and 94,000 in caliber .57 and .58 were taken in good condition, plus 31,000 for the Mississippi .54 rifles, and 50,000 more in damaged condition, requiring sorting and possible remanufacture. The damaged guns were also picked up, 1,406 of assorted types, but only half of these, 692, were shipped on to Richmond. The balance might have been cannibalized for repairs on the spot by unit ordnancemen. While Colonel Baldwin did not so state, it may be that many of the non-standard or older guns were abandoned by the Rebels, in favor of a good Springfield .58 only to appear again in their ranks as "Yankee souvenirs" picked up by their comrades.

The spirit of "do it yourself" prevailed in the camps and lines when a battle was in the offing. Even soldiers who ordinarily might expect to be supplied with fixed (rolled paper) ammunition spent time in readying their ammunition boxes for the fray, while among most Southern regiments each man had to be a "handloading specialist" and make his own ammunition.

"The question of ammunition was one of the most important and serious," wrote Brigadier General N. R. Pearce, CSA, some years after the war in discussing the preparations of Arkansas troops, at the battle of Wilson's Creek, *Battles & Leaders,* Vol. I, pp 299. "As the Ordnance Department was imperfectly organized and poorly supplied, the men scattered about in groups, to improvise, as best they could, ammunition for their inefficient arms. Here, a group would be moulding bullets—there, another crowd dividing percussion caps, and, again, another group fitting new flints to their old muskets. They had little thought then of the inequality between the discipline, arms, and accoutrements of the regular United States troops they were soon to engage in battle, and their own homely movements and equipments. It was a new thing to most of them, this regular way of shooting by word of command, and it was, perhaps, the old-accustomed method of using rifle, musket, or shot-gun as gamesters or marksmen that won them the battle when pressed into close quarters with the enemy."

Had General Pearce been able to read the Senate "roasting" of his counterpart, General Fremont, commanding the very troops that opposed him at Wilson's Creek, he might not have been so sorry for his boys. Perhaps there was inequality between the discipline of the "regular" United States troops and the rebels, but that inequality was in part the creation of such drillmasters as Fremont's Zagonyi, who turned plough-jockeys into swordsmen in six weeks. To listen to the Federal's complaints about Austrian muskets that kicked heavily and were as dangerous to the user as to the person fired at, General Pearce would have got the impression the opposing forces were a little more nearly equal than he claims. And, assisting his Arkansas troops in the early days, was a little known gunsmith of Fort Smith, John Pearson, who transformed numbers of flintlock sporting rifles to percussion and may have bored out a good many to .54 or .58 caliber.

John Pearson

Hailing from Baltimore, and originally from England where he apprenticed as a clockmaker, John Pearson made his mark on history when he and Sam Colt came together in 1834. As a practical gunmaker in Baltimore on Center Market Place, Pearson was called on by Colt to make models of firearms in perfecting the Colt revolver. While *The Story of Colt's Revolver* (W. B. Edwards, Stackpole Company, 1953) contains the first mention of John Pearson, and he is ignored by lists of gunmakers compiled by various authorities, Pearson was described in a brief obituary in the Fort Smith *Elevator* of Friday, August 3, 1883, as follows:

> Mr. Pearson was a gunsmith and we may well say master of his trade. He should have been, as we verily believe, the recipient of honors attributed to Colt for the Colt's patent firearms. He was one of the most ingenious of men, and a scientific workman, a sober, steady, industrious and honest man. He goes to his grave at the ripe age of 80, respected by all who knew him.

Pearson's sudden death at 10 a.m. August 1 was a surprise to many, including his fellow Masons of the Bellevue Royal Arch Chapter No. 8, of which he was a member. He became a Mason on January 28, 1853, in Fort Smith, but apparently appeared in that bustling border town prior to 1850, his second son Richard being born there in that year. Pearson's wife was Jenny Irvine, whose brother Alfred was colonel of the Royal Enniskillen Dragoons. Colonel Irvine later moved from Fort Smith to Canada where he served as a factor of the Hudson's Bay Company. It is possible, though not recorded so far as is known, that gunsmith Pearson might have supplied his brother-in-law with some "fusils" or Indian Trade rifles. Meanwhile, in Fort Smith, Pearson set up a gun shop in the 400 block on Garrison Avenue. At the rear of the shop, facing on North 4th Street, was his home. Pearson made single-shot guns and pistols; also presumably retailed. Family legend is that Pearson was given $30,000 in cash by Sam Colt as a final settlement for any claim which Pearson might have had with his early work on the Colt designs. Pearson used this money to buy Colt's revolvers which he sold in the West.

Circumstantial proof of this may appear in Mitchell's Colt book, on page 75. Colonel Colt in February, 1861, left Hartford for a Caribbean cruise; not for a vacation but in the essential need to relieve the pain of his illness with warmer weather. An important letter (probably to Hugh Harbison in Hartford) dated Havana, February 18, 1860, in Mitchell's book is an obvious error of year (see page 70, op. cit.) and begins: "We have just all landed here safe and sound and I improve the minute to say I drew a check for $30,000 while in New York in favor of the cashier of the Mechanics Bank which please enter upon your (company) checkbook and charge the same to my private account."

Several facts are in this brief statement: Colt wrote a Colt's Pat. Firearms Mfg. Co. check, but did not draw it in favor of anyone; instead, he cashed it at the Mechanics Bank, having drawn it in their favor instead of "cash," or "to bearer." He asked that this be charged

Gunsmith John Pearson lost fortune he obtained from Colt for revolver invention, by serving loyally the Lost Cause.

to his private account and not to the Company, because it did not relate to the Company affairs but to some other cause. It hardly could be assumed to relate to the Cuban cruise, for the ship was chartered, and so much in gold, enough to found a new armory, would not have been needed. That Colt paid this sum to another person is almost certain, for he certainly would not be so foolish as to carry $30,000 around in gold with him; and there seems no probable cause why he would want to do so. But, if he met John Pearson in New York on that occasion, Pearson perhaps buying for his own account or for the state authorities—this would explain the sum of $30,000 mentioned by Colt and the long-held family legend that Pearson was paid $30,000 by Sam Colt.

When he was paid this sum by Colt is not known by the family. Knowing Colt, one is safe in saying that he paid it only when it did not pinch him to do so, say in 1861 when business was booming with millions from musket contracts in sight on the horizon. *Why* Colt paid Pearson is another question: guilt? or generosity? or sincere recognition of a long-standing debt? or conclusion of some private agreement to reimburse Pearson from the eventual fruits of success? No one will ever know, for in any case, Colt would not have chosen to publicize the payment. We think it very probable this $30,000 drawn by Colt in February, 1861, was given in cash to Pearson. What he did with it was to turn around and immediately buy Colt's revolvers with it! The profits from business must have been good, for Pearson is said to have had $75,000 in gold at one time before the evacuation of Fort Smith by Confederates, buried in his yard for safe-keeping. When at last war began, in a burst of Southern patriotism, the gunsmith dug up the gold and invested the entire sum in Confederate war bonds. He put his shop at the disposal of the Confederacy, and seems to have held some position roughly equivalent to "Chief of Ordnance for the Confederacy in the Southwest." It is possible Pearson aided in setting up manufacture of some of the Colt-type pistols of "Confederate" origin, made in Arkansas or Texas. More probable, he stayed close to Fort Smith, repairing and percussioning, until the town was occupied by Federal troops and he had to flee. His shop was broken into and papers and records as well as equipment destroyed. Attempts to return home were made hazardous by bushwhackers in Arkansas, so he turned to smuggling. He went over to Kentucky and engaged in "the river traffic," carrying contraband, mostly medicinal drugs such as quinine and opium, from Ohio to the Confederate armies in the mid-South. At war's end, he returned home and tried to resume business as usual, which the obituary in the Fort Smith paper seems to indicate he did successfully.

An immigrant clockmaker from England, John Pearson helped invent one of the principal weapons of the Civil War, the Colt revolver. He wore himself out working for the South, poured his life savings down the drain of the Lost Cause, and wound up running drugs on a smuggler's errand of mercy. But Pearson was far from alone in such conduct: the "beau geste" but sincere sacrifices of thousands like him for the Southern cause were the real arms and armor that defended the Confederacy.

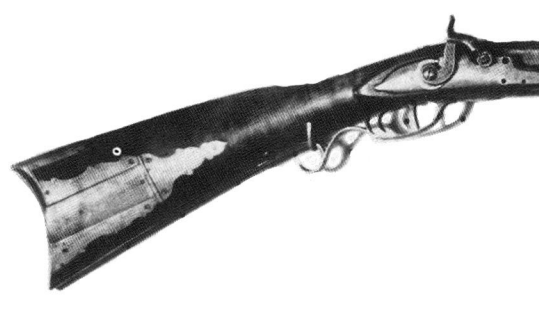

Virginia "Kentucky" with patchbox suggesting source near Harpers Ferry is percussion conversion done using drum with clean out screw patented in England by Colt in 1855. Unusual gun has 1763 French lock but half octagon .70 barrel is rifled with 12 grooves. Band midway is where front of forearm attached to barrel unbreeches when key is removed to take down for compact carry and also has added left side bar for sling ring for horseman's use. Piece symbolizes 45 "Sporting rifles" issued between Nov. 1, 1861, and 1862, from Richmond Arsenal. CSA Document No. VIII of 1863 tabulates issues:

44,692	flint muskets	542	flintlock pistols	7	Merrill's carbines
59,148	percussion muskets	1,997	US percussion pistols	9	Jenk's carbines
72	rifled muskets	531	flintlock rifles	1	Sharpe's carbine
361	Colt's rifles (believed revolving .44s)	1	Belgian rifle	140	single barrel shotguns
1,751	percussion rifles	1	John Brown's rifle	53	Double barrel shotguns
681	Hall's carbines	1,903	revolving pistols	50	musketoons
133	Sharpe's rifles (spelled with an "e")		with 94 stocks for same	199	cavalry percussion pistols
363	Minnie (sic) muskets	1,221	Read's rifles, (unidentified at present,	260	percussion rifles
1,105	Harpers Ferry rifles (M1841)		perhaps Wm. Read & Sons of Boston?)		
596	HF rifles with sword bayonets	472	Mississippi rifles (contract 41s?)		
4,000	Hall's rifles	122	North's rifles		
107	artillery musketoons	15	Derringer rifles		
76	Colt's revolving carbines	15	Enfield rifles		

Also listed are artillery, ammunition, shot and shell, forges, tents and other "ordnance, implements, accoutrements" issued from October 1859 through November 1, 1863.

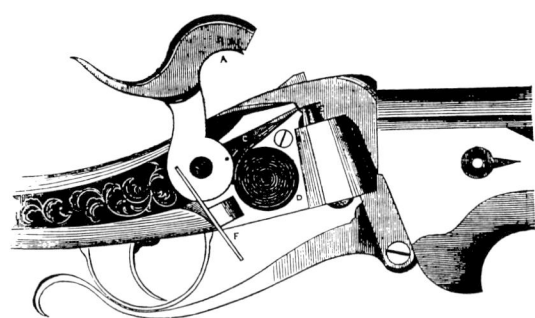

John Brown's rifle was issued from Virginia Armory in 1859-1861, and went to the collections of the U.S. Cartridge Company, and later to Maury C. Clark of L.A. as noted in the 1951 5th edition of *The Gun Digest*, just a century after 2nd Model Sharps was written up in the *Scientific American*, March 8, 1851, which probably persuaded Old Brown to buy one, only to lose it in Harpers Ferry raid of 1859.

CHAPTER 27

Long Arms For Lee

The Confederate Rifles and Rifle Muskets were of eight basic categories. Early in the war both the U. S. Rifle and Musket Model 1855-61 became standard issue as made in Southern armories. Copies of the Mississippi Rifle in .58 caliber, often adapted to take a sword bayonet, were another state ordnance favorite. The British Enfield, of both imported and domestic-made origins, had its influence. And to a limited extent the continental features appeared in some long guns, such as the Texas "Tyler" Rifle known as "Austrian." In front band-nose cap assembly and details of lock form and cone seat, it appears this gun (from one surviving specimen) was inspired in design by the Austrian Lorenz Rifle mated with a light French Minie. Such a cross of types also appeared in the Tallassee Carbine manufactured in Tallassee Armory, Alabama, and adopted in 1864 as the standard pattern for Confederate cavalry. In lock and fittings, it resembled the Enfield; but in the small of stock to butt plate it was U. S. Musket in form. A fifth "type" of Confederate long gun was the breech-loading cavalry carbine. Excellent copies of the Sharps slightly modified were turned out in Richmond, Virginia, and limited numbers of novel breechloaders of several descriptions were forged by eager and talented mechanics to arm the beloved Southland. Such were the so-called Confederate Perry, the still-unidentified "Rising Breech" model, and the simple and fundamentally excellent Tarpley cavalry arm.

The sixth group of Confederate arms is the imported rifle and rifle musket. Among these popularly tabbed as "Confederate" are such arms as the Calisher & Terry, a limited issue British gun passed over in the United Kingdom service in favor of the Westley Richards. The "worthless Belgians" had their share in arming the Stars and Bars. The finest Enfields ever made were regularly consigned to the blockaded posts in defiance of the Anaconda. Austrian rifles completed the score.

Battlefield salvage and reconstructions may be considered a seventh sub-type of C. S. long gun, if done officially and in the time period of the war. Numerous standard U. S. guns must be lumped in this category.

An eighth group is the standard U. S. musket and rifle, flint and percussion, of patterns from 1798 to 1861. Many of these were on hand in Southern state arsenals as a matter of course. These were issued to the militia under the Act of 1808 for equipping and arming them. Prior to the National Guard legislation subsequent to the Civil War, the organized militia of the several states were issued arms according to quotas. The quotas were based on the number of able-bodied men in the state, in respect to its population, as that population related to the total population for all the states. While the value of the arms quota was expressed in terms of U. S. Muskets, states could requisition artillery, cavalry harness, uniforms, or whatever other military stores, regularly adopted by the United States, they might desire, and the Chief of Ordnance would cause contracts or purchases to be made to the value of that state's quota, and charge the Militia Act appropriation. Annually since 1808, $200,000 had been appropriated for this purpose; after 1861 the amount had increased to $600,000. Some years, it was the custom of a state to let its quota "ride" for the next fiscal year, to increase the value it could draw against. Thus a state could allow its money to remain with the Ordnance Corps until it could afford, say, a complete battery of cannon; or enough arms of uniform type, to equip a regiment.

The importance of this Act in the arms history of the antebellum South is recognized; less recognized is the transition from Federal Arms Appropriations to the fiscal problems of equipping the state itself, through the means internally of its own citizens. This transition occurred abruptly, and at different times throughout 1860-61, as the several Southern states passed or signed their Ordinances of Secession. Suddenly freed from the obligations of Federal taxation and revenues, the South was initially in a prosperous condition. The cotton crop looked good. And martial fervor was everywhere.

Private Musket Makers

It was into this spirit that the Yankee private militia musket makers wandered. During the Cold War grand plans were laid for armories and arsenals all over the south. And oddly, the ones to suffer most when war finally came were the Northern munitions makers! The pattern of rifle most affected by these firms was a

Arms transferred to Southern U.S. armories or issued to States prior to 1860 included basic types shown here. Majority were flintlocks of 1821-22 pattern (top) but some had been converted to percussion in 1840's by U.S. (2d from top). M1842 smoothbore muskets, original percussion, were also in lot and same model had been made in Dixie in 1852 (3d). Rifles included the popular "Mississippi" (shown elsewhere in this book) and earlier standard arms such as this .54 "common rifle" M1817. Shown is rifle by contractor N. W. Starr, Middletown, Ct., transformed to percussion by "French method" with cone directly into barrel. Muzzle-loading carbines on hand in South included this type, the U.S. M1855. Arm shown is West Point Museum gun, one of two prototypes reported made 1848 cal. .54, but identical issue arm of 1855 was cal. .58. 300 made 1855, without Maynard primer.

version resembling the Model 1841 "Mississippi rifle" or the U. S. M1855 brass-trimmed Harpers Ferry rifle without the Maynard tape primer.

Eli Whitney

Kicking off the parade south seems to have been Eli Whitney who, under a contract with the state of Mississippi June 6, 1860, agreed to deliver 1,500 Mississippi Rifles with sword bayonets. By October 15, he expressed some fear at having the arms inspected. He sent 60 to Adjutant General W. L. Sykes of that state who reported to Governor John J. Pettus on January 18, 1861, in explaining why the state was short of arms, that "The arms were received and examined and proved to be old guns fixed up." None of the arms were received under the contract and "The affair is now being adjusted between a U. S. senator and said Whitney, but owing to the bad faith of Whitney the arms will probably never be received and the (volunteer) companies will have to resort to whatever can be furnished."

No specimen of these Mississippi State 60 Whitney rifles, unquestionably conforming to the pattern of the U. S. Rifle Model 1841, with sword bayonets attached, has so far been identified. The short and long "Enfield" rifle miscalled "Confederate Whitney" is described under "Enfields" (Chap. 21). Among Pennsylvania makers there seems to have been some contract current which we strongly suspect was a Southern order, from the style of the arms. Governor Curtin of Pennsylvania

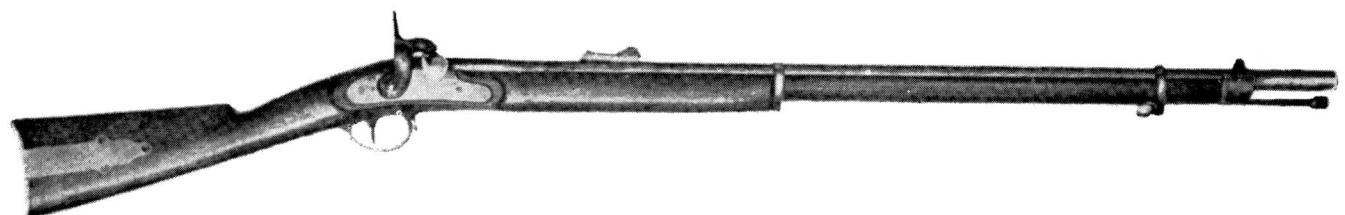

"Average" militia rifle of the late 1850's or 1860 is this J. Henry & Son short rifle cal. .58 with muzzle of barrel turned round for socket bayonet. Same bayonet adaptation is noted on S. Carolina marked Kentucky rifle though coincidence is not enough to justify claiming the Henry was intended for that Southern state. Similar arm was made by J. H. Krider with Sharps-type patchbox, but using Enfield-style lock.

stated definitely November 26, 1861, that his state had no contracts for arms. Guns of P. S. Justice, J. Henry & Sons, and J. H. Krider, all Philadelphia makers, have a basic resemblance one to the other. All use a Sharps-form brass patchbox which is not Robbins & Lawrence or Sharps make, although it is remotely possible some of the Sharps British Model Carbine tools might have gone into shaping the patchboxes. All resemble the rifle titled "Harpers Ferry Rifle."

Justice Rifle

A second type was the Justice Harpers Ferry Rifle, caliber .58, 35-inch barrel rifled with three shallow grooves, fitted with M1855 style rear leaf sight and bayonet stud without guide, on right of muzzle. Brass mountings, oval screw-clamp bands, and Justice special trigger guard; length overall 4 feet 3 inches; weight 9 pounds 2 ounces. Lock appears to be a Harpers Ferry transformed flintlock of 1822, with original flying eagle and also stamped P. S. Justice/Philada. No proof mark; Justice' name only. Serial number on trigger guard tang surmounted by a "P." The specimen Fuller illustrates is No. P/315, early in the manufacture of the Justice special model guns. The cone seat bottom is carved to fit pan-cut in the lockplate, but other Justice guns have the nipple holster of 1841-2 percussion form.

J. Henry Rifle

A similar rifle was made by J. Henry & Son, which was all-brass mounted. This 35-inch barrel short rifle is .58 caliber. The stock nose cap is of 1855 form, but the barrel is turned at muzzle for socket bayonet; the Sharps-style brass patchbox is let into the right of the buttstock. The cone seat resembles either an Enfield or an Austrian, and is notched into the lockplate. Two brass bands are screw-clamping. The lockplate, somewhat of Colt Special Model form, rather rounded and short, is stamped with maker's name which also is on the left side of the barrel, that is octagon at breech. A specimen is shown in Golden State Arms Company's sales catalog *World's Guns;* another specimen sold by Kelly & Malloy, July, 1962, has a Justice trigger guard.

Remington

There is a suspicion that one of the best-known makes of rifles also entered into this field of militia arms, that of the Remington Harpers Ferry Rifle. Delivery of this arm to the United States did not occur until April 18, 1863, under formal contract of August 11, 1862, with the United States Ordnance Department. But preliminary talks toward furnishing this arm began at the end of July, 1861. Eli Remington went to Washington about July 18 with specimens of the revolvers; after talks with Ripley, on July 29, 1861, an order was sent for 5,000 revolvers, and on July 30, another order for 10,000 rifles, caliber .58, "with sword bayonet stud similar to those of the Harpers Ferry rifle model of 1855, in other respects of the pattern of the rifles without bayonets (i.e., M1841) heretofore made by you for this department." While we may err in putting the Remington "Harpers Ferry rifle" into this class, it is not worse than lumping the Whitney Minie Rifles into the Confederate category. The possibility that both Whitney and Remington were interested in Southern contracts is not remote; that Whitney precipitously delivered junky old rifles worn out, while Remington sought to build a good rifle from the ground up, is characteristic of both their firms. Whitney lost the Mississippi contract by being too quick. Remington lost out on any Southern sales by being too slow; he ultimately sought acceptance by Ripley of the nonstandard rifle. Why Ripley accepted this rifle cannot be ascertained, but if Remington already had some capability to produce it, this would have been an important factor in Ripley's judgment. The expression "in other respects of the pattern of the rifles without bayonets heretofore made by you for this department" is not a demand by Ripley for uniform interchangeability with the US M1841 rifles. Parts of the Remington Harpers Ferry rifle, erroneously but popularly called "Zouave rifle," will not interchange with the M1841 rifle.

Krider

Closer to the form of M1841 rifle as manufactured in the South is the militia rifle of J. H. Krider, Philadelphia. Somewhat more common than others of this breed, the Krider rifle was "an exceptionally well-made piece, but does not conform to any U. S. Model." The patchbox is the Sharps-form of Justice and Henry. Brass mounted, with white-metal stock tip, the rear sling swivel is attached to the guard bow like the Enfield. The 33-inch barrel has seven-groove rifling, caliber .58, the fixed rear sight, no proof marks, a cone seat like the M1841-2 pattern, is browned finish, and is stamped PHILADELA. The Enfield-type lock is

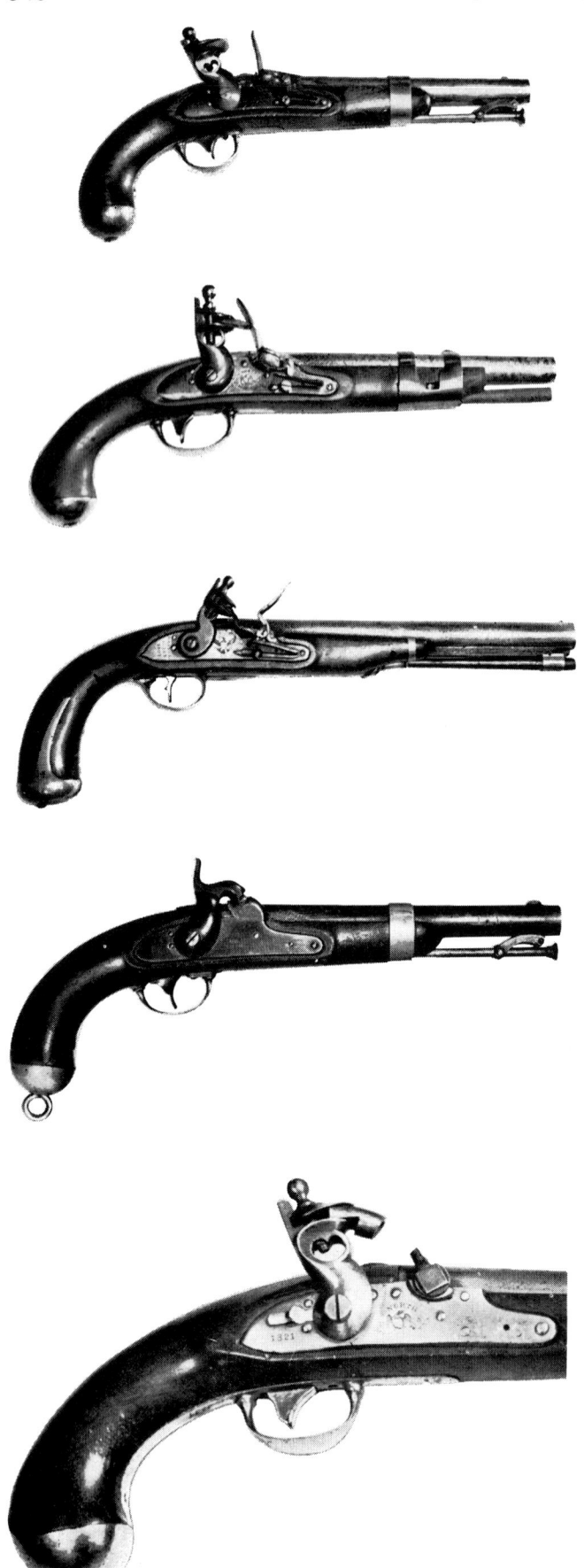

stamped KRIDER, and is casehardened. Lock and cone seat touch, and there is a sliver of stock wood surrounding lock under the cone seat. Length overall 4 feet 1½ inches; weight 8½ pounds.

There is a possibility it was this rifle of which Alabama purchasing agent J. R. Powell wrote on December 6 and December 7, 1860. He was at the St. Nicholas Hotel in New York travelling through New England and down to Washington and back. He had purchased a lot of "Minnie guns" already, but for a time the New York market was cleared of surplus, a "European order of which I telegraphed you has taken up all the Government arms and that the agents understood to represent Victor Emanuel have bought all the Minnie guns for sale in (the) trade." The Italians were also having a Civil War. On the 7th Powell stated positively: "I have contracted today for 365 more Minnie muskets, 5 grooves instead of seven which the others had, at $13."

That these were not Whitney arms is proved by his statement that "Whitney's factory of New Haven I have not visited from the prejudices with which you inspired me toward his guns before I left home. I understand he has served Mississippi worse than our state."

In addition to Mississippi and Alabama, another state which seems to have explored the possibility of Northern equipment prior to the final rupture in April was Tennessee. The only justification for this claim in particular is the recent finding "in Tennessee" of serial number "1" of the Orison Blunt Enfield Rifle Musket.

Orison Blunt Enfield Rifle Musket

At the time this arm was discovered, it was assumed to be a good long Enfield, and was sold as such by the finding collector at the Columbus, Ohio, gun collectors' show in October, 1961, to a dealer who priced it as a good shooting Enfield. The author had passed this display several times and seen nothing to interest him, when on the final pass he was asked by another customer if a spare parts sling swivel being offered for sale would fit an Enfield.

In responding, "Yes, it fits on the guard like this

Southern pistols included specimens of U.S. issue from early days. Most found were probably Johnson M1836 flintlock cal. .54, (top), but some North M1816 arms could be found (2d). Half-stock US M1806 pistol made at Harpers Ferry was popular and same model was made at Virginia State Armory early in century. Arm shown has been restocked, with country repair to ramrod guide. Major supplies of single shots were Aston or Waters U.S. M1842 percussion guns, also cal. .54. Butt ring is non-issue addition for lanyard. Southern conversions from flint were often simplest type possible, like this altered North 1819 model (dated 1822) with hammerhead gripped in jaws of original flint cock, and country rifle drum screwed into barrel. Pernicious habit of modern dealers in "putting back" old converted arms to flint using cast iron parts and clumsy fitting reduces genuine old examples of this transition era; frequently destroys Southern association of gun which could be revealed by study of conversion systems. (Top three pistols from collection at Independence Hall, Chicago.)

one here," he noticed that "this one" was of U.S. Rifle form, and a moment later picked up the gun to examine the proof marks. Instead of British marks, the barrel breech 1-9/16 inches forward of the back bore an oval proof mark ¼-inch long, encircling the initials DP/B. The oval is engraved, not stamped, and at the finish of the engraving circle the engraver cut a little inside the more gentle curve of the oval and had to put his tool again to the metal to finish the loop oval. It is generally considered this mark stands for "Definitive Proved, Blunt," in keeping with Blunt's recognized knowledge of British and continental gun-making practice as he testified later before the Holt Committee.

The barrel is exactly 40 inches long, the rear steel screw-clamping band exactly 10 inches on its middle from the barrel breech flat. The hammer of straight Enfield form is originally not checkered on the spur and is rather slender in the neck. The Enfield-type lockplate is border engraved but the engraver did not finish his job, doing little more than scratching the double guide lines in and that not completely around. Behind the hammer a crown is stamped, the die jumping for a double stamp. While this resembles the British St. Edward's Crown on Enfield locks, it is not the same stamp, for example, as on the Robbins & Lawrence "Windsor" Enfield locks.

Forward of the hammer the mark: 1860/TOWER is fraudulently engraved. That it is fraudulent is revealed by the lock itself: thicker in the plate than an Enfield lock, and with the rear boss where the "side nail" or rear lockplate screw is supposed to enter, undrilled. Instead, the rear lock screw is set forward about 1⅛ inch and the threads are cut in a hole drilled through the thin part of the plate forward of the hammer. Threads of both side screws are finer than Enfield threads. To clear the new location of rear screw, the spring stirrup and forward limb of the tumbler have been filed bright after final drawing to a bronzy temper after hardening. If they had not been filed down, they would perhaps wedge against the rear screw when installed.

All the lock parts are straw colored. File finishing is good, but the spring, of true Enfield form, has many scars on the surface and would never have passed the sharp inspectors at either Tower, in England. The lock, case hardened in smoky gray-blue colors, is entirely unmarked as to bona-fide maker's marks. To accommodate the new location of rear side screw, the stock is likewise drilled and the square-tipped brass escutcheons sunk there and in the regular place for the front screw. In the spot where the regular rear screw is on the ordinary Enfield, a plug of walnut has been inserted and the grain is a little cockeyed to the grain of the stock; inside, the fact that the screw hole was provisionally drilled in the wood is shown by it coming all the way through the wood in the usual place, but never had a piece of metal in it. The stock is of good, straight-grained military American black walnut, unmarked; the brass nose cap, trigger guard, and buttplate are of Enfield form. The trigger plate is like the Enfield, but squared at the ends instead of rounded. Beneath the butt plate a centerline and cross scribed marks appear, indicating hand work in the stock finishing. The bottom of the barrel near to the breech plug, and the stock inletting opposite, are both stamped 1. The tang screw passes through the location of the regular Enfield rear side screw, accounting for the relocation.

In relocating, the screw now passes across the line of the breech plug wedge, hence this section is notched to receive it. The barrel cannot be lifted free from the stock unless the rear lockplate side screw is removed. The ramrod fitted bears the name DEELEY lightly stamped near the regular Enfield-shaped head. The cone unscrewed readily with the fingers when this gun was first examined, and apparently has never been fired; the rifling, 3 deep grooves of half the width of the lands, was in perfect condition. Cap size was not for musket, but smaller as for rifle or pistol caps. The original bayonet, its existence revealed by marking in the finish at the muzzle, was not found; the regular Springfield type fits the sight-base stud better than the Enfield, which has too much sideplay, but the socket of the bayonet extends 1/16th of an inch forward of the muzzle so those shipped with these rifles must have had deeper slots and different locking rings, or else were cut flush with the muzzle when individually fitted.

The snapcap of Enfield form was attached to the rear swivel by prying the chain's last brass loop open enough to slip it over the swivel screw-base end, then crimping it tight after assembly. The interior of the hammer striking face is cut in a hemisphere shape with a deeper short cylindrical recess shrouding the nipple; this form is not found on Enfields generally. The barrel is browned by a rust-blacking process, now somewhat worn; the original metal surface of the barrel was not polished by emery, but finely file-finished.

While these minute details may seem redundant, they are cited because they reveal the emergency fitting up by non-standard methods of good military rifle parts to produce a good military rifle. If the Tennessee origins of this rifle mean anything, more than that some later collector bought the gun in the North at a junk shop and ultimately sold it in Tennessee, then it suggests this was Blunt's first pattern musket sent down to Tennessee as a sample. That samples were sent down is proved by J. R. Powell's letter cited, to Governor Andrew B. Moore of Alabama: "I send to you by express also a specimen of Colt's Navy pistol as a present for you. Also some samples of guns for your inspection." The Navy sent was the M1851, serial 95844 and is owned by a descendant of the governor today.

Another M1851 Navy Colt is the same period of sale, #94745, and was carried by, as near as can be made out from the marking, W. W. Edwards, Company B, of Terry's Texas Rangers. A Hartford-stamped gun, evidently the resistance to Hartford-marked products in some Texas circles, was not so much as

Hartley imagined. As J. R. Powell wrote to Governor Moore, "I think it would be well to let me order some more (arms) of Hartford manufacture."

It is not wise to generalize too much on the samples and pre-war purchased arms with which the South was sprinkled, lest one fall prey to such relic-creators as the chap who called on J. M. Shafer, a columnist for the present-day Altoona, Pennsylvania *Mirror*. As Shafer wrote to the author April 14, 1961, "People keep insisting I take a look at their Civil War relics. Last evening I saw a queer one. It was a Henry barrel attached to a Martini action and had a full American walnut stock. On the right side of the rifle butt was attached a brass name plate which read, 'This rifle is the property of James O. Swithley, Company B, 3rd Virginia Cavalry, 1863.' On the action is stamped 'Martini Patent No. 9354.' On the barrel is stamped 'Henry Arms Company, B7194.' The rifle is of .45-70 caliber. Also stamped on the action are a pair of crossed guidons with the letter "B" immediately below the guidons."

It is perhaps hardly worth commenting that the metallic cartridge rifle described was a development of the Swiss engineer F. von Martini modifying the breech from the American Peabody rifle of 1865, which was combined with the Scotsman Tyler F. Henry's rifling, and in .450 Martini-Henry caliber (not .45-70) was adopted in 1871 to replace the Snider breech-loading conversions in the British service. The crossed guidons is the British Army ordnance proof mark and the rifle so blithely carrying the date "1863" was manufactured some years after 1871. With this guidepost to the maxim of *caveat emptor* in the field of Confederate firearms, we may now proceed.

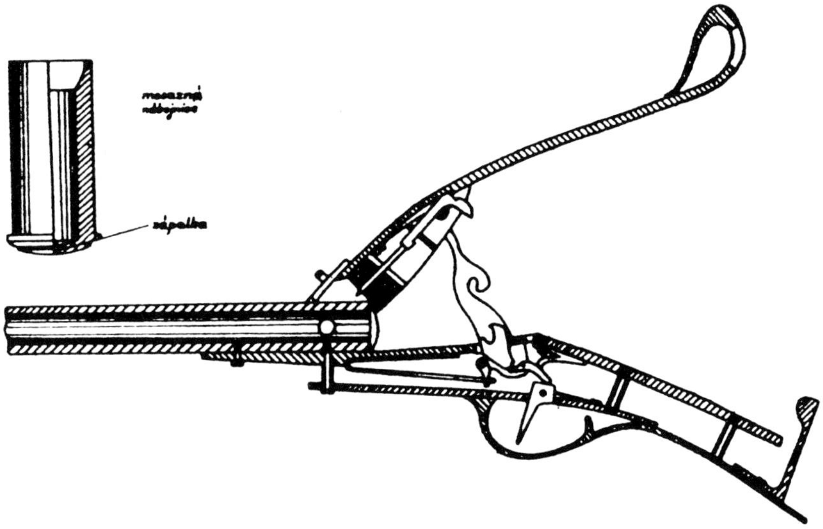

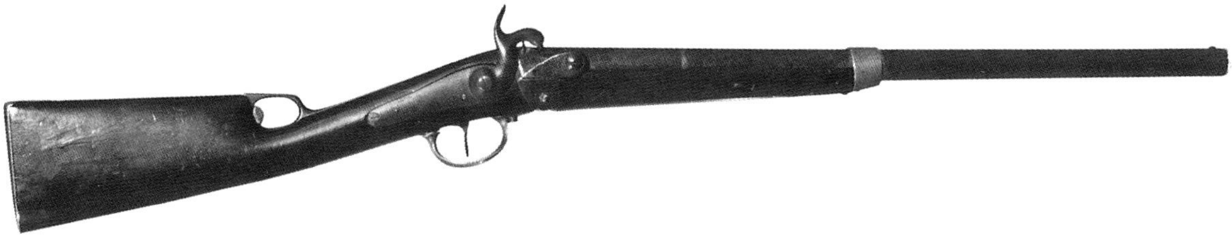

Reputed CSA smoothbore is unique Pauly system .70 cal. "mousqueton" of French design. Former owner said that his grandfather, who was in the Confederate cavalry, brought it across the Plains to California after the war. Gun's barrel is engraved, "Invention de LeFaucheux — Pauly." Monkey tail breechloader by J.S. Pauly was rejected by Napoleon I. Pauly died ca. 1820s in England, but his gunsmith-protege Casimir LeFaucheux continued to work in Paris. Cartridge is percussion variant of Desnyau patent May 4 and June 11, 1840, and gun's garniture and back action lock conform to French service models of that period. Gun was probably a sample sent to the South in hopes of contract for French inventor. Design reflects last effort of Pauly style and first tipping barrel breechloading before LeFaucheux perfected his T-type swing lever latch, used on European shotguns and rifles. Reloadable charger with percussion cone led to innovation of pin fire cartridges. Odd little gun is "missing link" in arms technology.

CHAPTER 28

Sidearms For Southrons

At a meeting of the Texas Gun Collectors Association several years ago this author got a terrible shock. He stopped at a table upon which were a number of percussion revolvers purported to be Confederate. They were not for sale; their proud owner had spent a pretty penny in amassing what is recognized as the best collection of Confederate revolvers in the world. But the shock came because the author, having some handiness with a file himself, was forced into the realization that if *he* couldn't do a better job of butchering up a pistol conglomeration composed of bits of Manhattan, Metropolitan, different vintages of Navy Colt, and turn the barrel round, ad nauseum, he would *quit!* The statement is not to give offense to the collector—he knows who he is, and he knows that his fellow collectors regard him with sincerity as a gentleman and a scholar. The statement is to point out three morals:

Three Rules For the Collector

1. Beware of any "unknown" Confederate revolver, for though aspirations and contracts or offers of arms to be delivered in the future were many, the actual number of going gunmakers who fulfilled their responsibilities were few.

2. The modern home handyman with more junk pistol parts and an equal helping of junk ethics is turning out Confederate pistols in quantity quite equal to the wistful cupidity of the collectors. There is more money around for Confederate sidearms than there are C.S.-made revolvers to buy. A typical Confederate revolver that in 1957 was referred to in awe as worth $300-$500, today cannot be bought for $1,500. One gun not even considered by many authorities to be "Confederate" (though it will be seen that we differ in this point of view) is the St. Louis-made Shawk & McLanahan. In 1958 we were queried as to the value of one; refused to say more than it is worth "several hundreds of dollars." When we checked into the status of the gun a year later, we were informed that "It is still for sale and the price is $6,000." Though of a limited production run, certain things did set it apart from the others of the same make. For a unique Confederate arm of importance, there is almost no limit to the prices asked. The destitute South has arisen again, not with money having 12-pounder Napoleons printed on the backs, but with good old United States Notes and Silver Certificates. Major market for the Confederate revolver is in the South, particularly among the better heeled Texans. To the buyer, *caveat emptor* is the maxim.

3. Unfortunately for the historian, the South had a demand for revolvers almost as pressing as the financial demand today to fake something up. Second-hand parts, components sold off as non-standard by a big factory, limited production runs of Northern arms unmarked or with Southern issue markings, all serve to confuse the serious researcher. Mingled with fakes of 40 or 50 years ago, now thoroughly aged, or refinished arms of two generations past now russetted into a semblance of "originality," are the genuine individual pieces made as prototypes, shop or promotion models, or as a gun to defend Ol' Massa when he went off to the war.

The skills of the Southern manor blacksmiths should not be underrated. Negro gunsmiths in the Carolinas, slave and free, worked before the war and their products recognized as such today are creditable pieces of workmanship. It was the black man at the forges in the Tredegar who shaped the sinews of war for Colonel Burton's rifle factory. The owner of a slave who was a skillful mechanic was a prosperous man, for the hire of the Negro to the local factory was a good source of income. Hence, among the fakes from the early days of gun collecting, and the confusion of the current crop of "Palmetto Armory" pistol handimen, exist genuine rarities. The still-unrecognized Confederate pistol is rare, because nearly all Confederate pistols have characteristics in common; they are copies of the Colt or the Whitney. But just as the fake "unique" piece should not be gobbled up too eagerly, so the collector should not be too quick to condemn a specimen of a hitherto unknown pattern reputed to be "Confederate." The bad habits of most collectors in failing to record, in the form of affidavits that would stand up in court, the known facts, and the relevant hearsay, when they kick up such a gun from "out of the bushes," is a serious loss to gun collecting, history of the South, and their own pocket books in that order.

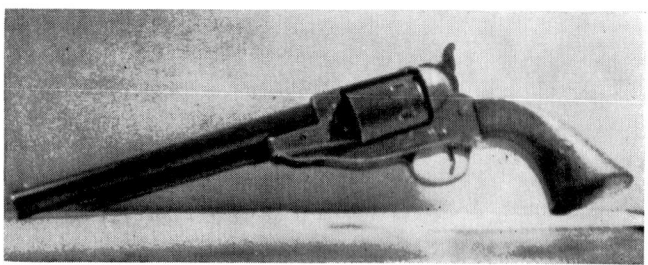

Shawk & McLanahan brass-framed revolver resembled the Whitney but had more support to barrel threads like later Southern Spiller & Burr, and was stronger on frame angle below barrel. Gun shown, No. 2, is marked WILLIAM TEGETHOFF, name of firm's backer.

The Shawk & McLanahan Revolver

The original Confederate Colt is considered to be the brass-framed revolvers of Colonel Griswold made near Macon, Georgia. But to touch on the original, it is necessary to backtrack to a period, as in the militia musket confusion, immediately prior to the war. Militant nervousness, distance from protection of the Federal forces in the East, and a spirit of taking care of one's own problems oneself, brought William Abel Shawk, of Pennsylvania, J. K. McLanahan of Cincinnati, and William Tegethoff, loan broker of St. Louis, together in Carondelet, Missouri. There was produced for a very short time the Shawk & McLanahan pre-Civil War Missouri revolver. A brass-framed .36 six-shooter somewhat resembling the Whitney, the "usual" specimen is marked on backstrap of butt, *Shawk & McLanahan, St. Louis, Carondelet, Mo.* But S & McL pistol serial No. 2 bears the mysterious stamping WILLIAM TEGETHOFF, a neat die stamp, on barrel, frame, and cylinder. Research by St. Louis gunsmith Robert H. Vaughn who owns this interesting pistol revealed that Tegethoff was in the loan business, either a pawn shop or the predecessor of today's "building & loan associations," and was a backer of Shawk in making these guns. No. 2 presumably was given to Tegethoff, who used the same die with which he might have marked silverware which he sold, to indicate ownership of this gun. No. 16 is recorded by Fuller; how many S & McL pistols were made is anybody's guess.

The link between Shawk and Charles H. Rigdon, of the St. Louis firm Rigdon & Harmsted, scale makers, is tenuous. Shawk had made a fire-engine and sold it to the city of St. Louis in 1855 and went there to demonstrate it. Rigdon later served as "engineer" of the fire-engine. That the two met seems probable. Albaugh says Rigdon supplied the machinery with which Shawk made the revolvers.

In 1858 Shawk petitioned the authorities of the St. Louis suburb of Carondelet to allow him to establish a factory for the manufacture of locks and fire-engines. The firm name was Shawk & McLanahan. There Shawk invented a rifling machine and there built the revolvers. Rigdon's "machinery" if there was any obtained by Shawk, may have been fixtures for making the gun. The weapon is well made and the skilled professional engineering hand of Rigdon seems evident in the S & McL pistol. The market for this weapon was big. The popular sentiment in the South was, that a man should be allowed to carry a gun if he wanted to. Perhaps the Code Duello was relied upon too heavily for disciplining hotheads, but pistol carrying while travelling as well as the right to "keep a gun around the house" was inborn in the population. Numerous state laws protected this right. While Richmond authorities later were to go around the country scavenging sporting arms and private weapons, the situation provoked Governor Clark of North Carolina to issue a proclamation that Confederate agents "have no lawful authority to seize your private arms, and you will be protected in preserving the means of self-defense." The conflict between a good Navy six for ol' Granny to protect the ol' manse, and the needs of the cavalry, fighting in a far state, were given substance by the Constitution of the Confederate States of America. Article I, Sec. 9, Par. 13 states: "A well-regulated militia being necessary to the security of a free State, the right of the people to keep and bear arms shall not be infringed."

The appointment of former presidential candidate John Charles Fremont as general commanding the Western Department with headquarters in St. Louis terminated Shawk's revolver venture. Shawk, a Pennsylvania Quaker (man of peace?) remained a loyal Union man; Rigdon sided with the South and took his machinery with him. The actual fixtures for shaping the S & McL pistol doubtless remained behind in Carondelet, ultimately to be junked. Rigdon's contribution to the South seems to have been a barge load of basic machine tools, and his engineering savvy.

Leech and Rigdon

Rigdon floated his gear downriver to Memphis. There he found Thomas Leech, gunsmith and sword maker doing business as the Memphis Novelty Works. Leech's "novelties" consisted of cavalry swords, rolled armor plate, and gun repair; of the latter, presumably making hammers and percussioning was the principal activity. Rigdon may have been engaged in setting up a revolver works, for the Memphis *Daily Appeal*, November 15, 1861, states that the "Eagle Foundry" of Streeter, Chamberlain & McDaniel was preparing to make "Colt revolvers." A "Colt revolver" was what Rigdon was eventually to make under his own name. Navy-type revolvers by Leech & Rigdon and Rigdon & Ansley were probably the best-manufactured mass-production revolvers of the South.

In partnership with Thomas Leetch, the name of the firm Leech & Rigdon first appeared in print May, 1862, advertising swords for sale. But the threat of Federal forces and the war on the Western waters was brought home to Memphis, caused Confederate authorities to urge the removal of arms-making potential further into the deep South. L & R had planned for this move in March, buying land in Columbus, Missis-

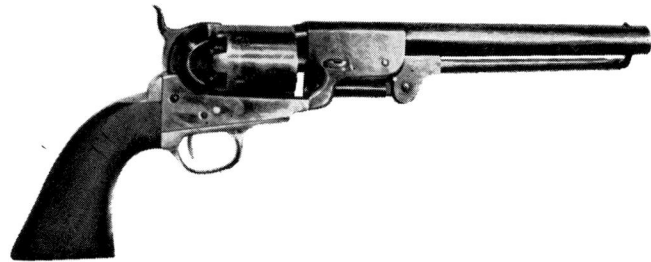

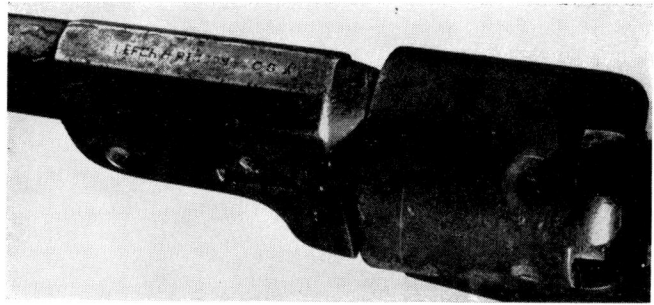

First type Leech & Rigdon had round barrel typical of Southern "Navy Colts" and conventional 6-notch cylinder. Barrel top (inset) was stamped with firm name until C.S. Government took over management; thereafter CSA was added. Serial of barrel-cylinder shown is 942 or 972: pieces are mounted upon Colt Navy frame and have been so for many years. Button-pin latch is characteristic of early production Leech guns under 1,000 serial.

sippi. To this site they shifted, departing from Memphis May 9, 1862. The order of General Beauregard to evacuate arms plants from Memphis doubtless affected the Eagle Foundry as well; no pistols have been identified as of this factory, and it may be that Rigdon first tried to work with them; failed and turned to Leech; was interrupted by the removal to Columbus. And in turn, this set-up was dismantled in December, finally moving to Greensboro, Georgia, about December 15. There in the Greensboro Steam Factory, which they bought, the first revolvers were made.

Set-up time apparently occupied them for two months only; on March 6, 1863, Leech & Rigdon received a contract to manufacture revolvers for the C. S. War Department. It is believed L & R guns made after this date bear the CSA stamp on the barrel. L & R ended their partnership December, 1863, and Rigdon moved to Augusta, Georgia. Some or all of the revolver tooling went with him; Augusta-made Rigdon revolvers have trigger guards of the same unique form as the earlier L & R pistol guards. In Georgia, Rigdon formed a partnership with C. R. Keen, and A. J. Smythe as minor shareholders, Jesse A. Ansley as a fourth investor, and Rigdon as principal.

Rigdon and Ansley

In January, 1864, Rigdon, Ansley & Company was formed, but in the South things are done, as Mrs. Margaret Mitchell said, "more leisurely." By a curious coincidence, the production delay in a baby and in a Colt-type revolver (the author has reason to know from making some thousands of the *latter* recently) is nine months. But in the South, as in Mrs. Mitchell's great book, the gestation period for both babies and revolvers apparently was longer. It was not until March 13, for example, that water power was arranged for the shop; when at last Rigdon began to put up finished revolvers is not known but apparently he began cutting metal in March for power would not have been needed before then.

Ansley, though described by Rigdon as essential to the revolver business, was not judged so by the local draft board. Early in 1864 he was conscripted and eventually in January, 1865, advertised his one-fourth interest in "the pistol factory—a very desirable paying investment," for sale. At the "desirable paying investment" Smythe organized the Rigdon Guards, himself as captain. The pistol workmen, some 60 hands, took part in the defense of another revolver factory, in the battle of Griswoldville, Georgia, November 22, 1864, and Smythe and others were wounded.

Another threat to the pistol factory by Yankee raiders in December made the plant a rallying point for home guards. Rigdon stuck to his guns and during February still was in operation, to judge from General Gorgas' order to Colonel Burton to assume supervision over work at the Macon, Athens, Columbus, and Tallassee Armories and "the contract establishment of Rigdon & Ansley at Augusta."

Rigdon's Colt-type revolvers differ obviously from the Colt Navy M1851 prototypes in having barrels turned round forward of the breech. Numbers are on butt strap front of guard strap, bottom of barrel breech, joining spot on frame like Colt, top inner flat of loading lever, and usually on the side of cylinder between two of the shoulders.

While the form of the handles is well shaped and very much like the Colt, the contour of the trigger guard differs and appears to be uniform throughout all known genuine Rigdon revolvers, of whatever place of origin. The radius inside is a little sharper at the rear of the trigger. A specimen in the author's collection, while much rusted on the steel parts, is clean on the brass and shows a good amount of "mechanization" in the manufacture. The width of the trigger guard

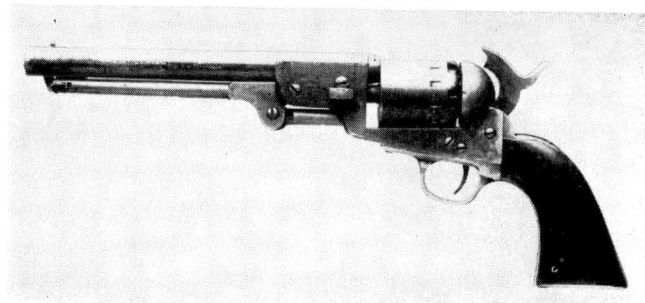

Twelve cylinder stops and Navy-type loading lever latch distinguish this later Rigdon & Ansley revolver from earlier production, but trigger guard roots reveal same milling cut as first pistols. Finish was originally casehardened, frame and lever, with blued barrel and cylinder. Handle straps are brass.

was cut by a straddle-mill set-up to judge from remaining tool marks, and the back of the strap to which the mainspring attaches was profile milled. Filing or "striking up" in the white stage was very skillfully done. The main spring, though not polished, has been filed its length (to avoid cracking from cross-file cuts) and is neatly tapered in width and thickness to give a good spring action to the hammer. The serial number 964 is stamped with the "9" one space *above* the line of the "6." An eighth inch below the serial is stamped D. Reading from the muzzle, the top barrel flat is stamped LEECH & RIGDON CSA and appears to set the production of the Confederate contract guns from at least this serial number. Albaugh states L & R are supposed to have made 350 pistols, approximately, in Columbus. Study of all Rigdon revolvers reveals there is no overlap and that apparently he began numbering in Columbus and continued in Greensboro and the same series in Augusta. The range recorded is as high as 2330, in the Milwaukee Public Museum.

With Jesse Ansley, Rigdon introduced a prominent design feature, an additional set of cylinder stop slots, making 12 in all. A further change, which had been introduced in the beginning of the CSA Leech & Rigdon contract, was the loading lever Navy latch. Early L & R revolvers have a latch captive in the lever with a cross pin for releasing, like the Yankee Starr pistols. No. 964 has the regular Navy latch, like a Colt Navy, but No. 899, carried by Colonel Harry Gilmor of the 2d Maryland (CSA) Cavalry, is the "Starr" latch. A further detail change seems to be in the exact filed-up profile of the front of the barrel breech; on Rigdon, Ansley & Company guns this seems to assume more of a forward slant than most of L & R pistols; but a few L & R pistols are found with this shape.

The Rigdon, Ansley & Company 12-stoppers (a safety feature but causing considerable re-timing of the lock work to function right) do not bear the firm name, only CSA. That these are the products of Rigdon, and a continuation of Leech & Rigdon, was not understood some years ago, but was surmised by the failure of serials to be found overlapping. Yet the trigger guard form, distinctive once it is understood this guard was made by machine and in quantity and all alike, is a far more important clue to the maker's identity.

Rigdon may have struggled to keep the plant going until the very end; at least one of these pistols is known with barrel and cylinder mounted upon a contemporaneous Colt Navy M1851 frame and handle. The use of genuine Colt parts, where they would fit, is not unique among Confederate handguns; though uncommon, it did happen.

Griswold & Gunnison

The factory that the Rigdon Guards fought to save was their competitor, that of Samuel Griswold and A. W. Gunnison. When war came, Griswold converted his cotton gin factory to arms making and by July, 1862, was in the pistol business. At this time 24 hands

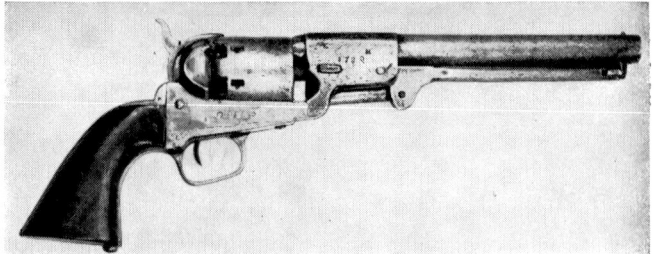

Col. E. C. Grier's brass-framed .36 Army pistol made at Griswoldville, Ga., was rugged and sturdy supplement to firepower of Southern chivalry. Factory was among most reliable producers in South in spite of harassment and eventual destruction by Kilpatrick's cavalry.

were working 22 machines; 100 pistols were in the works. Twenty-two of the workmen were slaves. From the time the shop began production to its destruction during the battle at Griswold 3,600 "Colt" revolvers were made there. The distinguishing feature of this series is the brass frame. Brass-plating an iron frame on an otherwise unidentified revolver purporting to be "CSA" has been noted, so checking an offered Griswold & Gunnison pistol with a magnet should be a routine collector's precaution today.

Because Colonel E. C. Grier, Griswold's son-in-law, had some connection with the enterprise, these pistols are sometimes called "Griswold & Grier." More often found heavily used, these guns were delivered under a contract to the C. S. Government entered into about August, 1862, "for as many as the manufacturers could produce." The machinery had taken from March to August to set up, but was quite simple and the casting of the frames with inner cuts already cored out greatly reduced the machinery needed. Only the saving in machine time and in tooling can account for this lavish use of even normally valuable brass when the Confederacy was in dire need of metal for making percussion caps. Production was anticipated to be five guns a day.

Years ago it was assumed by collectors that the brass-framed Colts were made at different points throughout the South, that they were "typical" of Southern revolvers. Evidence they were the output of one factory was gathered by E. Berkeley Bowie of Baltimore, whose gun collection is now deposited at the Fort McHenry National Monument, Baltimore. "Mr. Bowie at one time probably had more of these brass framed Colts than any museum or individual," writes R. D. Stuart in *Firearms of the Confederacy*. "He found that the brass in them was of the same quality and texture; that the rifling—six grooves right—was done with the same machine, and that there was no overlapping of serial numbers." Trigger guards of the G & G pistols are rather squarish in shape, and the handle gives an effect of being tilted very slightly backward; the difference between it and a Colt is quite pronounced. The depth of the brass frame at the front edge is also greater than the depth of the Colt at this same point; while the bullet loading cut-out is not so widely cut as the Colt. Early G & G's seem to have round barrel breeches; those made after serial No. 1500 (approximately) are octagonal breech. Frame, barrel, and cylinder are usually marked with the full serial number, boldly stamped on the frame right side, barrel right side, and side of cylinder (or all left side, but uniform). Exceptions to this require a good deal of corroboration in other manufacturing details before permitting the gun to be certified as a genuine G & G. Relics dug up at the site of the factory, burned by Kilpatrick's cavalry, indicate forgings and stampings were used; the first for the barrels, the latter for the hammers. The hammers were punched out of rolled iron sheet, as female profile die and hammer blanks in different stages of finish have been found at the site of the factory, much rusty but still recognizable. Use of World War II surplus mine detectors has given great stimulus to battlefield and factory-site explorations among gun cranks with an archeological turn of mind.

Spiller & Burr

While the G & G was purchased at about $50 each by the Confederacy, it was considered, in the eyes of Colonel Burton, to be inferior to the Spiller and Burr. Another brass-framed CS pistol, these were made by Edward N. Spiller of Baltimore and David J. Burr. The latter was owner of a machine works in Richmond, and at first there was some consideration given to setting up the pistol works in the Virginia capital. Chief promoter behind this move was James Henry Burton. That the man in public life most noted for the mechanical excellence of Southern arms should set up a private factory is not too strange. In June, 1861, he was commissioned a lieutenant colonel of Ordnance in the Virginia military establishment by Governor Letcher; not until December was he commissioned in the Regular Army of the Confederate States, with the same rank, as Superintendent of Armories. His offer to General Gorgas made in November, 1861, would seem to have had something to do with it. Gorgas had recommended Burton should set up a pistol factory; in response to this suggestion, Burton wrote:

> I propose to establish the manufactury in or near to the City of Richmond and have made arrangements to secure the most experienced talent to engineer the mechanical requirements of the enterprise. I beg to enclose herewith a draft of the conditions and terms on which I propose to embark in the business and contract with the War Department for the supply of revolving pistols . . .
> . . . I would not be justified in embarking in the business on a Government contract for a less number than 15,000 pistols . . .

Burton asked for an advance of funds scheduled at perhaps a total of $100,000, to be returned to the Government by deductions of 20% from the prices charged in pistol deliveries. The frames were to be of "good, tough brass properly electroplated with silver," but the model of gun was not specified. On November 20, 1861, Burton made an agreement with Spiller and Burr to obtain for them a contract for 15,000 Navy revolvers; agreeing also to superintend the machinery, preparation of buildings, and the general manufacturing.

On November 30, 1861, the C.S. War Department contracted with Spiller and Burr for 15,000 Navy revolvers in terms which included the idea of cash advances and repayment out of deliveries, as Burton had originally proposed to Gorgas. The model to be made is specifically described as "of a pattern substantially the same as that known as Colts, the model of which will be supplied by the said War Department." Spiller and Burr were to be given the preference in orders for more pistols by the War Department provided of course they could deliver; in this preferential treatment there is a hint of Colonel Burton's lack of disinterestedness, though the clause was a great incentive to Spiller and Burr to do well. Burton's interest was attacked in the Confederate Congress; Gorgas came to his support, but Burton promptly sent in his resignation. Secretary of War George W. Randolph refused to accept it, but evidently Richmond was too warm for the pistol makers and they decided to set up in Atlanta, Georgia. There is no evidence any pistols were made in Richmond.

The plant was shifted to Atlanta in the summer and fall of 1862, and by December, Spiller was ready with a sample of the revolver. What gun this sample actually was is rather well confirmed by a complaint which Burton raised with Spiller about the latter's handling of drawings of the pistol. Spiller had been asked by the Columbus Firearms Manufacturing Company of Columbus, Georgia, to help them in their tooling-up. Spiller spoke to Burton about this, as he wanted to make duplicate tools for them and give them copies of Burton's carefully executed drawings. Burton objected to this; Spiller ignored the objections. So it was that Burton, while on duty at the Macon Armory in November, discovered that Haiman & Brothers, of Columbus, were in possession of copies of some of Burton's drawings. As a Confederate States Ordnance Officer, Burton should have been mailing out complete sets of Colt's Navy drawings to anybody who could use them; as a silent partner in Spiller & Burr he took Spiller through the wringer about giving technical know-how to the competition.

These drawings may not have been of much use to Haiman, for from them Spiller made one pistol and took it up to Richmond. It was well approved, but the bore apparently was a little tight by comparison with a Colt Navy. Spiller informed Burton that his pistols were found to be a trifle smaller than the Colt Navy and that he would have to change this, although it would give him trouble to do so. Meanwhile, no pistols were being delivered and General Gorgas was getting worried.

A new contract, taking into account the rise in costs of labor and essential materials, was set up between Spiller & Burr and the C.S. War Department, approved by the new Secretary of War James A. Seddon on March 5, 1863. Apparently 600 pistols were delivered

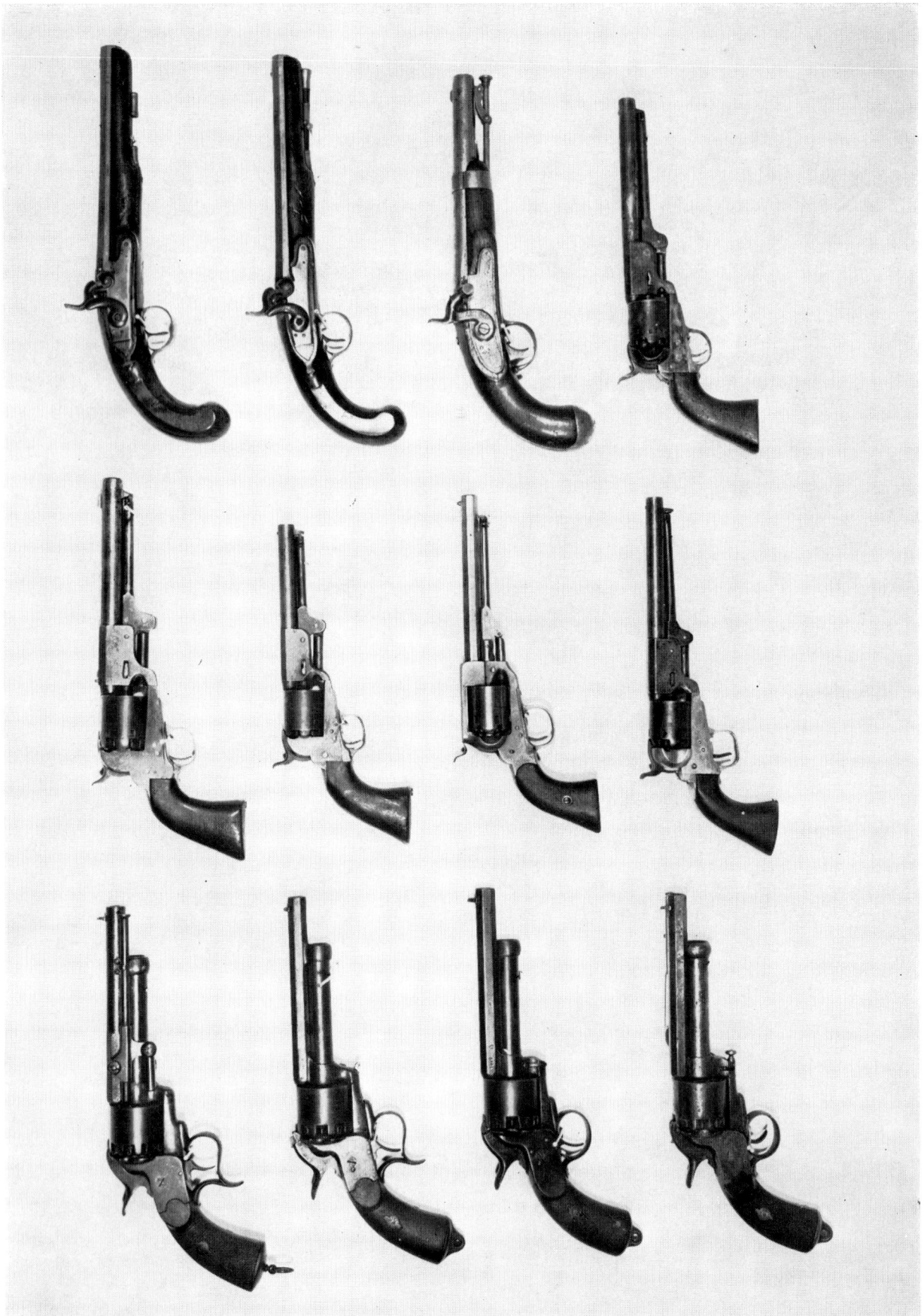

Confederate handguns in Forgett collection include LeMat first model with latch on barrel, transition type with improved lever, navy-guard types with different barrel latches. Middle column shows two Dance revolvers, .44 and .36, compared for size. Spiller & Burr is early issue before Burton took over factory and marked them CS; bottom is Griswold with frame made from church bell brass. Pair of duellers are Wogdon, London, style but have Southern conversion hammers; horse pistol is 1836 flinter rebuilt with new sporting lock and drum conversion by C. H. Slocomb & Co., New Orleans. Bottom, right, is Rigdon & Ansley 12-stop cylinder "navy" used in C. S. Army.

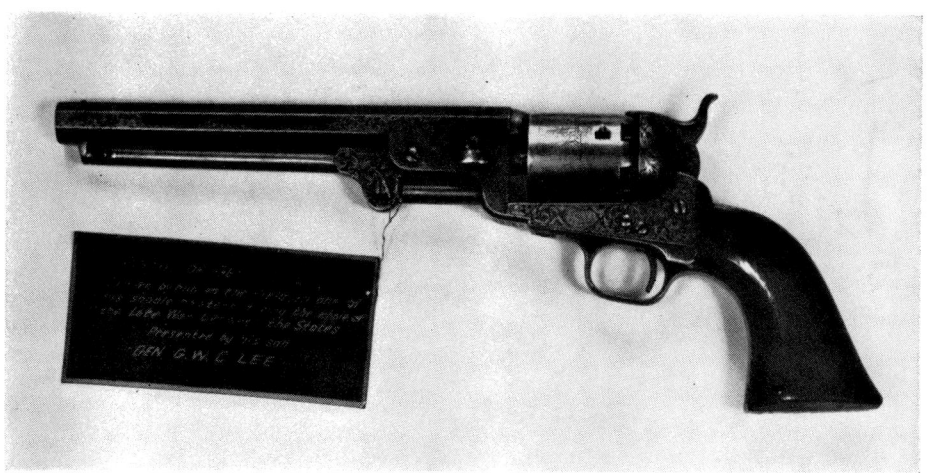

Colt Navy #37698 originally engraved was probably presented to General R. E. Lee by Sam Colt about 1854. Though tag affixed by Confederate White House Museum, Richmond, states arm was carried by General Lee in one of his saddle holsters during the War, probability is pistol was wrapped in oiled silk and never used during four years as condition seemed too good to reflect combat use.

during the month of February, for this curious March 5, 1863, contract specifies delivery of 600 guns in *February*, 1863, "and thereafter 1,000 pistols per month until the deliveries are completed."

The principal purpose of this contract seem to have been getting more money for Spiller, as the contract price was increased; the fact the firm did deliver and was now ready to deliver pistols may have had a strong influence in getting Gorgas to prepare the contract according to new terms. Under the March 5 contract, the old one was suspended, and with this suspension, contract terms calling for Colt-type revolvers were also suspended. For it seems that the remodeling of Spiller's tools to make a Colt-type arm of correct dimensions was too costly, and in a period prior to February, 1863, they resorted to casting the frames. A cast brass frame can be made in a mould of Whitney shape as easily as Colt, and the solid frame gun is cheaper to manufacture than the Colt type, by a factor of about 20% less cost at least. Moulder's patterns are more quickly made by hand from basswood, than are fixtures for attaching to machine tools.

Burton's insistence now that the contractor himself get up a model, and make gauges and drawings from it, suggests the preparation of the Whitney-framed Spiller and Burr as commonly known was an attempt to overcome some obstacle in manufacturing. But production did not continue regularly. By February, 1864, they were so far behind that Colonel Burton obtained an appropriation of $125,000 on the 29th to complete the purchase of the machinery, tools, fixtures, and materials of Spiller & Burr, the Government having advanced $60,000 already to help finance their beginning.

Up to this time about 700 revolvers had been fabricated in Atlanta; the equipment was moved to the Confederate States Armory at Macon, Georgia, and there Colonel Burton managed the business directly. Existing records for the Government portion of this enterprise have survived and indicate that exactly 689 revolvers were made at Macon. About 1,400 Spiller & Burr guns were made of Whitney form, plus at least one "too small" of Colt Navy pattern. An unmarked pistol of obvious Spiller & Burr form exists, with burl walnut grips; it is supposed to be the model Burton required Spiller to make. The Whitney-type loading lever is attached to the cylinder pin, and that in turn is retained by a common screw entering from the right of the frame below barrel. Since it was desirable to have the cylinder out to clean the pistol, the design was modified to a turning lug, which when twisted, released the cylinder pin. Cylinders, originally intended with barrels to be of steel, were exempted from this in the contract if steel could not be obtained. They were made of iron, apparently twisted while hot, as the pistols have a spiral grain to the cylinders. The 6⅛-

Revolver presented to Stonewall Jackson by his men and now preserved in "White House" museum in Richmond is elaborately etched Lefaucheux double action pinfire 7mm probably purchased at Hartley, Schuyler & Graham and smuggled down from New York. Confederacy was not enthusiastic about metallic cartridge arms, imported few if any pinfires officially.

Famed guerrilla chief Quantrell is said to have carried two Dragoons at the saddle bow and two more in the belt, but this M1862 Colt New Police Pistol .36 caliber is at Ohio State University museum and recorded as carried by Quantrell.

inch octagon barrels are stamped (reading from muzzle) SPILLER & BURR; frame right front corner below bullet loading cut is stamped C.S. The barrel nipple, that is, the threaded rear portion, is entirely surrounded by the brass of the frame which comes flush to the front of the cylinder. It is possible that delays in getting these guns into production may have been caused by some trouble like splitting of the barrel at the breech if barrels were iron and soft. The original model would have been a Whitney pistol and on the Whitney, the barrel threads are partly exposed, unsupported, as the Whitney barrel is of strong cast steel. The iron Spiller & Burr barrels might crack at the breech until someone, presumably Burton, modified the design to shroud all with brass. If such a change occurred, it is not surprising no specimens exist with exposed barrel threads; as defective models, barrels split from firing, they would have been tossed back into the melting pot to make good guns.

The move of the Spiller & Burr equipment to Macon Armory was not followed by immediate resumption of production. Not until October, 1864, was the equipment set up anew. On the 5th, Burton telegraphed Gorgas saying Colonel Cuyler had no more arms for repairing and asked if he ought to unpack the pistol machinery and set it up to give the hands something to do. Gorgas at once replied that day by telegraph, "Put your pistol factory in operation & push the works;" by the 13th Burton could report resumption of production on the Spiller & Burr.

Cost of manufacture at Macon of the Spiller & Burr was high, reflecting depreciation of the value of the money: $62.21. This included $8.00 interest on capital invested, $200,000 at 8 per cent, revealing a production plan to make 2,000 revolvers, but failing to include any figure for plant renewal of worn machinery. Perhaps it was calculated at the end of producing 2,000 revolvers that the factory would still be worth the $200,000. Material cost $19.59, and labor and supervision was $34.62. One lucky member of the Texas Gun Collectors' association prizes a Spiller & Burr that he bid in at an auction, in a bucket of junk iron, for $1.50 the lot. Current value a century later is perhaps $600 or more; an appreciation on the Confederate currency in which Burton figured the revolver's worth of just about 1,000 per cent. If war-weary Southrons had saved their Confederate money invested in Confederate arms, verily the South could rise again! An odd S & B, formerly Richard Steuart's, now in the Norton Asner collection, is unmarked, frame corners are rounded, with rubber grips. Said to be original, they are unique.

Haiman Brothers, Louis and Elijah, fared less well in their efforts to make arms. As L. Haiman & Bro. they were highly successful in supplying general military stores, swords, sabers, but when they tried to make revolvers they failed. On August 26, 1862, Richmond gave them a contract to make 10,000 revolvers. They applied to Spiller & Burr for drawings and tools, and Spiller gave them some drawings for the Colt Navy, as made by Colonel Burton. What they made seemed never to conform to the drawings. No. 7 of their pistols exists: it is a 5-shot pocket .36 with approximately a 4½-inch octagon barrel. The pistol resembles one model of Manhattan without the customary 12-cylinder stop slots, and is reputed to be a "promotion model." Distinctive feature is the capping cut, which is low on the curve of the frame, as on certain Manhattans. No. 23 of the Columbus Firearms pistols is more "normal," with octagon breech round barrel. The capping cut out is rather small and the bottom edge is on a line drawn above the nearby percussion cone, when the cylinder is in the normal position, hammer down on a cone. No. 46 has a larger capping cut out, as does No. 50; the curve of the cut out spans approximately the distance between the outside edges of the two cone cutouts in the cylinder.

It is a little misleading to say, as Albaugh has stated, that these are "very similar in appearance to the Leech & Rigdon product." It is true both patterns have iron frames and round barrels, but the trigger guard of the Haiman revolver is a little more like the small guard Navy Colt, if generalizing on the basis of a few existing specimens is fair. Collectors estimate less than 100 revolvers were made before Columbus Firearms sold out to the Confederacy in the move, in late 1863, to put the manufacture of revolvers on a "professional" basis.

Haiman, as an old workman, David Wolfson of Columbus, Georgia, recollected to E. Berkeley Bowie in 1924. ". . . had two people from Virginia who were experts in the manufacture of Colt's revolvers or pistols, they built machinery to make the several parts of these pistols and we made quite a large number of them in exact imitation of the Colt army pistol . . . The pistol was made with round barrel and every part was made by machinery. The inspecting officer was a man in Captain Humphrey's office. I do not remember his name."

The "two men" may be Burton and Spiller, of Richmond. That "every part was made by machinery" is probably a correct recollection, for Burton's emphasis on precision manufacture and his knowledge of tooling was the bed-rock of know-how upon which the Confederacy built her arms. Though Columbus Firearms continued as a factory producing swords, the pistol tools appear to have been transferred to the Columbus Armory. There a "model" pistol was prepared and sent to Macon Armory for inspection in the spring of 1865; additional pistols were ready to ship, and Columbus asked Macon for shipping boxes. Macon, according to Albaugh, responded by saying Spiller & Burr boxes would not be suitable for shipping—the reason can only be guessed at. If these C.S.—Columbus Armory pistols differed from the Haiman product, their differences have not been noted.

The Cofer

One of the most ingenious revolvers of the South, rarest, and most impractical was the invention of Thomas W. Cofer. His was one of few Confederate patents on inventions of firearms, and was granted August 12, 1861. A gunsmith of Portsmouth, Virginia, engaging in selling ordinary sporting guns, Cofer conceived of a pre-loaded metallic cartridge for revolvers which could be used, and re-used, by the soldier in the field. The brass cartridge had an iron nipple screwed into the back, taking a common percussion cap. The cylinder was bored straight through, and when the cartridges were inserted, a rim held them in place. The square-shouldered nipple extended back and these were shielded by a rear plate which fitted over them closely enough to turn the cylinder as the plate was turned. The plate was notched for cylinder stops and had the ratchet. A spring latch on the frame beneath the barrel permitted sliding the cylinder pin forward to remove the cylinder for, presumably, quick loading. The cartridges were to be saved and re-used, and probably the relatively cheap cylinder, simply six chambers and a central arbor hole, could have been supplied as an inexpensive accessory to be used pre-loaded. What is perhaps a patent model of this first model Cofer is in the collection of B. D. Munhall, Bel Air, Maryland, who first recognized what it was. The gun has had an accident: the barrel and top of the frame is blown off, but the top stamping (some of which remains) probably was T. W. COFER'S PATENT/AUGUST 12, 1861. The marking appears to be individually hand stamped.

Perhaps it was after Cofer blew up his first model, that he turned to more conventional ideas. The same brass frame, with stub trigger, and a removable left

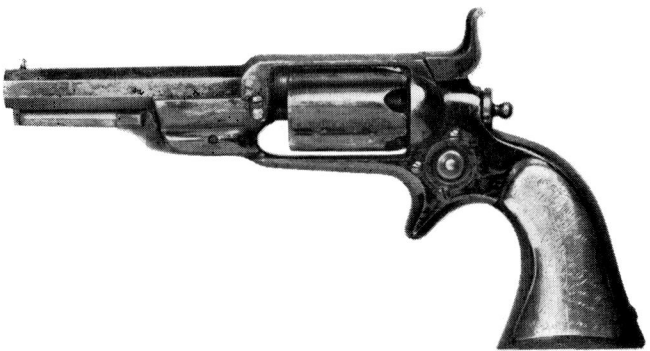

Sidehammer, 1855 Colt, .31 cal. revolver, No. 400 was owned by Major Wm. L. Bailey, C.S.A., on Joe E. Johnson's staff, as indicated on silver handle plate.

side plate was used, but the cylinder is conventional percussion and a Colt-type lever is hung below the barrel.

An exceptionally fine Cofer percussion model with the Colt-style loading lever was found about 1954 in Freeport, Maine, by collector Clifford Young. Mr. Young tracked the gun back, found it had been in one family since the Civil War, descendants of one S. H. Merrill who tagged the pistol's original flap leather holster "21 July 1864. This revolver and holster was captured from a rebel signal officer by Capt. S. H. Merrill, 11th Main Reg't." Aside from the name marking the only other marks are the letter L in two places on the frame, while the loading lever assembly is marked with the numeral 1. An apparently identical specimen, also in a holster but of different form, is No. 13 once owned by William Albaugh, who took a good description of it:

Six shot, .36 caliber, cylinder length 1¾ inches with six cylinder stops which are oblong. Barrel length 7 7/16 inches octagonal, right hand rifling seven grooves. Frame brass, width at the barrel ¾ inch. Top of frame stamped T. W. COFER'S/ PATENT in two lines; barrel stamped PORTSMOUTH, VA. all stamping reading down the barrel. Serial # 13 found on following parts—frame plate screws, hammer screw, rear of cylinder, front of frame under loading lever plunger, front left side

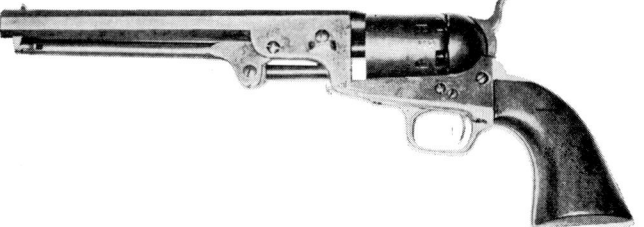

Thought of as somehow a Confederate-association piece is the Metropolitan Arms—H. E. Dimick St. Louis series of revolvers. Shown is a marked Metropolitan including naval scene on cylinder resembling Colt's but dated New Orleans, April, 1862, on cylinder, date of capture of that city, by Admiral Farragut. Unmarked specimens of this type are considered Dimick revolvers, while a few bear barrel marking "made for H. E. Dimick." It is presumed that Yankee Horace E. Dimick was not above selling guns down the river, a promiscuous trade in those days in the strongly Southern-sentiment city.

of loading lever, top of cylinder pin, under barrel next to the frame, inside of both wood grips, left side of hammer, hammer screw head, and inside of side plate.

That there may be some connection between the Cofer and the Spiller and Burrs is suggested by the use, by both makers, of a cast brass frame which in its rougher state is "like the Whitney," and by the Colt-type loading lever appearing on both series of arms. Though five or possibly only six Cofers of the percussion series and one blown-up cartridge model exist, yet a sub-type can be differentiated among the percussion guns on the basis of loading levers—cylinder pin assemblies. This Colt-type lever also appears on the Spiller & Burr. Whitney levers are fitted, for example, on Spiller & Burrs Nos. 128, 131, 150, 214; Cofers Nos. 1, 13, "L" ... A Cofer stamped only E. B. GEORGIA has a Whitney lever. "Why?" is one of those frequent puzzles of Confederate ordnance supply.

The blown-up Cofer has checkered grips; No. 1 regular Cofer has plain walnut grips. Less than fifty of these guns are believed made; there is no record of Cofer's having a C. S. contract.

Other Producers

Two partners in Memphis need to be mentioned here though their productivity was nil, their influence on the war nothing, so far as military arms are concerned. Two revolvers of Colt 1851 type exist, identified as output of this partnership. One has a full octagon barrel and a brass frame, with "6." stamped as a serial (?) on cylinder, backstrap, trigger guard, barrel, hammer, and rammer. The top of the barrel is marked SCHNEIDER & GLASSICK, MEMPHIS, TENN. in one line. It is said this marking is with a die, not individually hand stamped.

While the author once made such a promulgation about a pistol he had examined very carefully (page 365, *The Story of Colt's Revolver*) it appears in this case he was wrong. Another advanced collector with a knack of keeping check on fakery stated he had been present and seen such stamping applied, with individual

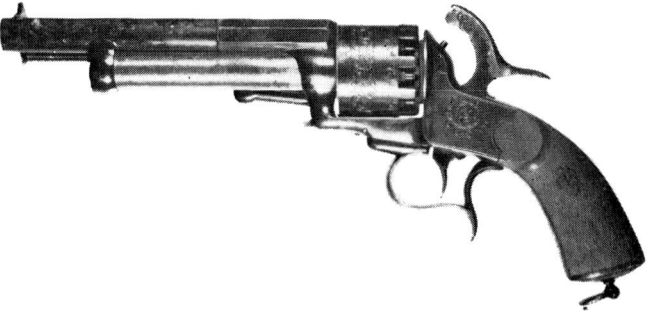

First Model LeMat carried by General P. G. T. Beauregard has "cavalry" spur guard and compound loading lever on right side of half-round barrel. Hammer nose has tiny studs on sides of movable tip. Barrel latch is pivoted in frame above trigger guard base.

letters, in as neat a line as if put on with a roller die. Further, with values of C. S. pistols sky-high, it is even potentially profitable to make up a name-stamping die in the old fashion to give a semblance of authenticity; hence such statements must be considered and reconsidered, in examining the authenticity of any odd Confederate relic. All we know is what we read in the papers—the Memphis *Daily Appeal* again, for December 8, 1861:

Memphis Manufacture. We were yesterday shown by Messrs. Schneider & Glassick, of Jefferson street, between Front and Main streets, a six-shooter Navy pistol of their own manufacture. It is a beautiful weapon, not inferior to the Colt's make in any particular. The finish of the whole, the accuracy of the parts and the excellent working of the mechanism are admirable. Iron, brass work, and wood work are all specimens of skill. We are proud that Memphis can turn out such splendid workmanship.

It will be remembered that three weeks before (November 15) the *Memphis Daily Appeal* was making big noises about the machinery being set up in the Eagle Foundry "for the manufacture of Colt revolvers." It appears Memphis was a scene in November of '61 of just the sort of speculative spirit which in New York at that time threw the Yankees' contracts into confusion

Unique First Model LeMat engraved on octagon breech of half-round barrel COL LEMAT'S PATENT is serial No. 8, bears special LeMat trade cypher unlike later "star-LM" mark. Gun is said to be one of dozen sent to Gen. Beauregard for gifts to Confederate big-wigs. Photo courtesy Maj. L. P. Henderson, Jr., Savannah, Ga.

and called for Holt and Owen. Alas for Southern arms collectors, there were no "Holt and Owen" in Dixie to come to the aid of later researchers. How much of the Schneider & Glassick pistol was made by them; how much pieced together from parts; how much borrowed from the Eagle Foundry or from Rigdon or from the little known gunmaker Frank J. Bitterlich, of Nashville, Tennessee, is impossible to surmise. Bitterlich definitely did make pocket pistols for S & G to sell with their names on them; whether Bitterlich also sub-contracted the fabrication of a few pistols to be shown around as specimens of Memphis handiwork is anybody's guess. Exact uniformity was not attained in the Schneider & Glassick product, apparently. No. 20 exists of this series, and the trigger guard is more nearly the size of the Colt small guard, smaller than No. 6.'s guard. The trigger, adapted for a larger guard, has been bent slightly to fit. An additional specimen is marked 12M in several places and in one place 12Mdl. The meaning of these marks is not known. The barrel breech was hand-made by filing, not on a lathe, as the rear edge is not at right angles to the axis of bore as would normally be the case. The bullet cut-out is small, not the large cut of the 1860's. Each shoulder is notched and a nose on the hammer rests in a slot to lock the cylinder between chambers for "safety." Individually hand-stamped SCHNEIDER & GLASSICK, MEMPHIS, TENNESSEE on the top flat of the part-round barrel, it resembles the others about as much as it resembles the Colt. The trigger guard is more ovaled, as if stretched a little to fit over a long trigger.

These few arms were the total of revolvers produced in the Eastern Confederacy which achieved any recognizable production. That even the Schneider & Glassick, with three reputed specimens and Cofer with less than 10 are mentioned, indicates the extremely low productivity of the South in this respect. Probably not over 7,500 revolvers of Confederate origin were ever produced in the Memphis-Richmond-Columbus-Macon complex of industries.

That they were good guns, is attested by the surviving specimens. That out of such a small number a goodly amount should have survived, is no great surprise. They were objects of local pride when fabricated, and were retained near there. In later years when "junque" dealers would remodel them into attractive desk lamps, or sell them at auction for old brass, there were enough collectors around to help preserve the remains.

Today, because of the demand, faking is common in this field. Opportunities to buy "Confederate" guns are greater than the guns themselves; hence any purchase should be carefully considered. The natural cupidity of the collector in refusing to share his fortune with his friends until *after* title passes will permit a good many hasty buyers to get stung in the future. For the lucky collector who does own an example of "the Confederate Colt," he can be proud he has a memento of brave men and brave days, long gone by.

CHAPTER 29

"Sans Guarantie Du Gouvernment"

The "grapeshot revolver" of Confederate Colonel Jean Alexander Francois LeMat was an arm "formidable." With 9-shot .40 caliber cylinder surrounding a huge central bore taking a 16-gauge buckshot charge, the LeMat revolver was a weapon admirably adapted for the hand-to-hand fighting of the naval boarding party, or the close-in charge of cavalry. It was single action, needing to be cocked for each shot, but a flick of the finger could switch the movable hammer nose to the "shot" position and fire the devastating blast of a short barreled shotgun for close fighting.

LeMat's Early Activities

LeMat's history as an arms designer is obscure. He was listed as Dr. LeMat in New Orleans at 188 Dauphine Street, in 1853, and was connected with firearms. In 1856 he patented the grapeshot revolver, October 21. One model pistol survives, made by Krider in Philadelphia. He continued to develop his ideas and in 1859 received the first of four British patents. The 1859 London document applies to both muzzle-loading and breech-loading (cartridge) revolvers, but no cartridge guns were made, it is believed, until after the war. His second patent, No. 1081, issued 1862, shows the ramrod moved to the left side, a characteristic of Transition and Second Model LeMat revolvers. Postwar British patents cover breech-loading ideas and an improved hammer.

The worthy doctor's patent activity was warning of his plans to manufacture the big revolvers. A former complimentary colonel on the staff of a former governor of Louisiana, LeMat dropped his medical title with the coming of war and hobnobbed with the military. Albaugh says he had as partner in his pistol enterprise none other than General P. G. T. Beauregard. This is not confirmed by *Napoleon in Gray,* biography of Beauregard, but is not unlikely. Both men were prominent New Orleans citizens of French descent. Both were of a military inclination. The fact that LeMat followed up his 1856 patent with further patenting and experimenting, indicated his serious interest in successfully producing his revolver. Unfortunately, he lacked the mechanical ability to make the project an entire success. Supplementing the good doctor's own lack, was his known partner, C. Girard, formerly of the Smithsonian Institution.

Girard established an office in Paris, at No. 9, Passage Joinville, known as C. Girard & Company, for the manufacture of LeMat revolvers. Where these firearms were actually made is not known—doubtless later researchers will delve into the French records, if any have survived three wars, and finally divulge the whole story of LeMat. But the colonel seems to have been more of an inventive and business agent, while Girard carried out the manufacture. His prospective purchaser was the belligerent South, but records of arms delivered suggest fewer guns were officially received than has been supposed.

LeMat revolvers were definitely ordered by the C.S. Army and the C.S. Navy. For example, when the Confederate ironclad *Atlanta* was captured June 30, 1863, three LeMat revolvers were among the ship's arms.

The colonel's plans originally called for domestic production of the big revolvers at the New Orleans works of F. W. C. Cook, Cook & Brother, who initially undertook also to produce Enfields for the Confederacy. But the threat to the city ultimately realized in Farragut's running past Forts Jackson and St. Philip and taking New Orleans, persuaded LeMat his fortunes and future were in France.

He worked with merchants Gautherin & Company of New Orleans. As their agent, he disbursed $2,500 "as a bribe." This was in connection with their illegal trading with the Confederacy after the fall of the city to the Federal forces and installation of General "Silverspoon" Ben F. Butler as Yankee commander. Butler was irritated by the warlike trading of alleged French firms, continuing their dealings with the Confederacy under cover of the French flag. He was especially annoyed when Gautherin, to pay for goods imported from France, managed to convey $400,000 in specie, packed in barrels, from a local bank to the French consul in the city, "for safe keeping." This effectively removed the gold from Butler's control, and its shipment abroad aided the Confederate cause. Gautherin, ordinarily a tobacco broker, was dealing in uniforms for the Confederacy, and the gold may have been related to whatever finance arrangements Colonel LeMat made with

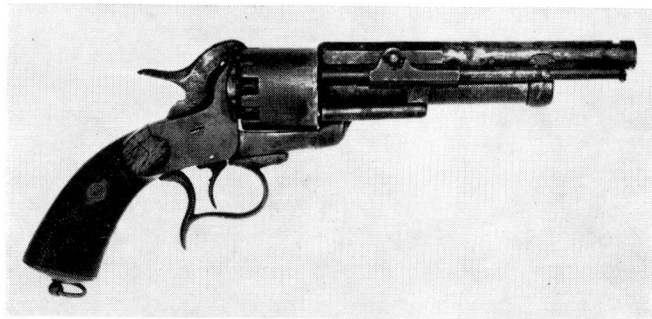

Possibly first LeMat production revolver made is this First Model having the first type barrel latch, a catch pivoted in bottom curve of barrel instead of attached to frame. Side of barrel near cylinder is stamped "1" and no LeMat proof mark of "star over LM" can be seen.

Richmond authorities for payment of his revolver accounts.

In September, 1862, reference to money for LeMat is made by C.S. agent Edwin De Leon, writing directly to Judah Benjamin from Paris. His lengthy epistle brings Benjamin up to date on many matters, and toward the end declares:

> The establishment of credit here would save the Government from great embarrassment and the enormous loss on exchange which it now suffers, as well as relieve the agents abroad from the difficulties of which they complain. I have been requested by Messrs. C. Girard & Co., who are making LeMat's revolvers for the Government under contracts with the Navy and Army Departments with Colonel LeMat, a partner in the factory, to forward their correspondence with the agents of those Departments in Europe, and to request that effectual steps may be taken to fulfill the Government obligations in that respect. They complain of the loss of both time and money in consequence of the failure of Captain Huse to co-operate with them or carry out his instructions in spirit as well as in letter.

In what manner Huse failed to cooperate with LeMat is not known; possibly he was not so prompt in furnishing payment or advances of funds, or in some other way hindered the work. But LeMat himself seemed to be giving more time to "commuting" via blockade runner to New Orleans and conniving with Gautherin, than giving his attention to the business. Whether he was a practical gunmaker, or even a skilled amateur, is not known; he may have had professional gunsmiths do all his model making. But he must have had considerable practical knowledge about the details of manufacture of his gun, and to this gunmaking project he was not devoting enough time.

The contract which LeMat had with the C.S. Navy, according to Secretary Mallory, required that "the pistols are to be delivered and inspected in London," and after passing inspection, they were to be paid for by Navy Agent Commander James D. Bulloch and re-shipped to the South. Up to July 30, 1862, just 200 of the Navy LeMats had been accepted, having been forwarded to Richmond and paid for there. (The inference is that these were not proof tested in London nor inspected there. Possibly they were Transition Model revolvers with round guards, "Paris" markings?)

Bulloch proposed to C. Girard & Company that they arrange to ship the revolvers to him and he would make arrangements to inspect them. He explained that he had no funds at the moment with which to pay, and suggested they might have some ideas of security he should offer. They replied, evidently after debating the whole summer what to do, that they would waive payment in London, and started to ship pistols to the Navy representative.

Bulloch ordered his inspecting officer, Lieutenant Chapman, to "ask for a sample of the pistols already delivered to the War Department and to get a written certificate from the manufacturer that the one furnished him was identical with those previously accepted." Chapman procured the sample but turned it over to his successor, Lieutenant Evans, without doing any inspecting. Evans approved 100 guns and reported to Bulloch they were as well finished as the sample, but that "the barrels, lock frames and hammers, are of cast iron; that the contact between barrels and cylinders is so loose as to permit much escape of gas; and that the cylinders, not being provided with springs, as in other repeating arms, are apt to revolve too far when the pistols are rapidly cocked, so that the hammers are likely to fall upon the divisions between the nipples when the firing is quick."

These mechanical defects were serious to Bulloch, who refused to receive any more LeMats under that contract, preferring to ship them on to Richmond for the Ordnance officers there to pass or reject. This method of shipment seemed satisfactory for a time to Girard. The record book of Colonel John M. Payne, Ordnance officer in charge of imported arms received at Wilmington, North Carolina, from the blockade runners, notes 150 LeMat revolvers coming through during July, 1863, "which were not approved." The probability is that LeMat felt small obligation to the Confederacy because of the unusual pay-later plan, and decided to run these guns in to sell privately if the Army wouldn't accept them.

Meanwhile, Bulloch took a walk over to the London Armoury Company and got a quotation. "The grapeshot revolver Messrs. C. Girard & Company are now supplying can be manufactured by the London Armoury Company for something less than £5 each," he wrote

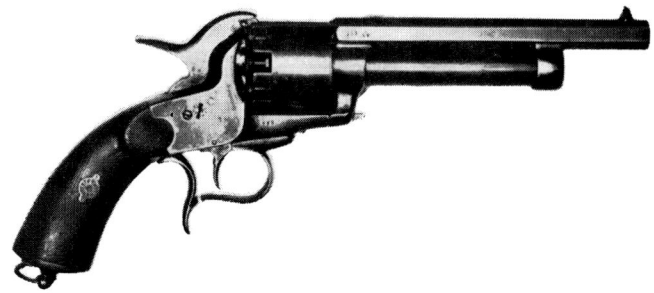

Transitional LeMat possibly made for C.S. Army has spur guard for cavalry use and barrel is not full-octagon. Loading lever is of simpler form, but studs are still made on sides of hammer nose. Butt ring is delicate, made in separate pieces. Serial 755.

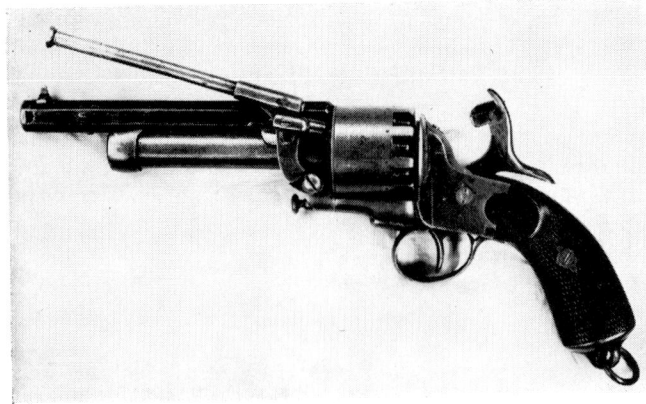

Probable Navy LeMat is this improved Second Model with Rigby-type loading lever on left side of full-octagon barrel. Gauge mark "18" and Birmingham proofs appear on barrel and cylinder. Barrel latch is screw pin which has to be unscrewed before barrel can be turned off of fixed shotgun barrel. Hammer nose is turned down in position to hit shot barrel nipple.

to Richmond. In spite of this, there seems to be no specimen of LeMat which finish and manufacturing characteristics would assign to London Armoury or any other English maker. The British-proved LeMats bear Birmingham marks but are wholly Paris-manufactured, finished and stamped there. Still, LeMat did not give up, and during early spring of the next year, negotiated another contract with the Confederate Government, this time the Navy Department.

Direct reference is made to a Navy contract "with Mr. LeMat" as early as July, 1862. After supplying a few revolvers on this contract—no complete record exists to say how many—a second contract is mentioned. Writing to Commander Bulloch April 7, 1864, Commander John M. Brooke, Chief of the Navy's Ordnance, stated, "Herewith you will receive a copy of a contract with Messrs. C. Girard & Company, for 2,000 'grapeshot revolvers' for the use of the Navy, to be delivered and inspected in England." More efficient payment terms were set forth with this contract, funds to be made available from Fraser, Trenholm & Company upon presentation of certificates of inspection by some officer in England appointed by or acting as agent for Commodore Barron. The pistols were to be shipped in lots of 250 or 500, each gun accompanied by ten cartridges and ten percussion caps. This suggests the existence of packets of LeMat cartridges—nine .40 caliber conical ball loads for the revolver cylinder, and one buckshot charge for the shotgun barrel.

The terms of the contract including requirement for ten shots each were passed on to Lieutenant W. H. Murdaugh, CSN, the officer appointed to inspect the LeMat guns.

Murdaugh Condemns the Revolver

Murdaugh, who was stationed in Paris, varied the terms to the extent of inspecting the first run of Navy guns at the Girard Factory. His report of June 23 was highly unflattering, confirming the trouble found with these guns two years earlier by Bulloch.

> Paris, June 23, 1864
>
> Sir: In obedience to your order of the 13th instant, I have inspected the pistols made by C. Girard & Co. under contract with the Navy Department and have the honor to report that from the general bad character of the workmanship I have declined to receive those which they had on hand ready for delivery. As a specimen of the workmanship, I would state that of the first seven examined, six had defects, as follows, viz: In one the grape-shot barrel went off at the fourth or fifth fire of the revolving cylinder from a defect in the hammer. On the next the cylinder would not revolve from defect in spring of revolving apparatus. In the next the hammer at times would miss striking the nipple altogether, seriously damaging it. In the other three the fixed and revolving barrels were not true with one another when in position for firing, and in one of these the hammer did not strike fair.
>
> Of all those examined, none appeared to be reliable, and almost all of them had serious defects, such as those enumerated. In all the metal of which the faces of the hammers were made was too soft.
>
> Very respectfully, your obedient servant
> W. H. Murdaugh
>
> Flag Officer S. Barron,
> Paris

Murdaugh's condemnation sealed the fate of LeMat's relations with the Confederacy. Judging by a letter of the following February, 1865, the intervening time was partly occupied in getting approval from Richmond to annul the Girard contract, and equally in trying to get serviceable revolvers delivered by Girard on his contract. The original document committed Girard to deliveries of 500 guns per month, the first delivery to begin 500 in November, 1863. Declared Barron in his letter of above date to Girard, "The terms stipulated in this agreement have by no means been complied with by you up to this day; nevertheless, so long as there was a chance of getting these arms into the Confederacy and cotton out to pay for them, I did not hesitate to take upon myself the responsibility of ordering the inspection and payment of such as were received."

Barron said to Commander Brooke, February 7, 1865, that only 100 revolvers under this contract had been reported ready for inspection. No indication of how many actually were received, though Lieutenant Murdaugh's provisional inspection report five months

Paris-finished Navy Second Model LeMat No. 1666 in M. Clifford Young, Boston, collection, has screw-barrel latch of simple form with spring on side attached to barrel. Hammer nose has tail through hammer head slot.

before was not encouraging about quality. Accordingly, Barron notified Girard the contract was void and that there was no need to extend themselves further on any account of the Confederacy. The fall of Fort Fisher and the cotton shortage, plus money shortage, made Commander Bulloch more anxious to pay contractors who had been more diligent in fulfilling their obligations to the Confederacy.

All C.S. LeMats Were Alike

Some collectors have assumed that the "Navy LeMat" is the smallest type having a rifled barrel of .35 caliber and shot barrel about .50 caliber. But one of the guns of the type "formerly furnished to the Army," used by Navy Inspector Lieutenant Evans as a pattern for his viewing the Navy arms, shows conclusively that both military Southern LeMat revolvers were of the same general type, size, and caliber.

LeMat's .40 caliber 16- or 18-gauge revolvers were for both C.S. Navy and cavalry. J. E. B. Stuart carried a handsome engraved spur guard First Model First Type pistol of the form, evidently supplied for cavalry use. Those with round guard it would appear were for the Navy, though no marks other than the "star over LM" for LeMat, plus a variety of company names engraved on the barrel, are on these revolvers; and of course the proof marks of Birmingham testing are sometimes found. The .35 Baby LeMats, of which some exist, do not reveal any more information about the good doctor and his enterprise than do the marks on their bigger brothers. The Baby model, of which specimen No. 35 is pictured, conforms to the round guard Second Model First Type design. This is borne out by the only Baby with barrel engraving, shown; use of the word "System" also occurs in .40 cal. Second Model arms above 950 rather than in those first made.

The purpose of the Baby LeMat can only be conjectured. Probably the colonel intended to fabricate this smaller sized model for belt and pocket use, to supplement his heavy holster or military pistols which were the ones initially in demand. Extant is another "Baby," but pinfire, No. 20, listed in the Golden State *World's Guns* catalog. But the ups and downs of LeMat manufacture never permitted him to establish a stable trade during the war.

Two Categories

Dr. LeMat's revolvers have been grouped into two categories by collectors heretofore, mainly on whether the gun does, or does not have a spur to the trigger guard. (The alternate shape is a round or oval guard.) But the guard is a minor difference, since it is nonfunctional; that is, either guard could be fitted to any of

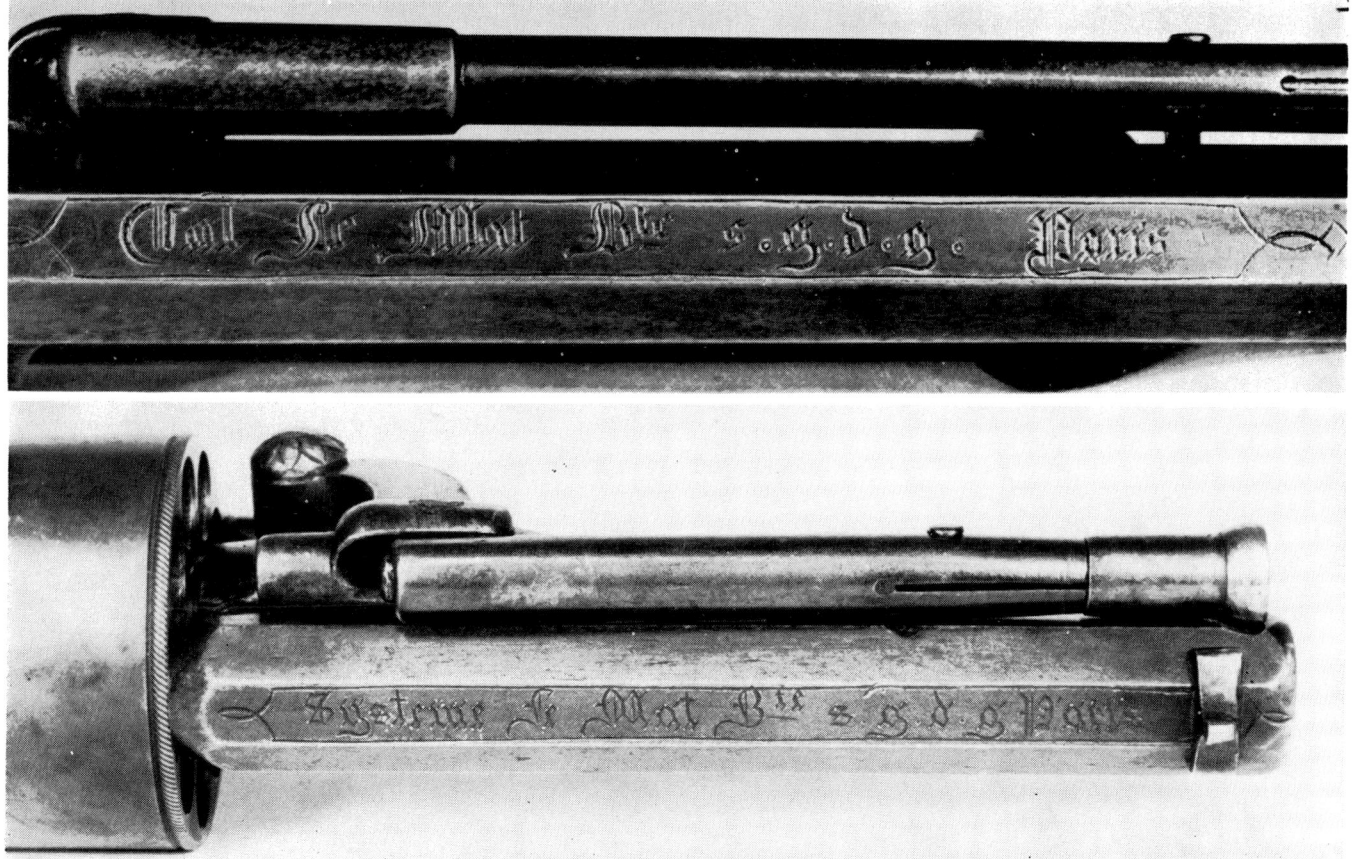

Typical Second Model LeMat, marking was hand engraved on top barrel flat. Significance of various LeMat markings is not understood by today's collectors, though there should be some reason for distinctions between "Systeme" and "LeMat's Patent." etc. variations. Bottom view shows Baby LeMat marking. Gun is Second Model pattern, consistent with phrasing of mark.

the several models or sub-types of LeMat handguns. The purpose of the spur to the guard was to permit the cavalryman to place his trigger finger there, as he rode at the charge with his pistol raised and cocked. Spur guards appear on all LeMat firearms, alternately with the round guard.

The inference is unmistakable: those with spur guards are the LeMats consigned to the Army authorities at Richmond. We have found no cavalry anecdotes of the use of the LeMat. This may be because the guns spent time in some Nassau warehouse waiting to run the blockade. The round guards were for the Navy. Since the Marine was not astride a jouncing horse, with pistol cocked, there was no requirement for the spur guard.

Basic differences separate the LeMat handguns into two general classifications: those of the early production with fragile swivel loops fitted separately into the bottom of the butt frame, and half-round half-octagon barrels, and those with full octagon barrels and a heavy lanyard loop cast as a lump integral with the butt frame. In the early model, the loading lever is a compound type having two hinges, and works on the same lever principle as the Colt lever, though it is attached at the right side of the barrel. The later type of lever is attached to the left of the barrel, and works somewhat like the British loading levers, with the plunger sliding more or less in a straight line and with a cut in either the lever or the plunger to allow for the motion of the hand lever as it is swung through its arc. Both LeMat levers are held in place by the rammer head of the shotgun barrel loading rod. This rod, having its smaller end split to spring out and hold it inserted, is slid inside the main rammer from the front for carrying. In loading, it is easily pulled loose when the rammer is swung away from the barrel, and the shot bore is then charged like a common muzzle-loading shotgun.

LeMat seems to have been uncertain of the best method of fastening the barrel, which had to be removed for take-down in cleaning. Of course, all the LeMats had barrels which screwed around the central shotgun bore into place. But their vertical positioning was done by a catch of some sort at the front of the frame.

A LeMat No. 21 pictured by Albaugh has a large and easy lever, pivoted in the base of the barrel lug, and snapping into a frame front end cut to index. The lever is big enough to be easily snapped back by the thumb. The No. 21 revolver has the early characteristics: half-round barrel, first type complicated lever on right side, fragile lanyard loop boss inserted in butt frame. On the whole, LeMat seems to have made improvements in the strength of details of his guns and in the convenience of their manufacture. As a general rule, spur guard guns predominate through the early production; round guards in the Second Models. Between First and Second models there is a definite Transition series.

The Several Models

LeMats break down into models with the following general details:

First Model, First type
Serial Numbers: 1-456.
Barrel: Half octagon, usually 7 inches long.
Guard: Spur.
Loading Lever: Right side of barrel.
Swivel: Separate in butt cap.
Hammer: Nose has two protective pegs, one each side; back curve smooth.
Barrel latch: Thumb type, pivoted in barrel lug.
Barrel marks: LeMat's Patent
    Col. LeMat's Patent
    Col. LeMat Bte. s.g.d.g. Paris

First Model, Second Type
Serial Numbers: Up to 450-460.
Barrel Latch: Finger type, pivoted front of lower frame and notching into barrel leg.
Hammer: Pegs but back curve has upturn or "hook" profile.
Transition Model
Serial Numbers: 450-950.
Barrels: Half octagon; full octagon; 7"; 6⅞".
Guard: Spur.
Loading Lever: Right side compound; left side simple type.
Swivel: Separate in butt; cast integral with butt frame.
Hammer: Smooth side, no pegs; back curve has upturn.
Barrel latch: Finger, pivoted in frame.
Barrel marks: Col. LeMat's Patent
    Col. LeMat Bte. s.g.d.g. Paris
    Col. Lemat Bte. s.g.d.g. Paris

Second Model
Serial Numbers: About 950-2500.
Barrel: Full octagon, 6-7/8".
Guard: Round (may find spur type also).
Loading lever: Left side of barrel. Plunger screwed to groove in lever moving arm; simple type.
Swivel: Cast integral with butt frame.
Hammer: Smooth side, rear upturn.
Barrel latch: Knob screw pin. Barrel lug new shape to accommodate.
Barrel marks: Col. LeMat Bte. s.g.d.g. Paris
    Syst. LeMat Bte s.g.d.g. Paris
    Systeme LeMat Bte. s.g.d.g. Paris
    SYSTme LEMAT Bte. s.g.d.g. PARIS (Birmingham proof)
    LeMat & Girard's Patent, London (Birmingham Proof)

Second Model, Second Type
Cylinder Retard: Has spring screwed frame left side that retards too rapid throw of cylinder.
Loading Lever: Left side, new simple style, of flat lever arm, not round. All foregoing have round lever arm for shot plunger inside.
Barrel: May have screw-in extension for rifled or smoothbore tube.

Rifle
Loading lever: Left side.
Shotgun Rod: Right side in thimbles.
Barrels: 38" long, both shot and rifled. Rifled barrel is half octagon and half round. Shot barrel to muzzle.
Guard: Special shotgun type, flat in front.
Butt: Shotgun style.

Small details distinguish or individualize many LeMats. In the Val Forgett, Jr., collection, four LeMats show interesting variations, though all conform to the correct pattern for serial numbers, allowing for production overlap in serial numbering.

The earliest is a Model 1, Type 1, with thumb latch on the barrel lump and spur guard, "Army" model. Right side compound lever, of course; serial high for the type, No. 456. Distinctive is an irregular notch cut in the side plate with a corresponding shape of the frame, to help hold the plate in place. This is not uniform in all guns and suggests two things about LeMat production facilities. First, that considerable shaping of major parts was done by individual craftsmen with files. Secondly, that no fundamental attempt at interchangeability was planned, though major components such as barrels and cylinders will more or less interchange.

Forgett's next LeMat is marked on the short octagon breech of its half-round barrel, "Col Le Mat Bte sgdg Paris." The swivel is separate, but the turned barrel and loading lever placed on left side, as well as frame-pivoted latch, style this one a Transition model: serial No. 478. No frame-sideplate joint notch. Hammer nose has lugs. Spur "Army" guard.

Still in the Transition series, but with solid swivel lug is the next Forgett gun, No. 803, "Army" spur guard. Instead of lugs, the hammer movable nose piece has a spur sticking up through the blade of the hammer, so the shooter's finger can move it quickly into firing position for the shot barrel. The barrel is engraved in Old English, capital and lower case letters, with "Col LeMat Bte s.g.d.g. Paris." A loading lever catch was placed on the barrel forward of the shot bore positioning ring. This catch is a spring hook, not very permanent, and often damaged.

The last gun in the Forgett group is serial No. 943, and still a transition model, tending to bracket correctly the figure set forth by M. Clifford Young (*American Arms Collector*, July, 1957) as to range of numbers for the Model 2, from 950 up to 2500. Without a lever safety catch or spring, its barrel is engraved identical (by hand) to No. 803. The butt is moulded with a solid swivel base; spur "Army" guard. The sideplate is fitted to the frame by a variant of the notch seen on gun No. 456: this one has a groove filed in the sideplate top edge with a tongue integral with the frame.

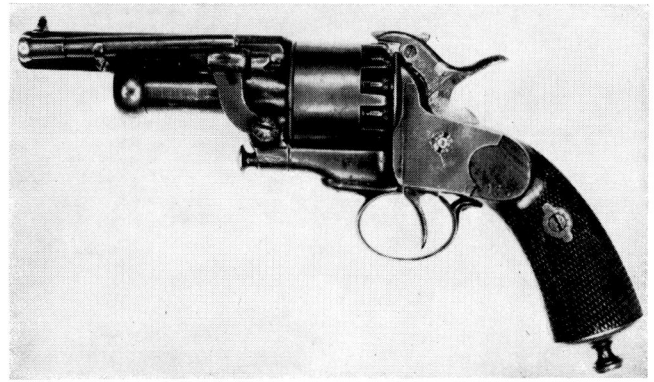

Distinctive "Baby LeMat" No. 35 in William Bacon collection, Richmond, was bought from Yankee gun collector dealers by present owner but where it fits into LeMat story is unknown. Though marked "Systeme" on barrel gun was not a contract-made piece but actually was made by LeMat and barrel side is marked star/LM.

Examples of the rounded guard gun appear in the higher serials. One such in the Robert Abel's collection bears the surcharging of 1763. T. MERCOTT, 68 HAYMARKET LONDON SW in one line on the right side of the shot barrel. Serial 2412, this bears clearly the usual LeMat factory stamp of $\overset{\star}{_{LM}}$ on the right breech of the octagon barrel. With the "Navy" round guard, this model is marked SYSTME LEMAT BTE SGDG PARIS but is Birmingham proved. Bearing so high a serial number, it suggests either that LeMat delivered the last of the lot to London gun shops when the Confederacy's chances ran out, or that the gun was resold later by T. Mercott, he having possibly purchased it from some member of the late Confederate States Navy interned in London at the end of the war. Mercott is not listed in the usual compilations of London gunsmiths and gunmakers. One LeMat, with extension shot barrel, has a Tranter-type lever at left. Big LeMats are scarce enough. Whether the several are remaining items of regular production, prototype samples, remains for some later researcher to find out. Somewhere in France may remain records to tell us the full story of Dr. Jean A. F. LeMat and his formidable Confederate revolvers.

CHAPTER 30

Texas Fights Alone

In the Trans-Mississippi area after the fall of Vicksburg, supplies to Confederate forces in the West were cut off. But the western Confederacy was very much self-sustaining. More capacity for manufacturing existed there than has generally been recognized. Small manufactures in part owed their genesis to the large German population of thrifty and skilled farmers and craftsmen who had settled there in the 1840's. By the end of the war one of the largest armories in the South had been begun at Tyler, Texas; construction plans for 1866 were surprisingly large. In a town which is now a suburb of Dallas, Lancaster, a pistol factory was started which had a capacity of 200 Colt-type revolvers monthly. Southwest of Galveston at Marion (now East Columbia) good-quality revolvers were made by machinery in quantity.

Actual production levels reached were far short of the needs of the times. But domestic manufacture in any war has only been supplementary to the arms in being at the commencement of the war. It is an axiom of warfare that weapons not in being at the beginning of the conflict, or procured or produced very soon thereafter, will be of little effect and influence during the next few years. In Texas, production lead time, spiralling prices or machinery and metals, and impressment of skilled hands into the Army, all contributed to low production rates.

Distance had created the autonomy of Texas and the autonomy had created the will of Texans to handle their own affairs. Thus the Act of January 11, 1862 created the Military Board of Texas, an Ordnance committee to spend $500,000 for buying and manufacturing arms; to establish a cannon foundry, and to appoint agents to oversee these operations. The board members were Governor F. R. Lubbock, Comptroller C. R. Johns, and Treasurer C. H. Randolph of Texas. This board was to greatly affect the fortunes of a Northern engineer, A. S. Clark, the family of Labon E. Tucker, Joseph E. Sherrard, and Pleasant Taylor. Embroiled in their activities was the Lieutenant Governor of Texas, John M. Crockett, ultimately concerned with the very peculiar failure of the Lancaster pistol makers.

The Lancaster Revolver

There are few extant specimens of Lancaster revolvers; most of them are unmarked. All so far identified seem to be of Colt dragoon size. While it is popular to illustrate this "type" with a photo of a pistol having a squareback guard, two marked pistols of definite Clark and Sherrard association bear round guards. Discernible cylinder etching in a decorative pattern on these two revolvers reveals an attempt at playing on state loyalties in their sale; while their crude construction and the absence of a bullet loading cut on the right side of the barrel frame suggests their primitive nature.

In evaluating Confederate handguns it is always wise to keep in mind that the Confederacy had a supervisory staff of engineers that ranked among the best in the world. That Colonel Burton, for example, should be "imported" into England from Virginia and then "reimported" for the cause of the South in 1861 was not an accident. It reflected the fact that he was among the best men in the world for this sort of work: setting up factories for the manufacture of arms. C.S. engineers were old Springfield men; the officers were from West Point. Standards of the Confederate and state authorities were high; they knew what they should make, even if they were not able for one cause or another to make enough.

With this in mind we take the risk of asserting that the Texas Arms dragoons, of the pattern called generally "Tucker & Sherrard" are the primitive or first model pistol of Lancaster make. Of several extant specimens, Nos. 120, 126, and 2120 bear legible cylinder marks. These are not roller engraved with a die, but put on by acid etching. The complete cylinder bears a scrollwork pattern over its surface, broken by three motifs: along the leading edge a name (No. 126, J. P. LAWRENCE; No. 2120, L. S. PERKINS) with a large star to the right marked above and below, TEXAS/ARMS and to the right, an armorial shield bearing on itself an oval, 13 stars inscribed, supported by two halberdiers; the whole surmounting crossed cannon over a cannon ball.

The muster roll of Texas state troops which went into Confederate service has been reduced to a card file at the Texas State Archives; to Vic Friedrichs of Austin we are indebted for the information on one J. P. Lawrence:

Lawrence, J. P., Private, enlisted in the Mesquite Light Horse, Dallas County, commanded by Captain Asher W. Carter, January 6, 1861, 13th Brigade State Troops. This company consisted of 50 men, rank and file; when formed, was tendered to the State of Texas with the condition that each man be provided with a good Sharps rifle and an army Six Shooter.

Another J. P. Lawrence is listed as of Kaufman County, enlisting in the Trinity Guards Cavalry Company, Captain Obediah Van Pool, on July 6, 1861. Only a J. P. Perkins has been noted; Friedrichs speculates as to whether J. P. Perkins could have been carelessly inscribed "L.S." by the engraver. The nature of the work, perhaps put on by rolling the cylinder across a wood block wetted with acid-resisting paint, shows the background etched out over the cylinder surface, the markings raised. Using such a stamp, it would be easy to fit in the owner's name, thus individualizing the gun.

Of pistols credited to the Tucker & Sherrard group, the main distinction has been in the absence of the loading cut out on the barrel frame. Pistols known of this type have differences:

Serial No. 3, squarebacked guard, oval cylinder stops.
Serial No. 23, squarebacked guard, oval cylinder stops.
Serial No. 193, squarebacked guard, thin rectangular stops.
Serial No. 106, squarebacked guard, thin rectangular stops.
Serial No. 126, round guard, rectangular stops, lead grooves.
Serial No. 241, round guard, rectangular stops, lead grooves.
Serial No. 249, round guard, rect. stops, lead groove, cyl. engr.
Serial No. 404, squareback guard, thin rectangular stops.
Serial No. 2120, round guard, rect. stops, lead groove, cyl. engr.

These oddly follow the basic changes in the Colt series of 1st, 2d, and 3d model dragoons to some extent; No. 404 seems out of phase. The serial range apparently covered by this group, if indeed it is still correct to assume them all to be the products of the Lancaster pistol makers, does not seem to jibe with the records.

Collectors generally consider that the Texas authorities gave Tucker & Sherrard a contract for 3,000 pistols, and that according to a newspaper notice about 400 were completed. Except for the No. 2120 specimen, (excellently fabricated, closely resembling a Colt product, but apparently definitely not a botched-up Colt) the extant serials do not check with this alleged historical record of only 400 guns produced. But a look at records unearthed by Vic Friedrichs in *The Texas Gun Collector* (issues 51, 52, 67) suggest that all is not as previously supposed.

The Dallas *Herald*, February 19, 1862, seems to contain first mention of Joe Sherrard as a gunmaker, stating "Messrs. Sherrard, Killen and Brunie, of Lan-

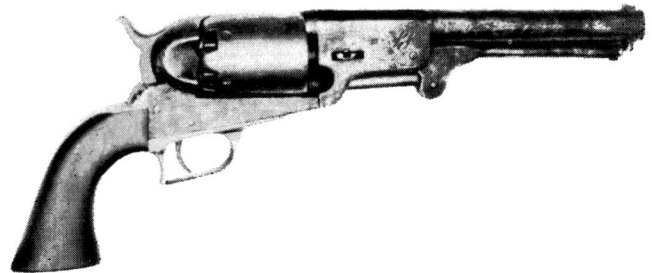

So-called Texas Dragoon appears to be a copy of regular Colt M1848 but varies in minor dimensions. Specimen shown is one of three similar guns found in northern Mexico. Pattern usually associated with early Dallas (Lancaster) production has no bullet-loading cut and probably pre-dates Civil War.

caster, in this county, have formed a co-partnership for the purpose of manufacturing Colts and other revolving pistols." Their combining seems to have been inspired by knowledge of the $500,000 which the Military Board was authorized to spend; they had between 50 and 100 subscribers who pledged to buy their pistols at "$40 each for Navy pistols and $50 for the Army size." News of this enterprise filtered back to Austin, and on March 6 the Military Board directed Lieutenant Governor John M. Crockett to "interview immediately with gentlemen in your county who are constructing revolving pistols, and learn from them the extent of their ability to manufacture pistols—whether the Board can in any way aid them to increase their results, and whether they can build guns for use in the Army." The Board offered to advance money if this would "materially increase the rapidity of making arms."

Crockett reported March 17 from Dallas that "There is no establishment of this kind in this county, but there are about 20 gunsmiths, some of whom are first rate . . . They are willing to go into a shop at any time." Crockett induced a few of the better gunsmiths to open a shop and with their available tools they believed a production of 30 revolvers a week was possible.

"I have seen a specimen of the workmanship of one of the men, a very fine revolver. They are of such a class they could not be made for less than forty or fifty dollars apiece. But I suppose this government would not desire such polish and complete finish as the one I saw." We feel this refers to the ornate etching on the Clark, Sherrard pistols, which bear the two maker's names etched on the barrels, and the cylinder decorated. This is a somewhat higher price for these guns than Perkins was paid, if it was the same Perkins. When Pvt. J. P. Perkins of the 9th Regiment Texas Cavalry, who enlisted August 31, 1861, at Lamar County, was transferred to the C.S. Army, he was paid for the value of his horse $180, saddle $40, rifle $60, and pistol $25.

Crockett's Unsuccessful Venture

Crockett organized the pistol makers and on March 20, 1862, reported they would be ready to contract

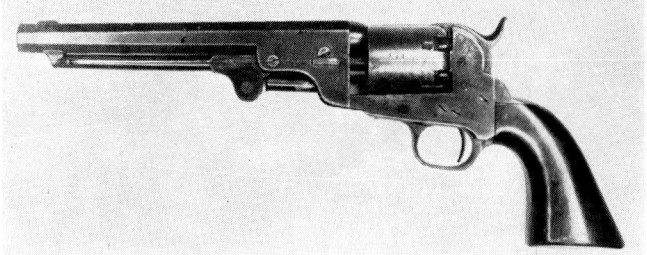

Remarkably fine specimen of .44 Dance Brothers is No. 121 in Vic Friedrich's collection. Flat frame is distinctive characteristic of this series of Texas pistols made near Galveston. Sometimes called "Dance Dragoon," title is misnomer since full-octagon-barreled pistol is more nearly what might be termed "army size."

after an outlay of several thousand dollars. Spurring on their efforts was the bad news of Pea Ridge, Arkansas, where the Confederate general, Van Dorn, was beaten and the Texas forces lost two of their bravest leaders, General Ben McCulloch and General McIntosh.

The firm organized by Crockett was styled Tucker, Sherrard & Company, and on April 11, 1862, the Military Board signed a contract. By its terms, the Military Board agreed to "take by purchase of them all the pistols they shall make within one year and after the first of May next, not to exceed 3,000." This is no contract to make 3,000 pistols, but only up to 3,000, or such less number as may be delivered. The contract bound the makers to deliver 100 in May, the pistols to "be subject to inspection at said shop before delivery." As to the description of firearms proposed to be made by Tucker, Sherrard & Company, "That said pistols are to be of the kind and quality of Colt revolver, but the exact form and style being immaterial so that said pistols are good and substantial arms of the size and after the manner of said Colt revolver. That one-half of said pistols shall be of Colt Army size and the other half of the Navy size." Signatory to the contract for the firm were Labon E. Tucker, J. H. Sherrard, W. L. Killen, A. W. Tucker, Pleasant Taylor, and last but not least, John M. Crockett.

Crockett now devoted his whole time to the project, in which it was obvious he had a financial interest. But workmen engaged to be employed had not come in, and the draft took some of the men. The younger son of Labon Tucker, Elihu McDonald, was constantly explaining that he was on "war work," but one day 12 armed men marched him off to the nearest recruiting station. After he joined the Army, the authorities apparently returned him to the Tucker shop. But Crockett says in a wholly misleading fashion to the Military Board on May 19, 1862, "We are forging pistols and will begin to finish within a few days." By June 30, he has to report to the Board, "We are not ready to deliver 100 pistols," though they should have been ready in May.

Crockett planned to set the works up as a major factory, not a tiny job shop. By hand work, 100 pistols could have been completed, but there was risk of impressment of the guns by the military. He states positively June 30, "We have several hundred on the way and could finish 100 at very short notice & perhaps a much larger number but we desire to be advised." In making these "several hundred" he had forged up all the cast steel on hand, and could get no more. On July 3 he asks the Military Board if iron would do; "Our pride is sufficient to impel us to use the best material, but if we should fail to get steel, we would like to be advised of your opinions." By July 21, the importunate local commander, Colonel Buford, had been badgering the factory to let him have some pistols, but still they refused to assemble any for fear of having them seized.

Tucker, Sherrard & Company wanted the Board to give orders on them for guns; then they would assemble these in a short time and deliver. To have guns lying around waiting, was too much of a temptation to the gun-hungry cavalrymen.

The Board replied, sending out Major George Dashull to pick up 200 pistols, but their letter of advice arrived Saturday, August 2, and Dashull arrived Monday, and had to go back to Austin empty-handed. On the 18th, Crockett wrote a most important letter, admitting that even if they had known in time, they could not have given the major any pistols:

We are now at work on the third hundred pistols and our expectations is to complete the four hundred during the month of September. A very large portion of our labor, perhaps one half, ever since we began, has been best used on tools and machinery, being unable to procure them in any market. We might have finished a hundred perhaps if our exertions had been directed alone to that object, but it would have interfered with our system & carried us to losses at some other point, so as to fail completing 100 per month. Besides, we could not think that a small lot would be of any great importance. We expected from the beginning to cast the breech pieces, and consequently did not proceed to forge them, so as to complete a part of the pistols. We did not succeed well at first with the foundry and all the pistols were delayed on account of it.

Crockett remarks on the low price the state was paying, how they could finish up the pistols and sell at retail for $60 to $100 locally. The Tuckers were fearful of their mounting investments and were bought out of the company, probably by Crockett; but they continued to work as hired hands. By September 2, Crockett noted that "The three hundred pistols we now have approaching completion we will hasten to the finishing and will advise you. The fourth hundred we fear will be delayed for want of the arrival of material." Crockett asked for $5,000 further advance; and informed the Board that the Tuckers having withdrawn from the company, they did business now as Sherrard, Taylor & Company. While the letter speaks of Crockett impersonally it was obviously written or drafted by him.

Crockett persistently puts off the Board on the times of pistol deliveries. He needs money to tide them over the winter. The hands beg off to go to the harvest, "They are Texans, farmers, and will thrash and sow their little grasses." The prices offered locally for pistols mount to $100. On September 24, 1862, the remaining members of the firm sign a bond in the sum of $10,000 that they will deliver 300 pistols in October. The Board then gives them the $5,000 advance requested. But during October Crockett burdens the mails with problems of impressed workmen—inability to get artisans from the Army, though the Board and the C.S. authorities in the beginning had told him he could get them.

Crockett again writes, on November 20, now weeks past the delivery of 300 pistols as promised under bond:

> The writer has devoted his whole time to the business since it began & for the last three months has remained in the shops from little after sun up till sundown every day, except Sunday, urging the hands and the superintendents to the most diligent & energetic exertions. In that time the most has been done that it was possible to accomplish with the number of hands employed & the writer acquired much information both of the theory & practical operations. He has kept a register of the amount of labor best owed on every part of the pistol & can demonstrate the time necessary to make a certain number with any number of hands. Our operations are tedious for want of the preparations spoken of above ($25,000 investment and an early start). It is easy to see how Colt with certain facilities could make the article for nearly one third of our price and make money. We could have completed 100 parts, perhaps 200 by this time, but we did not begin to do a tinkering business, and large operations move slow.

Crockett furnishes some astonishing information concerning the manufacture of Colt revolvers, as it was conceived to be in Texas:

> Colt's pistols are not pure cast steel and scarcely a piece of them [is] hammered—they are either cast, or cut out. They answer a good purpose, but are not as good as ours. He cast his cylinders, barrels and breech pieces of iron converted to steel in his own foundry. We are failing to find material and are now preparing to melt our own ore and do all we can to secure material by our own resources.
>
> We beg leave to assure the Board that out of, we hope, the purest patriotism we are doing our utmost to complete the pistols . . . As soon as it is possible to get off a lot we will advise you. We think that ten days will develop what we can do and we will then advise you.

By January 28 matters had not improved. Though Crockett had planned to make 200 guns a month, with machinery employing about 50 men, the most employed at any one time was 25, and the average for the period was about 12. The first five months was spent in making tools, including apparently basic machine tools which they could not buy in the market. The fall of New Orleans (April, 1862) stopped the supply of iron and steel. To try his case in the papers, and stave off disciplinary action by the Military Board, Crockett obtained the insertion of a notice in the *Texas Almanac*, Austin, February 28, 1863:

> SIX-SHOOTERS. We were shown the other day a beautiful specimen of a six-shooter, manufactured in Dallas by Col. Crockett, who has a large armory now in successful operation. The pistol appears, in every respect, quite equal to the famous Colt's six-shooter, of which it is an exact copy, with the exception of an extra sight on the barrel which we think is a decided improvement.

> We learn that Col. Crockett has now 400 of these pistols on hand, which he has manufactured within the last six months, and which he has offered to the Governor at remarkably low figures.

In an attempt to jack up the ante from the Board, Crockett had Texas Senator Guinn introduce a memorial on March 2 in the legislature, calling for an increase of the state price of the pistols to $80. During March, Crockett tried to talk to both Mr. Randolph and Major Johns about increasing the price, but not until the day he left to return to Dallas did Major Johns unofficially say it would be best if he sold the guns privately. The conclusion of the affair came in June. The legislature in view of the failure to deliver decided to cancel the contract upon repayment of the $10,000 advance, "and in July last the parties repaid the loan in Confederate Treasury notes with $814.00 interest."

Possible cause for Crockett's bringing the contract to this conclusion is offered by the endorsement to this result: "The difference in the specie value of this money at the time it was advanced and at the time of its return was very considerable, but from the language of the law the Board has no alternative but to receipt the tender made, and cancel the bond."

Finis cannot be written to the story of the Tucker-Crockett pistols. Analysis of the above testimony reveals that Crockett did not forge the frames, expecting to have them cast. In spite of his protestations of putting 100 pistols together "soon," the deadline is each time advanced or ignored. Difficulty in getting materials is frequently stated—iron suitable for casting the frames, we assume. The local coal was not suitable for melting this iron, and the smelting cupola they made would have to be completely torn down and rebuilt to a reverberatory furnace for different grades of ore or fuel.

A. S. Clark, maker with Sherrard of the dragoon-size revolvers, seems to have worked with Crockett. According to an old resident of Lancaster, Mr. A. B. Rawlins, whose manuscript is quoted by Fuller:

> I was born in the town of Lancaster, Texas, in 1855, and at the beginning of the Civil War was probably six years old. Among the things that first impressed my mind was the erection of what we called the pistol factory on the banks of the branch on the west side of Lancaster, about two stones throw west of the public square. In later years I became aware that this pistol factory belonged to the Confederate states of America. My chief interest in boyhood days was the workmen. First in my memory was A. S. Clark, who was reputed by our community to be a Yankee. Next was a man named Fitzsimmons, not a native Texan, but a fine pattern maker; likewise Jim Cary, a scientific blacksmith, and another blacksmith, whose name was Sherrod (sic.). Both these men were native Texans. There was also employed in the factory a cousin of mine named Virgil Kellar, a young man about 16, who became very expert as a pattern maker . . . Virgil Kellar often brought his work at night and worked on it, and I recall his having exhibited a pattern of a six-shooter which he had made out of cedar. Virgil Kellar worked with the factory about two years and was called to the colors in Ross' Brigade in the Trans-Mississippi Division and never returned, having been killed in battle.
>
> A. S. Clark never left Lancaster to go into the Army and remained a resident of Lancaster until his death about 1905.

In later years of my life, being related to him by marriage, I became intimately acquainted with him and have often heard him relate his connection with the pistol factory.

It seems he was brought to Lancaster from Michigan, or some other Northern state, by the Confederate States authorities, and placed in charge as superintendent of the factory, was furnished all the money he could spend in its operation ($10,000?—W.B.E.), with instructions to make all the guns he could, which he proceeded to do, and in carrying out these plans often recited to me trips he would make to Galveston for the purpose of purchasing steel and other supplies and necessary tools for the making of guns. I recall one item, files, of which he had difficulty in finding a sufficient number, having bought the entire supply in Galveston.

The Dance Revolvers

While there is nothing in the foregoing inconsistent with the sad chronicle of Mr. Crockett, the fact of Clark's going to Galveston raises a logical surmise, based unfortunately on nothing but the existence of another class of Texas Civil War era revolvers; those of the three Dance brothers, James, David, and George.

Produced at the Dance blacksmith shop a little west by south of Galveston near the old capital of Texas, Columbia, these guns exist in two basic sizes, .36 and .44. The .36 is a round-barreled Navy of Colt size. The .44 is not, as often surmised by those who have never handled one, a dragoon pistol; it is a scaled-up Navy, basically an Army-sized pistol, not dragoon. The distinctive feature of all Dance revolvers is the absence of the round part of the frame or standing breech; the frame is thought of as "milled flat" at this point.

The Dance smithy is known to have made plows, farm implements, and feed mills. But the degree of capital mechanization of this factory is not at present known. Apparently it was not until 1863 at the earliest that the Dance brothers turned to making firearms, if so early. As one collector who has done what research *can* be done on Dance, Paul C. Janke of Houston, puts it,

> About 300 of the Dance revolvers were made, as nearly as we can figure. Mile C. Bell, a soldier of the Confederacy, was issued one of these revolvers while home on sick leave, in Kenney, Texas. Before he was able to return to duty, the war was over, and Dance Brothers revolver No. 317 never saw action. No. 317 was evidently one of the last revolvers made before the manufacture of revolvers was discontinued at the close of the war.

The Tucker

Another revolver resembling the .36 Dance in points of manufacture but with a complete rounded frame boss, a la Colt, is known with the Tucker marking: L. E. TUCKER & SONS etched on top of the barrel. It has NO. 72 on the cylinder. The thoughtful reader will now be way ahead.

We surmise that Crockett, upon paying off the debts of the factory in inflated currency, was left with unfinished parts on hand. These parts were of all pieces except the frames. Initially, he expected to cast the frames and admittedly did not forge them. Casting proved unsuccessful. Clark may have gone to Galveston to buy out the town of files to use in the finishing; or Crockett may have taken the desperate step of buying up files to melt down into frames.

Not many frames were made that way, you can be sure! A file, melted down, would be reduced by uncontrollable oxidation in the furnace, with the huge area of its rippled surface, to probably half or less in metal; and that would be contaminated and need blowing off of the impurities with an air draught. That Clark might have stopped to see Dance as a source of metal seems almost a certainty. Also a certainty is that Crockett was working up *both* sizes of pistols, for at the conclusion of the contract 1,500 of each size were due. That no one has ever recognized a Navy-size Tucker, Sherrard & Company pistol is hardly strange; but the existence of the L. E. Tucker & Sons revolvers serves to confirm the surmise: Crockett sold out the frameless sets of parts to Dance, maybe liquidating his investment and making a profit.

The parts were good parts, well machined, made with the excellence his fulltime attention to detail warranted. The basic machines were also easily sold. The inference is that Crockett and the Tuckers did not get along too well as co-equal administrators, and the Tuckers were content to let Crockett run it and pay them wages, since they had got their money out long before the demise. Hence, with the contract annulled by the board and the debts paid off, Tucker took over what frames *had* been made, and fitted up the L. E. Tucker revolvers.

In East Columbia, Dance commenced making frames for the pistols. Without forging dies to stamp a lump of iron with the round frame, the Dances did the next best thing, they cut the frames from plates of rolled iron. If the Dance revolver was made from "whole cloth" and the tools advanced in each part of the work from time to time, no benefit would be gained by making the frames flat. But with a pile of parts finished ready for frames, there was some point to making the frames as quickly and as cheaply as possible. The frames were not "milled flat"; the frame raw material was that thickness to begin with. Adding 317, for the Dance number, to 72, for L. E. Tucker and his boys, we reach 389 units production, agreeing with Crockett's candid statements of the progress of the Tucker, Sherrard & Company and Sherrard, Taylor & Company pistols.

Perhaps Clark and Sherrard, who started the whole business, may have returned to making the dragoon size guns. In spite of the Perkins name on Dragoon No. 2120, the identification with a Perkins of 1861 is not necessarily complete. The finish and execution of this pistol is superior and reflects considerable experience in their manufacture. As Mr. Rawlins, the Lancaster old-timer, said to Fuller, "When the war ended, of course the pistol factory ended, and who fell heir to it I am unaware. I can still see in mind's eye that old factory with its old melting furnace, filled with charcoal and scraps of all kinds of iron and pouring its liquid metal through a spout into a ladle to be carried by laborers to moulds . . . As to who fell heir to this machinery, I have no knowledge, but naturally suppose it fell into the hands of Mr. Clark."

CHAPTER 31

The Southern Armories and Superintendent Burton

The word "beleaguered" had not been heard. Riding high on a wave of patriotic ardor, Southern forces were triumphing wherever they clashed with the Federals. Brash Southrons proclaimed they would "whip the Yankee's with cornstalks," but after Virginia's legislature passed the Ordinance of Secession on April 18, the state authorities acted on somewhat more responsible measures to ensure production of weapons. Capture of the United States' Arsenal and Hall's Rifle Works at Harpers Ferry was ordered.

Capture and Burning of Harpers Ferry Arsenal

In the event of attack on this arsenal, the commander had orders to destroy it. John Brown's capture revealed how indefensible the position was. It meant losing half the North's arms-making capacity, but the sacrifice was deemed essential.

"Finding my position untenable, shortly after 10 o'clock last night I destroyed the arsenal, containing 15,000 stand of arms, and burned the armory building proper," reported First Lieutenant Roger Jones, U. S. Mounted Rifles, commanding at Harpers Ferry on April 19, 1861, "and under cover of the night withdrew my command almost in the presence of 2,500 or 3,000 troops." He concluded his report to General Winfield Scott by stating "I believe the destruction must have been complete." But within the hour Virginia and Maryland secession troops swarmed through the gate and past old John Brown's firehouse, out into the Armory alleys and roadways to the square two-story arsenal storehouse and to the flaming Armory factory buildings.

The arsenal was beyond hope of saving. Though the rivers rushed by, there was not water and pumps enough to consider trying to stop the flames. Dipped in varnish for protection, or oiled with thick tallow, the 15,000 new M1855 Rifled Muskets and Rifles, together with experimental arms, transformed flint locks and other weapons in storage made a pyre that flamed high, illuminating the sleepy mechanical town of Harpers Ferry on the hillside. Then the floor timbers gave way above, and with a crash the second floor cascading sparks like some monster pinwheel subsided to the street level; then, overburdened and weakened by the fire, the first floor collapsed and all fell through into the deep basement to burn until all was consumed. Today, a century later, the National Park Service is conducting an archeological survey of these strata of buried muskets.

At the manufactory were two lines, for producing the Rifle Musket, and the Rifle, and a somewhat less important set-up for fabricating the M1855 Pistol Carbine. Valiant work by the Marylanders saved the tools, thousands of parts in all stages of manufacture, and a great quantity of the rifle stocks. In storage at Harpers Ferry in 1859 had been 130,000 seasoned musket stocks; hard, dense, straight-grained black walnut three years or more old, dry and of top quality. Though the estimated annual production of 12,000 per year might have reduced the total to 100,000 or less, by the time of General Jackson's raid there were a good many left.

Jubilant Maryland troops took 17,000 gun stocks which they saved from the flames and shipped them in gratitude to the armory at Fayetteville, North Carolina. Major Bradley T. Johnson (ultimately brigadier general) was on the staff of the 1st Maryland Volunteer Infantry, C.S.A., and through his charming wife, who was a native of North Carolina and a friend of the Governor, the Maryland Line had been equipped with Mississippi rifles. The actual weapons could have been made by any one of the several contractors of Harpers Ferry itself; but the probability is that they were the famed Palmetto Rifle, the M1841 U. S. Rifle as made by William Glaze & Company at the Palmetto Works in Fayetteville, on contract for the state in 1852. The 17,000 salvaged stocks appear to have been, probably, those for the M1855 Harpers Ferry rifle. This arm later, with the type 1861 lockplate (without Maynard primer) and with a special "S" shaped hammer was the main rifle fabricated at Fayetteville.

Photos like this one taken after Jackson's Raid reveal considerable damage to government arms factories there (rifle works, left; and rifle musket main armory, right arrow) but Confederates ran shops for several weeks making rifle muskets while remainder of stores and machinery were being moved South.

The Harpers Ferry Arsenal, with between 4,000 and 5,000 finished rifles and rifle muskets, and the carpenter shop, were totally destroyed by Lieutenant Jones' bombs. But Pollard (*Lost Cause*) states that 5,000 rifles in an unproved state, and 3,000 not finished (assembled but not inspected as finished?), were seized by Virginia troops. Fourteen thousand burned rifle muskets were fitted with new stocks at Richmond. Virginia helped herself to the machinery, the basic machine tools, and the sets of fixtures for making parts of the Rifle and the Rifle Musket, as well as quantities of unfinished and semi-finished parts. Much of this materiel was at once sent via railroad to Winchester; then by wagons to Strasburg, and from there via Manassas Gap Railroad to the Richmond Arsenal.

On May 7, 1861, Colonel T. J. (Stonewall) Jackson reported to Lee that "Mr. Burkhart, who is in charge of the rifle factory, reports that he can finish 1,500 rifle muskets in thirty days. I have, in obedience to the orders of Governor Letcher, directed the rifle machinery to be removed immediately; after that the musket factory. My object is to keep the former factory working as long as practicable without interfering with its rapid removal."

The Richmond and the Fayetteville Rifle Muskets

Under direction of Burkhart, Harpers Ferry continued to make rifle muskets for a period of two months; by June 18 all the former United States Arsenal materiel had been removed to Richmond and Fayetteville. Splitting the machinery between two factories gave rise to what are essentially two different series of arms: the Richmond Rifle Musket and Carbines, which are cut-down variations, and the Fayetteville Rifle. The major difference, generally, is in the lockplate form. That of the Richmond guns is a forging shaped to take the recess for Maynard tape primer, a "humpbacked" lockplate. The Fayetteville is the basic U. S. 1861 shape of plate; the stocks for both types conform to the respective patterns in their inletting.

The Richmond lockplate is an obvious attempt to employ forgings and forging dies which stamped out the Maynard type of lockplate. Richmond locks are known dated for 1861, '62, '63, '64, and '65; toward the last, skimping on the metal which does not fill the die completely can be observed; the humpback shape is not so full or complete as in the early locks. A few of the "humpback" lockplates are seen on Fayetteville rifles; these were selected from Richmond-destined spare parts, to fit up into the 17,000 gun stocks taken by the Maryland troops and sent to North Carolina. Or it is possible that the former Master Armorer of Harpers Ferry, Ball, had not sorted out the tools until late in 1861 to begin work on the regular Fayetteville rifles? While the lockplate tools could have been made in Fayetteville by Ball or someone else skilled in toolmaking, there is a hint in coincidence of some dates that the fixtures for making the new U. S. lockplate, without Maynard primer, may have existed in the Harpers Ferry shops at the time of capture.

In fiscal year ending June 30, 1860, Superintendent Alfred M. Barbour, a strong secession man, reported on the fabrication at Harpers Ferry of "one set patchbox gauges for the rifle musket." To be included in this report, the gauges must have been made subsequent to June 30, which is logical as the patchbox is recorded in the Ordnance Manual for 1861 as having been added to the Rifle Musket July 9, 1859. But a new and cheaper patchbox was designed, and the model from Springfield Armory is marked A—117/60 (now in Fuller collection). If this mark means "Allin, January 17, 1860," a possible translation, it conforms to the report and recommendations of the Springfield Armory board of officers which on May 18, 1860 recommended changes in the Rifle and Rifle Musket pattern, but okayed preserving the patchbox, suggesting adoption of an improved round form. The same board also recommended abandoning the Maynard primer. While Springfield and existing Harpers Ferry records have not been examined for this moot point, it seems Springfield was given the task of making up the patchbox, and Harpers Ferry, innovator of the Maynard primed M1855 pattern in the first place, the job of modifying the lock.

Capture of the provisional tooling for a modified plain lock by Jackson's force in April of 1861 would account for the delay in Springfield Armory finally abandoning the Maynard primer, George Dwight not initiating that change at Springfield until April 30.

The idea that Harpers Ferry had been supposed to redesign the lock gives some reasonableness to the idea which then arose, after the capture of Harpers Ferry, of completely redesigning the Springfield pattern to the 1861 Special Model; the rise of the South's military power rapidly revised the Federal notions, and Harpers Ferry settled, as did Fayetteville arsenal, for chopping off the top of a plain lock for the new pattern. But Fayetteville, we think, had the tools from Harpers Ferry for the new lockplate; Richmond kept the tools for the old.

The Virginia State Armory

The Virginia State Armory at the south end of Fifth Street, bordered by the James River and fronting on the Kanawha Canal, had an ancient and honorable history. As the Virginia Manufactory it had fabricated flintlock muskets and rifles, and some pistols, for the forces of the commonwealth. Authorized to be erected by act of the legislature in 1797, the armory was in production by 1802, turning out 2,151 muskets by October 13, 1803, of the Charleville-Springfield modified pattern. Flintlock rifles, full-stocked with brass patchboxes, of military Kentucky form, were also made, and two types of pistols, the latest type resembling the U. S. Harpers Ferry 1806 model, but with a swivel ramrod. Thousands of these arms were on hand to be transformed to percussion; many being cut down for cavalry issue, in 1861. With the increase in production and distribution of Government armory guns, and the decrease in Indian warfare within the commonwealth, the demands on the Richmond factory diminished. In 1820 it was shut down, and the buildings converted to the use of a school. In 1860 the buildings, which from their appearance in old prints reflected the institutional architecture of 1840-50, reverted to state uses and a company of militia cadets was billeted there.

The move to refit the establishment as a manufacturing armory began stirring in February of 1859. On the 18th, Adjutant General William H. Richardson received a circular from Colt informing him of the values of Colt's percussion arms in terms of U. S. muskets. The purpose of the circular was to enable the state official to calculate how many Colt arms he could get instead of the state's annual quota of U. S. muskets under the Militia Act of 1808. To Richardson, this seemed like a godsend and he asked Colt if the colonel would take "a large number of the old flintlock muskets, pistols, rifles" in a depot at Richmond in exchange for original percussion arms, at the rate indicated in the circular.

Colt did not reply directly, at least he did not accept the proposition. But he did, during the year, consider other possibilities and had the Colt company secretary, Major William M. B. Hartley, on duty in Washington, check into the Richmond situation.

Hartley was authorized to present a proposal of four points to Governor Wise of Virginia concerning rearming the state troops. First, Colt would agree to exchange the old arms for new Colt's Patent guns, but not at the circular equivalent, only at a fair value, and he would deliver the Colts only "as fast as I can make sale of the old arms." He considered this point "decidedly preferable for all parties and especially so for a few years until some of the other propositions can be carried out." These are the words of a man who neither expects nor wants war!

Second, Colt would contract exclusively with Virginia for a fixed length of time to make any of his arms at the U. S. prices. Third, was one of the most interesting: he proposed to supply "machinery and tools," the complete plant, for making annually 10,000 rifled muskets "of the United States pattern," for $250,000. The fourth proposal was to supply machinery to rifle and sight, and alter to percussion, the old Virginia Manufactory arms, for $50,000; the plant to have a capacity of 10,000 arms per year.

Hartley at once went to Richmond, and made a critical examination of the premises. Virginia, resisting the idea of putting out money, had countered with an offer that Hartley was in favor of: a stock company should be formed, Colt to take 9/16, putting up machinery to pay for his share and control. A new arsenal of granite should be built, using 200 laborers from the penitentiary, to be in a more defensible position. The waterpower of the Kanawha Canal impressed

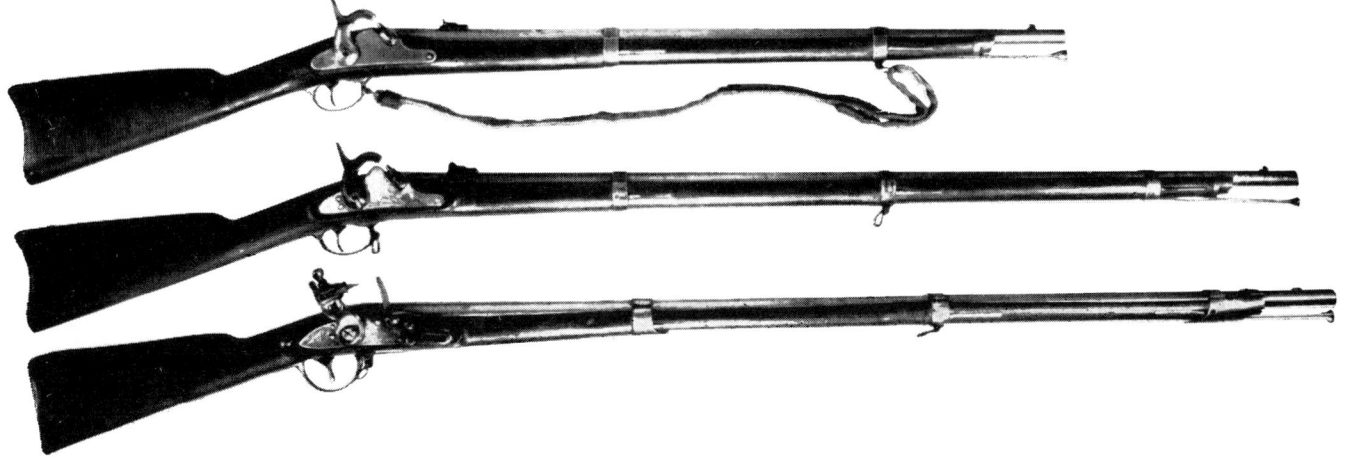

Short rifle and rifle musket of M1855 type but minus Maynard primer were made at Richmond Armory. Guns shown are stamped CS, were produced for Confederacy after South's armory system was placed under Col. Burton's supervision. Bottom is smoothbore, flintlock, 1808 pattern musket made at Virginia Manufactory in Richmond, 1813. There were 50,000 of these issued by Virginia State Ordnance Chief, Dimmock, in first days of War. From Jac Weller collection.

Richmond also assembled guns using captured and salvaged parts. Shown here is unique version with Special Model 1861 U.S. barrel (flat cone seat bolster) mounted to 1855-type stock, bands and lock. Plate is dated 1864; has 1864-type U.S. bevel edged hammer.

Hartley; the water "can be used three times," i.e., drive three separate sets of power wheels, and "it would almost drive the works of Lowell," referring to the enormous consumption of power in the textile industries of Lowell, Massachusetts.

After January 1, 1860, Colt continued to be sanguine that some arrangement could be made with the state. After the alarm of John Brown's raid, which had alerted not only the state but the whole South to the prospect of similar madcap uprisings, legislatures everywhere appropriated surplus money for arms. Virginia appropriated an additional $150,000 for the purchase of arms, and more for putting the armory into operation. Hartley would not give up the notion of making Colt's arms of some description in Richmond. He suggested leasing the old armory; it is in his letter to Colt of February 7, 1860, that Hartley states: "A cheap rifle should be made for the militia at from $10 to $15 each, say .52 or .50 caliber and I believe many thousands would be ordered."

While Colt had adherents in the Capitol, and master gunmaker Samuel Sutherland was a sales agent for his new guns, plans for the Northern arms maker to revitalize the Southern factory fell through. Instead, the state's newly appointed Master Armorer Solomon Adams was sent back to Springfield Armory, where he had labored for the United States for the preceding 15 years, to make copies of drawings and to prepare a model arm as a pattern for Virginia.

Adams and his assistants were engaged in this work in November, 1860, but required a little greater liberty than the work of making the model musket allowed, and found Colonel Craig dead set against assisting Virginia. On petitioning Secretary of War John B. Floyd, a staunch Virginian, for permission to "use some of the armory patterns for the Richmond machinery, and the privilege of taking drawings of fixtures, tools and etc.," Adam's desire was granted.

James Henry Burton

With Adams was another long-time employee of the United States Arsenal at Harpers Ferry, James Henry Burton. Born at Shenondale Springs, Virginia, August 17, 1823, Burton attended school in Pennsylvania, but entered the machine trade in Baltimore at the age of 16. In 1844 he took a job at the rifle works under John Hall and in 1845 was appointed foreman. He rose to Master Armorer within 10 years, and attracted the attention of the British who came to the United States, inspecting arsenals in 1855, in connection with the Sharps rifle contract. Offered a good position he resigned from Harpers Ferry and from then until 1860 was Chief Engineer of the Enfield Royal Small Arms Factory. While there, he became acquainted with the tool-making firm of Greenwood & Batley in Leeds, from whom Enfield purchased gunmaking equipment; this contact was to be renewed when Burton worked for the South.

He returned to Virginia in 1860 and accepted a position with Joseph R. Anderson at the Tredegar Works, in connection with their contract to make the machinery for the Richmond Armory. By June, 1861, the Tredegar machinery and the Harpers Ferry equipment were in operation; on July 12, George W. Munford, Secretary of the Commonwealth, tendered the services of the booming Richmond Armory to the use of the Confederate State Government.

Prior to the setting up of machinery, the Armory had issued 10,000 U. S. flintlock muskets to both state and C.S. troops, and 50,000 "Virginia flintlock muskets, these last plainly known by the stamp 'Virginia' upon the lock." With Colonel Burton as Superintendent of Armories of the Confederacy, was Solomon Adams as Master Armorer of the state, General Gorgas moving in with his family as the Government shifted north from Montgomery. The Richmond Armory was ready for full-scale manufacture of Rifle Muskets by Springfield Armory standards.

To use in making muskets, Adams had 20,000 seasoned musket stocks obtained in an exchange from Harpers Ferry before the raid, plus such quantities of parts of arms as were salvaged. In June of 1860, parts of arms in progress were valued at $93,573. At the time of Jackson's raid, there were 4,287 arms in store, of different types, valued at $60,000. Cannibalized, finished up, placed into seasoned stocks, these parts of arms and burned guns made bright were among the first issues from Richmond's newest arms factory. Said General Gorgas:

> The machinery of the rifle musket (caliber .58) retained at Richmond, got to work as early as September, 1861. If we had possessed the necessary number of workmen this "plant" could have been so filled in as to have easily produced 5,000 stands per month, working night and day. As it was, I don't think it turned out more than 1,500 in any one month.

The Richmond Rifle Musket

The basic rifle musket was the major production in Virginia. With flat iron bands and the regular 1855 cone seat, it resembles at a short distance the standard U. S. service arm. The absence of Maynard primer is noticeable because the plate is solid in this area. There are actually the production of three factories concerned in this picture. First, there are the M1855 Rifle Muskets fabricated under Virginia supervision (Colonel Jackson) at Harpers Ferry during the two months after its capture. At least 1,500 arms may be considered to have been made there; possibly more. They are assumed to be standard M1855 guns, type of 1859 with patchbox. As noted, Pollard records 5,000 guns being seized which were "unproved." Possibly these bear the usual Harpers Ferry marks but lack the VP-eagle barrel stamps.

The second "transition" Confederate Richmond Rifle is that made prior to August 23, 1861, in a temporary set-up by Burton in a tobacco warehouse. The Harpers Ferry equipment could not be moved into the Richmond Armory because Tredegar's contract had called for a complete suite of machinery, and all the space had been appropriated. Burton built muskets mostly from captured parts, waiting the beginning of work at the Armory proper. As General Gorgas notes, the Armory began turning out arms by September, 1861.

In the interim, the Burton-Virginia State guns bore only the mark RICHMOND VA. 1861 on the lockplate, and sometimes visible the stamp of Burton, JB on the stock behind the trigger guard tang as on Enfields. In the fall, the C.S. authorities, particularly Gorgas, wanted to shift the Harpers Ferry equipment deeper into the South; the state refused. Their gift was to be used by the Confederacy in the Richmond works, or not at all. Gorgas acquiesced and phased in the Harpers Ferry equipment and placed Burton in charge. William Albaugh III, leading authority on Confederate arms, expresses the opinion (*Confederate Arms*, Albaugh & Simmons) that the Tredegar machinery is

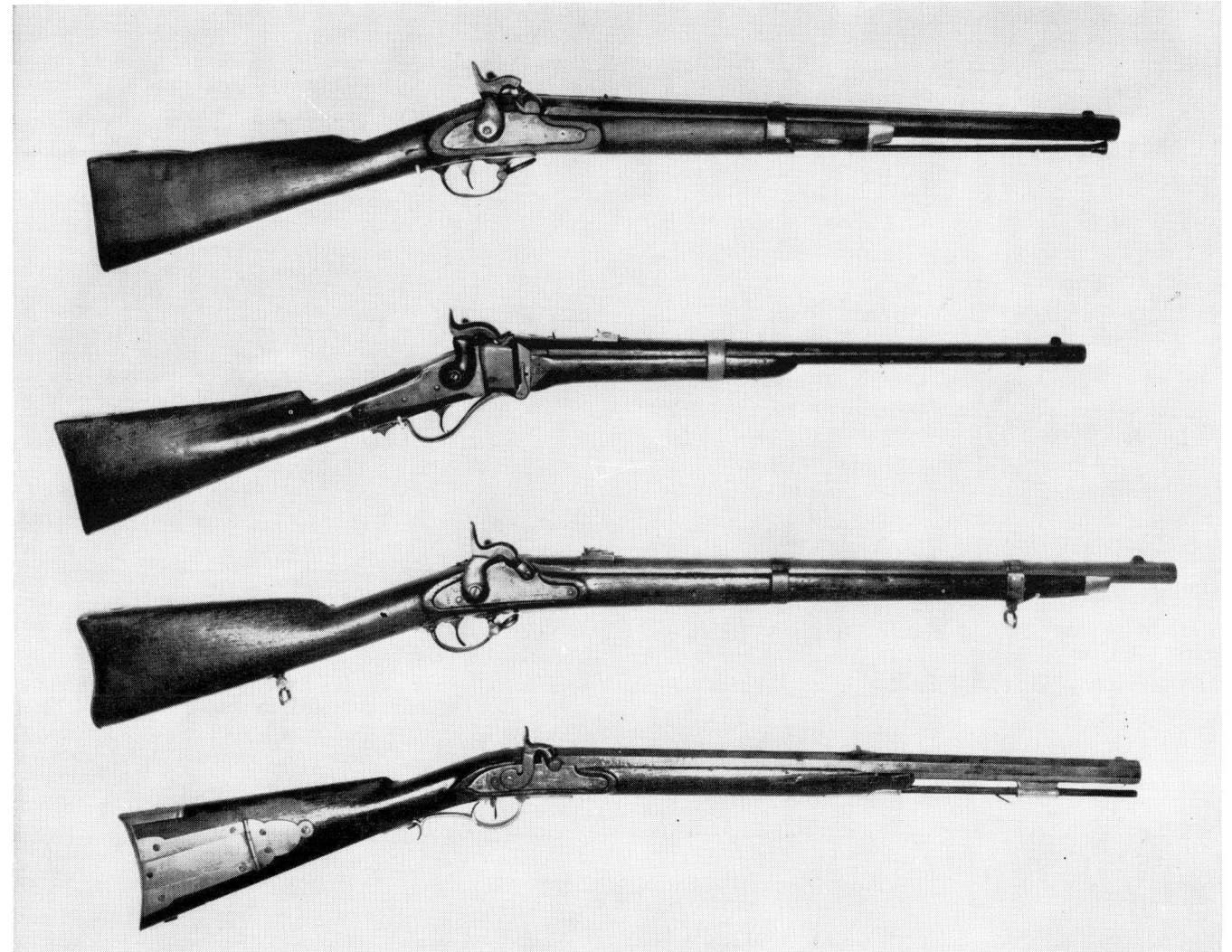

Both D. C. Hodkins and J. P. Murray copied the U.S. M1855 Carbine. Gun shown is not marked and ramrod swivel formerly mounted below muzzle is gone. Second is Richmond Sharps carbine, No. 8729, with no trace of Robinson's mark usually found on lockplate. Well machined, the buttstock may be a replacement. Hinged-leaf rear sight. Third is Richmond Armory carbine or musketoon dated 1863 with extra sling swivel in belly of stock. At bottom is Virginia Manufactory rifle made 1815 as a long "Kentucky" and then cut short in 1861 by James Walsh for cavalry issue. Val Forgett collection.

thought to have been for the fabrication of the Model 1842 muskets.

This seems hardly likely, in view of Solomon Adams' trip to Springfield to make a pattern arm and the employment of Burton to supervise the Tredegar machine contract. All the emphasis was on the best arm, not the abandoned and discarded gun. The state did purchase 5,000 altered percussion muskets from the United States for $2.50; these were roughly equivalent to the M1842 percussion guns when properly altered, and it seems most unlikely that Virginia, after dickering with Colt and trading around for the "best repeaters" of the time would contract with Anderson for machinery to make a musket model a generation old.

Except for the addition of the mark CS above the name, signifying the rifle musket was made for the Confederacy at Richmond, the guns continued to be the same. When it became necessary to fabricate some parts completely, the Harpers Ferry captured stores having been exhausted, brass was substituted for cast iron. Richmond rifle muskets are found with brass nose caps and butt plates. Issues throughout the war included captured gun parts, accounting for mixed models, such as one example pictured with the U. S. pattern of 1863 hammer and barrel fitted to a Richmond lock and stock group.

The Fuller & Stuart "Humpback"

A curious version of this arm with "humpback" lockplate marked E. WHITNEY/NEW HAVEN is pictured by Fuller & Stuart; the rear sight is the 1855 type and buttplate is of brass. Whitney did have a contract for the original 1855 Rifle Musket, which was never fulfilled. Whitney's penchant for putting up odd mixtures of non-standard parts to peddle here and there, and "old arms finished up," is well known. Whether Whitney actually fitted up this arm for the South, or stamped a Burton-Richmond musket bought at a surplus sale after 1865, is not known.

Two short models of "humpback" lock guns were made at Richmond, not to salvage parts further but as definite models, apparently. The "Navy musketoon" is so-called from having been bored smooth to about .62, presumably for the use of buck-and-ball which has some practical application in boarding tactics at close range. Barrel is 30 inches long, two bands held by springs.

The front band is about where the middle band fits on the musket. The cavalry carbine is similar but shorter, 25-inch barrel, caliber .58, with the front band set back and the nose cap fitted immediately forward of the band spring. Brass buttplate and nose cap may appear on these arms, and the sights on all three may be the 1859 leaf type or the 1861 pattern with rounded sidewalls at the leaf hinge screw. The cavalry carbine has not only the front band and trigger guard sling swivels found on the other two, but may have a sling swivel fitted on a base in the belly of the stock about 7 inches from the butt.

Semmes' Activities

While the Richmond works readied itself to produce the Rifle Muskets, the machinery for the .54 Harpers Ferry 1841 rifle, and some equipment for the M1855 rifle, were passed along to the State of North Carolina Armory at Fayetteville. Meanwhile, Captain Raphael Semmes had been working in the North prior to Sumter, under assignment from President Jefferson Davis. In addition to procuring percussion caps and many other vital stores, Semmes was assigned to track down some very interesting rifle-making machinery offered for sale by Ames in Chicopee Falls. President Davis wrote to Captain Semmes February 21, 1861:

A short time since the most improved machinery for the manufacture of rifles, intended for the Harpers Ferry Arsenal, was, it was said, for sale by the manufacturer. If it be so at this time, you will procure it for this Government, and use the needful precaution in relation to its transportation. Mr. Barbour, the superintendent of the Harpers Ferry Armoury, can give you all the information.

Barbour evidently informed Semmes that this machinery was for the conversion of muzzle-loaders to the Morse-system breechloader, for in Washington, Semmes spoke with Morse on the subject. In some surprise, Morse, thinking he was authorized to go after the machinery, wrote to President Davis on March 6, 1861:

In pursuance of my understanding with you respecting the machinery for arms, I immediately, on my arrival here, went to work to find out the facts relative to the business, and had prepared a letter to you as the result of my investigations which I took on Sunday evening to Captain Semmes for delivery, as I learned he was going direct to Montgomery. Much to my surprise, he informed me that he had been sent here fully authorized to transact the same business, and instead of going to Alabama, he was on his way to the East to see Mr. Ames . . . I hope that Captain Semmes may succeed in the enterprise, for then I shall have the satisfaction of knowing that my exertions and honest endeavors to benefit the Confederacy will have been crowned with success.

George Washington Morse

George W. Morse was in many ways the co-equal of James Henry Burton. Inventor of a toggle-joint breech-loading rifle or transformation for a muzzle-loader, somewhat like the Jenks and Merrill arms, the Morse gun tools apparently were made by Ames. General Ben McCulloch came east for the purpose of buying 1,000 Colt's revolvers and 1,000 Morse rifles for Texas. In getting the Colts, he was successful. But no operating plant for the Morse arms was in being, though tooling existed and plans were many. Morse's was the earliest successful military cartridge rifle, and used a reloadable centerfire musket-capped cartridge. As a Southern rifle, less than 1,000 were made, but they command the respect of the present for the ingenuity of the past.

A South Carolinian, Morse had lived in Baton Rouge and it is from that place that his patents, October 28, 1856, and June 5, 1858, were issued. The

Contract militia rifle by J. J. Henry when located at Boulton, Pa., was issued in SOUTH CAROLINA to judge by mark stamped on barrel flat. Muzzle is round to take socket bayonet. Enormous quantities of Southern sporting rifles were bored out to take .54-inch rifle bullets and then burst on proof-testing, accounting for relative scarcity of Southern Kentuckys today. Forgett collection.

Patent Office model for the 1856 specification has a compact toggle joint action with a top lever folding forward; the cartridge is a stubby .58 bullet, largely filled with powder in a big base cavity, and stuffed into a short rimmed case. Variations on this idea were made by Morse, but first production was set up at the works of the Muzzy Rifle & Gun Manufacturing Company, Worcester, Massachusetts. One hundred handsome cased sets of Morse breech-loading sporters were made by this firm; these cases included one stock and action, with interchangeable .54 caliber carbine, .50 caliber rifle and 16 gauge .69 caliber) shotgun barrels. Morse was backed up in this speculation by an order from the War Department for 100 military carbines ordered March 5, 1858, but apparently none were made. Instead, Morse sold the United States the right to alter 2,000 guns to breech-loading under his patents at a royalty of $5 for each gun. Of 1,000 arms drawn for the purpose, only 56 U. S. muskets of the Model 1840 were altered for test in 1859 to Morse breech and rifled with long range sights added. Apparently a full set of tools had been made for this work, since 544 more were partly converted. The remaining 400 were returned to store, unaltered, when the appropriation was exhausted.

Springfield also altered four .54 caliber rifles (M1841 presumably), one .58 rifle (M1855?) and started on three carbines, left uncompleted. The .58 rifle was sent to Harpers Ferry as a model in 1860. Of the 56 completed Morse conversions, one was sent to the Muzzy firm as an ammunition test gun, two were held at the Ordnance Office as presumably inspection models, and 53 were delivered to the Washington Arsenal for test. As a result, the Army decided to standardize the Morse conversion, changing all percussion muskets to breech-loading rifles. The system would work equally well on flint arms since the hammer was reduced to a cocking lever, the breech block carrying its own inside firing pin and two extractors.

While Colonel Lewis notes *(American Rifleman,* March, 1955) that "Machinery was being installed for that purpose at Harpers Ferry, where it was captured by Confederate troops before production started," it seems that tool-maker Ames had some of the Morse equipment which Semmes managed to get South via his own channels. Morse was a mechanical genius. Perhaps he did not have the administrative abilities to organize manufacturing on the same large scale as Colonel Burton. But the carbine of his production was practical and reasonably cheap, and his single shot muzzle-loading musket might have doubled the capacity of Confederate armories if it has been standardized in the beginning of the war. The Morse musket is a novelty because it is one of the very few applications of intelligent invention to what usually is a centuries-old pattern of side lock musket.

The Morse musket did not have a lockplate. The hammer was hung on an arbor that passed through the stock from side to side; at each end it was guarded by a brass oval plate but in the center passed through the tumbler. The tumbler was hung in a frame of bent strap iron, cheaply made. The frame was roughly the length of the trigger guard tang and removed from the bottom of the stock when the tang was unscrewed in the usual way. The mainspring leaf bore against the tumbler, and was fixed at the back of the folded sheet-iron "frame." The trigger, mounted in the sheet iron assembly, bore directly against the tumbler, instead of using a separate sear. The whole outfit was a "package deal" that could have been fabricated in enormous quantity at a properly equipped shop and shipped out all over the nation to musket and carbine makers, if anybody had been foresighted enough to see its merits. Unfortunately, Morse seemed more interested in making guns for state defense than in volume production.

When war began, Morse shelved plans to build the 3,000 carbines which the United States had contracted to manufacture in 1860. The tools were either at Ames, or at Harpers Ferry; as he later testified, he plotted with the Armory master armorer Ball to steal the carbine tools; eventual production of the Morse carbine at Greenville seems to indicate he was successful. While Gluckman *(American Arms Makers)* states he was in charge of cartridge making machinery taken from Harpers Ferry and put into service at Nashville, Morse on July 18, 1861, wrote to Secretary of War L. P. Walker asking for machinery that definitely was for making small arms, not merely cartridges. He desired to obtain on loan a trip hammer for welding barrels, planers, screw machines, a cone machine, lathes eight milling machines, a rifling machine, punch press, and many other items. The bill of machines would fit up a shop sufficiently to turn out Morse muskets; General Polk had indicated that Morse could probably obtain the loan of these machines and with that understanding the state of Tennessee had bought buildings and grounds for an Armory. Perhaps Morse got the equipment he desired; when Nashville was evacuated in April, 1862, Morse and machinery went to Greenville, South Carolina. In March, ex-Governor William H. Gist of South Carolina had been made chief of a Department of Manufacturing and Construction, with duties to encourage foundries, workshops, and arms factories. South Carolina decided to build an arsenal, and David Lopez was chosen superintendent. Temporary shops were set up on the state house grounds at Columbia while a permanent arsenal and armory was being erected in Greenville. Choice of the site was dictated by the gift of Vardry McBee of 20 acres near the Greenville & Columbia Railroad. With Morse now in Greenville, his wife joined him, she having left Washington, D.C.

The state spent over $500,000 on the Greenville works, and an inventory in the latter part of 1863 placed the value of the plant at $283,000. This was a far step from the machinery Morse wanted to borrow earlier, which he appraised at $8,000 to $10,000 value. At the factory, Morse produced breech-loading brass-framed centerfire cartridge carbines. Numbers on specimens are found as high as 548 on one in the Confederate Relic Room of the State House at Columbia. Another Morse carbine in this display is numbered 474. A card attached to the gun says it was given to Relic Room by F. W. Huseman, who was a gunsmith of Columbia and worked for Peter Kraft. Huseman it is

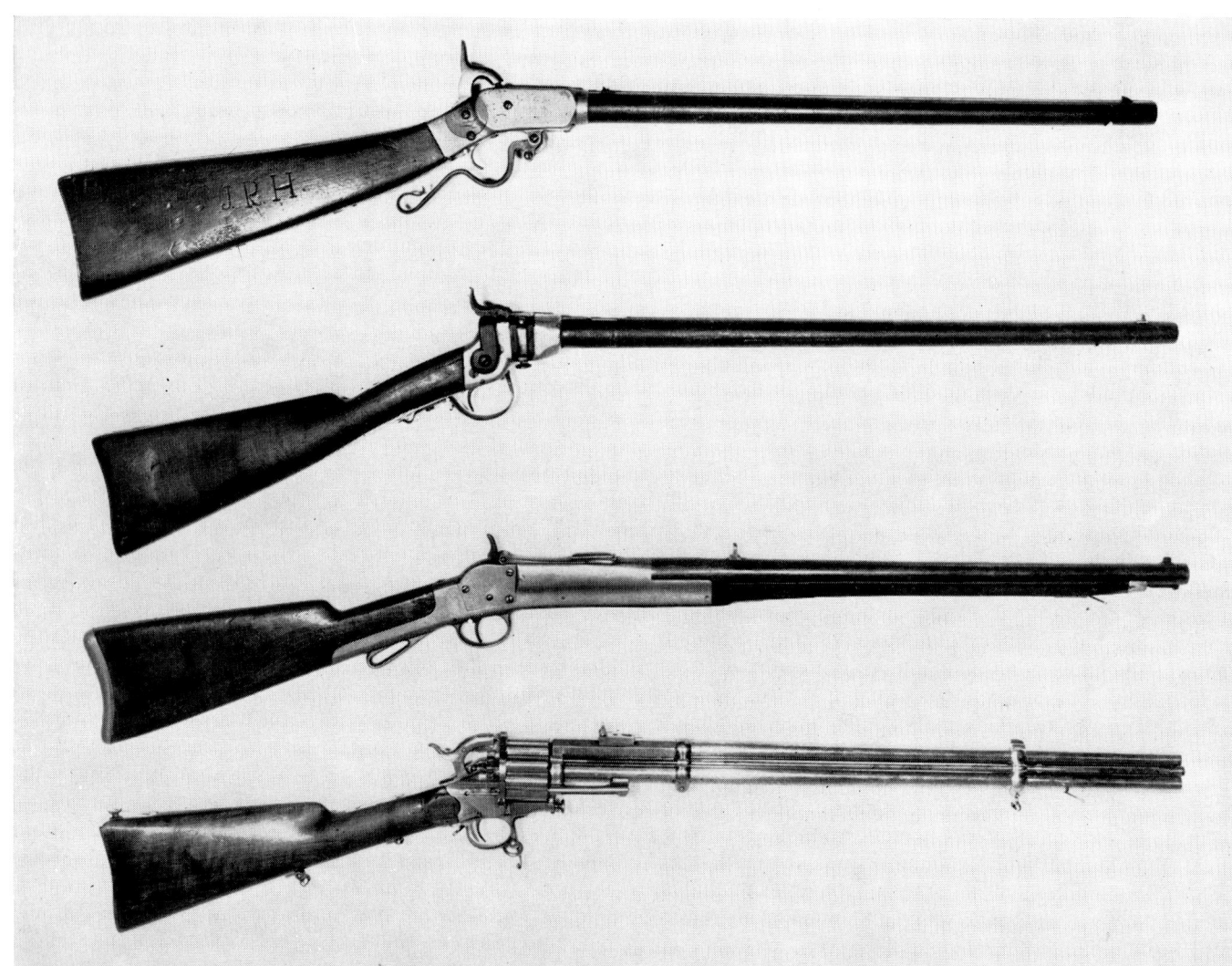

South's carbines showed ingenuity and manufacturing skill. So-called "Maynard" or "Perry" combines stock of one and tipping breech of another. The author thinks brass-framed Tarpley, 2nd, may be evolution from Alexander's patent breech gun. The 3rd is Morse Carbine made at State Works, Greenville, S. Carolina. Breech hinges up like Merrill to load metallic cartridge. LeMat revolving rifle is shown only because it is popularly thought to be Confederate association but no records show use of any percussion LeMat rifles in the South, and this bright pinfire specimen is definitely post-war. Val Forgett collection.

said also worked for Morse, probably in Greenville.

By the fall of 1862, the State Works at Greenville was well established, manufacturing shot and shell, gun carriages, caissons and ammunition chests, pikes, rammers, railroad spikes and rails, and other equipment. Orders were given for making revolving cannon though it is not known if any were built. By April of 1863 the Morse carbine plant was in operation and continued for 18 months. The extent of the factory is described by preliminary remarks on September 2, 1862 of the sub-committee reporting to Gist:

> It is said that by the 1st of October next the works will be in condition to cast said shot and shell and soon afterward to cast cannon, but not to make small arms for six months afterwards, unless the emergency of the service should require them sooner, which could be done by multiplying labor at increased expense.
>
> It is not contemplated to establish a first class armory, but upon a scale commensurate with State means, which may be increased if necessity should require it thereafter.

Under these conditions it is not surprising that less than 1,000 Morse carbines should have been built there. The arm built for South Carolina was supposed to be for the beginnings of a complete rearming of Union forces in 1860-61 with breechloaders. Governor Bonham reported to the Legislature November 23, 1863, that he had contracted for 1,000 and "A part of them have been completed, and I regard them the best cavalry weapon in use. The compensation to Colonel Morse has not been determined upon, and I recommend this matter to your consideration, as something more than the mere value of the article manufactured it may be thought proper to allow."

Odd in form, the Morse rifle was eminently practical as a work of machinery. The top lever opened the breech by collapsing a toggle joint, and the gutta-percha wad in the base of the cartridge sealed around the musket percussion cap and prevented gas leakage; the front of the breechblock slightly entering into the rear of the cartridge to help make the seal. The frame of cast brass extended through the weak part of the stock small, usually easily broken in rough service on other guns, and was carried forward some below the 20-inch barrel; overall length about 40 inches. Butt stock and forestock were of butternut; the weight only 6½ pounds, though seeming "hefty" owing to the center of balance being the center of mass of the brass frame. Usually marked only with the serial number, one gun in the Val Forgett collection obtained in the region of Clemson, South Carolina, is stamped MORSE on the right side of the receiver directly below the hammer. The gun's cast brass frame has been repaired during process of manufacture, the re-brazing being noticeable only under close examination.

Powered by coal, not cheap water, the productive State Works was unprofitable. In December, 1863, the legislature authorized the Governor to dispose of the State Works if he could except that he was to keep materialized, and on November 2, 1864, the *Daily South Carolinian* of Columbia announced the State Works would be sold at public auction on November 15. Bids were apparently not high enough and no sale was consummated; Governor Bonham recommended that month moving the State Works to Columbia to use the canal water power, but apparently this was not done, for Governor Magrath placed J. M. Eason in complete charge of the State Works at Greenville in February, 1865. Said the Governor, "Hitherto they have not been productive; now they must be so." The State Works at Greenville escaped the notorious burning of Columbia which destroyed so much capital enterprise; in 1866 the legislature again attempted to sell the establishment.

Morse remained decidedly unreconstructed. At the close of the war numbers of U. S. rifles were transformed to breechloaders by the Allin system. Modifications of this system were adopted as successive U. S. standard arms. In 1875 he brought suit against the Government and Winchester Repeating Arms Company as co-defendants in infringements of his cartridge patents, claiming a royalty of $5 on each of the 130,000 breech-loading Government rifles made to that date. Ultimately the decision was made in his favor. For a short time the lever action rifles made by the Whitney Arms Company were counterstamped after manufacture on the tops of the barrels with G. W. Morse's Patent, 1854. This marking has puzzled many who wondered how an 1854 patent could affect an 1875 rifle. A House Report on Morse in 1878 recommended compensation, and the ultimate payment was made to his widow, for Morse died before it was finally paid. The notice was brief in the New York *Tribune* of March 9, 1888:

> Washington, March 8—Col. G. W. Morse, the inventor of the Morse cartridge and breech-loading gun, and a nephew of Professor Morse, who invented the telegraph, died at his home in this city today. His funeral will take place Saturday.

The Mississippi Rifle

The "Mississippi Rifle" was a very popular Southern state contract arm. Numerous would-be makers obtained contracts and appear briefly in records. Some of their output has been identified, sometimes only tentatively. One of the best-made copies of the 1841 rifles was that produced by the Shakanoosa Arms Company in Alabama, known more commonly by the name of Dickson, Nelson & Company.

Two distinct variations of the Dickson, Nelson & Company short rifle were made, according to Jim Blackburn *(Gun Report,* October, 1961). Superficially both are two-band short rifles, .58 caliber, along the lines of the U. S. M1841 with Enfield overtones, brass bands. The first type, usually dated 1863, has spring-retained bands on a cherry-wood stock. Though esteemed by cabinet makers, cherry is not always as strong as walnut, and the makers preferred walnut in their second "issue." The nosecap is of Enfield type, not the two-loop band of the M1841 model. There is of course no patchbox. Rear sight is of two-leaf type, possibly 300- and 500-yard notches. Buttplate is curved, of conventional rifle-musket form.

In the second form, found dated 1864 and 1865, the D. N. & Company seem to have made minor attempts to strengthen the arm, in the stock, especially. The wood is walnut, while the tang of the trigger guard plate is extended to the rear more than the 1st type; the back tang is 5½ inches long, 9 inches long overall. In both types, front bands and guard bows carry the sling swivels; the second type has narrower, clasping bands. In one arm owned by Blackburn, the appearance of the stock at the place for the rear band suggests that in fact no rear band was fitted; an emergency economy in parts, perhaps. The second type rear sight is a simple dovetail blade, V notch. The buttplate is more primitive, flattened and at an angle like the 1841 Rifle or U. S. Musket 1842. Vertically to the rear of hammers on first and second types the lockplate, of U. S. 1841 form, is marked ALA./1863 (or '64, or '65) in two lines; forward of the hammers the plates are marked in three lines: DICKSON/NELSON & COMPANY C.S.

These well-made arms were produced in a limited quantity, though the "Shakanoosa Arms Company," proprietors, William Dickson, O. O. Nelson and silent partner Dr. L. H. Sadler, had evidently tooled up to make 5,000 Mississippi-type rifles for the state of Alabama. They delivered at least 645 of these to the state, receiving $90 each in somewhat inflated currency in payment.

Dickson and Nelson were from Tuscumbia, Alabama, and Dr. Sadler lived at Leighton. Deliveries were supposed to begin May 2, 1862, but the advance of the Union forces caused their withdrawal to Rome, Georgia, where they found haven to produce arms for Alabama. They had been in Rome a short time when the plant was burned, causing them to take up new quarters at Adairsville, Georgia, and, finally, a further move to Dawson as the tides of war washed close to them. It is possible the cherry stock guns are associated with their first production in Rome. Later production in Dawson included plans to fabricate a carbine.

Many carbine stocks and blanks of walnut were found there and remained on hand in the wood trade there for many years until recent discovery by collectors snapped them up as souvenirs of this peripatetic factory. Made on order for the State of Alabama, in a factory which produced most of its rifles in the neighboring commonwealth of Georgia, it seems likely that many of the arms produced were actually used by a Missouri regiment. Blackburn reports (*op. cit.*) that of three Dickson, Nelson & Company rifles he has owned, two came from Jefferson City, Missouri, one from St. Louis.

The Cook & Brother Factory

One of the largest ordnance establishments in the South was the factory of Ferdinand W. C. and Francis L. Cook, known as Cook & Brother. First located in New Orleans, the works was shifted the day before the fall of the city, April 24 and 25, 1862, and ultimately re-established at Athens, Georgia. While in New Orleans, the firm contracted with the State of Alabama which took the total production of the works, about 25 rifles a day with 400 men at work. Louisiana interests endeavored to increase the production to 100 rifles a day, with the balance to Louisiana, but the capture of the city prevented this expansion.

Enfield rifles were made and examples exist marked COOK & BROTHER NO, but the anonymous ordnanceman who for six weeks was attached to the Confederate Ordnance Department, stated very positively: "New Orleans turned out the best rifles I ever saw in the South. They were similar to the French Minie rifle, furnished with fine sword bayonets. The Louisiana troops were mostly armed with these." Apparently he was in error, considering that the short Type M1859 sergeant's rifle with sword was "like the French minie," as it also had a sword bayonet. When F. W. C. Cook commandeered a steamboat to carry his machinery up river, he gave 200 rifles to a local defense officer and retained 200 for his own crew which manned the boat. Later, bribing a Federal guard with a $10 bill, he managed to get a schooner full of steel out of the city also, to forge into rifles for rebellion.

Prior to evacuating New Orleans, Cook dallied with the prospect of making the LeMat revolver; doubtless he examined the doctor's heavy octagon-barreled prototype made by Krider of Philadelphia, and then decided against it; such was a factor in sending Dr. LeMat aboard the *Trent* to England and eventual production on the continent. Cook stuck to Enfields, and on April 1, 1862, contracted to supply the Confederate Government with 30,000 Enfield rifles, "complete with sabre-bayonet, sheath and frog," at $30. July, 1862 was the date of the scheduled first delivery, the contract to be completed by December, 1863. Apparently Cook did not propose to expand much; this still averages a delivery of 750 rifles monthly.

The move to Athens caused a renegotiation, with first delivery date scheduled for January, 1863. Purchasing Carr's three story grist mill and 25 acres on Trail Creek outside of Athens, the Cooks put up a fine 2-story armory of two wings flanking a castellated center tower which served as offices. While some trouble was noticed by Confederate inspectors with the spring temper of the locks and their inletting, they were pronounced "the finest that I have seen of Southern manufacture." Stamped on the case-hardened lock plate with a Stars & Bars behind the hammer and COOK & BROTHER ATHENS, GA. in front, over the date, together with the gun serial number by the front lock screw, they are a well made article with stock of local walnut and brass from donated and confiscated brassware.

Four patterns of Enfields were made, all conforming very closely to the British original. An inspector

Stars and Bars signed lockplate of Cook & Bro. carbine made at Athens, Ga., in 1864. Gun serial No. 6130 was made at one of best-equipped arms plants in South.

had urged that Cook be provided with a set of gauges, but it is unlikely this was done. All have brass trim, clamping bands, and while differences can be noted in shape of cone seat, all follow the Enfield pattern. The long Cook Enfield has three bands, 39-inch barrel of Enfield type. The Cook short rifle has 33-inch barrel, and two versions exist: with sword bayonet stud and with the front sight base serving as socket bayonet stud. Late in 1864 it was ordered that the manufacture of sword bayonets be discontinued, and the differences in the Cook series are in line with this order. A cavalry carbine with ramrod attached by a muzzle swivel like the M1842 pistols was also made, barrel about 21 inches, and an artillery carbine, 24-inch barrel. Rear sights were fixed, and the barrels are often marked PROVED, as well as the date.

Cook barrels were of unusual construction, of wrought Swedish iron which had been forged 1½ inches square, then twisted while hot to lay the inclusions which would cause weakness at right angles to the line of bore. Instead of a seam being exposed to the force of the powder and bullet contact throughout its length, it would be twisted spirally, giving a better support to barrels of fundamentally inferior metal. While Cook lacked barrel rolling machinery, he bored these from the solid, using a battery of vertical boring machines he had developed, from which the chips fell out of the muzzles, eliminating the need to back off the cutting tools. Evidently the barrels were upright in the most approved Hartford fashion, spun around the stationary drills and cutting from their own weight.

Shortage of skilled labor gave Cook many problems, and in 1864 the C. S. Government considered buying the factory. Colonel Burton reported it to be: "... the best fitted-up and regulated private armory that I have yet inspected ... The establishment reflects much credit upon the senior proprietor and he has exhibited a much better appreciation of the requirements of an armory than any other person who has attempted a like enterprise in the Confederacy."

Burton wanted to buy the factory. Under his expanding authority, it was to come within his power to move workmen and tools from one place to another, to continue the flow of guns at the optimum rate. Cook and Brother would be a valuable link in this chain of production. But the works had to shut down when this did not come about, and the Government began to renege on its payments for arms delivered. Meanwhile the Cooks, having been commissioned Major F. W. C. Cook and Captain F. L. Cook, organized a reserve force of their workmen. Among fights the battalion engaged in was the battle of Griswoldville, when they united with the men of the revolver factories in the defense of the Griswold & Gunnison works. Near Hardeeville, South Carolina, Major Ferdinand Cook was killed on December 11, 1864.

In February and March, Colonel Burton proposed to move the entire carbine factory at Tallassee to Athens. On April 10, he informed Master Armorer Charles Henry Ford, who had re-opened the Cook factory for small arms repairs, that the move had begun. Ford was to find billeting for over 100 white workers and their families, but within a few days the matter was to become academic for Ford; the Confederacy was no more.

Francis Cook recovered control of his armory from the United States authorities long enough to have it ordered sold by the Clarke County, Georgia, sheriff to pay his personal debts. The building was bought for $18,000 by the Athens Manufacturing Company and today is a cotton mill.

Cook & Bro. copied the Enfield faithfully in most models. Long arm was adapted for angular bayonet. Short rifle in New Orleans make may have been fitted for sword bayonets, but few specimens found reflect order of 1864 discontinuing issue of sword bayonets in South. Carbines were fitted with hinged rammers in early production, later used simple swell-end rod. Bottom carbine in Smithsonian Institution, is like-new specimen, shows twist pattern of iron barrels invented by Burton to increase strength in poor materials.

Enfield Rifle Factory Set Up in Macon

Colonel Burton had a great interest in the Enfields of Cook, and in supplying them with gauges. But the central government had a plan to set up an Enfield works abroad, then ultimately transfer it to the South. Secretary of War Walker, on May 7, 1861 called the attention of Governor Howell Cobb, who was President of the Confederate Congress, to this idea. Referring to the manufacture of arms, he said:

> At London a complete set of machinery exists, which was made in this country, after the pattern of the machines at Springfield, in the United States. It would, I think, be no difficult matter to get these machines copied and executed on the spot with great rapidity. Triplicate machines should be ordered to ensure the chances of delivery of at least one set. For this purpose an additional appropriation of $300,000 may be needed . . . for the three sets of machinery. Should they all arrive, they will, even if not required by the government, be easily disposed of. The amount already asked for under the head of armories and arsenals, would also require to be increased by an item of $75,000 for a suitable building.

It was not until 1863 that Colonel Burton was able to accomplish this, the machinery to be set up at Macon, Georgia. He returned to Leeds, England, to Greenwood & Batley, machinery builders. Burton was welcomed by his friend Arthur Greenwood, a director. G & B had considerable experience in furnishing the specialized machinery needed for gunmaking, and had set up Enfield rifle factories, since their founding in 1856, for: East India Council, 1859; Royal Small Arms Factory, 1860, Elswick Ordnance (Armstrong) 1860, Royal Laboratory (ammunition machinery) 1860, Birmingham Small Arms Co., 1861 and London Armoury, 1862.

As can be seen, rifles obtained by the Confederacy had been made on all the above set-ups except those of the East India Company, probably established in India, the Royal Laboratory, and Elswich.

In 1863 a contract was negotiated between Greenwood & Batley, and Fraser, Trenholm & Company for a complete Enfield rifle factory, to be installed in one of the largest small arms factories in the world which the Confederacy was building at Macon, Georgia.

At present no description of this machinery exists,

Master armorer, James H. Burton, worked to set up factory at Macon, Ga., for making of Enfield rifle. Specimen shown, from Enfield Royal Small Arms Factory pattern room, is type adopted by South early in War as standard.

but its production rate was to have been 10,000 rifles a month, or approximately 300 rifles a day. An almost identical contract was negotiated by G & B with the Russian Imperial Government in 1871, with Colonel Burton called in to supervise planning the machinery. It was to make the Russian "Bredan II" bolt action single shot rifle, .42 caliber, and is probably very similar to the Enfield plant:

> The actual contract was for a complete factory, capable of producing 300 complete (Berdan II) rifles and bayonets in a 10 hour working day. About 950 machines of varying types were made and delivered, coupled with the necessary jigs—fixtures—tools and cutter gauges—compound gauges—drop stamping and hot forging dies, including a complete department to cover maintenance and the replacement of worn out equipment. All inspection—interoperational—tool and cutter gauges were made and tested at (Greenwood & Batley) on the actual production of the rifle and bayonet.

Land had been obtained for the Macon Armory when in May, 1862, the mayor and city council gave a vast tract of land to the Confederate States Government. The conveyance was made "in consideration of the patriotic devotion of the people of Macon to the government of their choice," for a token sum of $5, "and the further consideration of the advantage to accrue to the city from the erection of an armory within its limits." The Confederate authorities took possession and began the erection of a large armory; the walls were completed and a number of lesser buildings finished when the city was surrendered to Major General James H. Wilson, U.S.A. The unfinished two-story armory was 45 by 620 feet, of brick from a nearby 27-acre brickyard that had been once Union property, and was to be again. A second building of brick was completed, two stories, 45 by 165 feet. A new brick laboratory of one and two stories, 25 to 80 feet wide and 700 feet long, had also been completed, and a number of other buildings including a brick one-story proof house.

The tools for the C.S. Enfield were completed, boxed, and shipped for the account of Fraser, Trenholm & Company. They were in Bermuda at the time the war ended. Their whereabouts today is a mystery. Equally fascinating is the thought that Greenwood & Batley, before shipping the factory, must have set it up experimentally and run off a batch of parts; these parts were finished and assembled into completed guns, for the approval of Colonel Burton, Major Anderson or Huse, one of whom certainly was "riding herd" on the project. The foregoing is speculative, but common practice, and there is no reason to think Greenwood & Batley deviated from this plan. What these rifles were, how they were marked, is a question to stump the experts. Bonafide Confederate rifles, they never reached the Confederacy.

Today Greenwood & Batley flourish, surviving defaults of cotton crop failures, collapse of national creditors, and a thorough pasting in World War II when a stick of Jerry bombs laid the factory low. But they still cherish memories of the gentlemanly Colonel Burton, one of the most knowing men when it came to gun tools. They employed him after the war in preparing tooling for the Russian Government on a rifle designed by the famous Yankee, Hiram Berdan. Ironic that former enemies should come together in building rifles for yet another strange land.

Richmond and Fayetteville Production

While Burton preferred the Enfield, the Springfield influence of the tools at Richmond and Fayetteville persisted in Confederate small arms design. At Fayetteville Armory, the M1855 type machinery had been in production. The first issue of arms was put up on the stocks from the Maryland troops, which appear to have been fully finished for the long range rifle; the two-band model with the patchbox mortised out to hold a special front sight ring with crossed wires. This ring slipped over the muzzle, fastened with a set screw, and placed crosshairs on the foresight for super-accurate aiming. As some stocks had been mortised for the Maynard primer lockplates, sufficient profiled but un-mortised lockplates were sent along of the "humpback" variety to finish up these rifles. If a modified 1861 lockplate was fitted to the cut-out M1855 stock, there would be great danger of water getting into the lock mechanism, to its considerable detriment.

More common an example of the Fayetteville rifle is that found with the distinctive S hammer. Suggesting a modified continental form of hammer, the style also suggests the workmanship of some A. H. Waters & Company percussion pistols resembling the M1836, converted, that collectors have discovered recently. Whether the complete set of forging dies for hammer was of North Carolina origins, or bought in the North, cannot be determined. That it is characteristic, cannot be denied. The author once owned a Deringer-marked Common Rifle, much polished, that had been bought in a Liege gun shop. From indications it was assumed the rifle had been imported as Civil War surplus years ago. However, it had been transformed to percussion by a bolster conversion. The hammer was a diminutive Fayetteville hammer, scaled down a little for the smaller rifle-sized lock of the 1817 Common Rifle.

One or two examples of pistol-carbines are found with the same humpback lockplate of the earliest arms, and a special hammer of rather straight form, not curved like the M1855, nor of the S shape. The lockplates are obviously of the 1855 tape primer form but without the mortising for Maynard works; otherwise, they are common M1855 pistol carbines. Locks are dated at the rear, 1862, and before the hammer the word *FAYETTEVILLE* and an eagle stamp, unlike the Harpers Ferry Pistol-Carbine eagle stamp, the eagle facing dexter. The H-F eagle faces sinister, but is turned away from the arrows, sign of war. This eagle appears also on the *FAYETTEVILLE* rifles, in both cases surmounting C.S.A. An old tale of Bannerman's is that the die was from Harpers Ferry and the USA was cut out and CSA substituted. This die appears to be like the Harpers Ferry M1842 stamps.

Richmond and Fayetteville supplied the majority of long guns of Confederate manufacture. Brass bands on Fayetteville rifles, iron M1855-61 type on Richmond arms is the rule; both series may have brass buttplates, the existing iron ones believed to be captured plates and forgings worked up. In spite of the scarcity of copper in the South, skilled labor was in even shorter supply. Eventually the manpower scale was to overbalance in favor of the North and the South went under. But this shortage of men, not arms, was recognized early on the production front.

The decision to use brass, valuable for percussion caps and eventually planned to be used in cartridge

Extensive gauging was to be introduced in South's production scheme by Macon Enfield factory. Gauge set shown is from Enfield Armory.

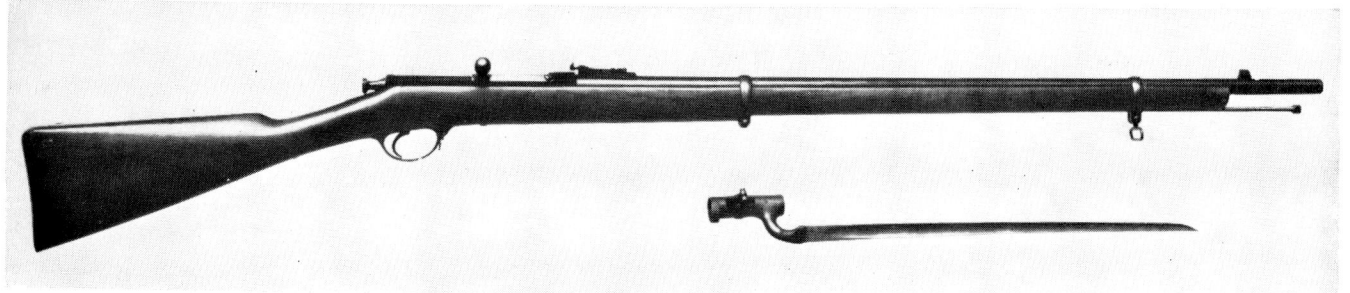

Col. Burton contracted with Greenwood & Batley for South's armory. Tools were shipped to Nassau before war's end. Later, Southern ordnance genius worked with G. & B. on Russian rifle contract making Berdan II breechloader (above) of 1871.

manufacture, was based on the shortage of skilled labor. Cutting tools adapted to steel and iron will last two or three times longer without sharpening or re-grinding, when used against brass. Pouring brass to form was also a time and manpower saver; this may have dictated the use of brass for even the lockplates of some arms, as the virtually unique George Todd Springfield-type rifle musket preserved in the Battle Abbey collection at Richmond, Virginia. Lockplate, hammer, bands, guard and plate, butt and nose cap, all are of brass. Its barrel has U.S. proofs and either typifies the salvage of U.S. parts by the South, or the creation of a non-existent pattern of Type 1861 rifle musket for the benefit of the collectors of yesteryear. It is stamped on the lockplate Geo. H. Todd, Montgomery, Ala., and behind the hammer, C.S.A. 1864.

To augment the workman shortage, Gorgas tried importing English mechanics as he imported Enfields:

To supplement this scarcity of operatives, Colonel Huse was authorized to engage for us a number of skilled workmen, used to work on small arms, and to pay their passage over. They came in through the blockade at Wilmington without difficulty, but we could do nothing with them. They had been engaged to be paid in gold, which meantime had risen to such a price as to make their pay enormous, and would have produced utter disintegration among our own operatives. I offered to pay one-half of the wages promised them in gold, to their families in England, if they would take the remainder in Confederate money, which would support them here. I brought the British consul to confer with them here. But they stood upon their bond, and foreseeing that their presence would do more harm than good, I simply, with their consent, reshipped them by the next steamer, and paid their passage back. The experiment cost us something like £2,000 in gold, and made us shy of foreign workmen, especially English . . . Of all obstinate animals I have ever come in contact with, these English workmen were the most unreasonable . . .

With the ordinary workmen at Richmond, Gorgas fared better. Under the close supervision of Major W. S. Downer, C.S.A., the Armory was understaffed but turning out guns. For the first three months after transfer of the armory to the Confederacy by the state, Downer was engaged in phasing-in the Harpers Ferry machinery. The exact nature of this equipment was described by Colonel Dimmock, chief of Virginia Ordnance Department, in an order to Colonel Burton dated June 15, 1861. Having decided to lend the Harpers Ferry rifle machinery to North Carolina, Dimmock ordered Burton to deliver it to any authorized agent to transport to Raleigh, "taking care to retain all and any machines or parts thereof that may be necessary for the making up of muskets. The barrels and stocks suitable for the rifle and not fit for the muskets you will also turn over to said agent." The reference to "muskets" is of interest, for the scavenging of arms-making tools from the United States Arsenal was done by experts, many of them master workmen who knew at a glance what was the purpose of some unimaginable piece of metal work.

Without the aid of armorers Ball and Barbour, Burton and others intimately acquainted with the workings of the Harpers Ferry establishment, and the fixtures needed, the coup of its capture by Stonewall Jackson would have been but a capture of a junk pile. Engineers of any other profession than that of fabricating the actual models of arms made at the Arsenal would have been entirely stymied in trying to determine the functions and the set-up of this equipment. But Solomon Adams—oh, wise named man!—had made copies of the Springfield drawings and by constant reference between drawings, master workmen, and obvious details, the jumble of machinery was sorted out. It was this, in detail, which occupied the three months after August 23, 1861, when the Virginia authorities ceded the use of the armory to the Confederacy.

Meanwhile, on January 25, 1862, the Virginia Advisory Council recommended that Colonel Dimmock set up the musket machinery in the State Armory. There is definite confusion over the exact nature of these different sets of machinery. State machinery was made by Anderson at Tredegar under the personal direction of Burton, as a complete contract for the state. What was ultimately turned out under Confederate Army Major Downer's supervision tells only a part of the story. From about October, 1861, to October 1, 1863, according to an interrogatory of Downer made at that time, the Richmond Arsenal had turned out since its transfer to the Confederacy the following arms:

Rifle muskets	11,762
New rifle carbines .58, muzzle loading	2,791
New smoothbore carbines, .69	651

These carbines used up all the stocks and barrels damaged so as to render them unfit for muskets. The

Several sets of gunmaking machinery existed in South by 1861 which influenced models of arms chosen and locations of factory sites. Top and second are Palmetto musket and rifle made on tools supplied by Benjamin Flagg of Millbury, Mass. to South Carolina in 1852. Third is Fayetteville rifle of most common form with typical "S" shaped hammer reminiscent of some A. H. Waters mid-fifties commercial conversions or percussion pistols. Harpers Ferry rifle stocks were sent to Fayetteville as gift from Maryland troops. Bottom is enigmatic muzzle-loading Hall rifle believed made by J. B. Barrett at Wytheville, Va. Piece is clever engineering to use parts already made for long Hall breechloading rifle while stock suggests entirely new pattern was made for turning out new stock. Center hammer is of Hall form but adapted to strike nipple set into breech plug; Hall barrel appears to have been new and not yet fitted with side ribs for holding receiver. Separately for comparison is shown flintlock Hall rifle of standard form dated 1839, but bearing silver presentation plate by order of Congress bestowed on Gustavus A. Bird for gallantry at siege of Plattsburg, Sept. 14, 1814.

.69 carbines appear to have been .58 barrels bored rather thinly, in the thick back portion of the tube. Downer was rather unclear in his figures, however, for later on, December 29, 1863, he gives a further recapitulation which indicates the rifle musket section was running full blast. From October, 1861, to November 30, 1863, there were manufactured at Richmond:

Rifle muskets, model 1855 23,381
Muskets, model 1842 1,225
Rifle carbines, caliber .58 . . . . 2,764 (?)
Rifle muskets or carbines repaired or
   made of old parts with new added . . . 12,212

Why Downer reduced the number of .58 carbines made in his later tally is not known; presumably he had the facts at hand. Whether the Muskets, Model 1842, were from a new run of parts on tooling actually set up, or the assembly of Harpers Ferry captured parts, is another question.

Arming the Cavalry

Woven into the legend of the South is the gallantry and courage of the Southern horsemen. The chivalry of the Southland has had its many chroniclers, and the story of Dixie cavalry cannot be told in detail here. That it was a major force in the early years of the war was reflected by the rapid organization of an adequate Northern force of efficient cavalry to oppose Johnny Reb on horseback. When Custer's Spencer-repeater armed cavalrymen from Michigan met the Confederate

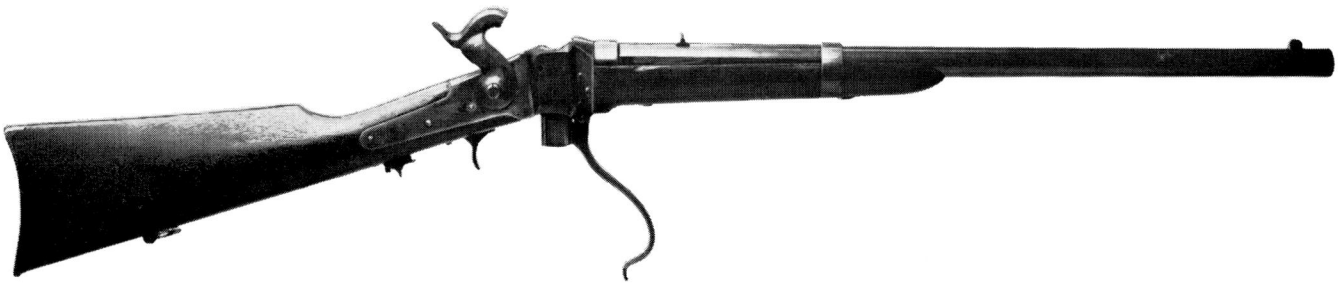

Sharps carbine was designed by Burton for production in Richmond by S. C. Robinson. Plate of specimen shown bears stamp S. C. ROBINSON/ARMS MANUFACTORY/RICHMOND VA/1862, and at rear, serial number 168.

troopers armed with double shotguns or revolvers, the encounters were brisk and bloody. The "arme blanche" grew red but later medical records of saber wounds revealed far fewer than the retelling of flashing-blade encounters might lead one to expect.

In reporting on the arms of one major figure of Southern chivalry, Nathan Bedford Forrest, the Ordnance Officer at Memphis, William R. Hunt wrote to Secretary of War Judah P. Benjamin in March, 1862:

> Requisitions are daily made upon me for pistols for cavalry service in this department, but I can find none for sale at any point in the Confederacy. Many have been bought up by the infantry (officers and privates), and I respectfully suggest that you disarm the infantry and let the cavalry get the pistols now in the hands of the former. In this way enough pistols could be obtained for all the cavalry in this section, and the infantry could get money for an arm that is of no service to them. Colonel Forrest, the most efficient cavalry officer in this department, informs me that the double-barrel shotgun is the best gun with which cavalry can be armed, and that at Fort Donelson one discharge of his shotguns, at close quarters, scattered 400 of the enemy whom three of our regiments had vainly tried to dislodge from the stronghold in a ravine.

Not the discharge of shotguns, the discerning reader will observe, but the shock effect of a cavalry charge at close quarters, was the tactic which dislodged the enemy. Though recommending the shotgun, Forrest did not always have uniformity of arms in his command. Carbines, muskets, and pistols were reportedly used by Forrest's men, in the following testimony:

(Woodford Cooksey, Co. A, 13th Tennessee (U.S.) Cavalry):
Q. Do you know who shot you?
A. It was a white man. He shot me with a musket loaded with a musket ball and three buck shot.
Q. Did you have any arms in your hands when you were shot?
A. No, sir.
Q. Did the one who shot you say anything to you?
A. I was lying down. He said, "Hand me up your money, you damned son of a bitch." I only had four bits—two bits in silver and two bits in paper. I handed it up to him.
(Lieutenant McJ. Leming, Adjutant, 13th Tennessee (U.S.) Cavalry):
A. About this time they shot me . . . I saw there was no chance at all and threw down my sabre. A man took deliberate aim at me, but a short distance from me, certainly not more than 15 paces, and shot me.
Q. (By Mr. Gooch) With a musket or pistol?
A. I think it was a carbine; it may have been a musket but my impression is that it was a carbine. Soon after I was shot I was robbed . . . Some of the colored troops jumped into the river, but were shot as fast as they were seen. One poor fellow was shot as he reached the bank of the river. They ran down and hauled him out. He got on his hands and knees, and was crawling along, when a secesh soldier put his revolver to his head, and blew his brains out. It was about the same thing all along until dark that night.

Confederate Ordnance Chief Gorgas condensed into one paragraph the frenetic activity of Southern artificers to supply cavalry carbines:

> The want of cavalry arms caused me to make a contract with parties in Richmond to make the Sharps carbine—at that time the best cavalry arm we had. A set of machinery capable of turning out 100 arms a day was driven to completion in less than a year, nearly all the machinery being built up "from the stumps." The arms were never perfect, chiefly for want of nice workmanship about the "cut off." It was not gas-tight. We soon bought out the establishment, and converted it into a manufacture of rifle carbines, caliber fifty-eight, as the best arm our skill would enable us to supply to the cavalry.

Gorgas' recollection is not entirely correct: the Richmond arms were well made and show, in the rare new specimens existing in U.S. Government museums, good finish and fit. But it is said some had Sharps-Hartford breechblocks, either battlefield replacements or evidence of cannibalization in the emergency; hence some at least were no worse than the Hartford guns in being gas-tight. The gas leakage did give rise to some problems. It was shown by experiments following reports the carbines "blew up" that the metal of the guns was not defective, nor was their design. What happened was not uncommon with other Sharps rifles; it was caused by failure to keep the breechblock flash-hole clean.

When the Sharps mis-fired, to clear the charge necessitated dropping the breechblock and eventually

At Enfield Armory, Burton in late 1850s supervised modification of Sharps carbine to placement of nipple directly on barrel; then actually made at least two Sharps Carbines at Enfield, one of which shown has cone flashing into chamber without complicated channels in breech block. Experience was drawn upon by Burton in setting up Richmond factory.

punching out the ball from the muzzle. In dropping the lever, the loose powder that had collected inside the cavity in the block face (the cavity was a part of the Lawrence style breech sealing design) was carried down and a few grains would fall into the forearm mortise of the lever spring. Powder would accumulate there so even minor gas leakage might set it off, blowing the forearm out at that point and putting splinters in the shooter's arm. Many things in the mechanical construction of the Sharps could contribute to this trouble. Failure of the breech sealing plate to move as freely as it should might have been one cause.

Making the Sharps carbine in Richmond was a project of Colonel Burton, though he is not so firmly identified with it as the eventual contractor, Samuel C. Robinson. In the spring of 1861 Mr. C. W. Alexander brought to Burton's attention a breech-loading rifle with a segment of the barrel breech that was pivoted on an axis parallel to the bore, and could be swung aside to be chamber-loaded. Burton suggested omitting the chamber and inserting the charge directly into the barrel, using only a solid swinging breech part. He later brought Alexander into the Richmond Armory and gave him a Sharps carbine from which to copy the Lawrence gascheck, and Alexander made a model carbine paid for by the Confederate States Ordnance Department. Albaugh supposes (*Texas Gun Collector,* issue 62, September, 1955) that the model gun made by Alexander differed but little from Sharps carbine with the R. S. Lawrence "gas-check pattern." But the model carbine having disappeared, we must turn to Burton's own description (as quoted in *Firearms of the Confederacy,* p. 203), that the Leetch patent breechloader of 1853, which Burton examined in 1857 in England, "embraced substantially the same breech-loading arrangement as that originally submitted by Mr. C. W. Alexander in the spring of 1861." Alexander seemed not to meet with success, but the use of the Sharps as a model for him to study must have struck Burton later on as foolish. Why fiddle around with odd-ball guns when the Sharps could also be copied? A meeting of minds occurred when South Carolinians Thomas E. McNeill and William Glaze (owner of the old Palmetto Armory), and importer T. W. Radcliffe, formed the "Confederate States Armory & Foundry Co.," hoping to achieve a capital of $1,000,000 to fabricate ordnance and ordnance stores at Macon, Georgia. With great expectations, McNeill then engaged Colonel Burton to assist him, and they obtained a contract with the Confederate States Government May 5, 1862, for 20,000 breech-loading carbines of Sharps patent.

Burton's Methods

Burton was a talented general engineer, it is true, but there was a reason why McNeill joined with him in contracting to make the Sharps carbine. Burton had special experience in engineering a set up for the Sharps, as experimental Sharps guns had been fabricated under his superintendency at the Enfield Royal Small Arms Factory in 1858. Enfield's chief contribution to Sharps design had been to omit the Maynard primer, and fit the percussion cone directly into the top of the chamber, avoiding the complicated flash channels through the breechblock. Redesign of the breech linkage was too complicated for Burton to do on short notice, but to omit the Maynard primer was easy, and it was this arm which the Confederate armory ultimately built. McNeill obtained both machinery and cash advances under this contract but seems not to have performed. Burton had been working with Samuel Robinson to set up equipment to make the brass framed

Confederate arms in Smithsonian collection reflect industrial resources of men and machines little suspected by later historians. 1: Mendenhall, Jones & Gardner M1841-55 with Lancaster sword bayonet; 2: Cook short rifle; 3: Richmond rifle musket; 4: Palmetto musket; 5: Morse patent lock muzzle-loading musket; 6, 7, 8: Sharps, Tarpley and Cook carbines; 9, 10: Richmond and Cook carbines; 11: Tallassee C.S.A. regulation carbine combining butt of U.S. rifle form with Enfield lock and barrel; 12, 13: Sharps and "Perry" carbines; 14: long Enfield rifle, maker undertermined but probably English, though lock is without Tower or Crown marks. Leaf elevator sights are uncommon among C.S. guns.

Whitney pistol ultimately built by Spiller & Burr. Regardless of the personal interest which this remarkable engineer seems to have had in too many arms plants, it was a system of merit.

Burton seems to have associated himself with potential manufacturers in an arms contract. He would then develop the tools and get ready to build. But Burton himself was only one man, and it was not to his liking to spend his time exhausting himself in travelling about the country. It was almost easier to transfer the contract, ship the machinery down stream to another group of would-be fabricators, and turn to a new task close to home in Richmond. Thus, he was responsible for the founding of a number of arms factories, without actually having spent much time in them to set up the machinery. With Robinson he built the revolver machinery; then Robinson disposed of it to Spiller & Burr and began anew to make Sharps carbines, a contract for the supplying of which Colonel Burton just happened to have in his pocket. They must have commenced working on it not later than May-June, 1862, for by December 8, 1862, Major W. S. Downer reported to General Gorgas that as the firm of Robinson was about to start turning out arms, it might be to the advantage of the Ordnance Department to rent or buy the works.

Under government supervision, Downer estimated savings on government orders might be made enough to pay for the factory. Robinson seems to have been agreeable to selling out, but Downer was not easily taken in by the high prices Robinson quoted for both the cost of manfacture and the complete factory. Meanwhile, guns were rolling off the line and between December and March, 1863, a production of at least 1,500 Sharps carbines was reached. This production record of 500 guns monthly was fantastic, but not remarkable when the competency of the man behind the scenes, Colonel Burton, is considered. On March 1, 1863, the Confederate States Ordnance Department concluded the purchase of the Robinson factory.

Guns made by Robinson are found marked "S C. Robinson Arms Manufactory, Richmond, Va.," on the lockplate in four lines, and "S. C. Robinson Arms Manufactory" on the barrel in front of the rear sight and "Richmond, Va. 1862" to the rear. Such a gun, #1642, was once listed by dealer Stephen Van Rensselaer in 1935 as being elaborately engraved. It was said to have been a prize won by a Confederate sniper and later captured by a Union soldier and brought to New Hampshire. The highest carbine bearing Robinson's name, found by researcher Albaugh, was #1882. While a carbine has been seen the first two numbers of

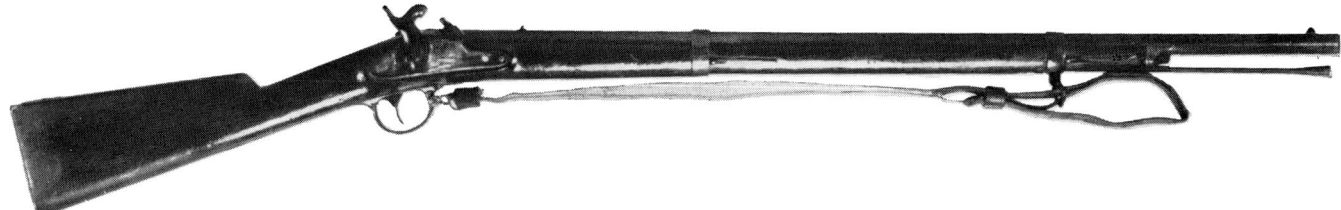

J. P. Murray rifle, like Mendenhall, Jones & Gardner, is combination of M1841 and M1855 U.S. styles.

which may be read "88—," it is believed the stamps are not clear and the numbers are "33—." On September 30, 1863, Gorgas reported that 3,000 carbines had been made at the now C. S. operated plant since September, 1862.

Though the Robinson shop represented a high degree of efficient mechanization, producing 500 carbines monthly once it got started, the administrative branch of the Confederate Ordnance Department was less effective. Production fell off from conflicts in the program.

New Carbine Ordered

In July, 1863, General Robert E. Lee ordered that a new muzzle-loading carbine be made for cavalry use. Several ingenious breechloaders had been developed, other than the Richmond Sharps. The Tarpley at Greensboro, Georgia, was being manufactured. A swinging breech design, it is of the mechanical form that the Burton-modified Alender design might have taken, though the actual shape of the missing Alexander model carbine is not known. Alexander obtained a Confederate States patent a month or two after Tarpley patented his gun in February, 1863. Another oddity, bearing no marker's name and at present not verified as to location of manufacture, is the "rising breech" model; while another with a tipping breechblock and a board stock like the Maynard is variously called "Confederate Maynard" or "Confederate Perry." These and other small-production weapons proved unreliable and Lee recommended that all efforts be placed on procuring a good supply of standard muzzleloaders of a fundamental Enfield pattern.

By August 5, a new model carbine was ready in Richmond, and A. L. Bargamin was instructed by Downer to convey the model carbine to General Jeb Stuart for his examination, report and, it was hoped, approval. The brilliant cavalry leader of the Army of Northern Virginia mixed arms field trials in with his other duties, when the Federals permitted. On August 14, Bargamin having returned to Major Downer with the results, Downer instructed Solomon Adams to make another model meeting the objections of Stuart's men. The butt was to have more drop, like that of a Smith's carbine returned by Stuart as a sample. The length of stock was correct but the barrel was wanted 1½ inches longer. Brass bands, Enfield lock. The sights were to be corrected, and "It is desirable that special pains be taken to make a weapon for accurate shooting at a moderately long range that we may be able in some measure to compete with the Sharps carbine in the hands of the enemy which are very accurate at 800 yards." The second model made had a sliding ring on a sling bar; this was objected to as the gun, being a muzzle-loader, should not be carried slung muzzle down for fear of losing the charge. Swivels for a sling were to be attached, the cavalryman to carry the loaded arm across his back. "The inspectors of this arm will be rigid in their inspection," Downer instructed, "allowing no work to pass which will in any way impair the durability and service of this arm."

The manufacture of the new Richmond .58 carbine was undertaken at a time when the crumbling ramparts of the Confederacy exposed every city to Northern raiders. Perhaps there were those who had not given up hope; maybe a few were not conscious that before them was to be a "last ditch" stand and then utter dissolution. But the dangers of Richmond as a location for this important mass-production works of basic cavalry arms was obvious to all. By the end of April, 1864, Gorgas had instructed Burton and Captain C. P. Bolles to visit several locations offered for the new carbine factory, including Tallassee, Alabama.

"The town of Tallassee consists entirely of the cottages of the factory operatives," Burton reported, the factory being the cotton mill of Barnett, Micon & Company. Leases were arranged and into one of the buildings, and new sheds put up by the Confederate authorities, the carbine machinery from Richmond was being shifted. By August, 1864, Captain Bolles was able to report progress in setting up the machinery, but materials were in short supply. Not until September 8, 1864, did Burton order bar iron for the barrels at Tallassee. But in spite of not having money to pay the hands, and the dissatisfaction of city workmen transported to a rural existence, Bolles began cutting metal. In February, 1865, the one thing lacking was the stock; but 500 gunstocks were located at Macon Armory intended for rifle-muskets, and these were sent to Tallassee.

Commanding the C. S. Armory at Tallassee now was Major W. V. Taylor, and in the face of threatened evacuation he began to prepare packing cases for the machinery. Burton informed him (March 22, 1865) "If the removal be effected, it will be to Athens, Georgia, where there is shop room and power ready for your use." But during all this time, Taylor kept the men at work assembling carbines and by April 3 informed Burton he had 500 carbines ready and wanted to know where to deliver them. Efficient as ever, Burton acknowledged this the same day instructing him to "turn over and forward at once to Colonel Cuyler, Macon Arsenal, the 500 carbines."

A Virginian, William New, had been detailed to work at the Tallassee carbine factory. He later said after the war that when the Federal troops occupied Tallassee, "the machinery was destroyed together with all completed guns and material." Whether any shipment of the 500 carbines to Macon was accomplished is doubtful.

Across an Ordnance Department daily record ledger of the Macon Arsenal Laboratory is a final entry dated: "June 15, 1865. Played out. Done gone, quit. Turned over to U.S. forces, and taken an everlasting receipt."

Thus did the Confederacy fall.

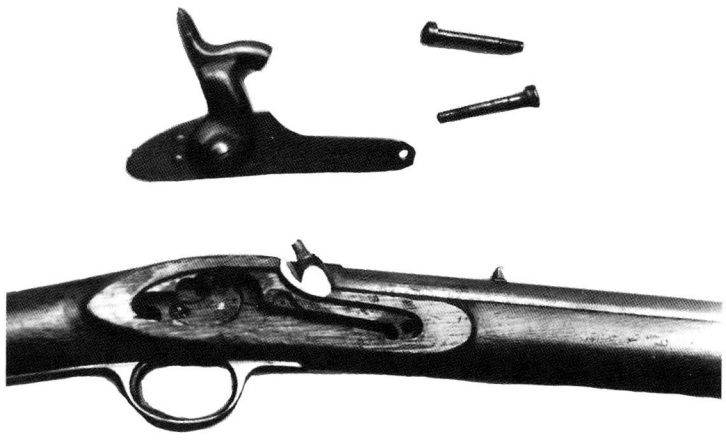

Crisp inletting of lock mortise in mint Cook & Bro. Athens Ga. two-band Enfield CS rifle symbolizes immense threat to New England industry from upsurge of manufacturing and communication in the South in the 1850s. With capital, brains and skill the South could compete with goods from any source. Southerners today consider that the Civil War was an attack on economic progress to save markets for the North.

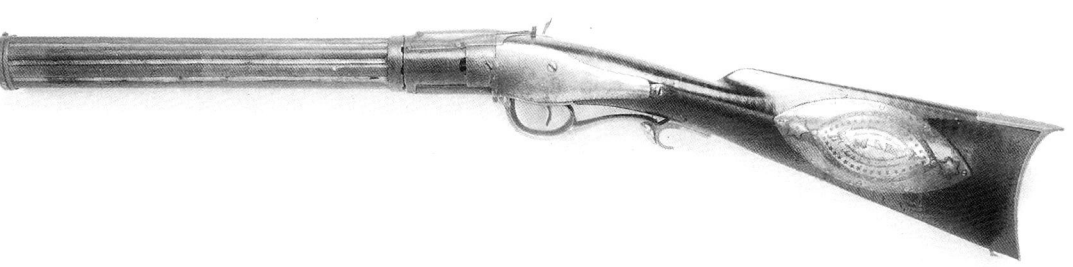

Lorenzo Sibert's "Virginia Pacificator" 48-shot carbine was for Staunton Arms & Ordnance Co. The silver plate on the patent model was engraved "union forever." Harpers Ferry made a .40 cal. army model tested in January 1861. In March Col. Burton estimated the cost to make 3,000 Sibert rifles yearly with bayonets would be $41,405. Design of "open chamber" was revived circa 1900 and in the 1950s for cannon.

Facade of Macon C.S. Arsenal, nearly 800 feet wide, was front to numerous shop buildings housing what South expected to be the world's largest machine works. Enfield tools were built by Greenwood & Batley in Leeds to Col. Burton's specifications. Shipment of some tools reached Bermuda, but the war ended. What would have made the South an industrial rival to the North is now under city streets.

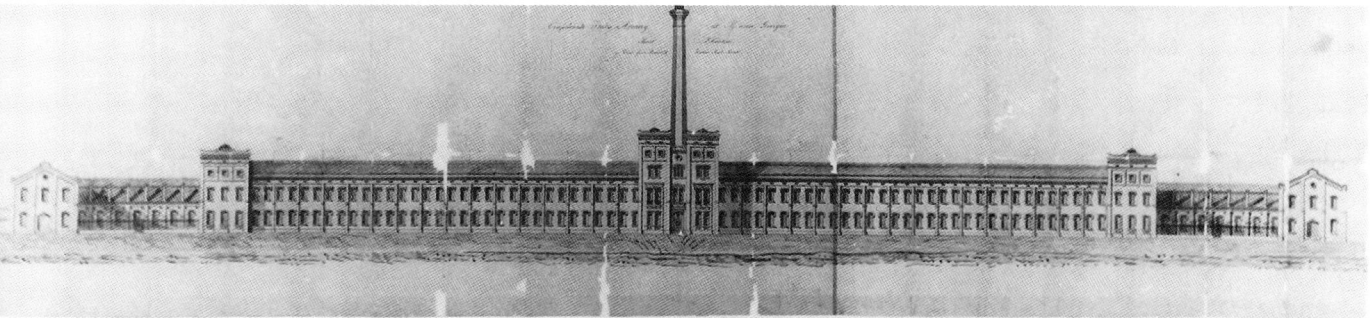

Macon photo courtesy James Henry Burton Papers, Manuscripts and Archives, Yale University Library.

CHAPTER 32

The Southern Pistol—The Derringer

Generically, the Deringer pistol, or "Derringer" as it came to be known, is a small defensive pistol of large bore. Gun maker Henry Deringer, listed in the Philadelphia City Directories as early as 1811 at 29 Green Street, did not at first achieve fame as a maker of pocket pistols. His M1808 U. S. military holster pistols are eargerly sought after by collectors; they command prices that now range into the "fabulous" category. He moved to 374 North Front Street in 1813, remained there until 1823. Presumably from the Front Street shop he shipped at least a few of the 2,000 Model 1817 flintlock Common Rifles he contracted to supply the United States on April 3, 1821. This lot was evidently a continuation of business which began with his making Common Rifles of the 1817 pattern on a contract dated July 23, 1819. Even before this time he had a contract of 1814 to furnish 980 rifles to the Government, while, in December of 1828, after moving to a new factory "entry from 93 Race Street," he agreed to supply 600 Hall breech-loading rifles. Due to production difficulties, Deringer asked permission to change this order to 400 muskets of the M1816 pattern. Although it is believed some or all were delivered, no Deringer muskets of this lot have been located.

In 1842 or '43, the plant was relisted due to renumbering of that part of town, and became known as 612 North Front Street. In 1843, he undertook again to supply the Government with pistols, of the Navy Boxlock percussion pattern. Flintlock rifles by Deringer, while highly prized, are relatively common; flint pocket pistols by him are unknown. An explanation may be that the percussion system was well established by 1820 among sporting gun users, while governments clung to flint and steel for 20 years thereafter.

Deringer sporting guns, or defense pistols, included large holster or duelling types, but all followed a form borrowed from the English pocket pistols of the 1830's.

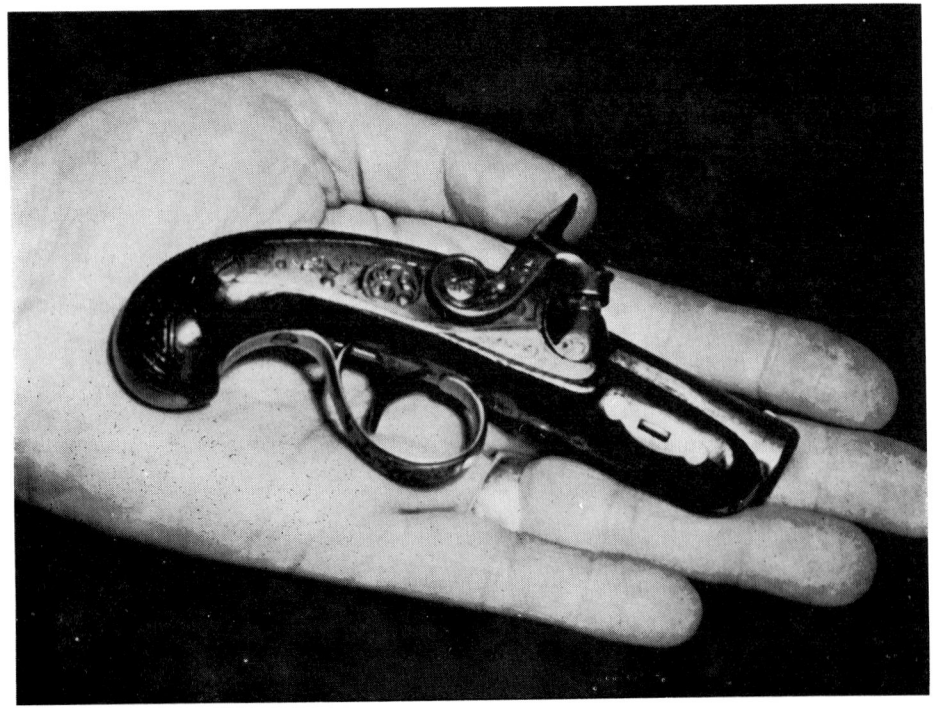

Small as the palm of his hand, John Wilkes Booth affected the deadly big-bore, .44 caliber Deringer pistol which put end to shooting war of '61-'65.

The back action lock was adopted as standard. While it removed wood from the curved portion of the handle, it left more wood under the barrel and in general permitted a stronger stock where it counted.

Big pistols, other than Government models, had octagon barrels, and ramrod ribs below. As the size got smaller, the barrel got rounder, retaining the top flat but being formed smoothly without the octagon corners through the rest of its dimension. A style point carried through most pocket Deringer pistols was a silver plate set forward of the lock and below the nipple bolster, to protect the stock from cap burning. Most Deringer arms, like that with which Booth assassinated Lincoln, were easily concealed pocket pistols shooting round bullets of approximately .40 to .45 bore. With barrels hardly longer than two calibers, in the smallest specimens which have survived, they were rifled; and truly rifled with grooves, not just notched at the muzzle like some of the cheap Belgian or English single shots of the period. But holster pistols as large as .54 and tiny vest pocket Deringers of .36 caliber are recorded.

The variety of even the "genuine Derringer," as trade agents advertised old Henry's pistols, leads one to suspect that his failure on the Hall Rifle contract was because he simply could not or would not adhere to John Hall's strict requirements of interchangeability in all the parts.

Genuine Deringer pistols of pocket size so far as is known were always sold in pairs; almost always (if new) equipped with a powder flask, common single ball mould, and little chamois draw-string or tie end pouches to preserve the pistols in the pocket from lint and tobacco grains. But though sold in matched pairs, it is fair to say as regards the system of their manufacture, that no *three* Deringer pistols were ever alike.

Differences in Derringers

When the Deringer moved south and west, an even wider latitude of minor style points appeared which tend to localize the maker or area of manufacture of some of these important little pistols. Alabama collector Jay P. Altmayer, who manages to sandwich an amazing amount of scholarship into an active life not connected with the gun field, other than as a hobby, has noticed enough differences in Southern derringers to comment on this.

"Although more derringers were sold in the Far West, than there were sold along the Mississippi," Altmayer notes, "out of the Mississippi gun trade grew a chain of rare makers. The collector will emphasize the minor variations of stock shape and lock shape that developed from St. Louis all the way to Houston.

"There are Houston derringers, one known by Mendenhall of North Carolina, and a rare pair of Louisiana derringers. Bitterlich of Nashville contributed to this Southern derringer evolution. Such arms have different decoration and design than the Philadelphia derringers, and possibly are improvements.

"The stock seems to be a little stronger and while

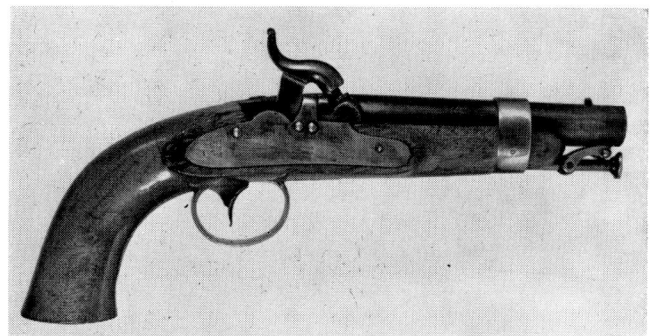

Deringer contractor for U.S. for years, made this well-machined M1843 "boxlock" Navy pistol with inside hammer on interchangeable parts plan. Belt pistol was first percussion arm issued to U.S. forces, actually made and in service before the brass-trimmed M1842 Cavalry pistol. Specimen shown is dated USN 1847, and marked on lock DERINGER/PHILADEL'A. Finish was blue barrel with casehardened lock and brass guard and band.

their ornamentation may not be quite as fine, it would be analogous to comparing a Hawken rifle to a Tryon rifle made at the same time. The Tryon would be much the jazzier looking, and the Hawken would be the sturdier and more functional."

The Bitterlich Derringer

Details found on unmarked derringers, or pistols bearing a name which is plainly that of a sales agent or owner, may help tie down a Southern origin for the gun. A nut instead of a hammer cap screw is one characteristic of pistols made by Frank J. Bitterlich, 16 Deaderich Street, Nashville, Tennessee. Bitterlich pistols are characteristic in having octagonal barrels, though there are of course exceptions. Southern-made pistols seem to have the cheaper, easily taken down detail, which Deringer himself used sparingly, of fastening the rear of the lockplate by the edge or flange of the wood screw which merely holds a notched end of the plate. Many true derringer pistols, especially the better quality ones, have the lockplate rear tip drilled cleanly through for a screw that more solidly holds the plate, but also must be removed completely to disassemble.

Bitterlich pistols have one clue which, marked or unmarked, would seem to correctly identify an arm as being made by this celebrated pistol smith. This is the detail form of the bottom edge of the lockplate (back action of course), and the rounded shape of the plate which is blended into the cross-section curve of the wood handle. The bottom edge of the plate is a broken curve with a sort of corner to it, approximately in line vertically with the front edge of the hammer. While Philadelphia derringers are usually scroll engraved on lock, hammer, and trim, Southern-made pistols are more often completely plain. Of the few Bitterlich pocket persuaders so far identified, some have edge engraving, a line of triangular-shaped chiseled indents, as a decorative border to the lockplates, and along the flat-shanked hammers. Bitterlich also seems to have pioneered in flat-butt derringers, and made a few which have metal sheath triggers like the "Root patent" Colts and common stub-trigger cartridge guns of the succeeding decades.

Schneider & Glassick

Though Bitterlich is little known today, two of his customers became famous when they combined to supply revolvers for the Confederacy. These were William S. Schneider of Memphis, and Frederick G. Glassick of the same city. Derringer-type pistols having the Bitterlich characteristics are known with the trade names of both Glassick and Schneider applied, indicating they were separate and competitive merchants, in the ante bellum days of this gambler haunted Mississippi River port. Schneider pistols may have wedge-fastened barrels, with oval silver stock escutcheons; the Bitterlich derringers for Glassick have a 4-leaf escutcheon on the bottom of the stock, and the barrel is held by a screw from the bottom.

After war began, Schneider and Glassick merged into a new firm, advertised for all persons who had left guns for repair longer than 3 months, to get them, for they would turn the remainder over to the Confederate Government as of March 15, 1862. The two had embarked upon the manufacture of revolvers, and proposed to furnish the Confederacy with Colt-type revolvers of local manufacture. Schneider & Glassick revolvers are exceedingly rare, 14 having been made, and of three surviving specimens, two are iron-framed while one is brass framed. Barrels are Colt-type octagon. It is thought that these revolvers may actually have been made by Bitterlich for his erstwhile derringer distributors. A Bitterlich-type derringer, hammer fastened by a narrow nut instead of cap screw, and barrel held by the Glassick-type stock screw, is known marked "J. Hausmann." His address is unknown, other than that the pistol has a Southern origin.

Certain Characteristics

Over the South, derringer suppliers had a brisk sales day. From Houston, Texas, came specimens of the pocket blasters having at least two features which many collectors consider "characteristic." First, is the presence of a rather rounded and pronounced schnabel fore-end tip, more rounded than that of true derringers, yet definitely present, unlike the Bitterlich type which seem to have little or none. Less definitely characteristic is the barrel wedge escutcheon of nickel silver, fastened by two side screws finished flush with the plate and stock. Pineapple finials are rare on these, which are more commonly ovaled. Genuine derringer escutcheons of course are often pineapple-shaped in their ends, and usually set in with wire brads soldered to the backs, instead of a visible screw or pin.

A handsome pair of G. Erichson, Houston, derringers in the Pugsley collection show the "Houston schnabel" as well as screw-fastened escutcheons. The shape of the escutcheon is more curved around the

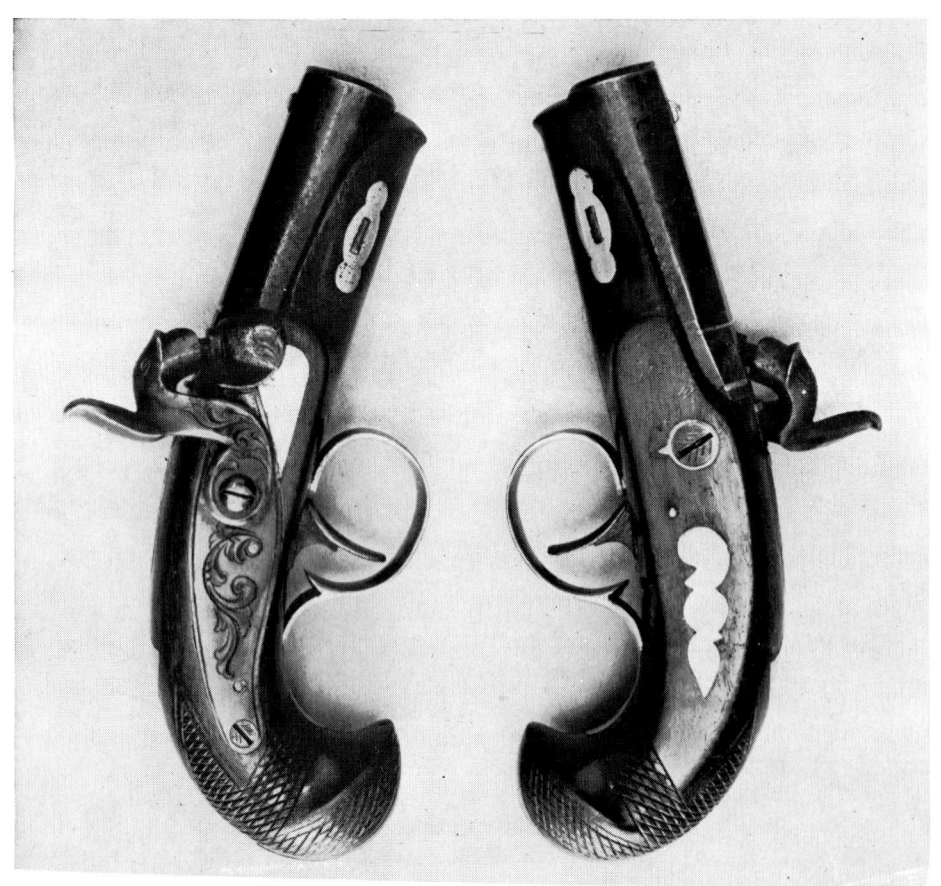

Pistols by Henry Deringer were sold in pairs. Some were cased with mould, flask, loading rod, but often they were carried in chamois bags in the pocket, or loose and ready to go. Specimens shown from C. C. Snook, Richmond, Va. collection are like new and unmarked except for numbers 6 and 7 stamped under barrels and in fore-end. Two dealers consider them unmarked but genuine Philadelphia Deringers. Possibility is, that gunmaker did not mark some guns shipped South after 1860 to avoid giving evidence he was trafficking with Secession States.

screws than the plain ovals on an E. Schmidt, Houston, derringer in the Metzger collection at Texas A & M College.

Who actually made these pistols is still in doubt, but the Erichson pair offer a "style suggestion." This exists in the arbitrary profile of the hammers, flattened on their outter sides and shaped with a sort of "plateau" or ridge, nicely convexed along the edges and smoothly faired into the form of the hammer head and spur. The hammer nose which drops over the cone is quite long, shrouding the cone to protect the finish from cap-flash. On top of the hammer nose is a functionless style point, a little curved pad or curlicue which is a vestigial form of the lip that on an earlier pistol might have been a "dolphin hammer."

The details are exactly like their counterparts on a 10-gauge W. Greener "Warranted Indestructible By Gunpowder" double barreled shotgun in the author's collection, the barrels of which are dated "1850." Regardless of the absence or presence of British proof marks, it would appear that some Southern derringers were of predominantly Birmingham, England, make. Testimony of one of Birmingham's principal gunmakers before a Parliamentary committee about 1854 indicates that up to the mid-century at least 95 per cent of all commercial or civilian gun locks consumed in the United States had been made and exported by British shops. As research continues, even more ties between the Southern derringers and British makers may be found. The Erichson pistols with their hammer forms do not mean that Greener made them; rather, that both had hammers and, probably, locks from the same (as yet unidentified) Birmingham lock maker.

Belgium in the old days apparently made a few of the worthy Henry Deringer's competitive imitation pistols. The presence of the oval ELG proof stamp on the bottom of the barrel, hidden when stocked up, suggests that this mark was placed out of the way so the pistol could be sold as a genuine Deringer arm. This mark was seen by me on a "Lincoln-sized" pistol, otherwise plainly finished, unmarked, and apparently in new condition, which was examined nearly 20 years ago before the present replica business had begun. I have always viewed this specimen, whereabouts unknown now, as a "genuine" old pistol of the imitation Deringer breed. A Liege revolver maker, J. Berenger, also made "Deringer" pistols: the name coincidence may have inspired him as a copyist.

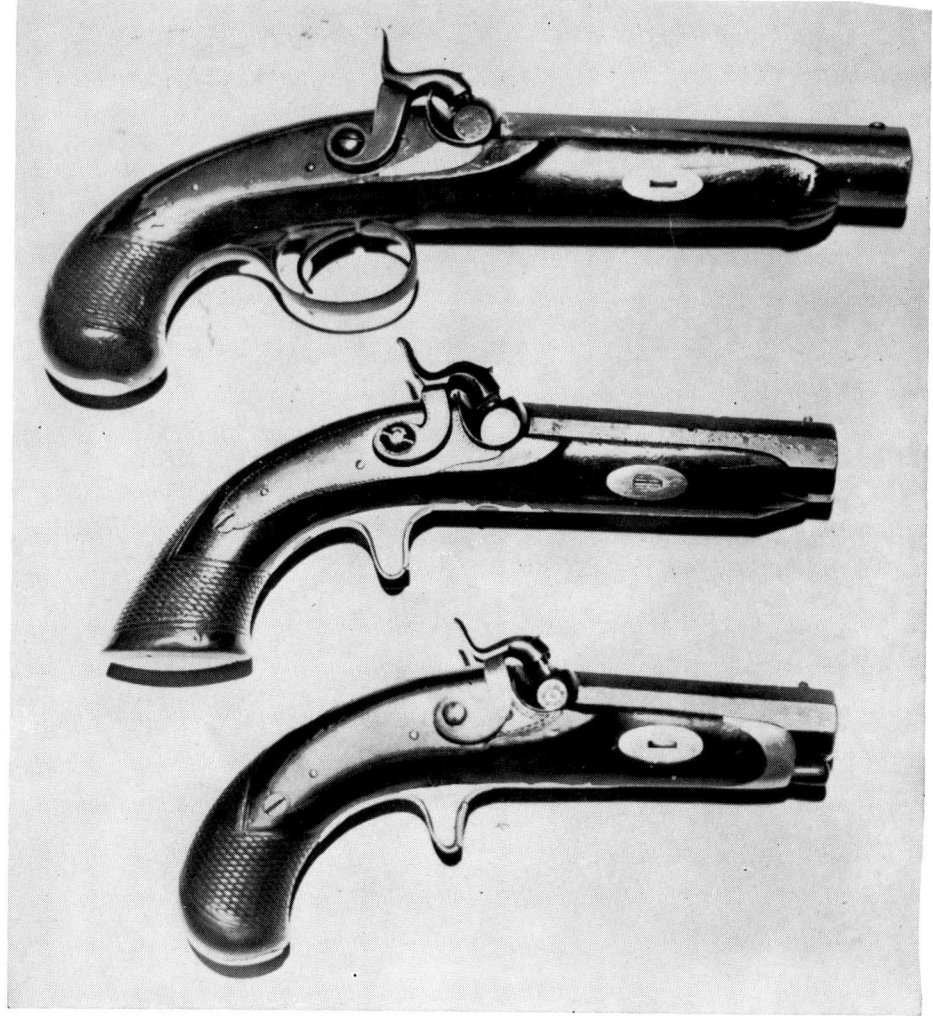

Three Memphis "derringers" by Schneider & Co., who also proposed to make Colt-type revolvers, reveal certain style points often found in Southern derringers. Big pistol is ordinary style though large size; middle has spur trigger with oddly curved lockplate and split nut on hammer. Flat butt is rare but characteristic. Bottom pistol has stubby ramrod. Octagon barrels also are "tip off" to Southern origins of a derringer pistol. Philadelphia Deringer pistols had rounded barrels flatted on top.

The assassin, John Wilkes Booth.

The martyred President, Abraham Lincoln.

Derringer pistol used in the assassination of Lincoln.

The .44 caliber Colt pistol carried by Booth.

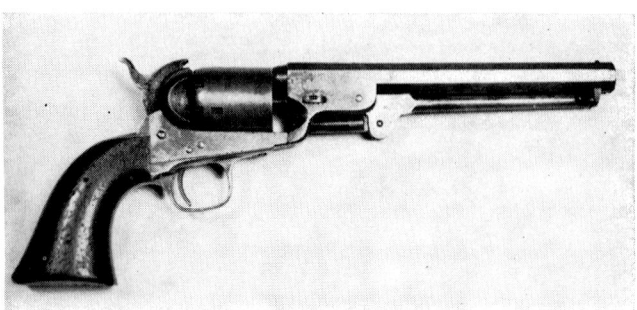

The .36 caliber Colt carried by Booth.

The tall man slumped forward, his head sagging upon his breast, the tension in his mind suddenly ended by the smashing trauma of the small lead ball from a Derringer pistol which had entered his skull at the hairline. Labored breathing and a trace of brain oozing from the hardly noticeable point of entrance were the only signs he was still living.

Below, the theater audience wondered if this was some strange part of the play, for, on the stage, limping from the pain of his twisted foot stood a man whom they all knew, the celebrated thespian, John Wilkes Booth. He brandished a knife; called "bowie" by the press it was in actuality a Rio Grande Camp Knife with spear-point blade instead of clipped blade like the true bowie style. His ringing shout, "Sic semper tyrannis," 'still seemed to hang in the thick theater air. It was recognized as the motto of the State of Virginia by many, but a few translated it literally, and gradually a horrible surmise arose in the crowd: The President is dead.

To horse, then hooves clattering on the cobbles in the alley behind Ford's Theater, and away into the night. The chase was on. Puzzle upon mystery mounted in the wake of the event, in the accumulation of evidence. Why was the door to the President's box unguarded? Why had General Grant stayed away? What was the strange connection between the events of that terrible April night and the strange and ruthless ambitions of Secretary Edwin M. Stanton? But most people overlooked the obvious: that Booth's handsome visage with its drooping mustaches was his free ticket to any performance, his passport back stage in virtually any theater in America. No one could anticipate that he would call upon a tiny single-shot pistol of Henry Deringer to do a deed that, strangely, gave him a more positive, though hated, immortality than his stage career

Right: Ford's Theater in Washington, D.C., where the President was shot. Now a museum.

Below: Right, pocket knife found on Booth when shot in Garrett's barn. Left, dagger used by Booth to stab Maj. Rathbone.

had done. And as for the gaunt tired man with the rough-hewn face and the polished mind: was he truly a tyrant to thus perish? Many persons, in Government and out, thought so; surely he had usurped vast power through his exercise of executive prerogative and single-handed control of people and events. But was this bad? Historians still cannot unravel the answer in the light of a hundred years of time.

From the theater, Booth fled into Maryland. He sought sanctuary, was given medical aid, eventually was trapped in a blazing barn. One report says he took his own life, another gives Sergeant Boston Corbett the dubious honor, a distinction which haunted the blue-coated noncom to his grave. All that now remain as relics from this dazzling moment in history are some guns, some knives, the testimony of witnesses who contradicted themselves with every paragraph, a diary mysteriously stripped of vital entries.

Today, Ford's Theater is a museum, a sober monument to this black night in America's growing up. There is The Pistol: inert, potentially defective with its broken hammer cap screw and split stock. There are Spencer carbines, the carbine Secretary Stanton refused to see tested on the day President Lincoln remarked, "They do pretty much as they have a mind to, over at the War Office." Was ever a truer word spoken in jest? There are two Colt pistols: a .44 1860 Army No. 20407 with four-screw frame, and a .36 1851 Navy No. 111685. The knives are there, too: the big 9½-inch long Rio Grande Camp Knife, made by Wm. Jackson & Co., Sheaf Island Works, Sheffield, England, and the little gentleman's folding blade pocket knife, found on Booth's body in Garrett's barn. And there lingers on, too, the question posed by Booth when he uttered his cry as he jumped from the President's box onto the Ford's Theater stage: how much power must a man assume, before a madman assumes he is mad? Sic semper tyrannis? It is a sobering instruction from history.

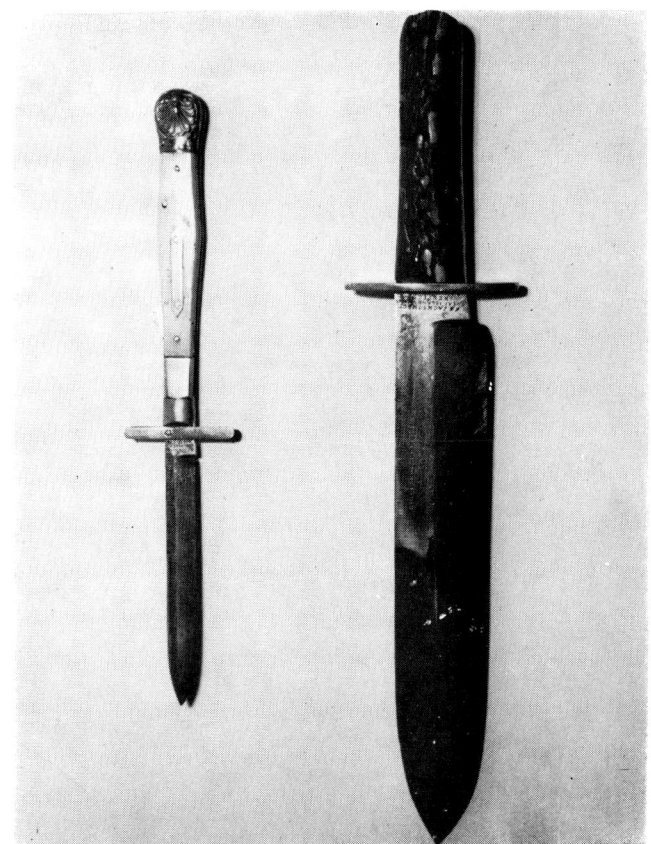

CHAPTER 33

What Happened to the Guns, Post War

In the wake of the terrible conflict lay broken lives, piles of dead men "groaning for burial," and the smoldering bricks and gaunt, solitary chimneys of a Southland laid waste. In its wake lay, too, stacked in piles like cordwood, or in armory chests of twenty muskets, twenty bayonets, with appendages, the most fantastic conglomeration of assorted small arms ever to be collected together on the face of the earth. Half these were Union arms; but the immense Confederate ordnance establishment fell almost entirely into the hands of the Federal Army in 1865. The polyglot minions of Peter the Hermit, slashing through the ranks of Saracens to protect the Holy Sepulchre from infidel defilement, never carried a more varied lot of arms and weapons.

Disposal of "War Surplus"

Some of the guns remained in storage until long after they had been obsoleted by superior designs. Then many were sold at auction, while others, battlefield relics, or remnants of post-war selling through Montgomery Ward & Company and other large firms, filtered out through the normal trade channels. Often some old Civil War musket remained in attic or barn until the rise of the little old lady antique dealer. The gun collector is often offered muskets "carried by my grandfather at Bunker Hill" which bear the dates of Civil War manufacture conspicuously stamped on lock, on barrel, on bayonet, or saber blade. The collector will scoff at these dealers who cannot even tell when the gun was made, though the date is marked on it. They should not scoff—the failing was not uncommon in Civil War Times. Consider the position of General Butler, after he had occupied New Orleans and decreed amnesty for all holders of deadly weapons, if they would turn them in to the provost marshal. One gentleman of the South was brought before Butler, some time after the amnesty period had passed, on a charge of possessing weapons, including a saber. He pleaded that the weapons were family relics. "That, General, was my father's sword," he declared.

"When did your father die, sir?" Butler queried. "In 1858," replied the man. Butler looked at the blade where the hilt joined, saw the U. S. inspector's stamp and date of manufacture. "Then he must have worn this sword in hell, sir," he replied, "for it was made in 1859."

Less humorous, more exciting, was the career of Mr. Hartley's firm after the war. In 1870 those very thousands of guns which he helped import were in turn bought by him for export. Just ending was a five-year postwar boom for expanding America, with the cattle country growing to dominate the economic scene. But for thousands of steers only a few cowboys were needed. Though the range opened up, the prosperity did not involve vast migrations westward. True, hundreds of thousands of people did move west, but they were not rich people. They were poor, and remained so, with notable exceptions, throughout the buffalo shooting decade till 1876. Indians, not pioneers, ruled the plains then. And the commercial market for mass sales of sporting firearms was not as prosperous as external conditions would warrant. There were too many war surplus guns on the market, specifically of two brands, the Spencer and the Sharps. Both names had achieved "consumer acceptance," both were good, solid serviceable rifles. The Spencer, and the cartridge conversion of the Sharps in .50 caliber were issued to soldiers on the frontier. Sergeant Bullhead's Indian police carried Sharps converted rifles the day they slew Sitting Bull in 1890, so for a long time war surplus Civil War guns supplied the limited wants of the frontier. From 1866 to 1870 this was especially true of the Spencer guns.

Spencers were in demand but the Government had almost 100,000 of them. Spencer's own production could not compete in price with his war-surplus guns from Government sources. Arms which he had sold for $30 were now being hawked about the trade for five to seven dollars. J. H. Johnston, proprietor of the Great Western Gun Works of Pittsburgh, advertised "I will pay the following prices in cash or trade, and express charges, for second hand arms in working order; if broken or rusty, they will suit me as well, but I will make a fair reduction for the missing parts: Spencer rifle or carbine, 7 shooter, cash $7.00, trade $9. Henry rifle or carbine, 16 shooter, $12 cash, $16 trade." He gave no cash value on Colt 1860 Army or

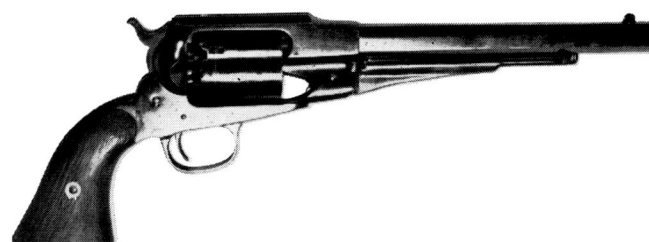

Off to Cowes and market went brand new Remington .44 revolvers, much liked by French ordnance officers. Author bought new specimen of U.S. Civil War pistol in small French gunshop in Rennes in 1949 for $6.00. Butt had been drilled for lanyard swivel base but gun had never been used.

Colt Navy revolvers, nor for Sharps army rifles, 30-inch barrel, but he gave $5 trade-in on those three items.

Johnston, among others, wanted these to sell to France. Probably Great Western was gathering arms on commission for the New York firm of Schuyler, Hartley & Graham. Hartley's firm had large contracts with the French Government in 1870, and if it were known in the western parts of the country, western Pennsylvania and farther west, that the gun firms were buying for France, prices would have rocketed. Certainly Johnston planned to rebuild and cannibalize guns to make complete ones. His low prices on non-metallic cartridge guns was possibly because he planned to convert them to cartridge before shipping to France.

Arms Conversion

Converting the Sharps' guns was done by altering the hammer to flat face and fitting a new breechblock, carrying a center-fire or rimfire pin. The barrel was sometimes re-lined and the gun chambered for the rimmed metal shell. An extractor was also fitted, working on the same pin as the block lever hinge.

Colts could be converted by the gunsmith, in Great Western's own shops, or by the Colt company. Usually the job involved fitting a cylinder which had had the nipple bolsters turned off and the space taken up in the frame by a thick plate or ring, which was permanently attached, and carried a spring-flip loading gate. On the barrel was fitted a side rod ejector. Patents of William Mason, a former Remington and Winchester employee, and C. B. Richards, later professor of mechanical engineering in Yale, figure in this conversion era 1868-73.

Spencer's Company Fails

By 1869, Christopher Spencer's company folded, and the manufacture of the lever-action repeating rifles ceased. Commercially, it was too bad, for the company assets were taken over by the Winchester Repeating Arms Company of New Haven, while the remaining stock of arms was merchandised through Hartley, Schuyler & Graham. If Spencer had survived for one more year (he did go back into business making shotguns in Brooklyn), it might have been his firm that took over Winchester, instead of vice versa. For with the start of the Franco-Prussian War, Spencer guns received as much use as ever they saw in the Cumberland Valley or the farmlands of eastern Pennsylvania.

Shipment to France

Headed "Off to France," was a notice in the New York *Herald* in 1870.

The steamer *Ontario*, of Boston, cleared from the Custom House yesterday for Cowes and a market, with a full cargo of arms and munitions of war, as follows:
73,620 muskets
20,950 carbines
   500 rifles
   500 army revolvers
17,785,352 cartridges
1 case moulds
55 pieces artillery
The total value of the warlike material, $1,853,497, three-fourths of which is shipped by one house . . . There were no passengers reported at the Custom House, but it would be singular if there were not a few enthusiasts accompanying such an important addition to the resources of France. The Ontario cleared for "Cowes and a market" which means that she will stop there to get a convoy of French men-of-war in case any enterprising German war vessel took a fancy to try whether such a cargo was contraband of war.

The allusion to a passenger was not far from the mark. Probable supercargo in charge of "three fourths of which is shipped by one house," was W. W. Reynolds, of Schuyler, Hartley, & Graham. With power of attorney signed over to him by the firm, Reynolds' job was to see to the safe delivery of the guns, and bring back the gold which the French promised to pay for guns delivered in Paris.

Reynolds had a valuable cargo to oversee: 72 cases holding 1,440 Sharps carbines; 138 cases of Sharps rifles, 2,760; 168 cases of Spencer carbines, 3,360; and 145 cases of Spencer rifles, 2,900 guns, figuring on the usual 20 arms per chest. In addition were 2,090 cases of ammunition, over two million rounds in cartridges. Additional cargoes included Remington New Model .44's, new stock, and used; Colt 2-band .56 caliber rifles. These last had been experimented with in 1868 by the French army test board, seeking to adopt a breechloader. Additional thousands were

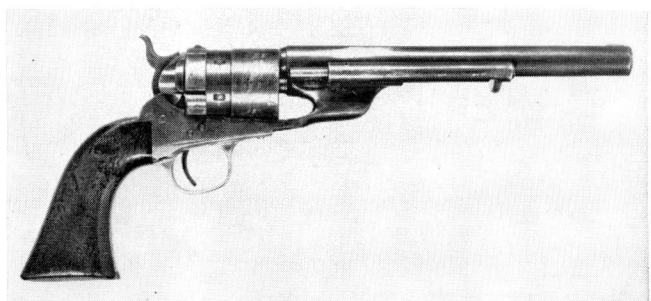

Percussion Army revolvers were converted in small quantities to metallic cartridge for reissue to the post-war cavalry. This regular M1860 Army Colt has been fitted with ejector-rod housing that fills loading plunger hole, and special breech piece carrying floating firing pin and loading gate. Several thousand regular New Model Army Colts were returned to factory by Ordnance to have this change made.

Behind scenes of surplus buying was Marcellus Hartley, whose military goods firm emerged from Civil War as one of the largest businesses in nation, controlling cartridge factory at Bridgeport and ultimately Remington Arms Co. itself.

shipped to Paris for the war. Colt and Army revolver paper packets of cartridges were sent over by the ton—I got a dozen such packets, assorted makers such as Hazards, Johnston & Dow, Watertown Arsenal, in 1951 from a French gun collector. "These I found in the basement at Versailles palace," he told me.

Reynolds got the guns to Paris, safely inside the French lines before the Germans completed their encirclement of the City of Light. The French paid Reynolds for the guns and shipping cases. Then came the problem: How to get out?

Recalling the adventures of Professor Lowe's balloon corps, and knowing something of the popular fad of free ballooning, Reynolds decided to buy a gas bag.

Armed with a permit from Peard, the Finance Minister, he sought out an old theater which had been converted into a balloon factory; to complete one balloon took ten days, and cost $1,250 in gold.

At this point word was received from the government that M. Gambetta, the great War Minister, must leave Paris for reasons of state (the Germans were too close) and the use of the American's balloon was requested. A period of bad weather followed, from day to day Gambetta was forced to delay his start, so that the second balloon was finished before the first one left. Friday the morning of the departure, came. An immense crowd of people drew together; the members of the government were present, and both balloons bore the French tricolor. Gambetta and his companions climbed into the wicker basket attached to one. In the other were seated Mr. Reynolds, his friend Mr. C. W. Way of New York, a French officer M. Cuzon, and the aeronaut Durevilio. At eight minutes past eleven the ropes were thrown off, and the balloons shot high into the clear sky. A breeze bore them toward the Prussian lines; soon there were puffs of smoke far beneath them. Bullets whistled through the air; cannon, musketry, and rockets were turned upon the adventurers, and for a time they were in the greatest danger. Swiftly moving specks—mounted Uhlans—galloped along the threadlike roads below, expecting the voyagers would be forced to descend; but fortune favored, and the freshening breeze finally bore them out of range.

Then there came a new peril. Gambetta's engineer lost control of his balloon which dropped close to the ground and then shot up swiftly again directly beneath Mr. Reynolds' car; for a few minutes it looked as though a fatal collision could not be avoided. A sudden breath of wind changed its course, and once more the two swept onward together.

Gambetta attempted to land at Criel but discovered just in time that it was a Prussian camp. He escaped by throwing his baggage overboard and was wounded in his hand by a shot. Later he came down into a tree top near Amiens. The Americans kept on for ninety-five miles, and made a safe landing at Ville Roy whence they, too, went by rail to Amiens. (From *A New Chapter in an Old Story*, Remington Arms Company, N.Y., 1912.)

In token of this remarkable feat, and commemorating the successful end of a tricky business deal, the grateful Hartley gave a party for Reynolds on his return to New York. He was presented with a handsome gold watch, engraved on the hunting cover with a picture of a balloon, the date of the escape, "Oct. 7, 1870," and the motto "Dieu protege," God protects. Inside it bore an inscription of presentation to William W. Reynolds from Hartley, Schuyler & Graham.

Recently in Illinois an unusual Smith & Wesson .32 revolver was bought from a dealer by collector Archer L. Jackson, Jr. The revolver was carved with a balloon, and the interlaced cypher of "WWR." Gold and silver finished, and handsomely engraved, it, too, was a memento of this incident in the life of a munitions salesman, presumably also presented by Hartley & Graham. And so thrillingly did this incident captivate the popular mind at the time, that a form of powder flask design was created, and sportsmen carried the bag flasks, inverted by their sides, embossed in the crossed rope design of a gas or hot air balloon.

Hartley's sales to the French in 1870 were the subject of a Congressional investigation, which examined the entire picture of War Department surplus arms and ordnance disposed of between 1870 and 1872. An early purchase by Hartley, Schuyler & Graham consisted of 500 Bormann fuses and tools, and 10,000 Sharps cartridges at $10 per thousand, delivered on September 1, 1870. Later that month, on the 28th more ammo including 660,000 musket cartridges, 1,318,000 rounds for Spencers, and 420,000 Sharps primers, were turned over to the partners. Schoverling & Daly, later Schoverling, Daly & Gales, importers and originators of the brand name "Charles Daly" on fine shotguns, bought 10,000 Henry cartridges for $11.50 a thousand. Deliveries to E. Remington & Sons during September included 400,000 Spencer cartridges at $18/M, 604,800 Spencer cartridges for only $16/M, 2,241,024 pistol cartridges (presumably combustible .44 loads for cap and ball revolvers) at $9/M and 2,502,622 pistol cartridges at only $8/M. Herman Boker & Company also got into the act, buying 500 cavalry saddles, "unserviceable," which if the term means what it does today were probably perfectly brand new saddles, which had not within the past ten years had the benefit of Government inspection.

Sales of War Surplus

It is the habit of the Ordnance Department to automatically classify any goods as "unserviceable" after some specified period of time, providing that the goods may be inspected and reclassified "serviceable" if found to be so in fact. But the act of inspecting is needed to reclassify ordnance stores to "serviceable" grade. Post World War II sales of surplus small arms has often involved delivery to the purchaser of brand new guns, never removed from the factory boxes, which were classified as "unserviceable" simply because they had been in storage, not inspected, for more than a decade. Boker's purchase of "unserviceable" saddles was probably in this category, though he paid only $2.50 each for the saddles and a half buck each for 1,000 halters.

The arms sales were widely advertised, and held at posts located in various parts of the country. Though not listed in the 1870's, a somewhat later purchaser of considerable quantities of surplus was Colonel W. Stokes Kirk of Philadelphia. He used to make his bids and when successful, at once rent a large, temporary emporium in the city where the sale was held. Striking off large hand bills, he paid boys a few pennies to plaster the town with them. These bills tabulated everything he had bought, and gave low prices, for cash. After a few weeks of this he would close down the store, having liquidated a good deal of the more salable parts of the lot, and would then ship the remainder back to his depot for sale over a longer period of time. Colonel Kirk's warehouses in Philadelphia up until the decade after World War II used to be a "gold mine" for enterprising merchants and gun fans who could get into the "back room."

Another firm which grew to prominence in later years before the turn of the century was that of the White Brothers, at 3 South Water Street, New York. Until 1950 it was possible to assemble a new Remington .44 revolver from parts found there. The West Point Museum about 1956 made a very large purchase at very moderate prices of a great variety of Civil War uniform trappings, epaulettes, chevrons, belts, and other gear which the White's had preserved for a century in a like-new condition.

Even at this present time it is possible to obtain new components for the favorite arms of the war, Springfield Rifles of every model, Sharps and Spencer carbines and rifles, new Hall carbine stocks and new Starr revolver parts. Firms specializing in these components are just now breaking into the reservoir of parts which accompanied ever large contract. The tabulated cases of muskets, for example, which were in the sale list, had long since been sold off; now the "gravy" of the

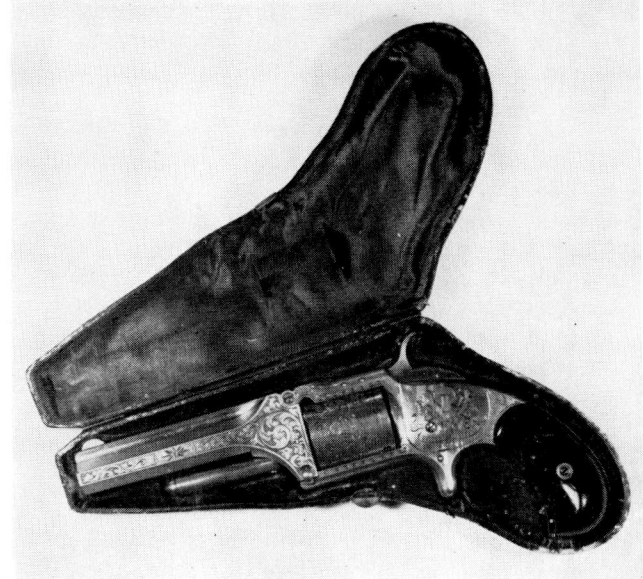

Hartley & Graham salesman William Reynolds was bag-man for arms selling syndicate which negotiated purchases for France after Remington was forbidden to buy at U.S. sales. Reynolds was in Paris to pick up the cash, and escaped in a balloon. Exploit of Oct. 7, 1870, coincided with War Minister Gambetta's flight from capital; was commemorated on pistol Reynolds received at testimonial dinner on his triumphant return to New York. Odd Smith & Wesson shown is unusual transition model having barrel and cylinder of late Civil War pocket .32 model but round butt of post-war type.

purchase, the spare parts chests, were being looked into. This writer in 1961 purchased from several sources enough parts, new, for the Sharps New Model 1863 Rifle, to complete a used receiver with barrel attached that he bought from yet another merchant. He selected the Sharps parts from two competitive lists, taking a buttstock from one and a forestock from another, because the parts were lowest, though each vendor offered practically identical lists of parts. That competition should exist 100 years after the contracts, in the sale of parts of Civil War arms, is a remarkable commentary upon the tremendous quantities of materiel actually produced for that conflict.

The sale lists of 1870 would send a modern collector into a frenzy of buying. On November 25, 1867, at Leavenworth Arsenal, Kansas, condemned ordnance stores including 19,551 small arms were sold. Listed were Colt's revolving rifles, "United States Rifles Model 1840" (sic), Enfield and Belgian rifle-muskets, Enfield rifles, Sapper's rifles, U.S. rifle muskets, Austrian and Belgian rifle muskets, U.S. smooth bore muskets, Austrian rifles, Adams, Lefaucheaux, Savage, Starr, and Whitney pistols, Prussian rifle-muskets, carbines by Burnside, Cosmopolitan, Gallagher, Green, Hall, Joslyn, Maynard, Merrill, Smith, Starr and Wesson, and Austrian carbines. On May 26, 1868, another sale of artillery materiel took place at Watervleit Arsenal, "West Troy," New York. On August 26, 1868, Springfield Armory advertised their September 29 sale of such oddments as "lot of window-frames, lot of window shutters and blinds," but such less well tabulated and enigmatically listed items as "small arms, various models;" and "parts of arms, various models." Catalogs of these sales were available on application.

Four days before the sale, the Government suspended the sales at Springfield and another at St. Louis of "carbines, muskets, rifles, pistols, shot-guns, swords and sabers" among other equipments, scheduled for October 5. The Congress was taking a long look at the method of selling surplus.

They reappraised the conditions of such sales, and a tender put out at the time lists a number of businesslike terms the purchasers had to comply with. Then the Springfield sale was resumed "by order of the President," set for 10 a.m. December 14, 1868. Other sales were scheduled for December 17 at Watertown Arsenal near Boston, and December 21 at Frankford near Philadelphia. A week later, doubtless following the wishes of the regular sales attenders who preferred to go south for the winter, Fort Monroe Arsenal at Old Point Comfort was the site, December 28, of the sale of 217 cast-iron guns of various descriptions and two bronze guns. Interesting to contemplate and wonder about, were "36 foreign model arms of various calibers," evidently purchased by Major Mordecai or other European travellers over the years for the benefit of our Ordnance Department's engineers to study, and then relegated to Fort Monroe when their period of usefulness had passed.

Three offerings were sufficiently varied to be of importance in their own time, and to have some points of interest for the modern student. Chronologically, the first and most important sale was a proposal issued by Colonel Crispin, from his office of the Ordnance Agency at Houston & Greene streets (PO Box 1811) in New York, on July 3, 1869. He declared that up till August 4, offers would be received for:

- 100,000 Springfield rifled muskets, caliber .58, new
- 100,000 Springfield rifled muskets, caliber .58, cleaned and repaired
- 5,000 Spencer carbines, new model, caliber .50, new
- 5,000 Spencer carbines, old model, caliber .52, new
- 5,000 Spencer carbines, accouterments, "Blakesley's," new
- 5,000 Spencer carbines, accouterments "other models," new

The second offering by Colonel Crispin on November 22, 1869, was to be opened as to bids on December 22, 1869. It included:

- 40,000 Enfield rifle muskets, cal. .577, new
- 3,000 United States flintlock muskets, cal. .69, serviceable
- 5,000 Remington carbines, cal. .44, new
- 15,000 Starr's army pistols, cal. .44, new

There were also sabers and many thousands of pounds of small arms and cannon powder in this lot.

On October 17, 1870, a further offer was made public, bids to close October 29. This offer was made by General Dyer, Chief of Ordnance, directly and not through Colonel Crispin. The Government proposed to sell:

- 2,500 breech-loading muskets, caliber .58, with cartridges for same.
- 1,000 Ball's repeating carbines, cal. .50, with ammunition.
- 2,500 Gallagher's carbines, adapted for Spencer ammunition.
- 4,000 Maynard's carbines, with 400 rounds of ammunition per gun.
- 1,000 Palmer's carbines, caliber .44, with ammunition.
- 3,600 Remington carbines, caliber .44, with ammunition.
- 2,500 Warner's carbines and ammunition.
- 2,700 Joslyn's carbines & ammunition, caliber .52.
- 40,000 sets carbines accouterments, serviceable, Blakesley's and other patterns.
- 70,000 sets infantry accouterments.
- 20,000 Starr's revolvers, caliber .44, with ammunition.
- 5,000 Rogers & Spencer's revolvers, with ammunition, caliber .44.
- 10,000 Remington Army revolvers, caliber .44, with ammunition.
- 35,000 pistol holsters.
- 40,000 cavalry sabers.
- 1,000 Spencer rifles.
- 20,000 sets horse equipments.

Remington was a heavy buyer in October, 1870, purchasing 50,000 Springfield rifled muskets, cleaned and repaired and fully serviceable, at $5 each. Then on November 30, the Ilion Company bought back from the Government nearly the entire complement of split-breech carbines supplied on their contracts of September 30, 1865, and May 24, 1866. Contract price on the carbines, caliber .56-.50 Spencer chambering, was $23 each, and 14,999 were delivered. The November, 1870, repurchase at $15 each, together with 19,434 Spencer carbines of similar caliber, and 17,517,822 Spencer cartridges, gave the company a handsome profit on their transactions.

Spencer carbines were a heavy favorite among the export Franco-Prussian War buyers. A total of 94,196 Spencer carbines was delivered to the War Department between January 1, 1861, and June 30, 1866. Of these, 35,028 were disposed of in the 1870-72 sales, most of them destined for Paris through Remington or Hartley; 31,269,746 Spencer shells also were sold, about two-thirds of the total number of 58,238,924 Spencer cartridges procured from '61 to '65.

In selling surplus, the custom of the Government officers was to call for bids for small lots of arms at a price. Then, if the buyer desired, the bid could apply to a much larger lot, sometimes as many as 250,000 Springfield muzzle-loaders at a crack. Because of the huge quantities of this war materiel being put into the market by Uncle Sam in 1870, the newspapers leaped on the sales as food for sensational articles. Boosting the circulation of their sheets also depressed the circulation of the Remington brothers, who would have been much happier if this business had not reached the light of public notice.

Unable to control the newspapers, the Remingtons were suddenly spotlighted with articles which were deliberate editorializations against their business. Inevitably, a Congressional committee was called to inquire into the arms business and sales by the Ordnance Department. Remington, among all the other large buyers and sellers to the Government, was outlawed. By order of Secretary of War W. W. Belknap, late in 1870, no more arms were sold to Remington, since it was known that Remington was shipping rifles to France.

Sales to France

The realities of the case are interesting, by contrast with the later events in disposing of the Civil War surplus. The cabinet's decision to stop shipping arms to France was at the insistence of the State Department, which felt that the fact the United States was known to be supplying guns on an "official" basis to one of the belligerents would endanger our relations with the other power, Germany. At that time a weak imperialistic nation emerging from a heterogeneous confederation of princely states, the Germany of Kaiser Bill might have been postponed a generation by a more active aid of the United States to our sister republic France. If France, with publicly avowed assistance of Uncle Sam, had been able to throw back the German invasion of 1870, a defeated Germany would not have been in such a strong position in 1914. The Great War would have, instead, been of the minor magnitude of the Franco-Prussian War, and the global devastation of World War II might have been confined to the struggling of a minor power, Germany, for "lebensraum" on the continent of Europe. Fearful of arousing Germany against us, the United States, having just fought the biggest war the world had seen, having just disbanded the biggest armed force ever to march, having in her store houses millions of serviceable muzzle-loading rifles, was afraid to risk the displeasure of Germany which was in fact the acknowledged aggressor against France.

France, unlike the United States, had no such vast store of arms in her arsenals. Stripped of serviceable, man-killing muzzle-loaders by the scavenging buyers of Uncle Sam and Jeff Davis, the Republique had only just begun to rearm with an improved breech-loader about 1866. Germany, flushed with triumph at Koeniggratz against the Austrians in 1866, was bent on national growth by force of arms.

The new German rifle, introduced in 1840 to the Prussian service, was the famous and semi-secret "Zundnadelgewehr," or needle gun.

Against this weapon the French were rapidly introducing their own breech-loading arm, the Chassepot. This employed a slightly similar cartridge, self consuming, made of glazed linen with a more elongated bullet than the needle gun. French research on bullets had always tended to be in the advance of the world reductions to small bore, and the Chassepot rifle, of 11mm, was in advance of the German, as the needle gun's caliber was .64. But French ordnance officers, having shipped all their 1820-1850 period muzzle-loaders to Yankees and Rebels, were eager to buy the improved Springfield muzzle-loaders which Uncle Sam, through a generous Ordnance Department, was offering to their friends, the Remingtons.

Competitive Bidding on Surplus Ordnance

Invitations for proposals to bid on Ordnance supplies were sent out October 12 by General A. B. Dyer, Chief of Ordnance, to A. B. Steinberger, John Absterdam, and Remington & Sons, as follows:

Sealed proposals, to be opened at the Ordnance Office at 12 m. tomorrow, October 13, are hereby invited for the purchase of—

Two hundred thousand Springfield muskets, new; 110,000 Springfield muskets, serviceable and in good order, .58 caliber, muzzle-loaders, with 150 rounds of ammunition for each gun; 40,000 Enfield muskets, new more or less; 40,000 Enfield muskets, cleaned and repaired; 30,000 Enfield muskets, unserviceable.

Bids will be entertained for any one of the above lots of arms, with ammunition for the same, and the privilege is reserved of rejecting any bid that may not be deemed sufficient.

A margin of 20 per cent must be paid at the time of the award by any and all bids, and the residue upon the delivery of the stores.

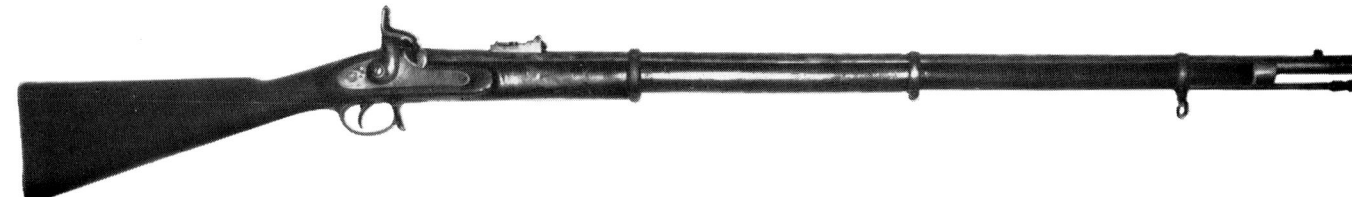

"Bid $7.50 for Enfield" wired Franklin of Colt's to Ordnance office. Gun shown was brought back from France by arms importer Museum of Historical Arms, Miami.

Realizing, perhaps, that his clerk had not notified his friends in Hartford, General Dyer telegraphed to General William B. Franklin, president of Colt's Patent F. A. Manufacturing Company, early the following morning, advising him of the sale: "Sealed bids will be opened at noon today at this office. Bid by telegraph for all new Enfields on hand. Seven insufficient and declined."

Franklin acted and by 2:20 p.m. Dyer's office had received his reply: "Will give seven dollars fifty cents for all new Enfields. Answer."

While the Chief of Ordnance might be considered as unduly favoring his friend General Franklin, the fact was that Ordnance, with the approval over the years of the Secretary of War, wished to get rid of the surplus. New arms were being made at Springfield on the improved patterns of master armorer E. S. Allin, and while the U. S. Army had been reduced in force to only 30,000, there were more than ample arms on hand and being made. Dyer, in notifying Franklin, was just showing good sense.

Colt's had been a prime supplier of Enfield rifles during the war, and Dyer, knowing of the Colt Company's depot and former factory in England, doubtless supposed that Colt's through their world-wide commercial connections could dispose of the Enfields. His telegram, while it stated a base price below which the Government would not consider a bid, was not unfair. Rather, it put Franklin, if he wanted the guns, in a position of knowing what sort of figure the Government had in mind to accept, and thus he could sell the guns at a profit, at the same time being able to bid with some confidence that he would be awarded the rifles. In fact, he wanted so much to ensure himself of getting the guns, that he replaced his $7.50 bid with one of $7.75 for each gun.

Activity on the Springfields was brisk, but many possible purchasers wished a couple of days' delay in the closing date. Accordingly, Dyer set the date up to October 15; then to the 18th. Franklin, having apparently a firm order from London at the beginning, had to cable his party that there was delay. Since the firm order doubtless was from someone hoping to supply the French Government, a particular move of that body, a decree, radically altered the plans of international munitions merchants hoping to sell to France. By decree of October 12, communicated to Remington Arms secretary, son-in-law W. C. Squire, who was staying at the Arlington House in Washington till the bids should be opened, the Government of France was likely to seize arms imports of arms and pay for them at their own terms. Samuel Remington, president of E. Remington & Sons, was on the spot in Paris and cabled to Squire:

If you have not yet bought for the government you will be able to do so on better terms. By decree of the government issued (Oct. 12) all arms entering France are liable to be taken as national property, and paid for according to appraisement. Speculators in arms intended for France will find their profit small. Competition with you has been forced and fictitious.

This man, Samuel Remington, was a curious person to have abroad as representative of so august a manufacturing firm. He was the middle brother of three, the others being Philo and Eliphalet Remington III. These two, according to the official Remington story by Alden Hatch, "puritanically disapproved of Samuel Remington, (but) they realized that he was the perfect emissary to the 'dessolute' capitals of Europe." Sam, characterized as a night owl and not adverse to a drink now and then, was "their best salesman." He was "a gregarious, polished gentleman, quick of wit, with a warmth and charm that were to make him fast friends among all nations."

Linked overseas with young Sam was Samuel Norris, caliber .58 rifle-musket builder and sub-contractor of Springfield, Massachusetts. Norris, "of London" as he was characterized in the late 1860's, was one of several former Civil War contractors who labored abroad where war continued. Among others, bidding on the same lot of arms which attracted the Remingtons' attention, was another old friend, Caleb Huse, former Confederate purchasing agent in Europe. Located at 17 Broad Street, New York, Huse replied to Dyer's Springfield rifle offering with: "I offer ten dollars seventy-five cents each for fourteen thousand new Springfield rifles; twelve dollars fifty cents per thousand for two million eight hundred thousand cartridges. Request reply by telegraph."

But Sam, whose profligate nature is said to have affronted his "puritanical" brothers, was to get a shrewd lesson in duplicity from his puritan family and their long-time business associate, Marcellus Hartley. For Remington & Son, prevented officially from being awarded any guns at Ordnance sales, proceeded to scurry around in the market and obtain the assistance of their competitors in making successful bids. Strangely, they were successful in the face of one major bid by a mystery man who on examination proved to have adequate capital.

The successful bidder, Charles Wright, offered a top

price of $15.25 for 200,000 new Springfields, but when Dyer tried to learn something about him, the facts were difficult to elicit. The Ordnance general on October 18 sent a very courteous note to Wright, who was staying at Willard's Hotel, asking Wright to call at the Ordnance Office the following morning "at 9½ o'clock," or offering to welcome Wright at Dyer's home, "No. 1530, immediately back of the Arlington, on I Street" at 7 p.m. that evening. Meanwhile, Dyer wired the Ordnance chief clerk in New York: "Ascertain who is Charles Wright, of No. 10 Pine St., room fourteen, and report by telegraph, or, if possible, by to-night's mail."

Chief Clerk Charles J. McGowan checked out Wright, found at first that he was unknown. Subsequently, McGowan located "A party named Thurston, said to be Wright's partner, knows all about him, but refuses information. Refers to George S. Gideon, at Washington, and says the arms are for a large banking house here, but refuses names."

Who Mr. Wright was and for whom he was working remains to this day a mystery. It is possible some speculator in France was his patron, and the decree of the French Government cut off his source of profit. Pressure for awarding the sale to the other bidders was strong. Dyer informed Crispin on October 20, 1870, that the bids had been accepted and the awards made as follows:

To Austin Baldwin & Co.:
40,000 new Springfield muskets, cal. .58, at $12.30 each; 110,000 cleaned and repaired Springfield muskets, cal. .58, at $9.30 each.
25,000,000 cartridges, cal. .577, at per thousand $16.30.

To Herman Boker & Co.:
50,000 new Springfield muskets, cal. .58, at $12.05 each.

To Schuyler, Hartley & Graham:
100,000 new Springfield muskets, cal. .58, at $12.05 each.

To A. B. Steinberger:
About 6,300 cleaned and repaired Enfields, at $5.30 each.

To General W. B. Franklin:
All new Enfields, (between 30,000 and 40,000) at $7.75 each.

The not-so-fine hand of the Remingtons was also evident later in the deal between D. B. Trimble and Thomas Poultney, of Poultney and Trimble, of Baltimore, and the Navy Department. Under oath General William B. Franklin in April, 1872, testified to his knowledge of the matter. Franklin was at the time vice president of Colt's, who also acted for Remington in helping the acknowledged agent of France avoid if not actually evade the United States neutrality declaration.

A Government Arsenal Fills a Foreign Order!

The Navy Department had ordered 10,000 rifles to be built at Springfield Armory on the Remington Rolling Block breech-loading system, .50 caliber. These arms were finished with casehardened frames, and blued 32⅝-inch round barrels, of Springfield Model 1868 type, rifled with three broad grooves, and fitted under the muzzle with a stud for attaching the fish-scale brass hilted sword bayonet. The fore stock is held by two spring-bands.

As first issued, this rifle had the rear sight mounted quite close to the receiver, over the chamber. The Secretary of the Navy condemned these rifles and Thomas Poultney made an offer to buy them from Springfield Armory, paying the Navy a sum equal to the fabrication cost of 12,000 more rifles with the rear sights properly located.

It is entirely possible the relocation of the rear sight was an important technical objection. The drilling for screws to attach it may have been thought by Navy ordnance men to have weakened the barrel at the chamber. With the offer of Poultney in hand, it was a better deal for the Navy to give Springfield Armory an additional order for 12,000 rifles, than have them called in and new barrels fitted.

A mysterious Mr. Markley of New Jersey was fingered by General Franklin as having received $10,000 from Poultney to arrange the matter. While the United States did not suffer economically, the international prestige of the country, in its relations with Germany, was jarred a little. For not all the rifles of the Navy's first 10,000 had been fully completed at the time the sale was made. Additional rifles were fabricated at Springfield Armory on the first Navy order, to be tested, marked with the United States inspectors' stamps, packed and shipped, directly out to New York harbor, to go aboard a freighter destined for France! While this was not the only time that the United States Armory at Springfield was to manufacture for a private purchaser, it was the first on record.

That Poultney suspected things were not entirely on the up and up was revealed by his partner, Trimble, several days later. He knew that $10,000 had been paid by Poultney to Markley, but he disclaimed knowledge of what it was for; said this was not "his branch of the business." He claimed that while he knew of the payment, his own side of the affair was to attend to the fancy goods and hardware line, while Poultney attended to the guns. To Senator Schurz' cogent question, "Do your books show anything about this transaction with Mr. Markley?" Trimble answered damningly, "No, sir."

Poultney received the 10,000 Remington-Springfields in bright condition though they were originally put into production casehardened and blued. The French wanted bright muskets; and some 900 which had been issued to the Marines at scattered fortresses and depots when called in were sent back to the Springfield shops to be burnished clean of their bluing.

Poultney Trys Again

Undaunted by the possibility of disapproval of his Remington purchase, Poultney kept at the Ordnance Department, seeking more arms. He was a heavy purchaser of all types of surplus equipment, and some not so surplus. He preferred National Armory products, new make or rebuilt. Learning that the Armory had been conducting experiments in rebuilding Spencer carbines into rifles, fitted with Springfield "Eagle-V-P" barrels and new forestocks, he tried to buy them. His expectations were not unfounded. Silas Crispin, now a brevet colonel, was on duty as usual in New York, office at Houston and Greene streets. To General Dyer, Chief of Ordnance, on January 6, 1871, he telegraphed: "Benton has 500, more or less, Spencer rifles on hand. Please authorize sale at 30 dollars."

Replied Dyer, "Sell Spencers at 30 dollars each."

The demand continued, and Crispin wired Washington again, the afternoon of the 7th, seeking to learn if the Navy had any Spencers. Dyer fired back at once: "Commander Navy Yard instructed to issue to you Spencer rifles."

Certainly with Spencer rifles being sold so briskly at $30, Poultney was justified in thinking he, too, could have some if he could sniff them out. The transformed Springfield-Spencers were by way of being an experiment and any junior Ordnance officer could have told him they served more as an engineering study than as any important step forward in reequipping the Grand Army.

The President Stops the Fun

But in between this brisk business someone stepped in and put a halt to the fun:

> Ordnance Office, War Department
> *Washington, January 23, 1871*
>
> Major S. Crispin,
>   Corner Houston and Greene Streets, New York
>   The President directs that sales of ordnance and ordnance stores be discontinued.
>   Acknowledge receipt.
>
>   A. B. Dyer,
>   *Chief of Ordnance*

The same day Dyer sent a follow-up clarifying telegram, saying that Crispin could deliver all stores sold previous to his receipt of the Presidential stop-sale telegram. This led to some loop-hole searching. Smith, Crosby & Company had put up margin for Parrott rifled field batteries, which purchase they had transferred to C. K. Garrison. Crispin sought to deliver to Garrison a suitable quantity of ammunition. To his and Dyer's surprise, J. Schuyler Crosby declined to receive the ammunition, saying he did not want it. In another instance, Alfred Steinberger had put up margin and been awarded 6,300 Enfield rifles in October, 1870, but these had not been taken by him up to January 25, 1871. Crispin sought instructions as to whether he should deliver these arms. Dyer did not feel too much in favor of the presidential proclamation: "Consummate sale of Enfields made in October to Steinberger," he responded.

But Poultney was left out in the cold. By February 14, he sent off a little St. Valentine's note to his good friend General Dyer: "I am ready to take, on account of my purchase of the 19th of January, of carbines altered to rifles, the 1,200, more or less, Spencer carbines on hand at national Armory, altered to rifles, at 30 dollars per arm."

Dyer was adamantine; to Crispin fell the unpleasant task of informing Poultney, "that the Secretary of War declines to authorize alteration and sale of Spencers." The golden flood had been shut off, and now the Congress stepped in to investigate. The honeymoon was over.

Congressional Investigation

Hannibal Hamlin was appointed chairman of the Select Committee to Investigate Sales of Arms, Etc. under a Senate resolution of February 20, 1872:

> Resolved, That a select committee of seven be appointed to investigate all sales of Ordnance Stores made by the Government of the United States during the fiscal year ending the 30th of June, AD 1871, to ascertain the persons to whom such sales were made, the circumstances under which they were made, the sums respectively paid by said purchasers to the United States, and the disposition made of the proceeds of such sales; and that said committee also enquire and report whether any member of the Senate, or any other American citizen, is or has been in communication or collusion with the government or authorities of any foreign power, or with any agent or officer thereof, in reference to the said matter; and, also, whether breech-loading muskets, or other muskets capable of being transformed into breech-loaders, have not been sold by the War Department in such large numbers as seriously to impair the defensive capacity of the country in time of war; and that the committee have the power to send for persons and papers; and that the investigation be conducted in public . . ."

The testimony and report of the committee proceed through 857 fascinating pages of secret deals with Springfield Armory, offers by noted Civil War contractor Hermann Boker to buy arms for the Germans to oppose the French, condemnation of good arms in favor of their being sold at reasonable prices to would-be international munitions runners, and charges and attacks upon President Grant and others.

The subject is entirely too lengthy to do more than outline in this book, which has as its fundamental approach the arms of the American Civil War and, in this chapter, what happened to some of them. But the spirit of the testimony, and the parties to it in 1870-72, are strikingly parallel in some ways, and antithesis in others, to situations in the arms trade of America in the late 1950's and early 1960's. For example, one of the most outspoken condemners of the sales of arms was Massachusetts Senator Sumner. Another Senator from Massachusetts, Mr. John F. Kennedy, representing the small arms industry "lobby" of that state, in the 1950's was outspoken against the sale of surplus arms. On the Ordnance level, today's (1961) Ordnance Department prefers to acquire half a million, more or less, semi-modern automatic rifles of good quality—the M14. A plea or justification made for this in the international cold war emergency is that "The perfect is the enemy of the good," i.e., a search for superior infantry weapons designs can handicap the acquisition of second-rate but good arms at the time.

Back in 1870, the complaint was that the Ordnance officers had disposed of half a million or more acceptable muzzle-loaders, which were capable of being transformed into breechloaders economically. Although better arms (the Winchester repeaters, the innumerable bolt-actions which led to magazine loaded arms in the following decade) were successfully in use, Ordnance preferred the course of economy in altering muzzle-loaders to breechloaders by inserting a "trap door" breechblock in the back of the barrel.

Associated with Senator Sumner was Senator Carl Schurz who alleged great harm to the United States from the sales. In beginning the inquiry, Hamlin approached Schurz concerning some statements he had made; Schurz replied that "The witnesses to be examined in this case will almost all be unwilling witnesses, whose testimony will depend upon the manner of their examination, where one point will suggest another." Such "unwilling witnesses" included Trimble, already noted, Colt's vice president General Franklin, Richard Jordan Gatling himself, and a host of others whose names were familiar to the Ordnance Department from the preceding ten years as sellers of the very ordnance stores they now sought to repossess, for shipment to a foreign belligerent power, France.

The gross amount received during fiscal year 1871, the period of greatest sales, was $9,748,943.13, nearly $10,000,000. In gold, in 1871, at the prevailing purchasing power, this was a very great sum of money. Deducting costs of the sales, which amounted to $219,634.47, including the manufacture of cartridges at Frankford Arsenal to fill out some quantities, and money already on hand, the Ordnance Department received nearly 9½ millions of dollars, all of which was paid into the Treasury. The ratio of income against expenditures was about 10¢ on the dollar, the ordnance stores bought during 1861-65 totalling $130,266,364.79.

Two Acts related to the conditions of the sales. The first, of March 3, 1825, provided that the President could order sold any arms "which, upon proper inspection or survey, shall appear to be damaged or otherwise unsuitable for the public service, whenever, in his opinion, the sale of such unserviceable stores will be advantageous to the public service."

The Act clearly related to those arms, among other articles, which had been found, upon proper inspection, to be unserviceable or damaged. A lot of brand new arms, properly preserved and in mint condition can acquire the grading of "unserviceable" by reason of the passage of time. But this was not considered in the Act referred to; the inspection had to be made and upon inspecting if damage or other cause for declaring unserviceable was found (as for example brand new but clearly obsolete flint muskets), the President in his discretion could authorize their sale.

While many of the complaints raised at the vast disposal program of the Ordnance Department were based upon current constructions of this Act, there was another law in effect more directly relating. As Secretary of the Committee Carpenter noted:

On the close of the late war, in 1865, the Government found itself in possession of a large amount of muskets and other military stores, not damaged and unserviceable within the meaning of the Act of 1825, but unsuitable in the sense that other and improved arms were more desirable; and thereupon Congress, in 1868, passed an Act under which the sales in question were made, as follows:
"That the Secretary of War be, and he is hereby authorized and directed to cause to be sold, after offer at public sale on thirty days' notice, in such manner and at such times and places at public or private sale as he may deem most advantageous to the public interest, the old cannon, arms and other ordnance stores, now in possession of the War Department, which are damaged or otherwise unsuitable for the United States military service, or for the militia of the United States, and to cause the net proceeds of such sales, after paying all proper expenses of sale and transportation to the place of sale, to be deposited in the Treasury of the United States."

The Committee found in the wording of this Act, opportunity for unjust or undesirable conduct on the part of the War Department. Since it was passed in 1868, it would have been possible in complying with the letter of the law for the War Department to have put the whole fantastic accumulation of Civil War surplus munitions up for sale on 30 days' notice in one lump. The condition of the market alone would have produced no takers; the quantity would have frightened away all buyers, even governments. Then, according to the letter of the law, the Department could have peddled bits and pieces here and there at any old price at private treaty.

The actual course pursued was far different, a "soldier's construction" of the law, rather than a lawyer's interpretation, as the Committee found. Parcels of armaments were offered from time to time and thus the market was "felt out" by the sales officers, and they were kept abreast of the times. When it became known that France, for example, in 1870, was to be a purchaser of surplus Springfield muskets, General Dyer deliberately raised the price of the arms.

He claimed that France had charged the United States high prices for muskets ten years previously when the Union had been in danger, and he hardened his heart to the protestations of the French agents, fixing a price of $12 for new Springfield Rifle Muskets (which had cost as little as $14 a decade before and been "written off" the account books by the fact of Northern victory), and $9 for "C & R," or Cleaned and Repaired Springfields. "Free" Confederate Enfields and other arms were priced in proportion. As the committee reported, in determining if the sales were to the best interests of the United States, "The testimony upon this subject is all one way ... prices received by the Government were higher than could have been expected, and much higher than the same stores would now command." Only in one point does the testimony and the Committee seem at variance, and then only because the Committee were directed to find out facts at certain levels, and not absolutely.

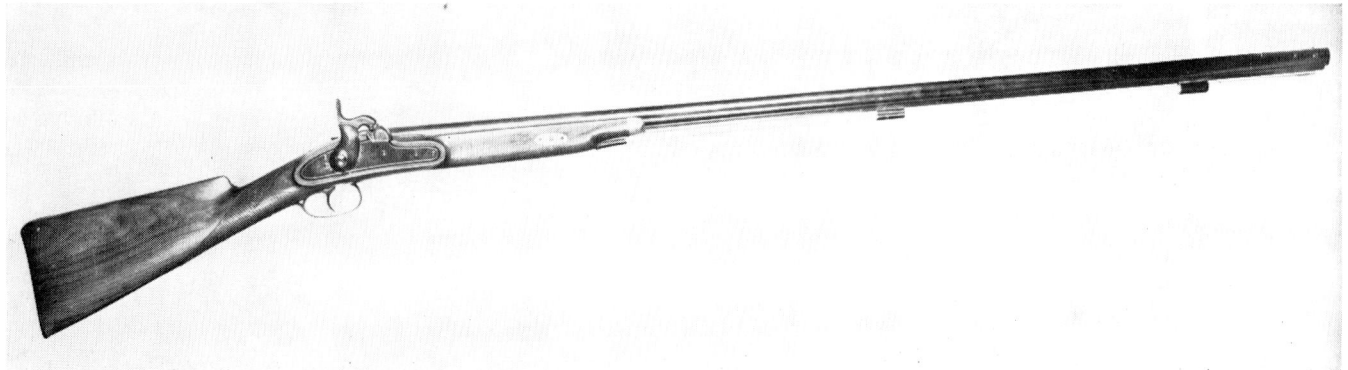

Surplus parts went into "sporterized" arms. Shown is controversial "forager's shotgun" using Springfield M1842 lock and barrel, in West Point Museum. Controversy is pointless as old catalogues quite clearly show variety of shotguns offered by different firms, based on Government surplus arms or parts.

This area of discord surrounded the government order excluding persons known to be agents of France, from directly purchasing after the fact of their agency became known. But witness after witness testified to the fact that arms purchased by Schuyler, Hartley and Graham, by Austin Baldwin & Company, by Hermann Boker and others, all were delivered to one French ship in the harbor and there checked from the lighters into the hold by a man named Starbuck, who was the official representative of Remington Arms.

Seventeen shiploads of munitions went out alone on vessels of the General Transatlantic Company, including the *St. Laurent,* the *Ville de Paris,* the *Lafayette,* the *Periere,* and the *Washington,* between September 3, 1870, and April 22, 1871. Cases bore marks of the consignees, but two sets of marks in particular elicited comment: ER & S, and RF. The ER & S were obviously destined for E. Remington & Sons, whose agent and member of the family Samuel Remington was resident in Paris at the time. The marks "RF" were more enigmatic; some witnesses thought they meant "Remington Freres," studiously avoiding the fact the mark was quite obviously the cypher of the belligerent power *Republique Francaise.*

Among the guns shipped to France were nine of the caliber .50 Gatling Guns made by Colt's at the end of the war. General Hagner of Watervleit Arsenal received in exchange nine new caliber .50 guns from Colt's, conducting the business of the transaction directly with General Franklin and Hugh Harbison, Colt's treasurer-secretary. The exchange deal was naturally worked out, following the pattern of the .50 Remington rolling block rifles bought by Poultney and Trimble, to give the French agents arms in being, quickly, when time was short. Then Colt's could finish the nine improved guns at their leisure.

The deal, "avoiding" complying with the directive stopping sale aided the cause of research and development by giving both Colt's and the Ordnance officers experience with a new type of curved feed case for ammunition. This feed case had been developed for use with the bottleneck caliber .42 Berdan Gatling guns made on the Russian order. At least nine such guns, but in caliber .50, were delivered to General Hagner together with 240 of the special curved feed cases. The replacement guns afforded an opportunity to observe that the cartridges misfired, and the cases failed to feed certainly, unless an assistant kept his thumb upon the follower. Less sensitive primer compounds used in the Frankford cartridges, were claimed by Franklin to be the cause of the one defect, as ammunition made by Union Metallic Cartridge Company and by Colt's Cartridge Works did not misfire in the .42 Russian Gatlings. Modifications of the feed case follower was discussed and the experiment had value in its "new look" at the Gatling batteries of our frontier service.

The arms sales investigation was concluded without anybody getting cashiered or shot. Some of the testimony led to "whitewashing," but the matter took on the aspects of comedy when Boker testified that he, as a sympathetic German-American, had telegraphed to the German Government asking if he should buy arms to keep the French from having them. Bismarck replied that he could get all the arms in France he wanted, "As we shall pick them up on the banks of the Loire cheaper." The German troops did just this and concluded after the end of hostilities an interesting sale of 100,000 Springfield rifle muskets, captured from France, to the Turkish government at $1 each— some 8 per cent of the cost paid out by the French to obtain them!

The minority view in the Senate was not fully in agreement. Filed by John W. Stevenson, it made some detailed criticisms about the Poultney & Trimble purchase, noting that in this the Baltimore partners were fronting for Remington. Further, the matter of Starbuck checking in the cases and issuing receipts in his name in behalf of an obvious syndicate of buyers conspiring to purchase for France was set forth precisely by Stevenson:

> . . . The Remingtons, after they had become known as the agents of the French government, still maintained a lively intercourse with the Ordnance Department and its officers, in connection with the sale of arms through intermediaries, and that in some of the transactions above referred to, the fact that such third parties were not the real purchasers, but were acting for the Remingtons, could, by

vigilant inquiry, have been early ascertained by the officers making the sales. What unprejudiced mind can doubt it?

The testimony develops other facts worthy of note in this connection. The arms were delivered by lighters in the pay of the ordnance agency, on certain piers at New York, partly at the pier of the French Transatlantic Steamship Company, partly at pier No. 3, where steamships were loaded, known by common report to have been chartered by the French consul. The cases were sometimes hoisted immediately from the lighters on board those ships. While still in the lighters, the cases were marked "R.F." which meant, Republique Francaise, one of the employees of the ordnance agency, sent there to keep an account of the deliveries, taking part in thus marking the boxes. The receipts for delivery were signed and given to the employee of the ordnance agency by one and the same man, in the name of Remington & Sons, Austin Baldwin & Co., and Thomas Richardson, thus tending to create a presumption that the arms really went into the hands of one and the same party. This man (Starbuck) had been charged with this business, and his receipts were accepted at the ordnance agency in pursuance of a letter addressed by Colonel (W. C.) Squire, Remington's known agent, to Colonel Crispin. A French officer, Captain Guzman, openly inspected large quantities of artillery on the wharf at New York, and that French officer received there from an employee of the ordnance agency, certificates as to the quality and condition of the goods delivered.

(This requirement for certificates was in conformity to the proposal of Remington to the Ordnance Department to buy up to 19,000 Spencer carbines, accompanied by certificates as to their quality and condition signed by an ordnance inspecting officer. WBE.) The same French officer was seen by Mr. (C. K.) Garrison at the ordnance agency in conversation with Colonel Crispin about ordnance stores.

But Garrison, though he doubtless testified truly concerning the rapport between Captain Guzman and Colonel Crispin, was not too knowledgeable a man himself when it came to arms sales. One of the heaviest buyers of weaponry, especially Parrott 10- and 20-pounder rifled field artillery, Garrison furnished the Committee with an odd bit of comic relief.

Cornelius K. Garrison did not enter into the arms sales with a view to actually purchasing anything. He took part, doubtless in consideration of a sum of money, which in the contract he assessed at only "$1 and certain other valuable considerations" to be surety on behalf of several Americans who were contracting to supply arms to France. Frederick Billings, W. J. Valentine, and William Saint Laurent November 28, 1870, at Tours, France, agreed to supply the French government with arms. A stipulation of their contract involved depositing 1,000,000 francs with some banking house in New York as security for performance of their contract. Not wanting to put up this money in cash, they turned to Garrison as a wealthy man of New York to offer his own means as surety. This was acceptable to J. S. Morgan & Company of London and Dabney, Morgan & Company of New York, through whom the transaction was channeled.

Garrison was to advance the money needed to pay for the guns. He was to have the right of veto on such arms as he felt were not in accordance with the contract between Billings, Valentine and St. Laurent, and the Government of France. He was also to charter a vessel or vessels as necessary to fulfill the transportation of the arms abroad. While the original contract called for delivery of arms at Bordeaux by December 20, 1870, the French not only extended it in favor of the Americans but made a deposit of six millions of francs, about $1,200,000, in their favor at J. S. Morgan in London to be used to pay for the purchases.

The French Government tried to abrogate the contract during the spring; the Chancellor of the Exchequer of England refused to allow the money to be withdrawn from J. S. Morgan & Company, alleging it had been deposited there for a specific purpose. The matter was brought to suit, but back in the United States, Garrison, for the consideration of $100,000 from the contracting trio, had been paying out for arms purchased in the names of half a dozen other firms and buyers.

A. B. Steinberger had turned over Enfields to Garrison, and from other buyers, as well as in his name, he had acquired some 40,000 Enfield rifles and 20 batteries of field artillery. The French reneged on their contract because of the military situation abroad; the country had been invested by the German Army. But at last they agreed to accept delivery of the arms at Algiers. Meanwhile, Garrison had tried to obtain a refund of his $60,000 deposit or margin put up on the Enfield purchase.

His reasoning was accepted by Colonel Crispin, who noted in correspondence that the purpose of a margin or earnest money was to protect the seller against loss in the event the option to one party prevented a sale in the interim to another party. No such potential loss could have been shown, and he recommended compliance with Garrison's petition to have a full refund on the Enfields. But the Parrott rifled guns were another matter, he having bought and paid for them, even obtaining five batteries from an outside source.

As Garrison told Senator Carl Schurz under oath, "In these statements about the arms business, I want it distinctly understood that I am not speaking as an expert. I do not know a shotgun from a rifle, scarcely." (As Captain Garrison, he seemed once to have known a good deal about the value of Chasseur de Vincennes carbines shown to Fremont!)

He then went on to speak of the Parrott rifled guns. "My understanding was that the goods were all to be had at two places, at Washington and Watervleit (Arsenals). Afterward, on account of the rejection of a number of these pieces, they fell short, and, as I understand, some pieces of artillery had to come from St. Louis, some saddles, bridles, harness, etc., from Rock Island, and from different parts of the country, and it was during the time of snowstorms, and, as I said before, my lay-days were running out. We had so many lay-days, after which I had to pay £200 per diem demurrage, and that was my anxiety."

Garrison had chartered a steamer for shipping the guns, at £11,000 a trip, plus the £200 per diem demurrage. He had so many days at the dock without charge for the charter fee; then he had to pay £200 for each day overtime that the SS *Ontario* lay idle at the wharf.

"I would almost rather do anything than ship batteries" pleaded Garrison and view here of U.S. heavy artillery ready for transportation at Yorktown during Peninsular campaign shows why. Big 30-pounder Parrott rifles in background are grouped with quantity of "impedimenta," such as field forges and ammunition waggons which accompanied gun in the field. Pieces shown probably were included among Garrison's purchase in 1870 which overflowed from biggest steam freighter afloat. Guns are in travelling position, trunnions unseated and tubes pulled to rear to balance in draught.

"I was dealing with a thing I knew nothing about," pleaded Garrison as he, metaphorically, clutched his sheaf of a $100,000 commission: "I supposed all these batteries would not measure more than 400 or 500 tons, and I found they measured 2,500. I did not know anything about a battery. I chartered the largest ship in the United States, and I thought she could carry twice the quantity of freight, but I found I was very much mistaken." Brokenly, he concluded, "I would rather do almost anything else than ship batteries."

What Garrison had neglected to determine was that his 20-pounder Parrott cannon came in lots of eight pieces per battery, plus ammunition wagons, field forges, and complete harness to hook up six or eight horses for draught. There were additional saddles, "valise" saddles, for the artillerymen to ride the horses, and ton upon ton of accessory leather and ironware that accompanied these 20 batteries of field cannon, fully found and ready for war. Bulky and uncrated, the rolling mass of the 160 pieces of field artillery more than filled the *Ontario's* hold.

Smith Crosby & Company actually paid the Ordnance Department for the 20 batteries of Parrott guns. They were taken out of the *Ontario,* though Garrison later found it cheaper to buy the ship than pay the charter. They were reshipped via sailing vessel during June or July, 1871, to Algiers.

The location of these cannon today is a mystery. Of iron, it is to be hoped that they were not so valuable as scrap iron to cause diligent and thrifty French ordnance officers to have them melted down, as was done with so many valuable old bronze and brass guns. In the dry air of Algeria they might still repose in some French-Algerian artillery park, unused, in good condition. If some eager surplus dealer of today should find them and ship them back to the United States for sale to Civil War cannon buffs, we hope that he has better luck than Mr. Garrison, who would "rather do almost anything else than ship batteries."

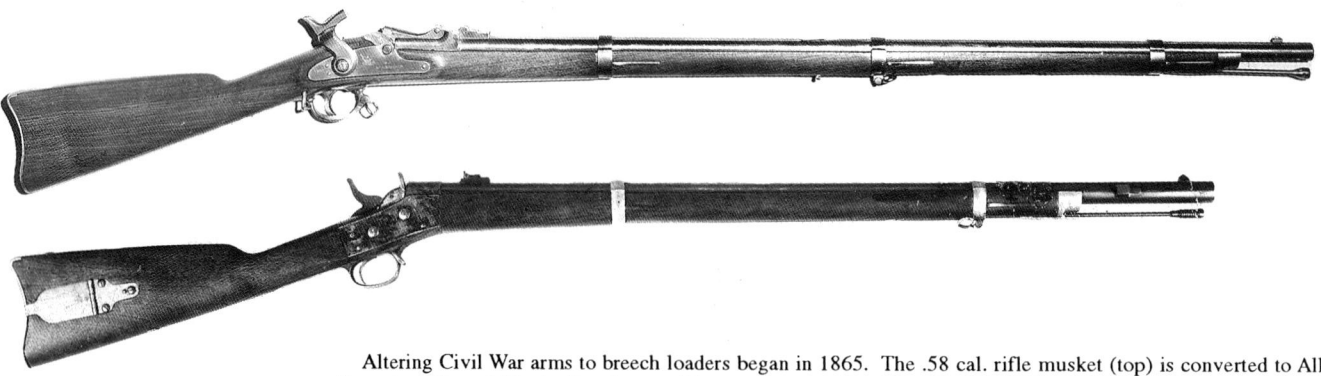

Altering Civil War arms to breech loaders began in 1865. The .58 cal. rifle musket (top) is converted to Allin "trap door" breech block. Remington rifle was altered with rolling block breech, possibly for Vatican Zouaves.

CHAPTER 34

What's on Bannerman's Island?

The power launch which had brought us across the Hudson from Cornwall, New York, churned nearer to Polopel Island. I could see the square mass of the castellated warehouse looming out of the morning haze. The breakwater was awash with the tide, but we rounded the long southern arm and chugged between the guard turrets, passed a worn sign which proclaimed "Keep Out—Explosives—Armed Guards." In quiet excitement I waited for the boatman to bring the launch alongside the wharf. I could wait patiently. Along with millions of passengers on the New York Central's water level route up the Hudson, along with thousands of gun collectors who know the fabulous Bannerman arms business and its incredible catalog (which after 90 years is still a standard reference work for gun students)—I, too, had long wondered "What's *on* Bannerman Island?"

The firm of Francis Bannerman Sons was a legend in the gun collecting field. Their 300 page catalog is a treasure trove of data on Civil War artifacts, everything from the binnacle of Admiral Farragut's *Hartford* to the guns of the *Kearsarge*. Colt 1860 Army revolvers at $2.85 once appeared in this incredible catalog; and in the 1950's I spotted a price tag reappearing on a coveted Gatling gun for a fraction of the actual value. Alas, the gun had been sold by the time I realized what had occurred; Bannerman had unearthed in their vast storehouses of ancient Civil War and postbellum arms, a forgotten Gatling gun and priced it in line with their original pricings. What else lay on their island warehouse in the Hudson?

Since that day in 1942 when I wandered into the long, narrow shop on lower Manhattan, the building at 501 Broadway with its antique "Bannerman—Firearms" and the gold bullion letters on the facade proclaiming "Army & Navy Outfitters" which has hardly changed in a half century; since that day when I bought a rusty Spencer rifle on their "Specials" table for $2, Bannerman's catalog and company had been a moulding factor in my collecting of old guns. With the tremendous post-World War II interest in arms collecting, some other merchants have tried to imitate Bannerman, with more or less success. But it is not easy to imitate a legend. And legend Bannerman's has become, largely because of the Island. Now I was to be the third outsider in a generation to set foot on the Island. The first was an Army colonel who visited the Island after World War II. The second man was sitting by me in the launch. Valmore Forgett, late PFC, Ordnance Corps USA, now owner of the Service Armament Co. I was there as a reporter. Forgett was there to see if he could avoid getting blown up.

Bannerman bought the island in 1900 from one Thomas Taft, who had bought the rocky crag in Newburgh Bay to keep it from being used as a depot for untaxed whiskey. Taft cut out the bootlegging and, when Taft was told that Bannerman had voted the Prohibition ticket, not to win but just to register his vote dry, the deal was made. Taft entailed the title with one condition, that no liquor be sold on the Island. This became one of the most ironic twists in the story of the Island Arsenal, for as it turned out, the condition should have read, "No whiskey shall be *used* here."

On that Island, Francis Bannerman erected a rambling, castellated warehouse five stories high, rising some fifty feet above the level of the Hudson. He needed the Island to store 20,000,000 rounds of captured Spanish 7mm Mauser ammunition, as well as thousands of Mauser rifles captured in the Spanish-American War. Ultimately he moved other munitions to the Island, including case after case (possibly as many as a hundred thousand at one time) of Civil War Springfield rifles. Of most interest to Forgett professionally, were tons of Civil War and Spanish War artillery shells, corroded into dangerous condition. In addition, Bannerman, to build a foundation on which to place his arsenal, sank barges in the Hudson— barges filled with live Civil War artillery projectiles. As we disembarked and walked across the crumbling concrete walk, I noticed that the overgrowth of poison ivy was tangled about the nose studs of fused Parrott rifle shells.

The potentially dangerous condition of the age-old munitions stored on the Island became apparent to the Bannerman people recently, and they tried to locate

Imposing pile of Bannerman's Island Armory is seen by New York Central passengers on route from Big Town up to Albany. Building is somewhat smaller than grotesque architecture makes it appear. Signs warn of fierce dogs on guard but recent caretakers shot them because they stole the Collie puppy's food.

an ordnance expert who would deactivate the unsafe munitions. They contacted West Point's Museum and were told, "Go see Val Forgett." They also wrote to Aberdeen Proving Ground. "Only man in civil life we know who would tackle that job is Forgett," they were told. Thus warmly recommended, the engaging proprietor of Service Armament Company was willing to risk life and limb to take a look. With an ever-present possibility of stepping on some ancient fuse rotten with verdi gris that would detonate from the pressure of a foot, we trod Bannerman's Island.

The breakwater (composed of thousands of .45-70 musket barrels dumped in and mortared over) led to a north ground-level door. Beside the entrance I suddenly paused, scooped down into a tin box filled with the pine needles of decades, and pulled out a 1-inch Gatling Gun cartridge case that crumbled in my fingers from corrosion. That case, in "keepable" condition, would be worth from $5 to $10 to a collector. There must have been a hundred in the box once—now gone beyond recall.

Inside the first floor of the main warehouse, we walked past stacks of ammunition cases. These chests, each about two by one by three feet in cube, contained some of the 20,000 rounds of high explosive Spanish War cannon ammunition that Bannerman wanted deactivated. In addition, there were round metal canisters, Navy gray, holding an even two dozen two-pounder brass case cartridges. The shells were painted red, high explosive, and the fuses were of a type that is "armed" by the shock of discharge, ready to fire on impact. These shells were condemned, so the story goes, because they had been dropped once in transport. We shook one slightly—something rattled inside. I looked at the piles of ammo chests rising twice as high as my head into the dimness of the unlighted warehouse vault, and wondered how easy it would be to "shock" them a second time for detonation. I certainly did not envy Forgett his job.

We continued to probe. My gun-hunting instincts were all primed to find a 20-musket armory chest, or one of those chunky square boxes containing fifty New Model Army Colts, the way Uncle Sam used to ship them. But rust and dust covered everything. There was no system, no order, just chaos.

To the rear on the first floor, Island caretakers had laid out a hundred cases of .45-70 ammunition for one dealer order. More cases held tens of thousands of the brass-bullet Spanish Remington cartridge. Off in a corner by a rickety, dangerous stairway were three big chests, lids smashed. Each contained Spanish Mauser cartridge clips, once-bright with fresh nickel plate for

From gun shields on battlements Francis Bannerman surveyed Hudson River. Arms magnate once discharged a 37mm explosive round to demonstrate lot of ammo was serviceable and later received complaint from shore dweller.

tropical issue, now spotty and stained with age.

On the second floor we discovered more interesting relics. A pile of scrap resolved itself into a tangle of rifle barrels. We apparently had stumbled on to Bannerman's "factory" area where, long years ago, skilled workmen had remodeled long Army rifles into cadet muskets for private military academies. In another section of this floor, we came upon hundreds of sword hilts—just the hilts and about a foot of blade, and scabbards chopped in half, all of the American Civil War pattern. North-South Skirmish fans would have liked that cache before someone chopped 'em in half. Further on, we came to artillery carriages, with the wood-spoke wheels smashed, and the bronze hubs missing. One trunnion cap remained; its fellow had been hammered off. "What is this, battlefield salvage?" I asked. "Heck no," Forgett snorted. "A former caretaker was an alcoholic, and he took boatloads of brass over to the mainland to peddle for booze!" In sorrow, I counted Gatling carriages. Each was damaged, the guns gone, their heavy brass housings melted years ago. A few barrels, a damaged set of trunnion arms or two, some gears, a bent feed case—all that remained of a dozen fine Colt Gatlings.

I took the light and decided to pass to the highest point quickly, get the lay of the land, and then continue the search working down. The top was a huge "captain's walk" ringed by a parapet and with gun shields set in embrasures, for the Navy quick-firers—light guns shooting the two-pound shell, that old Francis had bought from the Spanish War sales. Even these guns were gone, more probably unlimbered and sold for scrap, since they had no military value for over a generation.

The castle roof was tarred, and sagging. One side sloped a good four feet lower than the other, and I did not dare trust my weight to the middle. I edged around carefully, caught the view downstream where West Point's gray granite barracks clustered on the hillside, saw farther down stream where Cornwall was a sprinkling of white window frames and blue roofs. Then I started downstairs. The three top floors were empty of heavy gear, the top two stripped clean. Through the concrete floors I could see daylight as the sun shafted through some window on the floor below. Wire net and rods showed where the concrete had sloughed off, leaving nothing but reinforcing metal.

The third floor level had a southern exit to a castellated walkway that slanted down abruptly to ground level. Strewn about and tumbled into the rank garden below, were dozens of U. S. Army white cork helmets. "Rudy Vallee bought 600 of those a few years back," I was told. "His band wore them, and then they were auctioned off for charity." Today—anybody want a pith helmet? They're up there on the Island, rotting in the rain.

The second floor came in for another careful search. I shuddered to look at a carefully piled stack of Civil War army knapsacks, forming a huge cube possibly fifteen feet high and thirty feet on a side, which had begun to tip. A single rope passed in front of the pile, the topmost tiers of which had now sagged out as much as five feet over the base. The rope had frayed to a single strand or two. If that pile collapsed, it might have force enough to bring down the whole tottering old building!

Though Bannerman built for the ages, his castle has hardly lasted a lifetime. A reason why is found in Bannerman's story of a potential customer. "A party came to us," recounted the late Frank Bannerman VI "and wanted to purchase a large lot of military cartridges. The price was satisfactory and the sale was almost made, when he requested the privilege of using our island to repack the cartridges into nail kegs." Bannerman refused. "We will not sell you the cartridges," he told the revolutionary agent. "You haven't money enough to induce us to break the law." The ammunition buyer then went to another firm, bought the cartridges he needed, had the boxes wrapped in excelsior and packed in kegs of dry cement. The shipment was seized by customs officers, the ammunition impounded and sold at auction. "We were the pur-

Breakwaters at Polopel Island were pleasuredom for Bannerman family, who gaily disported in swim togs unmindful of barges of artillery shells which had been sunk to provide foundations for construction.

chasers," Bannerman added smugly. "The cement we used in building our island storehouses, and the cartridges were sold to the President of Santo Domingo."

El Presidente got a better deal with his cartridges than Bannerman got with the cement. It occurred to me that, if I were a revolutionary, shipping ammo in cement barrels as a disguise, I too would buy the *cheapest cement* I could find. To judge from the state of Bannerman's castle, that is what happened. The 20-inch thick main walls have developed cracks through which daylight passes, and weeds are starting to push their way into the building.

We walked outside again, and it was like walking out of the 19th into the 20th century. Piles of gummy knapsacks, chests of unfinished Krag Jorgenson rifle parts, rusted cartridge clips and broken artillery carriages were the heritage of the 19th century to the 20th. Outside, a shattered Civil War 3-inch iron rifle needed a thousand dollars worth of woodwork to make it useful. And, still looking up stream, defending the Island from the holiday boaters who often oar close for a look, a monster Dahlgren gun rested on its iron barbette carriage, frozen solid with red, immovable, but as grand in its silence as when it frowned from the gunwales of Flag-officer Farragut's *Hartford* and challenged the Confederacy on the western waters.

I had brought with me several old Bannerman catalogs, two dating back to 1903 and 1905, and here in the shadow of the firm's memories, it amused me to look through them and see what was once offered. Take the Hall rifles, for example.

"First American Breech-Loading Flint Lock Rifle made in America," reads the 1905 catalog. After a thrilling description of the guns, calculated to speed the purchaser's pulse, comes the kicker: "We expect to get $50 each for some of these guns . . . but for the present we will pack gun in case ready for express (buyer pays expressage) for $10.00 each." Though this lot of Hall rifles has long since been sold, Bannerman has left us a story of how he obtained them. At the Government auction sale, 300 Hall's rifles were offered. In 1873, Bannerman had bought such guns in unserviceable shape at 3½¢ each. About 1900, he had paid as much as $8 a gun. Puzzled over the market value of these guns, Bannerman dreamed three days before the sale that he was in his Broadway store, selling a man a Hall rifle for $1.71. He took this figure as his bid. When the bids were opened, it was found that Bannerman's competitors, Hartley & Graham, had also bid $1.71. Bannerman and H & G's business friend, William Read of Boston, cut the lot three ways. Even at $10.00, Bannerman could afford to sell them.

The founder of this fantastic arms business (which, as early as the turn of the century, "requires 15 acres for storage") was the sixth Francis Bannerman, a vigorous Scottish nationalist born in Dundee, Scotland, in March of 1851. With his parents, he arrived in America in 1854, and grew up in Brooklyn, where his father ran a ship's chandler store near the Navy Yard.

The business, managed by his father and later by Frank, grew during the 1870's and 1880's, but did not take on its character of a general munitions firm until near the turn of the century. In 1897, Bannerman moved to 579 Broadway, a spot that served as major outfitter for many of the Spanish American War volunteer regiments.

Young Frank had accompanied his father to the Government auctions which siphoned off the tremendous Civil War surpluses and, with native Scottish sagacity and some acquired Yankee acumen, became a shrewd bargainer in the surplus sales then being held in New York. A newspaper ad of about 1900 showed three steam trains and the heading, "Three train loads of army goods sold to Francis Bannerman," with revolvers at .50 up, carbines at $1.00 up, muskets slightly higher.

Though Bannerman's later catalogs intimated he had purchased guns at the end of the Civil War, his name is conspicuous by its absence from the Congressional report of sales made in 1870-71. Then a half million Springfields, plus tons of cannon and harness, were sold off to arm the French in the Franco-Prussian War. Though Bannerman may not have been personally active in those sales, his firm was to have a long association with foreign munitions houses. By World War I he had consolidated small arms storage and sales at 501 Broadway, with the Island Arsenal off Cornwall, a warehouse at the Erie Basin Stores on the Brooklyn water front, and a Belgian agent in Liege at 79 Rue Lairesse. "Our agent in Belgium" said Bannerman, "acted for the firm of Hermann Boker & Co. who supplied the U. S. Government . . . during the Civil War. He informed me he altered over 60,000 Austrian tube lock guns into regular percussion cap muskets . . . Consequently tube lock guns are now rare." Concluded Bannerman with the "hard sell" approach, "Every gun-collector needs one."

Not bothering to communicate the whole story to his readers, Bannerman neglected to tell them that he had commercial connections with the German-Belgian munitions firm of Adolph Frank of Hamburg. To judge from the overlapping offerings of identical muskets and rifles, Bannerman did a brisk business bidding in guns for ALFA and the European munitions traders, reserving a stock for his store. Collectors shudder to recall the picture of the Colt rifle musket in Bannerman's catalog where, in addition to reassuring every collector that he needed one, Bannerman remarks that his Liege agent altered 50,000 of them to *flintlock* for the African trade, and they are "now rare." There seems to have been considerable reciprocity between Bannerman in New York and the German and other foreign munitions brokers. Offered in Bannerman's catalog as well as those of European dealers, were the identical souvenir trinkets—desk weights, ink stands, and button hooks, made from a variety of small arms cartridges and small-caliber cannon shells.

The small-caliber cannon shells, 37mm or Hotchkiss

Three trainloads of army goods bought by Scottish munitions king at turn of century included Rogers & Spencers for 25¢ and various non-standard guns for which no market had existed earlier. At prices of nearly $5 for a Perrin and $6.50 for a Joslyn, Bannerman had hard time selling off many guns until collector interest increased in period of World War II.

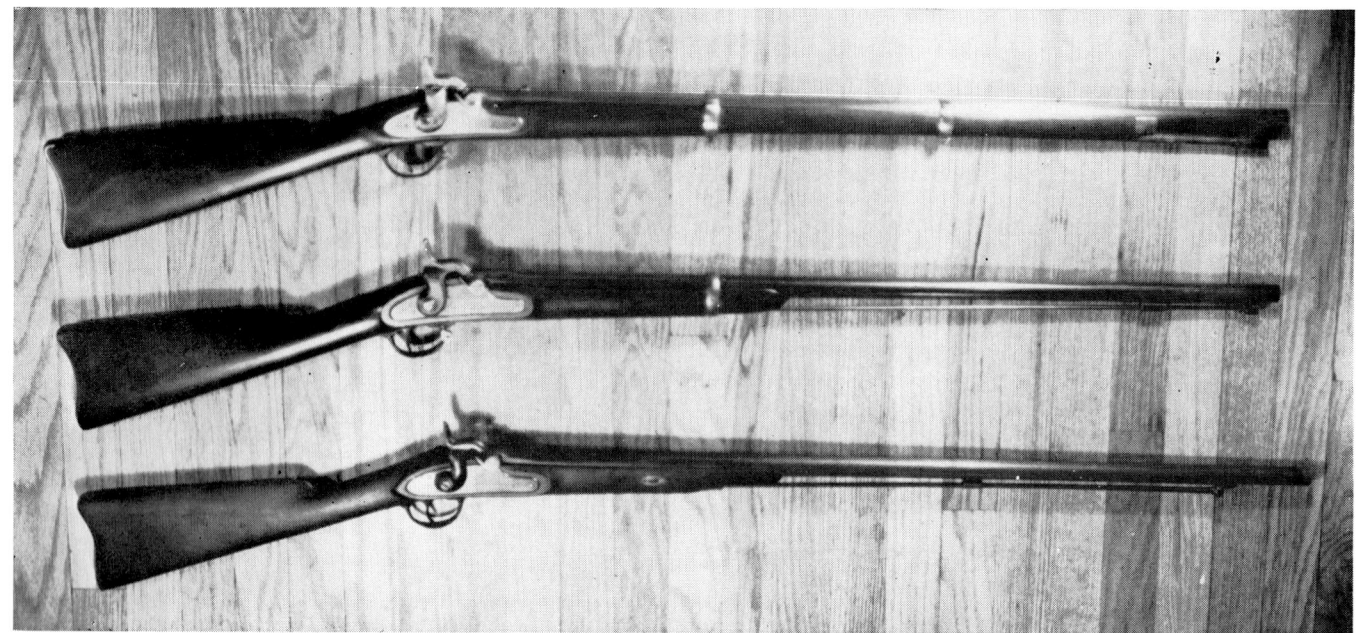

Transformed Civil War muskets were poor-man's shotgun in 1880s. Top is Colt Special Model cut to short rifle, but middle is Bannerman-Hartley-Daly-Great Western 1863 Springfield transformed to shotgun using condemned parts. Gun is nearly new, shows seam in barrel blue not visible if bright. Bottom is one of Bannerman's 50,000 Colt Special Models shipped to Liege and changed to shotgun by correspondent M. Ancion & Co., now Ancion-Marx.

one-pounder projectiles, were souvenirs from Bannerman's biggest commercial coup, when he purchased 90 per cent of the captured Spanish war material acquired by the United States in the Spanish-American War. Over 20 million rounds of small arms cartridges, plus a tremendous pile of other munitions already on hand, made the New York fire marshal take a dim view of the business, and so Polopel's Island was purchased. To it came barge loads of munitions, including the Spanish Mausers. Many of Bannerman's Mauser rifles were cleaned and repaired at Springfield Armory. The armory business was a little slow in 1900 since the Army boards were considering adopting a new magazine repeating rifle, ultimately the famous "03 Springfield," and Bannerman paid the men. Bannerman then bought 14,000 guns and offered them at $10 each, with 7,000,-000 rounds of 7mm ammo. Master of the "hard sell" in a gentle 19th century sort of way, Frank wrote, "Any day our Agent may send us cablegram ordering shipment of the whole lot (for export). If you contemplate purchasing a good rifle do not put it off. Every one is pleased with the Mauser." Some of his customers were more than pleased! they went stark, raving mad with joy. Surely only a madman would write, as one testimonial declared, "The Mauser is the only gun made for use in hunting big game, mountain sheep, elk, etc., at 1,500 to 2,000 yards. The .30-30 rifles are not in it. The Mauser is superior to any American-made sporting gun." Even for 1900, that was a real "gone" shooter.

Bannerman lived an adventurous life. The Mausers did not make him any money sitting in New York, and he decided to go abroad to sell them. Complained Bannerman frequently, "The American Government does little or nothing to help their merchants trade in foreign countries." He had shipped a sample Mauser and cartridges to King Alexander of Serbia, via American Express. But the King was assassinated and the transaction slightly delayed. The gun remained in the American Express office in Hamburg until Bannerman asked the new King Peter if he was interested. Said Bannerman, "The Serbian agent cabled 'Yah!' but no business could be done without samples."

Quickly, Bannerman took passage for Europe, entrained to the Balkan kingdom with his rifle and cartridges. He met the Serbian agent in Liege and gave him the package of cartridges to smuggle through, while Bannerman decided to take the Mauser rifle to King Peter personally. At the German border the customs officer reached for the gun but the Scotchman, game to the last, cried out, *"Nein Zoll, Deutsche Mauser,"* ("no duty, German Mauser") and showed the guard the "Loewe-Berlin" stamp on the gun. But the customs officer levied a duty of 72¢, which the munitions magnate gladly paid, and continued on his way to Serbia. The ironic finale to the excursion was that Serbia agreed to buy the rifles, but Austria-Hungary refused to allow shipment, and the deal fell through.

Dealer in second-hand goods, Bannerman often tried his hand at manufacturing. In the 1880's, he became associated with Christopher M. Spencer, rifle inventor then making a pump shotgun, first of its kind and one liked by Annie Oakley. The Spencer business fell apart in 1887, and Bannerman for the next twenty years listed the Spencer factory in his catalog as "for sale."

By World War I Bannerman had grown to be the

Specialist at rebuilding long guns into short ones, Bannerman devoted a page of his 1905 catalog to short rifles which he made up for sale to cadet organizations. Piece second from top is typical of Civil War two-band rifle of Springfield type called by collectors "artillery rifle," but Bannerman's catalog makes plain fact that he built these rifles himself and they were not Civil War issue. Interesting is Sharps cadet rifle shown. Not listed under Remington, cadet rifles is special gun Bannerman made up using .50 cal. U.S. Navy pistol actions.

largest house of its kind in the United States. A cooperative bidder with rival firms like W. Stokes Kirk and Hartley & Graham, he had a better sense of publicity and appealed more to the gun crank and collector than to the revolutionary agent. Though he spiced his offerings with phrases like "special bargain prices to government war ministers," his primary appeal was to the curio collector. Remington revolvers, new at $1.85, he suggested could be grouped with brass drumstick holders (20¢), U. S. Marine brass shield (15¢), crossed sabers (10¢), and U. S. brass bridle monogram (10¢), or "All the above articles for $2.40, not including the board." The happy purchaser was supposed to make his own mounting placque, drill a hole through the revolver frame, and bolt it to the board as a "den decoration."

But Bannerman did turn out some unusual models of guns for shooting purposes. Cadet corps were outfitted with Bannerman cut-down Springfield rifles, or Remington single shot pistols converted to small infantry muskets. For the more delicate cadets, he offered "Quaker guns," his own original design, using U. S. muskets with wooden barrels. Once he owned 125,000 Springfield musket stocks, and he could make up these items from time to time from spare parts. A thousand type 1903 rifles, bored .303 caliber with complete cartridge belts and bayonets, were delivered to the British as a gift in 1914 from their Scot friend. His Majesty's Government said thank you, tried out the rifles at Hythe, found that the first shot would hit the mark, but found also that the second shot would not feed into the chamber. The big .303 rims jammed in the Mauser-type magazine. So they stamped all the guns "DP" for "Drill Purposes," and not one of them saw combat. But the spirit was there. An old British soldier told me that the Bannerman Springfield was one of the most accurate rifles he had ever handled, with that .303 cartridge on the front-lug action, for the first shot. For the founder of the firm, the first shot was the last; the sixth Francis Bannerman died in 1918.

After World War I Bannerman's firm kept active, and such deals as Civil War Smith carbines, which they sold by the thousands through Gimbel's New York store for as little as 29¢, kept them in business. They bid in thousands of the Russian Nagant rifles and proudly proclaimed that buyers should order, "as our prices are half what the ammunition companies charge." They even converted Russian rifles to .30-06, but few people care to talk about that nowadays. Such guns were definitely unsafe.

And through the years the Broadway store sold the Springfield rifled muskets, the Colt revolvers as "complete outfit, including flask, mould, caps, just $7.50." But today, with the 501 Broadway address now cleared for a parking lot, and the Island crumbling into the weather, gun fans want to know what is left at Bannerman's. The question is not easily answered. The New York store ran through the depth of a city block, had basements and sub basements, and from personal experience I know that something nobody expected always seems to crop up there. With the Island and the store, I still cannot answer the question "what's left at Bannerman," except to say "plenty." Bannerman's is full of surprises.

While Bannerman doesn't have cases of muskets left, the impossible does happen. Said the Island's caretaker, "We found a box of .50-70 rifles here last month and sent them down to the store." And from the sub basements of the store, cases and chests of parts, accouterments, artillery components, and ammunition came in bewildering confusion. The old firm, ready for a facelifting, was re-established at Blue Point, Long Island (Box 26). An aggressive selling program has put more of the Civil War relics before the collector, and Bannerman's is booming again. But they are still a little leery of that island. There is enough ammunition on that rocky crag to make it boom all by itself.

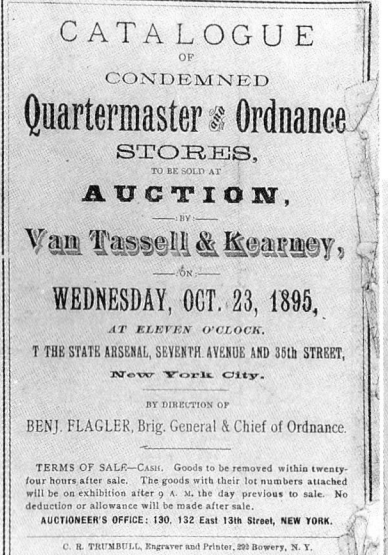

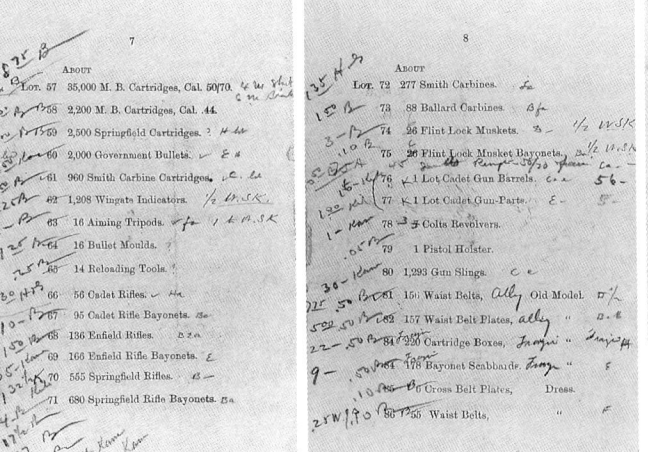

Bannerman profited by buying 88 Ballard carbines for lot price of $1, and 26 flintlock muskets for $3. He sold half to W. Stokes Kirk of Philadelphia, who with Hartley & Graham fixed auction prices in their bidding. The 1888 Bannerman catalog listed "present regulation" .45/70s but also .58s from the 1860s. No prices are shown. Guns offered "refinished" were done at Springfield Armory.

CHAPTER 35

The Rage Over Replicas

Among Civil War arms collectors there is no controversy quite so strong as that of the manufacture of replica Civil War arms. Recognizing, understanding, and sympathizing with collector friends who are opposed to this trade, I have to say that I am not in complete accord with their doctrines. The "advanced collector" argues that he is jealous of the genuine value of his genuine rare guns. He believes that the value of the genuine articles into which he has put money as much for "investment" as for collecting love, is harmed by the production of numerous copies.

Replicas, "Si;" Fakes "No"

It is true that this argument applied to currency is the motive behind the suppression of counterfeiting. Issuing additional paper money tends to debase the original issue in value. Whether issuing, say, 6,500 fluted-cylinder Army Colts by copies in this century debases the value of the genuine pistol made in 1860 is the current question. The collectors are widely split on the topic. But only a few, a vocal and respected minority, are influencing far-reaching policy decisions. For example, advanced Colt collector John S. duMont told me that he had persuaded the *American Rifleman* journal to refuse advertising from a maker of "replica" arms, Penrod O. Musser. Whether duMont had ever got stuck on the purchase of a Walker Colt hand-crafted by modern replica machinist Penrod O. Musser of California is not known to me. I doubt it, for John owns or has owned several genuine Walker Colts and knows his guns pretty well. But even the expert, when the conditions are just right, can get "taken." Yours truly paid out good money for a squareback Navy Colt which proved to be less than genuine. The odd thing was that the often-faked detail of squareback guard was entirely correct, but it had been renumbered and marked to place it in a rarer series of currently faddish popularity. The "experts" get taken,

Lack of war surplus shooting irons, such as Bannerman once sold, sparked renaissance of percussion firearms fabrication on mass scale in Italy and Belgium in late 1950s. Arms shown are products from the firms Navy Arms Co. and Centennial Arms Corp., both productions being set up abroad by author.

In Brescian shop of Vittorio Gregorelli fine Italian hands put together copies of Colt Navy revolvers. Workman standing takes whisker of metal off brass "Reb" backstrap while man with file shapes curve of 1851 barrel frame.

if unwary or too eager. Whether the wholesale manufacture of replicas of classic firearms encourages this possibility is the current debate. My own choice on the matter is, "No." I back it up by my own activities in founding and in engaging in the current business of making old-time Civil War guns for those high-priced vacant gaps in many a collection, and for the modern shooter who wants to try out the old guns. Of this business it cannot be claimed nostalgically that "They don't make them like they used to," for we do!

My first notion of replica manufacturing occurred in 1947 when from Civil War surplus parts I was able to build up a brand new Colt M1851 Navy revolver. I used the gun for shooting, even filed its bright blued barrel to fit a crosswise BAR sight blade for better aiming at short ranges. Texas collector Jimmy Voulgaris badgered me to sell him the gun, for he sought to mount the parts again on a display board to show the ingredients of the original Colts in new condition. At the time I had some hazy notion, incapable of fulfillment, that it would be fun to make the Navy Colt again. I liked the looks of the gun and it certainly was famous enough. Briefly employed by Colt's, I even conjectured if the old Hartford firm would get up steam on such a project; but other, more pressing matters of making a living intervened. Later, oddly, Colt's was to use my own make copy of one of their classics as a model from which they constructed a current $7/8$ scale replica of their own gun. But this gets too confusing too soon.

The idea and the parts-Navy stuck with me. After getting started in the gun writing game I reverted to the project casually. In 1956 Val Forgett, who was then about to found the machine gun business known as "Ma Hunter," gun importer Sam Cummings, then vice president, later president of Interarmco, and I were talking about the gun business at the latter's warehouse in Alexandria. I mentioned to Sam the prospect of having the Navy Colt manufactured. Sam replied that he had asked Erma Werke (Munich, Germany) for costs but that it would be $20 each and then 5,000 would have to be ordered. The price was prohibitive; but in a couple of years Colt prices so skyrocketed that the price no longer seemed excessive. It was in the Albergo Vittoria in Brescia, gunmaking city of Italy, in October of 1957, that Forgett, an Italian businessman, and I decided to resurrect the Navy Colt.

Navy Arms Company

"You can have anything you want made in the gun shops in Brescia," our friend told us. "What shall we make?" Val asked me. "The Navy Colt can be made for $20 in Germany; maybe it can be made for the same or less here," I replied. On a handshake a deal was made and Navy Arms Company came into being. I was to supply the model and get the business going, for I had ways of transferring the pistol to Italy quickly and could follow up on the manufacturing details.

A full study was prepared by me of manufacturing all parts of the Navy Colt. Since I possess the first prototype and the first production model I flatter myself that their attention to the fitting of the lock work, the "lock timing," is a consequence of translation and study of my manufacturing prospectus. The document included sketches of possible manufacturing set-ups, photos of engraved guns, and drawings of engraving layouts on the pistols.

Meanwhile, we tried to mail a Navy Colt to Brescia. The pistol was borrowed from a collector friend in

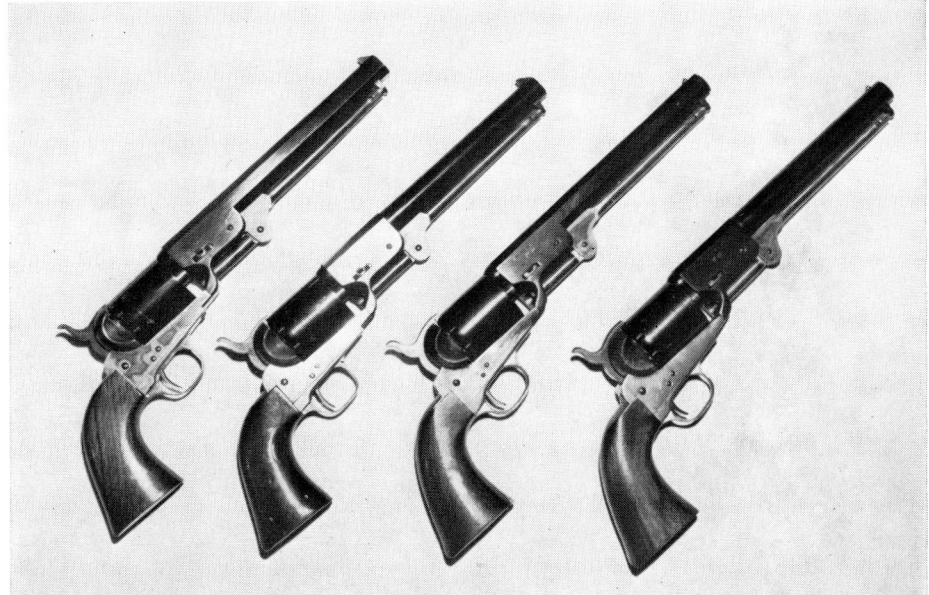

Model arms in author's collection include prototype Navy Arms pistols No. 1 "Yank" and No. 13 "Reb," left and second; third and 4th pistols show *Made In Italy* stamping on barrel, are serial numbered Yank 1, and Reb 2. Brass-framed pistol is simulation of Griswold & Gunnison, though differences are at once obvious in handle and frame shapes.

France and taken secretly to England, where it was delivered to an arms company for export directly to Italy. Though clearly marked as an antique, the pattern pistol was refused by the Italian customs authority because the addressee did not have a license to manufacture firearms. The addressee was the firm of Vittorio Gregorelli, a subcontractor to the Beretta factory on M-1 Garand and on Beretta .30 caliber carbine parts, and general machinsts to the gun trade. But, Gregorelli did not make complete guns. The pistol was returned to England.

Desperate, Val turned to me and I promised to get my model pistol No. 82 over to the Italians. In the spring of 1958 I flew to Berchtesgaden, Germany, to cover the convention of the Association of Rod & Gun Clubs, U. S. Forces, Europe. There, I turned the pistol over to Johnny Neumyer, genial outdoor writer for Stars & Stripes. Johnny was fascinated by the project and promised to deliver the gun to his brother, Major Neumyer, stationed in Italy. He did, the Major got it to Brescia, and Gregorelli began cutting metal.

To be sure that the manufacture of the pistol was perfectly understood, Gregorelli was required to make 12 model arms (for promotional and display purposes). He made not 12, but 16 guns. I believe 10 of these were copies of the Colt Navy M1851 pattern which I had supplied him, and the rest were with brass frames and round barrels, copies of the Confederate Griswold & Gunnison .36 Army revolver.

I received No. 1 of the Colt, the "Yank" and No. 13 of the "Reb" at my office only four or five days before I departed for Europe again. The models were excellent, brilliantly blued, but there were many details incorrect. "For gawdssake get over there, Bill, and get those details straightened out with the Italians," was Val's happy sentiment when I phoned him before my departure. This I did, and duly noted were some dozen changes between the prototypes and what should be produced by machine.

Most of the changes were subtle; two are obvious. The front sight in the prototypes was a blade dovetailed in from the front of the flat muzzle. This was decreed altered to a bead screwed into the top like the original Colt. Also, the screw heads of the guard screws were too large, and the brass of the guard plate had been left wide at the rear screws to surround the bigger heads. This caused the brass to project out slightly, not being flush with the thickness of the frame at that point. Also, the end of the guard plate was chopped just beyond the front guard screw; this was corrected to more nearly conform to the model. The handles on both "Yank" and "Reb" are like the Colt but not quite. I deliberately did not have them copy the inner curve and beveled angle on the back of the guard plate, since this made a quick distinction between the modern copy and the old original. The barrel tops from No. 1 of the production series were marked NAVY ARMS CO; the prototypes are unmarked.

I was later glad the grips were so different; at a meeting of the Wisconsin Gun Collectors Association several years later I saw a neatly rusted brass framed pistol tagged "Confederate, $300.00". I thought this price was a trifle unfair since Navy Arms Company only charged $89.95 list price for their pistols and that was with all the original blue and markings, not rusted and filed-off as this specimen of "Reb" that I saw before me. I did not bother to inform the advanced collector of his choice; the grip shape was a dead giveaway. Internally, of course, the tight and shallow rifling for 9mm is another giveaway. The prototypes had 7 grooves right hand (clockwise) twist; the production pistols from the first, 6 grooves.

Characteristic of the Navy Arms pistols is the absence of the Colt safety pins on shoulders between the nipples, and consequently lack of the tiny cut in hammer face to slip over these pins. The lip of hammer

First of Mississippi replicas is shown by Bernardelli worker as Edwards inspects initial production in Gardone, Brescia, in 1970. Recreation of historic arm was first discussed by author in Feb. 1946 with Edwin Pugsley of Winchester who hoped to build the rifle in the old Whitney Armory then standing unused.

has a square notch rear sight instead of Colt's Vee, a copy of the sighting notch I had filed in my own pistol for better aiming.

It was almost ten months from my visit in the summer of 1958 that corrected the production error, to the delivery of the first pistols to Navy Arms in New Jersey. From then to date the fabrication of these guns has been a steady business. Forgett thought it desirable to make a rifle, and I suggested the Remington "Zouave" rifle as being the most colorful of the Civil War patterns to be available for copying. While originally this manufacture was to be undertaken by one shop in Brescia the Italian agent of Navy Arms did not agree with the contractor as to terms, and the job was given to another maker, Zoli.

Navy Arms also contracted for the Remington .44. At about the time the Italians began to work on the Remington revolver, I learned that a Pennsylvania gunsmith and machinist, Witloe Precision, Incorporated, of Collingdale, proposed to fabricate a copy of the New Model Remington .44 and price it at $125. I happened to know that cost estimates on the Navy Arms Remington ran approximately 10 per cent of that and also, that Witloe didn't know of the pending release of the Navy Arms gun. I notified a go-between that in my opinion Witloe would lose his shirt on trying to build 5,000 of these guns to sell at $125, and let it go at that.

Witloe was too deeply committed in parts stock to stop, and for a time it appeared that he and Navy Arms might make some deal in which Navy Arms would buy him out of the Remington business. But this folded and Witloe decided to go it alone. He has produced a bronze framed model, somewhat after the Spiller & Burr Confederate guns, calling it the "Lee," with the iron framed pistol the "Grant." All are .44, 8-inch, blued finish and exceedingly well made, to justify the quite high price. Perhaps because the model of Remington copied is of most interest to the black powder target shooter, due to the sights being more in a fixed relation than the Colt style, the Witloe guns will probably not fall afoul of special markings and faking.

Mars Equipment Company

During these affairs, I was called in as a consultant to Shore Galleries, an auction firm specializing in firearms sales, and remained with this activity when the auctioneer, Sig Shore, formed a company to deal in surplus military rifles and ammunition, and secondhand guns generally. While the original concept of MARS Equipment Corporation was to engage in buying from primary importers and resell as jobbers and dealers in the United States, the market conditions dictated an expansion of the company funds into other channels. The course of manufacturing presented itself and a series of coincidences launched the now-popular Centennial Arms Corporation line of percussion shooting replica revolvers, pistols, and pistol-carbines. The success of Forgett in Navy Arms, with which Shore had dealt in the auction business, led him to decide to manufacture the Model 1860 or Colt's New Model Revolving Holster Pistol—the Colt New Model Army .44.

My work on this was at first less, ultimately considerably more effort than with launching the Navy Arms project. Shore and myself on a trip to Germany passed through Liege, Belgium. There we made the acquaintance of Mr. Paul Hanquet, great grandson of one J. Hanquet who in 1852 had signed an agreement with Sam Colt authorizing him to manufacture Colt's Patent (Colt Brevete) revolvers in Liege. Associated with Mr. Paul was his cousin, Mr. Albert Hanquet, in a company the trade mark of which is "Centaure." The rampant centaur is quite clearly lifted from the cylinder engraving of one of Colt's Paterson pistols, and "Centaure" had been handgun and musket makers in Liege for generations. Shore bought a number of muskets from these people and later, upon returning to the United States and casting about for additional work for MARS money, hit upon the idea of having them make the copy of the Colt 1860. Other people were interested in this venture and to distinguish the military and modern firearms sales business of MARS from the new venture, a new firm was organized, appropriately titled by me, Centennial Arms Corporation.

Centennial Arms Corporation

The evolution of Centennial Arms Corporation to its present position of volume producer of quality hardware was not without its "moments." The models supplied to Centaure were two: a mint parts-assembled

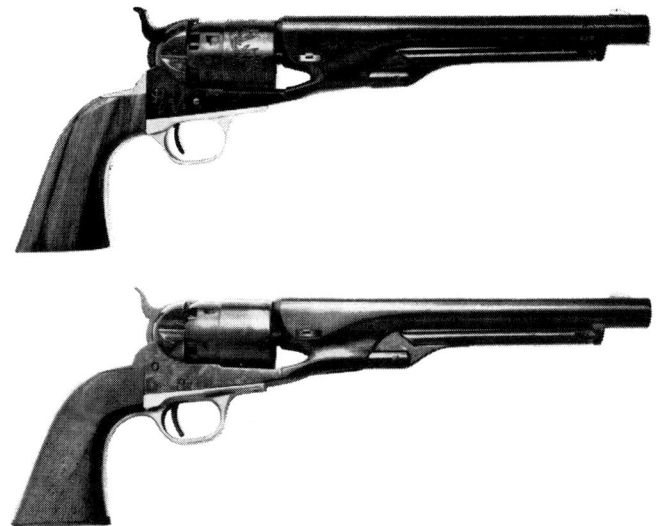

First regular Armys had plain cylinders but engraving was added copying Colt-type ship scene at about time silver plated handle "Civilian Model" was added to line late in 1960. A fluted cylinder model with attachable shoulder stock was made for sale after National Rifle Association had laws changed regarding stocked pistols.

Army 1860 that had a slightly bent trigger guard but was otherwise perfect, and a rusty but not much worn, "crisp" Army with a perfect trigger guard. The parts Army gave details for finishing, type of polishing, color of blue and such. I mistakenly assumed the contractor would recognize the scars on the guard, as if the pistol had been dropped on concrete, and take the perfect but rusty specimen as the model. Instead, as an expression of the faithfulness with which he desired to execute our wishes, the guard was copied including the dent. Thousands of guards were cast up with egg-shaped bows! Fortunately, I was in Liege to inspect the first pistol made, and caused two corrections to be introduced. The guards were all swedged to the correct shape by a steel plug and secondly, the curved line on the side of the barrel was preserved, the first pistol having been polished a little "soft" along his contour. Guns were numbered from "1" up in the series which began to duplicate the regular NMA. This was the three screw frame, cut for stock and with the toe of the butt notched for stock. Cylinder belts were plain up to about 1,400; thereafter the Navy scene was regularly furnished on regular cylinders. The first gun, unnumbered, was kept by Hanquet. The second gun stamped MODEL was given to the present president of Colts. It was engraved by me on the barrel, ADDRESS FRED ROFF, HARTFORD, CT.

As a variation after about 500 of the regular NMA had been received by Centennial Arms, the so-called "Civilian Model" was made available. This has a round frame not cut for stock, no notch in toe of butt, and the straps are silver plated. Serial numbers in this series, unlike the Colts in which they are concurrent with all other variations, run also from "1" up but prefixed by a letter to indicate the series; thus: "C1, C2, C3 . . ." Both these pistols have 8-inch barrels, rather shallow regular rifling constant twist and slow, and bear the barrel stamping 1960 NEW MODEL ARMY. The civilian cylinder bears a Navy scene engraving like the Colt but with less background detail. About 500 of these guns were made with the legend ENGAGED 16TH MAY 1843 as a part of the engraving but this was removed at the suggestion of the Ohio Gun Collectors Association board of directors to inhibit possible use of these cylinders in fakery. Actually, there are so many detail differences in the fabrication of these guns that only the most unsophisticated collector with larceny in his heart need fear getting taken by one of the Centennial pistols as an original. The boring and rifling, for example, are adapted to the .451 round ball; using the Lyman mould. For the regular Colts, Lyman offers the .457 round ball, a considerable difference in bore size.

In the spring of 1961 the first Fluted Stocked Army was turned out. As a pattern, Centaure was furnished with a rough-condition genuine 1st Model 1860 Army, 7½-inch barrel, full-fluted cylinder, four screw frame cut for stock. The first pistol completed was F9 (a prefix and numbering from 1 up being the rule also,) and it was delivered to me at a dead run by Roger Vryens of the Centaure firm as I waited for the train up to the airport to return to the United States in June,

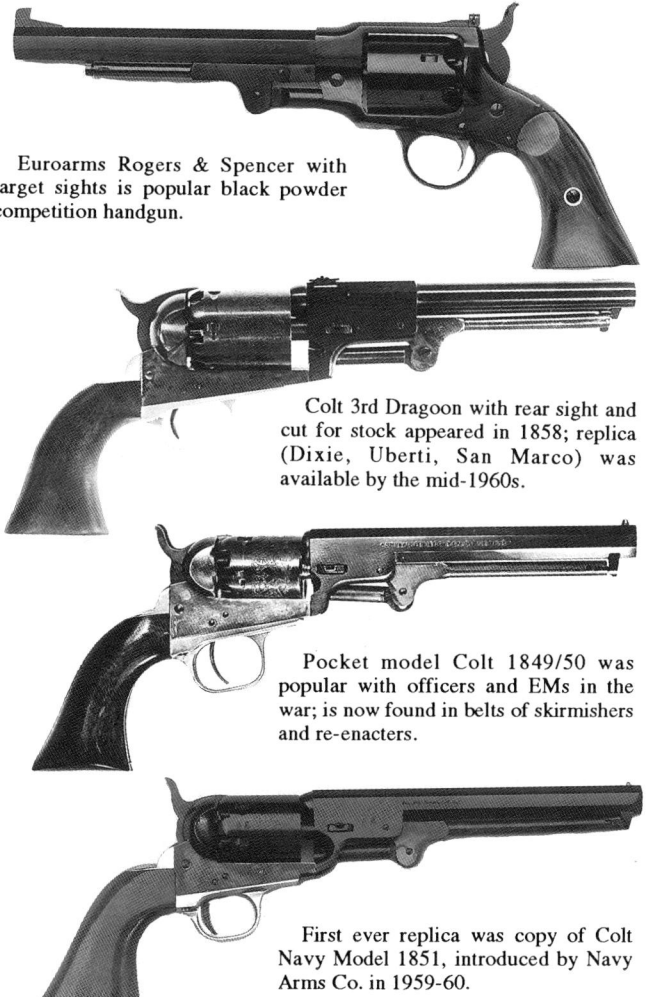

Euroarms Rogers & Spencer with target sights is popular black powder competition handgun.

Colt 3rd Dragoon with rear sight and cut for stock appeared in 1858; replica (Dixie, Uberti, San Marco) was available by the mid-1960s.

Pocket model Colt 1849/50 was popular with officers and EMs in the war; is now found in belts of skirmishers and re-enacters.

First ever replica was copy of Colt Navy Model 1851, introduced by Navy Arms Co. in 1959-60.

Hartford pistol makers resurrected lineaments of their old Model 1860 Army in cast-zinc, .22 single-shot, scale model of big cap and ball pistol. Colt's obtained two Centennial revolvers, copies of their own old M1860, to copy in turn for making their new replica of an old favorite.

1961. The backstrap had been polished and not yet blued after final fitting; I subsequently blued it in my gas stove and sold the pistol and stock at an Ohio show.

Among efforts to improve the basic form of the pistol, Centaure electro-brazed the loading lever lug to the barrel. This produced a problem which was not solved for some time. It was noticed that slight spotty rust would form about 2 inches from the muzzle, marring the otherwise brilliantly burnished swedged rifling. Repeated attempts were made to solve the cause of this, including instructions to the proof house about oiling after cleaning. Still, light rust persisted. Then I noticed in a rack of barrels not yet sent to the proof house, the same kind of rust! When this was called to the attention of the works manager he explained that to keep the heat from spoiling the bore, the workman sticks a piece of raw potato in the muzzle while brazing the lug. My only instructions were "No more raw potatoes!"

As usual with the Liege fabricants, even the larger ones, work is done here and there and then put together. Consequently the barrels are forged and drilled, rifled and turned outside, and supplied to the machine shop for further finishing. Frames are machined from a solid forging; cylinders lathed from stock. The backstrap, one piece in the Colt, is constructed in three pieces, at lower cost by avoiding use of special machinery. The top is one part, welded to the back strap, and the butt strap is then jig-welded in turn. In the event of a rare presentation engraving from Colonel Colt to General Smorgasbord appearing on a suspect backstrap, X-Ray will easily reveal the two welds and the fraud. If, in order to successfully fake up one of the Centennial arms it is necessary to attach genuine Colt parts, it is easy to see that the advent of the Centennial reproductions has added nothing to the faker's basket of tricks that wasn't in the junk pile already.

The Fluted Stocked Army owes its being to the National Rifle Association's efforts in amending existing outmoded laws, the National Firearms Act (Internal Revenue Code of 1934, 1957, 1960). Prior to 1957 the law prohibited the transfer without payment of $200 tax of any revolver or pistol to which a stock was attached, under the construction that this became a rifle having a barrel length less than 18 inches, a prohibited and taxable article. Recent pictorial publicity on collectors possessing old .44 Colts with stocks had given some of them embarrassment of a Federal investigation; while an importer risked jail and fine when it was observed by the New Orleans Customs authority that he was importing an 18th century blunderbuss having a barrel less than 18 inches in length.

Amendment to Internal Revenue Code

Accordingly, conferences were set up, through the insistence of the N.R.A. Gun Collector committee and the newly appointed Gun Collector staffman, C. Meade Patterson, to solve some of these perplexities. The result was an amendment to the code which exempted arms "not firing fixed metallic ammunition." This at one stroke simply and conclusively exempted the whole sweep of collector arms. As Patterson said in an address before the Wisconsin Gun Collectors Association that year, "So now all you collectors don't have to hide away your shoulder stocked Dragoon Colts."

While Meade charitably made it appear that the members were in possession of vast hordes of stocked Dragoons, I knew positively that the effort of the majesty of Congress in revising that bill had been in favor of perhaps five or ten collectors in the country who owned the surviving few genuine stocked Dragoon Colts, and the slightly larger group which owned the Army 1860 fluted cylinder pistols with stocks. I felt this was unfair, and that a vastly larger number of collectors and shooters should realize some benefit from the work of the N.R.A. and accordingly strengthened my resolve to build percussion guns at that moment. With the advent of the Fluted Stocked Army the mission was complete.

Curiously, the N.R.A. made possible the sale of these guns but at the same time restricts its membership from having any knowledge of them. The sale of replica arms is forbidden by the executive committees of this organization, which purports to represent the interests of the shooters of America. Advertising of replicas is rejected. A complete censorship of anything relevant to replicas in the pages of the Association's journal, *The American Rifleman*, contrasts most strangely with the plastering of pages of the other gun magazines which the replica makers do by advertising and which the gun writers do out of the interest in the subject, by feature articles. Gradually the details of the replicas, how to tell them from the real guns, etc., emerge as a body of literature builds up in the other firearms magazines. But the great body of the shooting public, allegedly the 450,000 members of the N.R.A., remain in ignorance of these facts. The N.R.A. management seems content to deprive them of the opportunity for learning how to avoid getting stung, all the while crying out that replicas are a menace to the gun collector fraternity.

Actually, the sentiment is hardly uniform within the N.R.A. on these things, but minor powerful cliques can control major aspects of policy. It is evident that is the case here. The dangers of ignorance are not too great; most of the N.R.A. members are readers of one or more of the competitive journals and perhaps on the pages of the several other gun magazines they will find that information they miss on the pages of the N.R.A. journal.

Meanwhile, the production of replica arms continues. Fabricants include other Belgian and Italian contractors for several different American sales outlets. One of the biggest general firms is Dixie Gun Works of Union City, Tennessee. Owned by Turner Kirkland, Dixie sports one of the most diversified lists of muzzle gun parts to be found. Major components for almost every percussion and flint gun ever made can be duplicated or modified from existing items in Kirkland's great stock. His "Dixie" squirrel and Kentucky rifles are great favorites, and the call for a really deluxe arm has caused him to add a fancy silver engraved Kentucky of Liege make selling for hundreds of dollars.

In this he is but returning to the fold, for Liege was the source of an astonishing number of so-called "Kentucky rifles" sold here in the 1860's and later. Duplicating the American patterns exactly, the Liege hand-made fabricants supplied the wants of the nation moving westward as industry founded on the growth of the Civil War turned to machine work in mass production. Today, some few of this nation which in recreation and hobbies delights on looking backward to the post-Civil War West, again turn to Liege to supply rifles and pistols of the same type that fought the Civil War.

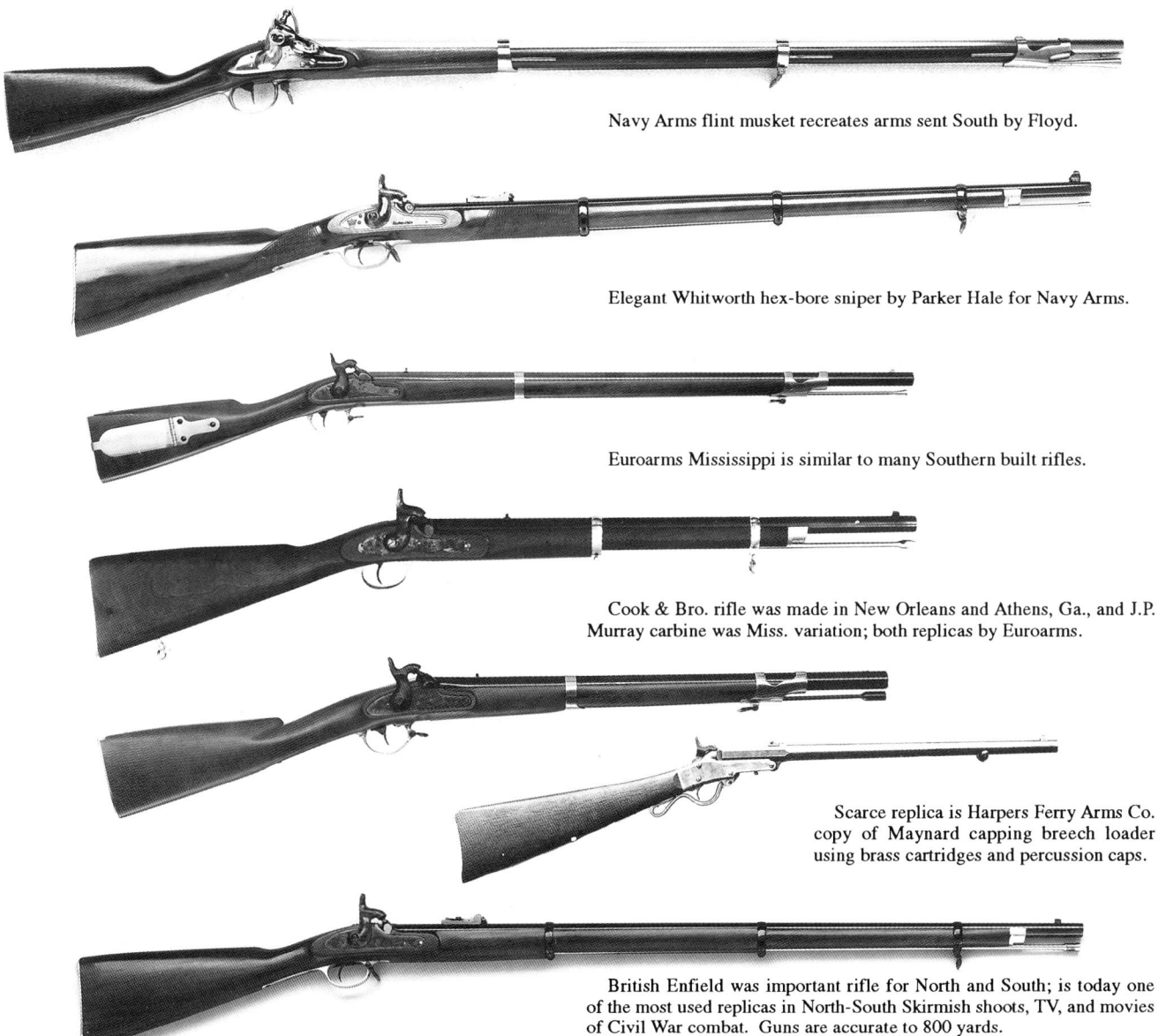

Navy Arms flint musket recreates arms sent South by Floyd.

Elegant Whitworth hex-bore sniper by Parker Hale for Navy Arms.

Euroarms Mississippi is similar to many Southern built rifles.

Cook & Bro. rifle was made in New Orleans and Athens, Ga., and J.P. Murray carbine was Miss. variation; both replicas by Euroarms.

Scarce replica is Harpers Ferry Arms Co. copy of Maynard capping breech loader using brass cartridges and percussion caps.

British Enfield was important rifle for North and South; is today one of the most used replicas in North-South Skirmish shoots, TV, and movies of Civil War combat. Guns are accurate to 800 yards.

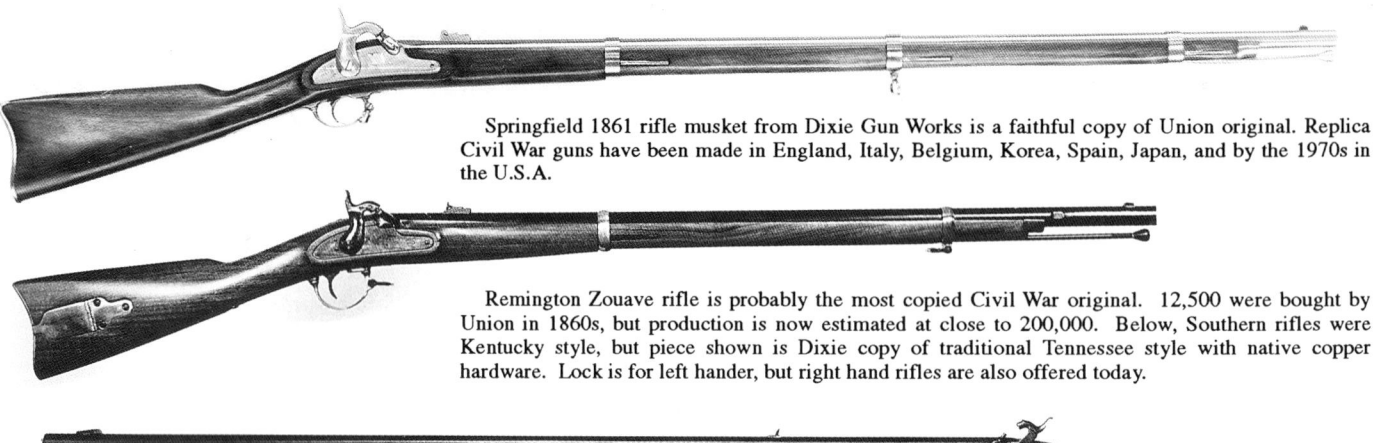

Springfield 1861 rifle musket from Dixie Gun Works is a faithful copy of Union original. Replica Civil War guns have been made in England, Italy, Belgium, Korea, Spain, Japan, and by the 1970s in the U.S.A.

Remington Zouave rifle is probably the most copied Civil War original. 12,500 were bought by Union in 1860s, but production is now estimated at close to 200,000. Below, Southern rifles were Kentucky style, but piece shown is Dixie copy of traditional Tennessee style with native copper hardware. Lock is for left hander, but right hand rifles are also offered today.

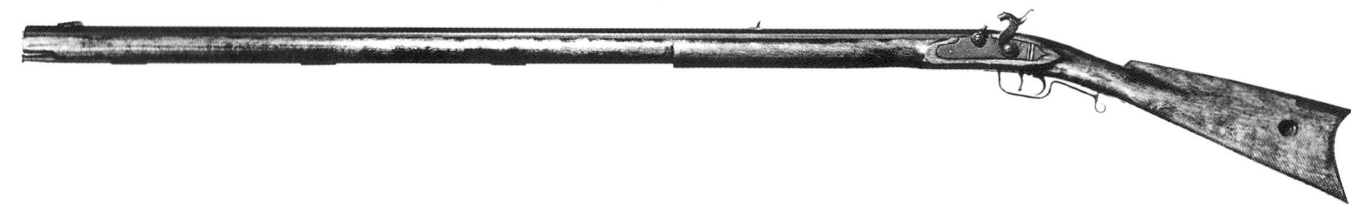

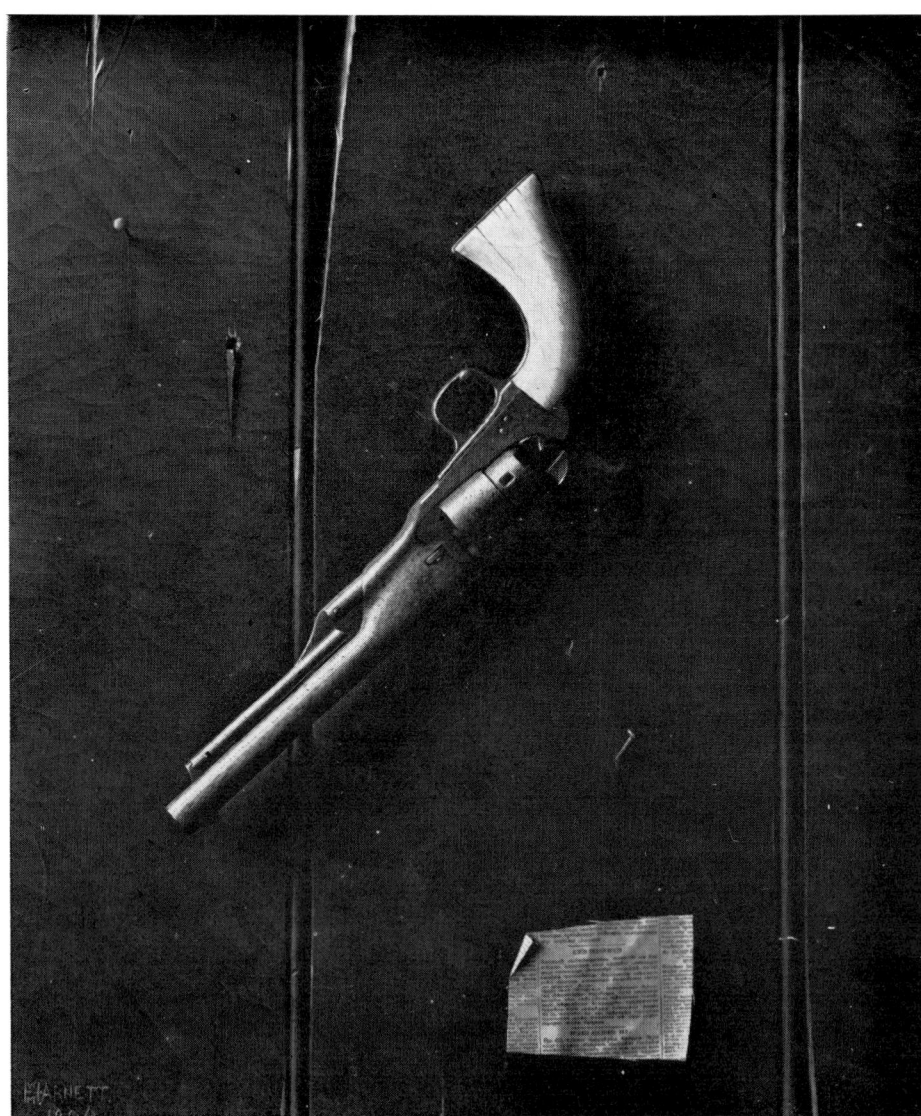

Noted painter, William Harnett, in 1890 portrayed Model 1860 Army Colt, themed nostalgia of "they don't make them like they used to" which lasted until now, when they do!

CHAPTER 36

The War Was For Real

Death took on a new face in the Civil War. It was the same family, there was the same family resemblance; the keening wail of real pain, the hopeless sobbing of the dying, gut-shot, calling in vain for cooling water as the pitiless rain splattered, churning the red Georgia dust into a soup-like mud . . . the sobbing ended on the third or perhaps the fourth day, when, without aid, Corpsmen, Sanitary Commission nor Red Cross help, the few survivors, Blue or Gray, of some nameless battle in some forgotten state finally choked to death on the rising flood of muddy water in some ditch where they had fallen, seeking shelter. All this was familiar; and the strange blue color of frostbite that shortly turned to sickening sweet gangrene, the buzzing of thin-bladed saws in hastily improvised operating "theatres" while the heavy-bodied horses stamped and sniffed nervously the smell of blood from the adjoining stall, all this would have been familiar to the veteran of Napoleon's Peninsular Campaigns or the Swedish stalwarts who fought with Gustavus Adolphus.

Effect of Minie Ball

But to the large, easily-probed holes gouged out of living flesh by round slow-moving blobs of lead of 3/4-inch diameter, a new dimension had been added—the Minie ball.

At nominal ranges, velocities were higher and were better sustained than with the round bullets. Terminal velocity—which is the dispassionate name that the ballistician gives to the "thwack" that to the living is the sound of death—terminal velocities were higher. Methods of preserving cadavers from the battlefield for study did not exist; nor would it have been a socially acceptable practice to explore the bloated mounds of flesh for causes of death. Better to bury them, sometimes without identification in mass graves, and turn your talents toward succoring the living, Doctor.

It was on the living, those who survived the trauma that the Richmond Laboratories or the bullet-stamping machine at Crittenden and Tibbals or Frankford Arsenal sought to inflict; on the living that the research was carried out to determine why they were the lucky ones, and their partners, the dead.

So it is that the literature of the era speaks of "Gunshot wounds" as if no one had died; the carefully detailed illustrations in the Medical & Surgical History of the War are of living targets, men who, broken in body, still lived. Perhaps because less extensive exploration was done than pure science might have wanted, the literature of the period is incomplete. The effect of a small missile suddenly introduced into the living system was described in extrinsic detail, but the phenomena of the wounding process itself remained much of a mystery until many wars later.

For the nature of the Minie ball wound was often so terrible, so blasting to tissue, that the cry arose "The (Rebels, Yankees; cross out one) are using explosive bullets." A shot in the extremities would, on being cleansed, reveal fragments of shattered bone several inches distant from the source of the injury. What should have been a penetrating wound (some as neatly as if a lancet were thrust between radius and ulna) became a terrible, crippling, smashing invasion of the sacred machine, splitting bones like green twigs and extravasating blood in a vast volume of tissue about the path of the projectile. War, in the Wilder-

The sacred machine stopped. Ballistic shock, hemorrhage, brought life's end to unknown Confederate soldier of Ewell's Corps during attack of May 19, 1864. Bad luck, not bad armament, caused death, for his fine Enfield long rifle, good as the North's best, lay near when Brady took this photo.

ness, at Pittsburgh Landing, at Manassas, was indeed hell.

Most Common Cause of Death

The most common cause of death was tetanus, lockjaw, indirectly, from gunshot wounds. Not all gunshots were immediately fatal. Some were complicated by bacterial contamination, often introduced into the wound later. For example, at First Manassas, where wounded were put into a farm shed or barn lively with the manure of generations of horses, the dread lockjaw was omnipresent. Yet an equally bloody battle, Shiloh or Pittsburgh Landing, had far fewer tetanus casualties; almost none. This was occasioned by the kind of soil they fought over. In the East, fields worked for seasons were dangerous with tetanus. In the West, the virgin land along the Mississippi had its share of dangers, but tetanus was one of the least of them.

Gunshot wounds reflected the changing armament of the times. One survey of 4,002 Union cases of gunshot wounds of the scalp broke down as follows: 2,612 were reported at "conoidal musket ball" or high velocity Minie-Burton type; 384 as round musket ball at low velocity, and two as explosive ball.

Explosive Bullets

The use of explosive ball ammunition in rifles has an interesting history. Such projectiles were definitely not anti-personnel missiles. The bullet was hollow, with a cavity filled with a few grains of black powder. Sometimes a conventional percussion nipple was fitted into the nose, recessed below the curve or ogive of the tip. A percussion cap was put on the nipple. Since this cap was below the level of the bullet, the projectile was not set off when it was rammed home. Or, as in the original Jacobs rifle, the ramrod was recessed inside for clearance.

British General Jacobs, of the East India Service, is recorded as being a pioneer in the practical application of explosive shell to small arms. While no Jacobs Rifles were obtained for regular issue by either side in the war, a digression on this famous rifle is worthwhile

Col. M. B. Walker, U.S., gave order for his brigade to charge after firing volley with bayonets fixed. In distance, Rebel skirmishers were deployed in the advance to draw Union fire while main body of troops stood ready in woods. Range appears about 100 yards but the Minie rifles both sides used were man-killers at 800.

here. The explosive bullet is tied up with an understanding of the savagery of the conflict, while a few Jacobs rifles could reasonably have been used by Southern chivalry as double-barrel shotguns in the early days of the war. It was deemed of sufficient importance to be fully described by Wilcox (*Rifles and Rifle Practice,* pp 208, et seq.) and was commonly known by military men in the late 1850's.

"The Jacobs rifle, so called from its maker, General Jacobs, of the East India service, is double barreled, with four deep grooves, of breadth equal to that of the lands; length of barrel 24 inches, weight of barrel six pounds; the grooves of uniform depth and twist, making four fifths of a turn in the length of the barrel; diameter of bore, .529 inches. The ball has four projections or ridges to fit the four grooves of the barrel; these projections have the same inclination as the grooves of the rifle, extending throughout the length of the cylindrical part of the ball, which is used with a thin greased patchin (sic); diameter .524 inches; it has no hollow, the base being flat and smooth; length, 2½ diameters; weight, 754 grains, charge, 68 grains.

"General Jacobs reports excellent practice with this rifle at 2,000 yards, both with the solid ball and with the shell, which is of the same exterior form as the ball. At 1,000 yards, he says that a soldier tolerably instructed, can strike a target the size of a man *once* out of *three* times. Firing at 1,200 yards, with his shells, they penetrate a brick wall several inches, and bursting, tear out large fragments. In the rammer to this rifle the head is hollow, in order that in pressing down the shell no accident may occur. A copper tube, containing the powder, and having the fulminating composition at its upper extremity, is inserted in the shell."

The use of the rifle in this period, prior to the war, when Jacobs was at work, was attractive to infantrymen who sought to disable the enemy's artillery ammunition wagons. British ordnance boards were at the time characteristically composed of artillery officers and, according to J. N. George, *British Guns & Rifles,* they took a dim view of anything tending to discredit their arm of the service. An earlier explosive ball, developed by a Captain Norton in 1824, had seven studs on it to engage the grooves of a 7-grooved Baker rifle, standard British Light Infantry arm. Norton argued, says George, that "riflemen would in future wars engage and silence enemy batteries at ranges far beyond those at which the solid bullet was effective, since by firing at their powder caissons they would be able to blow them sky-high when at a distance at which it would be next to impossible to pick off an individual gunner."

The early explosive bullet experimenters were not above using their projectiles on soldiers, since it was found that the pointed ball on rupturing presented a greater area in its passage through the body, like the old round ball, and so created a more severe wound. Because the explosive bullets were generally of large caliber anyway, the wound differences attendant on velocity increases of a "forced ball" were not at first recognized. Further, other than the Indian Mutiny and the Crimea, war-time experiences using the new Enfield "minie" bullet, actually the Pritchett bullet, were few.

Norton's bullet was studied by a British committee of artillerymen who concluded that the studs on the bullet body would be worn away by the projectiles rubbing against each other in the soldier's bullet pouch and render it useless in accuracy; they therefore reported against the use of the Norton bullet and generally condemned the principle of the explosive bullet thereby. But the principle remained a challenge to experimenters.

It was Colonel John Jacobs, founder of the Scinde Irregular Horse Regiment of Indian cavalry and the town of Jacobabad, who pushed the explosive rifle shell to the front and forced it upon the military as well as to the attention of sportsmen. The great game of India were the first proving ground of the rifle shell, but it was on a special range built wholly at his own expense at Jacobabad that (later) General Jacob performed his tests. Says J. N. George:

Some idea of the extent of Jacob's experiments will be gathered from the fact that his practice range at Jacobabad . . . extended for over two thousand yards, with massive targets of whitewashed brick, some of them as much as 50 feet wide and 40 feet high, spaced out at irregular intervals. More than fifty single and double barreled rifles and bullet moulds innumerable had to be made in London, and thence shipped to the General's Indian headquarters, before these experiments were completed and powder and lead were consumed literally by the ton in testing these weapons and projectiles. His experiments with the rifle shell alone accounted for some thousands of pounds of gunpowder, which was packed, hundreds of pounds at a time, into wooden cases or wagons meant to represent military caissons, and was successfully exploded by rifle fire at ranges varying from twelve hundred to two thousand yards.

Of the rifles themselves "Stonehenge" records that:

The recoil is by no means pleasant. The gauge is 32. This rifle does not seem to have any advantage at sporting ranges; but for military purposes it has been strongly recommended, especially in reference to the explosive shells which are used with it. In 1856, a report upon General Jacob's rifle was made to the Indian Government, which states, "that at ranges from 300 to 1200 yards the flight of the shell (used with this rifle) was always point foremost, and the elevation at the extreme range inconsiderable. The shells which struck the butt invariably burst with full effect; and practice was made by the many officers who attended, at distances which could not have been attained with any other missile." The shells alluded to in the report require a short stout barrel, and cannot be used with a long thin one, like the Enfield. For killing large animals, like the elephant or rhinocerous, they are peculiarly qualified; and I should strongly recommend elephant hunters to examine into the merits of this rifle, as made by Mr. Daw, of Threadneedle-street, London, who received his instructions from the late General Jacob.

Something of an anomaly, these short, powerful two-barrel guns for use at extra long ranges, have a stud attached to the right tube at the muzzle for attaching a bayonet like the sword bayonet of the Baker rifle, for close-in fighting!

Sixth Maine Infantry overran Confederate lines at Fredericksburg at this point, even though gray soldiers were behind stone wall. An 1855 Rifle Musket and 1856 Enfield lie in foreground. Indignity of death was heightened by comrades and thieves who turned pockets of dead inside out: former to send mementos home to loved ones, latter for gold.

The Jacobs bullet was a massive shell, thick walled, and with a not always safe type of nose primer. But experimenters continued to work, knowing that a bullet for the Enfield or Springfield type of rifle musket would have far wider an application to the battlefield, than a special projectile requiring its own species of shoulder howitzer to propel it. Although Wilhelm's *Military Dictionary*, 1883, notes "There is a strong sentiment against use of these bullets in firing at troops," this sentiment was not respected by Confederate troops at Vicksburg.

In his *Memoirs,* Grant conjectured that the defending Southern riflemen used explosive musket balls, because they thought the balls would burst over the Union trenches and do some damage. The wound damage was considerable:

"A solid ball would have hit as well. Their use is barbarous because they produce increased suffering without any increased advantage to those using them."

Officially, the Confederacy did manufacture some explosive bullets for small arms. According to Commander Minor, C.S.N., "Lt. (Beverly) Kennon ordered the manufacture of 100,000 rounds of musket shells at 15 cents apiece, of which 39,000 rounds are now at the Naval Laboratory at Atlanta, Georgia. Many were lost in New Orleans. They were of no use in the Navy and a dangerous projectile, and many exploded in the operation of ramming. Their sole value lay in the components of lead and fulminate of mercury. As Ordnance officer, I would not authorize their use."

Perhaps Lieutenant Kennon envisioned their value being fired from marksmen in the fighting tops of the ships, to set off the powder barrels beside the enemy's cannon, in a close-and-board battle. Commodore Preble noted that "C. S. Sharpshooters used explosive balls. Dr. Burton has one. A conical ball, pointed and charged with fulminate." It appears this "Kennon-shell" had no small primer but was entirely filled with fulminate; a most dangerous conception. Kennon had shells made in .69 musket caliber and .54 for Mississippi rifle, but there is no record of their practical use by the miniscule Confederate Navy.

The C. S. bullet may have been inspired by a West Point manual used in 1862 which summed up the popular experience on the subject. The manual described how "percussion bullets may be made by placing a small quantity of percussion powder, closed in a copper envelope, in the point of an ordinary rifle-musket bullet, or by casting the bullet around a small iron tube, which is afterward filled with powder and surmounted with a common percussion cap. The impact of the bullet against a substance no harder than wood is found to ignite the percussion cap or charge and produce an effective explosion. These projectiles can be used to blow up caissons and boxes containing ammunition at very long distances."

Improving on this general description of a high explosive rifle bullet was the development of Samuel Gardiner, Jr. He patented (November 23, 1863) an explosive shell which was a tiny copper vase case inside the bullet, with the neck protruding at the base. The interior was filled with powder, and the neck closed with a slow-burning powder, timed for 1¼ seconds. Ignited on firing, the projectile burst in the air without needing to hit. A total of 33,350 of these shells were issued to Federal troops in calibers .54 (363 grains), .58 (451 grains) and .69 caliber. Total purchased were 110,000 of the "Gardiner musket shells" of which 10,000 rounds were abandoned in Virginia and 10,000 used at Gettysburg.

Some of these were fired by Confederate troops. General E. L. Dana, U.S.A., informed H. E. Haydon that C. S. troops fired explosive balls at his command, and Dana's ordnance officer reported that they were Union ammunition which had been lost the day before. A form of Gardiner shell made by the South has, according to Colonel B. R. Lewis, characteristics of make and wrapping which suggest Richmond Arsenal as the place of manufacture, though the package does not conform to C. S. Government orders requiring date and arsenal of fabrication, and is marked simply "ca. .577 Enfield" in ink. The fact the ammunition packages contained explosive ammunition was revealed by the color code, the colors of string used in tying—two strands, purple and brown.

Though evidence proves explosive bullets were issued by both sides, the post-war charges that the South was barbarous by so doing were not particularly well-founded. Isolated use of musket shell against personnel were few. But there were enough to demand some consideration at the St. Petersburg, Russia, convention of 1867 which tried to get warfare back to a gentlemanly basis. The convention, to which the United States was not a party, agreed to limit explosive projectile weight to a minimum 400 grams. The American Benjamin Berkeley Hotchkiss had been developing a rapid fire gun of rifle caliber—a specimen with nine barrels in approximately .45 caliber was tested by the U. S. Navy about 1869—but the St. Petersburg convention bound him to use larger calibers for explosive projectiles. He accordingly took an extra margin for his minimum shell, and designed a projectile of "ideal" form which coincidentally measured 37 millimeters diameter when he turned one up. Thus did the 37mm caliber come into existence, one of the most popular sizes of light ordnance of all time. Honor being put into the discard after World War I, explosive projectiles again returned in small calibers, 20mm for aircraft cannon and, in World War II, many nations used rifle bullets carrying a bursting charge. German "B-Patronen" 8mm fired at a steel plate at 50 yards distance makes a blinding blue flash on impact, and if deflected will leave a sky trace visible in daylight for several seconds. The Gardiner musket shell evidently left a sky trace, too, but the possible value of a tracing projectile for spotting rifle fire or locating targets for artillery did not occur to the Blue and Gray soldiers.

Other Causes of Severe Wounds from Bullets

Not all the explosive wounds were caused by gunpowder-filled musket shells. Little understood at the time, though recent research has shed some light on the subject, was the existence of a temporary wound cavity of enormous proportions during the passage of the bullet. This temporary cavity was caused by a transfer of energy from the bullet point tangent to the body, to the fluids of the body. Since water is incompressible, the result is to accelerate the water, hence the flesh, rapidly away from the projectile due to the lighter inertia of the body tissue. This energy imparted to the tissue caused development of a cavity which expanded to many times the size of the bullet, flexing several times as the elasticity of the muscle fibers tried to restrict the cavity against the force of the energy-transferred fluids. The effect was to cause a secondary rending and tearing of the flesh.

The passing of the bullet excavated, by physically destroying flesh equal to the diameter of the bullet. The temporary cavity ruptured blood vessels, extravasated blood, and "pulped" flesh throughout a far greater volume. This pulping or secondary damage from the temporary cavity was proportional to the velocity of the bullet.

Though the truly high velocities of today's light sporting rifle bullets, pencil-like jacketed pellets of 150-200 grains weight average travelling at 3,000 feet per second, were not approached, the real velocity of the Minie bullet or the long, slender Whitworth sniper slug of .45 caliber were from 20 per cent to 100 per cent higher at termination than the round ball musket projectiles. The wounding effect, though not as extreme as the pulping from a high velocity modern expanding bullet that "spoils too much meat," as the hunter says, was still terrible by contrast with common experience.

Accusation of being explosive bullets lay with such experience, resulting from improved ballistics of the new weapons. Medical science of the day had no understanding of the phenomenon. Only at the time of the Korean War, by using high speed X-Ray movies of dogs shot with steel bullets at high velocities, has this temporary cavity effect been reduced to understanding. At the time of the Civil War, experience with various kinds of gunshot wounds was slight—indeed, experience in military medicine, and medical personnel, were in short supply.

Medical Techniques of the Civil War

A few of the Regular Army medical officers had some experience in the Mexican War and Indian border incidents. Others had observed combat casualties or served as volunteers in the Crimea. City surgeons knew gunshot wounds from the police clientele, or gentleman duellists. But prompt diagnosis of the extent of injury, skillful surgery, the initiative and ingenuity to use poor instruments or ill-adapted apparatus, and the techniques of dressing in the prospect of long delays before bandages could be renewed—in all these skills the new Army medics were weak. Fortunately (for the less-severely wounded) the well-informed military surgeons were often in positions where they could help instruct the volunteers, and the current works of medical literature were relied upon.

The most valuable instruction was a series of pocket manuals issued by the Sanitary Commission on the more important operations, camp and field diseases. Indeed, except for the Bull Run casualties and a few injuries from occasional skirmishes in Virginia in the opening days of the war, the Union doctors had little to do except examine recruits and enforce hygiene in camps. Meanwhile, the volunteer surgeons and assist-

Dramatic Kurz & Allison litho of battle of Kenesaw Mountain, June 27, 1864, between Sherman and Gen. Moody McCook on Union side and C.S. General Johnston seems corny but is realistic presentation of point-blank musketry duels engaged in by soldiers generally armed for first time in history of warfare with accurate rifles. Foolhardy tactic explains, but does not excuse, record bloodbaths of battles.

ant surgeons, approximately 4,000 of them throughout the war, studied the Sanitary Commission handbooks until they knew the fundamentals of battlefield repair. As the war wore on, back from battle rolled the ebb-tide of broken bodies.

To the problems of repair and treatment after gunshot wounds, a whole new generation of sawbones gave their devoted, Herculean attention. Wounds received in battle were almost always attended with considerable —often dangerous or fatal—hemorrhage. Checking bleeding before it induced shock was of first importance. Adapted from the French service, some form of tourniquet was used: a tie, suspenders, an old rope. But risk of damage from gangrene by shutting off the flow too long caused Dr. Alexander B. Mott of the Sanitary Commission to devise a tourniquet of two strips of metal, strapped at the ends. This left the blood vessels at the sides, as of the leg, free to carry the load, since the pressure was exerted by a pad on one strip, and at a point opposite when the strips were drawn up.

"The use of powerful styptics," states a contemporary account, "has been recommended by some surgeons, and soldiers were advised to carry a small bottle of some of these styptics with them; but the most eminent surgeons disapprove of their use in wounds of the limbs whenever the tourniquet can be substituted for them, as their use is almost invariably followed by extensive sloughing and ulceration, and they are often unsuccessful in checking the hemorrhage, forming only a huge clot, which, falling away after a short time, leaves the orifice larger and the hemorrhage more profuse than at first."

In head wounds or places where a tourniquet could not be applied, the styptics, such as persulphate or perchloride of iron, or alum styptic, were useful. A piece of lint which in more glamorous though less sanitary accounts may have been the undergarments of some Southern belle, shredded into fibers, was saturated with the solution and laid over the bleeding. A larger fold of dry linen was put on top and moderate pressure applied for a short time to hold it in place. Uniform and moderate pressure with a roller bandage snugly applied was generally enough to close the smaller blood vessels and inhibit bleeding from the larger. "In the field hospitals there is so much difficulty in the proper application of roller bandages that they are seldom used, a piece of cloth or lint wetted in cool water being the usual application," said the *American Annual Cyclopedia* for 1864.

More equipment than a roller bandage and torn handkerchief was needed for the increasingly devastating wounds caused by the Minie ball. So similar was the appearance of the Minie wound to that of an explosive ball, that the two were often lumped together in medical discussions of wounds as two phases of the same problem.

The round musket ball, even of large diameter—.69 or .70 calibers—was readily thrown from its course on striking bone, tendon, even firm muscle tissue. Velocity was low and in spite of mass, the inertia was less; therefore less easily deflected. The Minie ball at greater velocity had two points in its favor. As to mass, it was equal to that of a round ball considerably larger in diameter, or much greater than a round ball of equal diameter. It was also thrown at a higher average velocity and, due to the form of the bullet, the velocity was disproportionately higher at the target, than a round ball of the same caliber. The Minie in its passage drove straight on through muscle, tendon, and bone, leaving a jagged, ugly wound. The temporary cavity effect, though not so large in proportion as the pulping caused by a modern high velocity bullet, was yet far greater than the neat wound channel of a spent round ball.

Contemporary Studies of Bullet Wounds

Considerable brain power was spent in studying this new aspect of medicine on the battlefield. At best an inexact science, medicine had no quick answers for the changed diagnosis and prognosis for Minie wounds, but doctors North and South were probing the problem. Surgeon E. Lloyd Howard, 27th Regiment North Carolina, Cooke's Brigade, published a thought-provoking if not entirely correct study of the matter in the *Confederate States Medical and Surgical Journal,* June, 1864:

Art. VI—The Effects of Minie Balls on Bone.
Since the introduction of the Minie ball into warfare, surgical writers, with entire unanimity, have agreed that wounds of bony structures, inflicted by this missile, are characterized by extensive fissuring and comminution, such as was rarely, if ever, seen when the old smooth-bore musket was the weapon of the soldier. In every recent work on military surgery, we are told that the adoption of the improved weapon has "revolutionized" this branch of the science, and these writers would have us believe that this supposed extensive fissuring of bone is a new element, which should materially modify our prognosis and treatment of this class of injuries.
This doctrine I believe to be false in theory, and directly contrary to the teachings of experience.
The difference in the effects of the two balls depends upon their different rates of velocity; consequently, we should naturally expect that the missile having the greater degree of force, would cause the lesser splintering of bone—just as we see a bullet from a rifle pierce a pane of glass, leaving a clean, round orifice, without radiating fractures, while the same projectile, thrown with less velocity, as from the hand, will shatter the glass into fragments.
In a late publication, "A Manual of Military Surgery," prepared for the use of the Confederate States Army, by order of the Surgeon-General, we find, in the chapter on gunshot wounds, the following passages:
"When a cannon ball, at full speed, strikes, in direct line, a part of the body, it carries away all before it. If it be part of one of the extremities which is thus removed, the end remaining attached to the body presents a stump with nearly a level surface of darkly contused, almost pulpified tissues. Minute particles of bone will be found among the soft tissues on one side, but the portion of the shaft of the bone remaining in situ is probably entire . . . In ricochet firing, or in any case where the force of the cannon shot is partly expended, the extremity, or portion of the trunk, may be equally carried away; but the laceration of the remaining parts of the body will be greater. The surface of the wound will be less; even muscles will be separated from each other and hang loosely, offering, at their divided ends, little appearance of vitality; spiculae of larger size will probably be found among them, and the shaft may be found shattered and split far above the line of the transverse division."
The description of the difference in wounds, caused by balls at great and lesser velocity, is well drawn and true to nature. But, though admitting this difference in the case of cannon-balls, the writer alleges a directly opposite condition to exist in wounds from musket balls. At page 41 occurs the following: "A rifle bullet which splits up a long bone into many longitudinal fragments, inflicts a very much more serious injury than the ordinary fracture effected by the ball from the smoothbore musket."

Why should not here, also the projectile of more rapid flight produce the cleaner section, just as has been admitted to be the case with cannon shot? It may be said that there are other points of difference between the two missiles than that of velocity—as the conical form, and the rotary motion of the Minie ball—two features wanting to that of the smooth-bore.
How the rotary motion could have any influence in producing the fissuring, is not apparent. The form of the conical ball gives it, it is asserted, the peculiar power of the wedge, and that it is by virtue of this power that it produces the supposed fissuring. That this wedge-like shape gives the ball easier passage through the air or other obstacles of slight molecular tenacity, which it may encounter in its flight, may be true. On meeting with an object of greater density and of fibrous structure, that the fibres should rather be separated in their length than torn across by such a missile, giving it passage through the rent, would seem a natural supposition, and such separation be apt to extend beyond the immediate point struck. But that such is not the fact in the case under consideration, experience abundantly proves. When a conical ball strikes a plank, we find as little splitting of the wood as from a round ball; and here the fibrous character of the substance is far more marked than in the case of bone.
That this wedge power is not exercised, is partly due to the fact that immediately, on contact, the leaden missile is somewhat flattened out of its original shape, (even by substances of less density than its own), but principally because great velocity robs the wedge of its peculiar force, which is essentially slow in its action (sic!).
Wounds from the smoothbore musket are now but rarely seen by the army surgeon (June 1864), but we often have presented to us injuries of a similar character from fragments of shell, balls from spherical case shot, and the rifle ball, whose force has been partly expended by distance, etc., and the similarity of this last to wounds from round balls is an additional argument, if any were needed, against the theory of wedge-action. In these cases I have almost invariably found more extensive comminution than in those where the limb has been pierced by the Minie ball in full flight.
When you have a ball impacted in the shaft of a bone, you will generally find fissures extending for a considerable distance both upwards and downwards. I have frequently seen this in wounds from the round leaden ball, musket-size, from spherical case, whose velocity is seldom sufficient to carry it entirely through a limb.
On the other hand, where we have a limb pierced by the Minie ball, with the orifices of entrance and of exit of the same size and appearance—which is an indication that the ball passed at great velocity, with unimpaired force, we may feel assured that a clean cut has been made through the bone, and that there is no great fissuring around the immediate vicinity of the point struck. In the large number of amputations and resections for wounds of this nature, which I have witnessed upon the different battle-fields, rarely, if ever, have I seen fissures extending along the shafts of the bone.
Both the Minie and the round ball, in passing through a bone, destroy everything in their paths; but the missile of the lesser velocity exerts its destructive influence over a wider sphere around that path than that of the greater speed, whose injurious effects are confined to its immediate track, just as I have before illustrated, in the case of the pane of glass.

Internal Repairs not Attempted

How many gallant North Carolinians Surgeon Howard killed with his bungling analysis of gunshot wounds is a toll of death no rolls record. But he should perhaps be forgiven his faulty diagnosis of high velocity wounds and their supposedly slight bone damage between those neat holes of entrance and exit, for little exploratory surgery was ever resorted to on the battlefield dressing table. Surgeon Howard preferred in his practice of the inexact science to draw exact inferences and make generalizations good for all cases. That such an approach to medicine is impossible was not revealed to him in his study of gunshot wounds, because he overlooked one branch of preservative surgery to which more modern medicos have, often broken heartedly, devoted their career. This is repairs of gunshots within the body cavity itself.

The doctor brave enough to rip open an abdominal wall and go in and stitch the little holes in a perforated intestine might have existed, but the new work of Pasteur was but a medical journal report, not reduced to practice, and Lister's antiseptics had not yet gained any general acceptance though gallons of rot-gut were poured into festering wounds in a dim-sighted understanding that this was "cleaning" them. Death for sure sat on the shoulder of any doctor who did such drastic surgery under the battlefield conditions of sanitation; death probably claimed its victim in the presence of all the clean towels and "hot water" the students could prepare at the most advanced medical college. Howard's experience in dealing actively with gunshot wounds, as was the experience of most other physicians, related strictly to the arms and legs; in working with these, was the most success to be found. For success, read: the patient lived, even though a multiple amputee. Howard's appraisal of internal damage from higher-velocity bullets was quite incorrect and must have led to a great deal of suffering. Repairs effected without proper surgery were but a tribute to the tenacity with which the physiognomy of the injured soldier repaired itself.

Some Ignorance Persisted Until Very Recently

Such confusion over gunshot injuries remained a part of Army medical gospel and was shared by some surgeons even as late as the 1950's. During the Korean War the small-caliber high velocity (1,300 f.p.s. M/v) Russian PPSH-41 submachine guns were in great use by the Chinese Communist Forces. It was not uncommon for an American soldier to be brought in by medical corpsmen with five or six bullet holes across his body, from the small .30 caliber Mauser pistol bullets the Russian burp gun fired. The relatively undamaged area about the holes, often appearing to be nothing more than little blue punctures, entrance and exit, caused a great many men to be given only temporary aid, when they needed a complete opening up and repair of the very extensive internal damage done by what was discovered experimentally to be the temporary cavity effect.

The death tolls from these insignificant-appearing wounds were out of proportion to their seeming severity, and extensive studies were conducted at Princeton University on the mechanics of gunshot wounds. High speed motion pictures using X-Ray film were hooked up to illustrate the passage of a steel ball through the leg of a live, anesthetized dog or cat; body shots were also studied.

The small bullet at velocities around 4,000 feet per second would create a prodigious cavity many times its own diameter. Enlargement of the photographs showed the ball to be tangent to the interior of this cavity only at one point: the point on the surface of the ball that was in the direction of the line of flight. The cavity extended actually *forward* of the position of the ball, the point of tangency internally appearing as a stem. The ball appeared to rest on this like a golf ball on a tee.

The presence of this cavity, and its form, was explained by the hydraulic nature of the mechanical damage being wrought by the bullet. Perhaps if hydraulic machinery manufacturer Colonel James T. Wilder had been approached by doctors as to why his Spencer-armed brigades were such butchers, he might have come up with an answer at least more scientific than Dr. Howard's essay. For the fluids in the muscle are accelerated away from the ball, due to their lighter mass,

Modern skeptics are convinced of Minie ball's devastation when exhibitions of shooting between military men armed with Garands conclude with victory to North South Skirmish Association members armed with Civil War rifle muskets. Target, 2 x 4 stake, is cut in half by bullets, recalls forests chopped off breast high by rifle fire in Civil War. Scene pictured is from annual fete at Ford museum's Greenfield Village, Dearborn, Mich.

momentarily faster than the ball itself and hence the creation of the "stem" when the temporary cavity extended beyond the position of the ball momentarily. These phenomena were clearly visible at ultra high velocities, but that they existed in moderate form at lower velocities is indisputable. Nevertheless, that phenomena in physics which is known as the rate of propagation of stresses, or the speed with which the physical smashing effect (avoid use of the word "shock") of the bullet is transmitted to the bones struck, created confusion in the minds of Dr. Howard and his contemporaries.

Bone Damage

Howard noticed that round balls made a seemingly more severe wound, greater comminution of bone. The word describes bone made small or fine as by grinding. What was overlooked by Howard but not ignored in the official histories of Civil War medicine was the shattering effect sometimes found in Minie wounds which caused a wound much more severe than the neat entrance-exit holes other times observed. For when the round ball hit, it sheared and chopped its way through the leg; when the Minie hit *with enough speed,* the bone might be split and shattered into large fragments, each one of which proceeded off in a direction roughly spherical to the point of impact, causing severe secondary lacerations. Howard's views are interesting; they were not authoritative for diagnosis.

If the word is not challenged as inappropriate, the subject of death had its wryly humorous aspect. One was in the oft-repeated "accident" of getting one's foot knocked off by a cannon ball. Though slow moving, less than sonic velocity and of size to make them plainly visible as they neared, the popular 12-pounder round ball of about 4½-inch dameter sent a good many voluntary injuries to the rear. So leisurely did a cannon ball bound along as it skipped through wagons, mules, and infantry ranks seemingly undeterred by the gory mass piled up behind it, that the soldier was not above sticking his foot out to "stop" it. "Comminuted" is a good description indeed for the hash that remained as the stump of the soldier's leg. At good speed, the shock was not transmitted through the leg because the rate of motion of the projectile was faster than the propagation of stresses through the limb. The wound was a sheared wound. At slowest speeds, the leg might be torn off at the hip or smashed at the knee. The "joke" was on the man who sought to escape battle and be returned to the rear with a "minor" wound.

Head Injuries

Dr. Paul Steiner, writing in *Military Medicine,* May, 1956, gives some interesting notes on head injuries, evidently at relatively low velocities. "Was it worth while having men with head wounds carried from the field?" was a topic of interest to surgeons in the spring of 1864. Brigadier General Alexander S. Webb and Brigadier General James S. Wadsworth discussed the matter; both were to fall victim of head wounds, Wadsworth to die, Webb to remember and to write about it.

Matthew Brady's ubiquitous bright rifle musket adds incongruous note to grim lesson of war: the silent brutality of death which the living too soon forget. Bounding lazily like a ball, spent 12-pounder shell has disembowled Federal soldier.

Webb noted to Wadsworth that in his experience a case was past cure if, with a head wound, when he slowly lost his vertical position he was incapable of making a movement of his head from the ground. Webb, wounded at Gettysburg at the head of his brigade while repelling Pickett's Charge, was a second time hit at the "Bloody Angle" in the Battle of Spotsylvania Court House, May 12, 1864.

"The bullet passed through the corner of my eye and came out behind my ear," he recalled. "While falling from the horse to the ground I recalled my conversation with General Wadsworth; when I struck the ground I made an effort to raise my head, and when I found I could do so, I made up my mind I was not going to die of that wound, and then I fainted." General Webb recovered slowly, and though not again assigned to command it was not from any lack of mental ability. As chief-of-staff to Meade, then commanding the Army of the Potomac, Webb finished the war as a brevet major general, U. S. Army, and was honorably discharged at his own request in 1870.

His colleague General Wadsworth fared less easily. On May 6, 1864, the second day of the battle of the Wilderness, General Wadsworth led his men in a charge up the Plank Road and fell from a bullet in the head. His last day was recorded by a young physician, Z. Boylston Adams, of Massachusetts, a captain of G Company, 56th Massachusetts V. I., who had been injured in the leg and captured at the time General Wadsworth's body was recovered by the Confederates. In attendance on the wounded were Doctors Miner and Gaston, of Mahone's brigade, A. P. Hill's corps. Says Adams of the doctors, "both smelled pretty strongly of whisky," which was as much a tonic for a doctor elbows deep in blood after the carnage of a typical Civil War battle, as it was a soporific for the injured to help knock out the pain as the saws bit deeper. When Adams regained consciousness after a leg amputation he saw he was lying beside a Union general with a tag in his hand reading "General James S. Wadsworth."

"I lifted his eyelids, but there was 'no speculation in

those eyes,'" Adams relates. "I felt his pulse, which was going regularly. His breathing was a little labored. There was no expression of pain, but occasionally a deep sigh. His noble features were calm and natural, except that his mouth was drawn down at the left side. His right arm was evidently paralyzed, which indicated that the injury was to the left brain. Examining further, I found that a musket ball had entered the top of his head a little to the left of the median line . . .

"The surgeons came Saurday night and examined General Wadsworth's wound, removing a piece of the skull, and then probing for the ball; (the latter struck me as bad surgery). One remarkable thing about the case was that the ball had entered near the top of the head, had gone forward, and was lodged in the anterior lobe of the left side of the brain. One can only conjecture how such a wound was received, but I have since learned that his horse was shot and fell with him, and it may have been that he was hit as he fell forward, or bent forward his head in anticipation of a volley from the advancing enemy. He seemed to be unable to swallow, for if more than a teaspoonful was put into his lips, it ran out of the corners of his mouth upon his beard. Occasionally he heaved a deep sigh, but otherwise lay in calm slumber. On Sunday the 8th, he became comatose, with rising and falling respiration and ceased to breathe finally at near two p.m. having lived about forty-eight hours since his wounding."

The Human Spirit Endures

Of the treatment for the wounded available even in the last months of the war, Adams had little praise. He was taken to another part of the field where he lay without shelter, almost unnoticed among the hundreds of other wounded collected there. So diligent was the North in certain aspects of the blockade that medicines and drugs were "countraband." The "Anaconda" systematically prevented shipments of drugs and surgical instruments to the South, a "measure which did not shorten the conflict by a day, but cost the Southern troops untold agony," as Allen Nevins observes in his essay "The Glorious and the Terrible" *Saturday Review*, September 2, 1961. Adams had been among the lucky: he had been operated on under benefit of chloroform anesthetic. When he came to, "Of what happened about me during this ten or eleven days that I lay on this part of the Wilderness battlefield, I have but a vague rememberance. It seems like a horrid nightmare. The groans and complaints of the wounded sufferers, the foul stench, the tormenting gnats and flies, the pain and fever, thirst, vomiting and diarrhea, the sense of loneliness and abandonment, every one around me being utter strangers, the back raw from lying on the ground, the hot sun against which the scanty foliage of the trees afforded little protection, the maggots which got into my wounds—how can I tell all the horror of that time! . . ."

This then was the end product of the guns of the Civil War. The 620,000 dead in both armies, North and South, were the lucky ones. Those who picked up a Minie ball and lived to regret it carried the terrible memories to the end. Yet somehow the fraternal strife to many was truly over, once the peace at Appomattox was signed. The tales of hospitality on the part of the Southern survivors in their later regimental fraternal associations, to the regimental survivors of their enemies who travelled over many of the battlefields in the 1880's and even after, and the courtesy and spirit of forgiving friendship with which Northern veterans welcomed Southern parties of visitors, is an incredible sequel to the greatest conflict in the Western Hemisphere. The Nation divided against itself did not fall. Guns North and South boomed defiance and, ultimately, for one side victory and for the other, a curiously honorable defeat. It is this story which the collector, the student, the historian finds today in records of the guns of the Civil War.

Confederate flag flies high honoring 3,364 dead and over 52,000 P.O.W.s held at Yankee Point Lookout, Md., camp. At right, replica Enfields on Memorial Day salute Rebs at Staunton, Va., CSA monument.

Photo courtesy Charles Culbertson, Staunton

APPENDIX

Bibliography

A SELECTED READING LIST

Albaugh, William A. III, *The American Arms Collector*, Jan. 1958
———, and Simmons, Edward N., *Confederate Arms*, Harrisburg, 1957
American Annual Encyclopedia, 1864
An Impressed New Yorker, *Thirteen Months in the Confederate Army*
Battles and Leaders of the Civil War, Century Co., N. Y., 1887
Blackburn, Jim, *The Gun Report*, October 1961
Blanch, H. J., *A History of Guns*, London, 1909
Bruce, Robert V., *Lincoln and the Tools of War*, New York, 1956
Buckeridge, J. O., "Abe and His Secret Weapon," *The Saturday Evening Post*, March 31, 1956
Burnside, Graham, *The Gun Report*, December 1959
Butler, Benjamin F., *Butler's Book*, Boston, 1892
Chinn, Col. G. M., *The Machine Gun*, Washington, 1951
Confederate States Medical Journal, June 1864
"Correspondence on the Purchase of Arms," *Proceedings of Commission on Ordnance & Ordance Stores*, Ex. Doc. No. 72, 37th Cong., 2d Sess.
Crump, Irving, *How a Boy Made the First Remington*
Daily South Carolinian, November 2, 1864
Davis, Glenn, *Butler and His Cavalry in the War of Secession*
De Forest, W. H., *A Volunteer's Adventures*
Edwards, William B., *The Story of the Colt Revolver*, Harrisburg, 1953
Freedley, Edwin T., *Philadelphia and Its Manufactries*
Fremantle, A. J. L., *Three Months in the Southern States*, Mobile, S. H. Goetzel, 1864
Ford, A. P., *Life in the Confederate Army*
Fuller, Claud, *The Rifled Musket*, Harrisburg, 1958
———, and Steuart, Richard D., *Firearms of the Confederacy*, Huntington, 1944
George, J. N., *English Pistols and Revolvers*, New York, 1962
———, *English Guns and Rifles*, Harrisburg, 1947
Golden State Arms, *World's Guns*
Gluckman, Col. Arcadi, and Saterlee, L. D., *American Gunmakers*, Harrisburg, 1953
Greener, W. W., *The Gun and Its Development*, London, 1881
Gun Report, January 1959
Harris, Clive, *History of the Proof House*
Hartford Courant, March 15, 1874

Hatch, Alden, *Remington Arms in American History*, N. Y., Rinehart, 1961
Haw, S. B., *Army Ordnance*, Jan.-Feb., 1938
Heitman, Francis B., *Historical Register and Dictionary of the United States Army*
Horan, James D., *Confederate Agent*
Lewis, Col. B. R., *Notes on Ammunition of the American Civil War*, Washington, 1959
Longstaff, Maj. Frederick V., *The Machine Gun*
Memphis Daily Appeal, November 15, 1861
Mitchell, James H., *Colt, the Man, the Arms, the Armory*, Harrisburg, 1959
Nevins, Allan, *Saturday Review*, September 2, 1961
New York Herald, 1870
New York Tribune, March 9, 1888
Nutter, Waldo E., *Manhattan Firearms*, Harrisburg, 1959
Official Records of the Rebellion, GPO, 1891
Ordnance Contracts, Ex. Doc. No. 99, 40th Cong., 2d Sess.
Parsons, John E., "New Light on Old Colts," *The Texas Gun Collector*, March, 1951
Peterson, Harold, *The American Gun*, Winter 1961
Pollard, Edward A., *The Lost Cause*
Pollard, Maj. H. B. C., *A History of Firearms*
"Remington Arms, A New Chapter in an Old Story," *The American Rifleman*, New York, 1912
Remington Centennial Book
Report on Arms Sales, 1870, Report No. 183, 42nd Cong., 2d Sess.
Ripley, Col. William, *Vermont Riflemen*
Sawyer, Charles W., *John Metcalf, Old-Time American Rifleman*
———, *Our Rifles*
Schumaker, Perry, *Colt's Pocket Pistols*
Smith, Winston O., *The Sharps Rifle*, New York, 1943
Southern Historical Society Papers
Stevens, Capt. C. A., *History of the Sharpshooters*
Suydam, Charles R., *The American Cartridge*
Texas Gun Collector, September 1955
Tice, James, *Shotgun News*, December 15, 1961
U. S. Army, *Instructions for Making Quarterly Returns of Ordnance and Ordnance Stores*, 1865
Walsh, J. H., *The Shot-gun and Sporting Rifle*, London, 1862
Wilcox, Cadmus M., *Rifles and Rifle Practice*
Wiley, Bell I., *The Life of Billy Yank*, Indianapolis, 1951
Williamson, Harold F., *With Sherman to the Sea*
Young, Clifford M., *American Arms Collector*, July 1957

Index

A

Accessories, 42; 119; 122; 127; 137; 142; 148
Adams, Hon. Charles Francis, 65
Adams Express expedites Fremont arms, 133
Adams Revolving Arms Co. of N.Y., 96
Adams, Robert, of LACo., 85; and Huse, 86; revolver, 72; 96-8
Adams, Solomon, of Va. visits Springfield, 376
Adams, Dr. Z. Boyleston wounded, 437-8
Ainslee & Cochran, Louisville, rifles, 29
Alabama cadets, before legislature, 83
Alabama, receives arms samples, 349
Alabama, University of, 82
Alabama troops, 10th Inf. charges USSS, 226
Albert, Col. former officer Austrian Army, 134
Alden, Capt. James Dean, and Colt, 307
Alexander, C. W., CS carbine by, 390
Allen, Brown & Luther, S & W meet, 168
Allen, Ethan, 4
Allen & Thurber pistol illus., 171
Allen & Wheelock 4-5; revolvers, 282
Allin, E. S., 20; 46; 316
Almy, Albert H., helps Mowry, 45; 57
Almy, J. H., Asst. QM Gen. Conn., 45
Alsop, Charles R., revolver, 280
Amber, John T., 189; 222
American Arms Co., 108
American Enfields, 31-2; 48; 57; 252
American Machine Works (see Tyler, Philos B.), 44; 102; 107
American Ordnance Association, 12
Ames Arms Co., maker Adams revolver, 96-7
Ames, James T., founds Mass. Arms, 104
Ames Mfg. Co., machinery from, 86
Ames, Nathan Peabody, 103; Jenks, 184
Ammunition all used up, 226
Amoskeag Mfg. Co., 52-3, Lindners, 122
Ancion-Marx, 29; altered muskets, 260
Anderson, Maj. Edw. C., CS, 86-88
Anderson, Joseph R. of Tredegar, 336
Andrews, E. W., 54
Andrews Sharpshooters, at Antietam, 224
Ansley, Jesse A., partner of Rigdon, 353
Anthony, Jacob, takes arms, Indiana, 204
Anthony, John B., 36; spare parts, 53
Archer, Dr. Junius L., cannon maker, 336
Armorers, impressment of, 370
Arnold, Andrew R., Supt. Manhattan, 206
Arrowsmith, George A., Hunt patents to, 168
Artillery model Springfields, 59
Ashmun, Hon. George, helps Colt, 314
Assault fire, tactic, 156; 162
Aston & Co., 56
Atkinson, Pvt. Geo., illus., 259
Atlanta, CS ironclad, LeMats aboard, 362
Augustin, Gen. Baron Vincent, 260; 292
Augur's brigade, 224
Austrian arms, 29; 66; 69; 74; 89; 94; 135; 256-62; 264; 269; 292
Avis, Capt. John, given Brown's guns, 2

B

Bacon, Thomas, 206
Bailey & Co., Enfields, 248
Bailey, Maj. Wm. L., CSA, gun illus., 359
Baldwin, Austin, 139; 277; 407
Baldwin, Lt. Briscoe, CSA, 342
Ball, Albert, carbine manufacture, 127
Ball carbine, 128
Ball, Charles, inventories Volcanic, 176
Ball, R., 126
Ballard, Charles H., rifle, 124
Ballisticians, study Volcanic accur., 175
Ballistics, internal, 16; 313
Balloon, motif on powder flasks, 402
Ball & Williams, 25
Baltimore, Merrill guns made in, 119
Baker, J. S., comdg DC Cavalry, 163
Baker, Col. Lafayette C., of DC Cav., 161
Banks, Gen. Nathanial. US, 14
Bannerman, Francis, 59; 260; 277; 281; 413-420
Bapty's, gun dealer, 106
Barbour, Alfred M., 374
Barber, Capt. G. M., used Spencer, 148-9
Barber, Rev. Lorenzo, USSS, 211
Bargamin, A. L., CS armory workman, 392
Barkalow, W. V., Enfields 33, 248
Baring Brothers, bankers, 66; 68; 70; 72
Barnett, minie rifle by, illus., 249
Barrels, 179-80; 183; 189; 308
Barry, Capt. Richard P., inspector, 277
Barstow, Col. C. W. A., orders Merrills, 120
Bartless, Joseph & Robert S., gun locks, 187
Bateman, lock maker, N.Y., 4
Bavarian arms, 68; 122; 266-7; 292
Bayonets, saw edge, possible use, 255
Bay State Arms Co., 35
Beach, Albert, deposition value, 205
Beals, Fordyce, revolver, 192

Beauregard, Gen. P. G. T., 360; 362
Beauregard & Slidell, 282
Beckett, Wm., with Cosmopolitan, 111
Beecher's Bibles, 3
Beecher, Rev. Henry Ward, on Brown's raid, 2
Belcher, Benjamin, 103
Belgian gun, CSA, 92; 120; 261; "Enfield," 266
Belonna Foundry, makes US cannon, 336
Benet, Capt. S. V., 40; 286
Bennett, R. B., trustee Volcanic, 176
Benton, Lt. J. G., 19-20; 232
Benzoni, Sgt. Louis, US, 10
Berdan, Col. Hiram, 210; 240; 298
Berenger, J., pistol maker, 397
Bermuda, CS activity at, 94
B. FA Co., 185
B.F.A., 187
Bigelow, Hiram, 39, 56
Billinghurst, William, Requa gun, 228-9
Billings, Frederick, to sell French, 411
Bird, Gustavus A., Hall rifle to, 388
Birge's Sharpshooters, 141
Birmingham, England, 68; 73; 79; 242; 254
Birney, Gen. David B., orders Sharpshooters on, 225
Bismarck, Count von, surplus arms, 410
Bitterlich, Frank J., 361; 395
Blaine, Hon. James G., boosts Spencer, 146
Blair, Charles, of Collinsville, 1
Blakeslee Quick-Loader, 154
Blue Springs, CS rapid fire gun at, 233
Blunt, Orison, 31-33; 124; 349
Bodine, F. L., 43; 54
Bohemian carbines, bought by Schuyler, 70
Boker, Herman, 28; 74; 205; 260-72; 407-10
Boker, M. H., Jr., 271
Bolles, Capt. C. P., at Tallahassee, 392
Bolt action carbine, Palmer, 127
Bomford, Col. George, 11; Hall, 138
Booth, John Wilkes, 5; 156; 398-399
Boston Arms Co., 40
Bourne, John Tory, 94, 98
Boutet à Versailles, 8
Bowie, E. Berkeley, CS revolvers, 354
Bowie knife, bayonet, 51; worn CS, 339, 342
Bragg, Braxton, fights Mexicans, 103
Brass, to test manufacture, 279; CS, 340
Bray, Edward P., Ballard improve, 125
Breech Loading Gun Co., 250-52
Bridesburg, 33
Bristol Firearms Co. organized, 114
British contract, LACo, 87; Greene, 106
Broadhead, Col. U.S., orders Lindners, 122
Brockway, C. J., Colt rifles from, 214
Bronson, Lt., M.V.B., 210; 217
Brooks, Wm. F., Springfield, 37; and Gibbs, 123
Brown, A & F, 48
Brown Bros. & Co., Enfields, 248
Brown, Corp. Al, of Vermont, 211
Brown, John, 1; 2; 4; 106
Brown, John W., agent Henry rifle, 159
Brown Mfg. Co., 127
Brown, Plumb and Ralph, 47
Brown & Sharpe, 46
Brown, W. E., bayonet on Enfield, 249
Browning, Jonathan, made Miller gun, 183
Brucker, Wm. Wilbur, Sec. of War, 12
Bruff Brothers & Seaver, Joslyn car., 129
Bruff, R. P., gen. mgr. Joslyn, 130
Brunswick rifle, 16
Bryant, David M., 103
Buckland, Cyrus, at Spfld, 20; stock, 55
Buckland, T. W., 103
Buckley & Co., Enfields, 248
Buckner, Gen. Simon Bolivar, 233
Buffington, Lt. H. R., on Hall carbines, 138
Buford, Maj. John, 62
Buist, Capt. G. L., had Belgians, 92; 340
Bulkley arm, 28
Bulkley, Samuel & Co., Enfields, 248
Bullet moulds, various, 324
Bulloch, Comdr. James D., CSN, 93; 95; 368
Burkhart, CS armorer at Harpers Ferry, 374
Burnside, Gen. Ambrose E., 114-18; 155, 56
Burnside, Graham, Vendetti theory, 168-9
Burr, David J., CS pistol maker, 355
Burt, Addison M., 46
Burt, Hodge & Co., 46
Burt, O. F., 46
Burt, O. T., 47; 52
Burton, James Henry, Harpers Ferry, 17-19; at Enfield, 67; blue print, 355; Spiller & Burr, 357; at Macon, 357; Haiman, 359; biographical, 376; with Tredegar, 376; inspection mark, 377
Bushnell, Cornelius S., surety Joslyn, 130; surety Lindsay, 286 (*Cyrus* error, 130)
Butler, Gen. Benjamin F., 96; 237; 362; 400
Butterfield, Joseph B., Springfield rifles, 57; revolvers, 282 (*Josiah* error, 282)

C

Cabeen, Robert B. (Jenks), 34
Cabot, Silas, 3
California Joe, see Head, Truman
Calisher, B. J., Enfield rifles, 248
Calisher & Terry, breech-loading rifle not CS, 248
Callender, Capt. F. D., with Fremont, 134
Cameron, New York police captain, 124
Cameron, Simon, 24; 26-7; 268
Campbell, Sheriff John W., 5
Canning, E. W., Enfields, 248-9
Cannon, 11; 154; 215; 217-18; 412
Carabine à tige, development, 263
Carabine Chasseurs de Vincennes, 9; 67
Carbine Board, evaluates calibers, 126
Carbines, CS, illus., 377, 380, 384; 389; 391
Carnmann, Frederick W., with Mowry, 44, 45
Carr & Avery, sells machine guns, 230
Carrier, J., and S & W, 172
Carter, Timothy W., 103
Cartoon, of Yankee soldier, 438
Cartridges, 23; illus., 80; Austrian rifle, 257; Ballard, 125, 126; Burnside, 114, 117, 118; Confed. making, 342; Cofer, 359; Colt, 324; Consol-Augustin, 260; Flobert, 163; Greene, 105; Hunt "rocket ball," 166; Maynard, 118; Perrin, 290; Pettengill, 275; Raphael, 291; Remington, 195; Requa battery gun, 229; silver plated, 117; S & W handmade, 172; Spencer, 154; Burnside Spencer, 156; makers of Spencer, 149; Spencer no CS make, 155; Spencer rifle, 144, 147; Spencer sporter, 152; Starr, 202; various, .44, 126; Vendetti, pistol, 169; Warner, 131.
Cary, Jim, Texas pistol workman, 371
Cases omitted, list, 27
Cast steel, in Burnside barrels, 116
Cavalry, 100; 122; 154; 236; 323
Cedar Creek, Battle of, 15
Cenature muskets illus., 427
Centennial Arms Corp., 421
Chaffee, C. C., 44
Chamberlain, Enoch, 40
Chambers gun, 273
Chandler, Capt. R., approves Spencer rifle, 149
Chapin, Charles O., with James Warner, 130
Chapin, Chester W., forms Mass. Arms Co., 104
Chapman, R. W., forms Mass. Arms Co., 104
Charter Oak stock, 318
Chase, John, 103
Chasseurs d'Afrique, 9-10.
Chauncy, Capt. John S., USN, inspector, 148
Cheney, Charles, finances Spencer, 146
Chickamauga, Spencer rifle at Battle of, 154
Chickering, Col. T. E., used Spencer, 149
Chicopee Falls Mfg. Co., 102-3
Cisco, Hon. John J. aids Ketchum, 136
Clapp, Everett, treasurer Starr Arms, 197
Clark, A. S., in Texas, 368; from Michigan, 372
Clark false muzzle, 182; 210; 222-24
Clark, F. J., trustee Starr Arms Co., 197
Clark, M. C., of Los Angeles, 3
Cloudman, Maj. Joel W., approved Henry's, 158
Cochran turret revolver, 273
Cofer, Thomas W., 359; revolver, 360
"Coffee Mill Gun," 234
Cole & Brother, 39
Coleman, E. P. & Brother, 39; 43
Collier, Elisha, 273
Collins & Co., 40
Collins, Wm., partner H. Smith livery, 173
Colorado arms, 41
Colored troops, 312
Colt carbines, accidental discharge, 97
Colt Enfield rifle, 309
Colt factory, 58; 307; 328
Colt, Judge James B., 305
Colt revolver, ivory grip, 6; marks, 197; London parts, 207; Lion-eagle, 288; Alabama, 304; Mass. issue, 319; light Dragoon, 319; nickle plated, 326; London barrel, 328; hinge frame, M1863, 329; postfire, 329; pocket Navy, 330; Navy 1861, 330; war production, 330; Hartford make from England, 331, 333-5; Lincoln Navy, 333; New Police, 335; cased 334; Hartford, 334; US Police, 335; Hartford, 349; R. E. Lee, 357; pocket 1855, 331, 359; making 371; conversion illus., 401.
Colt revolver, M1860 series; model, 318, 320; burst, 320; CS 320; nickle, 321; Floyd approves, 321; quantities, 322; cased set, 322; details, 322; Hartford, 322; price reduced, 322; stocked model, 323; regular, 323; Hagner gets, 323-4; South, 324-5; Hawley, 325; Zollicoffer shot, 325; Kentucky, 325; Navy, 326; interchangeable, 327;

440

Index

final delivery, 327; civilian, 328; fire, 328; Sweden, 333; Tiffany grip, 335; offered CS, 339; painting, 428
Colt rifle, Berdan, 212-15; Army 1857, 306; militia, 307; English locks, 308-9; 314; Harpers Ferry conversion, 317; HF delivery, 326
Colt, Samuel, 5; Mass. Arms, 105; Winchester, 174; Remington, 179; London factory, 206; Sharps, 299; colonelcy, 305-06; Cuba, 307; Enfields, 312; Canada, 314; 1st contract, 316; unlimited pistols, 318; death, 318; governor, 330; worker politics, 331; bookcase presentation, 331; employee policy, 333; pays Pearson, 343; rearms Virginia, 375
Colt shotgun cartridge, 324
Colt Special Model musket deliveries, 307-18
Common rifle, 346
Confederate agents compete with Hartley, 81
Confederate revolvers, various, 351-72
Confederate rifles, 339; 340; types, 345
Confederate States Armory & Foundry, 390
Congdon, barrel importer, 44
Conn. troops, 1st Conn. Colt's Rifles, 305
Consol, Guiseppe, 94; 134; 260
Constitution, CS, right-to-keep-and-bear-arms clause, 352
Constitution, US, 6
Conway, Martin F., 4
Cook & Brother, CS rifle maker, 382-3
Cooper Firearms Mfg. Co., Gatlings, 239
Cooper & Hewett, barrel maker, 35
Cooper, Joseph, 206
Cooper, Peter, 54
Cooper & Pond, Enfields, 248
Copperheads, alleged use of Henrys, 159
Coppoc, Andrew, Brown conspirator, 1
Cosmopolitan Arms Co. carbines, 110-14
Cost calculation of rifle musket, 44
"Cotton Clads," Spencer rifles on, 148
Cotton warrant, 82
Cranpin, Herzberg rifle maker, 266
Crawford, Capt., used Ballard rifle, 125
Craig, Col. H. K., 12; 17; 20; 136
Craig & Koch barrels, 48
Creeping lever ramrod of Roots, 318
Crescent Firearms Co., 58
Crispin, Capt. Silas, 28; 108; 261
Crittenden & Tibbals, 149; 172
Crockett, Lt. Gov. John M. of Texas, 370
Crown Hill Cemetery, Gatling slave in, 241
Cummings, Col. Arthur, 33d Va., 91
Cummings, Sam, costed new Navy revolver, 422
Cunard, E., Enfields, 248
Curtis, Maj. of DC Cavalry, 162
Custer, Brig. Gen. G. A., and Spencer, 155
Cushing, Hon. Caleb, recognizes Huse, 84
Cutter, Dr. Calvin, 3

D

Dabney, Morgan & Co., finance surplus, 411
Dagget, saber maker, 43
Dahlgren, John A., 51; 146; 237-8
Dalton, Hon. C. H., 52
Damnyankee Rifle, 158
Dance Bros. revolvers, 356, 370, 372
Dandov, C., Liege arms seller, 74
Danville Va., CS gun captured, 231
Dashull, Maj. Geo., Texas arms, 370
Davies, John M., partner Winchester, 174
Davis, Hon. Jefferson, 12; 16; 21; 83; 92; 115; 192
Davis, Jeff, target fired Berdan, 212
Day, James I., surety Joslyn carbine, 130
Dead soldier, 429; 437
Deane, Adams & Deane, 96
De Forest, Col. O., 5th NV Cav., 282
Delvigne rifle, 9
Devendorf, Lewis, on Rem. rifle, 186; 188
De Forest, Wm. Henry, quoted, 13-14
DeMeir, Juan C., 47
Deringer, Henry, 11; biographical, 394-5
Derringer pistols, copy, 395; Belgian, 397
Devil's Den, 217
D-G/Anchor mark on guns, 266
Dichell, Col. wants Merrill carbines, 119
Dickel, Col. N. Y. Mounted Rifles, Merrill, 120
Dickerson, Edw. N., lawyer for Colt, 105
Dimick, Horace E., revolver (see Metropolitan Arms Co.), 359; Fremont rifles, 142
Dingee, Silas, Austrian rifles, 259
Dinslow & Chase, barrels, 47; locks, 52; 123
Dinsmore, S. P., Merrill agent, 119
D C (1st Baker's) Cavalry, 158
Dix, Gen. John A., Merrill carbines, 120
Dixie Gun Works, replica arms, 427
Dixon, C. P., agent Jennings rifle, 166
Dixon, Nelson & Co., rifles, 381-2
Dixon, Wm., CS rifle maker, 382
Douglas, Sen. Paul H. of Ill., 57
Douglas, R. A., barrels, 40
Dow, W. H., of Illinois, 77
Downer, W. S., 387; 392
Draft Riots destroy Marston shop, 124
Dresden Enfields believed Thouvenin, 263
Dresden rifles, 69

Dreyse system, 100
Duffy, James, offers rifle, 28
Dunkirk, St. Louis emergency likened, 134
Durant, C. W., arms Coloradans, 41
Durrie & Rusher, Enfields, 36; 249
Dwight & Co., 39
Dyer, Alex. B., 46; 51; 130; 195; 202; 239; 275; 405; 409
Dyer, Thomas, to get Savage an order, 280

E

Eagle Foundry, Memphis arms factory, 352
Eagle Mfg. Co., 25; 43; 45
Eagle, spread, Whitney trademark, 59
"Eagleville" musket, 46
Early, Lt. Gen. Jubal A., CSA, 15
Eason, J. M., at Greenville, 381
Eastman, Arthur M., and Hall carbines, 136
Eaton, A. K., 54
Eaton & Kittredge, 54
Edwards, W., Colt revolver illus., 326
Edwards W. W., Texas Hartford Colt, 349
Egypt, Viceroy Guard rifle, 92
Elliott, Wm. H., Remington revolver, 193
Ellsworth's Zouaves, 8
Empire works, 47; 56
Enfield Rifle, lockplate, 32; machinery, 67; Schuyler, 68; N. Y. price, 70; Liege, 77; standard CS, 82, 87; LACo price, 86; CS price, 95; disassembled, 95; by Indians, 120; Ohio, 149; Union, 242-55; Windsor, 247; analysis marks, 242-56; US make, 246; Eagle-M mark, 252, 33; Francotte, 255; Colt delivery, 308-11; Springfield pattern, 309, 312; Souths captured North, 339-40; American walnut, 349, 384; CS contract machines, 384; gauges, 386; carbines, 384, 391; surplus bought by Colts, 406
Enfield Sharps carbine, illus., 390
English workmen, imported by CS, 387
Erichson, G. Houston derringer by, 396
Erie Canal, transportation breakthrough, 183
Essler & Bro. locks, 38
Essler, Robert, locks, 47
Evans, Lt., CSN inspector, 365
Explosive bullets, 429-35

F

Fales, Thomas J., sec. Colt's Armory, 314
Falmouth, Va., skirmish at, 224
False muzzle, See Clark
Farlee, G. W., claims loss Marston, 124
Faucet breech gun system, 119
Fayetteville rifle, 373; 385
Ferris, George H., partner M. James, 183
Ficklin, Maj. B., CSA, accuses Huse, 98
Fingal, CS blockade runner, 93
Finish on arms; Austrian, 256; Enfields, 244, 246; Gatling, 239; nickle, 192; Pettengill, 275; Remington, 192; Savage, 277; Spencer, 155; Starr, 199, 202; Springfields, 53; Zouave, 180
Firing pin, Smith & Wesson use, 165
Fish, Henry H., surety Remington, 191
Fisher, Warren, offers Spencer rifle, 147
Fisk, Capt., used Ballard rifles, 125
Fitch, J. P., Enfield order canceled, 36
Fitzsimmons, Texas pistol workman, 371
Flagg, Benjamin, tools for Palmetto, 388
Flare pistol, US, 125
Flint, Charles, 81
Flintlock muskets, mortality with, 92
Flobert, Louis Nicholas Auguste, 163-4; 169
Folsom, Charles, 58; 206
Folsom, H & D Arms Co., 58
Foote, Hon. S., pres. of Senate pro tem, 56
Forager's musket, 59; illus., 410
Ford, A. P., criticized Belgian gun, 92
Foreign arms, Belgian inaccurate, 340; cartridges, 80; CS on Fingal, 338; by Bermuda, 341; tabulation CS, 93; Tower marks, 341; Hartley production estimate, 77; specifically requested, 133; tabulation Boker, 272; desirable characteristics of, 71-2; illus., 75
Foreign carbines, 128
Foreign musketoons, 128
Forgett, Valmore Jr., 413; 423
Forrest, Gen. Nathan Bedford, CSA, arms, 389
Forsyth, Rev. Alexander, detonater, 182
Forsyth, John, offers CS Colts, Sharps, 339
Fort Monroe, 62
Fort Pillow massacre, arms used at, 389
Fort Sumter, relatively undamaged, 84
Foster, G. P., improves Burnside, 115
France, war in Algiers, 8; 401; 406
Francotte, August, 72, 77, 96
Frank, Adolph, with Bannerman, 260
Franklin, Gen. Wm. B., buys surplus, 406
Fraser, Trenholm & Co., 69; 82; 84-5
Fraternity, post-war, 438
Fraudulent rifle, Va. cavalry mark, 350
Fredericksburg, Battle of, 13; 342; 432
Freeman, Austin T., revolver, 273-4
Freeman, William, 47; 128; 277
Fremont, Gen. John C., buys arms, 28; 65; 66; 133
Fremont Hussars, sabers, 134; gallantry, 141

French arms, descr., 66; types, 262; 264
Friedrichs, Victor, Texas records of, 369
Fruwirth, Ferd., helps Hartley, 75; gun, 265
Fruwirth, Joh., carbines, 258
Fuller, Claud E., 31; 96
Funke, partner Boker, 270
Funkhauser, Col., 158

G

Gallagher, Mahlon J., carbine, 121
Gallaher, John S. & Co., 40
Gallaher, R. H., 40
Gardner, W. W., use of Henry, 158
Garibaldi rifles, 75; 266; 267
Garrison, Capt. Cornelius K., 28; 40; Enfields, 249; charter Ontario, 412
Gas seal revolvers, 279
Gaston, Nelson H., of Volcanic Arms, 173-4
Gatling, John W., reminiscence, 237
Gatling, Richard Jordan, gun, 233; Ben Butler, 235; riots, 235; Petersburg, 236; disloyal, 238; profits, 240; exchanged, 410
Gauges, 325-6; 386
Gaupillat, cartridge earlier than Volcanic, 169
Geary, Col. John W., 60
Geiger, Leonard M., rolling block gun, 195
Georgia buys muskets, 88
German "Enfields," 42; Springfield, 256-8
Gestapo, Baker's Cavalry like, 161
Gettysburg, Battle of, 150; 225
Gibbs, Lucius H., carbine, 123; in riot, 124
Gill, John, Enfields, 249
Girard, C. & Co., 362-65
Gist, Wm. H., of South Carolina, 380
Glaze, William, organizes CS factory, 390
Gluckman, Col. Arcadi, cited, 125
Goddard & Brother, Enfields, 249
Goodman, J. D., 78; 96; offers Enfields, 253
Goodnow, A. F., 35
Gordon, Castlen & Gordon, arms Kentucky, 41
Gorgas, Gen. Josiah, on Huse, 82; 338
Gorloff, Gen., inspects Gatlings, 240
Gorman's brigade, 224
Graham, Malcolm, 71
Grant, Gen. U. S., 92; revolver, 209; rifle, 213
Great Western Gun Works, 400
Greeley, Horace, used Gatling guns, 236
Green Rifle Works, and Warner carbine, 131
Greene, Lt. Col. James Durrell, 102; 105
Greener, W., 67; 107; 397
Greenwood & Batley, Enfield contract, 384
Greenwood, Miles & Co., Gatling gun, 235
Gregorelli, Vittorio, replica arms, 423
Gregory, Col. 91st Penn. Vols., 62
Grier, Col. E. C., CS pistol, 354
Griffing, Frederick, 56
Griffith, John & Son, Colt wholesaler, 329
Griffiths, John, defaults 1841 contr., 184
Griffiths, Navy sub-inspector, 148
Griswold, Samuel, revolver, 354; 356; 423
Gross, Charles B., revolver, 112
Gross, Henry, breech-loader, 110; 112
Gruler, Joseph, Manhattan Arms design, 206
Gunnison, A. W., Griswold partner, 354
Gutta percha, grips, 193; 356
Guzman, Capt., French inspector, 411
Gwyn, Edward, carbines, 110

H

H-mark on cartridge, 178
H-mark on Kerr revolver, 90
Hagner, Maj. P. V., 55; 110; 129; 268-9
Hahn, Wm., sells German Springfields, 256
Haiman & Bro., revolver like Manhatn, 358
Hall carbines, Fremont purchase, 135
Hall rifle, CS muzzle loader, 388
Hall, Joseph, 48
Hamilton, Archibald, 86
Hamlin, Hon. Hannibal, on arms sales, 408
Hampshire Riflemen, 91
Hampton, Gen. Wade, Colt cylinder flute, 319
Hanquet, J., made Colt revolvers, 424
Harbison, Hugh, sells Colt rifles, 212-4
Harpers Ferry Arsenal, 1; 17; 373; CS mfg., 374; Morse, 378; machinery, 387
Harpers Ferry Rifle, M1855, 22; 91; 142; 167; 191
Harrington, Jubal, 206
Harrington, Stephan H., of Indiana, 204
Hart, B. F., 206
Hartley, Marcellus, 70-79; 206; 249; 254; 402
Hartley, Maj. Wm. B., 307; 331-2
Hartshorn, Isaac, of Burnside Rifle Co., 115
Haskell, Samuel, Enfields, 249
Hatch, Alden, cited, 183
Hawken rifles, 142
Hawkins, Rush, recruits Zouaves, 10
Hawley, Gen. Jos. R., and Spencers, 150
Hay, John, describes Spencer-Lincoln, 151
Hayes, Wm., 48
Hays, John, 40
Hayward, Washington, B & O porter dead, 2
Head, Truman, Sharpshooter, 215-6
Heath, James, carried heaviest rifle, 223
Hedden & Hoey, case investigated, 29
Henderson, US musket speculator, 73

Henry, Benjamin Tyler, 163; 170; 177-8
Henry, J. J., Kentucky militia rifle, 379
Henry, J. & Son, militia rifle, 347
Henry rifle presented Welles, 146; 158-63
Hewes & Phillips, machinery, 199
Hewett, Charles; see Hewett & Cooper
Hewett & Cooper, 40
Hewett & Randall, 38
Hicks, Wm. C., 40; 172-4
Hill, Lt. R. M., inspects Justice arms, 62
Hoard, Hon., Charles B., 43; 55; 273
Hodge, James T., 46
Hoe, Robert & Co., 44
Hoey, John, Enfields, 249
Hoff, John, Austrian rifles, 37
Hoffman, Marvin, cited on CS marks, 89
Holt, Judge Joseph, 27; loss on Halls, 140
Hoover's Gap, battle, Spencer rifle, 149-50
"Horizontal Shot-tower," 144; 149
Horse pistols, 291, 2; Southern, 348; 356
Hoskins, Capt., lauds Austrian arms, 135
Howard breech-loader, 118
Howard, Surgeon E. Lloyd, on minie ball, 435
Howard, Gen. O. O., on Spencers, 150
Howland & Aspinwall, Enfields, 249
Huger, Col. Benjamin, rifle test, 18
Huger, Lt. CSN, comdg *McRae*, 95
Hume, Alexander, with Cosmopolitan, 111
Humor, battlefield, 227
Humphreyville Mfg. Co., 39
Hunt cartridge for S & W pistol, 172
Hunt, Walter, invents "Volition repeater," 166
Hurlbut, Brig. Gen. S. A., requests Minies, 133
Huse, Caleb, 67; 82; 90; 98; 99; 406
Huseman, F. W., CS gunsmith, 380

I

Ibbotson, Henry J., Enfields, 35; 249
Ide, Pvt. John S. M., 'scope rifle, 216
Ilion Gulph, 179
Illinois troops, Governor's Legion, 110; 2d Cav., 296; 21st Vol. Inf., 209; Birge's Sharpshooters, 143
Independence Hall Asso., Chicago rifle, 184
Independent Grays, 91
Indiana, buys Burnside carbines, 116
Indiana Troops, 1st Mt. Bgd. 17th Vol. Inf., 149; 21st Vol. Inf. wants Merrills, 120; secret CS regiments raised in, 238
Indians, in US service, 92
Inspection, 2d, 3d. 4th quality, 48; 72
Irwin, Richard & Co., Enfields, 250

J

Jackson, Charles, of Bristol Firearms, 115
Jackson, Maj. Thomas J., 5
Jacobs, Col. John, invents rifle, 431
Jacquith, Elija, patent revolver, 104
James, Morgan, rifle, 183; 187; 212
Jarvis, John S., to England, 308
Jarvis, Elisabeth, Gatling letter, 233
Jefferys, Charles & W. D., Enfields, 250
Jenks, Alfred & Son, Springfields, 33; 48; 56
Jenks, Barton, 34
Jenks carbine, 103; 119; 121
Jenks, Wm. develops Navy carbine, 184
Jennings, Lewis, breechloader, 165
Johnson, M. Rene, 36
Jones, Lt. Catesby Ap, at Norfolk, 336
Jones, Gen. Edward F., pays freight, 197; 203
Jones, Loren, Supt. Marston, 123
Jones, 1st Lt. Roger, burns HF Arsenal, 373
Jones, R., inspects Justice muskets, 62
Jones, R. L., 35
Joslyn, Benjamin F., 128; 130; 277
Joslyn, Milton, at Colt's, 128
JS-Anchor, 85; 89; 90; 91; 95-96; 98; 255; 311
Justice, Philip S., 60-64; 250; CS 347

K

Kabyle tribes, 8-9
Kagi, J. H., with Old Brown, 4
Kane, John, at Marston Armory, 123
Kautz, Cavalry Div., used Henrys, 161
Keen, C. R., partner Rigdon, 353
Keene, John W., foreman Marston, 123
Kellar, Virgil, makes wooden Texas gun, 371
Kellinger, deWitt C., surety Warner, 131
Kendall, Nicanor, makes 5-shot bar rifle, 167
Kendrick, Green, Springfield, 53; 173
Kendrick, John, 53
Kennedy, Sen. John F., opposes arms sale, 408
Kentucky troops use Ballard rifle, 125; Henry rifle, 158; Co. M, 12th US Cav, 159; 19th US Vols., 29
Kerr revolver, 90; 95-6
Kerr rifle, 87
Ketchum, Morris, supports Treasury, 136
Kibitzers, Lincoln-Spencer shooting, 152
Kimball, W. G. C., on Chicopee rifle, 102-3
King, John L., and James Warner, 130
King, Hon. Preston, helps Hoard, 44
Kingsbury, machine tool, 46
Kinsman, J. B., sells "breech-loading rifle," 250

Kipp, Peter, of Sharpshooters, 226
Kirk, Col. W. Stokes, surplus arms, 403
Kirkland, Turner, makes replicas, 427
Kirkpatrick, J., Enfields, 250
Kittredge, Ben, 131; 206; 209
Klein, Philip H., needle gun, 115
Knabb, Capt. 88th Penn Vols., 62
Knights of Golden Circle, 238
Knives, hunters, illus., 186
Kraft, Peter, CS gunsmith, 380
Krider, J. H., militia rifle, 347; LeMat, 362
Kruse, Drexel & Schmidt, and Fremont, 134

L

Labor, shortage, 128; troubles, CS, 387
Laidley, Major T. T. S., 52; 62
Lainhart, Little George, 221
Lakeman, Col. M. B., 3d Maine, 225
Lamb Knitting Machine Co., 109
Lamson, Ebenezer G., 35; E. G. & Co., 127
Lamson, Goodnow & Yale, 35
Lang, W. Baily & Co., Enfields, 252
Laurent, William St., sells arms to France, 411
Lawrence, J. P., Texas pistol owner, 368-9
Lawrence, Richard S., 105; 144; 167
Lawson, F. H., Enfields, 252
Leavett, Daniel, 102
Lee, James Paris, carbines refused, 128
Lee, Robert E., 5; 357; 392
Leech & Rigdon, 352-3
Leetch B/l rifle, 250-51; Alexander carbine, 390
Leetch, James S., rifle, 250
Lefaucheux, Eugene Gabriel, revolver, 65; 69; 249; Gettysburg, 289; Jackson, 357
LeMat, Dr. Jean, revolver, 356-366; 380
LeMille, Liege barrel maker, 311
Leonard, L., military storekeeper, 117
Letter of marque for Huse, 93
Lexington, Mo., Battle of, 135
L, G & Y Springfield muskets, 35
Liege Arms Assoc., 74
Lightning Brigade, Wilder's, 149-50
Lincoln, Abraham, 151-2; 212; 229; 234; 268; 398-9
Lincoln, George S. & Co., machinery, 46
Lincoln, Robert, 151
Lindert, Albert W., on Mass. Arms guns, 4
Lindner, Edward, carbine, 122
Lindsay, John P., 284-86
Litchfield, 183
Loading tools, Flobert, 165; Gallagher, 122
Loaded to the muzzle, rifle, Spencer, 150
Lock plates, CS rifle differences, 374-5
Lombard, Sgt. Francis O., Spencer, 148
London Armoury, 73; 78; 85; 245; 249; 363
London Pistol Co., 207
Longfellow, Henry Wadsworth, quote, 26
Longstreet, Gen. James, delayed by Sharpshooters, 225
Lopez, David, Supt. Columbia Arsenal, 380
Lorenz Rifles, Carbines, see Austrian Arms
Loron, cartridge earlier than Volcanic, 169
Lower, John P., 206
Lynch, Capt. J. A., defeats Rebels, 222
Lyon, Gen. Nathaniel, needs muskets, 133

M

M-14 rifle, characterization of, 408
Machine Guns: Bombards, 228; cartridge, 229; Ager, 229; CS use of, 231; Requa, 228; at Battery Wagner, 228-9; CS, 231; Gorgas, 231-33; at Danville, 231; Vandenberg, 232; Williams cannon, 232-33; Gatling, 233-41
Machinery, duplicate at Harpers Ferry, 22; for Springfields, 44; Trenton, 46; barrel, 52; drill, 53; Remington, 183; Starr, 199; typical inventory, 208
Mack, John, surety Starr contracts, 197
Macon Armory, 385; 393
Madrid, Enfield-type rifle, 271
Magruder, Lt. Col. John H., USMC, 266
Maine troops; 3d Inf. and Longstreet, 225; 6th Inf. at Fredericksburg, 30; Weldon, 161
Maitland & Auchincloss, 54
Malleable iron, 117; not in Spencer, 148
Mallory, Hon. Stephen H., Sec. Navy CS, 83; 95
Malvern Hill, Sharps at Battle of, 218
Manassas, gunshot wounds at, 430
Manhattan Firearms Co., 40; 204-209
"Manton" Springfields, 57
Manton, Joseph, 58; invents tube lock, 182
Manufacturers, regular for Ordnance Department, 200
Manufacturing, 168; 194; 355; 371; 374; 383; 426
Marcy, Gen. Randolph Barnes, 212
Cyrus Manville, Lindsay factory(?), 284
Marines, USMC, 1; 97; 175; 266
Markley, mystery man arms sales, 407
Marks, supposed CS, 88-89
Marlin Firearms Co., 124
Marlin, John Mahlon, 127
Martini-Henry rifle, supposed CS use, 350
Marseilles muskets, Wright inspects, 270-71

Marsh, S. Wilmer, breech-loading rifle, 40
Marshall iron, 36
Marston, William W., 30; 37; 125; 138
Martin, CS agent, 74-5
Martini, F. von, 36
Maryland troops, 6th Vol. Inf., 2; and Merrill guns, 120
Maryland, Cumberland, Spencer used at, 148
Mason, Hon. James M. and Huse, 98-99
Mason, William, 39; Springfields, 42
Mason, William, conversion revolvers, 401
Massachusetts State Committee, 1; 4
Mass. Arms Co., 2; 3; 4; 97; 101-2; 104; 105; 108-9
Massachusetts, State of, and Spencer, 126; 148
Mauser, 76; 77
May, C. W., 77
Maynadier, Col., 28; and Lindner, 122
Maynard Arms Co., 101
Maynard, Dr. Edward, 16; carbine, 101-106; 188; 316; CS, 380
Maynard Rifle Co., 101
McCulloch, Gen. Ben, CS, buys Colts, Morses, 378
McFarland, William F., 86; 109
McKay, James, 40
McClellan, Gen. George, and Spencer, 146
McKeever, Capt. Chauncy, Austrian arms, 135
McLanahan, J. K., with Shawk, 352
McLaurin, Archibald, guns to South, 96
McLean, Samuel & Co., Enfields, 253
McMillan, Col., of Indiana, 220
McNeill, Thomas E., CS factory, 390
McRae, CS financier lauds Huse, 98
McRae, CS sloop of war, 95
McWhinney, James, 236; Ridnge & Co., 236-7
Medicine, at time of CW, 433
"Melting column," infantry and Spencers, 154
Mendenhall, Derringer pistol, 395
Mendenhall, Jones & Gardner, rifle, 392
Mercott, T., London gun seller, 367
Merrill, James H., perc. Ballard breech, 125 carbine, 119-21; Latrobe & Thomas, 119; Patent Firearms Co., 121
Merrimack Arms Co., 127
Merwin & Bray, 124
Merwin, Joseph, perc. Ballard breech, 125
Metcalf, Capt. John H. III, mythical, 220
Metcalf, Capt. John T., of McMillan, 220-2
Metcalf, John, of Wayback, 221
Metropolitan Arms Co. revolver, 359
Michigan troops, 1st Regt., 92; 9th Inf., 284; Sharpshooter wins match, 211
Mickles & Hopkins, Prussian muskets, 38
"Milbury" muskets, 39
Mile-long shot, 221-22; 226
Militia Act, 11; Lindners bought, 122
Militia Rifle, Ohio, 7; South, 347-49; 379
Militia system, 7
Miller, J. pill-lock revolver, 182
Miller, Wm. Henry, and Stevens gun, 104
Mills, Ben, sights rifles of Ky. Vols., 29
Mills, J. D., sells machine guns, 230
Millward, Charles, barrel mark, 63; 244
Minie ball, medical aspects, 434-5
Minie, Capt., 9; British pay, 15; rifle, 67
Minnesota troops, Co. F, 9th Vol. Inf., 259
Mississippi Rifle, 12; 193; Whitney, 346; 381; 392
Mississippi troops, Toby-Maynard anecdote, 101
Mitchell, John M. (Jenks), 34
Mitchell, John T., Enfields, 253
Mitchell, Joseph G. (Jenks), 34
Moore, George G., 206
Moore, John P., Enfield rifle order, 32; 252
Mordecai, Maj. Alfred, 76; 260
Morgan, John P., and Hall deal, 136
Morgan, J. S., (sic) finance Garrison, 411
Morris, Tasker & Co., 46; 48
Morse, George Washington, CS rifle, 378-81
Morton, Gov. Oliver P., 116; 204
Mosby, Gen. John Singleton, on Henry, 161
Moses & Co., CS agents, 74
Motley, U.S. Minister, arms, CS, 94
Moulton, Manhattan revolver of, 209
Mowry, James D., Springfields, 44-45
Muir, William & Co., Springfields, 47; 51
Mulholland, James, Springfields, 54
Muller, Louis, Liege arms seller, 74
Multiple discharge, explanation of, 97
Murdaugh, Lt. W. H., inspects LeMats, 364
Murray, J. P., rifle, 392
Muskets, British, 85; 88-89
Musser, Penrod O., makes replica arms, 421
Musson, J. W., merchant Bermuda, 98
Muzzy Rifle & Gun Mfg. Co., 379

N

Napoleon III refuses sell arms, 69
National Firearms Act amended, 426-7
National Rifle Association and replicas, 426-7
Navy Arms Co., 421
Navy, U.S., 111; 146; 148; 275
Naylor & Co., Enfields, 78; 235
Needle gun, 100; 115
Nelson, Lt., USN, Colt pistol for, 326
Nelson, O. O., CS rifle maker, 382
Nessler bullet, recommended, 30
Neumyer, Johnny, and replica guns, 423
Newcombe, Mrs. Albert, on Gatling, 234; 241

INDEX

New England Emigrant Aid Committee, 3
New Hampshire troops, Spencers, 151; 156
New Haven Arms Co., 161; 176
"New York" Springfield musket, 48
New York troops, 1st Mounted Rifles, 120; Ira Harris Guard 5th Cav., 282; 9th Inf. "Hawkins Zouaves," 8; 14th Brooklyn Zouaves, 92; 22d Militia w/Enfields, 243; 144th Inf. had CS Enfields, 339; Duryea's Zouaves and Sharps, 296
New York State, Enfields, 254; 268
New Yorker, impressions of, in CS, 340-41
New, William, at Tallassee, 393
Newson, Henry, and Volcanic, 176
Nicholas, Czar, and Gatling, 240
Nicholson, W. F. & Co., 39
Nippes, Albert S., Sharps, 1
"Norfolk" Springfield musket, 47
Norris, Samuel, 39; 44; 46; 57; 195; 286; 406
North, C. B., 39
North, Capt. James H. CSN, and Bulloch, 95
North, James, endorses Savage deposition, 139
North, Col. Simeon, 11; 37
North Carolina troops, 5th Inf. & Colt, 216
North & Savage, 278
Norton explosive bullet, 431
Norwich Arms Co., 44-5; make Schubarth musket, 57
Nugent, Edward; see John H. Schenck
Nunnemacher, Rudolph J., Ballard rifles, 125

O

Oakley, Annie, used Spencer shotgun, 157
Oberndorf, a/N, mark on musket, 68; 77
Ohio, Starr revolver, 199; carbine, 110-14
Ohio troops, Spencer, 149; Enfields, 149
Opdyke, George, buys Marston shop, 123
Oppen, Baron F. A. K. W. von, 311
Order of American Knights, Gatling member, 238
Osgood, bayonet maker, 43
Otard, Frank, Enfields, 254
Overland Expedition, 125
Overman, Wm. W., 122
Owen, Hon. Robert Dale, 27; Hartley, 71

P

"Pacific Ballard," 127
Palmer, John Courtlandt, 139; 168
Palmer, William, carbine, 127-8
Palmetto Guards, 92; 340
Palmetto Armory, arms, 346; 388
Parker, Charles, 54
Parker, Snow, Brooks & Co., 54
Parrott, Capt. P. R., 200
Parts issued by Springfield Armory, 48
Patch, Nathan M., US inspector, 103
Payne, Col. John M., mentions LeMats, 363
Peace, pacification by Spencers, 150
Pearson, John, paid by Colt, 343-44
Peck, H. J., lends rifle to Lincoln, 212
Pecksmith Mfg. Co., 56
Pegram, Capt. CSN, 93
Penno, W. L., merchant Bermuda, 98
Pennsylvania, no contracts by State, 347
Pennsylvania troops, 28th and Justice, 60; 62
Percival, Orville, gun made by H. Smith, 168
Perkins & Livingston, Enfields, 254
Perkins, L. S., Texas revolver mark, 368
Perrin & Co., revolvers, 290-91
Perry, CS carbine, 380
Petheridge, Col. Md., officer US, 120
Petrikin, B. Rush, 54
Pettengill, C. S., revolver, 274-76
"Philadelphia" muskets, 34; 39
Philadelphia, muskets rifled at, 134
Piedmont rifled muskets, 74
Pierce, Andrew J., shoots Colt rifle, 215
Pill-lock priming, 167; 182
Pirko, of Vienna, 89; pistol, 291
Pistol-Carbine, Springfield, 1855, 20-21
Pistols, tabulation US purchased, 273
Plan For Militia, book by Col. Martin, 6
Pleasant Hill. Metcalf at, 222
Pleasanton, Capt. Alfred, and Spencer, 146
"Plymouth Rifle" (Dahlgren), 9; 50-51
Poirier Freres, 77
Pomeroy, Lemuel, 11
Pomeroy, Gen. Sam C., 3
Pond, Charles H., 206
Pondir, John, case investigated, 28; Enfields, 254
Post, Col. Henry A., issued Colt rifles, 224
Post, J. W., & Wheeler, agents Volcanic Arms, 175-6
Potomac Guards, 92
Potts & Hunt, Enfields, 243-45; 309
Poultney & Trimble, 107; 407-8
Powell, J. R., agent Alabama, 348
Preston, Francis, of Manchester, 36
Prevost, A. G. M., of Trenton, 46
Price, Gen. Sterling, CSA, 134
Primers, special musket exploded, 134
Pritchett bullet, 19
Private armories, 11; contracts end, 12
Proof, Spencer, 148; Springfield, 48
Proof mark, DP/B Blunt, 31

Providence Tool Co., Springfields, 35-36
Prussian arms, 47; 75; 76; 89; 120; 266; 267; 292
Pryse & Redman, Enfield rifle, 85
Publicity, Volcanic pistol, 175
Purchasing agents, Union, 27
Purnell, Col. Md., US officer, 120
Pusey, machinery from, 48
Putnam Phalanx, 8

Q

Quantrell, revolver carried by, 358

R

Rack, storage for rifle muskets, 26
Radcliffe, T. W., and CS factory, 390
Rains, Gen. J. G., CSA, 156
Ramsay, Gen. George D., 121; 126; 130; 201
Ramsdell, G. W., case investigated, 28
Raphael, George, revolvers imported, 290-1
Rawlins, A. B., reminiscence, 371
Raymond, Edward A., revolver, 274
Ream's Station, Henrys at battle of, 158
Rebetey, Augustus, Manhattan arms by, 206
Redfield, stock maker, 36
Reed, William, 206
Remington, Merrill carbine, 119; Jenks carbine, 121; J. W. Keene, 124; Eli Jr., 179; 1st rifle, 180, a fraud, 182; Zouave, 180; revolver .44, 180; family, 180; sporting rifles, 180-189; 211; 1841 rifle, 184; flintlock muskets, non-existent, 185; assembled rifles, 188; Sam before Committee, 190; Eli dies, 190; Philo, 190, 196; Zouave rifle, 190-191, for South, 191; 347; revolvers, 191-95; condemned, 191; rolling block carbine, 195; French sales, 401-7; forbidden buy surplus, 405; Remington-Springfield rifles polished bright, 407; replica, 421
Replica arms, 422; 427
Revolvers, tabulation US purchased, 273
Reynolds, W. W., 401; 402; 403
Rhode Island troops, Burnside carbine, 115
Rhuleman, August, 67; 69; 270
Rice, Hon. Alexander H. and Spencer, 147
Rice, John, supplied by Jenks, 34; Springfield rifles, 38; 43
Richards, C. B., revolver of, 401
Richards, Westley, rifle illus., 250-51
Richardson, George J., 122
Richardson & Overman, carbine, 121
Richmond, industrial center, 336-8
Richmond rifles, 338; variations, 375-77; 387
Rider, Joseph, rolling block rifles, 195; revolver, 195
Rifle musket, M1855, 5-load pressure test, 23
Rifle musketoon cal., 69 ammo, 23
Rifle pit descr., 216; illus., 217
Rifles, accuracy, 13; 15; pre-1855, 18-19
Rigby flats, 186
Rigby, John & Co., 187
Rigdon & Ansley revolver, 353; 354; 356
Rigdon, Charles H., 352
Riley, Robert, Blunt essay cited, 31
Rimfire cartridge, predecessor, 164
Rindge, I., 236
Ripley, E. J., executor Wesson, 103
Ripley, Gen. James W., Chief of Ordnance, on program, 25; examines Duffy rifle, 28; Blunt musket, 31; vetoes Schubarth, 55-56; to Nassau, 70; arms available, 71; Smith, 107; Merrill, 119; sells Halls, 136; and Spencer, 147; instruction foreign arms, 268; suggests alterations Springfield model musket, 316
Ripley Waterproof Rifle, 170
Ripley, Lt. Col. Wm. F., 210; Reb sniper, 216; anecdote Yankee captures Reb, 226
Roberts, Gen. Benjamin S., 36
Roberts, Wm. S., 47
Robbins, H. E., 54
Robbins & Lawrence, Enfields, 35; 168; 247; 315
Robinson & Cottam, Vandenberg gun, 231-32
Robinson, Edward, 40
Robinson, Samuel C., revolver, 391; Sharps, 391-2
Robitaille, Charles, revolver, 274
Rodman, Capt., inspects Burnsides, 116
Roff, Fred A. Jr., of Colts, 425
Rogers, Henry S., revolver, 274-5
Rogers & Spencer, Springfields, 54; 277; revolvers, 274-77
Rogers, T. Robinson, Springfields, 54
Roper, Sylvester, aided by Spencer, 157
Root, Elisha King, and Colt, 314
Rowand, Dr. Charles L., and Butterfield, 282
Ruffin, Edmond, 5
Rusk, Texas senator, and Colt, 104
Ryder, James M., 56

S

Sabers, use in battle, 141
Sadler, Dr. L. H., CS rifle maker, 382
Saloon pistol, 165
Sanford, Hon. Henry, Belgian muskets, 65; has Wright inspect guns, 268

Sanitary Commission, pistol at fair, 331; medical booklets, 433
Sarson, John B., 47
Sarson & Roberts, and Jenks, 34; Springfields, 47; Enfields, 255
Satterlee, cited, 125
Saunders, G. G., US inspector, 32
Savage Arms Corp., 109; acquires brand name, 130
Savage, Edward, 37; deposition, 139; 280
Savage, Josiah, 139
Savage, R. F. A. Co., 37; revolver, 277-79; Springfields, 281
Sawyer, Charles Winthrop, on short muskets, 59; long range shot, 221; Lindsay, 285
Saxon rifles, 69
Schenck, Courtney, 54; 277
Schlesscher, of Boker & Co., 271
Schneider & Glassick, revolver, 360; derringer pistols, 396
Scholefield, J. Sons & Goodman, 96
Schroeder, carbine, 100
Schubarth, Caspar D., Springfields, 55
Schurz, Sen. Carl, investigation sales, 409
Schuyler, Col. George L., 38; 59; 66
Schuyler, Hartley & Graham, 42; 131; 254; 401; 407
Schuyler, Jacob Rutsen, 71; 206
Scott, Asst. Sec. Thomas A., 28; 122; 212
Scott, Gen. Winfield, 12
Scrugham, Judge Warburton, Warner, 131
Scudder, Linus, 40
Searer & Hay, Enfields, 254
Sea Service Rifles, 95
Seaton, Lt. C. W., of Vermont, 210
Seaver, W. A., "tower mark" Enfield, 38
Sebenius, Harald C., on Spencers, 152
Sebor, Charles R., pres. Savage R. F. A., 278
Semmes, Capt. Raphael, CSN, buys arms, 378
Senatorial interest in contracts, 56-7
Sergeants, U. S. S. S., scope rifles, 224
Seth, "Old Seth," captures cannon, 218
Set trigger, Spencer, 152
Seven Pines, Williams gun at, 233
Seymour, Hon. Thomas H., 8
S. G. D. G. (sans guarantie du gouvernement), 362
Shakanoosa Arms Co., 381
Sharps carbine, 1-4; Shutts, 2; CS, 389-91; Indian carbine, 294; carbine orders tabulated, 296; 1863 model, 297; coffee mill stock, 300
Sharps, Christian, 206; 283-303
Sharps rifle Ripley first orders, 295; artillery musket, 295; Ben Butler, 295; Berdan serials, 299; pellet primer, 300; and Hankins carbine, 302; contract, 302
Sharpshooters, Spencer rifle, 147; recruitment of, 210; breechloaders, 211; CS, 219; at Gettysburg, 226; like squirrel hunting, 227
Shaw, Capt. Joshua, percussion cap, 182
Shawk & McLanahan, revolver, 352
Shenandoah Sharpshooters, 92
Schenck, John H., agent Union machine gun, 236
Schenkl carbine, 100
Sherman, Brig. Gen. W. T., Kentucky arms, 41; Henry rifles with, 159
Sherrard, Joseph, Texas pistol maker, 369
Shingle Lincoln shot at, 151; 152; 154
Shore, Sigmund, makes replica revolvers, 424
Shotguns, popular in South, 341
Shoulder stocks on Alsop revolver, 280
Shutt, Col. Augustus P., 2
Sidehammer mechanism, 182; 185
Side knives, see Bowie Knives
Sight elevation, improvised, 226
Signal pistol, US, 125
Silver grip Colts, 332; 335
Simmons, Senator James F., and Schubarth, 55
Simon(s) H. and Son, 38; Enfields, 254
Sinclair, Lt. Geo. T., at Norfolk, 336
Sinclair, Hamilton & Co., 86
S & K, 266
Skerrett, Lt. Cmdr. J. S., Starr revolver, 202; tests Gatling gun, 238
Skinner, Chauncy D., 278
Skirmishers, deployed, illus., 430
Small Arms, CS opinion of, 340
Small-bore Enfield, 87
Smith, partner of Kendall, 168
Smith, Amos D. & J. Y., 55
Smith, Crosby & Co., buy surplus arms, 412
Smith, David, sells Requa guns, 229
Smith, Frederick H., 205
Smith, Gilbert, carbine, 106-8; 121
Smith, Horace, biography, 103-5; Jennings, 165; makes Flobert pistols, 164; abroad, 168; livery stable, 173. See Smith & Wesson
Smith, Samuel B., 28; 37; 122
Smith, Sam, on London Pistol Co., 207
Smith & Wesson, 103; founded metal cartridge industry, 109; invent Flobert cartridge, 165; toggle joint not patented, 169; wouldn't work, 177; Herman Boker, 206; gauges for Russian revolver, 240; 273
Smith, Young & Co., 71
Smythe, A. J., partner Rigdon, 353
Snaphaunce lock, 8; 59
Solid frame, Starr, 202; Colt, 192-3

South Carolina buys Remingtons, 193
Spanish Enfield, used CW, 271
Special Model Musket, 35; 52-3; see also Colt Special Model; Amoskeag; Lamson, Goodnow & Yale
Speed, Hon. J. F., approves Prussian arms, 30
Spencer, Christopher Miner, 144; total rifles, 144; in Hartford, 145; cal. .58, 147; endurance, 149; insignia, 150-54; Lincoln, 151; sporting rifle, 152; CS capture, 155; by Burnside, 156; Spencer-Lee, 157; sold to Winchester, 157; 401
Spies, John J., 206
Spiller & Burr, CS revolver, 356; 390
Spiller, Edward N., 355
Sprague, Gov., surety for Burnside, 119
Springbok, CS blockade runner, 93
Springfield Arms Co., 130
Springfield carbine, 346
Springfield musket, 346
Springfield rifle musket, Maynard, 19; to make Special Model, 35; from Wm. F. Brooks, 123; SPRINGFIELD, 129; defective arms issued, 151; low price, 190; locks made England, 314
Squires, Col. W. C., 196
Stabler, Edward M., cut-off to Spencer, 157
Stansbury, Maj. Smith, CS ord. at Bermuda, 94; 98
Stanton, Edwin M., 27; 28; 30; 156
Starbuck, of Remington Arms, 410
Starr, Nathan, 11
Starr, Eben T., revolver, .36, 197; carbine, 199; Springfield rifle, 199; Navy test, 202-3; derringer, 203; and C. B. Hoard, 274
Staten Island Steel Works, 47
States require arms, 70
Stealing arms under truce flag, 92
Stearns, George L., 4
Steinberger, A. B., surplus arms, 407
Steiner, Dr. Paul, cites CW wounds, 437
Stephen Hart, blockade runner, 93
Stephens, of Butterfield, 57
Stephanson, J., Gibbs carbine parts, 123
Stevens, Aaron C., with Old Brown, 1
Stevens Arms Co., 100; 124
Stevens, Joshua, 102; 104
Stevens, Simon, offers Halls, 135; carbine rifling, 138; claim okay, 141
Stevenson, Hon. John W., minority view arms sales, 410
Stills, copper from for perc. caps, 156
St. Louis Arsenal, muskets rifled at, 134
Stockwell, Pvt. Elisha, likes Belgian gun, 92
Stone River, Battle of, 430
Stoneman, Gen., wants Merrill carbines, 119
Stonewall Brigade, 92
Stout, T. B., secy. Starr Arms Co., 197
Stowe Mfg. Co., 39
St. Petersburg Convention, explosive bullets limited at, 433
Straw, E. A., supplies Lindner carbines, 52; 122
Streeter, Chamberlain & McDaniel, 352
String measure, target scoring, 211
Strobell & Co., Gibbs carbine, 35
Stuart, I. W., 318
Stuart, Gen. Jeb, and Terry carbine, 248; LeMat revolver, 365; 392
Stuart, John, Enfields, 254
Stutler, Boyd B., 4
Suhl musket, 267
Suhl rifles, 42; 255
Sumner, Senator Charles, arms sales, 408
Surplus arms, sold to Huse, 99; 406; 277; 400 et seq
Surplus parts, propose to make, 318
Suter, Thomas, 159
Sutherland, Samuel, Colt agent, 376
Swiss militia, 6
Sword bayonet, approve Craig, 19
Sykes, W. L., of Mississippi, 346
Syms, Wm. J., 206
Symmes carbine, 16; 100
Syracuse Fire-Arms Co., 54
Syrus, Wm. J. & Brother, Enfields, Belgian, 255
Swinburn & Son, 242

T

Tactics described, 14
Talbot, Jones & Co., Gatling gun, 239
Talcott, Col. George, court-martial, 12
Talcott, Samuel, and D. B. Wesson, 173-4
Tallassee carbine, 392-3
Tallman, Edward D., 275
Tallman, George C., partner Rogers & Spencer, 275
Tallman, Henry, 275
Tambeur Freres, 74
Tanner & Co sells rifles to Hartley, 77
Target rifles, used by Sharpshooters, 211
Tarpley, CS carbine, 380
Taunton Locomotive Works, and Hall, 138
"Taunton" musket, 42
Taylor, Mrs. Vesta Spencer, 146; 151
Taylor, Maj. W. V., at Tallassee, 392
Tegethoff, Wm., finances Shawk revolver, 352

Telepathy, Huse convinced of, 85
Telescope sights, 212-227
Tennessee troops; 5th US Cav. used Henrys, 159; Carroll's brigade used bayonet hunting rifles, 341
Texas, Austrian muskets for, 94; military board, 368-71; revolver, 369
Texas troops, Gildner's brigade and rapid fire cannon, 233; Terry's Texas Rangers, 349
Thomas, Gen. George H., and Union guns, 236
Thomas, Philip E. & Lewin W., gunmakers, 119
Thornton, Col. Wm. A., 32; 130; 300
Thouvenin rifle a tige, 9; 67; Saxony, 69; 263
Tiffany & Co. Enfields, 255
Tige, description chamber "a tige," 18
Tillet, Antoine Paul Regnier, and Flobert, 165
Tin, for finishing cartridges, 117
Todd, George H., brass mounted musket, 387
Tomes, Francis, 70-71
Tomes, Son & Melvain, Enfield ramrods, 255
Tourniquet, 434
Tower Junction Shops, Joslyn carbines, 130
Tower mark, Birmingham, 69; Blunt, 349
Tower rifle, 242; 245
Tracers not used CW, 433
Transportation, public, 84
Treadwell, Lt. James T., Ordnance, 60
Tredegar Iron Works, makes Williams cannon, 233; railroads, 337; offers to arm South, 337; Richmond Armory, 378
Trenholm Bros., 84
Trenholm, John, meets Hartley, 81
Trent, LeMat aboard ship, 382
Trenton Arms Co., 46
Trenton Iron Co., 46
Trenton Iron Works, see Hewett & Cooper
Trenton Locomotive & Machine Mfg. Co., 46
"Trenton" musket, 36; 46
Trepanning, attempted on battlefield, 438
Triple cross, British obsolete mark, 106
Triplett & Scott, carbines, 128
Trouax, Pvt. Robert, with Spencer, 150
Truberth (Fruwirth) helps Hartley, 75
True magazine, false story in, 221
Tube-lock ignition, 260
Tubular magazine, first use of, 166-7
Tucker, Labon E., pistol contract, 370
Tucker, L. E. & Sons, revolver by, 372
Tucker & Sherrard revolver, 368-72; possible sale to Dance, 372
Tuckerman, George, surety Remington contract, 191
Turkey, buys Enfields, 78; surplus arms, 410
Tuscaloosa cadets, 83
Tweed, Harrison, 138
Tyler, Daniel, to buy arms, 65
Tyler, Philos B., gauge maker, 43; 108
Tyler, Sgt. Richard W., 1st USSS, 225

U

Uniforms, CS, 69; US, 100; Cav., 155
Union Arms Co., revolvers, rifles, 40-41; 208
Union Defense Committee, Enfields, 255
"Union and Fremont," war-cry, 141
Union Metallic Cartridge Co., origins, 71
Union Rifle, 110-14
Union Volley Gun, 229; 231-32
United States District Court, Enfields from, 255
Unsold, John C., 4
"Untembery" (Wurtemburg) musket, 68; 77
U.S. Police, Baltimore, 296
Utica, Remington barrel rifled at, 183

V

Valentine, W. J., sell arms to France, 411
Vance, Gov. given Vandenberg gun, 231
Vaughn, Robert H., and Tegethoff, 352
Velocity, M1855 arms, 24; Delvigne, 264
Vendetti pistol, and Volcanic, 168
Venus, blockade runner, 94
Vermont troops, Co. F, USSS, 210; Colts, 215
Vicksburg, Enfields captured at, 92; explosive bullet at, 432
Vienna Arsenal, 69-70; 94; 270
Virginia Manufactory musket, 375; 376; 348
Virginia mark on Starr pistol, 202
Virginia State Armory reactivated, 375
Virginia Troops, Richmond Howitzers, 218-9; equipment at start of war, 338
V.M.I., 5-6
Volcanic Arms Co., pistols and rifles, 168; 172-76
Vulcan, modern Gatling gun, 233; 239-41

W

Wadsworth, Brig. Gen. Jas. S., 437-8
Wagner, Lt., 88th Penn. Vols., 62
Wagner, Fort, Whitworth rifles used, 219
Walch, John, multishot revolver, 283-4
Walker, Hon. Leroy Pope, CS Sec. War, 83
Walker, Col. M. B., at Stone River, 430
Wallis & Wallis, catalog cited, 197
Wapping Heigths, Sharpshooters skirmish, 226

Wardwell, Jeremiah M., Enfields, 255
Warner, James, carbine, 130-31; 206
Warner, Samuel L., surety Savage, 281
Warner, Thomas, 104
Warren & Steele, Albany gunmakers, 188
Washburn, N., barrels, 35; 39; 43; 44
Washington Arsenal issues Springfields, 62
Wass, Col. 41st Mass., 149
Waters, Asa H. and Co., 11; Merrill, 129
Waters, S. H. & Co. (A. H. & Co.?), 43
"Watertown" Springfield rifle, 43-4
Watson, Asst. Sec. War. P.H., 34; 71
Webb, Brig. Gen. Alexander S., head wound, 437
Webley, revolver discharge, 97
Weed, Thurlow, libels Opdyke, 124
Welch, Brown & Co., 47
Welch, Wm. W., Springfields, 47
Welles, Hon. Gideon, 146; Gatling, 240
Wellsman, senior partner Trenholm, N. Y., 85
Werder, Johann Ludwig, Lorenz rifles, 257
Wesson, Daniel Baird, 103; Jennings, 168
Wesson, Edwin, buys revolver maker, 103
Wesson, Frank, 104; carbines, 131
Wesson & Leavitt, 103
Wesson, Stevens & Miller, 104
Weston, Capt. Edmund, of Vermont, 210
West Point, Gibbs carbine at, 123; Huse lived near, 82
Wheeler, Henry F., pistols, 108
Wheeler, Robert & Sons, 244
Wheeler, William A., 36-37
Wheelock, James A., 37
Wheelock, Thomas P., 206
Whitaker, Wm. (Jenks), 34
White Bros., surplus arms, 403
White, Rollin, patent a fraud, 205
Whiteley, Capt. R. H. K., 10; 137; 198-99
Whiting, C. B., friend of Moulton, q.v., 209
Whitney, Eli, 11; 48-51; Arms Co., 59; odd Springfields, 59; Enfield, 61-3; Volcanic, 176; revolver, 286; thin lockplates, 316; bad reputation, 348; CS pattern, 378
Whittmore, Nathaniel, rifle by, 213
Whitworth Rifle, 219-220; 250
Wiard, Norman, 33
Wide-Awakes, influence Colt revolver mark, 332
Wigert & Otard, French rifles, 38
Wigert, Arthur, Enfields, 254
Wilcox's brigade, CS, and Sharpshooters, 226
Wilder, Col. John Thomas, Spencers, 149; at Chicamauga, 154; Henrys, 161
Wilkeson, Samuel, 25
Williams, Abe, 221; 223
Williams Ball, zinc washer ammo, 41
Williams, C. H. & Co., 38; 39; 44; 46; 47; 56
Williams, Capt. D. R., rapid fire cannon, 323
Williams, P. K., use of Henry, 158
Williams, Senator W. S., and revolvers, 277
Wilsons' breech-loading rifle, 96
Wilson, Capt. James M., exploits Henry, 160
Winchester house, 158
Winchester, Oliver Fisher, buys Smith & Wesson, 173; shirtmaker, 174; Volcanic, 176; Henry, 177
"Windsor Locks" Springfields, 39; 52; 54
Windsor Mfg. Co., 35
Winther, Oscar C., "load on Sunday," 159
Wisconsin "Eagles," 265
Wisconsin troops, 14th Inf., 92; 3d Cav., 120
Witloe Precision, makes replica revolvers, 424
Wogdon style duellers, 356
Wolcott, C. P., agent for Ohio, 42
Wolff, Eldon G., monograph cited, 125
Wolfson, David, reminiscence Haiman, 358-9
Wood, Gen. John, and carbines, 110
Woodcock, W. W., Enfields, 255
Woods, Col. I. C., aide to Fremont, 134
Woodward & Cox, to supply machine guns, 229
Woolcott, H. H., pres. Starr Arms Co., 197
Wounds, Minie ball, 429; explosive, 429; 430; tetanus, 430; Kennon shell, 432; Gardiner at Gettysburg, 432; temporary cavity, 433-36
Wright, Charles, bids Springfields, 407
Wright, George, inspector, 72; 268-72
Wright, Lysander, machinery, 199
Wycoff, Henry, Savage middleman, 281

Y

Yale, B. B., 35
Yankees sell guns to Rebs, 159
Yorktown, Battle of, 215; artillery, 412
Young, Daniel J., of Harpers Ferry, 40

Z

Zagonyi, Maj. Charles, of Fremont Hussars, 141
Zella-Mehlis, musket lock, 267
Zimmer, Capt. Louis, smuggles caps, 338
Zoli, makes Zouave rifle, 424
Zollicoffer, Gen. Felix, 325
Zouave regiments, arms of, 196
Zouaves, French, 263. See also Militia